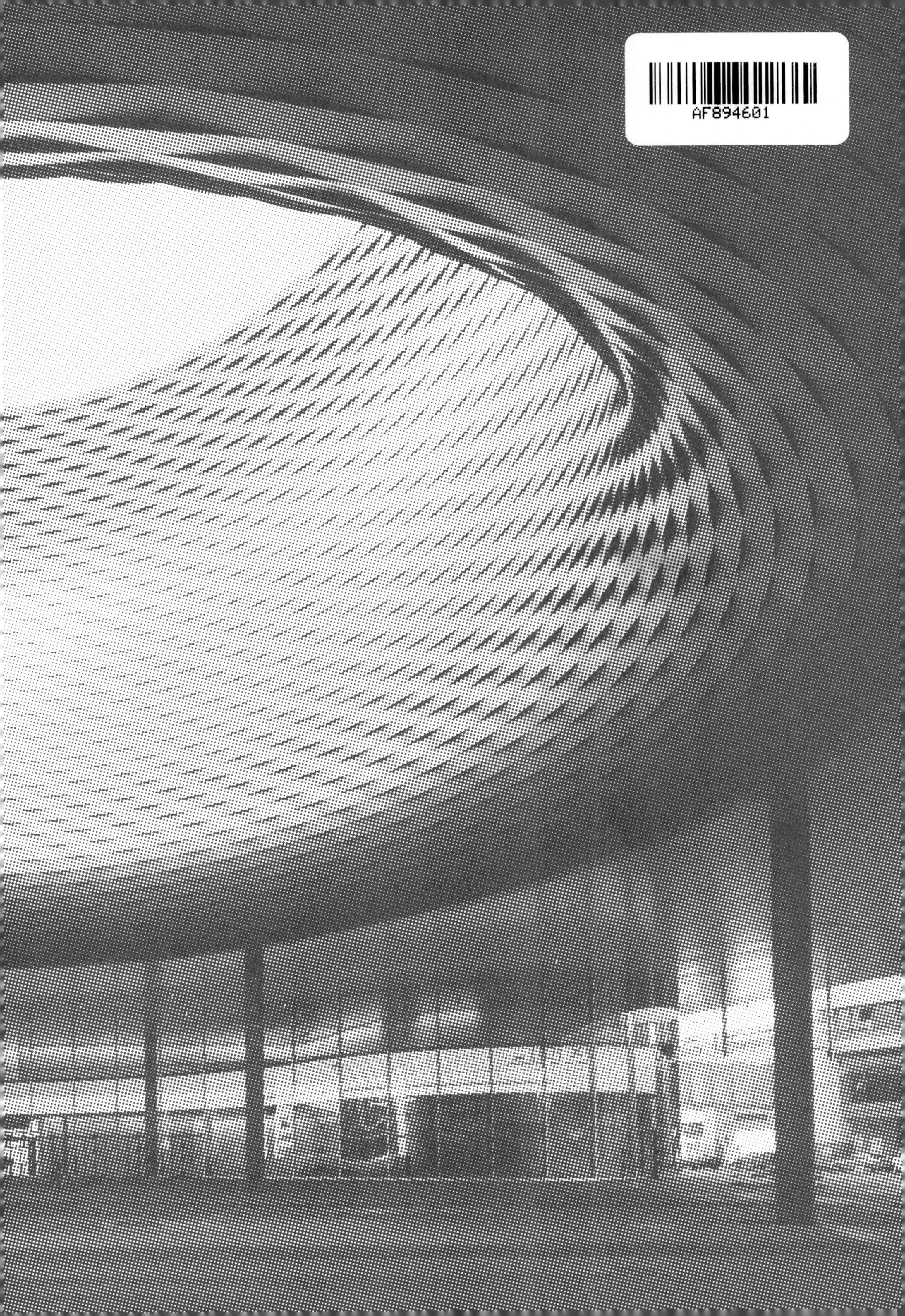

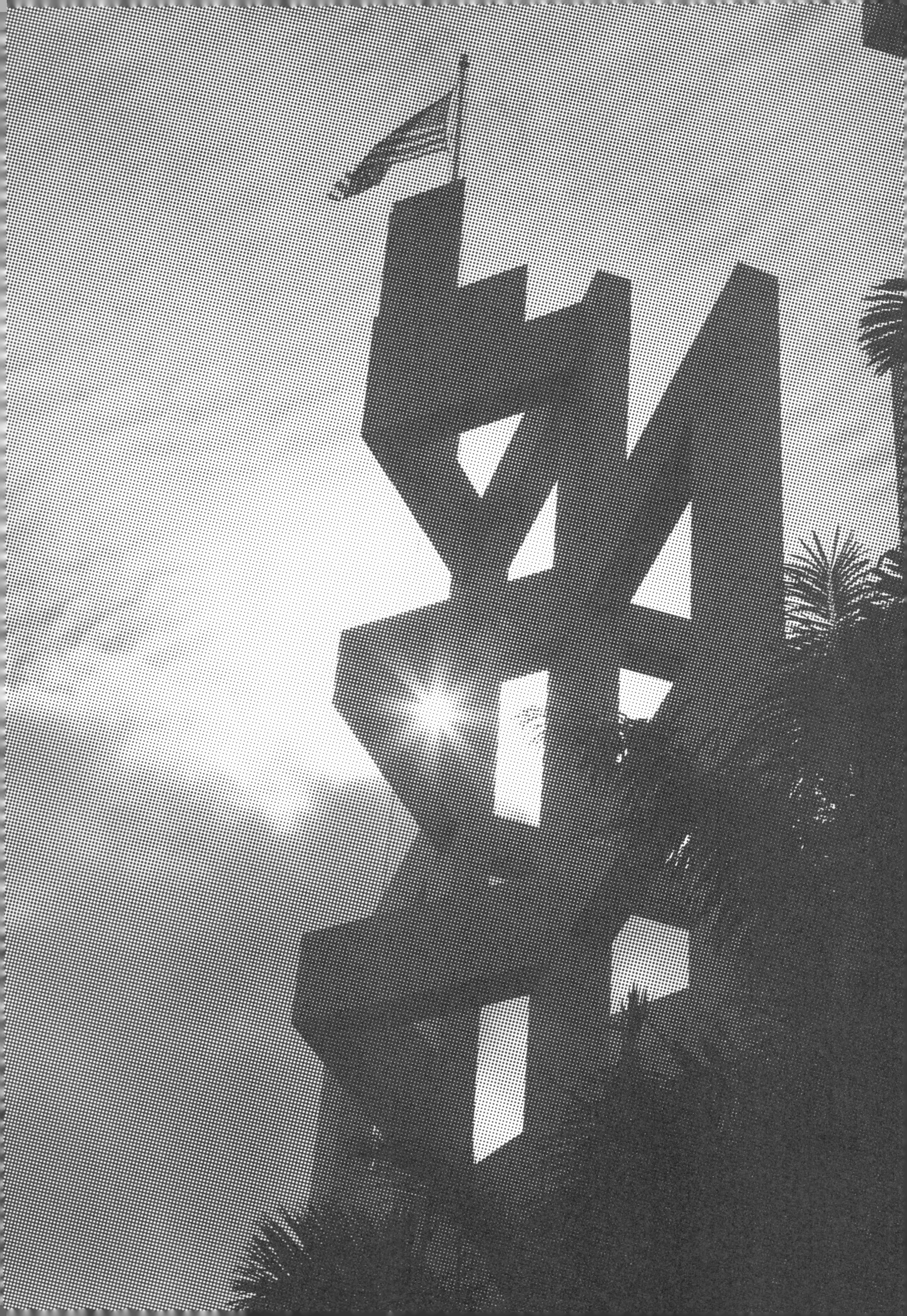

Art | Basel

YEAR 44

A–M

Hong Kong
Basel
Miami Beach

Table of Contents

#

N

O

P

Q

R

S

T

U

V

W

X

Y

Z

Galleries

Tour d'horizon: Harald Falckenberg

Every Era Gets the Art World It Deserves

The renowned Hamburg collector dissects the last few decades in the art world, which are marked by a growing complexity and mutability—and declares that retreat is not an option.

Harald Falckenberg, born in 1943, is a Doctor in Law, and Professor of Art Theory at the Hamburg Academy of Art since 2008. His collection of contemporary art, which comprises over 2,000 works, is shown in cooperation with renowned exhibition house Deichtorhallen/ Hamburg. Falckenberg is associated with the publishing houses Philo Fine Arts and Merve, and has written numerous essays on art and artists, collected in the anthologies *Ziviler Ungehorsam* (Civil Disobedience), 2002, and *Aus dem Maschinenraum der Kunst* (From the Engine Room of Art), 2007.

The term "art world" was coined in the mid-1960s by Arthur Coleman Danto, the influential American critic and pioneer of art theory who died on October 27, 2013, at the age of 89. Unlike the traditional art of representation, which sought to manifest the power and influence of the Church, the aristocracy, and the haute bourgeoisie as beautiful, good, and true, the art world stands for the complex referential system of contemporary art that is only accessible and explicable in the framework of economic, socio-political, academic, and philosophical contexts. Art's transgressive orientation found its programmatic expression in Joseph Beuys' notion of an "expanded concept of art." Danto dated the fall back to April 21, 1964, when Andy Warhol first presented the Brillo boxes at New York's Stable Gallery as the American consumer version of Marcel Duchamp's readymades. Pop art, "And that's supposed to be art?" was the outraged response, particularly among the representatives of the New York School of Art around Clement Greenberg, who wanted to establish a specifically American art with Abstract Expressionism and, in a second phase, Color Field paintings, in contrast to the Eurocentrism of the École de Paris. But there were many alternative models to the New York School in the 1960s and 1970s, in the form of Minimalism, Land art, and Conceptual art. In Europe, the Viennese Actionists and Fluxus came onto the scene, seeking to establish a free society defined by art.

Naturally, this is but a cursory overview of postwar art. But certainly Danto was right when he argued that the decisive impulse came from Warhol and of course Duchamp, who as the "godfather" of this development, celebrated a highly regarded retrospective of his works understood as anti-art in 1963 in Pasadena—50 years after the emergence of the first readymade, and after more than four decades of silence and absence from the art world. And still today—another 50 years later—Duchamp's influence on postmodernist art that deals with the object remains omnipresent among the latest generation of artists.

On the one hand, there is a political "critical art" that subverts the art world with strategies of intervention and techniques of deconstruction. It is interested in the framing conditions of artistic practice, with the goal of humanizing society. Feminism, gender, AIDS, urbanity, post-Fordism, and postcolonialism are the central questions treated in now almost 100 biennials and triennials around the world. documenta 10 under Catherine David (1997), and documenta 11 under Okwui Enwezor (2002), were platforms for such critical art. Its orientation and organization are defined by a network of internationally organized curators. The slanderous accusation of "curatism" is circulating as a new art form, with impresarios and virtuosos of concepts that use individual artists as living arguments and evidence of their own ideas.

The challenge against the art market welcomed by many critics in the run up to documenta 12 under Roger Buergel/Ruth Noack (2007) was no surprise. It is the art market that has played a decisive role in developments, up until today. The starting point was in the 1980s, a decade when conservative leaders such as Ronald Reagan, Margaret Thatcher, and Helmut Kohl defined the world's political climate. After many years of discourse in cultural theory, painting—called *Flachware*, literally "flatware," in the jargon of the art market—was once again in demand under the slogan of the "hunger for images." Neo-Expressionism, Transvanguardia, the Junge Wilden, the Pictures Generation, and Appropriation art drove the prices to heights that were previously inconceivable. Artists such as Richard Prince, Jeff Koons, and Haim Steinbach became leading figures in a movement that abandoned all scruples about the commercial use of art, and aggressively courted the art market, no longer wasting a thought on the elite notion of an artistic body of a life's work, an oeuvre. Bad Painting, deskilling, and fast-paced careers modeled after showbiz defined the art world. If Joseph Beuys' creed from the early 1970s, "Every person is an artist," reflected his romantic fusion of art and life, "Every artist is a person" was the laconic answer of punk artist Martin Kippenberger scarcely ten years later.

The art boom of the 1980s—it is claimed that there was more art sold during this decade than in all previous centuries combined—collapsed entirely in early 1990. The blame was attributed to the megalomania of Japanese investors and the future branch of a speculative market in new technologies. But it's not that simple. The international business world is closely linked to political and social developments. It's about power and counterpower, in the art world positions of resistance as propagated by the counterculture of Beatniks and Hippies and Pop art in the 1950s and 1960s. The Venice Biennale in 2013 under Massimiliano Gioni brought with it *Abart*, outsiders, and anthroposophists like Rudolf Steiner, fans of alternative societies, into a contemporary context with the art market. Developments since the Second World War have taken place at a ten-year rhythm. The boom in the art market in the 1960s under John F. Kennedy's motto of the "New Frontier" was followed by the crash of the 1970s with defeat in the Vietnam War and the oil crisis. Then there was the spectacular rebirth in the 1980s and the collapse of 1990, which has primarily to be traced back to the Western world's need to reorganize itself entirely and to use financial means to integrate the Eastern markets after the surprising end of the Soviet empire. As a result, under Presidents Bill Clinton and George W. Bush the financial markets and an unleashed banking system determined the course of events. Huge amounts of money were freed, generating a boom in the art market that began in 1998, far surpassing the turnover of the 1980s.

Today's art system involves many diverse forms of dependency and manipulation, all the way down to the level of the tabloid. It seems irrefutable that the artist is being rediscovered as a subject and person of resistance. And quite in the sense of long suppressed political art.

A key influence at the end of 1999 was the decision of international auction houses to include young contemporary art in their programs. The auctions were a shock, for they undercut the constructive work of the galleries. Many, not least the artists themselves, saw this as a betrayal. But the anger of the gallerists was short-lived. They quickly recognized the chance to keep the prices of young art stable by targeted bidding or, even better, driving up the prices just in time for planned openings. A decisive influence was played by the masters and billionaires Bernard Arnault, François Pinault, and Charles Saatchi, who with their eyes wide open, moved toward instrumentalizing art for their global market strategies. And with them the many speculators and financial jugglers who bet on young art, over the long term investing in dubious funds and in the short term throwing art back on the market at auctions.

The developments in recent decades are not free of irony. After starting with the goal of the avant-garde to anchor art beyond elitist notions and in people's lives, things have finally returned to that very point. Ours is now a society of the spectacle with sponsored happenings and large scale events that degrade art as a means of feeding the culture industry, and an art market with top prices for important works that only a few wealthy people and exquisite art institutions can afford. This can be understood as a step back toward the re-feudalization of art. Significant in this perspective was Jeff Koons' show at Versailles in September 2008, financed by Pinault. Just a week later, September 15 made history by highlighting the links between art, commerce, and speculation: this was the day when Damien Hirst, side-stepping his galleries and key supporters Charles Saatchi, Jay Jopling, and Larry Gagosian, delivered more than 200 works to Sotheby's London, created especially for the auction, and sold them for the miraculous sum of £111 million. And it was the very same day that Lehman Brothers in New York had to declare bankruptcy, with knock on effects that are still being felt by international economies today.

However much the end of art has repeatedly been asserted, it will not take place: art is always open to new developments. Every serious collection has to face this challenge.

In the meantime, most of the speculators have disappeared, and with them an art market that relied excessively on the hype of the young and the new. The program galleries are having a hard time. And yet, the media again and again announce new record prices for art. The world's rich are little affected by the crisis. They place their money in recognized art that they purchase at auctions or top-notch galleries that more and more often make a large part of their yields as art dealers on the "secondary market." For the rich, art is an investment; there is talk of a general flight to material assets in times of low interest rates and money laundering, but first and foremost art is seen as a luxury accessory and status symbol. Art in today's society has risen to become a new dominant culture, and like sport and showbiz is anchored in the system of international companies and the mass media. Products and news undergo an increase in value due to art. At issue are desires, longings, and personal individuality. The boundaries of design, fashion, and advertising have long since been transgressed. As creative potential, art and culture are tapped on all layers and marketed. Recently, the German tabloid *Bild* reported on the opening of Art Cologne: "Important art, even more important VIPs! Art has become the religion of high society. A guest of honor at the opening was Gabriele Inaara Begum Aga Khan. She was even more beautiful than much of the art on offer."

The development is relentless and not just a passing hype, as some steadfast optimists might like to think. Art as a religion—and this position is not only taken by the tabloids—seems absurd, but hits the nerve of a society that beyond the weary power pragmatics of Western politics dominated by the latest polls, and the unresolved world-wide cultural struggles, looks for salvation in the postmodern era. It's about meaning and greater significance. Money, power, and prestige stand as hard currency. The art world is a model of participation in the spirit of the old Surrealist slogan "Dreams that Money Can Buy." The dream factory of art is accessible to all, regardless of the size of their wallet. But for top artworks, as in sport or showbiz, top prices are being paid. The oft-cited art bubble is not going to burst.

During the course of this development, the artist has undergone an enormous increase in value to the point of idolization. But success has come at a high price, with the affirmation of the art system, the adjustment to taste guidelines, and the dependence on galleries and curators. To create something new all one's own, while remaining in the game, is a balancing act that only few succeed at mastering. We can notice art's return to style, ability, and technique, typical of the representational art that had been frowned upon for so long. We are confronted with pictures and works that are politically correct, but hardly have a chance of finding their way into mass media networks that rely on violating taboos and transgressing limits. Indubitably, the stars of the scene are the artists who take the fate of their art into their own hands, and create their own institutions that they control and administer with paid staff. Artists like Matthew Barney, Olafur Eliasson, Damien Hirst, and Jeff Koons represent this development, which takes the model of the artist-prince from past ages as its starting point.

Private collectors, due to their personal relationships with artists, gallerists, auction houses, museums, and critics, are among the most important networkers of the art system. But they are participating in a game of role-playing under the conditions of an art system that has a temporary character. Museums and other art institutions are now financially and time-wise so taxed with their exhibition programs, that there is little room for activities in the realm of their collections. They no longer want complete collections. Only a few works, or groups of works, are preferred. The reticence of institutions is one important reason why so many private museums have emerged in recent years. But this solution is limited to only few collectors, personally and financially. The desire of so many collectors to leave behind a monument of their long-term engagement with art is a dream far beyond the reality of the current art world.

The result of this study is disillusioning—which is not necessarily a bad thing. Art is a mirror of society. Every period gets the art it deserves. We see professional dealmakers, speculators, seduced collectors, and exhausted artists. Art as a counterpower? Since the early 1960s, there has been a struggle against the subjective. Today's art system involves many diverse forms of dependency and manipulation, all the way down to the level of the tabloid. It seems irrefutable that the artist is being rediscovered as a subject and person of resistance. And quite in the sense of long suppressed political art. How fragile the political systems are is revealed by the many struggles for freedom, and the revolts of current times. The powerful Chinese state can only defend itself against Ai Weiwei through house arrest. Strangely, he is allowed to keep his mobile phone and access to the Internet, in the hope that at some point there will be nobody left listening, and he can become a mere fiction. Weiwei, with his daring political protest, deserves the greatest respect, and yet he is part of the market-oriented and financial system of today's international art. His works are sold at top prices. At the Venice Biennale in 2013, he was exhibited in the French pavilion as a German contribution in exchange for the French contribution of the Albanian artist Anri Sala. Apparently this deal was worked out by German and French cultural officials, who naturally covered the lion's share of the cost. This has little to do with free art.

My aim is not to categorize art by attitude, authenticity, and creativity, or even by autonomy and freedom. These are empty terms of the seemingly ever-new that only gain importance in the context of history, as has been exemplarily outlined in the development of postwar art. However much the end of art has repeatedly been asserted, it will not take place: art is always open to new developments. Every serious collection has to face this challenge.

And it is certainly not my intention to speak for other collectors, who have different interests and convictions, but the focus of my collection always was and remains grounded on counterculture and Conceptual art. Currently I am exploring how these positions expand in the newest developments of contemporary art, as much through painting as through photographic-based or multimedia works.

My collection started with Punk, with young people who don't believe in anything anymore. Personally I'm neither a believer nor a pessimist: I'm convinced of evolution and, while others might think that evolution always leads to something better, to me there is no morality in that process. Just change.

Marc Spiegler
Director
Art Basel

Dear Reader,

The book you are holding represents an entirely new publication approach for Art Basel. Unlike past catalogues and show guides specific to a single fair, this book embodies a year in the art world as seen through our lens.

This was a landmark year for us—one during which Art Basel went truly global—and we have aimed to capture its vibrancy via our three shows, the art lovers attending them, and the host cities: Hong Kong, Basel, and Miami Beach. You will find photographs not only of individual artworks, but also of entire fair stands, revealing the architectures and juxtapositions that make great pieces resonate off each other. Likewise, we also asked eminent art world players to choose their favorite moments, pieces, and places from each show week. Of course, every exhibiting gallery is also spotlighted, in ways that give insights into the history and character of each. Finally, the book extends beyond the shows, covering people and places across the broader art world.

Why the new direction? Because what defines our shows is people. Whether they are artists, gallerists, curators, writers, museum directors, or private patrons, the art world within which Art Basel exists is constantly catalyzed by these personalities, people whose lives are driven forward by art.

Space constraints sadly preclude a detailed thanking of the galleries, cultural allies, partners, and team members who make Art Basel's year-round activities possible. Yet I would like to express gratitude to the two people who have most contributed to making this book a reality: Annette Schönholzer, Art Basel's Director of New Initiatives, and Lionel Bovier, Director of JRP|Ringier.

Wishing you many delights and discoveries over the following 774 pages.

Marc Spiegler, Director
Art Basel

Liebe Leserin, Lieber Leser

Wir freuen uns, Sie mit diesem Buch überraschen zu dürfen, denn wir haben hier einen ganz neuen Ansatz zugrunde gelegt. Im Unterschied zu den vorheriger Katalogen und Show Guides, die sich nur auf eine Messe bezogen, blicken wir in diesem Buch durch unsere ganz persönliche Brille auf das vergangene Jahr in der Kunstwelt zurück.

Das Jahr 2013 ist ein Meilenstein für uns – ein Jahr, in dem Art Basel weltweit zum Begriff geworden ist. Die Kraft und Vitalität dieses Jahres wollen wir in Bildern von den drei Messen, von deren kunstbegeisterten Besuchern und den Messestädten Hongkong, Basel und Miami Beach dokumentieren. Deshalb finden Sie hier nicht nur Fotografien einzelner Kunstwerke, sondern auch ganzer Messestände, wo grosse Kunstwerke durch eine gelungene Messearchitektur und eine geschickte Gegenüberstellung in ihrer Wirkung noch gegenseitig verstärken. Ausserdem haben wir Persönlichkeiten der Kunstszene gebeten, uns zu sagen, welches ihre schönsten Momente, Objekte und Orte bei jeder Messe waren. Selbstverständlich präsentieren wir auch alle ausstellenden Galerien. Dabei ist es uns wichtig, Einblick in die Geschichte und den besonderen Charakter jeder Galerie zu geben. Und über die Messen hinaus möchte das Buch schliesslich Menschen und Orte der grossen Welt der Kunst näherbringen.

Warum aber dieser neue Ansatz? Weil die Menschen das Herz unserer Kunstmessen sind. Ob Künstler, Galeristen, Kuratoren, Museumsdirektoren oder private Mäzene – diese Persönlichkeiten, diese Menschen, deren Lebensmotor die Kunst ist, sind die Katalysatoren der Kunstwelt.

Leider ist es aufgrund des begrenzten Platzes nicht möglich, allen Galerien, Partnern aus Kultur und Wirtschaft und Teammitgliedern, die die Aktivitäten der Art Basel das ganze Jahr über erst ermöglichen, im Einzelnen zu danken. Dennoch möchte ich zwei Menschen meinen herzlichen Dank ausdrücken, die einen wesentlichen Beitrag zur Entstehung dieses Buches geleistet haben: Annette Schönholzer, Director of New Initiatives der Art Basel, und Lionel Bovier, Direktor von JRP|Ringier.

Lassen Sie sich von den folgenden 773 Seiten in den Bann ziehen.

Marc Spiegler, Direktor
Art Basel

Estimada lectora, estimado lector

El libro que tiene entre sus manos responde a un enfoque de publicación completamente nuevo para Art Basel. A diferencia de los catálogos y guías de los años pasados, que eran específicos de una sola feria, estas páginas abarcan un año en el mundo del arte visto a través de nuestros ojos.

Un año crucial para nosotros, durante el cual Art Basel trascendió su espacio habitual para salir al mundo. Y en estas páginas nos hemos propuesto capturar la vitalidad de nuestras tres ferias, de los amantes del arte que las visitaron y de las tres ciudades anfitrionas: Hong Kong, Basilea y Miami Beach. Encontrará aquí fotografías, no solamente de las obras expuestas, sino también de algunos stands de exposición íntegros, que relevan las arquitecturas y yuxtaposiciones que dieron más resonancia a las distintas obras de arte. También hemos pedido a eminentes personalidades del mundo del arte que escogieran sus momentos, obras y lugares favoritos de cada semana de exposición. Como es natural, este libro presenta lo más destacable de las galerías, evidenciando asimismo aspectos históricos y el carácter de cada una de ellas. Pero esta publicación trasciende el espacio de las tres ferias y nos lleva a descubrir a diversas personas y diferentes lugares del amplio universo del arte.

¿Por qué hemos adoptado este nuevo enfoque? Porque lo que define nuestras muestras es la gente. Artistas, galeristas, curadores y directores de museos o mecenas particulares: son estas personas, que viven impulsadas por el arte, las que catalizan constantemente el mundo del arte en el que existe Art Basel.

El limitado espacio disponible no nos permite agradecer en detalle a todas las galerías y a todos los aliados culturales, colaboradores y miembros del equipo que han hecho posibles las actividades de Art Basel a lo largo del año. Deseo, sin embargo, expresar mi agradecimiento a las dos personas que más han contribuido a la realización de este libro: Annette Schönholzer, Directora de Nuevas Iniciativas de Art Basel, y Lionel Bovier, Director de JRP|Ringier.

Le deseo que disfrute de agradables e interesantes momentos descubriendo todo lo que le ofrecen estas 773 páginas.

Marc Spiegler, Director
Art Basel

Chère lectrice, cher lecteur,

L'ouvrage que vous avez entre les mains est le fruit d'une approche complètement nouvelle pour Art Basel. À la différence des catalogues ou des programmes consacrés à une seule manifestation, ce livre incarne une année dans le monde de l'art depuis notre optique.

Cette année a été particulièrement marquante pour nous – Art Basel a pris une dimension vraiment globale – et nous souhaitions en capturer l'atmosphère unique à travers nos trois expositions, les amateurs d'art qui les ont visitées et les villes où elles ont eu lieu : Hong Kong, Bâle et Miami Beach. Vous y trouverez non seulement des photographies d'œuvres individuelles qui y étaient présentées, mais aussi de stands dans leur ensemble, révélant ainsi les architectures et la mise en scène permettant aux œuvres de se mettre mutuellement en valeur. Pour chacune des semaines de l'exposition, nous avons également demandé à des membres éminents du monde de l'art de choisir leurs moments, leurs œuvres et leurs endroits préférés. L'accent est bien sûr également mis sur les galeries participantes, dont on découvre l'histoire et le caractère particuliers. Enfin, l'ouvrage dépasse le cadre des foires en s'ouvrant sur des personnalités et des événements extérieurs.

Pourquoi avoir choisi cette nouvelle orientation ? Parce que ce sont les êtres qui sont l'essence même de nos expositions. Qu'ils soient artistes, galeristes, commissaires d'exposition, directeurs de musée ou collectionneurs, le monde de l'art dans lequel Art Basel évolue est façonné en permanence par ces personnalités, portées par leur amour de l'art.

Les contraintes d'espace empêchent de remercier individuellement les galeries, les partenaires culturels et les membres des équipes grâce auxquels les activités d'Art Basel peuvent se dérouler tout au long de l'année. Je voudrais toutefois exprimer toute ma gratitude aux deux personnes qui ont le plus contribué à la réalisation de cet ouvrage : Annette Schönholzer, Directrice des Nouvelles Initiatives d'Art Basel, et Lionel Bovier, Directeur de JRP|Ringier.

Je souhaite que les 772 pages qui suivent soient pour vous la source de nombreux plaisirs et découvertes.

Marc Spiegler, Directeur
Art Basel

Gentile lettrice, gentile lettore,

Il libro che tiene tra le mani rappresenta per Art Basel un approccio alla pubblicazione completamente nuovo. A differenza dei cataloghi e delle guide relative a una singola fiera pubblicati negli anni scorsi, esso racchiude un anno di arte visto attraverso i nostri occhi.

Un anno cruciale per noi, durante il quale Art Basel è realmente diventata una fiera di portata globale. Noi da parte nostra ci siamo posti l'obiettivo di catturarne l'energia con le nostre tre esposizioni, i loro visitatori amanti dell'arte e le città che le hanno ospitate: Hong Kong, Basilea e Miami Beach. Troverà fotografie non solo di singole opere d'arte ma anche di interi stand fieristici, che mostrano le architetture e le giustapposizioni che amplificano le vibrazioni dei singoli capolavori. Abbiamo inoltre chiesto agli attori più eminenti del mondo dell'arte di scegliere i loro momenti, le opere e i luoghi preferiti di ogni settimana di esposizione. Naturalmente si puntano i riflettori anche su ogni singola galleria, evidenziando aspetti della storia e della personalità di ognuna di esse. Questo libro infine va oltre le esposizioni, presentando persone e luoghi di un mondo dell'arte più ampio.

Ciò che definisce le nostre esposizioni sono proprio le persone. Questo è il motivo per il quale abbiamo deciso di cambiare approccio. Che si tratti di artisti, galleristi, curatori, direttori di museo o sostenitori privati, il mondo dell'arte in cui esiste Art Basel viene costantemente catalizzato da queste figure, persone che vivono per l'arte.

Per limiti di spazio non è purtroppo possibile ringraziare in dettaglio tutte le gallerie, gli alleati culturali, i partner e i collaboratori che rendono possibili le attività di Art Basel tutto l'anno. Desidero tuttavia esprimere la mia gratitudine alle due persone che hanno contributo più di tutte alla realizzazione di questo libro: Annette Schönholzer, Direttrice Nuove iniziative di Art Basel, e Lionel Bovier, Direttore di JRP|Ringier.

Le auguro di trovare spunti piacevoli e fare interessanti scoperte in queste 772 pagine.

Marc Spiegler, Direttore
Art Basel

尊敬的讀者：

您現在手上拿著的這本書，展現了巴塞爾藝術展的全新出版方式。與以往專門提供單一展會的目錄和參觀指南不同，本書收錄了我們在鏡頭之下藝術世界的全年傑作。

今年，我們正式踏入了新的里程——巴塞爾藝術展終於向全球邁進。我們已訂立明確目標，旨在以我們的三個展會、出席展會的愛好者，以及香港、巴塞爾和邁阿密海灘三個城市，捕捉美妙的活力時刻。您將會看到的相片，並非僅僅是個人藝術作品，書中還有整個展台的相片，展現出多種特色建築，並將各件偉大作品並置排列，使其產生共鳴，互相輝映。同樣，我們也會在展會期間的每個星期，邀請一眾藝術家前來挑選他們最喜愛的時刻、作品和地點。當然，每個藝廊都會得到注視，各種表現方式將能夠引導觀賞者深入探討每件作品的歷史和特色。最後，本書的視角更會延伸至展會之外，介紹廣闊藝術世界裡的人物和地點。

為何採用新的方向？正正是因為人的因素，才最能夠為展會賦予精彩意義。無論他們是藝術家、畫廊經營者、策展人、博物館總監還是私人贊助者，巴塞爾藝術展身處的藝術世界都不斷受到這些名人的催化影響——因為這些藝術家的生活，全部都以藝術來驅使前進。

因空間所限，我們惜無法列出詳細名單，完整表達對各個藝廊、文化同盟、合作夥伴和團隊成員的真切感謝，他們對巴塞爾藝術展的全年活動實在貢獻良多。但是我希望在此感謝兩位對製作本書作出最大貢獻的人：巴塞爾藝術展新措施總監 Annette Schönholzer 以及 JRP|Ringier 總監 Lionel Bovier。

希望您在閱讀隨後的771頁時，能夠洋溢出愉悦之情和找出各種精彩發現。

Marc Spiegler, Art Basel巴塞爾藝術展藝術總監

亲爱的读者:

您所持的这本书是了解巴塞尔艺术展的全新刊物。与以前的、针对单个展览的目录和展览指南不同，这本书透过我们的镜头表现艺术世界的一年。

这是我们具有里程碑意义的一年——巴塞尔艺术展真正走向全球的一年，通过在香港、巴塞尔和迈阿密海滩三地主办展览，艺术爱好者们参加展览，我们已朝着捕捉其活力的目标发展。不仅您会找到每个艺术品的照片，而且您会找到全部展览展台的照片，展现彼此共鸣的建筑风格和并置影像。同样，我们也邀请著名的艺术世界玩家从每个展览周中选择他们钟爱的瞬间、作品和场地。当然，每个展出的艺廊也被聚光灯照得通明，让各个艺廊彰显其历史和特色的韵味。最后，这本书延伸出展览之外，将更广阔艺术世界的人和场地囊括其中。

为什么这是新趋势? 因为不论是艺术家、画廊、馆长、博物馆院长，还是私人赞助人，决定我们展览存在的是人，巴塞尔艺术展所在的艺术世界是由这些人生被艺术推动

的人物不断促进的。

很遗憾，由于空间限制，无法逐一对支持巴塞尔艺术展全年活动的画廊、文联、合作伙伴和成员表示感谢。我还是想要特别感谢2个人，他们对这本书的出版做了最多贡献，他们是: Annette Schönholzer, 巴塞尔艺术展的新创意总监; Lionel Bovier, JRP|Ringier 的总监。

祝你们在接下来的771页有许多欣喜和发现,

Marc Spiegler
总裁
巴塞尔艺术展

Galleries by City

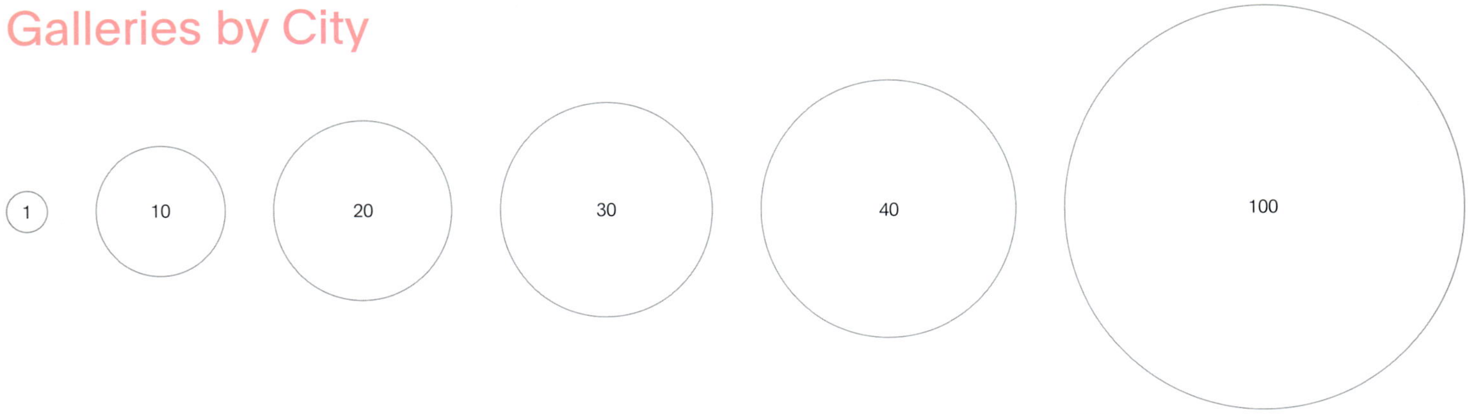

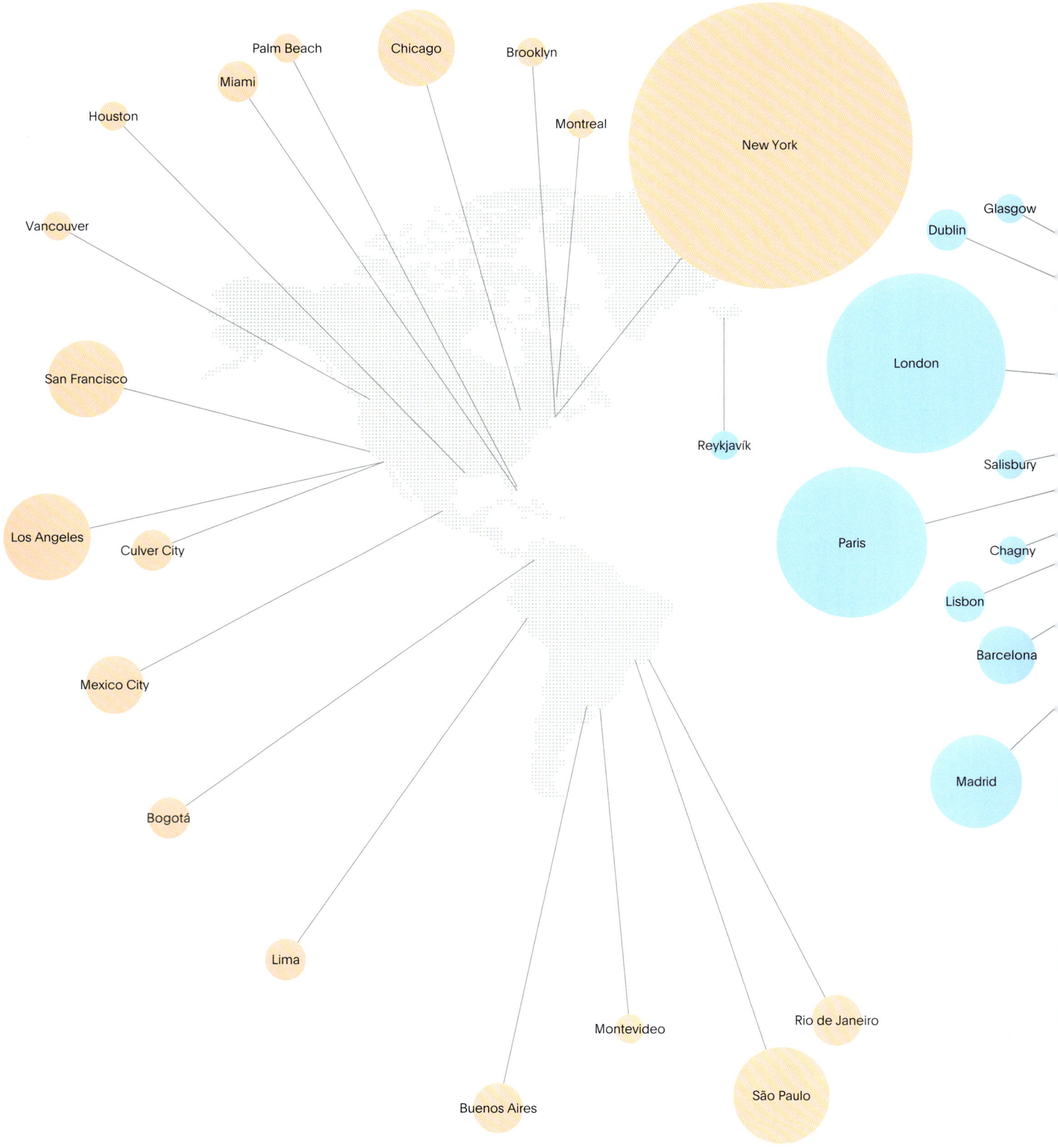

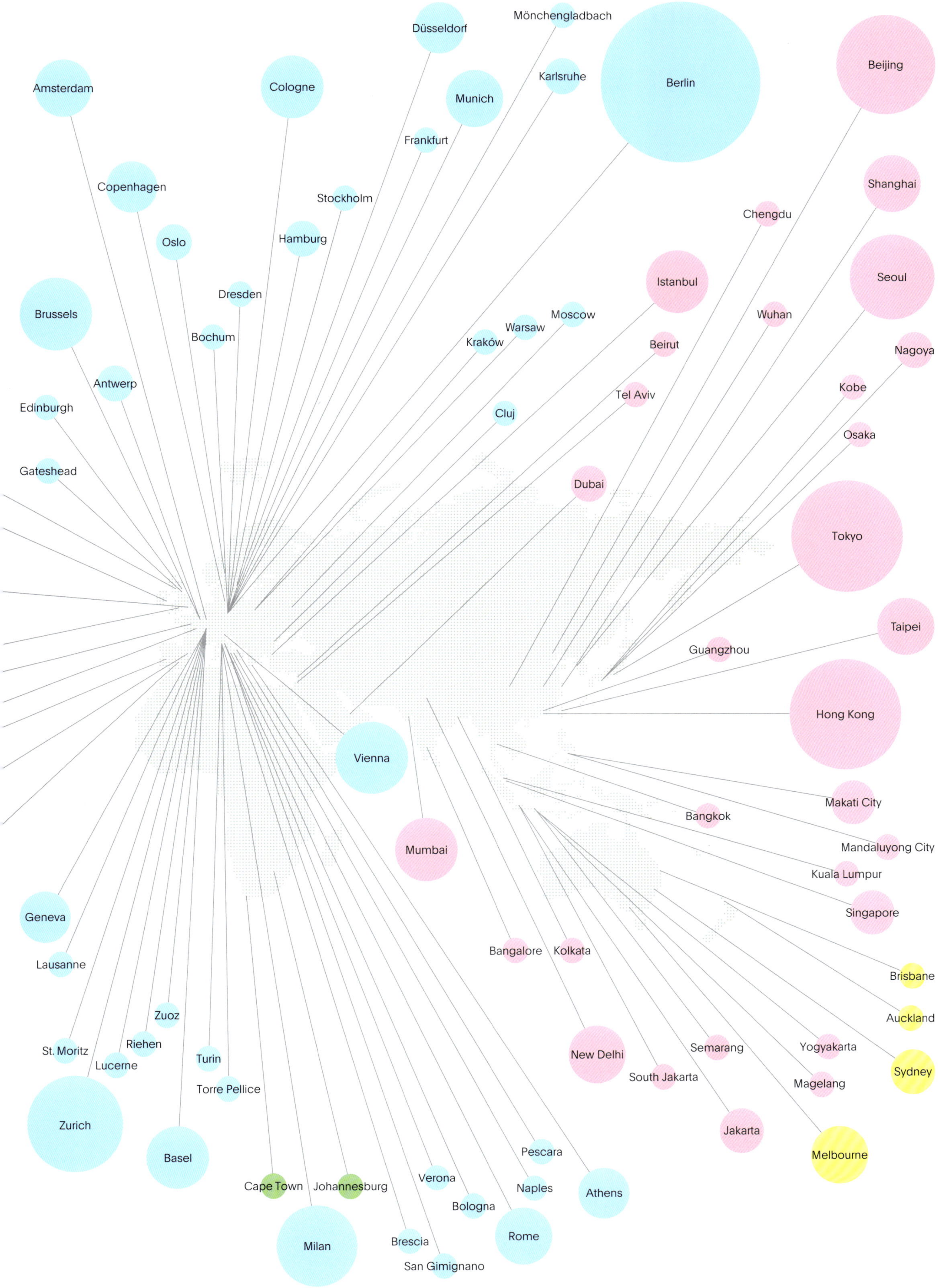
Mönchengladbach
Düsseldorf
Berlin
Beijing
Amsterdam
Cologne
Munich
Karlsruhe
Frankfurt
Copenhagen
Stockholm
Shanghai
Chengdu
Oslo
Hamburg
Istanbul
Seoul
Dresden
Brussels
Bochum
Moscow
Warsaw
Kraków
Wuhan
Beirut
Nagoya
Antwerp
Edinburgh
Tel Aviv
Kobe
Cluj
Osaka
Gateshead
Dubai
Tokyo
Taipei
Guangzhou
Hong Kong
Vienna
Makati City
Bangkok
Mumbai
Mandaluyong City
Kuala Lumpur
Singapore
Geneva
Bangalore
Kolkata
Lausanne
Brisbane
Auckland
Zuoz
Riehen
St. Moritz
Lucerne
Turin
New Delhi
Semarang
Yogyakarta
Sydney
South Jakarta
Magelang
Torre Pellice
Zurich
Basel
Jakarta
Melbourne
Pescara
Cape Town
Johannesburg
Verona
Naples
Athens
Bologna
Milan
Rome
Brescia
San Gimignano

Galleries by Country

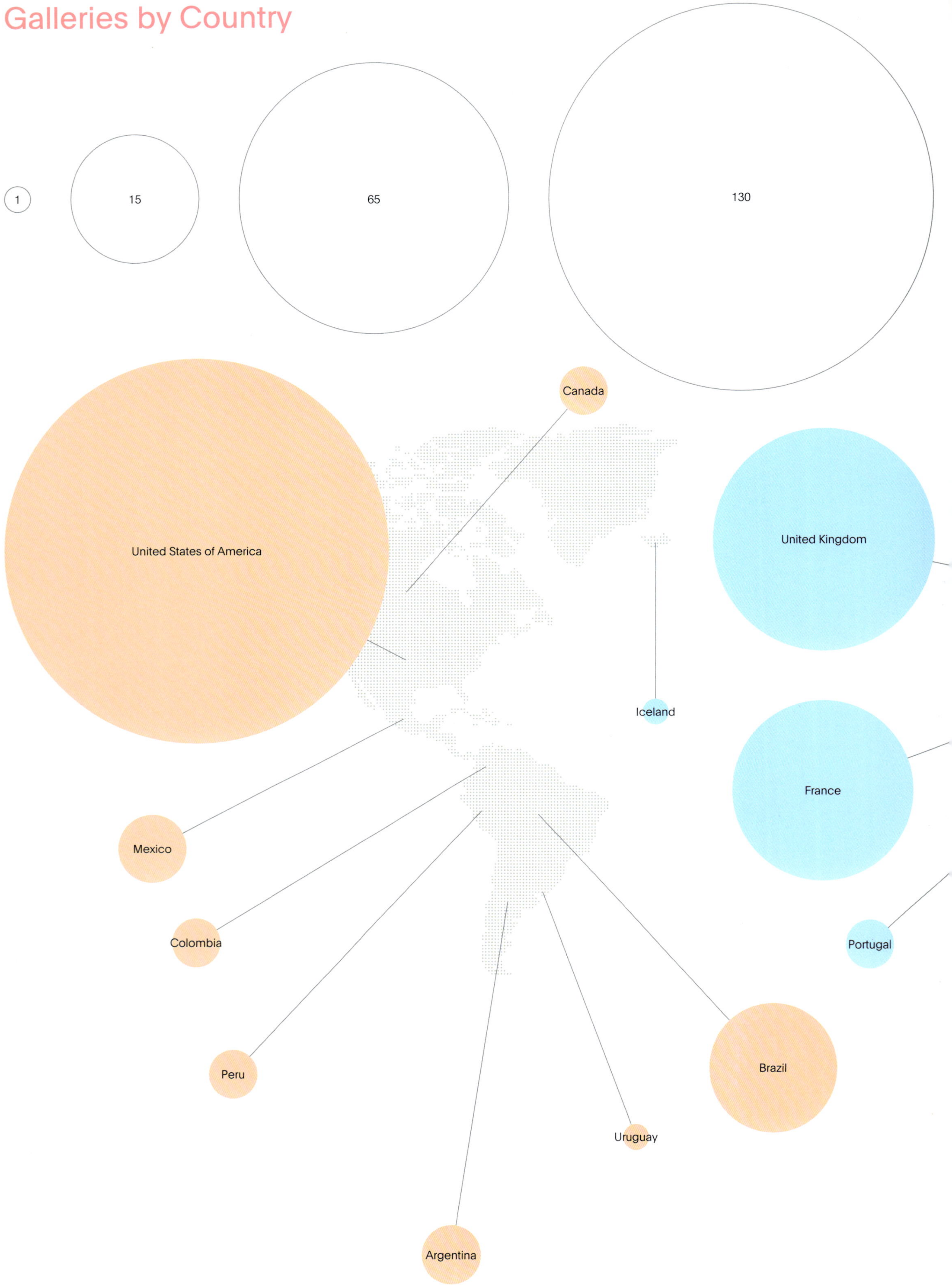

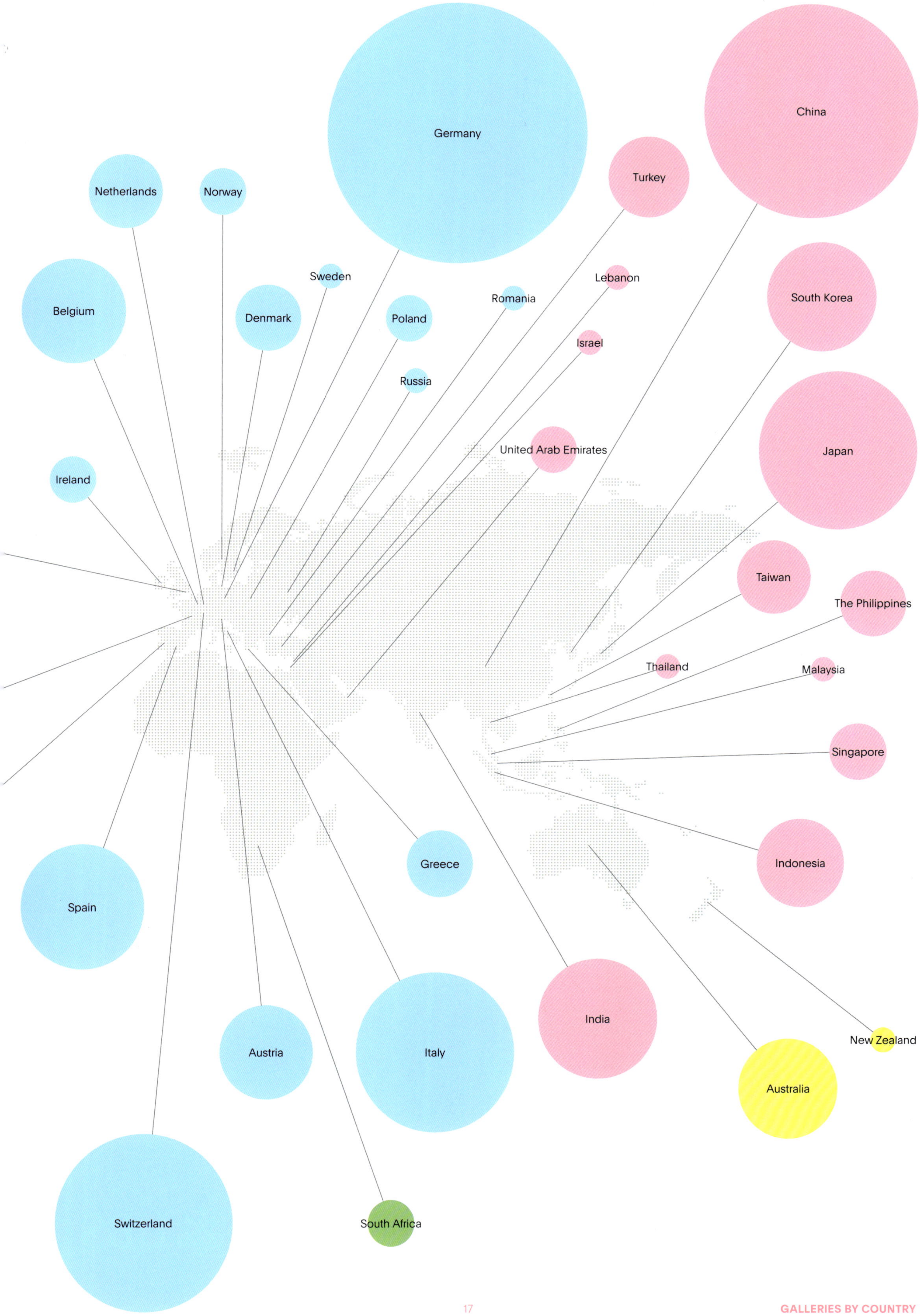
Germany
China
Netherlands
Norway
Turkey
Sweden
Lebanon
Belgium
Denmark
Poland
Romania
South Korea
Israel
Russia
Japan
United Arab Emirates
Ireland
Taiwan
The Philippines
Thailand
Malaysia
Singapore
Indonesia
Greece
Spain
India
New Zealand
Austria
Italy
Australia
Switzerland
South Africa

Art | Basel

Hong Kong | May | 15–18 | 2014

Art | Basel

Basel | June | 19–22 | 2014

M
.CH

UBS

Art | Basel
Miami Beach | Dec | 4–7 | 2014

Global Partners

Lead Partner

Associate Partners

Lounge Hosts

Official Partner

Automotive

Carrier

Local Partners

Hong Kong
Lounge Hosts

Official Hotel

Official Concierge

Basel
Show Partners

Lounge Host

Miami Beach
Official Hotels

Media Partners

Global

Hong Kong

Basel

Miami Beach

Statement by Sergio P. Ermotti
Group Chief Executive Officer
UBS

Whenever we are asked why UBS has enjoyed such a long association with Art Basel—going back to 1994—we always explain that this fair is a premier event for art collectors—which aligns very well with our own interest in collecting art as demonstrated by the UBS Art Collection.

Collecting contemporary art is an integral part of our corporate culture—a pursuit that brings innovative thinking and fresh perspectives into our offices every day. It connects us with key audiences at leading museums through loans and exhibitions from the world-renowned UBS Art Collection. It inspires and challenges us, in a way that meshes perfectly with our daily work in collecting knowledge, interpreting fast-changing situations, and exploring opportunities in the financial world.

For these reasons, we understand and share the passion that many of our clients feel for collecting contemporary art. Our clients, in turn, recognize UBS as a trusted partner in this exciting field. They look to us to provide them with information, insights, and a very high level of access to the best in contemporary art, whether they are enjoying one of the Art Basel shows, visiting an outstanding museum exhibition, or participating in the extraordinarily dynamic art market. Insight is also provided through our client services such as the UBS Art Competence Center or the UBS Arts Forum, which provide access to outside leading experts in the field of contemporary art.

Like so many of our clients, UBS wants to be wherever the art world gathers, contributing meaningfully to the dialogue about art. That is why we collaborate with several museums across the world and, first and foremost, why we have become the global Lead Partner of Art Basel, joining with the organization at its shows in Basel, Miami Beach, and now Hong Kong.

We congratulate Art Basel on its ongoing success and look forward to meeting again with our clients and friends, arts professionals, and fellow collectors at one of the great cultural gatherings in the world.

Mitteilung von Sergio P. Ermotti
Group Chief Executive Officer UBS

Die Frage, warum UBS die Art Basel seit 1994 als Partner unterstützt, lässt sich mit einem Satz beantworten: Die Art Basel ist eine der bedeutendsten Veranstaltungen für Kunstsammler. Damit entspricht sie unserem eigenen Interesse an Kunst, denn durch die UBS Art Collection gehört auch UBS zu den Sammlern.

Kunst zu sammeln ist Bestandteil der Unternehmenskultur von UBS. Die UBS Art Collection bringt mit zeitgenössischer Kunst täglich innovative Denkweisen und frische Perspektiven in unsere Räumlichkeiten und unsere Arbeit. Unsere renommierte Sammlung bietet durch Leihgaben und Ausstellungen in führenden Museen wichtige Anknüpfungspunkte zu unseren Zielgruppen. Die Sammeltätigkeit ist für uns Anregung und Herausforderung zugleich und fügt sich nahtlos in unser tägliches Bestreben ein, Wissen zusammenzutragen, Veränderungen rasch zu erfassen und neue Möglichkeiten in der Finanzwelt auszuloten.

Daher verstehen und teilen wir die Leidenschaft vieler unserer Kunden, die zeitgenössische Kunst sammeln. Unsere Kunden wenden sich an uns als zuverlässigen Partner, der ihnen Fachwissen, Marktkenntnisse und Zugang zu erstklassiger zeitgenössischer Kunst bietet. Das kann den Besuch einer Messe der Art Basel oder einer hochkarätigen Ausstellung beinhalten ebenso wie die Partizipation am ausserordentlich dynamischen Kunstmarkt. Unser Know-how vermitteln wir zudem über das UBS Art Competence Center und das UBS Arts Forum. Letzteres ermöglicht einen direkten Zugang zu führenden externen Experten für zeitgenössische Kunst.

Wie so viele unserer Kunden will UBS sich aktiv im Dialog über Kunst engagieren und vor Ort sein, wenn sich die Kunstwelt trifft. Deshalb kooperieren wir mit mehreren Museen weltweit. Insbesondere deshalb sind wir globaler Lead Partner der Art Basel und arbeiten mit dieser Organisation an ihren Kunstmessen in Basel, Miami Beach und neuerdings auch Hongkong zusammen.

Wir gratulieren der Art Basel zu ihrem anhaltenden Erfolg und freuen uns darauf, unsere Kunden und Freunde sowie Kunstexperten und gleichgesinnte Sammler bei diesen weltweit bedeutenden Kulturveranstaltungen zu treffen.

Comunicado de Sergio P. Ermotti
Group Chief Executive Officer UBS

Siempre que nos preguntan por qué UBS mantiene una relación tan prolongada con Art Basel, que comenzó ya en 1994, explicamos que esta feria es uno de los eventos más importantes para los coleccionistas de arte y que, como coleccionistas de arte que somos, es perfectamente compatible con nuestro propio interés, como demuestra la UBS Art Collection.

Coleccionar arte contemporáneo es una parte fundamental de la cultura corporativa. El arte contemporáneo lleva cada día ideas y perspectivas innovadoras a nuestras oficinas. Nos relaciona con públicos clave de importantes museos a través de las obras prestadas y de las exposiciones de la prestigiosa UBS Art Collection. Nos inspira y desafía de una forma que encaja a la perfección con nuestras tareas cotidianas, que consisten en reunir conocimientos, interpretar situaciones que cambian rápidamente y explorar las oportunidades del mundo financiero.

Por estos motivos, comprendemos y compartimos la pasión que sienten muchos de nuestros clientes por coleccionar arte contemporáneo. Nuestros clientes, por su parte, consideran que UBS es un socio de confianza en este ámbito tan emocionante. Esperan que les proporcionemos información y conocimientos y que les facilitemos el acceso al mejor arte contemporáneo, ya sea en uno de los festivales de Art Basel, mientras visitan una magnífica exposición en cualquier museo o mediante la participación en el extraordinariamente dinámico mercado del arte. Además, a través de nuestros servicios para clientes, como el UBS Art Competence Center o el UBS Arts Forum, ponemos a su disposición una serie de conocimientos que permiten acceder a expertos externos en el campo del arte contemporáneo.

Al igual que muchos de nuestros clientes, UBS quiere estar presente allá donde se encuentre el arte y contribuir significativamente al diálogo acerca de él. Es por esto que colaboramos con diversos museos de todo el mundo y, sobre todo, por lo que estamos orgullosos de ser el principal socio mundial de Art Basel, participando en la organización de sus festivales en Basilea, Miami Beach y ahora en Hong Kong.

Queremos felicitar a Art Basel por su exitosa trayectoria y expresar nuestro deseo de volver a encontrarnos con nuestros clientes y amigos, profesionales del arte y coleccionistas como nosotros en uno de los mayores encuentros culturales del mundo.

的致詞 Sergio P. Ermotti
集團行政總裁
瑞銀

每當被問及瑞銀集團與巴塞爾藝術展自1994年以來一直保持的長久聯繫時，我必會解釋，巴塞爾藝術展是藝術收藏界的盛事，這與瑞銀集團藝術收藏部在藝術收藏方面所表現出的濃厚興趣非常一致。

收藏當代藝術品是我們企業文化中不可或缺的一部分：藉此每日將創新的思維及新穎的觀點帶進我們的辦公室。世界知名的瑞銀集團藝術收藏部通過出借展品和舉辦展覽，將我們與頂尖藝術館的主要觀眾聯繫在一起。它為我們帶來啟發與挑戰，這正與我們在金融世界中匯集知識、解讀瞬息萬變的局勢并不斷探索機會的日常工作非常吻合。

因此，我們深深了解並分享客戶對收藏當代藝術的熱愛。客戶亦繼而在這一精彩的領域中視瑞銀為可信賴的夥伴。不論客戶參觀任何一個巴塞爾藝術展或一場傑出的藝術館展覽，或是參與那朝氣蓬勃的藝術現場，他們都倚賴我們提供資訊、觀點，以及眾多接觸頂級當代藝術的途徑。我們亦通過瑞銀集團藝術才華中心或瑞銀藝術論壇等服務為客戶提供觀點，並使其接觸到外界頂尖的當代藝術家。

正如我們許多客戶一樣，瑞銀希望與藝術界緊密合作，為藝術交流對話做出積極貢獻。因此，我們很榮幸與全球數家博物館進行合作，亦尤其榮幸成為巴塞爾藝術展的全球主要合作夥伴，并與其在巴塞爾、邁阿密海灘以及正在香港舉辦的展覽中進行合作。

瑞銀祝賀巴塞爾藝術展不斷取得成功，並期待將來在世界某個頂級文化聚會上，再次與各位客戶、朋友、藝術家及收藏家們見面。

Concentrated watercolors,
water-based acrylics, and water

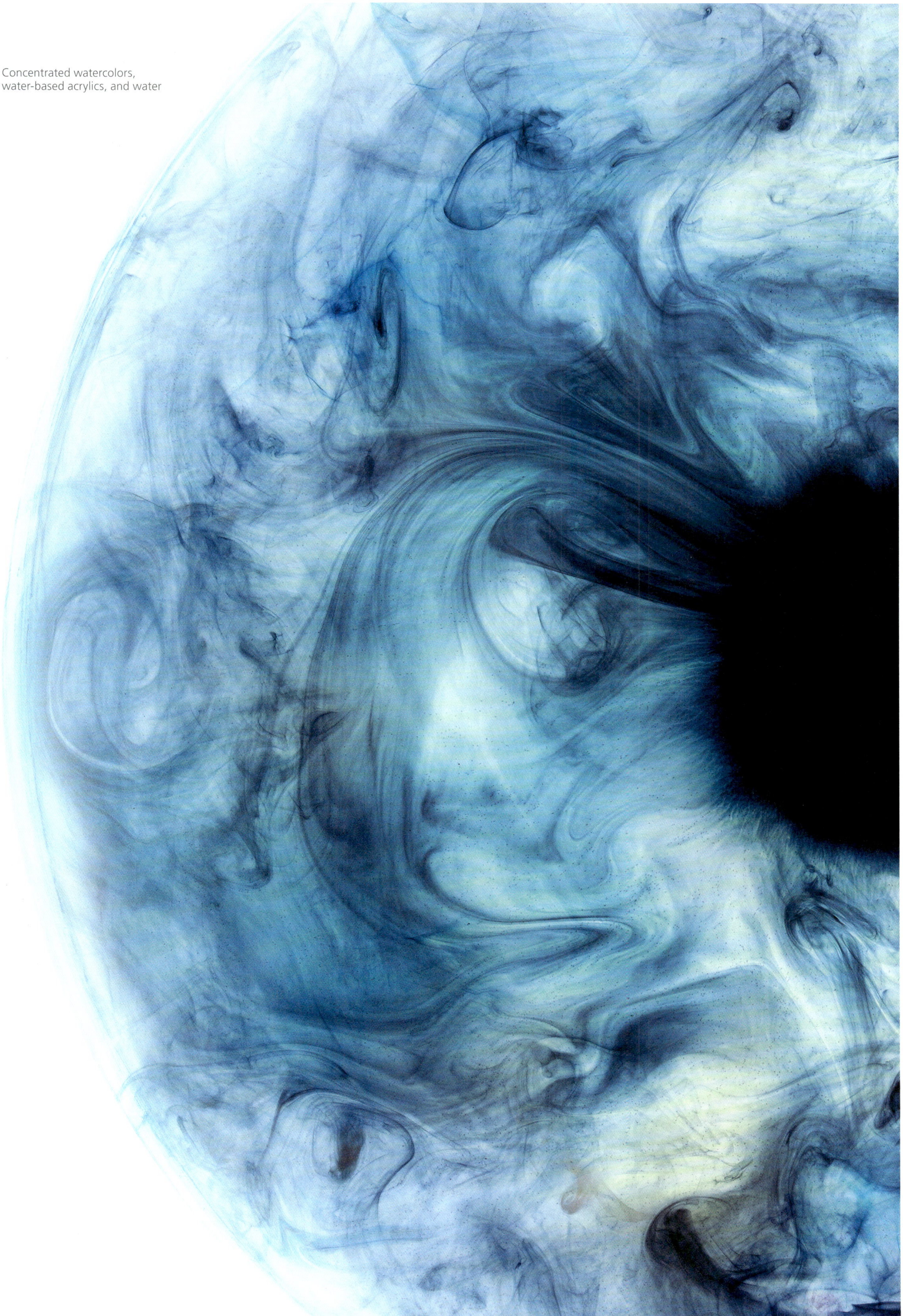

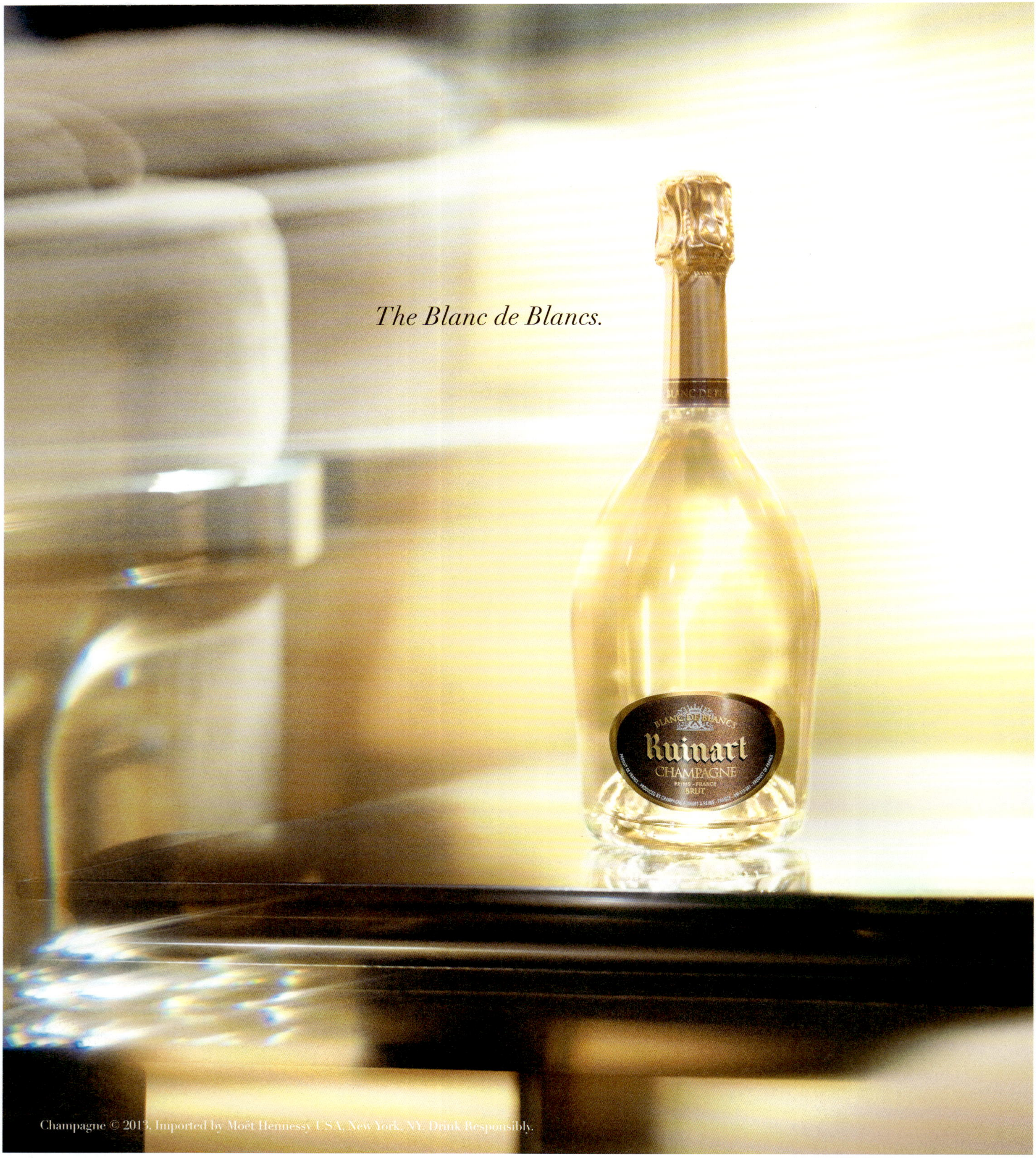
The Blanc de Blancs.
BLANC DE BLANCS
Ruinart
CHAMPAGNE
BRUT
Champagne © 2013. Imported by Moët Hennessy USA, New York, NY. Drink Responsibly.

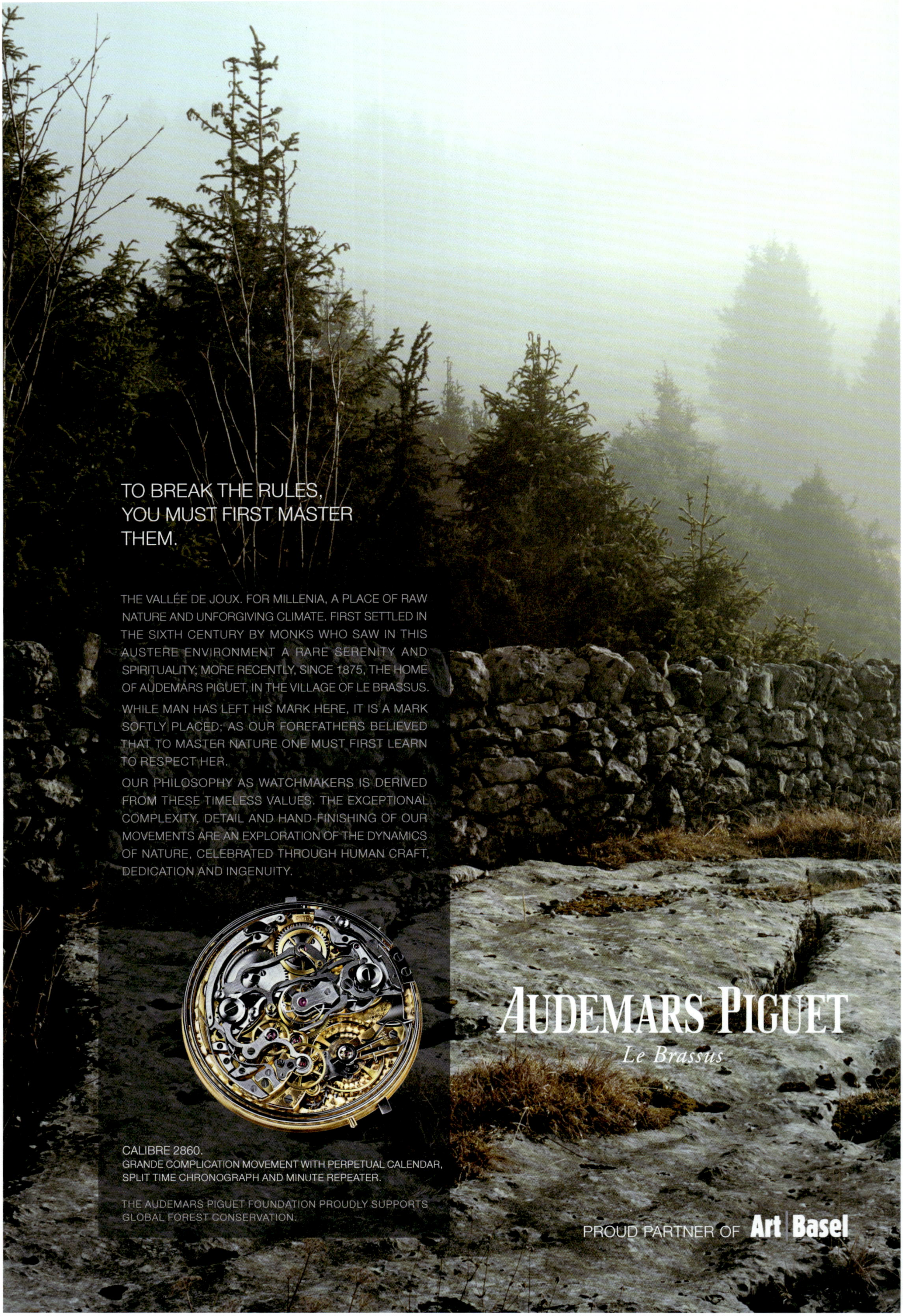
TO BREAK THE RULES, YOU MUST FIRST MASTER THEM.
THE VALLÉE DE JOUX. FOR MILLENIA, A PLACE OF RAW NATURE AND UNFORGIVING CLIMATE. FIRST SETTLED IN THE SIXTH CENTURY BY MONKS WHO SAW IN THIS AUSTERE ENVIRONMENT A RARE SERENITY AND SPIRITUALITY; MORE RECENTLY, SINCE 1875, THE HOME OF AUDEMARS PIGUET, IN THE VILLAGE OF LE BRASSUS.
WHILE MAN HAS LEFT HIS MARK HERE, IT IS A MARK SOFTLY PLACED; AS OUR FOREFATHERS BELIEVED THAT TO MASTER NATURE ONE MUST FIRST LEARN TO RESPECT HER.
OUR PHILOSOPHY AS WATCHMAKERS IS DERIVED FROM THESE TIMELESS VALUES. THE EXCEPTIONAL COMPLEXITY, DETAIL AND HAND-FINISHING OF OUR MOVEMENTS ARE AN EXPLORATION OF THE DYNAMICS OF NATURE, CELEBRATED THROUGH HUMAN CRAFT, DEDICATION AND INGENUITY.
AUDEMARS PIGUET
Le Brassus
CALIBRE 2860.
GRANDE COMPLICATION MOVEMENT WITH PERPETUAL CALENDAR, SPLIT TIME CHRONOGRAPH AND MINUTE REPEATER.
THE AUDEMARS PIGUET FOUNDATION PROUDLY SUPPORTS GLOBAL FOREST CONSERVATION.
PROUD PARTNER OF Art Basel

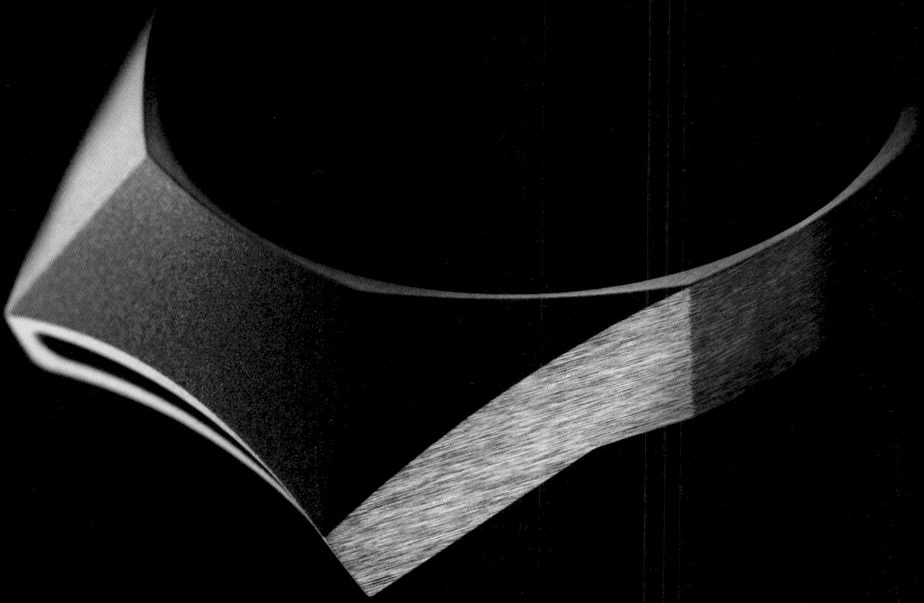

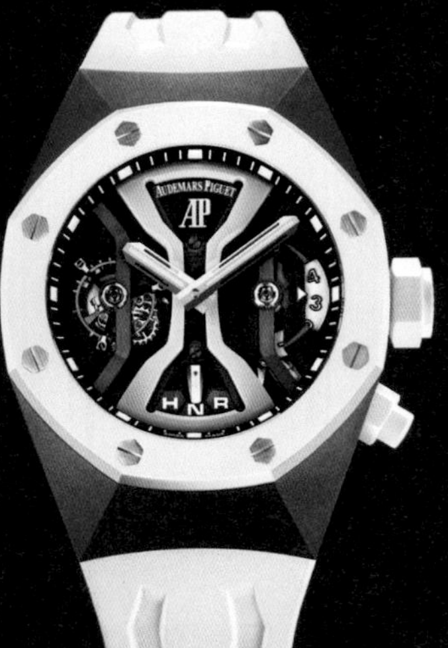

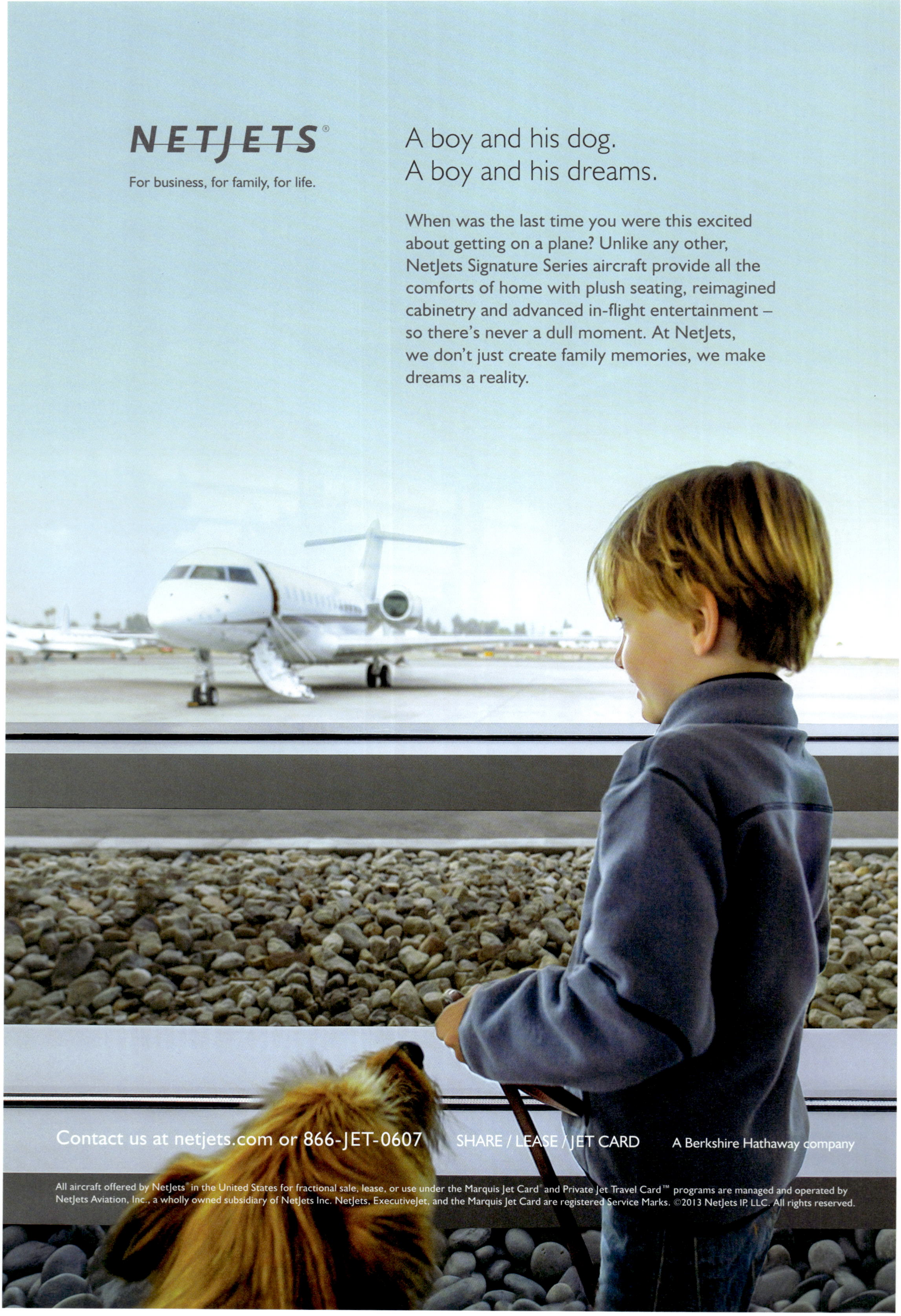
NETJETS®
For business, for family, for life.
A boy and his dog.
A boy and his dreams.
When was the last time you were this excited about getting on a plane? Unlike any other, NetJets Signature Series aircraft provide all the comforts of home with plush seating, reimagined cabinetry and advanced in-flight entertainment – so there's never a dull moment. At NetJets, we don't just create family memories, we make dreams a reality.
Contact us at netjets.com or 866-JET-0607
SHARE / LEASE / JET CARD
A Berkshire Hathaway company
All aircraft offered by NetJets® in the United States for fractional sale, lease, or use under the Marquis Jet Card® and Private Jet Travel Card™ programs are managed and operated by NetJets Aviation, Inc., a wholly owned subsidiary of NetJets Inc. NetJets, ExecutiveJet, and the Marquis Jet Card are registered Service Marks. ©2013 NetJets IP, LLC. All rights reserved.

A

A

- Hong Kong
- Basel
- Miami Beach

A

A Gentil Carioca

Rio de Janeiro — Galleries Kabinett

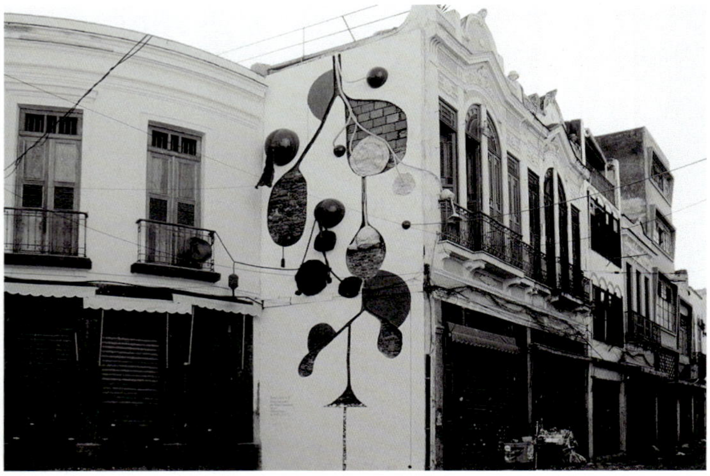

What first compelled you to open a gallery?
The need to have a space in Rio de Janeiro with a program that reflected the artists' way of seeing and thinking.

Who is the first artist you showed and what was most memorable about that show?
Fabiano Gonper, an artist from the northeast of Brazil; nobody knew him at the time in the Rio/São Paulo axis. Also no one knew what A Gentil Carioca was, which had opened in the blink of an eye, out of necessity, from an urgency we felt to have a new space in the city. The first work to be sold in Gentil's inaugural exhibition was to the Brazilian artist Antonio Dias—something symbolic to us!

When did you first participate in Art Basel and what was most memorable about that show?
In 2007, in Miami Beach, we presented a project in which Ricardo Basbaum transformed a container from Art Positions into a discussion of the art market and its globalization.

- **Contact** A Gentil Carioca
  Tatiana Bührnheim
  tatiana@agentilcarioca.com.br
  correio@agentilcarioca.com.br
- **Established** 2003
- **Owner(s) / Partner(s)** Laura Lima
  Marcio Botner
  Ernesto Neto
- **Team** 5
- **Space(s)** 106 m² + 141 m² + 64.5 m²
- **Artists at Art Basel** Ricardo Basbaum
  José Bento
  Botner & Pedro
  Carlos Bunga
  Cabelo
  Carlos Contente
  Guga Ferraz
  Fabiano Gonper
  Maria Laet
  Laura Lima
  Jarbas Lopes
  Renata Lucas
  Simone Michelin
  João Modé
  Paulo Nenflidio
  Maria Nepomuceno
  Hélio Oiticica & Neville D'Almeida
  Bernardo Ramalho
  Thiago Rocha Pitta
  Rodrigo Torres
  Pedro Varela
  Alexandre Vogler

A Thousand Plateaus

Chengdu — Insights

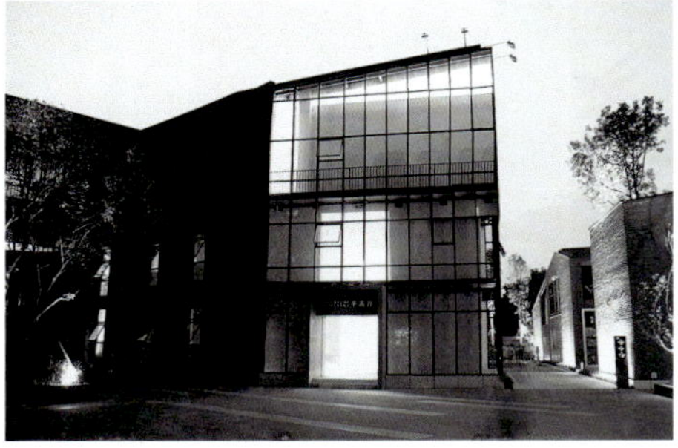

What first compelled you to open a gallery?
With its exhibition hall and screening room, A Thousand Plateaus Art Space is a professional gallery committed to presenting and promoting China's contemporary art. It is mainly about researching, presenting, and promoting outstanding works and experimental projects by emerging Chinese artists, and actively carrying out domestic and international cooperation projects.

Who is the first artist you showed and what was most memorable about that show?
Our first exhibition was *Disembedding*, a group exhibition including Fang Lijun, Shu Qun, Wang Yin, etc. The title of the exhibition fit in with our gallery name, A Thousand Plateaus, a reference to Gilles Deleuze's book. The artistic vision of the gallery runs parallel to the ideas formulated by the French philosophers Deleuze and Guattari. In line with their views, we want to provide a space where the artists and the artworks all form different independent entities ("plateaus") with their own rationale and right to exist, urging viewers to develop their personal understanding and interpretation of the artworks.

When did you first participate in Art Basel and what was most memorable about that show?
In 2013, in Hong Kong, at the Insights sector. It was really an honor to participate in the first edition of Art Basel in Hong Kong. It is a great platform to promote our artists and establish new relationships.

- **Contact** A Thousand Plateaus Art Space
  Yu Di
  info@1000plateaus.org
- **Established** 2007
- **Owner(s) / Partner(s)** Liu Jie
- **Team** 9
- **Space(s)** 1,200 m²
- **Artists at Art Basel** Chen Qiulin
  Wang Yin
  Zhai Liang
  Zhou Chunya
- **Further artists represented** Nicolas Grospierre
  He Gong
  Li Lang
  Liu Chuanhong
  Qi Lan
  Shen Xiaotong
  Shi Jindian
  Tu Hongtao
  Xiao Kegang
  Xiong Yu
  Zhou Bin

Abreu

New York

Galleries
Unlimited
Galleries

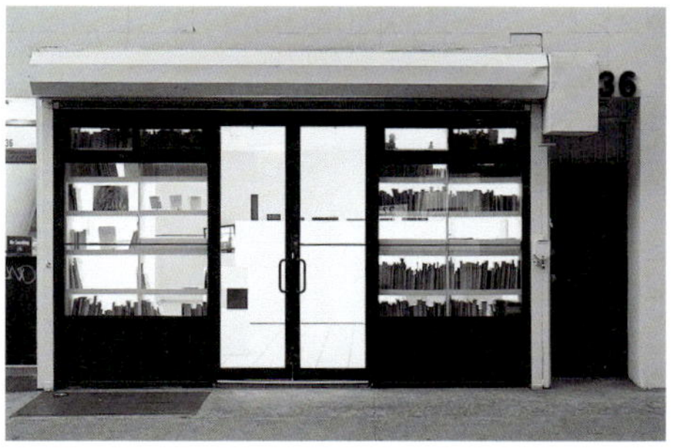

What first compelled you to open a gallery?
As a late bloomer, it seemed like the only business I might have a chance to succeed in, given my past experience and knowledge base.

Who is the first artist you showed and what was most memorable about that show?
The painter Blake Rayne. I invited him to make a series of paintings with the films of Jean-Marie Straub and Danièle Huillet in mind. We both admired these filmmakers who rigorously adapt carefully selected texts from history. The show featured two of their films, *The Death of Empedocles* and *Cézanne*, a series of 12 paintings by Rayne, as well as a text about Straub and Huillet by Dominique Paini. It integrated 2,500 years of Western history with a few works, and delineated the contours of a ground upon which the gallery's program could anchor itself.

When did you first participate in Art Basel and what was most memorable about that show?
Our first participation in Art Basel was in 2007 in the then-named Premiere sector. One of the most memorable aspects of that show is that it was the gallery's first participation in any art fair.

- **Contact** Miguel Abreu Gallery
  Liz Stamplis
  liz@miguelabreugallery.com
  post@miguelabreugallery.com
- **Established** 2005
- **Owner(s) / Partner(s)** Miguel Abreu
- **Team** 10
- **Space(s)** 1,300 m² (2014)
- **Artists at Art Basel** Rey Akdogan
  Liz Deschenes
  R. H. Quaytman
  Sam Lewitt
  Scott Lyall
  Florian Pumhösl
  Eileen Quinlan
  Pamela Rosenkranz
  Pieter Schoolwerth
- **Further artists represented** Hans Bellmer
  Gareth James
  Raha Raissnia
  Jimmy Raskin
  Blake Rayne

Acquavella

New York

Galleries
Galleries
Galleries

- **Contact** Acquavella Galleries, Inc.
  info@acquavellagalleries.com
- **Established** 1921
- **Owner(s) / Partner(s)** William R. Acquavella
  Eleanor Acquavella Dejoux
  Nicholas Acquavella
  Alexander Acquavella
  Tsutomu Takashima
  Esperanza Sobrino
  Michael Findlay
  Fiona Biberstein
  Ken Yeh
- **Artists at Art Basel** Francis Bacon
  Jean-Michel Basquiat
  Alexander Calder
  Willem de Kooning
  Edgar Degas
  Richard Diebenkorn
  Jean Dubuffet
  Lucian Freud
  Alberto Giacometti
  Jasper Johns
  Fernand Léger
  Roy Lichtenstein
  Damian Loeb
  René Magritte
  Brice Marden
  Henri Matisse
  Joan Miró
  Claude Monet
  Jean Paul Riopelle
  Enoc Perez
  Pablo Picasso
  Camille Pissarro
  Jackson Pollock
  James Rosenquist
  Ed Ruscha
  Wayne Thiebaud
  Cy Twombly
  Andy Warhol

Aike-Dellarco

Shanghai

Discoveries

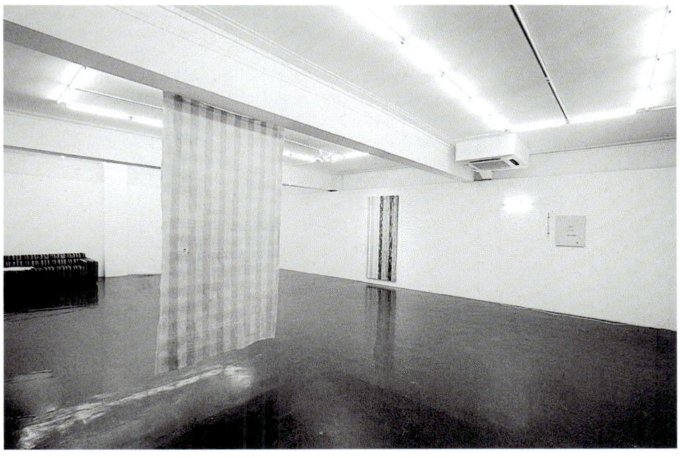

What first compelled you to open a gallery?
My father owns an art gallery specialized in European Old Masters; I started working in his gallery when I was a teenager, and when I was 25 years old I opened my own gallery.

Who is the first artist you showed and what was most memorable about that show?
The first exhibition was a solo show of the pioneering photographer Xiong Wenyun. Her photographs shot in Tibet in 1999 were a great example of performance and Land art in China.

When did you first participate in Art Basel and what was most memorable about that show?
Our first official participation in Art Basel was in 2013 in Hong Kong, with a solo show of the video artist Li Ran. We presented a new video installation, and all the copies were sold to institutional collectors during the fair. In 2012, when Art Basel had just taken over ART HK, we won the Art Futures prize with a solo project by Lee Kit.

- **Contact** Aike-Dellarco
  Roberto Ceresia
  roberto@aikedellarco.com
  shanghai@aikedellarco.com
- **Established** 2007
- **Owner(s) / Partner(s)** Roberto Ceresia
- **Team** 6
- **Space(s)** 350 m²
- **Artists at Art Basel** Li Ran
- **Further artists represented** Chen Zhou
  Ettore Favini
  Jiang Pengyi
  Jin Shan
  Lee Kit
  Li Shurui
  Tang Dixin
  Wang Sishun

Air de Paris

Paris

Galleries
Unlimited

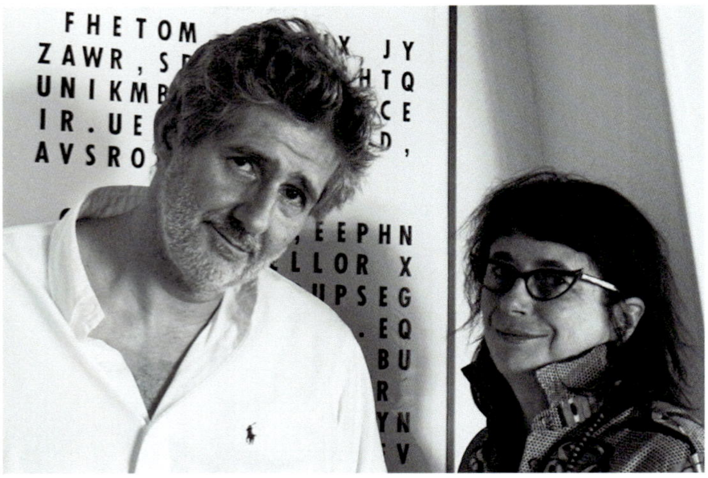

What first compelled you to open a gallery?
Art and adventure.

Who is the first artist you showed and what was most memorable about that show?
The first show was *Les Ateliers du Paradise*, amonth-longperformance-based project by Pierre Joseph, Philippe Parreno, and Philippe Perrin.

When did you first participate in Art Basel and what was most memorable about that show?
In 2000. Joy and excitement, and a beautiful Unlimited project with Dejanov/Heger, a collaborative duo that doesn't exist anymore.

- **Contact** Air de Paris
Vincent Romagny
vincent@airdeparis.com
fan@airdeparis.com
- **Established** 1990
- **Owner(s) / Partner(s)** Florence Bonnefous
Edouard Mérino
- **Team** 5
- **Space(s)** 300 m² (gallery) + 300 m² (storage)
- **Artists at Art Basel** Leonor Antunes
Thomas Bayrle
François Curlet
Stéphane Dafflon
Guy de Cointet
Brice Dellsperger
Trisha Donnelly
Claire Fontaine
Liam Gillick
Joseph Grigely
Guyton\Walker
Carsten Höller
Dorothy Iannone
Aaron Flint Jamison
Pierre Joseph
Ben Kinmont
Adriana Lara
Ingrid Luche
M/M (Paris)
Monica Majoli
Sarah Morris
Mrzyk & Moriceau
Philippe Parreno
Rob Pruitt
Torbjørn Rødland
Allen Ruppersberg
Bruno Serralongue
Shimabuku
Sturtevant
Lily van der Stokker
Jean-Luc Verna

Aizpuru

Madrid
Seville

Galleries

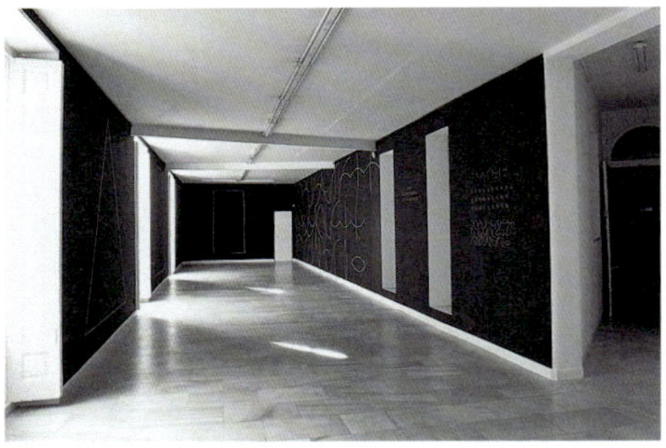

What first compelled you to open a gallery?
It was at the request of Sevillian artists with whom I used to spend a lot of time.

Who is the first artist you showed and what was most memorable about that show?
The first artist we showed was Soledad Sevilla. The exhibition was received with a lot of enthusiasm by the Sevillian and Spanish contemporary art world. My gallery immmediatelly became a meeting point for the most relevant people of Sevillian culture.

When did you first participate in Art Basel and what was most memorable about that show?
Our first year was in 1982 and since then we've been attending every edition—except in 1987, when I had to have eye surgery! Every year is memorable at this wonderful fair.

- **Contact** Galería Juana de Aizpuru
Juana de Aizpuru
juanadeaizpuru@juanadeaizpuru.es
aizpuru@juanadeaizpuru.es
- **Established** 1970 (Seville)
- **Owner(s) / Partner(s)** Juana de Aizpuru
- **Team** 6
- **Space(s)** 600 m² (gallery) + 300 m² (storage)
- **Artists at Art Basel** Art & Language
Miroslaw Balka
Eric Baudelaire
Tania Bruguera
Jordi Colomer
Sandra Gamarra
Dora García
Alberto García Alix
Cristina García Rodero
Pierre Gonnord
Rogelio López Cuenca
Cristina Lucas
Yasumasa Morimura
Albert Oehlen
Markus Oehlen
Tim Parchikov
Fernando Sánchez Castillo
Montserrat Soto
Wolfgang Tillmans
Heimo Zobernig
- **Further artists represented** Jonas Dahlberg
Georg Herold
Joseph Kosuth
Valeriano López
Andrés Serrano
Franz West

Alexander

New York — Edition

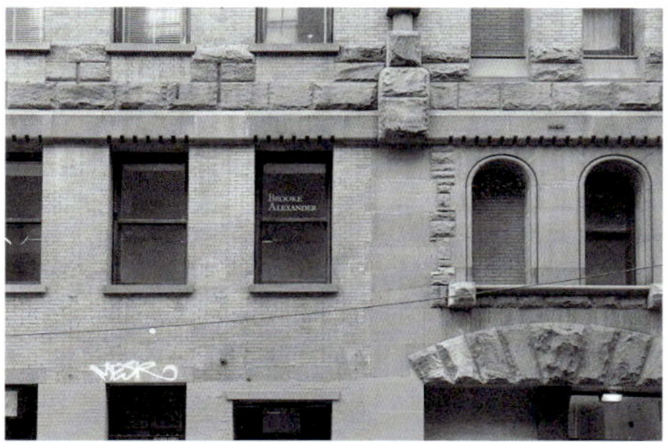

What first compelled you to open a gallery?
The art world in the 1960s was focused on Pop art, and I thought there was an opportunity to publish and show artists who had another point of view: Josef Albers, Alex Katz, Richard Artschwager, Philip Pearlstein, to name a few.

Who is the first artist you showed and what was most memorable about that show?
Locations (1969) by Richard Artschwager, was the first multiple published by Brooke Alexander. The most memorable aspect of its showing was the general confusion of the audience …

When did you first participate in Art Basel and what was most memorable about that show?
In 1972. The art world at that time was much less familiar with editions of American artists and we were very much encouraged by the response to our offering of Alex Katz, Malcolm Morley, and Robert Rauschenberg.

- **Contact** Brooke Alexander
  Barbara Baruch
  bbaruch@baeditions.com
  info@baeditions.com
- **Established** 1968
- **Owner(s) / Partner(s)** Brooke Alexander
- **Space(s)** 650 m²
- **Artists at Art Basel** Josef Albers
  Richard Artschwager
  Donald Judd
  Ellsworth Kelly
  Sol LeWitt
  Bruce Nauman
  Barnett Newman
  Ken Price
  Markus Raetz
  Fred Sandback
  Richard Tuttle
  Franz West
- **Further artists represented** John Baldessari
  Philip Guston
  Jasper Johns
  Robert Longo
  Robert Mangold
  Allan McCollum
  Matt Mullican
  Raymond Pettibon
  Robert Rauschenberg
  Allen Ruppersberg
  Ed Ruscha
  Luc Tuymans
  Andy Warhol
  Rémy Zaugg

Alexander and Bonin

New York — Galleries Unlimited; Galleries

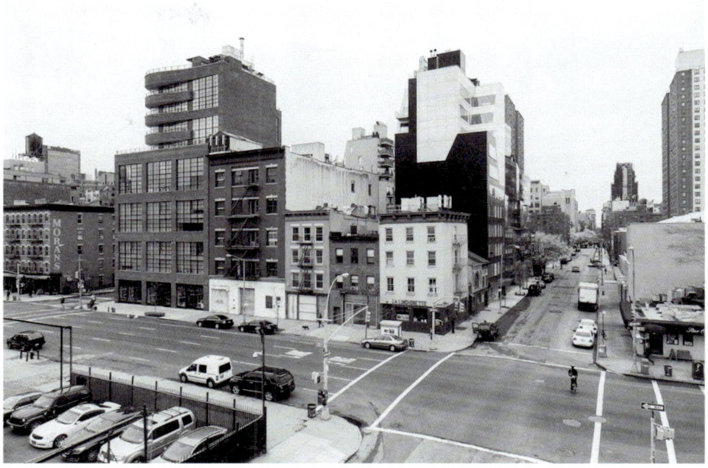

What first compelled you to open a gallery?
Alexander and Bonin was established with the primary purpose of representing a selected group of international contemporary artists, such as Willie Doherty, Mona Hatoum, and Doris Salcedo, whose works were exhibited in important museums and alternative spaces, but not yet represented by a New York gallery.

Who is the first artist you showed and what was most memorable about that show?
The first artist to have a solo exhibition in the gallery was Willie Doherty. Doherty's seminal video installation, *No Smoke Without Fire*, was presented for the first time in New York having premiered at the Reina Sofía as part of the 1994 landmark exhibition, *Cocido y crudo*.

When did you first participate in Art Basel and what was most memorable about that show?
The gallery's first participation at Art Basel was a Statements booth of Willie Cole's work in 1999. It was the first time we presented a solo booth of a gallery artist and the range of medium and reference in Cole's work was unique to the fair at that time. The artist responded with a strong group of work referencing his African-American background and the history of the African diaspora in North America.

- **Contact** Alexander and Bonin
  Kathryn Gile
  kg@alexanderandbonin.com
  gallery@alexanderandbonin.com
- **Established** 1995
- **Owner(s) / Partner(s)** Carolyn Alexander
  Ted Bonin
- **Team** 7
- **Space(s)** 372 m²
- **Artists at Art Basel** John Ahearn
  Matthew Benedict
  Robert Bordo
  Fernando Bryce
  Michael Buthe
  Willie Cole
  Eugenio Dittborn
  Willie Doherty
  Paul Etienne Lincol
  Victor Grippo
  Mona Hatoum
  Diango Hernández
  Emily Jacir
  Robert Kinmont
  Stefan Kürten
  Jorge Macchi
  Rita McBride
  Ree Morton
  Sylvia Plimack Mangold
  Doris Salcedo
  Paul Thek
- **Further artists represented** Peter Hujar
  Sean Scully

A

Alisan

Hong Kong ● Galleries

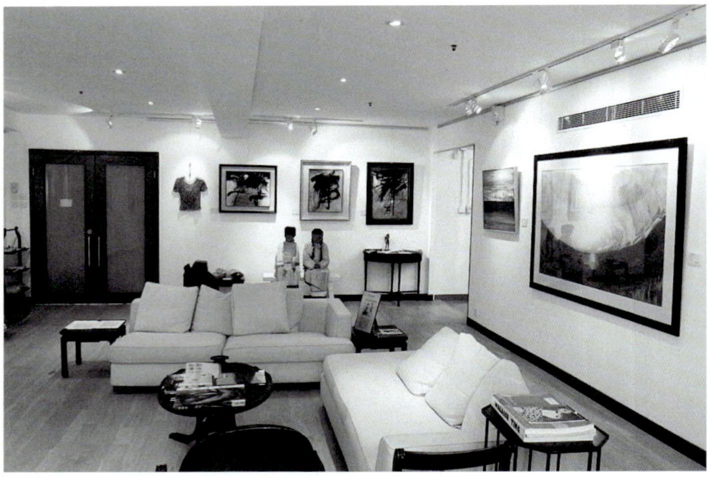

What first compelled you to open a gallery?
In the 1980s there were very few serious art collectors who focused on contemporary Chinese art, as China was still very closed to the West. Passionate about art, Alice King decided to introduce Chinese contemporary art to Hong Kong, as well as to international collectors with one of the first professionally run galleries in Hong Kong, Alisan Fine Arts. Due to the political situation at the time, it focused on introducing Chinese diaspora artists, such as Zao Wou-Ki, Chu Teh-Chun, Walasse Ting, and Chao Chung-Hsiang. As China opened up, the gallery organized the landmark exhibition *A State of Transition, Contemporary Paintings from Shanghai* in 1987. This show introduced to the world 14 artists, among them Chen Jialing, Li Shan, Zhang Guiming, and Zhang Jianjun, at the Hong Kong Arts Centre.

Who is the first artist you showed and what was most memorable about that show?
The first artist we showed was Chang Chieh in 1981, a Taiwanese artist who mainly paints vibrant and serene lotus flowers. The exhibition was a collaboration with the French bank Société Générale, and took place at their headquarters. It was very well received. The artist himself, with his long white beard, came from Taipei to attend the opening, followed by many interested collectors.

- **Contact** Alisan Fine Arts
  Kathleen Mak
  kmak@alisan.com.hk
  info@alisan.com.hk
- **Established** 1981
- **Owner(s) / Partner(s)** Alice King
  Daphne King
- **Team** 3
- **Space(s)** 280 m²
- **Artists at Art Basel** Chao Chung-hsiang
  Chu Teh-chun
  Gao Xingjian
  Man Fung-yi
  Walasse Ting
  Wang Tiande
  Wei Ligang
  Yang Jiechang
  Yu Youhan
  Zao Wou-ki
- **Further artists represented** Chinyee
  Chuang Che
  Fang Zhaoling
  Ming Fay
  Hsiao Chin
  Huang Rui
  Jiang Dahai
  Ju Ming
  Leng Hong
  Li Shan
  Lui Shou-kwan
  Luo Qi
  Shao Yan
  Shi Hu
  T'ang Haywen
  Tseng Yuho
  Wang Chuan
  John Way
  Wucius Wong
  Yang Qi
  Yang Xiaojian

Altman Siegel

San Francisco ● Nova

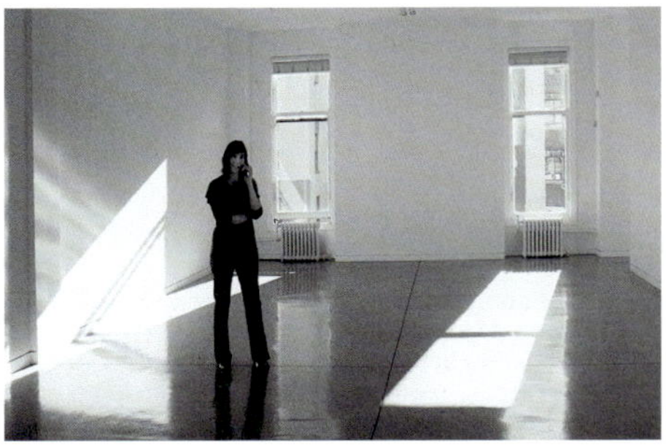

What first compelled you to open a gallery?
I was the senior director for more than 10 years of a large New York gallery. When I moved to San Francisco, a vibrant city but with a small art scene, I felt that someone with my skill set could make a major contribution.

Who is the first artist you showed and what was most memorable about that show?
My first solo show was with Trevor Paglen at the bottom of the recession in 2009. The framer thanked me for putting such a large order for frames into production because no one was doing any kind of ambitious production at the time. The show went up and was wildly popular. It made me think having a gallery was easy, until the next month when almost nothing sold.

When did you first participate in Art Basel and what was most memorable about that show?
Last year! We did a solo show with Matt Keegan in Positions. We made a huge sale of many works to an international client who we had only dreamed about before.

- **Contact** Altman Siegel
  Claudia Altman-Siegel
  claudia@altmansiegel.com
  info@altmansiegel.com
- **Established** 2009
- **Owner(s) / Partner(s)** Claudia Altman-Siegel
- **Team** 3
- **Space(s)** 609 m²
- **Artists at Art Basel** Shannon Ebner
  Chris Johanson
- **Further artists represented** Zarouhie Abdalian
  Nate Boyce
  Jessica Dickinson
  Liam Everett
  Laeh Glenn
  Fran Herndon
  Matt Keegan
  Shinpei Kusanagi
  Devin Leonardi
  Trevor Paglen
  Will Rogan
  Sara VanDerBeek
  Emily Wardill
  Garth Weiser

de Alvear

Madrid ● Galleries

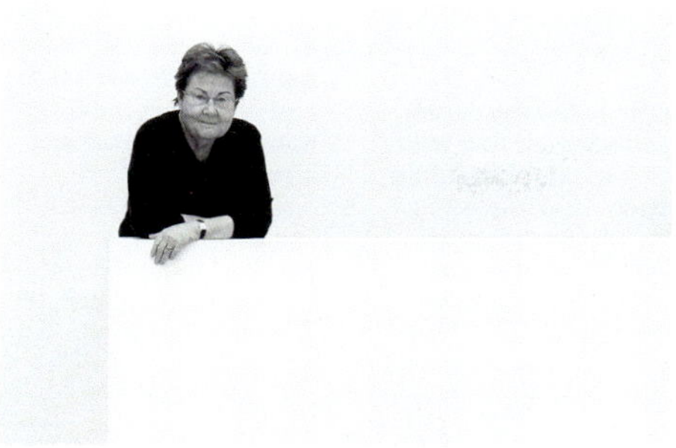

What first compelled you to open a gallery?
My passion for collecting and art was the main reason that prompted me to enter the world of galleries. Before having the gallery under my own name, I was the owner of Galería Juana Mordó from 1980 until 1995, when I opened Galería Helga de Alvear. Currently, my collection includes over 2,500 works exhibited regularly at the Centro de Artes Visuales Fundación Helga de Alvear in Cáceres, Spain.

Who is the first artist you showed and what was most memorable about that show?
I remember the exhibition of Nam June Paik I organized in 1989. I did not sell anything. They were fantastic pieces on show, but at the time nobody in Spain knew who Paik was …

When did you first participate in Art Basel and what was most memorable about that show?
For me Art Basel is the most important art fair. Juana Mordó was a member of the consultative committee from 1976 onward; when I joined her gallery in 1980 I was allowed to accompany her. I was a member of the committee myself from 1984 onward. In 1981 the Spanish borders were still quite closely sealed to artworks. Nevertheless, we took 21 drawings by Julio González with us to the fair in Basel—with an export permit limited to two weeks. We sold 17 drawings, but had to bring them all back with us in order to apply for a definitive export license. The upshot was that the Spanish state decided to purchase 13 of the pieces, a decision which we then, to our shame, had to communicate back to the original buyers. The rest were sold immediately on the black market. It was still like that then.

- **Contact** Galería Helga de Alvear
  Alberto Gallardo
  alberto@helgadealvear.com
  galeria@helgadealvear.com
- **Established** 1995
- **Owner(s) / Partner(s)** Helga de Alvear
- **Team** 6
- **Space(s)** 900 m²
- **Artists at Art Basel** Katharina Grosse
- **Further artists represented** Helena Almeida
  Slater Bradley
  Angela Bulloch
  José Pedro Croft
  Ángela de la Cruz
  Michael Elmgreen & Ingar Dragset
  Jorge Galindo
  Axel Hütte
  Prudencio Irazabal
  Isaac Julien
  Jürgen Klauke
  Imi Knoebel
  Dan Perjovschi
  Thomas Ruff
  Santiago Sierra
  DJ Simpson
  Jane & Louise Wilson

Ameringer McEnery Yohe

New York ● Galleries ● Galleries

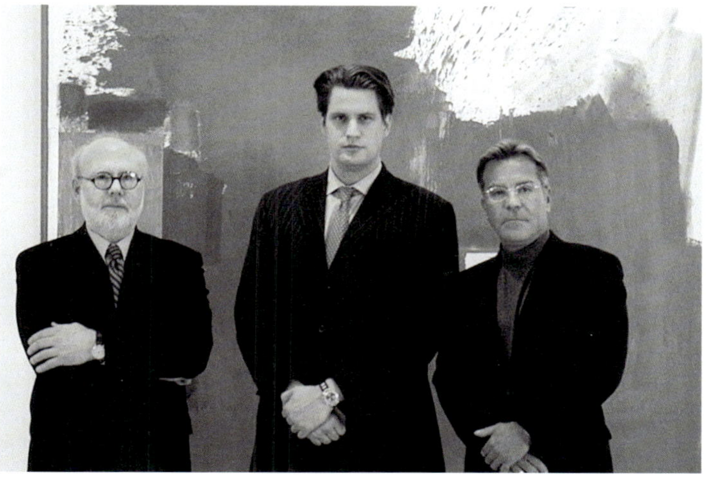

What first compelled you to open a gallery?
To follow in the footsteps of the legendary art dealers with whom we had previously worked, while contributing to the advancement of art history.

Who is the first artist you showed and what was most memorable about that show?
Hans Hofmann: Late Paintings From The Estate of The Artist. Many of the paintings in the gallery's inaugural exhibition had not been publicly shown since the artist's death in 1966 and exemplified the final, great flowering of Hofmann's 60-year career. Like the glorious late paintings of Monet and Matisse, the works celebrated the purity of color and light, and the sheer joy of painting.

When did you first participate in Art Basel and what was most memorable about that show?
Ameringer | McEnery | Yohe was proud to be selected for inclusion in the first edition of Art Basel in Miami Beach in 2002 and has exhibited annually ever since. In 2013, the gallery exhibited at the inaugural edition of Art Basel in Hong Kong and will participate again in 2014.

- **Contact** Ameringer McEnery Yohe
  Miles McEnery
  mm@amy-nyc.com
- **Established** 1999
- **Owner(s) / Partner(s)** Will Ameringer
  Miles McEnery
  James Yohe
- **Team** 14
- **Space(s)** 465 m²
- **Artists at Art Basel** Kevin Appel
  Oliver Arms
  Norman Bluhm
  Thomas Burke
  Rebecca Campbell
  Suzanne Caporael
  Rosana Castrillo Diaz
  Gene Davis
  Franklin Evans
  Helen Frankenthaler
  Iva Gueorguieva
  Frederick Hammersley
  Al Held
  Hans Hofmann
  Wolf Kahn
  Patrick Lee
  Markus Linnenbrink
  Morris Louis
  John M. Miller
  George McNeil
  Robert Motherwell
  Kenneth Noland
  Jules Olitski
  Rod Penner
  David Allan Peters
  Michael Reafsnyder
  Tam Van Tran
  Monique van Genderen
  Esteban Vicente
  Patrick Wilson
  Liat Yossifor

Ammann

Zurich — Galleries

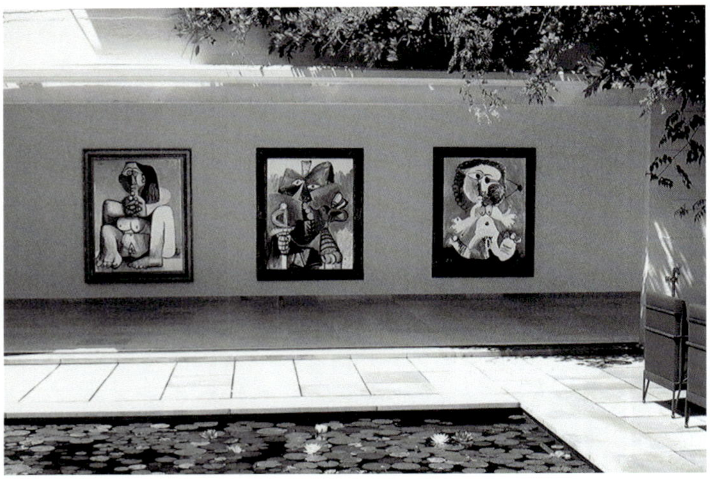

What first compelled you to open a gallery?
Thomas Ammann, the late brother of Doris Ammann, opened the gallery.

Who is the first artist you showed and what was most memorable about that show?
Pablo Picasso.

When did you first participate in Art Basel and what was most memorable about that show?
In 1995, Thomas Ammann Fine Art AG had the chance to show some important Modern Masters. Most memorable were Ernst Beyeler's excited comments when he visited the booth.

- **Contact** — Thomas Ammann Fine Art AG
  Han Byul Jung
  hj@ammannfineart.com
  da@ammannfineart.com
- **Established** — 1977
- **Owner(s) / Partner(s)** — Doris Ammann
  Georg Frei
- **Team** — 6
- **Space(s)** — 180 m²
- **Artists at Art Basel** — The Bruce High Quality Foundation
  Alexander Calder
  Willem de Kooning
  Eric Fischl
  Alberto Giacometti
  Martin Kippenberger
  Paul Klee
  Gregor Lanz
  Fernand Léger
  Brice Marden
  Agnes Martin
  Andrew Masullo
  Henri Matisse
  Joan Miró
  Albert Oehlen
  Pablo Picasso
  Sigmar Polke
  Robert Ryman
  Philip Taaffe
  Marc Tansey
  Cy Twombly
  Andy Warhol

Andersen's

Copenhagen — Galleries, Positions

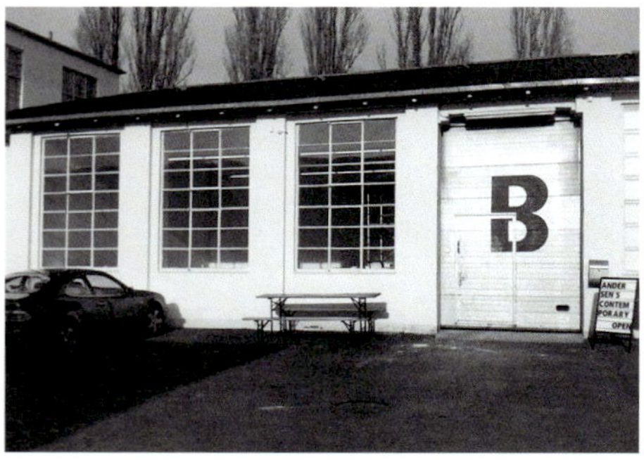

What first compelled you to open a gallery?
Well, it slowly drifted from artists showing in my apartment in Berlin to a gallery in Copenhagen.

Who is the first artist you showed and what was most memorable about that show?
The first show was actually a group show, where Jay Chung & Q Takeki Maeda were supposed to show some pins in memory of their South Pole expedition, but on the way to gallery the pins were thrown in a canal, as a performance that no one saw!!!

When did you first participate in Art Basel and what was most memorable about that show?
I guess Art Basel in Miami Beach, in a container on the beach. It was very very hot and difficult to sell anything in a swimsuit …

- **Contact** — Andersen's Contemporary
  Claus Andersen
  c@andersen-s.dk
  info@andersen-s.dk
- **Established** — 2005
- **Owner(s) / Partner(s)** — Claus Andersen
- **Team** — 5
- **Space(s)** — 500 m²
- **Artists at Art Basel** — Thilo Heinzmann
  Ulrik Heltoft
  Daniel Lergon
  Tomás Saraceno
- **Further artists represented** — Peter Bonde
  Jay Chung & Q Takeki Maeda
  Jason Dodge
  Simon Dybbroe Møller
  Olafur Eliasson
  FOS (Thomas Poulsen)
  Anna Fro Vodder
  Gæoudjiparl
  Albert Mertz
  Henrik Olesen
  Anselm Reyle
  Thiago Rocha Pitta
  Pia Rönicke
  Anja Schwörer
  Katja Strunz
  Theis Wendt
  Thomas Zipp

Andréhn-Schiptjenko

Stockholm — Galleries, Galleries

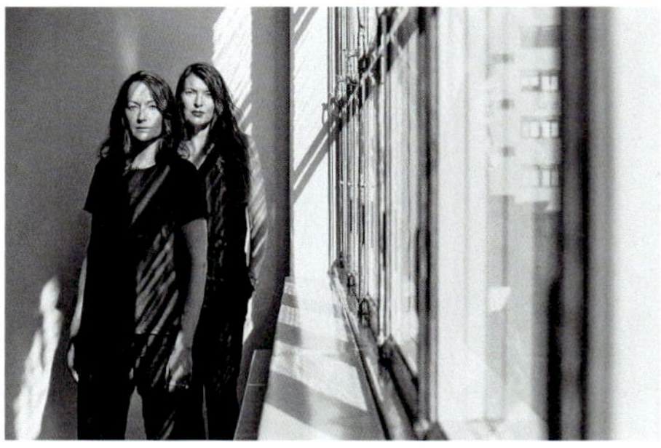

What first compelled you to open a gallery?
The acute sensation that there was a lot of interesting art being made and important conversations being held and that there was no space for either in the artworld landscape of Stockholm at the time. We met while working for another gallery and had an immediate strong professional connection, so when that gallery closed it seemed obvious to start out on our own.

Who is the first artist you showed and what was most memorable about that show?
Our first show was a group show with the title *Positions*, a statement as to the kind of work we wanted to show and artists we wanted to work with—some of whom we still represent. There were tons of people and a great opening party afterward, masked as a philosophical discussion club. No sales whatsoever.

When did you first participate in Art Basel and what was most memorable about that show?
In Statements, with a show by Annika von Hausswolff in 1998. She was a young artist but had nevertheless represented Sweden at the Venice Biennale in 1997. While we felt proud and excited to be part of Art Basel, indeed we had not anticipated how much it would mean for the gallery's further international development.

- **Contact** Andréhn-Schiptjenko
Cilène Andréhn
cilene@andrehn-schiptjenko.com
info@andrehn-schiptjenko.com
- **Established** 1991
- **Owner(s) / Partner(s)** Cilène Andréhn
Marina Schiptjenko
- **Team** 6
- **Space(s)** 325 m²
- **Artists at Art Basel** Uta Barth
Tony Matelli
Nandipha Mntambo
Julie Roberts
Xavier Veilhan
Cajsa von Zeipel
Gunnel Wåhlstrand
- **Further artists represented** Tobias Bernstrup
Jacob Dahlgren
Omid Delafrouz
Maya Eizin-Öijer
Carin Ellberg
Peter Hagdahl
Siobhán Hapaska
Katrine Helmersson
Martin Jacobson
Kristina Jansson
Lena Johansson
Brad Kahlhamer
Anna Kleberg
Annika Larsson
Matts Leiderstam
Katarina Löfström
Annika von Hausswolff
Johan Zetterquist

Approach

London

Galleries
Unlimited
Parcours

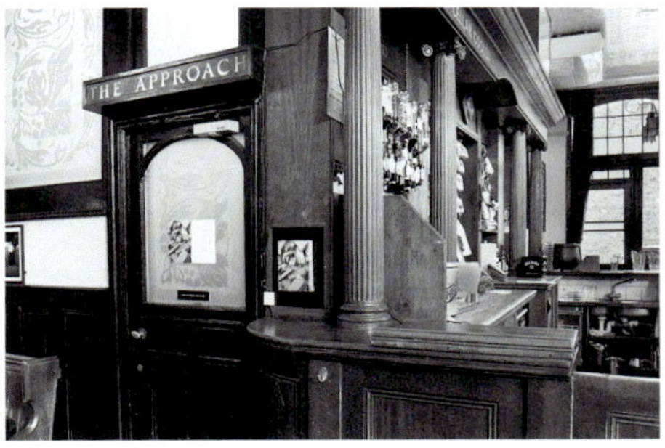

What first compelled you to open a gallery?
We were initially offered a nicely proportioned and well lit old function room above a pub to put on exhibitions. It was a great opportunity to enjoy the freedom of putting on shows in London's East End with little financial worry due to the patronage the gallery brought to the pub, especially on preview nights. It seemed like an offer too good to turn down.

Who is the first artist you showed and what was most memorable about that show?
The first show was a group exhibition featuring Liz Arnold, Jane Simpson, and Daniel Sturgis. Most memorable was the huge size of the crowd at the opening—drinking downstairs, upstairs, and outside. It felt like an instant success.

When did you first participate in Art Basel and what was most memorable about that show?
Our first participation was in Statements in Basel in 2003 with a presentation of one large Gary Webb sculpture on a rubber floor. When you sell the work almost immediately and you are with Gary Webb in Basel for a few days, memories are a blur.

- **Contact** The Approach
Mary Cork
mary@theapproach.co.uk
info@theapproach.co.uk
- **Established** 1997
- **Owner(s) / Partner(s)** Jake Miller
Emma Robertson
- **Team** 5
- **Space(s)** 90 m²
- **Artists at Art Basel** Alice Channer
Peter Davies
Evan Holloway
Germaine Kruip
Lisa Oppenheim
Amanda Ross-Ho
John Stezaker
Gary Webb
Sam Windett
- **Further artists represented** Phillip Allen
Helene Appel
Cris Brodahl
Stuart Cumberland
Patrick Hill
Jack Lavender
Edward Lipski
Dave Muller
Magali Reus
Evren Tekinoktay
Rezi van Lankveld
Sara VanDerBeek

Arario

Seoul
Cheonan

Galleries

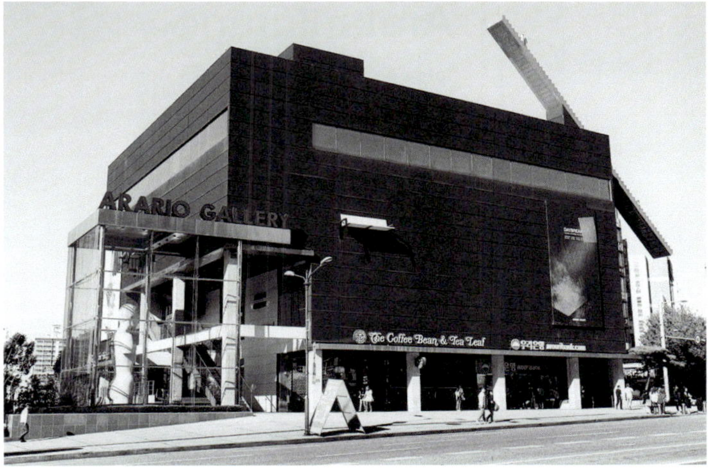

What first compelled you to open a gallery?
Since reopening its doors in Cheonan in 2002, Arario Gallery runs two branches in Cheonan and Seoul, and an office in Beijing. Arario Gallery has always endeavored to explore new grounds that have never previously been looked at by other institutions in Korea, promoting hybridization and diversity in a regionally localized art world through its active interactions with the international art world. The gallery has been introducing and proclaiming the excellence of Korean contemporary art to the rest of the world. On the basis of experience in China's art industry, the gallery currently presents various artists from India and Southeast Asia.

Who is the first artist you showed and what was most memorable about that show?
The Cheonan gallery has contributed to the advancement of regional cultural industry and extended vision of the art world through thought-through and diverse exhibition programs, including Keith Haring's solo exhibition (2002), Sigmar Polke's solo exhibition (2004), a group exhibition for artists based in Leipzig (2005), a solo exhibition by Hyung Koo Kang (2007), a group exhibition of young Chinese artists (2011), etc.

When did you first participate in Art Basel and what was most memorable about that show?
In 2013 in Hong Kong.

- **Contact** Arario Gallery
  Henna Joo
  henna.joo@ariogallery.com
  info@ariogallery.com
- **Established** 2002
- **Owner(s) / Partner(s)** Changil Kim
- **Team** 12
- **Space(s)** 300 m² (Seoul)
  750 m² (Cheonan)
- **Artists at Art Basel** Christine Ay Tjoe
  Leslie de Chavez
  Subodh Gupta
  Osang Gwon
  Sungpil Han
  Yan Heng
  Geraldine Javier
  Hyung Koo Kang
  Dongwook Lee
  Kohei Nawa
  Eko Nugroho
  J. Ariadhitya Pramuhendra
- **Further artists represented** Byoungho Kim
  Gao Lei
  Jitish Kallat
  Hanna Kim
  Inbai Kim
  Tallur L. N.
  Jihyun Lee
  Jinyong Lee
  Li Qing
  Nalini Malani
  Miao Xiaochun
  Insane Park
  Sun Yuan & Peng Yu
  Thukral & Tagra
  Yuan Yuan

Arataniurano

Tokyo ● Insights

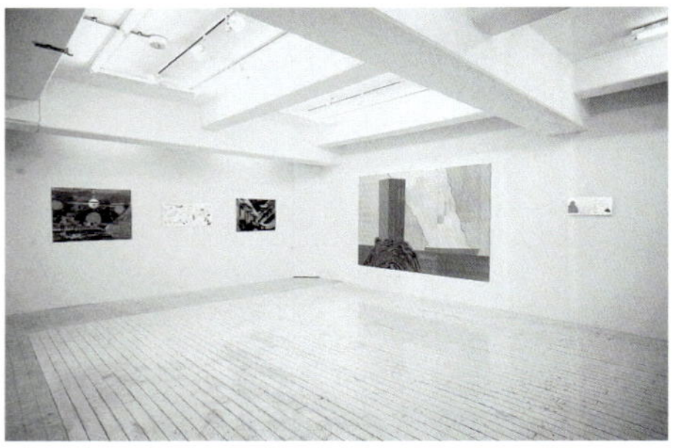

What first compelled you to open a gallery?
I worked for SCAI The Bathhouse in Tokyo for about 10 years and wanted to try to run my own gallery and work with artists of my own age.

Who is the first artist you showed and what was most memorable about that show?
Izumi Kato. When his paintings were included at the 2007 Venice Biennial, we held a solo show at our gallery.

When did you first participate in Art Basel and what was most memorable about that show?
We exhibited Takahiro Iwasaki's big sculpture in the Statements sector in Basel in 2010.

- **Contact** Arataniurano
  Mutsumi Urano
  u@arataniurano.com
- **Established** 2007
- **Owner(s) / Partner(s)** Mutsumi Urano
- **Team** 2
- **Space(s)** 40 m² (not including office and storage space)
- **Artists at Art Basel** Takahiro Iwasaki
  Tatzu Nishi
- **Further artists represented** Yusuke Asai
  Keiji Izumi
  Akiko Kinugawa
  Mana Konishi
  Toshiyuki Konishi
  Hiroyuki Oki
  Tadasu Takamine
  Youichi Umetsu
  Go Watanabe
  Yuichi Yokoyama

Ark

Yogyakarta ● Galleries

- **Contact** Ark Galerie
  contact@arkgalerie.com
- **Established** 2007
- **Owner(s) / Partner(s)** Ronald Akili
- **Artists at Art Basel** Wimo Ambala Bayang
  Ade Darmawan
  Davi Linggar
  Melati Suryodarmo
- **Further artists represented** Agustinus 'Jompet' Kuswidananto
  Eko Nugroho
  Dewa Gede Ratayoga
  Wedhar Riyadi
  Tromarama

Arndt

Berlin
Singapore ● Galleries
Encounters

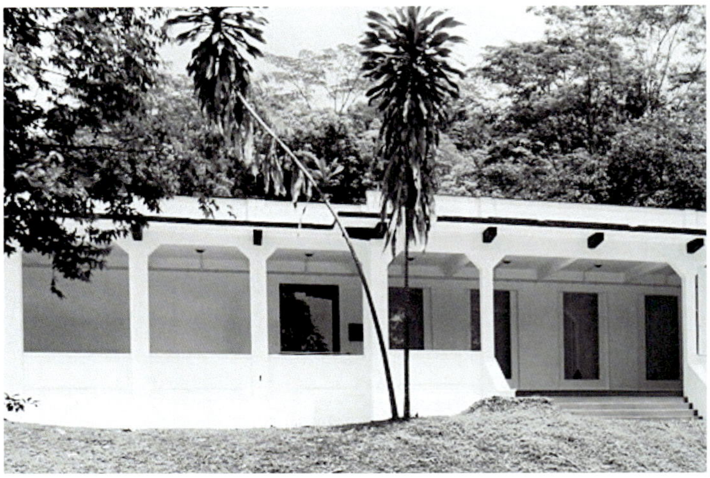

What first compelled you to open a gallery?
I always wanted to work in art and with living artists, because their critical vision on society and our world opens our minds and perspectives. Berlin, such a short time after the fall of the Wall, seemed to us the future art center and creative workshop of Europe. So I followed the inner "call from Berlin" and started my gallery in Berlin, despite Cologne and Duüsseldorf being the center of Germany's art market at the time.

Who is the first artist you showed and what was most memorable about that show?
We opened the gallery with a show of the photo-work by the musician David Byrne. Among the guests was Sophie Calle who came to visit Berlin for the first time in her life to start working on our first project, *The Detachment*—about the disappearance of symbols of the East-German past in former East-Berlin. The opening dinner was held in the ruins of a 19th-century ballroom—a surprise guest, attracted by Sophie Calle's presence, was the Minister of Culture at that time, to whom we could show Berlin's new art landscape.

When did you first participate in Art Basel and what was most memorable about that show?
We first participated with a Statements by Max Mohr in 1997, which marked the first of 12 consecutive years of participation in Art Basel. I remember that all our means went into the production of this first booth, and there was such excitement when all works and the entire installation were placed in major private collections and museums.

- **Contact** Arndt
  Lisa Polten
  lisa@arndtberlin.com
  info@arndtberlin.com
- **Established** 1994
- **Owner(s) / Partner(s)** Matthias Arndt
- **Team** 10
- **Space(s)** 650 m²

- **Artists at Art Basel**
  Christine Ay Tjoe
  Joseph Beuys
  Sophie Calle
  Gilbert & George
  FX Harsono
  Thomas Hirschhorn
  Jitish Kallat
  Heinz Mack
  Eko Nugroho
  Mike Parr
  Otto Piene
  Qui Zhijie
  Chiharu Shiota
  Nedko Solakov
  Agus Suwage
  Natee Utarit
  Entang Wiharso
- **Further artists represented**
  Erik Bulatov
  Hahan (Uji Handoko, Eko Saputro)
  Geraldine Javier
  Julian Rosefeldt
  Rodel Tapaya

Arratia Beer

Berlin

Positions

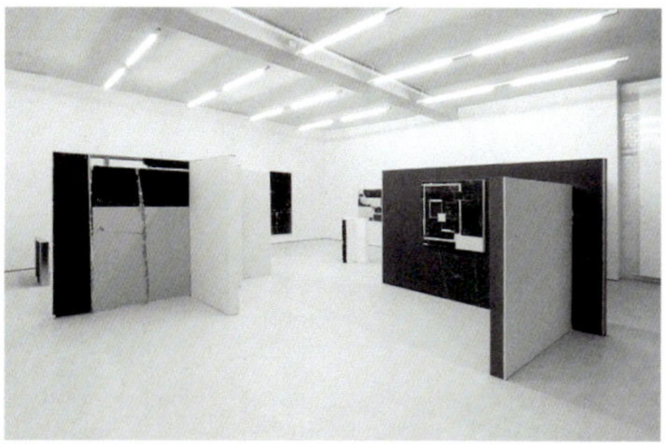

Who is the first artist you showed and what was most memorable about that show?
Patty Chang.

When did you first participate in Art Basel and what was most memorable about that show?
Our first participation was in 2012.

- **Contact** Arratia Beer
  Julia Staszak
  info@arratiabeer.com
- **Established** 2006
- **Owner(s) / Partner(s)** Euridice Arratia
  Elizabeth Beer
- **Team** 4
- **Space(s)** 200 m²
- **Artists at Art Basel** Gabriel Acevedo Velarde
- **Further artists represented**
  Patty Chang
  Omer Fast
  Fernanda Fragateiro
  Jennie C. Jones
  Matthew Metzger
  Pablo Rasgado
  Katerina Šedá
  Javier Téllez

Art : Concept

Paris

Galleries
Galleries Kabinett

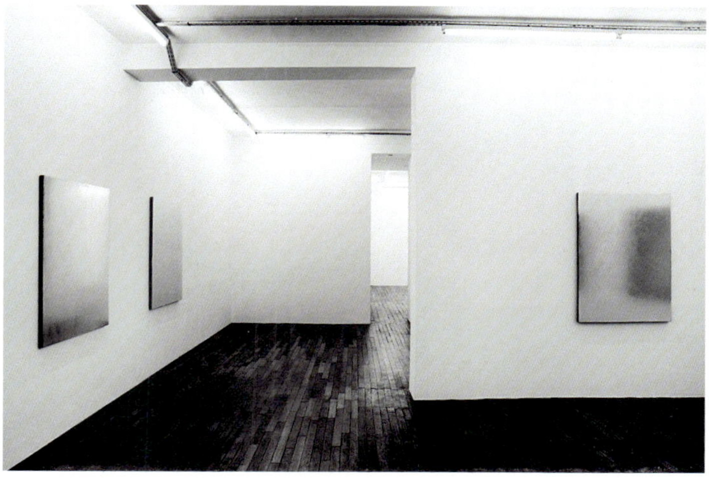

What first compelled you to open a gallery?
Nobody compelled me to open a gallery … I've always been interested in art, and after my law studies I decided to open a gallery.

Who is the first artist you showed and what was most memorable about that show?
I think it was a drawing exhibition by Roland Flexner or Ben, but I'm sure that the most memorable thing about the show was my inexperience in the art world.

When did you first participate in Art Basel and what was most memorable about that show?
It was in 1993 when the fair created a new section dedicated to young galleries. I couldn't access my booth for the opening because I hadn't paid for it. I tried to get in with my technical pass but you know the ladies at the Messe, no way to get in … In the end everything went well, thanks to the Art Basel team.

- **Contact** Art : Concept
  Aurélia Bourquard
  aurelia@galerieartconcept.com
  info@galerieartconcept.com
- **Established** 1992
- **Owner(s) / Partner(s)** Olivier Antoine
- **Team** 6
- **Space(s)** 140 m²
- **Artists at Art Basel**
  Martine Aballéa
  Pierre-Olivier Arnaud
  Julien Audebert
  Francis Baudevin
  Whitney Bedford
  Jean-Luc Blanc
  Michel Blazy
  Jeremy Deller
  Hubert Duprat
  Richard Fauguet
  Vidya Gastaldon
  Geert Goiris
  Lothar Hempel
  Nathan Hylden
  Jacob Kassay
  Andrew Lewis
  Adam McEwen
  Philippe Perrot
  Pietro Roccasalva
  Gedi Sibony
  Roman Signer
  Alexandre Singh
  Ulla von Brandenburg

Art:1

Jakarta ● Insights

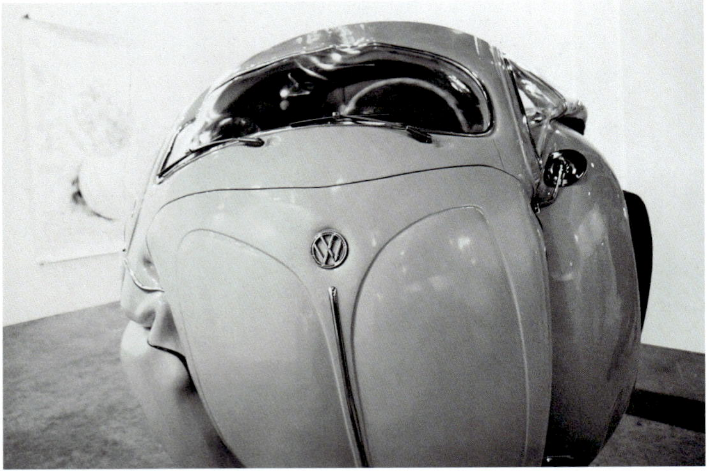

What first compelled you to open a gallery?
The need to introduce contemporary fine art to an Indonesian audience.

When did you first participate in Art Basel and what was most memorable about that show?
2013. Great experience for us as a new participant in Art Basel. We were impressed how well it was organized, the audience it covers, and the detailed planning prior to the event.

- **Contact** Art:1 by Mondecor Gallery
elena_lens@hotmail.com
info@mondecor.com
- **Established** 1983
- **Owner(s) / Partner(s)** Martha Gunawan
Monica Gunawan
Ricky Gunawan
- **Team** 30
- **Space(s)** 4,000 m²
- **Artists at Art Basel** Ichwan Noor
- **Further artists represented** Heri Dono
Tisna Sanjaya
Farhan Siki
Yudi Sulistyo

Artcourt

Osaka ● Insights

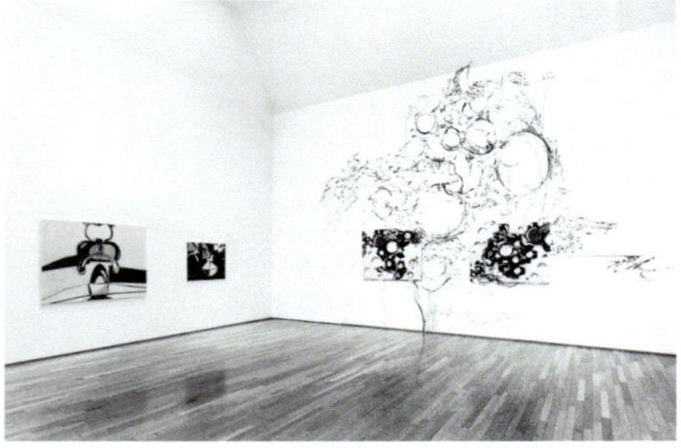

What first compelled you to open a gallery?
There are many wonderful artists in Kansai region (Osaka, Kobe, Kyoto, and other cities) who maintain international standards. I wish to promote their activities and bring their works to the global market.

Who is the first artist you showed and what was most memorable about that show?
I organized a group exhibition to celebrate the launch of the gallery: the show consisted of works by 15 emerging artists including Osamu Kokufu, Tomoko Sawada, Kohei Nawa, and Aiko Tezuka. Those artists led their generation and sprouted up afterward.

When did you first participate in Art Basel and what was most memorable about that show?
In Hong Kong, in 2013. Compared to ART HK before 2012, the participating galleries were more carefully selected by Art Basel.

- **Contact** Artcourt Gallery
Ami Fukuda
info@artcourtgallery.com
- **Established** 2003
- **Owner(s) / Partner(s)** Mitsue Yagi
- **Team** 4
- **Space(s)** 230 m²
- **Artists at Art Basel** Hitoshi Nomura
- **Further artists represented** Yo Akiyama
Yasuyoshi Botan
Norio Imai
Osamu Kokufu
Shiro Matsui
Saburo Murakami
Kozo Nishino
Akira Yanagisawa

Artiaco

Naples ● Galleries
● Galleries

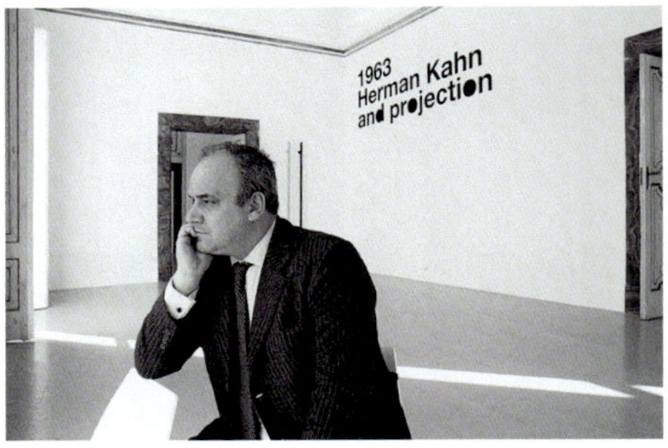

What first compelled you to open a gallery?
My personal interest in contemporary art together with a growing passion as young collector.

Who is the first artist you showed and what was most memorable about that show?
Giuseppe Penone in October 1988. The most memorable aspect of the show was strictly related to the artworks which Penone produced with the sand taken from the Solfatara volcano (still active near Naples) and dark earth from Cuma (an important archeological site near Naples). Penone filled two big glass boxes with those elements, leaving the impression of his hand while pouring the sand and earth into the boxes.

When did you first participate in Art Basel and what was most memorable about that show?
It was in 1994. I remember my satisfaction with the display of the booth and the excitement of the first sale, shortly after the opening of the fair. The following public days of the fair passed by without any particular event but, on the last day, while the end bell was ringing, three people entered the booth and bought three important artworks. Such a thing never happened again in the following 27 years of my career.

- **Contact** Alfonso Artiaco
Anna Caterina Bleuler
info@alfonsoartiaco.com
- **Established** 1986
- **Owner(s) / Partner(s)** Alfonso Artiaco
- **Team** 4
- **Space(s)** 530 m²
- **Artists at Art Basel** Darren Almond
Carl Andre
Giovanni Anselmo
Robert Barry
Botto & Bruno
Alan Charlton
Gilbert & George
Liam Gillick
Laurent Grasso
Thomas Hirschhorn
Craigie Horsfield
Ann Veronica Janssen
Melissa Kretschmer
Wolfgang Laib
Sol LeWitt
Lello Lopez
Raffaele Luongo
Vera Lutter

Rita McBride
Marco Neri
Gioberto Noro
Giulio Paolini
Giuseppe Penone
Perino & Vele
Anne & Patrick Poirier
Sergio Prego
Glen Rubsamen
Anri Sala
Niele Toroni
David Tremlett
Juan Uslé
Lawrence Weiner

- **Further artists represented** Victoria Civera
Jannis Kounellis
Gerhard Merz
Davide Minuti
Albert Oehlen
Ulrich Rückriem

Artinformal

Manila — Insights

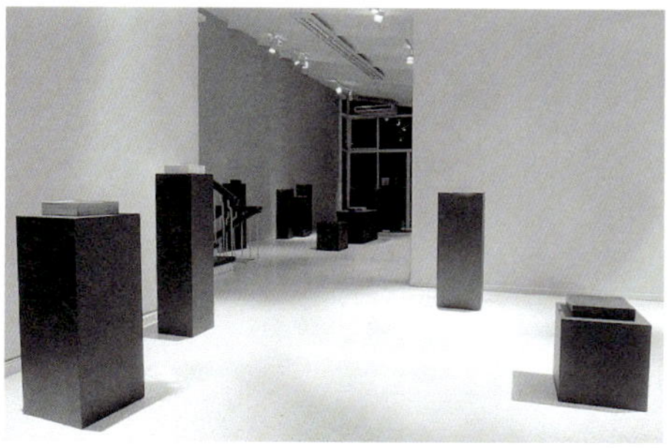

What first compelled you to open a gallery?
I noticed a need for a space that would focus on presenting serious exhibitions and at the same time help to educate the audience about contemporary Filipino art. I felt it was time to present exhibitions that were not common then among the existing galleries, that were mostly mall-based and highly commercial. Together with a group of dedicated contemporary artists, we felt that we should present art in a way that would widen the viewers' perspective. The work would not necessarily sell at first, but with exposure to new forms of art, and by speaking with the artists, the public would get it, and later purchase. Since then, it has been a very successful formula and it has caught fire.

Who is the first artist you showed and what was most memorable about that show?
We first did a group show with a dozen artists. The most memorable thing about it was that it was also the day when a very strong typhoon hit Manila and there was no electricity. We were able to borrow a power generator and since we were one of the few places with light, we had a full house and all the pieces were sold.

- **Contact** Artinformal
Tina Fernandez
tinafernandez.ai@gmail.com
info@artinformal.com
- **Established** 2006
- **Owner(s) / Partner(s)** Tina Fernandez
- **Team** 4
- **Space(s)** 170 m²
- **Artists at Art Basel** Marina Cruz
Pam Yan-Santos
- **Further artists represented** Eugenia Alcaide
Salvador Alonday
Zean Cabangis
Pablo Capati III
Erwin Leaño
Lui Medina
José Santos III
Mark Valenzuela

Atlas

London — Galleries

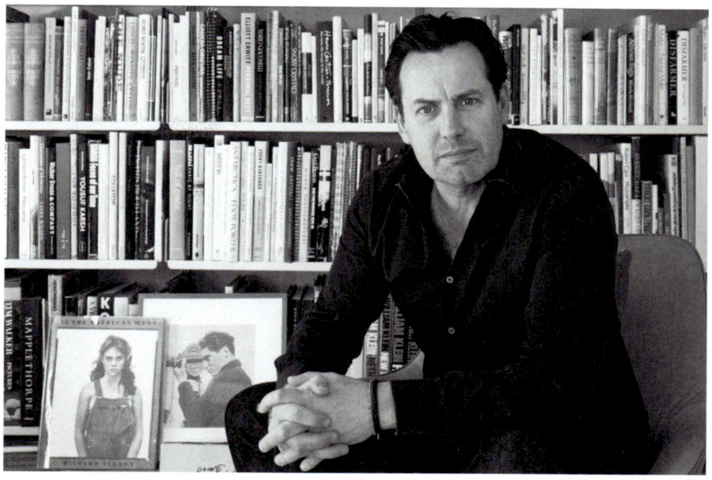

What first compelled you to open a gallery?
I started my career working with antiquarian and rare books. Atlas Gallery was founded in 1994 with strong ties to my personal interest in vintage photographs, as well as my roots in the rare book trade.

Who is the first artist you showed and what was most memorable about that show?
The first exhibition at Atlas Gallery was a show of vintage works by Frank Hurley from Ernest Shackleton's *Imperial Trans-Antarctic Expedition*, dating from 1911–1916. In the spring of 2012, Atlas Gallery had the pleasure of exhibiting vintage works by H.G. Ponting from Captain Robert F. Scott's ill-fated Terra Nova Expedition of 1912. Although the gallery has evolved to a much more contemporary program, this exhibition was a return to the founding genre of the gallery.

When did you first participate in Art Basel and what was most memorable about that show?
Atlas Gallery first participated in the inaugural Art Basel in Hong Kong in 2013. We showed a selected program of both our vintage and contemporary artists. We had the pleasure of exhibiting the iconic works of Magnum photographer René Burri in a large-scale contemporary format for the first time in Asia.

- **Contact** Atlas Gallery
Kathlene Fox-Davies
kathlene@atlasgallery.com
info@atlasgallery.com
- **Established** 1994
- **Owner(s) / Partner(s)** Ben Burdett
- **Team** 5
- **Space(s)** 90 m²
- **Artists at Art Basel** Bill Brandt
Nick Brandt
René Burri
Henri Cartier-Bresson
Frauke Eigen
Jeremy Hunter
Floris Neusüss
Irving Penn
Sebastião Salgado
- **Further artists represented** Robert Capa
Elliott Erwitt
Mario Giacomelli
Ernst Haas
Philippe Halsman
Nathan Harger
Thomas Hoepker
Frank Hurley
Adam Jeppesen
William Klein
Michael Light
Steve Macleod
Trent Parke
Herbert G. Ponting
Leni Riefenstahl
Dennis Stock
Paul Strand
Paolo Ventura

Aye

Beijing

Galleries

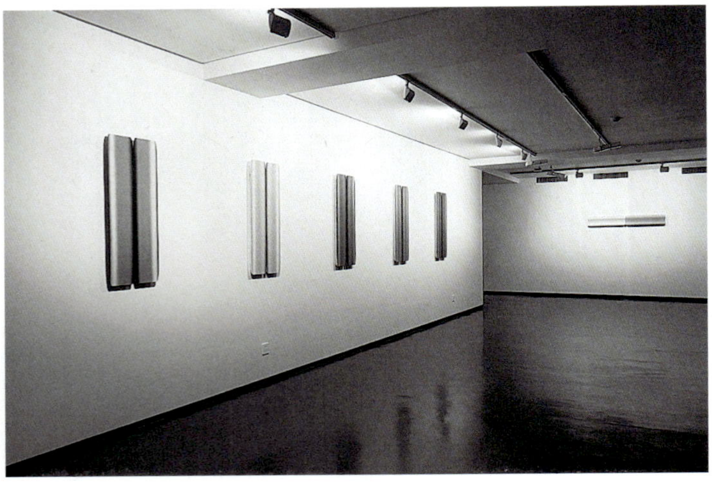

What first compelled you to open a gallery?
The love of contemporary art, and to organize our existing collection more systemically.

Who is the first artist you showed and what was most memorable about that show?
Our first exhibition was a group show, and the first artist we showed was Shi Benming. What was most memorable about that show was the main wall: it hosted almost 100 portrait images. It was amazing!

When did you first participate in Art Basel and what was most memorable about that show?
Our first participation at Art Basel was in Hong Kong in 2013. We aim to attend Art Basel in Basel in 2014.

- **Contact** Aye Gallery
Ziyan Meng
juliameng2003@gmail.com
aye@ayegallery.com
- **Established** 2005
- **Owner(s) / Partner(s)** Yan Qing
- **Team** 5
- **Space(s)** 300 m²
- **Artists at Art Basel** Chen Wenji, Chen Yufan, Ji Dachun, Liu Wei, Mu Boyan, Xia Xiaowan, Zhao Gang
- **Further artists represented** Hoo Mojong, Jiang Fang, Sheng Tianhong, Shi Xinji, Wang Mai, Wang Yabin, Xiao Yu, Yang Qiong

Arndt

Interview with Matthias Arndt

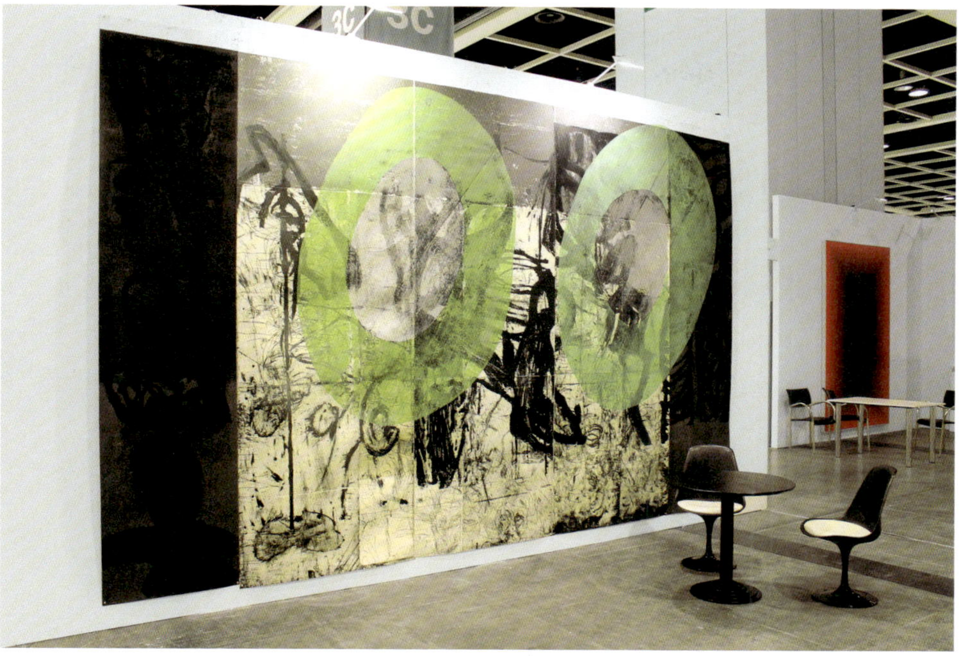

Art Basel in Hong Kong, 2013

You settled in Berlin 20 years ago. You opened a second gallery in Singapore in January 2013. Could you please tell us about the history of your gallery, and particularly about what led you to open a branch in Singapore?

During the first 15 "foundation years" in Berlin I ran my business as a traditional gallery, focusing on identifying key artists of my time (such as Thomas Hirschhorn, Sophie Calle, Nedko Solakov, Jitish Kallat, Julian Rosefeldt), and then establishing these artists in the local and international context and building a market around their work. In 2010, following a two-year process of analyzing the artists' and our major clients' expectations of the function and operation of a 21st-century gallery in a globalized market, I changed the format slightly: still working directly with the artists and mainly in the primary market, we would formulate precise missions and regions for the artists' collaborations, and define mandates with public, corporate, and private clients. This includes advisory and curated exhibitions in both the public and the corporate context. In addition to the Berlin gallery space opened in 2010 in the new Potsdamer Strasse gallery district, we started pop-up curated shows worldwide. These first major projects in Singapore, Sydney, and Melbourne allowed me to carry our international profile to the Asia-Pacific region, and over the past four years we have started collaborations with some of the key artists, and built relations with the major museums and private collections in Southeast Asia and the Australia Pacific region. Opening a space in Asia has been integral part of this strategy, allowing us to bring international art to Asia, and the best of Asia (mainly from the Southeast) to Berlin/the West. In January this year we opened Arndt Singapore in Gillman Barracks with a show of the ZERO Group [a European art group from the 1960s].

Why did you choose Singapore over any other city in the region?

Hong Kong is undoubtedly the center and international turntable of the Asian art market, with the leading Asian art fair Art Basel in Hong Kong, a thriving auction market, and many major international galleries setting up shop there. But Singapore also has considerable wealth and the government is dedicated to making Singapore another important art destination. Geographically Singapore is located between our European premises and Australia, where there's a lucrative art business advising museums, foundations, and a number of private collections. Most importantly Singapore is the gate to Southeast Asia: Indonesia, the Philippines, Thailand, and many new art landscapes, some in the recent focus of the international markets, many others yet to be discovered. In my practice I've always headed toward opening up new markets and audiences, anticipating trends, and showing the upcoming generations within a current international and established program. I also instantly sympathized with this Asian art hub in Gillman Barracks, with its 18 galleries, project spaces, and artists' studios together with the Center for Contemporary Art of Singapore, all on one site. So far I am very happy with my move; business has exceeded my expectations.

How did you get involved in the Asian scene? Was it through your participation in the Tate Asia-Pacific Acquisitions Committee?

Asian artists work much more independently than their Western colleagues, but the region lacks institutional infrastructures and professional organization of the market, which makes the distribution of their works more complicated. The network of artists, collectors, and the most important dealers therefore plays a major role. Our strategy, which is to build committed collaborations and open new markets, is meeting with a great response. The investment in building Arndt (formerly Arndt & Partner) as an international brand contributes to the brand-driven Asian markets, but my main focus is on our performance: numerous solo and survey shows accompanied by publications; e.g. the first, about Indonesian contemporary art, created awareness and a market for Southeastern Asian art outside Asia.

I find the art produced in Southeast Asia particularly rich and exciting. Artists in this region have not really detached themselves from society and their communities—so their work is very engaged, formally diverse, and technically extraordinarily developed. The Western audience needs to put this art and aesthetic, which is new for them, into context. So I was so pleased when I learned about the Tate Asia-Pacific Acquisitions Committee. An institution like Tate—a truly contemporary institution—can help tremendously in creating awareness for these new art landscapes.

In what way do your list of represented artists and your program reflect this double implantation? How did you conceive your first participation in Art Basel in Hong Kong? What approach did you adopt?

I try to show the best of both regions, both in the West and in Asia-Pacific. Since 2010 I have signed up 12 major artists from Indonesia, the Philippines, Thailand, and China, and I am currently looking further south in the direction of the Vietnamese and Cambodian art scenes. I am also looking toward Malaysia and Singapore. For Art Basel in Hong Kong 2013 we wanted to show our program in its entirety, giving both the international and the more recent Asian focus equal attention and space, and to establish dialogues between the different positions. The results have been rewarding: among many other transactions we placed Sophie Calle, Eko Nugroho, and Jitish Kallat in major Asian and Australian museums and foundations, and the centerpiece from our booth—by the Indonesian Entang Wiharso—went into the Olbricht Collection in Berlin.

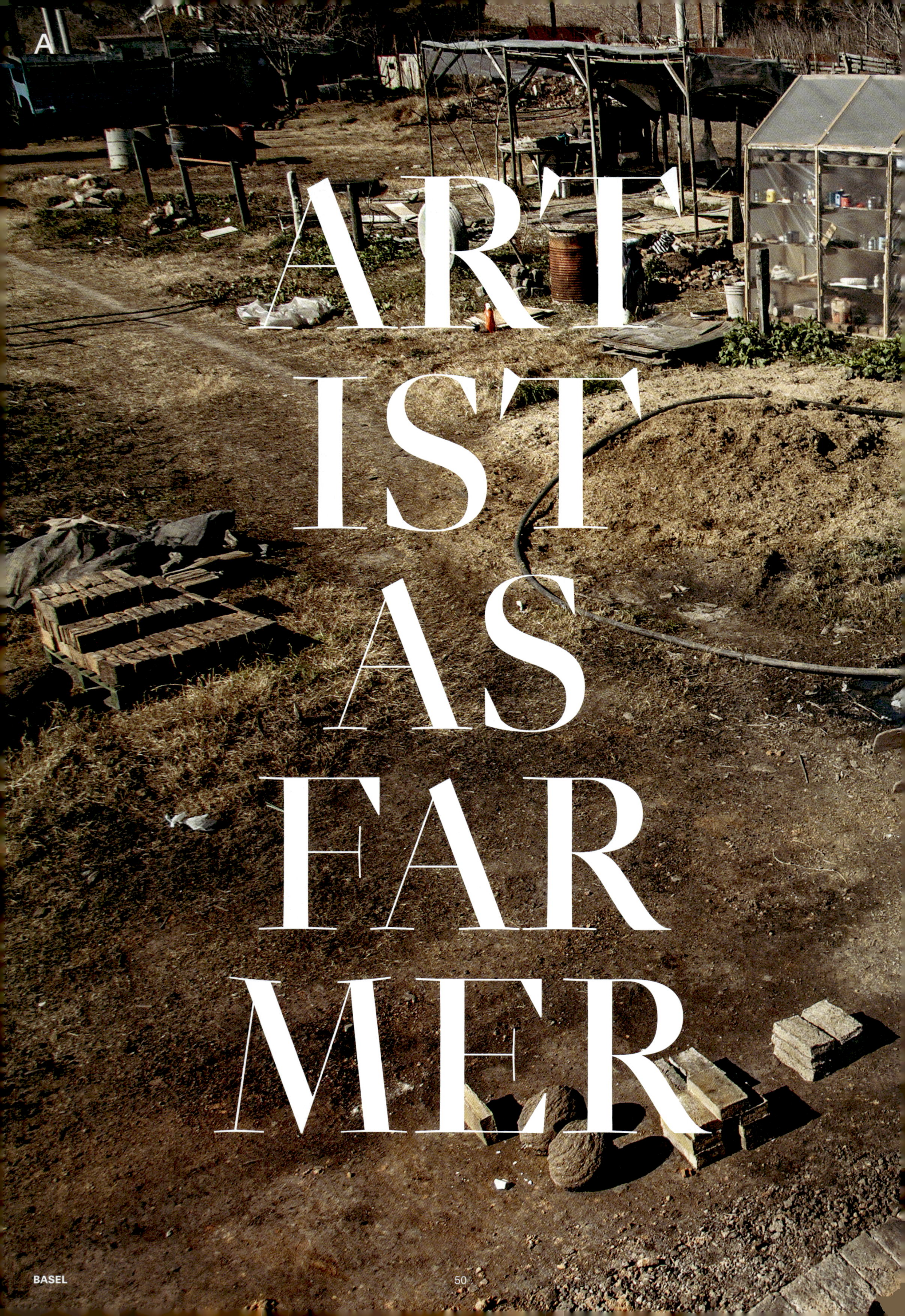

ARTIST AS FARMER

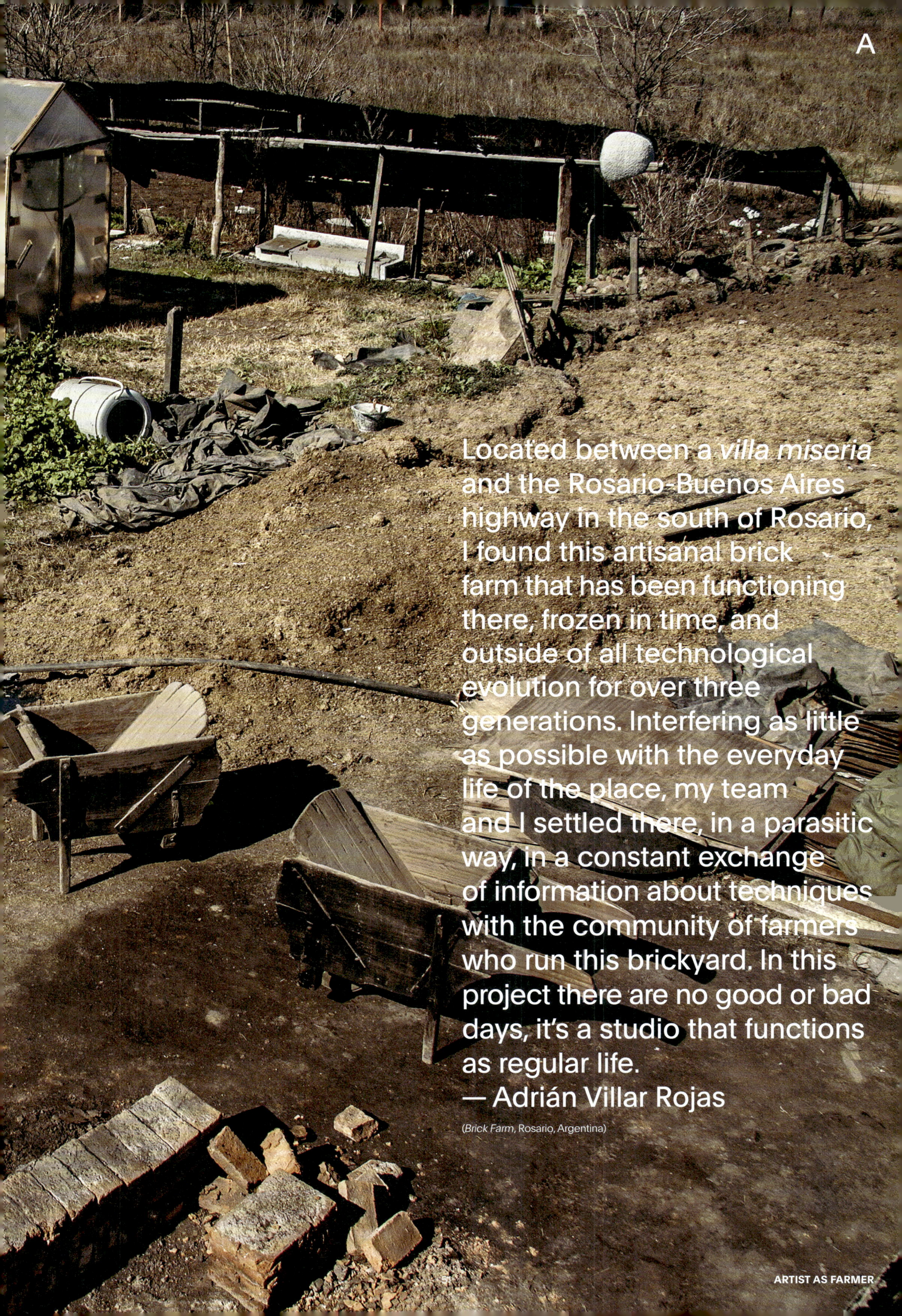

Located between a *villa miseria* and the Rosario-Buenos Aires highway in the south of Rosario, I found this artisanal brick farm that has been functioning there, frozen in time, and outside of all technological evolution for over three generations. Interfering as little as possible with the everyday life of the place, my team and I settled there, in a parasitic way, in a constant exchange of information about techniques with the community of farmers who run this brickyard. In this project there are no good or bad days, it's a studio that functions as regular life.

— Adrián Villar Rojas

(*Brick Farm*, Rosario, Argentina)

A

The Artist as Farmer by Hans Ulrich Obrist

Gianfranco Baruchello, Fritz Haeg, Agnès Varda, Adrián Villar Rojas, Zheng Guogu

Conversations
Artistic Practice

Basel
June 16, 2013

Gianfranco Baruchello, Artist, Rome

Fritz Haeg, Artist, Los Angeles

Agnès Varda, Filmmaker and Artist, Paris

Adrián Villar Rojas, Artist, Buenos Aires

Zheng Guogu, Artist, Yangjiang

Moderator: Hans Ulrich Obrist, Co-Director of the Serpentine Gallery, London

A complete version of the conversation is available at www.artbasel.com

This is dedicated to a pressing topic: the artist as farmer. It is part of a series of talks about artistic practice, and it follows "the artist as school maker," "the artist as urbanist," "the artist as activist," "the artist as poet," and "the artist as musician." The history of this panel has various origins. The trigger was a conversation with the architect Rem Koolhaas, who said, "the future is the countryside," and initiated questions on how to ruralize the urban. But the real origin goes back to Joseph Beuys and his lectures. Between 1972 and 1985, when I was a teenager, Beuys, invited by Baron Durini and Lucrezia de Domizio, stayed in a little village called Bolognano near Pescara in Italy. There he started his artistic ecological action, *La Difesa Della Natura*, the "defense of nature." This project was a manifesto for farming—it encompassed agricultural reformation, ecological awareness, environmental protection. It also addressed the question of extinction and endangered plants very early. He named the 15-hectares and its 7,000 planted trees of endangered species "Piantagione Paradise." It was of course a message he wanted to send out about environmental protection, but somehow it was also his proposition of an expanded notion of art.

Nowadays, environmental protection is related to activism, and often questions of farming have to do with the collective. Many agricultural projects have been developed, such as the temporary *Prinzessinnengarten* in Berlin, or online initiatives such as the *Open Source Ecology* (2003–) project, a global village construction set, a sort of do-it-yourself platform, originated by a network of farmers and engineers. It allows all kinds of structures to be built, which hopefully will guarantee a sustainable civilization for the future. Furthermore, some practitioners started their own agricultural projects and stopped all other activities to continue the project, like the Israeli conceptual artist Avital Geva, who retreated into a greenhouse and made it his main conceptual piece.

The talk today brings together practitioners for whom farming is a daily artistic practice, whether it represents an expression of social interaction, an act of artistic appropriation, the birth of a *Patatutopia*, a way of rethinking consumption, or a cultivation of entropy...

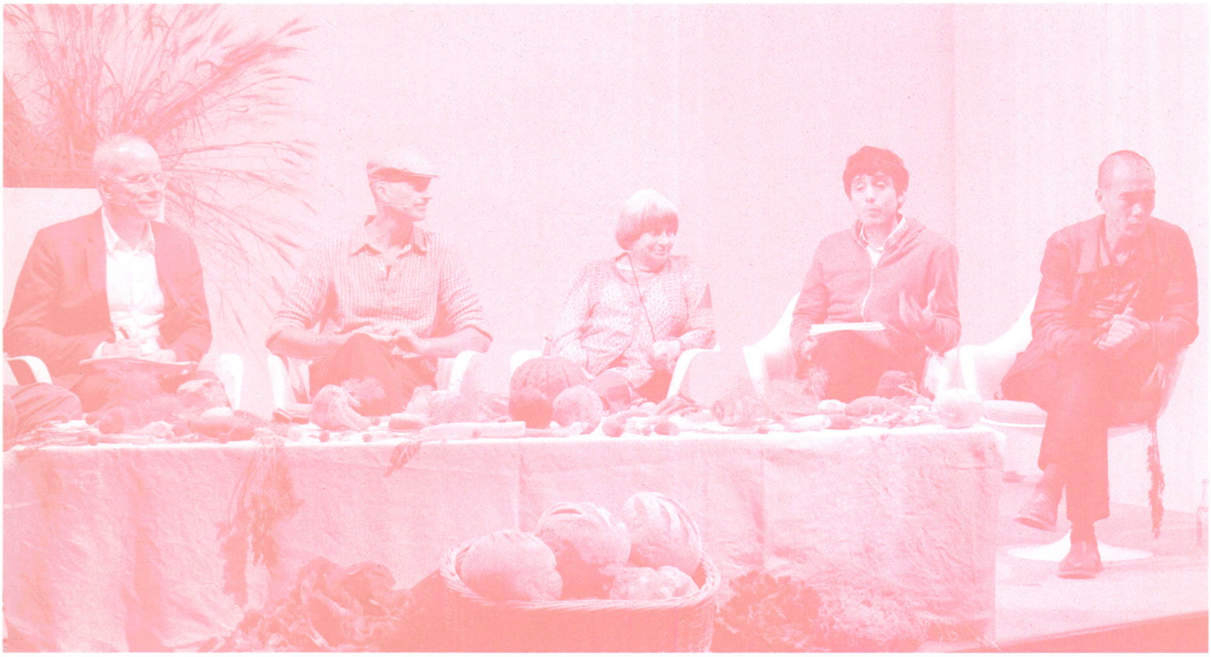

From left to right: Hans Ulrich Obrist, Fritz Haeg, Agnès Varda, Adrián Villar Rojas, Zheng Guogu

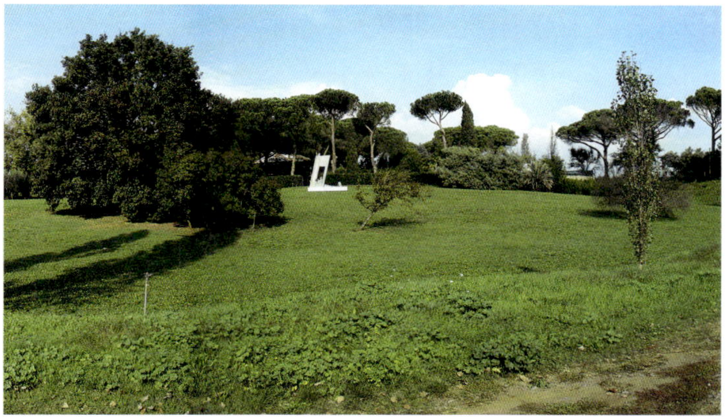

The land was found in an absolutely wild state and the problem was the noise coming from the highway. We started cultivating it to diminish the noise, and gradually transformed the place where I was living and working in into something different, the Baruchello Foundation. The property increased day by day and there are now 20 hectares of cultivated soil. It is dedicated to artists, encouraging interactions, creativity, and interdisciplinary reflections.
— Gianfranco Baruchello

(*The Garden*, 1985–2013 [formerly Agricola Cornelia], Baruchello Foundation, Rome)

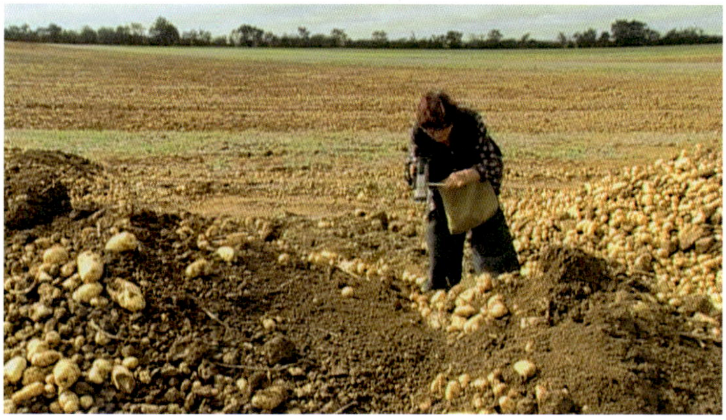

Inspired by the painting by Millet, I became interested in the action of gleaning. Today one gleans potatoes, and I was interested in the sociological reason for this action. How some people get what other people would throw away. On the second day of shooting I found a heart-shaped potato. This was a key to the movie. It meant that by making this film I would get the real feelings of people, and not only the agricultural side of it.
— Agnès Varda

(Agnès filming a field of potatoes, extract from *The Gleaners and I*, 2000)

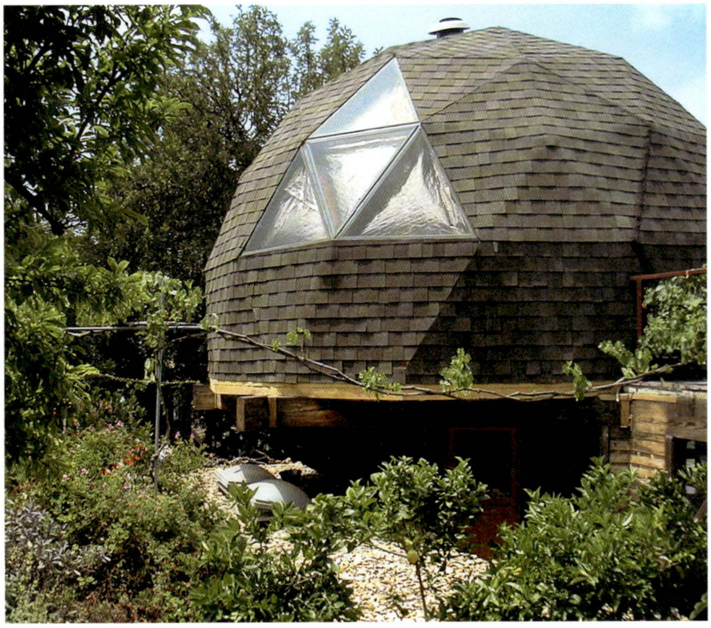

My own garden and home in Los Angeles, where I've been gardening and growing food for 15 years. This geodesic dome has now become the headquarters for a new kind of inquiry into domesticity and the domestic arts.
— Fritz Haeg

(Fritz Haeg's Los Angeles garden)

A

In the year 2000 I bought a piece of land from a farmer on the outskirts of Yangjiang, the town where I live. In 2005 I started the construction of my "ideal architecture." Like a seed planted by a farmer, it makes roots, germinates, blossoms, and bears fruit, developing from a simple to a complicated multi-dimensional project. Like a farmer who experiments with his cultivations on his very own piece of land, this is a long-term project.
— Zheng Guogu

(*Age of Empires*, 2000–)

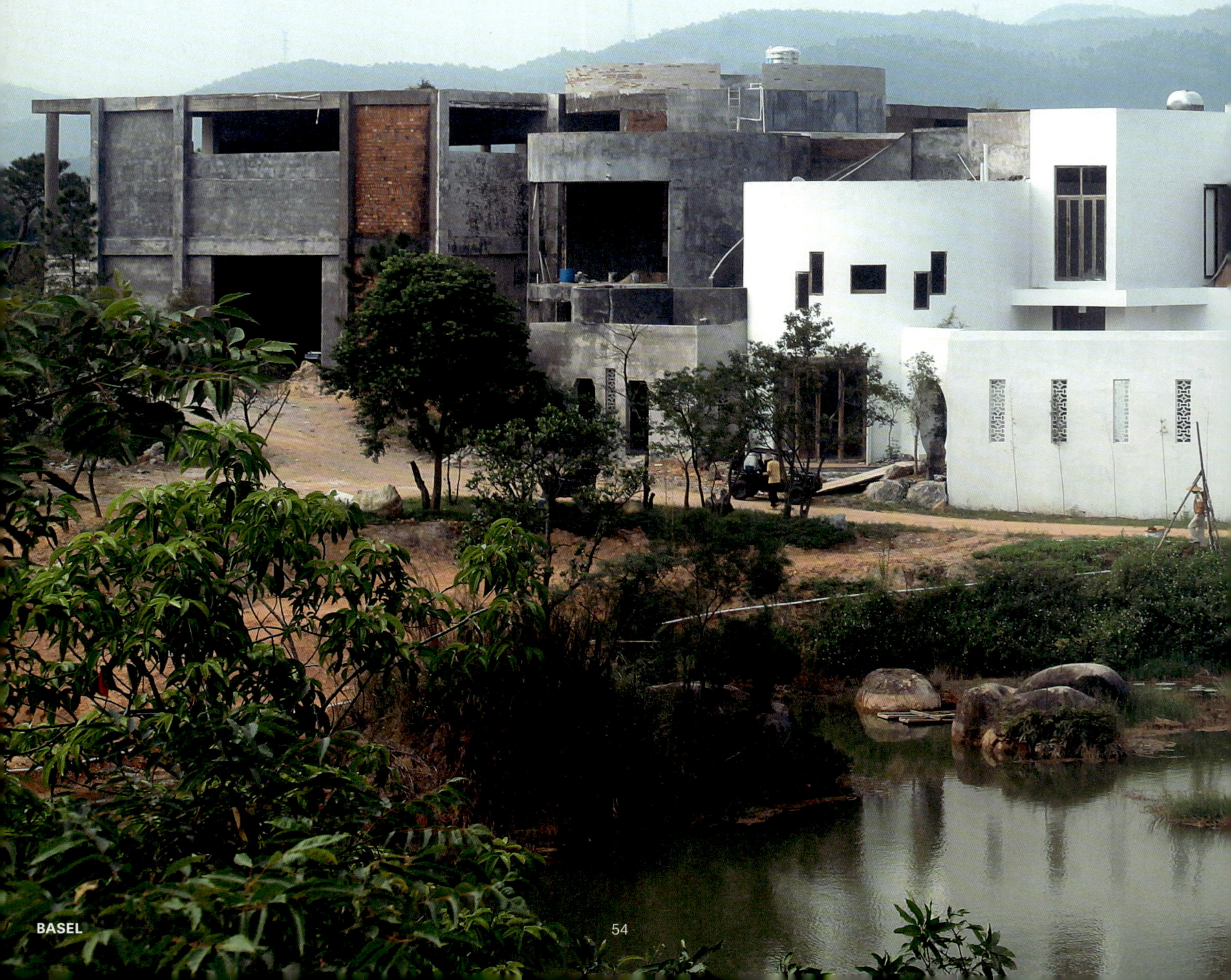

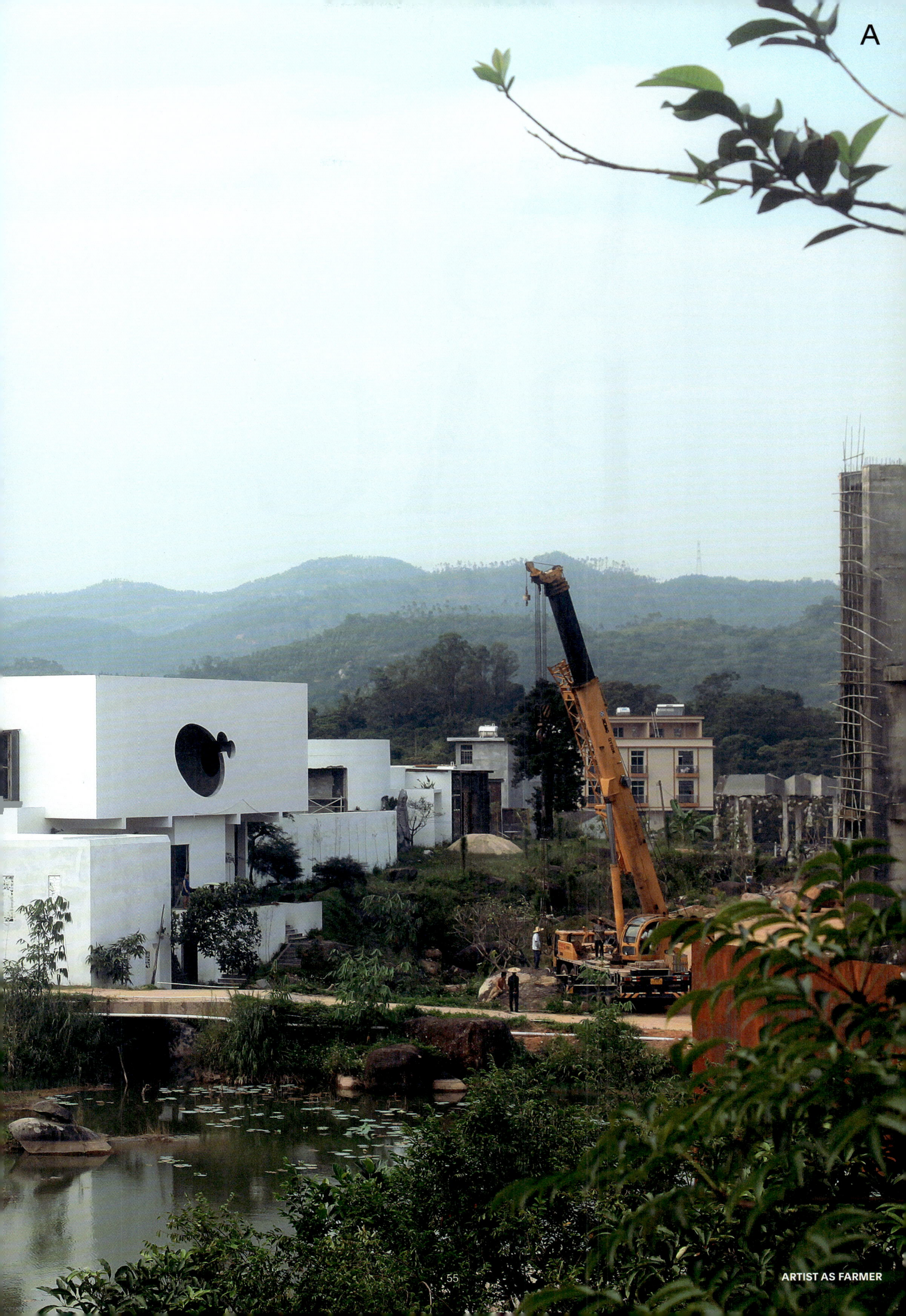

ASIA PAC IFIC RE GION

Collecting in the Asia-Pacific Region

Elaine Ng Talks with Marcel Crespo, Alan Lau, and Dick Quan

ELAINE NG Collecting in Asia is a long tradition. What is special about Asian collecting in the past 40 or 50 years is how countries producing the most active collectors have changed. For example, Japan led the region in most categories in the 1960s, 1970s, and 1980s, and often broke world auction records. This coincided with Japan's economic growth and political stability, which are major factors in stimulating both collecting and art production in almost any country or region. In the late 1980s we saw the rise of South Korea, Hong Kong, Taiwan, Singapore, and somewhat later, China.

At the beginning of this growth cycle there were few collectors, and most of them were conservative in terms of their buying, gravitating toward historical works produced in their own cultures and traditional materials such as jade, bronzes, ceramics, as well as other iconic cultural relics. In the contemporary art market, the circle was even smaller, and tended to be led by expatriates living in Asia and non-Asian collectors regularly traveling to Asia. These collections have since become historically important: many of the artists are now blue-chip, and their works are highly coveted by individuals and institutions. In the world of collecting, the past is the father of the future: art is long and life is short. On that note, I would like to introduce the three young pioneers who have joined this panel.

Mr. Marcel Crespo is a self-made entrepreneur active in many industries such as computer distribution, newspapers, outsourcing, telecoms, gaming, and hospitality. He's an active collector in Manila, and his collection includes both international Western art and contemporary art from the Philippines. He's a patron of Ateneo Art Gallery, widely considered the first museum of modern contemporary art in the Philippines. He's also instrumental in the Ateneo Art Award, which offers Philippine artists under 36 years old studio residencies worldwide (in the US, Australia, Europe, and Singapore).

Conversations
Collectors Focus

Hong Kong
May 25, 2013

Marcel Crespo, Collector, Patron of Ateneo Art Gallery, Manila

Alan Lau, Collector, Member of Tate's Asia Pacific Acquisitions Committee, Board of Directors at Para/Site Art Space, Hong Kong

Dick Quan, Collector, Board Member of Museum of Contemporary Art Australia Foundation, Board Member of Art Month, Sydney

Moderator: Elaine Ng, Editor-in-Chief, *ArtAsiaPacific*, Hong Kong

A complete version of the conversation is available at www.artbasel.com

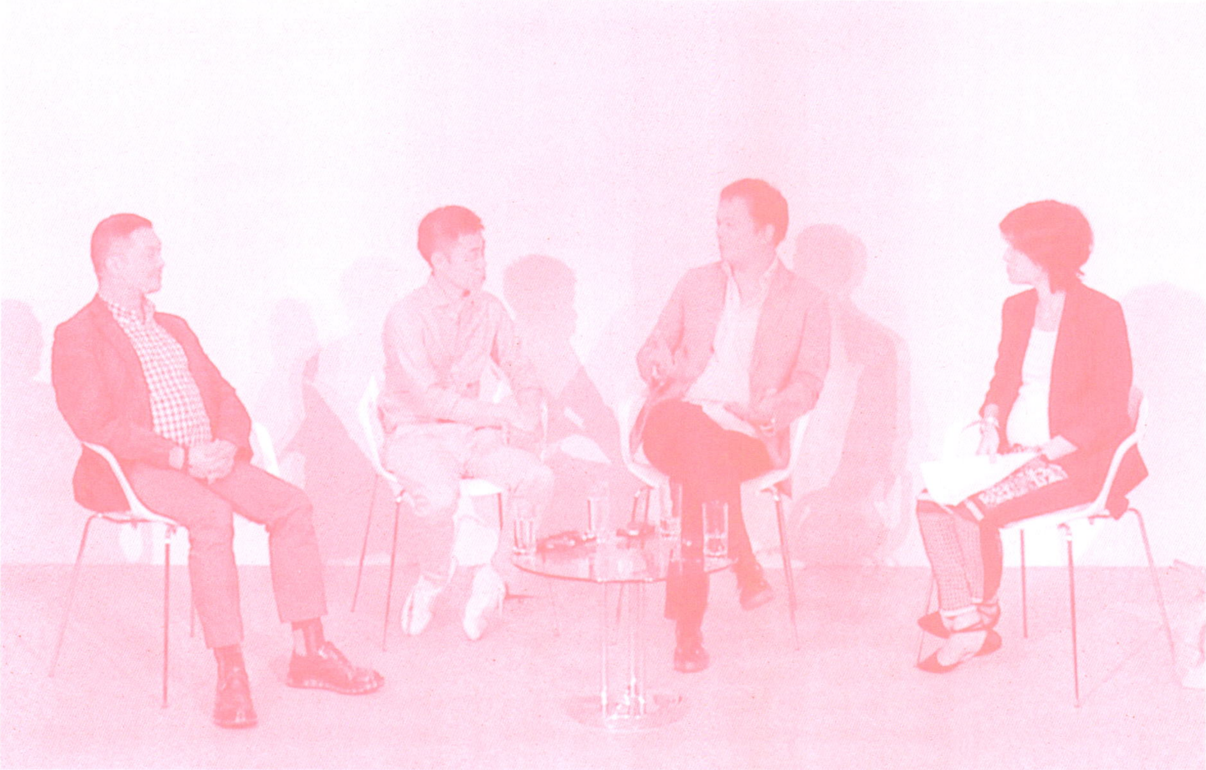

From left to right: Dick Quan, Alan Lau, Marcel Crespo, Elaine Ng

Mr. Alan Lau is head of the High Tech, Media, and Telecommunications Practice at McKinsey & Company's Greater China office. He also heads up the CFO Service Line for the Corporate Finance Practice in Asia. He previously worked at Citibank, London, in the investment banking division, and graduated from Oxford with a Masters degree in engineering. He is an active collector in Hong Kong, and is a member of the board of the non-profit art space Para/Site. He also sits on Tate's Asia-Pacific Acquisitions Committee.

In the world of collecting, the past is the father of the future: art is long and life is short.
— Elaine Ng

Dr. Dick Quan is Founding Director of Holdsworth House Medical Practice in Sydney. He's a prominent art collector, and has sat on many boards such as the Art Gallery Society of New South Wales, the Start Committee of the Museum of Contemporary Art in Australia, and currently serves as a board member of Sydney's Museum of Contemporary Art, the Art Gallery of South Australia, and Art Month Sydney.

How did you begin collecting, and how did you get to where you are today? And how would you describe your own taste in art?

MARCEL CRESPO I started buying art in my early 20s. I had bought my first home, and it felt cold. Something was missing. That's when I decided I wanted to buy art, and bring it into my life. I wouldn't call myself a collector at that point; I was still very young. On the other hand, collecting has always been part of my life. When I was younger I would collect things like coins, stamps, even knives. I have the collecting bug, if you want to call it that. My collection today is basically based on Filipino and Western art. It's a reflection of who I am. I was born in the Philippines and lived half my life in the United States.

I started collecting where most collectors start, with figurative works. I was looking for works where I could see that the artist had spent a lot of time and effort on the artwork to achieve technical excellence; artists like Ronald Ventura, Martin Eder, Damian Loeb. Then I moved into a phase where I started collecting 1980s artists from the West. I was very interested in the Pictures Generation, artists like David Salle, Robert Longo, and Richard Prince.

I'm currently exploring abstraction, process-based work, and video, for example Maria Taniguchi, Matias Faldbakken, Piotr Uklański, etc. You know, when you invited me onto this panel, I did a little bit of retrospection looking back at my collection; I realized that I might have ADD (Attention Deficit Disorder), or something. My tastes have changed so frequently …

ALAN LAU I started collecting around eight years ago. It started with the very simple idea that I wanted something for my new office wall. I wanted something very Hong Kong. There was only one person who came to mind, and actually he was not even recognized as an artist at the time. It was Tsang Tsou Choi or the "King of Kowloon," a Hong Kong graffiti calligraphy artist. But of course, my exposure to art started earlier, mostly when I was studying in the UK. I remember seeing a shark in a tank, and a pool of oil, wondering if it was art, and not really understanding it. Things finally made sense when I started collecting, because I started researching a lot more, especially about Hong Kong and China artists.

There are a couple of things that fascinate me: artists who work with text and language, not just because of the power of words, but also the way it can translate into something graphic and visual, such as Xu Bing, or Tsang Kin-Wah. Probably because of my professional work, I'm also interested in new media and technology: I love what Cao Fei has done with *RMB City*, and if you draw the line a little bit earlier, what Nam June Paik has done with media art. Thirdly, I also collect things that I think are helping to document what we are currently experiencing in urbanization, the social and political changes that we are witnessing in China, but also in the rest of the world; artists like Ai Weiwei and Takahiro Iwasaki.

Before this panel, we talked a little bit about whether we have regional, local, or global collections. In my opinion, you always stand in the cultures that you started in—which means for me, Hong Kong and Europe—I look at the world from that point of view. It's something I learned from the Tate in London, which has a global collection, but always stands in London, and looks at the world this way.

DICK QUAN I must say that I was genetically bred to collect art. I come from a family of completely mad collectors! Like Mr. Crespo, I started by collecting stamps and coins as a kid, but very soon the "disease" took over. I started collecting art at 21, when my father gave me an Edo Japanese print for my birthday. Then I went to university and met a lot of young artists like Lindy Lee; but the real trigger was at the 1986 Venice Biennale, at the exhibition *Futurism and Futurisms* held at the Palazzo Grassi. I had an awakening: I decided I was going to be an art collector. I started in Australia, where I collected artists in very regional and remote places. Then, after a tour to different Biennales, I decided to collect at Biennales. At one of them, in 1997, I met Mariko Mori, who showed me the work that she presented at the Danish Pavilion of the Venice Biennale: *Nirvana*. I thought, "*that*'s what I want," new media, the things for the future!

My collection is about what I consider to have cross-relevance and resonance for me and with the rest of the world. So I mainly collect what I call the "PRACCAs"—Pacific Rim Aesthetic Climate Change Artists. I believe that in Asia at the moment we are going through an aesthetic climate change, as relevant and startling as when the Impressionists displaced the Academy artists, when Pop jumped on top of Abstract Expressionism, or when cynical realism jumped on top of Social Realism. Recently I've been very impressed by Indonesian and especially post-Reformasi artists. I believe good art always comes from struggle.

I also extensively collect works from art collectives—another emergence in the PRACCA revolution. In my opinion, multiple minds are better than one; they offer a group vision. I'm interested in BirdHead, who redefines Chinese calligraphy through the medium of photography, and MadeIn Company, AES+F, teamLab from Japan, Elmgreen & Dragset.

I also collect artists from the Melbourne School of Model Making in Australia (MSMM) in Australia (such as Ron Mueck, Patricia Piccinini, Kate Rohde)—artists that have either lived or worked in Melbourne at some point and engage in model-making. For me these are very important artists, because their aesthetic is Western-based, but at the same time relates to Asian cultures.

EN In countries such as Hong Kong and the Philippines, where collecting is not institutionalized, do collectors have a responsibility to the society they live in, in comparison to support provided by the government?

DQ Especially in a place like Australia, where sport is the cultural supreme, collectors do have an important responsibility. It is up to collectors to support artists via the primary market, by investing in the cultural infrastructure of the community, purchasing artworks, and maintaining a dialogue with them. This will drive them to make better work, and avoid turning them into industrial producers of endless art products.

I believe it's my responsibility to make art accessible in places where it is not present. It changed my life: I want to give people the possibility to have that same feeling, and then be as passionate as me. I also believe I never own a work of art. I buy it because I think that it should be given to the next generation or to someone else because I see value in it. If I can't buy a work, I would like to see the institutions, where more people would see it, get the work.

I believe it's my responsibility to make art accessible in places where it is not present. — Dick Quan

MC In the Philippines, things are complicated because it's still developing. Art has taken a backseat in terms of priority, so that's where collectors have to get involved, to somehow try to support the local infrastructures and the local community. A lot of people have grand ideas of what being part of the community is, like building a mammoth museum or making huge donations to institutions, and I don't think it's about that. It's actually more about community building. For example, it's about communication and contact with Western institutions, galleries, and collectors, inviting them to see what there is in the Philippines, introducing them to the art community there, building dialogues between institutions and artists. A simple gesture such as introducing an artist to a gallery over lunch can lead to a show in New York! So, yes, there is a responsibility, and if you love art you can invest in it in more ways than just buying it.

AL I think the government can definitely do more and should do more. People donate, especially traditional art in Hong Kong (and also worldwide), but they don't donate in the contemporary art field. I hope it's simply because of the fact that we don't really have a contemporary art-dedicated institution in Hong Kong yet, which will change with the opening of M+. They will have their own budget, and hopefully it will really be a catalyst to draw people there. I agree with Dick, art needs to be seen and appreciated by others. And only institutions can do that. A lot of private museums are opening in China, but what a public institution can do is definitely different.

I hope that once M+ is built, a culture of donating artworks will develop.
— Alan Lau

DQ For many of my European friends, the language of these Asian artists I collect is not something they are familiar with. So it's also part of my responsibility to inform them about what I see in it and articulate those things. With the aesthetic climate change we are going through, I feel we have great opportunities, and art fairs are another place for them to happen. They are the spot where thousands of collectors converge, and in that sense they facilitate sharing, and you will always find someone who understands the work more than you do. I've learned much more in fairs and biennales through speaking with other collectors, artists, gallerists, etc. than by spending endless nights surfing the Internet!

EN You recently donated the performance *Guards Kissing* (2002) by Tino Sehgal to M+. It is a quite challenging and unusual artwork for Hong Kong …

AL I saw his work at documenta, and then at Tate Modern, and started to talk to Marian Goodman about acquiring a piece. I realized it didn't really make sense for me to own it because Tino's work, unlike any other work, is not allowed to be photographed or filmed. It is even more important for that kind of art to be presented in an institution. We spent time trying to find the right piece. We decided on something based on body language. It can be set up in any room, and when you walk in, you see two museum security guards kissing. *Impromptu*, right? And it can be a male and a female guard, it can be two men, it can be two women. It challenges so many things: What is art? How would people react to an intimate act? How would a *Chinese or Asian audience* react to such an intimate act? Recently there has been a lot of talk about gay and lesbian issues in Hong Kong. How would people react if there are two men and two women acting out? It's so challenging in so many ways, and really makes sense within a public institution. I suppose this donation I made shows local support to the museum. I hope that once M+ is built in Hong Kong, a culture of donating artworks will develop.

EN In communities lacking art infrastructures—museums, art schools, foundations, kunsthalles, archives of local art history—how many people does it take to get things moving?

AL I was actually surprised to realize how few people and resources it takes to start an art project. When Para/Site started about 15 years ago, it was a couple of artists coming together into an art collective … now it has grown to be a very important institution in Hong Kong.

MC Obviously you want as many people as you can get, but it really just takes one. I don't know if one single collector can change a situation alone, but I think a community formed by individuals coming together as a group can. In the Philippines I'm beginning to see that contemporary art has entered into the consciousness of a lot of people over the past ten years. In the past two or three years I've seen a lot of changes in people actually coming together and really trying to support local institutions. My generation of Filipinos is much more active than the generations of the past. That's all part of its growing process.

DQ In Australia we have the infrastructure—the government built all the museums often 100 years ago, and also very recently as well—but they don't support putting the art into the museums' collections. They give money to buy the paper clips. So it's the responsibility of individuals like us, passionate individuals. I know that our presence on this panel will stimulate friends and others to contribute.

EN Could you tell us about some of your most exciting recent purchases?

DQ I have bought a lot of works by Eko Nugroho, Hahan [Uji Handoko], and other Indonesian artists recently.

AL I recently bought works by Sun Xun, Zhao Zhao, and Koki Tanaka, who's representing Japan this year at the Venice Biennale.

MC At the fair here I purchased works by Ming Wong, David Ostrowski, and Svenja Deininger.

EN What would your suggestions and advice be to a new collector?

MC I think the most important thing is to be patient.

DQ You have to collect what really resonates with you. One of the mistakes collectors make is to buy names. For me, it's important to look at a lot of works, decide what I like, ignore the name, ignore the gallery.

MC Yes, you really have to look as much as you can. That's the key.

AL Go see, do research, speak to curators, gallerists, but at the end of the day, don't just listen to them, because as you can imagine people in the art world are all very opinionated! Listen to yourself, and you're going to end up collecting things that speak about your own story.

AUDIENCE How do you deal with editing or selling of parts of your collection?

DQ For me a work is only good when it's alive, and it's only alive when other people see it. It's not good for the artist if you pile his/her works in the storeroom. To have the work seen is part of my contract with the artist. Therefore, sometimes, if an auction house asks me to put one up for auction, I'll say yes, because weirdly enough that's also helping the artist. Nevertheless, I have more difficulty selling artworks I commissioned. They were part of a dialogue between the artist and myself, and so there's some part of me that lives in the work.

MC I have a big family, and sometimes when I don't have enough space at home, I *place* art in their homes. [Laughs] I agree with Dick. Even though I do have works in storage, they should be out there, and people should see them.

AL Personally, I've only sold pieces that I've bought at auctions, because there's a lot less attachment to them. If you buy a work from a gallery or an artist, you almost feel a moral obligation to keep it, even if it means keeping it in storage …

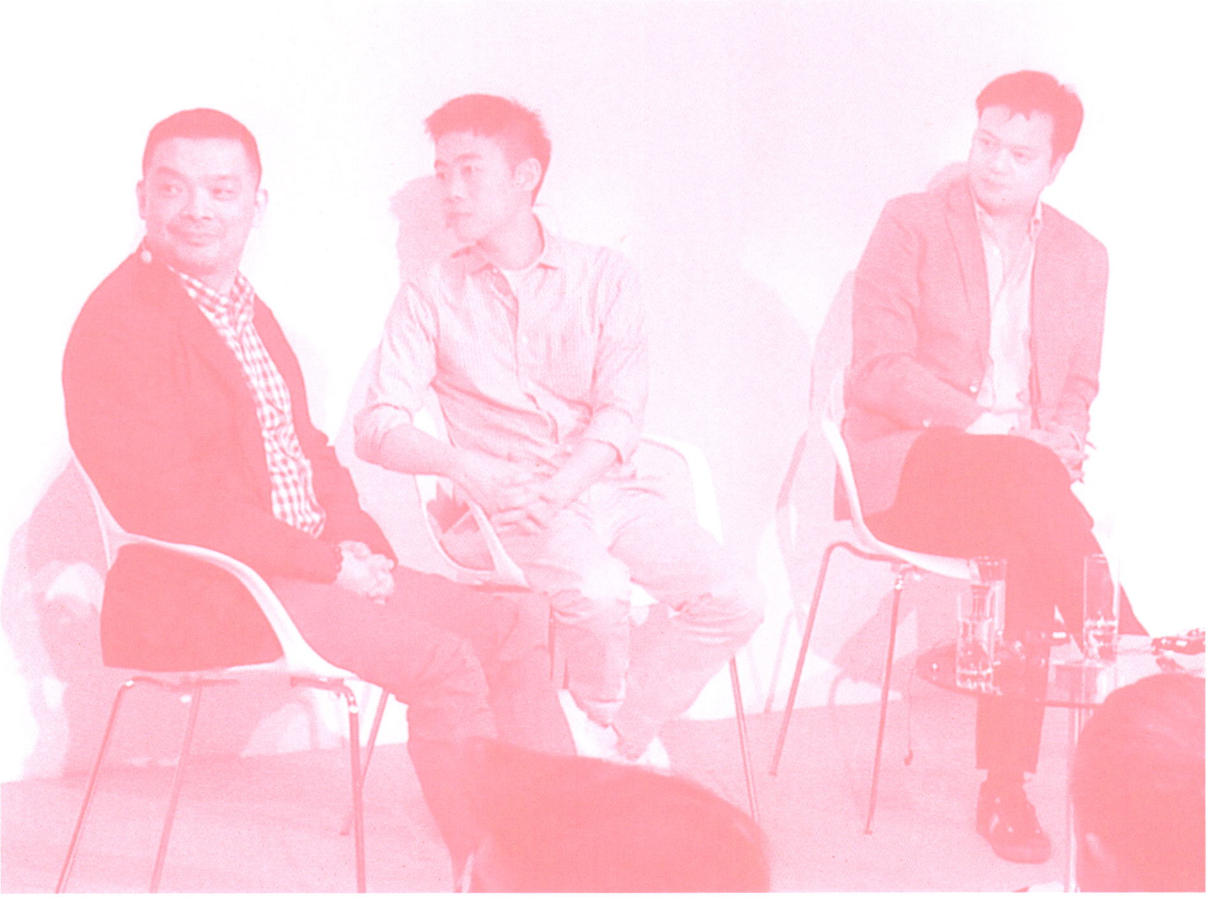

From left to right: Dick Quan, Alan Lau, Marcel Crespo

B

Balice Hertling

Paris ● Discoveries

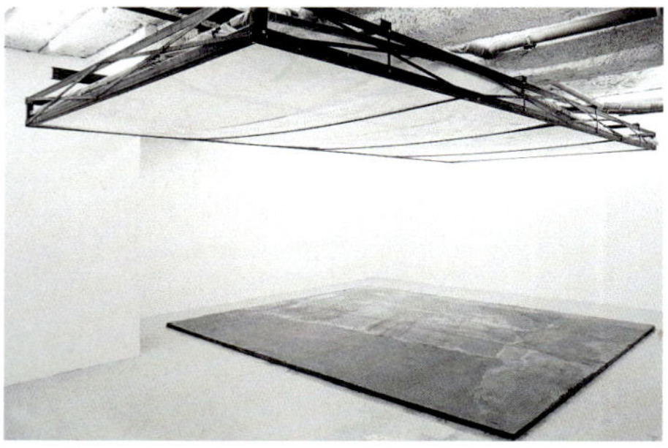

What first compelled you to open a gallery?
In 2007 there were not many young galleries in Paris. We started the gallery in collaboration with castillo/corrales (a curator-run exhibition space that was also co-organized by Oscar Tuazon. one of the artists we work with). It was a very dynamic group and this situation compelled us to launch a gallery.

Who is the first artist you showed and what was most memorable about that show?
Falke Pisano in January 2008. Lots of discussion around that exhibition and three quite different reviews in the publications *Artforum*, *Flash Art*, and *Frieze*, among others.

When did you first participate in Art Basel and what was most memorable about that show?
In 2009 we did Statements in Basel with Luca Frei, and Unlimited with Falke Pisano.

- **Contact** Balice Hertling
Daniele Balice
daniele@balicehertling.com
gallery@balicehertling.com
- **Established** 2007
- **Owner(s) / Partner(s)** Daniele Balice
Alexander Hertling
- **Team** 4
- **Space(s)** 90 m^2
- **Artists at Art Basel** Alexander May
- **Further artists represented** Neïl Beloufa
Kerstin Brätsch
Isabelle Cornaro
Mary Beth Edelson
Luca Frei
Nikolas Gambaroff
Charles Mayton
Greg Parma Smith
Reto Pulfer
Samuel Richardot
Oscar Tuazon
Stephen Willats

Baró

São Paulo ● Positions

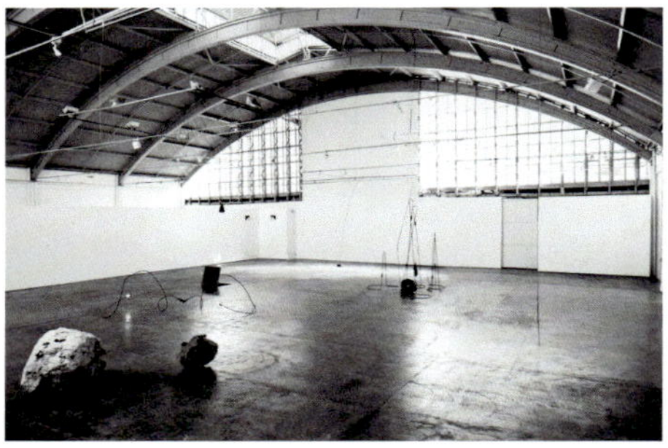

What first compelled you to open a gallery?
The intense art flux in Latin America and also the contemporary art background of the two gallerists were some of the few reasons that made us create Baró Galeria.

Who is the first artist you showed and what was most memorable about that show?
The first show was curated by us and titled *Arsenal*. The idea behind this show was to exhibit our "artsy guns," established Latin American artists, such as José Resende, Carlos Fajardo, Jac Leirner, Hélio Oiticica, Pablo Siquier, Roberto Jacoby, Iván Navarro, among others, with the new generation: Wilfredo Prieto, Henrique Oliveira, Dario Escobar, Tomás Espina, Yoshua Okón, etc.

When did you first participate in Art Basel and what was most memorable about that show?
We first participated in Art Basel in Miami Beach in 2011, with a solo project by the Brazilian artist Rosana Ricalde. The booth was filled with sentences from the book *Invisible Cities* (1972) by Italo Calvino, reproducing the world map with all these sentences and generating a complex and poetic reinterpretation of the book. The most memorable effect of this project was that it created a common "sense," where all the cultures, countries, and languages combined harmoniously in the space suggested by the artist.

- **Contact** Baró Galeria
Adriano Casanova
adrianocasanova@barogaleria.com
info@barogaleria.com
- **Established** 2010
- **Owner(s) / Partner(s)** Maria Baró
Adriano Casanova
- **Space(s)** 1,500 m^2
- **Artists at Art Basel** Lourival Cuquinha
- **Further artists represented** Norbert Bisky
Toby Christian
Nicola Costantino
Elena Damiani
Felipe Ehrenberg
Dario Escobar
Fabiano Gonper
Patrick Hamilton
Roberto Jacoby
Claudia Jaguaribe
Flavia Junqueira
Daniel Lannes
Rafael Lozano-Hemmer
David Medalla
Jorge Menna Barreto
Moris
Ivan Navarro
Yoshua Okón
Tulio Pinto
Enrique Radigales
Pablo Siquier
Mariana Sissia
Courtney Smith
Eduardo Srur
Tatiana Trouvé
Massimo Vitali

Baronian

Brussels

Galleries Unlimited

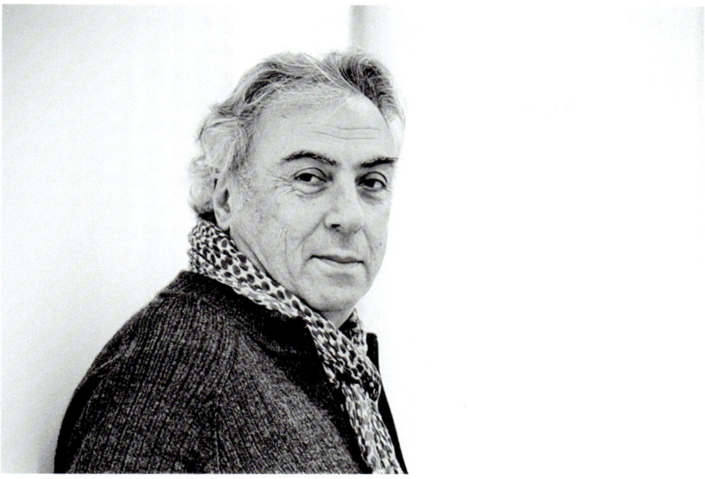

What first compelled you to open a gallery?
I started as an editor of silkscreen prints by contemporary artists, but I felt the need to meet with an audience.

Who is the first artist you showed and what was most memorable about that show?
Antonio Dias. The intention was that he would present silkscreen prints but he arrived with original drawings. The audience was composed only of some acquaintances and family members.

When did you first participate in Art Basel and what was most memorable about that show?
It was in 1978 and I sold my first work (Gilberto Zorio) to Harald Szeemann (who offered it to his wife for her birthday).

- **Contact** Albert Baronian
  Albert Baronian
  albert@albertbaronian.com
  info@albertbaronian.com
- **Established** 1973
- **Owner(s) / Partner(s)** Albert Baronian
- **Team** 5
- **Space(s)** 290 m²
- **Artists at Art Basel** Thomas Bogaert
  Marie José Burki
  Lionel Estève
  Olaf Holzapfel
  Tony Oursler
  Eric Poitevin
  Stanley Whitney
  Gilberto Zorio
- **Further artists represented** David Brognon
  Robert Crumb
  Robert Devriendt
  Michel Frère
  Gilbert & George
  Chris Johanson
  Florian Maier-Aichen
  Joseph Marioni
  Xavier Mary
  Benoit Platéus
  Emmanuelle Quertain
  Ry Rocklen
  Yvan Salomone
  Charles Sandison
  Alain Séchas
  Bruno Serralongue
  Helmut Stallaerts
  Achraf Touloub
  Marc Trivier
  Wang Du
  Robert Wilson
  Thomas Zipp

von Bartha

Basel
S-Chanf

Galleries

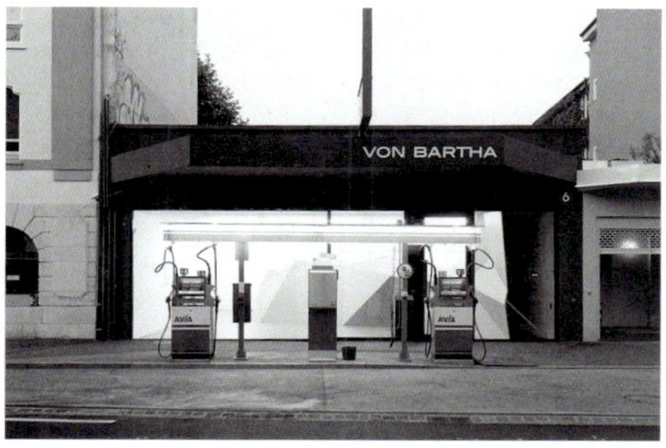

What first compelled you to open a gallery?
A strong urge to show art that fascinated us and was not given a wide recognition at the time.

Who is the first artist you showed and what was most memorable about that show?
November 1970 was the opening exhibition (a group show). In March 1971, we exhibited Johannes Grützke and Marcello Morandini: the largest contrast of artistic expression but it worked!

When did you first participate in Art Basel and what was most memorable about that show?
In 1978. Showing a wonderful still life by Amédée Ozenfant.

- **Contact** von Bartha
  Stefan von Bartha
  stefan@vonbartha.com
  info@vonbartha.com
- **Established** 1970
- **Owner(s) / Partner(s)** Margareta von Bartha
  Miklos von Bartha
- **Team** 8
- **Space(s)** 1,750 m²
- **Artists at Art Basel** Christian Andersson
  Andrew Bick
  Camille Graeser
  Terry Haggerty
  Daniel Robert Hunziker
  Imi Knoebel
  Perrine Lievens
  Bernhard Luginbühl
  Karim Noureldin
  Sarah Oppenheimer
  Boris Rebetez
  Jesús Rafael Soto
  Sophie Taeuber-Arp
  Magnus Thierfelder
  Jean Tinguely
  Victor Vasarely
  Bernar Venet
  Gerhard von Graevenitz
  John Wood & Paul Harrison
  Beat Zoderer

Baudach

Berlin

Galleries
Galleries

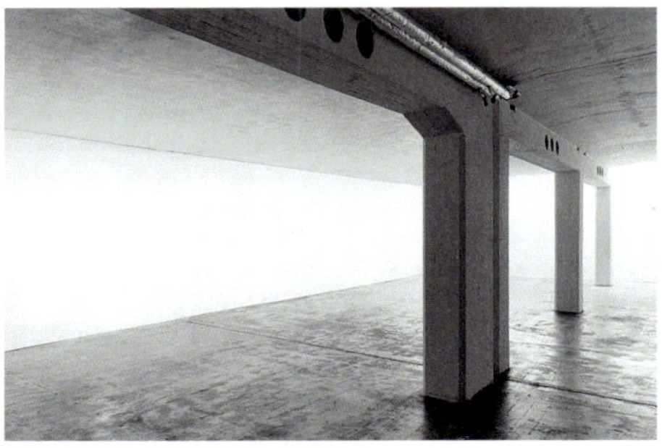

What first compelled you to open a gallery?
With a background in philosophy, history, and politics, and aiming at an academic career, I was always interested in art and the exchange of thoughts and ideas with artists. I understand art as an alternative sort of knowledge, and artistic practice as a form of research; therefore I am

glad and thankful that I did not become a professor but a gallerist, working with and for my artists.

Who is the first artist you showed and what was most memorable about that show?
The first show at the gallery was a solo presentation by German artist Andy Hope 1930. The exhibition consisted of a painting with pictographic human figures looking up at a burning sky, hanging alone on the most prominent wall. A few days later the 9/11 attacks occurred. It seemed as if the work had predicted the disaster and was then overpainted by the artist.

When did you first participate in Art Basel and what was most memorable about that show?
The first time that we participated in Art Basel was in 2011. We were showing a juxtaposition of works by Jürgen Klauke from the early 1970s and recent works by Thomas Zipp in the Feature sector. Both artists worked on transformation of self-identity physically (Klauke) and psychologically (Zipp). I remember being completely overwhelmed by the number of well educated visitors. Also, I remember the wonderful and sublime booth of Galerie 1900–2000 focused on art creation and the collection of André Breton.

- **Contact** Galerie Guido W. Baudach
  Elisa Freudenreich
  elisa@guidowbaudach.com
  galerie@guidowbaudach.com
- **Established** 2001
- **Owner(s) / Partner(s)** Guido W. Baudach
- **Team** 5
- **Space(s)** 400 m²
- **Artists at Art Basel** Björn Dahlem, Thilo Heinzmann, Andy Hope 1930, Rashid Johnson, Erwin Kneihsl, Markus Selg, Thomas Zipp
- **Further artists represented** André Butzer, Thomas Helbig, Jürgen Klauke, Bjarne Melgaard, Aïda Ruilova, Erik van Lieshout

Beck & Eggeling

Düsseldorf ● Galleries

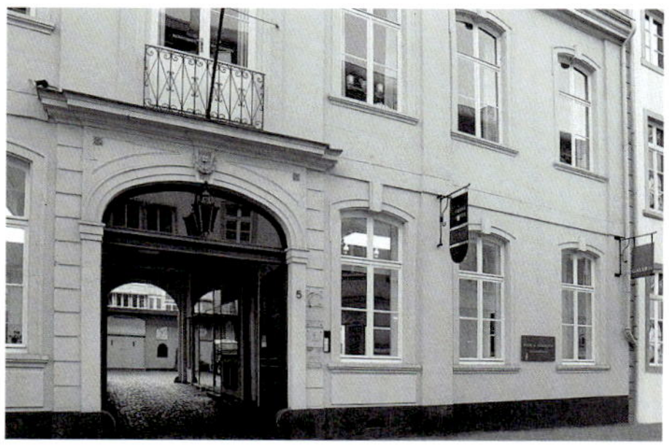

What first compelled you to open a gallery?
The passion for art.

Who is the first artist you showed and what was most memorable about that show?
Lyonel Feininger—works from Weimar and Dessau. Besides the great artworks, the exhibition was most memorable to us because in the accompanying catalogue we were able to publish the exchange of letters between Lyonel Feininger and his wife for the first time. This was an art historical highlight.

When did you first participate in Art Basel and what was most memorable about that show?
We first participated in Art Basel in Hong Kong in 2013. We showed outstanding ZERO pieces by Heinz Mack, Otto Piene, Günther Uecker, and others. Our booth was elected one of the Top Ten booths at the fair by Louise Blouin Media's *Artinfo*—but we did not sell a single piece.

- **Contact** Beck & Eggeling
  Katja Ott
  katja.ott@beck-eggeling.de
  info@beck-eggeling.de
- **Established** 1994 (Leipzig)
- **Owner(s) / Partner(s)** Michael Beck, Ute Eggeling
- **Team** 12
- **Space(s)** 300 m²
- **Artists at Art Basel** Hermann Bartels, Lucio Fontana, Heinz Mack, Piero Manzoni, Otto Piene, Günther Uecker, Gerhard von Graevenitz
- **Further artists represented** Magdalena Abakanowicz, Bertozzi Casoni, Marc Chagall, Gehard Demetz, Lyonel Feininger, Ernst Ludwig Kirchner, Paul Klee, August Macke, Emil Nolde, Heribert C. Ottersbach, Pablo Picasso, Manolo Valdés

Beijing Art Now

Beijing ● Galleries

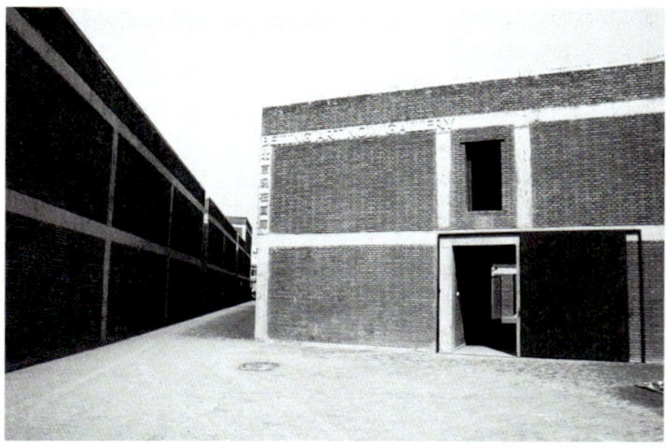

What first compelled you to open a gallery?
The hope of finding good Chinese contemporary art and presenting it to the world.

When did you first participate in Art Basel and what was most memorable about that show?
In 2008 in Basel.

- **Contact** Beijing Art Now Gallery
  Yudi Zhang
  yudiarts@gmail.com
  angallery@vip.sina.com
- **Established** 2004
- **Owner(s) / Partner(s)** Huang Liaoyuan
- **Team** 8
- **Space(s)** 800 m²
- **Artists at Art Basel** He Sen, Hong Shaopei, Song Chen, Yang Liu, Yang Shaobin, Yao Peng, Yu Xiao, Zhang Fazhi, Zheng Wei, Zhou Jie
- **Further artists represented** Fan Anxiang, Gao Yansong, Han Lei, Huang Jinming, Lei Benben, Li Bo, Liu Chuan, Lu Hao, Ma Liuming, Qin Qi, Qu Fengguo, Song Yonghon, Tan Qizhi, Wang Mai, Wen Ling, Wu Xiaohai, Xin Haizhou, Zhang Runshi, Zhang Xiaogang

Beijing Commune

Beijing

Galleries
Statements

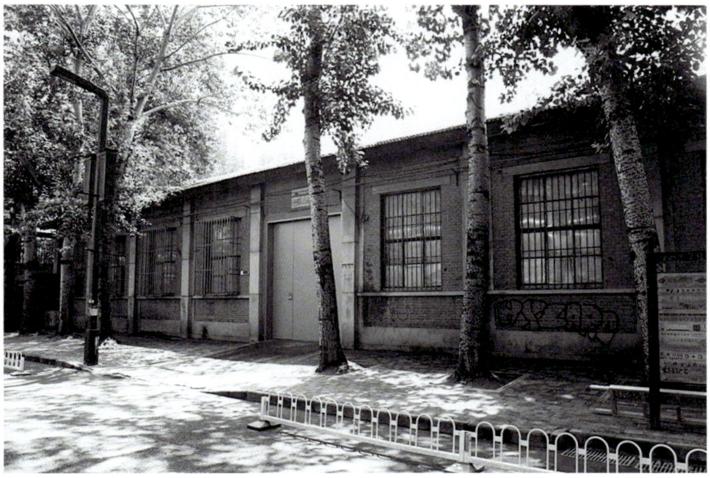

What first compelled you to open a gallery?
In 2004, the survival of China's contemporary art prompted me to establish Beijing Commune. The Chinese galleries have actually facilitated the emergence of China's contemporary art from a semi-underground situation, and won it gradual acceptance by the public.

Who is the first artist you showed and what was most memorable about that show?
The first program of Beijing Commune was a group exhibition, *The Game of Realism*, in 2005. At that time, there was no contemporary art museum, in the real sense, in China. Therefore, art galleries in China have been playing multiple roles in the development of the community. Here a gallery is not just a place to showcase art, but also the witness and the interpreter of contemporary art in China. The most memorable thing about this first exhibition was the recognition of the exhibition by the artists, and an audience wishful of better understanding China's contemporary art.

When did you first participate in Art Basel and what was most memorable about that show?
Beijing Commune first participated in Art Basel in Basel in 2013, and in the first edition of Art Basel in Hong Kong also in 2013.

- **Contact** Beijing Commune
  Jingjing Lu
  lvjingjing@beijingcommune.com
  info@beijingcommune.com
- **Established** 2004
- **Owner(s) / Partner(s)** Leng Lin (Owner)
  Lu Jingjing (Partner and Director)
- **Team** 5
- **Space(s)** 600 m²
- **Artists at Art Basel** Hong Hao
  Hu Xiaoyuan
  Huang Yuxing
  Liang Yuanwei
  Liu Jianhua
  Ma Qiusha
  Wang Guangle
  Xie Molin
  Zhao Yao
- **Further artists represented** Polit-sheer-form Office (PSFO)
  Song Dong
  Tang Hui
  Xiao Yu
  Yin Xiuzhen
  Zhang Xiaogang

benítez

Madrid

Galleries

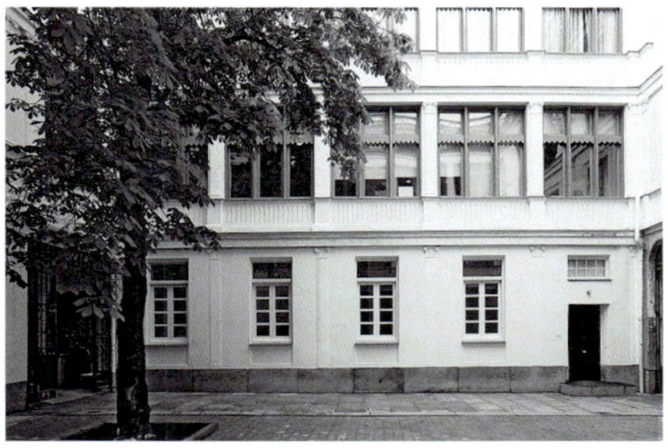

What first compelled you to open a gallery?
To be part of the creative process in the visual arts.

Who is the first artist you showed and what was most memorable about that show?
Ignasi Aballí. We developed a strong friendship, and he is still represented by the gallery today.

When did you first participate in Art Basel and what was most memorable about that show?
In 2002.

- **Contact** galería elba benítez
  Elba Benítez
  info@elbabenitez.com
- **Established** 1990
- **Owner(s) / Partner(s)** Elba Benítez
- **Team** 7
- **Space(s)** 143 m² (gallery) + 54 m² (office)
- **Artists at Art Basel** Armando Andrade Tudela
  Claudia Andujar
  Carlos Bunga
  Fernanda Fragateiro
  Carlos Garaicoa
  Mario García Torres
  Cristina Iglesias
- **Further artists represented** Ignasi Aballí
  Miriam Bäckström
  Cabello/Carceller
  Gintaras Didžiapetris
  Hreinn Fridfinnsson
  David Goldblatt
  Vik Muniz
  Ernesto Neto
  Francisco Ruiz de Infante
  Francesc Torres

Benzacar

Buenos Aires

Galleries
Unlimited
Galleries

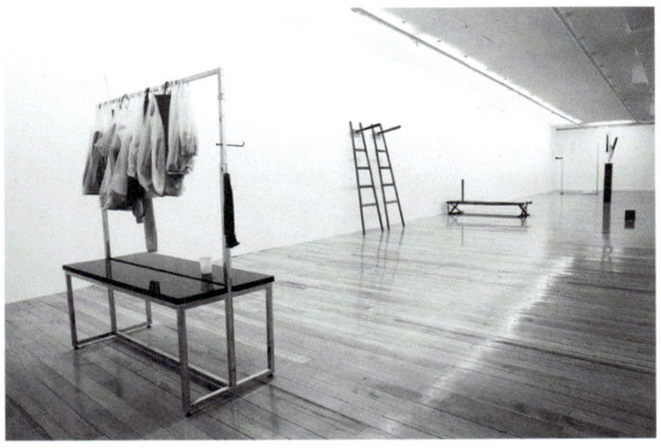

What first compelled you to open a gallery?
The gallery was founded in 1965 by Ruth Benzacar. In 2000, after she passed away, her daughter Orly Benzacar took over the gallery and as a family legacy continued her mother's project of supporting art from Argentina. Today Orly runs the gallery together with her own daughter Mora Bacal.

When did you first participate in Art Basel and what was most memorable about that show?
In Miami Beach, in 2002. The most memorable thing was the feeling that we were being part of a very important event.

- **Contact** Ruth Benzacar Galería de Arte
Valeria Pecoraro
valeria@ruthbenzacar.com
info@ruthbenzacar.com
- **Established** 1965
- **Owner(s) / Partner(s)** Orly Benzacar
Mora Bacal
- **Team** 8
- **Space(s)** 600 m²
- **Artists at Art Basel** Eduardo Basualdo
Marina De Caro
Max Gómez Canle
Carlos Huffmann
Luciana Lamothe
Valentina Liernur
Jorge Macchi
Liliana Porter
Miguel Rothschild

de la Béraudière

Geneva ● Galleries

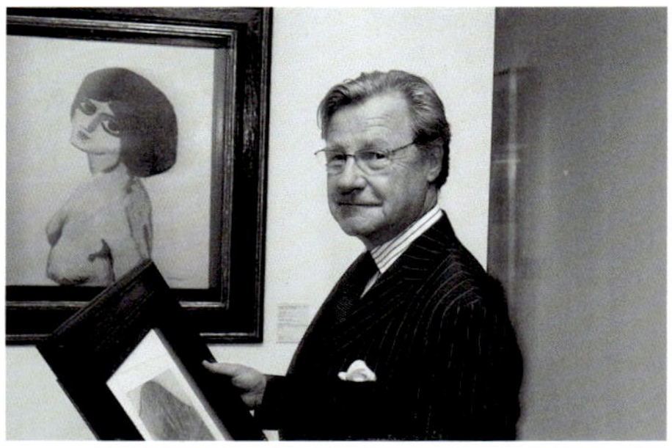

What first compelled you to open a gallery?
A passion for art and its market were the triggering factors that compelled me to open a gallery. Being a collector and coming from a family who has been collecting works of art since the end of the 19th century, I took up art dealing to continue this family tradition. Building a successful client-dealer relationship based on trust, knowledge, cooperation, and understanding was also a decisive factor.

Who is the first artist you showed and what was most memorable about that show?
What was most memorable at the opening of the gallery in Paris was the show dedicated to Pierre Bonnard, in 1994–1995. The exclusive selection of more than 150 drawings and watercolors by the artist contributed to gather, for the first time, his entire family around this event. This exhibition brought a happy end to their long disputes and it was reported as a significant show in the French media.

- **Contact** Galerie Jacques de la Béraudière
Paula Rey
paula@delaberaudiere.ch
galerie@delaberaudiere.ch
- **Established** 1994 (Paris)
2009 (Geneva)
- **Owner(s) / Partner(s)** Jacques de la Béraudière
- **Team** 3
- **Space(s)** 101 m²
- **Artists at Art Basel** Miquel Barceló
Victor Brauner
Marc Chagall
Salvador Dalí
Oscar Dominguez
Jean Dubuffet
Max Ernst
Sam Francis
Juan Gris
Wassily Kandinsky
Paul Klee
Yves Klein
Franz Kline
Fernand Léger
Richard Lindner
René Magritte
Marino Marini
Manolo Millares
Joan Miró
Joan Mitchell
Pablo Picasso
Martial Raysse
Germaine Richier
Chaïm Soutine
Yves Tanguy
Jean Tinguely
Maria Elena Vieira da Silva
Wols

Berggruen

San Francisco ● Galleries
Public

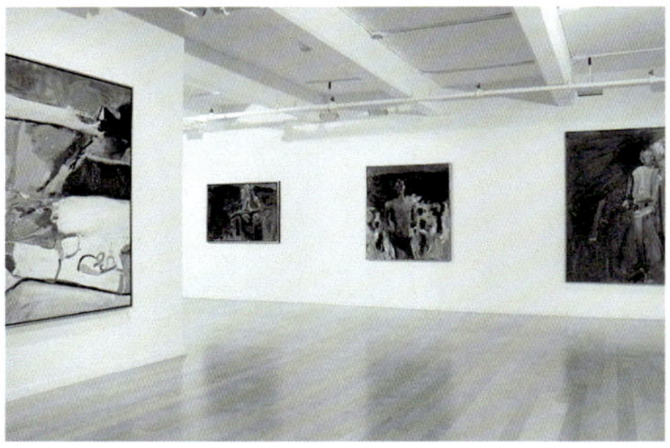

What first compelled you to open a gallery?
John Berggruen became an art dealer after reconnecting with his father Heinz Berggruen in the 1960s. Heinz Berggruen was an art dealer and collector who founded the Berggruen Museum in Berlin. He owned a gallery on the Île Saint-Louis in Paris. During this time he became acquainted with Pablo Picasso and eventually became his dealer. Berggruen resigned as director of the Paris gallery in 1980 in order to devote himself to collecting and dealing. In 1988 he donated 90 Klee works on paper to the Metropolitan Museum of Art in New York. In 1995, he finally left the art collection in a generous gesture to the Prussian Cultural Heritage Foundation. The collection, then comprising 118 works, opened to the public in 1997. In 2000, Heinz Berggruen's collection, which included 165 masterpieces by 20th-century masters such as Braque, Matisse, Klee, and Giacometti, with a unique group of 85 works by Picasso, was sold to the PCHF at about a quarter of its value. John says of his father's influence, "I wanted to get to know my father, and the easiest way do that was through his love of art and his work. He was passionate about his work. I found that I had an affinity for art. Maybe it's intuitive or genetic."

- **Contact** John Berggruen Gallery
Tatem Read
tatem@berggruen.com
info@berggruen.com
- **Established** 1970
- **Owner(s) / Partner(s)** Gretchen Berggruen
John Berggruen
- **Space(s)** 1,115 m²
- **Artists at Art Basel** Doug Aitken
John Baldessari
David Bates
Christopher Brown
Chuck Close
Willem de Kooning
Mark di Suvero
Richard Diebenkorn
Helen Frankenthaler
Alexander Gorlizki
Antony Gormley
Isca Greenfield-Sanders
Stephen Hannock
Donald Judd
Anish Kapoor
Ellsworth Kelly
Anselm Kiefer
Yayoi Kusama
Los Carpinteros
Morris Louis
Enrique Martínez Celaya
Tom McKinley
Julie Mehretu
Beatriz Milhazes
Nathan Oliveira
Martin Puryear
Ed Ruscha
Richard Serra
Joel Shapiro
Wayne Thiebaud

Berinson

Berlin

- Galleries

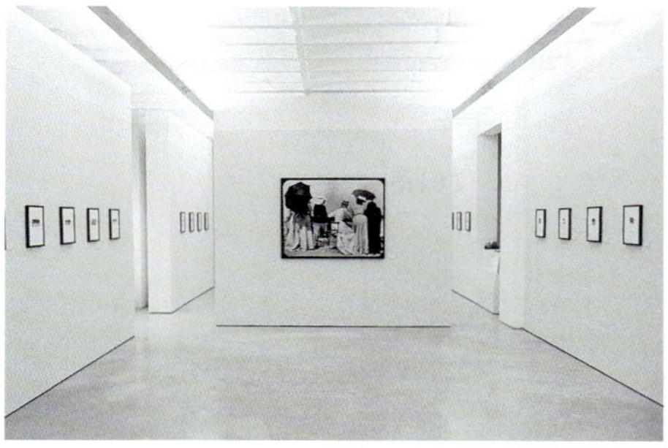

What first compelled you to open a gallery?
My favorite gallery space in an old Berlin apartment became available and I decided to open a gallery from one second to the next.

Who is the first artist you showed and what was most memorable about that show?
Weegee. It was the first comprehensive Weegee exhibition in Germany.

When did you first participate in Art Basel and what was most memorable about that show?
In 2002.

- **Contact** Galerie Berinson
  Natalia Kazmierczak
  natalia@berinson.de
  info@berinson.de
- **Established** 1988
- **Owner(s) / Partner(s)** Hendrik A. Berinson
- **Team** 4
- **Space(s)** 170 m²
- **Artists at Art Basel** Jankel Adler
  Hans Bellmer
  Max Ernst
  Hannah Höch
  László Moholy-Nagy
  Kurt Schwitters
  Stanisław Ignacy Witkiewicz
  Unica Zürn
- **Further artists represented** Willi Baumeister
  Karl Blossfeldt
  Marianne Brandt
  Claude Cahun
  Walter Dexel
  Otto Dix
  Hugo Erfurth
  Otto Freundlich
  Carl Grossberg
  George Grosz
  Raoul Hausmann
  John Heartfield
  Auguste Herbin
  Kurt Kranz
  Alfred Kubin
  Helmar Lerski
  El Lissitzky
  Man Ray
  Moriz Melzer
  Lee Miller
  Pierre Molinier
  Johannes Molzahn
  Georg Muche
  Oskar Nerlinger
  Richard Oelze
  Hans Richter
  Alexander Rodchenko
  Franz Roh
  Werner Rohde
  August Sander
  Oskar Schlemmer
  Rudolf Schlichter
  Arthur Segal
  Samuel Szczekacz
  Friedrich Vordemberge-Gildewart
  Weegee
  Wols

Bernier/Eliades

Athens

- Galleries
- Galleries Unlimited
- Galleries

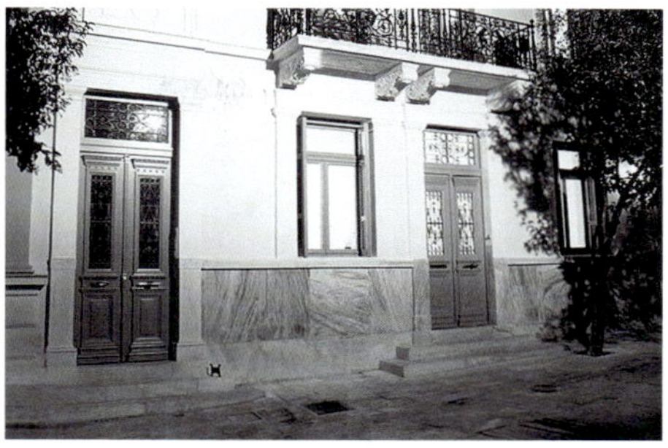

What first compelled you to open a gallery?
After starting in the publishing business with Parasol Press we wanted to present the international art scene that was then unknown in Greece.

Who is the first artist you showed and what was most memorable about that show?
Jannis Kounellis.

When did you first participate in Art Basel and what was most memorable about that show?
We had been showing with Parasol Press since 1974, and our first show with the gallery was in 1977.

- **Contact** Gallery Bernier/Eliades
  Elina Giannitsiotis
  elina@bernier-eliades.gr
  bernier@bernier-eliades.gr
- **Established** 1977
- **Owner(s) / Partner(s)** Jean Bernier
  Marina Eliades
- **Team** 5
- **Space(s)** 320 m²
- **Artists at Art Basel** Giovanni Anselmo
  Pier Paolo Calzolari
  Wim Delvoye
  Lionel Estève
  Edy Ferguson
  Gilbert & George
  Hannah Greely
  Cameron Jamie
  Dionisis Kavallieratos
  Jannis Kounellis
  Richard Long
  Valérie Mannaerts
  Jonathan Meese
  Marisa Merz
  Annette Messager
  Tony Oursler
  Lari Pittman
  Daniel Richter
  Susan Rothenberg
  Ulrich Rückriem
  Charles Sandison
  Thomas Schütte
  Jim Shaw
  Keith Sonnier
  Christiana Soulou
  Anup Mathew Thomas
  Wen Ling
  Entang Wiharso
  Yan Pei-Ming
  Zhang Hui
  Zhu Yu
- **Further artists represented** Haluk Akakçe
  Phillip Allen
  John Baldessari
  Herbert Brandl
  Stéphane Calais
  Alan Charlton
  Tony Cragg
  Carroll Dunham
  Donald Judd
  Moshekwa Langa
  Justin Lieberman
  Juan Muñoz
  Nikos Navridis
  Ry Rocklen
  Ed Ruscha
  Jeffrey Vallance
  Marnie Weber
  Sue Williams
  Robert Wilson

Fondation Beyeler

Riehen/Basel ● Galleries

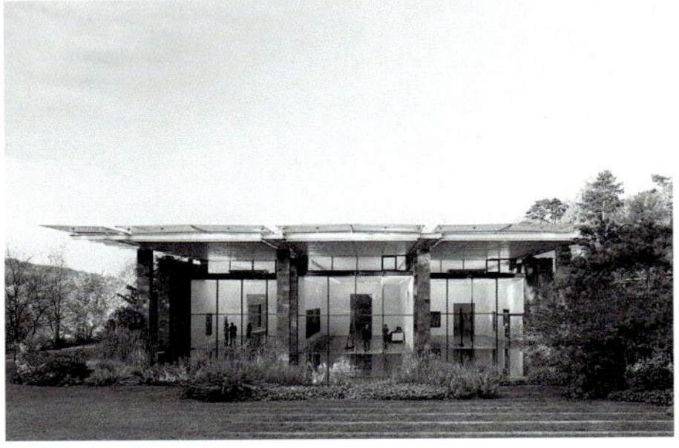

What first compelled Beyeler to open the foundation?

Ernst and Hildy Beyeler wished to make their outstanding art collection accessible to the public.

Who is the first artist the Fondation Beyeler showed and what was most memorable about that show?

Jasper Johns. Loans from the Artist and *Renzo Piano. Building Workshop*, both 1997–1998. The exhibitions highlighted the personal relationship of the founders and the museum to internationally renowned artists, as well as the close cooperation with the architect who built the museum.

- **Contact** Fondation Beyeler Elena DelCarlo elena.delcarlo@fondationbeyeler.ch info@fondationbeyeler.ch
- **Established** 1997
- **Owner(s) / Partner(s)** Ernst & Hildy Beyeler (Founders) Sam Keller (Director)
- **Team** 170
- **Space(s)** 3,800 m²

bitforms

New York ● Feature

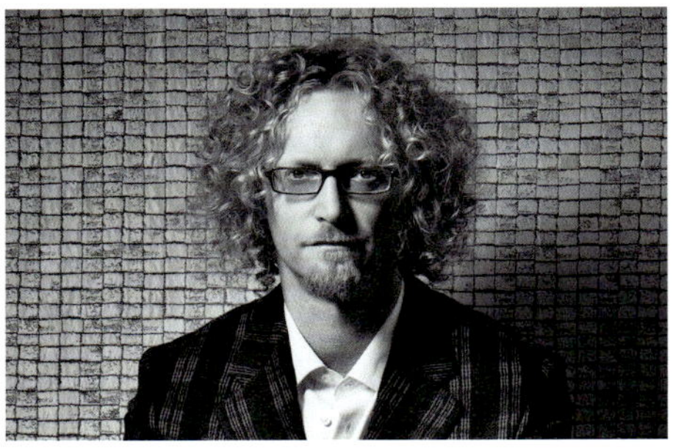

What first compelled you to open a gallery?

After running an online advertising company for many years, I desired to work more closely with the visually creative side of the business. I founded bitforms gallery after researching the new media art field, which was experiencing a tremendous amount of growth and attention. bitforms gallery is very much inspired by my research during this period, and the great number of museum survey exhibitions covering the topic. At that time in New York, the Guggenheim and Whitney both began commissioning net artists for the their permanent collections. The 2000 Whitney Biennial was the very first to really embrace the creative potential of technology. Other exhibitions influencing me were the SF MoMA's *010101*, Guggenheim's *Moving Pictures*, *BitStreams and Data Dynamics* at the Whitney, and P.S.1's *Animations*, all between 2000–2002. It was an incredible moment for this field, especially at the institutional level in New York.

When did you first participate in Art Basel and what was most memorable about that show?

In 2013. We showcased 50 years worth of work by Manfred Mohr, a German artist who started working with software in 1969. This moment not only recognized his accomplishments as a conceptualist and painter-turned-software artist, it was also a time to reflect on the tremendous cultural shifts surrounding new media art.

- **Contact** bitforms gallery Laura Blereau laura@bitforms.com info@bitforms.com
- **Established** 2001
- **Owner(s) / Partner(s)** Steven Sacks
- **Team** 5
- **Space(s)** 81 m²
- **Artists at Art Basel** Manfred Mohr
- **Further artists represented** Jeffrey Blondes, Daniel Canogar, U-Ram Choe, R. Luke DuBois, Claudia Hart, Yael Kanarek, Tim Knowles, Beryl Korot, Lynn Hershman Leeson, Rafael Lozano-Hemmer, Quayola, Casey Reas, Erwin Redl, Daniel Rozin, Björn Schülke, Siebren Versteeg, Peter Vogel, Zimoun, Marina Zurkow

Blau

London
Munich ● Galleries

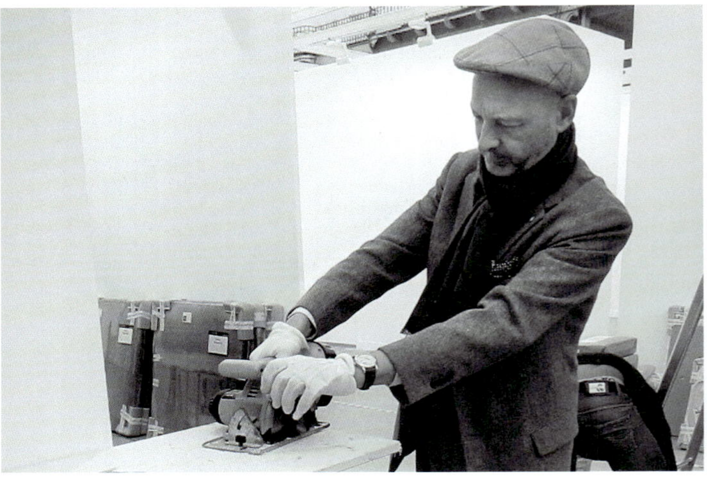

What first compelled you to open a gallery?

I was collecting an artist's work that nobody wanted to show, so I turned my photo studio into a gallery.

Who is the first artist you showed and what was most memorable about that show?

Karl-Heinz Schwind. We actually sold some drawings. Some of the clients we sold to are still clients of ours, 23 years down the road.

When did you first participate in Art Basel and what was most memorable about that show?

In 1994.

- **Contact** Daniel Blau Laura Seiler laura@danielblau.com contact@danielblau.com
- **Established** 1990
- **Owner(s) / Partner(s)** Daniel Blau
- **Team** 9
- **Space(s)** 400 m²
- **Artists at Art Basel** Andy Warhol

Blindspot

Hong Kong ● Insights

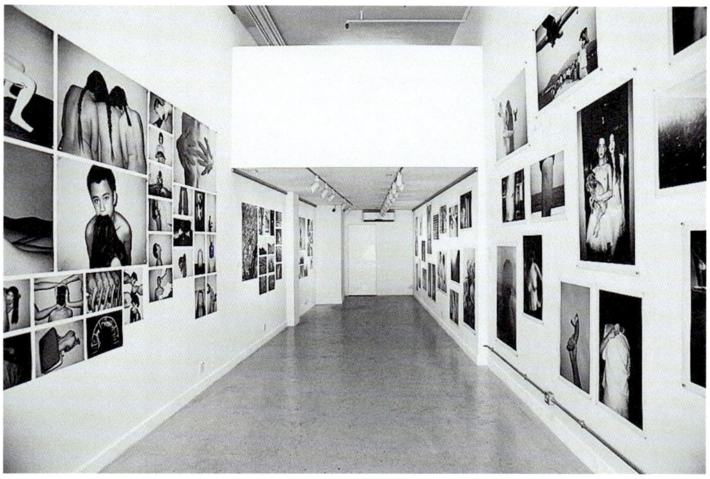

What first compelled you to open a gallery?
I was first compelled to photography when I studied film and photography, and aspired to be a photographer myself. I was inspired to open a gallery focusing on this area because photography was relatively under-represented in Hong Kong's art scene and art market.

Who is the first artist you showed and what was most memorable about that show?
The first artists we showed are a combination of Mainland Chinese and Hong Kong artists presented in a 3-part exhibition curated by Janet Fong: part I, with Miao Xiaochun and Enoch Cheung presenting their panoramic photography and video works; part II with Ng Sai Kit and Lai Lon Hin presenting their landscape and cityscape photography taken in Hong Kong; part III with Maleonn and Jiang Pengyi presenting their conceptual photography concerning personal and social issues in today's China. This debut trilogy represents to a large extent our direction at the beginning. Each show is memorable in its own way, sometimes because of its success, and at other times because of its challenge.

When did you first participate in Art Basel and what was most memorable about that show?
Our first participation in Art Basel was Art Basel in Hong Kong in 2013.

- **Contact** — Blindspot Gallery
Mimi Chun
mimi@blindspotgallery.com
info@blindspotgallery.com
- **Established** — 2010
- **Owner(s) / Partner(s)** — Mimi Chun (Director)
- **Team** — 3
- **Space(s)** — 750 m²
- **Artists at Art Basel** — anothermountainman
- **Further artists** — 223 (aka Lin Zhi Peng)
Enoch Cheung
Cui Xiuwen
Ho Siu Nam, South
Shu Ikeda
Jiang Pengyi
Ken Kitano
Kurt Tong
Lai Lon Hin
Ma Liang (Maleonn)
Miao Xiaochun
Annysa Ng
Ren Hang
RongRong & inri
Cozue Takagi
Wong Wo Bik
Yangjiang Group
Paul Yeung

Blondeau

Geneva ● Galleries

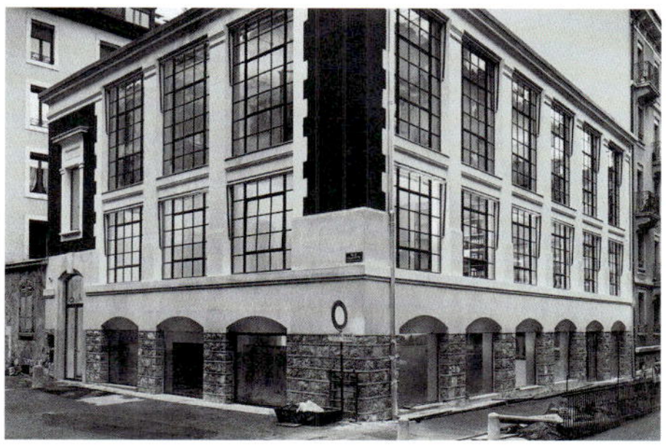

What first compelled you to open a gallery?
To be able to show contemporary art in Geneva. To go further in the comprehension of the artists exhibited.

Who is the first artist you showed and what was most memorable about that show?
Louise Lawler.

When did you first participate in Art Basel and what was most memorable about that show?
In 2011.

- **Contact** — Blondeau & Cie
Philippe Davet
philippe@blondeau.ch
muse@blondeau.ch
- **Established** — 2000
- **Owner(s) / Partner(s)** — Marc Blondeau
Philippe Davet
- **Team** — 5
- **Space(s)** — 1,000 m²
- **Artists at Art Basel** — Jean Arp
Alex Brown
Michael Cline
Jean Dubuffet
Mike Kelley
Martin Kippenberger
Louise Lawler
Sol LeWitt
Henri Matisse
Albert Oehlen
Raymond Pettibon
Jerry Phillips
Pablo Picasso
Peter Saul
Jim Shaw
Sophie Taeuber-Arp
Alessandro Twombly
Jean-Luc Verna

Blum

New York ● Galleries ● Galleries Unlimited

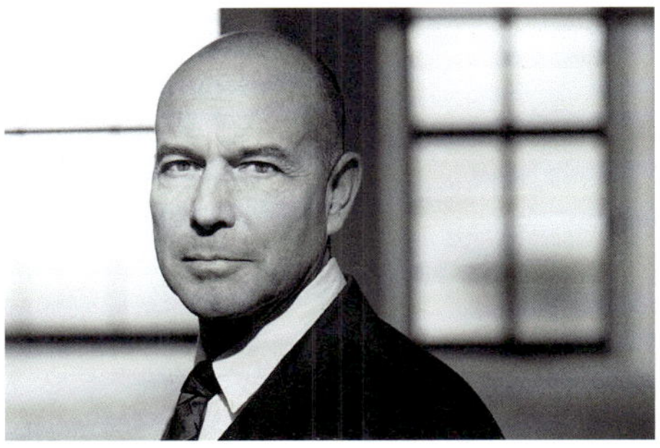

What first compelled you to open a gallery?
After six years at the Galerie Beyeler in Basel I decided to work in New York independently. For 12 years, from 1980 to 1992, I published editions, portfolios, and limited edition books exclusively, and became one of the original publishers of *Parkett* magazine. It then felt right to open a gallery after initially working with the artists I had published with: Louise Bourgeois, Alex Katz, David Rabinowitch, Helmut Federle, and others. I continued the publishing activity but the gallery exhibitions became my main focus after 1993.

Who is the first artist you showed and what was most memorable about that show?
The first artist I exhibited was David Rabinowitch. It was during this show that I understood that having a gallery was what I really wanted. I presented in this show the 12 prints of *The Collinasca Cycle*, each measuring 200 × 80 cm; it became a clear and memorable transition from the editions to gallery exhibitions.

When did you first participate in Art Basel and what was most memorable about that show?
I first participated at Art Basel as a co-worker of the Galerie Beyeler in 1970. This also was my introduction to the art world. In 1978, I participated as a publisher of editions—with artists such as Clemente, Cucchi, Disler, Penck, and others. This was my first independent experience at Art Basel.

- **Contact** Peter Blum Gallery, Blumarts Inc.
  David Blum
  art@peterblumgallery.com
- **Established** 1993
- **Owner(s) / Partner(s)** Peter Blum
- **Team** 6
- **Space(s)** 200 m²
- **Artists at Art Basel** Louise Bourgeois, Willem de Kooning, Jean Dubuffet, Alberto Giacometti, Philip Guston, Alex Katz, Kimsooja, Yves Klein, Yayoi Kusama, Agnes Martin, Jackson Pollock, Daniel Rich, Mark Rothko, Robert Ryman, Su-Mei Tse
- **Further artists represented** John Beech, Huma Bhabha, Helmut Federle, Rosy Keyser, Esther Kläs, Chris Marker, Richard Allen Morris, Adrian Paci, Luisa Rabbia, David Rabinowitch, David Reed, SUPERFLEX, Robert Zandvliet, John Zurier

Blum & Poe

Los Angeles
Tokyo
New York

Galleries
Galleries
Unlimited
Galleries

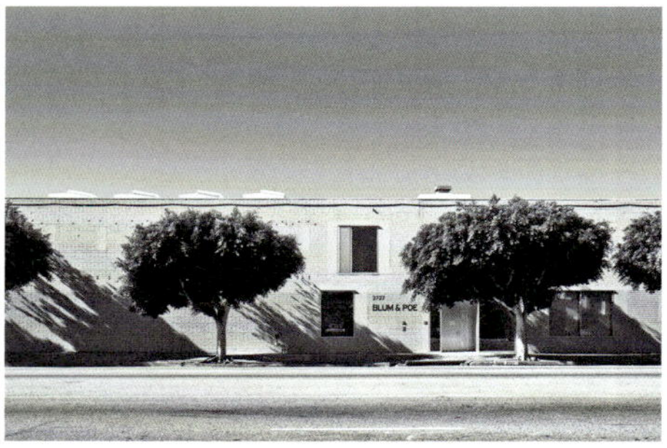

What first compelled you to open a gallery?
The gallery opened with the intention of exhibiting international contemporary art in all media, remaining strongly committed to working closely with artists to produce works of significant ambition. Blum brought over five years of immersion in the Japanese art world, and Poe provided a strong sense of the emerging artists in Los Angeles. Together, they have since represented an increasingly influential roster of artists.

Who is the first artist you showed and what was most memorable about that show?
Anya Gallaccio.

- **Contact** Blum & Poe
  Liz Hull
  liz@blumandpoe.com
  info@blumandpoe.com
- **Established** 1994
- **Owner(s) / Partner(s)** Tim Blum, Jeff Poe
- **Team** 17
- **Space(s)** 2,050 m² (Los Angeles)
- **Artists at Art Basel** Chiho Aoshima, J.B. Blunk, Jennifer Bornstein, Slater Bradley, Chuck Close, Nigel Cooke, Carroll Dunham, Sam Durant, Koji Enokura, Anya Gallaccio, Mark Grotjahn, Tim Hawkinson, Drew Heitzler, Julian Hoeber, Matt Johnson, Susumu Koshimizu, Friedrich Kunath, Shio Kusaka, Lee Ufan, Linder, Sharon Lockhart, Florian Maier-Aichen, Victor Man, Dave Muller, Takashi Murakami, Yoshitomo Nara, Matt Saunders, Hugh Scott-Douglas, Nobuo Sekine, Jim Shaw, Dirk Skreber, Kishio Suga, Henry Taylor, Keith Tyson, Chris Vasell, Michael Wilkinson, Zhang Huan, Zhu Jinshi

Boers-Li

Beijing

Galleries
Feature

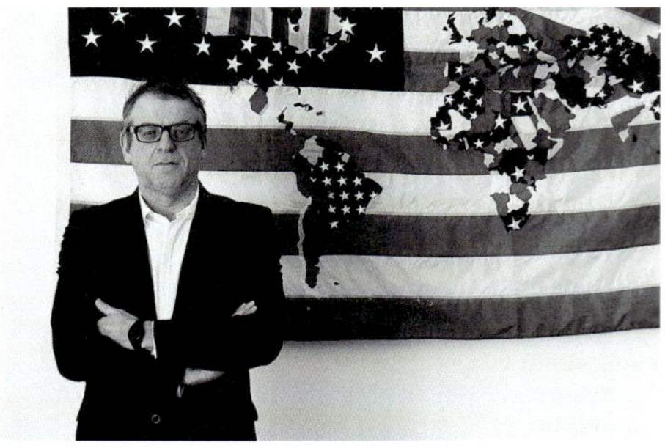

What first compelled you to open a gallery?
Showing upcoming artists in China.

Who is the first artist you showed and what was most memorable about that show?
It was an international group show, which showed art in a transitional state in China.

When did you first participate in Art Basel and what was most memorable about that show?
At Art 39 Basel, in 2008, we showed two young artists who made site-specific works.

- **Contact** Boers-Li Gallery
  Sui Fong Yim
  yim.suifong@boersligallery.com
  info@boersligallery.com
- **Established** 2005
- **Owner(s) / Partner(s)** Waling Boers
- **Team** 8
- **Space(s)** 800 m²
- **Artists at Art Basel** Chen Yujun, Huang Rui

Qiu Anxiong
Qiu Xiaofei
Song Kun
Xue Feng
Yang Xinguang
Zhang Peili
Zhang Wei

- **Further artists represented** Angela Bulloch
Chen Shaoxiong
Gade
Gong Jian
Hou Yong
Ji Lei
Lei Benben
Liao Guohe
Wang Wei
Xie Zhengli
Zeng Hong
Zhan Rui

Boesky

New York

Galleries
Galleries
Galleries

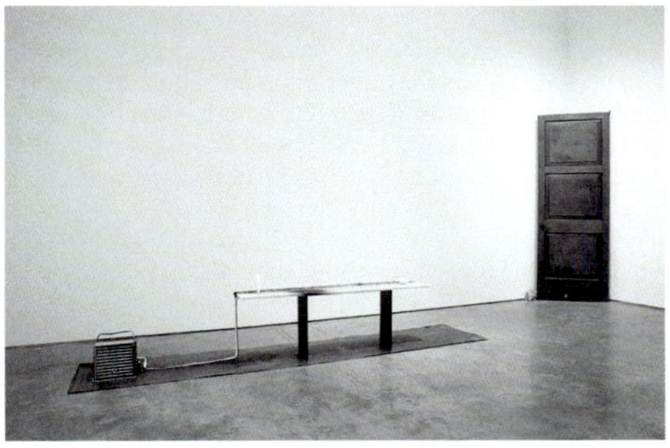

What first compelled you to open a gallery?
I was exposed to art at a very young age and from the time I was a child I dreamed of working with artists and opening an art gallery.

Who is the first artist you showed and what was most memorable about that show?
Lisa Yuskavage is the first artist I really represented. The most memorable about this experience was how powerfully conflicted I felt about her paintings.

When did you first participate in Art Basel and what was most memorable about that show?
In 1999 we were accepted in the Statements sector with Rachel Feinstein. The most memorable part about that presentation was how insanely nervous we both were!

- **Contact** Marianne Boesky Gallery
Adrian Turner
adrian@marianneboeskygallery.com
info@marianneboeskygallery.com
- **Established** 1996
- **Owner(s) / Partner(s)** Marianne Boesky
- **Team** 15
- **Space(s)** 2,000 m² (Chelsea)
1,500 m² (Uptown)
- **Artists at Art Basel** Diana Al-Hadid
Pier Paolo Calzolari
Svenja Deininger
Rachel Feinstein
Barnaby Furnas
Donald Moffett
William O'Brien
Hans Op de Beeck
Roxy Paine
Kon Trubkovich
Hannah van Bart
- **Further artists represented** Andisheh Avini
Matthias Bitzer
Jesse Chapman
Sue de Beer
Robert Elfgen
Melissa Gordon
Jay Heikes
Adam Helms
Yuichi Higashionna
Jacco Olivier
Anthony Pearson
Salvatore Scarpitta
Mindy Shapero

Ted Stamm
John Waters
Claudia Wieser

BolteLang

Zurich

Discoveries

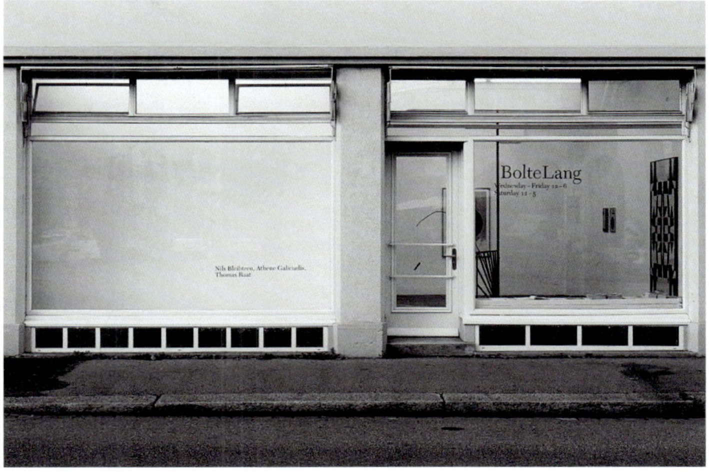

What first compelled you to open a gallery?
Friendship with great artists and the discovery of an amazing space led us to open our gallery.

Who is the first artist you showed and what was most memorable about that show?
Our first show was with Swiss artist Vanessa Billy, with whom we still work. The opening of that first exhibition was so well attended that we could not enjoy a minute of it—we were so scared for Vanessa's fragile works.

When did you first participate in Art Basel and what was most memorable about that show?
Our first participation was at Art Basel in Hong Kong in 2013. The whole experience was so memorable, starting with Benjamin Senior's amazing proposal, the acceptance letter, and then the entire stay in Hong Kong, which was made extremely easy by the fair management.

- **Contact** BolteLang
Anna Bolte
anna@boltelang.com
info@boltelang.com
- **Established** 2008
- **Owner(s) / Partner(s)** Anna Bolte
Chaja Lang
- **Team** 3
- **Space(s)** 130 m²
- **Artists at Art Basel** Benjamin Senior
- **Further artists represented** Vanessa Billy
Bianca Brunner
Claudia Comte
Daniel Gustav Cramer
Patrick Hari
Dagmar Heppner
Jill Spector

Bonakdar

New York

Galleries
Galleries

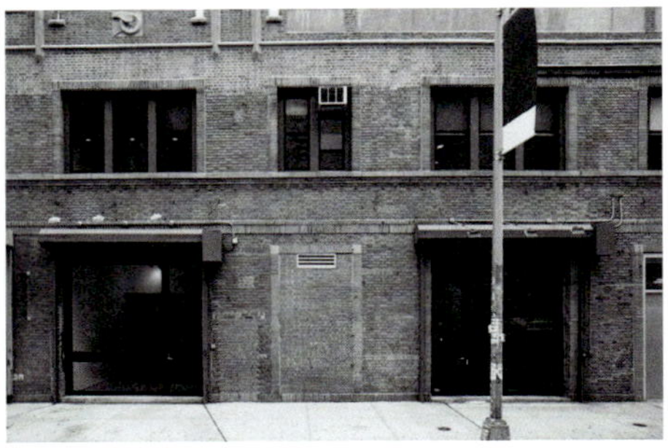

What first compelled you to open a gallery?
During the time I began my first job at Anthony d'Offay in London, a key group of YBA artists was emerging from Goldsmiths. It was then that I saw works for the first time by people like Damien Hirst, Sarah Lucas, Mat Collishaw, and Gary Hume, and quickly realized that I wanted to work with artists from my own generation.

Who is the first artist you showed and what was most memorable about that show?
Mat Collishaw and Damien Hirst. Mat's first exhibition took place in 1992 and was called *In the Old Fashioned Way*, which was very controversial and thought-provoking. That same year, Damien showed his iconic *Pharmacy* work, which continues to be one of his most important installations to date.

When did you first participate in Art Basel and what was most memorable about that show?
The gallery first exhibited at the fair in 1997. It was an exciting time during which we met many interesting collectors whom we continue to work with today.

- **Contact** Tanya Bonakdar Gallery
Ethan Sklar
mail@tanyabonakdargallery.com
- **Established** 1994
- **Owner(s) / Partner(s)** Tanya Bonakdar (Founder)
- **Team** 13
- **Space(s)** 512 m²
- **Artists at Art Basel** Uta Barth
Martin Boyce
Sandra Cinto
Phil Collins
Mat Collishaw
Mark Dion
Olafur Eliasson
Meschac Gaba
Siobhán Hapaska
Sabine Hornig
T. Hubbard/A. Birchler
Carla Klein
Liz Larner
Charles Long
Rita Lundqvist
Mark Manders
Jason Meadows
Ernesto Neto
Rivane Neuenschwander
Susan Philipsz
Peggy Preheim
Analia Saban
Tomás Saraceno
Thomas Scheibitz
Hannah Starkey
Haim Steinbach
Dirk Stewen
Jack Strange
Sarah Sze
Neal Tait
Jeffrey Vallance
Gillian Wearing
Nicole Wermers

Boone

New York

Galleries

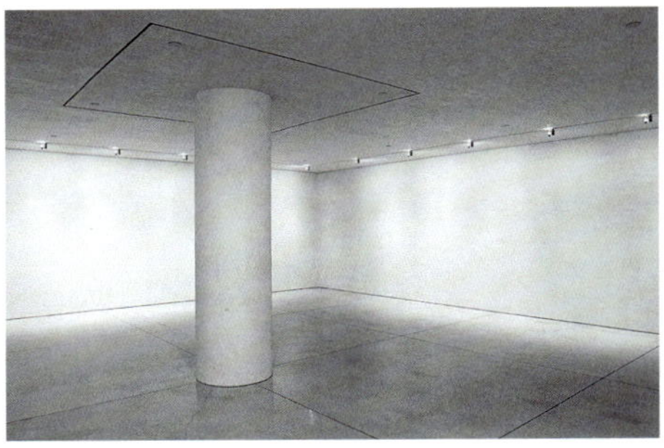

What first compelled you to open a gallery?
Mary Boone opened the gallery to show innovative young artists of her own generation. The gallery now shows prominent artists of different generations.

Who is the first artist you showed and what was most memorable about that show?
Julian Schnabel, who in the late 1970s was making work unlike anything else being shown.

When did you first participate in Art Basel and what was most memorable about that show?
Art Basel in Miami Beach in 2006 was the gallery's first participation in an art fair. Each day the booth was changed entirely, presenting the work of a single artist.

- **Contact** Mary Boone Gallery
Ron Warren
ron@maryboonegallery.com
info@maryboonegallery.com
- **Established** 1977
- **Owner(s) / Partner(s)** Mary Boone (Founder and Owner)
Ron Warren (Partner)
- **Team** 10
- **Space(s)** 316 m² (745 Fifth Avenue)
335 m² (541 West 24 Street)
- **Artists at Art Basel** Ai Weiwei
Joseph Beuys
Ross Bleckner
James Lee Byars
Patty Chang
Francesco Clemente
Will Cotton
Eric Fischl
Luis Gispert
Tomoo Gokita
Peter Halley
Hilary Harkness
Jacob Hashimoto
Jim Isermann
KAWS
Mel Kendrick
Barbara Kruger
Barry Le Va
Sherrie Levine
Liu Xiaodong
Andrew Masullo
Aleksandra Mir
Olivier Mosset
Marc Quinn
David Salle
Peter Saul
Keith Sonnier
Joe Zucker

Borch Jensen

Berlin
Copenhagen

- Edition
- Edition Kabinett

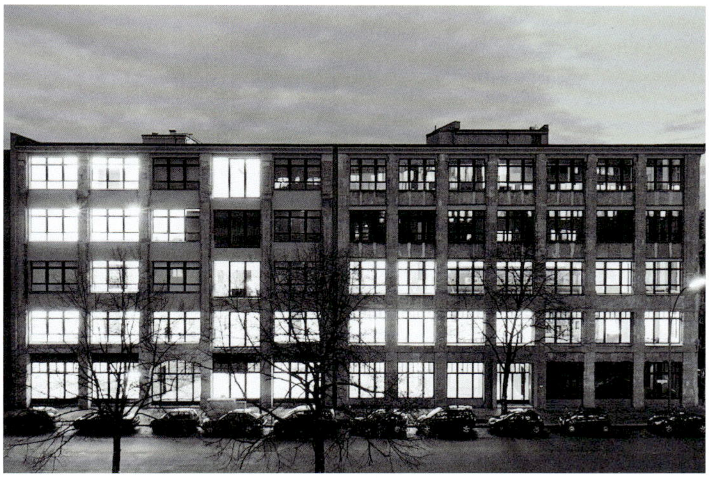

What first compelled you to open a gallery?
I am a publisher of fine art editions and wanted to show the prints that I published.

Who is the first artist you showed and what was most memorable about that show?
Baselitz, and nobody came.

When did you first participate in Art Basel and what was most memorable about that show?
In 2004.

- **Contact** Niels Borch Jensen Editions
  Lone Weigelt
  lone@nielsborchjensen.dk
  info@nielsborchjensen.dk
- **Established** 1979
- **Owner(s) / Partner(s)** Niels Borch Jensen
- **Team** 3
- **Space(s)** 300 m²
- **Artists at Art Basel** Iñaki Bonillas
  Tacita Dean
  Michael Elmgreen & Ingar Dragset
  Carsten Höller
  Tomas Saraceno
  Thaddeus Strode
  Al Taylor
  Sandra Vásquez de la Horra
  Danh Vo
- **Further artists represented** Georg Baselitz
  Thomas Demand
  Olafur Eliasson
  Douglas Gordon
  Rodney Graham
  Keith Haring
  Anton Henning
  Clay Ketter
  Martin Kippenberger
  Per Kirkeby
  Takehito Koganezawa
  Bjarne Melgaard
  Albert Oehlen
  João Penalva
  Tal R
  Robin Rhode
  SUPERFLEX
  Rosemarie Trockel
  Alan Uglow

Bortolami

New York

- Galleries
- Parcours
- Galleries

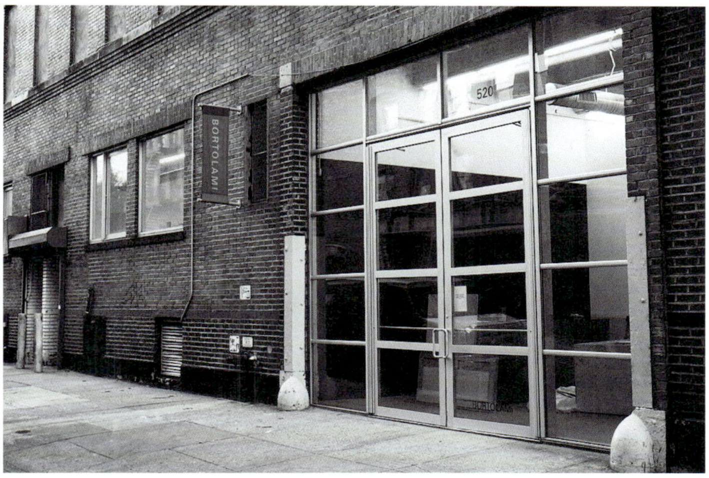

What first compelled you to open a gallery?
After three years with Anthony d'Offay and six years with Larry Gagosian, I wanted to try it on my own.

Who is the first artist you showed and what was most memorable about that show?
When I opened the gallery, our first exhibition was a group show called *Closing Down*. We were really just experimenting with the space in relation to artwork. The first solo show at the gallery was with Michel François, an artist who became part of my program. He made a hole in the gallery through to the exterior—in January!

When did you first participate in Art Basel and what was most memorable about that show?
We participated in the Statements sector with Richard Aldrich in 2009. It was Rich's first time in Basel, and he was amazed by the high level of cultural activities and the quality of artworks exhibited in the fair. Every artist should go to Basel once.

- **Contact** Bortolami
  Emma Fernberger Logsdail
  emma@bortolamigallery.com
  info@bortolamigallery.com
- **Established** 2005
- **Owner(s) / Partner(s)** Stefania Bortolami
- **Team** 10
- **Space(s)** 260 m²
- **Artists at Art Basel** Richard Aldrich
  Daniel Buren
  Tom Burr
  Michel François
  Jutta Koether
  Gary Webb
- **Further artists represented** Avner Ben-Gal
  Shane Campbell
  Morgan Fisher
  Michel François
  Piero Golia
  Thilo Heinzmann
  Patrick Hill
  Piotr Janas
  Barbara Kasten
  Scott King
  Jonathan Meese
  Anna Ostoya
  Peter Peri
  Ben Schumacher
  Eric Wesley
  Aaron Young

Bortolozzi

Berlin

- Galleries Unlimited Parcours

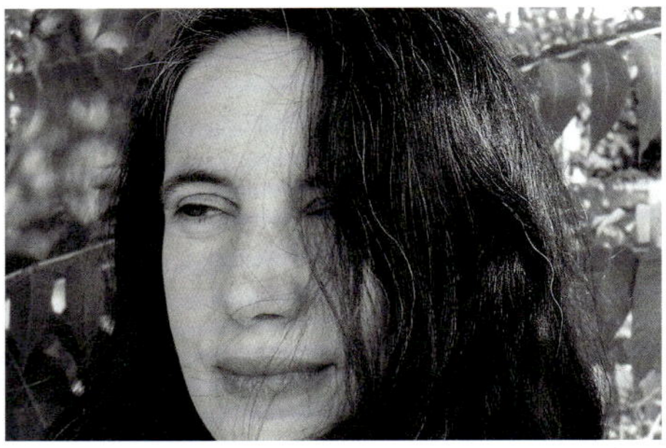

What first compelled you to open a gallery?
I naively believed in the transformative possibilities of contemporary art and wanted to work with people who shared this vision. And I still do.

Who is the first artist you showed and what was most memorable about that show?
Július Koller, and his question marks.

When did you first participate in Art Basel and what was most memorable about that show?
In the Statements sector of Art Basel with Turner Prize winner Susan Philipsz in 2007. She was presenting a work at the *Skulptur Projekt Münster 07*, which was happening around the same time. In 2008 I did another Statements presentation with Danh Vo.

- **Contact** — Galerie Isabella Bortolozzi, Saehee Hwang, info@bortolozzi.com
- **Established** — 2004
- **Team** — 7
- **Space(s)** — 140 m² (main space), 220 m² ("Eden Eden")
- **Artists at Art Basel** — Leonor Antunes, Ibon Aranberri, Ed Atkins, Juliette Blightman, Andrea Branzi, Jay Chung/Q Takeki Maeda, Jos de Gruyter & Harald Thys, Maria Lai, Danny McDonald, Oscar Murillo, Susan Philipsz, Seth Price, Carol Rama, Stephen G. Rhodes, Yorgos Sapountzis, Nora Schultz, Danh Vo, Betty Woodman

Borzo

Amsterdam

- Feature

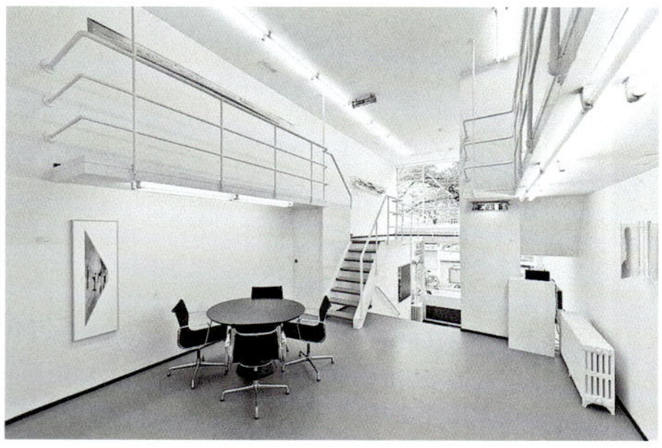

What first compelled you to open a gallery?
I grew up among paintings, as my father did … and his father …

Who is the first artist you showed and what was most memorable about that show?
Heinrich Campendonk. We presented works from the artist's estate (he died in Amsterdam, 1957) in cooperation with his widow. We sold nothing!

When did you first participate in Art Basel and what was most memorable about that show?
In 2013. A solo presentation of the ZERO artist Jan Schoonhoven. Great reception of the exhibition by the public, colleagues, and the press (*The New York Times* and other major media: "One of the ten must-see-stands").

- **Contact** — Borzo modern & contemporary art, Paul van Rosmalen, paul@borzo.com, info@borzo.com
- **Established** — 1924
- **Owner(s) / Partner(s)** — Paul van Rosmalen
- **Team** — 3
- **Space(s)** — 200 m²
- **Artists at Art Basel** — Jan Schoonhoven
- **Further artists represented** — Armando, Bram Bogart, herman de vries, Ad Dekkers, Jan Henderikse, Ewerdt Hilgemann, Henk Peeters, Ger van Elk, Bram van Velde, Geer van Velde

BQ

Berlin

- Galleries
- Galleries

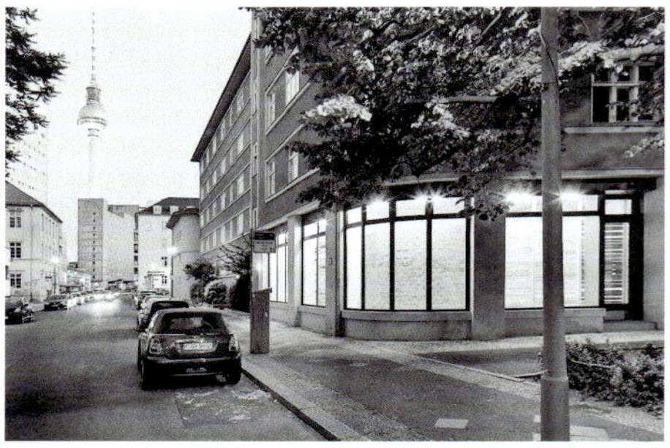

What first compelled you to open a gallery?
To work with artists.

Who is the first artist you showed and what was most memorable about that show?
In 1995, Walter Dahn and Philip Pocock before we opened BQ. It was a lot of fun to do our first show. We did everything we wanted to do: poster, catalogue, bar, video lounge, screenings …

When did you first participate in Art Basel and what was most memorable about that show?
Probably in 2004. It was a great opportunity to show our artists next to all the other established artists.

- **Contact** — BQ, Jörn Bötnagel, info@bqberlin.de
- **Established** — 1998
- **Owner(s) / Partner(s)** — Jörn Bötnagel, Yvonne Quirmbach
- **Team** — 3
- **Space(s)** — 200 m²
- **Artists at Art Basel** — Dirk Bell, Alexandra Bircken, Matti Braun, Andrew Kerr, Friedrich Kunath, Bojan Sarcevic, David Shrigley, Marcus Steinweg
- **Further artists represented** — Carina Brandes, Owen Gump, Kriwet, Reinhard Voigt, Richard Wright

Breeder

Athens
Monte Carlo

Galleries

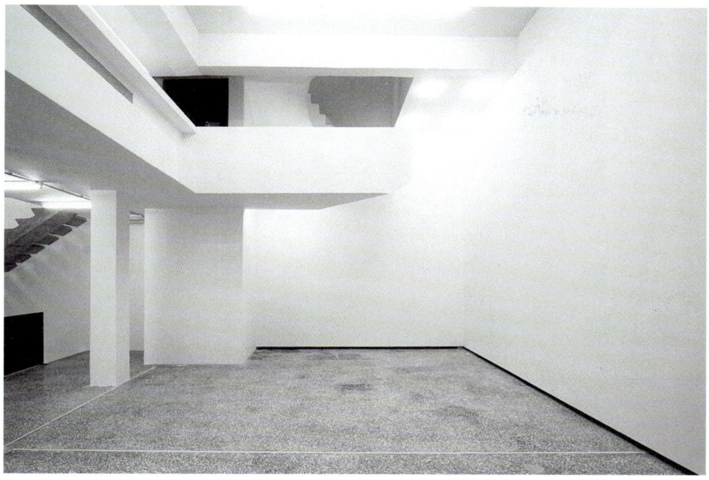

What first compelled you to open a gallery?
The Breeder gallery came to life almost by itself, it was the succession of a non-profit exhibition space on the premises of the *Breeder* magazine (2000–2002).

Who is the first artist you showed and what was most memorable about that show?
The inaugural show of our space as a commercial gallery was a solo exhibition by Scottish artist Jim Lambie. Lambie also DJ-ed on the night of the opening at an open party inside and outside the gallery space. It attracted the ultimate mixed crowd of museum directors, curators, and collectors rubbing shoulders on the dance floor with illegal immigrants living in the neighborhood.

When did you first participate in Art Basel and what was most memorable about that show?
Our first participation was in Miami Beach in 2004. The energy of that fair was unlike anything else the art world had experienced up until then. We vividly remember brisk business at the beach. Out first participation in Basel was in 2010. We were impressed by the active involvement of such a high percentage of visitors who became part of our installation *Boudoir* (1974) by Vlassis Caniaris.

- **Contact** The Breeder
Nadia Gerazouni
nadia@thebreedersystem.com
gallery@thebreedersystem.com
- **Established** 2002
- **Owner(s) / Partner(s)** Stathis Panagoulis
George Vavmakidis
- **Space(s)** 650 m² (Athens)
100 m² (Monte Carlo)
- **Artists at Art Basel** Markus Amm
Andreas Angelidakis
Marc Bijl
Vlassis Caniaris
Antonis Donef
Stelios Faitakis
Uwe Henneken
HOPE
Kalup Linzy
Andreas Lolis
Ryan McGinley
Irini Miga
Scott Myles
Angelos Papadimitriou
Jennifer Rubell
Shirana Shahbazi
Mindy Shapero
Daniel Sinsel
Gert & Uwe Tobias
Alexandros Tzannis
Jannis Varelas
Gabriel Vormstein
Xue Tao

Brito

São Paulo

Galleries
Kabinett

- **Contact** Luciana Brito Galeria
info@lucianabritogaleria.com.br
- **Established** 1997
- **Owner(s) / Partner(s)** Luciana Brito
- **Artists at Art Basel** Marina Abramović
Ricardo Basbaum
Rafael Carneiro
Leandro Erlich
Pablo Lobato
Anthony McCall
Tobias Putrih
Caio Reisewitz
Tiago Tebet
Héctor Zamora
- **Further artists represented** Lucas Bambozzi
Saint Clair Cemin
Waldemar Cordeiro
Rochelle Costi
Geraldo de Barros
Fabiana de Barros & Michel Favre
Thomaz Farkas
Paula Garcia
Gaspar Gasparian
Alex Katz
Allan McCollum
João Luiz Musa
Mônica Nador
Fyodor Pavlov Andreevich
Liliana Porter
Eder Santos
Regina Silveira
Delson Uchôa
Raphael Zarka

Ben Brown

London
Hong Kong

Galleries

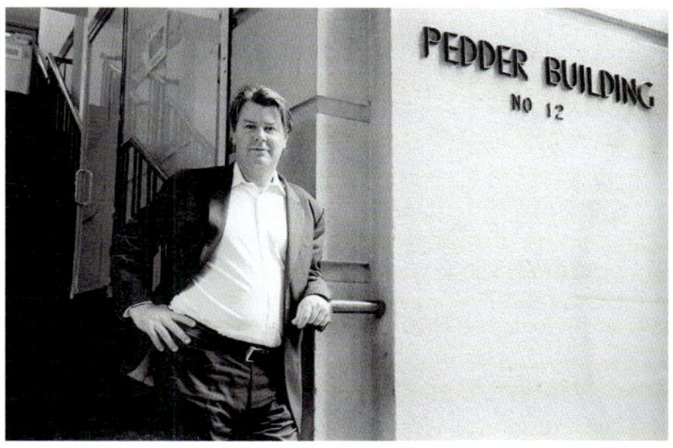

What first compelled you to open a gallery?
I was lucky to have parents who were great supporters of the arts and avid collectors. I opened my first gallery in January 2004 after spending ten years as a director of Sotheby's Contemporary Art department, and two years as co-managing director at Waddington Galleries. I couldn't imagine doing anything I'm more passionate about!

Who is the first artist you showed and what was most memorable about that show?
Candida Höfer.

When did you first participate in Art Basel and what was most memorable about that show?
In Hong Kong, in 2013: we had some fantastic works by the gallery artists and it was very exciting to be a part of the first Art Basel in Hong Kong, having been established in Hong Kong for many years.

- **Contact** Ben Brown Fine Arts
Emilie Ortolan
emilie@benbrownfinearts.com
info@benbrownfinearts.com
- **Established** 2004
- **Owner(s) / Partner(s)** Ben Brown
- **Team** 14
- **Space(s)** 500 m²
- **Artists at Art Basel** Ron Arad
Frank Auerbach
Miquel Barceló

Tony Bevan
Alighiero Boetti
Cai Guo-Qiang
Caio Fonseca
Lucio Fontana
Keith Haring
Candida Höfer
Claude & François-Xavier Lalanne
Jonas Lipps
Heinz Mack
Martin Mull
Vik Muniz
Nabil Nahas
Frank Stella
Tseng Kwong Chi
Gavin Turk
Not Vital
Yunizar

Gavin Brown

New York

- Galleries Unlimited
- Galleries

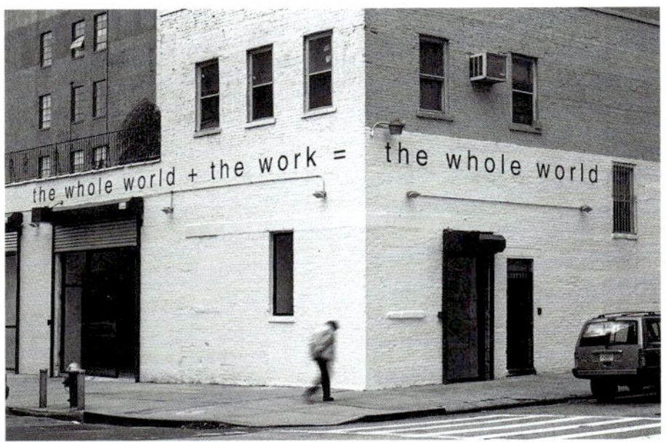

What first compelled you to open a gallery?
Need of $$.

Who is the first artist you showed and what was most memorable about that show?
Steven Pippin; staying up for 48 hours finishing the installation.

When did you first participate in Art Basel and what was most memorable about that show?
In the Statements sector with Elizabeth Peyton; that we were accepted!

- **Contact** Gavin Brown's enterprise
gallery@gavinbrown.biz
- **Established** 1994
- **Owner(s) / Partner(s)** Gavin Brown
- **Team** 16
- **Space(s)** 930 m²
- **Artists at Art Basel** Franz Ackermann
James Angus
Uri Aran
Thomas Bayrle
Dirk Bell
Jennifer Bornstein
Joe Bradley
Kerstin Brätsch
Martin Creed
Verne Dawson
Jeremy Deller
Peter Doig
Urs Fischer
Dara Friedman
Mark Handforth
Jonathan Horowitz
Alex Katz
Christopher Knowles
Udomsak Krisanamis
Ella Kruglyanskaya
Mark Leckey
Bjarne Melgaard
Silke Otto-Knapp
Laura Owens
Oliver Payne
Elizabeth Peyton
Steven Pippin
Rob Pruitt
Nick Relph
Steven Shearer
Frances Stark
Katja Strunz
Sturtevant
Spencer Sweeney
Rirkrit Tiravanija

Buchholz

Berlin
Cologne

- Galleries Unlimited
Parcours
- Galleries

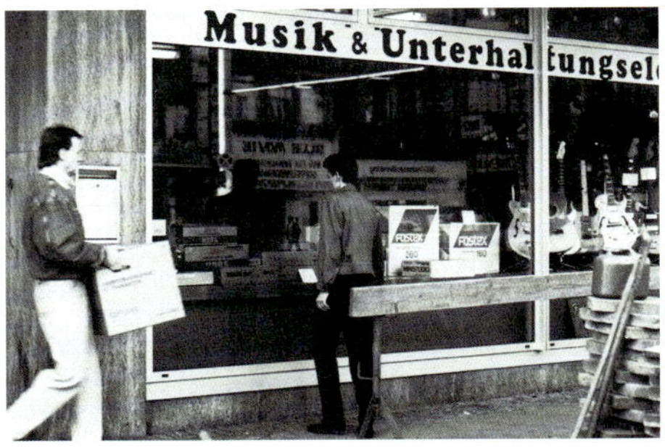

What first compelled you to open a gallery?
Daniel Buchholz: I was an apprentice at Walter König in Cologne and was always very interested in art. After my apprenticeship I spent some time in New York working for Jaap Rietman, learning a lot about the contemporary art scene of that moment. When I came back from New York, I worked for Walter's brother, Kasper König, and was his assistant for some exhibitions. It was somehow by chance or by accident that I opened the gallery, but already very early on I organized shows and events in my apartment. For example, the Cologne-based painter Udo Lefin once showed an incredibly psychedelic painting in my apartment in 1985.

Who is the first artist you showed and what was most memorable about that show?
One early and important exhibition project for me was my first collaboration with Isa Genzken. For our first project, I rented out the shop window of a Hi-Fi audio supply store in which Isa presented a large group of concrete radios.

When did you first participate in Art Basel and what was most memorable about that show?
Our first participation at Art Basel was much later, after I ran the gallery together with my partner Christopher Müller. In 1999 we showed an installation of Jeroen de Rijke and Willem de Rooij in the Statements sector. For this occasion, the artists had produced a three-minute preview for their incredible film project *Banter Gebang*, for which they were awarded the Art Baloise Prize.

- **Contact** Galerie Buchholz
Peter Currie
peter@galeriebuchholz.de
post@galeriebuchholz.de
- **Established** 1987
- **Owner(s) / Partner(s)** Daniel Buchholz
Christopher Müller
- **Team** 16
- **Space(s)** 70 m² + 90 m² (Cologne)
200 m² (Berlin)
- **Artists at Art Basel** Tomma Abts
Lutz Bacher
Nairy Baghramian
Tony Conrad
Willem de Rooij
de Rijke/de Rooij
Simon Denny
Lukas Duwenhögger
Thomas Eggerer
Vincent Fecteau
Morgan Fisher
Isa Genzken
Jack Goldstein
Julian Göthe
Richard Hawkins
Cameron Jamie
John Kelsey
Jochen Klein
Jutta Koether
Michael Krebber
Mark Leckey
Sam Lewitt
Lucy McKenzie
Henrik Olesen
Paulina Olowska
Silke Otto-Knapp
Mathias Poledna
Florian Pumhösl
R.H. Quaytman

Frances Stark
Josef Strau
Stefan Thater
Cheyney Thompson
Wolfgang Tillmans
Danh Vo
Cosima von Bonin
Martin Wong
Katharina Wulff
Cerith Wyn Evans

Buchmann

Berlin
Lugano

Galleries
Galleries
Galleries

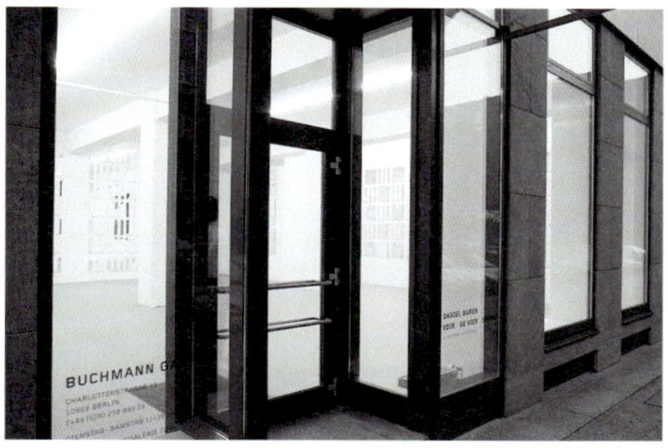

What first compelled you to open a gallery?
It was a passion for art and a personal relationship with artists that led to the decision to open a gallery.

Who is the first artist you showed and what was most memorable about that show?
In 1975: it was a painting exhibition by Swiss artist Matias Spescha, with works that he had previously shown at his retrospective at the Kunstmuseum Chur. In addition, he presented new works that transformed the gallery space into an architectural piece. A light installation by Michel Verjux was the inaugural exhibition of the gallery in Cologne in 1995, and the current gallery space in Berlin opened in 2005 with an in-situ installation of large mirror works by Daniel Buren.

When did you first participate in Art Basel and what was most memorable about that show?
Our first participation at Art Basel was in 1981 when we presented a large, almost five-meter-long table piece by Dieter Roth, and an installation by Mathias Spescha.

- **Contact** — Buchmann Galerie
  Andre Buchmann
  andre@buchmanngalerie.com
  info@buchmanngalerie.com
- **Established** — 1975 (in Switzerland)
  1995 (in Germany)
- **Owner(s) / Partner(s)** — Elena Buchmann
  André Buchmann
- **Space(s)** — 280 m² (Lugano)
  400 m² (Berlin)
- **Artists at Art Basel** — Lawrence Carroll
  John Chamberlain
  Tony Cragg
  Martin Disler
  Raffi Kalenderian
  Wolfgang Laib
  Tatsuo Miyajima
  Wilhelm Mundt
  Bettina Pousttchi
  Gerda Steiner & Jörg Lenzlinger
  William Tucker
  Emilio Vedova
  Clare Woods
- **Further artists represented** — Anna & Bernhard Blume
  Daniel Buren
  Sean Dawson
  Zaha Hadid
  Dennis Hollingsworth
  Des Hughes
  Mario Merz
  Arnold Odermatt
  Fiona Rae
  Joel Sternfeld
  Felice Varini
  Lawrence Weiner

Bureau

New York

Positions

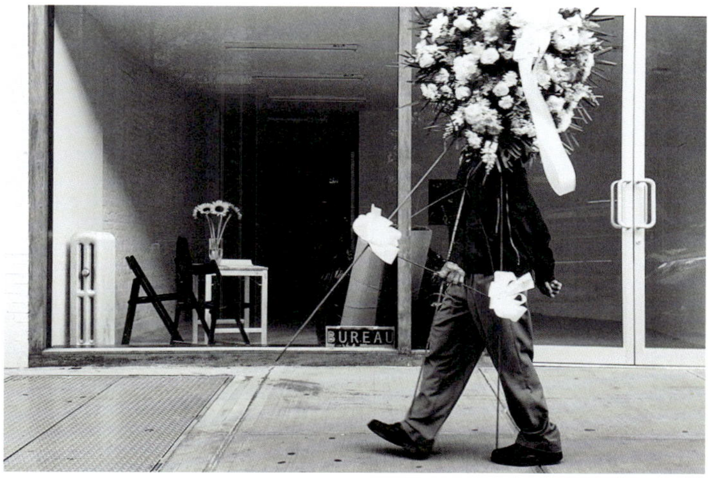

What first compelled you to open a gallery?
The gallery grew out of my curatorial practice and a desire to work closely with artists on developing their careers.

Who is the first artist you showed and what was most memorable about that show?
The first project at Dispatch, which was the curatorial space I co-owned with Howie Chen (and a prototype for Bureau) was an event with artist Ellie Ga before she departed for a trip to the Arctic aboard the polar schooner, the Tara. It was memorable because it was the beginning of a wholly unique project, which hinged on the exceptional correspondence between curator and artist.

When did you first participate in Art Basel and what was most memorable about that show?
This year in Miami Beach is my first participation at Art Basel.

- **Contact** — Bureau
  Gabrielle Giattino
  giattino@bureau-inc.com
  office@bureau-inc.com
- **Established** — 2010
- **Owner(s) / Partner(s)** — Gabrielle Giattino
- **Team** — 3
- **Space(s)** — 160 m²
- **Artists at Art Basel** — Tom Holmes
- **Further artists represented** — Erica Baum
  Ellie Ga
  Vivienne Griffin
  Matt Hoyt
  Viktor Kopp
  Lionel Maunz
  Julia Rommel

Borzo modern and contemporary art
Interview with Paul van Rosmalen

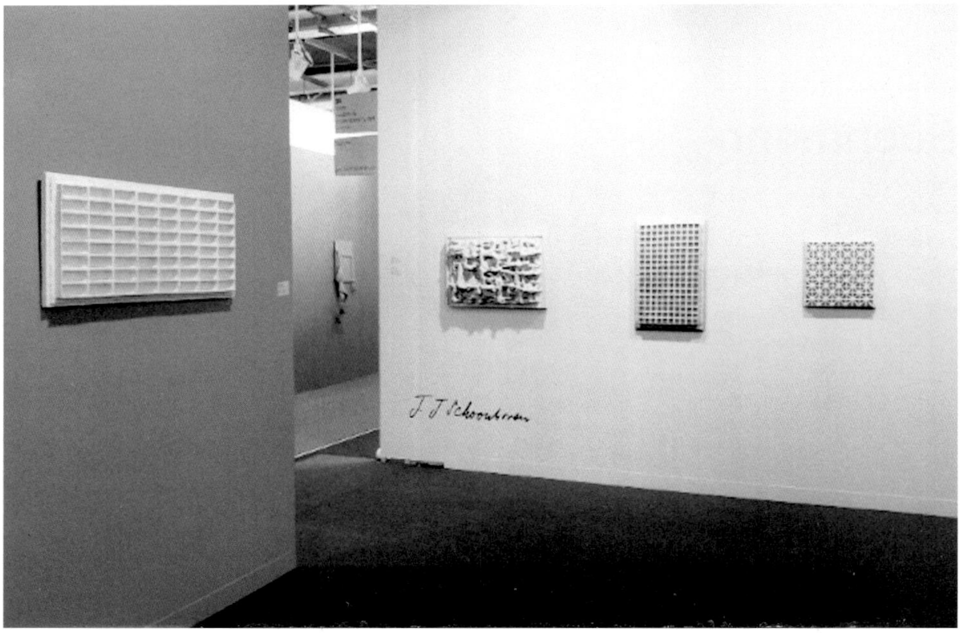

Art Basel in Basel
(Feature), 2013

Borzo modern and contemporary art is one of the oldest galleries in the Netherlands, with a history stretching back several centuries. Could you please briefly tell us about your past, and the gallery's current program, which is mainly devoted to the avant-gardes of the 20th century?

In 1824, Joseph Borzo, who was born in Italy, settled in 's-Hertogenbosch, the capital of Brabant in the Netherlands. Borzo manufactured mirrors, frames, and barometers as generations of Italian craftsmen had before him. Later he started dealing in prints. Exactly one hundred years after it was founded, my grandfather took over the gallery from the Borzo family and continued dealing in prints and old master paintings. In the postwar decades my father expanded the gallery, acquiring paintings from the 19th and early 20th centuries.

After I left Sotheby's Amsterdam in 1978 I started working with him, and my interest was soon directed toward modern and contemporary art. Historically important movements such as De Stijl and postwar ZERO, Minimalism, and Conceptual art soon became our core business. In 2005 the gallery moved to a Canal House on the famous Keizersgracht in Amsterdam with an original 1930s De Stijl interior.

At Art Basel 2013 you participated in the Feature sector with a solo presentation of Jan Schoonhoven, an important Dutch artist from the 1960s and 1970s. Why is his role in the avant-gardes of this period major? How did you conceive the presentation in Basel? And how do you comprehend the current revival of interest in this generation of artists?

At Art Basel 2013 we showed the rare white reliefs of Jan Schoonhoven (1914–1994), the most prominent member of NUL, the so-called Dutch branch of the international ZERO movement started in the late 1950s. The ZERO artists had a specific goal in mind: to eschew painting, and to produce art with a serial and repetitive character and with the absence of any personal emotion. ZERO was a reaction to the vibrant, colorful, and emotional Abstract Expressionism of the 1940s and 1950s.

ZERO was a truly international movement of related artists, mostly friends, with "representatives" in France, Italy, Germany, Belgium, and Holland. As one may expect from every truly new art movement—certainly with an identity that crossed borders—the artists who participated in ZERO achieved immediate and international recognition through their vision.

To conceive a solo presentation of Jan Schoonhoven at Art Basel has been a major effort that took us many years of experience and knowledge in this art historical field.

You also follow the new generation of artists, as shown by exhibitions such as *After ZERO* organized in 2011. What is your approach to the young Dutch art scene?

One of the aims of our exhibition policy is to make a link between modern art from the recent past and contemporary art. We do this by organizing art historical exhibitions such as *Na NUL (After ZERO)*, focusing on Conceptual art and Minimalism of the 1970s, and solo presentations by Dutch contemporary artists such as Ger van Elk, Marc Mulders, and Koen Vermeule. One thing the artists we work with have in common is their respect for the past, the history of art.

Artists of today are standing on the shoulders of their predecessors, in spite of the considerable contrasts.

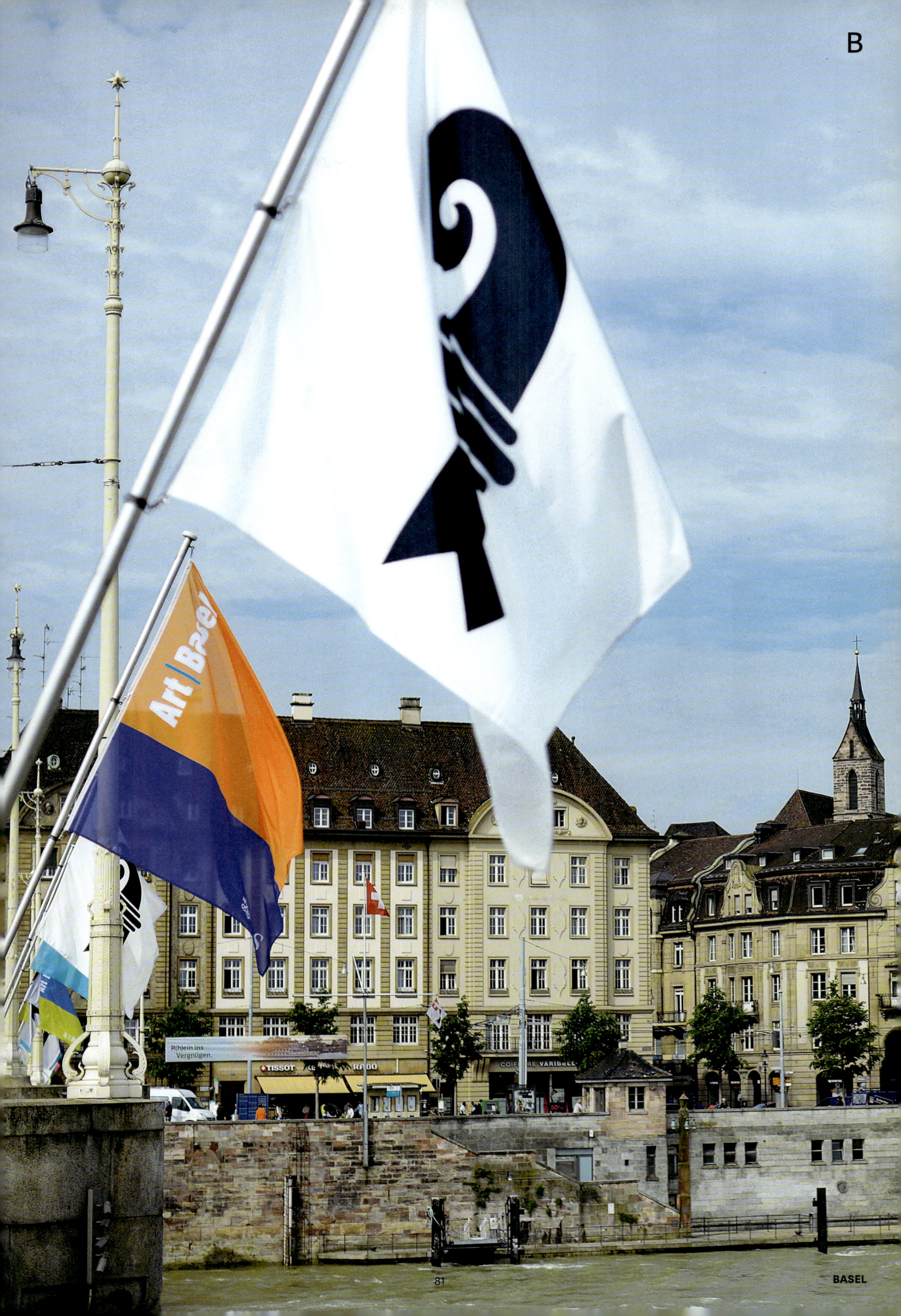
Art Basel
R(h)ein ins
Vergnügen.
TISSOT
RADO

B

City population	Population density	Fair founded in	Visitors in 2013	Number of exhibitors in 2013	Number of artists exhibited in 2013
195,100 (including Riehen and Bettingen)	7,590 inhabitants per square kilometer	1970	86,000	305	over 4,000

BASEL

Basel Exhibition Partners: Museums & Cultural Institutions

Antikenmuseum
Art and Ancient Civilizations of the Mediterranean Region

Fondation Beyeler
Max Ernst; Maurizio Cattelan

House of Electronic Arts
Semiconductor—Let There Be Light

Kunsthalle
Stories, Myths, Ironies, and Other Songs: Conceived, Directed, Edited, and Produced by M. Auder; Paulina Olowska: *Pavilionesque*

Kunsthalle Palazzo, Liestal
Nature? Swiss Photography from 1870 until Today

Kunsthaus Baselland
Christopher Orr: *Light Shining Darkly*; Laurent Grasso: *Disasters and Miracles*; Manuel Graf: *Commercials, Mosques & Ceramics*

Kunstmuseum
The Picassos Are Here!; Ed Ruscha: *Los Angeles Apartments*

Kunstmuseum—Museum für Gegenwartskunst
Some End of Things

Museum der Kulturen
POPCAP '13

Museum Tinguely
Tinguely @ Tinguely; Zilvinas Kempinas: *Slow Motion*

Schaulager
Steve McQueen

Vitra Design Museum, Weil am Rhein (DE)
Louis Kahn; Archizines

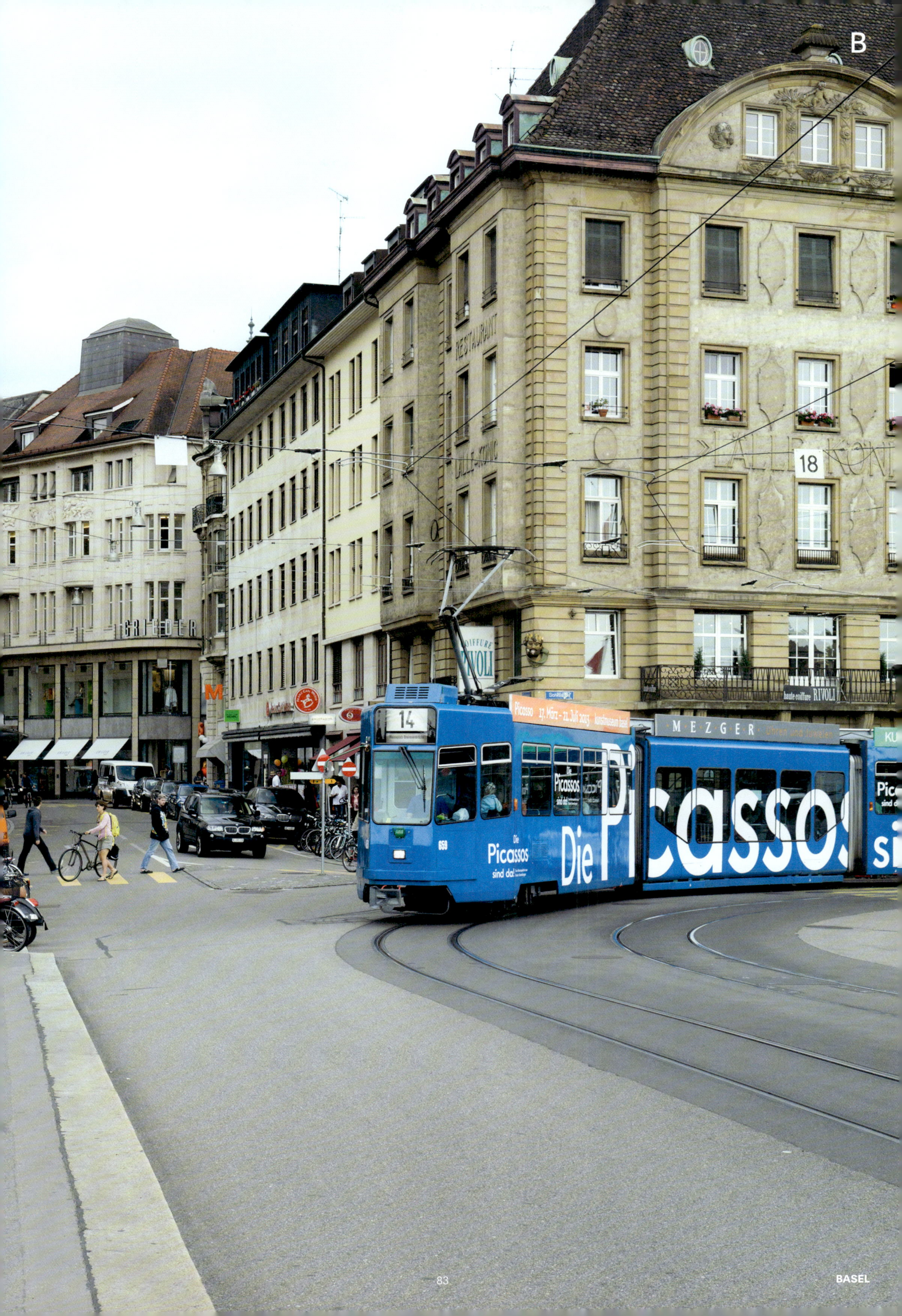
RESTAURANT
GRIEDER
18
RIVOLI
14
MEZGER
Die Picassos sind da!
Die Picassos

Jonathan Horowitz in his *Free Store*
Unlimited

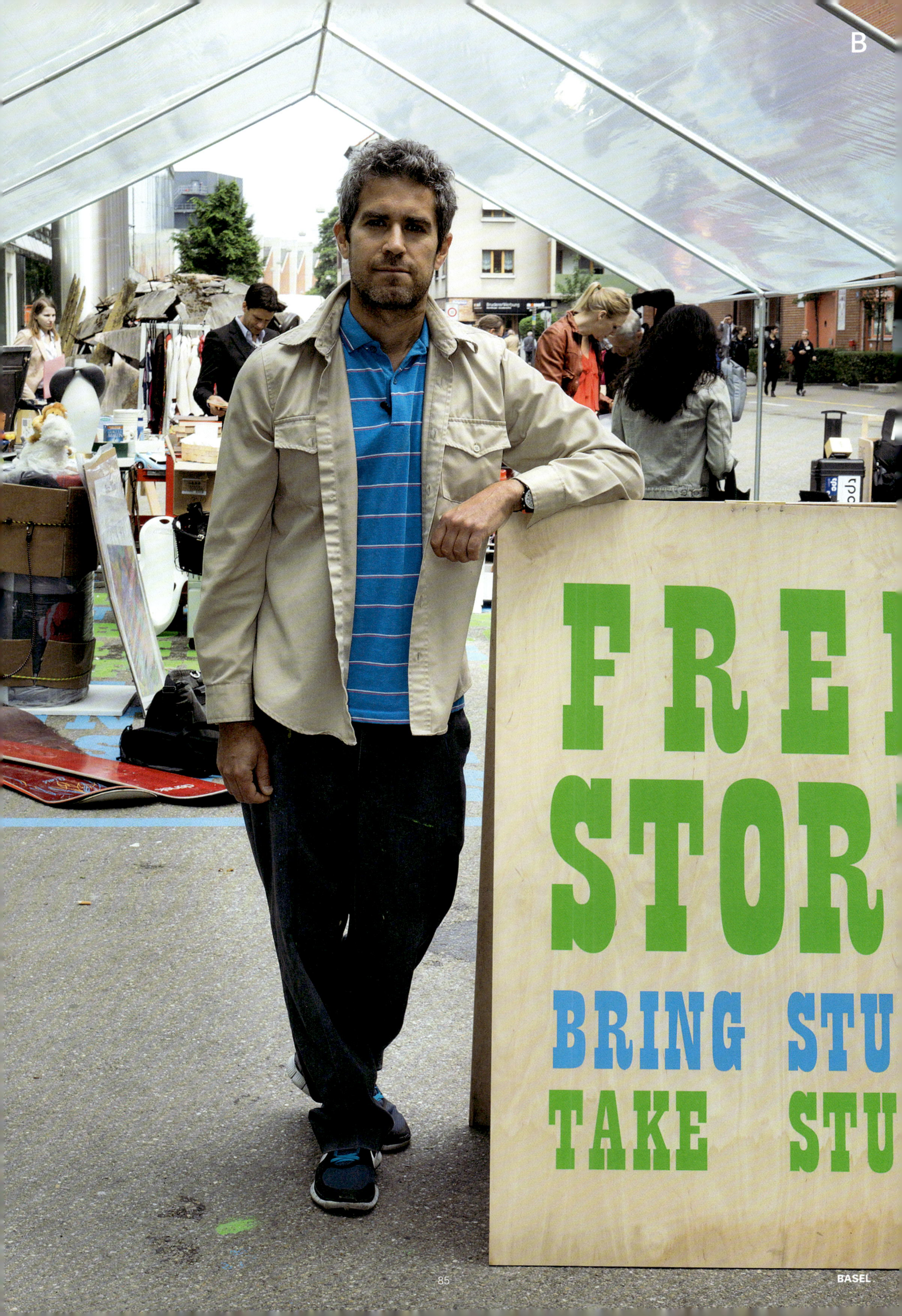
FRE
STOR
BRING STU
TAKE STU

B

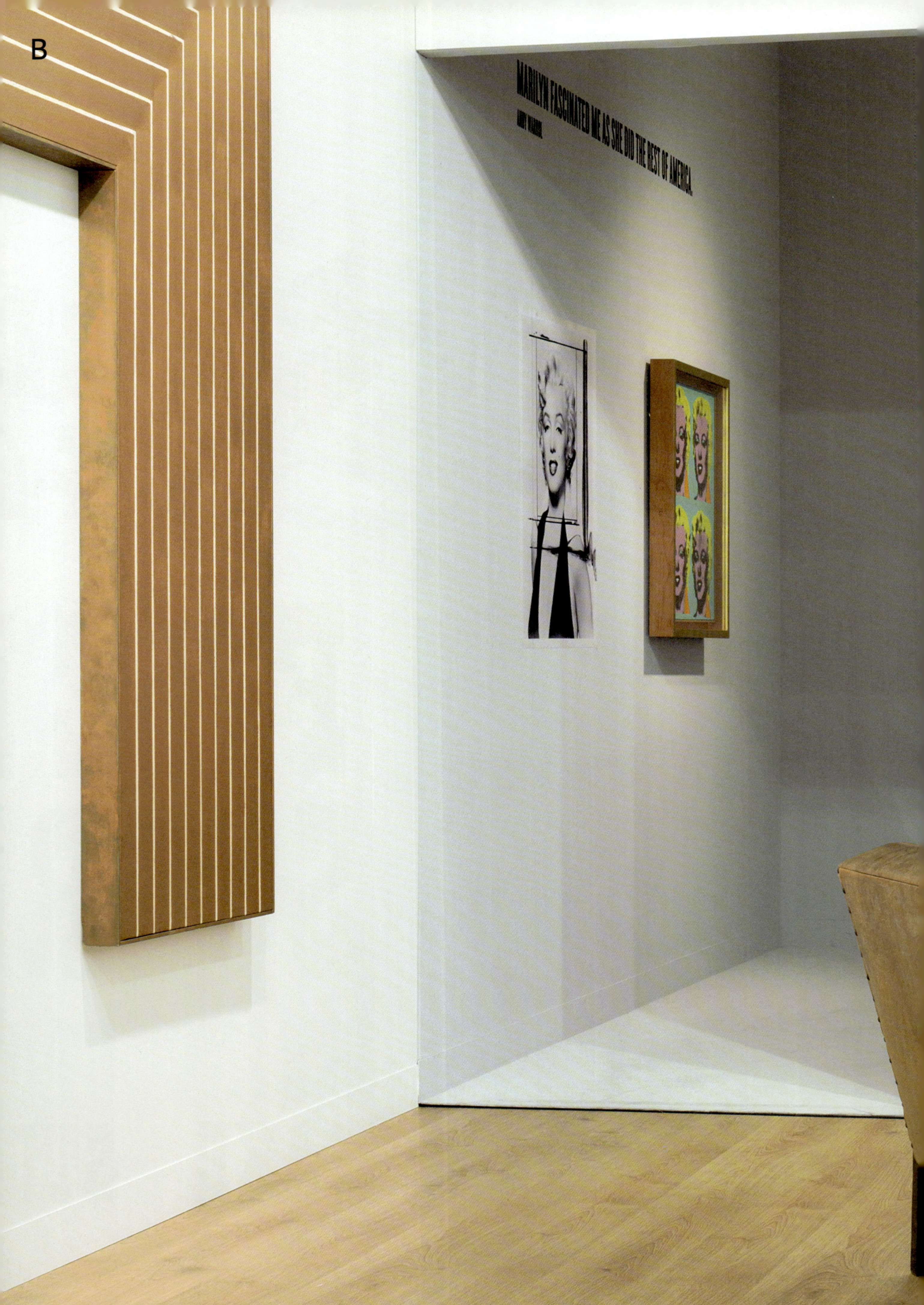

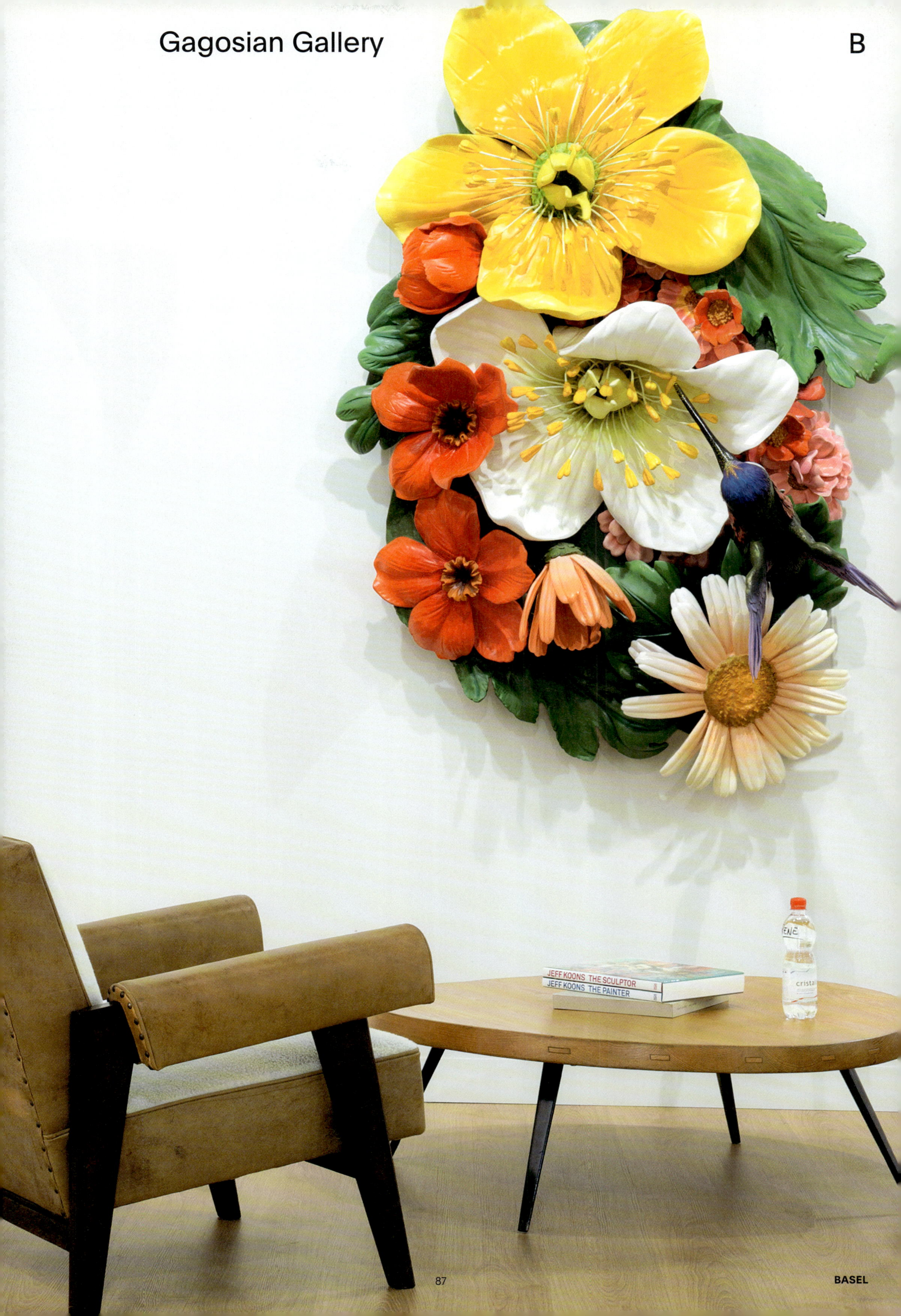
JEFF KOONS THE SCULPTOR
JEFF KOONS THE PAINTER

Fondation Beyeler

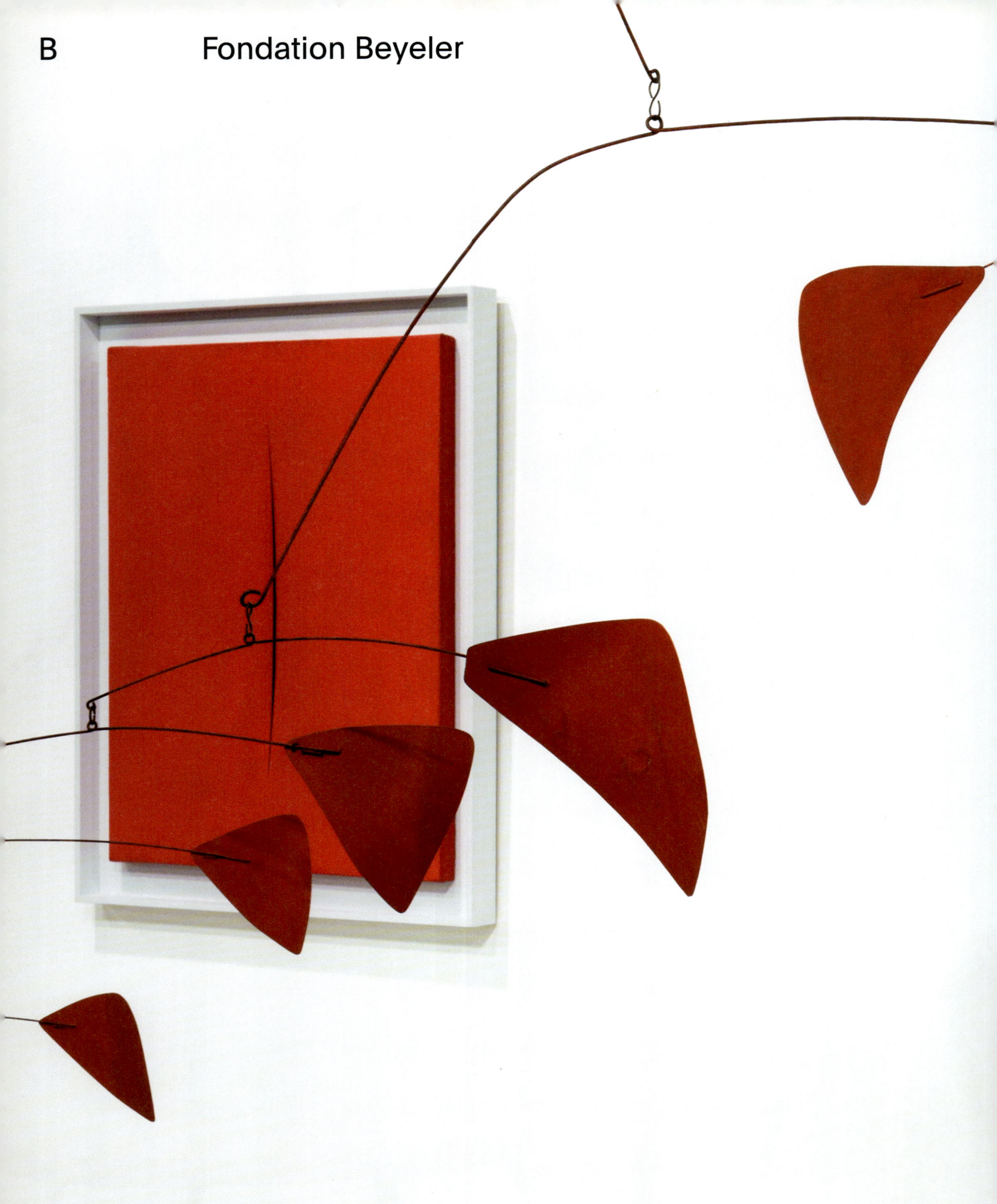

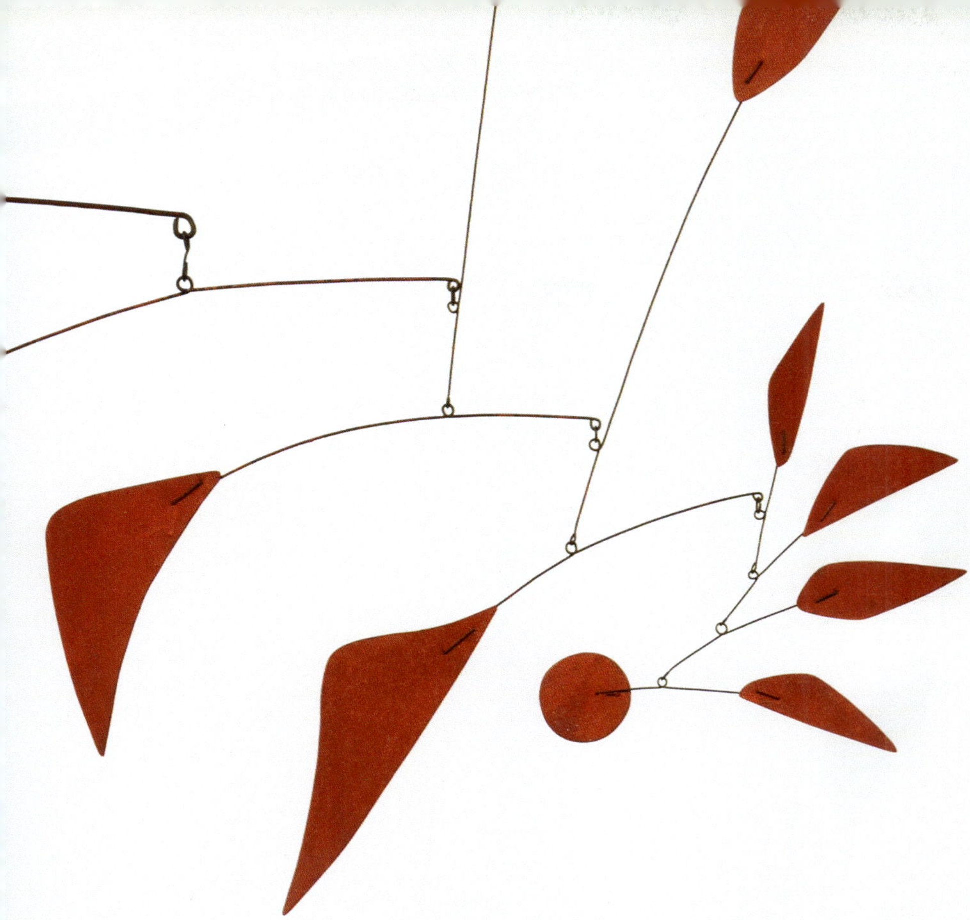

B

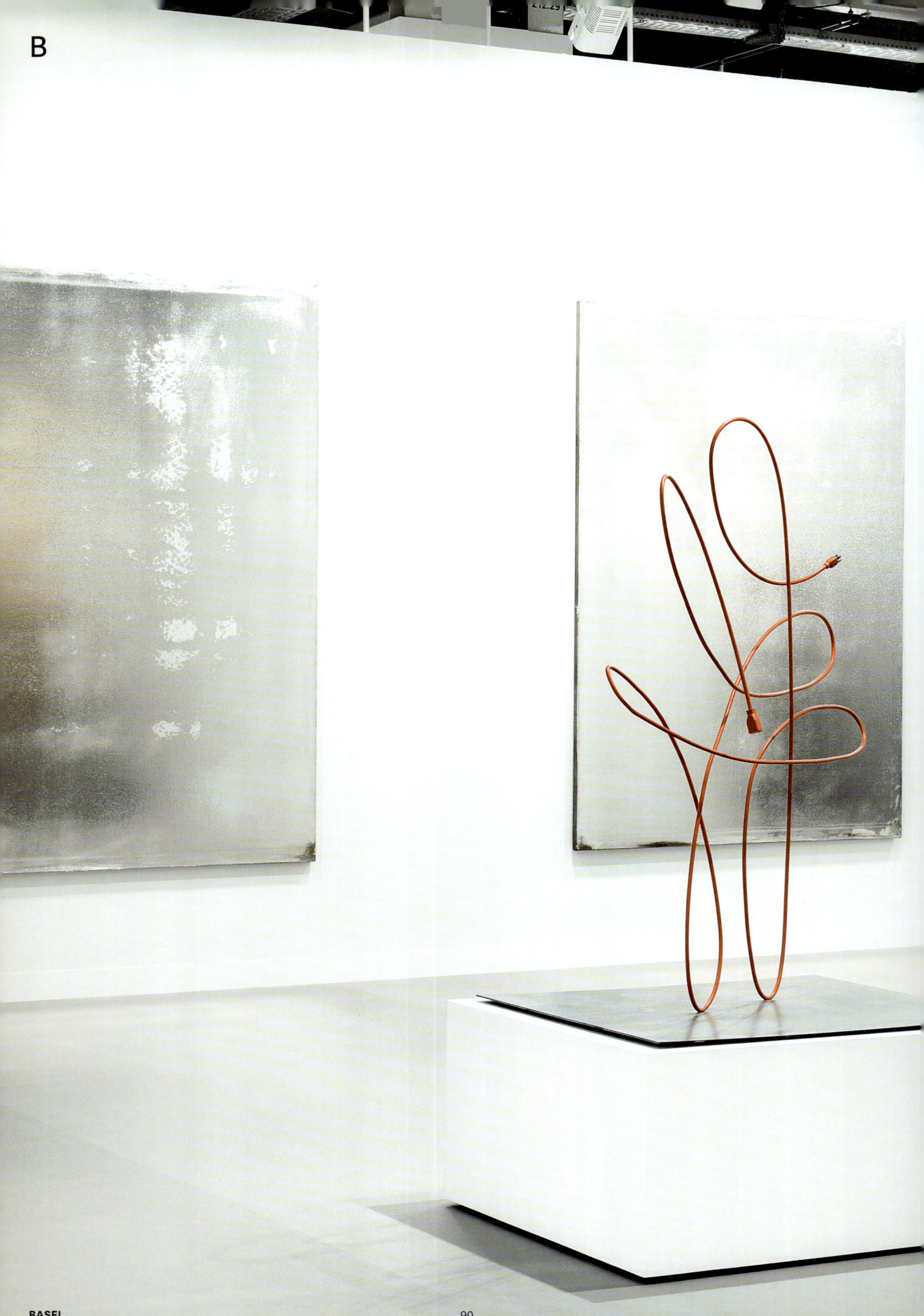

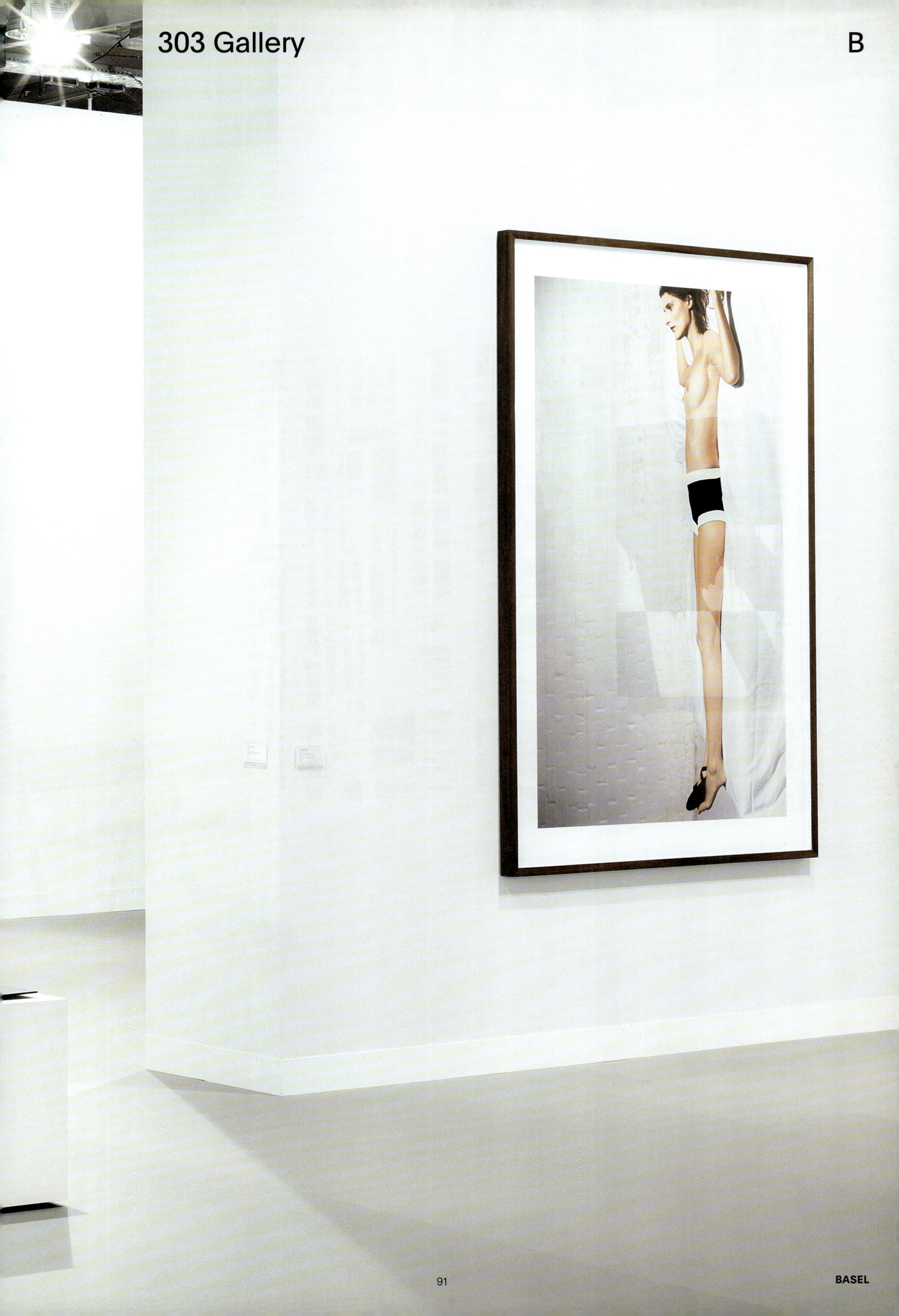

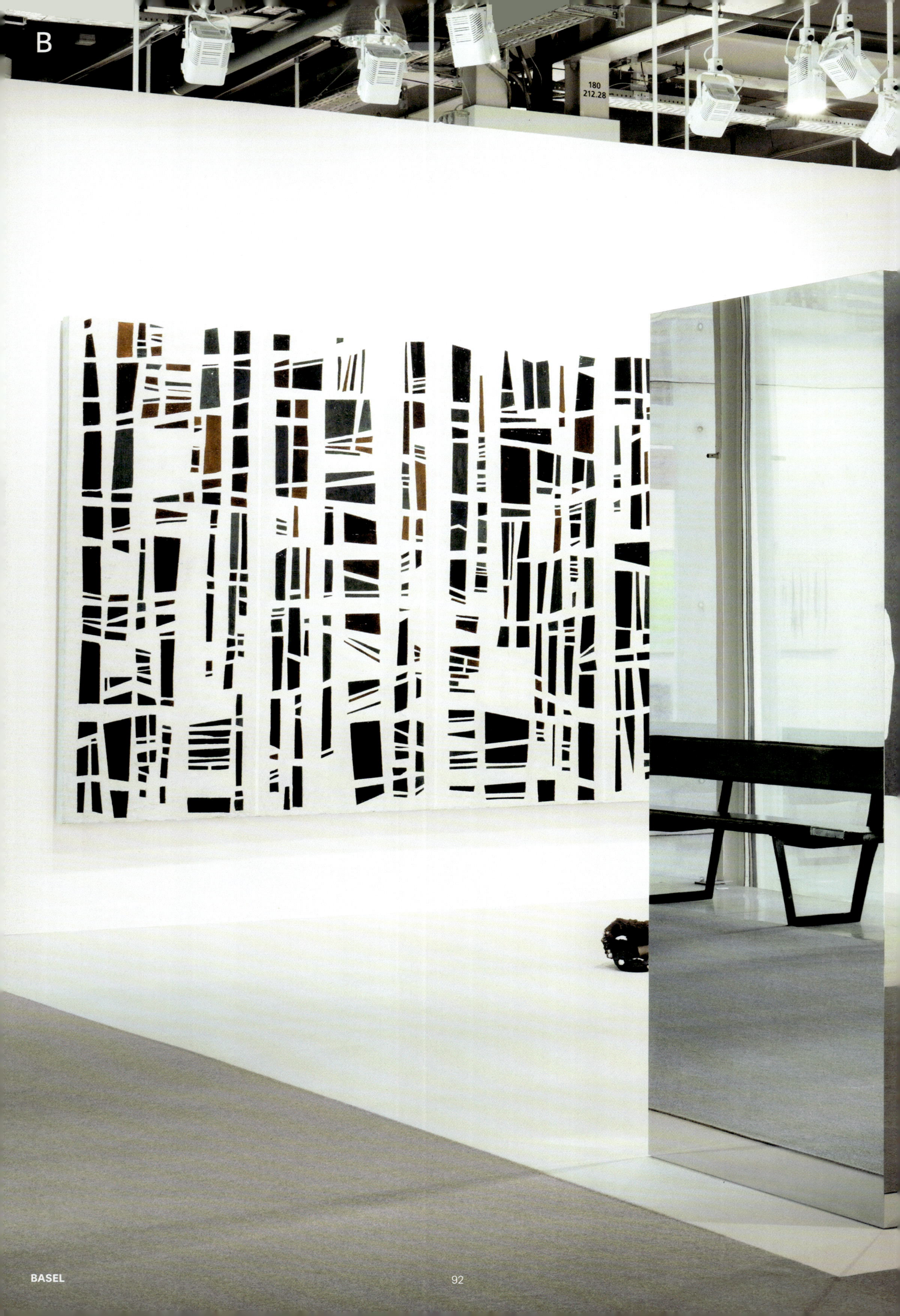
B
180
212.28

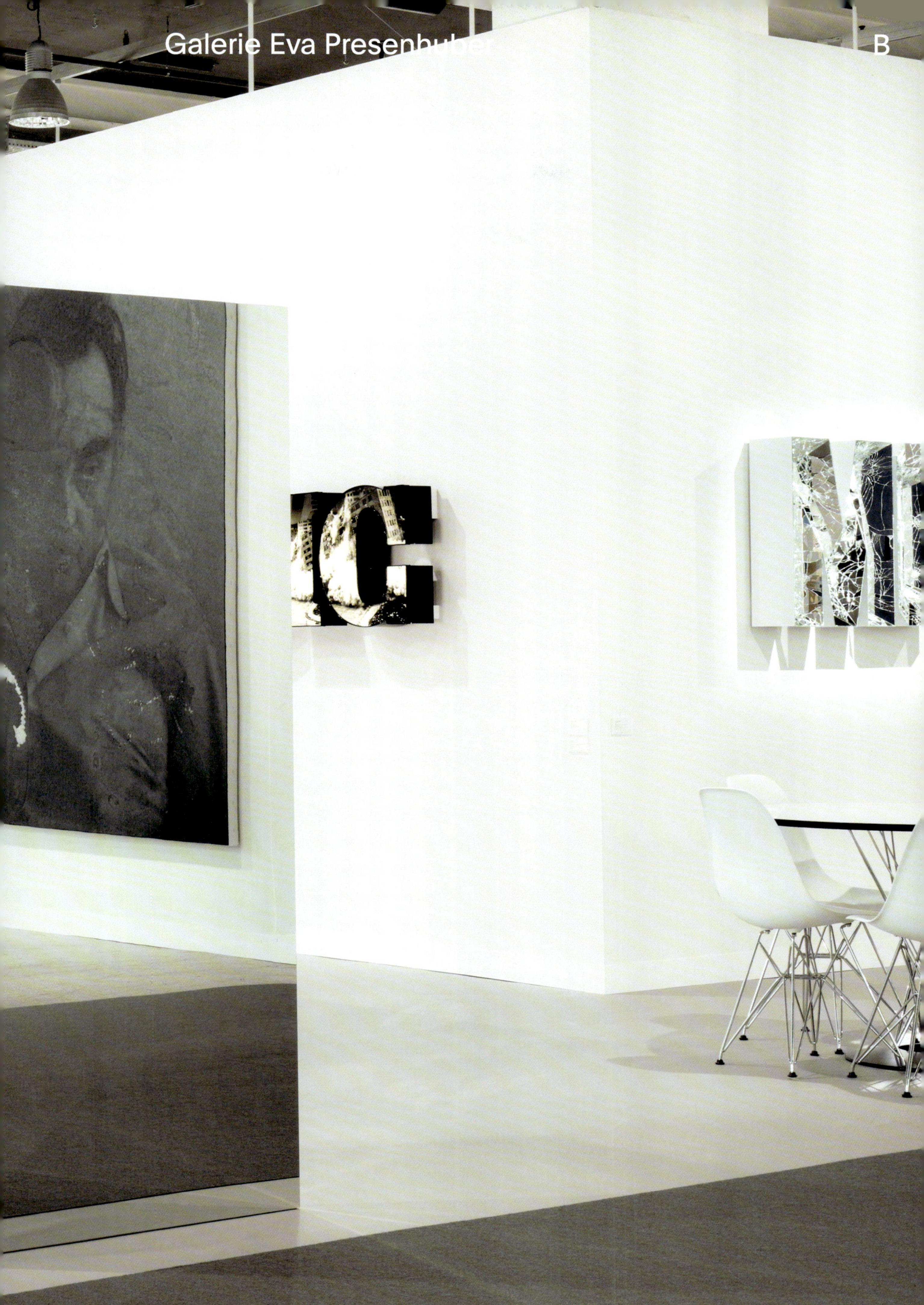

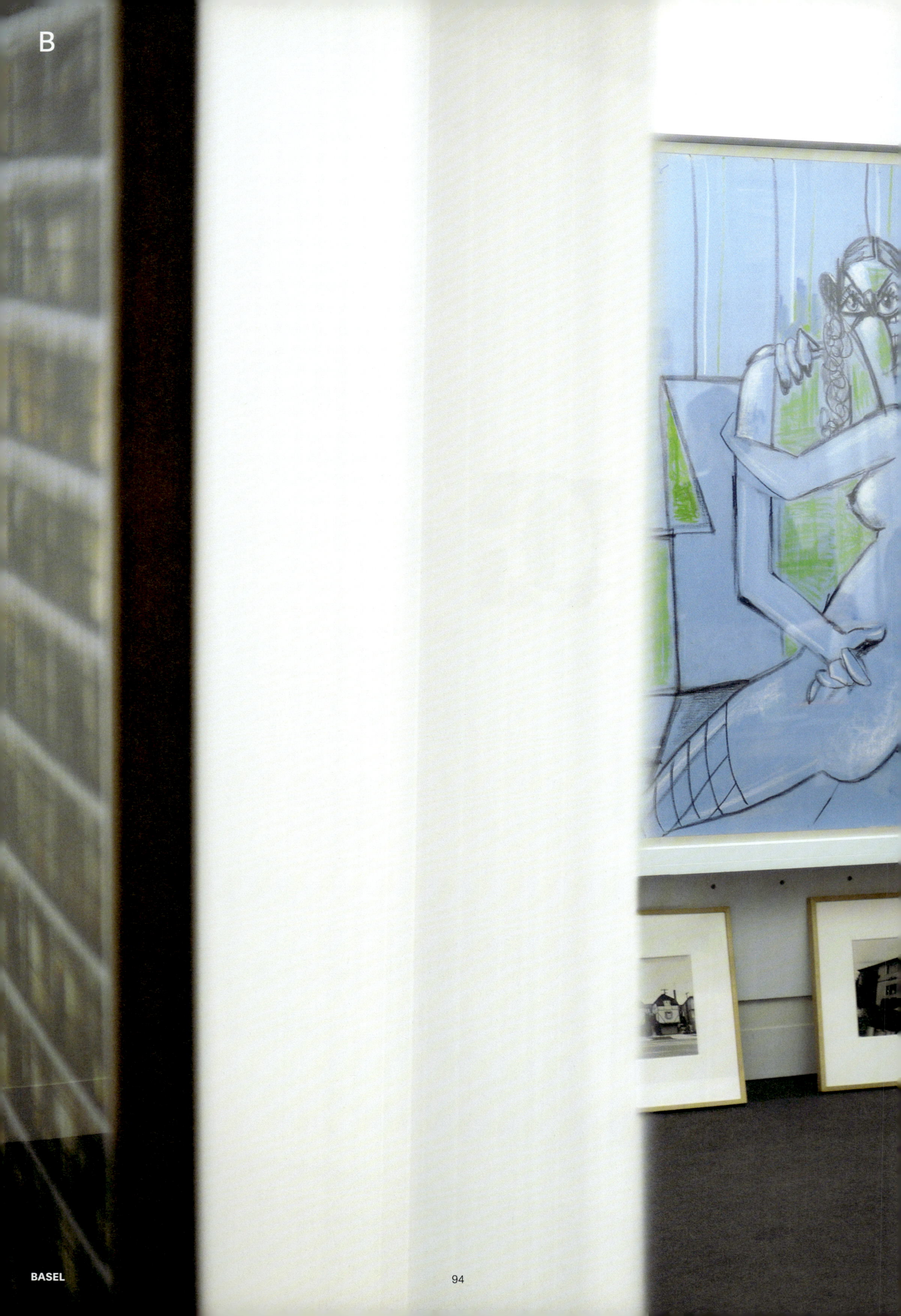

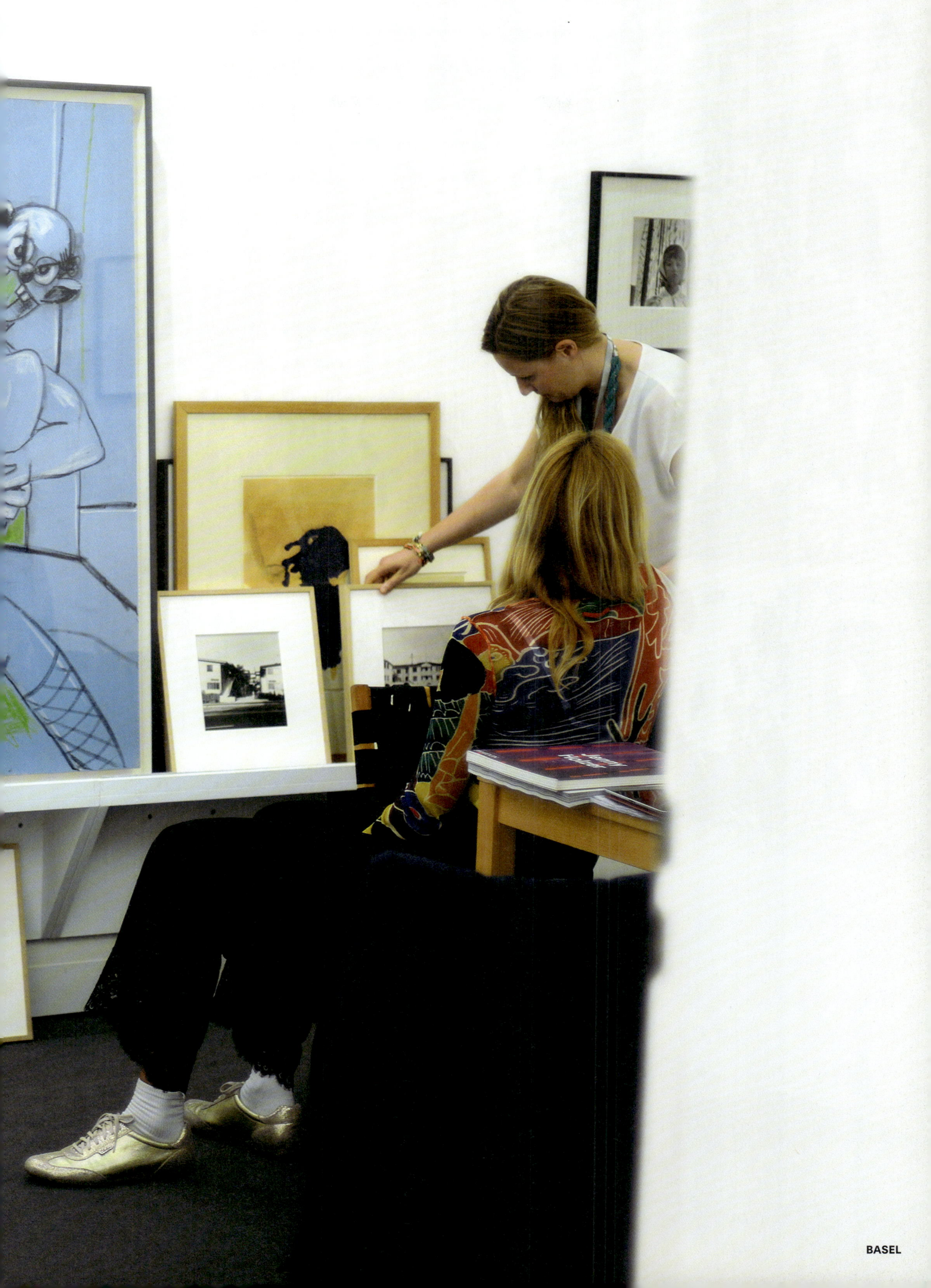

B

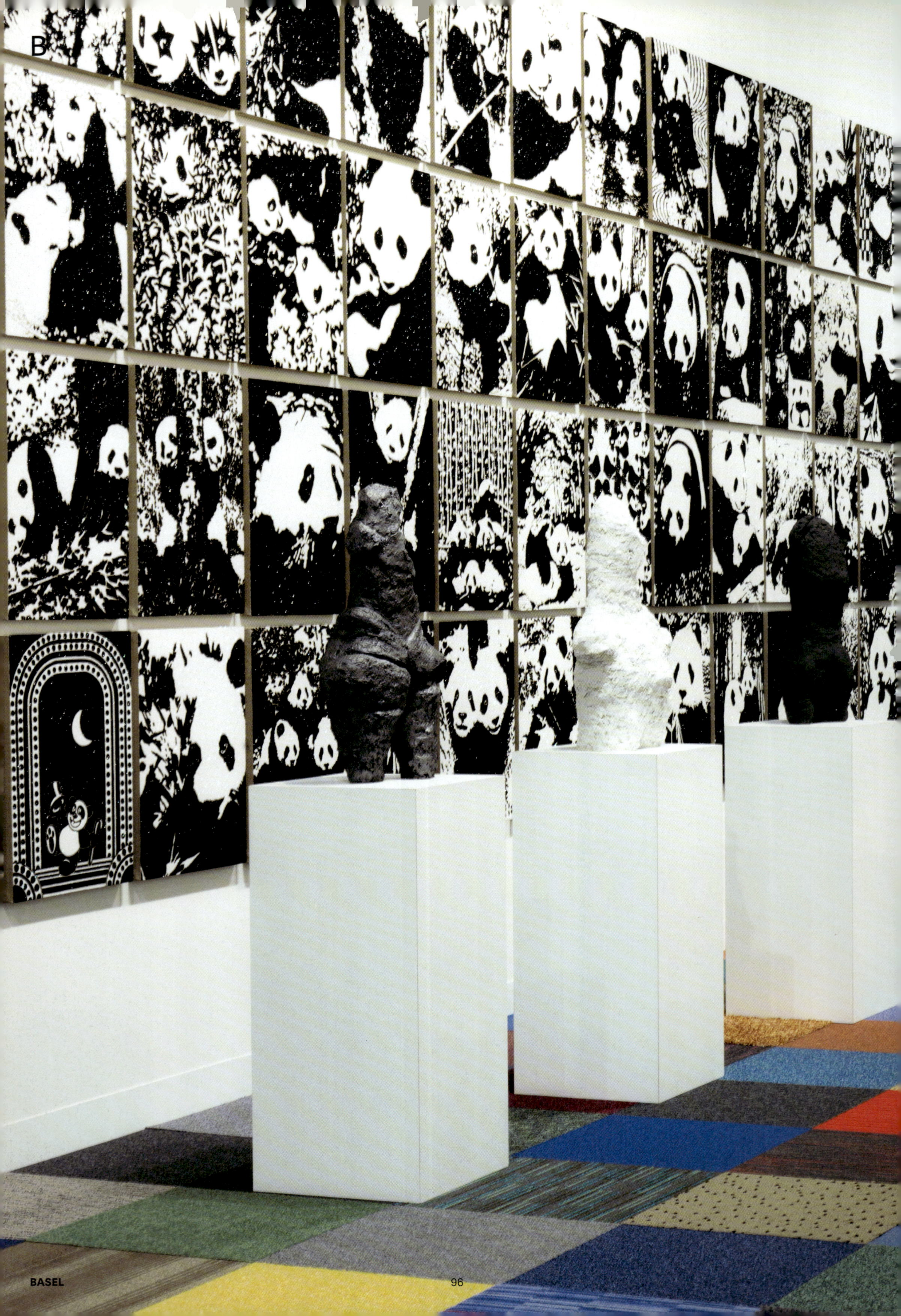

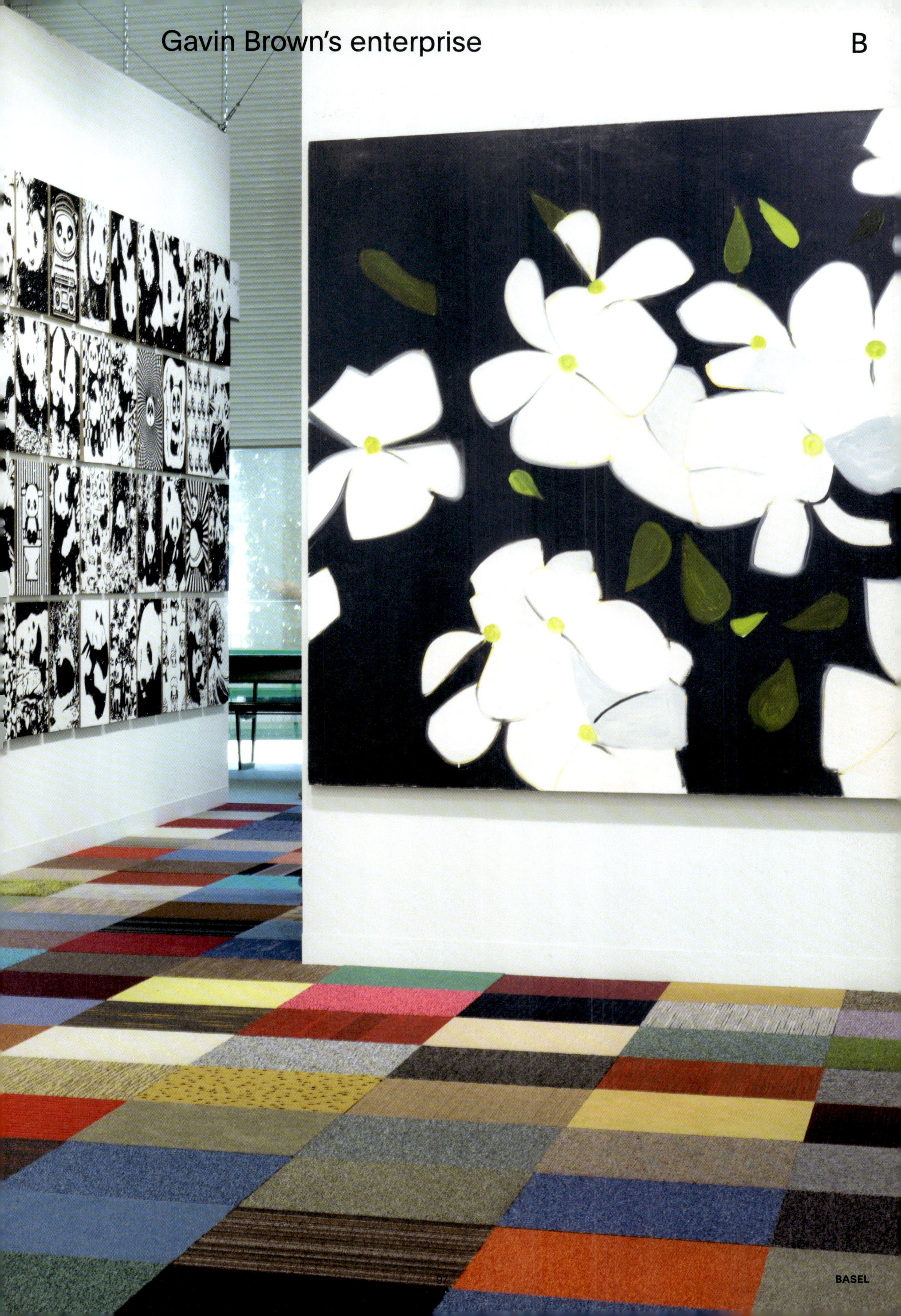

B neugerriemschneider

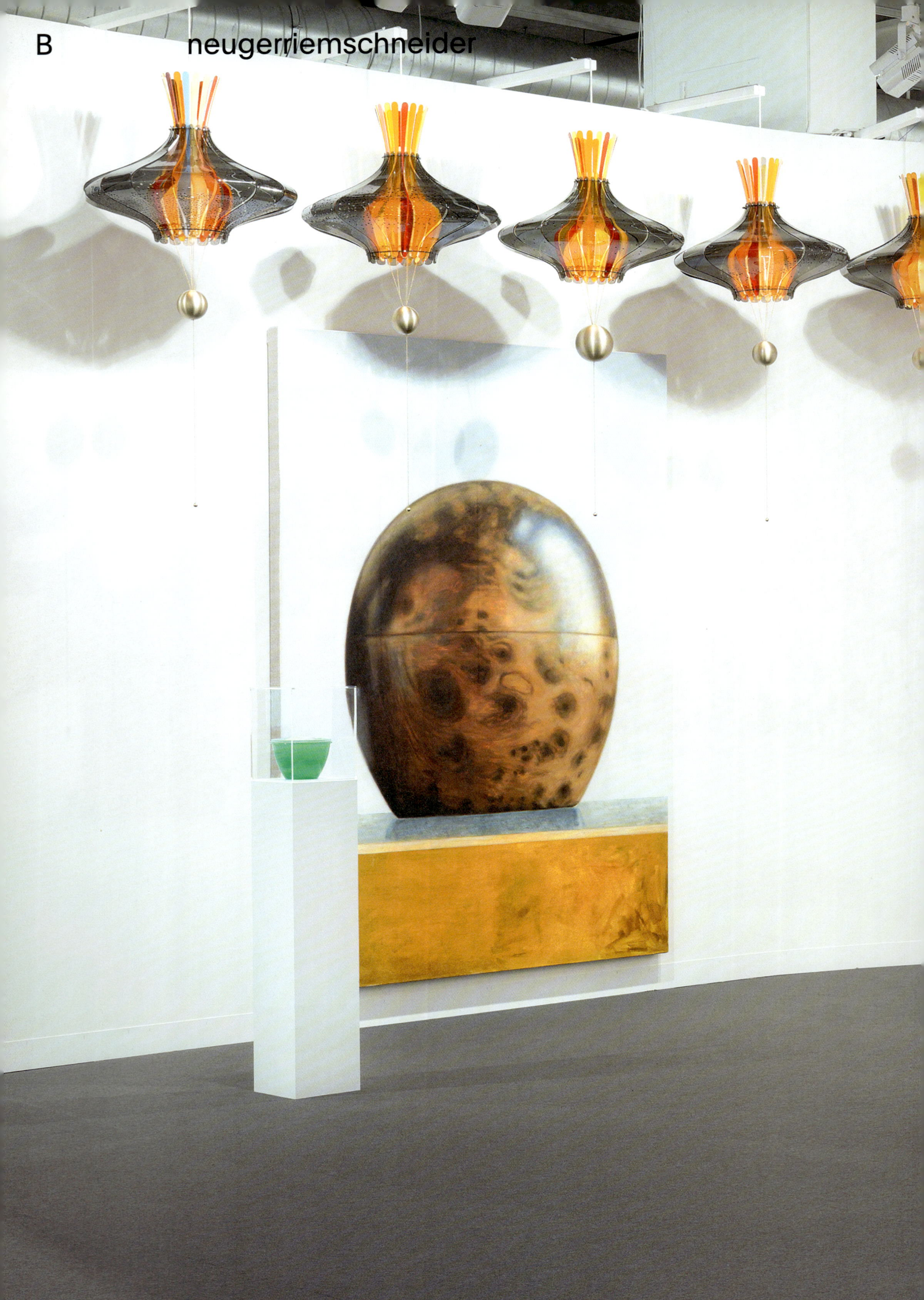

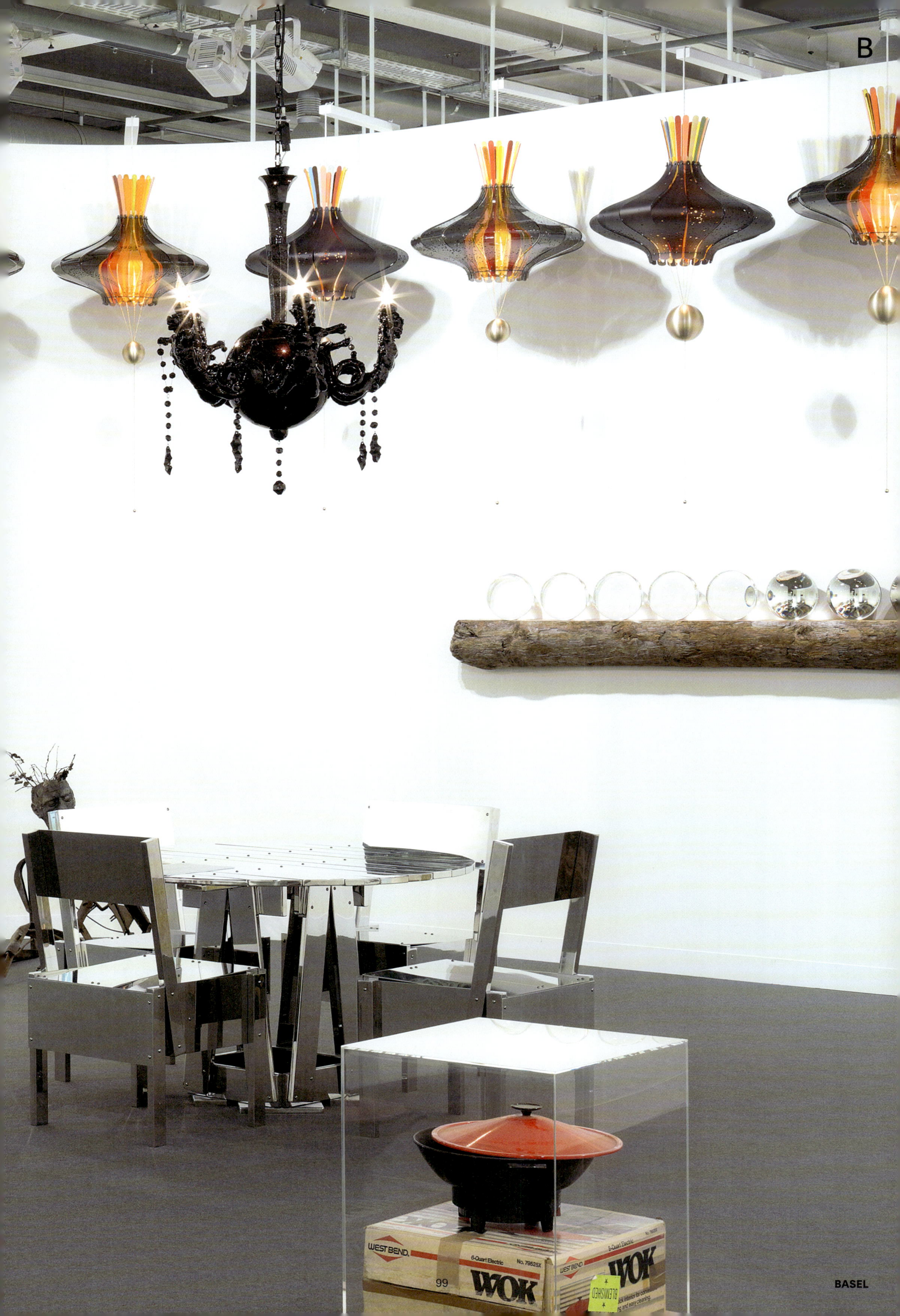
WEST BEND
6-Quart Electric
No. 79525X
WOK
WEST BEND
WOK
BLEMISHED

Galerie Hans Mayer

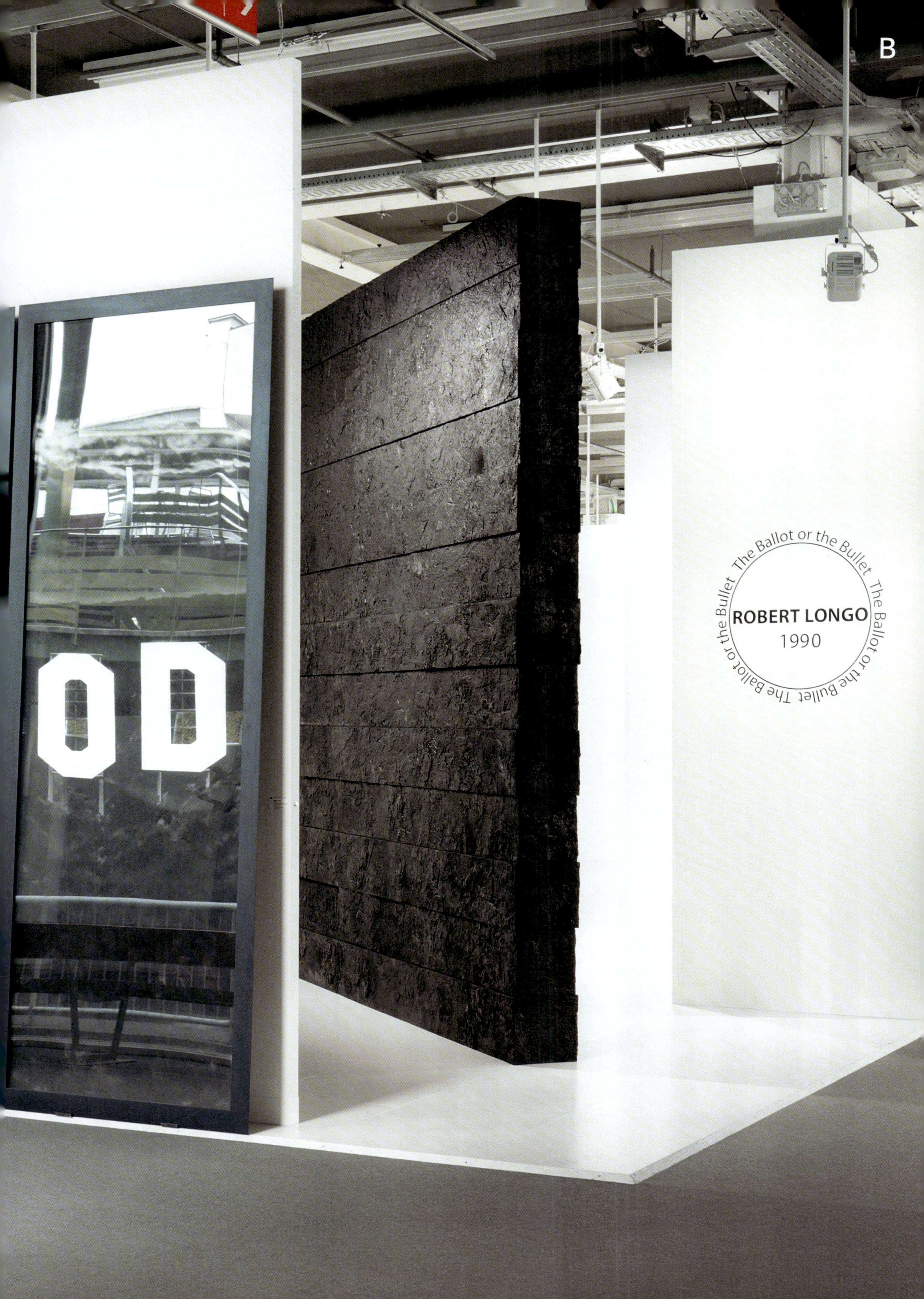
B
The Ballot or the Bullet The Ballot or the Bullet The Ballot or the Bullet
ROBERT LONGO
1990
OD

B

Friedrich Petzel Gallery

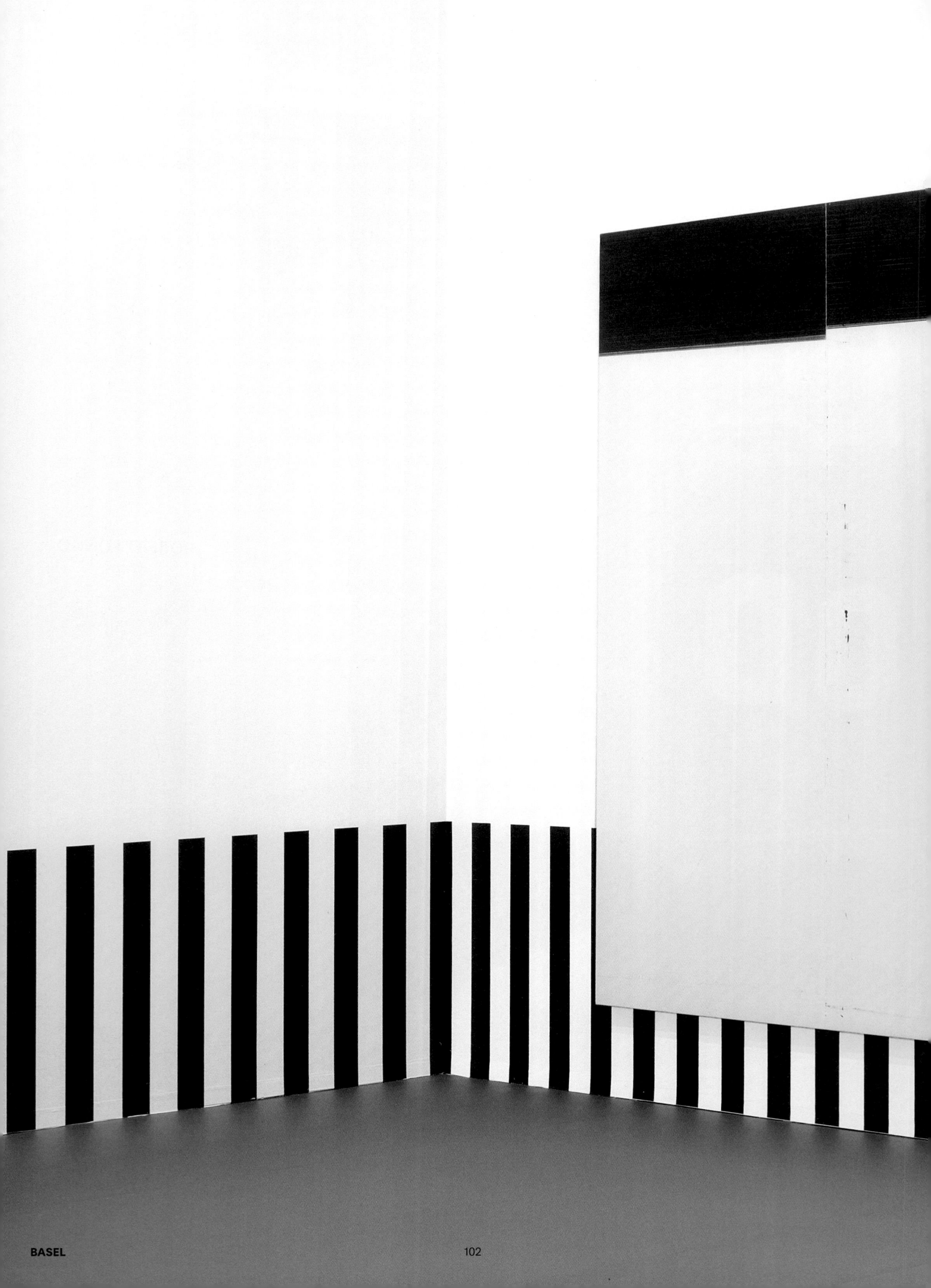

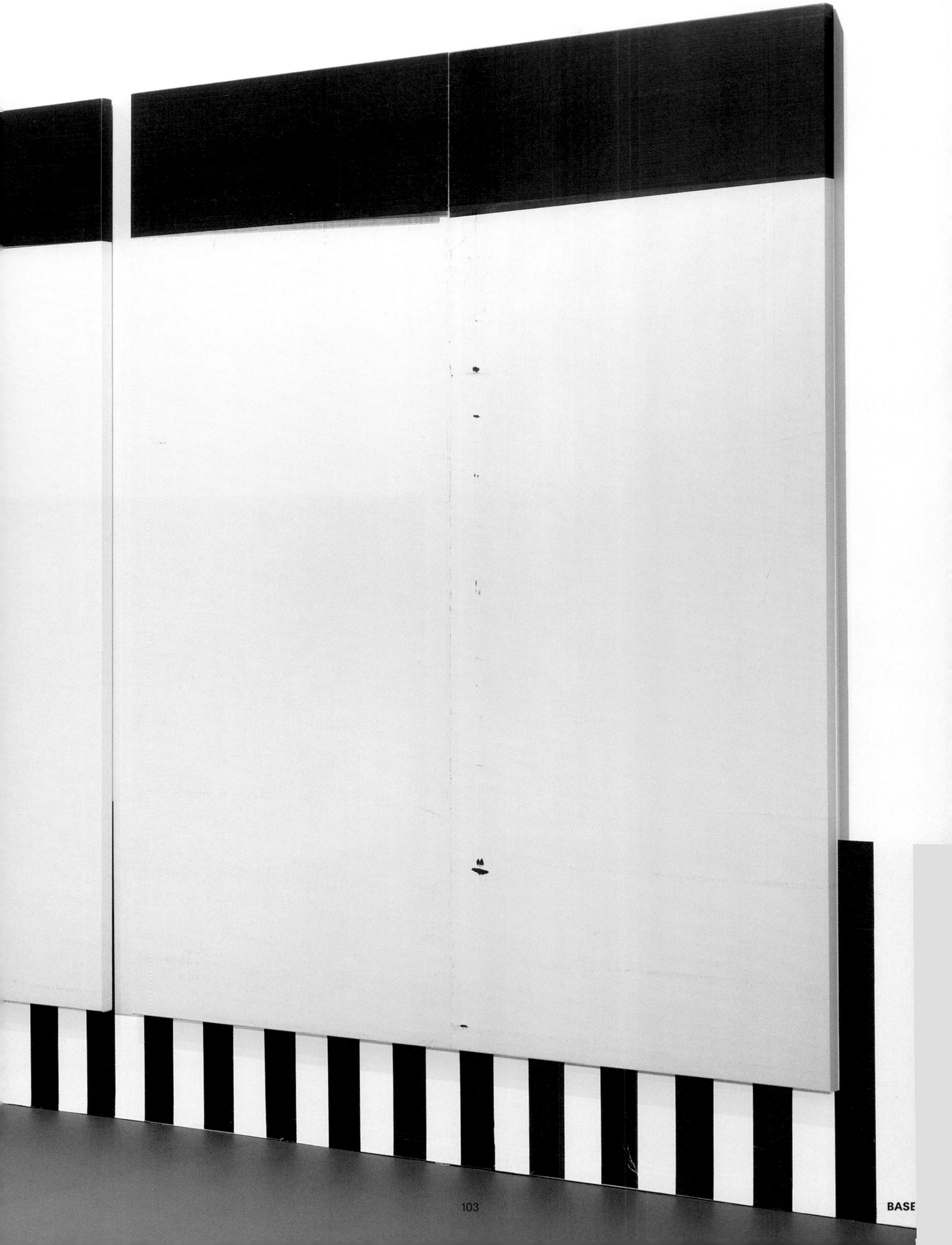

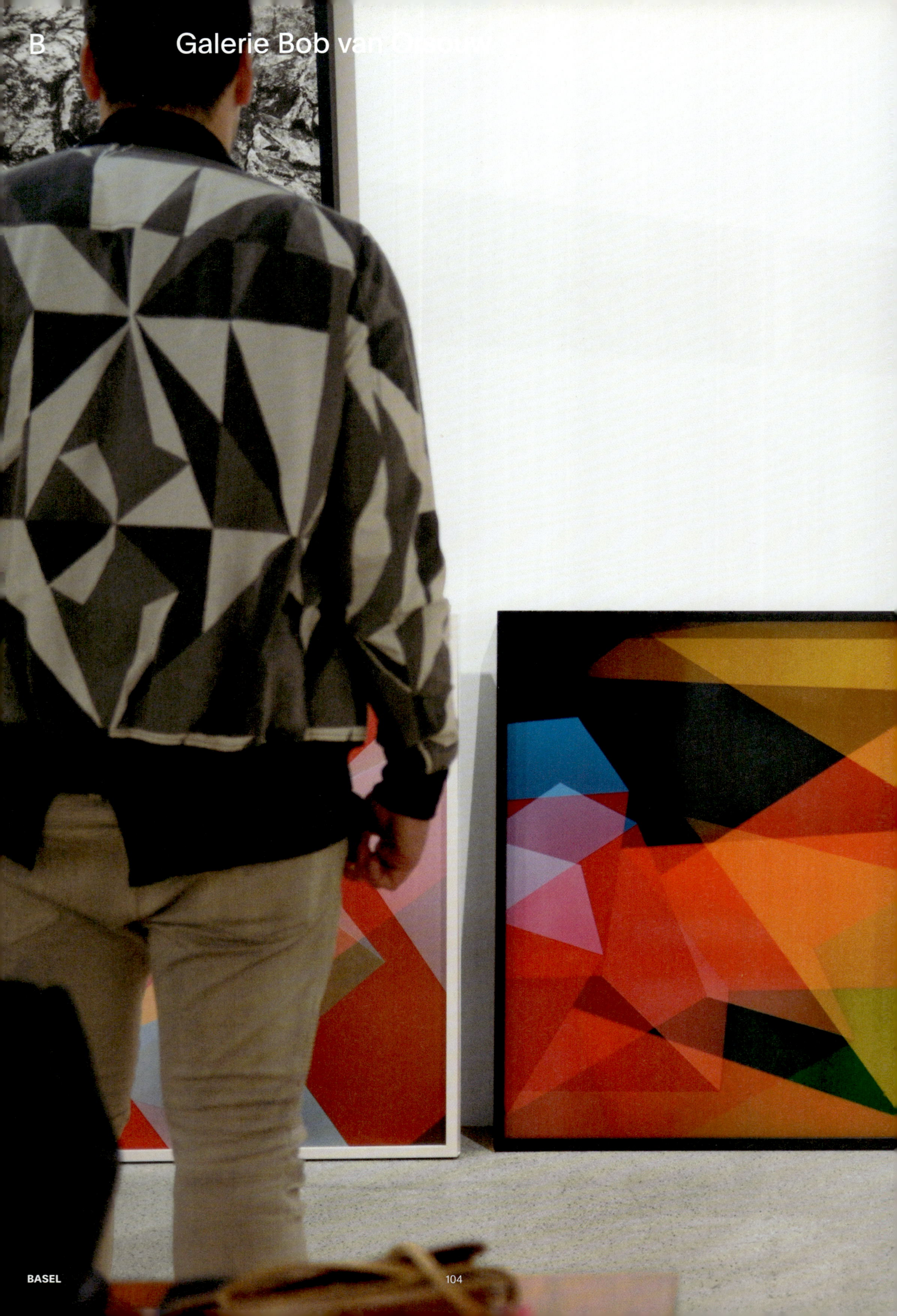

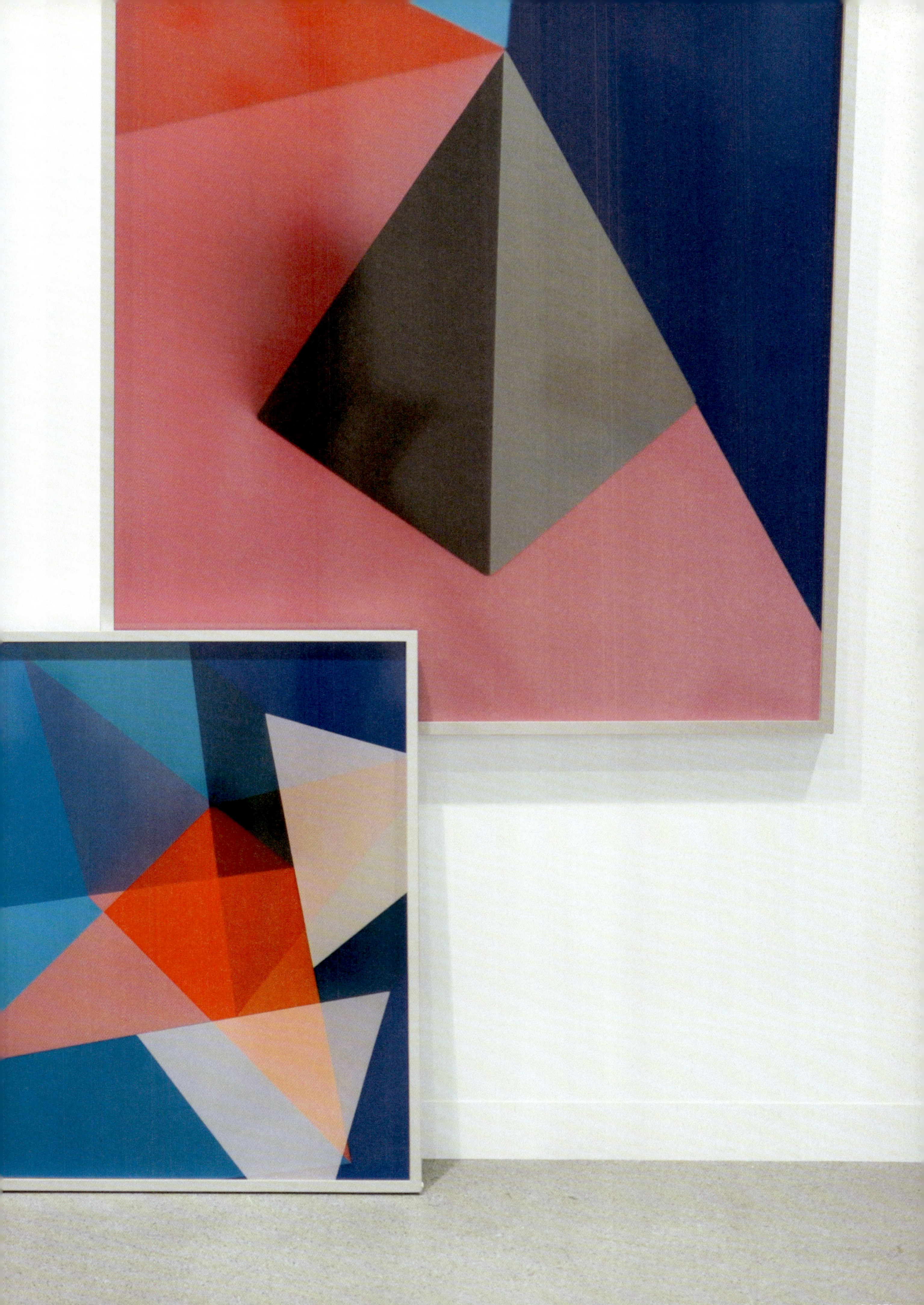

Galerie 1900–2000

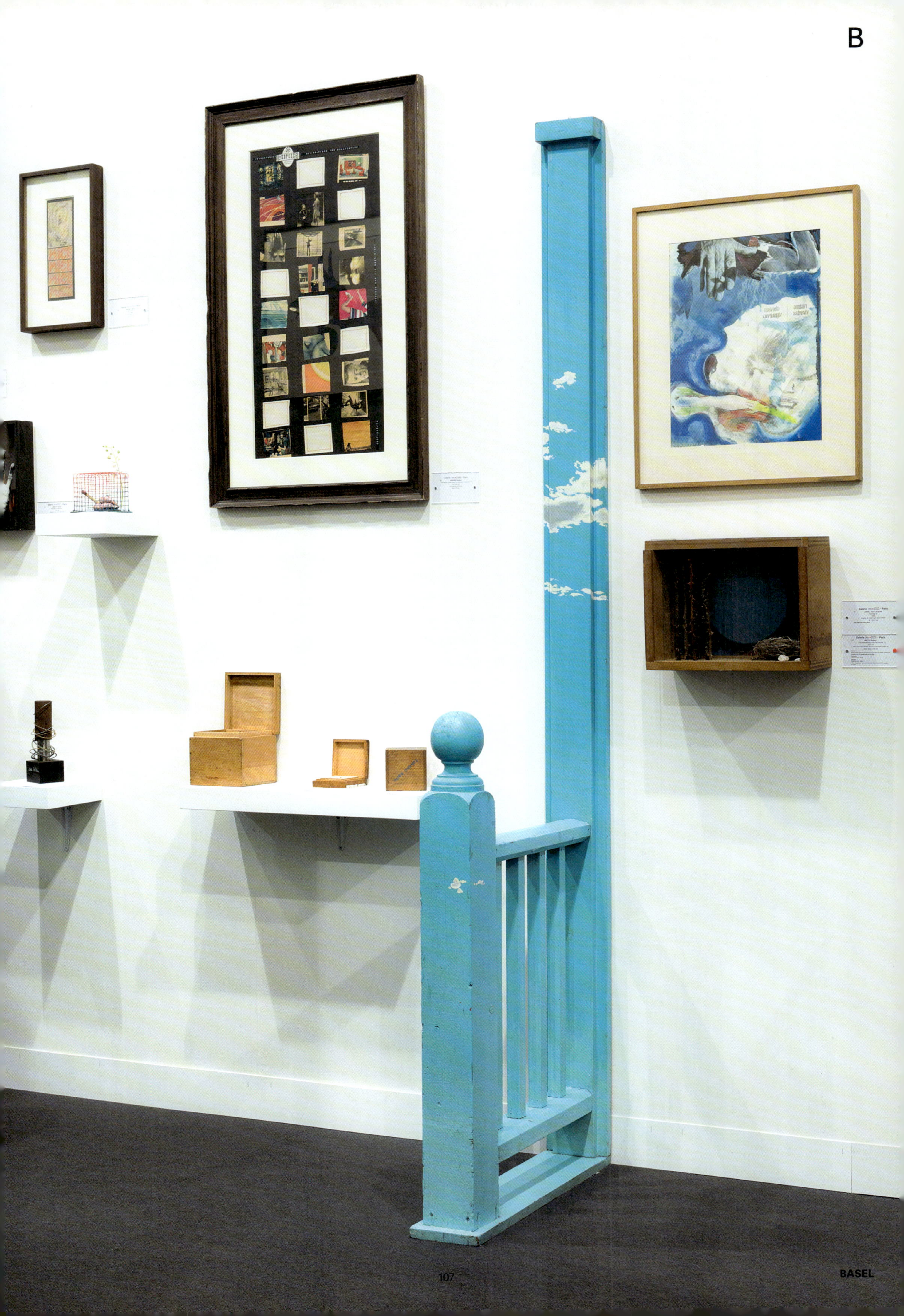

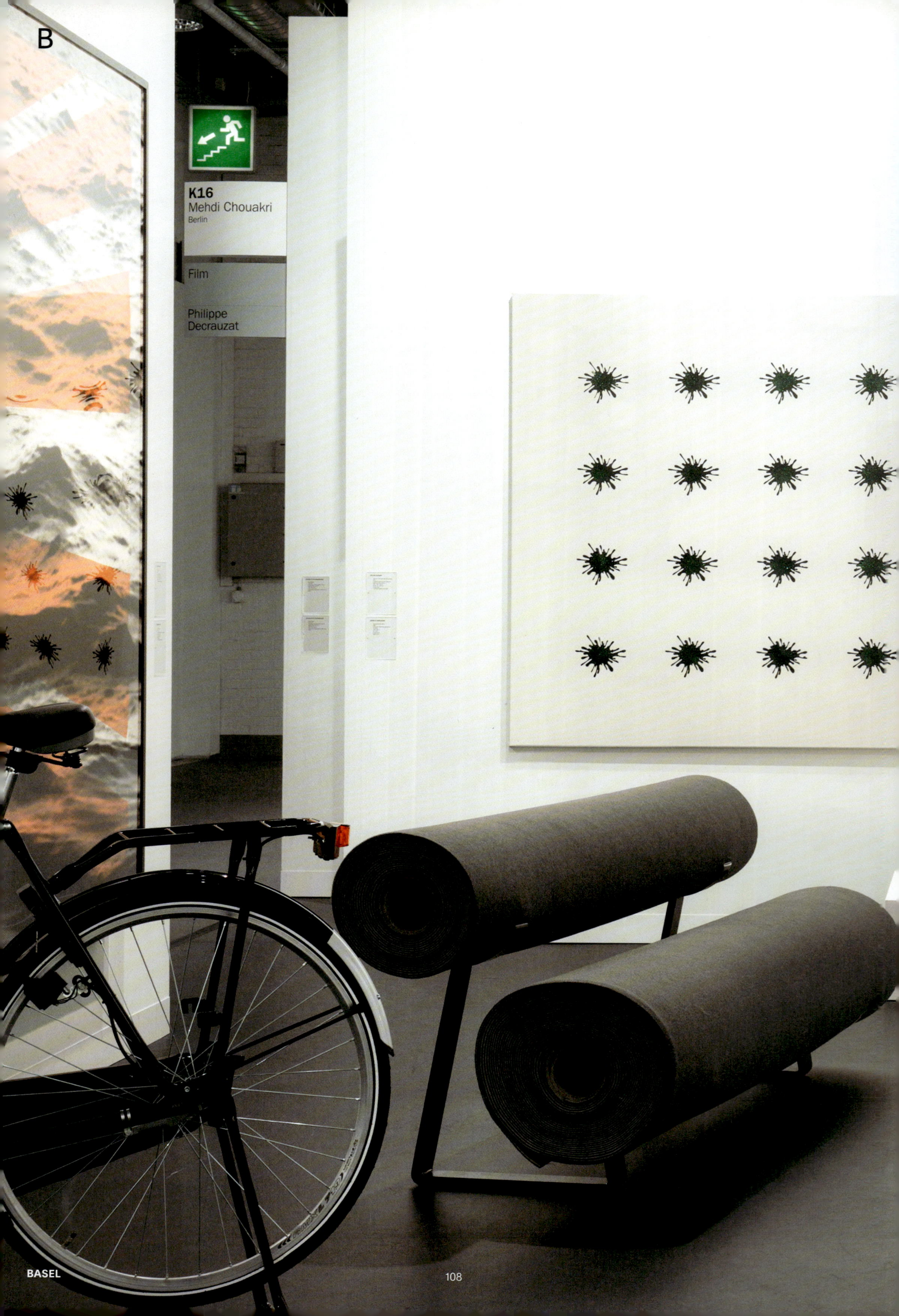
K16
Mehdi Chouakri
Berlin
Film
Philippe
Decrauzat

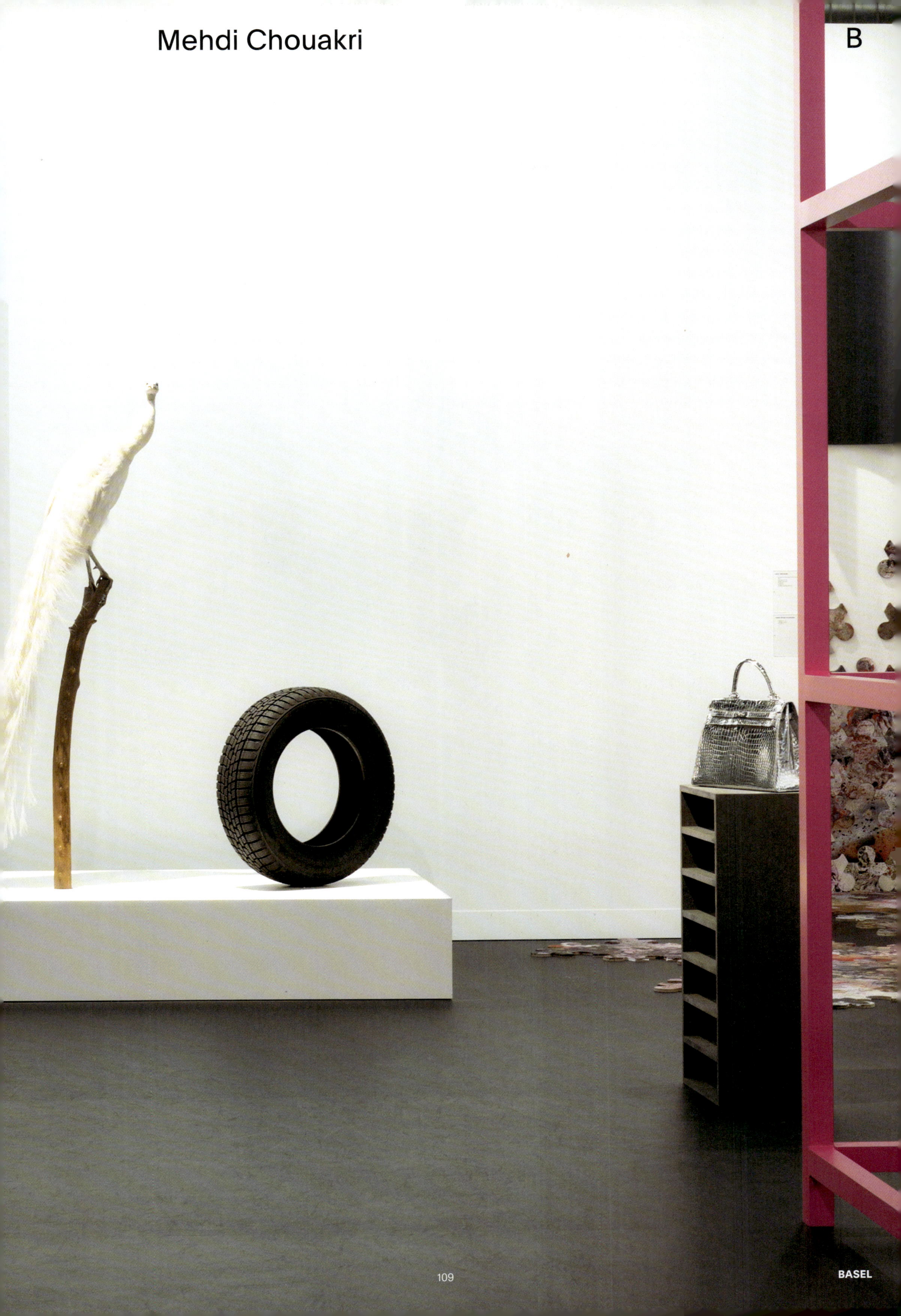

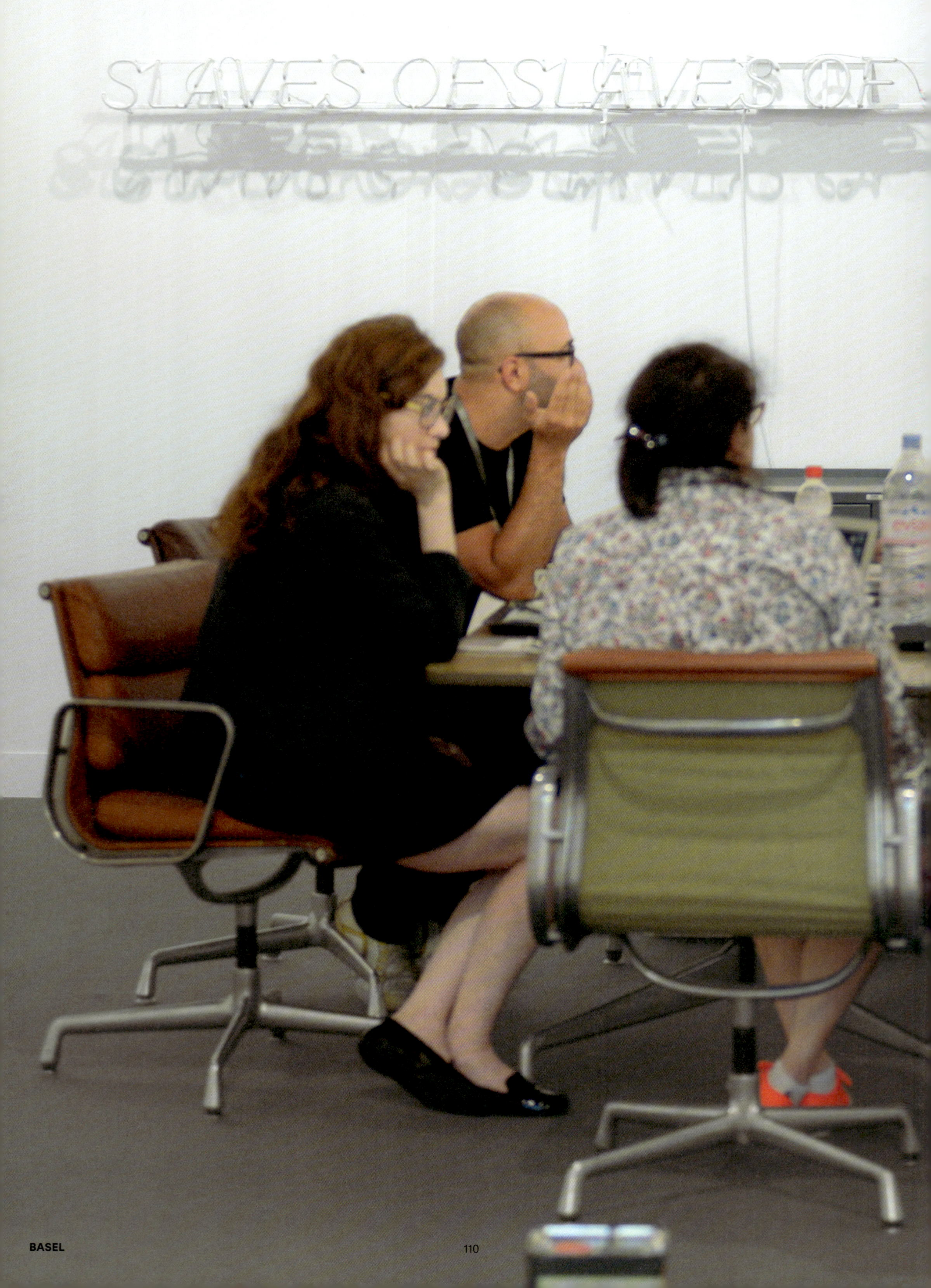
SLAVES OF SLAVES OF

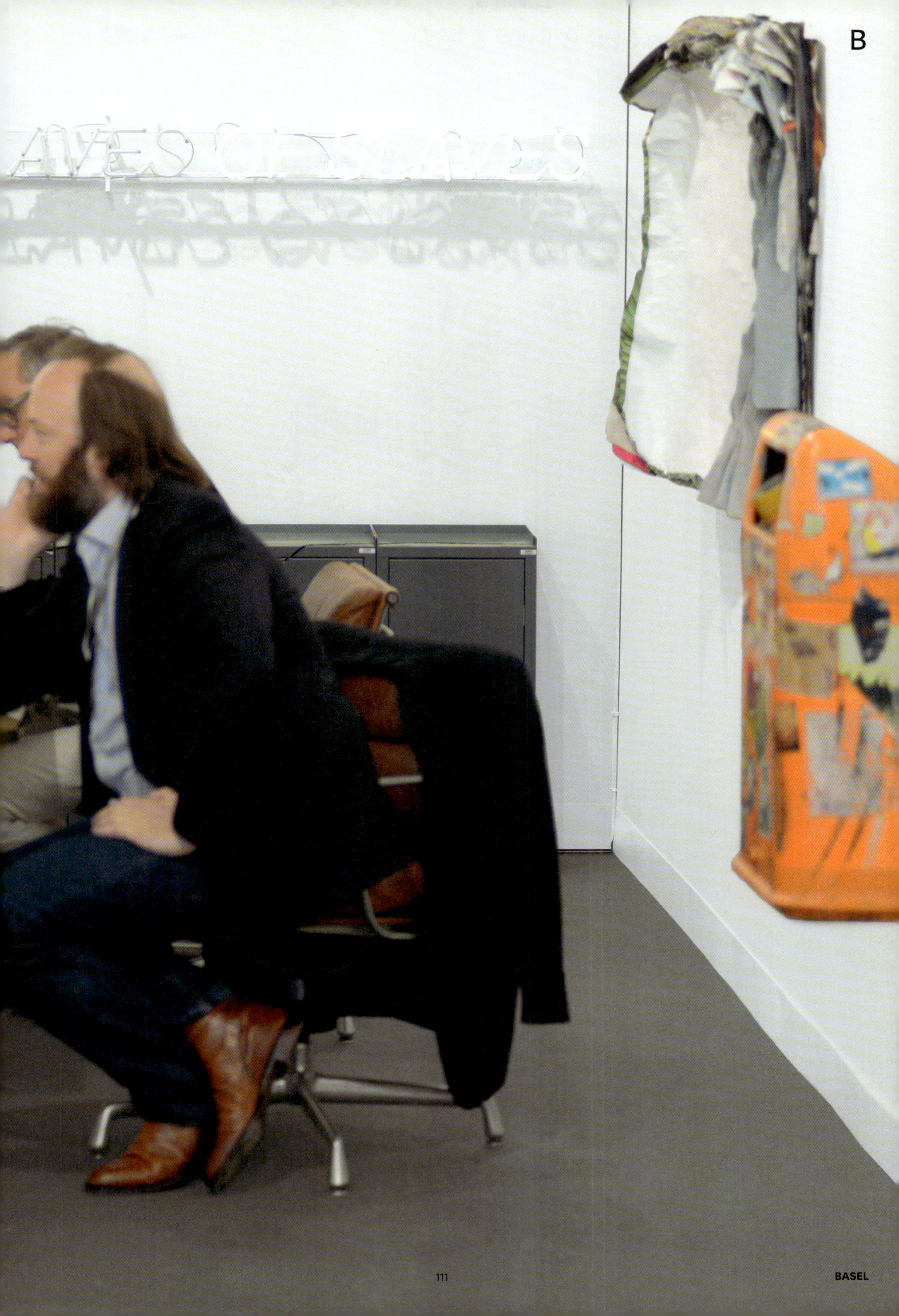

B

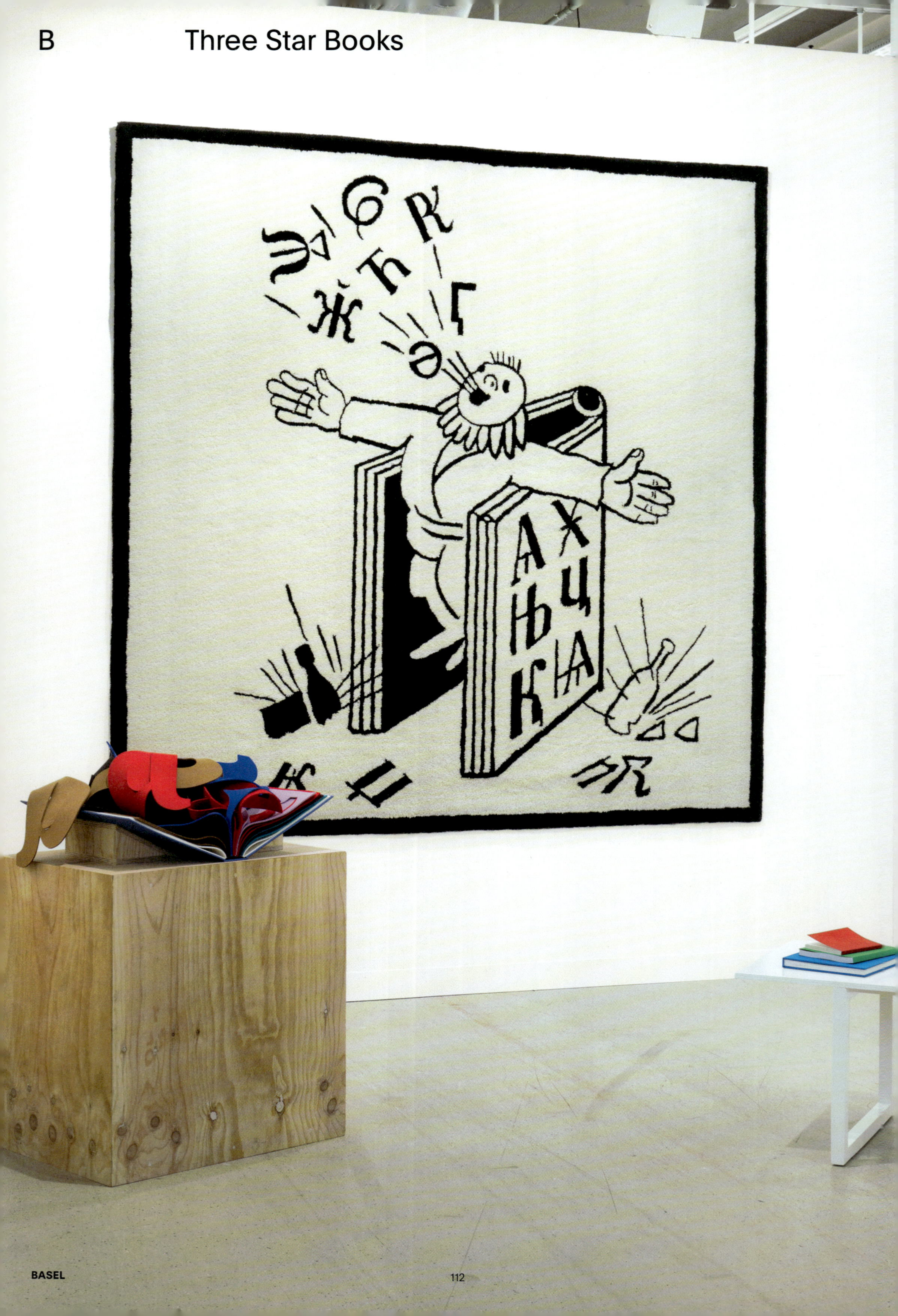

BIENNALES 2014

Berlin
Gwangju
Marrakech
Sydney

B

8th Berlin Biennale, May 29–August 3, 2014

Curator: Juan A. Gaitán

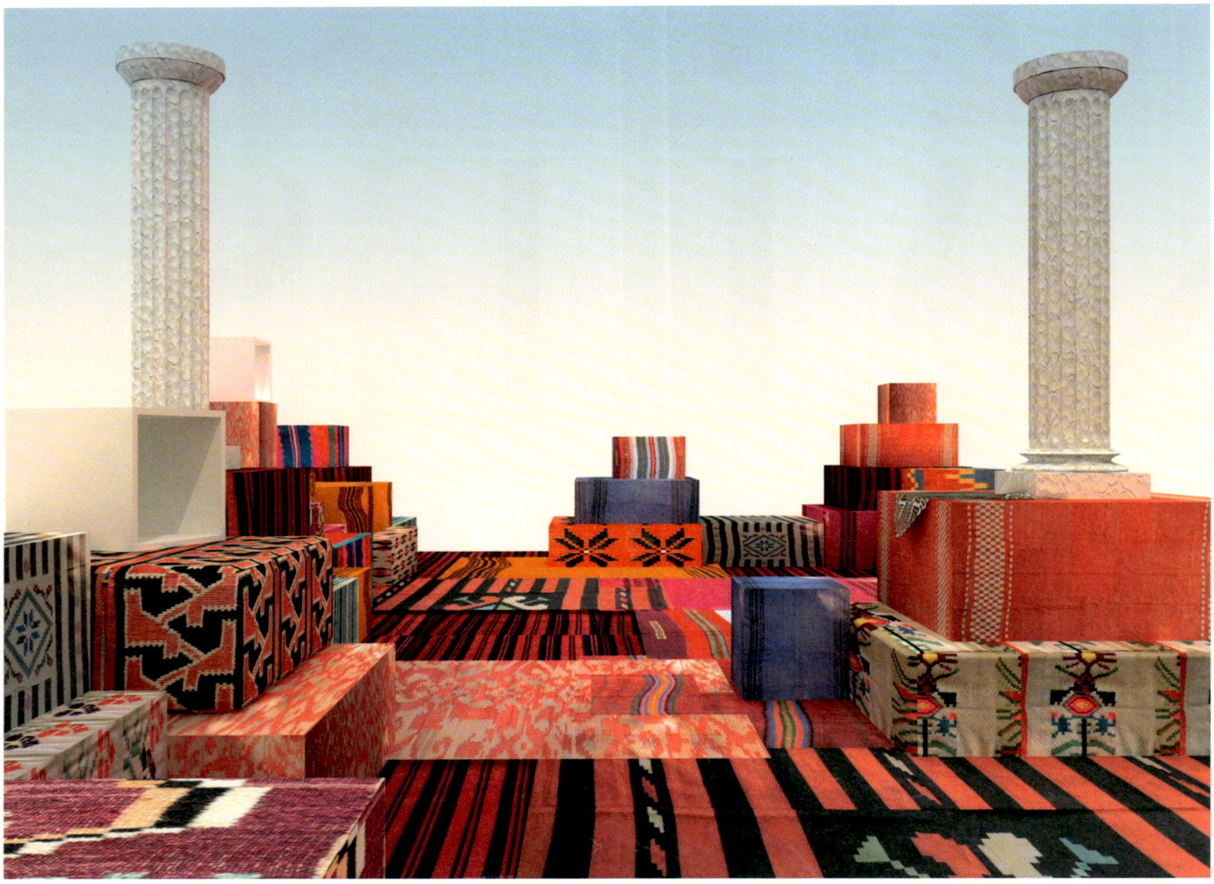

Andreas Angelidakis
Study for
Crash Pad, 2013

What are the main topics you are addressing in your Biennale as far as you could tell by December 2013? How would you phrase its differences, its singularities, both in terms of structure and contents?

The main interest for this Biennale is the empirical relationship to history, or how each individual positions themself in relation to the writing of history, and particularly the history that directly relates to their place and time, and then how this translates into their work as artists. Another way of putting this is to say that I am interested in an affective dimension, which is the dimension in which nothing can be seen as definitively settled in the rationalist charts. But this cannot be said to be the theme of the Biennale. It is, so to speak, a criterion for approaching contemporary artistic practices. Some works deal with the image in itself, as a phenomenon; other works deal with what the image can or cannot do when attempting to represent something, such as labor, or violence, and so on.

This Biennale is neither a continuation of nor a departure from former ones. I think of the Berlin Biennale as an ongoing experiment that each curator gets a chance to work out and take further. It has consistently been focused on Berlin, each time in terms of the city's present composition. The 8th Berlin Biennale is no exception in this respect, and we are considering how history appears or does not appear in the present city of Berlin, in 2014.

Could you give us some details of specific projects, some of the artists invited, that would exemplify the specificities and topics of your Biennale?

I can give you one. On the January 25 we will open a room designed by the Greek/Norwegian architect Andreas Angelidakis, titled *Crash Pad*. It's a functional room, but it's also meant to evoke two important historical moments: the invention of Antiquity in the late 18th century (which is to a large extent also the beginning of art history as we know it today) and the first Greek financial crisis in the 19th century, which promoted the invention of the system of financial monitoring that led to the formation of the International Monetary Fund. It is, in this sense, a work/installation that deals directly with Greece's place in Europe today, and in the history of Europe.

This year's Venice Biennale was considered by many as breaking away from the Biennale model to propose a museum-like exhibition. How much does this interfere, influence, or contradict your own Biennale's definition?

Actually the Venice Biennale of 2013 didn't contribute much to my own thinking about the Berlin Biennale. I visited it twice, but it didn't resonate with my own approach. I saw several very good works there, but I think of the Venice Biennale as a thing of its own kind that, other than the name, has little to do with other types of biennials around the world.

10th Gwangju Biennale: *Burning Down the House*, September 5–November 9, 2014

B

Artistic Director: Jessica Morgan

Burning Down the House explores the process of conflagration and transformation, a cycle of obliteration and renewal witnessed throughout history. Evident in aesthetics—the rotation of media, subject, and form—historical events, and an increasingly rapid course of redundancy and renewal in commercial culture, the Biennale reflects on the often violent events of destruction or self-destruction—burning the home one occupies—followed by a promise of the new and the hope for change.

In the 1930s Walter Benjamin coined the term "Tigersprung" (the tiger's leap) for the potential of commodities to leap back in time, cite from their own source book, and activate a form or look of the past for the present—all under the auspices of the "eternal return" within the culture industry where the merry-go-round of fashionable styles and movements continues apace. What can the "Tigersprung" mean for today's "tiger economies" like South Korea? It seems as if its culture is destined to continually re-run its history, due to the confluence of economic and political powers, which ask for the eternally new of fashionable commodities and industrial progress, while eschewing its cultural past. The very new in the guise of the old—stylistically as well as conceptually—becomes both a boon and a curse; and the art Biennale with its emphasis on the latest visual and plastic trends plays an ambiguous role within this process.

Burning Down the House celebrates the universal role of the artist as detractor and provocateur of cultural institutions and society at large, simultaneously acknowledging the aesthetic possibility and impossibility within art to deal directly and concretely with politics, and it looks to the act of renewal and revitalization that this spiral implies. At the same time, the 10th Gwangju Biennale shows the often raucous and joyous roles of artists who upset the given order and resist containment through a hedonistic exploration of sound, movement, and performance. The notion of burning—inherently suggestive of transformation and dynamism—can be applied equally to the radical demolition of perceptions of identity, race, nationality, and gender. *Burning Down the House* speaks, too, of the transformative powers of fire: the manner in which material is changed or destroyed by flames, manifest as residue of vivid interventions or remnants of celebrations. Combining the notion of fire as celebration with its use in protest underscores the dialectical role of art to show itself most expressively in the negation of its forms and institutions.

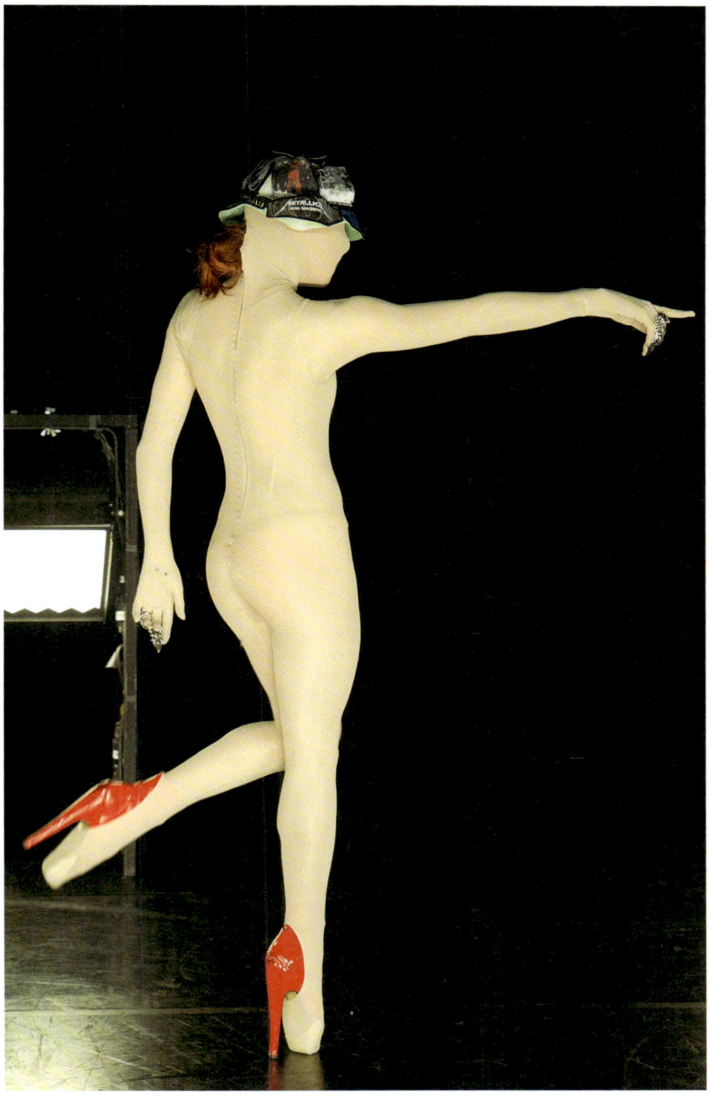

François Chaignaud & Cecilia Bengolea
(M)IMOSA, Twenty Looks or Paris is Burning at The Johnson Church (M), 2013
Produced by Vlovajob Pru

Including contemporary practice, as well as select examples from the Korean War era and after from Asia, Africa, Middle East, Europe, and the US, *Burning Down the House* will provide a critical reading of the relationship between artists and their social and cultural environment, in which engaged institutional critique and the playful assault of the establishment, with all their contradictory expressions, animate artworks.

The 10th Gwangju Biennale examines the potential of art *as movement*—simultaneously, to display the efforts made by contemporary artists to address subjective and public issues through individual and collective engagement, as well as demonstrating how challenging these efforts and their impacts have become. Contrary to museums with their often hegemonic cultural policies and their interests in denoting legacies and traditions, the Biennale is a mobile and flexible event, which offers a spectrum of creative expressions that are immediate, contemporary, and topical, making the proposed debate of art as movement fitting for the space of Gwangju—both geopolitically as well as in terms of institutional alternative.

5th Marrakech Biennale: *Where Are We Now?*, February 26–March 31, 2014

Visual Art Curator: Hicham Khalidi

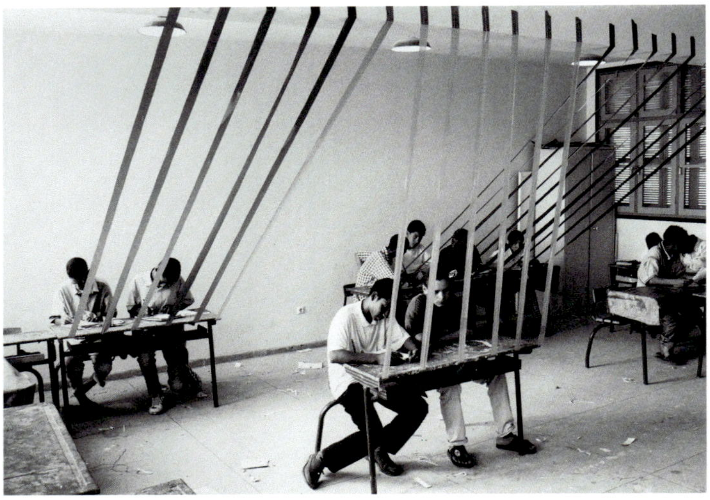

Hicham Benohoud
La Salle de classe,
1994–2002
Photograph

What are the main topics you are addressing in your project?

Where Are We Now? addresses first the status of today's Morocco. What does the country consist of? How was and is the country related to other countries, regions, and continents? Another question is how the shift of the West to the East and the Middle East is taking place. As a Moroccan who grew up outside of Morocco I feel there is a gradual shift happening from the Northern and Western toward the Southern and Eastern. One fact that makes this very clear is the number of re-migrants one meets in Morocco. Also, despite its political loyalty to the West, Morocco has maintained closer relationships with the Middle East and Asia. I am interested in the roots and history of these connections, and what future lies ahead.

Then I reworked the questions into another concern, following philosopher Peter Osborne's ideas regarding the contemporary and the global transnational: what is the contemporary and how is it related to artistic strategies and (national and international) identity? In one of his most important lectures Osborne speaks of artists fictionalizing their own authorities and explains how these artistic strategies lead to a global, transnational fiction of art. The ideas behind these fictional models and identities interested me greatly. I asked myself how these artistic strategies could be used as a model for progress and change.

Could you give us some details about the Biennale's structure and contents, and about specific projects, which would exemplify the specificities and topics of your Biennale?

The Biennale is a multi-disciplinary event that, as well as a visual arts exhibition, also presents literature, outdoor performances, and cinema screenings. The idea behind the Biennale setup was to fully engage the city and create a route for the public that starts in the mountains (from the Yagour Plateau where one can find ten-thousand-year-old Berber engravings) and follows the water flow down to Marrakech and subsequently ends in the industrial areas of the city. This route, as well as being a geographic trajectory, forms a timeline from the past and present to the future.

I chose to have the main visual arts exhibition situated in three venues: Palais Badii (the old palace of Ahmed Al Mansour), Dar Si Said (the old Berber museum of Marrakech), and Bank du Maghreb (the old central bank of Morocco). The location for each artist was chosen through dialogue with the artists. Many of the artists took the local situation as a basis and worked toward a narrative or discourse with the local people, the venue, or the Biennale itself. What I find surprising is how naturally the work of the artists coincided with the context.

One of the Moroccan artists invited to participate is Hicham Benohoud. In the 1990s he was a teacher at a primary school. Interestingly, he decided to document this period of teaching in a very peculiar way. Every day he would ask the students of his class, who were between 6 and 12 years old, to make props. These props were used to make several installations in the classroom. Sometimes he would use the tables or chairs by stacking them in different formations. Subsequently he would photograph the constellations of props, classroom furniture, and the students. This resulted in a series of hundreds of photographs called *La Salle de classe* that document an eight-year performance by Hicham and his students. Hicham will make a new work dealing with the aim of the Moroccan government to reach 20 million tourists in Marrakech by 2020.

This year's Venice Biennale was considered by many as breaking from the Biennale model to propose a museum-like exhibition. How much does it interfere, influence, or contradict your own Biennale's definition?

Massimiliano Gioni's choice to give a great deal of space to Outsider art only emphasizes the wide scope of artistic production in my opinion. It is a way to depoliticize the artistic; the hierarchy of what is artistic and therefore of what is true and what is not. By adding such an elaborate choice of Outsider art, a new encyclopedia is established, a new threshold given; or rather a reference of the absence of a threshold. It is very non-hierarchical in my opinion. Whether it is a real museum-like exhibition is for me not an issue (good or bad).

I think I am dealing with the same thing in Morocco. One of the most difficult things in making a selection of artists for the Biennale was the desire of the Biennale itself to add more Moroccan artists. Unquestionably one can feel a difference in the quality between artists in Morocco and artists in the West. But from what point of view am I saying that? The difficulty is based on my knowledge of what art should be, coming from the West. For that matter one could say the history of art is linear, but can there be any fixed point from which one can decide what art should be or should become? Any fixed point is by definition hierarchical and art is not. But still I felt there was a difference. I was looking for a specific Moroccan contemporary art. Was the quality of art based on the availability of educational platforms and the art sector in Morocco? The country only has three art academies as opposed to 17 in the country where I grew up. Next to that, there is no supportive infrastructure after graduation. Does infrastructure have anything to do with what art is or can become? What kind of contemporary art is possible regardless of any knowledge or system known to us as the system of contemporary art?

Another interesting thought about the flux between the local and the global came up at the Sharjah Biennale of 2013. As I was walking through the Biennale, suddenly it became apparent to me that Biennales have become world culture exhibitions. Walking through the exhibition I was looking at iterations of world culture in many different forms. With the entrance of so many countries into the Western art model, the subjects varied, but the form (the Western model) remained the same. World culture and art collide again.

18th Biennale of Sydney: *You Imagine What You Desire*, March 21–June 9, 2014

Artistic Director: Juliana Engberg

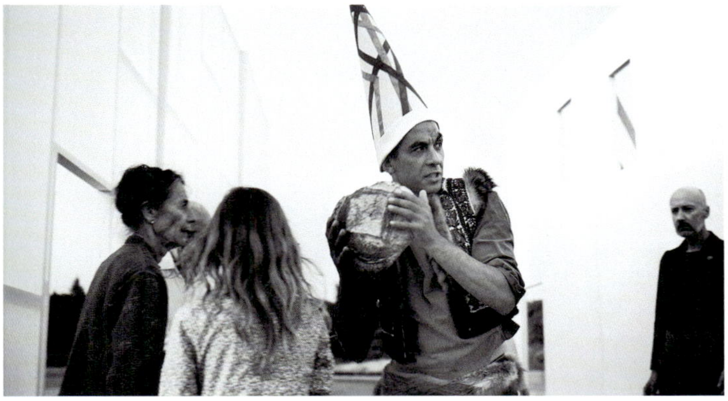

Ulla von Brandenburg
Die Strasse, 2013
HD video, 11'20, black and white, sound

What are the main topics you are addressing in your project? What is the context of the Sydney Biennale you are curating in 2014? How would you phrase its differences, its singularities, both in terms of structure and contents?

Energy and a tendency toward a kinetic feralness emerge strongly on my island setting. Psychological energy is very evident in the Museum of Contemporary Art venue. A raw energy, residual in the geo-political approach, can be found at the Art Gallery of New South Wales. Unconscious energy is captured in the distillations at Carriageworks, and finally a quiet energy is held in Artspace. Meanwhile, on the streets of Sydney, uncanny energy is delivered into the work-a-day lives of the urban dweller through performance and actions. This energy ignites through imagination, creativity, and desire on the part of artists and on behalf of audiences. *You Imagine What You Desire*.

The Biennale of Sydney is located in six different venues and spaces, each with a very particular atmosphere and set of physical conditions, which have been very strong and which were determined very early. On the island it is very important to meet the grandeur of the place and deal with the specificity of the conditions there, which are not at all museum-like. It is fairly mandatory to create projects for the island and respond to some of the site's history flows. Often the architectural preconditions of the venues inspired the approach. The Museum of Contemporary Art is an air/water space, suitable for liquid encounters. At the Art Gallery of New South Wales, which is a heavier, brutal space, a Promethian approach seemed necessary; there works tend toward an encounter with the now of politic and polis. At Carriageworks, once a film studio, previously a train yard, works that relate to the language of cinema have come together, and at Artspace, which is a beautiful wooden building, we take it back to nature.

You Imagine What You Desire is a hyper-visual Biennale and one that hopes to reassert the power of art for artists and audiences. Therefore the art is primary and not subordinate to some restricting theme, but finds its purpose in its ensemble and companionship with other works, and through the agency of the audience engagement. Happy anarchy and energy flow between art and audience.

Could you give us some details of specific projects, some of the artists invited, which would exemplify the specificities and topics of your Biennale?

Pipilotti Rist will make a new commission for the Museum of Contemporary Art. Her works, exuberant and joyful, but with a clear eco- and body-politic exemplify the kind of hyper-visual, immersive encounter that will captivate the audience. Gabriel Lester distills a mood moment, referencing film language in a large sculptural commission at Carriageworks. Callum Morton take us on a ride to the other side, a kind of ghost train for the technological age on the island, and Gerda Steiner and Jörg Lenzlinger encourage visitors to become their own generators in a set of whirly-gig and gizmo experiments involving kinetic movement. Nathan Coley will illuminate the nights and days with thoughts, and buff men will run in uniform choreographies through the city as part of Eglė Budvytytė's performance work. Ulla von Brandenburg will create a fictional street and community in her latest installation and film … and we are building a village with Randi og Katrine. This is the tip of a very large iceberg!

This year's Venice Biennale was considered by many as breaking from the Biennale model to propose a museum-like exhibition. How much does it interfere, influence, or contradict your own Biennale's definition?

I really enjoyed Massimiliano Gioni's Biennale, but I am not going the route of the museum, nor am I looking backward to formulate things through historical gatherings. I am pitching forward and have deliberately avoided a tight theme, which with six large venues and numerous site opportunities would wear a bit thin with constant repetition. Sydney is a large, grand-scaled Biennale and seeks a kind of discovery and experience to trigger the audience. I see it more as a set of spatial chapters really, where hopefully the aesthetic itineraries will be evident, and art will lead to art and idea to idea. *You Imagine What You Desire* leaves an open space for engagement and enquiry.

Eglė Budvytytė
Choreography for the Running Male, 2012
Performance, 30'

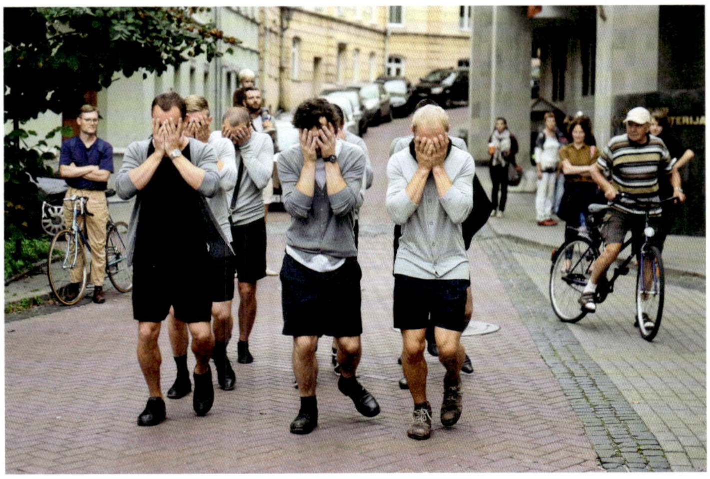

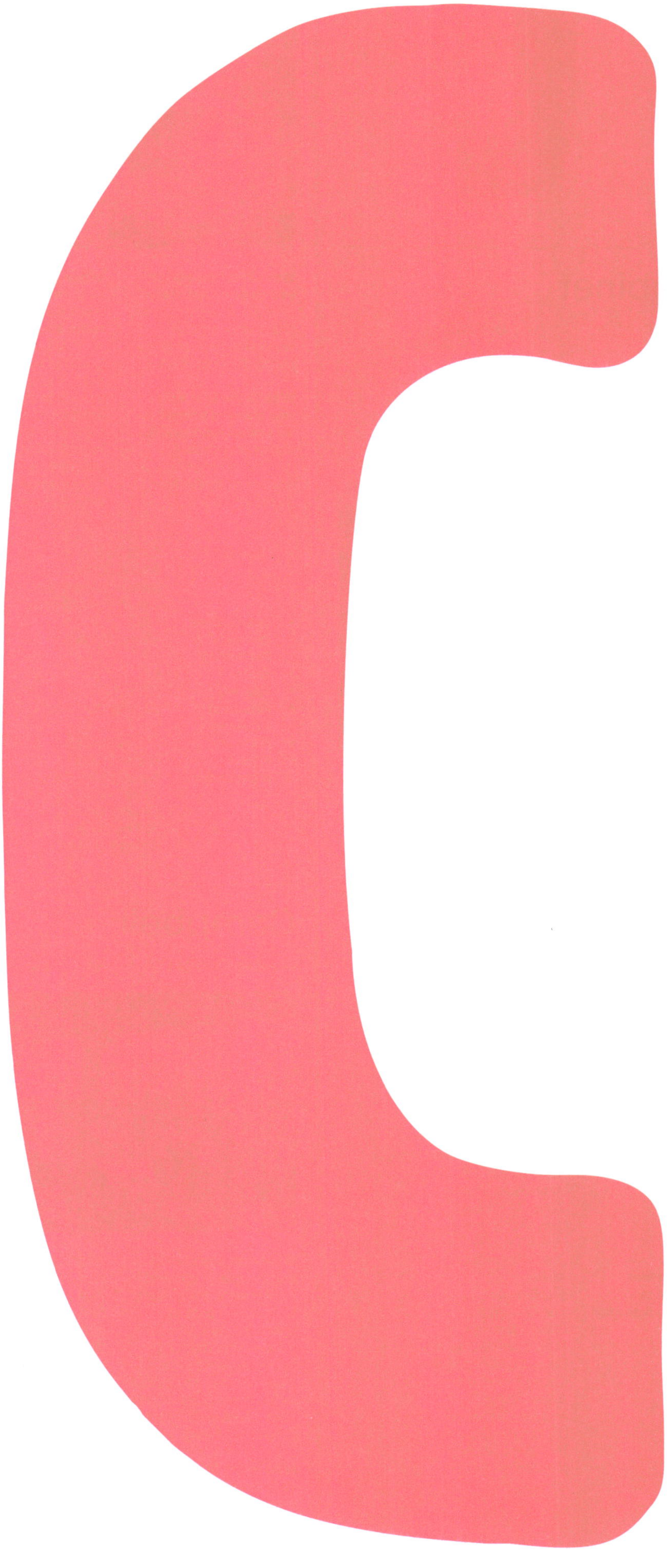

C

- Hong Kong
- Basel
- Miami Beach

Cabinet

London — Galleries Unlimited

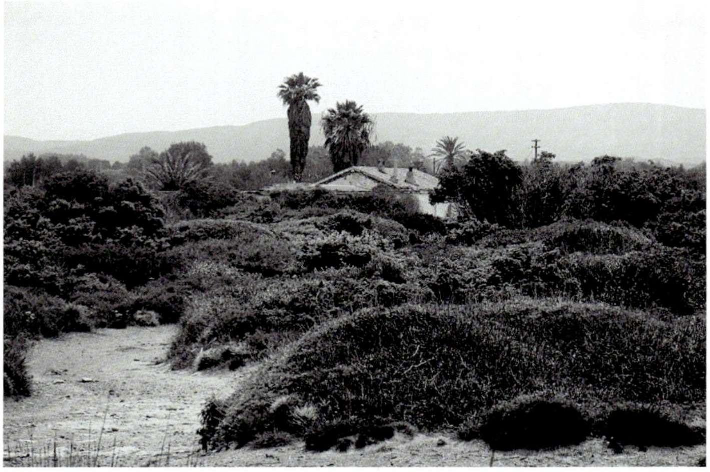

What first compelled you to open a gallery?
Boredom.

Who is the first artist you showed and what was most memorable about that show?
It was a book launch. There were no images.

When did you first participate in Art Basel and what was most memorable about that show?
In 2011. The smell of raclette.

- **Contact** — Cabinet
  Freddie Checketts
  art@cabinetltd.demon.co.uk
- **Established** — 1992
- **Owner(s) / Partner(s)** — Martin McGeown
  Andrew Wheatley
- **Team** — 4
- **Space(s)** — 268 m²
- **Artists at Art Basel** — Tariq Alvi
  Ed Atkins
  Bernadette Corporation
  Jay Chung & Q Takeki Maeda
  John Knight
  Mark Leckey
  Danny McDonald
  Lucy McKenzie
  Henrik Olesen
  Simon Thompson
- **Further artists represented** — Atelier
  Lutz Bacher
  Bonnie Camplin
  Gillian Carnegie
  Marc Camille Chaimowicz
  Lukas Duwenhögger
  Cosey Fanni Tutti
  Julian Göthe
  Anthony Symonds
  Lily van der Stokker
  Tris Vonna-Michell
  JD Williams

CAIS

Seoul — Insights

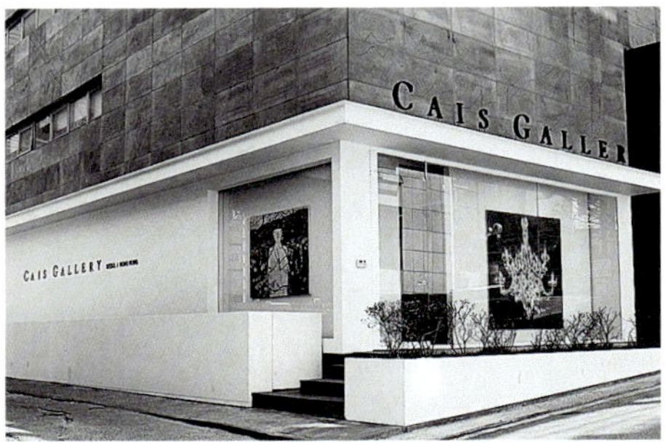

What first compelled you to open a gallery?
As a collector, I had a passion for art and wanted to be a contributer in the field of art.

Who is the first artist you showed and what was most memorable about that show?
The first show was a solo show by Gerhard Richter, in 1997.

When did you first participate in Art Basel and what was most memorable about that show?
CAIS gallery participated in Miami Beach for the first time in 2004. We introduced young Korean artists, and many people showed interest. Ten year later, Choi So Young who was among them, has became one of the most popular Korean artists.

- **Contact** — CAIS Gallery
  Boram Sohn
  boram@caisart.com
  caisart@caisart.com
- **Established** — 1997
- **Owner(s) / Partner(s)** — Myung Boon Yoo
- **Team** — 6
- **Space(s)** — 600 m²
- **Artists at Art Basel** — Seoung Won Won
- **Further artists represented** — So Young Choi
  Xooang Choi
  Kyoung Tack Hong
  BoMin Kim
  Kyoung Mi Lee
  So Yeun Lee
  Byung-Hun Min

Campbell

Oak Park (Chicago) — Statements

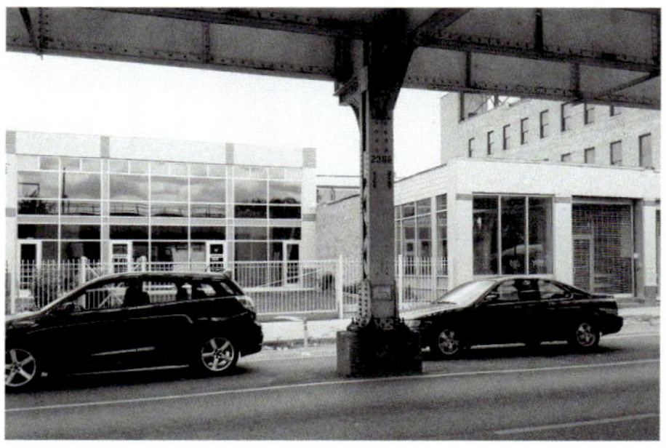

What first compelled you to open a gallery?
We were compelled to open our project space in September 2002 after visiting The Suburban, which is a small off-space operated by Michelle Grabner and Brad Killam in Oak Park (a suburb of Chicago).

Who is the first artist you showed and what was most memorable about that show?
Noah Rorem was the first artist we showed in our project space, which was our house in Oak Park. You never forget the first.

When did you first participate in Art Basel and what was most memorable about that show?
We first participated at Art Basel in the Statements sector in 2013. The most memorable thing was the line of Swiss riot police breaking up the people partying in the simulated favela on Messe Platz …

- **Contact** Shane Campbell Gallery
Eric Ruschman
eric@shanecampbellgallery.com
info@shanecampbellgallery.com
- **Established** 2006
- **Owner(s) / Partner(s)** Shane Campbell
Julie Campbell
- **Team** 7
- **Space(s)** 30 m²
- **Artists at Art Basel** Tony Lewis
- **Further artists represented** Chris Bradley
Jesse Chapman
Paul Cowan
Ann Craven
Kim Fisher
Michelle Grabner
Joanne Greenbaum
Mark Grotjahn
Jay Heikes
Patrick Hill
Shio Kusaka
John McAllister
Suzanne McClelland
Jason Meadows
William J. O'Brien
Alex Olson
Anthony Pearson
Adam Pendleton
Jon Pestoni
Zak Prekop
Amanda Ross-Ho
Lisa Williamson
Jonas Wood

Campoli Presti

London
Paris

Statements
Galleries

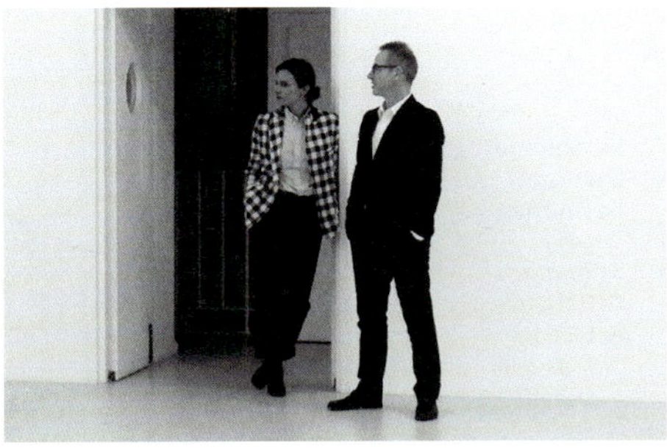

What first compelled you to open a gallery?
A desire to introduce a generation of artists based in the US to Europe, and cultivate their early exposure, establishing critical and institutional representation here. We are particularly interested in artists who explore the historical and material condition of their medium, and we wish to ensure the development of an ongoing conversation between European and American art.

Who is the first artist you showed and what was most memorable about that show?
The first artist we began to represent was Cheyney Thompson, with his first solo exhibition in the UK in 2003. This was the seed for developing an interaction between American artists and European discourses around the conventions of pictorial, sculptural, and photographic representation. This particular exhibition related Théodore Géricault's *Raft of the Medusa* and the genre of history painting to political and historical events in the US at the time.

When did you first participate in Art Basel and what was most memorable about that show?
Our first participation in Art Basel was in 2005. In the Statements sector we presented a project by Joanne Tatham & Tom O'Sullivan. What was most memorable for us about that show was that our presentation mixed seemingly glamorous elements with rougher, darker undertones. Presenting a singular, challenging work of this kind was a bold introduction of the gallery to the fair.

- **Contact** Campoli Presti
Cora Muennich
cora@campolipresti.com
info@campolipresti.com
- **Established** 2003 (London)
- **Owner(s) / Partner(s)** Emanuela Campoli
Gil Presti
- **Team** 5
- **Space(s)** 250 m² (London)
70 m² (Paris)
- **Artists at Art Basel** Jutta Koether
Daniel Lefcourt
Jason Loebs
Nick Mauss
Amy Sillman
Reena Spaulings
- **Further artists represented** Liz Deschenes
Roe Ethridge
Scott Lyall
Charles Mayton
John Miller
Olivier Mosset
Sean Paul
Pavel Pepperstein
Eileen Quinlan
Blake Rayne
Clément Rodzielski
Christoph Ruckhäberle
Nora Schultz
Joanne Tatham & Tom O'Sullivan
Cheyney Thompson

Canna

Jakarta

Insights

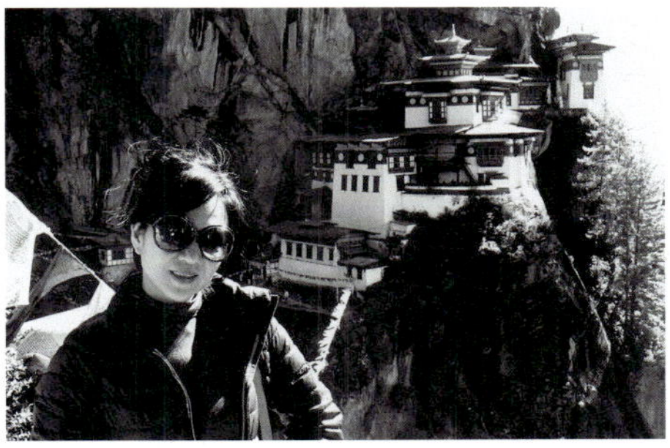

What first compelled you to open a gallery?
We started because of our love for the arts and collecting. We first wanted to educate friends and colleagues; then the bigger picture is to promote Indonesian art in Asia and Western countries.

Who is the first artist you showed and what was most memorable about that show?
Our first show was a group exhibition of modern and contemporary artists, such as Srihadi Soedarsono, Arie Smit, Sunaryo, Entang Wiharso, Nasirun, I Made Djirna. The nice memory was that we gained acknowledgement right away as a serious and reputable new gallery.

When did you first participate in Art Basel and what was most memorable about that show?
In 2013. We participated in the Insights sector, with a curated solo show by Entang Wiharso, a prominent contemporary Indonesian artist. We presented only one artwork, a massive 8-meter-long fence-like piece. Many visitors viewed it it as a brave and optimist gesture. But it paid off as our booth was chosen as one of the top ten booths in Art Basel.

- **Contact** Galeri Canna
Inge Santoso
ingecanna@gmail.com
canna@cbn.net.id
- **Established** 2001
- **Owner(s) / Partner(s)** Tommy Sutomo (Director)
- **Team** 5
- **Space(s)** 500 m²
- **Artists at Art Basel** Entang Wiharso
- **Further artists represented** Wisnu Auri
Oky Rey Montha
Suraji
Putu Sutawijaya

Capitain

Cologne
Berlin

Galleries
Unlimited

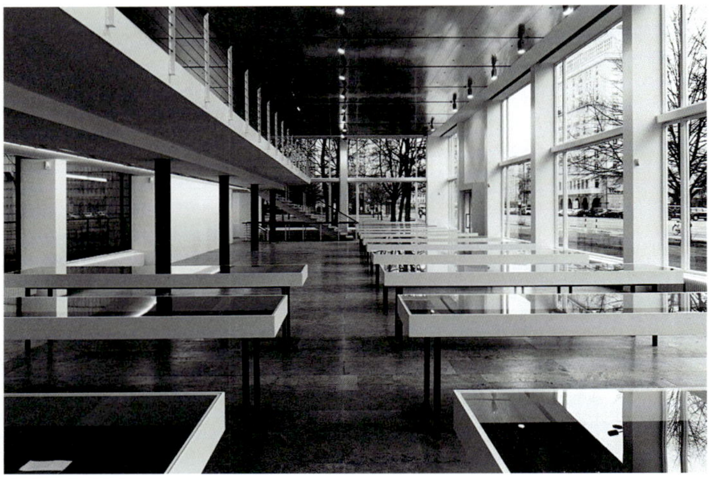

What first compelled you to open a gallery?
My friendship with Martin Kippenberger.

Who is the first artist you showed and what was most memorable about that show?
The first artist exhibited was Heimo Zobernig. Most memorable about that show was that A. R. Penck acquired the largest work on the first day of the exhibition.

When did you first participate in Art Basel and what was most memorable about that show?
The first participation in Art Basel was in 1987. It was exciting to be part of this international art fair.

- **Contact** Galerie Gisela Capitain
  Dorothee Sorge
  sorge@galeriecapitain.de
  info@galeriecapitain.de
- **Established** 1986 (Cologne)
  2008 (Berlin)
- **Owner(s) / Partner(s)** Gisela Capitain (Cologne)
  Friedrich Petzel (Berlin)
- **Team** 18
- **Space(s)** 440 m² (Cologne)
  1,300 m² (Berlin)
- **Artists at Art Basel** Karla Black
  Barbara Bloom
  Maria Brunner
  Gillian Carnegie
  Günther Förg
  Luke Fowler
  Anna Gaskell
  Wade Guyton
  Uwe Henneken
  Margarete Jakschik
  Rachel Khedoori
  Martin Kippenberger
  Zoe Leonard
  Meuser
  Marcel Odenbach
  Albert Oehlen
  Laura Owens
  Jorge Pardo
  Ascan Pinckernelle
  Seth Price
  Stephen Prina
  Sam Samore
  Elfie Semotan
  Monika Sosnowska
  John Stezaker
  Charline von Heyl
  Kelley Walker
  Franz West
  Christopher Williams
  Johannes Wohnseifer
  Christopher Wool
  Katsuhiro Yamaguchi

Carberry

Chicago

Galleries
Kabinett

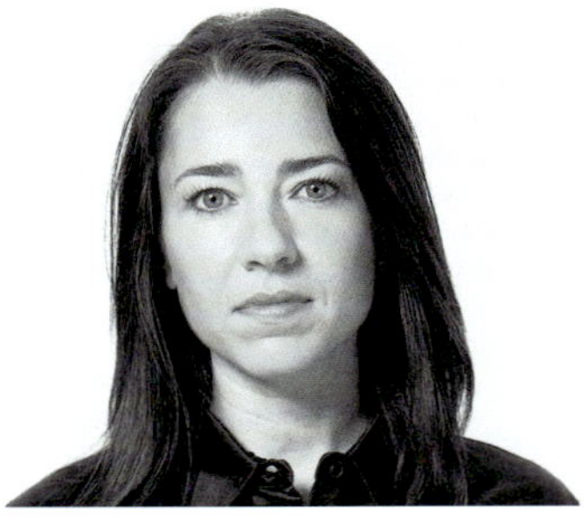

What first compelled you to open a gallery?
I had worked for a gallery for eight years, starting at an entry level position and advancing to director. Over time, I inevitably developed my own vision and sense of presentation and the time was right to forge out on my own.

Who is the first artist you showed and what was most memorable about that show?
José de Rivera, painting and sculpture of the 1930s. I was so proud of the installation, but also nervous, as it was my first opening, and I was afraid no one would come. The turnout was so great the crowd spilled into the hallway outside and we made sales that night! It was a great way to start.

When did you first participate in Art Basel and what was most memorable about that show?
In 2005. At one point during the VIP preview day we had a wait list three deep for one of the paintings in our stand. I couldn't believe it.

- **Contact** Valerie Carberry Gallery
  Susan Beagley
  susan@valeriecarberry.com
  info@valeriecarberry.com
- **Established** 2002
- **Owner(s) / Partner(s)** Valerie Carberry
- **Team** 4
- **Space(s)** 205 m²
- **Artists at Art Basel** Gertrude Abercrombie
  Charles Biederman
  James Brooks
  José de Rivera
  Dorothy Dehner
  Werner Drewes
  Herbert Ferber
  Arshile Gorky
  Philip Guston
  Charles Howard
  Knud Merrild
  Louise Nevelson
  Alfonso Ossorio
  Theodore Roszak
  Judith Rothschild
  John Storrs
  Vaclav Vytlacil
  John Wilde

carlier gebauer

Berlin

Galleries
Galleries

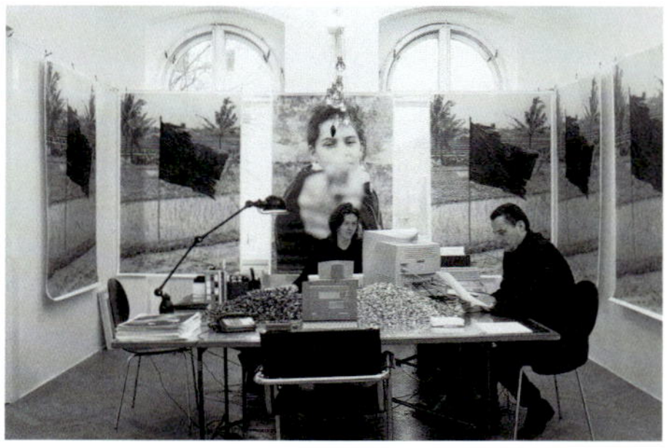

What first compelled you to open a gallery?
We didn't have enough contemporary art galleries in Berlin at that time.

Who is the first artist you showed and what was most memorable about that show?
Kirsi Mikkola, Michel François, Hans Hemmert. Two of the artists are still at the gallery and the show already marked the past for the future.

When did you first participate in Art Basel and what was most memorable about that show?
In 1996: (e.) Twin Gabriel with a huge basin for growing algae cultures.

- **Contact** carlier gebauer
  Sarah Miltenberger
  sm@carliergebauer.com
  mail@carliergebauer.com
- **Established** 1991
- **Owner(s) / Partner(s)** Marie-Blanche Carlier, Ulrich Gebauer
- **Team** 8
- **Space(s)** 600 m²
- **Artists at Art Basel** Michel François, Paul Graham, Asta Gröting, Tomasz Kowalski, Aernout Mik, Ming Wong, Kirsi Mikkola, Andreas Mühe, Erik Schmidt
- **Further artists represented** Huma Bhaha, Sebastian Diaz Morales, Dor Guez, Marcellvs L., Guillaume Leblon, Przemek Matecki, Julie Mehretu, Jean-Luc Moulène, Paul Pfeiffer, Jessica Rankin, Thomas Schütte, Peter Stauss, Fred Tomaselli, Janaina Tschäpe, Mark Wallinger, Emily Wardill, Kailiang Yang

Carzaniga

Basel ● Galleries

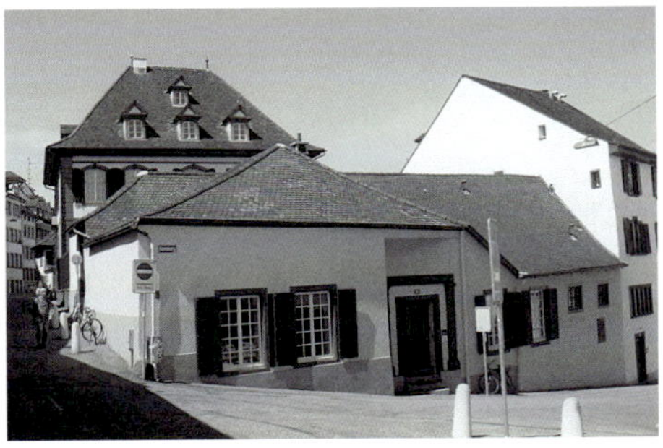

What first compelled you to open a gallery?
An interest in art and the relationship with one of the important artists in Basel at the time, Otto Abt.

Who is the first artist you showed and what was most memorable about that show?
Serge Brignoni. After many years of oblivion, this important Swiss artist and extraordinary personality was rediscovered by our gallery.

When did you first participate in Art Basel and what was most memorable about that show?
In 1982. The internationality and quality of the partcipating galleries and of the visitors.

- **Contact** Galerie Carzaniga
  Markus Rück
  markus.rueck@carzaniga.ch
  galerie@carzaniga.ch
- **Established** 1975/2004
- **Owner(s) / Partner(s)** Arnaldo Carzaniga, Philipp Hediger, Markus Rück
- **Space(s)** 500 m² (gallery) + 460 m² (garden)
- **Artists at Art Basel** Paolo Bellini, Julius Bissier, Walter Bodmer, Serge Brignoni, Samuel Buri, Paul Camenisch, Sam Francis, Rolf Iseli, Lenz Klotz, Wilfrid Moser, Albert Müller, Robert Müller, Meret Oppenheim, Flavio Paolucci, Marcel Schaffner, Hermann Scherer, Lorenz Spring, Albert Steiner, Niklaus Stoecklin, Mark Tobey, Varlin, Walter Kurt Wiemken
- **Further artists represented** Hermann Hesse, Giuseppe Spagnulo

Casa Triângulo

São Paulo ● Galleries ● Galleries

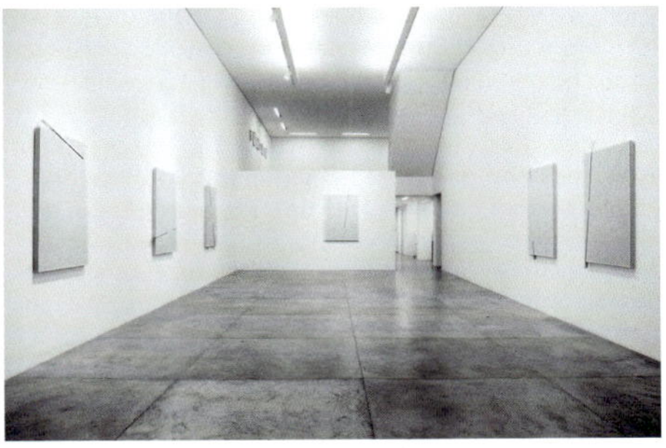

What first compelled you to open a gallery?
Back in the 1980s there was no space in São Paulo to show young artists. I was collaborating with a magazine and was thrilled about this potential, so I started an alternative space in a triangular house (that's where the name of the gallery comes from) in São Paulo downtown, for young artists to perform their most daring projects.

Who is the first artist you showed and what was most memorable about that show?
The first exhibition was a group show with artists Dora Longo Bahia, Carlito Contini, Fúlvia Marchezi, Roberta Fortunato, Vera Helena Ferreira, and Zulmira Amaral. The most memorable moment was the greatest effect of the opening—the gallery was absolutely full with an amazing public!

When did you first participate in Art Basel and what was most memorable about that show?
2003 was a very exciting year, we had just moved to a new space in São Paulo and it was our first participation in Art Basel in Miami Beach and the very first time we participated in an art fair in the US. The effervescence of the fair, it was booming! That is my greatest memory.

- **Contact** Casa Triângulo
  Rodrigo Editore
  rodrigo@casatriangulo.com
  info@casatriangulo.com
- **Established** 1988
- **Owner(s) / Partner(s)** Ricardo Trevisan
- **Team** 10
- **Space(s)** 300 m²
- **Artists at Art Basel** Sandra Cinto, Mariana Palma, Joana Vasconcelos
- **Further artists represented** Daniel Acosta, Albano Afonso, assume vivid astro focus, Eduardo Berliner, Tony Camargo, Flávio Cerqueira, Juliana Cerqueira Leite

Alex Cerveny
Stephen Dean
Valdirlei Dias Nunes
Yuri Firmeza
Max Gómez Canle
Vânia Mignone
Guillermo Mora
Nunca
Nazareth Pacheco
Reginaldo Pereira
Manuela Ribadeneira
Camila Sposati
Pier Stockholm
Jack Strange
Rommulo Vieira Conceição
Marcia Xavier

Casas Riegner

Bogotá

- Statements
- Nova

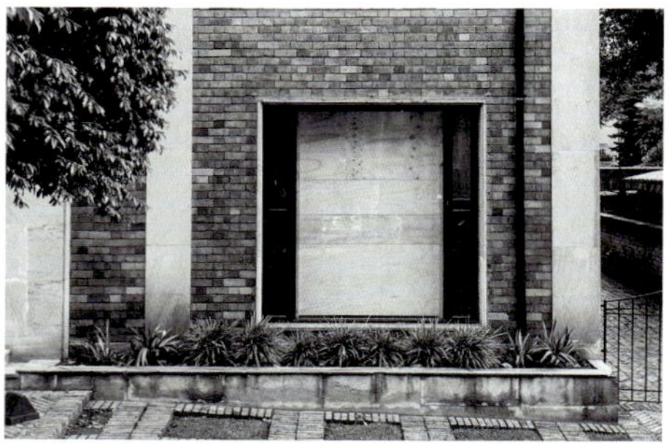

What first compelled you to open a gallery?
Our deep love and passion for art, and our desire to promote highly talented artists.

Who is the first artist you showed and what was most memorable about that show?
The first artist we showed in our Miami space (closed in 2004) was the Colombian painter Ana Mercedes Hoyos. The most memorable thing about the exhibition was that hardly anyone understood what was being exhibited.

When did you first participate in Art Basel and what was most memorable about that show?
Our first participation in Art Basel was in 2010. The most memorable thing was the project we exhibited involving Colombian master José Antonio Suárez Londoño and the emerging young artist Mateo López. It was a visual correspondence between these two artists from very different generations, which we titled *Ping Pong*. The project was extremely well received. Even nowadays people who saw the project come up to us asking about that wonderful presentation.

- **Contact** Casas Riegner
Paula Bossa
paula@casasriegner.com
info@casasriegner.com
- **Established** 2001
- **Owner(s) / Partner(s)** Catalina Casas
Alberto Casas Santamaria
- **Team** 7
- **Space(s)** 500 m²
- **Artists at Art Basel** Mateo López
Johanna Calle
José Antonio Suárez Londoño
- **Further artists represented** Leyla Cárdenas
Maria Fernanda Cardoso
Antonio Caro
Rosario López
Bernardo Ortiz
Maria Fernanda Plata
Miguel Angel Rojas
Luis Roldán
Liliana Sánchez
Rosemberg Sandoval
Gabriel Sierra
Wilger Sotelo
Angelica Teuta
Icaro Zorbar

Castelli

New York

- Galleries
- Feature

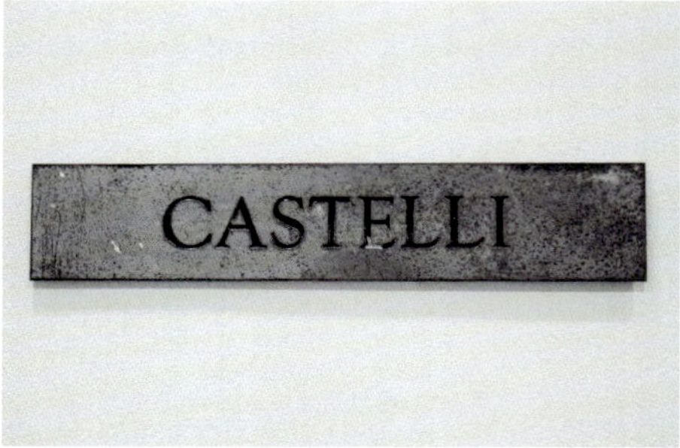

What first compelled you to open a gallery?
Castelli Gallery was opened by my husband Leo Castelli in 1957. I was educated as an art historian. I started to work at the gallery after meeting Leo; it just happened that way.

Who is the first artist you showed and what was most memorable about that show?
The first exhibition I organized was a show of works on paper by Jasper Johns in 1999. Johns had shown with the gallery since 1958. The most memorable thing about this show, on a personal level, was being young and being taught the job of running an art gallery by Jasper and Leo.

When did you first participate in Art Basel and what was most memorable about that show?
My first participation was in 2013. The gallery presented a show of works from the 1960s by Robert Morris. The most memorable thing about this show was the sincere enthusiasm with which it was received by visitors and colleagues.

- **Contact** Leo Castelli Gallery
Kristy Caldwell
kristy@castelligallery.com
info@castelligallery.com
- **Established** 1957
- **Owner(s) / Partner(s)** Barbara Bertozzi Castelli
- **Team** 4
- **Space(s)** 200 m²
- **Artists at Art Basel** Roy Lichtenstein
Robert Morris
Richard Pettibone
- **Further artists represented** Jasper Johns
Diana Kingsley
Joseph Kosuth
Keith Sonnier
Mike and Doug Starn

Cda-Projects

Istanbul

- Insights

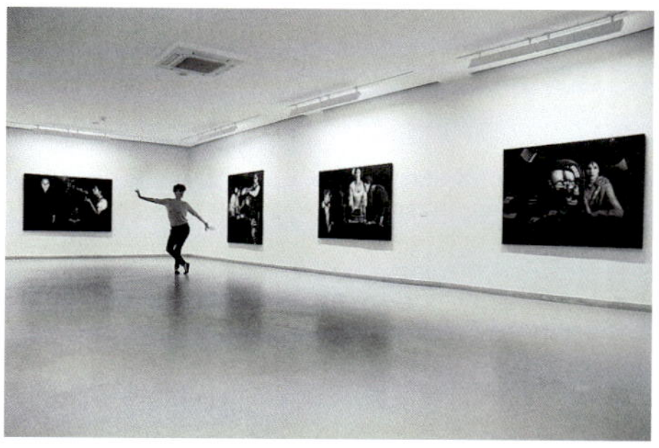

What first compelled you to open a gallery?
As a collector, I wasn't happy with the way galleries worked with artists and clients; I felt that I could contribute to improve this situation. I wanted to create a new model as a "commercial gallery supporting young artists and also working in the non-profit field."

Who is the first artist you showed and what was most memorable about that show?
It was a group show, we had almost 1,000 people at the opening!

When did you first participate in Art Basel and what was most memorable about that show?
We participated in

Art Basel in Hong Kong in 2013, with a curated booth of three female Turkish artists dealing with "violence against women." We were selected as one of the ten best booths by Time Out Hong Kong.

- **Contact** Cda-Projects
  Mine Erkmen
  mine@galerizilberman.com
- **Established** 2008
- **Owner(s) / Partner(s)** Moiz Zilberman (Founding Partner)
- **Team** 10
- **Space(s)** 540 m²
- **Artists at Art Basel** Ipek Duben
  Zeren Göktan
  Nazlı Eda Noyan
- **Further artists represented** Carlos Aires
  Selçuk Artut
  Janet Bellotto
  Burçak Bingöl
  Guido Casaretto
  Elif Varol Ergen
  Zeynep Kayan
  Fırat Neziroglu
  Jochen Proehl
  Özlem Simsek
  Funda Susamoglu

Cera

Lisboa

Galleries
Feature

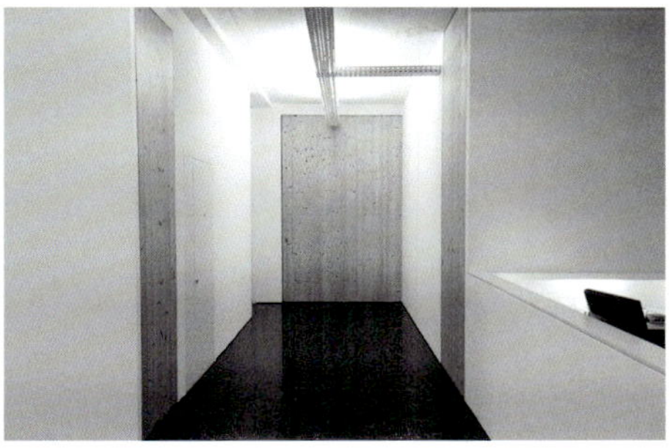

What first compelled you to open a gallery?
It started with an invitation from a local gallerist of whom I was a client, to become her business partner. It took me two years to say yes, and when I finally did so, she said she was planning to close. Once decided I had to try, and so I did it on my own.

Who is the first artist you showed and what was most memorable about that show?
Rosa Carvalho.

When did you first participate in Art Basel and what was most memorable about that show?
In the Statements sector in Basel with the piece *Film Festival* by Ricardo Valentim in 2007. In general we were thrilled to take part in the fair, to show alongside the best galleries in the world. In particular, we exceeded our best expectations for the fair as we sold the three editions of the piece to three different institutions.

- **Contact** Galeria Pedro Cera
  Vitória Guerra
  vguerra@pedrocera.com
  geral@pedrocera.com
- **Established** 1998
- **Owner(s) / Partner(s)** Pedro Cera
- **Space(s)** 350 m²
- **Artists at Art Basel** Gil Heitor Cortesão
  Pedro Neves Marques
  Adam Pendleton
  Gilberto Zorio
- **Further artists represented** Ana Cardoso
  André Cepeda
  Nuno Cera
  Matt Keegan
  Ana Manso
  Frank Nitsche
  Yves Oppenheim
  Paulo Quintas
  Tobias Rehberger
  Ricardo Valentim

Chambers

New York
Beijing
Salt Point

Insights

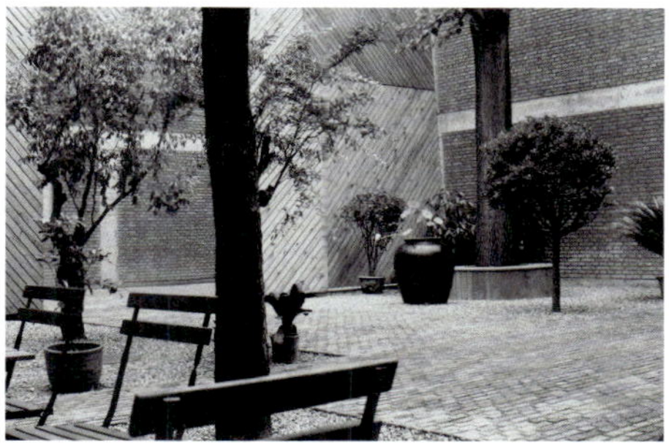

What first compelled you to open a gallery?
Before Chambers opened in New York in 2000, there were very few options for people in the US to see firsthand and learn about the rapid development of contemporary art in China. I felt this was a story that needed to be told and to which Western audiences would respond positively. Almost 15 years later the story has gotten much more complex, but we're just as excited to be a part of it.

Who is the first artist you showed and what was most memorable about that show?
The gallery's inaugural exhibition was with Lu Shengzhong, who was the first contemporary artist to use the traditional Chinese art of paper cutting. Many people said we were taking a big risk to open with such a show because it had never been exhibited in the US before. But *The New York Times* gave us a fantastic review and called the exhibition a "living temple," and the rest, as they say, is history.

When did you first participate in Art Basel and what was most memorable about that show?
Chambers has been exhibiting at ART HK since the very beginning and we were thrilled when the fair became part of Art Basel in 2013.

- **Contact** Chambers Fine Art
  David Clements
  dclements@chambersfineart.com
  bj@chambersfineart.com
- **Established** 2000
- **Owner(s) / Partner(s)** Christophe Mao
- **Team** 8
- **Space(s)** 1,500 m²
- **Artists at Art Basel** Zhao Zhao
- **Further artists represented** Ai Weiwei
  Cai Jin
  Chi Feng
  Cui Fei
  Feng Mengbo
  Guo Hongwei
  He Yunchang
  Hong Hao
  Hong Lei
  Lu Shengzhong
  Mi Mai
  Qiu Zhijie
  Rong Rong
  Shi Jing
  Shi Jinsong
  Song Dong
  Su Zhiguang
  Taca Sui
  Tan Dun
  Wang Jianwei
  Wang Tiande
  Wu Jian'an
  Xie Xiaoze
  Yang Jiechang
  Ye Nan
  Yin Xiuzhen
  Yuan Yuan
  Zhan Wang
  Zhang Dun
  Zhang Huan
  Zheng Guogu

Chan Hampe

Singapore ● Insights

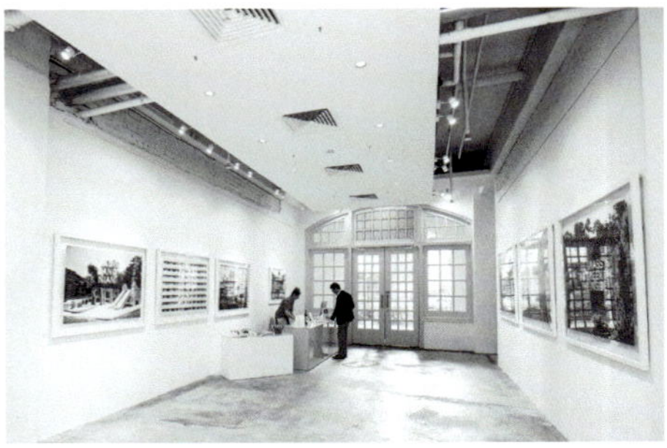

What first compelled you to open a gallery?
The result of a long-standing commitment to working with artists and in the arts.

Who is the first artist you showed and what was most memorable about that show?
Kirra Jamison and Alice Lang.

When did you first participate in Art Basel and what was most memorable about that show?
In 2013 in Hong Kong.

- **Contact** Chan Hampe Galleries, Benjamin Hampe, ben.hampe@chanhampegalleries.com, info@chanhampegalleries.com
- **Established** 2010
- **Owner(s) / Partner(s)** Angeline Chan, Benjamin Hampe
- **Team** 3
- **Space(s)** 1,400 m²
- **Artists at Art Basel** Dawn Ng
- **Further artists represented** Safaruddin Abdul Hamid (Dyn), Boo Sze Yang, Eric Chan, Chankerk, Belinda Fox, Yusof Ghani, Vincent Leow, Jahan Loh, Kumari Nahappan, Ruben Pang, Tay Bak Chiang, Wei Guan

Cheim & Read

New York ● Galleries Unlimited ● Galleries

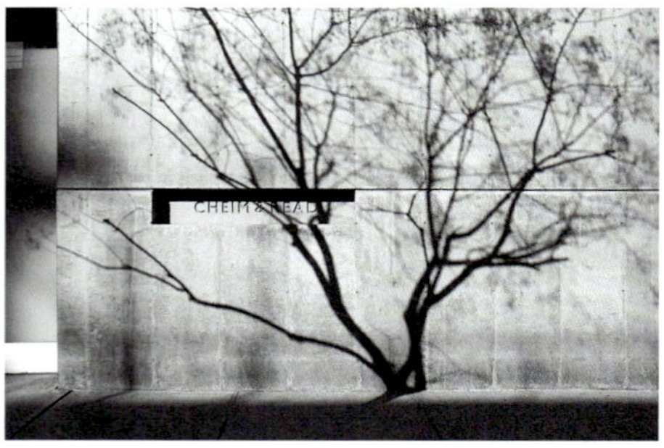

What first compelled you to open a gallery?
We met while students at the Rhode Island School of Design in the mid-1970s and quickly became friends—John Cheim majoring in painting, and Howard Read in photography. After running the Robert Miller Gallery for 20 years, we decided to take the artists we had identified with at Miller, such as Joan Mitchell, Louise Bourgeois, and William Eggleston, and open our own gallery in 1996.

Who is the first artist you showed and what was most memorable about that show?
Our first exhibition was a juxtaposition of a Louise Bourgeois *Spider* and a wall of *Truism* plaques by Jenny Holzer, which allowed the viewers to contemplate the shared interests of these two artists in terms of sexual identity, sexual politics, the structure of the family, and social mores.

When did you first participate in Art Basel and what was most memorable about that show?
Our first participation in Basel was in the year 2000. It was very exciting to present a Louise Bourgeois' *Cell* with Jenny Holzer's *Lustmord* photographs, a Man Ray *Natural Painting* of his name in red and a Jack Pierson word piece, *BLOOD*, and have them all make a connection across mediums and generations.

- **Contact** Cheim & Read, Ellen Robinson, ellen@cheimread.com, gallery@cheimread.com
- **Established** 1996
- **Owner(s) / Partner(s)** John Cheim, Howard Read
- **Team** 16
- **Space(s)** 550 m²
- **Artists at Art Basel** Ghada Amer, Don Bachardy, Donald Baechler, Lynda Benglis, Louise Bourgeois, William Eggleston, Louise Fishman, Adam Fuss, Ron Gorchov, Hans Hartung, Al Held, Jenny Holzer, Bill Jensen, Chantal Joffe, Jannis Kounellis, Jonathan Lasker, McDermott & McGough, Barry McGee, Joan Mitchell, Jack Pierson, Tal R, Milton Resnick, Sean Scully, John Sonsini, Pat Steir, Juan Uslé, Otto Zitko

Chemould

Mumbai ● Galleries ● Galleries Unlimited ● Galleries

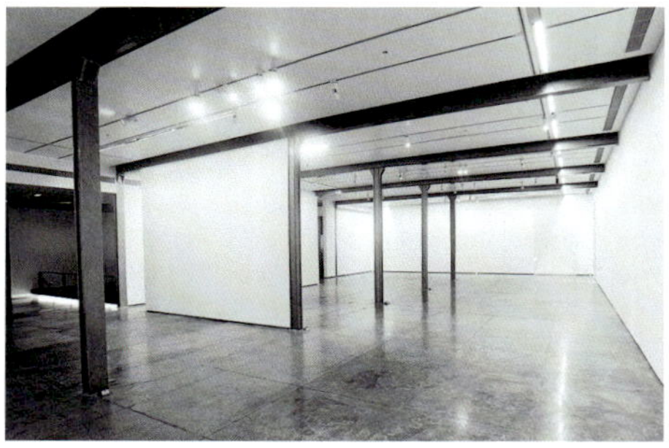

What first compelled you to open a gallery?
The gallery was opened by my parents in 1963. It is therefore a second generation gallery today, having celebrated 50 years of its existence in September 2013. I took over the running of the gallery 25 years ago, at first under the guidance of my parents, and then running it on my own with artists I developed an affinity with over the years.

Who is the first artist you showed and what was most memorable about that show?
The first artist I showed when I started running the gallery was Atul Dodiya, one of India's most important mid-career artists. Twenty-three years ago we were both starting out together, myself, organizing my very first exhibition, and he stepping into the arena with his first solo show in a gallery. Looking back, this was one of the most emtional and nurturing moments in my life as a gallerist.

When did you first participate in Art Basel and what was most memorable about that show?

My first participation was in Basel in 2010. We participated in the Feature sector with Atul Dodiya in conversation with one of our most important artists at the gallery, Bhupen Khakhar, a seminal artists of the 1970s, 1980s, and 1990s. There were three rather modest sized paintings by him, which nonetheless strongly attracted the eye of the visitors. In contrast, Dodiya's contribution were three life-sized rolling shutters, large, noisy, and extremely colourful. The juxtaposition of the two drew parallels between generations and practices (they were also very good friends) and was very well received. This was wonderfully rewarding!

- **Contact** Chemould Prescott Road
  Sandra Khare
  sandrakhare@gallerychemould.com
  art@gallerychemould.com
- **Established** 1963
- **Owner(s) / Partner(s)** Shireen Gandhy (Director)
- **Team** 9
- **Space(s)** 465 m²
- **Artists at Art Basel** Shezad Dawood, Shilpa Gupta, Jitish Kallat, Reena Saini Kallat, Desmond Lazaro, Rashid Rana, Gigi Scaria, Mithu Sen, Nilima Sheikh, Aditi Singh, Hema Upadhyay
- **Further artists represented** Dhruvi Acharya, Anju Dodiya, Atul Dodiya, Mehlli Gobhai, Bhuvanesh Gowda, Archana Hande, N.S. Harsha, Tushar Joag, Anant Joshi, Surekha K, Suhasini Kejriwal, Bhupen Khakhar, Shakuntala Kulkarni, Lavanya Mani, Ritesh Meshram, Pushpamala N., Jagannath Panda, Vivan Sundaram, L.N. Tallur

Cheng

Beijing — Insights

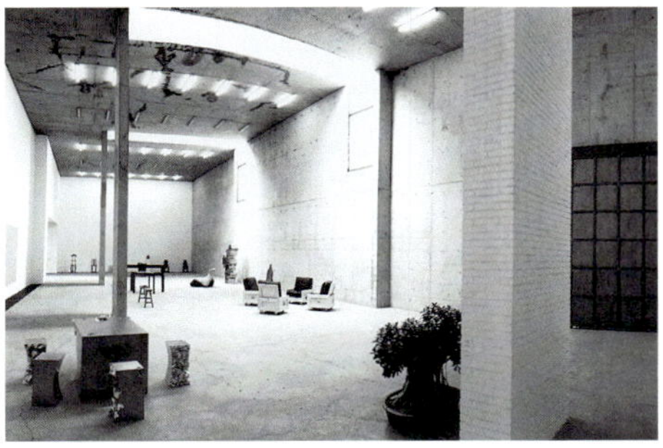

What first compelled you to open a gallery?
Expanding Chinese contemporary art's reception.

When did you first participate in Art Basel and what was most memorable about that show?
In 2013.

- **Contact** Xin Dong Cheng Gallery
  Alban Raysse
  contact@gmail.com
  contact@xindongcheng.com
- **Established** 2000
- **Owner(s) / Partner(s)** Xin Dong Cheng
- **Team** 3
- **Space(s)** 800 m²
- **Artists at Art Basel** Li Yongbin, Wang Gongxin
- **Further artists represented** Daniel Buren, Cang Xin, Chang Xugong, Roberto Diago Durruthy, Roberto Fabelo, Feng Zhengjie, Li Luming, Lu Hao, Luo Brothers, Martial Raysse, Rene Francisco Rodriguez, Shao Fan, Shi Jianmin, Wang Ningde, Wu Mingzhong, Yang Xun, Zhong Biao

Cherry and Martin

Los Angeles — Feature, Unlimited, Nova

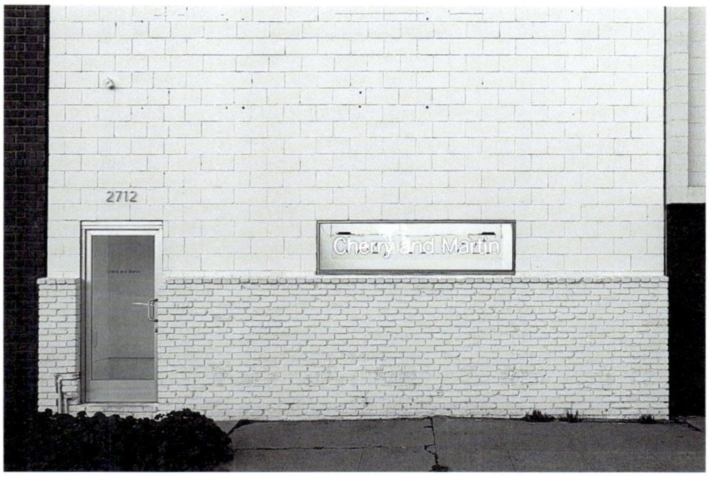

What first compelled you to open a gallery?
We wanted to show work that no one else was showing.

Who is the first artist you showed and what was most memorable about that show?
Our first solo show in the gallery was an 8-channel piece entitled *DMT* (2004) by Vancouver-based (now Berlin-based) artist Jeremy Shaw. It was very challenging technically and it looked great.

When did you first participate in Art Basel and what was most memorable about that show?
We exhibited a monumental bronze sculpture by Nathan Mabry in Miami Beach in 2008. I remember having to turn it sideways to get it into the space—and placing it with a great collection.

- **Contact** Cherry and Martin
  Philip Martin
  philip@cherryandmartin.com
  info@cherryandmartin.com
- **Established** 2006
- **Owner(s) / Partner(s)** Mary Leigh Cherry, Philip Martin
- **Team** 4
- **Space(s)** 370 m²
- **Artists at Art Basel** Matt Connors, Robert Heinecken, Bernard Piffaretti
- **Further artists represented** Brian Bress, Holly Coulis, Mari Eastman, Erik Frydenborg, Nathan Mabry, T. Kelly Mason, Florian Morlat, Robert Overby, Amanda Ross-Ho, Noah Sheldon, Alan Shields

C

Chert

Berlin

Statements

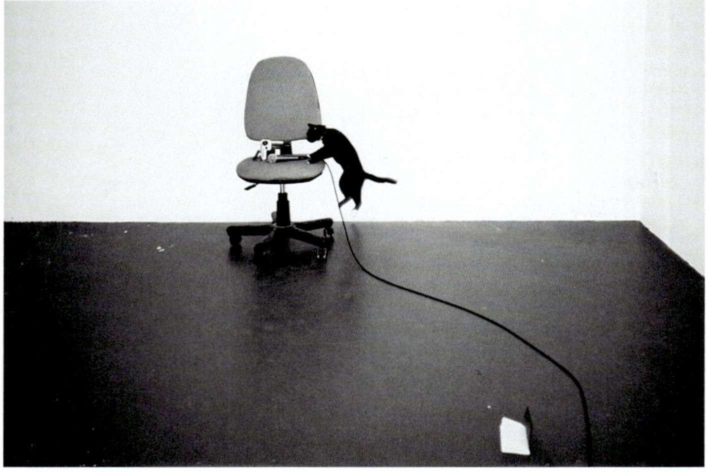

What first compelled you to open a gallery?
There is not one defining thing. It is more a consequence of the different experiences and encounters I had in the years prior to opening Chert, such as working for galleries in Italy and Germany, which shaped my decision to open my own.

Who is the first artist you showed and what was most memorable about that show?
Our first show was a group exhibition with four artists: Lucy Coggle, Hannah James, Petrit Halilaj, and Reto Pulfer. Petrit Halilaj lived in the gallery space, transforming it into a house, and invited his father from Kosovo to stay with him for a while. This was not visible to the public of course, but meant a lot for us and for the intention of the gallery, which since the beginning has aimed to develop a relationship with the artists that goes beyond what is apparent to the public.

When did you first participate in Art Basel and what was most memorable about that show?
Our first Art Basel participation was in 2011, again with Petrit Halilaj. We worked for over six months on the project, which consisted of transporting more than 60 tons of soil from Kosovo to Basel, completely filling the stand with dirt. This was a huge investment in every sense, a very risky project, whose difficulties we encountered only by working on it ... The memorable thing is that it finally worked out—the hill stood up for the whole week of the fair, and it even had a new white flower growing out of the top!

- **Contact** — Chert, Lilly Daniell, lilly@chert-berlin.org, post@chert-berlin.com
- **Established** — 2008
- **Owner(s) / Partner(s)** — Jennifer Chert
- **Team** — 2
- **Space(s)** — 74 m²
- **Artists at Art Basel** — David Horvitz
- **Further artists represented** — Alejandro Almanza Pereda, Lucy Coggle, Kasia Fudakowski, Jérémie Gindre, Petrit Halilaj, Hannah James, Heike Kabisch, Andrea Kvas, Vanessa Safavi, Carla Scott Fullerton, Erik van der Weijde

Chiba

Tokyo

Insights
Encounters

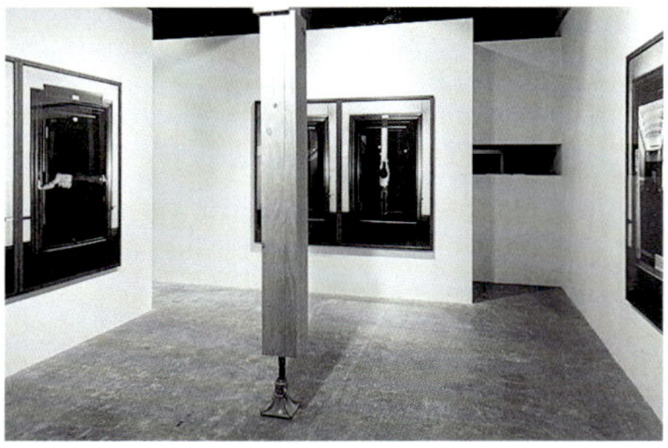

What first compelled you to open a gallery?
Yumiko Chiba thought that contemporary art brings new recognition, new notions, and a new sense of value to the world. She had been running a management office for contemporary artists since 1998 and decided to open a viewing space, where one could be in direct contact with the artworks. Yumiko Chiba wants to show the Japanese original culture and history in a contemporary manner in order to reconsider/reconstruct the Japanese culture in an international context. Also, she aims to introduce overseas artists into the Japanese market.

Who is the first artist you showed and what was most memorable about that show?
Yuichi Higashionna.

When did you first participate in Art Basel and what was most memorable about that show?
In 2013 in Hong Kong. Compared to the previous ART HK, the visitors' consciousness about art was definitely different. We observed a real development of collecting in Asia and a contemporary art market has definitely been built in Asia. It was a meaningful participation, and we are sure that we can base some of our future development on this success.

- **Contact** — Yumiko Chiba Associates, Yuki Miyanaka, miyanaka@ycassociates.co.jp, info@ycassociates.co.jp
- **Established** — 2010
- **Owner(s) / Partner(s)** — Yumiko Chiba
- **Team** — 5
- **Space(s)** — 42 m²
- **Artists at Art Basel** — Yuken Teruya
- **Further artists represented** — Emmanuel Guillaud, Yuichi Higashionna, Airan Kang, Dominik Lejman, Nobuhiro Nakanishi, Hiroko Nakao, Taishi Niimi, Shinji Ogawa, Ritta Paivalainen, Ari Saarto, Yusuke Shimura, Jiro Takamatsu, Ryudai Takano, Makiko Tanaka, Motohiro Tomii, Takuma Uematsu, Martin Walde, Chikako Yamashiro

Chi-Wen

Taipei — Galleries

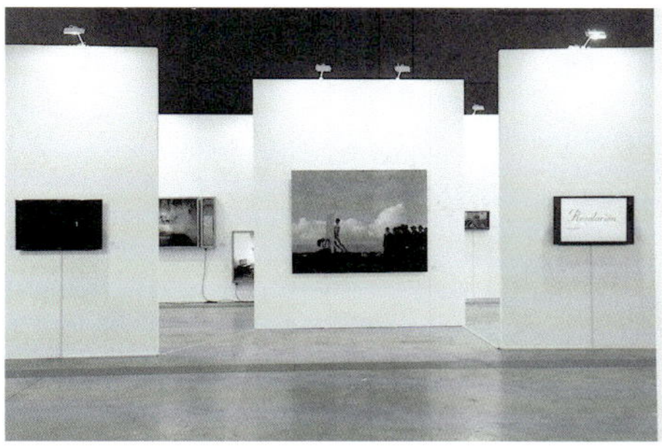

What first compelled you to open a gallery?
Video art.

Who is the first artist you showed and what was most memorable about that show?
Chen Chieh-Jen.

When did you first participate in Art Basel and what was the most memorable about that show?
In 2013 in Hong Kong.

- **Contact** Chi-Wen Gallery
  Chi-Wen Huang
  chiwen.huang@chi-wen.com
  info@chi-wen.com
- **Established** 2004
- **Owner(s) / Partner(s)** Joanne Huang Chi-Wen
- **Team** 5
- **Space(s)** 90 m²
- **Artists at Art Basel** Ivan Capote
  Chang Chien-Chi
  Chen Chieh-Jen
  Hsieh Chun-Te
  Liou Jawshing Arthur
  Ibrahim Miranda
  Ernesto Oroza
  Jose A. Toirac
  Yeh Wei-Li
  Yu Cheng-Ta
- **Further artists represented** Alterazioni Video
  Chen I-Chun
  Chen Shun-Chu
  Huang Chih-Yang
  Huang Hua-Chen
  Hung Tung-Lu
  Lee Kit
  Niu Chun-Chiang
  Peng Hung-Chih
  Tseng Yu-Chin
  Wu Chi-Tsung
  Wu Tien-Chang
  Yao Jui-Chung
  Yuan Goang-Ming

Chouakri

Berlin — Galleries, Galleries Kabinett, Public

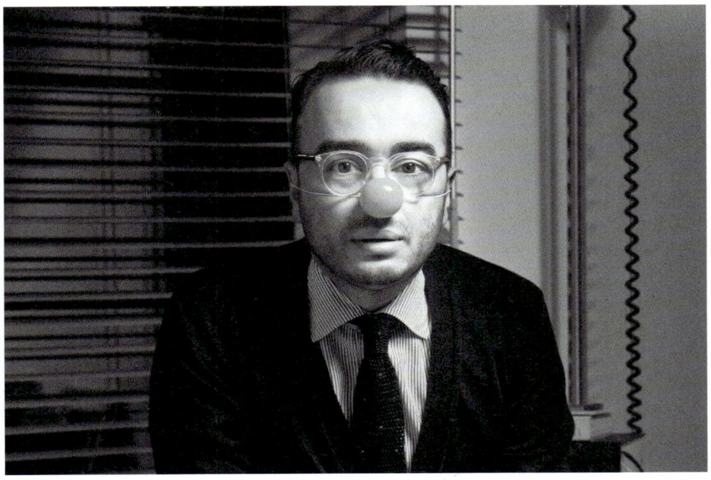

What first compelled you to open a gallery?
Simply because I enjoyed working with artists.

Who is the first artist you showed and what was most memorable about that show?
The first show was by Sylvie Fleury. We both spoke no German at the time and managed within two months to produce a major installation that afterward partly toured with a show curated by Sadie Coles and Eva Meyer-Herrmann at the Kunsthalle Nürnberg and the South London Gallery.

When did you first participate in Art Basel and what was most memorable about that show?
In 1999 we took part for the first time in the Statements sector at Art Basel. It was memorable as the installation we showed by Monica Bonvicini involved images of gay pornographic models dressed as construction workers (David Zwirner couldn't stand looking at it). We sold the installation before the fair ended.

- **Contact** Mehdi Chouakri
  Alexandra Alexopoulou
  galerie@mehdi-chouakri.com
- **Established** 1996
- **Owner(s) / Partner(s)** Mehdi Chouakri
- **Team** 6
- **Space(s)** 300 m²
- **Artists at Art Basel** Saâdane Afif
  John M Armleder
  Philippe Decrauzat
  Hans-Peter Feldmann
  Sylvie Fleury
  Mathieu Mercier
  Gerold Miller
  Charlotte Posenenske
  Gerwald Rockenschaub
  Peter Roehr
  Gitte Schäfer
  Luca Trevisani
- **Further artists represented** Claude Closky
  Isabell Heimerdinger
  Vincent Szarek

Cintra + Box4

Rio de Janeiro — Positions

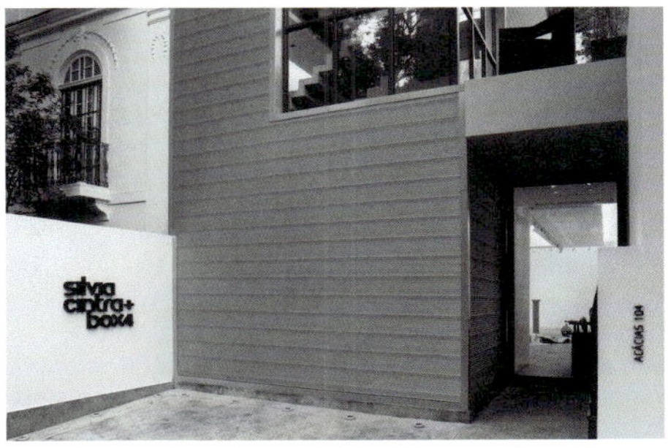

What first compelled you to open a gallery?
Silvia Cintra used to be an art advisor in the 1980s and early 1990s, and the close relationship she developed with many artists led her to open up her own gallery in 1992. Juliana Cintra, Silvia's daughter, founded Box 4 in 2006, a gallery focused on young artists. In January 2010 the gallery moved from its former location in Ipanema to a new three-story building specially built to host the gallery in Gávea, the new cultural spot in Rio de Janeiro; this caused the merging of the two galleries. With the merge, Silvia Cintra + Box4 Art Gallery seeks to concentrate the best of what is happening in the Brazilian contemporary art in one place, with an intense dialogue between established and emerging artists.

- **Contact** — Silvia Cintra + Box4
Juliana Cintra
jcintra@silviacintra.com.br
galeria@silviacintra.com.br
- **Established** — 1992
- **Owner(s) / Partner(s)** — Silvia Cintra
Juliana Cintra
- **Team** — 9
- **Space(s)** — 400 m²
- **Artists at Art Basel** — Laercio Redondo
- **Further artists represented** — Chiara Banfi
Cristina Canale
Carlito Carvalhosa
Leda Catunda
Marilá Dardot
Amilcar de Castro
Iole de Freitas
Luiz Ernesto
Marcius Galan
Mariana Galender
Renata Har
Maria Klabin
Lucia Koch
Nelson Leirner
Cinthia Marcelle
Rodrigo Matheus
Pedro Motta
Henrique Oliveira
Miguel Rio Branco
Daniel Senise
Ana Maria Tavares

Clages

Cologne — Statements

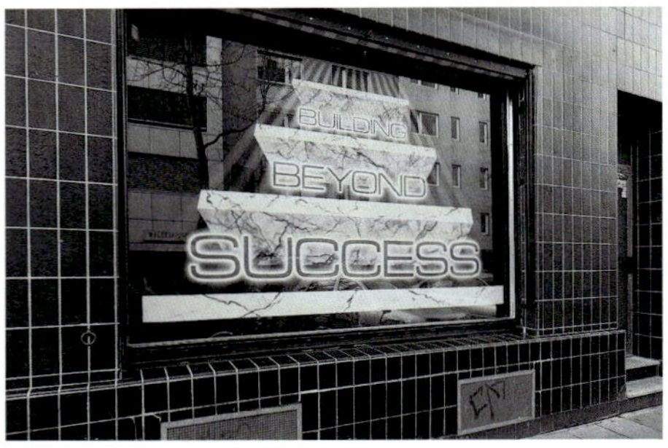

What first compelled you to open a gallery?
Clages emerged from the project space Büro DC. I decided to launch a gallery, a place of exchange and encounter, a site where alternative models and projects are introduced and mediated between various positions and subjectivities.

Who is the first artist you showed and what was most memorable about that show?
A group exhibition in the fall of 2007 with the gallery artists Juan Pérez Agirregoikoa, Anne Pöhlmann, Monika Stricker, and Bernhard Walter.

When did you first participate in Art Basel and what was most memorable about that show?
Our first participation was in 2013.

- **Contact** — Clages
Marietta Clages
office@mariettaclages.de
- **Established** — 2007
- **Owner(s) / Partner(s)** — Marietta Clages
- **Space(s)** — 50 m²
- **Artists at Art Basel** — Olivier Foulon
- **Further artists represented** — Juan Pérez Agirregoikoa
Shila Khatami
Sara MacKillop
Anne Pöhlmann
Claus Richter
Monika Stricker
Bernhard Walter

Cohan

New York — Galleries
Shanghai — Galleries

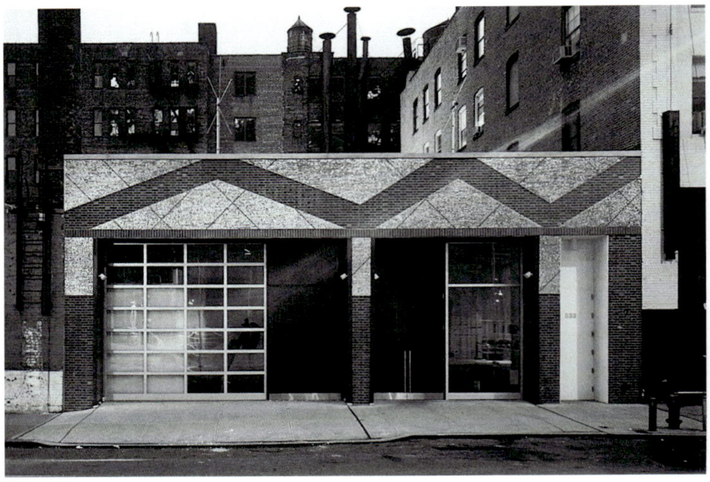

What first compelled you to open a gallery?
I was 17 years old and an intern at the New Museum, New York, which had just opened. For the next 20 years I worked for several great dealers including Paula Cooper in New York and Anthony d'Offay in London.

Who is the first artist you showed and what was most memorable about that show?
We opened the gallery with *Gilbert & George, Black, White and Red*. It was the early work dating from 1969 to 1980. The work looked as radical and fresh as the day it was made!

When did you first participate in Art Basel and what was most memorable about that show?
We were on the ground floor in 2004. We split our booth in half. On one side it was contemporary classics like Smithson, Nauman, and Paik, and on the other side it was younger gallery artists, Tomaselli, Viola, and Hancock.

- **Contact** — James Cohan Gallery
Laurie Harrison
lharrison@jamescohan.com
info@jamescohan.com
- **Established** — 1999
- **Owner(s) / Partner(s)** — James Cohan
- **Team** — 18
- **Space(s)** — 560 m² (New York)
260 m² (Shanghai)
- **Artists at Art Basel** — Helene Appel
Francesco Clemente
Simon Evans
Spencer Finch
Michelle Grabner
Trenton Doyle Hancock
Ji Yun-Fei
Beatriz Milhazes
Ou Yang Chun
Heather Rowe
Shi Zhiying
Yinka Shonibare
Shinique Smith
Fred Tomaselli
Bill Viola
Wang Xieda
- **Further artists represented** — Ingrid Calame
Folkert de Jong
Jesper Just
Byron Kim
Richard Long
Bill Owens
Katie Paterson
Hiraki Sawa
Robert Smithson
Erick Swenson
Tabaimo
Alison Elizabeth Taylor
Xu Zhen

Coles

London

- Galleries
- Galleries Unlimited
- Galleries

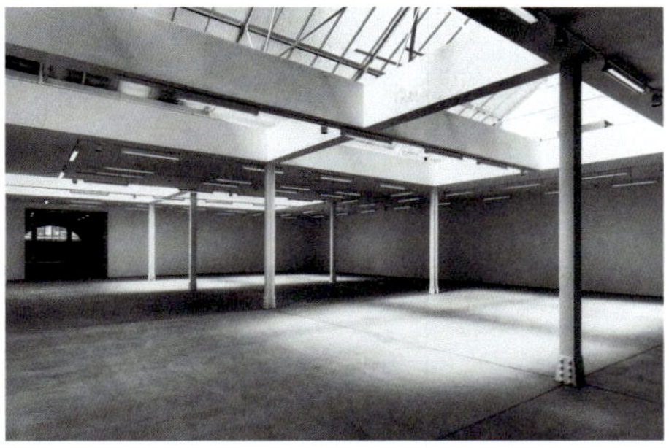

What first compelled you to open a gallery?
The artists Sarah Lucas and John Currin. They kept bugging me.

Who is the first artist you showed and what was most memorable about that show?
Sarah Lucas and John Currin. Sarah in an empty warehouse in St. John Street, and at the same time John, in my first gallery. Sarah's show, *The Law*, established a pattern for me, in that I like doing off-site projects in unlikely spaces. We returned to that way of working recently with her year-long *SITUATION* (2012–2013) in empty offices above the gallery. And John Currin hasn't changed a bit since that first show, but his painting gets better and better.

When did you first participate in Art Basel and what was most memorable about that show?
We did a Statements in Basel in 2000 with Simon Periton. We were so excited to participate. It felt like recognition or acceptance or something like that. There was a lot of euphoria. We got into the main fair the year after. Those were the days.

- **Contact** — Sadie Coles HQ
Lieselotte Seaton
lieselotte@sadiecoles.com
info@sadiecoles.com
- **Established** — 1997
- **Owner(s) / Partner(s)** — Sadie Coles
- **Team** — 16
- **Space(s)** — 280 m² (South Audley St)
560 m² (Kingly St)
- **Artists at Art Basel** — Carl Andre
Darren Bader
Matthew Barney
Dirk Bell
Avner Ben-Gal
Frank Benson
John Bock
Don Brown
Spartacus Chetwynd
Steven Claydon
William N. Copley
Adriano Costa
John Currin
Sam Durant
Shannon Ebner
Angus Fairhurst
Urs Fischer
Florian Hecker
Georg Herold
Jonathan Horowitz
David Korty
Gabriel Kuri
Jim Lambie
Hilary Lloyd
Sarah Lucas
Helen Marten
Victoria Morton
JP Munro
Laura Owens
Simon Periton
Raymond Pettibon
Elizabeth Peyton
Richard Prince
Ugo Rondinone
Wilhelm Sasnal
Gregor Schneider
Daniel Sinsel
Andreas Slominski
Christiana Soulou
Rudolf Stingel
Ryan Sullivan
Nicola Tyson
Paloma Varga Weisz
TJ Wilcox
Jordan Wolfson
Andrea Zittel

Contemporary Fine Arts

Berlin

- Galleries
- Galleries
- Galleries

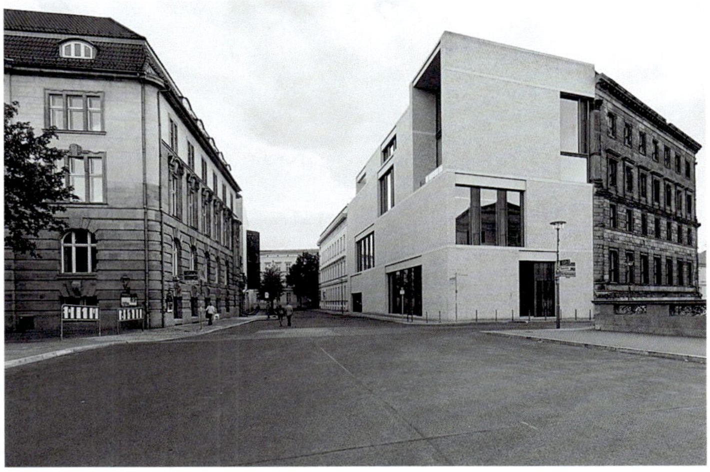

What first compelled you to open a gallery?
To work with artists and to become a serious member of the art world.

Who is the first artist you showed and what was most memorable about that show?
Michael Krebber. A lot of people came to Berlin from Cologne for the opening. At the time (20 years ago) this was really special, as Cologne was still the center of the German art world.

When did you first participate in Art Basel and what was most memorable about that show?
In 1993. I remember the enthusiastic reaction to the early Sigmar Polke paintings and drawings I showed.

- **Contact** — Contemporary Fine Arts
Imke Wagener
imke@cfa-berlin.de
gallery@cfa-berlin.de
- **Established** — 1992 (Bruno Brunnet Fine Arts)
1994 (CFA)
- **Owner(s) / Partner(s)** — Bruno Brunnet
Nicole Hackert
Philipp Haverkampf
- **Team** — 13
- **Space(s)** — 600 m²
- **Artists at Art Basel** — Markus Bacher
Georg Baselitz
Avner Ben-Gal
Peter Böhnisch
Marc Brandenburg
Cecily Brown
Bruce High Quality Foundation
Marcel Eichner
Max Frisinger
Georg Herold
Thomas Houseago
Thomas Kiesewetter
Michael Kunze
Jonathan Meese
Chris Ofili
Raymond Pettibon
Walter Pichler
Tal R
Anselm Reyle
Daniel Richter
Julian Schnabel
Dana Schutz
Norbert Schwontkowski
Katja Strunz
Gert & Uwe Tobias
Ralf Ziervogel

Continua

San Gimignano
Beijing
Boissy-le-Châtel

- Galleries
- Galleries Unlimited
- Galleries Public

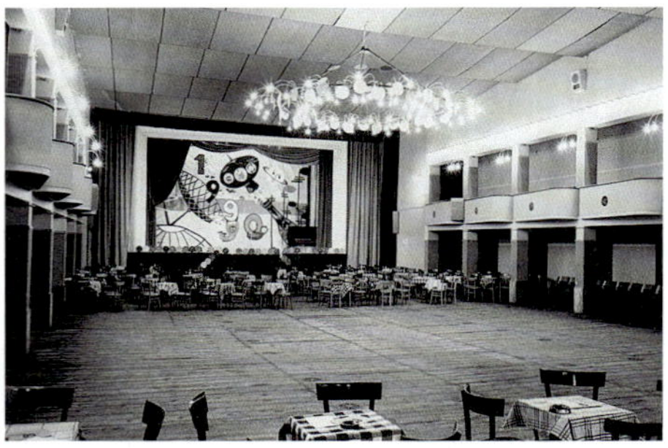

What first compelled you to open a gallery?
Galleria Continua opened in San Gimignano (Italy) in 1990, as the result of the initiative of three friends: Mario Cristiani, Lorenzo Fiaschi, and Maurizio Rigillo. Occupying a former cinema, Galleria Continua established itself and thrived in an entirely unexpected location, away from the big cities and the ultramodern urban centers, in a town—San Gimignano—steeped in history, timeless, magnificent. This choice of location provided scope for the development of new forms of dialogue and symbiosis between unexpected geographies: rural and industrial, local and global, art from the past and the art of today, famous artists and emerging ones. The gallery's presence in an area that is in a certain sense "forgotten," but which has a spirit and significant history of its own, has enabled it to create a reputation as a center capable of producing exciting and challenging contemporary work where it is least expected, unhampered by the spatial and temporal restrictions of classic contemporary art institutions. Remaining faithful to a spirit of perpetual evolution, and committed to interesting as broad a public as possible in contemporary art, over the course of 20 years Galleria Continua has created a strong identity for itself through its ties and experiences.

- **Contact** Galleria Continua
  Veronica Tronnolone
  veronica@galleriacontinua.com
  info@galleriacontinua.com
- **Established** 1990
- **Owner(s) / Partner(s)** Mario Cristiani
  Lorenzo Fiaschi
  Maurizio Rigillo
- **Team** 19
- **Space(s)** 2,500 m²
- **Artists at Art Basel** Ai Weiwei
  Kader Attia
  Daniel Buren
  Cai Guo-Qiang
  Loris Cecchini
  Chen Zhen
  Nikhil Chopra
  Berlinde De Bruyckere
  Leandro Erlich
  Meschac Gaba
  Carlos Garaicoa
  Kendell Geers
  Antony Gormley
  Gu Dexin
  Shilpa Gupta
  Subodh Gupta
  Mona Hatoum
  Ilya & Emilia Kabakov
  Zhanna Kadyrova
  Kan Xuan
  Anish Kapoor
  Jorge Macchi
  Sabrina Mezzaqui
  Margherita Morgantin
  Moataz Nasr
  Hans Op de Beeck
  Giovanni Ozzola
  Michelangelo Pistoletto
  Arcangelo Sassolino
  Manuela Sedmach
  Serse
  Nedko Solakov
  Sun Yuan & Peng Yu
  Pascale Marthine Tayou
  Nari Ward
  Sophie Whettnall
  Sislej Xhafa
  Yan Lei

Cooley

New York

- Discoveries

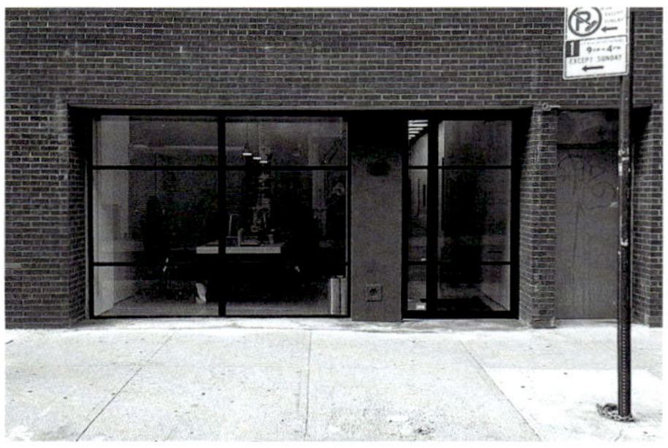

What first compelled you to open a gallery?
I felt unsatisfied with the level of interaction with artists in my former, albeit wonderful, job. I remember thinking this was a crazy idea. New York City boasts over 500 galleries, but then I remembered that there were maybe only eight or ten that I truly respected, and if I could create a gallery of high integrity and of that same caliber, then surely this idea was not quite so crazy.

Who is the first artist you showed and what was most memorable about that show?
Andy Coolquitt. His exhibition demonstrated to me that it's possible to make art about idealism despite the harsh pressures of the current art world. I cherish this possibility.

When did you first participate in Art Basel and what was most memorable about that show?
2013 in Hong Kong. I remember most the sense of excitement of exhibiting in Asia for the first time. The trip was filled with many firsts.

- **Contact** Lisa Cooley
  lisa@lisa-cooley.com
  frontdesk@lisa-cooley.com
- **Established** 2008
- **Owner(s) / Partner(s)** Lisa Cooley
- **Team** 4
- **Space(s)** 440 m²
- **Artists at Art Basel** Erin Shirreff
- **Further artists represented** Michael Bauer
  Alice Channer
  Andy Coolquitt
  Cynthia Daignault
  Josh Faught
  Frank Haines
  Alex Olson
  Scott Reeder
  Alan Reid

Cooper

New York

- Galleries Unlimited
- Galleries Public

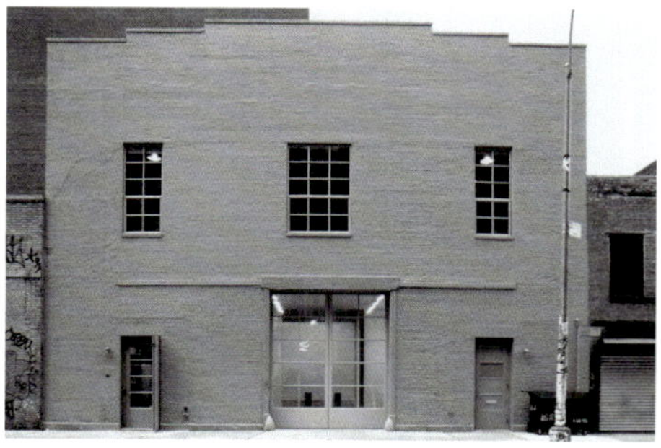

What first compelled you to open a gallery?
I really knew when I was 17 or 18 years old, when I was living in Paris, that I wanted to work with artists. Looking at art was preferable to doing anything else.

Who is the first artist you showed and what was most memorable about that show?
The opening for Walter De Maria was so memorable. It was the strangest thing: there were only about ten people and they were his closest friends—Robert Whitman, Simone Forti, La Monte Young. All of a sudden everyone sat on the floor around the perimeter of the room and became silent. It just happened and it lasted for five or ten minutes. Everything in the show was made out of wood—columns made out of wood in the hallway and a wooden arch at the end of the hall. There were two big frames made out of wood that were painted gold and silver, and there were works on paper.

When did you first participate in Art Basel and what was most memorable about that show?
Our first participation was in 1999, which is not so long ago considering how old the gallery is. I visited the fair every year and decided I wanted to do it before I died. I put up a series of Matisse watercolors by Sherrie Levine, and Michael Werner, who was across from us, came over, said "ah-hah," returned to his booth, and proceeded to put up the originals.

• **Contact**	Paula Cooper Gallery Ellie Levitt ellie@paulacoopergallery.com info@paulacoopergallery.com
• **Established**	1968
• **Owner(s) / Partner(s)**	Paula Cooper
• **Team**	16
• **Space(s)**	929 m²
• **Artists at Art Basel**	Carl Andre Tauba Auerbach Sophie Calle Bruce Conner Mark di Suvero Sam Durant Matias Faldbakken Charles Gaines Liz Glynn Wayne Gonzales Robert Grosvenor Douglas Huebler Sherrie Levine Sol LeWitt Christian Marclay Justin Matherly Claes Oldenburg Claes Oldenburg & Coosje van Bruggen Paul Pfeiffer Walid Raad Joel Shapiro Rudolf Stingel Kelley Walker Dan Walsh Carey Young
• **Further artists represented**	Jonathan Borofsky Céleste Boursier-Mougenot Dan Flavin Hans Haacke Michael Hurson Donald Judd Julian Lethbridge Jan Schoonhoven Meg Webster Robert Wilson Jackie Winsor Bing Wright

Corbett vs. Dempsey

Chicago • Galleries

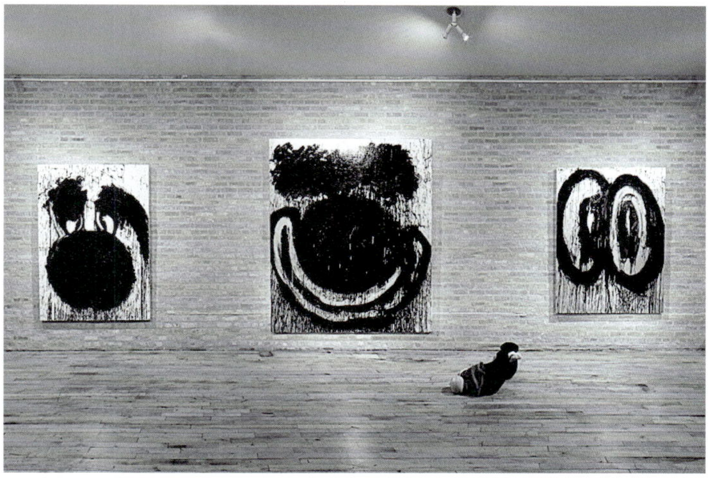

What first compelled you to open a gallery?
Curatorial interests.

Who is the first artist you showed and what was most memorable about that show?
Eve Garrison. The way the WPA-era cityscapes harmonized with the brick buildings visible outside our windows.

When did you first participate in Art Basel and what was most memorable about that show?
In 2013.

• **Contact**	Corbett vs. Dempsey Benjamin Chaffee ben@corbettvsdempsey.com info@corbettvsdempsy.com
• **Established**	2004
• **Owner(s) / Partner(s)**	John Corbett Jim Dempsey
• **Team**	3
• **Space(s)**	800 m²
• **Artists at Art Basel**	David Hartt Albert Oehlen John Sparagana Karl Wirsum Molly Zuckerman-Hartung
• **Further artists represented**	Ralph Arnold Morris Barazani Margot Bergman Peter Brötzmann Dominick Di Meo Robert Donley Ed Flood Art Green Walter Hamady Philip Hanson Arturo Herrera Thomas Kapsalis Gina Litherland Robert Lostutter Rebecca Morris Joyce Pensato Christina Ramberg Seymour Rosofsky Rebecca Shore Diane Simpson Charline von Heyl Christopher Wool Jimmy Wright

C

Corrias

London

Galleries
Unlimited

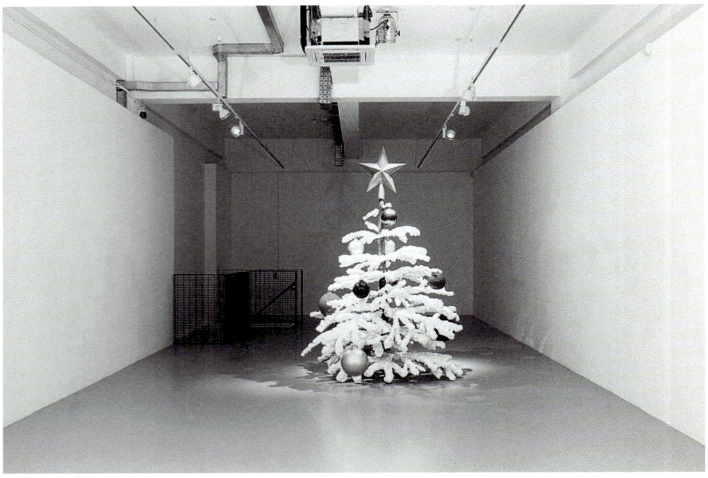

What first compelled you to open a gallery?
A passion for working with artists and the desire to contribute new ideas to the contemporary art discourse.

Who is the first artist you showed and what was most memorable about that show?
Pilar Corrias opened in London's West End on October 16, 2008, with an exhibition of new work by French artist Philippe Parreno, *Fraught Times: For Eleven Months of the Year it's an Artwork and in December it's Christmas (October)* (2008). The work consisted of a large scale, painted, cast aluminum sculpture of a decorated Christmas tree. Playing with the length of time we engage with something and with the concepts of celebration and desire, the Christmas tree marked the event of the opening of a new gallery. Parreno's work is known for challenging viewers by questioning authorship and perceptions of reality and illusion.

When did you first participate in Art Basel and what was most memorable about that show?
Pilar Corrias was the first gallery to present a solo project by Ulla von Brandenburg at Miami Beach, in the Positions sector in 2009.

- **Contact** Pilar Corrias
  Irina Stark
  irina@pilarcorrias.com
  sales@pilarcorrias.com
- **Established** 2008
- **Owner(s) / Partner(s)** Pilar Corrias
- **Team** 5
- **Space(s)** 350 m²
- **Artists at Art Basel** Koo Jeong A
  Tala Madani
  Philippe Parreno
  Tobias Rehberger
  Shahzia Sikander
- **Further artists represented** Charles Avery
  Keren Cytter
  Leigh Ledare
  Elizabeth Neel
  Mary Ramsden
  Mary Reid Kelley
  Julião Sarmento
  John Skoog
  Rirkrit Tiravanija
  Tunga
  Ulla von Brandenburg

Crèvecoeur

Paris

Positions

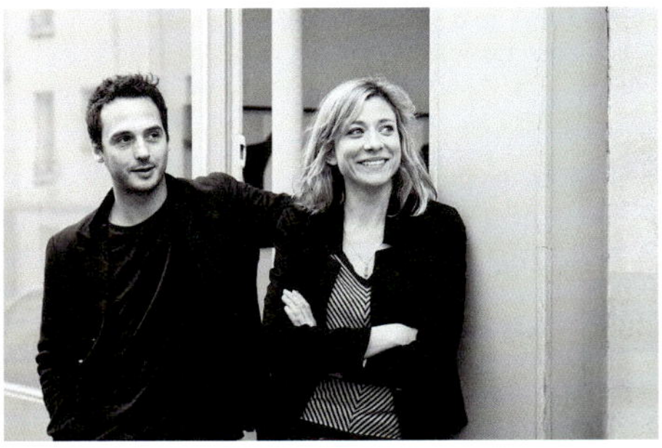

What first compelled you to open a gallery?
Being part of the contemporary creation, working closely with the artists.

Who is the first artist you showed and what was most memorable about that show?
Jorge Pedro Nuñez. Most memorable about his show was his wonderful collage series *Black Mountains in Color*, presented to the public for the first time. Fifty of them were shown, and all belong now to prestigious institutional and private collections.

When did you first participate in Art Basel and what was most memorable about that show?
Our first participation at Art Basel was in Miami Beach, in 2013, with a solo presentation of Jorge Pedro Nuñez's work in the Positions sector.

- **Contact** Crèvecoeur
  Axel Dibie
  axel.dibie@
  galeriecrevecoeur.com
- **Established** 2008
- **Owner(s) / Partner(s)** Axel Dibie
  Alix Dionot-Morani
- **Team** 3
- **Space(s)** 50 m²
- **Artists at Art Basel** Jorge Pedro Nuñez
- **Further artists represented** Xavier Antin
  Erica Baum
  Julien Carreyn
  Jochen Dehn
  André Guedes
  Shana Moulton
  Mick Peter
  Florian & Michael Quistrebert

CRG

New York

Galleries

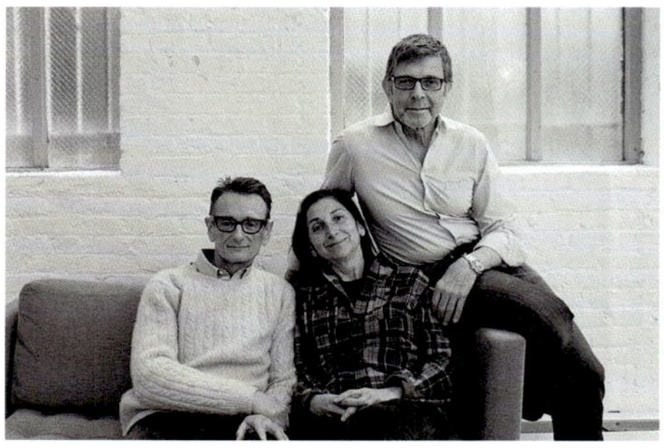

What first compelled you to open a gallery?
The belief that artists see the world differently, and that their art transports us to places we would never find ourselves.

Who is the first artist you showed and what was most memorable about that show?
Jean-Marc Bustamante. How the "known" terrain of the gallery space is transformed into a landscape of nostalgic desire by the intervention of common objects.

When did you first participate in Art Basel and what was most memorable about that show?
In 1994. At that time there was a worldwide economic crisis. I was impressed by how the "art world" endures.

- **Contact** CRG Gallery
Glenn McMillan
glenn@crggallery.com
info@crggallery.com
- **Established** 1991
- **Owner(s) / Partner(s)** Carla Chammas
Richard Desroche
Glenn McMillan
- **Team** 7
- **Space(s)** 400 m²
- **Artists at Art Basel** Tonico Lemos Auad
Saloua Raouda Choucair
Alexandre da Cunha
Tomory Dodge
Ori Gersht
Joana Hadjithomas & Khalil Joreige
Tom LaDuke
Jumana Manna
Steve Roden
- **Further artists represented** Eva Berendes
Steven Bindernagel
Colby Bird
Robert Buck
Russell Crotty
Angela Dufresne
Pia Fries
Lyle Ashton Harris
Butt Johnson
Siobhan Liddell
Melissa McGill
Kelly McLane
Carmen McLeod
O Zhang
Sam Reveles
Lisa Sanditz
Brian Tolle

Cristea

London

- Galleries
- Edition
- Edition

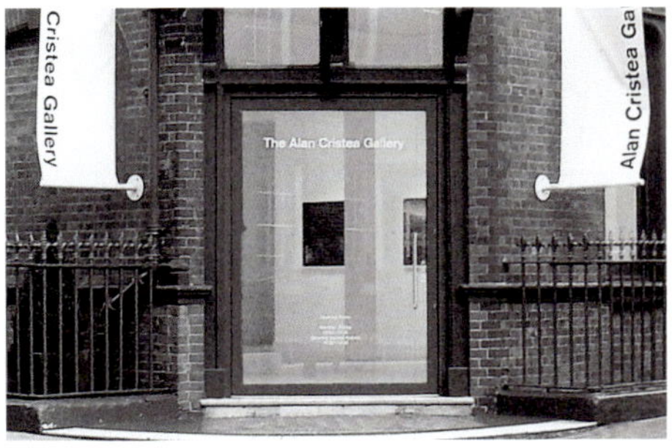

What first compelled you to open a gallery?
A desire to paper the world in original art and earn a living!

Who is the first artist you showed and what was most memorable about that show?
David Hockney. I mostly remember my nervousness about opening a gallery.

When did you first participate in Art Basel and what was most memorable about that show?
In 1997.

- **Contact** Alan Cristea Gallery
Ailbhe Clyne
aclyne@alancristea.com
info@alancristea.com
- **Established** 1995
- **Owner(s) / Partner(s)** Alan Cristea
Paul Chellgren
- **Team** 13
- **Space(s)** 170 m²
- **Artists at Art Basel** Josef Albers
Christiane Baumgartner
Gordon Cheung
Michael Craig-Martin
Dexter Dalwood
Ian Davenport
Edmund de Waal
Jan Dibbets
Jim Dine
Richard Hamilton
Marie Harnett
Howard Hodgkin
Ben Johnson
Allen Jones
Roy Lichtenstein
Henri Matisse
Joan Miró
Julian Opie
Pablo Picasso
Lisa Ruyter
Tom Wesselmann
Paul Winstanley
Richard Woods
- **Further artists represented** Anni Albers
Gillian Ayres
Georges Braque
Patrick Caulfield
Eduardo Chillida
Sam Francis
Naum Gabo
David Hockney
Ben Langlands & Nikki Bell
Sol LeWitt
Ian McKeever
Robert Motherwell
Ben Nicholson
Mimmo Paladino
Cornelia Parker
Vicken Parsons
Sean Scully
Joe Tilson
Andy Warhol
Catherine Yass

Crousel

Paris

- Galleries
- Galleries Unlimited Parcours
- Galleries

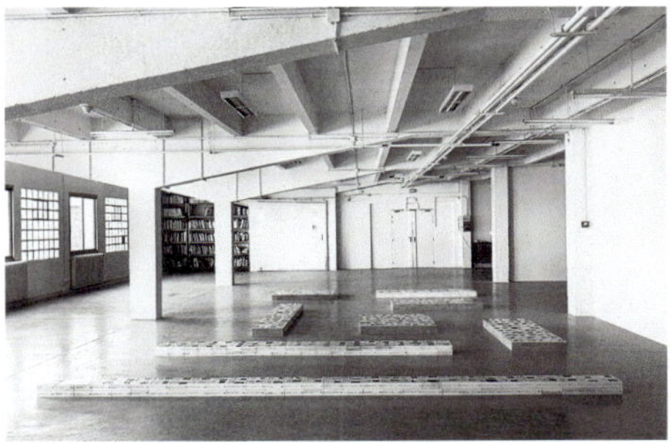

What first compelled you to open a gallery?
When in 1971 (still living in Brussels) I bought my first artwork without knowing anything about contemporary art, nor about Man Ray (the author of the work) from a lady who initiated me in such a pertinent and kind way, I decided that this was what I also wanted to do. Consequently, I studied art history, and familiarized myself with the gallery activities through several internships (a.o. at Galerie Alexandre Iolas, in Paris), and had a first experience with a colleague student in sharing a gallery, La Dérive, in 1976.

Who is the first artist you showed and what was most memorable about that show?
In 1980 I started my own gallery. The first artist shown was Tony Cragg. The whole exhibition was created on the spot. For one week, every evening, we would drive around Paris, preceding the garbage collectors so Tony could pick up the cardboard, wood, and plastic he needed to construct a perfectly geometrical stack of elements overnight that characterized the trash of the city. Or a huge blue moon made of blue plastic objects fixed onto the wall. Or a big tree made of elements of used wooden objects, laid out parallel on the floor. The exhibition was very generous in meaning, and introduced a totally original approach to sculpture making. It was the beginning of a new movement in sculpture in Great Britain, which would have wide impact on the young sculptors in Great Britain and worldwide.

- **Contact** Galerie Chantal Crousel
Jeremy Dessaint
jeremy@crousel.com
galerie@crousel.com
- **Established** 1980
- **Owner(s) / Partner(s)** Chantal Crousel (Owner)
Niklas Svennung (Partner)
- **Team** 12

C

- **Space(s)** 300 m² (10, rue Charlot)
750 m² (La Douane)
- **Artists at Art Basel** Jennifer Allora & Guillermo Calzadilla
Abraham Cruzvillegas
Willem de Rooij
Claire Fontaine
Isa Genzken
Wade Guyton
Mona Hatoum
Thomas Hirschhorn
Hassan Khan
Jean-Luc Moulène
Melik Ohanian
Gabriel Orozco
Seth Price
Clément Rodzielski
Anri Sala
Alain Séchas
Reena Spaulings
Wolfgang Tillmans
Rirkrit Tiravanija
Danh Vo
Haegue Yang
Heimo Zobernig
- **Further artists represented** Fikret Atay
Tarek Atoui
Wang Bing
Fabrice Gygi
Michael Krebber
José Maria Sicilia
Moshe Ninio
Sean Snyder
Andy Warhol

Crown Point

San Francisco

- Edition
- Edition

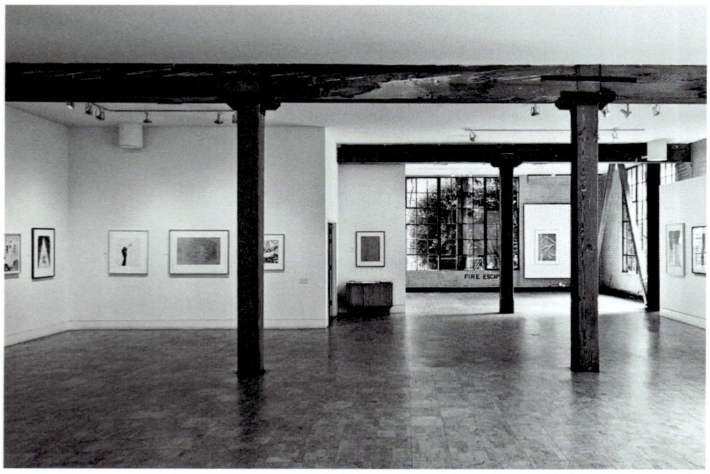

What first compelled you to open a gallery?
At first I simply wanted to give contemporary artists an opportunity to use the medium of etching hands-on. As our reputation became secure, we needed a gallery to show our artists' work in a professional setting and to promote the survival of our time-honored medium.

Who is the first artist you showed and what was most memorable about that show?
Daniel Buren and John Cage, 1979. Both came to California to make the work. We cut Buren's stripes into fragments and "exploded" them over the wall to "frame" Cage's delicate hand-engraved work.

When did you first participate in Art Basel and what was most memorable about that show?
In 1977. We showed Chris Burden's photo-etching facsimile Italian 10,000 lire note printed by us on both sides of the sheet, and early works by Vito Acconci. To announce our ambitions, we handed out compressed sponges as business cards.

- **Contact** Crown Point Press
Kathan Brown
kathanbrown@crownpoint.com
valerie@crownpoint.com

- **Established** 1962 (workshop)/1979 (gallery)
- **Owner(s) / Partner(s)** Kathan Brown (Founding Director)
Valerie Wade (Director)
- **Team** 10
- **Space(s)** 900 m² (gallery + workshop)
- **Artists at Art Basel** Tomma Abts
Vito Acconci
Darren Almond
Mamma Andersson
Anne Appleby
Robert Bechtle
Chris Burden
Daniel Buren
John Cage
Pia Fries
Katsura Funakoshi
Mary Heilmann
Anish Kapoor
Per Kirkeby
Sol LeWitt
Tom Marioni
Julie Mehretu
Jockum Nordström
Chris Ofili
Laura Owens
Markus Raetz
Tim Rollins and K.O.S.
Ed Ruscha
Alyson Shotz
Shahzia Sikander
Pat Steir
Richard Tuttle
- **Further artists represented** Richard Diebenkorn
Al Held
Dorothy Napangardi
Amy Sillman
Wayne Thiebaud
William T. Wiley
Fred Wilson

Cherry and Martin

Three Questions for Cherry and Martin

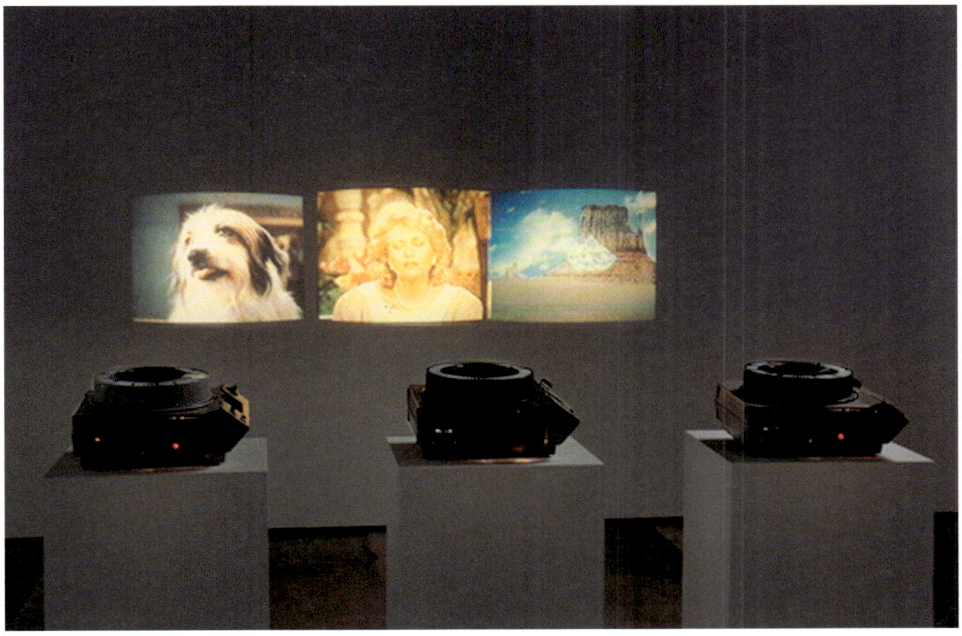

Art Basel in Basel (Feature), 2013

Your booth at Art Basel in Basel, in the Feature sector, was dedicated to an installation by the Californian artist Robert Heinecken. How has this presentation reflected the program and the "policy" of your gallery?

We first presented the work of Robert Heinecken (1931–2006) in an exhibition entitled *They Have Not the Art to Argue with Pictures* (2010). We asked viewers to consider his practice alongside that of several important artists working today. The various sectors of Art Basel have been a great platform for us to continue this intergenerational approach. There is good work being done by galleries like ours, who are examining artists of the recent past while at the same time considering the objects made by artists working now. For example, we exhibited work by Brian Bress, Matt Connors, and Mari Eastman; we did a project with Robert Overby (1935–1993); and mounted an exhibition reconsidering curator Peter Bunnell's landmark 1970 MoMA show *Photography into Sculpture* (for which we won the AICA-USA critics prize for Best Show in a Commercial Gallery Nationally).

Could you tell us more about this artwork and about Robert Heinecken's practice?

Surrealism on TV (1986) consists of projected 35mm slides, shot off the television by Heinecken. It is one of the most important works of the second half of his career, and like many of Heinecken's pieces, it had not been seen in Europe (prior to our exhibiting it at Art Basel). The images are almost exclusively "late night" television programming: televangelists; cranks; ads for consumer products that cost "only $9.99!"; aerobics instructors; animals doing people things; consumers testing their mattresses. Throughout it all, the image of a TV network newswoman—a favorite foil for Heinecken—appears constantly, perhaps legitimizing the madness. The piece consists of three variable-speed slide projectors. This variable speed introduces a chance-driven method: the combination of images is never the same thing twice. Our presentation was very stripped down—no bells and whistles, just the projectors and the booth—almost like what it must have been to see *Surrealism on TV* at a university like UCLA in the 1980s, when Heinecken's piece was first shown.

Heinecken plays a crucial and perhaps unique role in American art linking the found image in Surrealism with appropriation. He is now commonly referred to as a progenitor of [the] Pictures [Generation]. That's an intriguing idea that begs questions about expanded photography of the late 1960s and 70s generally. Should we be looking at conceptual artists using the camera (a trope we are all now comfortable with) vs. photographers that are conceptual? There's a difference there. Thanks to the touring solo exhibition of Heinecken's work (The Museum of Modern Art, New York, March 2014; travels to Hammer Museum), and his solo show at Wiels (Brussels, May 2014), there are exciting opportunities to think about the rich fabric of expanded photographic practice, both in the period in which Heinecken was working, and today.

In Miami Beach in 2013 you presented a "duo show" by associating two artists of different generations who use different mediums: Matt Connors and Bernard Piffaretti. Why this choice? How do these two artists' works dialogue with each other? For you, what is the interest of opening your program to non-Californian, and non-American artists?

Our presentation of Matt Connors and Bernard Piffaretti at Art Basel in Miami Beach is an example of how gallery shows and art fair presentations can work together to highlight genuine artistic exploration. Matt Connors first introduced me to Bernard Piffaretti's work. Piffaretti's solo show *Report*, at our gallery in January 2013, grew out of this, and our Miami Beach presentation further grew organically out of the conversation Connors and Piffaretti have had with one another, as well as the strides they have made in their own respective practices, working alone, in their respective studios.

French painting from the 1970s and 80s seems overlooked. Americans know the German artists from this period, but they know very little about the French—the Support/Surfaces movement, for example, who we will highlight in a gallery show in January 2014—or other French artists like Piffaretti, who first started showing with Jean Fournier in the early 1980s. It is intriguing in our historical moment to consider the work of another time, and the conversation between past and present. Matt Connors is a successful young American painter who has had several solo museum exhibitions in the US and Europe; last summer we presented a major project of his at Unlimited. Bernard Piffaretti is a French painter in his 60s who, before our recent gallery exhibition, had not shown in the United States in over a decade, and never before in California.

Clara Kim
Philippe Pirotte
Uli Sigg
Philip Tinari
Christine Macel
Adam Szymczyk
Jens Hoffmann
Theodora Vischer
Gabriela Salgado
Daniel Baumann
Beatrix Ruf
Alya Sebti
Franklin Sirmans

CURA TORS' CHOI CES

Clara Kim

Senior Curator of Visual Arts,
Walker Art Center, Minneapolis

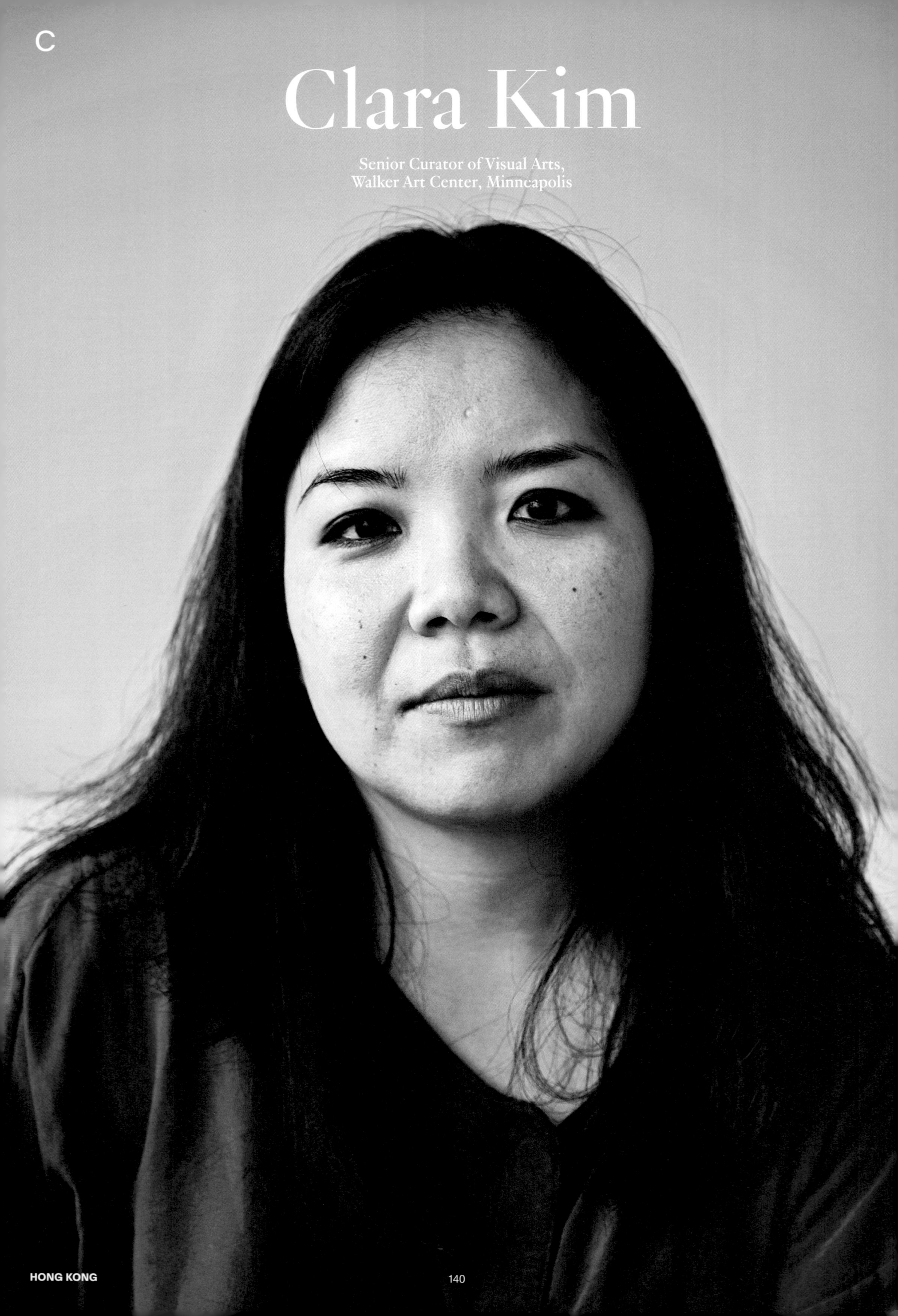

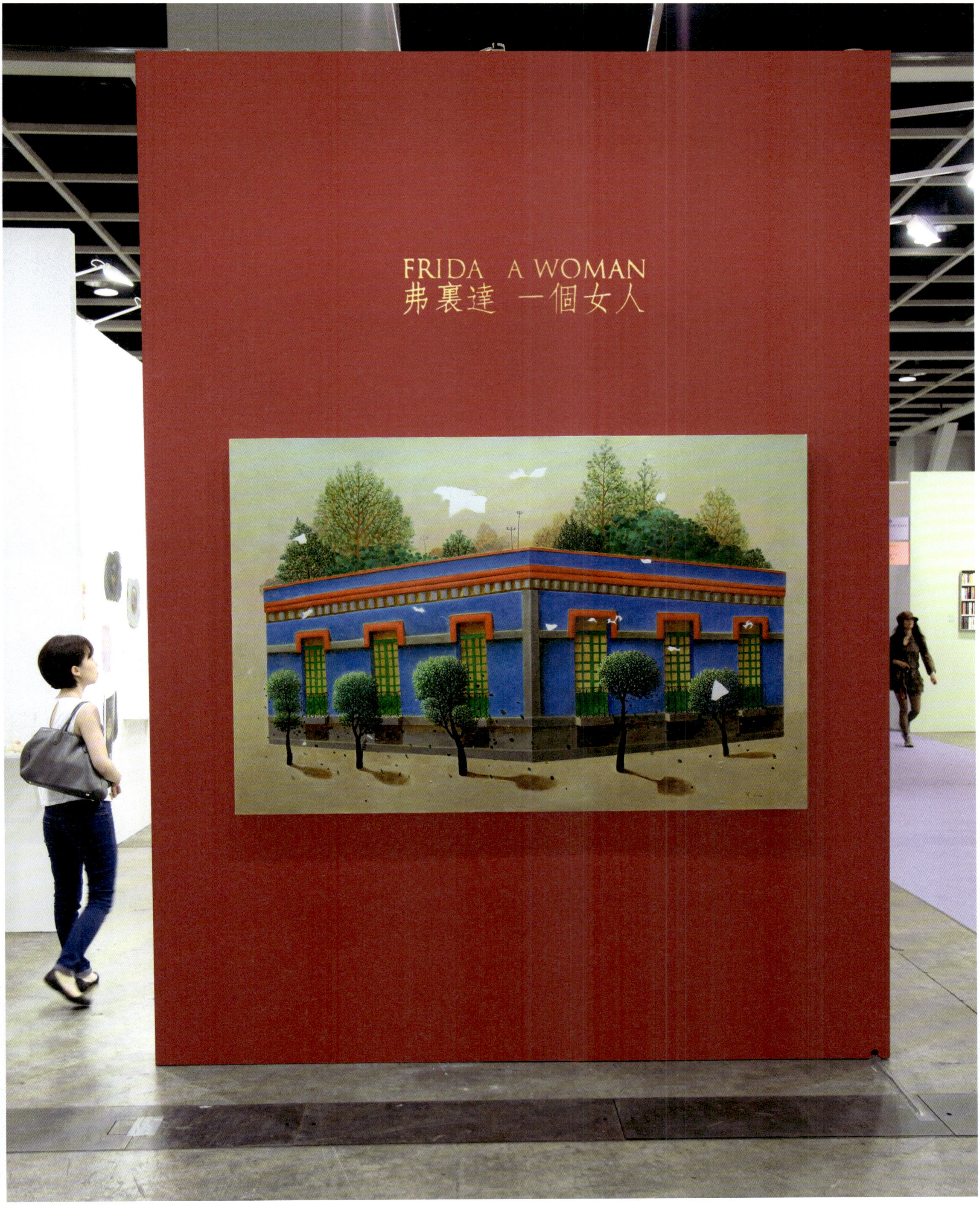

Chen Ke

Star Gallery (Insights)

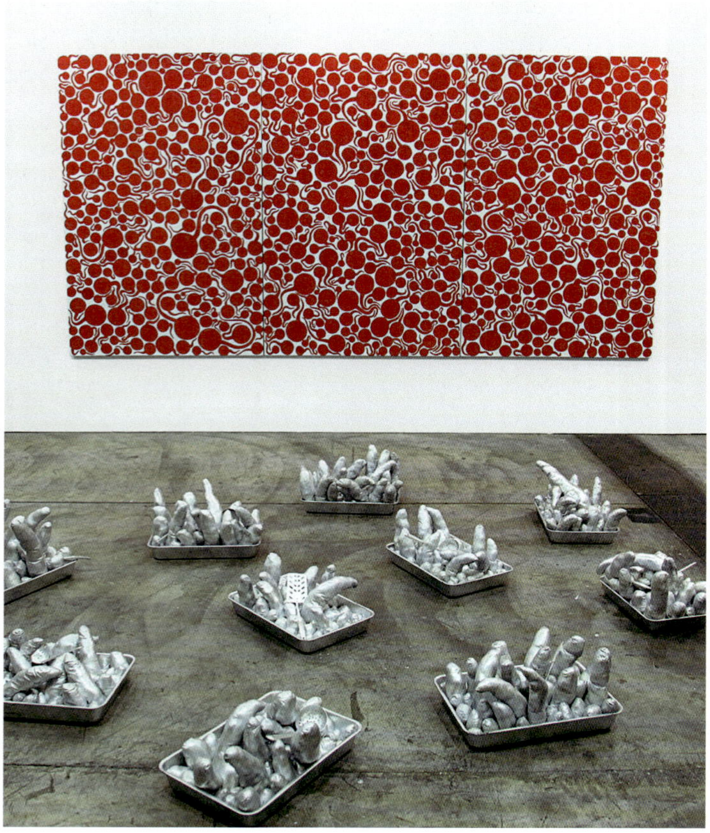

Yayoi Kusama

Victoria Miro/Ota Fine Arts

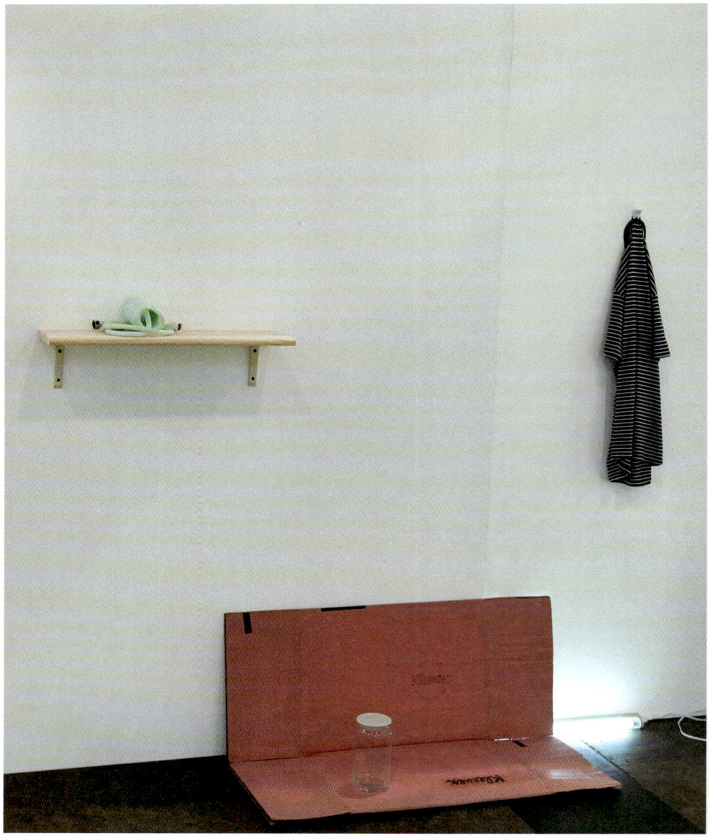

Lee Kit

Vitamin Creative Space

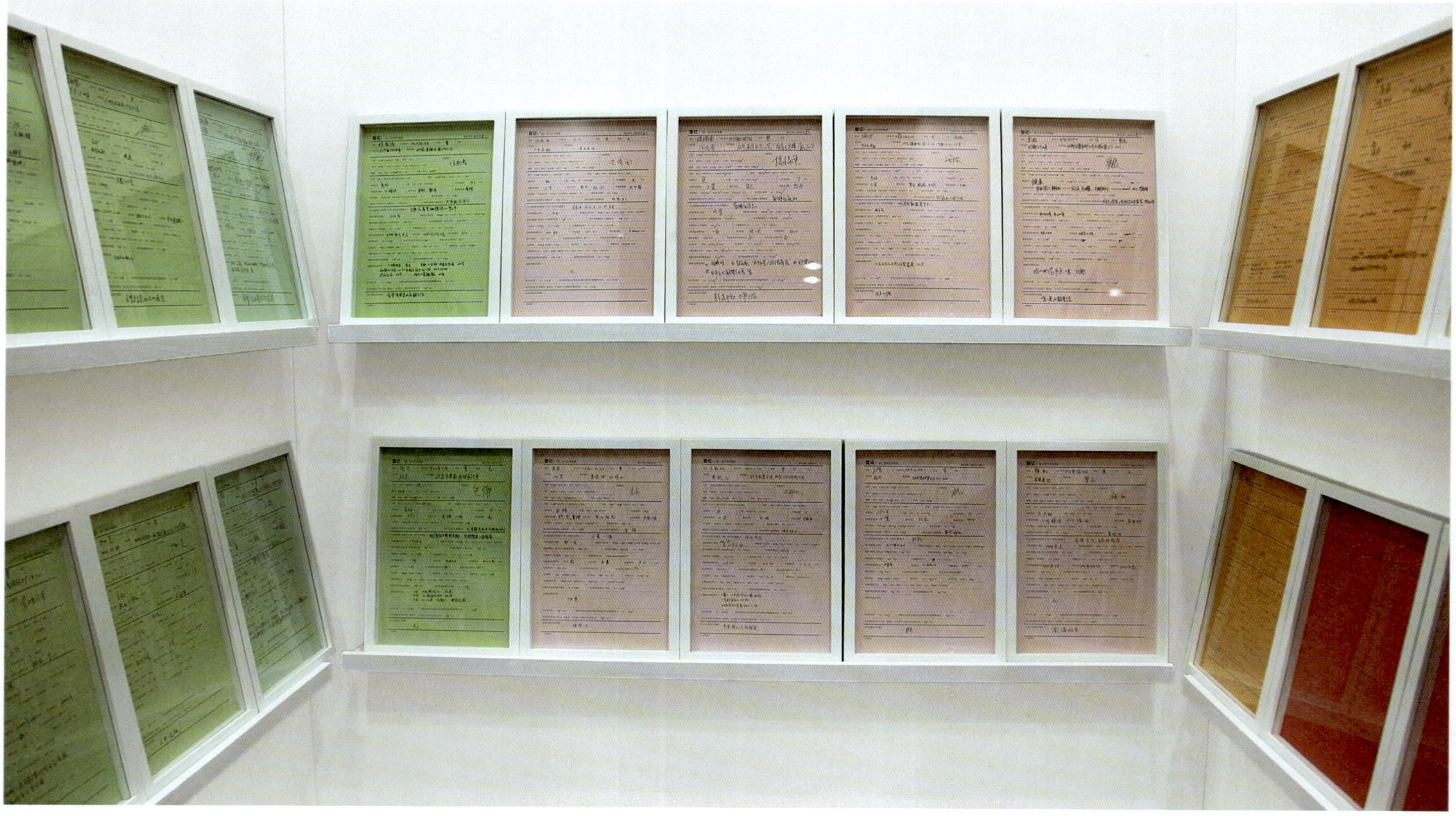

Geng Jianyi

ShanghART

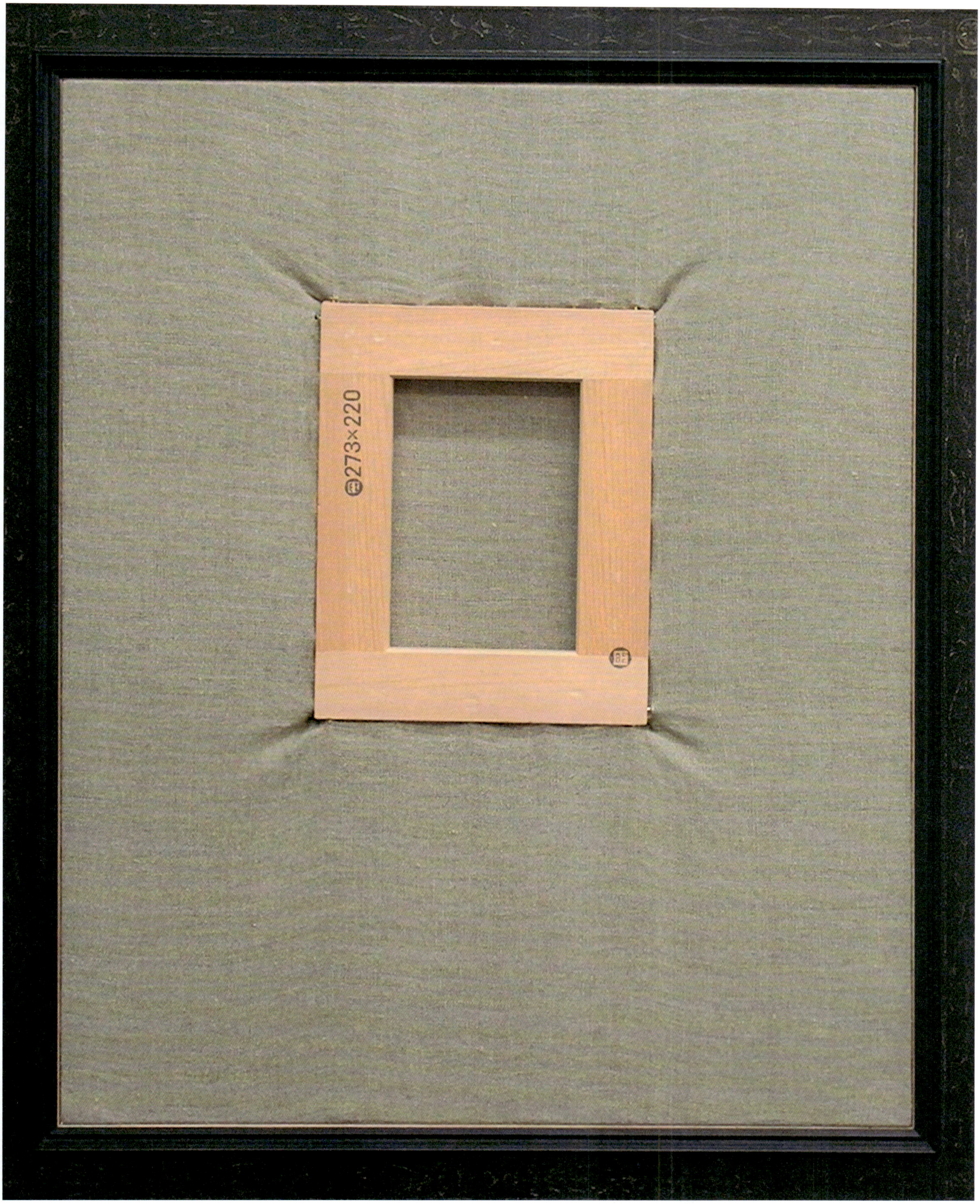

Susumu Koshimizu

Gallery Yamaki Fine Art (Insights)

C

Philippe Pirotte

Director Städelschule, Frankfurt, and Former Adjunct Senior Curator, Berkeley Art Museum & Pacific Film Archive, Berkeley

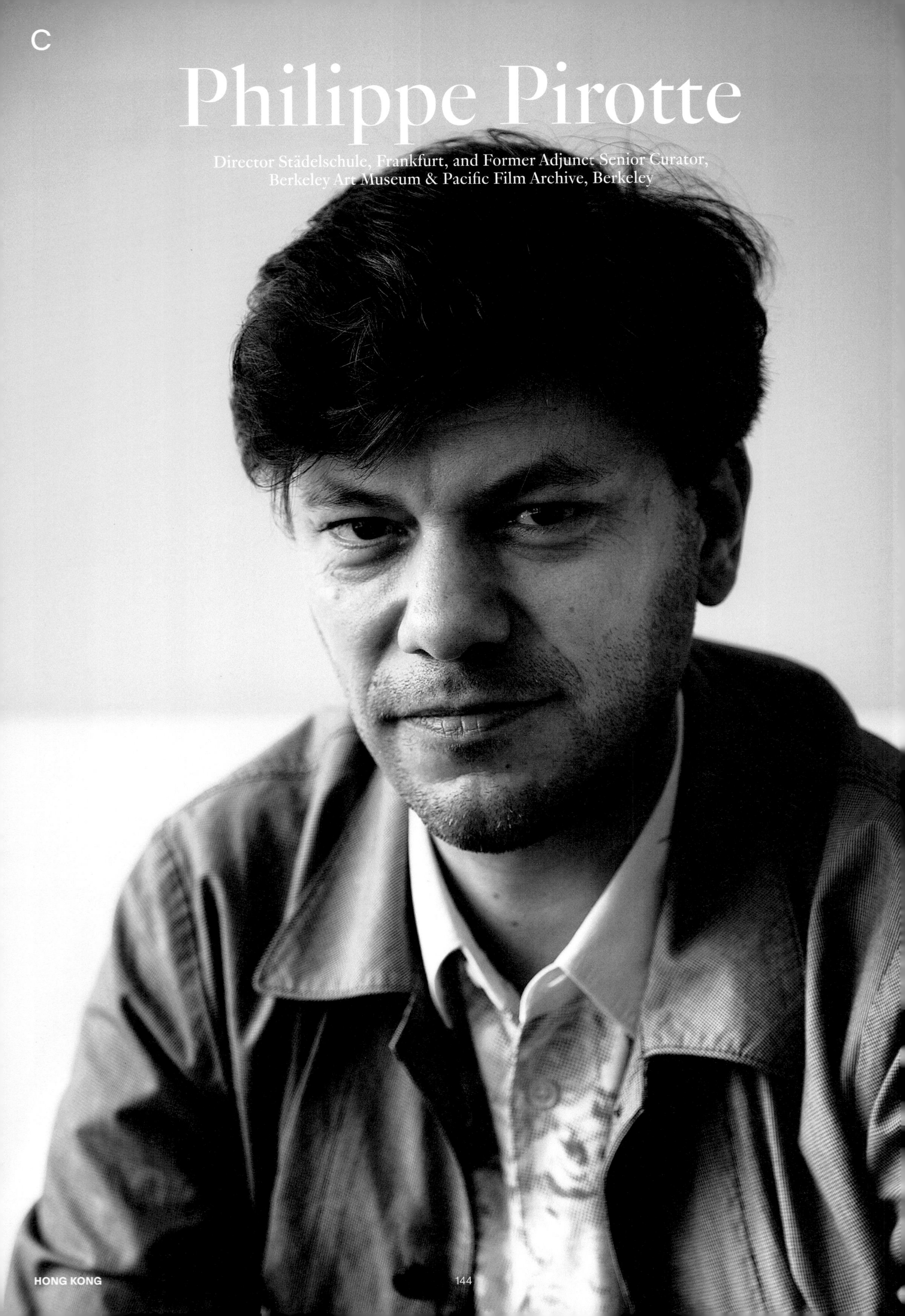

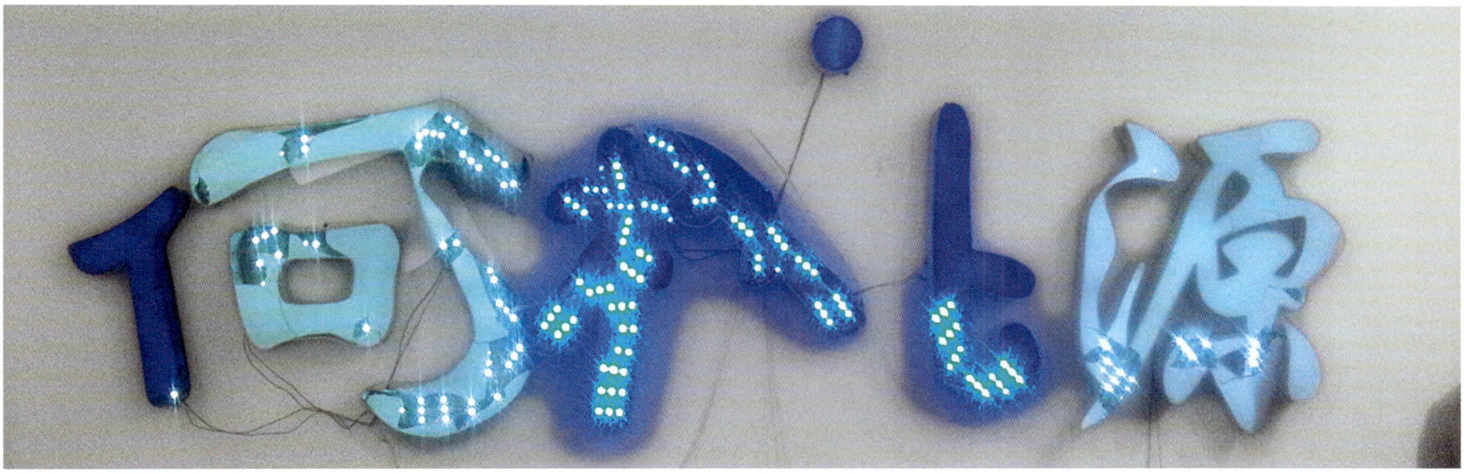

He An

Galerie Daniel Templon and Tang Contemporary Art

Fantastic Chinese artist writing very personal messages (the name of his father, love letters) in the stolen neon so present in Chinese metropolises at night.

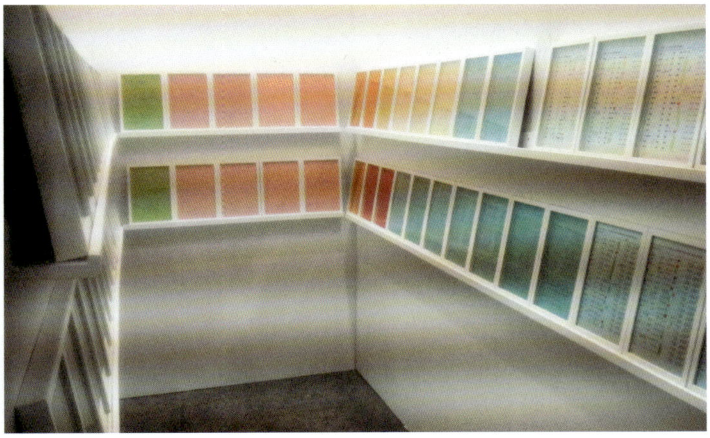

Geng Jianyi

ShanghART

An artist's questionnaire put up for *Home*, an exhibition organized in Shanghai in 2000. It gives us a humorous insight into the Shanghai artistic ecology of that time.

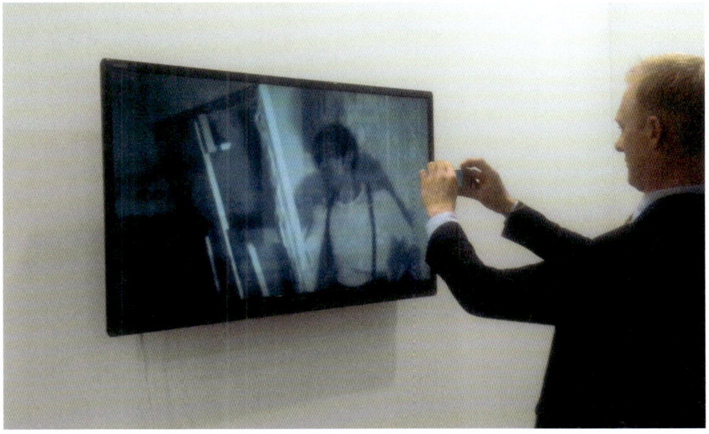

Li Ran

Aike-Dellarco (Discoveries)

A wonderful video in which Li Ran, who often engages in mimicry and the use of performance to parasite and change existing narratives, plays his father, a painter from the previous generation.

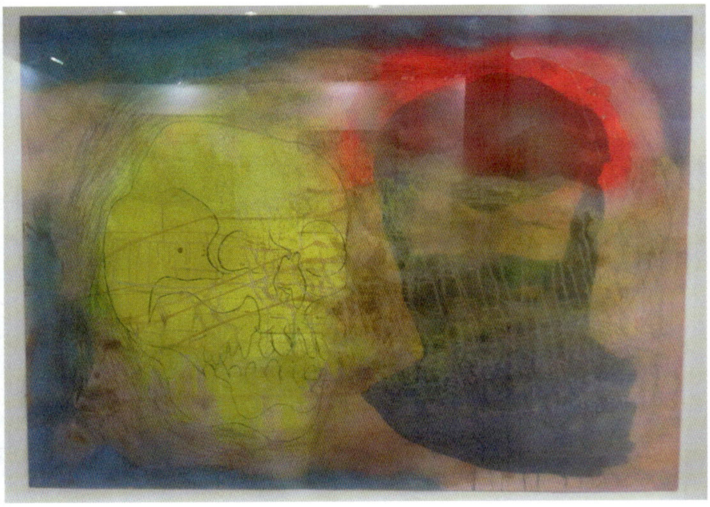

Moshekwa Langa

Goodman Gallery

Wonderfully succinct drawings based on personal memories, traumas, and reveries.

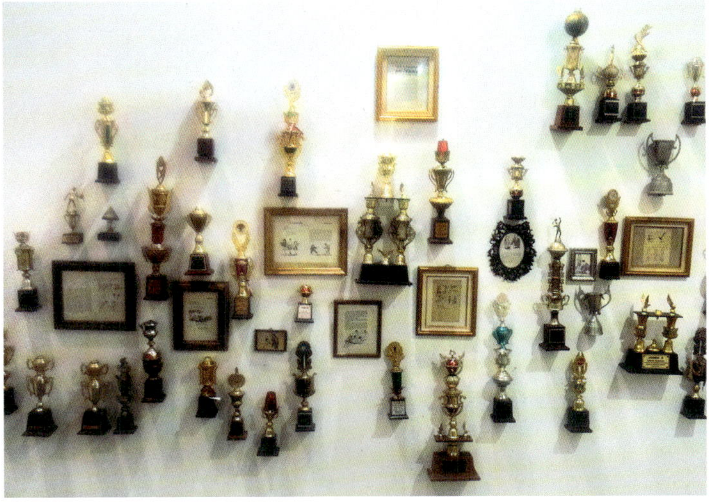

Ade Darmawan

Ark Galerie

Tournament trophies gathered at a fleamarket form a delusional and absurd narration of dreams and illusions.

Uli Sigg

Collector, Mauensee (Lucerne)

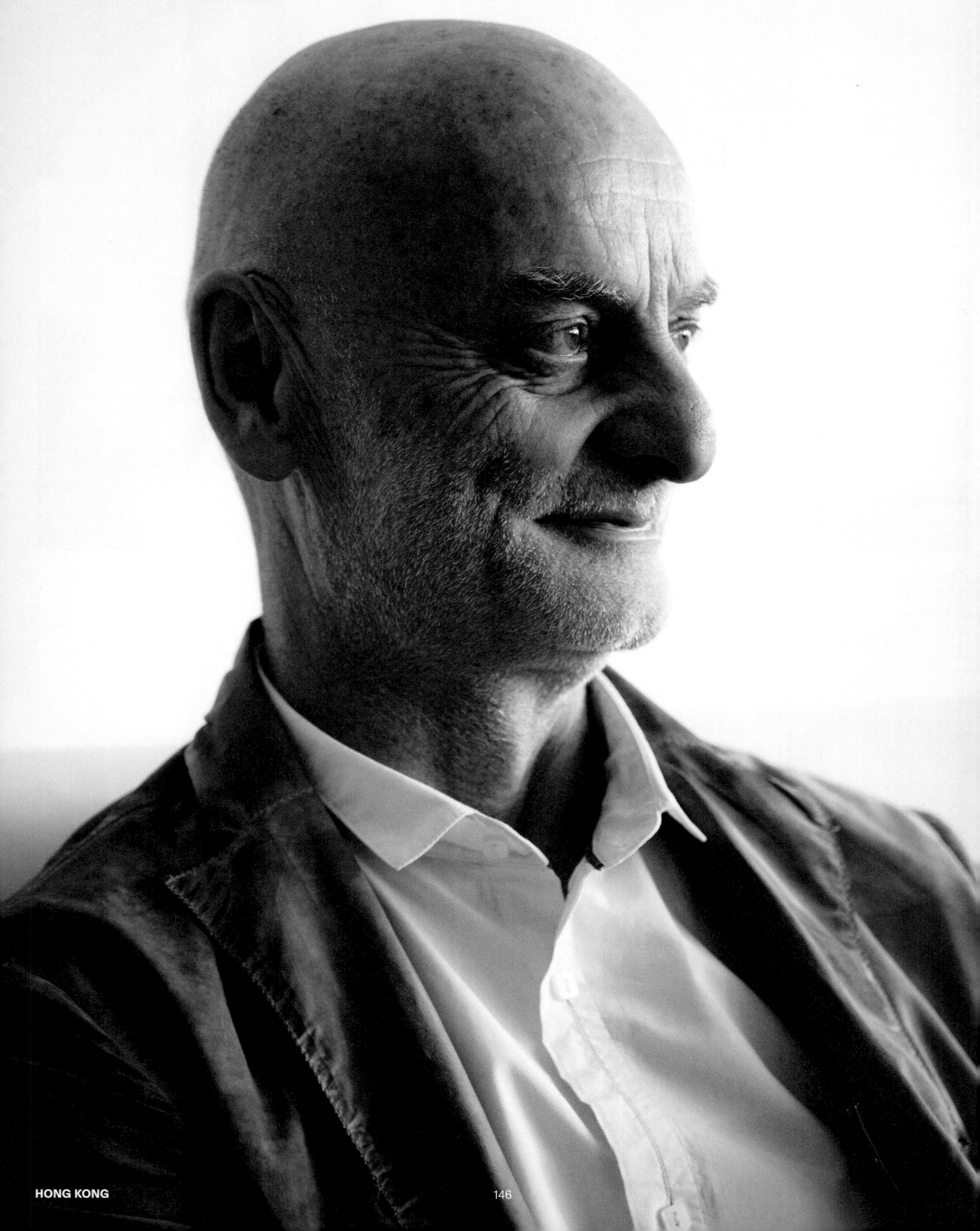

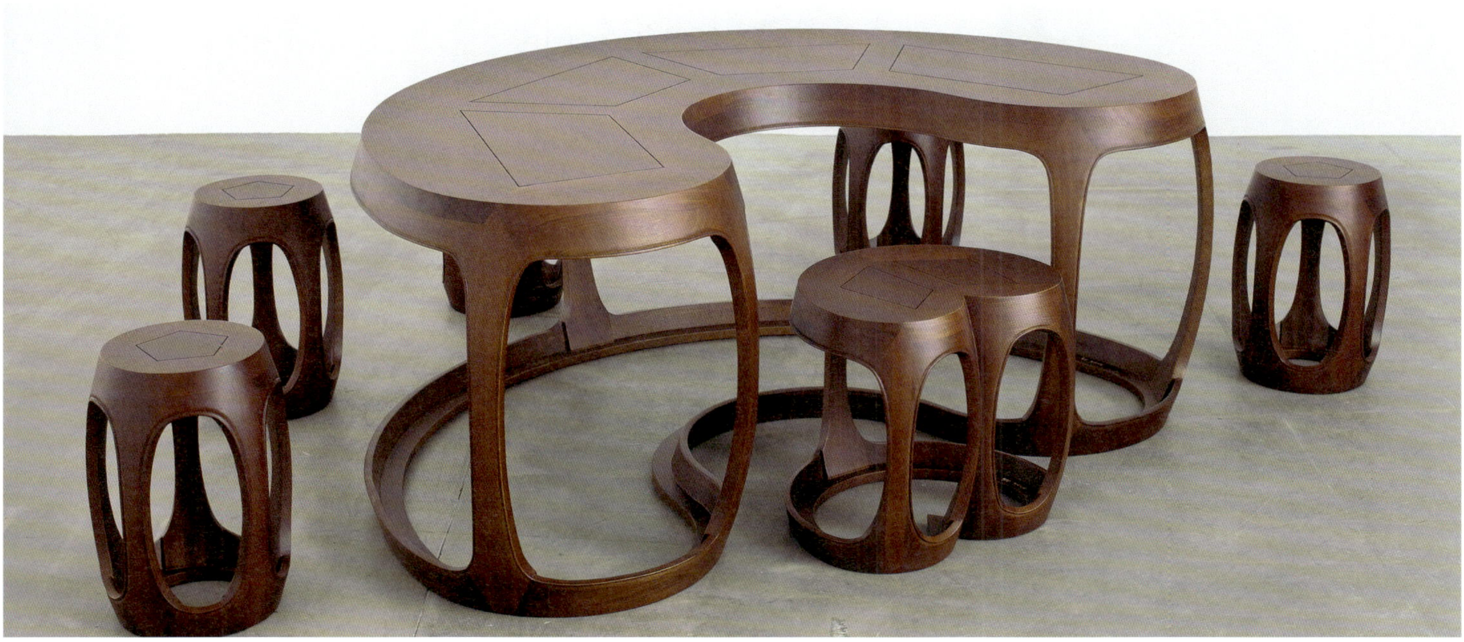

Shao Fan

Embroidered Tea Table - 2012, No. 3, 2013
Galerie Urs Meile

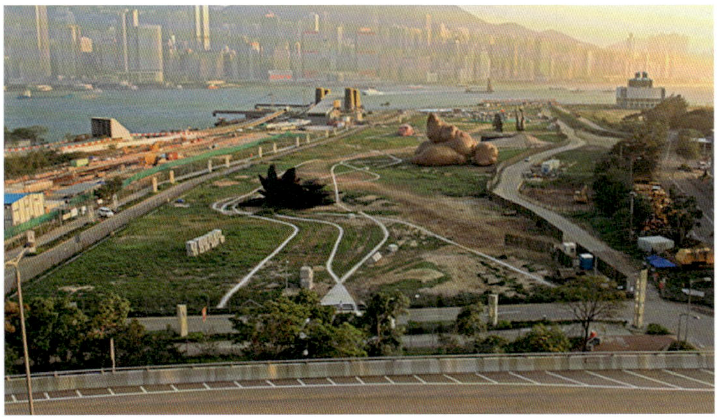

Paul McCarthy

Public commission *Complex Pile*, 2007, reinstalled in
West Kowloon Cultural District

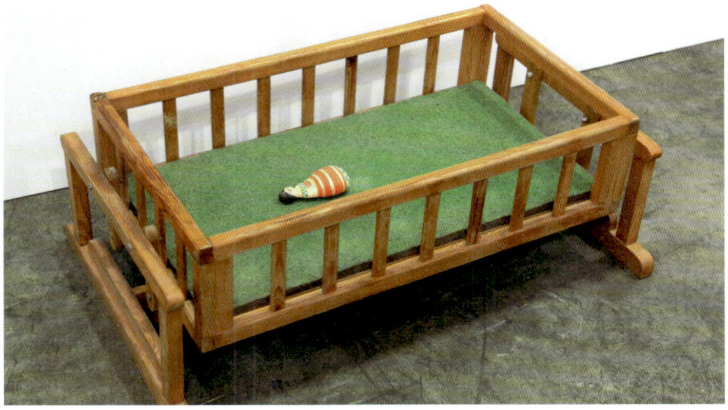

Chen Ke

Star Gallery (insights)

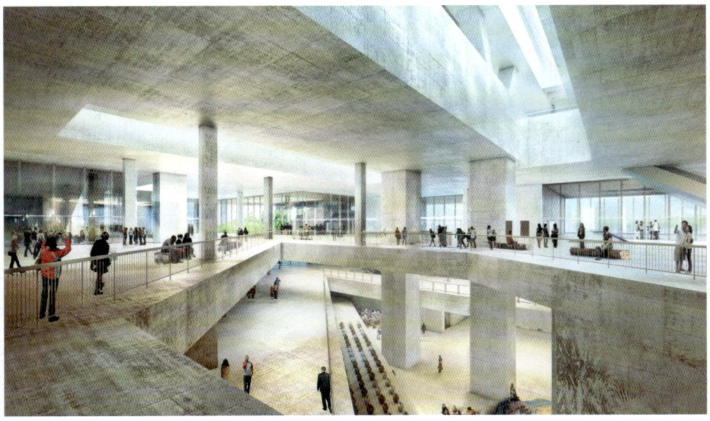

M+

The new museum for visual culture in Hong Kong,
located in West Kowloon Cultural District,
designed by Swiss architects Herzog & de Meuron

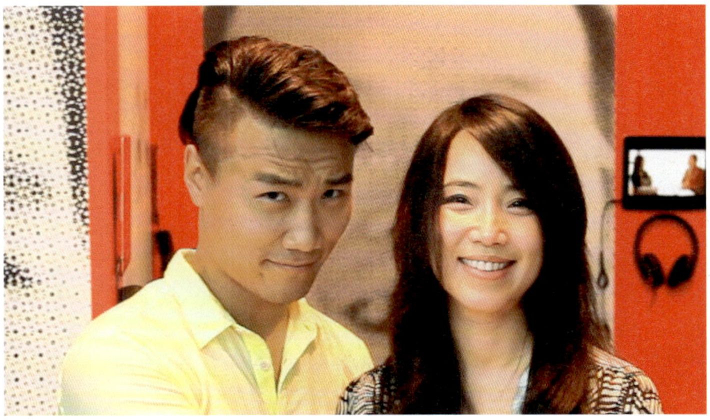

Chinese Contemporary Art Awards Booth

Yan Xing, 2012 Best Young Artist Award,
and Liu Li Anna, Director of CCAA

Philip Tinari

Director, Ullens Center for Contemporary Art, Beijing

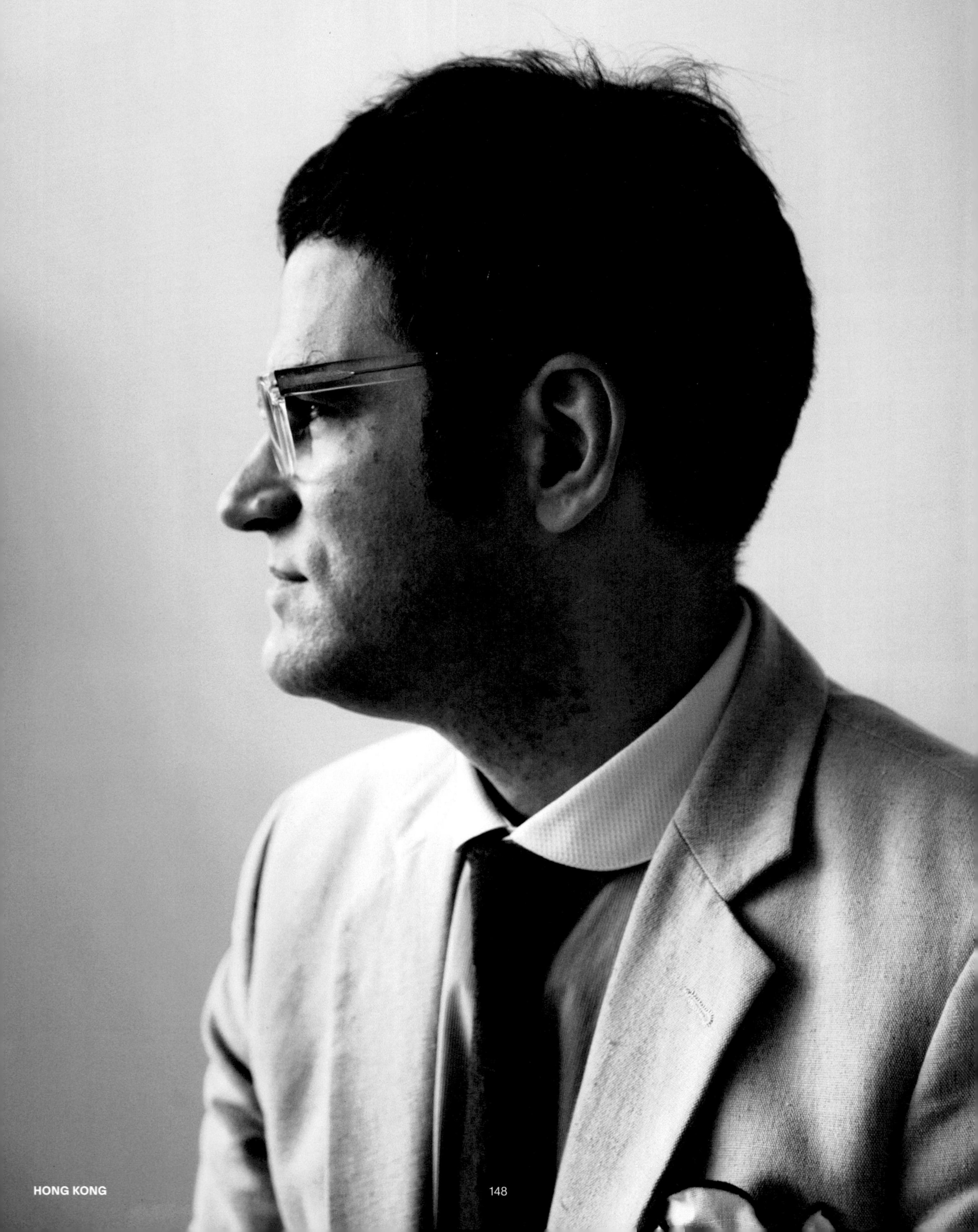

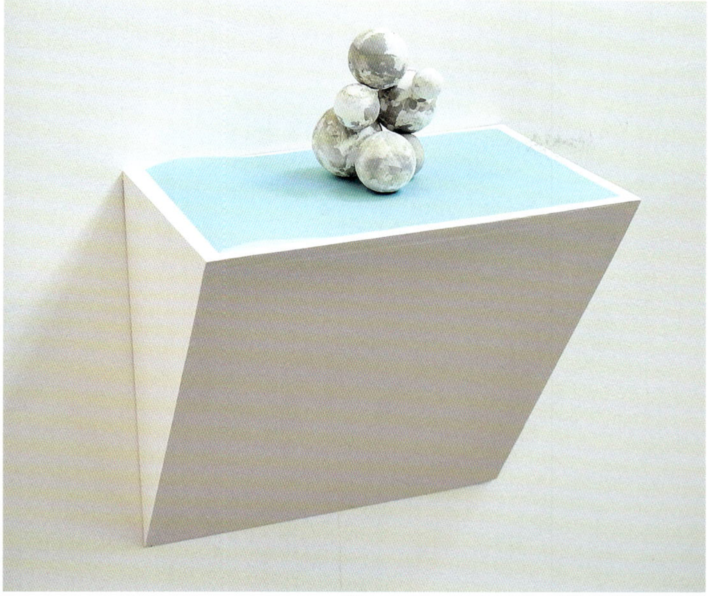

Brendan Earley

mother's tankstation (Discoveries)

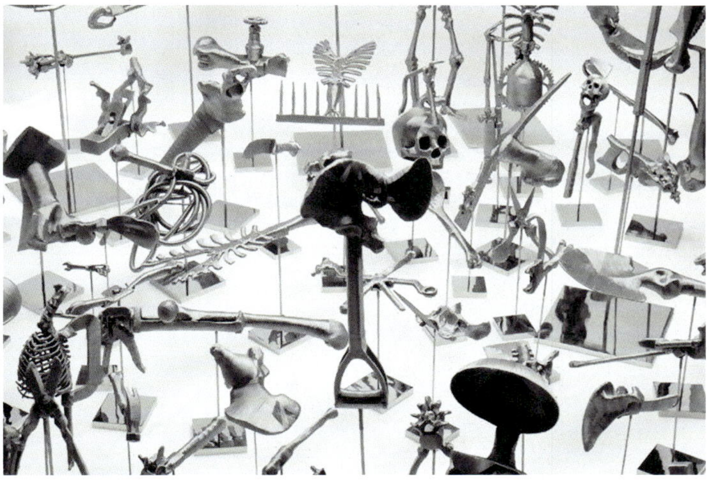

Lin Tianmiao

Galerie Lelong

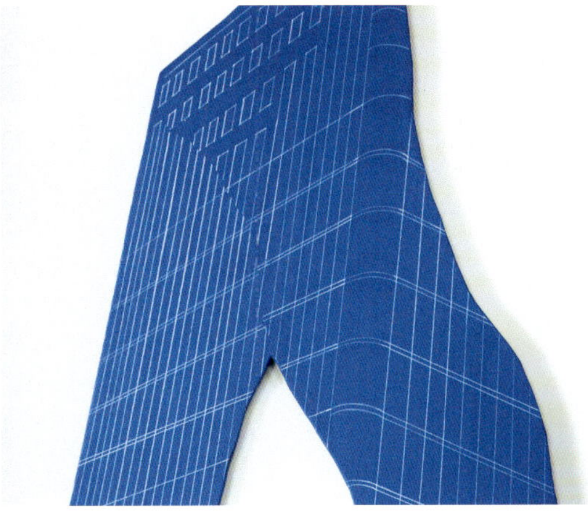

Praneet Soi

The Guild

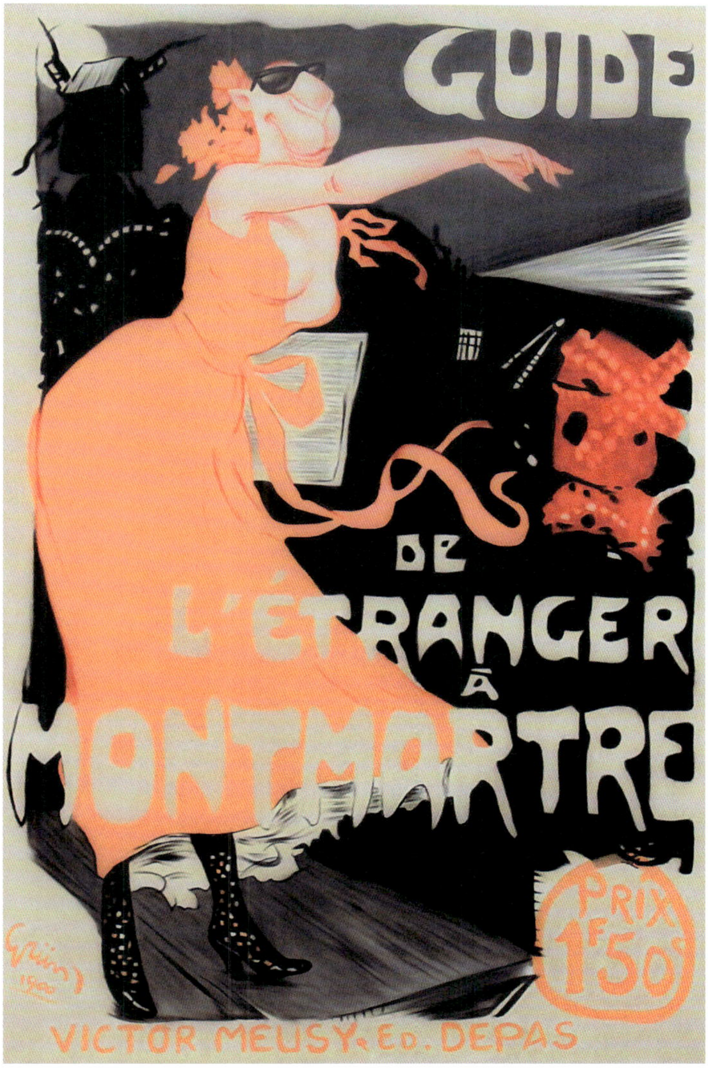

Zhou Tiehai

ShanghART

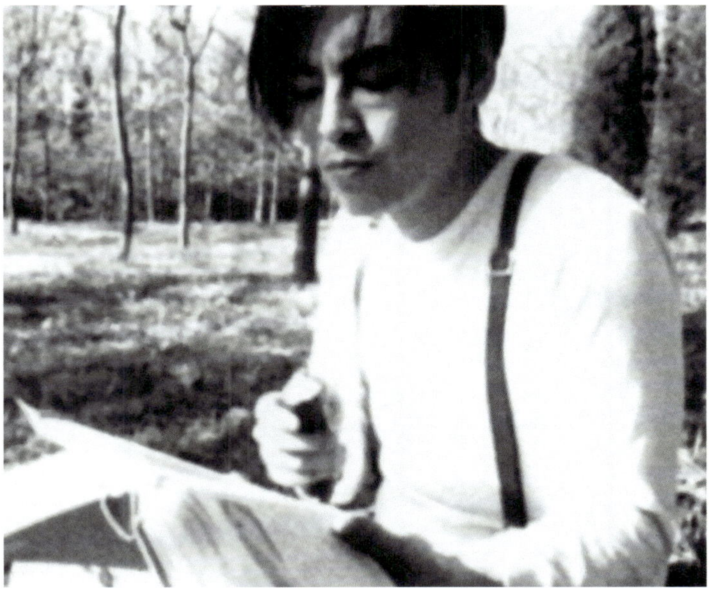

Li Ran

Aike-Dellarco (Discoveries)

Christine Macel

Chief Curator, Centre Pompidou, Paris

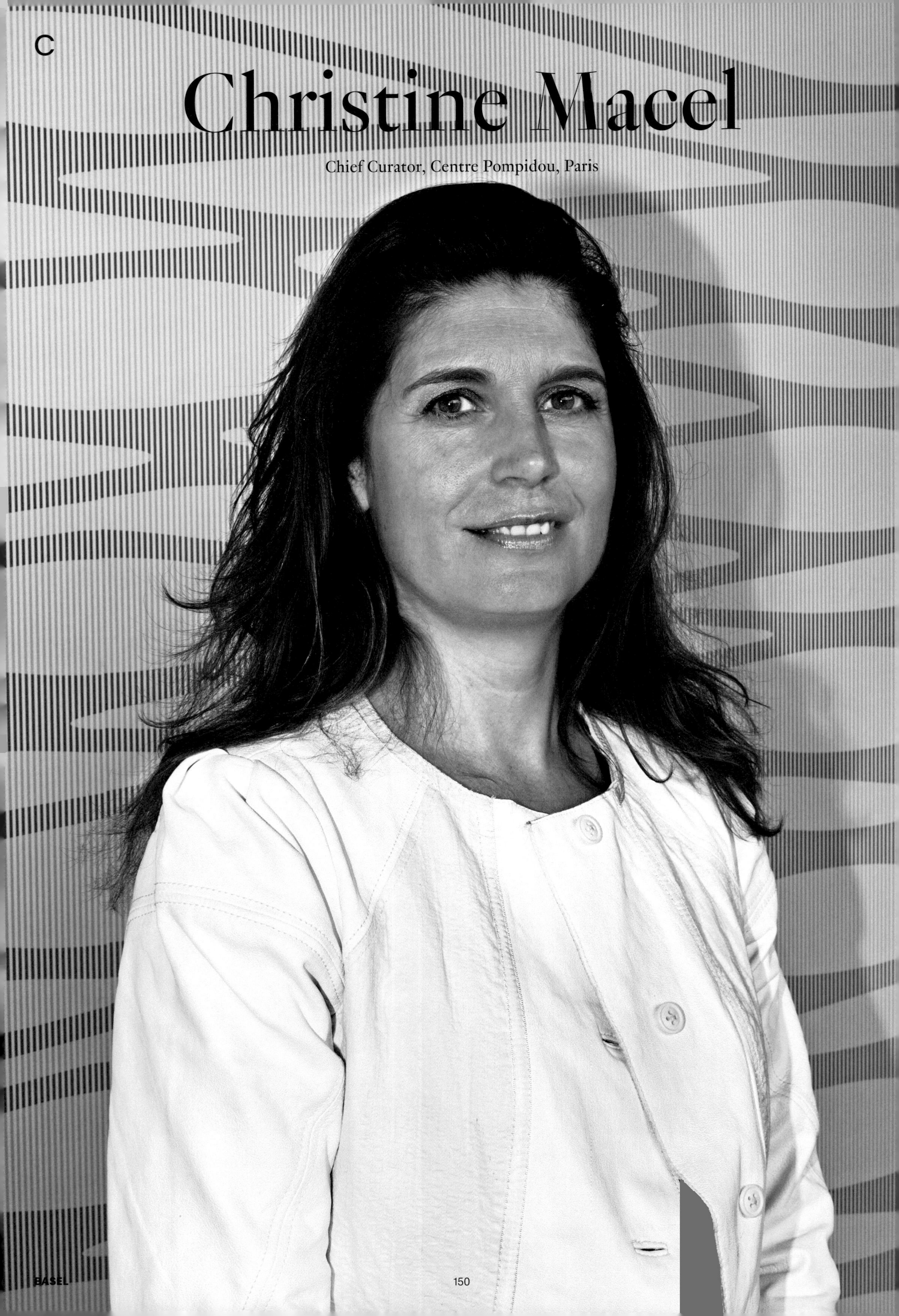

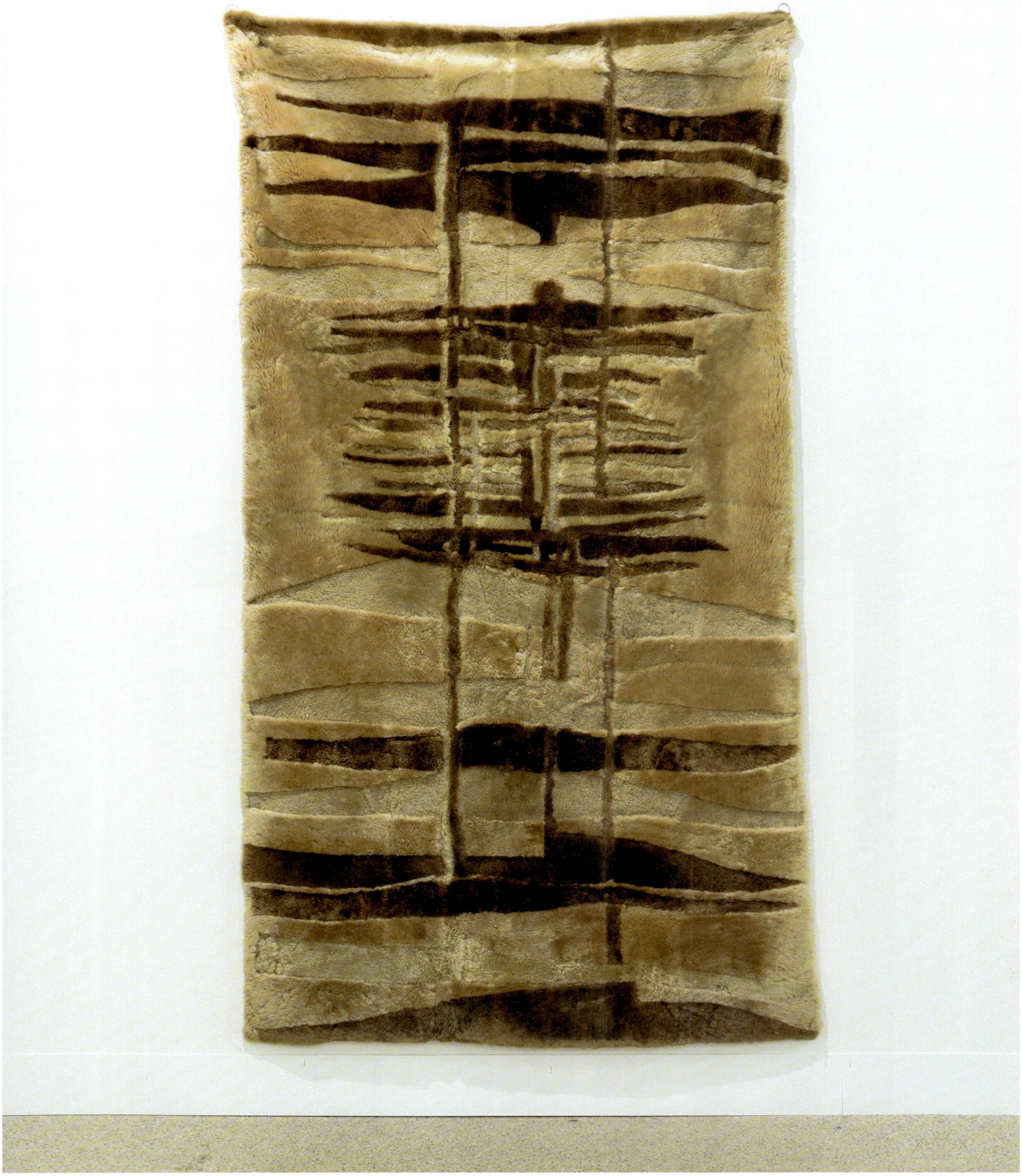

Carol Rama

La Pellicia, 1954
Galerie Isabella Bortolozzi

La Pelliccia (1954) qualifies as an unexpected artwork by this self-taught Turinese artist (the Golden Lion-winner at the 2003 Venice Biennale) who is nearly a hundred years old now, best known for her paintings and drawings that tend toward the erotic, and one could even say pornographic. This 1950s-tinted, furrow "drawing" on faux-fur reveals another aspect of Rama's palette.

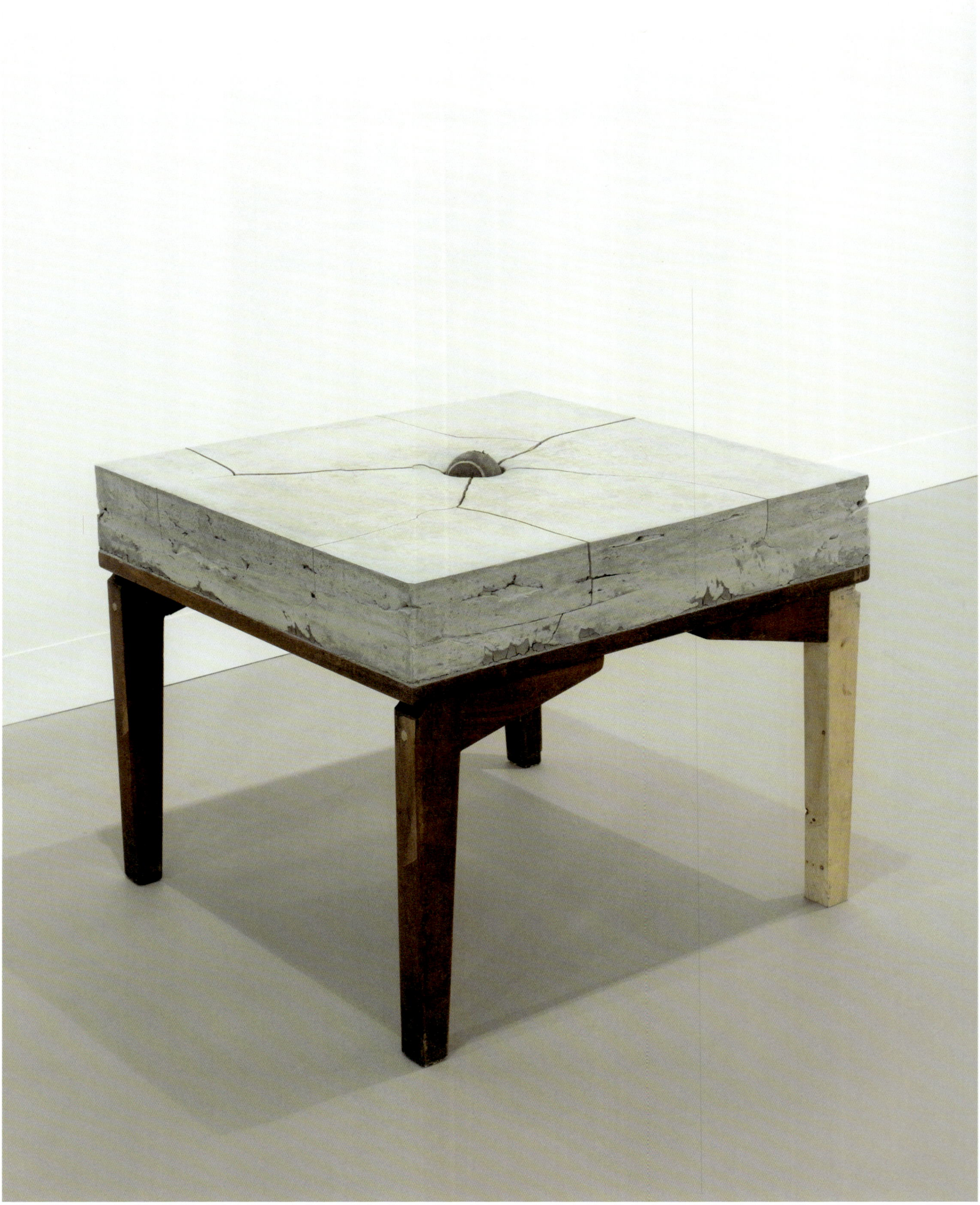

Adrián Villar Rojas

Los inocentes de los animales, 2013
Marian Goodman Gallery

What we usually see from this young Argentinian virtuoso are big dimension clay sculptures, such as his dropped column at the Tuileries in Paris or his sci-fi garden at the latest documenta in Kassel. All the poetic charm of his oeuvre is contained within this work, evoking fracture and irretrievable innocence, in the same manner as the title (which is also the title of his latest exhibition at MoMA PS1 in New York).

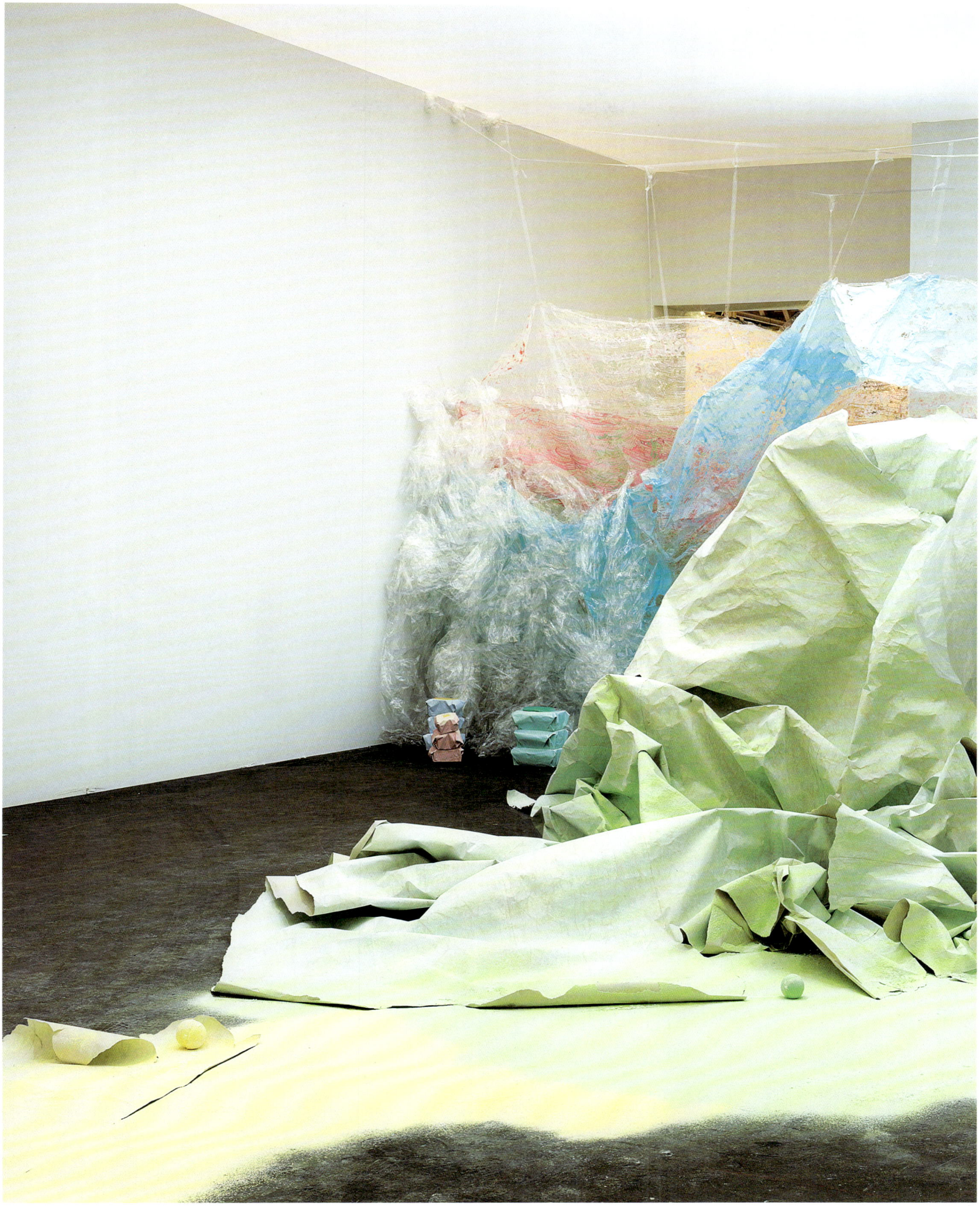

Karla Black

Doesn't Care In Words, 2011
Galerie Gisela Capitain and Stuart Shave/Modern Art (Unlimited)

This Scottish artist excels in haptic installations, a mix between sculpture and painting, halfway between the physicality and sensuality of materials, of moisturizing lotion and cosmetic powder. The materials that speak for themselves, as the title she has chosen reveals: *Doesn't Care in Words*.

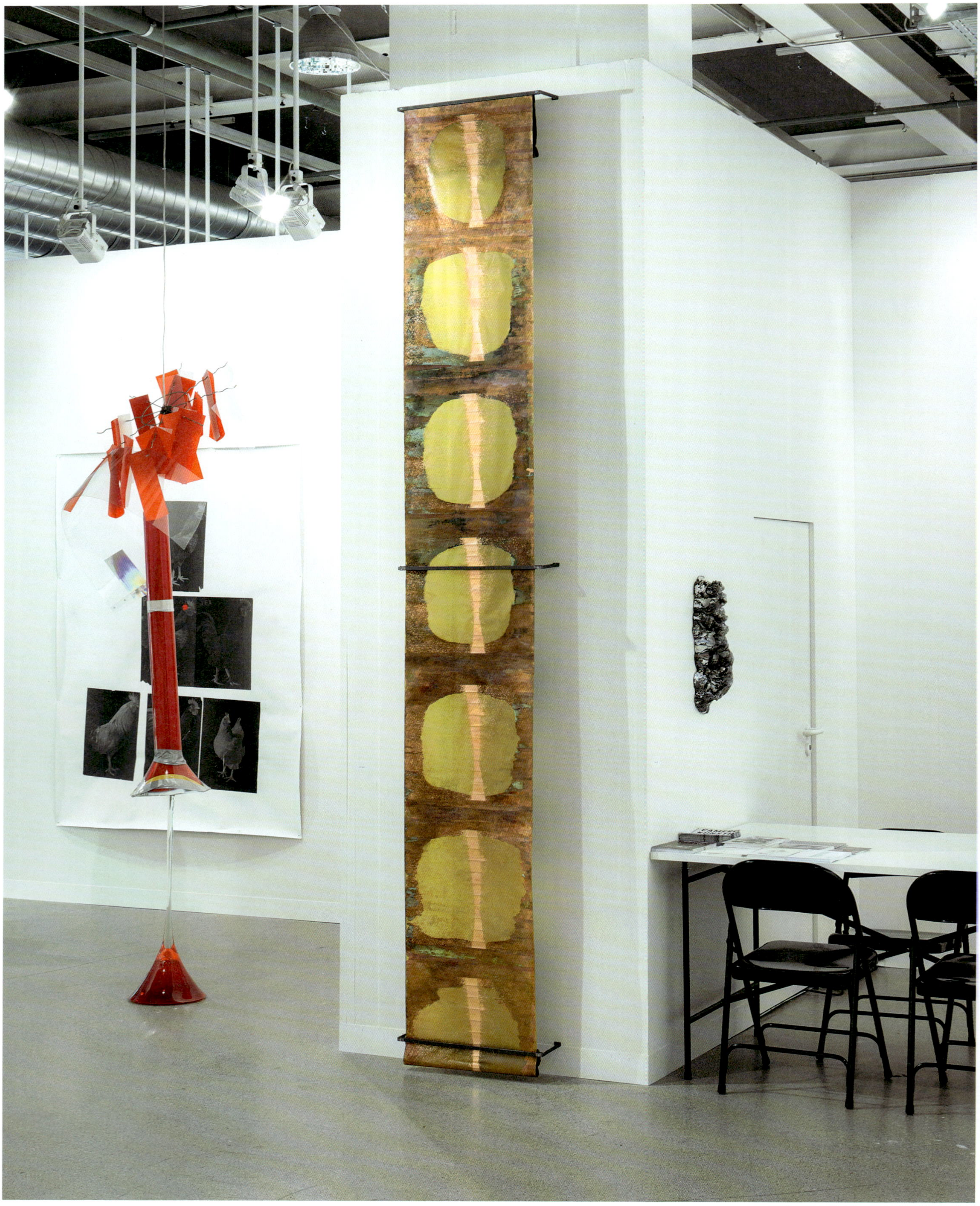

Sam Lewitt

Weak Local Lineament (ICF 05), 2013
Galerie Buchholz

Sam Lewitt (b. Los Angeles), completed the Whitney Program and is based in Brooklyn. He is best known for his "ferrofluid" installation at the last Whitney Biennial, which uses material found in computers. With a strong appetite for communication systems and technology, his piece comprises a partially corroded strip of copper, at once minimal yet sophisticated.

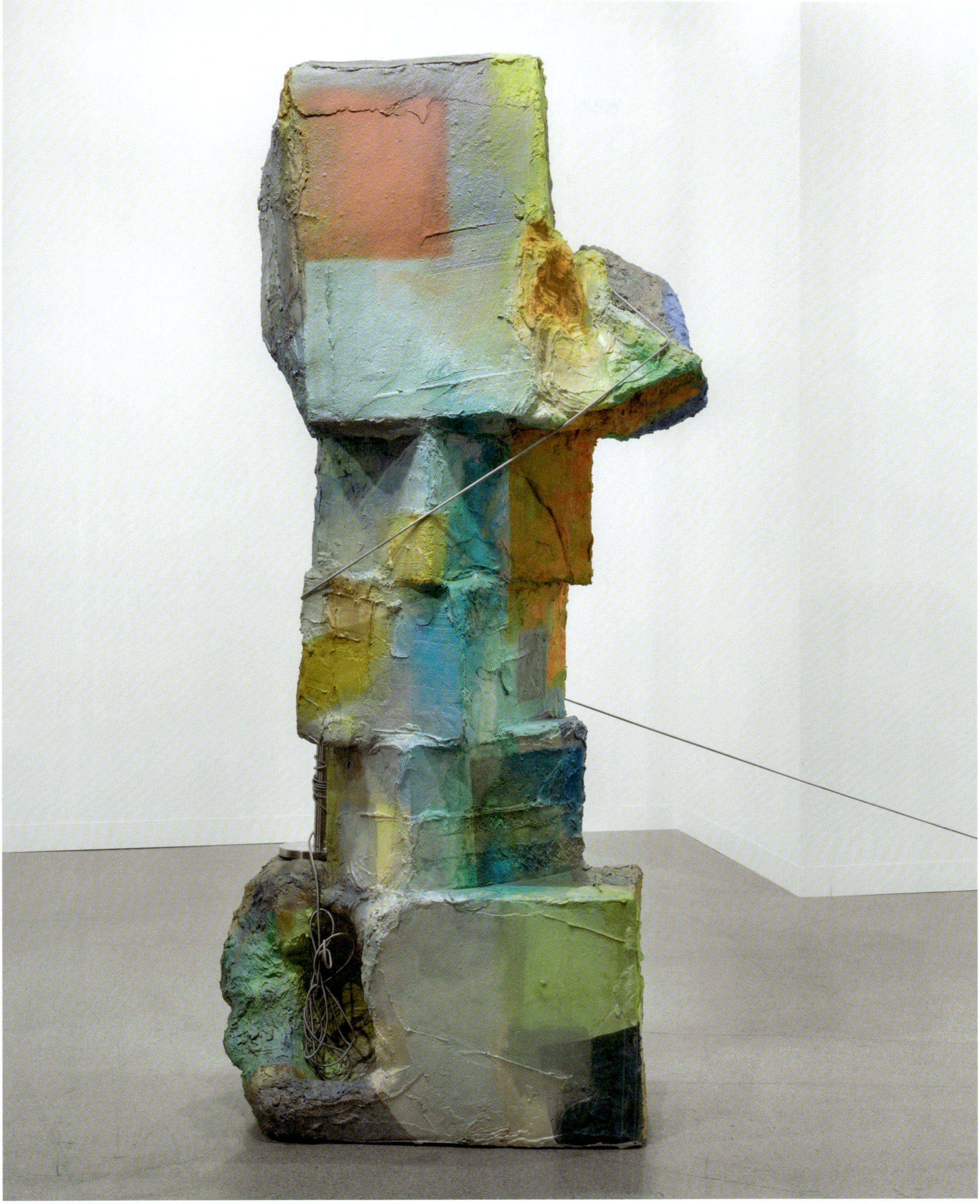

Rachel Harrison

XLT Footbed, 2013
Greene Naftali Gallery

The assembled polychromatic sculptures of New Yorker Rachel Harrison, combined with objects or images in an undeniable efficiency, play with various signs of contemporary culture as well as post-Pop sculpture, in the manner of Franz West or Isa Genzken. This assemblage integrates the museum's safety equipment in the work itself: the result is brilliant and hilarious.

Adam Szymczyk

Artistic Director of documenta 14, Kassel,
and Former Director, Kunsthalle Basel

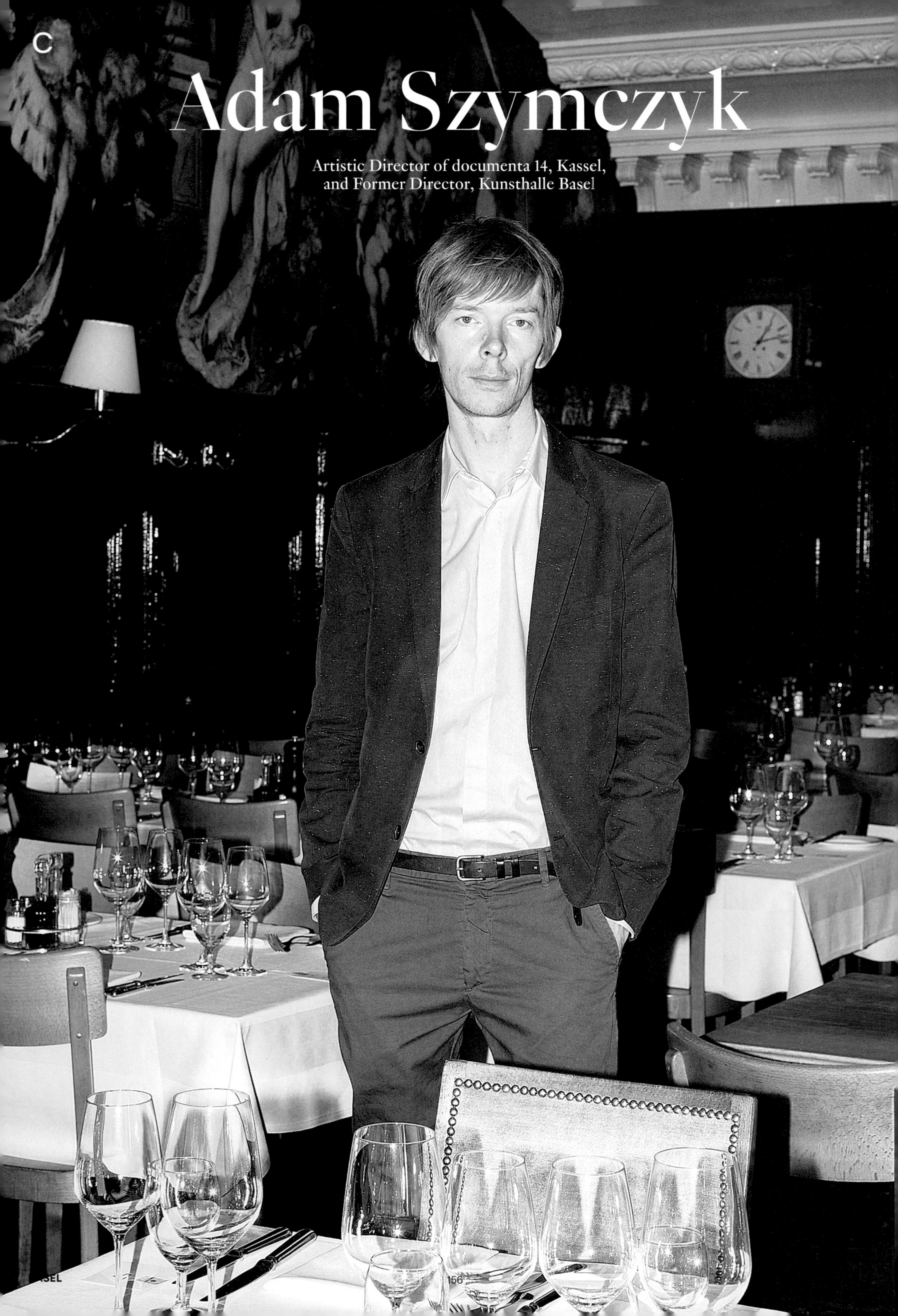

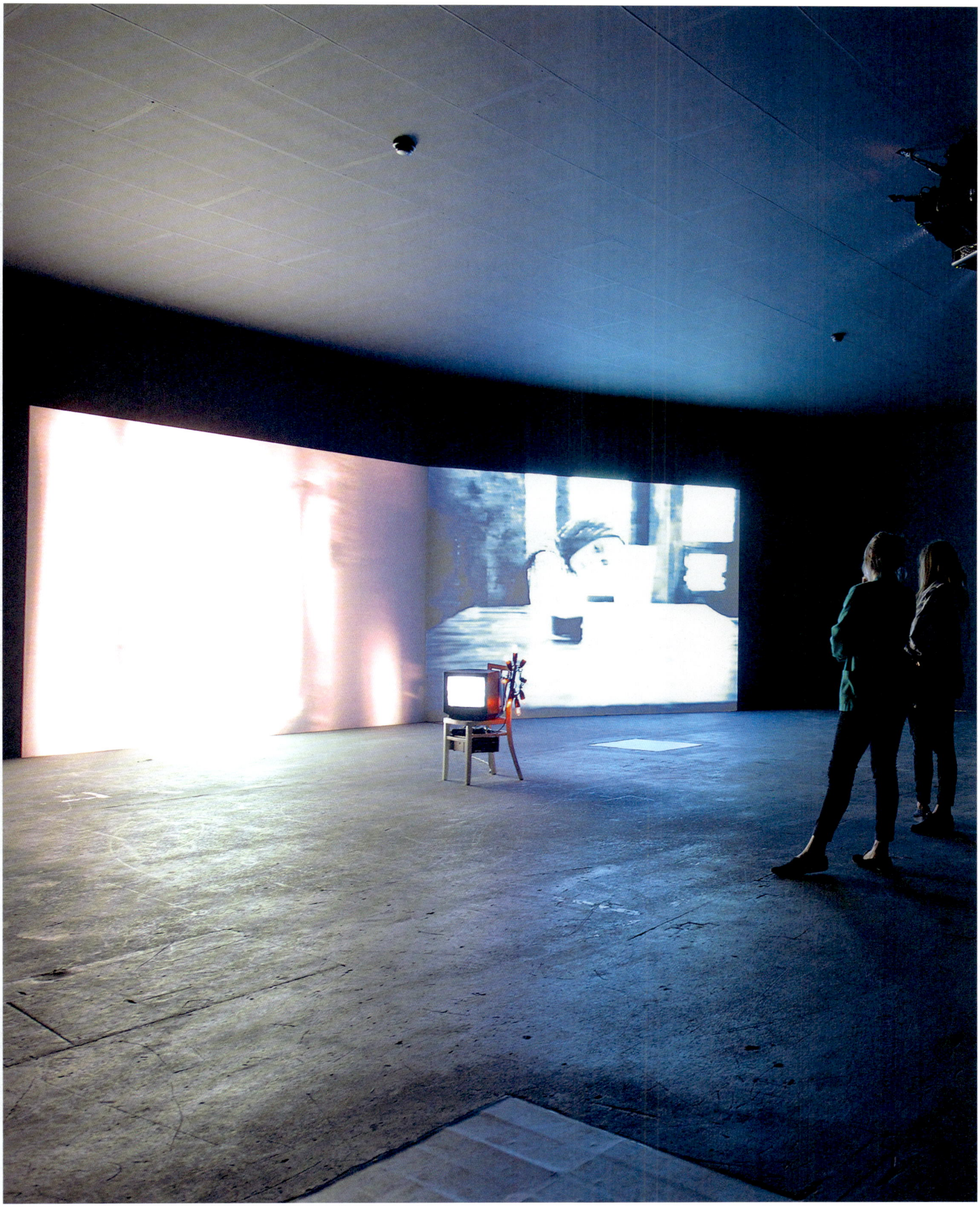

Susan Hiller

Wild Talents, 1997
Timothy Taylor Gallery (Unlimited)

Susan Hiller's video installation featuring Hollywood film excerpts of children demonstrating supernatural powers juxtaposed with documentary footage of believers during the pilgrimage to the sanctuary of Medjugorje in Herzegovina, where the Virgin Mary is said to appear, was the eeriest of all.

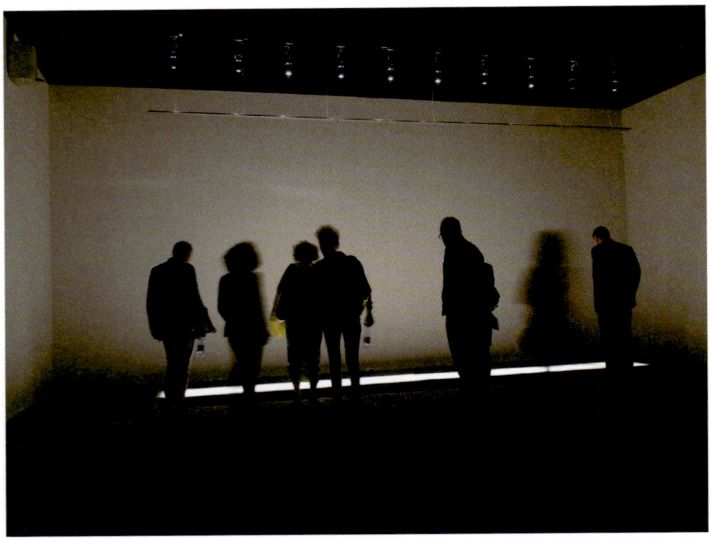

Teresa Margolles

Plancha, 2010
Galerie Peter Kilchmann (Unlimited)

Teresa Margolles' sculpture with water dripping and hissing on hot metal plates was thrilling, both minimal and mournful.

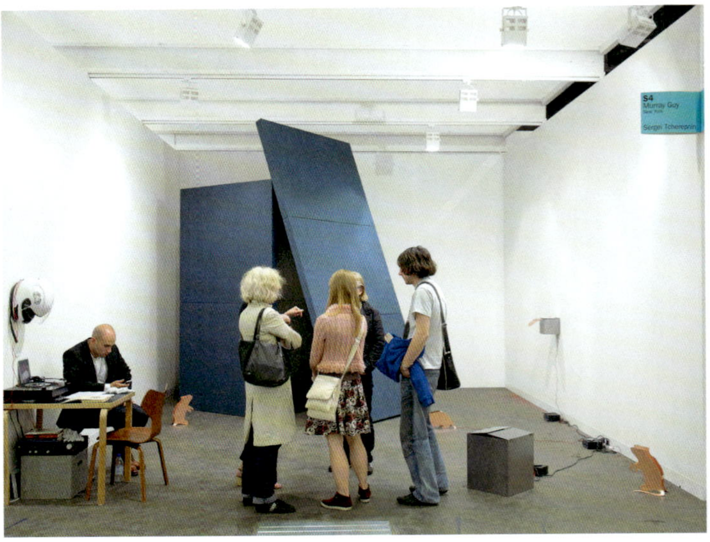

Sergei Tcherepnin

Pied Piper, Part Two: Ringing Rocks, 2013
Murray Guy (Statements)

An intriguing sound installation by musician and artist Sergei Tcherepnin.

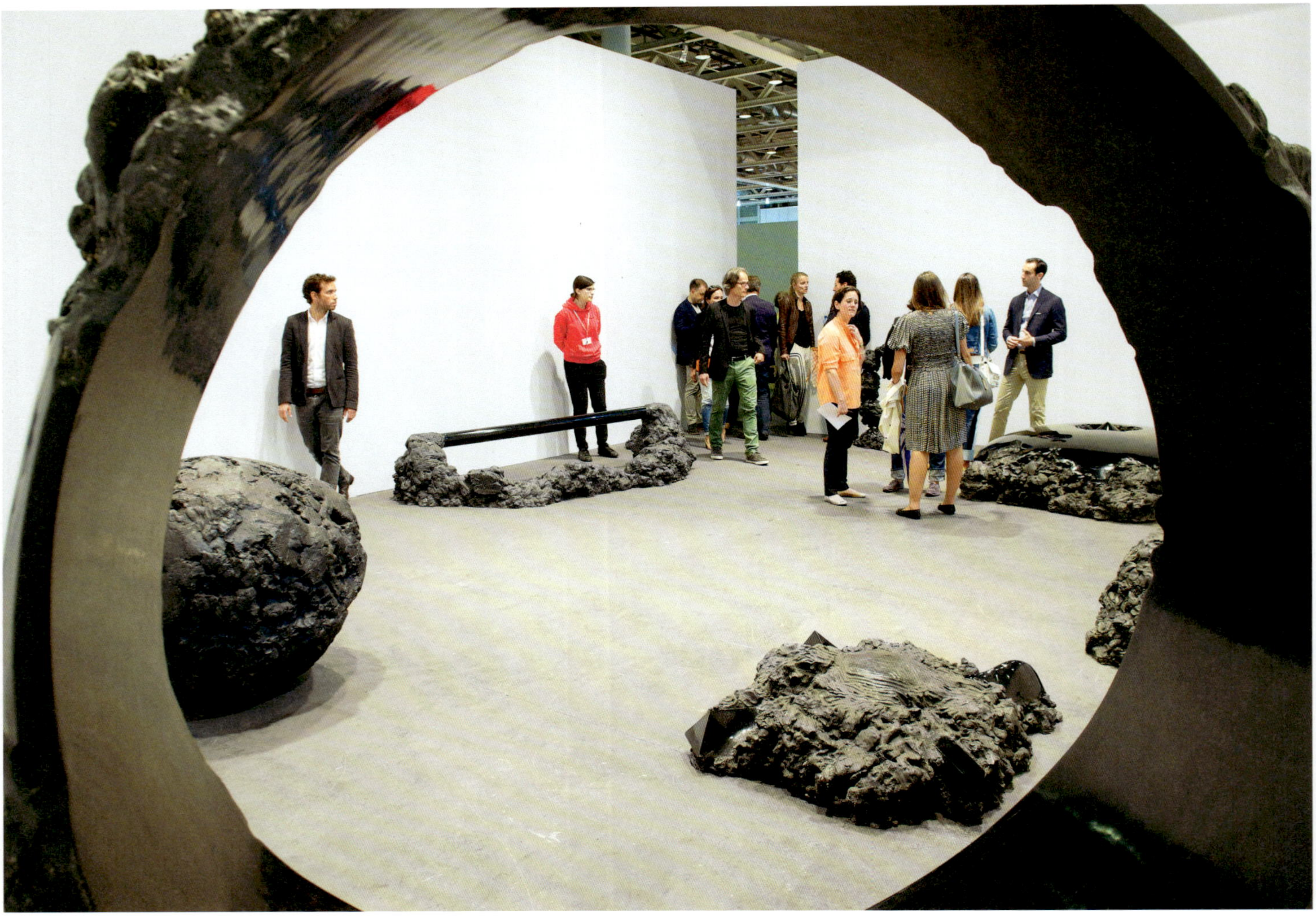

Nobuo Sekine

Phase of Nothingness–Black, 1977–1978
Blum & Poe (Unlimited)

A great, silent, and powerful ensemble of Nobuo Sekine's black sculptures.

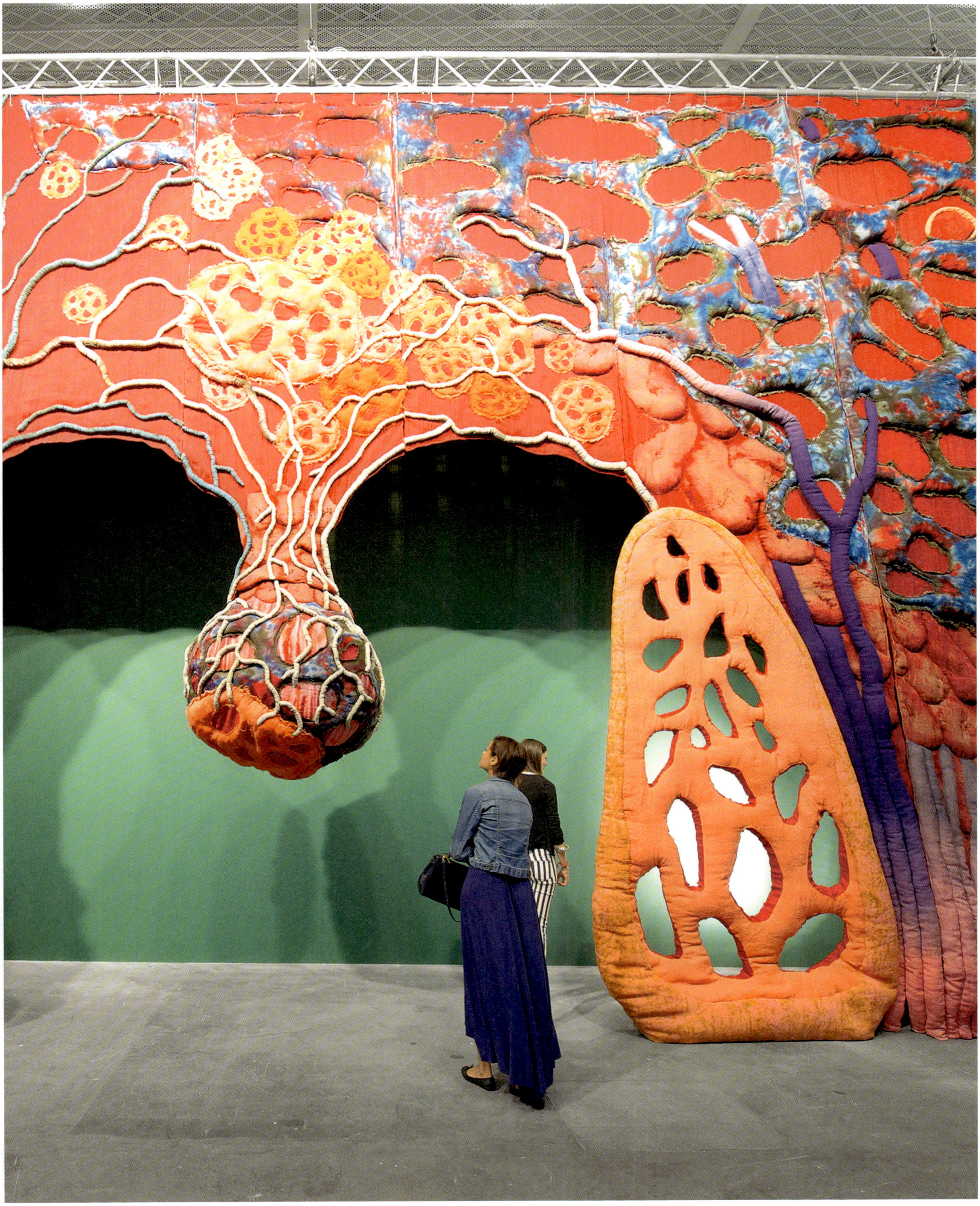

Piotr Uklański

Untitled (Open Wide), 2012
Massimo De Carlo and Gagosian Gallery (Unlimited)

Piotr Uklański's giant palate/throat tapestry at the rear end of the Unlimited sector made me nostalgic about Polish tapestry art that flourished during the Communist era.

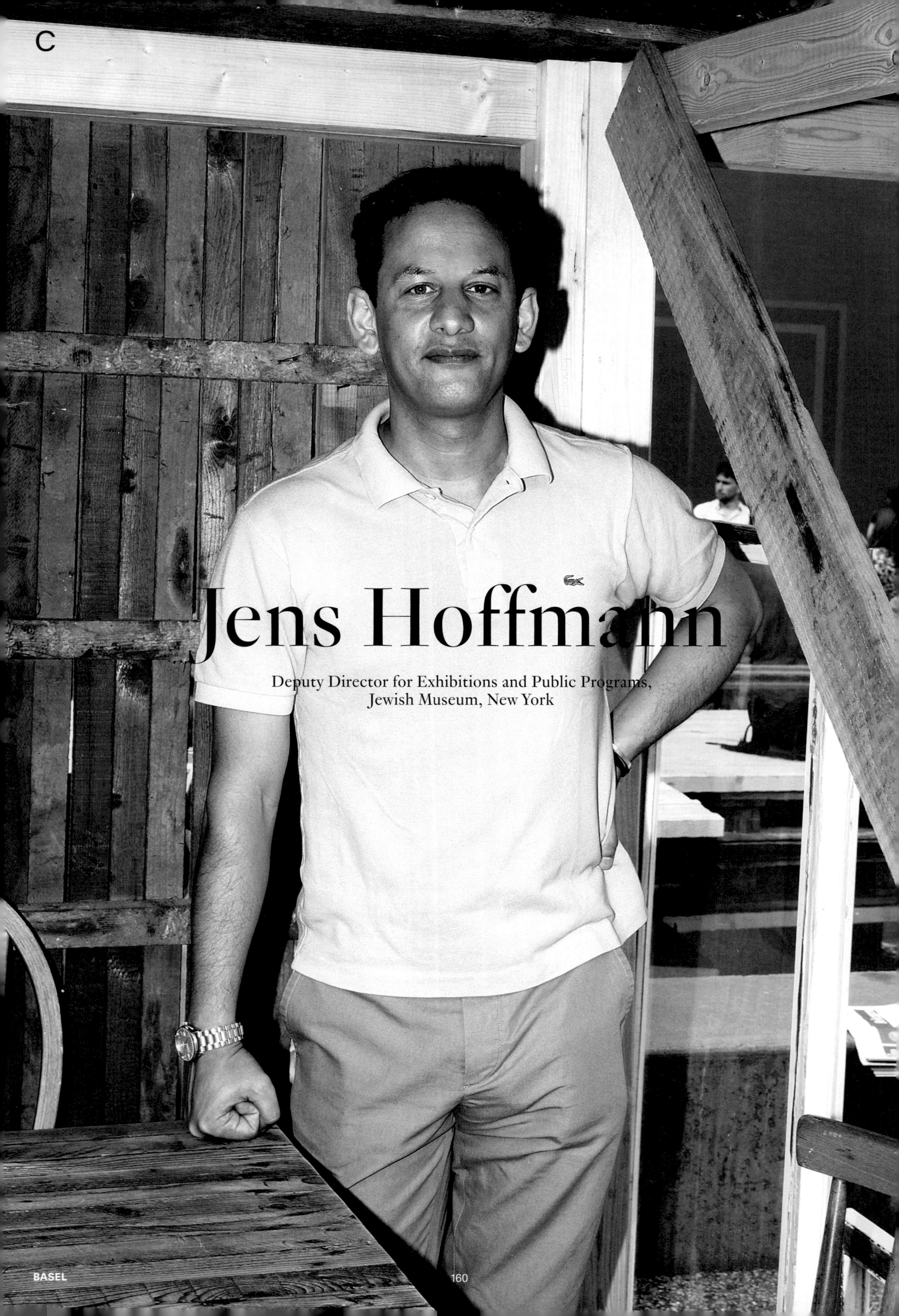

Jens Hoffmann

Deputy Director for Exhibitions and Public Programs,
Jewish Museum, New York

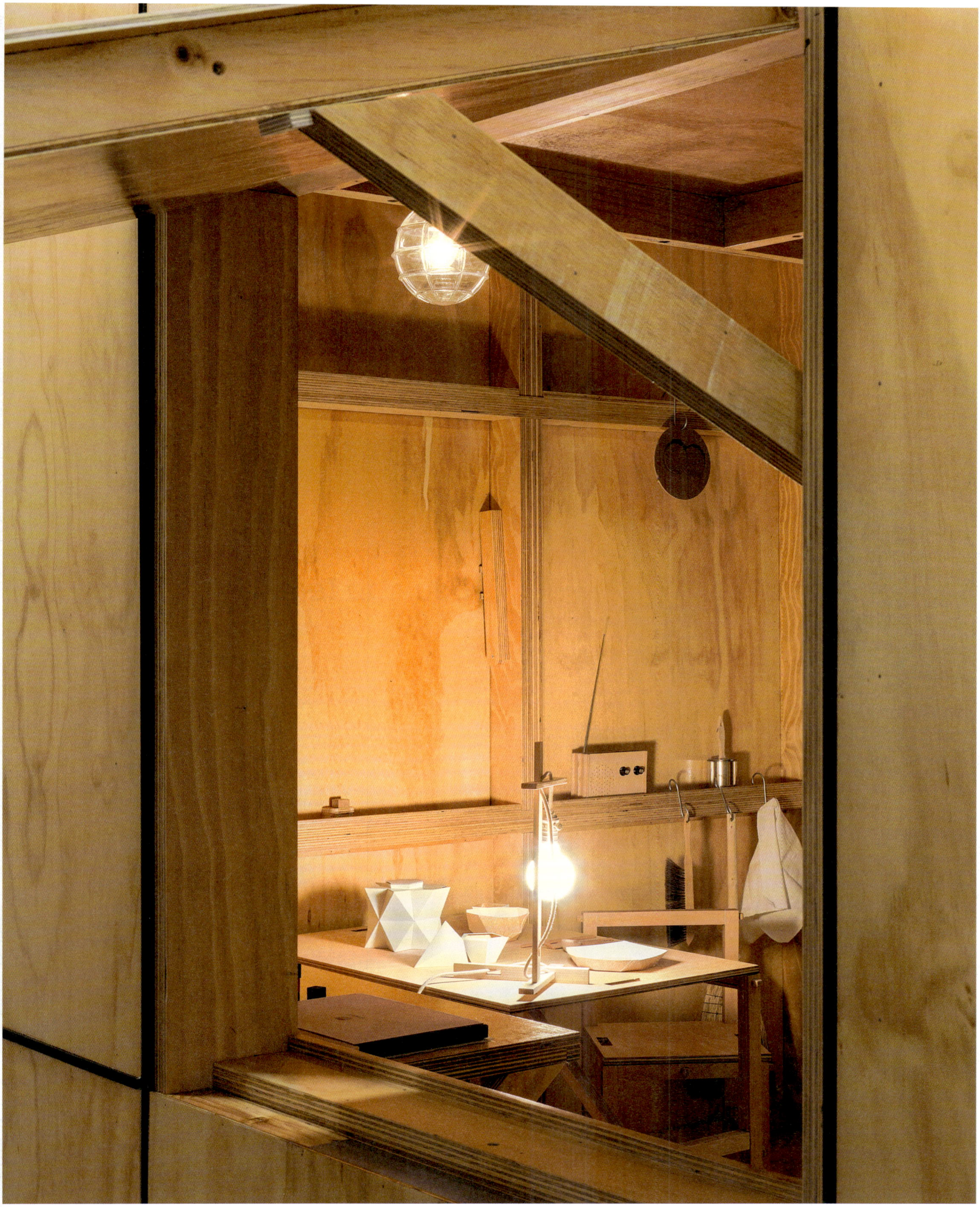

Mateo López

Casa Desorientada (Disoriented House), 2013
Casas Riegner (Statements)

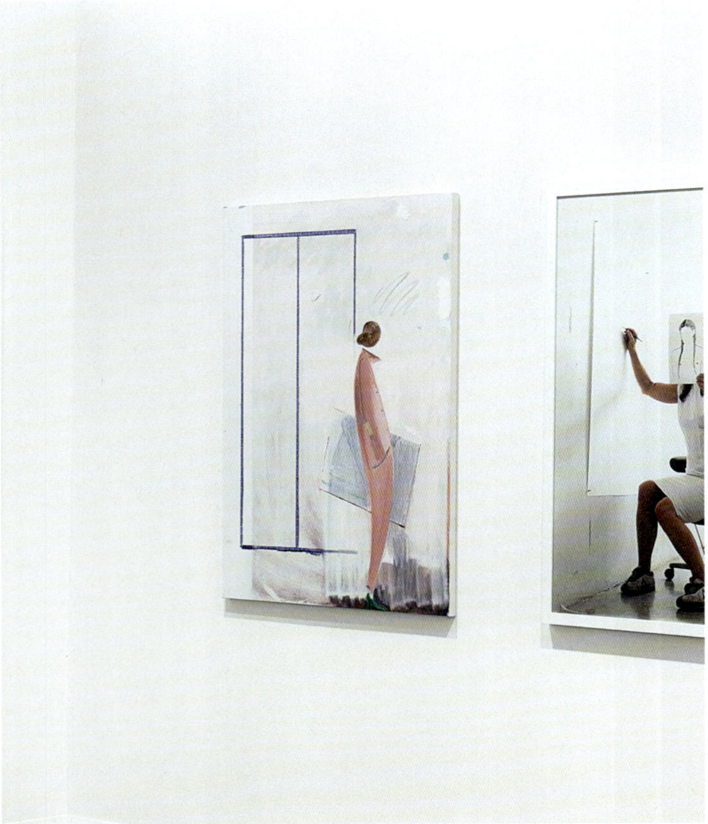

Sanya Kantarovsky

Marc Foxx Gallery (Feature)

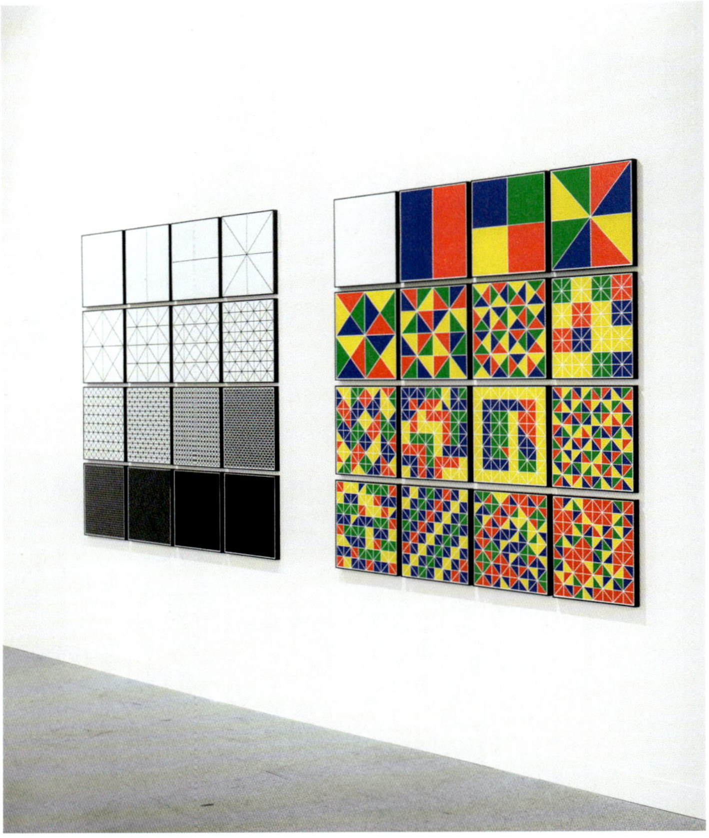

Eduardo Terrazas

Proyectos Monclova (Feature)

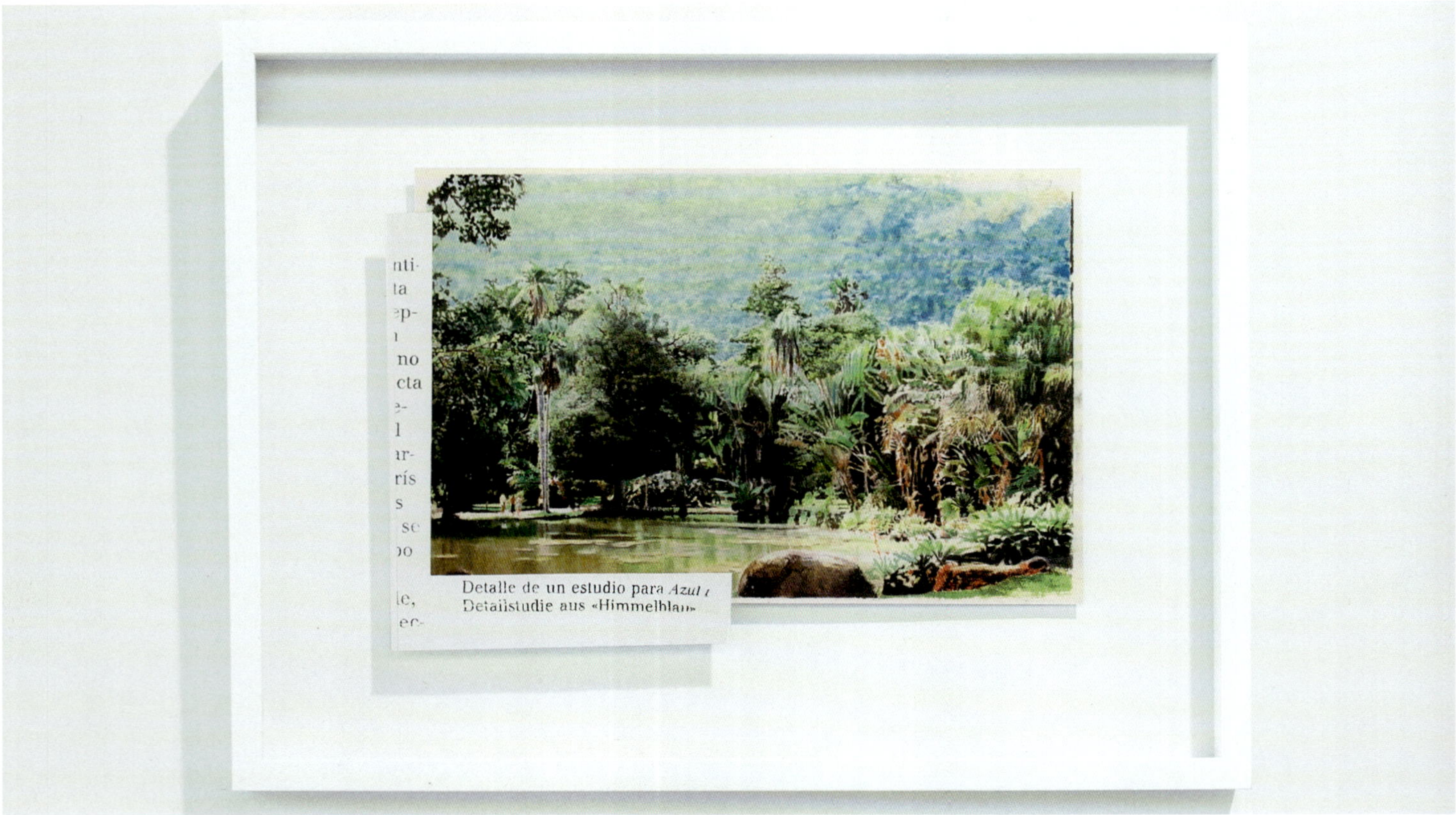

Juan Araujo

Cristina Guerra Contemporary Art

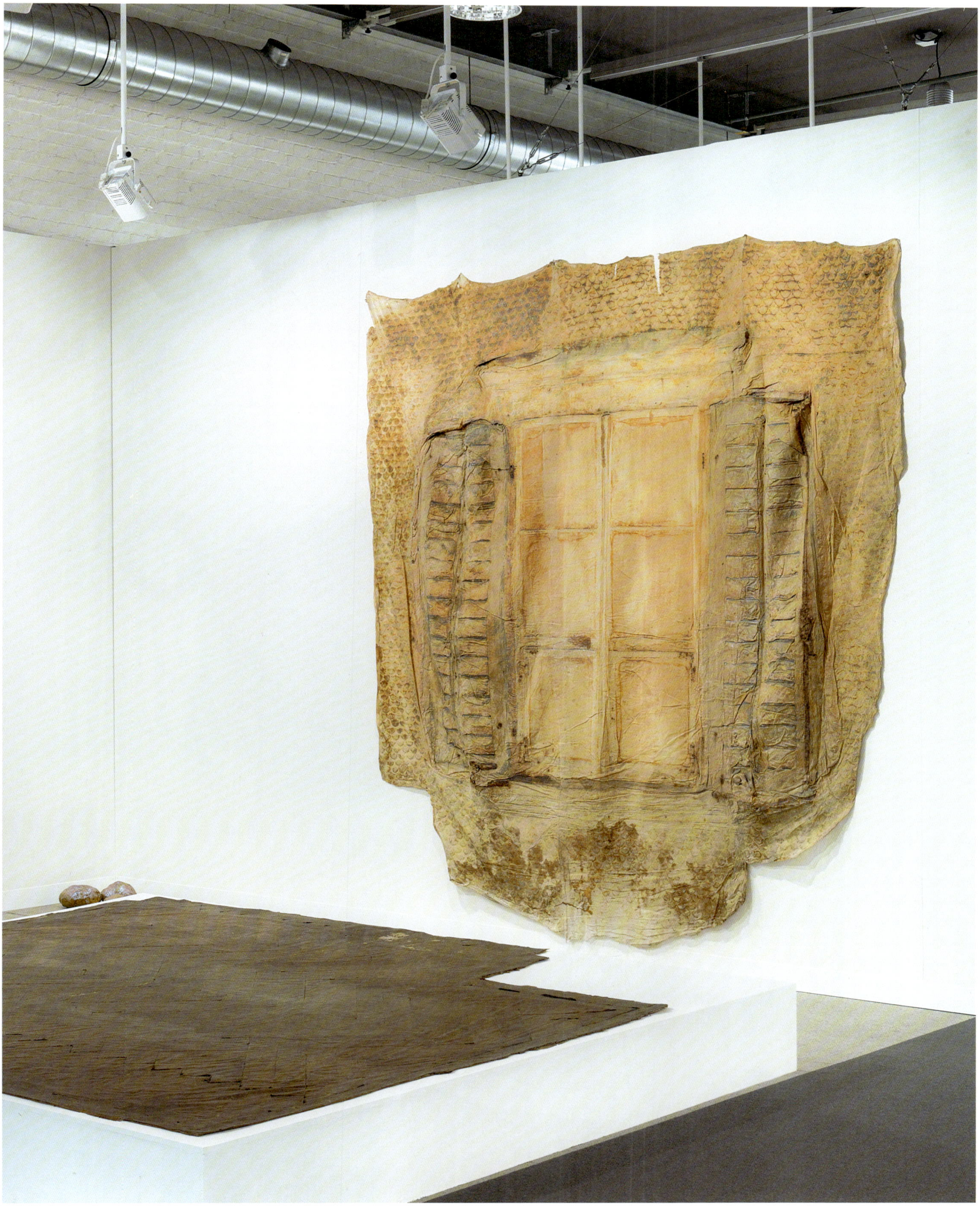

Heidi Bucher

Freymond-Guth Fine Arts (Feature)

Theodora Vischer

Senior Curator at Large, Fondation Beyeler, Basel

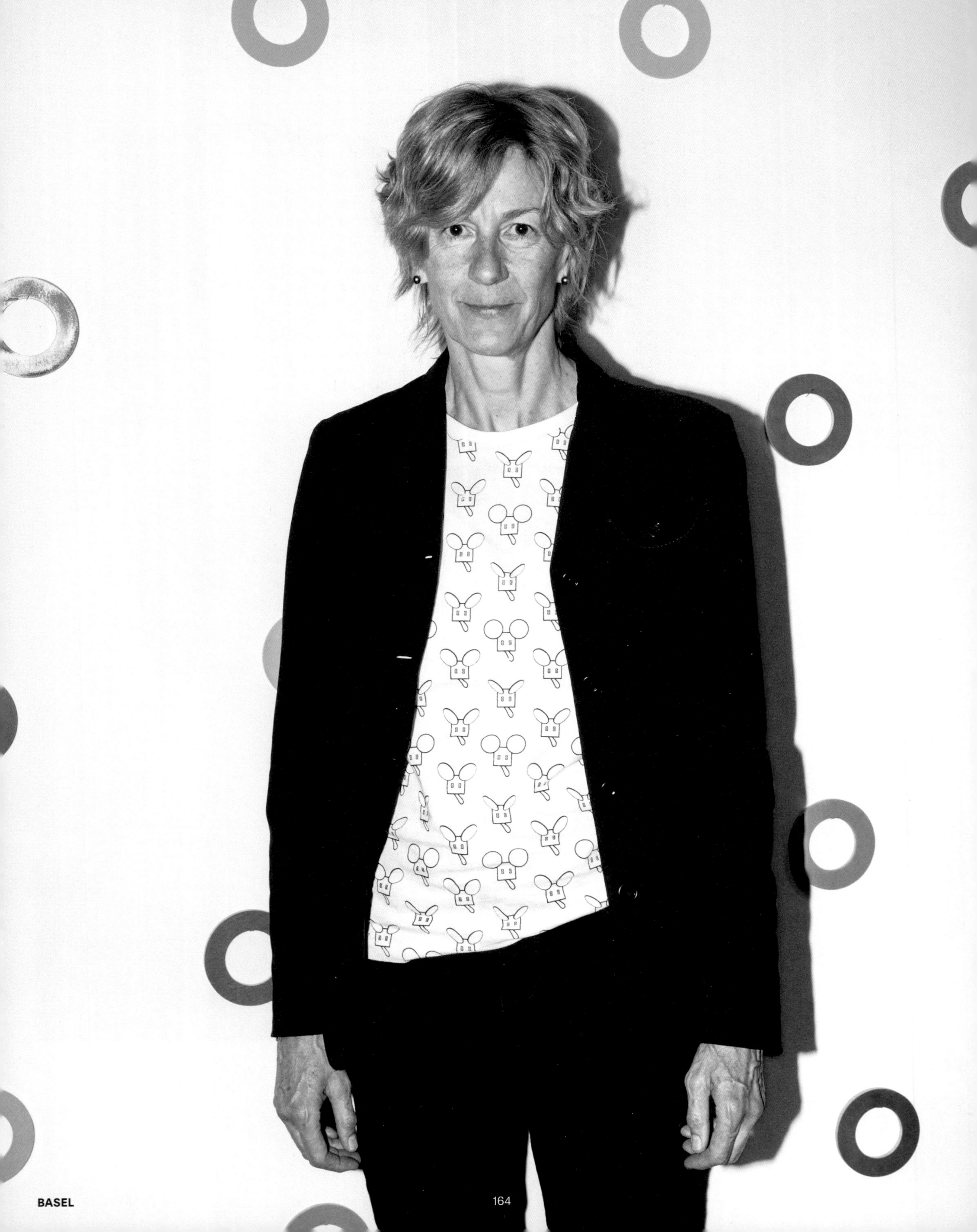

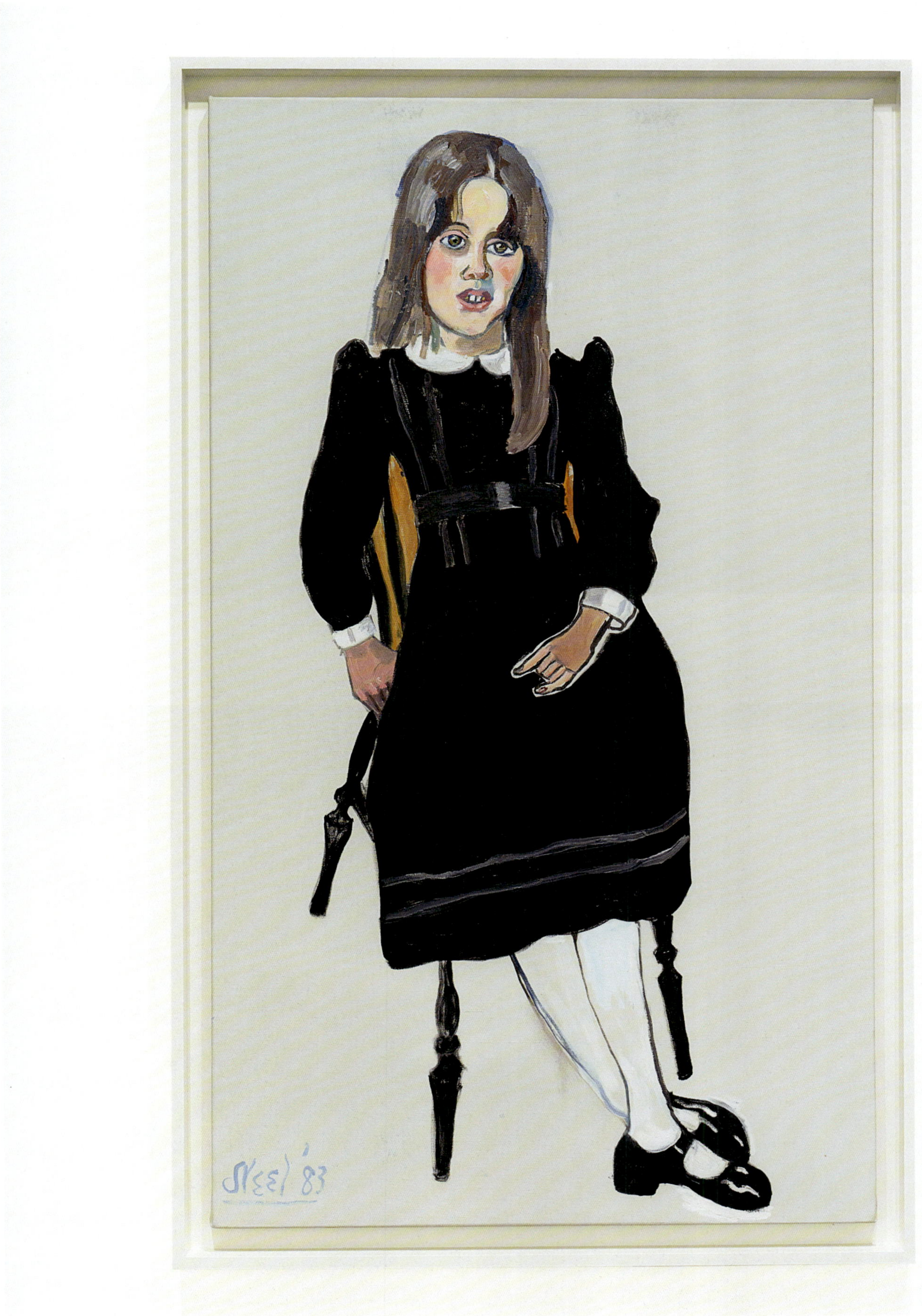

Alice Neel

Elizabeth, 1983
David Zwirner

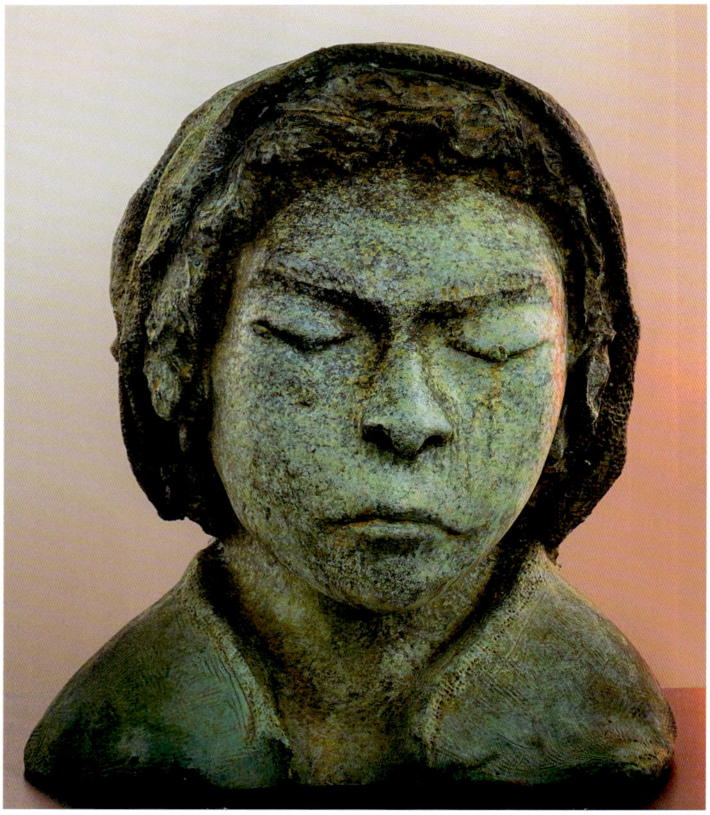

Thomas Schütte

The Third Sister, 2013, Galerie Pietro Spartà (Feature)

Robert Ryman

Dominique Lévy Gallery

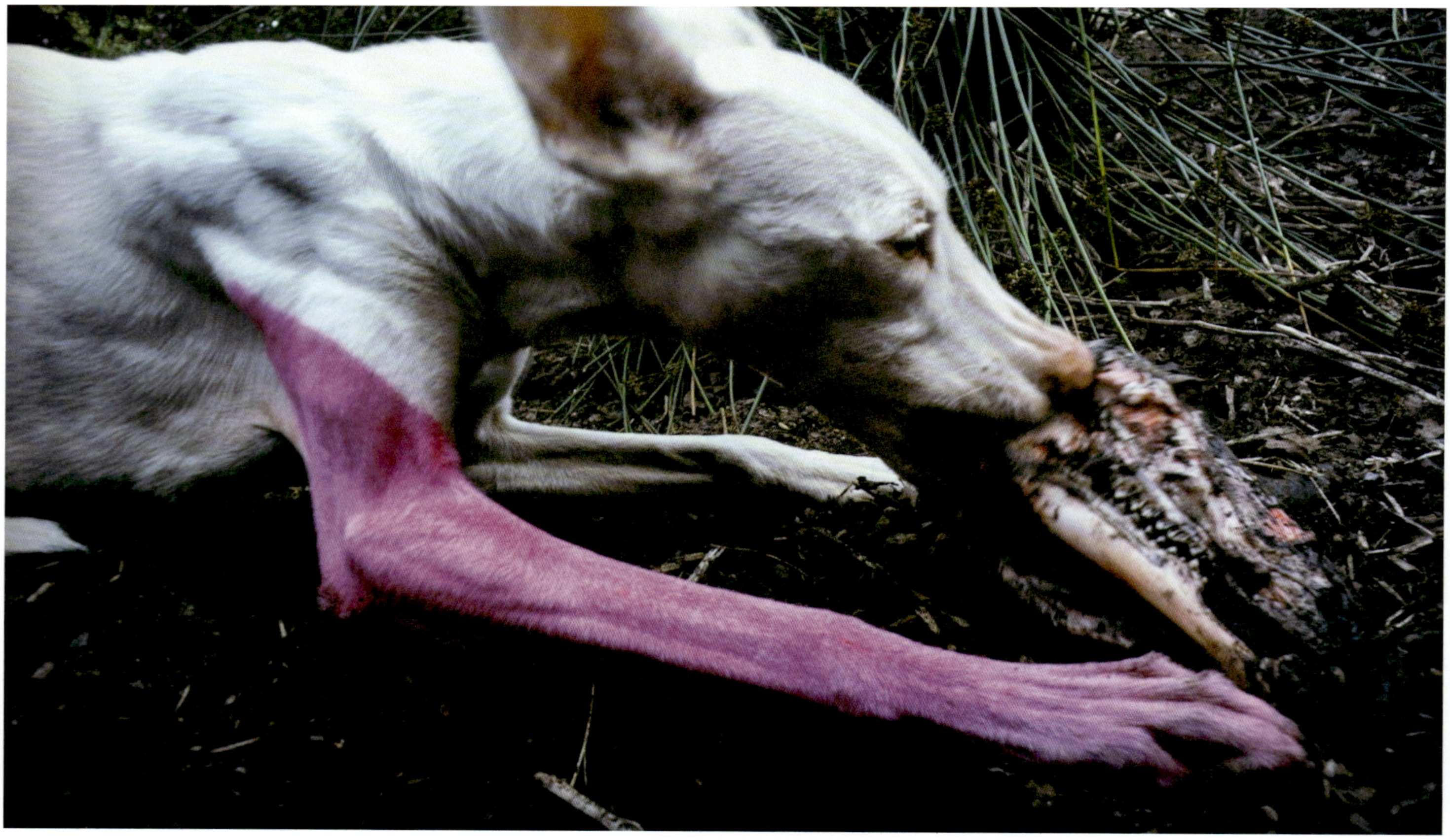

Pierre Huyghe

Untilled Film, 2013
Marian Goodman Gallery and Esther Schipper
(Unlimited)

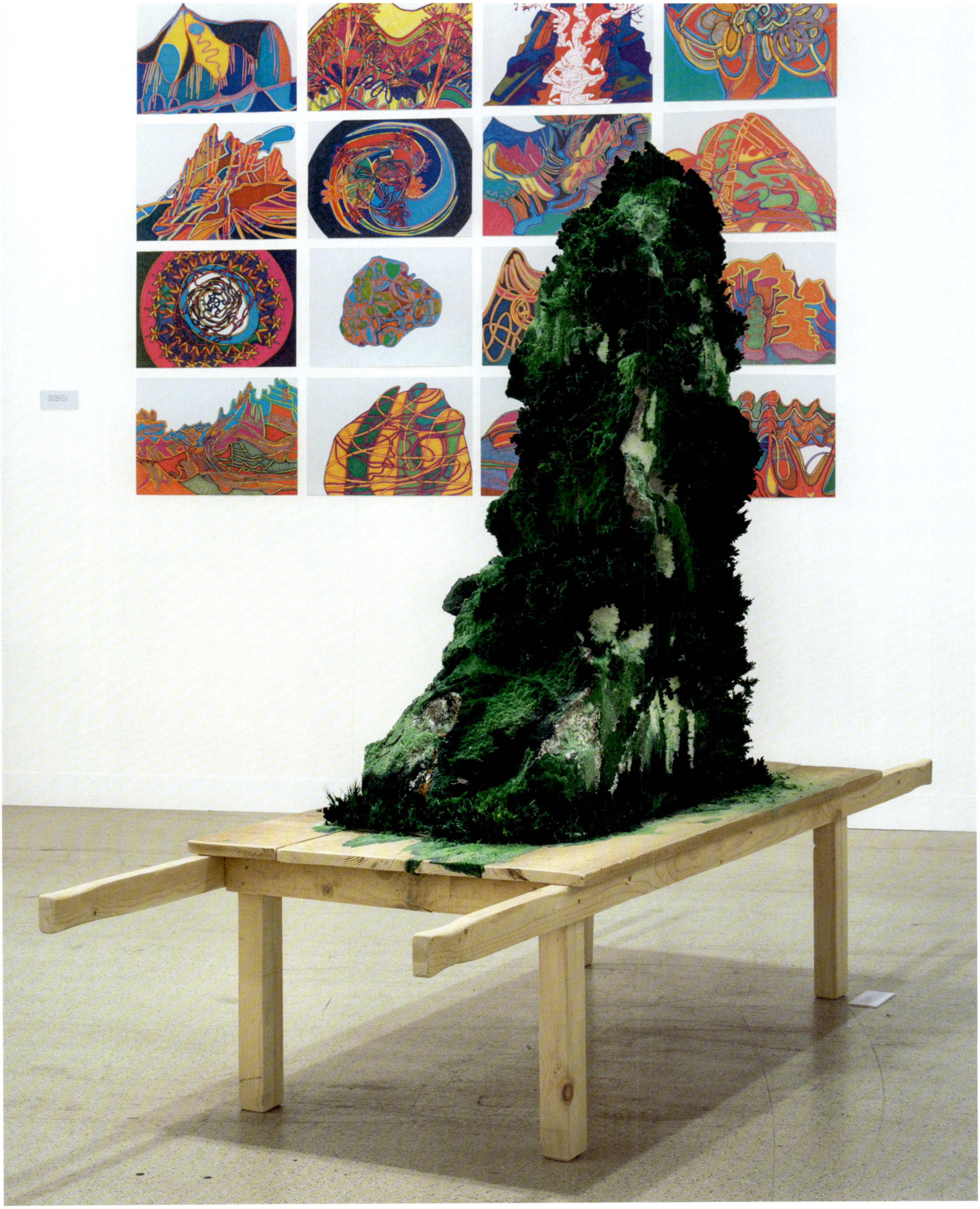

Steiner/Lenzlinger

Stampa

Gabriela Salgado

Curator, London, and Co-curator, La Otra Bienal 2013 (Bogotá)

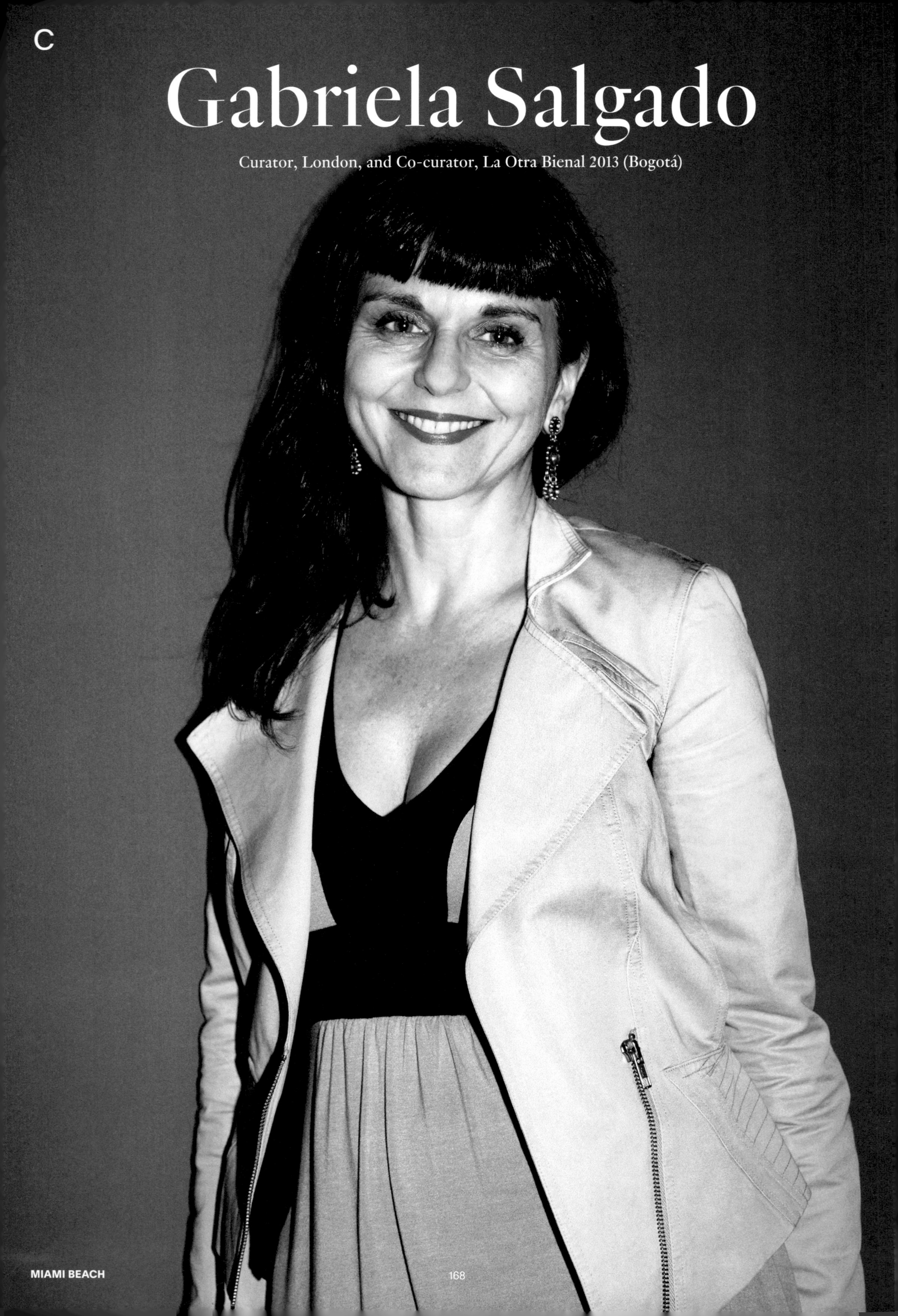

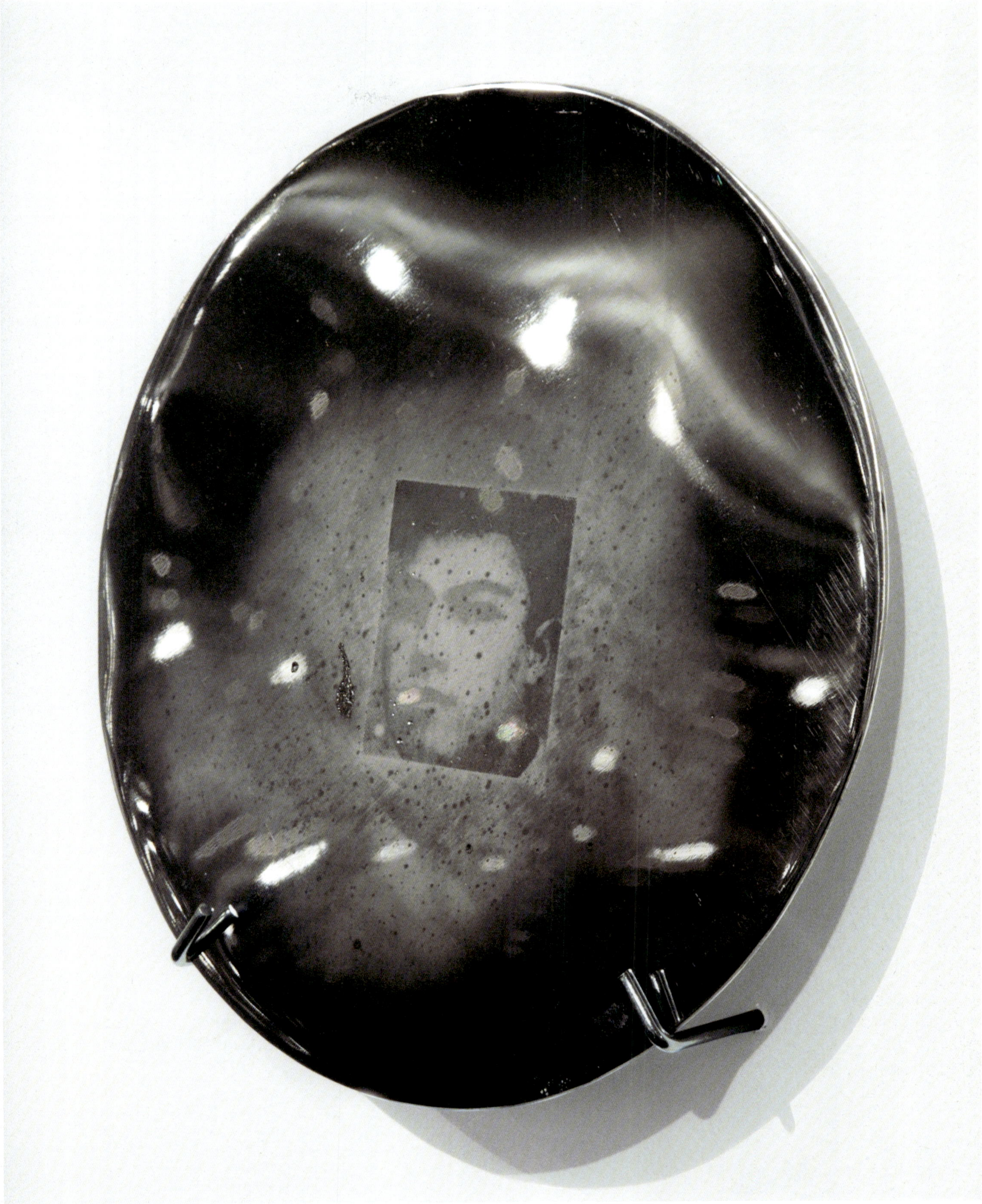

Oscar Muñoz

Aliento (Breath), 1995
UBS Collection, UBS Lounge

This wall-based work is a powerful metaphor for life and death: as we approach the 12 polished steel discs and breathe onto their surfaces, an intriguing image emerges—the photographs, rescued from newspaper obituaries, render an anonymous face that disappears as we inhale, revealing our own mortality.

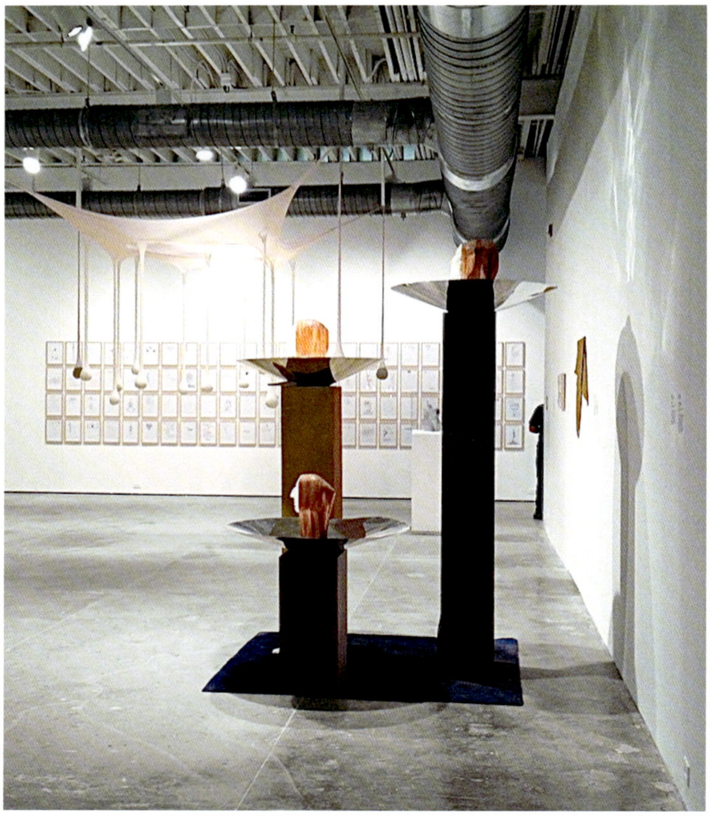

Permission to Be Global

Latin American Art from the Ella Fontanals-Cisneros Collection
Cisneros Fontanals Art Foundation (CIFO), Design District, Miami

An exciting exhibition articulated around four thematic sections served as a platform to present woks in all mediums by some of the most significant Latin-American artists. Featuring five decades of production, this collaboration with MFA Boston aspired to insert Latin-American art making into the Western canon.

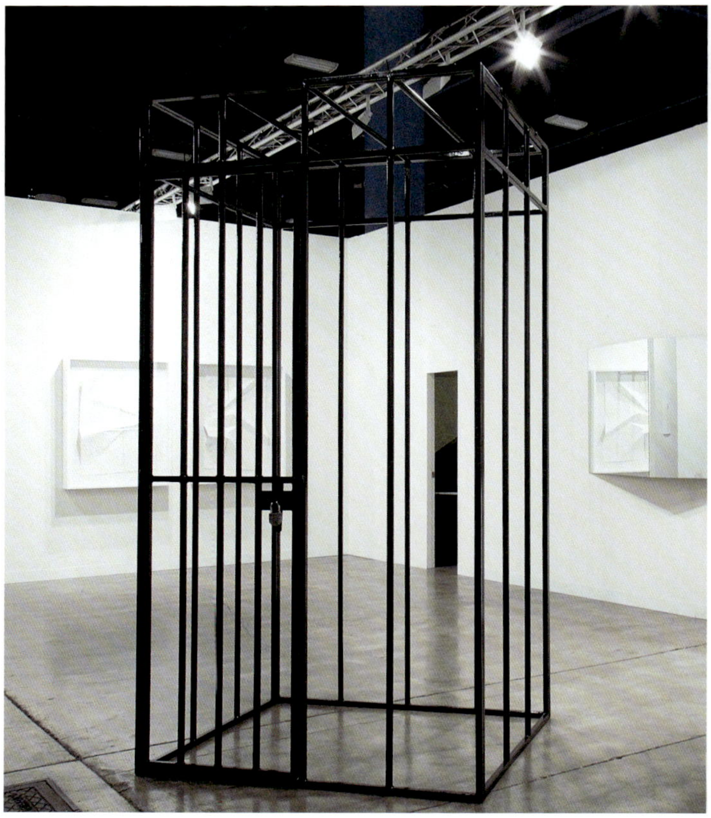

Ruth Benzacar Galeria de Arte

As a refreshing antidote to the usual bazaar-like format, the gallery offers a focused display of three Argentinean artists, covering emerging and established talents: Eduardo Basualdo's drawings and installation, Carlos Huffman's sci-fi paintings, and an intriguing site-specific work by Jorge Macchi.

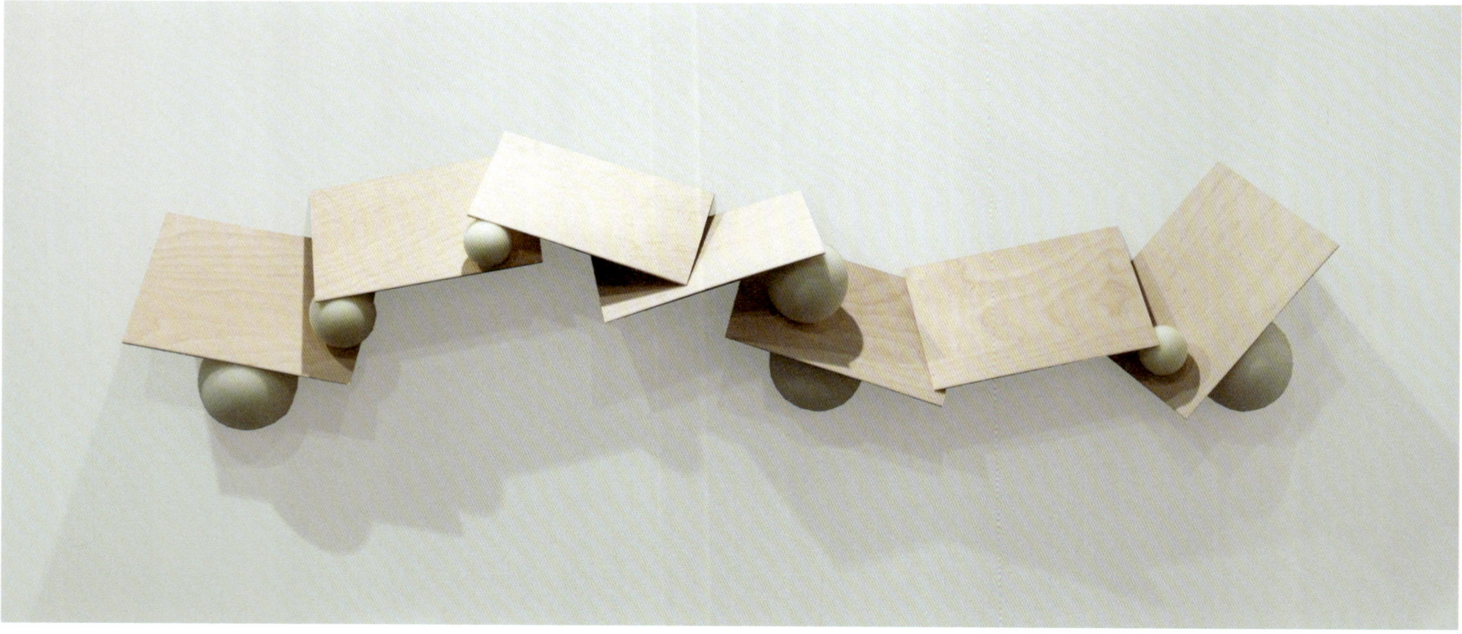

Carla Guagliardi

Partitura, 2013
Anita Schwartz Galeria de Arte (Nova)

Framed as a pristine historical overview of three generations of Brazilian artists dealing with Modernism from a local perspective, Carla Guagliardi's delicate sculptures, submitted to the effects of natural forces, evoke the experimental spirit inherited from influences as varied as Tropicalism and Constructivism.

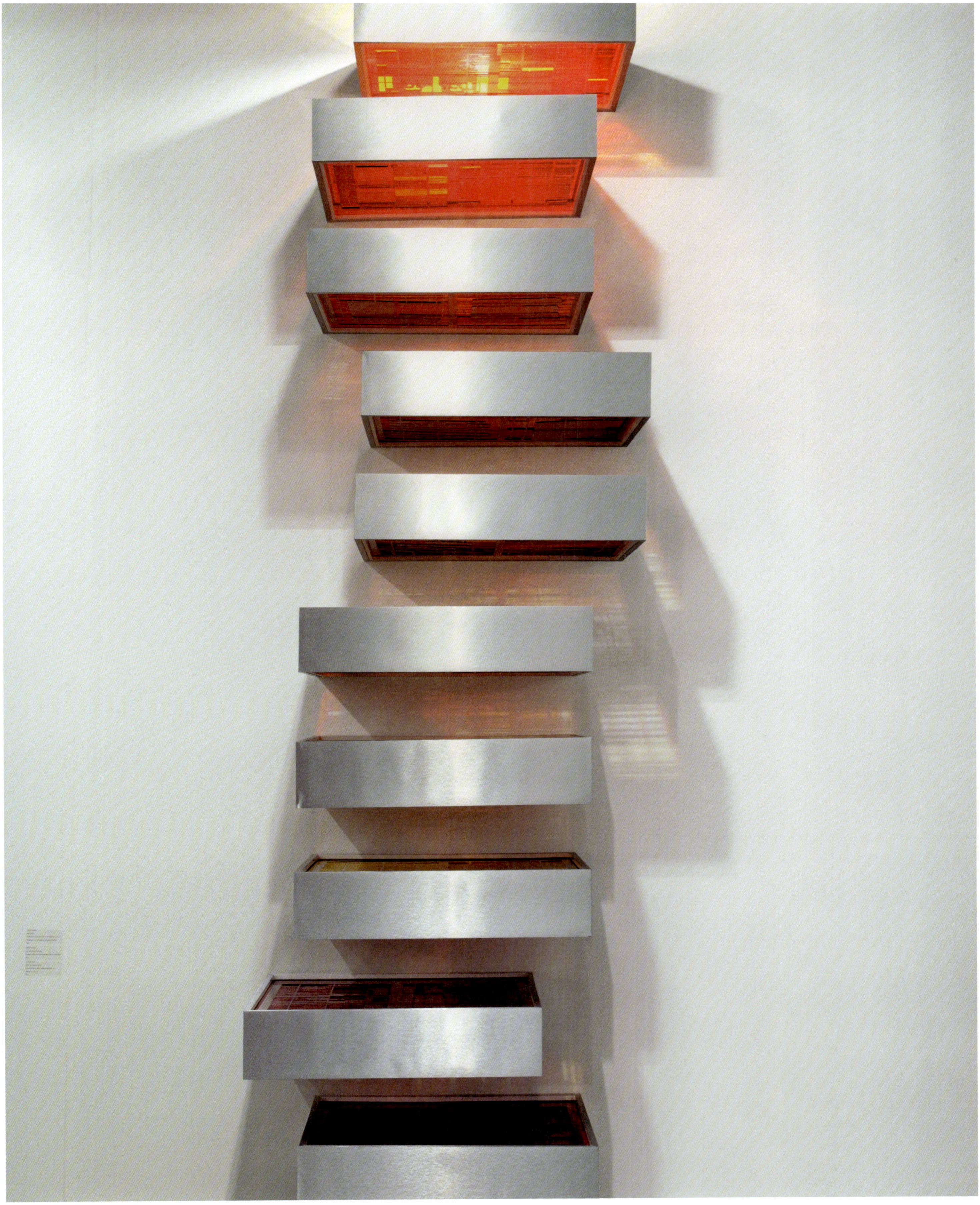

Voluspa Jarpa

What You See Is What It Is, 2013
mor charpentier (Nova)

With her take on Donald Judd's famous stacks of rectangular boxes, Voluspa Jarpa's new work revisits recently declassified CIA archives to implant traumatic political histories caused by South American dictatorships within the seemingly undisrupted beauty of Minimalism, conjuring up the contradictions of its ideology at a time of international crisis.

Daniel Baumann

Co-curator of the 2013 Carnegie International,
Director of the Adolf Wölfli Foundation, Pittsburgh and Basel

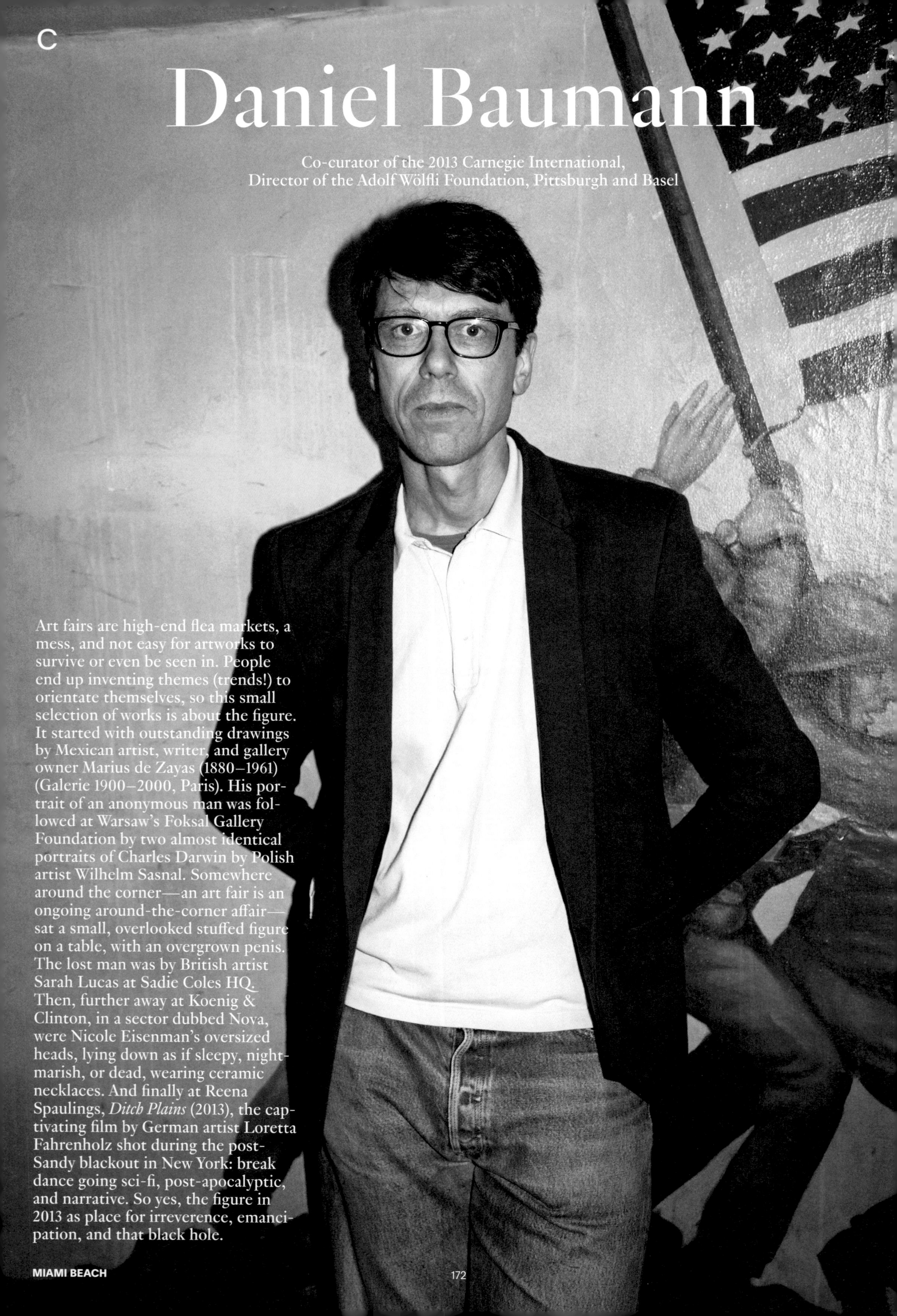

Art fairs are high-end flea markets, a mess, and not easy for artworks to survive or even be seen in. People end up inventing themes (trends!) to orientate themselves, so this small selection of works is about the figure. It started with outstanding drawings by Mexican artist, writer, and gallery owner Marius de Zayas (1880–1961) (Galerie 1900–2000, Paris). His portrait of an anonymous man was followed at Warsaw's Foksal Gallery Foundation by two almost identical portraits of Charles Darwin by Polish artist Wilhelm Sasnal. Somewhere around the corner—an art fair is an ongoing around-the-corner affair—sat a small, overlooked stuffed figure on a table, with an overgrown penis. The lost man was by British artist Sarah Lucas at Sadie Coles HQ. Then, further away at Koenig & Clinton, in a sector dubbed Nova, were Nicole Eisenman's oversized heads, lying down as if sleepy, nightmarish, or dead, wearing ceramic necklaces. And finally at Reena Spaulings, *Ditch Plains* (2013), the captivating film by German artist Loretta Fahrenholz shot during the post-Sandy blackout in New York: break dance going sci-fi, post-apocalyptic, and narrative. So yes, the figure in 2013 as place for irreverence, emancipation, and that black hole.

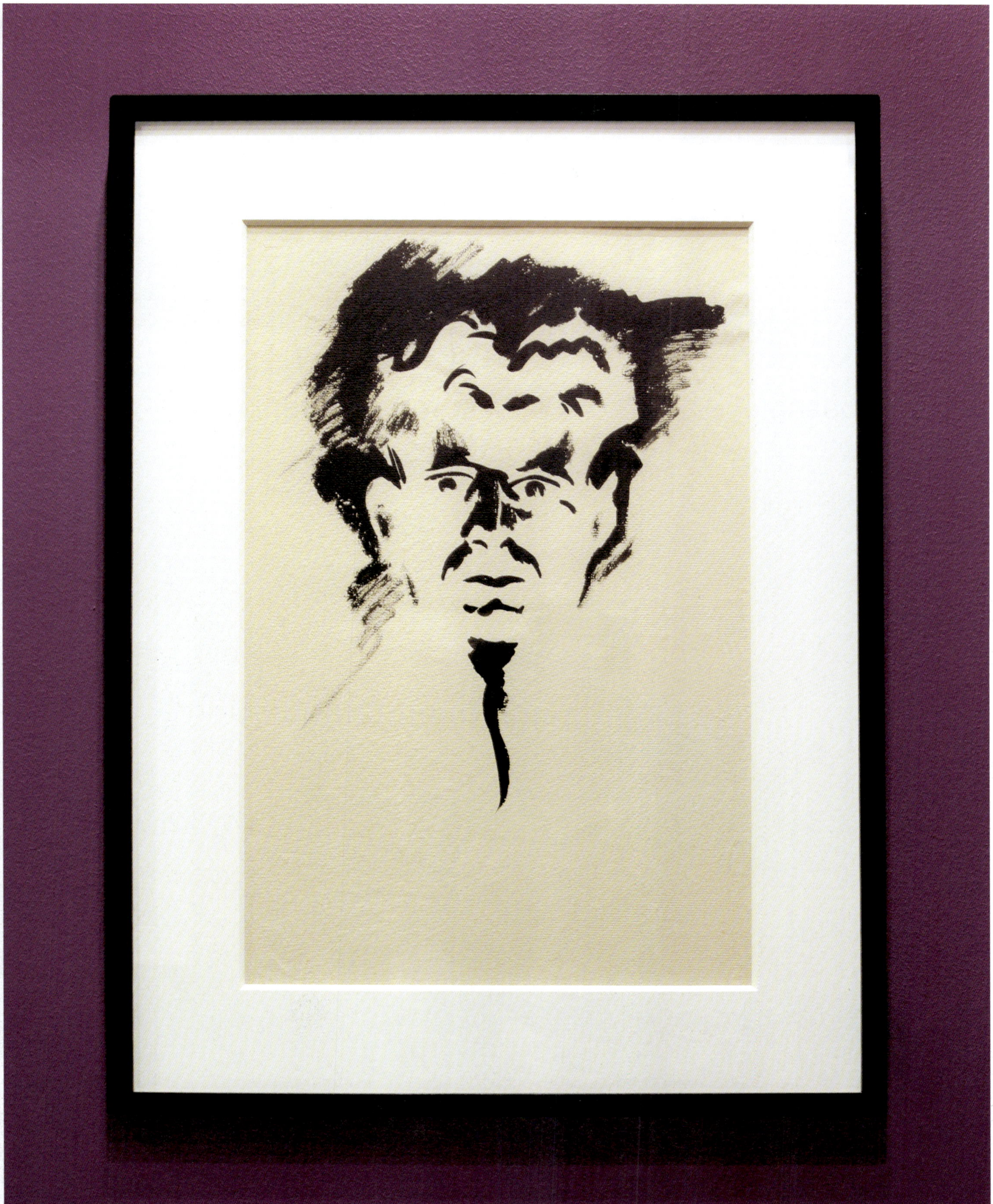

Marius de Zayas

Caricature of an unidentified man, undated
Galerie 1900–2000

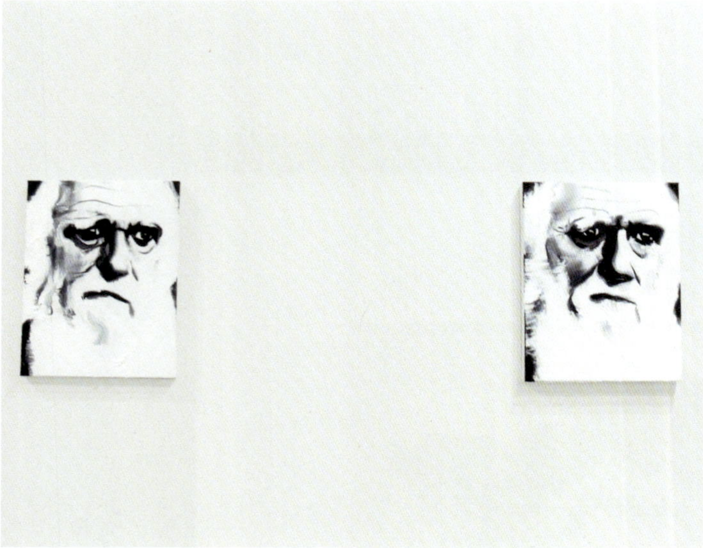

Wilhelm Sasnal

Darwin, 2013
Foksal Gallery Foundation

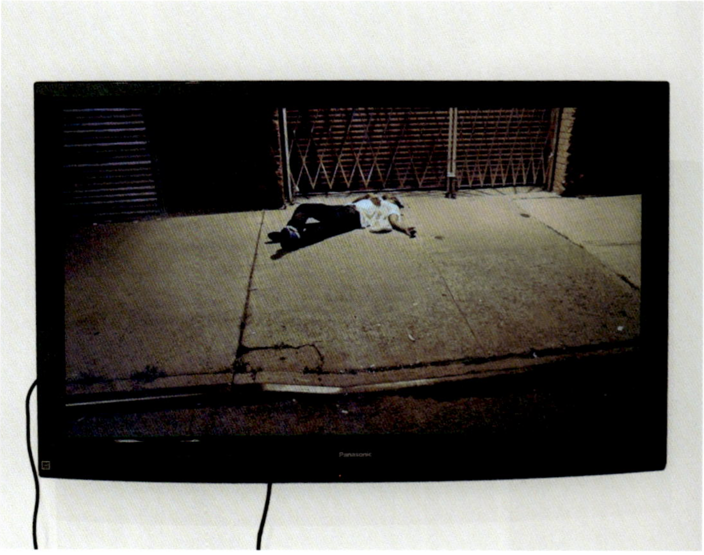

Loretta Fahrenholz

Ditch Plains, 2013
Reena Spaulings Fine Art

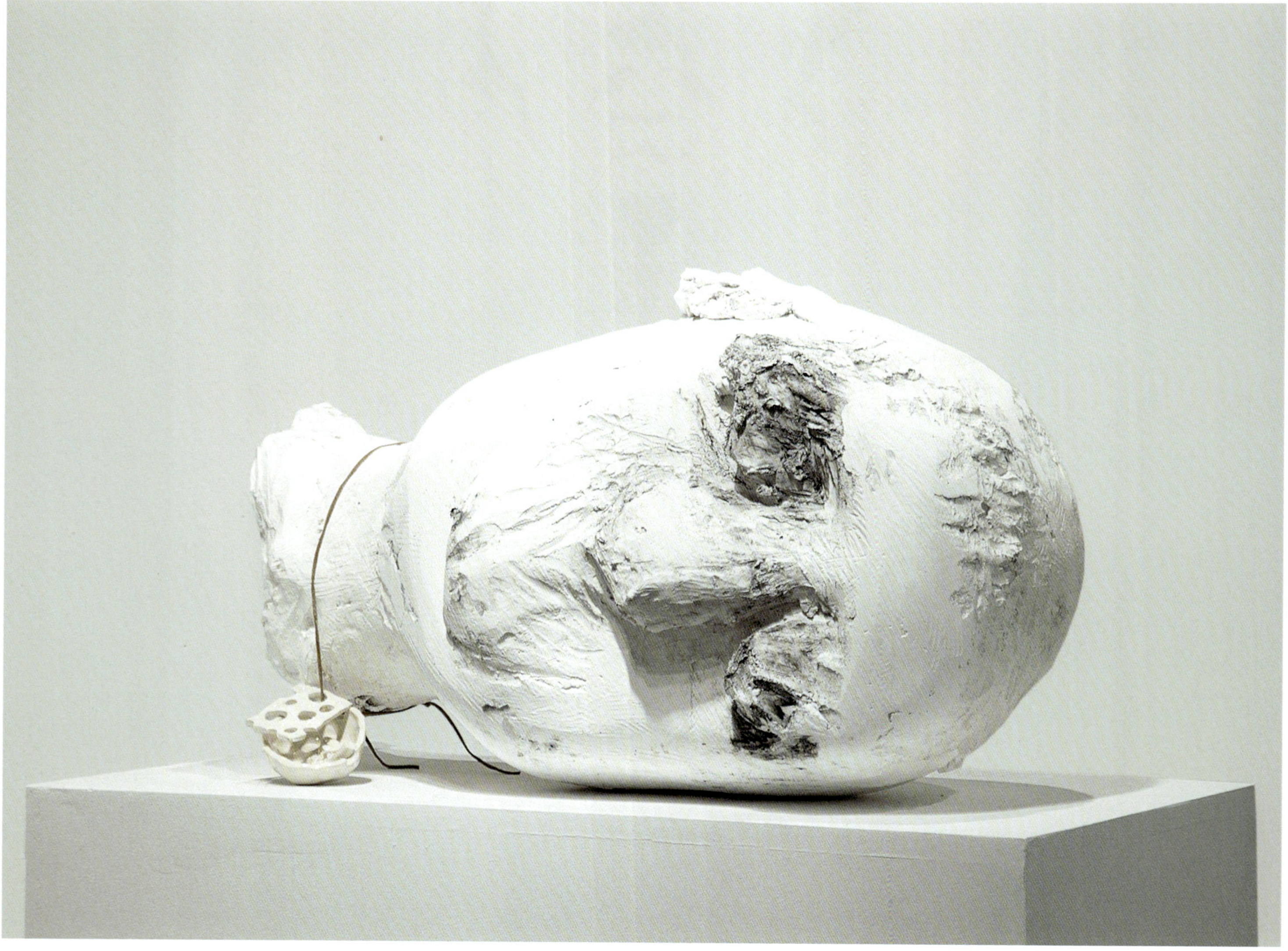

Nicole Eisenman

Koenig & Clinton (Nova)

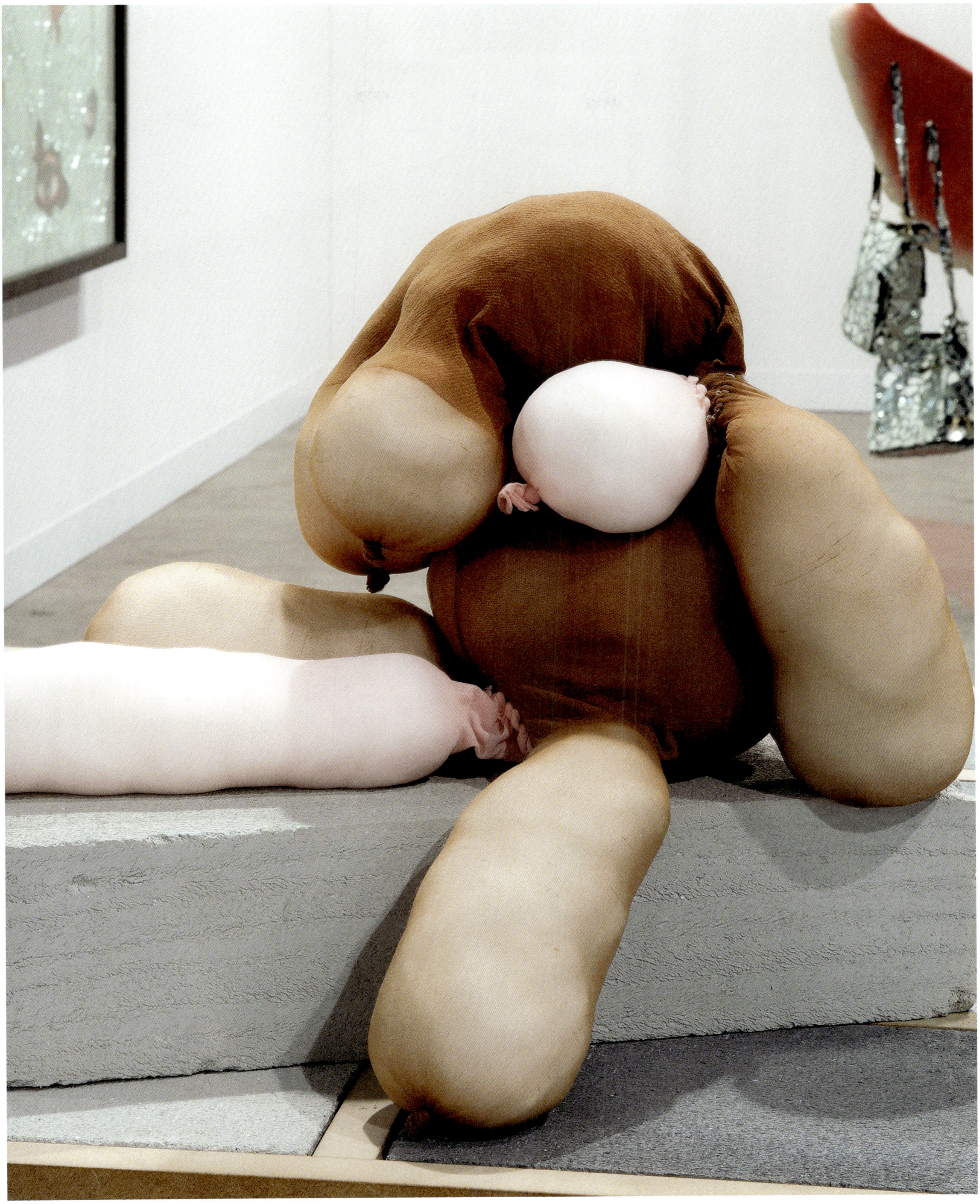

Sarah Lucas

Teenage Tit Teddy, 2013
Sadie Coles HQ

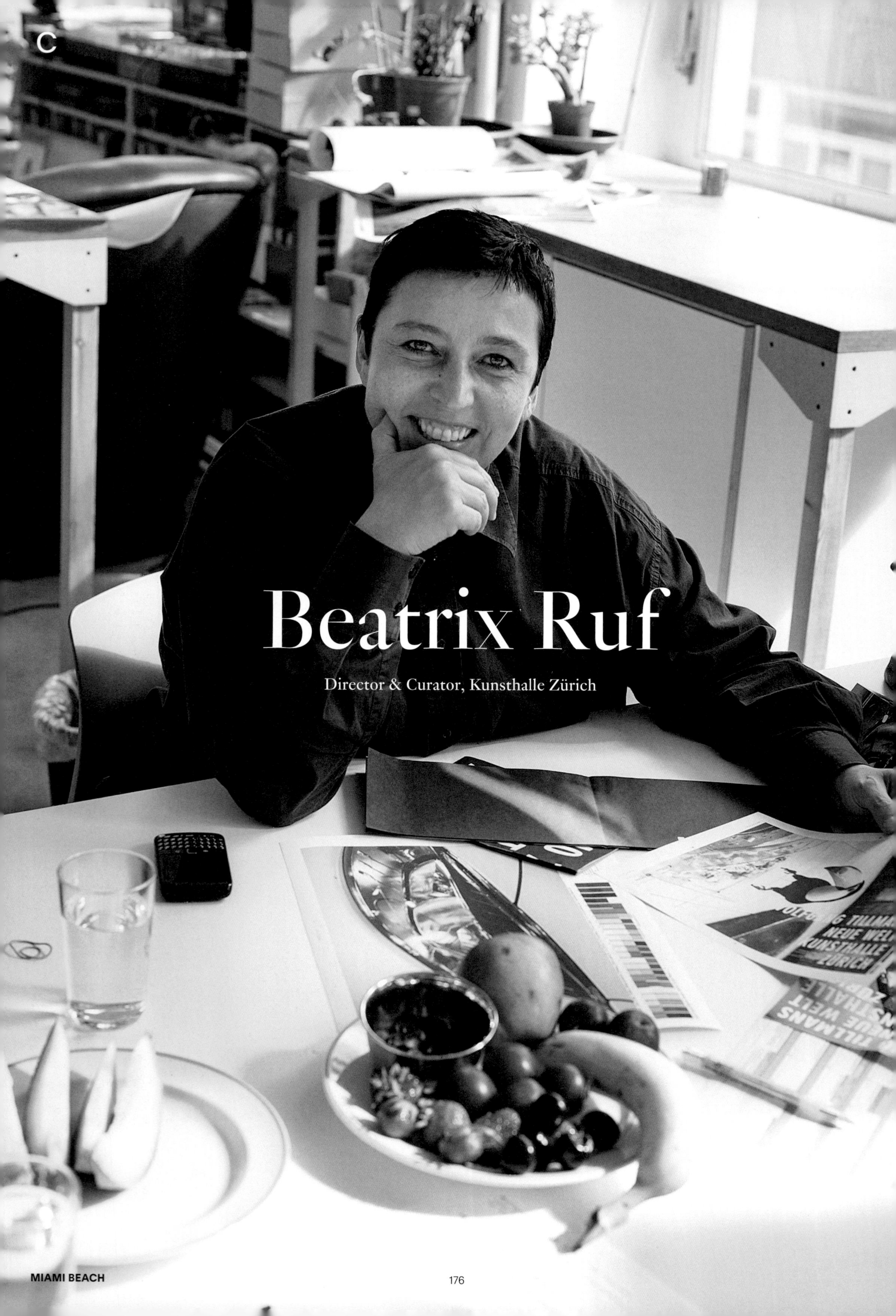

Beatrix Ruf

Director & Curator, Kunsthalle Zürich

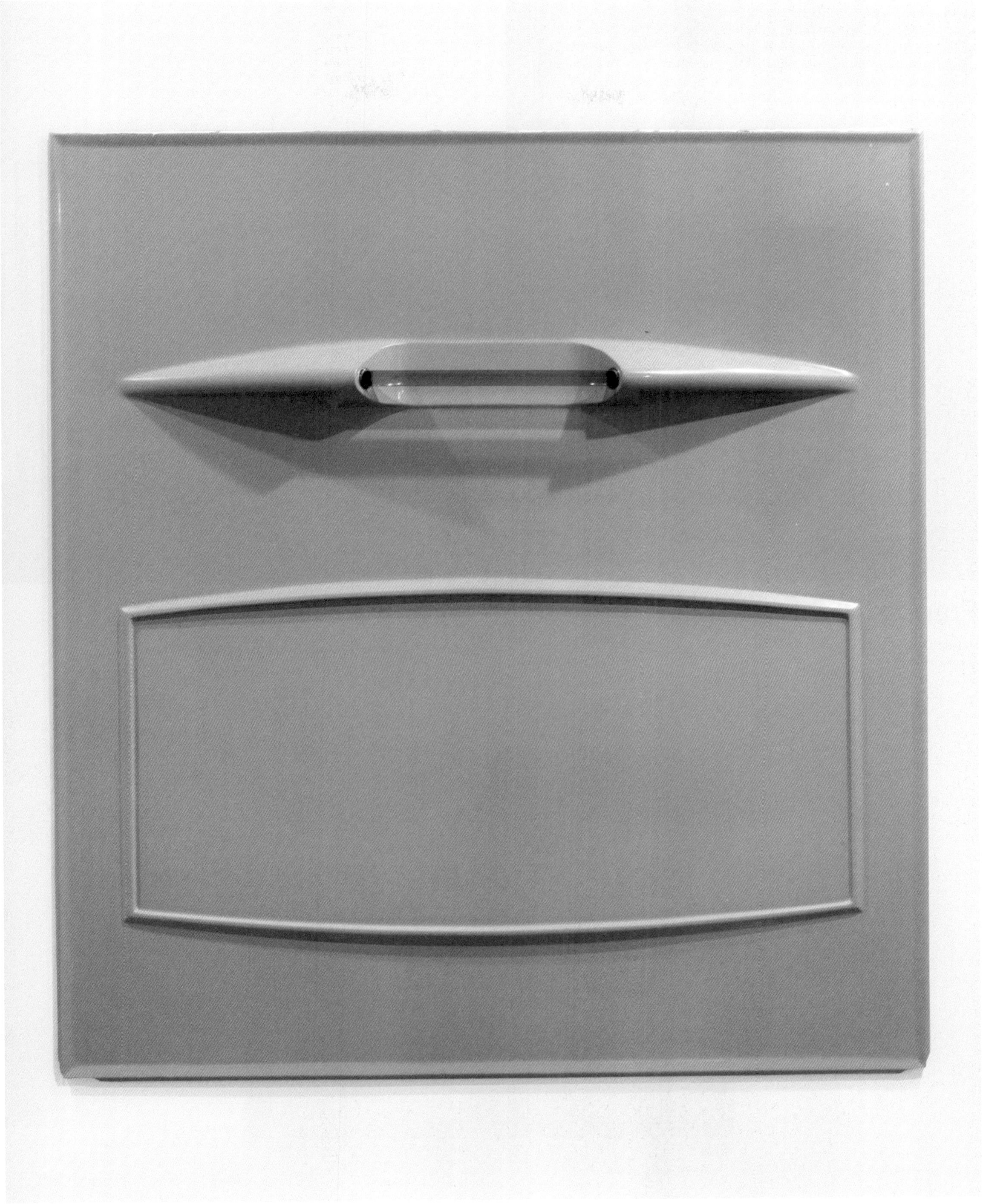

Lutz Bacher

Gog-Magog, 2013
Galerie Buchholz

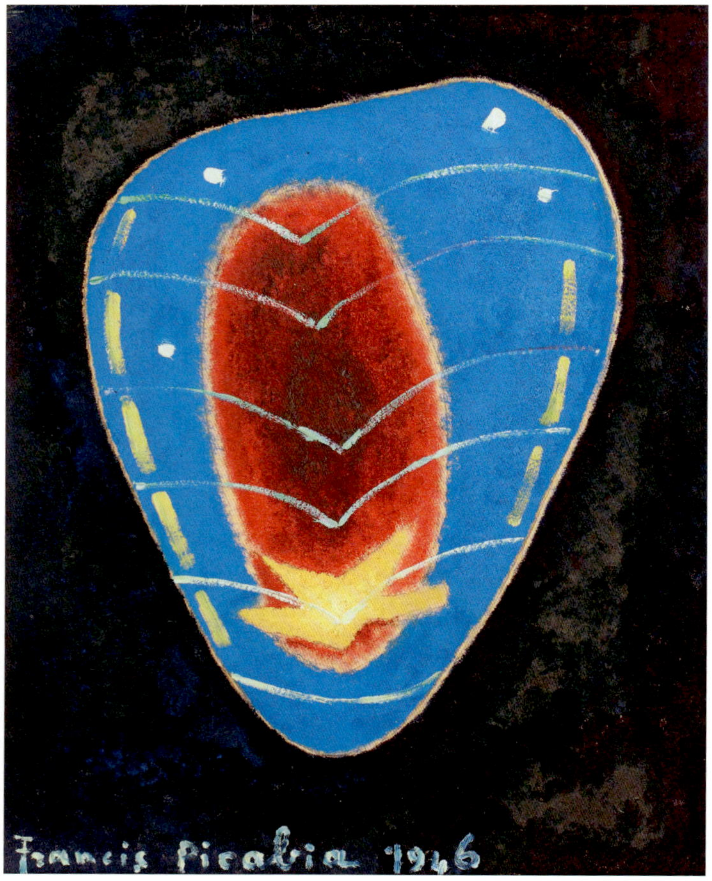

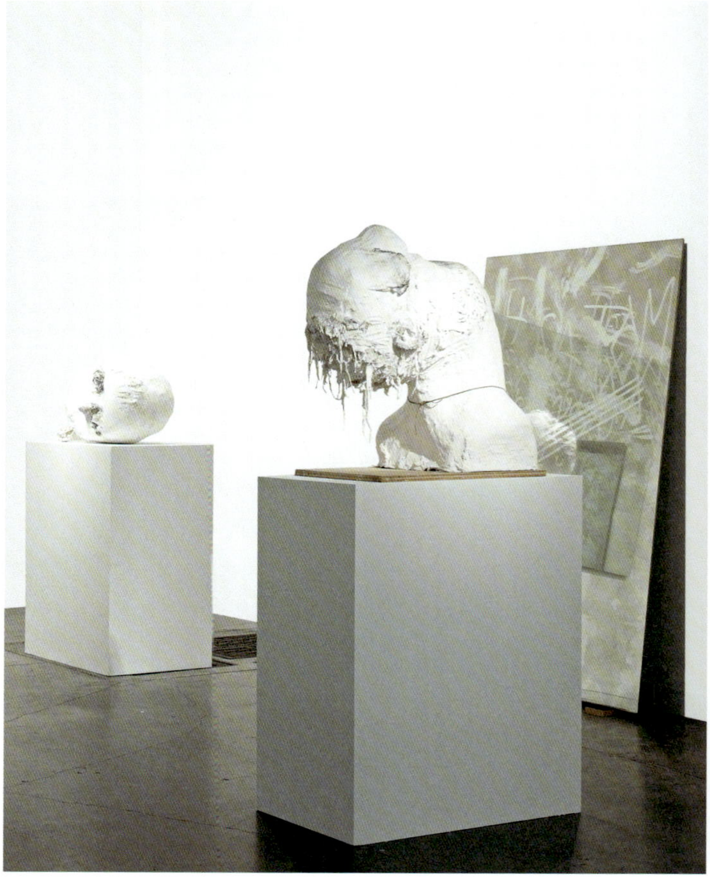

Francis Picabia

Chenille, 1946
Galerie 1900–2000

Nicole Eisenman

Koenig & Clinton (Nova)

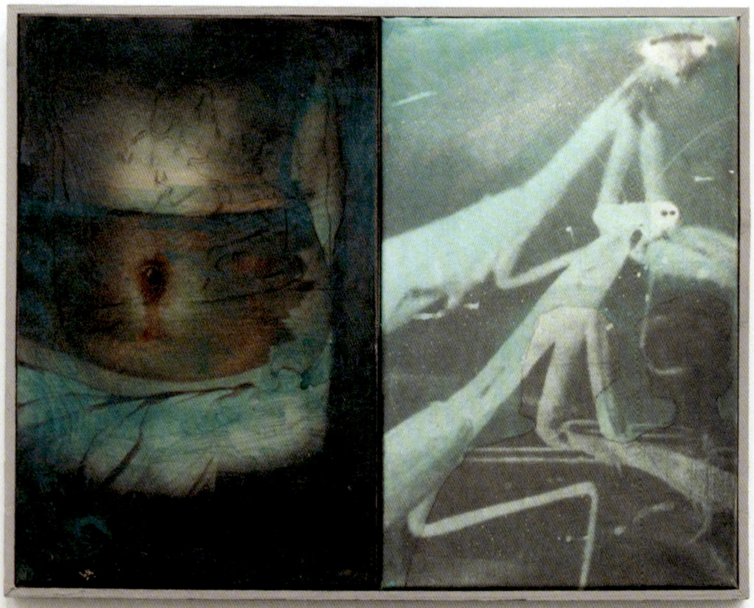

Birgit Jürgenssen

Kino/Cinema, 1987
McCaffrey Fine Art

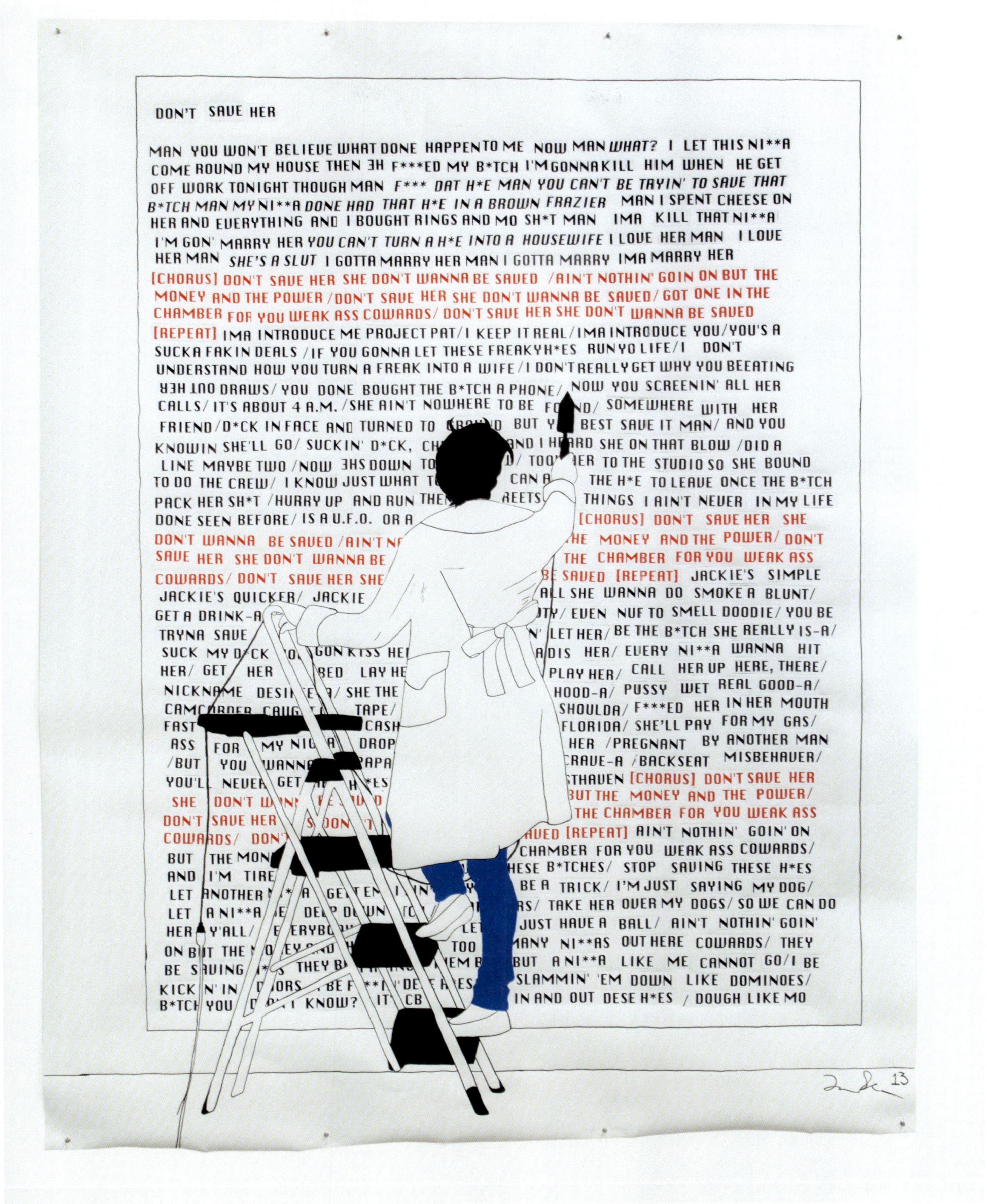

Frances Stark

Don't Save Her, 2013
Gavin Brown's enterprise

Alya Sebti

Artistic Director, Marrakech Biennale, Marrakech

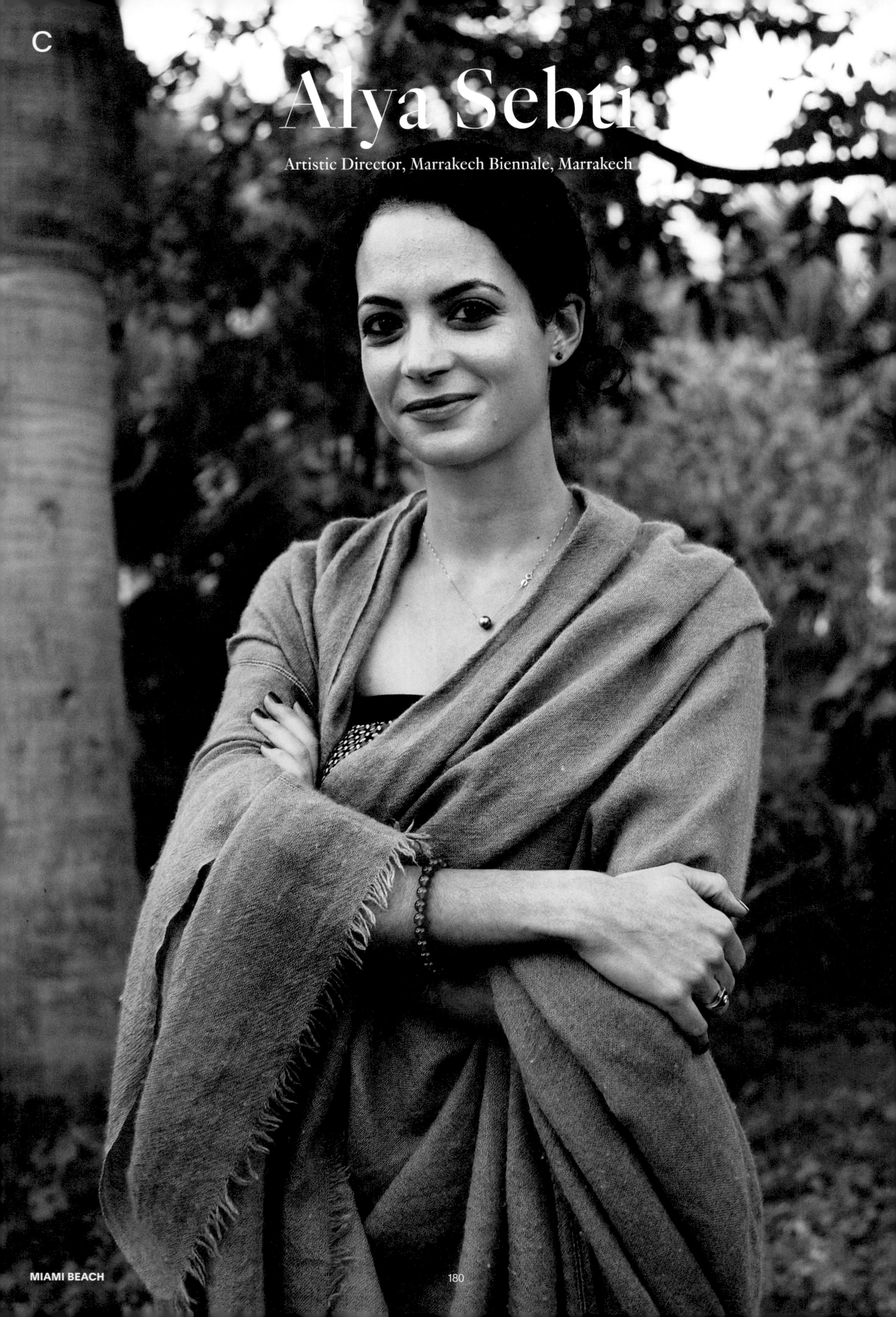

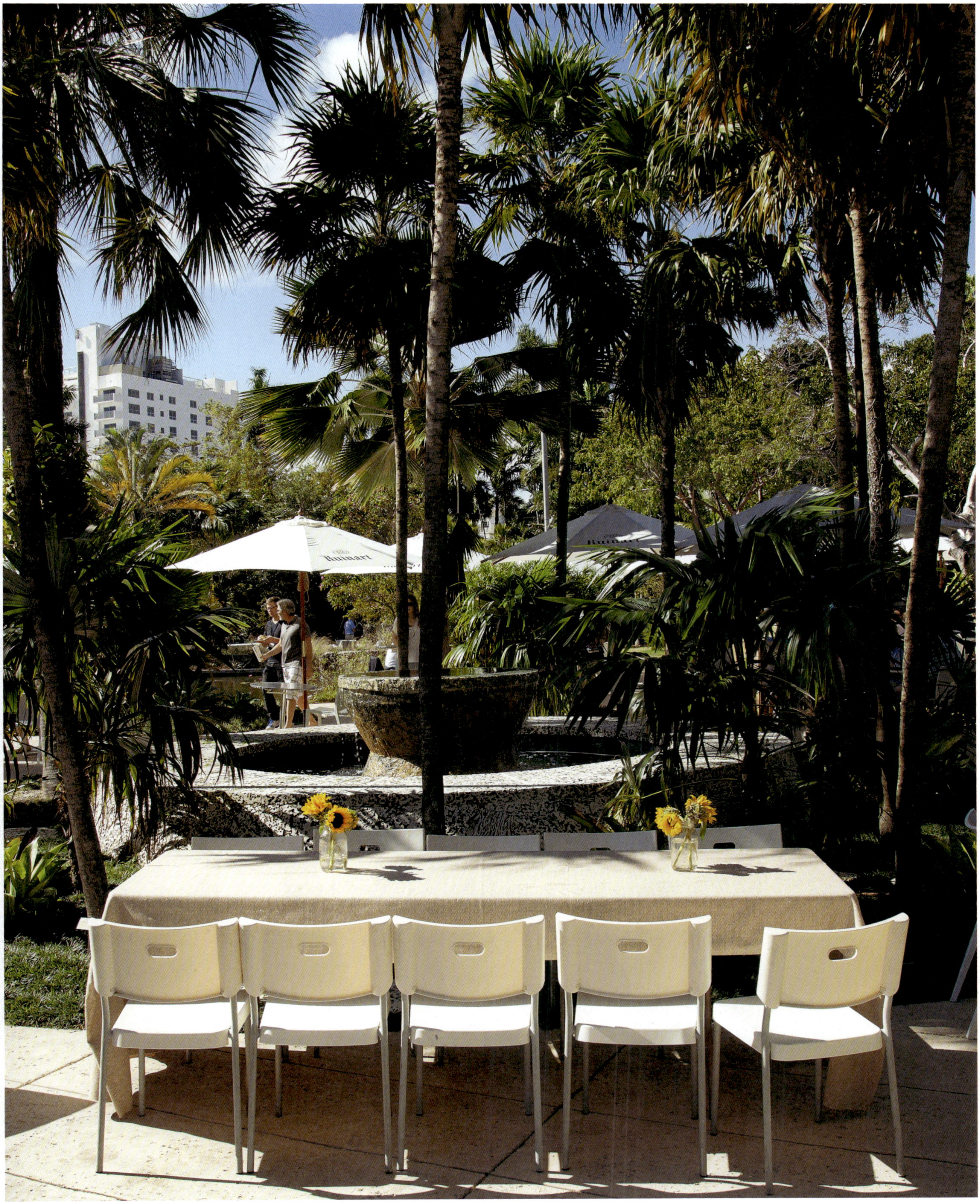

Miami Beach Botanical Garden

The Botanical Garden is located opposite Hall D in the Convention Center, making it not only the closest, but also the most enjoyable way to escape the joyously infectious hysteria of the rest of the show—a real breath of fresh air!

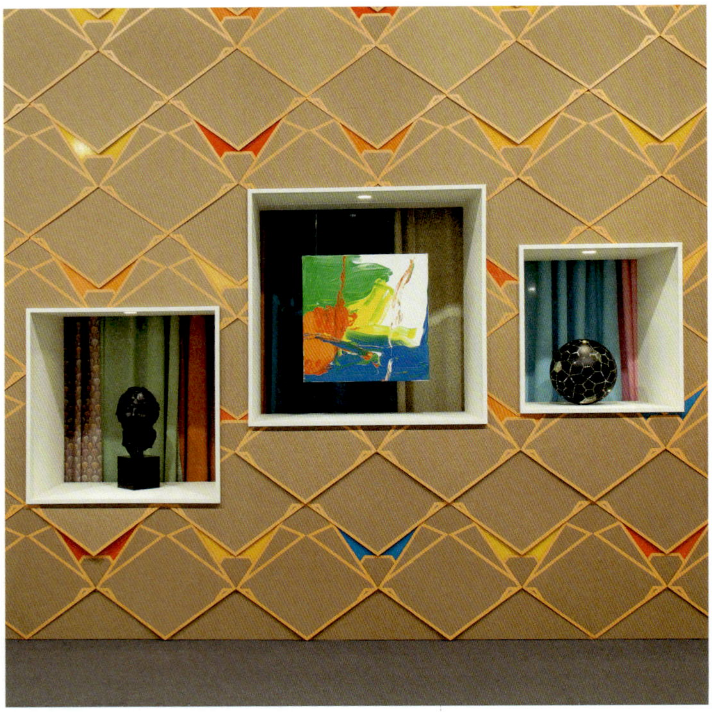

Jorge Pardo

The Booth/El Stand, 2013
neugerriemschneider

This gallery has he courage to hang a few select works to create a soothing, welcoming, offbeat, witty stand in the bustling art show, with a tequila bar right in the heart of the space. Designed by Jorge Pardo, the stand explores questions of hyper-consumerism and the acceleration of time, as visitors spend on average between 30 seconds and three minutes in any given stand; it invites visitors to take their time and come to the works at their own pace rather than being visually assaulted by them.

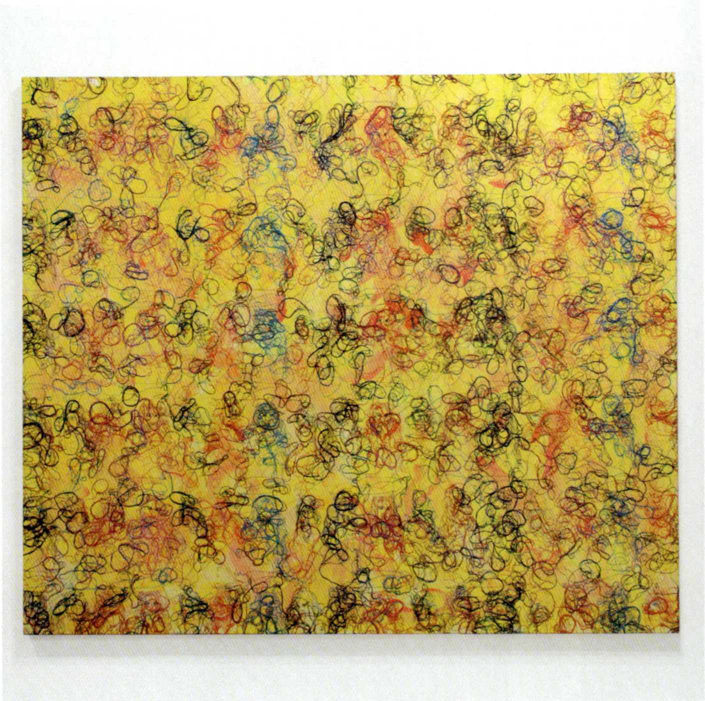

Ghada Amer

Sunflowers-RFGA, 2013
Kukje Gallery/Tina Kim Gallery

This is a highly intimate body of work that invites the viewer to come up close to engage with the work on several levels. Beyond the dangling threads, visitors gradually discern embroideries depicting women's faces and bodies. The Egyptian artist's work is sensual and feminine, yet also politically aware, striking a balance between seduction and feminism.

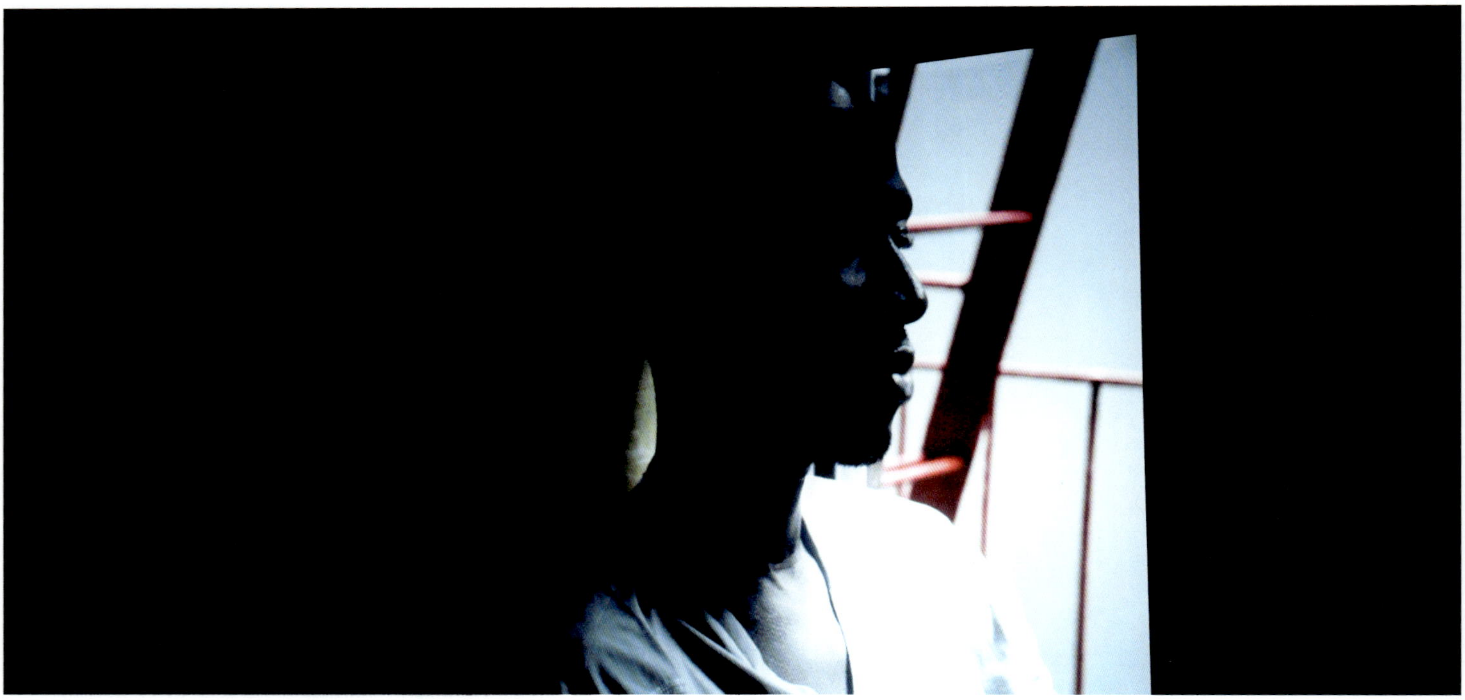

Bouchra Khalili

Speeches, 2012–2013
Pérez Art Museum Miami, Miami

Bouchra Khalili is a great artist and always a source of inspiration for me. She is a leading figure on the Moroccan cultural stage and a star of the 2014 Marrakech Biennale.

Gregor Hildebrandt

Pelz der Venus, 2013
Wentrup

Not quite a painting, not quite a video installation, but a blend of the two, this is a highly poetic work on the theme of memory. The artist has hand-assembled the individual tapes of a video installation, which he presses to the canvas, then removes, leaving behind the imprint of the negative, with all its imperfections.

Franklin Sirmans

Curator & Department Head, Contemporary Art,
LACMA, Los Angeles; Director of Prospect, New Orleans

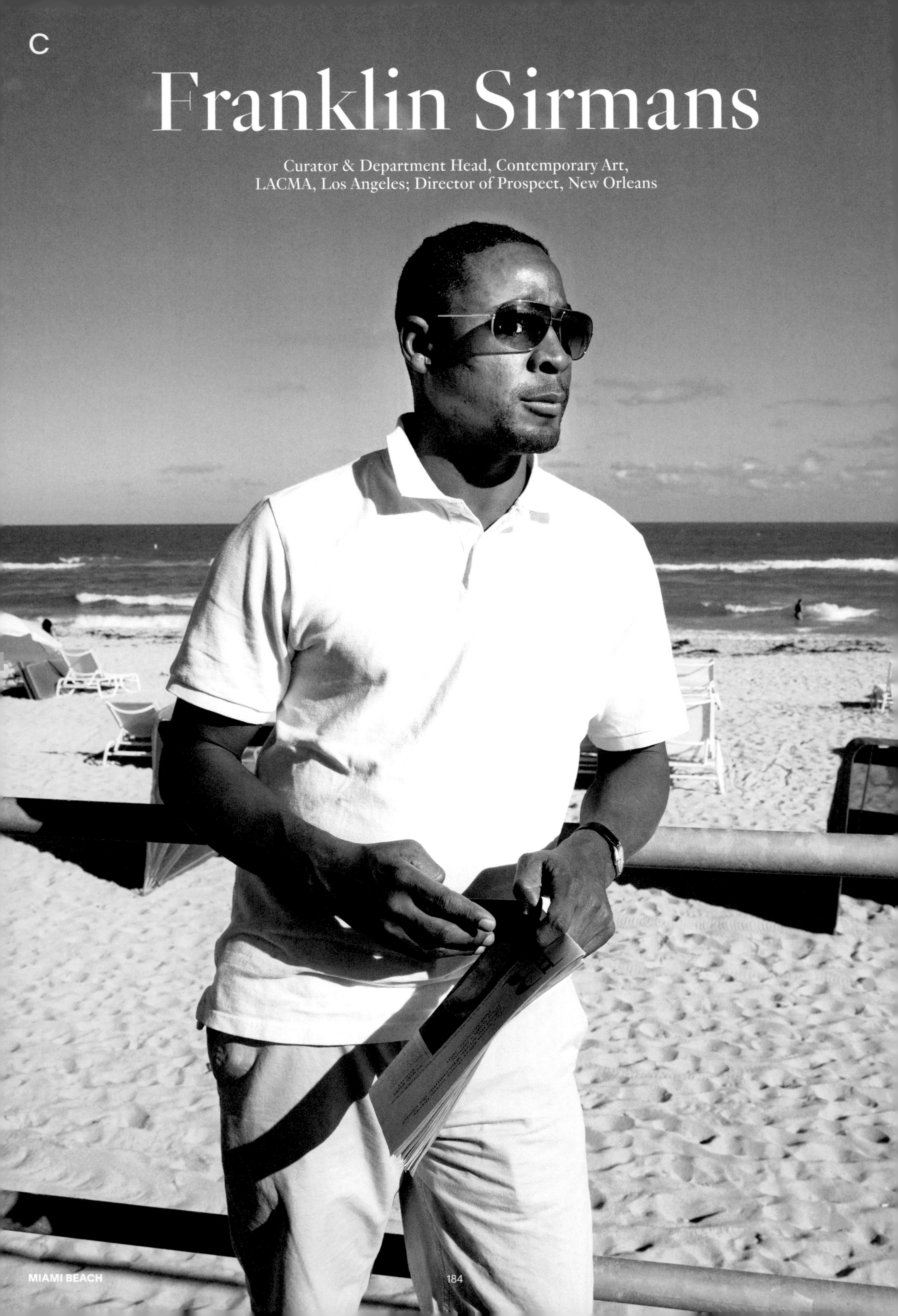

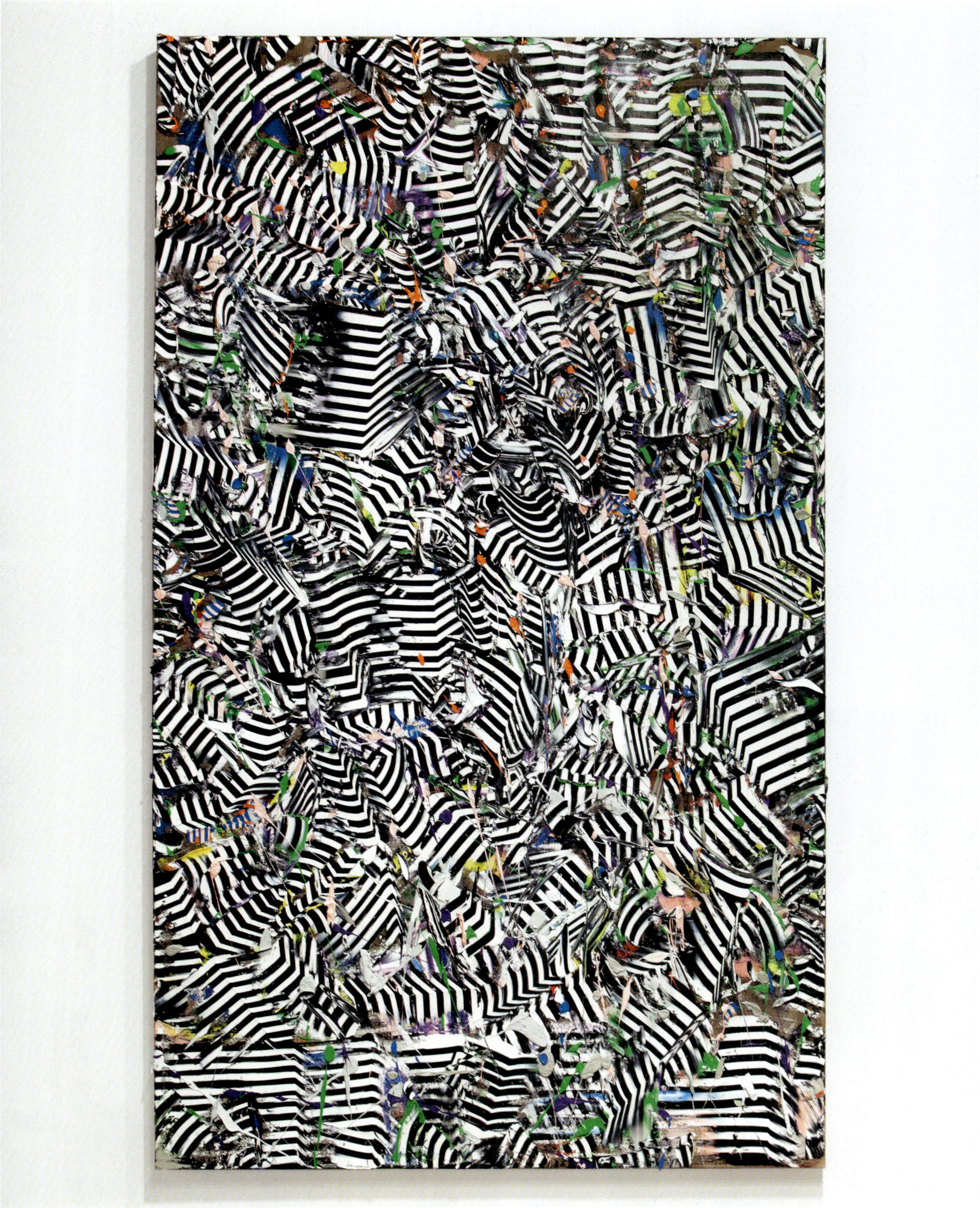

Zander Blom

Stevenson

Good abstract painting is collector crack. So, of course, by the time I got here, late afternoon on Day 1, everything was sold, including everything in the closet. Can't say curators aren't fiends as well. Although painterly and even expressionistic, there's something attuned to the moment that stood out at ABMB in Blom's paintings.

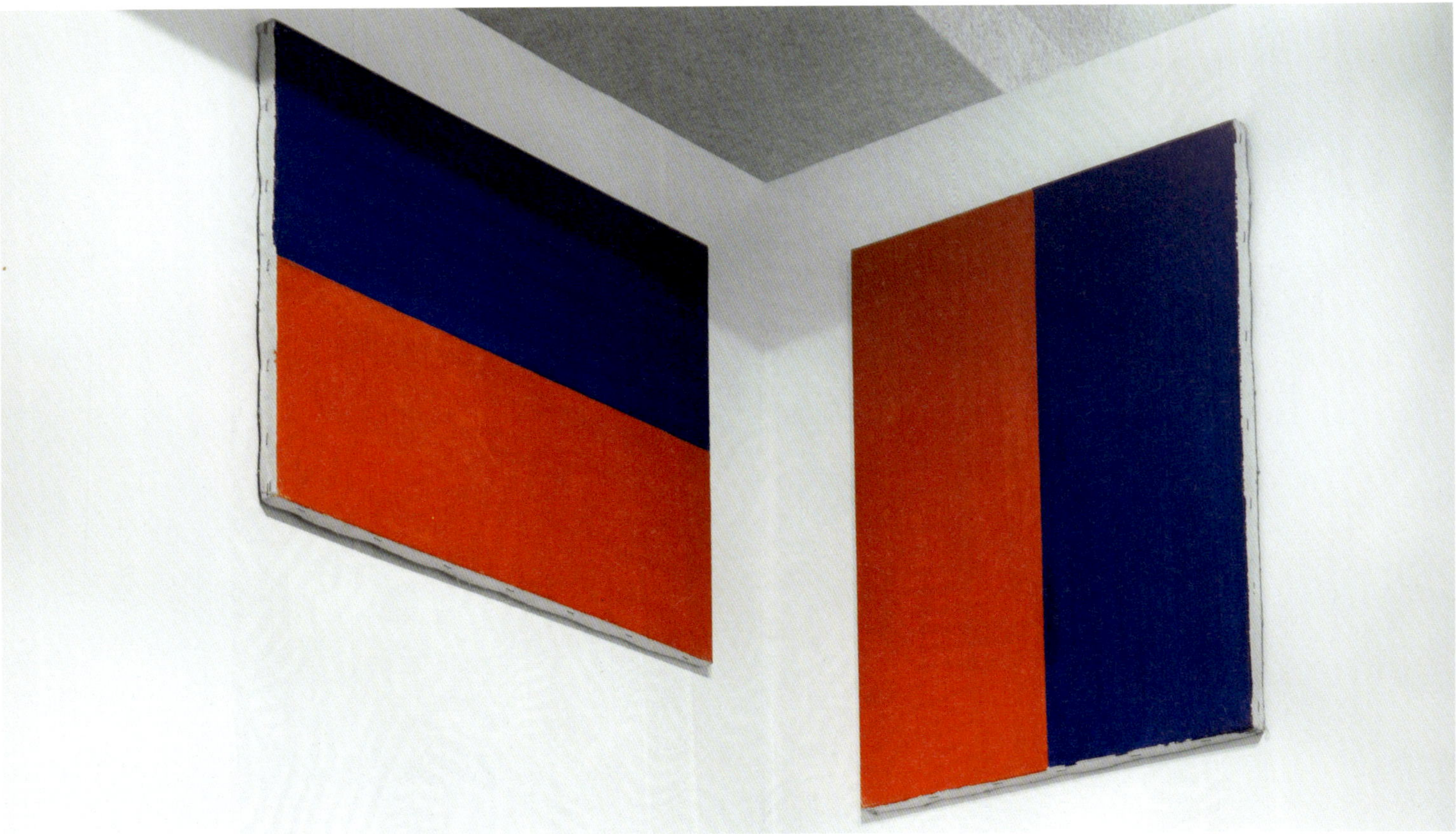

Albert Mertz

Tif Sigfrids, Nada Art Fair

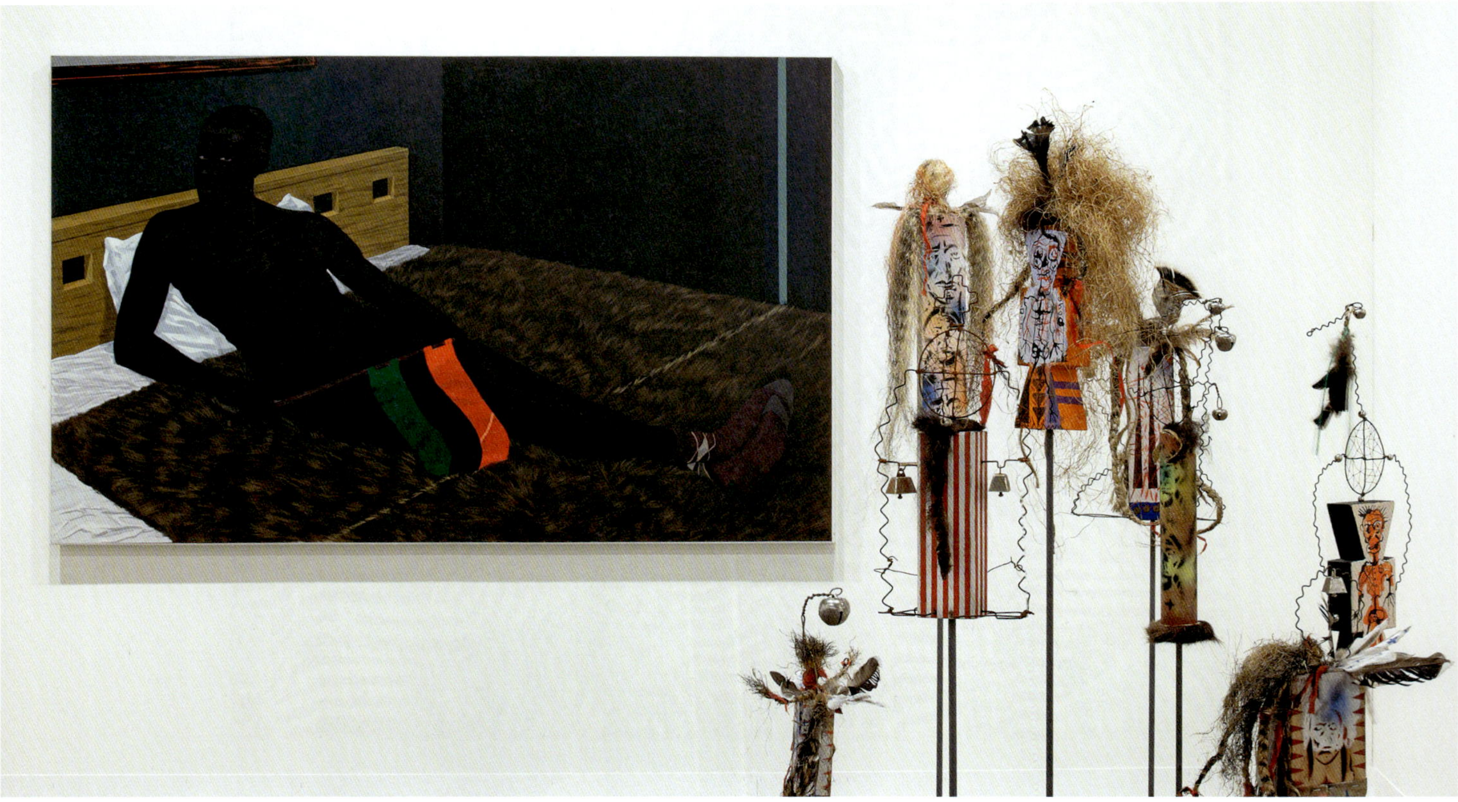

Jack Shainman Gallery

With artworks by Kerry James Marshall and Brad Kahlhamer

Great juxtaposition of two artists who paint human bodies in vastly different ways, though usually contested in their difference: black and Native American respectively. Where Kahlhamer works with a disjunctive lyrical line, especially in these sculptures, Marshall is all precision, as if he were re-painting the history books; both of their oeuvres make us reconsider.

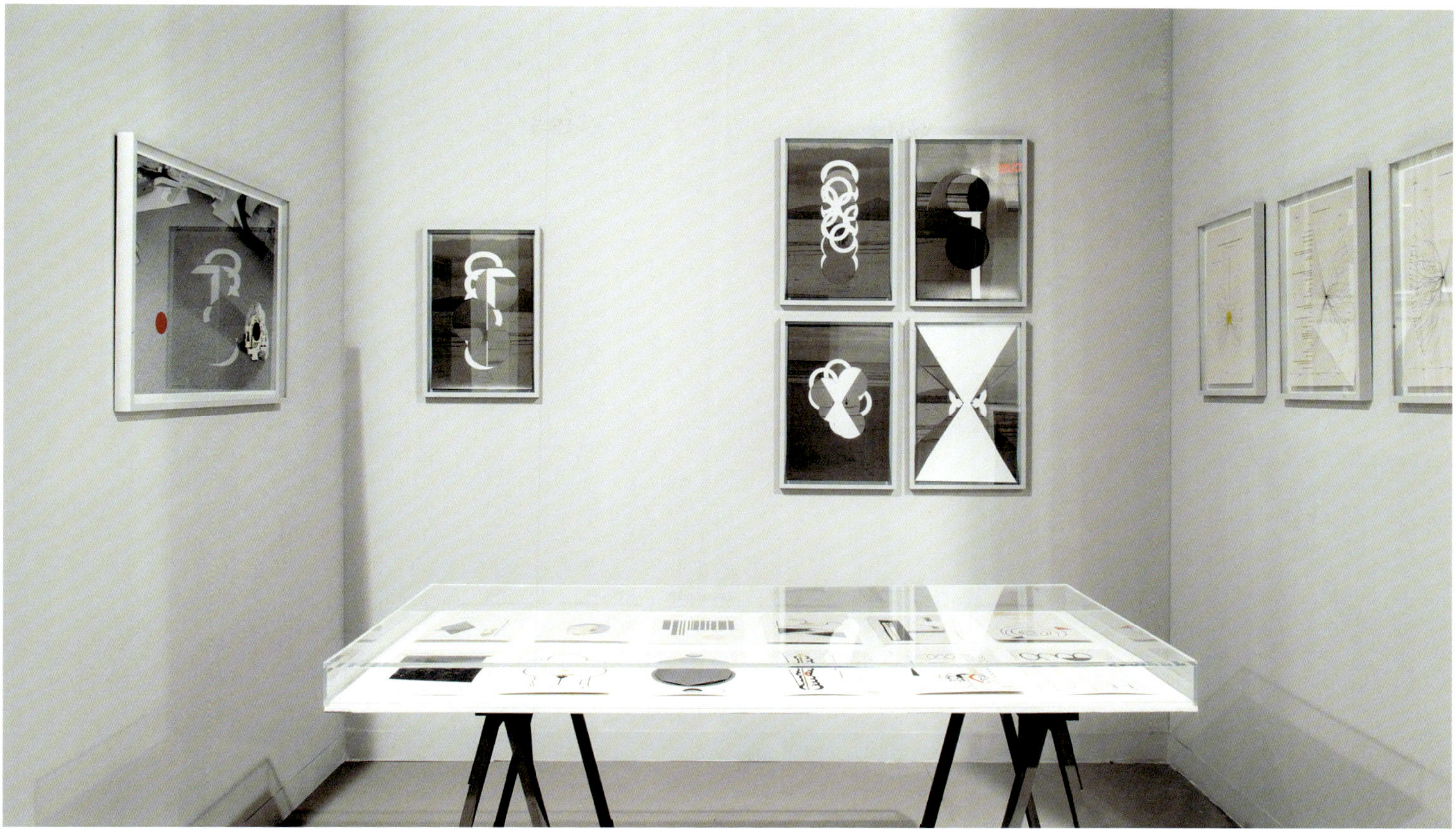

Damir Očko

Yvon Lambert (Kabinett)

Heavily influenced by the events surrounding the post-Yugoslavian transition in the 1980s, Croatian artist Očko was a featured artist for his gallery in the Kabinett section of curated exhibitions. Sure, that was part of the appeal. Someone willing to stand alone in an orgy of group play. Očko works with film, lightboxes, sound, drawing, and more. The bodies emerging from darkness in the films were hauntingly beautiful. That sounds clichéd, but its true.

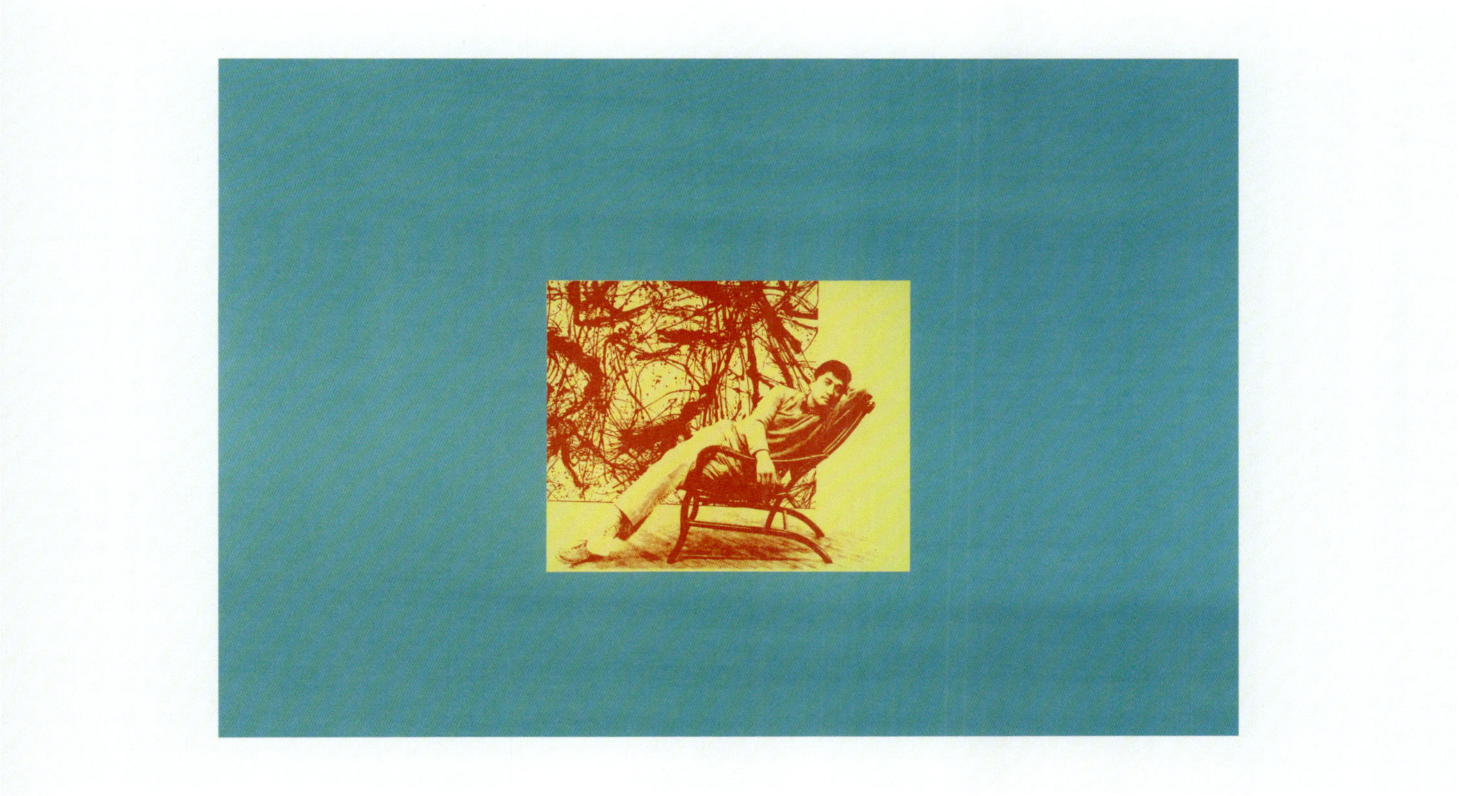

David Diao

Lying 1, 2000
Office Baroque (Nova)

D

D

- Hong Kong
- Basel
- Miami Beach

Daiter

Chicago ● Galleries

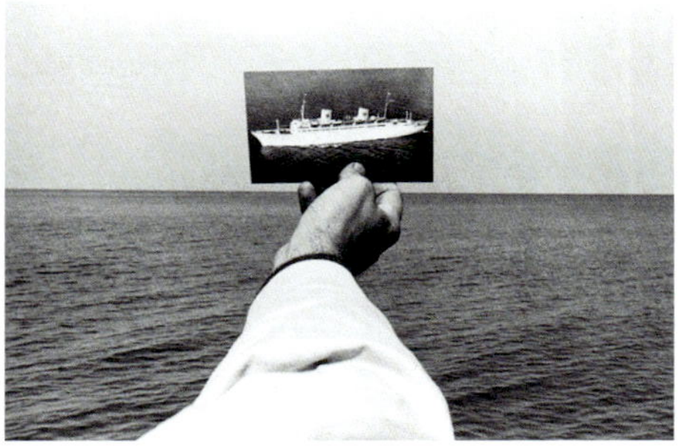

What first compelled you to open a gallery?
My interest in 20th-century photography—the avant-garde, experimental, documentary, and photojournalism, especially in America—led me to open the gallery. These very important and, at the time, generally underappreciated areas of photography became the primary focus of our exhibitions and publications, which have been by turns interesting, challenging, and controversial, but always strive to increase awareness of our artists and their works both in the photography and the general arts communities.

Who is the first artist you showed and what was most memorable about that show?
Our first exhibition was a group show and publication called *The American Century: Photographs and Visions Part 1: 1900–1935* in which we featured important vintage photographs by A.L. Coburn, Walker Evans, Lewis Hine, Dorothea Lange, Paul Outerbridge, Man Ray, Tina Modotti, Edward Steichen, Alfred Stieglitz, Paul Strand, and Edward Weston, among others. Most memorable was our publishing of a beautiful book on this exhibition. Also worthy of mention was our relief to have completed the building of our space, sent out the announcement cards, and hung the works—all in time for the opening night!

When did you first participate in Art Basel and what was most memorable about that show?
Our first year exhibiting at Art Basel was in 2005. Having visited Art Basel several times before exhibiting there, the experience was always wonderful—wandering the halls, taking in, and learning about all of these galleries' very fine works of art.

- **Contact** Stephen Daiter Gallery
  Stephen Daiter
  stephen@stephendaitergallery.com
  info@stephendaitergallery.com
- **Established** 1997
- **Owner(s) / Partner(s)** Stephen Daiter
- **Team** 6
- **Space(s)** 455 m²
- **Artists at Art Basel** Wynn Bullock
  Harry Callahan
  Lynne Cohen
  Robert Frank
  Kenneth Josephson
  Clarence John Laughlin
  Ralph Eugene Meatyard
  Barbara Morgan
  Vinicio Paladini
  Aaron Siskind
  Edmund Teske
- **Further artists represented** Dawoud Bey
  Bill Brandt
  Elliott Erwitt
  Walker Evans
  John Gossage
  Lewis Hine
  Yasuhiro Ishimoto
  Joseph Jachna
  György Kepes
  André Kertész
  Helen Levitt
  Ray Metzker
  Wayne Miller
  László Moholy-Nagy
  Marvin Newman
  Martin Parr
  Gary Schneider
  Arthur Siegel
  Art Sinsabaugh
  W. Eugene Smith
  Frederick Sommer
  Joseph Sterling
  Josef Sudek
  Charles Swedlund
  Alex Webb

DAN

São Paulo ● Galleries

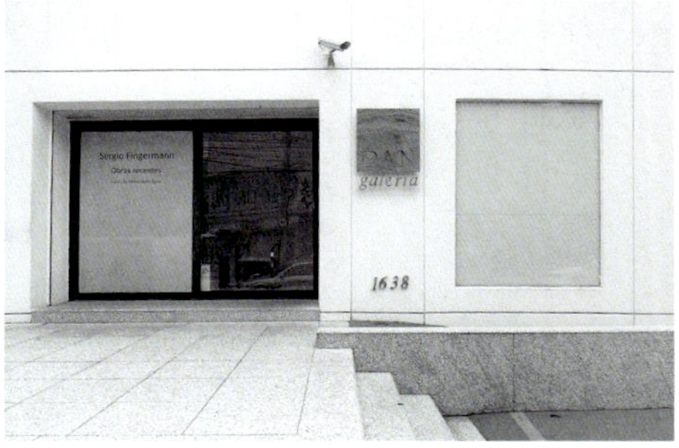

What first compelled you to open a gallery?
I was motivated by the contact with artists and collectors that came from my first activity as a partner in an art book publisher.

Who is the first artist you showed and what was the most memorable about that show?
The first significant exhibition at the gallery was of the artist Yolanda Mohalyi. This became a turning point in the history of the gallery, focusing on abstraction and Concrete art after this exhibition.

When did you first participate in Art Basel and what was most memorable about that show?
Our first participation was in 2011 at Art Basel Miami Beach, and the most memorable was the significant positive reaction we received from collectors and the general public about our presentation at the fair.

- **Contact** DAN Galeria
  Ulisses Cohn
  ulissescohn@dangaleria.com.br
  flaviocohn@dangaleria.com.br
- **Established** 1972
- **Owner(s) / Partner(s)** Jozsef Peter Cohn
  Gláucia Simonetti Cohn
  Flavio Isaias S. Cohn
  Ulisses Eliezer S. Cohn
- **Team** 14
- **Space(s)** 1,000 m² (including storage)
- **Artists at Art Basel** Josef Albers
  Ascânio M.M.M.
  Hércules Barsotti
  Max Bill
  Sérgio Camargo
  Lothar Charoux
  Lygia Clark
  Carlos Cruz-Diez
  Bill Culbert
  Geraldo de Barros
  Willys de Castro
  Norman Dilworth
  Hermelindo Fiaminghi
  Anthony Hill
  Macaparana
  Kenneth Martin
  Mary Martin
  Almir Mavignier

Luiz Sacilotto
Jesus Soto
Franz Weissmann
Alexandre Wollner

- **Further artists represented** Juan Asensio
José Manuel Ballester
Alejandro Corujeira
Christian Cravo
Dionisio Del Santo
Adolfo Estrada
Knopp Ferro
Sérgio Fingermann
Thomaz Ianelli
Linda Kohen
Cristiano Mascaro
Laura Miranda
Bob Nugent
Cesar Paternosto
José Spaniol
Eduardo Stupia
Amélia Toledo

Dane

London

- Galleries Unlimited
- Galleries

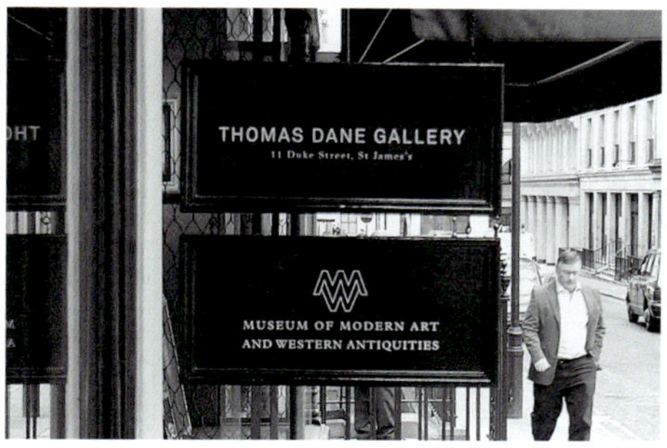

What first compelled you to open a gallery?
I was asked by Steve McQueen if I would work with him. I didn't have a gallery so it made sense to build one around him.

Who is the first artist you showed and what was the most memorable about that show?
Steve McQueen. The most memorable: having the opportunity to show two extraordinary works by Steve that are still as vital and relevant today as they were ten years ago.

When did you first participate in Art Basel and what was most memorable about that show?
June 2012. It was great to be showing alongside so many excellent galleries in what is the best fair in the world.

- **Contact** Thomas Dane Gallery
Elli Resvanis
elli@thomasdane.com
info@thomasdane.com
- **Established** 2004
- **Owner(s) / Partner(s)** Thomas Dane
Martine d'Anglejan-Chatillon
François Chatala
- **Team** 14
- **Space(s)** 400 m²
- **Artists at** Kutlug Ataman
Lynda Benglis
Walead Beshty
Abraham Cruzvillegas
Alexandre da Cunha
José Damasceno
Michel François
Arturo Herrera
Phillip King
Luisa Lambri
Glenn Ligon
Jean-Luc Moulène
Paul Pfeiffer
Kelley Walker
Akram Zaatari
- **Further artists represented** Hurvin Anderson
Anya Gallaccio
John Gerrard
Michael Landy
Steve McQueen
Lari Pittman
Jorge Queiroz
Amy Sillman
Caragh Thuring

Davidson

New York

- Galleries

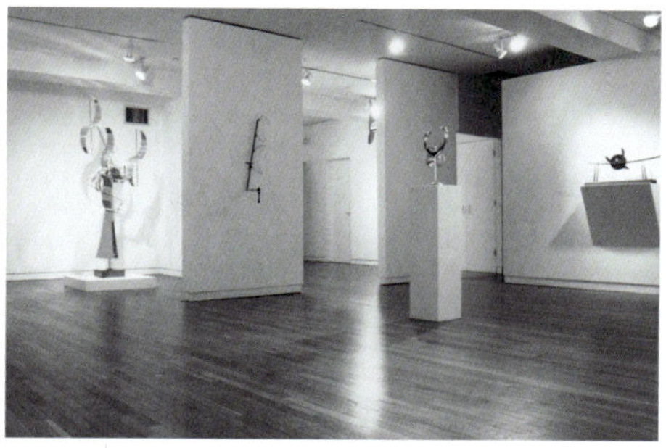

What first compelled you to open a gallery?
I wanted to use my degree in Art History, start a business, and work in a field I loved.

Who is the first artist you showed and what was the most memorable about that show?
Matta. The most memorable thing to me now is the availability of such beautiful works. The paintings were all from the 1930s and 1940s. It was a spectacular show.

When did you first participate in Art Basel and what was most memorable about that show?
In 1997 in Basel, and in 2005 in Miami Beach.

- **Contact** Maxwell Davidson Gallery
Brittany LoSchiavo
info@davidsongallery.com
- **Established** 1968
- **Owner(s) / Partner(s)** Maxwell Davidson III
E. Mary C. Davidson
Maxwell Davidson IV
- **Team** 6
- **Space(s)** 700 m²
- **Artists at** Harry Bertoia
Carlos Cruz-Diez
Pedro S. De Movellán
Kevin Osmond
Tim Prentice
George Rickey
Jesús Rafael Soto
- **Further artists represented** Christopher Brown
Ghost of a Dream
Sarah Hardesty
Kiel Johnson
Darren Lago
Sam Messenger
Mel Rosas
Kim Rugg
George Segal
Mary Ann Unger
Tom Wesselmann
William T. Wiley
Thomas Witte

De Carlo

Milan
London

- Galleries
- Galleries Unlimited
- Galleries

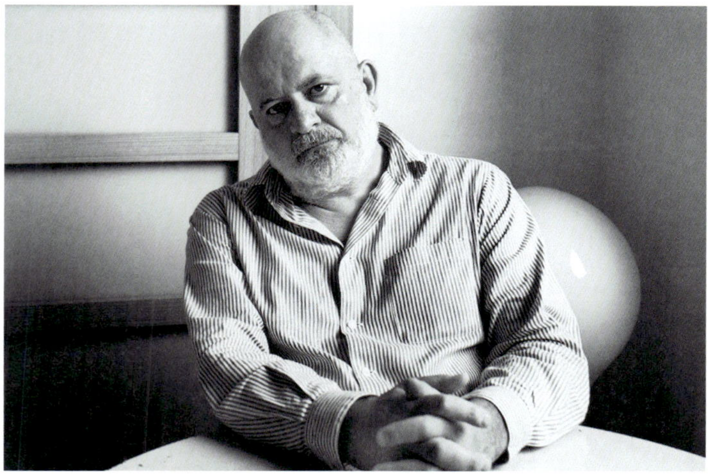

What first compelled you to open a gallery?
I wanted to be a musician, but once I realized that it was better not to, I decided to open my gallery.

Who is the first artist you showed and what was the most memorable about that show?
The first artist I showed in Milan was Olivier Mosset, whose influence was fundamental for my training as a gallerist. In fact for the opening the gallery wasn't even ready yet.

When did you first participate in Art Basel and what was most memorable about that show?
The first time the gallery took part in Art Basel was in 1993 and I can still remember the great excitement to be on a big and international stage.

- **Contact**
  Massimo De Carlo
  Stella Gianotti
  gianotti@massimodecarlo.com
  info@massimodecarlo.it
- **Established**
  1987
- **Owner(s) / Partner(s)**
  Massimo De Carlo
- **Team**
  25
- **Space(s)**
  500 m² (Milan)
  300 m² (London)
- **Artists at Art Basel**
  John M Armleder
  Massimo Bartolini
  Spartacus Chetwynd
  Steven Claydon
  Dan Colen
  George Condo
  Roberto Cuoghi
  Elmgreen & Dragset
  Gelitin
  Carsten Höller
  Christian Holstad
  Rashid Johnson
  Elad Lassry
  Liu Xiaodong
  Nate Lowman
  Matthew Monahan
  Diego Perrone
  Paola Pivi
  Rob Pruitt
  Rudolf Stingel
  Piotr Uklański
  Kaari Upson
  Yan Pei-Ming
  Aaron Young
- **Further artists represented**
  Sanford Biggers
  Chris Burden
  Maurizio Cattelan
  Paul Chan
  Roland Flexner
  Thomas Grünfeld
  Sol LeWitt
  Olivier Mosset
  Matt Mullican
  Steven Parrino
  Jim Shaw
  Josh Smith
  Ettore Spalletti
  Kelly Walker
  Andrea Zittel

de Montferrand

Beijing
Hangzhou

Insights

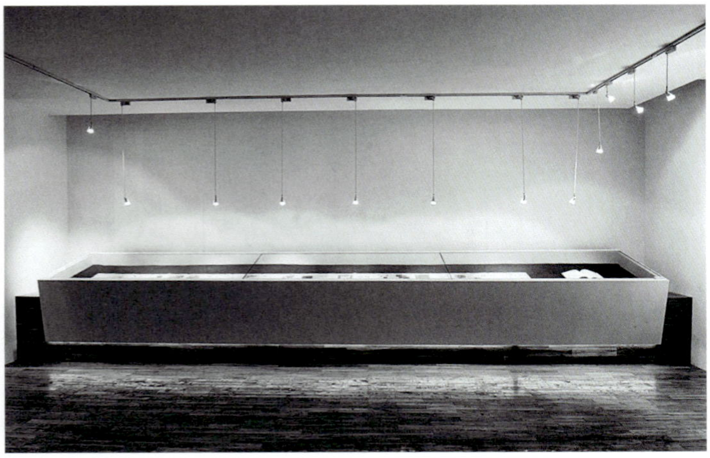

What first compelled you to open a gallery?
I was always amazed by the art market and I always wanted to open something of my own. After ten years in the art business, a great opportunity allowed me to open the first space.

Who is the first artist you showed and what was the most memorable about that show?
Liu Xiaodong was the first artist to trust me. I was touched!

When did you first participate in Art Basel and what was most memorable about that show?
In 2010. We presented the collection of an important European collector.

- **Contact**
  Hadrien de Montferrand Gallery
  Hadrien de Montferrand
  h@hdemontferrand.com
- **Established**
  2009
- **Owner(s) / Partner(s)**
  Hadrien de Montferrand (Founder)
  Laurent Dassault
  Olivier Hervet
- **Space(s)**
  180 m² (Beijing)
  160 m² (Hangzhou)
- **Artists at Art Basel**
  Ai Weiwei
  Chen Wenbo
  Ding Yi
  Guo Wei
  Hong Hao
  Huang Rui
  Li Guijun
  Ling Jian
  Liu Xiaodong
  Mao Yan
  Sui Jianguo
  Sun Xun
  T'ang Haywen
  Wang Du
- **Further artists represented**
  Dong Xiwen
  Fabien Mérelle
  Barthélémy Toguo
  Zhan Jianjun

de Osma

Madrid

Galleries

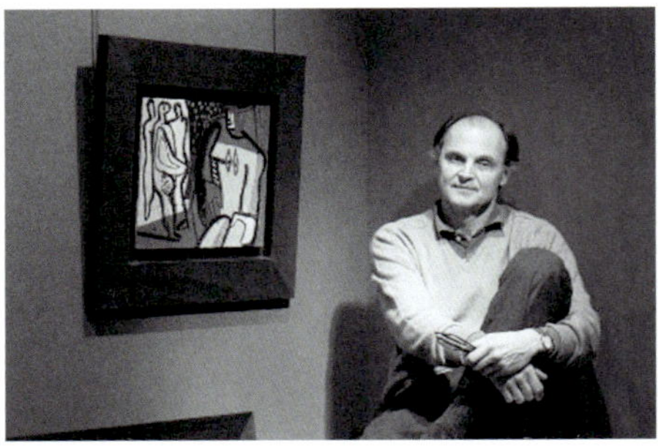

What first compelled you to open a gallery?
I had a gallery in New York until 1990, when I established myself in Madrid and decided I would open a gallery with my name.

Who is the first artist you showed and what was most memorable about that show?
My first exhibition was Barradas – Torres-García, two key figures of Latin-American and European Art. They met both in Barcelona in 1916 and were very influential for the Spanish and Latino avant-garde. We produced an important catalogue with unpublished correspondence of the artists and essays by major specialists.

When did you first participate in Art Basel and what was most memorable about that show?
In 2003, in Miami Beach. I shared the space with Galerie 1900-2000 of Paris. We had a great booth and the fair was small and beautiful.

- **Contact**
  Galería Guillermo de Osma
  Guillermo de Osma
  guillermo@guillermodeosma.com
  info@guillermodeosma.com
- **Established**
  1991
- **Owner(s) / Partner(s)**
  Guillermo de Osma (Director)
- **Team**
  3
- **Space(s)**
  220 m²

- **Artists at Art Basel** Josef Albers
Jean Arp
Antonio Bandeira
Washington Barcala
Rafael Barradas
Hércules Barsotti
Willi Baumeister
Max Bill
Victor Brauner
Lothar Charoux
Germán Cueto
Samson Flexor
Julio González
Juan Gris
José Gurvich
Le Corbusier
Esteban Lisa
Man Ray
Roberto Matta
Juan Melé
Joan Miró
César Paternosto
Pablo Picasso
Mira Schendel
Kurt Schwitters
Ivan Serpa
Richard Serra
Luis Tomasello
Joaquín Torres-García
Gregorio Vardanega
- **Further artists represented** José Alemany
Eduardo Chillida
Dis Berlin
Óscar Domínguez
Eugenio Granell
Sarah Grilo
Maruja Mallo
Francisco Sobrino

de Sarthe

Hong Kong — Galleries, Encounters

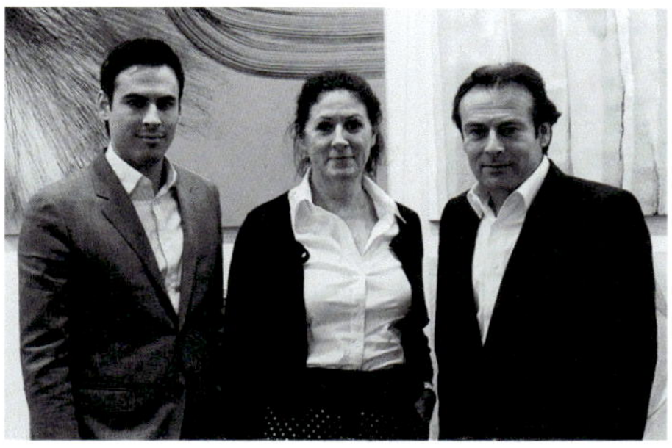

What first compelled you to open a gallery?
Passion for the art.

Who is the first artist you showed and what was the most memorable about that show?
It was in 1977. The artists were friends who were still at art school, and that was where I met my wife.

When did you first participate in Art Basel and what was most memorable about that show?
In 2013. The most memorable was being able to show Asian and Western masters alongside the younger generation of Chinese artists and receive such a positive response from collectors and the press.

- **Contact** de Sarthe Gallery
Suzanne Lau
hongkong@desarthe.com
- **Established** 1977
- **Owner(s) / Partner(s)** Pascal de Sarthe
Sylvie de Sarthe
- **Team** 10
- **Space(s)** 200 m²
- **Artists at Art Basel** Alexander Calder
Chen Zhen
Chu Teh-Chun
Hans Hartung
Lin Jing Jing
Joan Mitchell
Bernar Venet
Andy Warhol
John Wesley
Wu Guanzhong
Zao Wou-Ki

de Torres

New York — Galleries

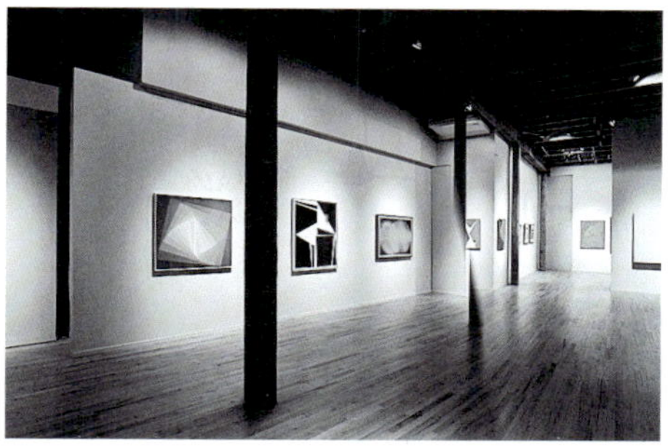

What first compelled you to open a gallery?
After co-curating the 1991 exhibition and catalogue, *El Taller Torres-García: the School of the South and Its Legacy*, that opened at the Museo Reina Sofía and traveled to other museums, I realized that without a gallery dedicated to Latin American geometric abstraction and Constructivism, the works of the show would disappear from sight. After more than a year of preparation, we opened the gallery in 1993.

Who is the first artist you showed and what was the most memorable about that show?
Francisco Matto was 82 when we opened the gallery with an exhibit of his unique totems, sculptures, and paintings, infused with the magic from Amerindian art.

When did you first participate in Art Basel and what was most memorable about that show?
In 2005 in Miami Beach. It was a very exciting experience. Our booth was always crowded and we met wonderful collectors and curators. We presented a selection of modern Constructivist works together with younger artists who were continuing the Modernist tradition into contemporary times, a theme that we continue to pursue. What was especially memorable was the enthusiasm of the visitors and the sales that we made.

- **Contact** Cecilia de Torres, Ltd.
Dan Pollock
dan@ceciliadetorres.com
mail@ceciliadetorres.com
- **Established** 1993
- **Owner(s) / Partner(s)** Cecilia de Torres
Dan Pollock
- **Team** 5
- **Space(s)** 140 m²
- **Artists at Art Basel** Julio Alpuy
Gustavo Bonevardi
Lidya Buzio
Miguel Chevalier
Marta Chilindron
José Pedro Costigliolo
Elias Crespin
Carlos Cruz-Díez
León Ferrari
Gonzalo Fonseca
José Gurvich
Louis Lim
Francisco Matto
César Paternosto
Eduardo Stupía
Augusto Torres
Horacio Torres
Joaquín Torres-García
Victor Vasarely
- **Further artists represented** Inés Bancalari
Eduardo Costa
Gustavo Díaz
María Freire
Sergio Gutman
Antonio Llorens
Jesús Matheus
Rogelio Polesello
Julián Terán

Dee

New York

Galleries

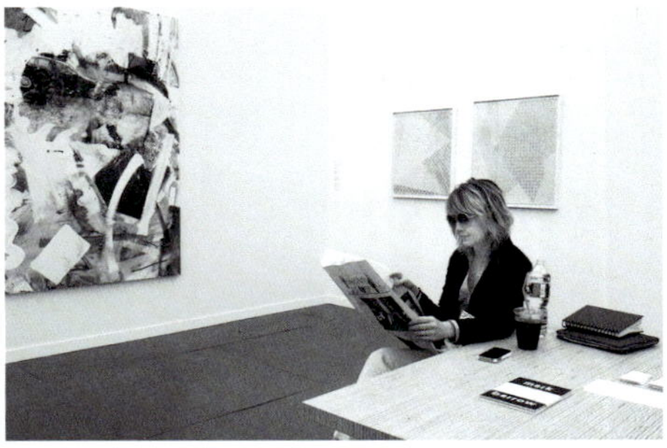

What first compelled you to open a gallery?
I love the creativity involved in playing a supportive role inside the studio as a strategist, agent, and curator. Initially in the late 1990s, I apprenticed in a 20th century gallery system, where I was extremely fortunate to have early on a number of important mentors. I was professionally raised by the older generation on a philosophy that the context for an artist's work in a curatorially rich program is the essential base from which the recognition and business for an artist would be built. I began a gallery to build that in a way that was meaningful for me, that sought to propose questions rather than provide answers. With the artists, we created a family built on that shared philosophy.

Who is the first artist you showed and what was the most memorable about that show?
We opened with a solo show of paintings by American artist Carl Ostendarp which is still one of my favorite shows to date.

When did you first participate in Art Basel and what was most memorable about that show?
Our first presentation at Art Basel was in 2009 with a two persons exhibition of Adrian Piper and Renée Green, presented together for the first time.

- **Contact** Elizabeth Dee
Jayne Drost Johnson
jayne@elizabethdee.com
info@elizabethdee.com
- **Established** 2002
- **Owner(s) / Partner(s)** Elizabeth Dee
- **Team** 5
- **Space(s)** 280 m²
- **Artists at Art Basel** Mark Barrow
Gabriele Beveridge
Philippe Decrauzat
Leo Gabin
Derek Jarman
Renaud Regnery
- **Further artists represented** Mac Adams
Miriam Cahn
Miranda Lichtenstein
Ryan McNamara
Carl Ostendarp
Adrian Piper
Julia Wachtel

Delhi Art Gallery

Delhi
Bombay

Galleries

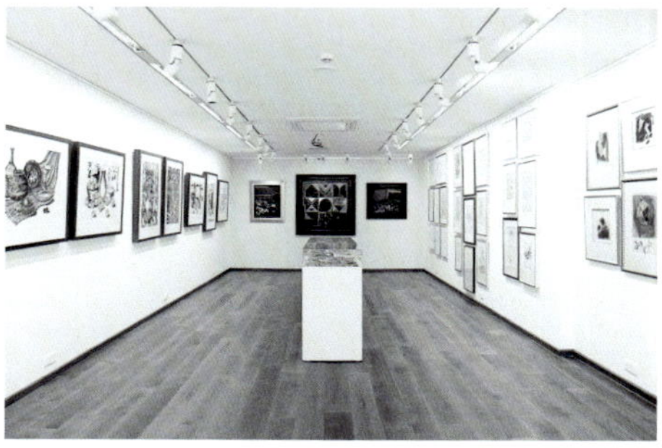

What first compelled you to open a gallery?
We saw tremendous business potential for an art gallery in India that would showcase works by old masters. In the two decades since it was established, Delhi Art Gallery has become distinguished for its focus on 20th century Indian art. Our efforts to preserve the artworks, document them, and ensure that buyers acquire the best, authentic works, have ensured our continued success.

Who is the first artist you showed and what was the most memorable about that show?
We showed works of artist GR Iranna in 1995. His work transcends the boundaries of time and space and has a profound quality. The sheer abstract force of his works at the exhibition is what made it so memorable.

When did you first participate in Art Basel and what was most memorable about that show?
Art Basel in Hong Kong gave us a platform to showcase some of our best works in front of connoisseurs, other galleries, and several other viewers. It also allowed us to demonstrate how we work with artists.

- **Contact** Delhi Art Gallery
Swapnil Avdhesh
swapnil@delhiartgallery.com
info@delhiartgallery.com
- **Established** 1993
- **Owner(s) / Partner(s)** Ashish Anand
- **Team** 75
- **Space(s)** 1,115 m²
- **Artists at Art Basel** K.H. Ara
S.K. Bakre
Bikash Bhattacharjee
Avinash Chandra
Jogen Chowdhury
K.K. Hebbar
M.F. Husain
Rabin Mondal
Akbar Padamsee
Sohan Qadri
S.H. Raza
G.R. Santosh
F.N. Souza
- **Further artists represented** Ambadas
Chittaprosad
Amitava Das
Haren Das
Sunil Das
Dhramanaryan Dasgupta
Prodosh Dasgupta
Gopal Ghose
Laxma Goud
Krishen Khanna
P Khemraj
Gogi Saroj Pal
Jamini Roy
Bireswar Sen
Paritosh Sen

didier

Brussels
Paris

Edition

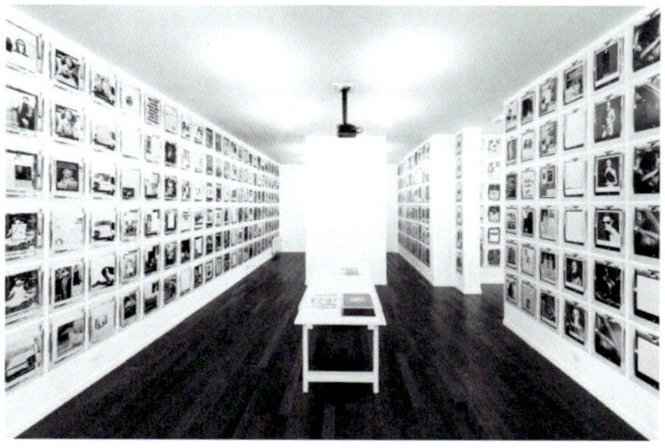

What first compelled you to open a gallery?
Mfc-michèle didier is first and foremost a publishing company. As an editor, my wish was to focus on production and publication of original works by contemporary artists. Acting as an intermediary between the artist and production professionals, I strive to keep intact the original project entrusted by the artist. In 2011, I opened a gallery in Paris as a place of reflection on the specific field of the artist's book.

Who is the first artist you showed and what was the most memorable about that show?
David Tremlett and Michelangelo Pistoletto were the artists I made my first publications with. Claude Closky was the first artist who was shown at the gallery in Paris, with the work Inside a *Triangle* (2011). It was really memorable because the artist's book was unfolded in a 44-meter long accordion.

When did you first participate in Art Basel and what was most memorable about that show?
My first participation was at Art Unlimited in 2004, where I showed the first part of On Kawara's *Trilogy*, entitled *I MET*. This 12-volume publication was shown with 12 On Kawara's *Date Paintings* from 1968 to 1979. The ensemble was really magnificent.

- **Contact** — mfc-michèle didier
Michèle Didier
micheledidier@gmail.com
info@micheledidier.com
- **Established** — 1987
- **Owner(s) / Partner(s)** — Michèle Didier
- **Team** — 3
- **Space(s)** — 85 m²
- **Artists at Art Basel** — Samuel Bianchini
On Kawara
Leigh Ledare
Allan McCollum
Annette Messager
Maurizio Nannucci
- **Further artists represented** — Dennis Adams
Carl Andre
Robert Barry
AA Bronson
Stanley Brouwn
Philippe Cazal
Claude Closky
Hannah Collins
David Cunningham
Charles de Meaux
Braco Dimitrijevic
Peter Downsbrough
Paul-Armand Gette
Liam Gillick
Joseph Grigely
Carsten Höller
Pierre Huyghe
Matt Keegan
Jutta Koether
Christian Marclay
John Miller
Jonathan Monk
Robert Morris
Antonio Muntadas
Philippe Parreno
Michelangelo Pistoletto
Hermann Pitz
Allen Ruppersberg
Joe Scanlan
Klaus Scherübel
Jim Shaw
Josh Smith
Lawrence Weiner
Christopher Wool

Dirimart

Istanbul

- Galleries
- Feature

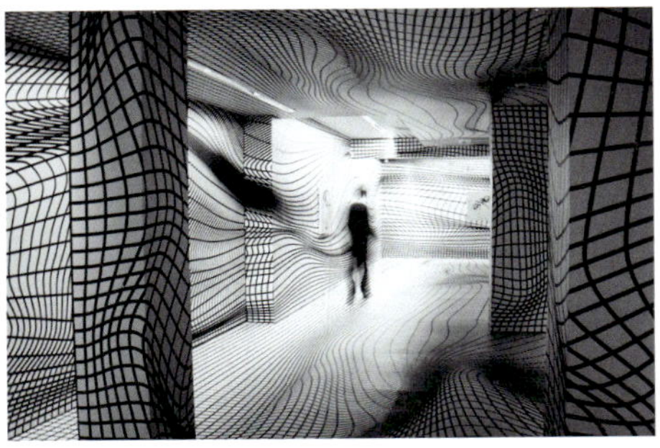

What first compelled you to open a gallery?
Our belief in a group of Turkish artists.

Who is the first artist you showed and what was the most memorable about that show?
Komet, Paris-based Turkish artist, born in 1940.

When did you first participate in Art Basel and what was most memorable about that show?
In 2013. While we were in Basel, a series of demonstrations and protests were taking place in Istanbul, and we were all trying to answer the visitors' curious questions about what is going on back home, rather than introducing Yuksel Arslan, the artist we put forward on our Feature booth.

- **Contact** — Dirimart
Tankut Aykut
tankut@dirimart.org
info@dirimart.org
- **Established** — 2002
- **Owner(s) / Partner(s)** — Hazer Ozil
- **Team** — 4
- **Space(s)** — 160 m²
- **Artists at Art Basel** — Yüksel Arslan
Sabine Boehl
Ebru Uygun
Ekrem Yalcindag
- **Further artists represented** — Franz Ackermann
Yesim Akdeniz
Ghada Amer
Neda Ismail Atar
Suzan Batu
Thomas Bayrle
Katharina Grosse
Özlem Günyol & Mustafa Kunt
Axel Hütte
Özcan Kaplan
Peter Kogler
Bjørn Melhus
Sarah Morris
Hermann Nitsch
Bill Viola
Wim Wenders
Necmi Zeka
O Zhang

Drawing Room

Manila
Singapore

- Galleries

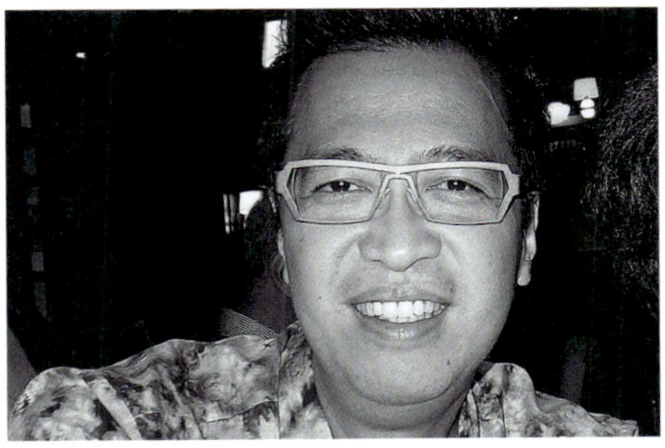

What first compelled you to open a gallery?
The Drawing Room began as a specialist venue that revitalised works on paper. Although works on paper is a major art form, they were not as collected as canvas works in the Philippines. I wanted to encourage collectors to take a second look at this important art form. Soon, this alcove of a particular medium expanded to various artistic formats that map the complex scope of thinking attributed to the contemporary terrain of Philippine art. In 2012, The Drawing Room opened its Singapore space in Gillman Barracks.

Who is the first artist you showed and what was the most memorable about that show?
It was a big group show of works on paper by artists working outside of Manila. It was an exciting combination of up and coming, mid-career and senior artists. Several soon became national artists.

When did you first participate in Art Basel and what was most memorable about that show?
We participated in the 2013 Art Basel in Hong Kong. We brought major works of artists we were working very closely with.

D

- **Contact** The Drawing Room
  Cesar Villalon
  cesarvillalonjr@gmail.com
- **Established** 1998
- **Owner(s) / Partner(s)** Cesar Villalon, Jr.
- **Team** 7
- **Space(s)** 200 m² (Singapore)
  80 m² (Manila)
- **Artists at Art Basel** Alfredo and Isabel Aquilizan
  Gaston Damag
  Kawayan De Guia
  Jose Legaspi
  Mark Salvatus
- **Further artists represented** Vermont Coronel II
  Roderico Jose Daroy
  Kiko Escora
  Roberto Feleo
  Alvin Gregorio
  Riel Hilario
  Troy Ignacio
  Diokno Pasilan
  Lirio Salvador

du Monde

Hong Kong — Discoveries, Encounters

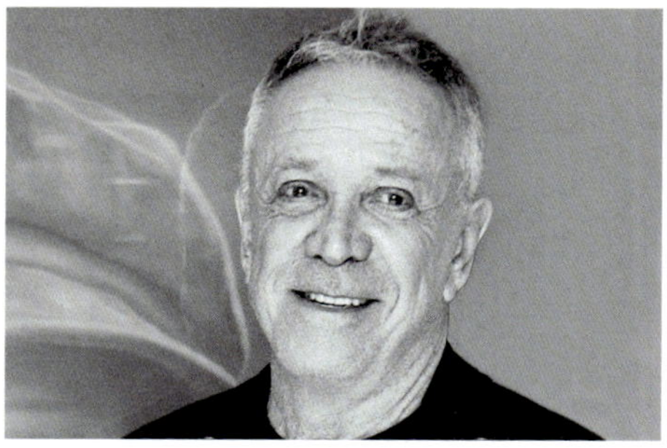

What first compelled you to open a gallery?
It was time to bring contemporary art to the people of Hong Kong, although in the mid-1970s, it was mainly expatriates interested in the visual arts. Interest by local people increased as a middle class started to emerge in the city, or colony as it was then known.

Who is the first artist you showed and what was the most memorable about that show?
David Hockney. The very positive interest shown by Hong Kong people in contemporary art, when collecting at that time involved mainly China School drawings and paintings or traditional Chinese ink paintings.

When did you first participate in Art Basel and what was most memorable about that show?
In 2013 in Hong Kong. In addition to showing a large installation (by Qin Chong) in the Encounters sector, we were showing a very conceptual installation in the Discoveries sector by the young Hong Kong artist Lam Tung-pang which most unexpectedly was sold during the fair to a private collector.

- **Contact** Galerie du Monde
  Fred Scholle
  fscholle@galeriedumonde.com
  fineart@galeriedumonde.com
- **Established** 1974
- **Owner(s) / Partner(s)** Fred W. Scholle
- **Space(s)** 300 m²
- **Artists at** Lam Tung-pang
- **Further artists represented** Feng Zhengquan
  Huang Yong
  Li Gang
  Liu Bolin
  Lu Yanpeng
  Qin Chong
  Qin Feng
  Qin Wen
  Shi Jinsong
  Sun Yi
  Wang Lifeng
  Yang Tao
  Zhang Xiaotao
  Zhu Yiyong

Dvir

Tel Aviv — Galleries

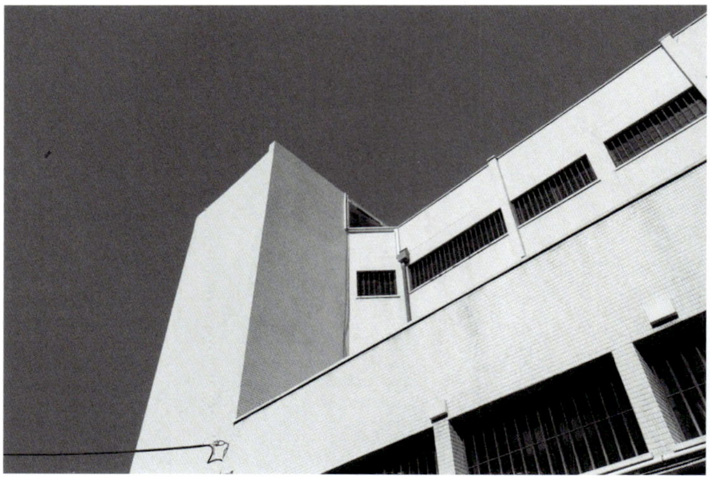

What first compelled you to open a gallery?
Dvir Intrator: My passion for art came from my parents who were enthusiastic art lovers and collectors. It was just natural for me to continue this line in the form of a gallery.

Who is the first artist you showed and what was the most memorable about that show?
David Reeb was the first artist the gallery showed. The most memorable about the show were Reeb's paintings of peaceful scenes that seemed to explode.

When did you first participate in Art Basel and what was most memorable about that show?
Dvir Gallery first participated to Art Basel in 2007. It was very exciting for us to be part of this prestigious art fair.

- **Contact** Dvir Gallery
  Yotam Shalit-Intrator
  dvirhangar2@bezeqint.net
  info@dvirgallery.com
- **Established** 1982
- **Owner(s) / Partner(s)** Dvir Intrator (Owner)
  Shifra Shalit (Owner)
  Yotam Shalit-Intrator (Director)
- **Team** 6
- **Space(s)** 1,000 m²
- **Artists at Art Basel** Adel Abdessemed
  Etti Abergel
  Nelly Agassi
  Miroslaw Balka
  Yossi Breger
  Mircea Cantor
  Claire Fontaine
  Latifa Echakhch
  Hans-Peter Feldmann
  Simon Fujiwara
  Douglas Gordon
  Dor Guez
  Shilpa Gupta
  Yudith Levin
  Boris Mikhailov
  Jonathan Monk
  Barak Ravitz
  Karen Russo
  Ariel Schlesinger
  Miri Segal
  Anna Shteynshleyger
  Taryn Simon
  Nedko Solakov
  Haim Steinbach
  Tavares Strachan
  Yanai Toister
  Naama Tsabar
  Lawrence Weiner
  Pavel Wolberg

Dirimart

Interview with Hazer Özil

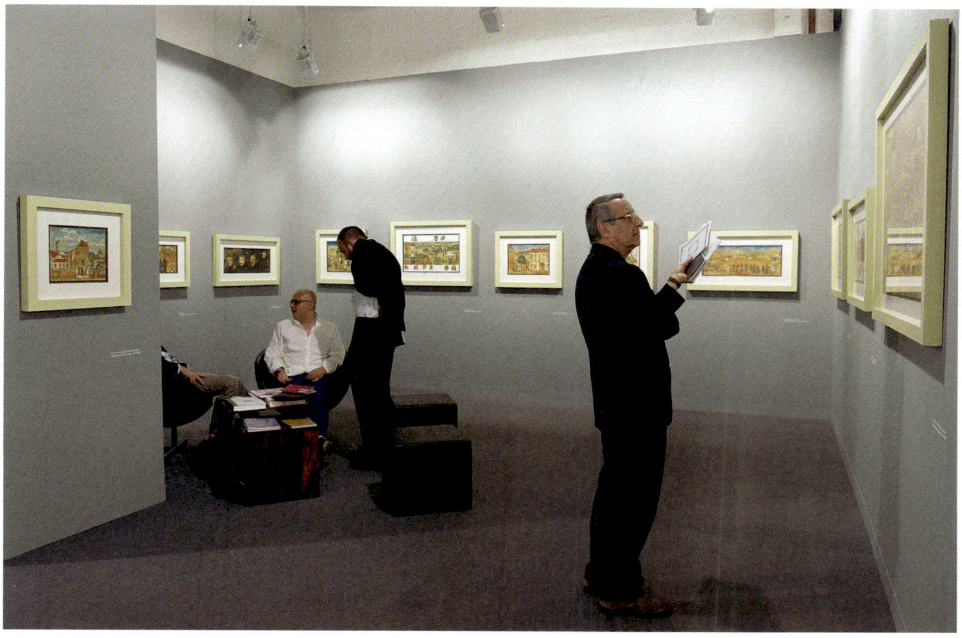

Art Basel in Basel
(Feature), 2013

You participated in Art Basel last June with a solo show devoted to Yüksel Arslan, an artist present at the 2013 Venice Biennale. Why did you choose this artist? How did you conceive the Feature booth?

Yüksel Arslan is an extraordinary Turkish artist who defies categorization. For more than 60 years he has been creating idiosyncratic images based on his extensive, highly personal studies of various visual and literary sources. We have always been keen admirers of his *sui generis* works, even though the international art community has only recently begun to recognize him as a unique master. In fact, the very first solo show at Dirimart gallery—ten years ago—was devoted to his amazing *Das Kapital* series. We were convinced that it would be a great idea to show his oeuvre in the Feature sector of Art Basel, not only because of his technical inventiveness, but also because of his courage to confront both sexual and political issues in a very uncompromising way.

When conceiving the booth, we tried to avoid an overcrowded, confusing representation. Instead of a pseudo-retrospective, we concentrated on designing a sleek, almost poetical show. Our main concern was to highlight his most characteristic fixations and provocations *in nuce*. Encouraging comments from visitors both familiar and unfamiliar with his work proved that our approach was right.

How do you build your program and selection of artists in terms of generational and geographical/cultural origin (Turkey/international)? Also, why is it important to you to publish a bi-annual magazine (*RES World Art/Art World*) and to thus be a cultural actor in the Turkish scene?

Dirimart is aiming not only to become the leading gallery in Turkey, but also a preeminent one in the international arena. In today's highly integrated art world, we think it is our duty to act as a resourceful enabler for both our collectors and artists. In that sense we try to work with cutting-edge artists with an ambition for wider recognition regardless of their nationality or age. While increasingly concentrating on world-renowned, established artists, we also keep an eye on exciting mid-career or young local artists. We feel very fortunate and privileged to be based in Istanbul, for the city's highly dynamic social and cultural life constantly inspires us to explore new avenues and broaden our horizon.

RES magazine, now in its sixth year, is an independent publication subsidized by Dirimart. We are very proud of its worldwide achievements and plan to continue our support to intelligent dialogue about art. In fact, we have recently decided to turn it into a quarterly and publish books as well.

This year, you participated in Art Basel and Art Basel in Hong Kong. How would you define these two fairs?

Both fairs were quite impressive in scope and magnitude. They definitely managed to attract enthusiastic audiences. Most importantly, their well-planned, highly professional designs facilitated meaningful communication and engagement. To a certain degree, Art Basel in Hong Kong appeared to be more spirited, with several inquisitive and open-minded visitors. Art Basel, on the other hand, stood out with its unparalleled, stimulating sophistication. We also felt a firm commitment to innovation and improvement, which boosted our optimism about the future.

D

The Discoveries sector, Art Basel in Hong Kong's global platform for emerging contemporary artists, allows galleries to show pieces by one or two artists from their program.

DIS COVER IES

2013 participants

Aike-Dellarco
Li Ran

Balice Hertling
Alexander May

BolteLang
Benjamin Senior

Cooley
Erin Shirreff

du Monde
Lam Tun-pang

Houldsworth
Francesca DiMattio

Jongma
Nina Yuen
Donna Huddleston

Kalfayan
Hrair Sarkissian
Raed Yassin

Karma International
Thomas Sauter
Ida Ekblad

Mendes Wood
Lucas Arruda

Francesca Minini
Matthias Bitzer
Becky Beasley

Monitor
Adam Avikainen

mother's tankstation
Brendan Earley

Mujin-to
Chim↑Pom
Sachiko Kazama

2P
Kwok Hin Tang

Paradise Row
Shezad Dawood

Plan B
Navid Nuur
Adrian Ghenie

RaebervonStenglin
David Keating

Rokeby
Sam Dargan

S.A.L.E.S.
Avish Khebrehzadeh
Shahryar Nashat

Seven Art
Rajorshi Ghosh

SKE
Mariam Suhail

Take Ninagawa
Ryoko Aoki

Utopian Slumps
Sanne Mestrom

Weingrüll
Benjamin Appel

Workplace
Marcus Coates

Xu
Wei Chen

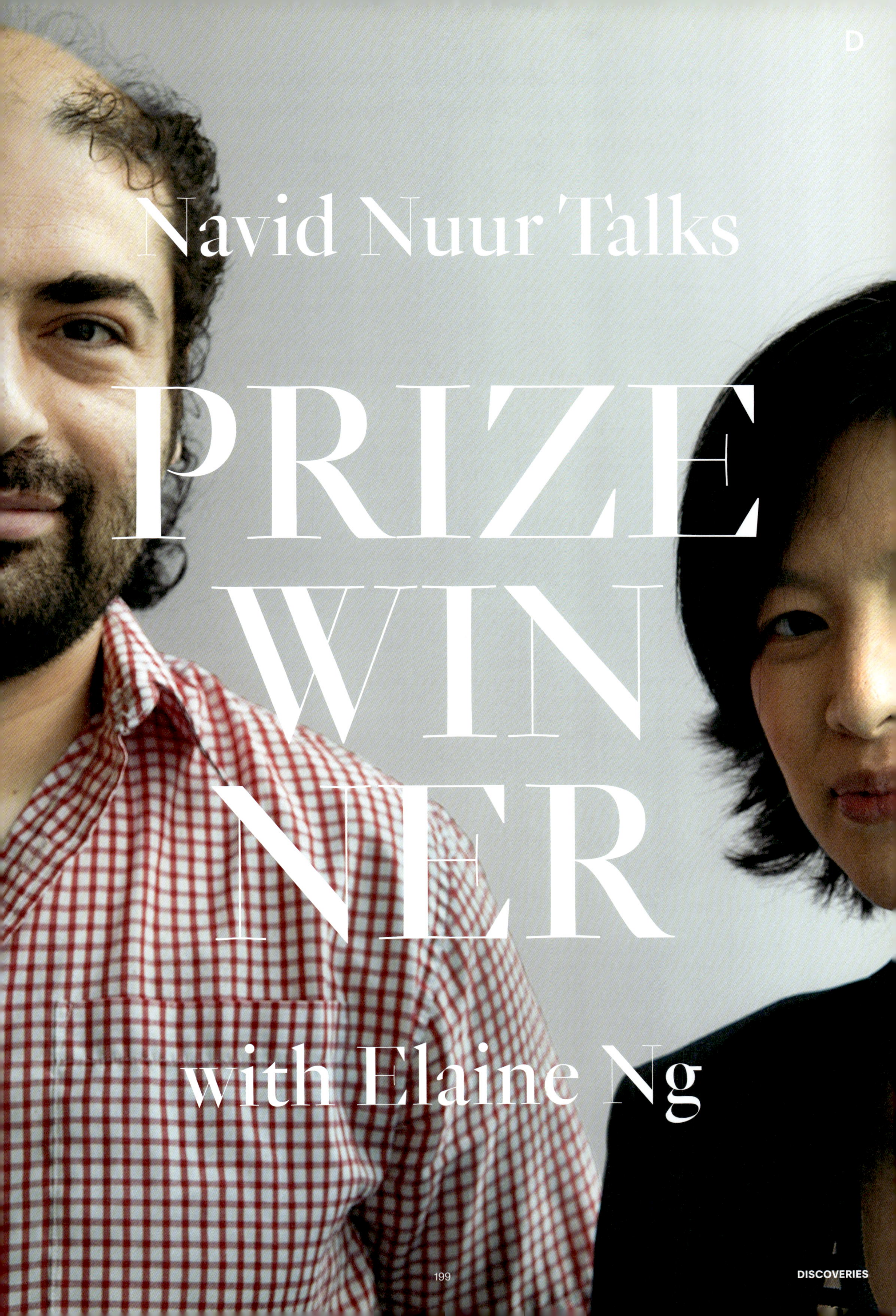

Navid Nuur Talks PRIZE WINNER with Elaine Ng

D

The Possibility of Purple

The first Discoveries Prize was awarded to Navid Nuur and Adrian Ghenie, presented by Galeria Plan B

Hong Kong
Discoveries

The prize consists of 25,000 US$. The artists were chosen by an expert panel of judges for their collaborative project, *The Possibility of Purple*, which questions the dematerialization of painting through a dialogue between the figurative and abstract.

Navid Nuur (1976, Teheran) lives and works in The Hague, Netherlands.

Adrian Ghenie (1977, Baia Mare, Romania) lives and works in Cluj and Berlin.

ELAINE NG You have been awarded the prize for *The Possibility of Purple* with Adrian Ghenie. Can you tell me how the collaboration came about?

NAVID NUUR Adrian and I are completely different in our practice: I do conceptual works and don't believe in any medium, while he is a figurative and historical painter. Visually it doesn't fit together. But, on a social level, we have lots of discussions about art.

One of our pieces consists of my voice accompanying the painting: I asked Adrian to paint, and as he was painting, like a commentary of a soccer game, I vocalized his actions and made the process clear. For a small dot, I went "blue," and a big dot I went "BLUE." Adrian could paint in any way he wanted with only the limitation to use red and blue. It left him the freedom to move into abstraction, and it was freedom for me as well because someone else was doing the work!

I think in a conceptual way with all my senses: not only with my mind, but with my nose, my mouth, and my hands.
— Navid Nuur

We both painted one half of the diptych *On the Road to Tarascon*. It is based on a Vincent van Gogh painting that was lost, and that inspired Francis Bacon to do his own version: a painter in front of a wheat field. Adrian did a third version based on the two previous ones, in a traditional way. Even though we used the same subject matter, my part is more static because it is based on research: I created a font on the computer by making a fusion of Vincent's and Adrian's brushstrokes and a grid that I colored with the paint Adrian had used for his part.

EN Somehow there is also action in Adrian's part. Could you tell us about it?

NN That's just Adrian's flow. Sometimes when he is not sure about a certain area, he smudges it, takes it off, and then maybe he sees a form, a face for example, that he keeps. There are abstract parts in his work, but they lead your eyes through the painting. The abstract parts in-between the narrative parts are not just random brushstrokes, they make you navigate through the painting. In my own interpretation of Adrian's and Vincent's paintings, I took these abstract elements into consideration. You will also find dots, but they appear more clearly as you walk further away from the painting. On the other hand, Adrian's part should be viewed close-up. My painting needs to be seen from a great distance, while Adrian takes you further in. This makes a complex optical relationship between our two paintings.

EN What about *Study 55/Ghenie* ...

NN It's from the Eye Codex of the Monochrome series. It results from years of studies about the phenomenology of colors, their emotional and optical impact. It's another collaboration: Adrian Ghenie made the blue color, and I made the painting. Actually I'm not so interested in the painting, or the final result, I am more attracted by all the side stuff that makes the painting, i.e. the way you perceive things with your eyes, how you can change knowledge into matter, how you can see the same painting from different conceptual points of view.

EN What about these little sculptures?

NN These small objects are made out of things produced when making the paintings, but which the painter doesn't need. For example, parts pushed out of the painting.

I've collected these bits in Adrian's studio, together with the rest of the residues I found in his studio, and put spy lenses on top and around them. They become this new microcosm, almost like a potential sublayer within his practice and my practice. I've made similar objects in 2006 with things that I found in my own studio, but this was the first time I've done it with somebody else's studio. These objects are called *These Are the Days.*

EN When did your collaboration start? And how did you know about each other's work?

NN We started the discussions about two years ago. We knew each other from the gallery where we both exhibited. We both knew that we had these respective gaps in our practices, and that we could use each other's energy to develop something. It was a genuine collaboration, where we both wanted to learn from each other. It wasn't something hip to do.

EN Were you attracted to the work?

NN No, not at all! For me he was just another traditional oil painter, but I liked him a lot as a person, and then I got more and more fascinated about the fact that his practice is so traditional. What did that mean? Limiting yourself to one thing, and positioning yourself in the history of painting.

EN Have you been thinking about the history of conceptualism and possibly where your practice fits in?

NN To be honest, the problem with conceptualism, especially in the 1960s, is that it's almost like being "über-catholic" … I think in a conceptual way with all my senses: not only with my mind, but with my nose, my mouth, and my hands. This represents a multi-layered intellect that I want to include in my work.

EN In 2011 you started the discussions, and in September 2012 you began to work in the studio. The discussions happened through emails and meetings in Berlin. Did you document that process?

NN We made a list and notes. We didn't document our discussions, but we would like to make a small publication to accompany the show at Galeria Plan B in September 2013.

EN What about the title of the show: *The Possibility of Purple*?

NN It was first about these two colors: red and blue. Together they become purple. I had worked with these colors in my clay works, in which you could hear me saying how the work was made. Purple is also the color of somebody smacked in the face. They are two colors that you have in your skin. As a painter Adrian was familiar with them as he used them to depict the skin. Used in different proportions, they show different emotions.

Navid Nuur with Adrian Ghenie, Galeria Plan B

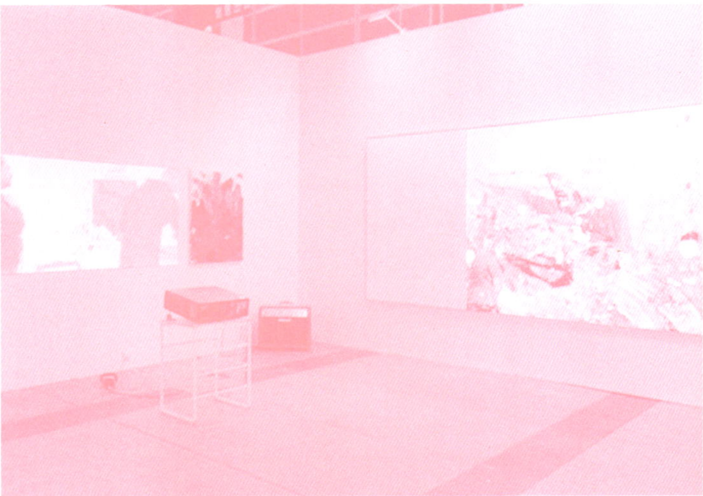

E

E

Ecart

Geneva — Galleries (Basel)

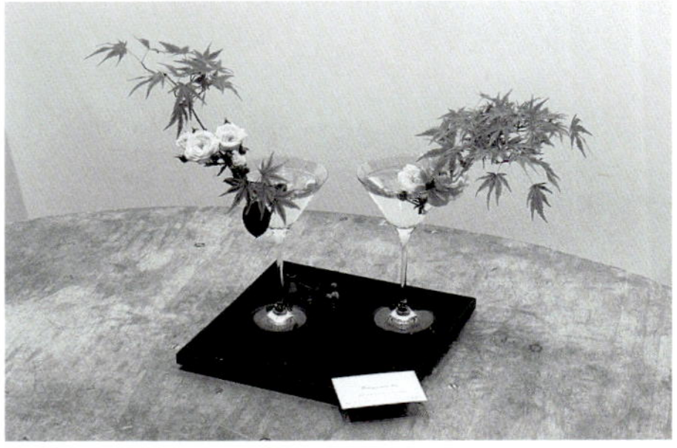

What first compelled you to open a gallery?
After opening an artists' cooperative under the name of Ecart in 1969 with a group of friends, we saw the necessity of making available current developments in art, in the form of a cooperative, artist-ran gallery.

Who is the first artist you showed and what was most memorable about that show?
John Armleder & Patrick Lucchini, *Events & Happenings* in December 1972.

When did you first participate in Art Basel and what was most memorable about that show?
In 1978.

- **Contact** Ecart
  Mai-Thu Perret
  mai-thu@bluewin.ch
  john.armleder@bluewin.ch
- **Established** 1972
- **Owner(s) / Partner(s)** John Armleder
  Mai-Thu Perret
- **Artists at Art Basel** Mimo Battista

Edwin's

Jakarta — Insights (Hong Kong)

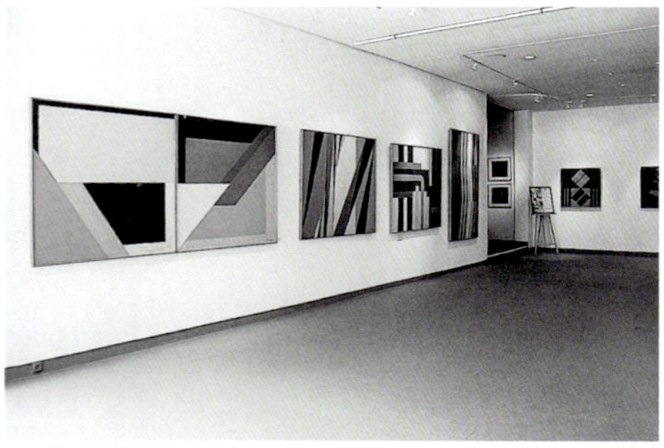

What first compelled you to open a gallery?
Passion.

When did you first participate in Art Basel and what was most memorable about that show?
In 2010, with Heri Dono's works.

- **Contact** Edwin's Gallery
  Edwin Rahardjo
  edwins_gallery@yahoo.com
  edwingaleri@cbn.net.id
- **Established** 1984
- **Owner(s) / Partner(s)** Edwin Rahardjo
- **Team** 30
- **Space(s)** 500 m²
- **Artists at Art Basel** Jumaldi Alfi
  Heri Dono
- **Further artists represented** Ayu Arista Murti
  Gusmen Heriadi
  Yi Hwan Kwon
  Hojatul Islam
  Piotr Jedrzejewski
  Bob Potts
  Edwin Rahardjo

Eigen + Art

Berlin
Leipzig

Galleries (Hong Kong)
Galleries (Basel)
Galleries (Miami Beach)

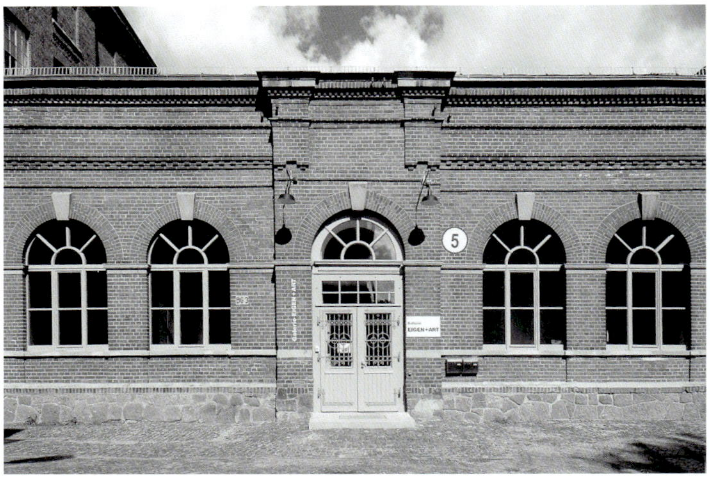

Who is the first artist you showed and what was most memorable about that show?
The first artists we showed during the early years were Olaf Nicolai, Carsten Nicolai, Maix Mayer, Jörg Herold, Uwe Kowski, and Neo Rauch.

When did you first participate in Art Basel and what was most memorable about that show?
In 1991, with works by Carsten Nicolai, Olaf Nicolai, and works of the Swiss artist Annelies Strba.

- **Contact** Galerie Eigen + Art
  Gerd Harry Lybke
  berlin@eigen-art.com
- **Established** 1983 (Leipzig)
  1992 (Berlin)
- **Owner(s) / Partner(s)** Gerd Harry Lybke (Owner)
  Kerstin Wahala (Partner)
- **Team** 22
- **Space(s)** 350 m² (Leipzig)
  220 m² (Berlin)
  230 m² (Berlin "Lab")
- **Artists at Art Basel** Birgit Brenner
  Marc Desgrandchamps
  Martin Eder
  Tim Eitel
  Jörg Herold
  Uwe Kowski
  Rémy Markowitsch
  Ryan Mosley
  Carsten Nicolai
  Olaf Nicolai
  Neo Rauch
  Yehudit Sasportas
  David Schnell
  Matthias Weischer
- **Further artists represented** Akos Birkas
  Nina Fischer & Maroan el Sani
  Stella Hamberg
  Christine Hill
  Maix Mayer
  Ricarda Roggan
  Annelies Strba

elbaz

Paris

- Feature
- Nova
- Public

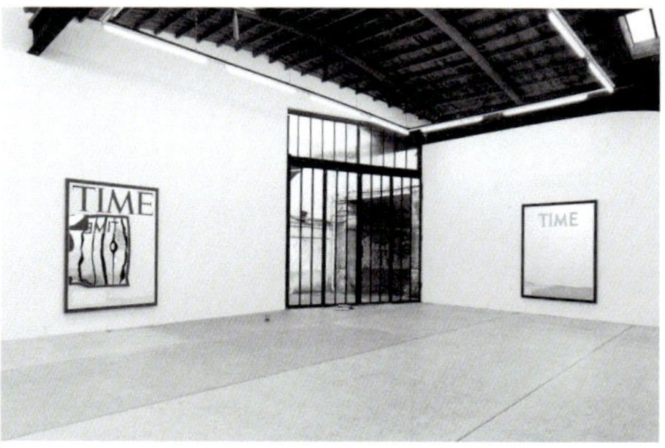

When did you first participate in Art Basel?
We started in 2009.

- **Contact** galerie frank elbaz
  Danka Sosic
  danka@galeriefrankelbaz.com
  info@galeriefrankelbaz.com
- **Established** 2002
- **Owner(s) / Partner(s)** Frank Elbaz
- **Space(s)** 200 m²
- **Artists at Art Basel** Davide Balula
  Mungo Thomson
  Blair Thurman
- **Further artists represented** Jesus Alberto Benitez
  Wallace Berman
  Tomislav Gotovac
  Julije Knifer
  Rainier Lericolais
  Mangelos
  Ari Marcopoulos
  Kaz Oshiro
  Gyan Panchal
  Bernard Piffaretti
  Meredyth Sparks
  Mladen Stilinovic
  Josip Vanista

EM

Seoul

- Insights

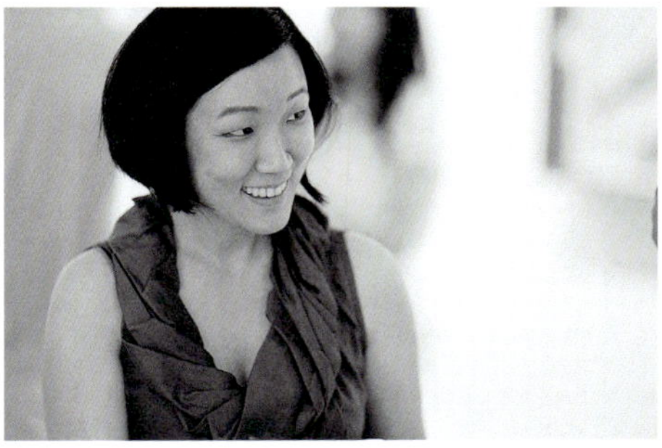

What first compelled you to open a gallery?
The passion for contemporary art, finding undervalued talents and growing with them.

Who is the first artist you showed and what was most memorable about that show?
It was a group show of young Korean and international artists. The show was a statement about the gallery's future direction, and having artists from different cultural and artistic backgrounds created wonderful stories.

When did you first participate in Art Basel and what was most memorable about that show?
This year at Art Basel in Hong Kong was my first participation. I showed Jae Yong Rhee. The visitors' reception of his work was quite wonderful.

- **Contact** Gallery EM
  Emma Son
  emma@galleryem.co.kr
- **Established** 2007
- **Owner(s) / Partner(s)** Emma Son
- **Team** 3
- **Space(s)** 116 m²
- **Artists at Art Basel** Jae Yong Rhee
- **Further artists represented** Hyuongsun Chang
  Siyeon Kim
  Yeowoon Kim
  Jeanie Lee
  Siwoo Lee
  Jörg Obergfell
  Jon Widman

Eslite

Taipei

- Galleries

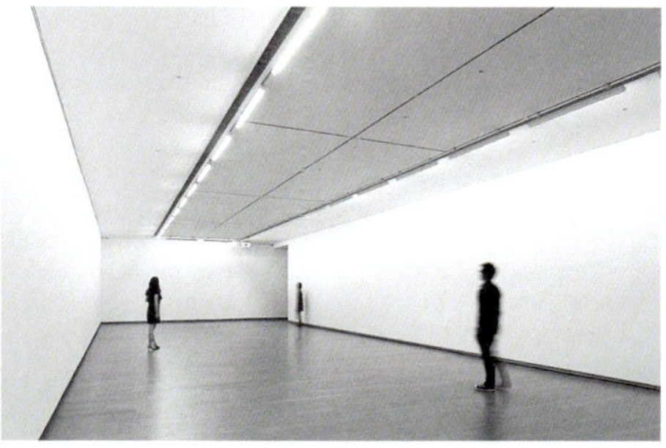

What first compelled you to open a gallery?
Emily Li Chao: In 1989, Taiwan's economy was on the rise; yet no place existed where people could find goods that were infused with art, design, and culture. At the time, Taiwanese art galleries were all presenting the same kind of art showing Japanese influences. Wishing to break from this mold, Robert C.Y. Wu imagined a more contemplative space that not only included books dedicated to art, but also a space for modern and contemporary art.

Who is the first artist you showed and what was most memorable about that show?
For the first six months, Eslite Gallery exhibited a series called *Appreciating Art* focusing on six artists—the works were not for sale, but for appreciation.

When did you first participate in Art Basel and what was most memorable about that show?
Our first participation was in 2009 in Basel in the Premiere sector. We showed Kuang-Yu Tsui and Michael Lin.

- **Contact** Eslite Gallery
  Casey Fan
  caseyfan@eslite.com
- **Established** 1989
- **Owner(s) / Partner(s)** Robert C.Y. Wu (Owner)
  Emily Li Chao (Director)
- **Team** 8
- **Space(s)** 1,000 m²
- **Artists at Art Basel** Liu Xiaodong
- **Further artists represented** Cai Guo-Qiang
  Tommy Chen
  Hsia Yang
  Ben-rei Huang
  Yi-Chen Hung
  Jeng Jundian
  Fu-sheng Ku
  Kuo Chwen
  Shida Kuo
  Lai Chih-Sheng
  Ai-Chen Lee
  Lee Ji-Hong
  Lee Mingwei
  Liao Chien-Chung
  Lien Chien Hsing
  Michael Lin
  Lin Yen Wei
  Su Wongshen
  Szeto Keung
  Su-Mei Tse
  Kuang-Yu Tsui
  Wang Yuping
  Jennifer Wen Ma
  Wong Hoy Cheong
  Xu Bing
  Tzu Chi Yeh
  Yu Hong
  Zhan Wang

Exhibit320

New Delhi ● Insights

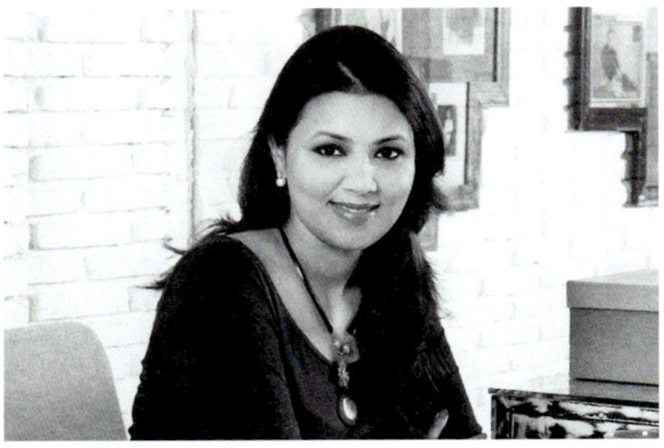

What first compelled you to open a gallery?
I've been collecting art from a very young age, and realized that in India there is immense talent accompanied by a lack of exhibition spaces. Seeing a major interest in contemporary art among the new generation of collectors, I opened a space, Exhibit320, in 2008. We have presented artists from India and from the Asia-Pacific region ever since. We are hosting now *Audible Forces*, a show curated by Diana Campbell Betancourt, in the gallery where we have shown for the first time in India artists such as Christian Marclay, Pedro Reyes, Amailia Pica, and Hannah Weinberger.

When did you first participate in Art Basel and what was most memorable about that show?
We first exhibited in 2011, with works by Nandan Ghiya and Muktinath Mondal. It was a great experience. I think our artists got a lot from the participation in terms of meeting new curators and museums.

- **Contact** Exhibit320
  Ranjita Chaney
  ranjitaraphael@gmail.com
  exhibit320@gmail.com
- **Established** 2009
- **Owner(s) / Partner(s)** Rasika Kajaria
- **Team** 7
- **Space(s)** 205 m²
- **Artists at Art Basel** Nandan Ghiya
- **Further artists represented** Bose Krishnamachari
  Muktinath Mondal
  Princess Pea
  Sandip Pisalkar
  Sachin George Sebastian
  Sumakshi Singh
  Priti Vadakkath

Exit

Hong Kong ● Galleries

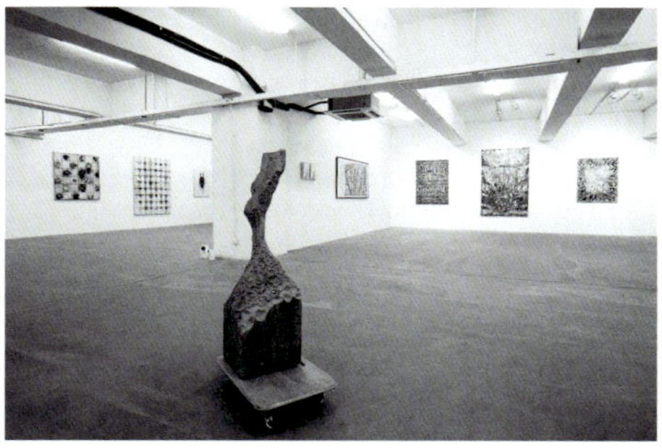

What first compelled you to open a gallery?
Hong Kong, with its unique culture, history, and dynamism has much to offer. We felt a need to identify, develop, and present emerging artists from the city and the region.

Who is the first artist you showed and what was most memorable about that show?
Lin Xue. We were touched that he would show his artworks again, after a ten year retreat.

When did you first participate in Art Basel and what was most memorable about that show?
We started by participating in ART HK back in 2009. The fair had already generated quite a buzz on an international level and we were glad to be one of the galleries to exemplify what this newcomer in the art world had to show.

- **Contact** Gallery Exit
  Joyce Lau
  joyce@galleryexit.com
  info@galleryexit.com
- **Established** 2008
- **Owner(s) / Partner(s)** Anthony Tao
- **Team** 3
- **Space(s)** 280 m²
- **Artists at Art Basel** Chihoi
  Hsu Yinling
  Kong Chun Hei
  Kwan Sheung Chi
  Sarah Lai
  Lewis Lau
  Lin Xue
  Ivy Ma
  Christine Ng Mien Yin
  Lulu Ngie
  Angela Su
- **Further artists represented** Nadim Abbas
  Chen Wei
  Cheung Szelit
  Genevieve Chua
  Silas Fong
  Makoto Fujimura
  Kong Yiu Wing
  Elise Lai
  Lam Hoi Sin
  Ng Ka Chun
  Roy Ng
  Cam Wong
  Trevor Yeung

Experimenter

Kolkata ● Feature

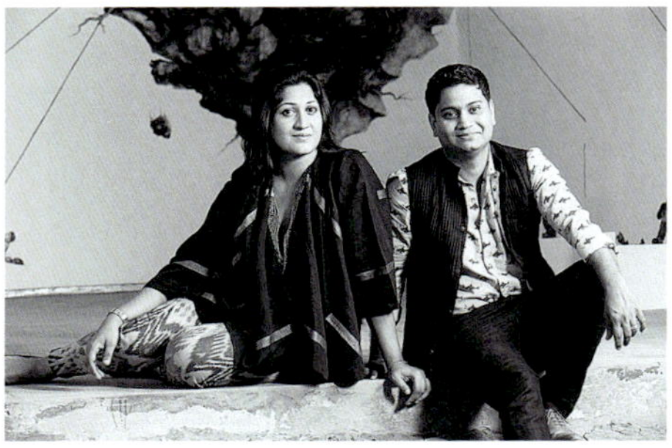

What first compelled you to open a gallery?
The need to show contemporary art that is relevant to the time we live in and is challenging to the viewers, in a way questioning the boundaries we set for ourselves.

Who is the first artist you showed and what was most memorable about that show?
For our first show, we had a group exhibition. We think it was a kind of show the city had never seen before. It set a longer-term association with the city and thereafter the region, far beyond our imagination.

- **Contact** Experimenter
  Prateek Raja
  prateek@experimenter.in
  info@experimenter.in
- **Established** 2009
- **Owner(s) / Partner(s)** Priyanka Raja
  Prateek Raja
- **Team** 6
- **Space(s)** 200 m²
- **Artists at Art Basel** Bani Abidi
  Naeem Mohaiemen
  Hajra Waheed
- **Further artists represented** Rathin Barman
  CAMP
  Natasha de Betak
  Adip Dutta
  Sanchayan Ghosh
  Nadia Kaabi-Linke
  Mehreen Murtaza
  Raqs Media Collective

Experimenter

Interview with Prateek & Priyanka Raja

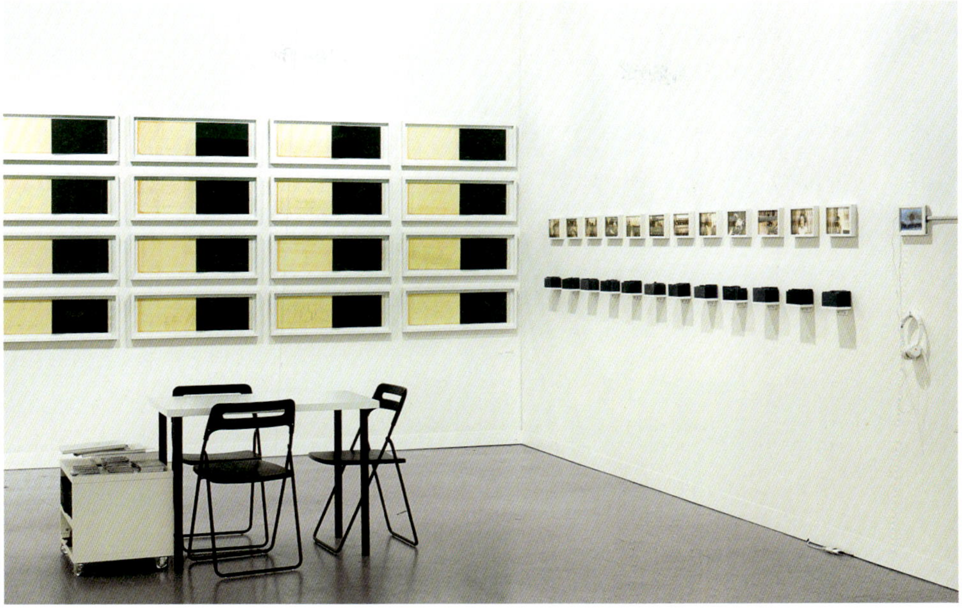

Art Basel in Basel (Feature), 2013

When did your gallery open and how would you define its program?

It opened in 2009 in Kolkata. It is focused on contemporary artists, mainly from South Asia, but also from across the world. We represent ten artists. Though it is not completely explicit, we do have a political bias in the program: a lot of the artists we work with have a sort of political intuition. In terms of medium we show photography, installation, drawings, sculpture, and quite a lot of film.

What led you to open a gallery? What is your background?

Prateek and I are married and we both had a different career previously: I worked for a shampoo manufacturer and Prateek was an art consultant. He wanted to open his own gallery for a long time, something cutting-edge, ahead of its time—so not so common in India.

It seems there aren't very many contemporary art galleries in Kolkata; are there more in New Delhi?

Actually there are more than 50 galleries in Kolkata, but their focus isn't on contemporary art. When Prateek decided to open a gallery, I quit my job and we found a nice space in Kolkata. We also had the desire to go back to the city we grew up in.

How would you describe the gallery landscape in India?

There are three categories of galleries: those focusing on classic masters with a secondary market program, which they either get from collectors, artists, or a dealer-to-gallery kind of trade. Then there is the category we fall into: focus programs, representing international artists, and attending art fairs; there are maybe 15 or 20 galleries of this type only in a country of one billion people. The majority of the galleries, unfortunately, are neither curated nor serious: they are just there, more like street-vendors.

Was this the first year you applied to Art Basel?

We applied last year for the first time, for a solo booth with Bani Abidi in the Statements sector.

And how did you decide to bring these three artists (Bani Abidi, Naeem Mohaiemen, & Hajra Waheed) together?

We do four fairs every year: Frieze London and Frieze New York, Art Dubai, and the India Art Fair. This year we dropped Frieze New York to do Art Basel, since we do not want to do more than four a year. Every fair is an extension of our program, it's part of a narrative that we gather together in an annual publication—so this booth is part of our book for this year. However, a fair booth of 30 meters square might not seem big enough for an exhibition. We consider each as a different part of a show: one big traveling show through the four fairs, with the same curatorial baseline, but different artists from the gallery, depending on the country. This one in Basel is about cities in crisis and the architecture of war, at different levels: state, personal, social, and political.

Could you tell me something about the three artists?

Bangladeshi artist Naeem Mohaiemen (who lives and works in New York) deals with a body of photographs that he found in his father's archives in the project *Rankin Street, 1953* (2013). There are personal stories attached to each photograph and he responds to them by making sandstone models that look like a city in ruins; but close up you realize that they are really the negative space of the photographs, like an architecture of memory loss.

Hajra Waheed is an artist of Indian origin who lives in Montreal. She was raised in Saudi Aramco, a gated community that produces 20% of the world's oil. She made the series *Expansion Charts* (2013), which looks at the growing size of the Mecca and the Medina (the two most important places of Islamic worship). She looked at 28 places within the Mecca and the Medina that were destroyed because of the fear of idolatry: in Islamic culture, there is this whole stronghold wanting the Mecca and the Medina to be the only sources of centralizing power and worship, and all these other places—important tombs or places where prophets have died—have not been allowed to coexist, and have actually been destroyed by religious leaders. Within the Muslim faith, there are two types of Salafis: the Shiites and the Sunnis. The Shiites believe that you can have multiple places of worship but the Sunnis believe that this is not possible.

So this is like Catholicism and Protestantism in Europe in some ways?

Exactly. In the Syrian war currently there are huge protests from the Shiites trying to protect the tombs of their religious leaders from the Sunnis. So Waheed's take on this is quite personal, she's thinking about the history of these people, wondering about the memory of these people. Some of the drawings are very simple, very childlike on this vintage Aero Type carbon paper, so there's almost a reflection of that space, the memory of the memory.

Bani Abidi is a very important Pakistani artist, currently living in Berlin. *A Table Wide Country* (2012) is a complex body of photographic works in which she assumes the role of this mad individual with an intense passion for collecting war toys. She imagines herself as a 70-year old man who locks himself up and plays with war toy models all day long. One clear political hint is that the good guys are all American soldiers and the bad guys are Muslims, but in general it plays with fact and fiction, and the viewer could believe that she's talking about an actual person, and a moment of history. All the works in the show have this type of connection between the personal and the historical, the real and the fictional, the represented and the figured.

E

A strong program since it launched in 1993, the Edition sector features leading publishers of editioned works, prints, and multiples.

EDIT ION

2013 participants

Basel

Alexander
Borch Jensen
Cristea
Crown Point
didier
Fanal
gdm
Gemini
Klosterfelde Edition
Knust
Lelong Editions
Nitsch
Pace Prints
Paragon
Polígrafa
STPI
Three Star
Two Palms

Miami Beach

Borch Jensen
Cristea
Crown Point
gdm
Gemini
Knust
Nitsch
Pace Prints
Paragon
Polígrafa
Stoiper
STPI
Twc Palms

John M Armleder

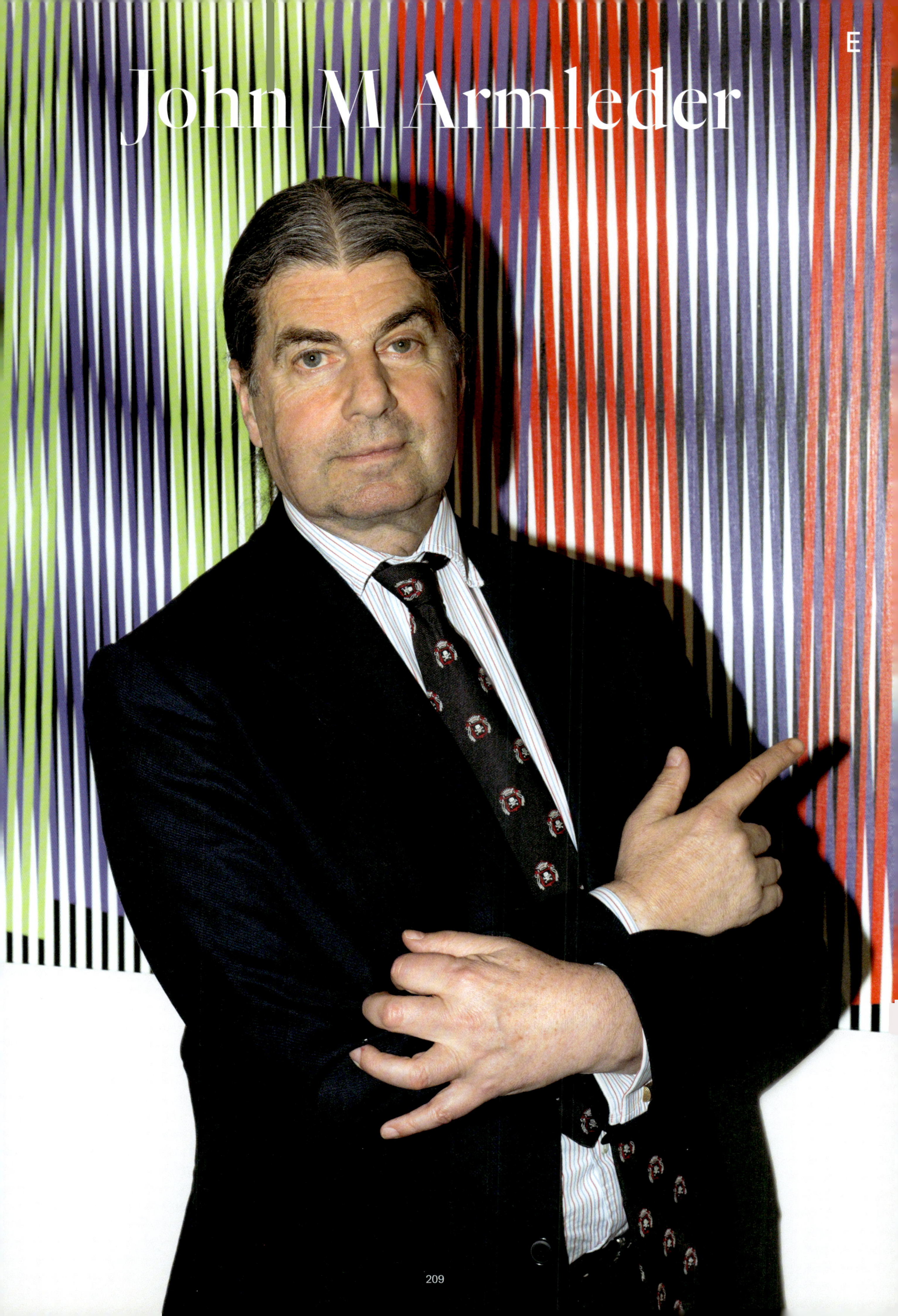

Lionel Bovier and Clément Dirié talk with John Armleder about the fair's beginnings, the Ecart booth, and the relativity of the concept of change

Interview conducted in Art Basel, on rhe Ecart booth, June 15, 2013

CLÉMENT DIRIÉ When did Ecart first take part in the Art Basel fair?

JOHN ARMLEDER In 1974, if my memory doesn't deceive me. First we took part in the Frankfurt Book Fair with artists' books that Ecart published. A stand then cost something like 500 DM: we thought we could afford that and we improvised a presentation, with absolutely no equipment. There were publishers from East Germany who brought us cushions so that we could sit down, they brought us coffee, saying the coffee in the café was too expensive, it was great—a golden era!

One day I thought to myself that since artists' books were published in Switzerland, we could perhaps show them at the Basel Art Fair, which had been created a few years earlier. I asked if we could have a table for the same price as a stand at Frankfurt—after thinking it over for some time, someone said yes. But just as we were getting ready to come with nothing but our books, an exhibitor pulled out, and they suggested that we should take over his stand; straight away I phoned all my artist friends to suggest that we should set up an exhibition that would change every day.

The following year I asked for a table again and the answer came that the fair had thought very highly of the way we had occupied the space the previous year, so they were offering it to us again for a very reasonable price. Things have changed a bit since then, but it has become an established tradition that Ecart is present. First on a stand mingled with other galleries, then between galleries and publishers, and today in the Edition sector. I pay the regular price per square meter but above all I have a smaller surface area. For a long time our geographic location made our presence at the fair stand out: we were like a fixed point on the fair's floor plan. The fact that we weren't a gallery with a shop window on the street, since the gallery had closed by then, was another unusual feature in the 1980s. There were murmurs of protest in the committee at one point: it was said of me that I was neither a gallery owner nor an artist, and I was reproached for giving 100% of the sale proceeds to the artist exhibited ... I simply relied on reimbursing myself by selling one of my pictures through another gallery ... It wasn't a very typical economic approach, but at that time things were less clear-cut. At the same time, that's still the case today, with the difference that everyone seems very happy to see me there still, at least up to this year.

CD So when the gallery closed, Ecart carried on existing thanks to Art Basel, in a way?

JA Quite. Even though I've organized various events under Ecart's name, its continued existence had been ensured every year in that form. To start with, we used to put on a solo exhibition by a different artist every day. Then we used to choose an artist and also publish a print, a multiple, an artist's book with him or her. On occasion we've also exhibited several artists. Generally speaking it's often had to do with artists who had not yet been represented at the fair, or rather unusual objects, or showing either a known artist who'd been somewhat forgotten, or an as yet unknown artist.

CD Can you give me some examples?

JA Among a great many others, we've exhibited Herbert Hamak, Karen Kilimnik, Pipilotti Rist, Fabrice Gygi, John Tremblay, the Klat, Amy O'Neill, Piero Golia, Carissa Rodriguez ... It's always the artists who decide what they want to show, except perhaps once or twice, like in the first or the second year, when we went out and bought anonymous paintings from a junk shop, and used them to make a hanging.

CD What about 2013?

JA I'm exhibiting Mimo Battista, an artist who originally came from Puglia, but he lived in Venezuela for a long time and was close to artists like Carlos Cruz-Diez and Julio Le Parc. He was active in the field of kinetic art for a certain number of years, and then came to Geneva—where he held two or three exhibitions—and decided to devote his time to his family. He completely stopped doing art to work in the clothing industry. He only started painting again last year. That interested me because his new works could equally well have been historicized by the renewal of interest in Op art. As it happens, they have the same value and the same interest. I've always been intrigued by the way a thing enters history or leaves it, and how perception of it changes according to the context.

CD There are myths surrounding the early days of any fair: was it really more of a "family affair" when Art Basel started up?

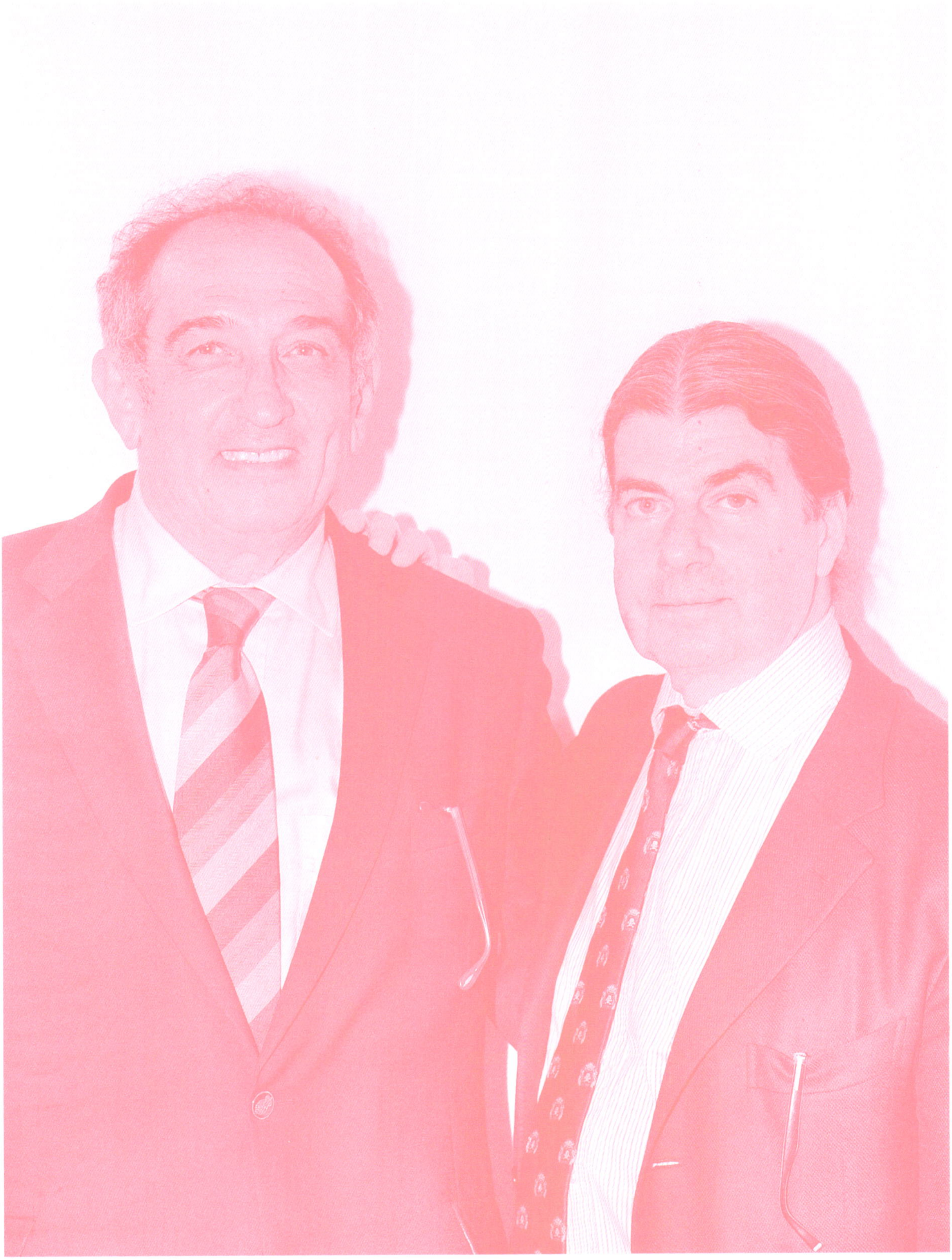

Mimo Battista and John M Armleder, Art Basel, Ecart, 2013

E

JA Yes indeed, that's not a myth. At first it was an initiative among friends, in a sort of wooden garage, on the present site of the Swisshotel, I believe. But that only lasted a few years. I've witnessed a great many changes, I remember times when the art market was rising, others when it was falling, but what's certain is that the art world has opened up to other people, in an exponential way, with ever more galleries, artists, works, visitors, and opportunities. At the same time that quantitative change doesn't imply a qualitative interpretation—something is changing, but we don't really know quite what. It's exactly the same as my health …

LIONEL BOVIER Multiples and artists' prints featured among Ecart's exhibition prerogatives. In the 1990s you showed a certain number of one-off works, but multiples were always there as a presence. Is the development of the Edition sector altering your relationship to the multiple?

Fifteen years ago I had the impression that it was very young artists who were presented on the Ecart stand, and that the galleries tended to present rather more established artists. There too, does the creation of Statements, of sectors for younger galleries, seem to you to have changed the situation, and your work with Ecart?

I often meet artists who say to me, "I never go to fairs," yet I generally meet them at fairs.
— John Armleder

JA I don't think things have changed that much, though at the same time everything's changed, for reasons of quantity. To tell the truth, in the very first years with Ecart, or even before I exhibited on any stand whatsoever, there were also a lot of young artists and quite a few publishers and multiples producers. The creation of sectors has had a federating effect—perhaps that's not the right way to put it …

There have also been other attempts to show publishers off to advantage: like that exhibition on a floor devoted to publishers of prints and multiples. Now there's a vogue for confusing the genres, which is one of the strengths of our present-day culture: one thing can replace another, even when we all have the impression we're making exclusive, unique items. It's an aspect people tried to fight against in a certain context at a given time, but it's a completely normal way of thinking today. That precipitate—in the culinary sense or the vocabulary of cocktail shaking—is extremely visible today, but it's not certain that the ingredients weren't in place right from the start … So I think that the more things change, the more they remain the same.

LB Even so, the presence of the artists has changed. I've seen the fair over a shorter period than you, but it's my impression that there weren't so many artists present at Art Basel 15 years ago.

JA That's both true and not true. Artists have always had a problem with the distribution of their work, and the platform that takes care of it. They've always been suspicious of the commodification of their work. Depending on the period, and that changes with the political or para-political discourse of the day, they assert that they don't want to be involved, while at other times that seems much less problematical. I often meet artists who say to me, "I never go to fairs," yet I generally meet them at fairs.

CD If we go back to the early years of the fair, at the time when there were only the Basel and the Cologne art fairs, what is it that made this fair a success?

JA I think one of the strokes of genius of the Basel fair was that it found the right date: when the art season, academic or other, is drawing to a close, before the summer. It's one of the great things about Basel. Now, as Lionel knows full well, there were projects that anticipated fairs, like the Salons for experimental galleries [The International Show of Pilot Galleries] in Lausanne (in 1963, 1966, and 1970), and the Basel and the Cologne fairs partly sprang from them; they demonstrated that period's need to create a sort of "galleries festival." We have to remember too that the gallery concept is relatively modern, just like the concept of the museum. Once this or that platform takes shape, it's both natural and easy to reproduce it. It's the enlargement of the public that justifies the increase in the number of fairs. The exponential side can be explained, as with the transformation from the small shop to the supermarket, then on to large-scale retail chains. In other words: there's nothing special about it.

Printed Matter,
Art Basel (Edition), 2013

Printed Matter

1970's

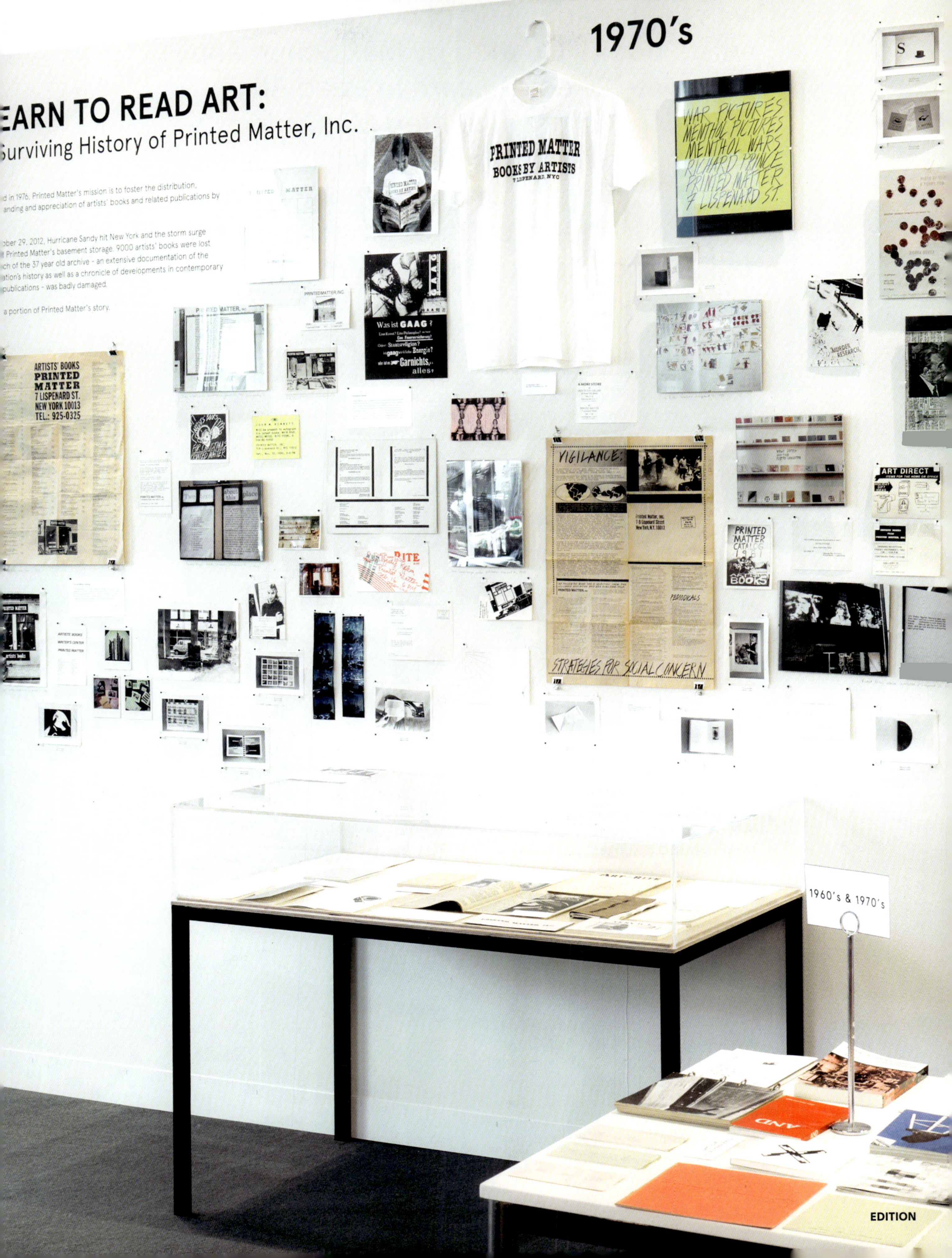

E

Printed Matter's presentation for Art Basel in Basel 2013 was engaging the documented history of the organization as it intersects with the broader field of contemporary artists' books. Curated by Max Schumann, Associate Director, *Learn to Read Art: A Surviving History of Printed Matter, Inc.* assembled a visually dense vitrine- and wall-based presentation featuring a broad range of material produced by the organization since its founding in 1976.

Borrowing its name from a text by Lawrence Weiner, *Learn to Read Art* has been used variously by Printed Matter, including for past exhibitions curated by former Director AA Bronson. The exhibition put on view material from the Printed Matter Archive that was damaged during basement flooding following Hurricane Sandy in 2012. The presentation focused around a chronological wall installation of announcement cards, flyers, press releases, posters, and other ephemera documenting the organization's programming history through artists' installations, book launches, panels, performances, and other events.

The show included images of the long-running window installations organized by Lucy Lippard, featuring early-career exhibitions by Jenny Holzer, Barbara Kruger, and Richard Prince, among many others. In addition, correspondence between administrators and artists/publishers gave a unique view into the early history of Printed Matter. In these papers the founding members are seen formulating the mission, founding strategy, and practice of the organization in the context of the broadening appeal and impact of artists' publications as a medium.

One text from Lippard, titled *Artists' Books: An Easy Way Out*, shows her edits on a manuscript that would appear in *Art in America* in 1977 under the header "The Artist's Book Goes Public." Also included was a survey of artists' publications, early book catalogues, and special editions published by Printed Matter through to the present. This was supplemented by an array of artists' books, distributed through the years by the organization, that exemplified the richness and diversity of forms, strategies, and processes encompassed by the field of artists' books.

Printed Matter,
Art Basel (Edition), 2013

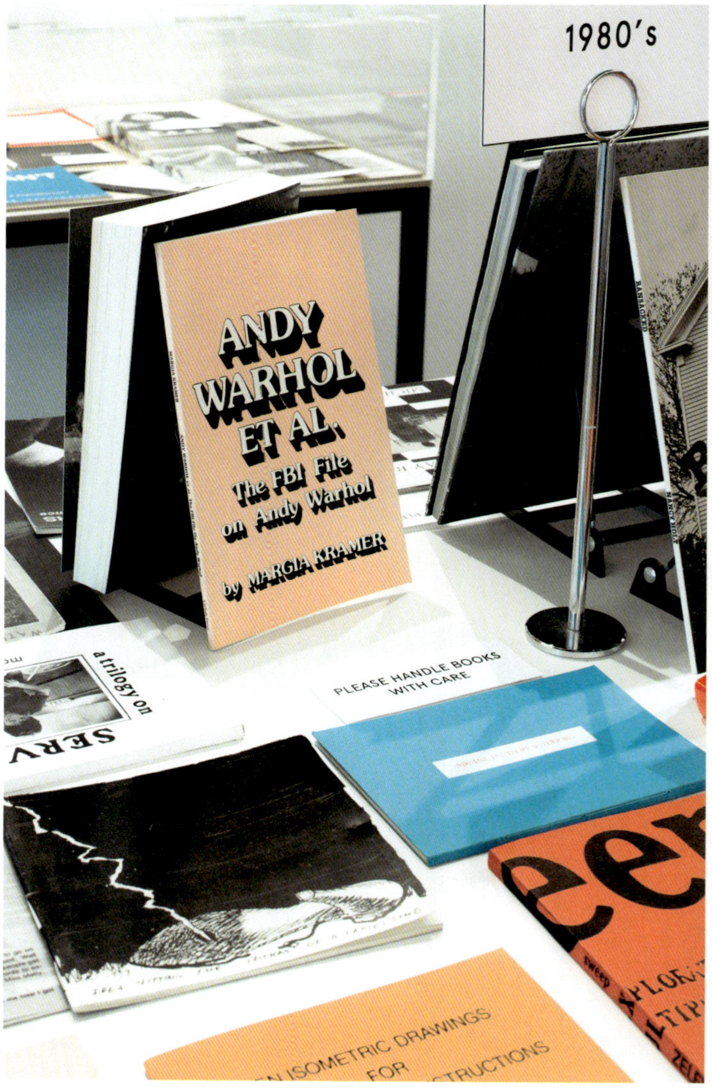

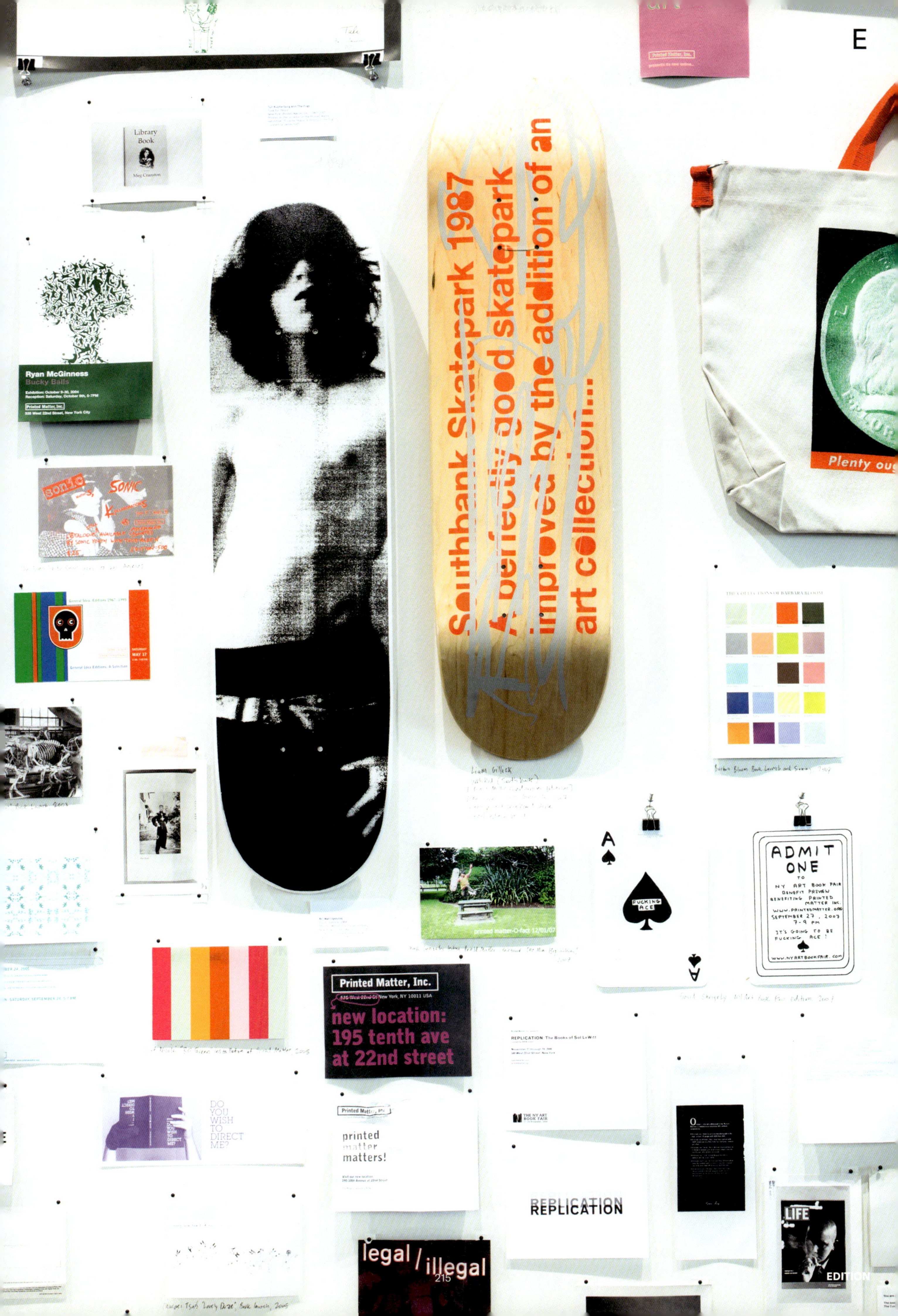
Library Book
Meg Cranston
Ryan McGinness
Bucky Balls
Exhibition: October 9–30, 2004
Reception: Saturday, October 9th, 6–7PM
Printed Matter, Inc.
535 West 22nd Street, New York City
SONIC
Southbank Skatepark 1987
A perfectly good skatepark
improved by the addition of an
art collection...
Plenty ou
General Idea Editions: A Selection
SATURDAY
MAY 17
printed matter-O-fact 12/01/07
A
FUCKING ACE
ADMIT ONE
TO
NY ART BOOK FAIR
BENEFIT PREVIEW
BENEFITING PRINTED MATTER INC.
WWW.PRINTEDMATTER.ORG
SEPTEMBER 27, 2007
7-9 PM
IT'S GOING TO BE FUCKING ACE!
WWW.NYARTBOOKFAIR.COM
Printed Matter, Inc.
535 West 22nd St New York, NY 10011 USA
new location:
195 tenth ave
at 22nd street
REPLICATION: The Books of Sol LeWitt
THE NY ART BOOK FAIR
DO
YOU
WISH
TO
DIRECT
ME?
Printed Matter, Inc
printed
matter
matters!
REPLICATION
legal / illegal
LIFE

E

Dedicated to large-scale sculpture and installation works by leading artists from around the world, Encounters provided Art Basel in Hong Kong visitors with the opportunity to see works that transcend the traditional art fair stand. The sector presented these works in prominent locations throughout the exhibition halls.

EN COUNT ERS

2013 participants

Arndt
Jitish Kallat

Chiba
Takuma Uematsu

de Sarthe
Chen Zhen

du Monde
Qin Chong

Hanart TZ
Guan Huaibin

Kerlin
Liam Gillick

Kukje/Kim
Haegue Yang

Lee
Marnie Weber

Long March
MadeIn Company

Magician Space
Zhuang Hui & Dan'er

Malingue
Laurent Grasso

Mizuma
Susan Philipsz

One and J.
Seung Yul Oh

Osage
Sun Yuan & Peng Yu

Project 88
Raqs Media Collective

S.A.L.E.S.
Flavio Favelli

Tang
Wang Yuyang

Qin Chong
Losing
2008

E

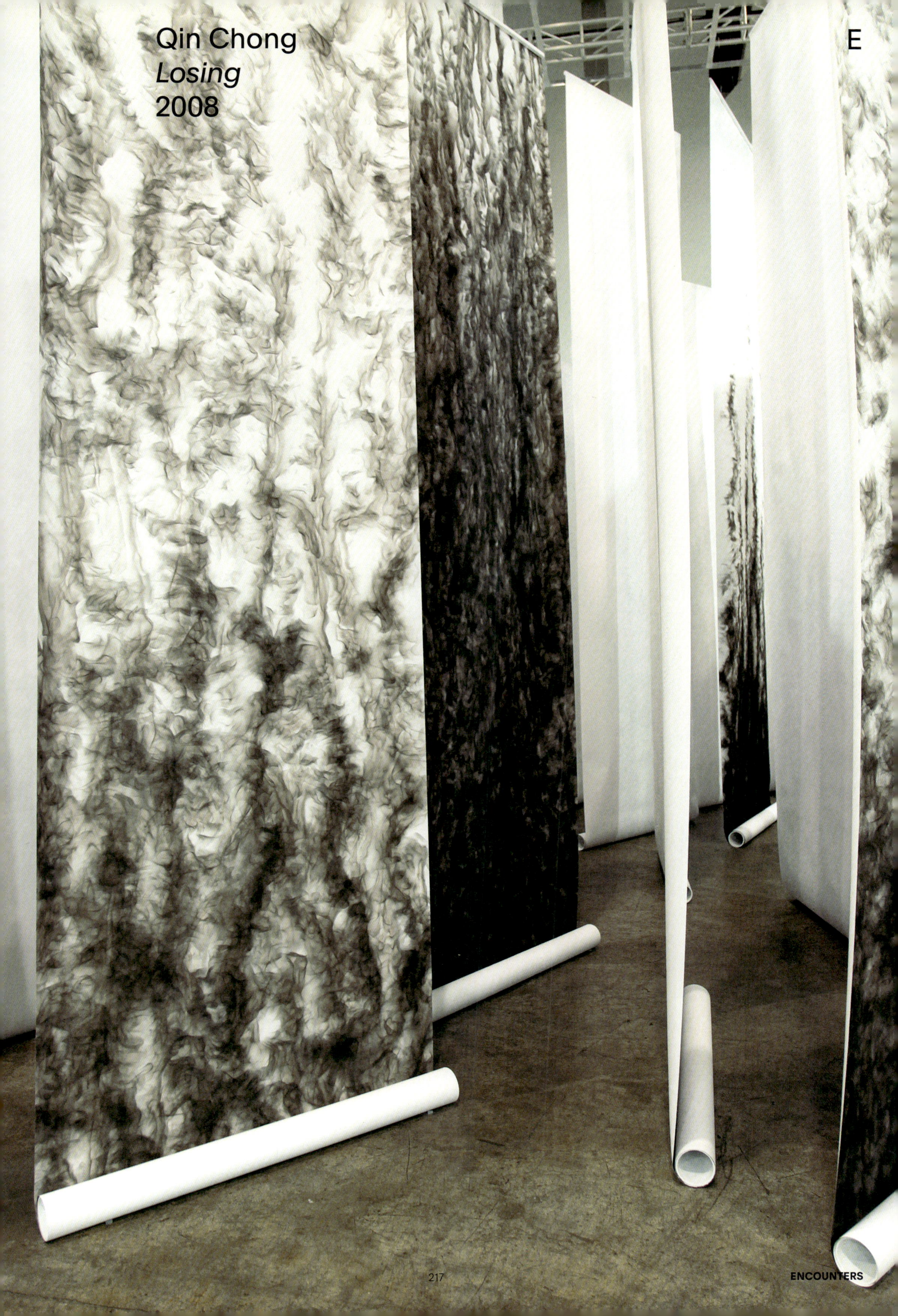

E

Laurent Grasso
Visibility is a Trap
2012

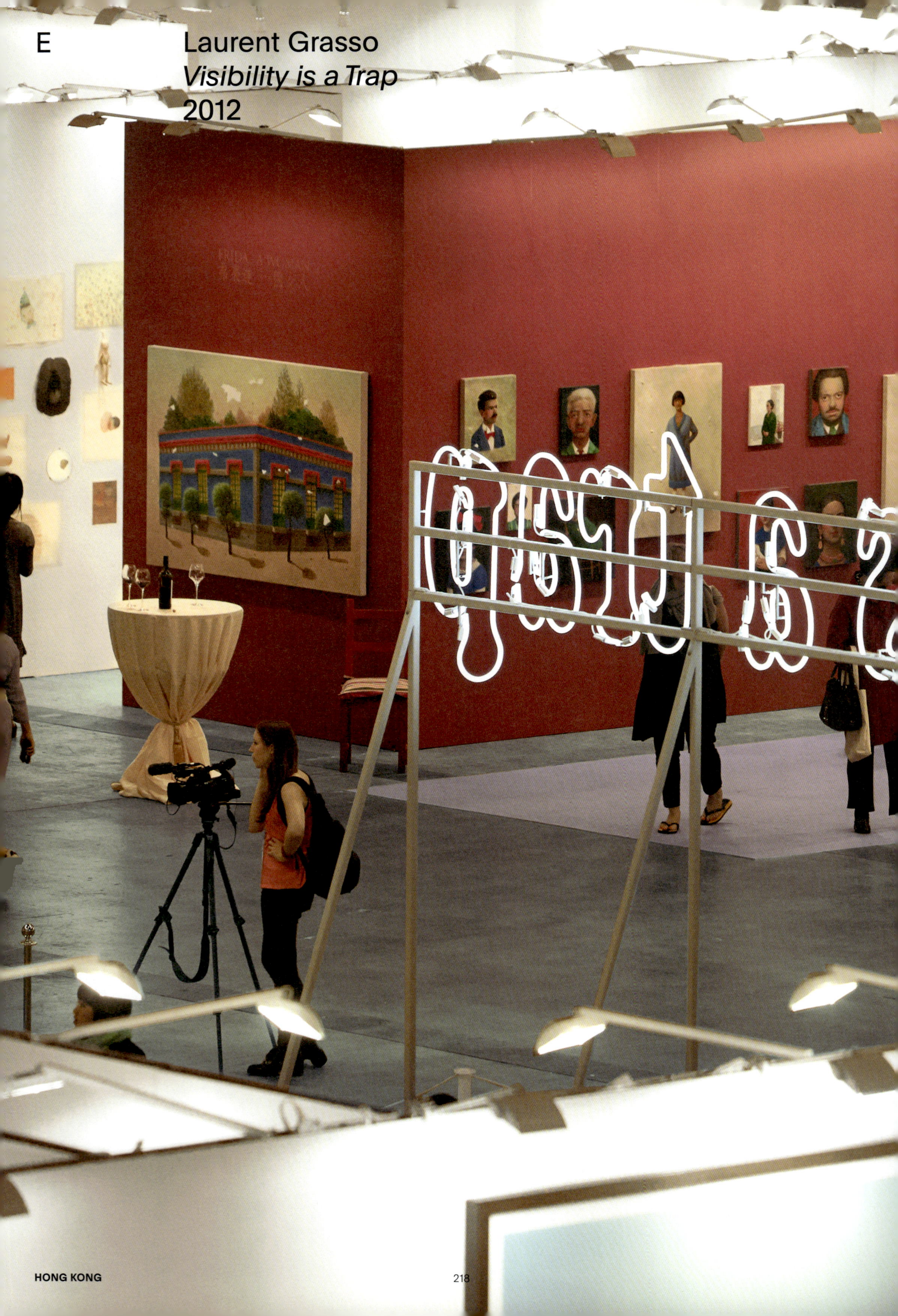

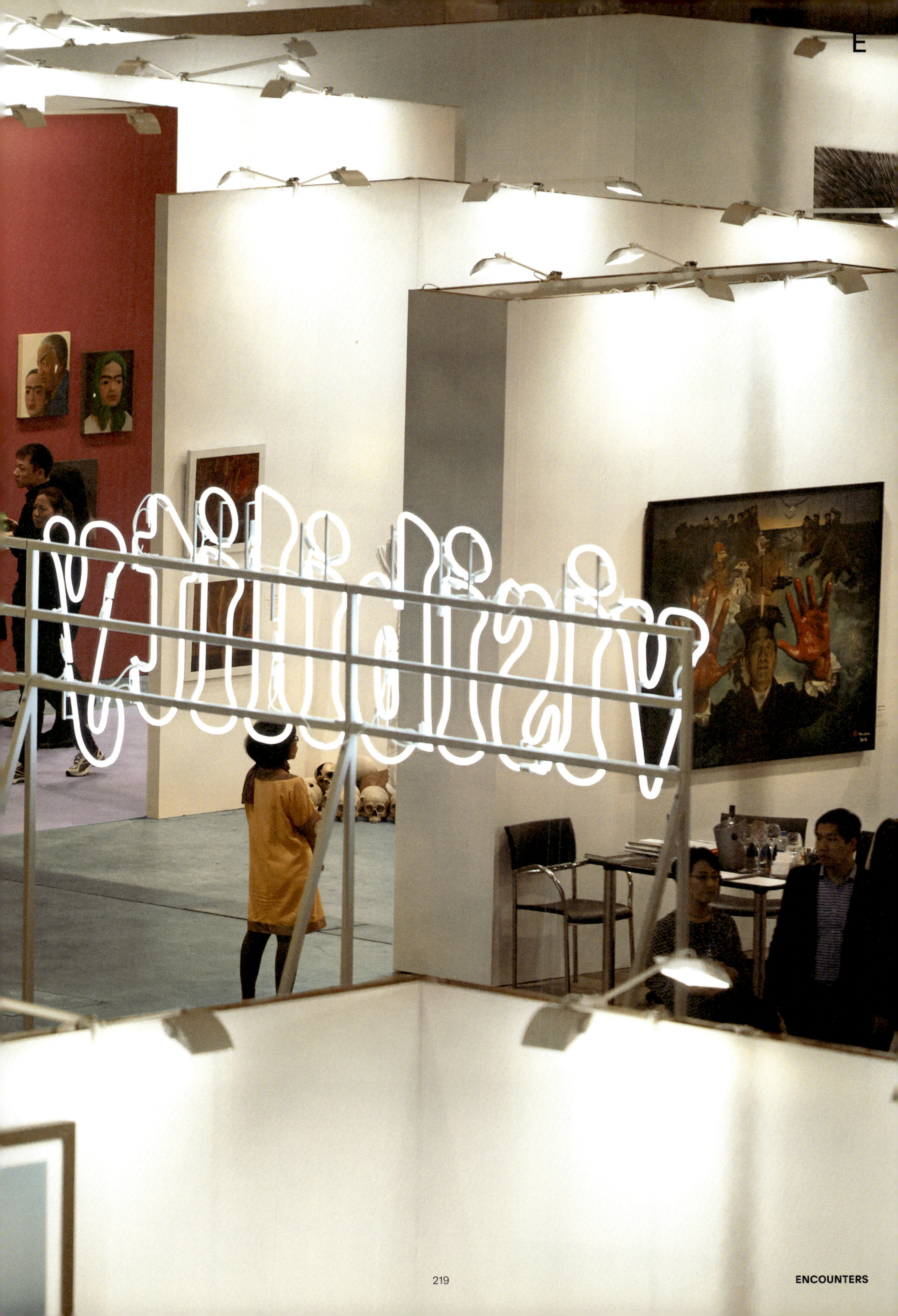

Flavio Favelli
China Purple
2010

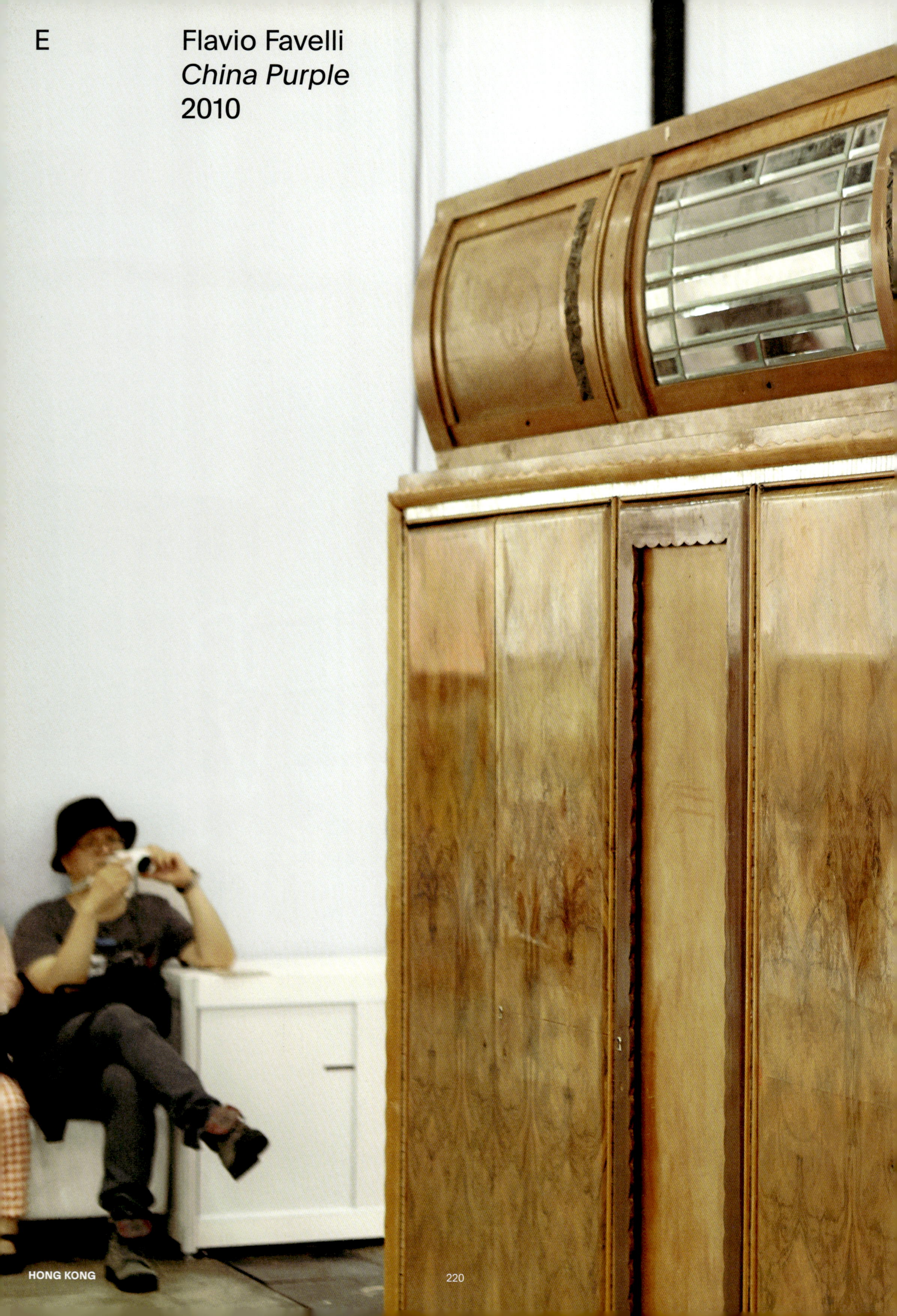

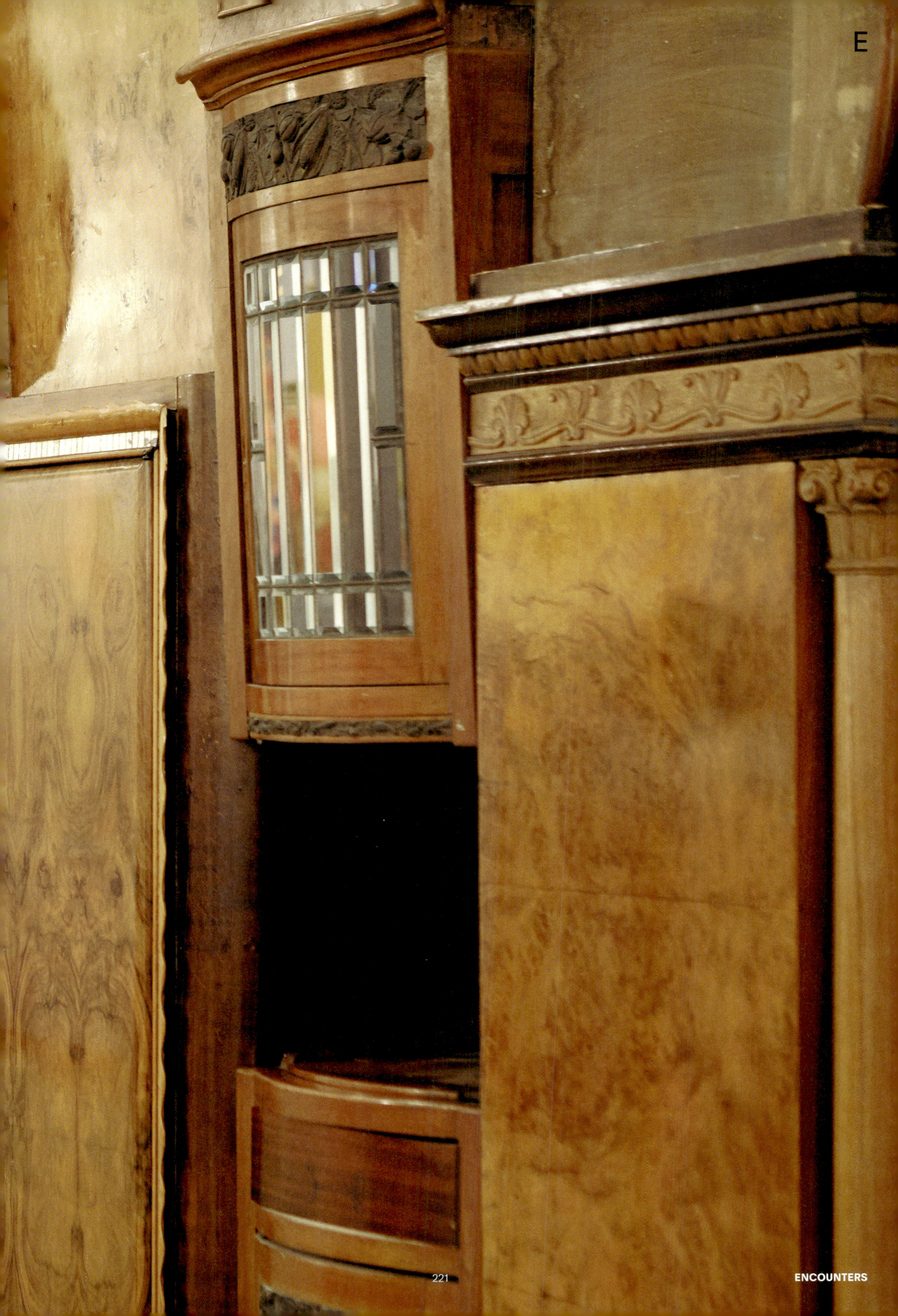

E

Liam Gillick
Complete Bin Development
2013

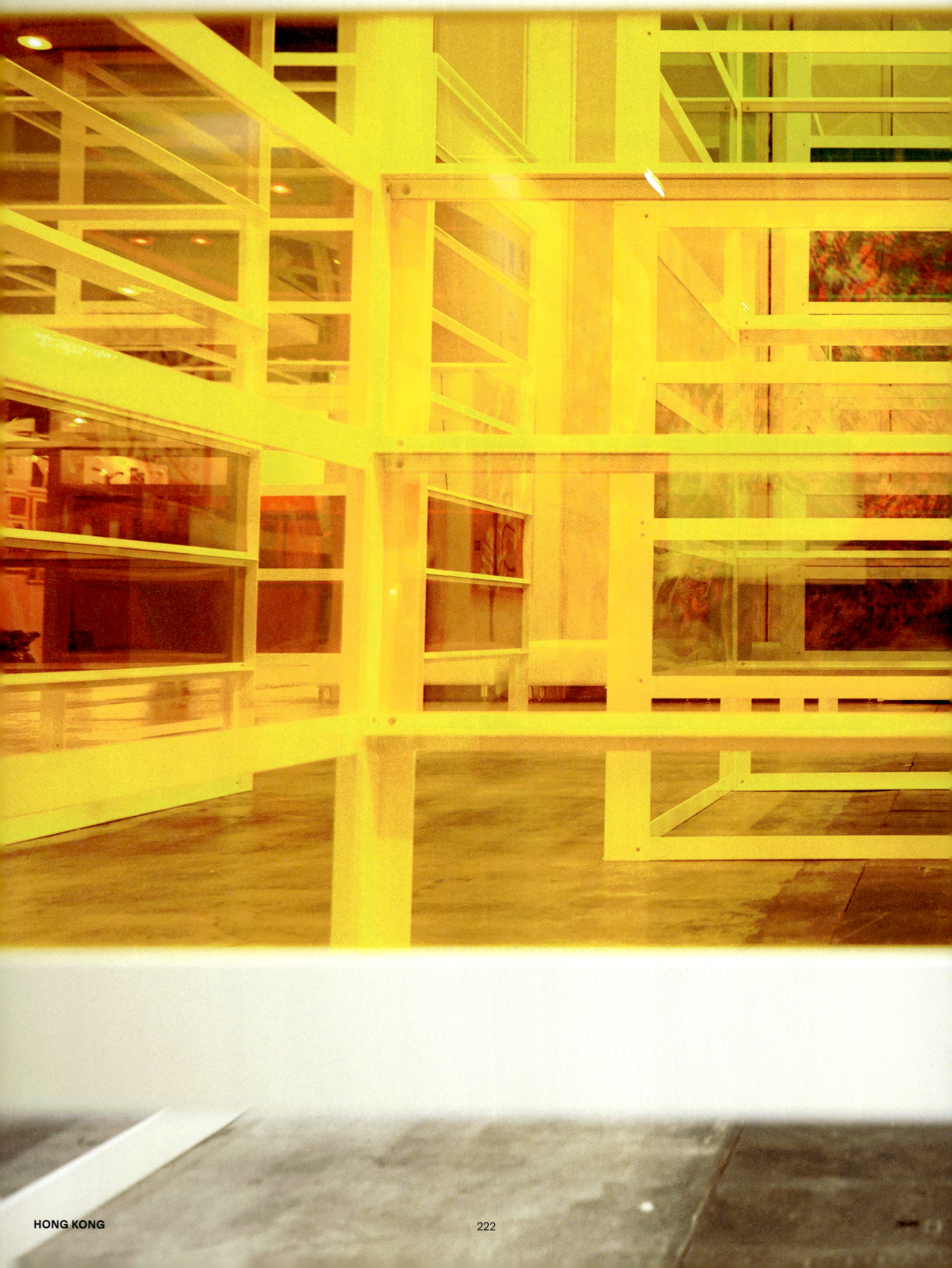

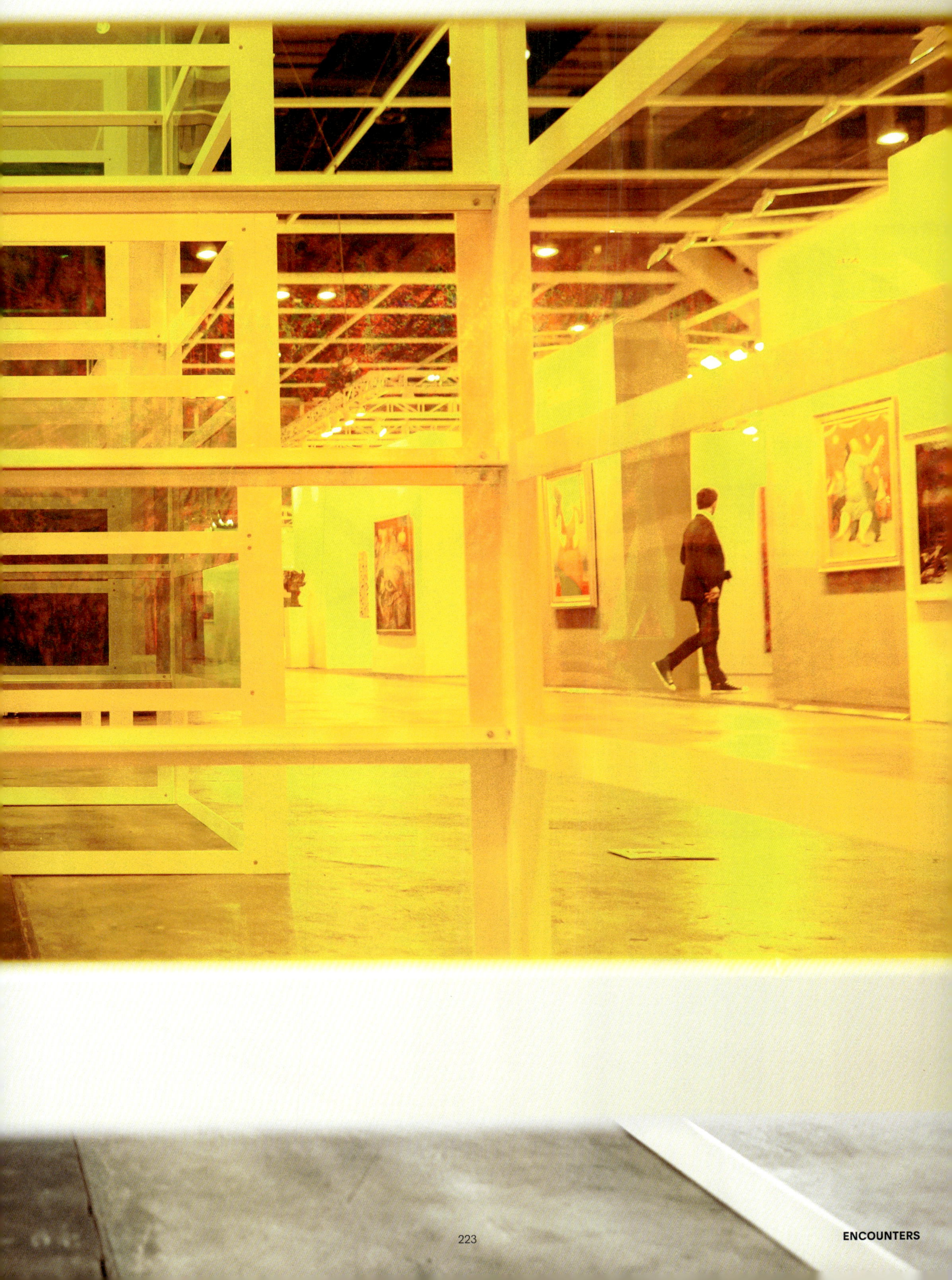

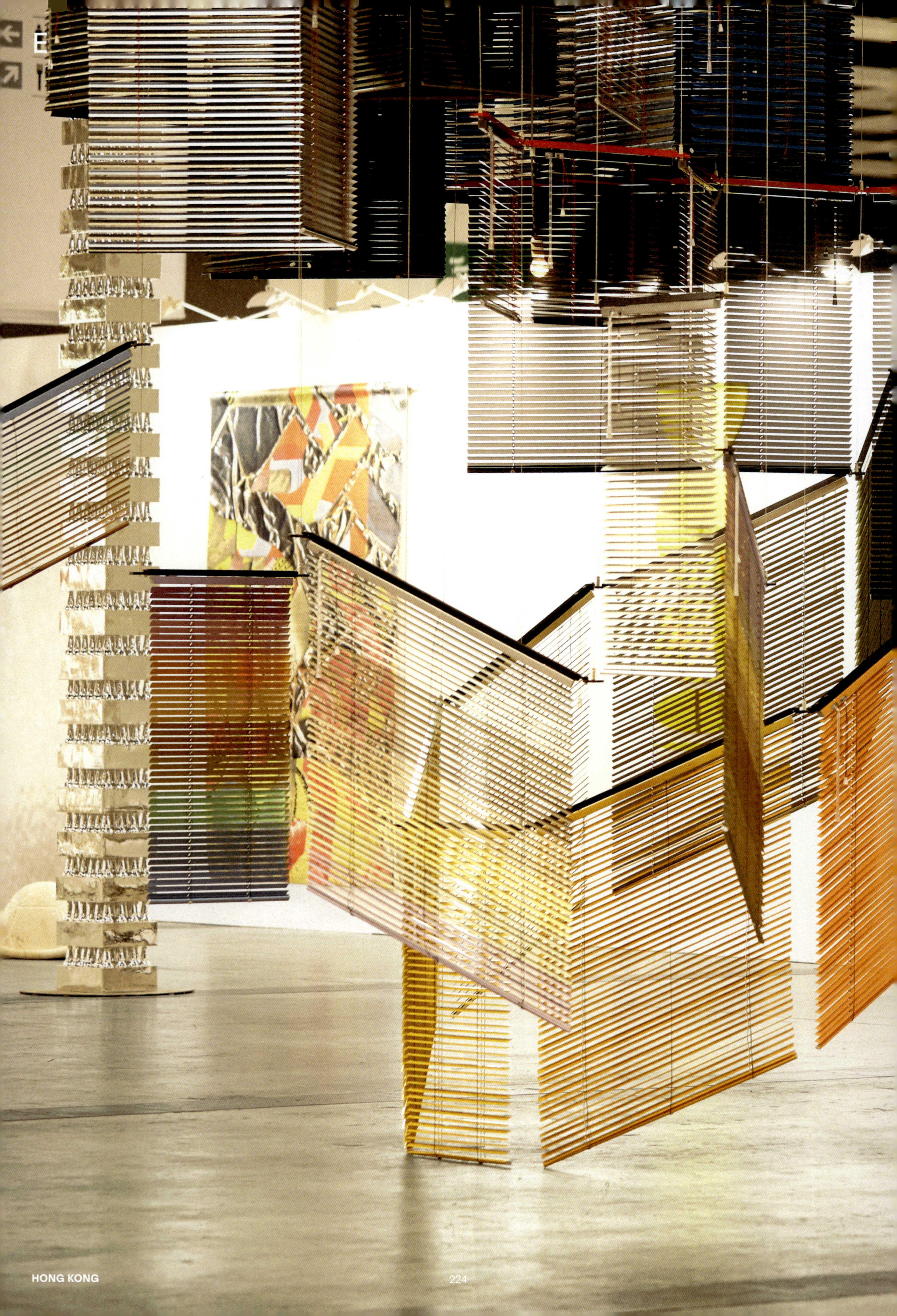

Haegue Yang
Journal of Mundane and Uncertain Days
2012

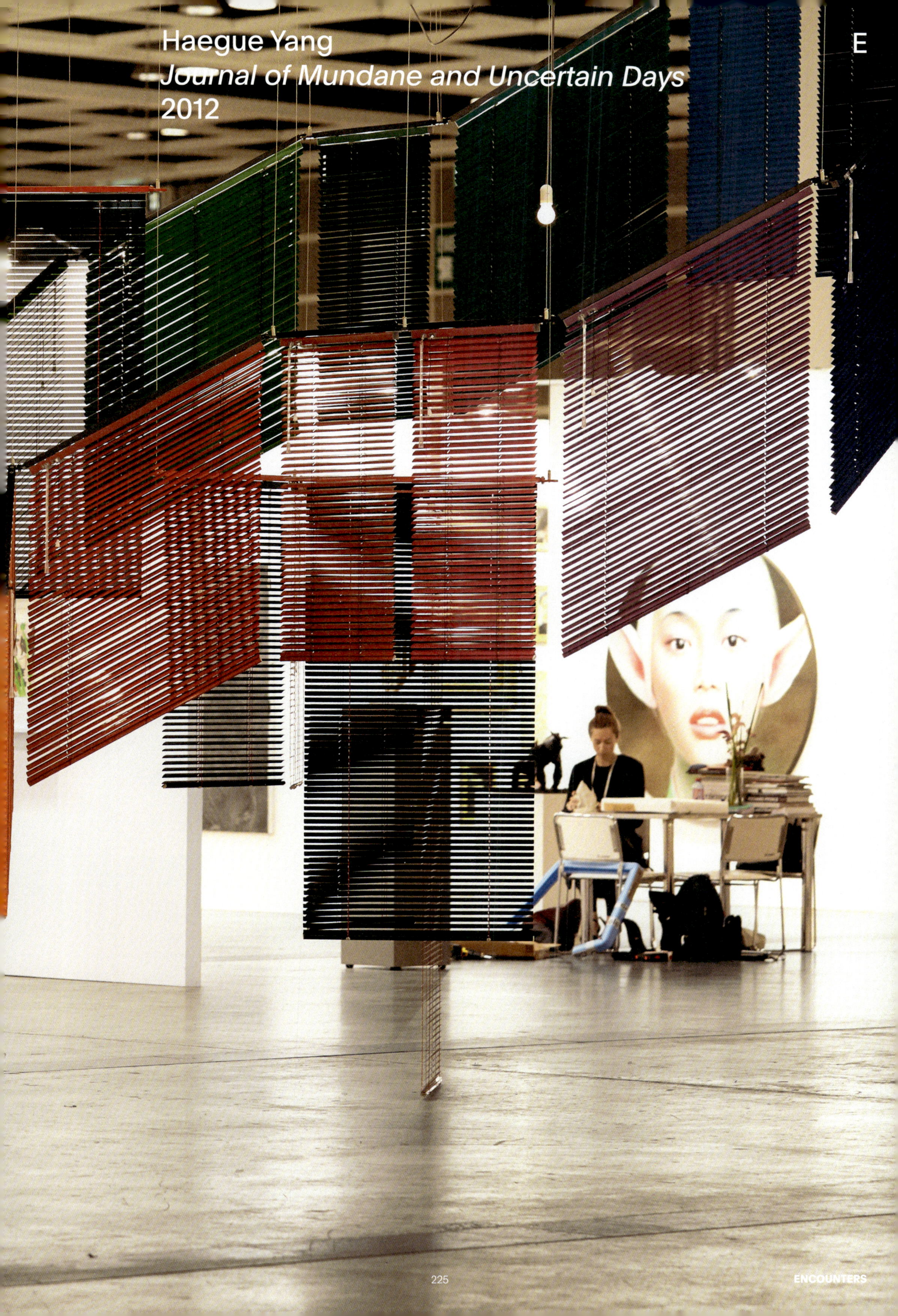

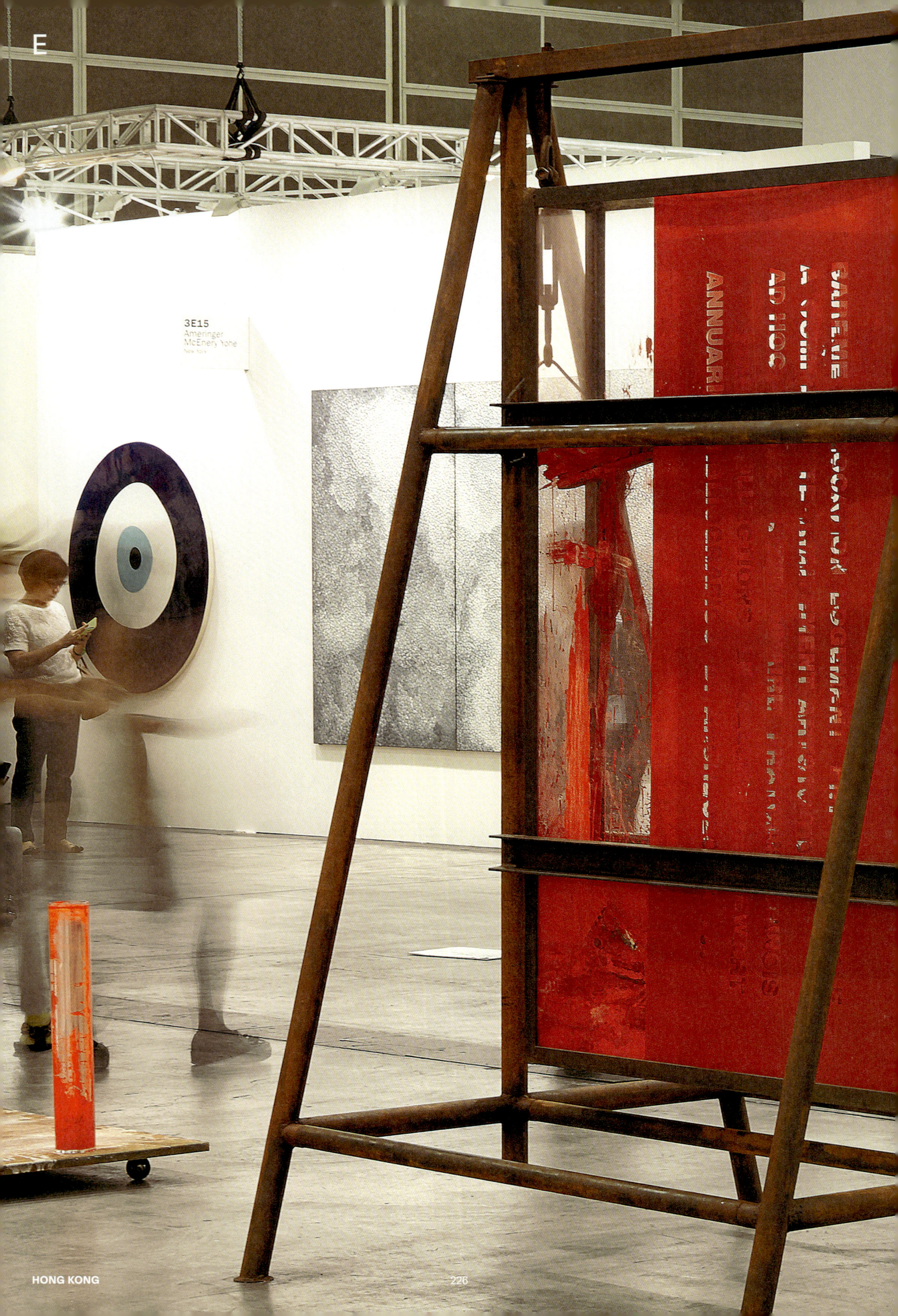
3E15
Ameringer
McEnery Yohe

Chen Zhen
Le Rite Suspendu/mouillé
1991

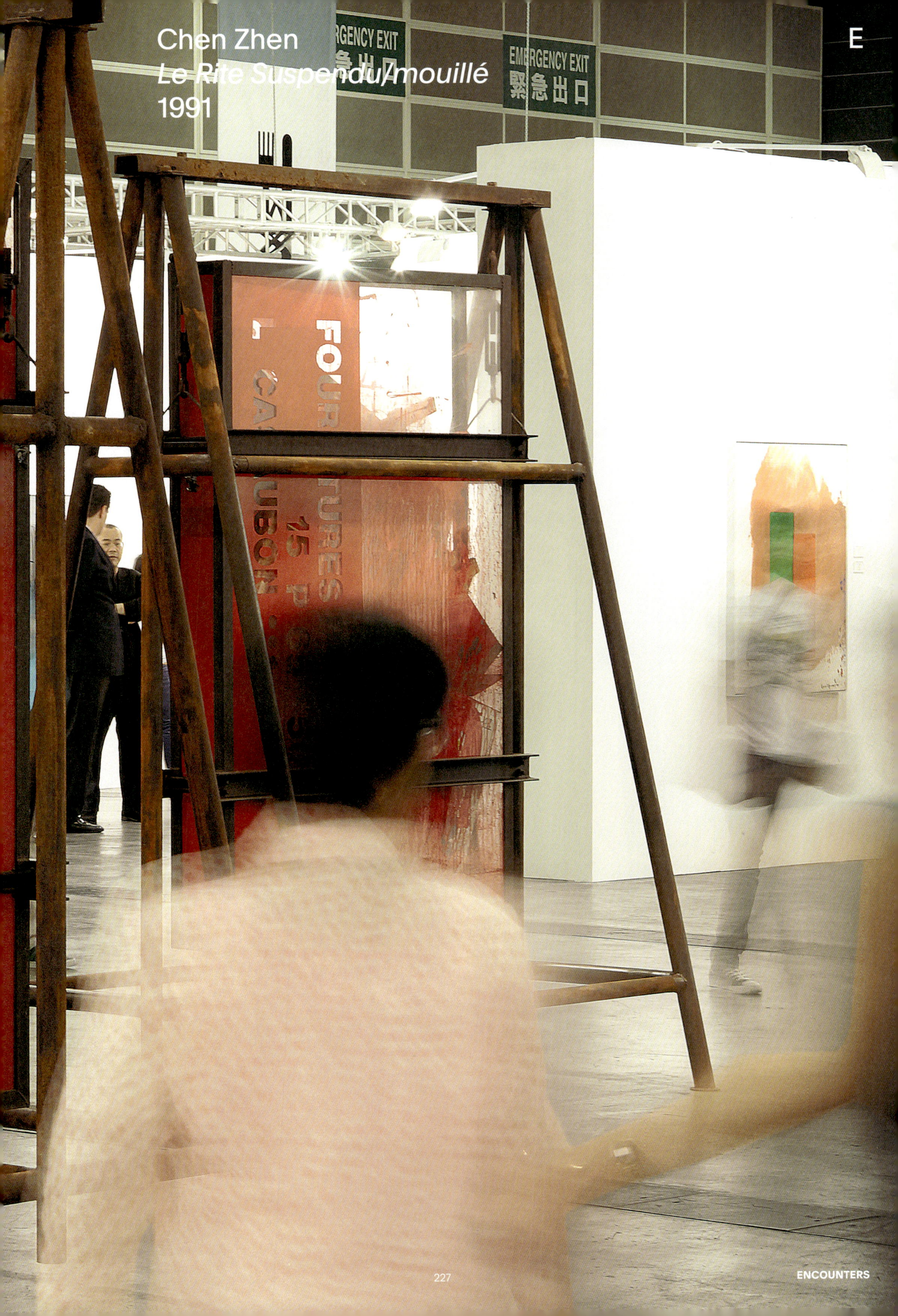

E

Jitish Kallat
Circa
2011

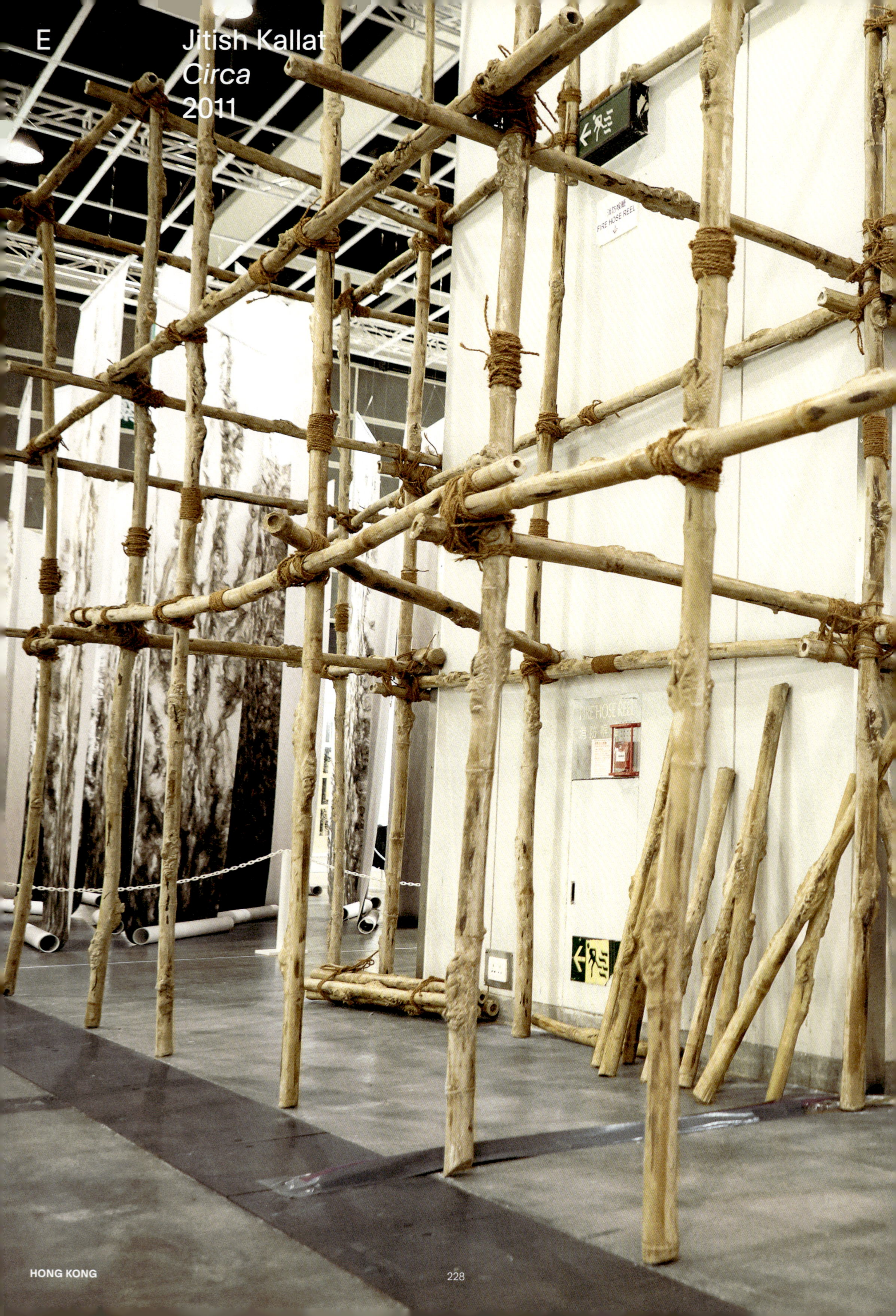

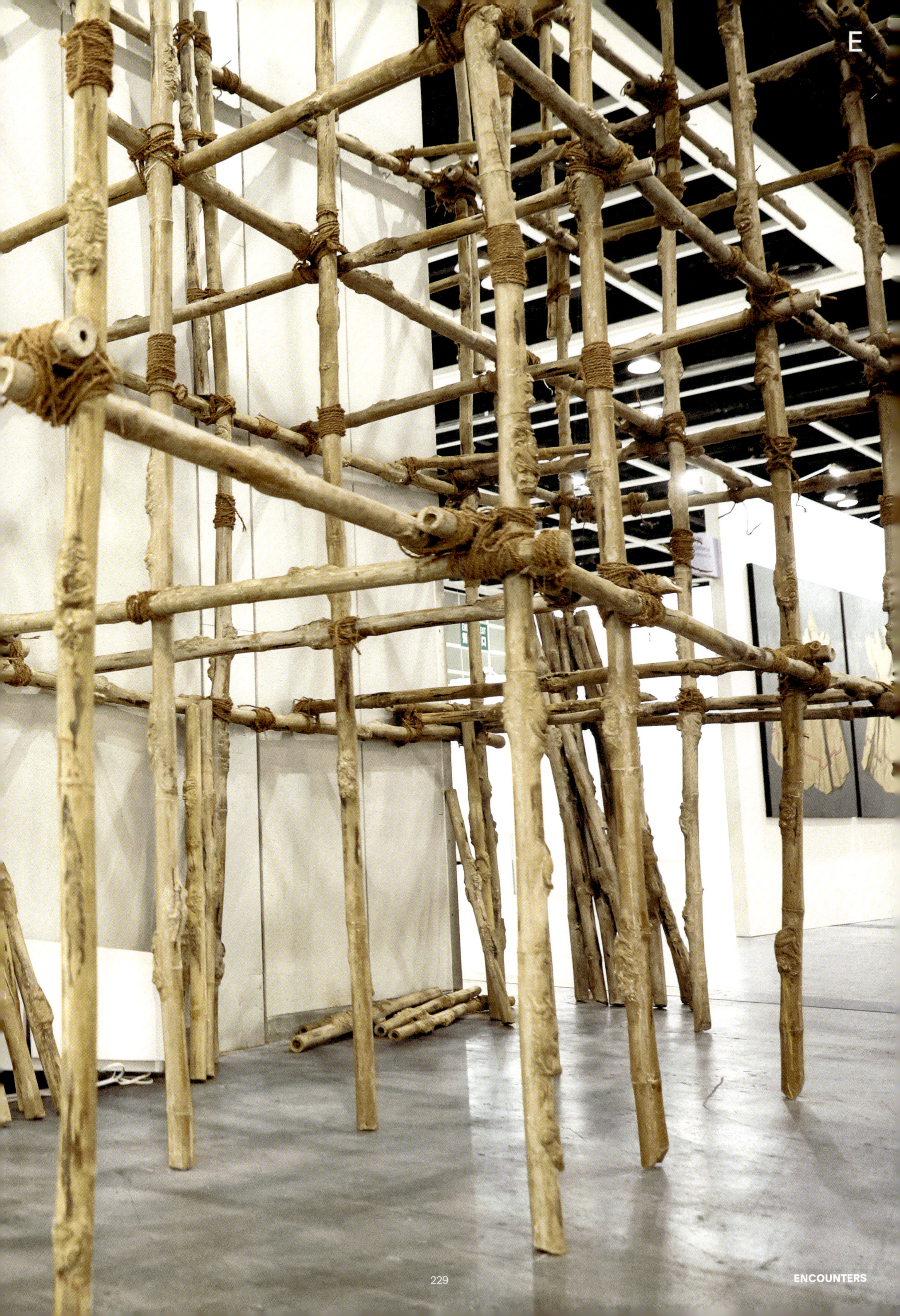

F

- Hong Kong
- Basel
- Miami Beach

Fanal

Basel — Edition

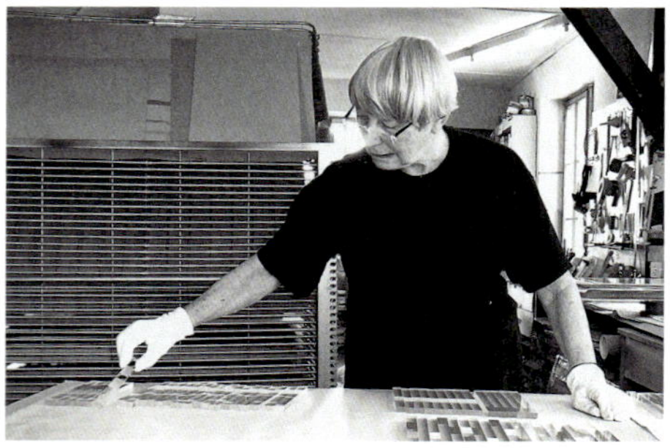

What first compelled you to open a gallery?
The desire to work and cooperate with other artists in the field of geometric abstraction.

Who is the first artist you showed and what was most memorable about that show?
Jean Gorin, it was the first edition work that was realized in our printing atelier with an artist.

When did you first participate in Art Basel and what was most memorable about that show?
Very early on; the connection with so many collectors and visitors interested in art.

- **Contact** Atelier-Editions Fanal
  Danielle Harder
  fanal@vtxmail.ch
- **Established** 1966
- **Owner(s) / Partner(s)** Danielle Harder
  Marie-Thérèse Vacossin
- **Team** 5
- **Space(s)** 650 m²
- **Artists at Art Basel** Serena Amrein
  John Carter
  Carlos Cruz-Diez
  Christoph Dahlhausen
  Helmut Dirnaichner
  Jean-Michel Gasquet
  Gottfried Honegger
  Verena Jeck-Zweifel
  Horst Linn
  Manfred Mohr
  Vera Molnar
  Michael Post
  Karin Radoy
  Sigurd Rompza
  Jocelyne Santos
  Reiner Seliger
  Klaus Staudt
  Sylvestre
  Jens Trimpin
  Marie-Thérèse Vacossin
  Thomas Vinson
  Jean-Pierre Viot
- **Further artists represented** Frank Badur
  Waldo Balart
  Ode Bertrand
  Charles Bézie
  David Bill
  Hartmut Böhm
  Andreas Brandt
  Jean Brault
  Marischa Burckhardt
  Pol Bury
  Geneviève Claisse
  Max Cole
  Daniel de Spirt
  Norman Dilworth
  Gerhard Doehler
  Bruno Erdmann
  Rita Ernst
  Christoph Freimann
  Kunibert Fritz
  Karl Gerstner
  Hansjörg Glattfelder
  Jean Gorin
  István Haász
  André Heurtaux
  James Juszczyk
  Renate Kasper
  Julije Knifer
  Tamas Konok
  Stefanie Lampert
  Verena Loewensberg
  madé
  MCBA
  Adalberto Mecarelli
  Christian Megert
  François Morellet
  Mehdi Moutashar
  Ben Muthofer
  Aurélie Nemours
  Susanna Niederer
  Meret Oppenheim
  Marta Pan
  François Perrodin
  Yves Popet
  Ruedi Reinhard
  Axel Rohlfs
  Vera Röhm
  Michael Rouillard
  Nelly Rudin
  Sato Satoru
  Maya Stange
  Erwin Steller
  Haruhiko Sunagawa
  Takashi Suzuki
  Ian Tyson
  Geert van Fastenhout
  Werner von Mutzenbecher
  Shizuko Yoshikawa

Faria

New York
Buenos Aires — Galleries
Kabinett

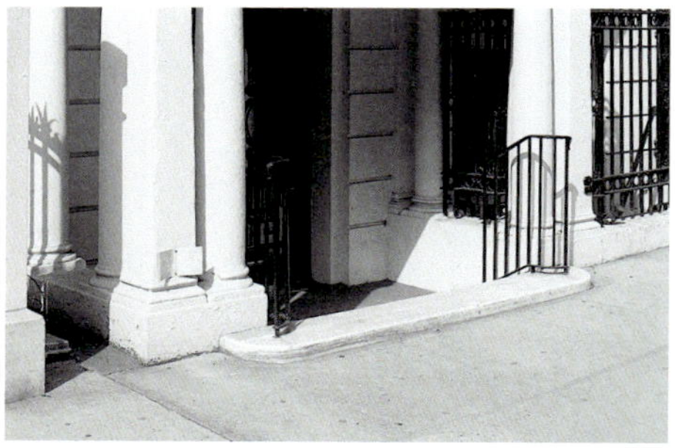

What first compelled you to open a gallery?
Henrique Faria opened an art cabinet on Madison in New York, in 2001, specializing in Latin American geometric abstract artists, such as Modern masters Jesús Soto, Raúl Lozza, Gego, Mathias Goeritz, and María Freire, as well as contemporary mid-career artists, such as Luis Roldán, José Bechara, and Eugenio Espinoza. In 2007 the gallery decided to venture into the much lesser known world of conceptual practices from Latin America (Juan Downey, Claudio Perna, Nicolás García Uriburu, and others). In 2009 we opened a new gallery with an exhibition by Argentine artist, poet, and filmmaker Leandro Katz. The next year, we doubled the size of the gallery, which allowed us to continue exhibiting historical Latin American works from the 1950s, 1960s, and 1970s in addition to contemporary artists such as Emilio Chapela, Alessandro Balteo Yazbeck, Miler Lagos, Javier Téllez. Since we opened the gallery, the demand for Latin American works has increased exponentially, and our client base has expanded from mainly Latin American collectors to international institutions, foundations, and museums.

- **Contact** Henrique Faria Fine Art
Eugenia Sucre
eugenia@henriquefaria.com
info@henriquefaria.com
- **Established** 2008/2010
- **Owner(s) / Partner(s)** Henrique Faria
- **Team** 5
- **Space(s)** 60 m²
- **Artists at Art Basel** Emilia Azcárate
Waldo Balart
Alessandro Balteo Yazbeck
Álvaro Barrios
Luis F. Benedit
Carlos Castillo
Emilio Chapela
Eduardo Costa
Jaime Davidovich
José Gabriel Fernández
Anna Bella Geiger
Carlos Ginzburg
Michael Gitlin
Terence Gower
Leandro Katz
Marta Minujín
Luis Molina-Pantin
Alejandro Puente
Luis Roldán
Osvaldo Romberg
Eduardo Santiere
Pedro Terán
Yeni & Nan
Horacio Zabala

Feast

Hong Kong — Insights

- **Contact** Feast Projects
info@feastprojects.com
- **Established** 2010
- **Owner(s) / Partner(s)** Philippe Koutouzis
- **Artists at Art Basel** T'ang Haywen
- **Further artists represented** Ron Arad
Chu Teh-Chun
Feng Shuo
Fensterbank
René Iché
Charles Jaulerry
Jeng Jundian
Liu Wei
Marlène Mocquet
Rashaad Newsome
Carr Patterson
Tie Ying
Xie Lei
Zao Wou-Ki

Feigen

New York — Galleries

When did you first participate in Art Basel and what was most memorable about that show?
The first time we participated in Art Basel we did a single booth of Ray Johnson, which created an enormous amount of excitement. It also introduced Johnson to a lot of the public. It was extremely exciting for Richard L. Feigen & Co., and for the Ray Johnson Estate.

- **Contact** Richard L. Feigen & Co.
Erin Hozack
ehozack@rlfeigen.com
info@rlfeigen.com
- **Established** 1957
- **Owner(s) / Partner(s)** Richard L. Feigen (Chairman)
Frances F.L. Beatty PhD (President)
- **Team** 10
- **Artists at Art Basel** Max Beckmann
Victor Brauner
Joseph Cornell
Jean Dubuffet
Max Ernst
Sam Francis
Ray Johnson
Roberto Matta
James Rosenquist
Peter Saul
Richard Smith
Yves Tanguy
- **Further artists represented** William Baziotes
Öyvind Fahlström
George Grosz
Pablo Picasso
Robert Rauschenberg
Pierre Roy

Fine Arts Literature

Wuhan — Insights

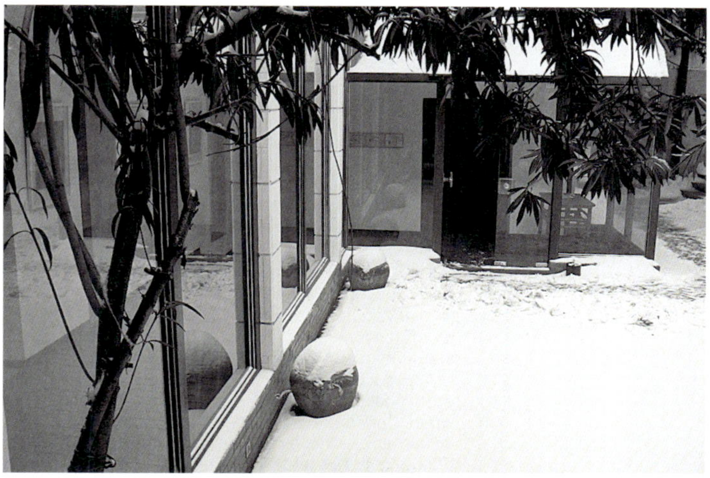

What first compelled you to open a gallery?
The city of Wuhan, in the middle of China, is a cradle and key place for Chinese contemporary arts, especially since the "Art Wave of 1985," which marked the beginning of Chinese contemporary art. Wuhan has fostered a batch of dominant artists, such as Wang Du and Zeng Fanzhi, as well as young artists driven by an experimental spirit. Artists in Wuhan have been recognized as a pioneering force. However, in the 1990s, many of them left for centers such as Beijing and Shanghai. As the first professional art gallery in Wuhan, established in 2003, we wanted to promote and introduce young artists to the international art scene and support them through their careers.

When did you first participate in Art Basel and what was most memorable about that show?
We participated at the first edition of Art Basel in Hong Kong in 2013, and were impressed by the collectors' and people's passion for art, as well as the good organization of the art fair. We sold all our works at the show.

- **Contact** Fine Arts Literature Art Center
Shuli Yan
meishuwenxian@163.com
- **Established** 2003
- **Owner(s) / Partner(s)** Ming Liu
- **Team** 10
- **Space(s)** 1,500 m²
- **Artists at Art Basel** Shi Jinsong
- **Further artists represented** Chen Bo
Fan Anxiang
Gong Jian
Jiang Zhilong
Li Jikai
WAZA Art Group
Zhang Quan

Fischer

Düsseldorf
Berlin

Galleries
Unlimited

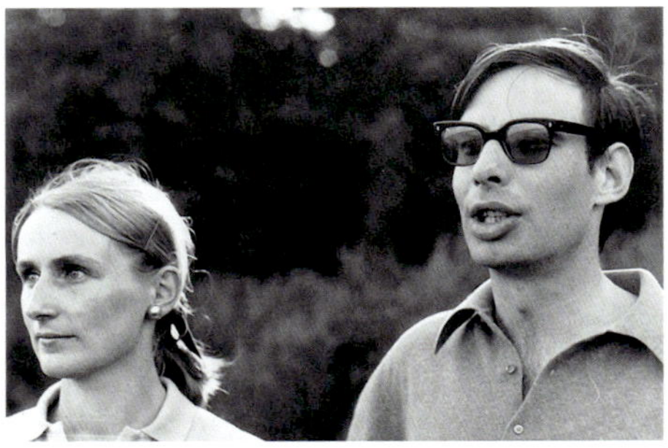

What first compelled you to open a gallery?
When we opened a tiny exhibition space in a disused alley in the center of Düsseldorf with a first exhibition by Carl Andre in October 1967, Minimal or Conceptual art were almost unknown in Europe and just a very small number of galleries focused on new developments in art. At that time, our prime objective was to introduce cutting-edge positions to the art world. One important instrument was to invite the artists to Düsseldorf to create a personal dialogue and to enforce the formation of an international network of artists and other people interested in art.

Who is the first artist you showed and what was most memorable about that show?
Carl Andre's *5 × 20 Altstadt Rectangle* (1967) consisted of 100 industrially produced steel plates of the same size covering almost the entire floor of the exhibition space. Many visitors walked across the artwork unknowingly and searched in vain for art on the empty walls.

- **Contact** — Konrad Fischer Galerie
  Dorothee Fischer
  claudia.pasko@konradfischergalerie.de
  office@konradfischergalerie.de
- **Established** — 1967
- **Owner(s) / Partner(s)** — Dorothee Fischer
- **Team** — 5
- **Space(s)** — 300 m² (Düsseldorf)
  260 m² (Berlin)
- **Artists at Art Basel** —
  Carl Andre
  Giovanni Anselmo
  Stephen Antonakos
  Bernd & Hilla Becher
  Guy Ben-Ner
  Marcel Broodthaers
  Stanley Brouwn
  Matthew Buckingham
  Peter Buggenhout
  Daniel Buren
  Nina Canell
  Alan Charlton
  Tony Cragg
  Hanne Darboven
  Jan Dibbets
  Hans-Peter Feldmann
  Gilbert & George
  Sofia Hultén
  Cristina Iglesias
  Zon Ito
  Stephen Kaltenbach
  On Kawara
  Harald Klingelhöller
  Jannis Kounellis
  Melissa Kretschmer
  Wolfgang Laib
  Jim Lambie
  Sol LeWitt
  Richard Long
  Robert Mangold
  Rita McBride
  Mario Merz
  Bruce Nauman
  Max Neuhaus
  Maria Nordman
  Claes Oldenburg
  Giuseppe Penone
  Manfred Pernice
  Magnus Plessen
  Wolfgang Plöger
  Charlotte Posenenske
  Thomas Ruff
  Robert Ryman
  Gregor Schneider
  Thomas Schütte
  Juergen Staack
  Yuji Takeoka
  Tatjana Valsang
  Paloma Varga Weisz
  Johannes Wald
  Lawrence Weiner
  Petra Wunderlich
  Jerry Zeniuk

Foksal

Warsaw

Galleries
Parcours
Galleries

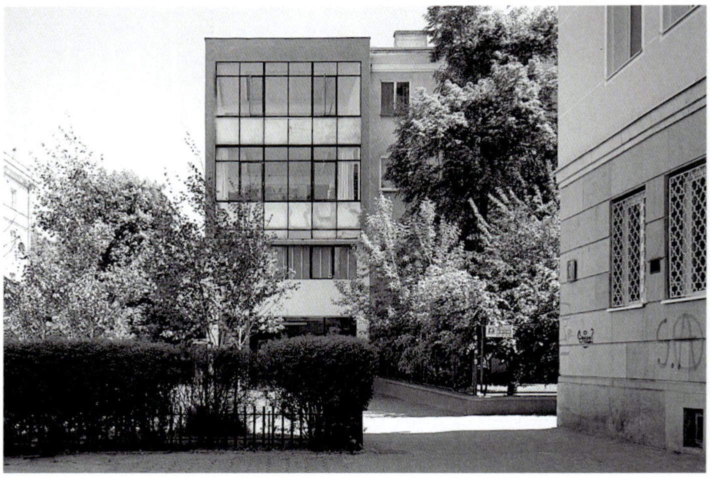

What first compelled you to open a gallery?
Dynamic collaborations with Polish and international artists in the 1990s, as well as Poland's political transformation.

Who is the first artist you showed and what was most memorable about that show?
Paweł Althamer—the exhibition was about escaping the format of the gallery as a white cube.

When did you first participate in Art Basel and what was most memorable about that show?
In 2003 in Basel's Statements sector. We got the Baloise Prize for Monika Sosnowska's *Corridor* installation with a great number of doors.

- **Contact** — Foksal Gallery Foundation
  Andrzej Przywara
  mail@fgf.com.pl
- **Established** — 1997
- **Owner(s) / Partner(s)** — Andrzej Przywara
- **Team** — 5
- **Space(s)** — 240 m²
- **Artists at Art Basel** —
  Pawel Althamer
  Cezary Bodzianowski
  Piotr Janas
  Katarzyna Jozefowicz
  Edward Krasinski
  Robert Kusmirowski
  Anna Molska
  Anna Niesterowicz
  Paulina Olowska
  Wilhelm Sasnal
  Monika Sosnowska
  Jakub Julian Ziolkowski
  Artur Zmijewski

Fortes Vilaça

São Paulo

- Galleries Unlimited
- Galleries

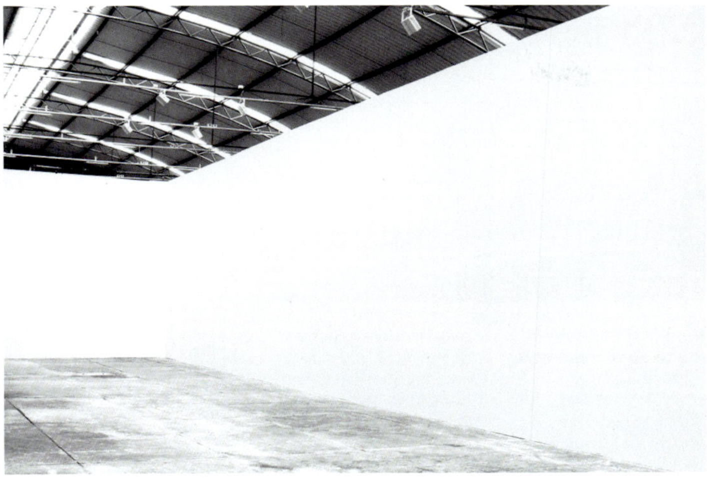

- **Contact** Galeria Fortes Vilaça
Gabriel de Souza
arquivo@fortesvilaca.com.br
galeria@fortesvilaca.com.br
- **Established** 2001
- **Owner(s) / Partner(s)** Márcia Fortes (Founding Director)
Alessandra d'Aloia (Founding Director)
Alexandre Gabriel (Associate Director)
- **Team** 23
- **Space(s)** 190 m² (gallery)
1,500 m² (storage)
- **Artists at Art Basel** Franz Ackermann
Efrain Almeida
Armando Andrade Tudela
Barrão
Carlos Bevilacqua
Tiago Carneiro da Cunha
Rodrigo Cass
Leda Catunda
José Damasceno
Iran do Espírito Santo
Simon Evans
Tamar Guimarães
João Maria Gusmão & Pedro Paiva
Marine Hugonnier
Sergej Jensen
Agnieszka Kurant
Lucia Laguna
Jac Leirner
Los Carpinteros
Rodrigo Matheus
Beatriz Milhazes
Gerben Mulder
Ernesto Neto
Rivane Neuenschwander
Damián Ortega
osgemeos
Sara Ramo
Nuno Ramos
Mauro Restiffe
Marina Rheingantz
Michael Sailstorfer
Julião Sarmento
Valeska Soares
Janaina Tschäpe
Adriana Varejão
Erika Verzutti
Cerith Wyn Evans
Luiz Zerbini

Foxx

Los Angeles

- Feature Unlimited

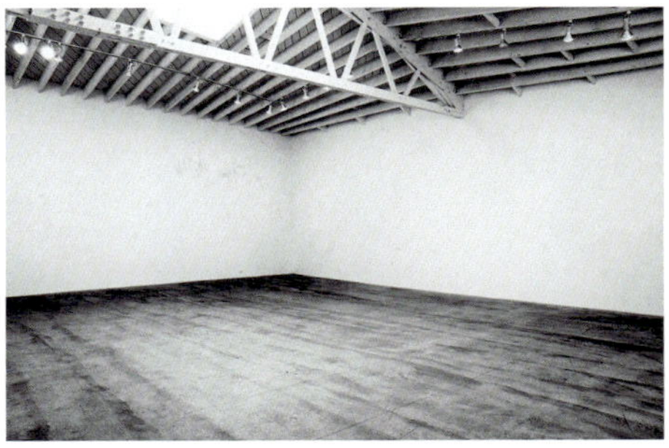

What first compelled you to open a gallery?

After working in the art world for nine years I borrowed $40,000 from my parents and opened my gallery in 1994 in order to make exhibitions with artists whose work I wanted to see but didn't sense would have an opportunity to exhibit in Los Angeles. At that time in Los Angeles it was very unusual for galleries to show international artists in an ongoing way. I made the first Los Angeles exhibitions with Olafur Eliasson, Hiroshi Sugito, and Martin Creed.

When did you first participate in Art Basel and what was most memorable about that show?

In 2012. After working in the art world for so long it's hard to find a new experiences, but it was like being at your first dance—very nervous and very excited at the same time. The exchange with the viewers and the level of engagement and interest is palpable and invigorating.

- **Contact** Marc Foxx Gallery
Samantha Longman
samantha@marcfoxx.com
gallery@marcfoxx.com
- **Established** 1994
- **Owner(s) / Partner(s)** Marc Foxx
Rodney Hill
- **Team** 4
- **Space(s)** 370 m²
- **Artists at Art Basel** Sanya Kantarovsky
Frances Stark
- **Further artists represented** Leonor Antunes
Cris Brodahl
Anne Collier
Andy Collins
William Daniels
Stef Driesen
Brian Fahlstrom
Roger Hiorns
Annette Kelm
Makiko Kudo
Luisa Lambri
Kris Martin
Jason Meadows
Carter Mull
David Musgrave
Alessandro Pessoli
Amalia Pica
Matthew Ronay
Maaike Schoorel
Hiroshi Sugito
Ricky Swallow
Mateo Tannatt
Guido van der Werve
Michael van Ofen
Sophie von Hellermann
Jennifer West
Sam Windett

Fraenkel

San Francisco — Galleries

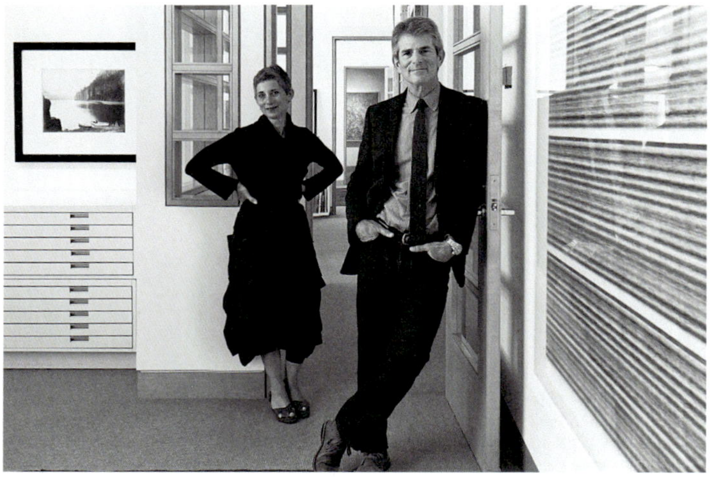

What first compelled you to open a gallery?
19th-century American landscape photographer Carleton Watkins was one important inspiration, in concert with a number of important photographers who, in 1979, were not well represented on the West Coast (and, in some cases, anywhere) such as Garry Winogrand, Lee Friedlander, and Nicholas Nixon. To this we added our ongoing interest in other types of photographs, such as 19th-century astronomical photographs, vernacular, and more. Today our photographers span the 1850s to 2013.

Who is the first artist you showed and what was most memorable about that show?
Carleton Watkins, an important album of his work from the 1860s. It is in every way the cornerstone of Fraenkel Gallery both literally and philosophically.

When did you first participate in Art Basel and what was most memorable about that show?
We started participating at Art Basel at the beginning of the 2000s. What is most memorable is the high level of every aspect of the show: the space, the walls, the philosophy, the museum exhibitions, the collectors, the larger audience, the colleagues, and of course the works represented. Everything.

- **Contact** — Fraenkel Gallery
  Jennifer Larsen
  jlarsen@fraenkelgallery.com
  mail@fraenkelgallery.com
- **Established** — 1979
- **Owner(s) / Partner(s)** — Jeffrey Fraenkel
  Frish Brandt
- **Artists at Art Basel** — Robert Adams
  Diane Arbus
  Lee Friedlander
  Adam Fuss
  Katy Grannan
  Peter Hujar
  Idris Khan
  Richard Learoyd
  Christian Marclay
  Ralph Eugene Meatyard
  Richard Misrach
  Nicholas Nixon
  Hiroshi Sugimoto
  Garry Winogrand
- **Further artists represented** — Eugène Atget
  Bernd & Hilla Becher
  E.J. Bellocq
  Mel Bochner
  Harry Callahan
  William Eggleston
  Walker Evans
  Robert Frank
  Nan Goldin
  Helen Levitt
  Sol LeWitt
  Irving Penn
  August Sander
  Andy Warhol
  Carleton Watkins
  Edward Weston

Freeman

New York — Galleries
Paris — Galleries, Public

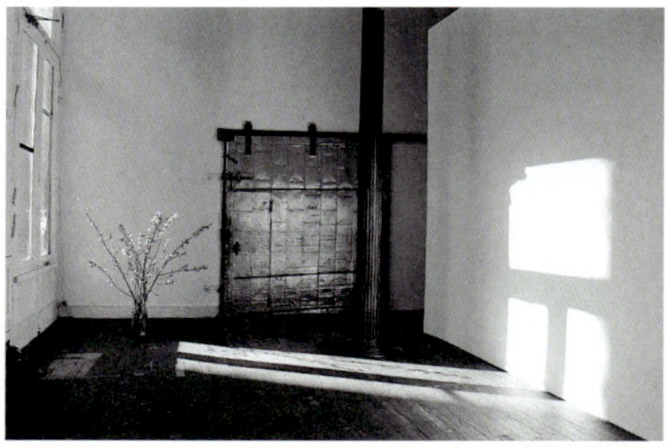

What first compelled you to open a gallery?
A desire to make exhibitions—initially exhibitions of historical works—that would put meaningful ideas and important art in front of people; finally the connections of historical works that remain influential to even the newest art of our time led the gallery to represent artists and estates from many generations.

Who is the first artist you showed and what was most memorable about that show?
The Ideal Object: Hiram Powers (1848) and Andy Warhol (1964) was the first exhibition, and was typical in many ways for connecting histories that had not previously been explored. Marble busts made in Rome of ancient goddesses by one of the greatest 19th-century American artists, side-by-side with stacks of Warhol boxes: both were really the same "ideal" object produced by the same culture 100 years apart. The differences in how each group of sculptures looked from the other disappeared once the shared formal qualities made themselves clear.

When did you first participate in Art Basel and what was most memorable about that show?
Peter Freeman, Inc. first participated in Basel in 2005; and in Miami Beach continuously from the first edition there in 2002.

- **Contact** — Peter Freeman, Inc.
  Suzanne Imber
  suzanne@peterfreemaninc.com
  info@peterfreemaninc.com
- **Owner(s) / Partner(s)** — Peter Freeman
- **Team** — 16
- **Space(s)** — 210 m² (New York)
  168 m² (Paris)
- **Artists at Art Basel** — David Adamo
  Dove Allouche
  Silvia Bächli
  Joseph Bartscherer
  Mel Bochner
  Marcel Broodthaers
  Pedro Cabrita Reis
  Alexander Calder
  Ernst Caramelle
  James Castle
  Jan Dibbets
  Helmut Dorner
  Lili Dujourie
  James Ensor
  Robert Filliou
  Pia Fries
  Josephine Halvorson
  Alex Hay
  Michael Heizer
  Donald Judd
  Ellsworth Kelly
  Harald Klingelhöller
  Mangelos
  Helen Mirra
  Matt Mullican
  Catherine Murphy
  Bruce Nauman
  Claes Oldenburg
  Eric Poitevin
  Sigmar Polke
  Charlotte Posenenske
  Gerhard Richter
  Fred Sandback
  Anne-Marie Schneider
  Jan Schoonhoven
  Thomas Schütte

Richard Serra
Lucy Skaer
Frank Stella
Richard Tuttle
Franz Erhard Walther
James Welling
Richard Wentworth
Rachel Whiteread

Freymond-Guth

Zurich

- Feature
Parcours

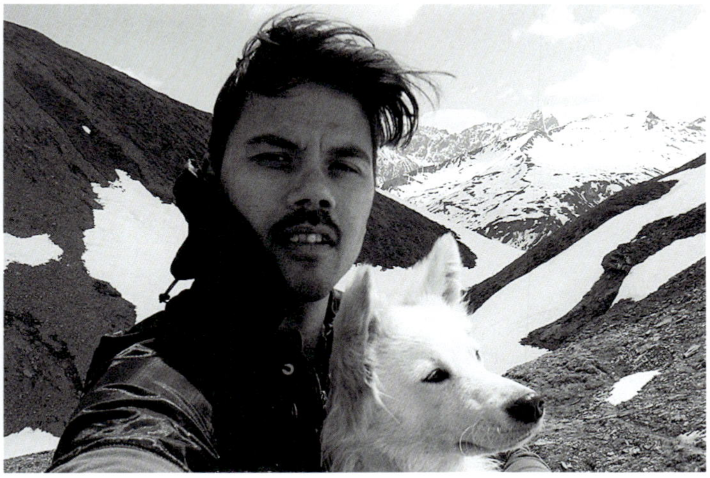

What first compelled you to open a gallery?
It was more of an artistic, playful concept with fellow artist friends from the context of my project space Les Complices, than a plan.

Who is the first artist you showed and what was most memorable about that show?
A group show with Loredana Sperini, Elodie Pong, Karin Suter, Philip Wiegard, and Ingo Giezendanner. Since the first gallery space was in a run-down building that had not been renovated for 40 years, all the artists and many friends helped painting, hanging, and making food for the opening that lasted ten hours.

When did you first participate in Art Basel and what was most memorable about that show?
In 2010 in Basel's Statements sector with Dani Gal. Realizing that the right context (Art Basel) makes it possible to sell a for 4-channel audio/slide installation with a silent film to a great international context—and that several times.

- **Contact** Freymond-Guth Fine Arts Ltd.
Jean-Claude Freymond-Guth
jeanclaude@freymondguth.com
office@freymondguth.com
- **Established** 2006
- **Owner(s) / Partner(s)** Jean-Claude Freymond-Guth
- **Team** 6
- **Space(s)** 250 m²
- **Artists at Art Basel** Heidi Bucher
- **Further artists represented** Marc Bauer
Sophie Bueno-Boutellier
Stefan Burger
Discoteca Flaming Star
Dani Gal
Virginia Overton
Elodie Pong
Tanja Roscic
Yorgos Sapountzis
Sylvia Sleigh
Loredana Sperini
Megan Francis Sullivan

Friedman

London

- Galleries
- Galleries
- Galleries
Public

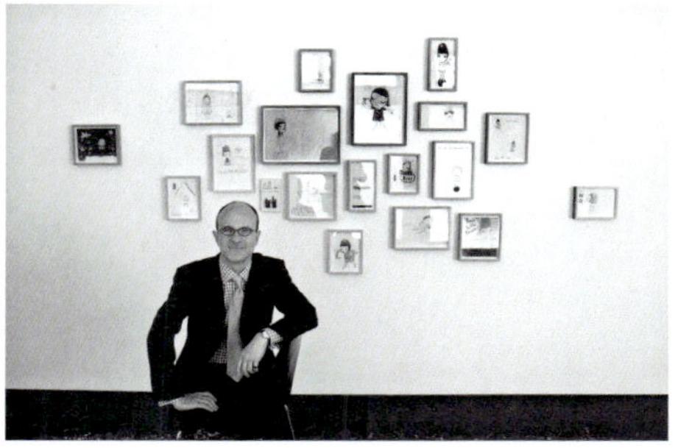

What first compelled you to open a gallery?
After a few years working as a private dealer, and then as a contemporary art specialist at Christies, I had a clear idea of the sort of gallery I wanted to start. It was my desire to work closely with the artists, nurturing them, and assisting them in realizing their visions. The timing was also fortuitous as I had a strong sense that London was on the cusp of becoming a credible international art capital.

Who is the first artist you showed and what was most memorable about that show?
Our first gallery show was by German sculptor Stephan Balkenhol. This show was the beginning of a very special and fruitful working relationship. Stephan remains as revered and popular today as he was almost 20 years ago and I look forward to future shows together.

When did you first participate in Art Basel and what was most memorable about that show?
Stephen Friedman Gallery first participated to Art Basel in 1997. I was grateful for being put on the waiting list as such a young gallery, having only been in operation for two years. I had very little notice to pull together a stand as I only found out two months prior to the opening that I was accepted. I knew I had to make an indelible impression. I arranged to secure a very beautiful abstract painting by Gerhard Richter from 1987. It was a showstopper.

- **Contact** Stephen Friedman Gallery
Kate Bradbury
kate@stephenfriedman.com
info@stephenfriedman.com
- **Established** 1995
- **Owner(s) / Partner(s)** Stephen Friedman
- **Team** 16
- **Space(s)** 269 m²
- **Artists at Art Basel** Mamma Andersson
Tonico Lemos Auad
Stephan Balkenhol
Claire Barclay
Huma Bhabha
Robert Buck
Andreas Eriksson
Tom Friedman
Kendell Geers
Wayne Gonzales
Daniel Guzmán
Thomas Hirschhorn
Jim Hodges
Judith Lauand
Li Tianbing
Paul McDevitt
Beatriz Milhazes
Yoshitomo Nara
Rivane Neuenschwander
Thomas Nozkowski
Catherine Opie
Cornelius Quabeck
Ged Quinn
Jennifer Rubell
Lucas Samaras
Yinka Shonibare
David Shrigley
Anne Truitt
Kehinde Wiley

F

Frith Street

London

● Galleries Unlimited

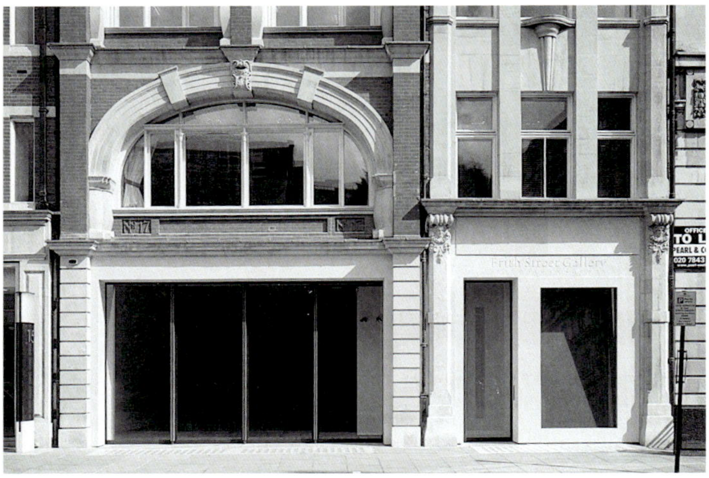

What first compelled you to open a gallery?
Frith Street Gallery opened in 1989 as a contemporary art gallery working in-depth with both young and established artists from the UK and abroad. Initially having an emphasis on works on paper, the gallery soon expanded its focus to represent artists working in other media (film, photography, sculpture, painting, etc.).

Who is the first artist you showed and what was most memorable about that show?
The first exhibition at Frith Street Gallery, in May 1989, was a solo show of works on paper by Luciano Bartolini. This was followed by an exhibition of etchings by two sculpture and installation-based artists, British artist Tony Cragg and Spanish artist Susana Solano.

When did you first participate in Art Basel and what was most memorable about that show?
Our first participation t Art Basel was in 1995, when we presented a selection of works by artists that have continued working with Frith Street Gallery over the past two decades including Thomas Schütte, Marlene Dumas, Juan Muñoz, and Callum Innes. Particularly memorable was the inclusion of Tacita Dean's *A Bag of Air* (1995) as part of the inaugural Art Video Forum. The piece, a 3-minute, 16mm black and white film taken from a hot air balloon, connects back to a childhood desire to bring clouds down to earth, and to suspend the belief that something so physical cannot be invisible.

- **Contact** Frith Street Gallery
  Dale McFarland
  dale@frithstreetgallery.com
  info@frithstreetgallery.com
- **Established** 1989
- **Owner(s) / Partner(s)** Jane Hamlyn
- **Team** 9
- **Space(s)** 620 m²
- **Artists at Art Basel** Polly Apfelbaum
  Fiona Banner
  Anna Barriball
  Massimo Bartolini
  Ingrid Calame
  Dorothy Cross
  Tacita Dean
  Marlene Dumas
  Callum Innes
  Jaki Irvine
  Juan Muñoz
  Cornelia Parker
  Raqs Media Collective
  John Riddy
  Thomas Schütte
  Dayanita Singh
  Bridget Smith
  Fiona Tan
  Juan Uslé
  Daphne Wright

Galeria Fortes Vilaça

Interview with Alessandra d'Aloia and Alexandre Gabriel

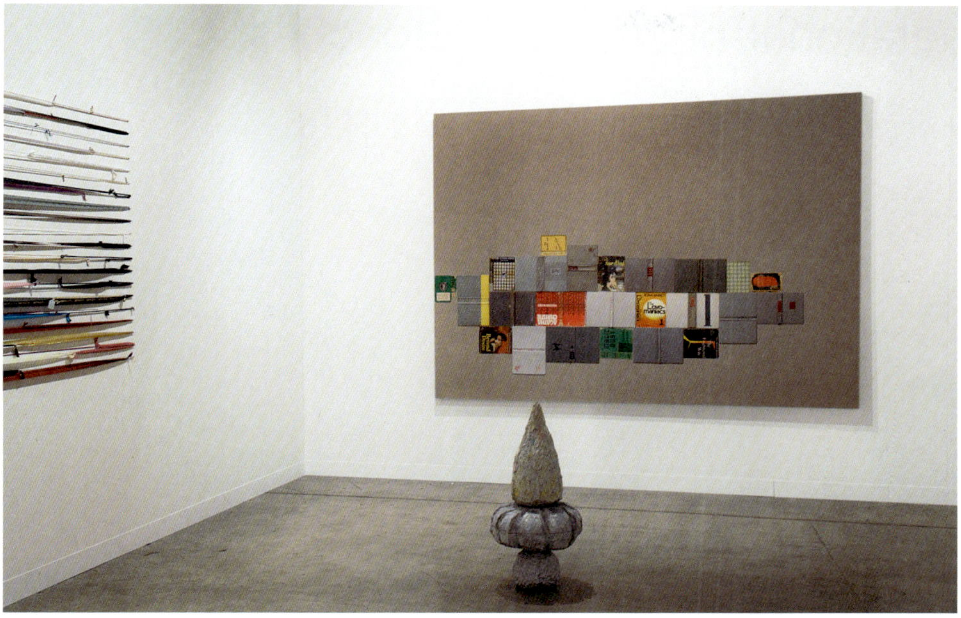

Art Basel in Miami Beach, 2013

Maybe we should start at the beginning, when you founded the gallery in 2001. How did it start?

Galeria Carmago Vilaça was founded in 1992 by Marcantonio Vilaça and Karla Camargo. Marcantonio passed away in 2000 and Márcia Fortes and I were asked by Karla Camargo to work as directors. Márcia was living in New York and I was Marcantonio's sister-in-law; we came to work and help Karla to run the gallery, but she decided to close the business in 2001, so we took it over under the name Fortes Vilaça. Alexandre Gabriel, Márcia, and I took it over together. The gallery retained most of the artists that Marcantonio had selected at the beginning. Only a few of them decided not to stay. There was a kind of continuity, because it was for us, and for Brazil at that time, a kind of legacy to continue this gallery, which has such an international approach. Marcantonio used to be one of the key gallerists on the international market, together with Luisa Strina and Thomas Cohn.

At that time the perception of Brazil was completely different than today. It was a lot of effort to participate in art fairs and to approach international collectors, museums, etc. It was quite hard for him and also for us at the beginning to be abroad. We were making almost 70% of our sales abroad at that time, which made us travel a lot. Around 2005 we decided to really focus on our internal market because we wanted to develop a larger group of collectors in Brazil. Brazil had already started to grow, the economy and a lot of the things in the world had changed, so we had a very good response. Nowadays the situation is the opposite of what it was when we started: we have a very strong local market in Brazil. But it is still our main goal to exchange ideas and be in dialogue with the international market.

How would you describe the specificities of your program, in terms of the artists represented?

I think we have a very diverse and intuitive selection of artists. We don't look for a specific group of artists, nor do we select something just because we don't have it represented already.

I think we were never in a position to form a specific group of artists, because the gallery itself started from another gallery. Of course we changed some of the artists, but we didn't start from scratch. As one of the biggest galleries in Brazil, you have to pay attention to the different stages artists are going through. We have to address difference: it's not just one generation, it's not one nationality, we have to bring international art to Brazil; and there's an institutional gap.

This has always been part of our agenda: bring young artists with fresh ideas to join the more established artists.

When did you first participate at Art Basel in Miami Beach?

Since the very beginning, the first edition. At the fair in Miami Beach there is a very strong Latin-American market, a lot of Latin-American collectors and institutions interested in this type of art, and Basel brings the Swiss structure, which I believe works perfectly because you have the balance of both things: being in Miami Beach, but having a very organized and institutional show, which is great. It has worked very well since the very beginning.

In terms of the collectors: these are people who follow our program and who know the artists, so it's not about introducing our program, it's more a continuous conversation about the development of careers. People like Ernesto Neto for instance, for years there was a huge installation at The Margulies Collection (Miami), and this was always a big thing for Neto, especially here, because people would see it there, understand the scale of the artist and then come here and see other works.

Everything is very connected.

Erika Verzutti took part in a talk yesterday in the Salon, as a participant of the 2013 Carnegie International, and you are showing some pieces by her. Could you tell us more about her?

Erika was one of the artists we brought to the gallery very early on, right after she graduated from Goldsmiths in London and moved back to Brazil. We gave her her first show, and several since then. At the beginning it was difficult to position her work within the context of Brazilian art because her practice is very different from everything else around her in Brazil. People often go to Brazil with an idea of what they are looking for in terms of art; for many years, Erika was not the person, or the kind of work, that matched the sort of preconception of what you would find in Brazil. But I think her own practice has developed toward something more connected to Brazilian contemporary art traditions. In her recent work that we are presenting here, you see a lot of references to modernist Brazilian art, which was something that caught the attention of many curators, and suddenly the work is understood in a different way. It's beautiful when you work with an artist for many years and see this development.

F

Focused on precisely curated projects, the Feature sector in Basel included thoughtfully developed solo presentations, as well as thematic exhibits built around a range of artists across diverse cultural, generational, or artistic approaches.

FEA TURE

2013 participants

Bani Abidi
Naeem Mohaiemem
Hajra Waheed
Experimenter

Yüksel Arslan
Dirimart

Pedro Barateiro
Bethan Huws
Joseph Kosuth
Vistamare

Barbara Bloom
Williams

Pablo Bronstein
Herald St

Heidi Bucher
Freymond-Guth

Luis Camnitzer
Parra & Romero

Marino Formenti
Stephen Prina
Mezzanin

Sonia Gomes
Mendes Wood

Robert Heinecken
Cherry and Martin

Sanya Kantarovsky
Frances Stark
Foxx

Robert Kinmont
Kilian Rüthemann
RaebervonStenglin

Julije Knifer
elbaz

Mario Merz
Thomas Schütte
Niele Toroni
Spartà

Manfred Mohr
bitforms

Robert Morris
Castelli

Ciprian Muresan
Plan B

Adam Pendleton
Gilberto Zorio
Cera

Jan Schoonhoven
Borzo

Joan Semmel
Alexander Gray

Sudarshan Shetty
SKE

Eduardo Terrazas
Monclova

Zhang Wei
Boers-Li

Tsuruko Yamazaki
Take Ninagawa

Robert Morris
Leo Castelli Gallery

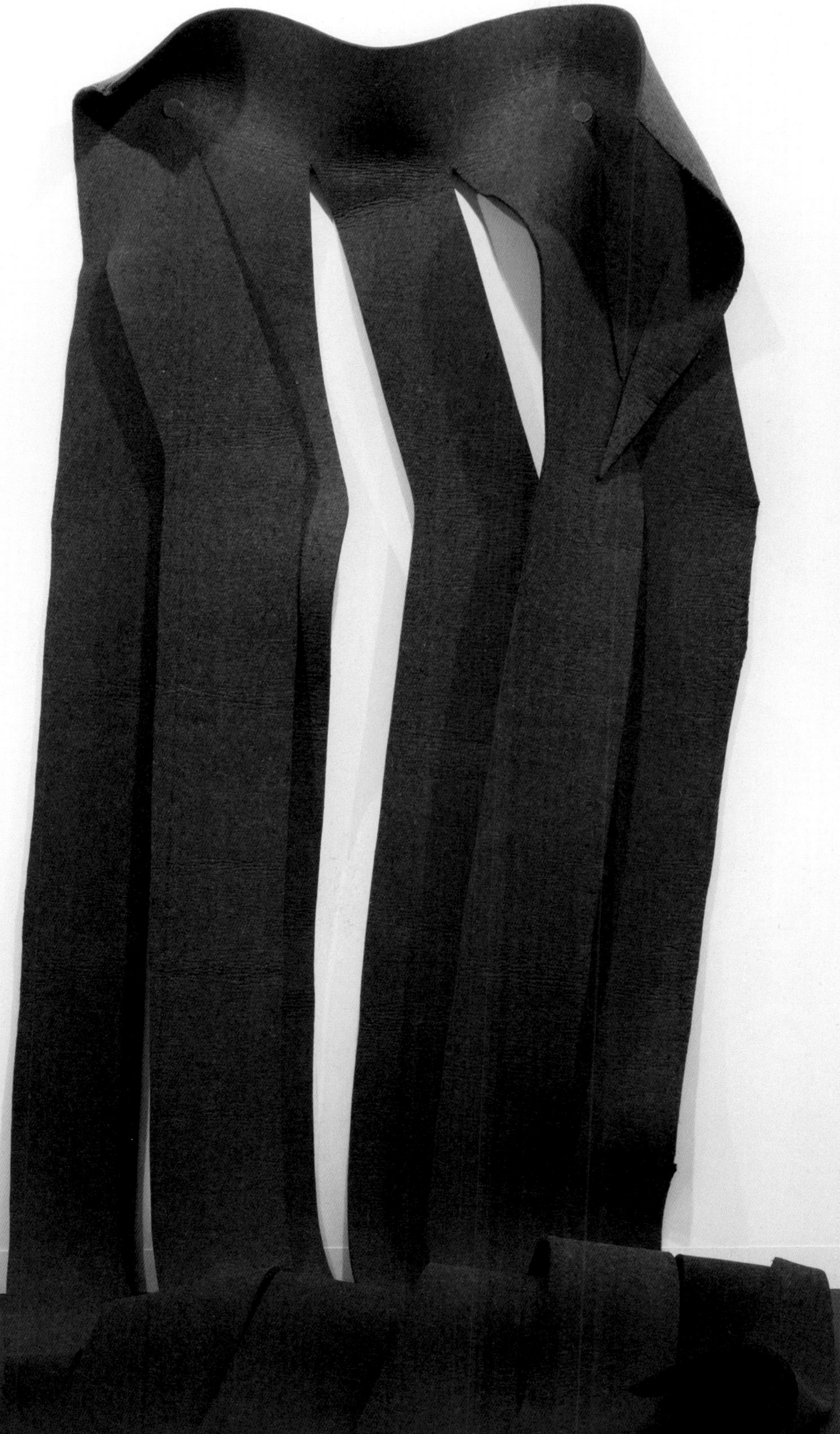

Tsuruko Yamazaki
Take Ninagawa

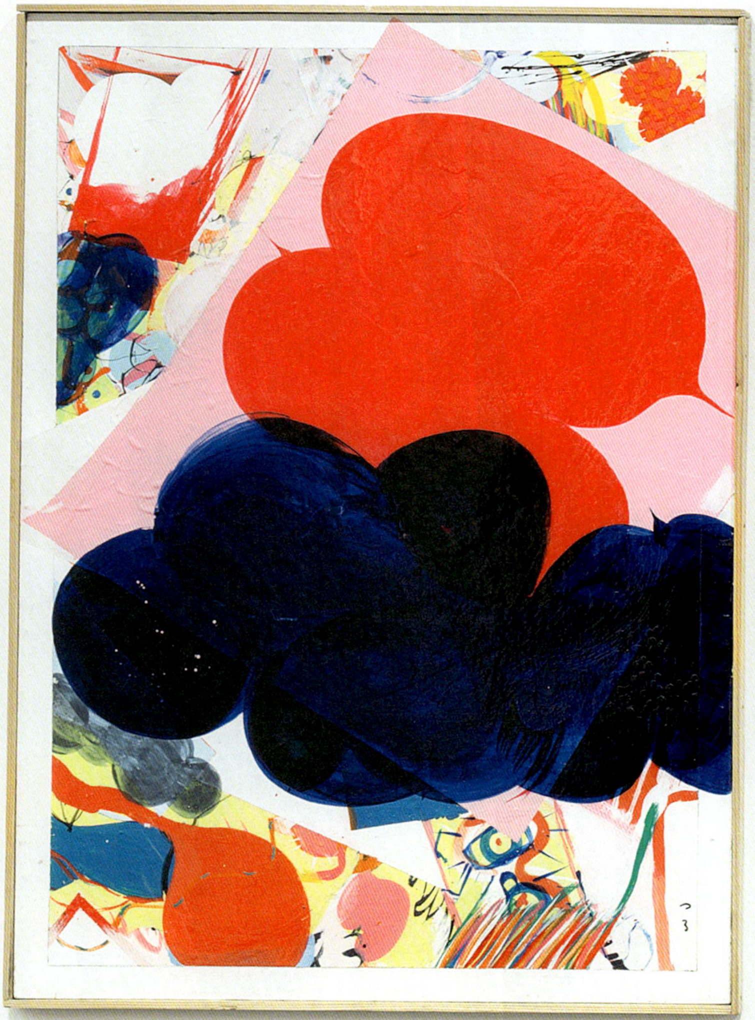

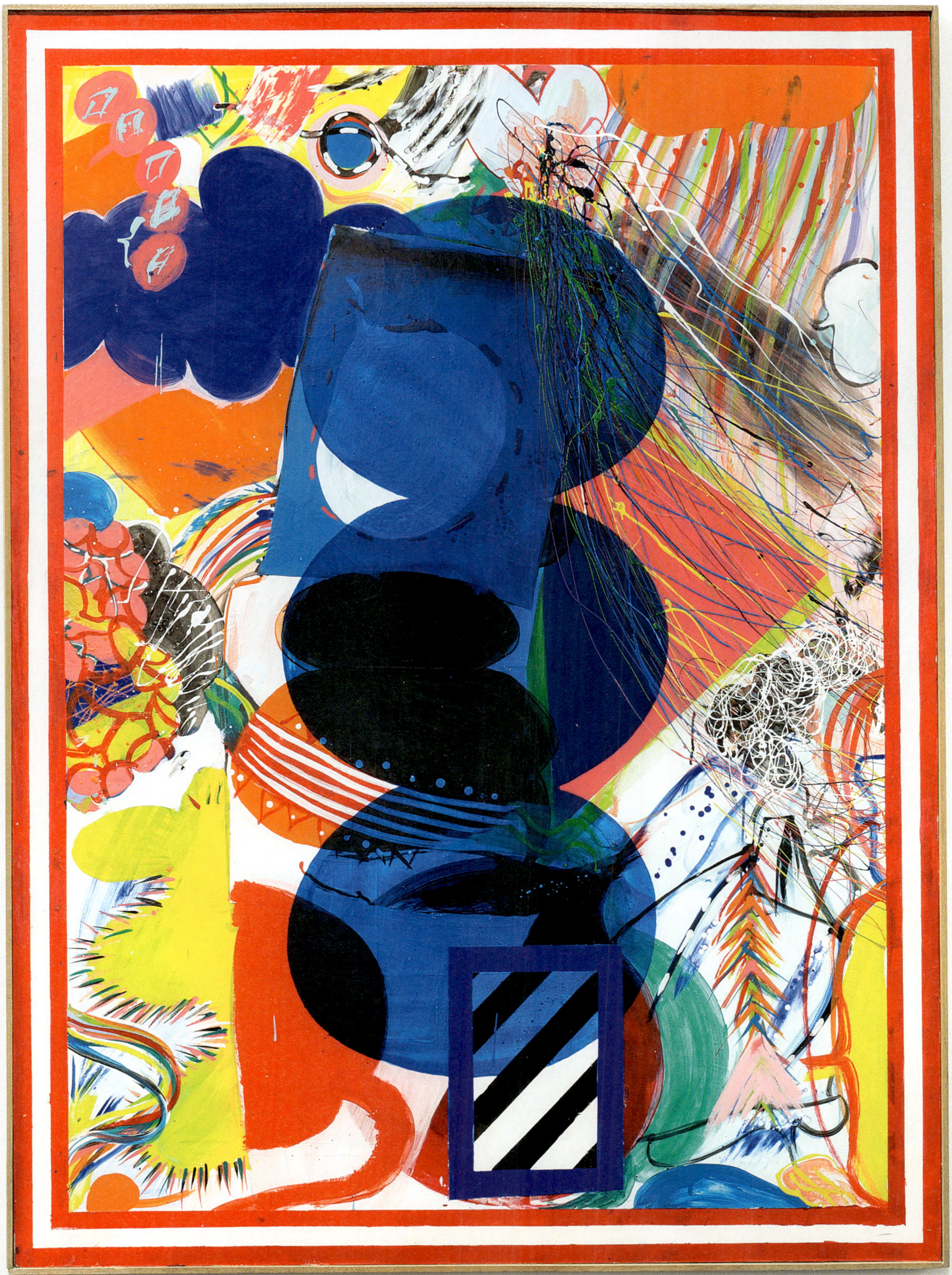

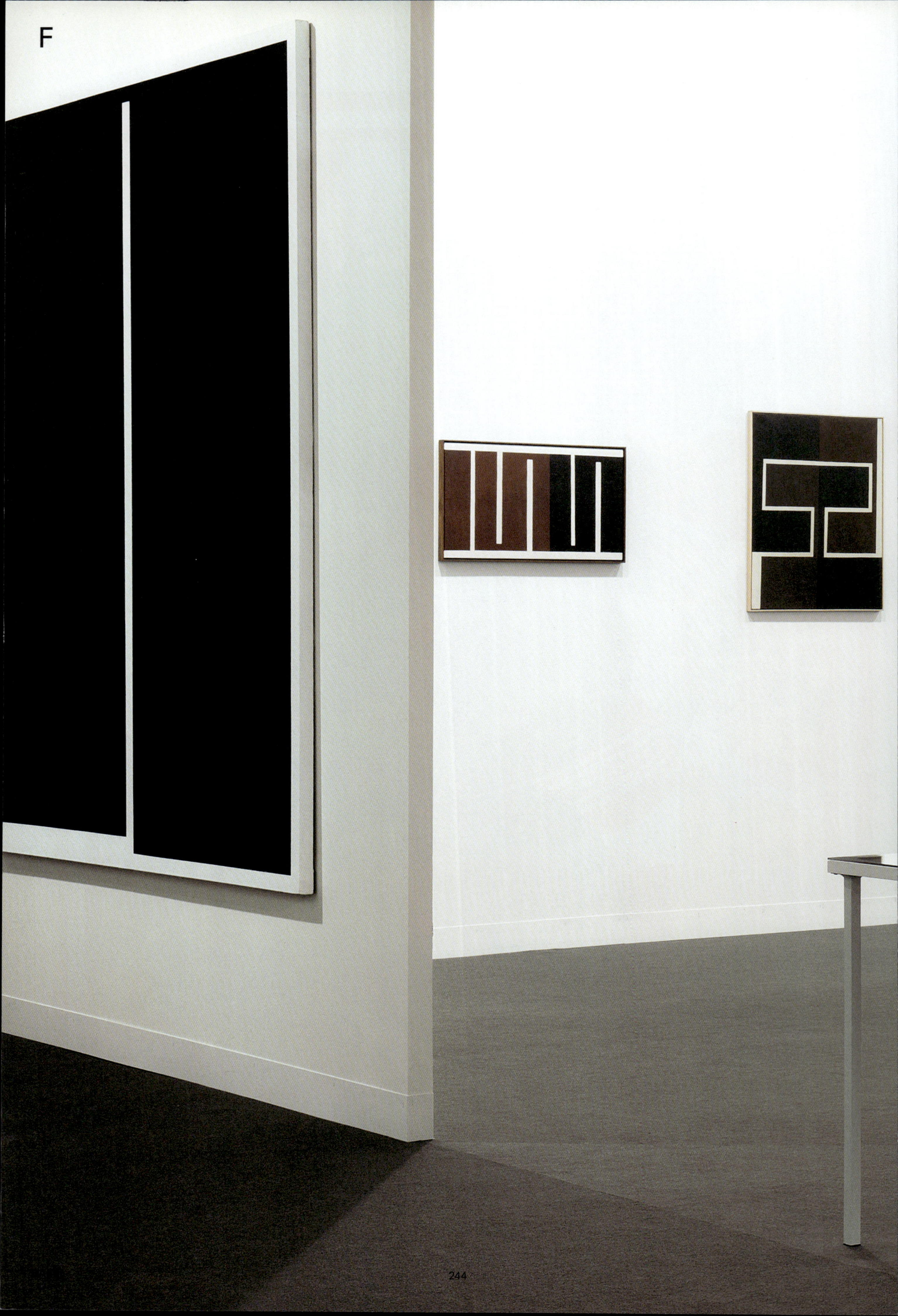
F

Julije Knifer
galerie frank elbaz

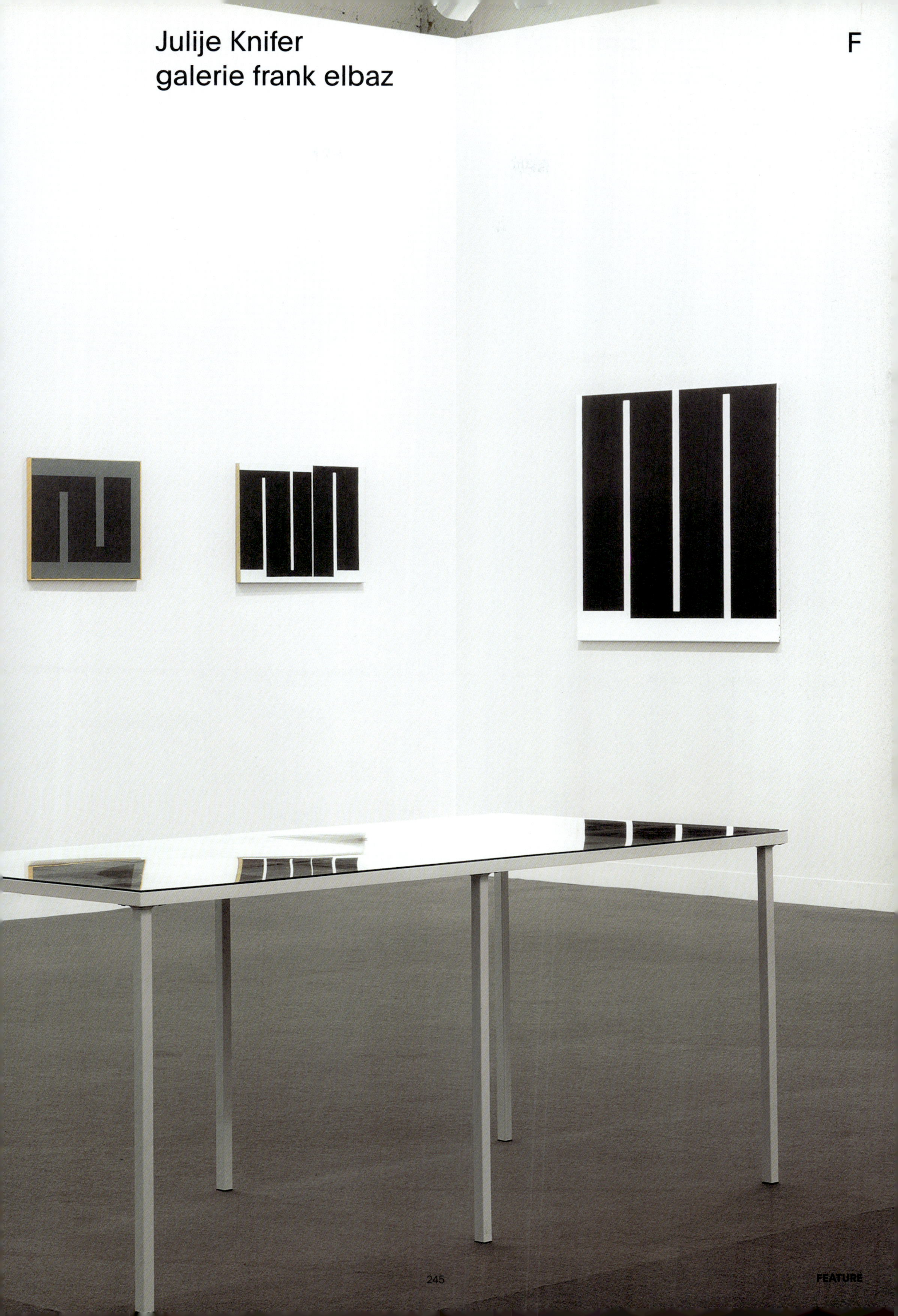

Luis Camnitzer
Parra & Romero

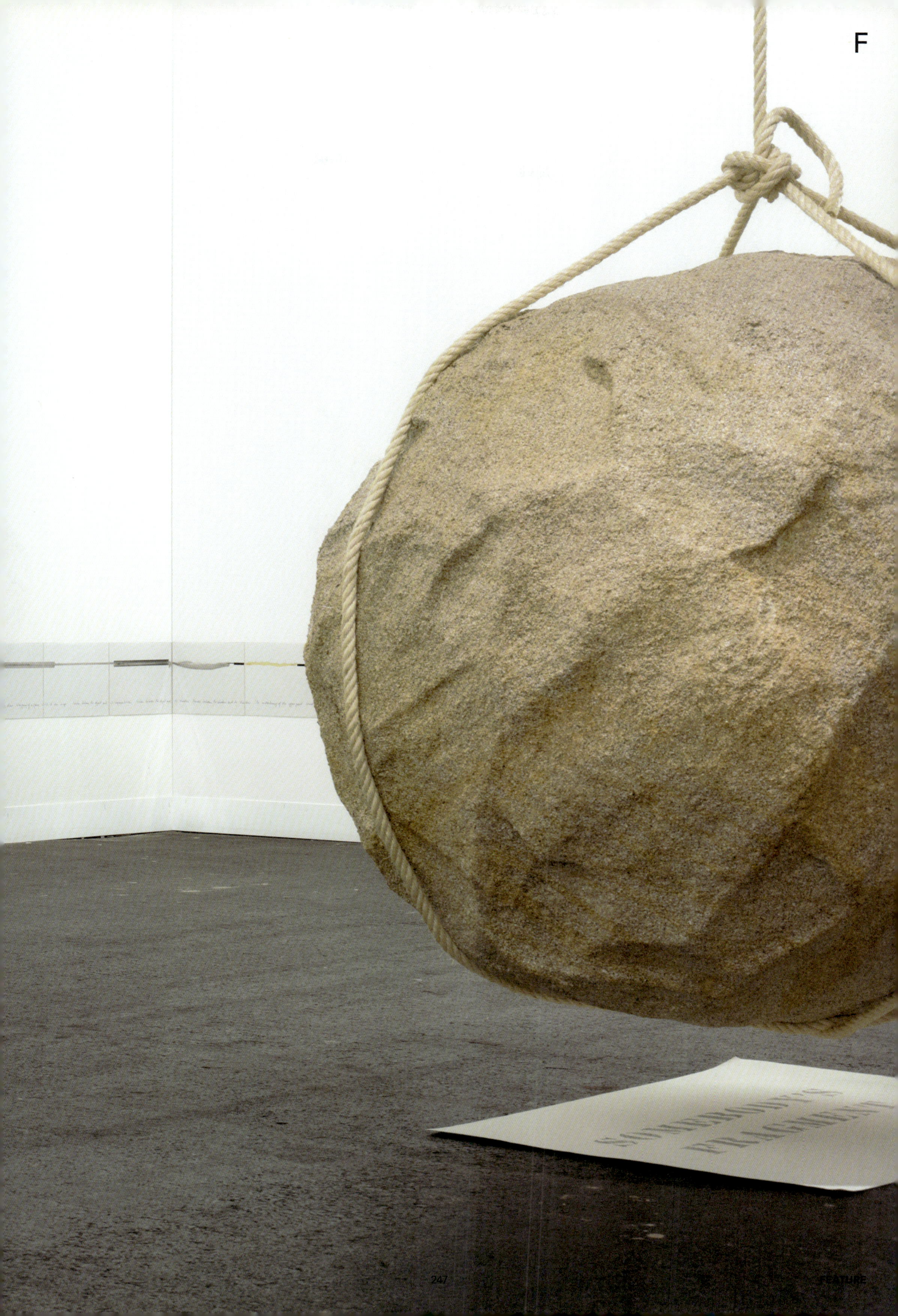

F

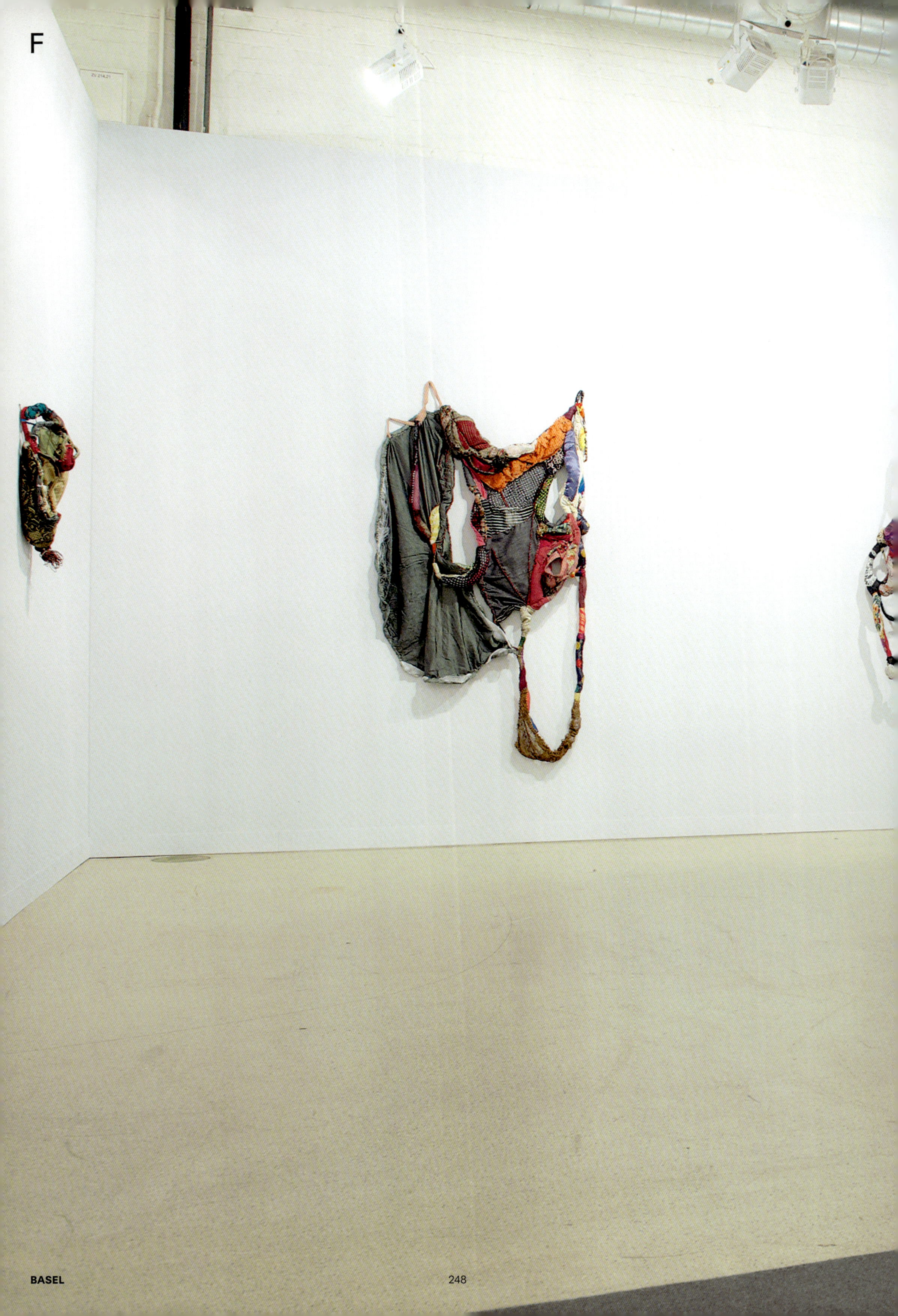

Sonia Gomes
Mendes Wood

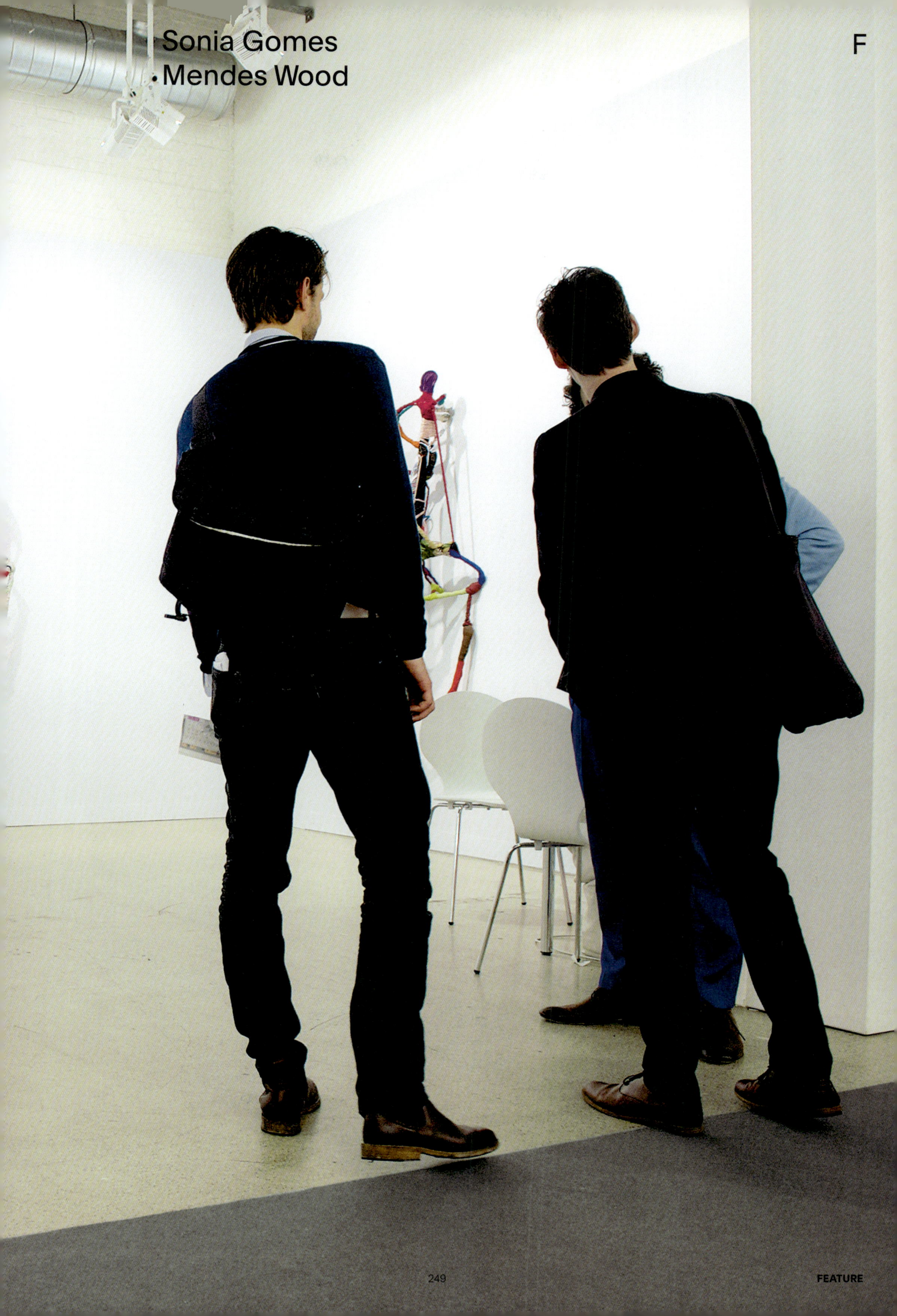

Ciprian Muresan
Galeria Plan B

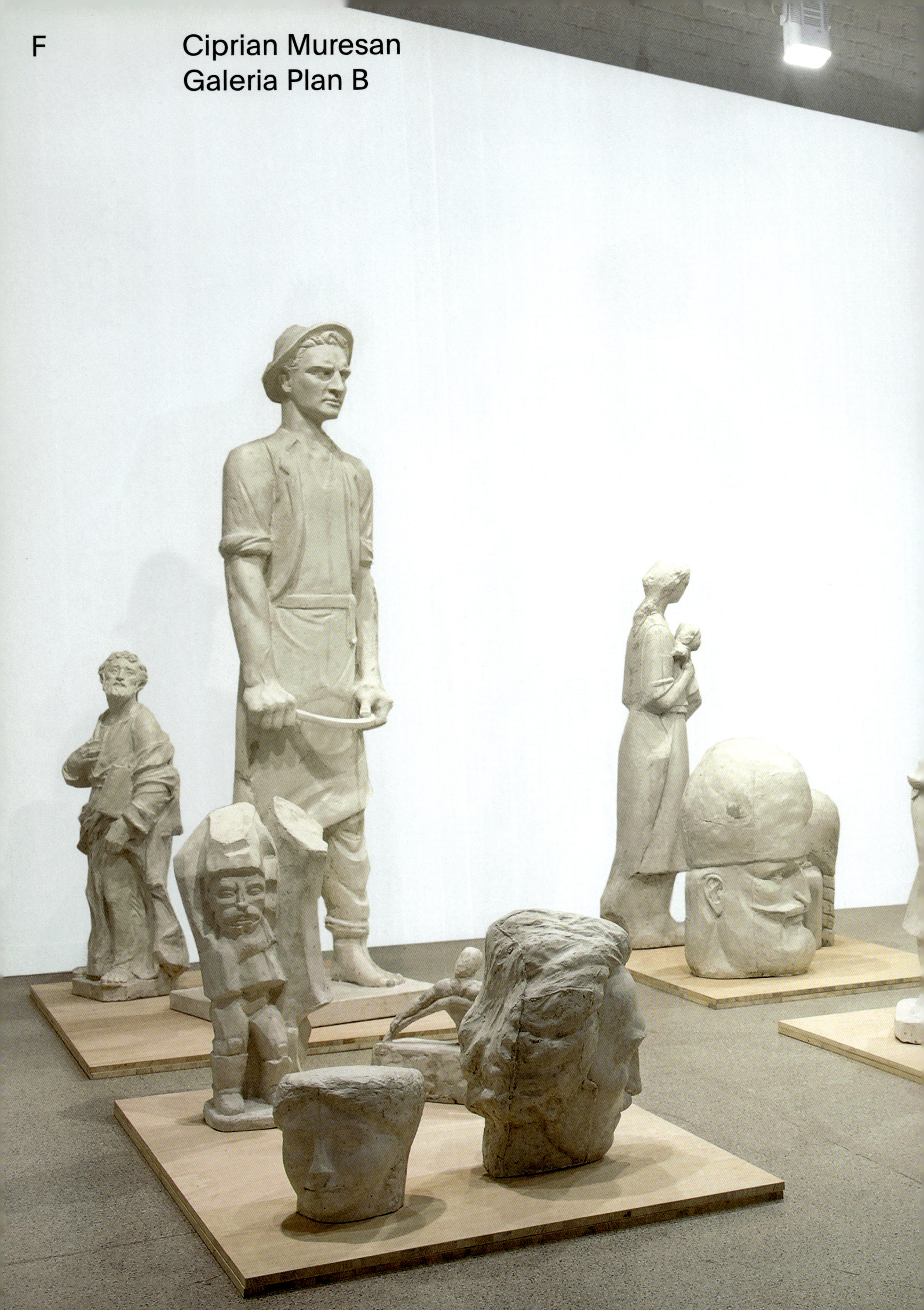

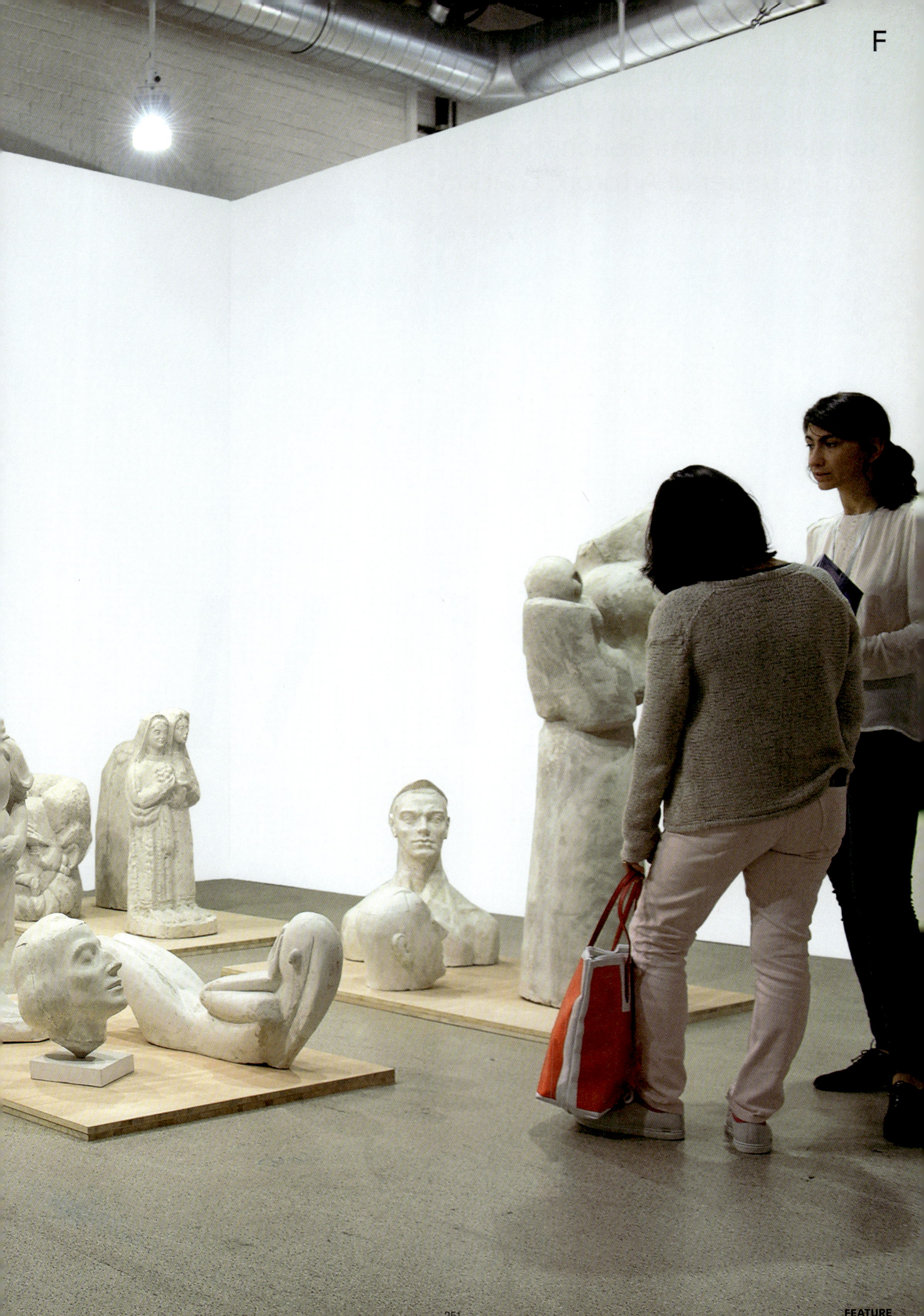

F

Basel's week-long program of films by and about artists is curated by Berlin film scholar Marc Glöde, and Zurich collector This Brunner. In Miami Beach the Film sector is organized by David Gryn, Founder of Artprojx, London.

FILM

2013 participants

Basel

Martin Arnold
Kader Attia
Michel Auder
Victor Burgin
Philippe Decrauzat
Peter Downsbrough
Isa Genzken
Zachary Heinzerling
Ho Tzu Nyen
Irwin
Christian Jankowski
William E. Jones
Hassan Khan
Idris Khan
Malcolm McLaren
Carsten Nicolai
Marcel Odenbach
Stephen Prina
Tom Sachs
Jim Shaw
Michael Snow
John Stezaker

Miami Beach

Nevin Aladağ
Brian Alfred
Carlos Amorales
with Julian Lede
David Austen
Bill Balaskas
My Barbarian
Luz María Bedoya
Dara Birnbaum
Martin Creed
Shezad Dawood
Mukul Deora
Rineke Dijkstra
Nathalie Djurberg
Cevdet Erek
Leo Gabin
Ana Gallardo
Nan Goldin
Christian Jankowski
Chris Johanson
Joan Jonas
William E. Jones
JR
Stanya Kahn
William Kentridge
with Philip Miller
Karen Kilimnik
Friedrich Kunath
Samuel Levack &
Jennifer Lewandowski
Sabine Lidl
Linder
Alice Maher
Mahony
Ari Marcopoulos
Bruce McLean
Oscar Muñoz
Takeshi Murata
Shirin Neshat
Rashaad Newsome
Tin Ojeda
Fyodor Pavlov-
Andreevich
Cheng Ran
Marco Rios
Pietro Roccasalva
Miljohn Ruperto &
SunTek Chung
Liliana Sánchez
Jeremy Shaw
Shimabuku
Yinka Shonibare MBE
David Shrigley
Regina Silveira
Lucien Smith
Mickalene Thomas
Nicola Thomas
Avinash Veeraraghavan
Kemang Wa Lehulere
Kehinde Wiley

Young Kim & Marc Glöde on Malcolm McLaren

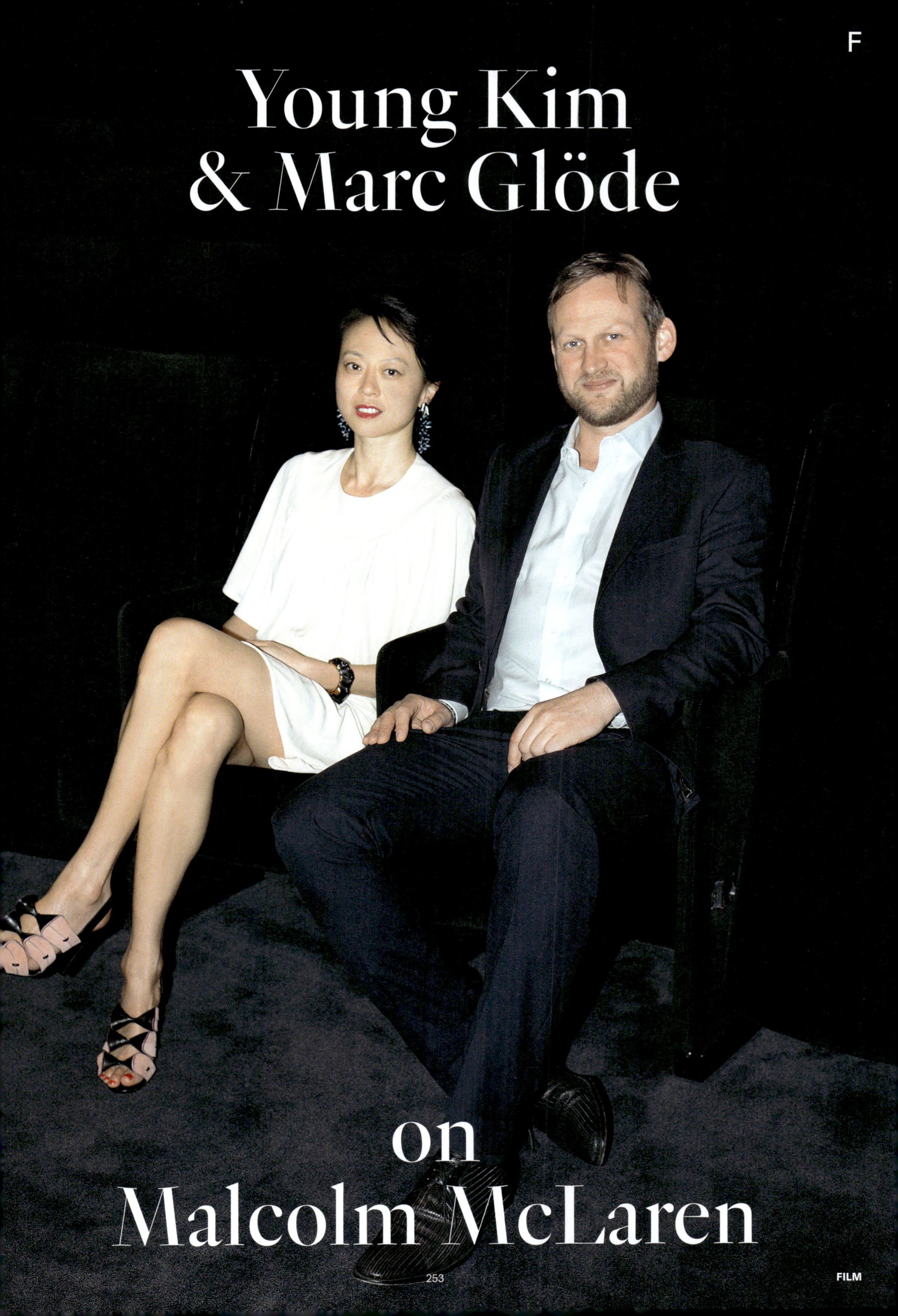

Young Kim interviewed by Marc Glöde about Malcolm McLaren

Malcolm McLaren's final film is a collage of ideal images of Paris. Using French film clips and commercials from the past hundred years, McLaren examines the intersections of art and commodity. The result is a beautiful visual poem.

Art Basel
Film

June 10, 2013
Stadtkino, Basel

Q&A with Young Kim, Malcolm McLaren's partner and head of the Estate of Malcolm McLaren, and Marc Glöde, Art Basel's Film sector curator, following the screening of Malcolm McLaren's *Paris, Capital of the XXIst Century* (2010)

MARC GLÖDE When did Malcolm McLaren start working on this film and how did this project evolve?

YOUNG KIM When I met Malcolm in 1998 he was based in London, but he still returned to Paris regularly. For him Paris was a home, it was a place of escape and refuge. He had gone to France in the late 1960s as an art student, and even earlier, in his late teens, he had won an internship to be a student of the automatist painter André Masson. It was during these years that he built up his interest in the Situationists and Guy Debord. That's where a lot of the material comes from.

The first time we met Sam Keller at a dinner in New York, he invited Malcolm to come to Basel to give a talk. To come here was something very special for Malcolm, because he had struggled throughout his life through commercial mediums (fashion, music, film), against structures and artistic limitations. The next year he was invited to show his artwork *Shallow 1-21* (2008), which is a similar work to the film *Paris* in its structure, in the sense that it has chapters, and it's also made out of what one could call the "detritus of culture." In *Shallow*, that meant pornography films that had been forgotten, discarded, and that he united together into something—one could say—quite magical.

For *Paris, Capital of the XXIst Century* (2010), Malcolm also took something that was normally considered garbage—old adverts—and turned that into something new. The research for this particular work started in the early 1990s. He was working on the *Paris* album (1994), on which a lot of this material is based, and stumbled upon this collection of archives of film and television ads, particularly French commercials shot in Paris. There were even ads from the Lumières brothers ... He was fascinated by them, and started to use bits of these ads' soundtracks in the *Paris* album, and then in the film. What fascinated him too, about these ads, was how many artists had used them as a new medium.

For the artists, film was this new magical material in the 20th century. Even great artists and directors like Max Ernst, Tati, and Jean-Luc Godard made ads. Like all great artists, he had a unique point of view on things. Certain ads were distasteful to me, or unusable, and somehow he would change them, he would put them in another context, find new combinations, and make something really great.

MG You mentioned Guy Debord ...

YK Malcolm was always fascinated by Debord and people of his generation, because today it's such a different world. Now everything is for sale, there's an ad for everything, and it's very hard to find a place where you're not hit with someone trying to sell you something. What is interesting is that the history of cinema—which the film is basically about—and then television, follow through a changing culture, this moment of transition when the culture of necessity evolved into a culture of desires, where you were buying things based on dreams, things that you didn't need to survive. This was something that started mainly in the 1920s and took off after WWII. Malcolm was part of the very last generation of people who experienced that shift. He was born in London in 1946, when there was still rationing. So obviously these ideas about what was happening with the commodification of culture, which was very much based on Debord's and also Marshall McLuhan's thinking, were very important to Malcolm.

MG Walter Benjamin was another influence. The title refers to his book *Paris, capitale du XIXe siècle* (1939).

YK Malcolm was reading Benjamin's book, which is basically about the development of the early commodity culture. He was very excited about it, but didn't know about Roman numerals very well, and so he said to me: "My God, Young, look, Walter Benjamin could tell the future. Paris *is* the capital of the 21st century!" and I said to Malcolm: "Actually Malcolm, that's the 19th century." He said, "Oh but I really loved the title." That's how it stuck.

MG How does he then relate to the whole question of rhythm, this idea developed by Walter Benjamin in "The Return of the Flâneur" about the rhythms of the city? In McLaren's movie, rhythm is key. It's created by music and the way it's edited.

YK The short length of the ads gives rhythm to the work. I suppose that his previous experience in pop music also influenced his editing. I mean, I always think that people read too much into the artists' artworks, but a lot of it is in the process and the experimentation. For Malcolm, the process was really organic. For him, the visual and the audio always went together. He believed in the look of music and the sound of fashion.

PUBLIC How did Malcolm want his films to be seen and presented? Did he want them to be seen in an art gallery context, or in a cinema context? Or in a kind of sculptural context? Did he want people to sit and be durational? At Unlimited, where *Shallow* was presented, people could come and go, it was a much more fluid way of viewing them.

YK He wanted them to be presented as art films, and with a projection system—he was against digital screens, but besides from that I can't really say … I think he would have been perfectly fine to have *Shallow* presented the way it is here, because they are in chapters, so you can jump in and out whenever you want. I don't think that he had to keep an audience captive at all, but he definitely wanted them to be treated as art films.

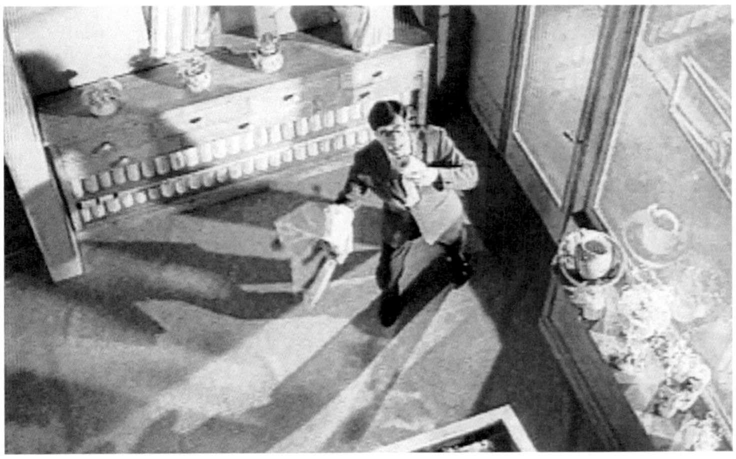

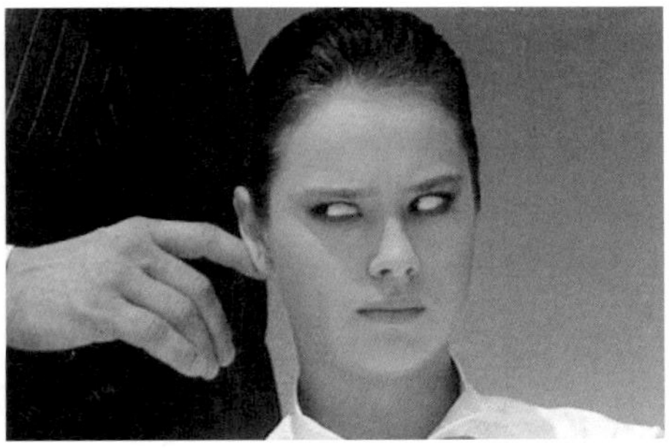

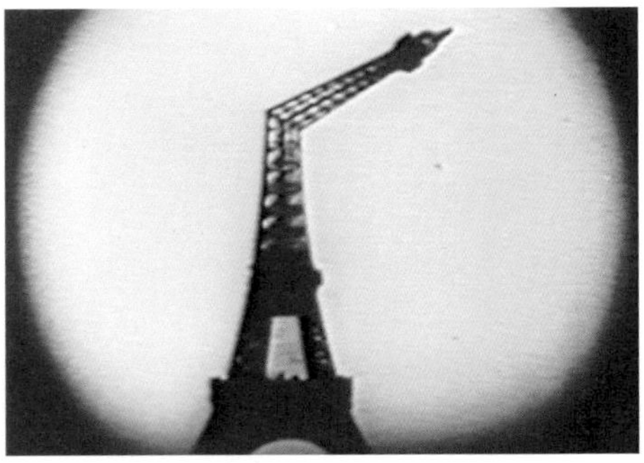

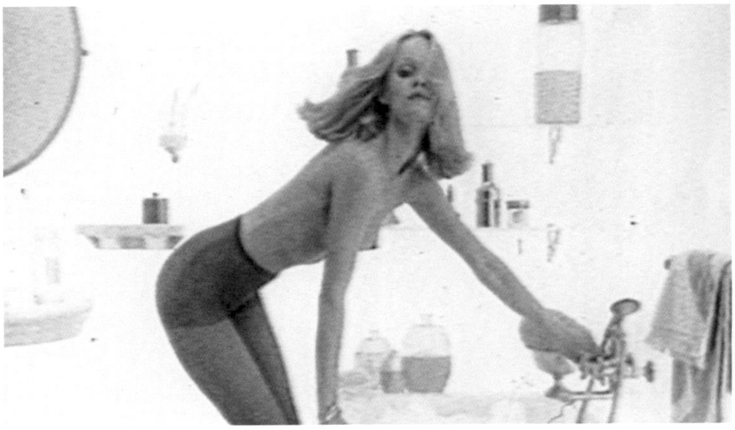

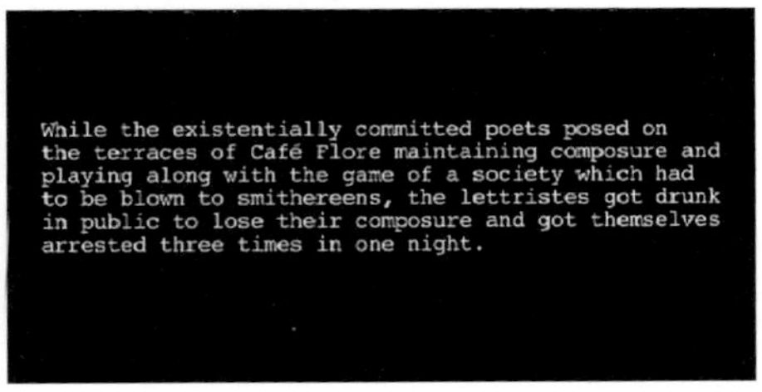

Malcolm McLaren
Paris, Capital of the XXIth Century, 2010

F

SoundScape Park
Miami Beach
Mickalene Thomas

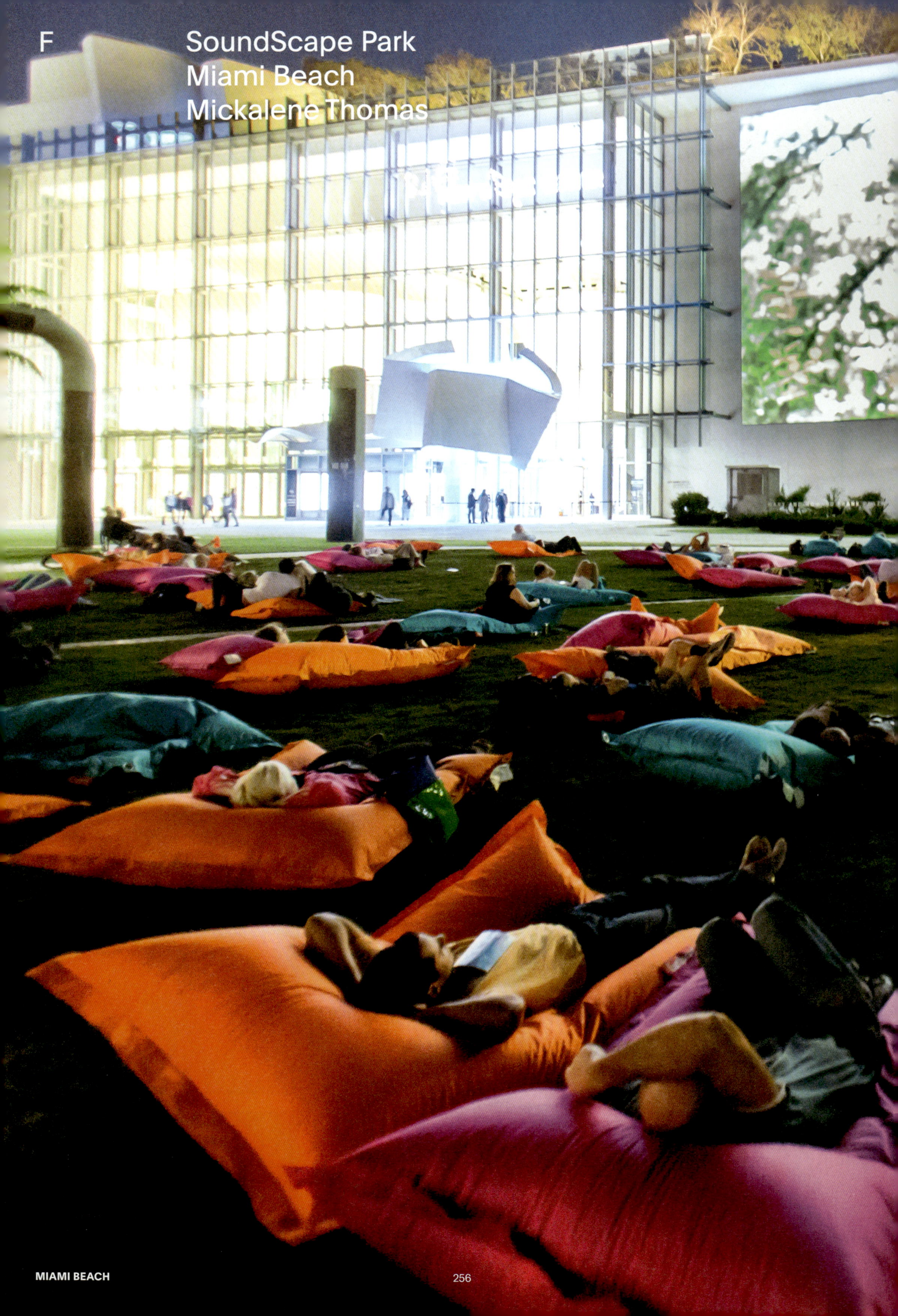

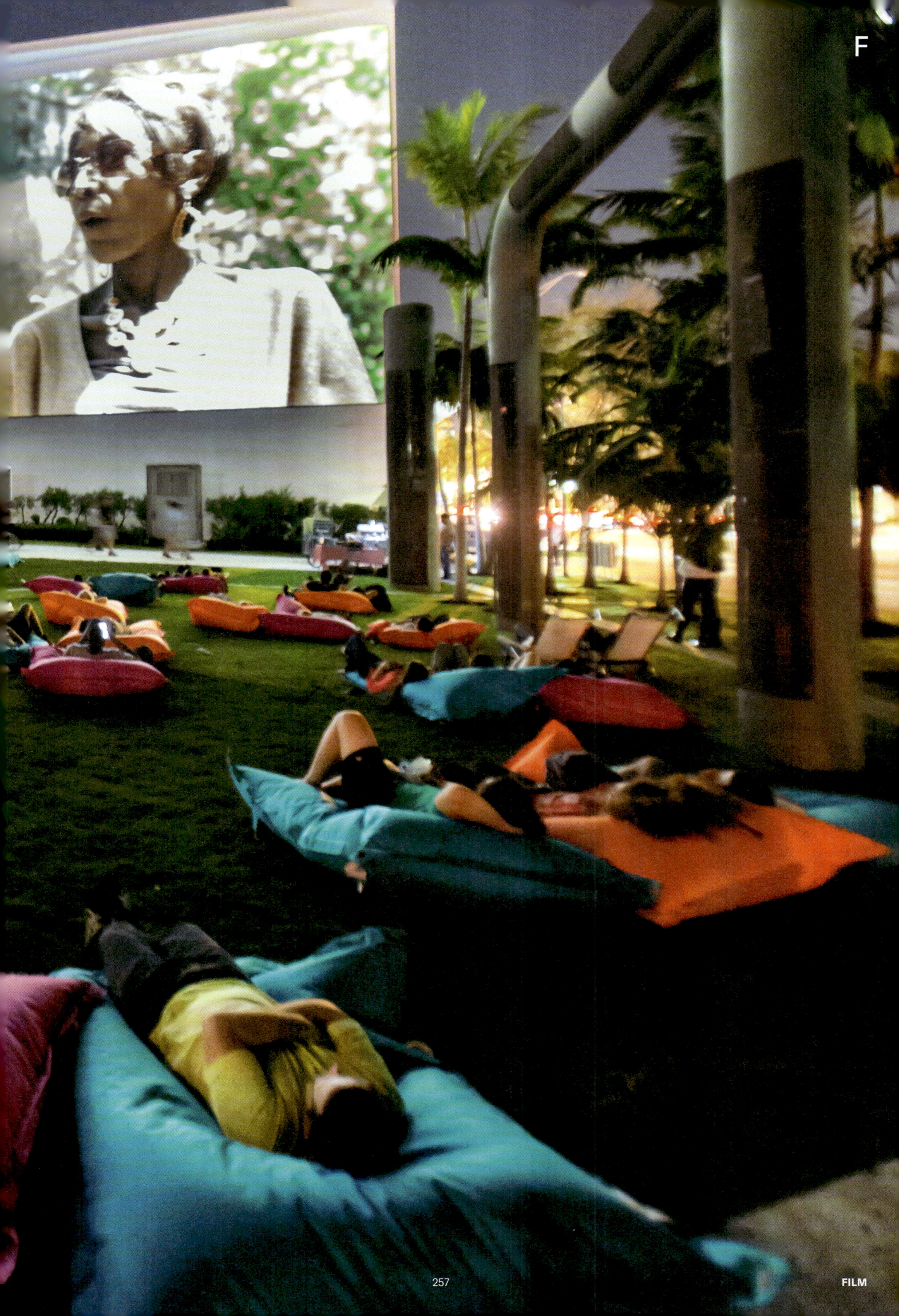

F

"Get Out of New York"—Dara Birnbaum

A Conversation with David Gryn, curator of Art Basel's Film sector in Miami Beach and Founder of Artprojx, London

Artist Talk
Dara Birnbaum

Art Basel in
Miami Beach
December 6, 2013

Dara Birnbaum,
Artist, New York

David Gryn,
Curator of Art Basel's
Film sector and
Founder of Artprojx,
London

A complete version
of the conversation
is available at
www.artbasel.com

DAVID GRYN This is the third year I have curated the Film sector for Art Basel in Miami Beach, which is projected onto the wall of the New World Symphony Center. Two years ago, when I discovered Dara Birnbaum's work at the South London Gallery in London, there was this piece entitled *Arabesque* (2011), a video installation sampling clips from YouTube of women performing Robert and Clara Schumann's respective piano compositions. It was shown on four screens, and I thought I couldn't even think about it for here, because we do a single screen projection. But I couldn't get it out of my head. To my delight, Dara Birnbaum agreed to make it into a single film projection. How was it for you to see it on the big screen?

There is a sense of timing that makes the works—even the early, appropriated works that might seem very simple are based on rhythmical patterns.
— Dara Birnbaum

DARA BIRNBAUM I was surprised! I was told that it's a 7,000 square-foot projection area and even though I have showed in a lot of clubs that were trying new technologies, and some with big screens, this is so different! First, because it has a real context, the symphony hall designed by Frank Gehry. A lot of my work is based on music. *Arabsesque* is actually a duo between a piece by Robert Schumann composed for his wife Clara, and another composed by Clara Schumann for her husband. A lot of artists want to bring their art into the public realm, but I thought this was very specific. Instead of putting sculptures in a garden, I liked this idea of a large screen acting almost like a mirror turned onto the Center itself. It was wonderful to be out in the open, with the sky, cars moving by, and occasionally the shadow of a palm tree, all adding something to the imagery and making a new montage.

DG One of the things I felt when looking at your work was that there's a roughness, a rawness, a "punkness"; it was like working with an artist who is very well esteemed and established, but it also felt fresh, raw, and contemporary. You make music with your work, there are repetitions, there's something of Steve Reich. How does that feel for you, this idea of making your own music?

DB I started very young (I actually did architecture before I did art) and I was thinking of going into music fairly early on, but felt I couldn't make it well enough. But the musicians I work with tell me that, for a video person, I have a very good ear! I see things as compositions that have to go together. There is a sense of timing that makes the works—even the early, appropriated works that might seem very simple are based on rhythmical patterns. I also grew up with Pop art and Minimalism, where there's a lot of seriality and repetition. I was always much more involved in the process than the product.

DG How is your position as a woman, and your relationship with feminism, thematized within *Arabesque*?

DB The earliest pieces I did were about two things: they tackled television as a language—there's a lot of appropriation there—and they were dealing with the images and the stereotypes of women, starting from *Technology/Transformation: Wonder Woman* (1978–1979). It's the thing that stayed with me thematically like a red thread. There was a period, around 1992 when the Gulf War started, when I could no longer relate directly to politics in my work as I had in *Tiananmen Square: Break-In*

Transmission (1990) or *Transmission Tower*: *Sentinel* (1992). I was driven back into gender politics by music, even before Clara Schumann, by *Erwartung* (1909), Schoenberg's opera written by a woman.

DG It's always a strange topic to talk about within an art fair, but how do you relate to the notion of art and commodity?

DB I'm getting old enough—I'm 67 now—to say that I feel the art world was a very different world when I started. One didn't deal with commodification right away. If anything one didn't look at galleries as role models. My main model was a sense of politically needing to find a voice for women. I hated the voice that was coming at me and that was the reason for appropriation: I thought everything was coming one way at me, so I was trying to grab things back. There were no home recording units back then, no one was carrying smartphones, we didn't used to get immediate information.

I grew up loving the arts, I had seen the earliest works of someone like Trisha Brown, and watching someone break through movement at that time wasn't even thought of that much. You couldn't put a price on that performance. Now, everything has to be priced. Even with appropriation, everything needs a release; I was doing it out of being a pirate—I went in and stole whatever I could, bought footage like I was buying illegal drugs. It wasn't as if I was bringing a commodity to people.

DG If there was a piece of advice you could give to a young artist, what would it be?

DB I would quote Patti Smith saying: "Get out of New York!"

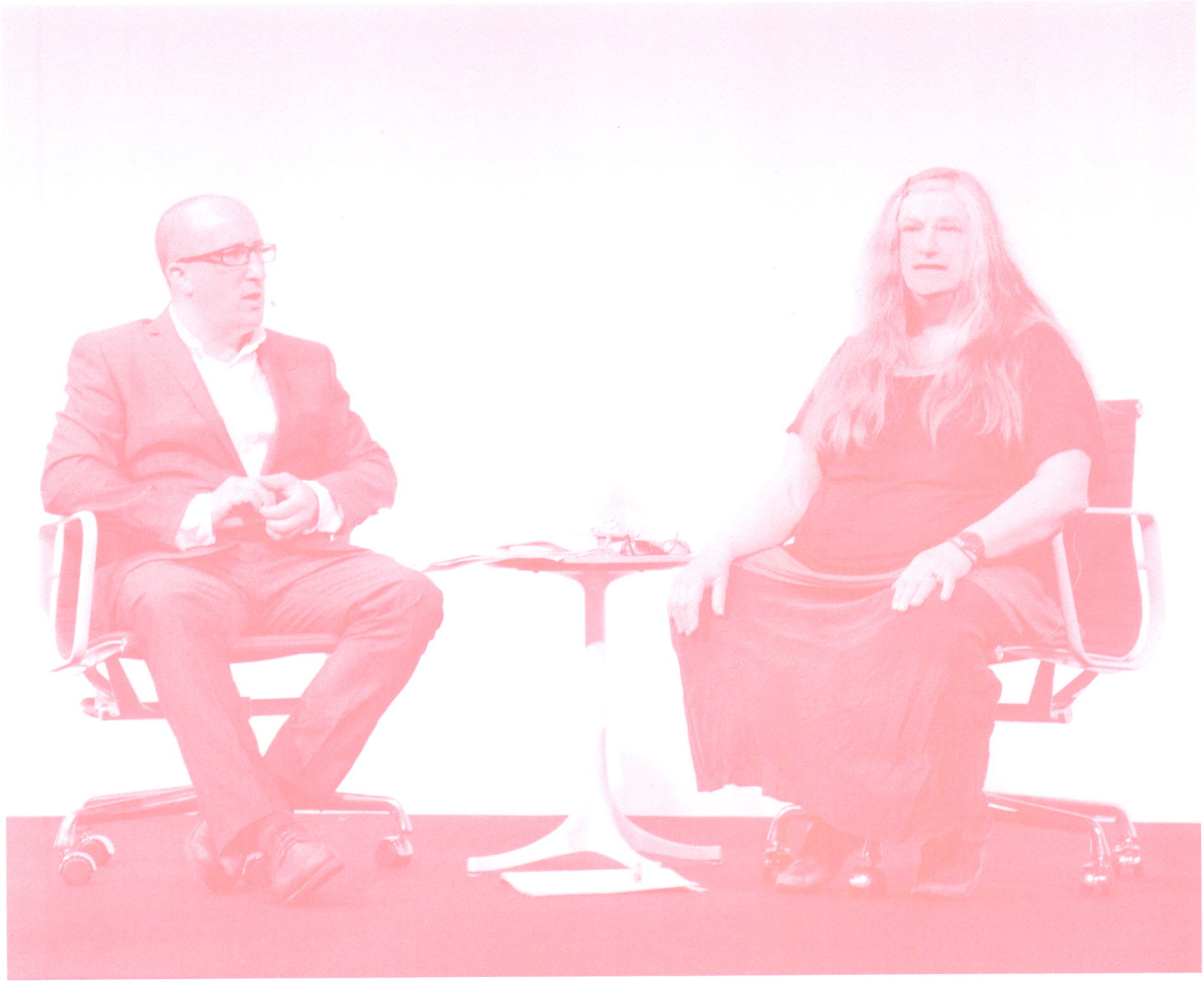

David Gryn and
Dara Birnbaum

G

G

- Hong Kong
- Basel
- Miami Beach

Gagosian

New York
Los Angeles
London
Paris
Rome
Athens
Geneva
Hong Kong

Hong Kong: Galleries
Basel: Galleries, Unlimited, Parcours
Miami Beach: Galleries, Public

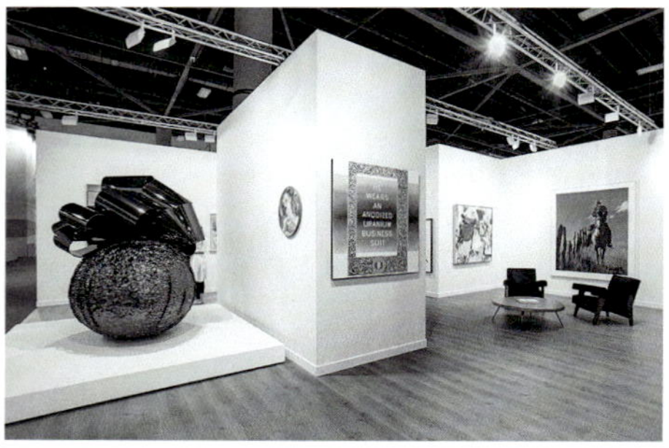

When did you first participate in Art Basel and what was most memorable about that show?
In 1995.

- **Contact** Gagosian Gallery, newyork@gagosian.com
- **Established** 1979
- **Owner(s) / Partner(s)** Larry Gagosian
- **Team** Approx. 200
- **Space(s)** 14,400 m² globally

Gajah

Singapore

Hong Kong: Galleries

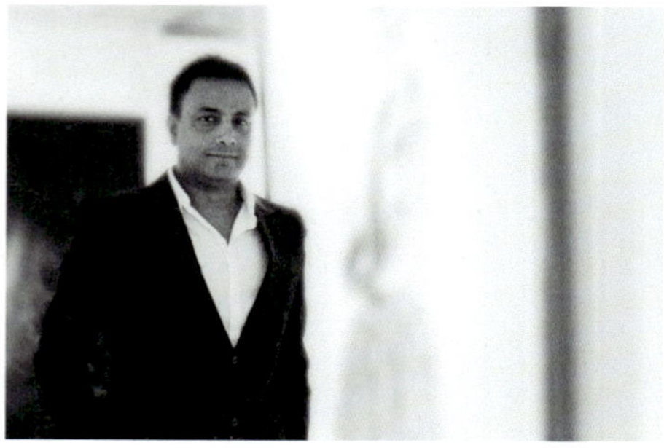

What first compelled you to open a gallery?
Back in the mid-1990s there was a dearth of galleries focusing on Southeast Asian art. There were a number of interesting artistic things happening in the region and I was drawn to this.

Who is the first artist you showed and what was most memorable about that show?
I showed Entang Wiharso and Narisun. The most memorable thing was that I hardly sold—it was tough!

When did you first participate in Art Basel and what was most memorable about that show?
My first participation was two years ago. The most memorable thing was walking into the hall of fame of who's who in the art world and certainly not feeling out of place.

- **Contact** Gajah Gallery, Aisha Amrin, aisha@gajahgallery.com, art@gajahgallery.com
- **Established** 1996
- **Owner(s) / Partner(s)** Jasdeep Sandhu
- **Team** 5
- **Space(s)** 211.5 m²
- **Artists at Art Basel** Ashley Bickerton, Nyoman Masriadi, Handiwirman Saputra, Yunizar
- **Further artists represented** Jumaldi Alfi, Teng Nee Cheong, Lotta de Beus, M. Irfan, Chua Ek Kay, Rudi Mantofani, Yusra Martunus

Galerist

Istanbul

Hong Kong: Galleries

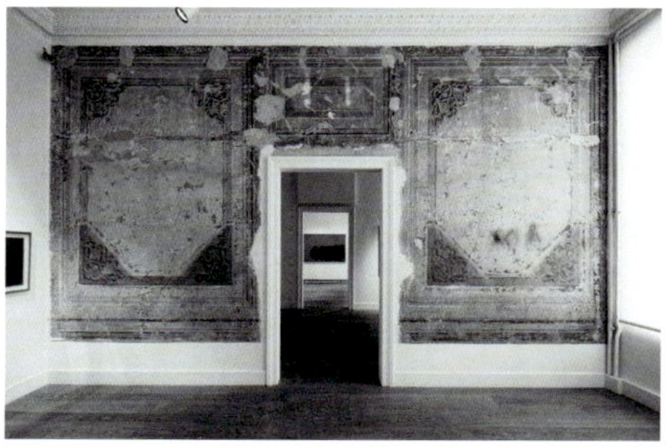

What first compelled you to open a gallery?
Galerist was founded with a mission to support Turkish contemporary art within Turkey and abroad. Participating in leading art fairs allowed the gallery and its artists to establish a strong presence on the international scene. During the accelerated development of Turkish contemporary art in the recent years, Galerist has begun to integrate established international artists in its program as well.

Who is the first artist you showed and what was most memorable about that show?
Haluk Akakçe was the first show at the gallery.

When did you first participate in Art Basel and what was most memorable about that show?
Galerist's first participation was at Art Basel in 2006. The interest of and enquiries from collectors and other galleries in Turkish art was eye-opening and inspirational.

- **Contact** Galerist, Doris Benhalegua Karako, dorisbenhalegua@galerist.com.tr, info@galerist.com.tr
- **Established** 2001
- **Owner(s) / Partner(s)** Melkan Gürsel Tabanlioglu, Taha Tatlici
- **Team** 10
- **Space(s)** 300 m²
- **Artists at Art Basel** Haluk Akakçe, Rasim Aksan, Francesco Albano, Idil Ikin, Arik Levy, :mentalKLINIK, Youssef Nabil, Arslan Sükan, Ayça Telgeren, Elif Uras, Nil Yalter
- **Further artists represented** Hussein Chalayan, Serkan Özkaya, Seza Paker, Ali Emir Tapan, Viron Erol Vert

Galleria dello Scudo

Verona ● Galleries

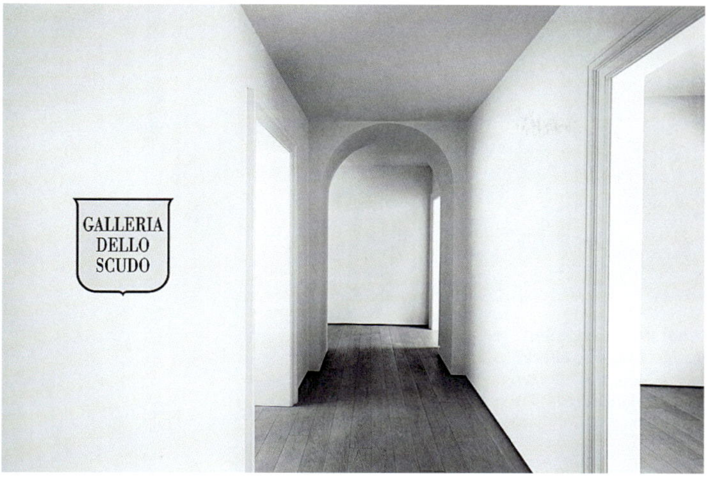

What first compelled you to open a gallery?
Family tradition is at the heart of our gallery activity.

Who is the first artist you showed and what was most memorable about that show?
A protagonist of Spatialism, Roberto Crippa, with paintings from the 1950s.

When did you first participate in Art Basel and what was most memorable about that show?
In 1997. The installation placed face-to-face the large-scale paintings by Giorgio de Chirico, part of his *Meubles dans la vallée* (1927) series, with some large plaster sculptures by Giulio Paolini—an impossible dialogue.

- **Contact** Galleria dello Scudo
  Laura Lorenzoni
  laura.lorenzoni@galleriadelloscudo.com
  info@galleriadelloscudo.com
- **Established** 1968
- **Owner(s) / Partner(s)** Massimo Di Carlo, Ettore Kovarich, Laura Lorenzoni
- **Team** 5
- **Space(s)** 300 m²
- **Artists at Art Basel** Afro, Alberto Burri, Pietro Consagra, Giorgio de Chirico, Piero Dorazio, Lucio Fontana, Leoncillo Leonardi, Piero Manzoni, Fausto Melotti, Giorgio Morandi, Gastone Novelli, Tancredi Parmeggiani, Antonio Sanfilippo, Salvatore Scarpitta, Toti Scialoja, Emilio Vedova
- **Further artists represented** Giacomo Balla, Umberto Boccioni, Giuseppe Capogrossi, Carlo Carrà, Marino Marini, Amedeo Modigliani, Giuseppe Santomaso, Alberto Savinio, Gino Severini

Gandhara

Karachi ● Galleries

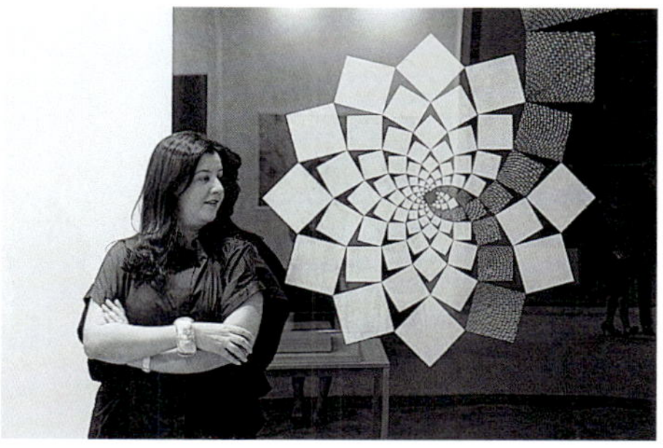

What first compelled you to open a gallery?
I collected a lot and spent a lot of time with artists, so it was a natural progression. I also wanted to show Pakistani contemporary art in the Asia-Pacific, as I felt it was shown in Europe and North America but did not have a voice here. The gallery space was set up, to bring well-curated exhibitions to Karachi audiences, both modern and contemporary art as well as new media and installation art.

When did you first participate in Art Basel and what was most memorable about that show?
Our gallery has shown from the first ART HK in 2008 and has continued every year including its metamorphosis into Art Basel in 2013. We have been pleased with the astounding response to Pakistani contemporary art we received in Hong Kong. Furthermore, this year the diversity of the collectors and the visitors was very apparent.

- **Contact** Gandhara-Art
  Irfan Baber
  info@gandhara-art.com
  irfan.baber@gandhara-art.com
  amna.naqvi@gandhara-art.com
- **Established** 2005
- **Owner(s) / Partner(s)** Amna Tirmizi Naqvi
- **Team** 6
- **Space(s)** 350 m²
- **Artists at Art Basel** Khadim Ali, Aisha Khalid, Atif Khan, Imran Qureshi, Adeel Zafar

Gaudel de Stampa

Paris ● Statements ● Positions

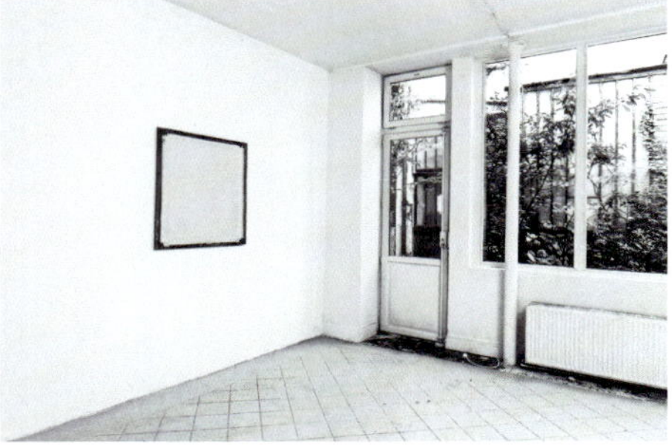

What first compelled you to open a gallery?
Denis Gaudel: I was an independent curator and then worked in a gallery for few years. I wanted to have freedom and support the artists I believed in.

Who is the first artist you showed and what was most memorable about that show?
We organized a solo presentation of Dove Allouche. The most memorable thing was that we didn't sell a single piece …

When did you first participate in Art Basel and what was most memorable about that show?
We did Art Basel in Miami Beach in 2011 with Jessica Warboys, whose work is now in the collection of the Pompidou.

- **Contact** Gaudel de Stampa
  Rany Gaudel
  rany@gaudeldestampa.com
- **Established** 2008
- **Owner(s) / Partner(s)** Denis Gaudel
  Rany Gaudel
- **Team** 3
- **Space(s)** 80 m²
- **Artists at Art Basel** Dove Allouche
  Jonathan Binet
- **Further artists represented** Mihut Boscu Kafchin
  Hildegarde Duane & David Lamelas
  Ida Ekblad
  Emil Michael Klein
  Andrea Romano
  Julia Rommel
  Lina Viste Grønli
  Jessica Warboys

Gavlak

Palm Beach — Galleries

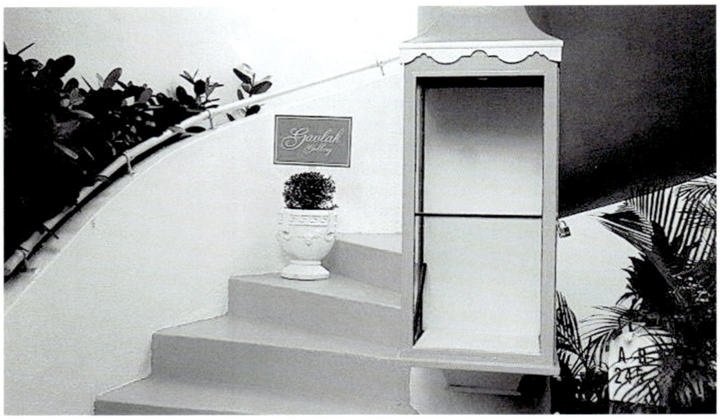

What first compelled you to open a gallery?
I moved from New York to open a gallery in Palm Beach (Florida), because there was no contemporary art gallery and so many great collectors in the region.

Who is the first artist you showed and what was most memorable about that show?
I opened my gallery with a solo exhibition of Wade Guyton.

When did you first participate in Art Basel and what was most memorable about that show?
I did a shipping container at Art Basel in Miami Beach in 2006 with Aleksandra Mir. We painted the entire container pink and installed carpet and a large crystal chandelier with her botanical print portfolio *The Meaning of Flowers*. Everyone went crazy for it! People told me I was radical. I always knew pink was the color of punk …

- **Contact** Gavlak Gallery
  Karene Telesca
  karene@gavlakgallery.com
  info@gavlakgallery.com
- **Established** 2005
- **Owner(s) / Partner(s)** Sarah Gavlak
- **Team** 3
- **Space(s)** 104 m²
- **Artists at Art Basel** Jose Alvarez
  Lisa Anne Auerbach
  Andrew Brischler
  Bovey Lee
  Simone Leigh
  Rob Wynne
- **Further artists represented** Florence Derive
  Phillip Estlund
  Orly Genger
  Wade Guyton
  David Haxton
  McDermott & McGough
  Marilyn Minter
  Jack Pierson
  Scott Reeder
  Alexis Marguerite Teplin
  Mungo Thomson
  Betty Tompkins
  Pae White
  T.J. Wilcox
  Bunny Yeager

gb agency

Paris — Galleries

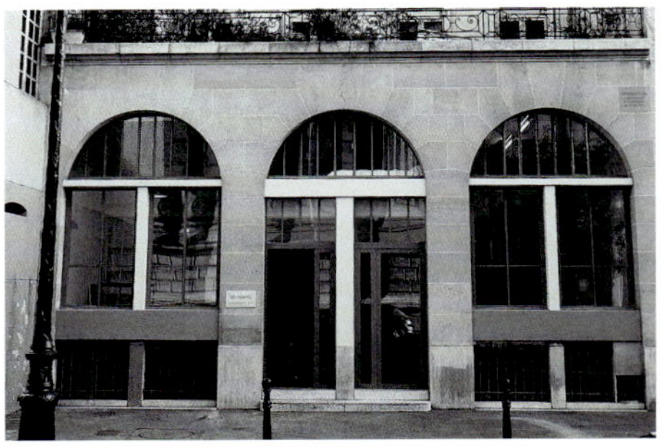

What first compelled you to open a gallery?
To have the freedom to show figures who for us have important things to say.

Who is the first artist you showed and what was most memorable about that show?
It was a group show titled *Hors-jeu* and it established the line of our program for the following years.

When did you first participate in Art Basel and what was most memorable about that show?
It was in Basel in the Premiere sector in 2006 and we tried to make a show around the notions of temporality. We were impressed by the quality of the public in Basel.

- **Contact** gb agency
  Nathalie Boutin
  nathalie@gbagency.fr
  gb@gbagency.fr
- **Established** 2001
- **Owner(s) / Partner(s)** Solène Guillier
  Nathalie Boutin
- **Space(s)** 320 m²
- **Artists at Art Basel** Mac Adams
  Robert Breer
  Ryan Gander
  Július Koller
  Jiří Kovanda
  Dom nique Petitgand
  Yann Sérandour
- **Further artists represented** Elina Brotherus
  Omer Fast
  Mark Geffriaud
  Deimantas Narkevicius
  Roman Ondák
  Pratchaya Phinthong
  Pia Rönicke

gdm

Paris — Edition
Edition

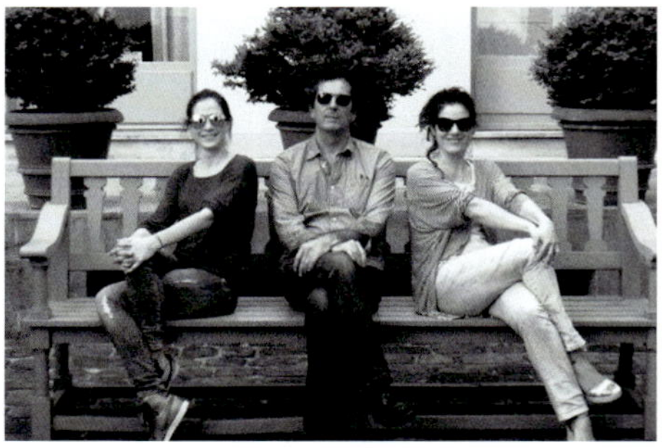

What first compelled you to open a gallery?
We created an edition gallery to distribute and make contemporary art accessible.

Who is the first artist you showed and what was most memorable about that show?
The first exhibition was a group show with Daniel Buren, Bertrand Parinet, and Louise Lawler. We found this memorable because from this first exhibition we had the possibility to make clear our purpose: to show international well-known artists as well as emerging ones.

When did you first participate in Art Basel and what was most memorable about that show?
Our first participation to Art Basel was in 2009.

The most memorable was an extraordinary meeting with a private museum director that found the gallery edition policy very interesting.

We also remember the wonderful welcome we received from all the other galleries in the Edition sector.

- **Contact** gdm
  Irene Varano
  galeriedemultiples@wanadoo.fr
- **Owner(s) / Partner(s)** Gilles Drouault
- **Team** 3
- **Space(s)** 60 m²
- **Artists at Art Basel** Saâdane Afif
  Neil Beloufa
  Stéphane Calais
  Claude Closky
  François Curlet
  Peter Downsbrough
  Ryan Gander
  Dorothy Iannone
  Julio Le Parc
  Robert Longo
  Matthew McCaslin
  Jonathan Monk
  Olivier Mosset
  Richard Prince
  Maxime Rossi
  Hans Schabus
  Franck Scurti
  Nedko Solakov
  Vincent Szarek
- **Further artists represented** Vito Acconci
  Boris Achour
  Elisabeth Ballet
  Lewis Baltz
  Virginie Barré
  Vincent Beaurin
  Jonathan Binet
  Dike Blair
  Monica Bonvicini
  Etienne Bossut
  Daniel Buren
  Julien Carreyn
  Viriya Chotpanyavisut
  Isabelle Cornaro
  Stéphane Dafflon
  Denis Darzacq
  Marcelline Delbecq
  Jason Dodge
  Noël Dolla
  Anders Edström
  Sammy Engramer
  Karin Hueber
  Véronique Joumard
  Regine Kolle
  Alix Lambert
  Renée Lévi
  Didier Marcel
  Stefan Nikolaev
  Damir Ocko
  Bill Owens
  Steven Parrino
  Bruno Peinado
  Mick Peter
  Jack Pierson
  Clément Rodzielski
  Bojan Sarcevic
  Robert Stadler

Gelink

Amsterdam

Galleries Unlimited

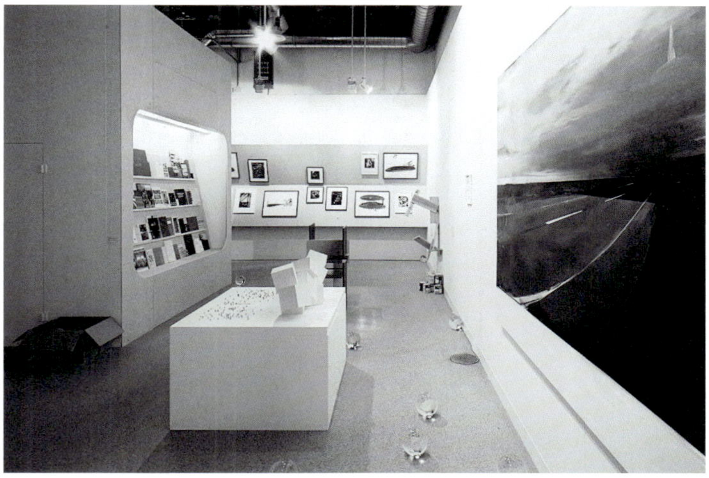

What first compelled you to open a gallery?
My motto is "I believe in miracles" and art is the closest to this.

Who is the first artist you showed and what was most memorable about that show?
Spanish artist Alicia Framis (born in 1967). For this first show in the gallery Alicia Framis invited several artists to think about and develop works and possible alternatives concerning the phenomenon of "loneliness in the city." Each artist had a personal angle on the subject. This exhibition set the tone of what people could expect form the Annet Gelink Gallery, and some of the artists introduced in this exhibition later had solo shows.

When did you first participate in Art Basel and what was most memorable about that show?
My first participation was in 1995, with my first gallery, Bloom gallery. That year I met Marc Blondeau, the best mentor in the art world.

- **Contact** Annet Gelink Gallery
  Floor Wullems
  floor@annetgelink.com
  info@annetgelink.com
- **Established** 2000
- **Owner(s) / Partner(s)** Annet Gelink
- **Team** 6
- **Space(s)** 275 m² (including office)
- **Artists at Art Basel** Yael Bartana
  Anya Gallaccio
  Ryan Gander
  Roger Hiorns
  Meiro Koizumi
  David Maljkovic
  Wilfredo Prieto
  Glenn Sorensen
  Erik van Lieshout
- **Further artists represented** Alicia Framis
  Carla Klein
  Kiki Lamers
  Dan McCarthy
  Muzi Quawson
  Ed van der Elsken
  Sarah van Sonsbeeck
  Marijke van Warmerdam
  Barbara Visser
  Erik Wesselo

Gemini

Los Angeles ● Edition
New York ● Edition

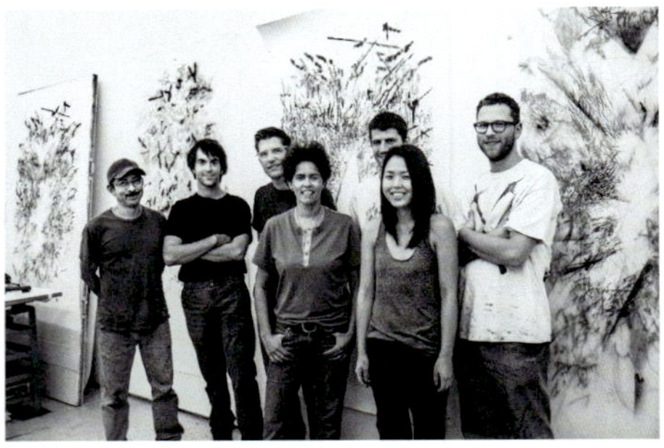

What first compelled you to open a gallery?
Gemini G.E.L. is an artists' workshop that makes limited edition prints and sculptures. The edition is hand-printed. Our purpose was to create a workshop that would produce high quality lithographs, etchings, and screen prints in limited editions—to bring artists from different locations in our country to Los Angeles, as well as work with several artists from the Los Angeles area.

Who is the first artist you showed and what was most memorable about that show?
Josef Albers, in June 1966. The next show was with Robert Rauschenberg, and the most memorable moment was his creation of the lithograph *Booster*, which was the largest hand-printed lithograph on record. It was 6 feet x 3 feet.

When did you first participate in Art Basel and what was most memorable about that show?
1973. We introduced Roy Lichtenstein's series entitled *Bull Profile* in our booth. The audience response was extremely positive. It was a great success.

- **Contact** Gemini G.E.L. LLC
Sidney B. Felsen
sidney@Geminigel.com
editions@geminigel.com
- **Established** 1966
- **Owner(s) / Partner(s)** Sidney B. Felsen (Co-Director)
Stanley Grinstein (Co-Director)
Joni Weyl
Rosamund Felsen
Elyse Grinstein
- **Space(s)** 167.5 m²
- **Artists at Art Basel** Josef Albers
Richard Artschwager
John Baldessari
Jonathan Borofsky
Cecily Brown
Chris Burden
Daniel Buren
Sophie Calle
Vija Celmins
John Chamberlain
Richard Diebenkorn
Sam Francis
Frank Gehry
Robert Gober
Philip Guston
Ann Hamilton
David Hammons
Michael Heizer
David Hockney
Jasper Johns
Ellsworth Kelly
Edward & Nancy Kienholz
Roy Lichtenstein
Brice Marden
Julie Mehretu
Malcolm Morley
Elizabeth Murray
Bruce Nauman
Isamu Noguchi
Claes Oldenburg
Darryl Pottorf
Ken Price
Robert Rauschenberg
James Rosenquist
Susan Rothenberg
Allen Ruppersberg
Ed Ruscha
Richard Serra
Joel Shapiro
Frank Stella
Richard Tuttle
Franz West
Terry Winters

Gerhardsen Gerner

Berlin ● Galleries
Oslo

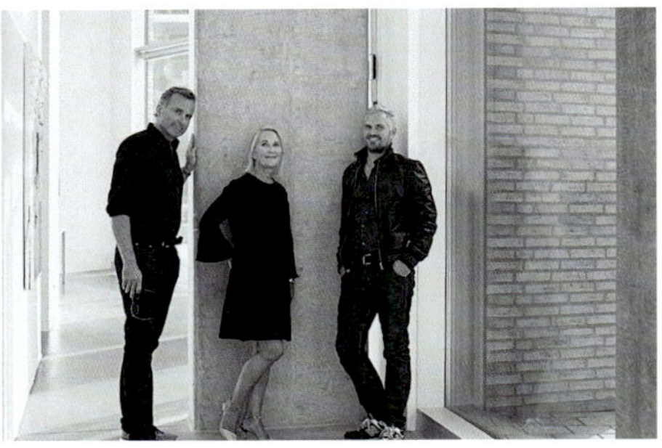

What first compelled you to open a gallery?
Atle Gerhardsen: It was an early premonition from when I was about 18 years old. I started going to galleries in Oslo about that time and eventually worked for a short period at Galleri Riis.
Marina Gerner-Mathisen: My father was a collector of European paintings. With a masters degree in art history I started a gallery in Oslo in 2001. When the exciting chance of working together with Atle and Nicolai came up, we decided to open up Gerhardsen Gerner Oslo.

Who is the first artist you showed and what was most memorable about that show?
Atle Gerhardsen: We did a series of opening shows in 1995 (such as with Norwegian artist Kjartan Slettemark). A memorable evening was Elin Wickström's one-night performance happening at the same time as the CIMAM (International Committee for Museums and Collections of Modern Art) conference in Oslo on July 4, 1995. They were upset that they could not jump Elin's queue. The queue was the work, entitled *One of The Most Fascinating and Thought-Provoking Exhibitions This Year* (1995). No one saw the exhibition that night …

When did you first participate in Art Basel and what was most memorable about that show?
After two years at Liste, we applied for the Statements sector at Art Basel in 1999, with Matthew Ritchie. We won the Baloise Art Prize and sold works to major collections. It was quite a leap from Oslo.

- **Contact** Gerhardsen Gerner
Maike Fries
maike@gerhardsengerner.com
office@gerhardsengerner.com
- **Established** 1995 (Oslo)
2001 (Berlin)
2007 (with Nicolai Gerner-Mathisen)
- **Owner(s) / Partner(s)** Atle Gerhardsen (Berlin)
Nicolai Gerner-Mathisen (Berlin)
Marina Gerner-Mathisen (Oslo)
Nicolai Gerner-Mathisen (Oslo)
Atle Gerhardsen (Oslo)
- **Space(s)** 370 m² (Berlin)
120 m² (Oslo)
- **Artists at Art Basel** Amy Adler
Edgar Bryan
Jan Christensen
Carroll Dunham
Lothar Hempel
David Korty
Jim Lambie
Shintaro Miyake
Markus Oehlen
Lari Pittman
Ingegerd Råman
Matthew Ritchie
David Salle
Dirk Stewen
Annika Ström
James White
Andrea Winkler
Yarisal & Kublitz

Gitlen

New York — Statements

What first compelled you to open a gallery?
I was working as a curator and writer when I started a project space in Portland (OR) in 2005, called Small A Projects. When I returned to New York in 2008, the Lower East Side was just starting to develop a gallery scene so I renovated a tiny storefront space on Broome Street.

When did you first participate in Art Basel and what was most memorable about that show?
Our first participation was in Basel Statements sector in 2013 with Jessica Jackson Hutchins. Hutchins first showed with me in Oregon in 2005 and her work was in the 2013 Venice Biennale so it was a real milestone for the gallery and for her.

- **Contact** Laurel Gitlen, gallery@laurelgitlen.com
- **Established** 2008
- **Owner(s) / Partner(s)** Laurel Gitlen
- **Space(s)** 167 m²
- **Artists at Art Basel** Jessica Jackson Hutchins
- **Further artists represented** Corin Hewitt, Bill Jenkins, Anissa Mack, Elizabeth McAlpine, Joseph Montgomery, Michael Patterson-Carver, Will Rogan, Allyson Vieira, Jesse Willenbring, Erik Wysocan

Gladstone

New York — Galleries
Brussels — Galleries, Unlimited, Galleries

- **Contact** Gladstone Gallery, info@gladstonegallery.com
- **Established** 1980
- **Owner(s) / Partner(s)** Maxime Falkenstein, Molly Epstein, Simone Battisti, Gael Diercxsens
- **Artists at Art Basel** Allora & Calzadilla, Kai Althoff, Miroslaw Balka, Matthew Barney, Robert Bechtle, Alighiero Boetti, Jan Dibbets, Carroll Dunham, Cecilia Edefalk, Cyprien Gaillard, R. H. Quaytman, Keith Haring, Gary Hill, Thomas Hirschhorn, Jim Hodges, Huang Yong Ping, Cameron Jamie, Anish Kapoor, Sharon Lockhart, Andrew Lord, Sarah Lucas, Victor Man, Mario Merz, Marisa Merz, Dave Muller, Wangechi Mutu, Jean-Luc Mylayne, Shirin Neshat, Damián Ortega, Walter Pichler, Lari Pittman, Magnus Plessen, R.H. Quaytman, Ugo Rondinone, Jack Smith Archive, Rosemarie Trockel, Paloma Varga Weisz, Andro Wekua
- **Further artists represented** Roe Ethridge, Dan Flavin, Lucio Fontana, Gilbert & George, Donald Judd, Mike Kelley, Martin Kippenberger, Sol LeWitt, Fausto Melotti, Anna Parkina, Raymond Pettibon, Elizabeth Peyton, Sigmar Polke, Richard Prince, Gerhard Richter, Dieter Roth, Robert Ryman, Gedi Sibony, Banks Violette

Gmurzynska

Zurich — Galleries
Zug — Galleries
St. Moritz — Galleries, Kabinett

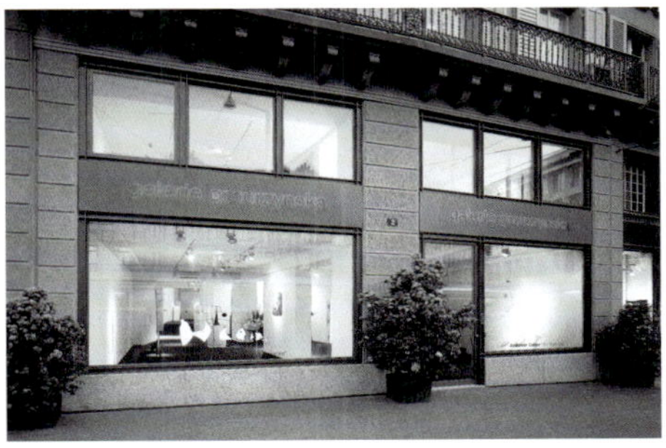

What first compelled you to open a gallery?
Becoming aware of a lack of understanding and knowledge of the Russian avant-garde in Europe led Antonina Gmurzynska to open the gallery in Cologne in 1965. The gallery specialized in the Russian avant-garde and classic Modern, showing scholarly and art-historically important exhibitions. After fully relocating to Switzerland in 2005 the gallery continues this tradition whilst also showing master artists of the 20th and 21st centuries. The gallery in Zurich occupies a building on Paradeplatz dating back to 1857 and in which one of the first Dada exhibitions took place. The opening of our fourth branch and second gallery in Zug in 2013, specializing in contemporary art, is a new chapter in the progression of Galerie Gmurzynska.

Who is the first artist you showed and what was most memorable about that show?
The first exhibition in Zurich was a solo exhibition by Alexander Calder, thoroughly endorsed by the Calder Foundation, who described it as "rare to experience a presentation of this quality outside of a museum." As with each exhibition at the gallery it featured a fully illustrated catalogue with important essays. The gallery has published more than 200 books and catalogues.

When did you first participate in Art Basel and what was most memorable about that show?
Galerie Gmurzynska has participated in every edition of Art Basel and it is some testament to this fact that Isabelle Bscher, the curator of the gallery, learned to walk in the aisles at Art Basel!

- **Contact** Galerie Gmurzynska, Mitchell Anderson, mitchell.anderson@gmurzynska.com, galerie@gmurzynska.com
- **Established** 1965
- **Owner(s) / Partner(s)** Krystyna Gmurzynska, Mathias Rastorfer
- **Artists at Art Basel** Fernando Botero, Alexander Calder, Scott Campbell, Marc Chagall, Lucio Fontana, Julio González, Robert Indiana, Mari Kasurinen, Yves Klein, Robert Klippel, Wifredo Lam, Henri Laurens

Fernand Léger
Jani Leinonen
Jacques Lipchitz
Kazimir Malevich
Joan Miró
Louise Nevelson
Marco Perego
Pablo Picasso
Alexander Rodchenko
Kurt Schwitters
David Smith
Joaquín Torres-García
Theo van Doesburg
Georges Vantongerloo
Andy Warhol
Tom Wesselmann

- **Further artists represented**
  Rudolf Bauer
  Anatol Brusilovsky
  Ronnie Cutrone
  Robert Delaunay
  Sonia Delaunay
  Lyonel Feininger
  Pavel Filonov
  Frantisek Kupka
  Karl Lagerfeld
  Mikhail Larionov
  El Lissitzky
  László Moholy-Nagy
  Liubov Popova
  Mel Ramos
  Karl-Peter Röhl
  Victor Servranckx
  Chaïm Soutine
  Sylvester Stallone
  Varvara Stepanova
  Nikolai Suetin
  Pat York

González

Madrid

Galleries
Galleries

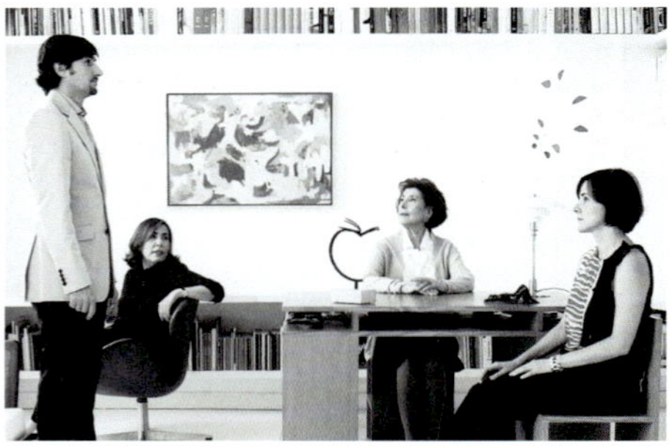

What first compelled you to open a gallery?
Galeria Elvira González opened in 1994 after having Galeria Theo with her husband Fernando Mignoni in Madrid since 1966. In 1966, Spain was not a democratic country, and the first exhibitions were of Spanish artists living in Paris, most of them in exile. The aim of Galeria Theo was to show those artists living abroad (including Picasso). In 1994, the situation was totally different and Elvira González decided to continue, with no partner at first, what inspired her first gallery. Shows by Picasso, Rothko, Juan Gris, Joan Miró, Tápies, Chillida, etc. followed.

Who is the first artist you showed and what was most memorable about that show?
Esteban Vicente.

When did you first participate in Art Basel and what was most memorable about that show?
In 1998. We sold a magnificent Joan Miró painting of 1938 to the Toyota Museum in Japan.

- **Contact**
  Galería Elvira González
  Isabel Mignoni
  imignoni@galeriaelviragonzalez.com
  info@galeriaelviragonzalez.com
- **Established** 1994
- **Owner(s) / Partner(s)**
  Elvira Gonzalez
  Elvira Mignoni
  Isabel Mignoni
  Fernando Mignoni
- **Team** 8
- **Space(s)** 400 m²
- **Artists at Art Basel**
  Juan Asensio
  Miquel Barceló

Alighiero Boetti
Waltercio Caldas
Alexander Calder
Antonio Calderara
Eduardo Chillida
Lucio Fontana
Robert Irwin
Donald Judd
Robert Mangold
Robert Mapplethorpe
Ed Ruscha
Richard Serra
Antoni Tàpies
Dan Walsh

- **Further artists represented**
  Elena del Rivero
  Adolph Gottlieb
  Jesús Rafael Soto
  Adolfo Schlosser
  Lee Ufan
  Esteban Vicente

Goodman Gallery

Johannesburg
Cape Town

Galleries
Unlimited
Galleries

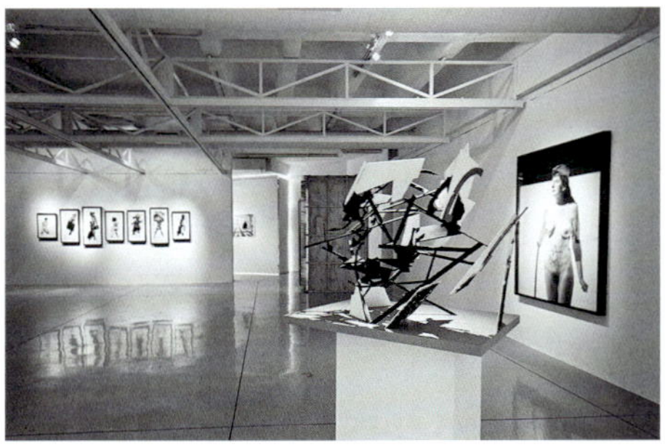

What first compelled you to open a gallery?
The Goodman Gallery has a long history in South African art. It was established by Linda Goodman (now Givon) in 1966 and, from the outset, supported and encouraged artists to exhibit despite the strictures of apartheid. In 2008, Linda Givon sold the gallery to Liza Essers who has brought several new artists into the Goodman fold and has maintained a strong international connection for the gallery.

Who is the first artist you showed and what was most memorable about that show?
The first artists to exhibit at the Goodman Gallery, such as Cecil Skotnes, were the pioneers of refusing to accept racism in the arts.

When did you first participate in Art Basel and what was most memorable about that show?
In 1984. We exhibited work by Judith Mason-Attwood and Marguerite Stephens. The exhibition, called *Monkey Shrine*, featured a collaborative work by Mason-Attwood and Stephens called *Catacombs*. The 2-meter high wall hanging woven in mohair featured animal bones and baboon skulls attached to it. The work caused surprise, dismay, and many questions among both Swiss customs and visitors to the fair.

- **Contact**
  Goodman Gallery
  Lara Koseff
  lara@goodman-gallery.com
- **Established** 1966
- **Owner(s) / Partner(s)** Liza Essers
- **Team** 24
- **Space(s)**
  300 m² (Johannesburg)
  200 m² (Cape Town)
- **Artists Art Basel**
  Candice Breitz
  Adam Broomberg & Oliver Chanarin
  Kudzanai Chiurai
  Jabulani Dhlamini
  Mounir Fatmi
  Kendell Geers
  David Goldblatt
  Alfredo Jaar
  William Kentridge
  Moshekwa Langa
  Walter Oltmann
  Mikhael Subotzky
  Nelisiwe Xaba &

Mocke J van Veuren
Clive van den Berg

- **Further artists represented**

Siemon Allen
Ghada Amer
Kader Attia
Jodi Bieber
Stuart Bird
Willem Boshoff
Lisa Brice
Carla Busuttil
Husan & Husain Essop
Claire Gavronsky
Frances Goodman
Haroon Gunn-Salie
Robert Hodgins
David Koloane
Liza Lou
Gerald Machona
Gerhard Marx
Thomas Mulcaire
Brett Murray
Sam Nhlengethwa
Kagiso Pat Mautloa
Stefanus Rademeyer
Tracey Rose
Rosenclaire
Rose Shakinovsky
Kathryn Smith
Gavin Turk
Minnette Vári
Nontsikelelo Veleko
Diane Victor
Jeremy Wafer
Sue Williamson
Hank Willis Thomas

Marian Goodman

New York
Paris
London

- Galleries
- Galleries
- Unlimited
- Parcours
- Galleries

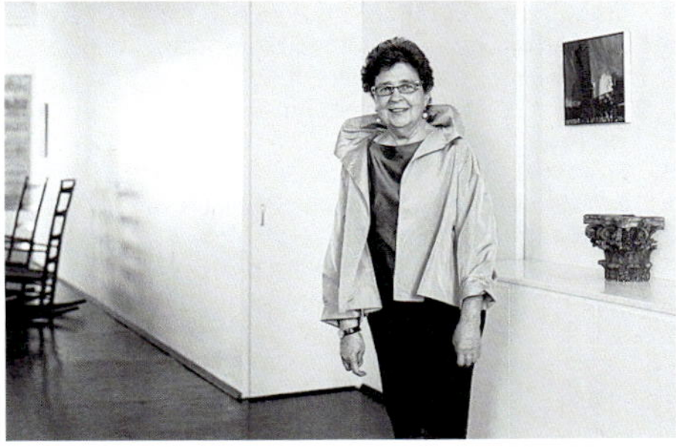

- **Contact** Marian Goodman Gallery
Alice Kim
alice@mariangoodman.com
goodman@mariangoodman.com
- **Established** 1977
- **Owner(s) / Partner(s)** Marian Goodman
- **Team** 30
- **Artists at Art Basel**

Eija-Liisa Ahtila
Chantal Akerman
Giovanni Anselmo
John Baldessari
Lothar Baumgarten
Dara Birnbaum
Christian Boltanski
Marcel Broodthaers
Maurizio Cattelan
James Coleman
Tony Cragg
Richard Deacon
Tacita Dean
Rineke Dijkstra
Yang Fudong
Dan Graham
Pierre Huyghe
Cristina Iglesias
Amar Kanwar
William Kentridge
Steve McQueen
Julie Mehretu
Annette Messager
Juan Muñoz
Maria Nordman
Gabriel Orozco
Giulio Paolini
Giuseppe Penone
Gerhard Richter
Anri Sala
Tino Sehgal
Thomas Struth
Niele Toroni
Adrián Villar Rojas
Danh Vo
Jeff Wall
Lawrence Weiner
Francesca Woodman

Grässlin

Frankfurt

- Galleries
- Galleries

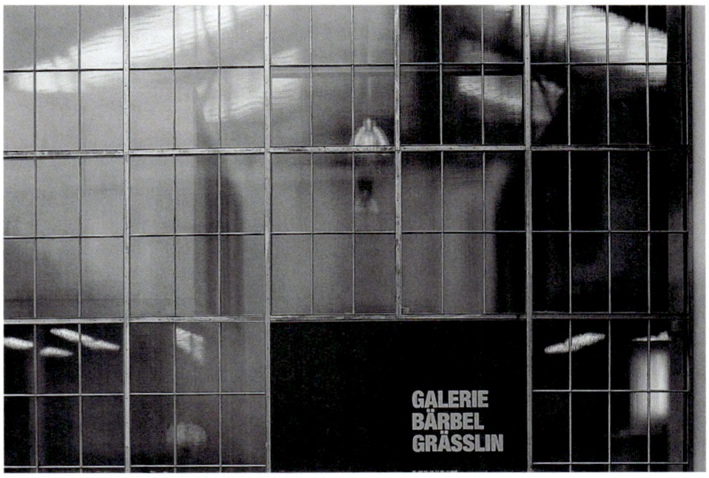

What first compelled you to open a gallery?
Passion for art.

Who is the first artist you showed and what was most memorable about that show?
Hubert Kiecol—the show was sold out at the opening.

When did you first participate in Art Basel and what was most memorable about that show?
In 1992.

- **Contact** Galerie Bärbel Grässlin
Klaus Webelholz
webelholz@galerie-graesslin.de
mail@galerie-graesslin.de
- **Established** 1985
- **Owner(s) / Partner(s)** Bärbel Grässlin
- **Team** 2
- **Space(s)** 250 m²
- **Artists at Art Basel**

Herbert Brandl
Helmut Dorner
Günther Förg
Georg Herold
Secundino Hernández
Martin Kippenberger
Imi Knoebel
Reinhard Mucha
Markus Oehlen
Tobias Rehberger
Franz West
Heimo Zobernig

- **Further artists represented**

Michael Beutler
Werner Büttner
Ika Huber
Hubert Kiecol
Imi Knoebel
Meuser
Stefan Müller
Christa Näher
Manuel Ocampo
Thomas Werner

Alexander Gray

New York

Feature
Galleries
Kabinett

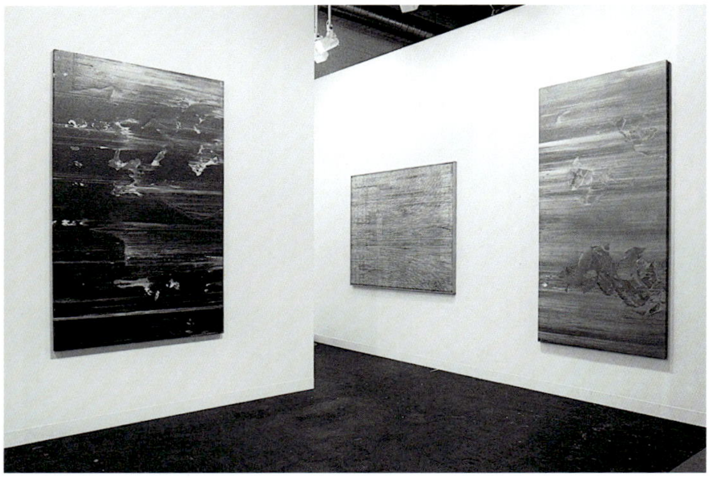

What first compelled you to open a gallery?
In 2006, we were concerned about a growing sense of amnesia in the contemporary art market. It was a moment of fascination with all things young, new, and emerging, that was overshadowing values tied to scholarship, precedent, and legacy. We noticed that established artists from the 1960s, 1970s, and 1980s, who had been influencers on a younger generation, were under-recognized in the market. This drove our mission, towards a recontextualization of these artists' significant contributions, and to platform their recent and innovative practices.

Who is the first artist you showed and what was most memorable about that show?
One of our first exhibitions was with the painter Jack Whitten. It was Whitten's first solo show in New York in over 13 years. The turnout of friends and artists was overwhelming and wonderful, filling our space beyond capacity.

When did you first participate in Art Basel and what was most memorable about that show?
In 2010, in Basel's Feature sector, the gallery presented a micro-retrospective of Jack Whitten's groundbreaking abstract painting, introducing his work to European audiences. That presentation resulted in the sale of an important historical work to the MoMA.

- **Contact** Alexander Gray Associates
  David Cabrera
  david@alexandergray.com
  alex@alexandergray.com
- **Established** 2006
- **Owner(s) / Partner(s)** Alexander Gray
  David Cabrera
- **Team** 9
- **Space(s)** 465 m²
- **Artists at Art Basel** Melvin Edwards
  Jeremy Gilbert-Rolfe
  Harmony Hammond
  Joan Semmel
  Hassan Sharif
  Jack Whitten
- **Further artists represented** Luis Camnitzer
  Coco Fusco
  Lorraine O'Grady
  Regina Silveira
  Hugh Steers

Richard Gray

Chicago
New York

Galleries
Galleries
Galleries

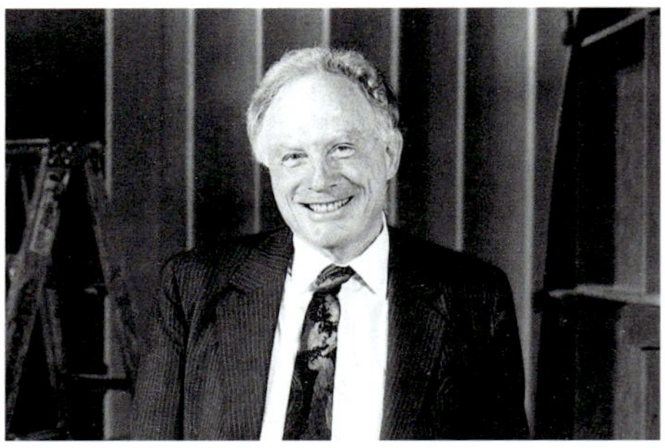

What first compelled you to open a gallery?
Friendships with the artists, restlessness, and a passion for collecting.

Who is the first artist you showed and what was most memorable about that show?
The gallery's first inventoried artwork was a painting by Jules Olitski followed over the next month by works by Willem de Kooning, Arshile Gorky, John Chamberlain, Albert Giacometti, Frank Stella, Louise Nevelson, and Lee Bontecou. The first exhibitions included shows by Robert Beauchamp and Fairfield Porter.

When did you first participate in Art Basel and what was most memorable about that show?
In 1991. In the middle of a global art market recession, we met amazing collectors, such as Ulla Dreyfus, Norman Braman, and many others, undaunted by circumstances, eager and open-minded.

- **Contact** Richard Gray Gallery
  Kelly Taylor
  kt@richardgraygallery.com
  info@richardgraygallery.com
- **Established** 1963
- **Owner(s) / Partner(s)** Paul Gray (Director)
  Andrew Fabricant (Director)
  Richard Gray (Founder)
- **Team** 10
- **Space(s)** 750 m²
- **Artists at Art Basel** Magdalena Abakanowicz
  Josef Albers
  Francis Bacon
  Georg Baselitz
  Olivia Berckemeyer
  Alexander Calder
  Joseph Cornell
  Willem de Kooning
  Richard Diebenkorn
  Jim Dine
  Jean Dubuffet
  Sam Francis
  Alberto Giacometti
  Ewan Gibbs
  Mark Grotjahn
  Philip Guston
  David Hockney
  Hans Hofmann
  Malia Jensen
  Jasper Johns
  Rashid Johnson
  Alex Katz
  David Klamen
  Franz Kline
  Fernand Léger
  Roy Lichtenstein
  Christian Marclay
  Brice Marden
  Henri Matisse
  Joan Miró
  Joan Mitchell
  Henry Moore
  Robert Motherwell
  Pablo Picasso
  Jaume Plensa
  Jackson Pollock
  Richard Prince
  Robert Rauschenberg
  Mark Rothko
  Ed Ruscha
  David Smith
  John Stezaker
  Marc Swanson
  Jan Tichy

Cy Twombly
Andy Warhol
Christopher Wool

Greenberg

New York

- Galleries
- Galleries

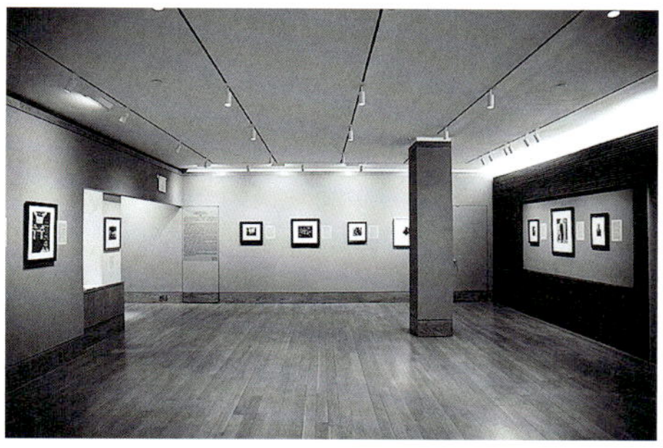

What first compelled you to open a gallery?
What first compelled me to open a gallery was the desire to demonstrate the importance of photography to the artists in my small community in Woodstock, NY, who didn't understand the significance of the medium.

Who is the first artist you showed and what was most memorable about that show?
The first major one-artist exhibition was devoted to Edward Steichen. I was able to put together a quality show of one of the most important photographers of all times. This exhibition set the stage for what was going to happen many years later when I got the chance to represent the estate of Edward Steichen.

When did you first participate in Art Basel and what was most memorable about that show?
Our first participation at Art Basel in Miami Beach was in 2006. In Miami, we were able to meet so many art collectors who had not been into photography before and to start new relationships with that kind of collector.

Contact Howard Greenberg Gallery
Theresa Forster
theresa@howardgreenberg.com
info@howardgreenberg.com

- **Established** 1981
- **Owner(s) / Partner(s)** Howard Greenberg
- **Team** 16
- **Space(s)** 600 m²
- **Artists at Art Basel** Berenice Abbott, Richard Avedon, Edward Burtynsky, Henri Cartier-Bresson, Bruce Davidson, David Goldblatt, William Klein, Jacques-Henri Lartigue, Saul Leiter, Vivian Maier, Joel Meyerowitz, Edward Steichen, Josef Sudek
- **Further artists represented** Eugène Atget, Bill Brandt, Roy DeCarava, František Drtikol, Walker Evans, Robert Frank, Jaromir Funke, Franke Gohlke, Eikoh Hosoe, Charles Jones, László Moholy-Nagy, Sarah Moon, Martin Munkácsi, Arnold Newman, Gordon Parks, Paul Strand, Miroslav Tichy, Roman Vishniac, Edward Weston, Minor White

Greene Naftali

New York

- Galleries
- Unlimited
- Parcours
- Galleries

When did you first participate in Art Basel and what was most memorable about that show?
In 2000.

- **Contact** Greene Naftali Gallery
Tara Ramadan
ramadantara@gmail.com
info@greenenaftaligallery.com
- **Established** 1995
- **Owner(s) / Partner(s)** Carol Greene
- **Artists at Art Basel** Lutz Bacher, Trisha Baga, Julie Becker, Paul Chan, Tony Conrad, Bernadette Corporation, Guy de Cointet, Jim Drain, Ida Ekblad, Harun Farocki, Günther Förg, Michael Fullerton, Gelitin, Lucy Gunning, Guyton\Walker, Rachel Harrison, Richard Hawkins, Jacqueline Humphries, John Knight, Joachim Koester, Michael Krebber, William Leavitt, Konrad Lueg, Helen Marten, Michaela Meise, Daniel Pflumm, Daniela Rossell, Allen Ruppersberg, Paul Sharits, Gedi Sibony, Michael Smith, Josef Strau, Daan van Golden, Sophie von Hellermann, Katharina Wulff, Haegue Yang

greengrassi

London

Galleries Unlimited

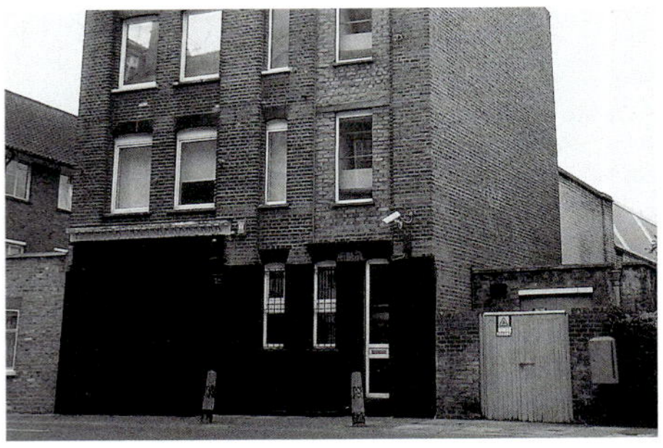

What first compelled you to open a gallery?
Passion.

Who is the first artist you showed and what was most memorable about that show?
Samuel Fosso.

When did you first participate in Art Basel and what was most memorable about that show?
In 2001.

- **Contact** greengrassi
Edwige Cochois
archive@greengrassi.com
info@greengrassi.com
- **Established** 1997
- **Owner(s) / Partner(s)** Cornelia Grassi
- **Team** 4
- **Space(s)** 110 m²
- **Artists at Art Basel** Tomma Abts
Jennifer Bornstein
Moyra Davey
Roe Ethridge
Vincent Fecteau
Giuseppe Gabellone
Joanne Greenbaum
Simon Ling
David Musgrave
Alessandro Pessoli
Jennifer Steinkamp
Pae White
Lisa Yuskavage
- **Further artists represented** Stefano Arienti
Gretchen Faust
Ellen Gronemeyer
Janice Kerbel
Shio Kusaka
Sean Landers
Margherita Manzelli
Kristin Oppenheim
Silke Otto-Knapp
Jennifer Pastor
Karin Ruggaber
Allen Ruppersberg
Anne Ryan
Frances Stark

Greve

St.Moritz — Galleries
Paris — Galleries
Cologne — Galleries

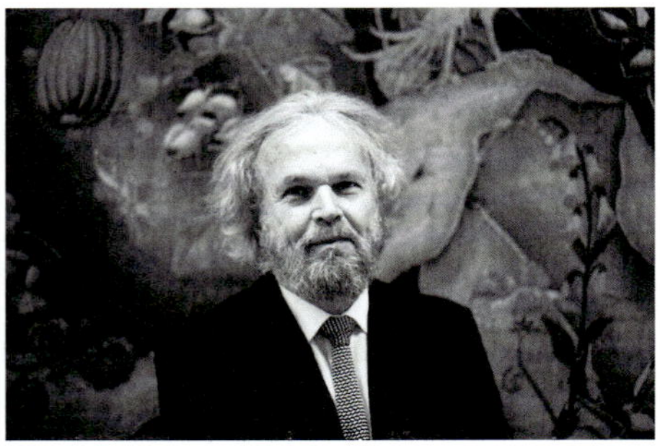

What first compelled you to open a gallery?
ART.

Who is the first artist you showed and what was most memorable about that show?
Yves Klein.

When did you first participate in Art Basel and what was most memorable about that show?
In 1972.

- **Contact** Galerie Karsten Greve AG
Bettina Haiss
b.haiss@galerie-karsten-greve.de
galerie.greve.moritz@bluewin.ch
- **Established** 1969/1973
- **Owner(s) / Partner(s)** Karsten Greve
- **Team** 15
- **Space(s)** 1,220 m²
- **Artists at Art Basel** Josef Albers
Pierrette Bloch
Louise Bourgeois
Alexander Calder
Lawrence Carroll
John Chamberlain
Joseph Cornell
Ding Yi
Lucio Fontana
Yiorgos Kordakis
Jannis Kounellis
Piero Manzoni
Fausto Melotti
Claire Morgan
Jean-Michel Othoniel
Robert Polidori
Gideon Rubin
Georgia Russell
Joel Shapiro
Pierre Soulages
Cy Twombly
Sergio Vega
Wols
- **Further artists represented** Eugène Atget
Ilse Bing
Brassaï
Thomas Brummett
Lynn Davis
Willem de Kooning
Jean Dubuffet
Adam Fuss
Gotthard Graubner
Leiko Ikemura
Mimmo Jodice
Paco Knöller
Catherine Lee
Sally Mann
Sigmar Polke
Norbert Prangenberg
Louis Soutter
Luise Unger

Grimm

Amsterdam

Galleries
Unlimited

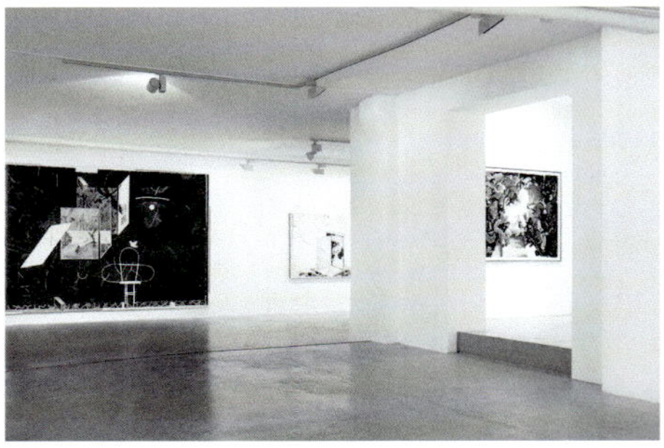

What first compelled you to open a gallery?
Grimm was established with the vision to bring international artists to the Dutch audience. The gallery has always strived to have an equilibrium between young, upcoming, and established artists.

Who is the first artist you showed and what was most memorable about that show?
George Condo. The most memorable was to represent and work with a great and internationally known artist.

When did you first participate in Art Basel and what was most memorable about that show?
The first participation to Art Basel was in Hong Kong in 2013. The most memorable of that show was the experience to present an overview of Desiree Dolron's *Xteriors* series to a new and diverse public.

- **Contact** Grimm
  Eva Coster
  eva@grimmgallery.com
  info@grimmgallery.com
- **Established** 2005
- **Owner(s) / Partner(s)** Jorg Grimm
  Hannah Reefhuis
- **Team** 2
- **Space(s)** 340 m²
- **Artists at Art Basel** Desiree Dolron
- **Further artists represented** Atelier Van Lieshout
  Charles Avery
  Larry Bamburg
  Huma Bhabha
  Matthew Day Jackson
  Alex Dordoy
  Angus Fairhurst
  Jess Flood-Paddock
  Brian Griffiths
  Adam Helms
  Gregor Hildebrandt
  Volker Hueller
  Jonathan Marshall
  Dave McDermott
  William Monk
  Ciaran Murphy
  Mick Peter
  Daniel Richter
  Norbert Schwontkowski
  Ger Van Elk
  Nick Van Woert
  Alexandra Verhaest
  Miguel Ybáñez

Grotto

Hong Kong ● Galleries

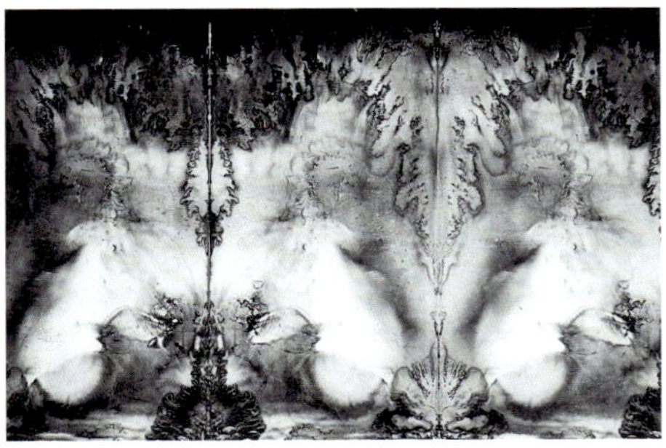

What first compelled you to open a gallery?
The lack of representation for Hong Kong artists.

Who is the first artist you showed and what was most memorable about that show?
The inaugural show featured Warren Leung, Fiona Wong, and Wilson Shieh. All of them went on to become the most successful professional artists in Hong Kong.

When did you first participate in Art Basel and what was most memorable about that show?
Our first edition of Art Basel was in 2013. It was its debut in Hong Kong, or Asia in general, and the energy and overwhelming response were memorable.

- **Contact** Grotto Fine Art Limited
  Henry Au-yeung
  henry@grottofineart.com
  info@grottofineart.com
- **Established** 2001
- **Owner(s) / Partner(s)** Henry Au-yeung
- **Space(s)** 168 m²
- **Artists at Art Basel** Koon Wai-bong
  Bovey Lee
  Danny Chin-fai Lee
  Joey Ka-yin Leung
  Wai Pongyu

Guerra

Lisbon ● Galleries ● Galleries

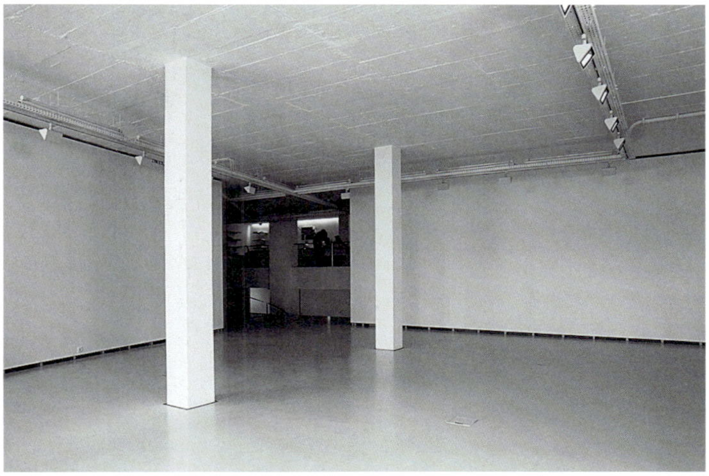

What first compelled you to open a gallery?
The internationalization of Portuguese contemporary art has been a major part of my life projects. I believe Portugal has a good geographical location, that can act as a platform between the north and south.

Who is the first artist you showed and what was most memorable about that show?
The first artist showed was the Portuguese João Tabarra, but I would also highlight Lawrence Weiner's exhibition the following year, as it was the first show of a foreign artist, who placed the gallery on the international art scene, one of the gallery's main goal.

When did you first participate in Art Basel and what was most memorable about that show?
In 2004. The most memorable moment was of course when I sold the first work of the Portuguese artist Rui Toscano.

- **Contact** Cristina Guerra Contemporary Art
  Inês Teixeira
  ines@cristinaguerra.com
  galeria@cristinaguerra.com
- **Established** 2001
- **Owner(s) / Partner(s)** Cristina Guerra
- **Team** 6
- **Space(s)** 450 m²
- **Artists at Art Basel** Christian Andersson
  Juan Araujo
  Michael Biberstein
  Angela Bulloch
  Filipa César
  Tatjana Doll
  Sabine Hornig
  José Loureiro
  João Louro
  Edgar Martins
  Matt Mullican
  João Onofre
  Rosângela Rennó
  Julião Sarmento
  Rui Toscano
  Lawrence Weiner
  Erwin Wurm
  Yonamine
- **Further artists represented** John Baldessari
  Luís Paulo Costa
  João Paulo Feliciano
  Daniel Malhão
  Jonathan Monk

G

Gupta

Chicago
Berlin

Galleries
Galleries
Kabinett
Public

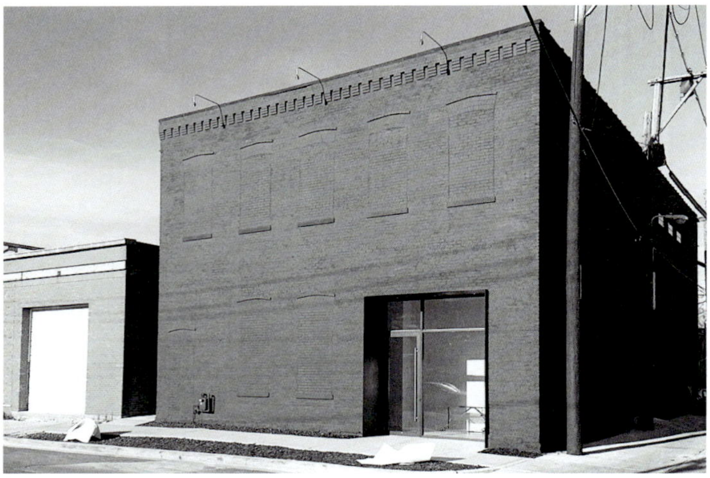

What first compelled you to open a gallery?

The contemporary art scene in Chicago was practically non-existent but there were some very interesting artists with unique practices that we thought needed exposure, so we started an alternative space to show these artists. Eventually our audience grew and the gallery followed suit. Today we have three gallery spaces with all of them emphasizing new projects and experimentation by emerging artists along with a few historical, museum-quality shows.

Who is the first artist you showed and what was most memorable about that show?

After a few group shows, we premiered an installation of Felix Gonzalez-Torres personal post-cards, over 1,000 of them installed hanging from the ceiling so the spectator had to walk through and engage with them. It was extremely heartfelt and sentimental to get a glimpse inside his personal world.

When did you first participate in Art Basel and what was most memorable about that show?

We were in the first Art Basel in Miami Beach in one of the containers for young galleries in the Positions sector. It was so fantastic to be on the beach and in a temporary space that compelled experimentation.

- **Contact** Kavi Gupta Gallery
  Kavi Gupta
  kavi@kavigupta.com
  info@kavigupta.com
- **Established** 2000
- **Owner(s) / Partner(s)** Kavi Gupta
- **Team** 11
- **Space(s)** 2,044 m²
- **Artists at Art Basel** McArthur Binion
  Theaster Gates
  Glenn Kaino
  James Krone
  Curtis Mann
  Angel Otero
  Roxy Paine
  Scott Reeder
  Claire Sherman
  Tony Tasset
- **Further artists represented** Johanna Billing
  Antonia Gurkovska
  Ari Marcopoulos
  Clare Rojas
  Melanie Schiff
  Scott Treleaven

Gemini G.E.L.

Interview with Joni Weyl

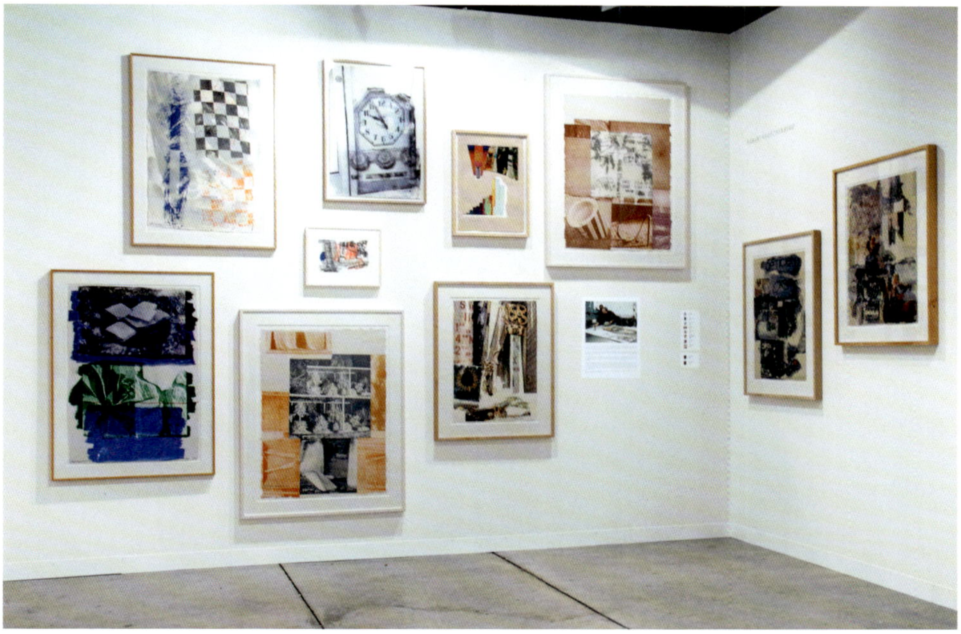

Art Basel in Miami Beach (Edition), 2013

Gemini G.E.L. (Graphic Editions Limited) was founded in 1966. What was the idea behind the creation of the gallery and how did you start?

It was started by three partners, two of whom had experience in the art world, through either collecting or making art as a hobby, and the third partner was a printer. It was created because while there were European print ateliers and workshops for artists like Picasso and Matisse, to their knowledge, nothing like that existed in the United States. As it turned out there was in fact an artists' workshop on the East Coast called ULAE (Universal Limited Art Editions), but they thought they were creating something new, and their vision was really about creating an environment where artists could come and make anything they could imagine, in collaboration with an atelier where the artists wouldn't have any financial restraints. They could come in and work freely and they wouldn't have to worry about the distribution of the work; all of this would be one entity (or publishing house), production as well as distribution under one roof. It clicked immediately. Robert Rauschenberg was the first artist to come into the workshop. Frank Stella was living in South California at the time and Bob encouraged him to make his very first prints at Gemini, and while Rauschenberg was at the workshop he got on the phone and talked to Claes Oldenburg saying "this place is great, the people are terrific, you should come out here and work with them." So, it very quickly built up a momentum whereby, by 1970, the core of artists that we have worked with in our history was formed.

One of the specificities of the gallery is that you have worked with the same artists since the 1970s, and you have managed to keep them working with you ...

Right, we have. Everything rests on a handshake; there are some contracts, but it's really the artists who decide to come because they like working with the staff. We've always made sure that we have the best partners we can possibly have, the most creative people. It's always been our intention to work in depth. We look at it as a marathon, not a sprint, and so we are very careful about the artists that we invite, and then we figure it's a life-long relationship.

From this point of view, how do you see the evolution of printing and edition making in the US? You started making prints, and you then turned toward more object-like editions. How do you understand this evolution? And how do you combine these two types of editions?

It started fairly quickly, in 1968: Claes Oldenburg asked if we could make a three-dimensional object and we said "sure." It was molded elastomeric urethane that went over a lithograph, so it was a combination of two media. It really launched us, and very quickly we did other three dimensional things with Oldenburg.

The workshop is in Southern California and we have resources available to us through the aerospace industry, the movie industry, all these little prototype shops, and things like that, so if we can't do it in-house we have lots of resources we can go to.

You started in Los Angeles; in the same building as today?

We started down the street about three, four blocks down, and within two or three years we had really outgrown the space. We shared it in a sort of old fashion way with a frameshop in the front, and we were in the back. Very quickly we were both outgrowing the space that we were sharing. So, the framing company stayed where it was and we moved down the street. We have a building that we bought, I think in 1969, and we bought the vacant property adjacent to it, so in 1979 we completed a Frank Gehry designed-building, which is part of our printing facility, and it has a gallery upstairs where we exhibit the prints and make exhibitions.

You are also working with the National Gallery of Art (Washington, DC) to construct a sort of printing archive ...

The first exhibition of this archive established at the National Gallery was in 1984. The object has always been to have a very scholarly, very thorough history of print making in America, and it started with the Gemini archive. They have expanded to a few other archives, but these are not as complete as ours. For ours, they have one example of every single print, and most of the objects that have been produced at Gemini. That's over 2,500 editions. It's a great resource; they also created an online catalogue raisonné, so scholars can go to the National Gallery website and study that object in-depth (how many proofs were made, what materials were used, etc.).

This is the first time Art Basel is doing an Edition sector in Miami Beach ...

It is the first time they formally acknowledge what they have been doing informally for many years. I mean, we have been exhibiting in Miami Beach almost since its inception. And we have been exhibiting in Basel since the beginning. There they always had a very important Edition sector. Here they just had a group of print dealers, and gradually they kind of gathered us together and eventually created a formal sector.

What do you feel the state of the print market is currently compared to the art market in general?

I think it has always been super-strong. Obviously when the economy dips there's always a little bit of a setback, but historically there has always been a great interest in prints. The great thing about limited edition prints, particularly by the artists that we are working with, is that it really affords people tremendous opportunity to buy a masterpiece by an artist at a fraction of the price that another of his/her artwork would be sold at.

GALLERIES MID LEVEL VS. MEGA

G

The Place of Mid-Level Galleries in the Age of the Mega-Gallery

Elizabeth Dee, Edward Winkleman, and Josh Baer

Salon
Art Market Talk

Basel
June 13, 2013

Elizabeth Dee, Founder and President, Elizabeth Dee Gallery, Co-Founder and President of The Independent, New York

Edward Winkleman, Founder and President of Winkleman Gallery, New York, and Co-Founder of the Moving Image art fair, New York/London

Moderator: Josh Baer, Art Advisor and Publisher of *Baer Faxt*, New York

A complete version of the conversation is available at www.artbasel.com

JOSH BAER We should dive right into the subject: what is a mid-level gallery? And are you one?

ELIZABETH DEE It's a gallery that has worked in a generational context, which has introduced or discovered artists who were not known to the public before. That can be emerging artists, but it also extends to mid-career ones. That's how I would define a mid-level gallery, and I will definitely say that I am one.

EDWARD WINKLEMAN We would definitely be considered as a mid-level gallery as well. You can distinguish a mid-level gallery from a mega-gallery or an emerging gallery. If somebody asks if you are a mega-gallery, you're probably not one ... There's a lot of romance about starting a gallery. I think you become a mid-level gallery when you realize that even Leo Castelli's gallery wasn't what its mythology is: there's an aspect of running a business that isn't necessarily romantic or fun, but important.

A mega-gallery would be a gallery that has either so many spaces or so many artists or so many directors that you can't really identify it as a mom-and-pop shop.
— Josh Baer

JB Is there another level that is in-between, that you could call the "top-level gallery"—and not necessarily "mega"?

EW Well, how would you define a mega-gallery?

JB A mega-gallery would be a gallery that has either so many spaces or so many artists or so many directors that you can't really identify it as a mom-and-pop shop. And then, I would say, a lot of the top-level galleries, you still walk in there, and—for the sake of argument—there's Marian Goodman sitting there and you identify with her, rather than 40 sales people in 20 locations.

EW Our aspiration would be to become *top-tier* but not *mega*.

ED I think I share that, but I see it as a much more complex agenda right now. What it means to be a *top-tier* gallery, for our generation, would be very different than for Marian Goodman's generation.

JB Who gets to make that decision? The artists? The collectors? The museums? Or the art-fair selection committees?

ED It means different things for different people. The art-fair selection reinforces and often legitimizes what I call "vertical hierarchy." But I see our generation rather working in a horizontal hierarchy.

JB Could you please develop that?

ED I think growing bottom-to-top is only one way forward: having the large space, the large staff, having more executive operations, that kind of professionalism is the narrative arc that we've seen in the last 20 years. I would certainly say that, from my perspective, coming through the recent recession, which was very significant for our generation, not having that level of capitalization at our fingertips, we've had to be more creative and more collaborative.
X Initiative, where I started to deal with the significance of the recession collectively, was the first time that I ever really moved into a lateral growth in my work as a gallerist.

EW I think it should be considered as a valid choice to *not* open 16 spaces

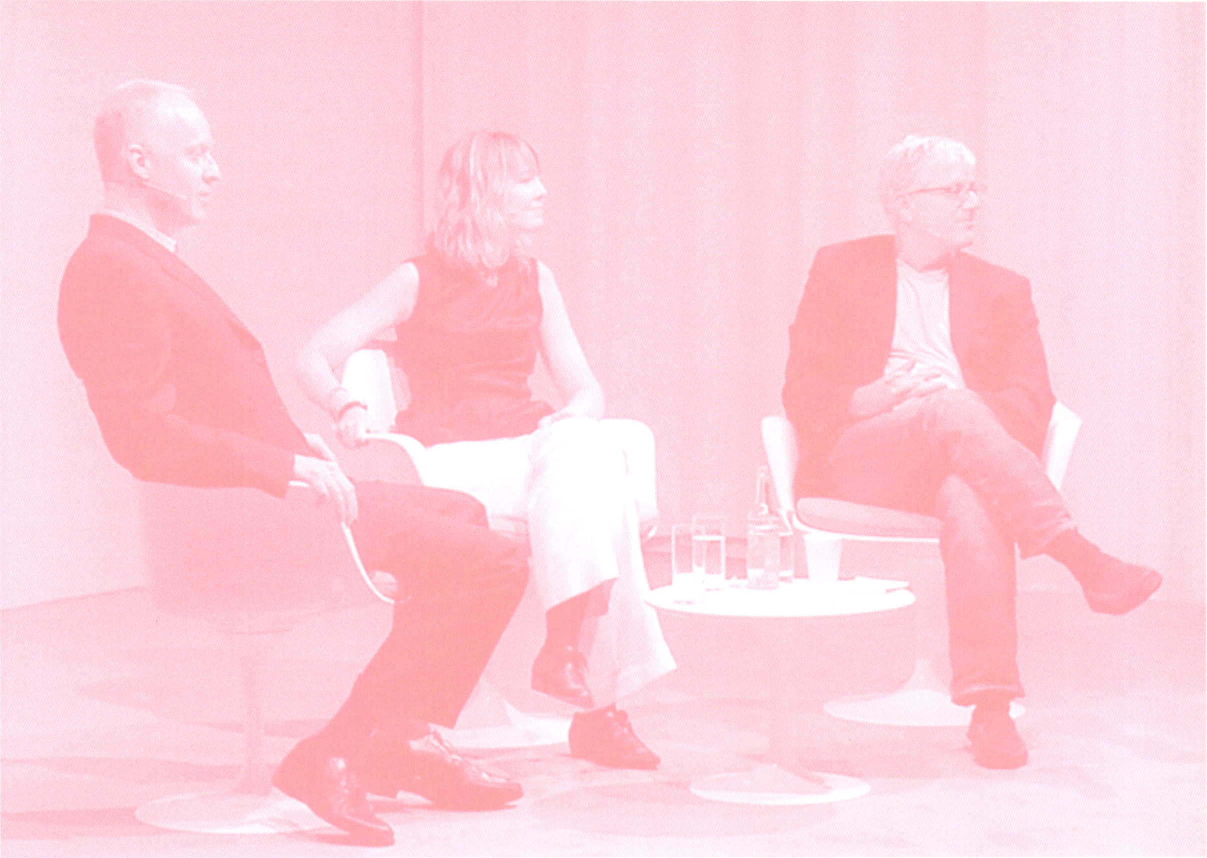

From left to right: Edward Winkleman, Elizabeth Dee, Josh Baer

all around the world, but instead to grow horizontally. For us as well, opening the Moving Image art fair was a choice to do something a little outside of our gallery space.

ED Building an artist's profile, from an emerging point to a place where they are performing well, including at auction, is a colleague-based strategic plan. We represent artists that have other galleries, we have regular discussions about museum shows, curatorial opportunities, collector opportunities; it's a very open discussion and it's very much built by the network of the galleries behind the artist. Having worked at a mega-gallery myself, before I started my own gallery, it was clear to me that my path was going to be more about collaboration.

EW To get back to your question specifically, I think whether you become a *top-tier* gallery or a *mega*-gallery is your own choice. You can exist as a top-tier gallery without necessarily having to open five or six spaces.

JB Don't you think you could be victim of your own success though? I mean, this is all sounding very utopian: we all get together, we all plan this, and everybody is in it together … and suddenly there's a lot of money! So, by becoming successful, you're kind of cannibalizing yourselves …

ED It already happens before the money actually becomes a major factor: emerging galleries are feeling frustrated because if they are successful, they get invited by the top art fairs, and as a result they are running from one city to the other, producing four-day exhibitions in this event culture which is driving their business, and they don't have time to go to the artists' studios anymore. So, already you are operating as some kind of mini-CEO and you have no staff to really assist you, you miss the time for reflection, etc. How do you manage a gallery into a global system as a company of four, doing six fairs around the world? I think those dilemmas happen earlier now than they used to. And then there's another level where you actually become fiscally successful with a group of artists and then you have to ask yourself, "Do I leverage this to the next gallery chapter?" and, "What does that gallery chapter look like?"

EW Whenever I start to think about challenges in the business, I always go back to basics: "What are my clients' needs?" I have two kinds of clients: collectors and artists. And so, trying to figure out how to navigate in this mega-gallery arena, I'm thinking about "What are my artists' needs?" I asked one of my artists today: "What are your needs?" and he said: "I actually need my dealers to be in my studio more."

JB Do you then need to keep up with the race, or do you want to go back to the tradition when I had a gallery, where ten or 15 artists was sort of the maximum that you could deal with, because you had to speak to each one of them every day?

I think you become a mid-level gallery when you realize that even Leo Castelli's gallery wasn't what its mythology is: there's an aspect of running a business that isn't necessarily romantic or fun, but important. — Edward Winkleman

EW I think that at a certain point artists should develop a dialogue with curators around the world as well, and that will replace the initial dialogue they had with the dealer. The problem is that everyone is super busy … In the curatorial community it's the same: they are so bogged down in the institution, trying to get projects going and the demands on them are so great that when they can come to Basel for four days, they want to have everything done. I planned a retrospective with a curator and an artist yesterday in four hours … That could never have happened otherwise. And you really feel that many of the museum shows that you sign up are actually only happening at the fairs. They're not happening in the studios. It never used to be like that: you would take the curator to the studio, there would be an ongoing dialogue, you would encourage the artists to have their own direct relationship with the curator on a creative level, and then, eventually, a project would emerge. Now curators are defining and picking artists with the galleries' help, and then moving directly into the production stage, without a lot of discussion in-between. I think that we can't underestimate the global situation, it's here, it's now, it's not just discussion anymore, and also the power of event culture—biennials, auctions, and art fairs—to drive all this activity, both for the market and the curatorial side.

EW I totally agree. And I think what emerges here for any particular players—the collectors, or the dealers, or the curators, or the artists—is a lack of time. A lack of time to do things in the way that they used to be done. I think collectors are very smartly using the art fairs as a way to catch up very quickly. What is lacking is the time they have to visit the galleries and have more in-depth conversations.

ED You also become accountable to the artists. You better have a huge list of top collectors you are offering works to. Back in Josh's days as a gallerist, if five collectors, maybe ten, were your potential key-audience for an exhibition, and you sent five or ten transparencies by FedEx, with a two page letter about the significance of this art object, that was enough to start the discussion. I came from that time, I started the last year or two, right before everything switched. And now, if I sit down with any artists and say: "Your show is fantastic, I've offered it to these five people," the reply would be: "You're not doing your job!"

JB Do you think that the art world or the gallery business will look different in five, ten, or 50 years? And if so, what might they look like?

EW If I had a crystal ball I would sell that information … [Laughs] Everybody is talking about this, and among the themes that emerge there is the idea that you don't need to have a physical space anymore. There's also a fair amount of discussion about switching to the entertainment model, where the dealer would be more like an agent or more like a manager.

JB Then you have to go from 50% to 10%. Most dealers don't want such a model for that reason …

EW Well, perhaps, but if you don't have the space to rent, then overhead is not such a big deal!

ED I think it's about a bifurcation: certain galleries are a platform and cultural producers, and some might leave the system to work exclusively with artists who interface with that platform. There has to be more with less, both time and money. There has to be some kind of evolution of the model because the model is really just not working.

H

- Hong Kong
- Basel
- Miami Beach

Haas

Berlin — Galleries

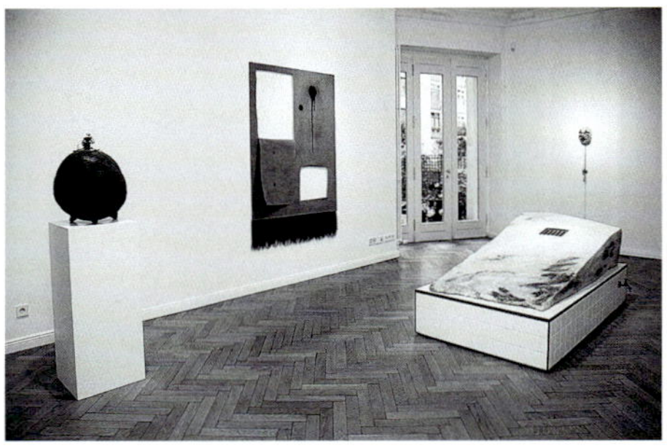

What first compelled you to open a gallery?
A fascination with art.

Who is the first artist you showed and what was most memorable about that show?
We showed German painting (Ernst Wilhelm Nay, Emil Schumacher, Wols, Willi Baumeister, etc.). Nowadays, these are some of the most sought-after paintings, but back then there was little interest in buying them.

When did you first participate in Art Basel and what was most memorable about that show?
In 1988. We met a client who still buys at our gallery today. The first show in Basel was a huge success.

- **Contact** Galerie Michael Haas
  Janna Oltmanns
  joltmanns@galeriemichaelhaas.de
  contact@galeriemichaelhaas.de
- **Established** 1978
- **Owner(s) / Partner(s)** Michael Haas
- **Team** 8
- **Space(s)** 400 m²
- **Artists at Art Basel** Jean Arp
  Giorgio de Chirico
  Paul Delvaux
  Otto Dix
  Jean Fautrier
  Marianna Gartner
  George Grosz
  Howard Hodgkin
  Ferdinand Hodler
  Ernst Ludwig Kirchner
  Paul Klee
  Henri Laurens
  Uwe Lausen
  Fernand Léger
  Charles Matton
  Paula Modersohn-Becker
  Francis Picabia
  Pablo Picasso
  Anton Räderscheidt
  Carol Rama
  George Rickey
  Georges Rouault
  Kurt Schwitters
  Louis Soutter
  Hans Uhlmann
  Félix Vallotton
  Bernar Venet
  Andy Warhol
  René Wirths
- **Further artists represented** Nicole Bianchet
  Stefan Bohnhoff
  Abraham David Christian
  Franz Gertsch
  Kerstin Grimm
  Julius Grünewald
  John Isaacs
  Richard Jordan
  Gustav Kluge
  Dirk Lange
  Stefan Mannel
  Arnulf Rainer
  Diana Rattray
  Pia Stadtbäumer
  Dimitris Tzamouranis

Hakgojae

Seoul — Galleries

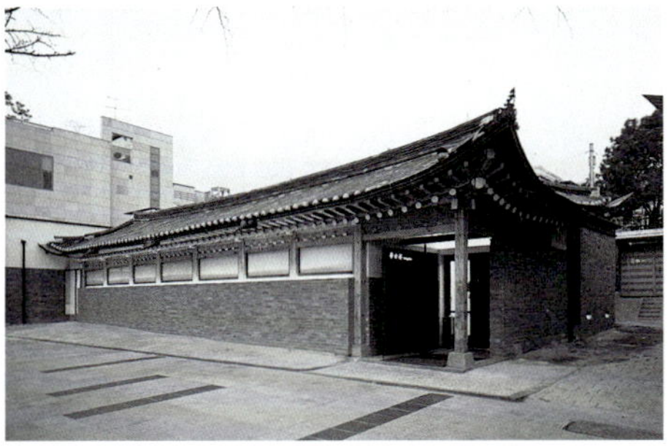

What first compelled you to open a gallery?
I studied Asian philosophy when I was young, looking for a way to make a contribution to both mankind and the world through academic studies. I was able to read books on art and aesthetics as I grew up. This led me to approach art and love it. It also inspired me to make the world more beautiful through art—this desire encouraged me to open a gallery.

Who is the first artist you showed and what was most memorable about that show?
I was deeply attracted to traditional Korean art. The golden age of Korean art history is from the mid-18th century to the early 19th century. I collected the representative works of academics at the time and opened an exhibition entitled *The Paintings and Calligraphy of Writers in 19th Century*. Although the exhibition was held in a very small space, it attracted many positive reviews from experts, as well as the press.

When did you first participate in Art Basel and what was most memorable about that show?
I have been participating at ART HK from 2008 on, and then when it became Art Basel in 2013. I was amazed by the diversity of the galleries and by the wonderful harmonization of programs, booth design, and works of each gallery. I am looking forward to being at Art Basel in Hong Kong in 2014.

- **Contact** Hakgojae Gallery
  Yookyung Hwang
  yookyung@hakgojae.com
  info@hakgojae.com
- **Established** 1988
- **Owner(s) / Partner(s)** Woo Chan-Kyu
- **Team** 9
- **Space(s)** 390 m²
- **Artists at Art Basel** Boomoon
  Tim Eitel
  Hyun-Sook Song
  Kyoung Tack Hong
  Lee Myoungho
  Lee Seahyun
  Lee Ufan
  Lee Yongbaek
  Lee Youngbin
  Jin Meyerson
  You Hyeonkyeong
  Zhang Huan
- **Further artists represented** Atta Kim
  Chen Wenji
  Choong Sup Lim
  Chung Hyun
  Chung Sang-hwa
  Ian Davenport
  Bernard Frize
  Jia Youfu
  Kang Yo-bae
  Kim Ho-deuk

Lee Bae
Lee Dong-youb
Lee Jong-gu
Noh Suntag
Oh Ryun
Jean-Pierre Raynaud
Shin Hak-chul
Suh Yongsun
Yangachi
Yin Qi
Yun Suk-nam

Hammer

New York — Galleries

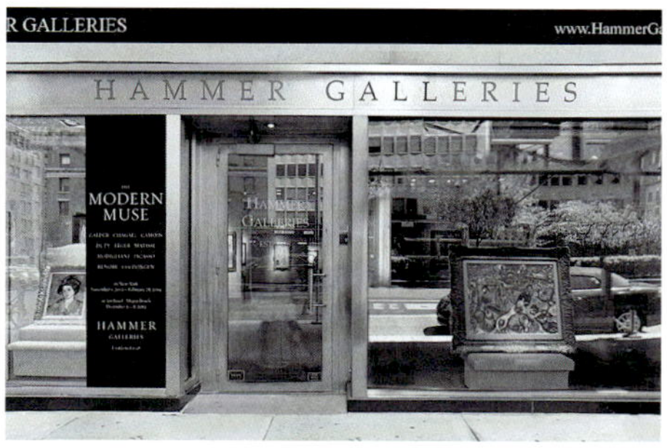

What first compelled you to open a gallery?
The gallery was founded in 1928 by industrialist and philanthropist Dr. Armand Hammer.

Who is the first artist you showed and what was most memorable about that show?
Hammer Galleries specializes in works by secondary market Modern masters, such as Alexander Calder, Marc Chagall, Fernand Léger, Henri Matisse, Joan Miró, Amedeo Modigliani, Pablo Picasso, Kees van Dongen, and others.

When did you first participate in Art Basel and what was most memorable about that show?
Our first Art Basel participation was in 2012 in Miami Beach. The energy of the fair, the quality of art works, and the number of serious collectors was all very memorable.

- **Contact** Hammer Galleries LLC, Howard Shaw, info@hammergalleries.com
- **Established** 1928
- **Owner(s) / Partner(s)** Howard Shaw
- **Team** 7
- **Space(s)** 200 m²
- **Artists at Art Basel** Alexander Calder, Marc Chagall, Salvador Dalí, Raoul Dufy, Alberto Giacometti, Fernand Léger, Henri Matisse, Amedeo Modigliani, Pablo Picasso, Kees van Dongen, Andy Warhol, Tom Wesselmann
- **Further artists represented** Pierre Bonnard, Mary Cassatt, Chen Yifei, Henri de Toulouse-Lautrec, Maurice de Vlaminck, Edgar Degas, Jean Dubuffet, Sam Francis, Paul Gauguin, Wassily Kandinsky, René Magritte, Edouard Manet, Claude Monet, Henry Moore, Berthe Morisot, Pierre-Auguste Renoir, Alfred Sisley, Chaïm Soutine, Yves Tanguy

Hanart TZ

Hong Kong — Galleries, Encounters

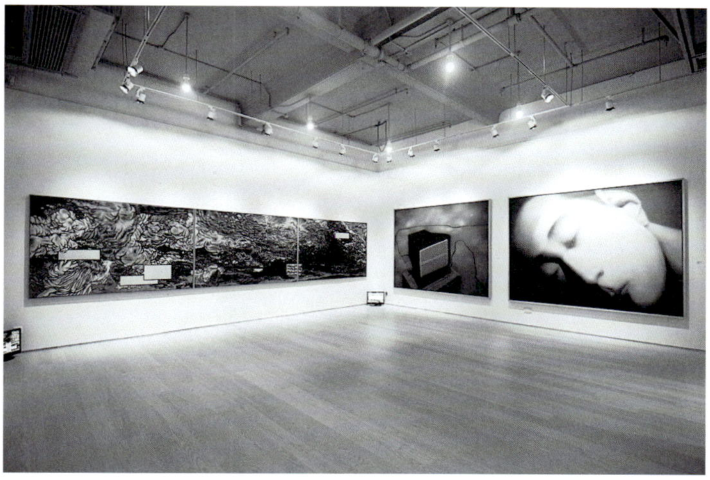

What first compelled you to open a gallery?
To take part in shaping Chinese modern art and to work with artists I believed in. The contemporary Chinese art world is a product of its efforts at modernization based on Western modalities and models—willingly adapted, copied, and sometimes even out-performed—yet Chinese contemporary art cannot be understood in such a limited framework because it straddles both sides of the Cold War, and also continues to have a dialogue with its own literati art history.
Following events such as an exhibition for the sculptor Ju Ming at the Hong Kong Arts Centre, I opened my gallery, Hanart, in December 1983, realizing I needed an independent platform for my own exhibitions. Before my first show I wrote art criticism, and worked as an independent curator of Hong Kong and Taiwanese artists.

Who is the first artist you showed and what was most memorable about that show?
I organized my first show for the artist Luis Chan, in 1980, as an independent curator.

When did you first participate in Art Basel and what was most memorable about that show?
We first participated in ART HK in 2008, and now at Art Basel in Hong Kong in 2013. Art Basel successfully brought together players who make the rest of the city believe that art and art collecting are important.

- **Contact** Hanart TZ Gallery, Arman Lam, hanart@hanart.com
- **Established** 1983
- **Owner(s) /** Chang Tsong-zung (Johnson Chang)
- **Team** 11
- **Space(s)** 100 m² (TZ Gallery), 380 m² (Hanart Square)
- **Artists at Art Basel** Gu Wenda, Qiu Zhijie, Wu Shanzhuan
- **Further artists represented** Gaylord Chan, Luis Chan, Chieh-jen Chen, Emily Cheng, Chow Chun Fai, Chu Hing Wah, Feng Mengbo, Ho Sin Tung, Michael Lee, Li Qing, Liu Dahong, Mao Xuhui, Wei Dong, Jennifer Wen Ma, Wong Chung-yu, Wucius Wong, Wu Shanzhuan & Inga Svala Thorsdottir, Yang Jiechang, Yao Jui-chung, Ye Wei-li

Harris Lieberman

New York — Galleries

- **Contact**: Harris Lieberman, gallery@harrislieberman.com
- **Established**: 2005
- **Artists at Art Basel**: Julia Dault, Lisa Oppenheim, Zak Prekop, Matt Saunders
- **Further artists represented**: Armin Boehm, Matthias Dornfeld, Stef Driesen, Daniel Guzmán, Karl Haendel, Julian Hoeber, Evan Holloway, Ohad Meromi, Rebecca Morris, Bernd Ribbeck, Tommy White, Thomas Zipp

Hauser & Wirth

London — Galleries
New York — Galleries, Unlimited, Parcours
Zurich — Galleries

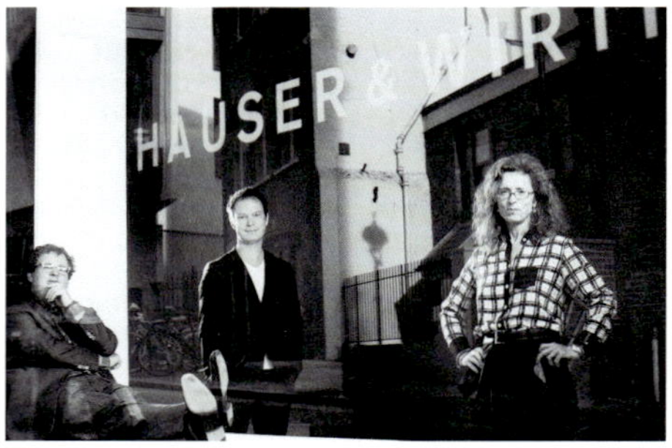

Who is the first artist you showed and what was most memorable about that show?
We had a group exhibition including Arp, Baselitz, Calder, Giacometti, Picabia, and others.

When did you first participate in Art Basel and what was most memorable about that show?
In 1999.

- **Contact**: Hauser & Wirth, Florian Berktold, florian@hauserwirth.com, zurich@hauserwirth.com
- **Established**: 1992
- **Owner(s) / Partner(s)**: Iwan Wirth (President), Manuela Wirth (President), Ursula Hauser (President), Marc Payot (Vice President)
- **Artists at Art Basel**: Rita Ackermann, Ida Applebroog, Phyllida Barlow, Louise Bourgeois, Christoph Büchel, David Claerbout, Martin Creed, Matthew Day Jackson, Berlinde De Bruyckere, Martin Eder, Zhang Enli, Ellen Gallagher, Isa Genzken, Dan Graham, Rodney Graham, Subodh Gupta, Mary Heilmann, Eva Hesse, Andy Hope 1930, Roni Horn, Thomas Houseago, Richard Jackson, Rashid Johnson, Hans Josephsohn, Allan Kaprow, Rachel Khedoori, Bharti Kher, Guillermo Kuitca, Maria Lassnig, Lee Lozano, Anna Maria Maiolino, Paul McCarthy, Joan Mitchell, Henry Moore, Ron Mueck, Caro Niederer, Christopher Orr, Djordje Ozbolt, Michael Raedecker, Jason Rhoades, Pipilotti Rist, Dieter Roth, Sterling Ruby, Anri Sala, Wilhelm Sasnal, Christoph Schlingensief, Roman Signer, Anj Smith, Monika Sosnowska, Diana Thater, Andre Thomkins, Philippe Vandenberg, Ian Wallace, David Zink Yi, Jakub Julian Ziolkowski

Herald St

London — Feature, Unlimited, Galleries

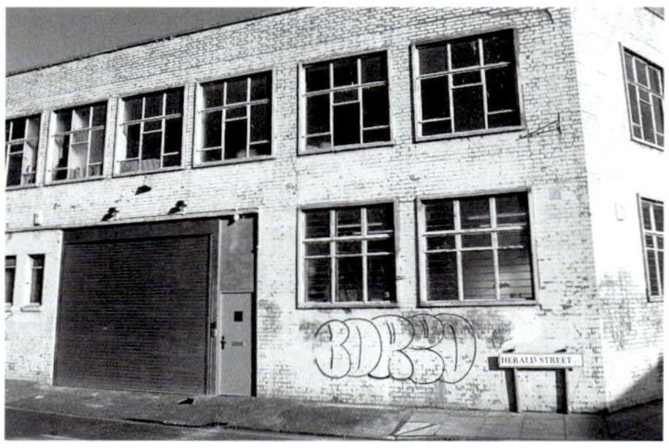

What first compelled you to open a gallery?
A tiny studio in Dalston.

Who is the first artist you showed and what was most memorable about that show?
Christina Mackie in 2005 was our first show.

When did you first participate in Art Basel and what was most memorable about that show?
The first time we exhibited was in the Art Premiere sector in Basel, it was exciting to be in the fair with a small booth to show our program so early on. There was a great generation of galleries in that sector.

- **Contact**: Herald St, Nicky Verber, nicky@heraldst.com, mail@heraldst.com
- **Established**: 2005
- **Owner(s) / Partner(s)**: Nicky Verber, Ash L'Ange
- **Team**: 5
- **Space(s)**: 200 m²
- **Artists at Art Basel**: Pablo Bronstein, Matt Connors, Matthew Darbyshire, Michael Dean, Ida Ekblad, Djordje Ozbolt, Amalia Pica, Nick Relph
- **Further artists represented**: Markus Amm, Alexandra Bircken, Josh Brand, Peter Coffin, Annette Kelm, Scott King, Cary Kwok, Christina Mackie, Oliver Payne, Tony Swain

Donald Urquhart
Klaus Weber
Nicole Wermers

Hetzler

Berlin

Galleries
Galleries

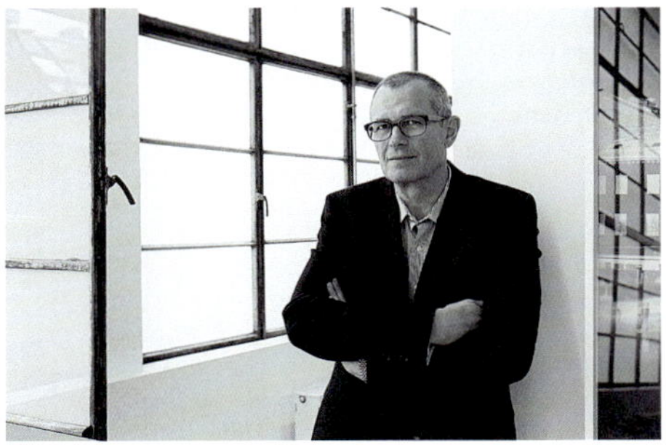

Who is the first artist you showed and what was most memorable about that show?
We showed Erwin Heerich.

When did you first participate in Art Basel and what was most memorable about that show?
In 1982.

- **Contact** — Galerie Max Hetzler
  Wolfram Aue
  wolfram.aue@maxhetzler.com
  info@maxhetzler.com
- **Established** — 1974
- **Owner(s) / Partner(s)** — Max Hetzler
- **Team** — 9
- **Space(s)** — 1,600 m² (Oudenarder Strasse)
  230 m² (Bleibtreustrasse)
  450 m² (Goethestrasse)
- **Artists Art Basel** — Darren Almond
  Glenn Brown
  André Butzer
  Rineke Dijkstra
  Günther Förg
  Mona Hatoum
  Jeff Koons
  Vera Lutter
  Marepe
  Beatriz Milhazes
  Ernesto Neto
  Frank Nitsche
  Albert Oehlen
  Yves Oppenheim
  Richard Phillips
  Michael Raedecker
  Bridget Riley
  Thomas Struth
  Rebecca Warren
  Christopher Wool
  Toby Ziegler

Hirschl & Adler

New York

Galleries
Kabinett

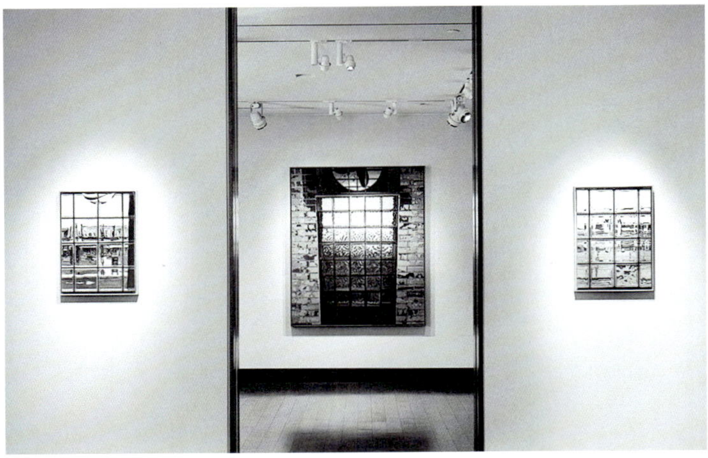

What first compelled you to open a gallery?
Hirschl & Adler Galleries was founded in 1952 and has long been a leader in the field of historical American Fine and Decorative Arts. In 1981 we expanded our business into the modern and contemporary field and decided it was best to do it under a different name. Thus, Hirschl & Adler Modern was founded.

Who is the first artist you showed and what was most memorable about that show?
We have represented American painter John Moore for over 30 years, and his first exhibition with the gallery was one of the first held at Hirschl & Adler Modern. The most memorable aspect of that show was just how quickly it sold out.

When did you first participate in Art Basel and what was most memorable about that show?
We first participated in Art Basel in Miami Beach in 2012, though the gallery had participated in Art Basel in Basel years ago. The most memorable aspect of our 2012 showing was observing the energy in the marketplace for American Modernism. We had been looking for a way to increase international awareness of American Modernist painting and sculpture, a longtime specialty of this gallery. While postwar American art is globally admired, this country's prewar artists are not well-known beyond our shores. Art Basel in Miami Beach draws more collectors from around the world than any other American fair, so we were thrilled to share this art with such a global audience.

- **Contact** — Hirschl & Adler Modern
  Dunham Townend
  dunhamt@hirschlandadler.com
  modern@hirschlandadler.com
- **Established** — 1981
- **Owner(s) / Partner(s)** — Stuart Feld (President & Director)
  Elizabeth Feld (Managing Director)
- **Team** — 19
- **Space(s)** — 1,022 m²
- **Artists at Art Basel** — George Ault
  Milton Avery
  Romare Bearden
  Thomas Hart Benton
  Oscar Bluemner
  Charles Burchfield
  Stuart Davis
  Charles Demuth
  Arthur Dove
  Marsden Hartley
  Edward Hopper
  Raymond Jonson
  Gaston Lachaise
  Blanche Lazzell
  John Marin
  Georgia O'Keeffe
  Winold Reiss
  Charles Sheeler
  Joseph Stella
  Max Weber
- **Further artists represented** — James Edward Deeds
  Arthur Wesley Dow
  David Ligare
  Richard Lonsdale-Hands
  John Moore
  Fairfield Porter
  Stone Roberts
  Bill Traylor
  Marc Trujillo
  Elizabeth Turk
  Stanley Twardowicz

Hoffman

Chicago

Galleries
Galleries Kabinett

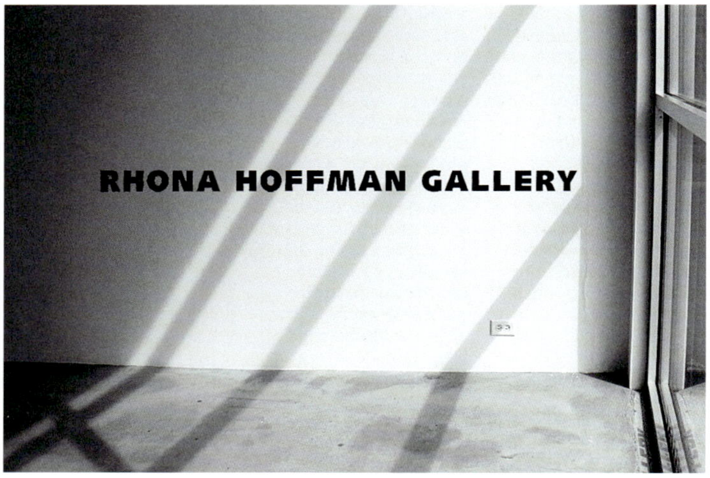

What first compelled you to open a gallery?
In 1974, I left working *pro bono* at the MCA and other art organizations and took a director position at Grace Hokin Gallery. In October 1976, Donald Young and I decided that we could fill a contemporary art void in Chicago by opening a gallery. Very contemporary art had no voice outside of museum exhibitions and we were mostly interested in the "now"! Great new art was being created and we wanted to be part of its disemination.

Who is the first artist you showed and what was most memorable about that show?
The first artist to make brand new work for the gallery was Donald Judd. He made a series of wall-hung plywood boxes with slants. Working with Don was memorable, as was having a magnificent work of art in our gallery's wall for a month. Memorable was also that many people thought it was furniture on which to put their empty wine glasses.

- **Contact** Rhona Hoffman Gallery
  Anastasia Tirari
  anastasia@rhoffmangallery.com
  rhoffman@rhoffmangallery.com
- **Established** 1976/ 1983
- **Owner(s) / Partner(s)** Rhona Hoffman
- **Team** 5
- **Space(s)** 370 m²
- **Artists at Art Basel** Vito Acconci
  Derrick Adams
  Todd Chilton
  Spencer Finch
  Julia Fish
  Hamish Fulton
  Luis Gispert
  Jacob Hashimoto
  Susan Hefuna
  Robert Heinecken
  Jenny Holzer
  Sol LeWitt
  Robert Overby
  Karthik Pandian
  Fred Sandback
  Xaviera Simmons
  Richard Tuttle
  Siebren Versteeg
  Carrie Mae Weems
  Anne Wilson
  Adrian Wong
- **Further artists represented** Mel Bochner
  Chris Garofalo
  Leon Golub
  Judy Ledgerwood
  Gordon Matta-Clark
  New Catalogue
  Richard Rezac
  Nancy Spero
  Brian Ulrich
  Kehinde Wiley

Hazlitt Holland-Hibbert

London

Galleries

- **Contact** Hazlitt Holland-Hibbert
  jhh@hh-h.com
- **Established** 2001
- **Owner(s) / Partner(s)** James Holland-Hibbert
- **Artists at Art Basel** Frank Auerbach
  Lucian Freud
  Barbara Hepworth
  Leon Kossoff
  Henry Moore
  Ben Nicholson
  Bridget Riley
- **Further artists represented** Francis Bacon
  Peter Blake
  Anthony Caro
  Naum Gabo
  Gilbert & George
  Richard Hamilton
  David Hockney
  Howard Hodgkin
  Allen Jones
  Richard Long
  Sean Scully

Hopkins

Paris

Galleries

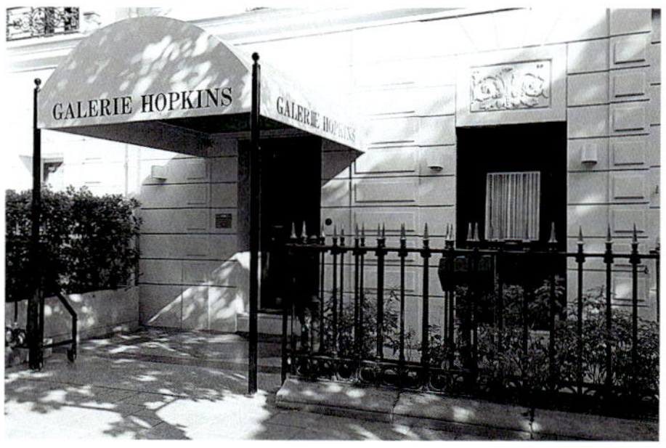

What first compelled you to open a gallery?
I had some wonderful paintings but no visibility in order to share them with others.

Who is the first artist you showed and what was most memorable about that show?
In the mid-1980s we were showing Impressionist works. It was a huge success and we had about 26,000 visitors, which was remarkable.

When did you first participate in Art Basel and what was most memorable about that show?
In 2006. What impressed us the most was the high interest shown by collectors from all over the world.

- **Contact** Galerie Hopkins
  Marie-Caroline van Herpen
  mcaroline@galeriehopkins.com
  hopkins@galeriehopkins.com
- **Established** 1984
- **Owner(s) / Partner(s)** Waring Hopkins
- **Team** 6
- **Space(s)** 240 m²
- **Artists at Art Basel** Josef Albers
  Jean Arp
  Victor Brauner
  Alexander Calder
  Nicolas de Staël
  Jean Dubuffet
  Max Ernst
  Julio González
  Hans Hartung
  Baltasar Lobo
  René Magritte
  Henri Matisse
  Manolo Millares
  Joan Miró
  Joan Mitchell
  Robert Motherwell
  Pablo Picasso

- **Further artists represented** Serge Poliakoff, Gerhard Richter, Pierre Soulages, Sam Szafran, Yves Tanguy, Maria-Helena Vieira da Silva, Marc Quinn

Houk

New York — Galleries
Zürich — Galleries

- **Contact** Edwynn Houk Gallery
  info@houkgallery.com
- **Established** 1977
- **Owner(s) / Partner(s)** Edwynn Houk, Julie Castellano, Daniel Blochwitz
- **Artists at Art Basel** Valérie Belin, Ilse Bing, Bill Brandt, Brassaï, Manuel Álvarez Bravo, Sebastiaan Bremer, Henri Cartier-Bresson, Lynn Davis, Elliott Erwitt, Lalla Essaydi, Sissi Farassat, Robert Frank, Gail Albert Halaban, Nadav Kander, André Kertész, Dorothea Lange, Danny Lyon, Man Ray, Sally Mann, David Michalek, Tina Modotti, László Moholy-Nagy, Abelardo Morell, Vik Muniz, Robert Polidori, Herb Ritts, Alexander Rodchenko, August Sander, Hannes Schmid, Stephen Shore, Alfred Stieglitz, Edward Weston

Houldsworth

London — Discoveries

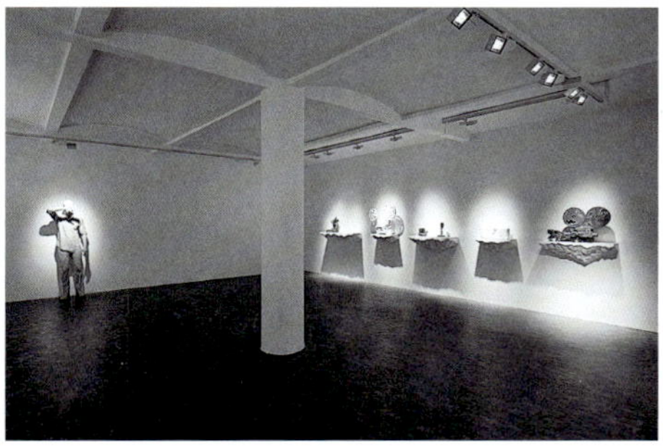

What first compelled you to open a gallery?
To support emerging artists.

Who is the first artist you showed and what was most memorable about that show?
Cameron Galt, a young Scottish artist—Charles Saatchi bought all the works.

When did you first participate in Art Basel and what was most memorable about that show?
Art Basel in Hong Kong in 2013.

- **Contact** Pippy Houldsworth Gallery
  Davina Brincat
  davina@houldsworth.co.uk
  gallery@houldsworth.co.uk
- **Established** 1999
- **Owner(s) / Partner(s)** Pippy Houldsworth
- **Team** 6
- **Space(s)** 185 m²
- **Artists at Art Basel** Francesca DiMattio
- **Further artists represented** Daniel Arsham, Ruth Claxton, Clem Crosby, Rachel Goodyear, Martin Kobe, Kirstine Roepstorff, Yuken Teruya, Zoë Walker & Neil Bromwich

Hufkens

Brussels — Galleries, Unlimited, Parcours
Galleries

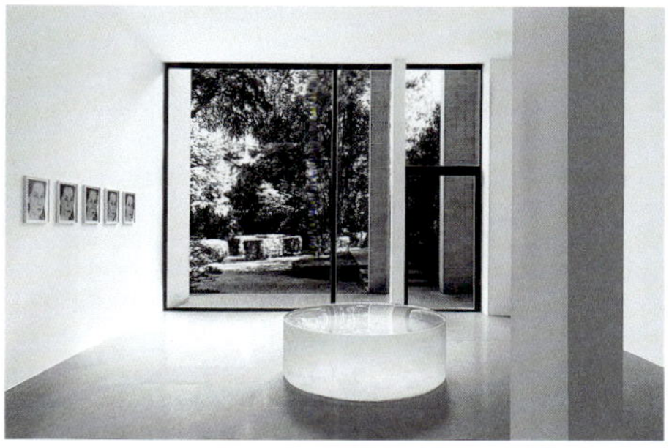

What first compelled you to open a gallery?
Already as a child I was interested in seeing art. I studied law to please my parents, but I was bored. I think I always knew I wanted to be an art dealer. When I started with my gallery at 22 it was the irrational decision of a young guy with a dream.

Who is the first artist you showed and what was most memorable about that show?
One of my first exhibitions was with Antony Gormley. I intuitively felt he was a great artist and I was very lucky that our paths crossed. Surprisingly he agreed to do a show with me. More than 25 years later we are still working together.

When did you first participate in Art Basel and what was most memorable about that show?
In the beginning I worked alone and I did everything by myself, from the installation to the dismantling. It was a real adventure.

- **Contact** Xavier Hufkens
  Elisabeth Van Caelenberge
  elisabeth@xavierhufkens.com
  info@xavierhufkens.com
- **Team** 15
- **Space(s)** 800 m²
- **Artists at Art Basel** David Altmejd, Harold Ancart, Daniel Buren, Thierry De Cordier, Michel François, Adam Fuss, Antony Gormley, Evan Holloway, Roni Horn, Thomas Houseago, Jacob Kassay, Robert Mapplethorpe, Malcolm Morley, David Noonan, Alessandro Pessoli, Jack Pierson, Ken Price, Tim Rollins and K.O.S., Sterling Ruby, Erwin Wurm
- **Further artists represented** Saâdane Afif, Philip Allen, Richard Artschwager, Louise Bourgeois, Cris Brodahl, Jean-Marc Bustamante, John Chamberlain, George Condo, Willem de Kooning

William Eggleston
Pierre Huyghe
Bertrand Lavier
José Lerma
Michelangelo Pistoletto
Robert Ryman
Padraig Timoney
Lesley Vance
Jan Vercruysse

Hutton

New York • Galleries

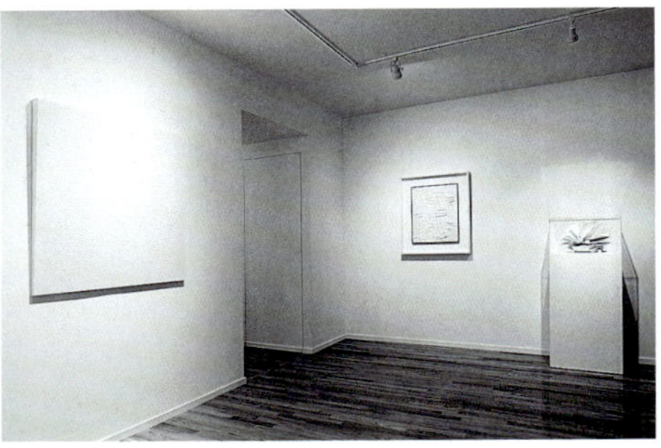

What first compelled you to open a gallery?
Leonard Hutton established the gallery because of his interest in Fine Arts and Antiques.

Who is the first artist you showed and what was most memorable about that show?
The first exhibition of a single artist was devoted to Gabriele Münter. It was memorable because Mr. Hutton collaborated with the artist directly and it was her first exhibition in America.

When did you first participate in Art Basel and what was most memorable about that show?
We first participated in Art Basel in 1973 and it was memorable in that it was our first ever participation in an art fair.

- **Contact** Leonard Hutton Galleries
  Ingrid Hutton
  art@leonardhuttongalleries.com
- **Established** 1957
- **Owner(s) / Partner(s)** Ingrid Hutton
- **Space(s)** 140 m²
- **Artists at Art Basel** Pier Paolo Calzolari
  Robert Delaunay
  Sonia Delaunay
  Sam Francis
  Helen Frankenthaler
  Sidney Geist
  Adolph Gottlieb
  Wassily Kandinsky
  Lee Krasner
  Fernand Léger
  Robert Motherwell
  Giulio Paolini
  Richard Pousette-Dart
  Ettore Spalletti
- **Further artists represented** Josef Albers
  Giacomo Balla
  James Brooks
  Anthony Caro
  Ilya Chashnik
  Niki de Saint Phalle
  Jean Dubuffet
  Friedel Dzubas
  Natalia Gontcharova
  Julio González
  Al Held
  Hans Hofmann
  Paul Klee
  Frantisek Kupka
  Mikhail Larionov
  Fausto Melotti
  Joan Miró
  David Nash
  Pablo Picasso
  Robert Rauschenberg
  Efim Rojak
  James Rosenquist
  Frank Stella
  Nikolai Suetin
  Natalia Udaltsova
  Tom Wesselmann

Herald St

Interview with artist Pablo Bronstein

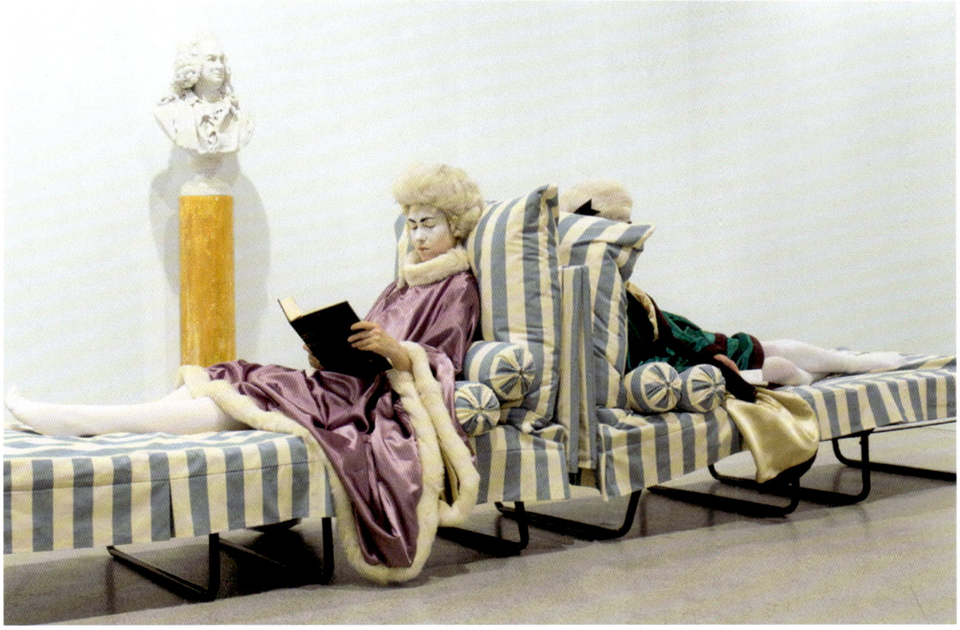

Art Basel in Basel (Feature), 2013

My piece for Art Basel is a minimal performance: just two people lying on a bed. It's a directional piece that is technically difficult to do for the dancers, because they have to hold positions and stay still for hours—with a few breaks. To frame this performance, I have chosen the 18th century, but this layer of history is in lots of ways false, as the title *Marie-Antoinette and Robespierre engage in an irritable post-coital conversation* illustrates. I'm supposing a hypothetical angry argument between them after having sex, but of course these two historical figures never met, and certainly never had sex. Furthermore, the costumes look as if they're from the 18th century, but they are a kind of 1940s or 1950s Hollywood version of 18th-century style. It's the same with the beds: they are a kind of Nancy Reagan style daybed.

In a way, you conceived this performance the way Sofia Coppola did for her own version of *Marie-Antoinette*, with anachronisms and fiction?

Better than she did! Indeed, there are very different sort of cracks and bits of lies superimposed onto this essentially minimal piece. One of the differences, of course, between this and a minimal performance is the fact that these dancers are in a kind of dandy pose. They are elegant, holding positions that look like they're lazy and easy, but which are actually quite difficult and annoying. It's a style that is very similar to ballet, where you look as if you're making less effort than you are actually making. I'm using this baroque physical language, that you would see in portraiture, on top of a minimalist performance structure.

In your work, you usually deal with dance and choreographic movements, but this piece is a "still performance."

Yes, but it's not a *tableau vivant*, because the performers are in "real time," in a sense. A *tableau vivant* would be, for example, two people running, but frozen in their run. Here it's two people reading and resting on beds in *real time*.

And they are really reading something.

Sure! They can choose what they read. They were both reading a Murakami novel for a while, but one of the dancers got bored and now is reading a book about me …

How did you choose the performers? Was it through a casting?

Rosalie Wahlfrid, aka Marie-Antoinette, is a dancer I've worked with for a long time. She's a very experienced Laban-trained dancer with some kind of classical background, making her very good at releases and improvisation. Because of her ballet training she has a natural *attitude*. This is the first time I have worked with Sy Simon, aka Robespierre. I needed someone that could embody the late 18th century in his face. I was more concerned with finding the right facial look with him than other things.

Tell us about the sculpture in the background.

It's a cheap 19th-century plaster imitation of an 18th-century bust of Rousseau, who is relevant to this in a wider historical sense because he unites both sides of the French Revolution.

Finally, what about doing this piece at an art fair?

I already have a presence within the fair, I show my drawings with Franco Noero, so it's exciting to be able to do a performance as well.

City population
7,184,000

Population density
6,620 inhabitants per square kilometer

Fair founded in
2013 (predecessor, ART HK, founded in 2008)

Visitors in 2013
60,000

Number of exhibitors in 2013
245

Number of artists exhibited in 2013
over 3,000

HONG KONG

Hong Kong Exhibition Partners: Museums & Cultural Institutions

Art Museum, The Chinese University of Hong Kong
Ancient Chinese Gold from the Mengdiexuan Collection

Asia Society Hong Kong Center
Light Before Dawn: Unofficial Chinese Art 1974–1985

Burger Collection and 1a space
I Think It Rains

Dr Sun Yat-sen Museum
Dr Sun Yat-sen and His Family

Flagstaff House Museum of Teaware
A Date with Chinese Tea

Goethe-Institut Hong Kong
João Vasco Paiva

Hong Kong Arts Centre
Cityscape: Music of the Mind—Hong Kong X Paris Comics Dialogue

Hong Kong Film Archive
The Cinematic Matrix of Golden Harvest; Morning Matinee Commemorating Wong Man-lei's 100th Birthday: Wong Man-lei, an Actor's Actor

Hong Kong Heritage Museum
Au Ho-nien: Free and Unfettered: Chinese Paintings and Calligraphy; The Heavenly Breeze: Selected Works of Gao Qifeng and His Disciples; Intelligence Infinity: Inspiration through Art

Hong Kong Museum of Art
A Hundred Chinese Paintings from the Hong Kong Museum of Art; The Origin of Dao: New Dimensions in Chinese Contemporary Art; Special Exhibition for the Twentieth Anniversary of Xubaizhai Gallery

Hong Kong Museum of Coastal Defense
Anti-Japanese War Heroes: An Exhibition on the Hong Kong Independent; Battalion of the Dongjiang Column

Hong Kong Museum of History
When Hillsides Collapse—A Century of Landslides in Hong Kong—Be Prepared for Danger in Times of Peace

Hong Kong University Museum and Art Gallery
Jao Tsung-I; René Burri: *Utopia*

Macao Museum of Art
Faces: Children's Art Exhibition; Napoleon and the Decorative Arts: Treasures of the Imperial Palaces; Yang Shan Shen—The Legacy: Commemorative Exhibition of the Centennial Birth Anniversary; Shiwan Ceramics Exhibition; Carol Kwok: *What you don't know can't hurt you*

Maritime Museum
We are Like Vapours; Wah Kwong at 60

Mobile M+
Inflation!

Parallel Contemporary Art
Hong Kong Eye

Para Site Art Space
A Journal of the Plague Year

Run Run Shaw Creative Media Center
40+4; Shanghai Soulmates; Pure Land

Savannah College of Art and Design, Hong Kong
Angel Otero: *Material Discovery*

Spring Workshop
Qiu Zhijie: *The Universe of Naming*

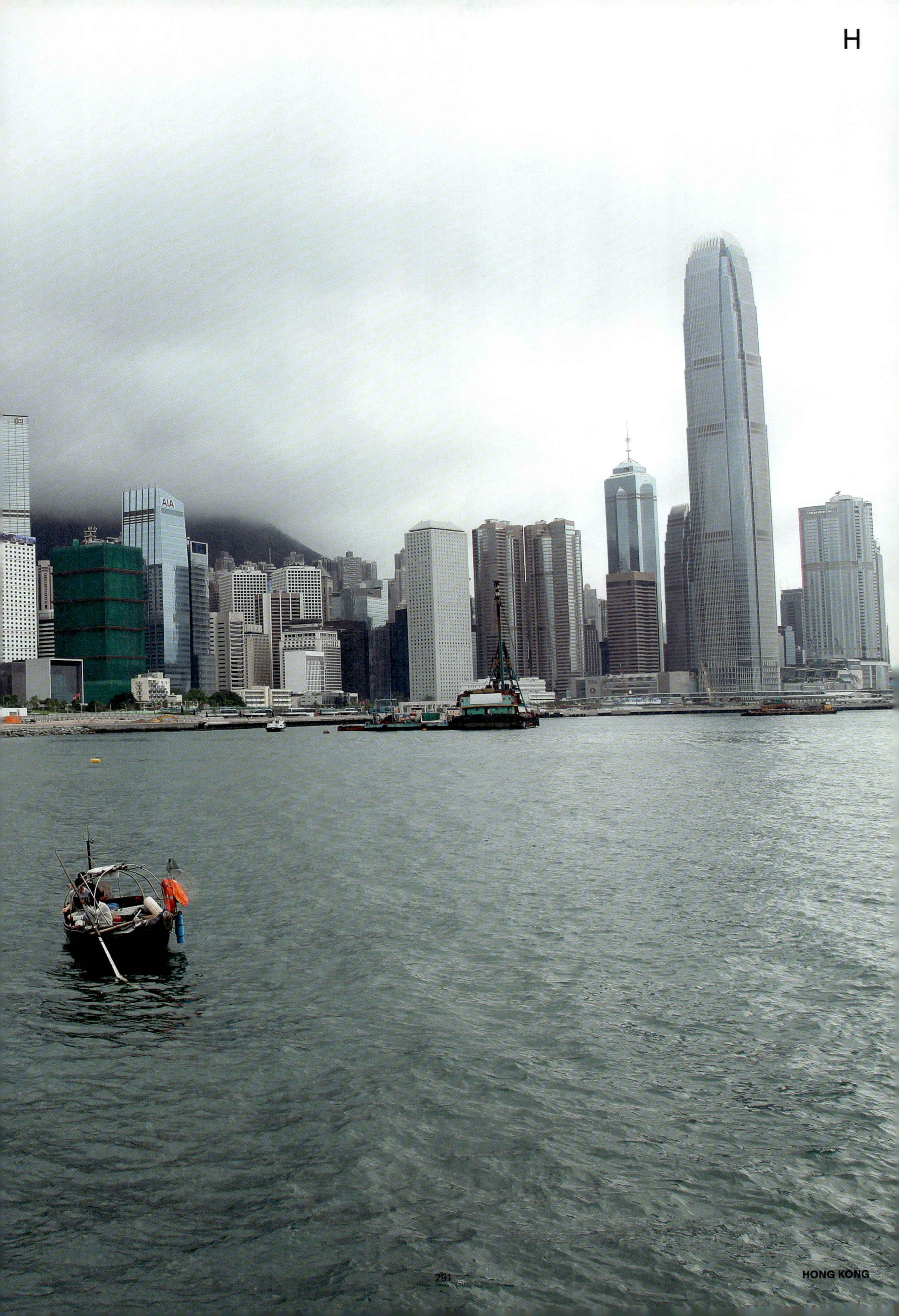
AIA

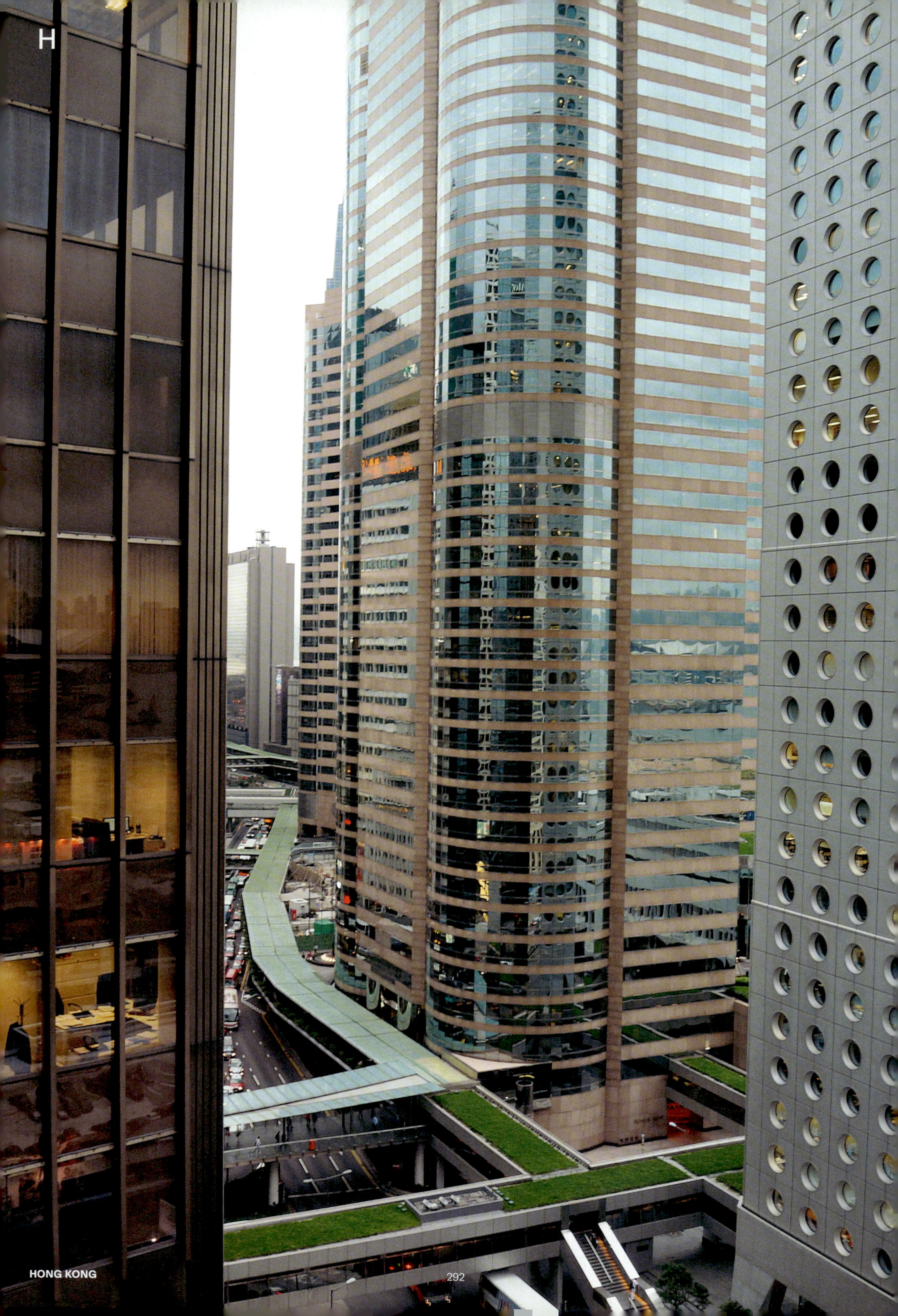

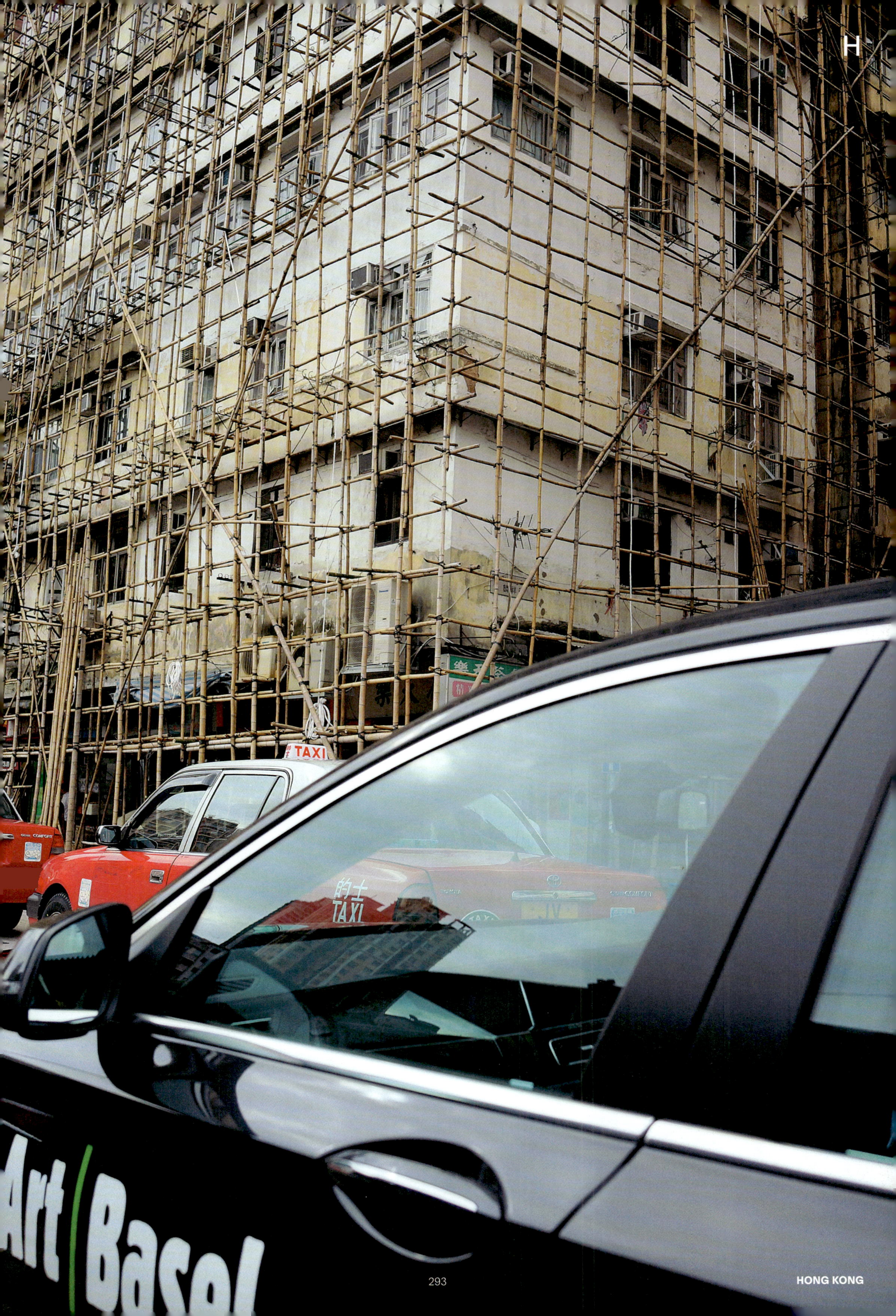
TAXI
的士
TAXI
Art Basel

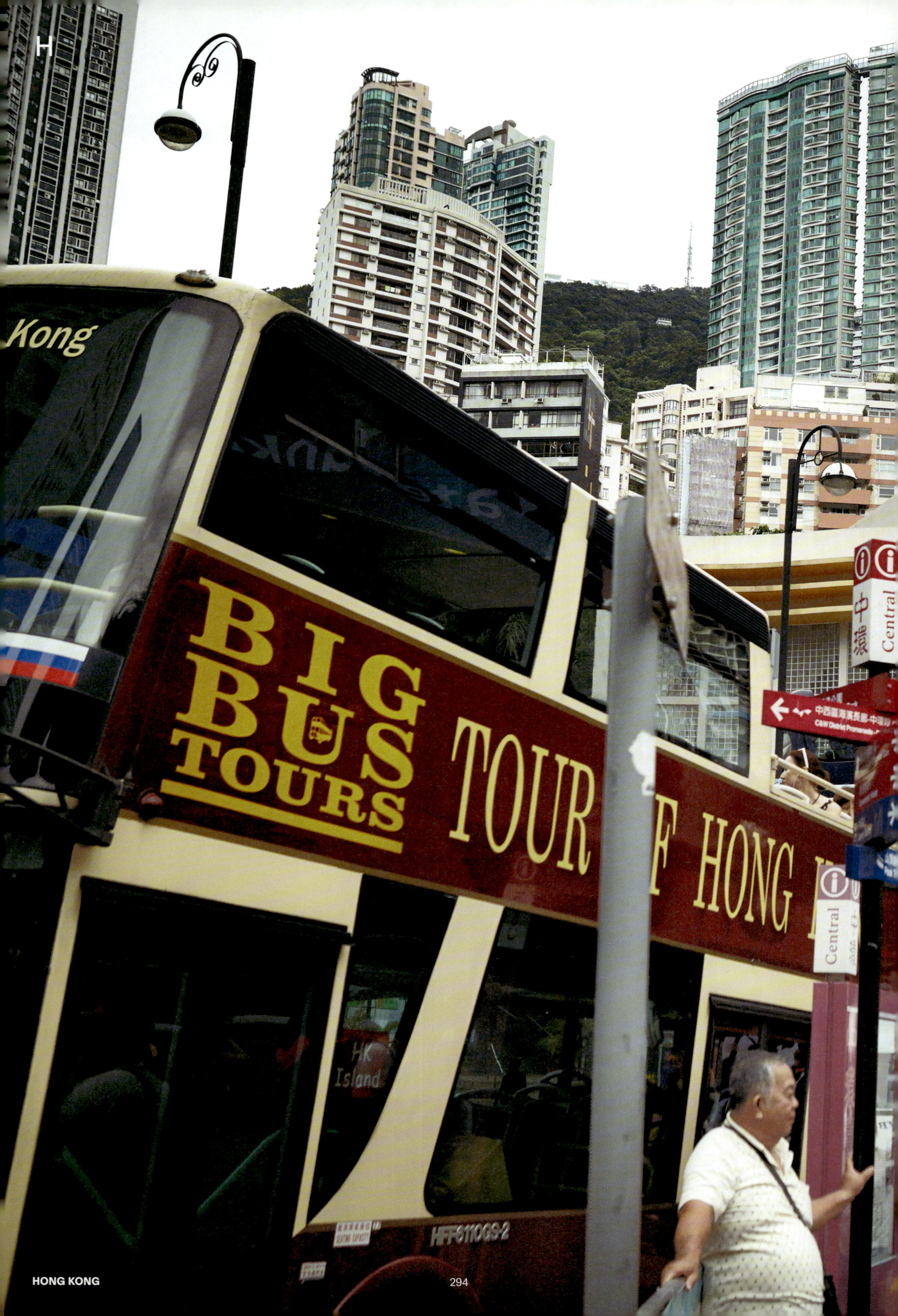
Kong
BIG
BUS
TOURS
TOUR
HONG
中環
Central
Central
HK
Island
HFF6110GS-2

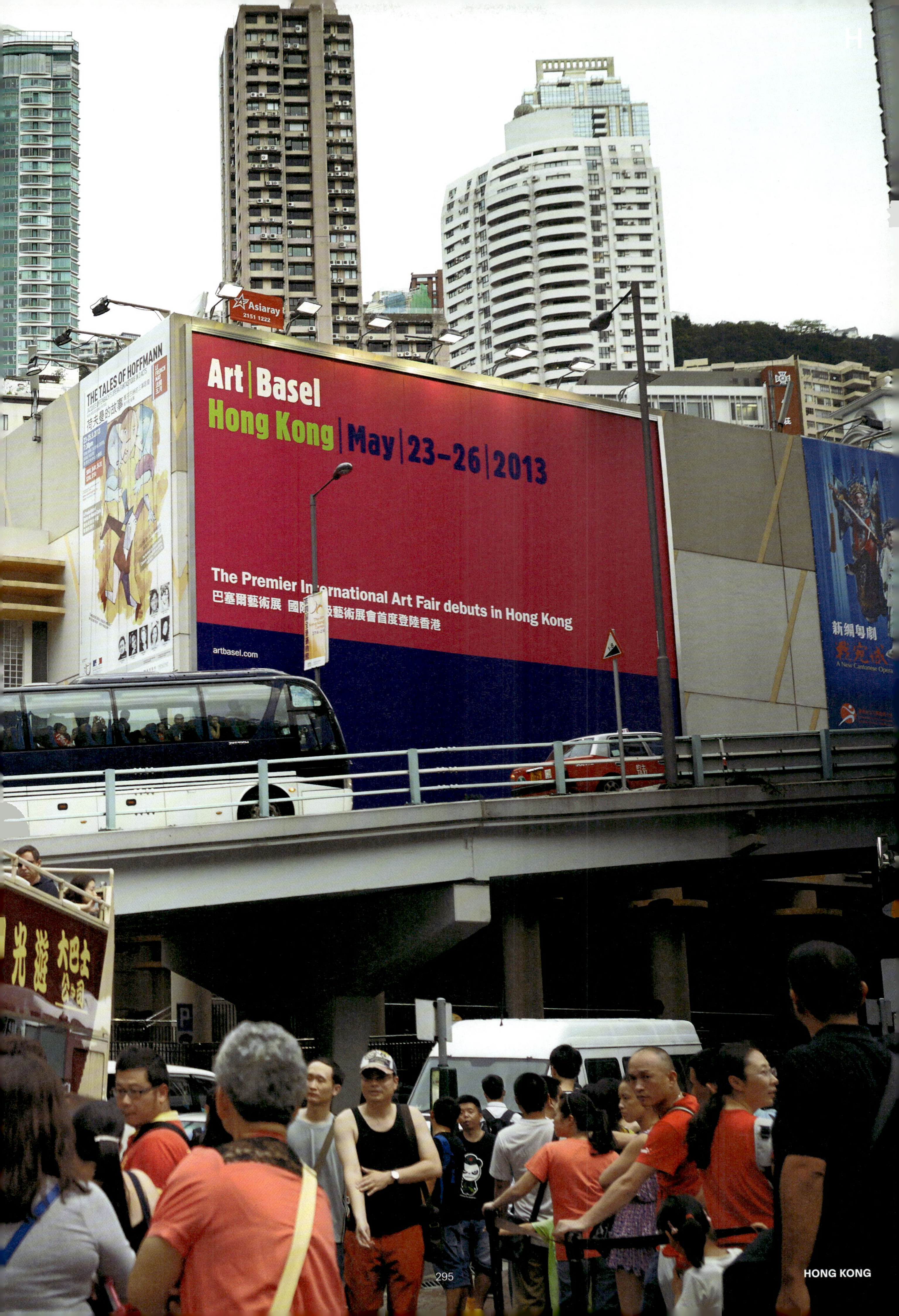
Asiaray
2151 1222
THE TALES OF HOFFMANN
荷夫曼的故事
Art | Basel
Hong Kong | May | 23–26 | 2013
The Premier In
ernational Art Fair debuts in Hong Kong
巴塞爾藝術展
藝術展會首度登陸香港
artbasel.com
新編粵劇
A New Cantonese Opera

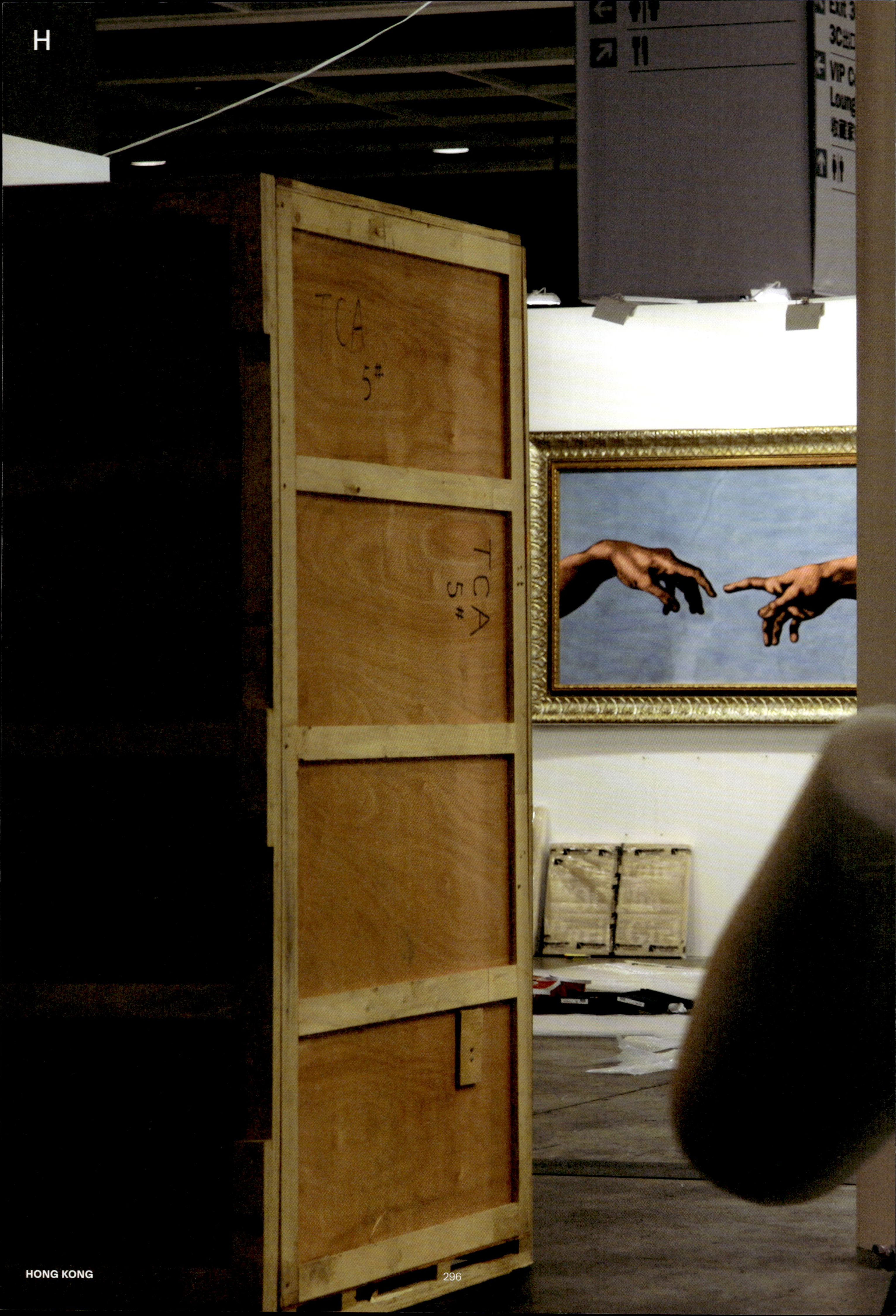
TCA
5#
TCA
5#

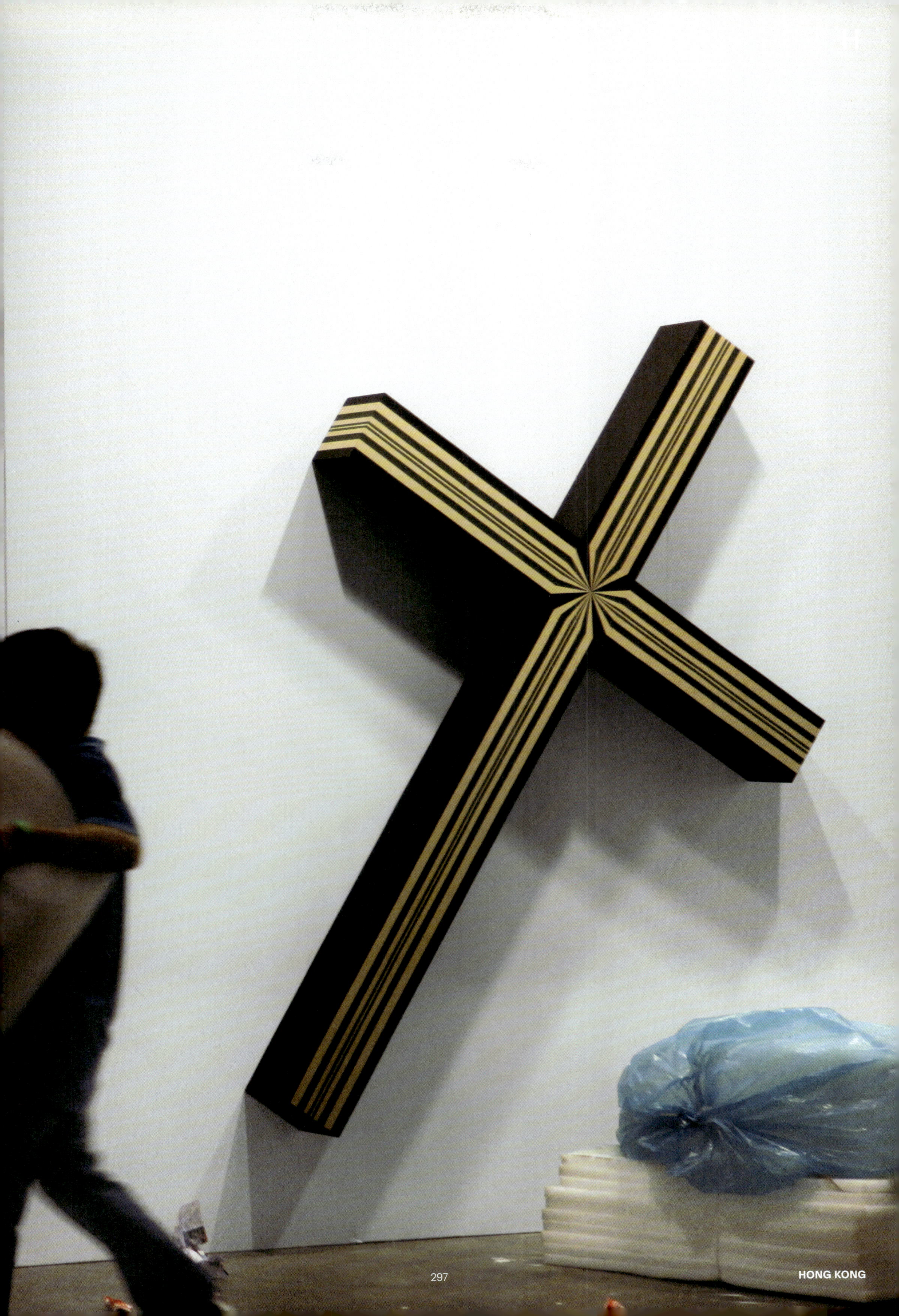

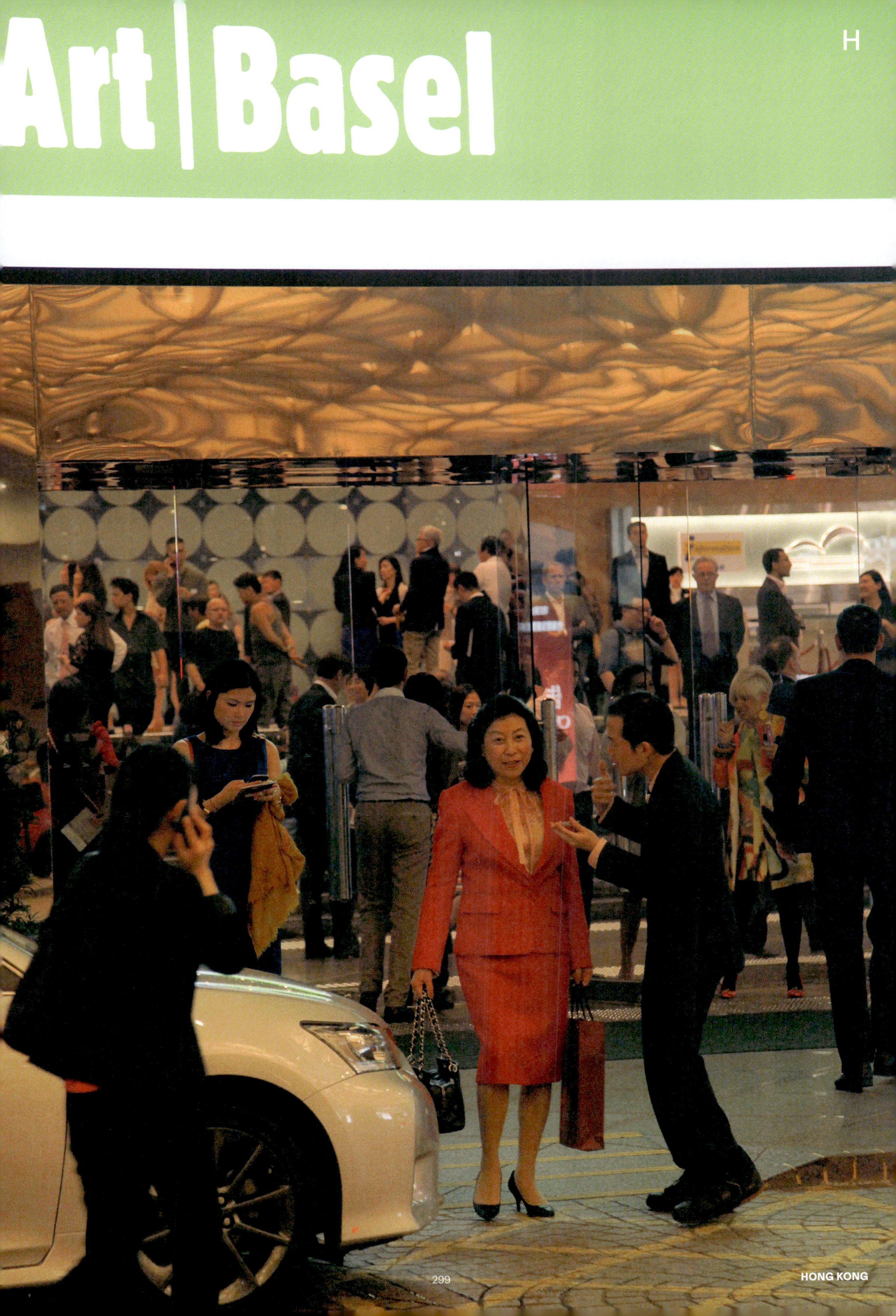
Art|Basel

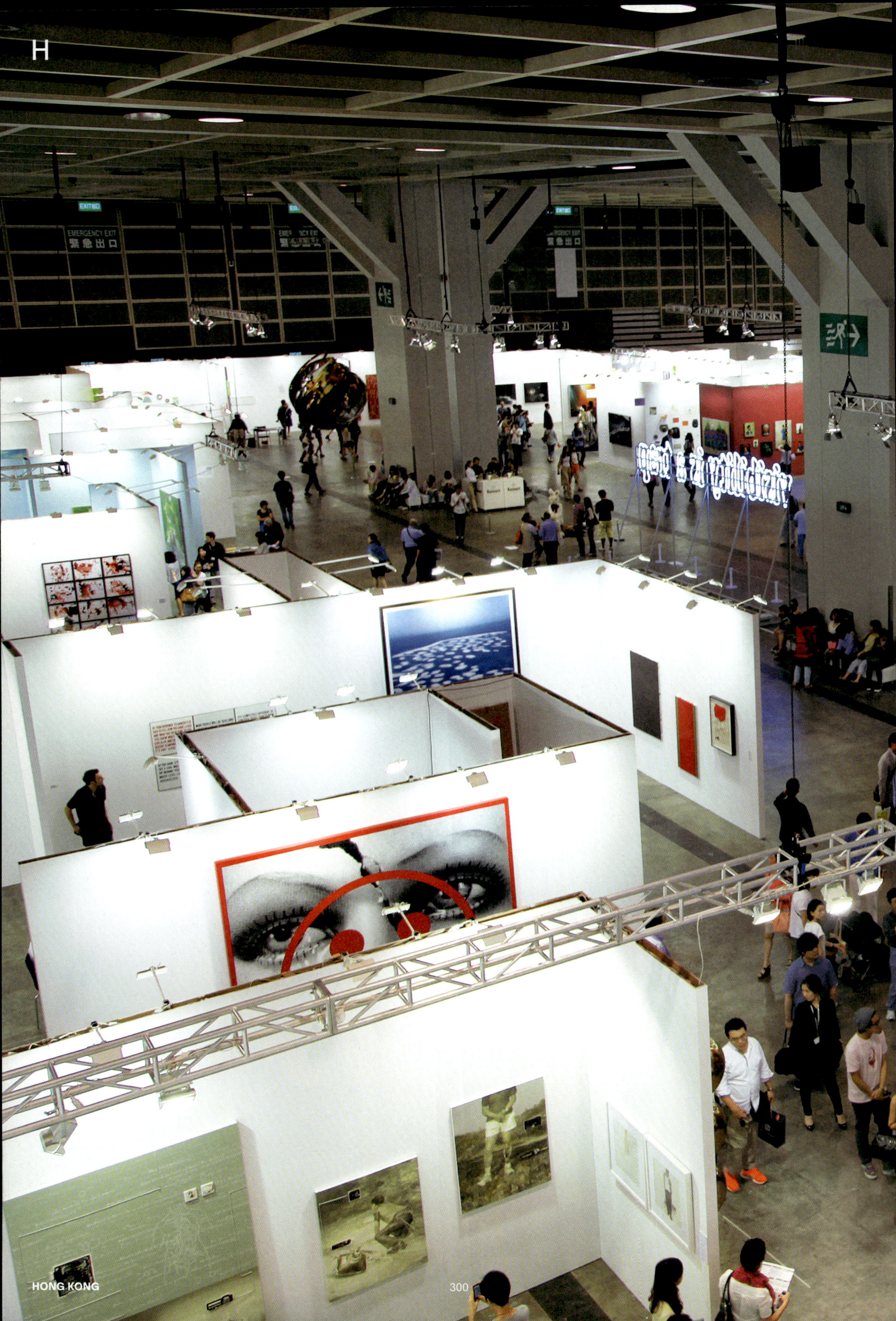

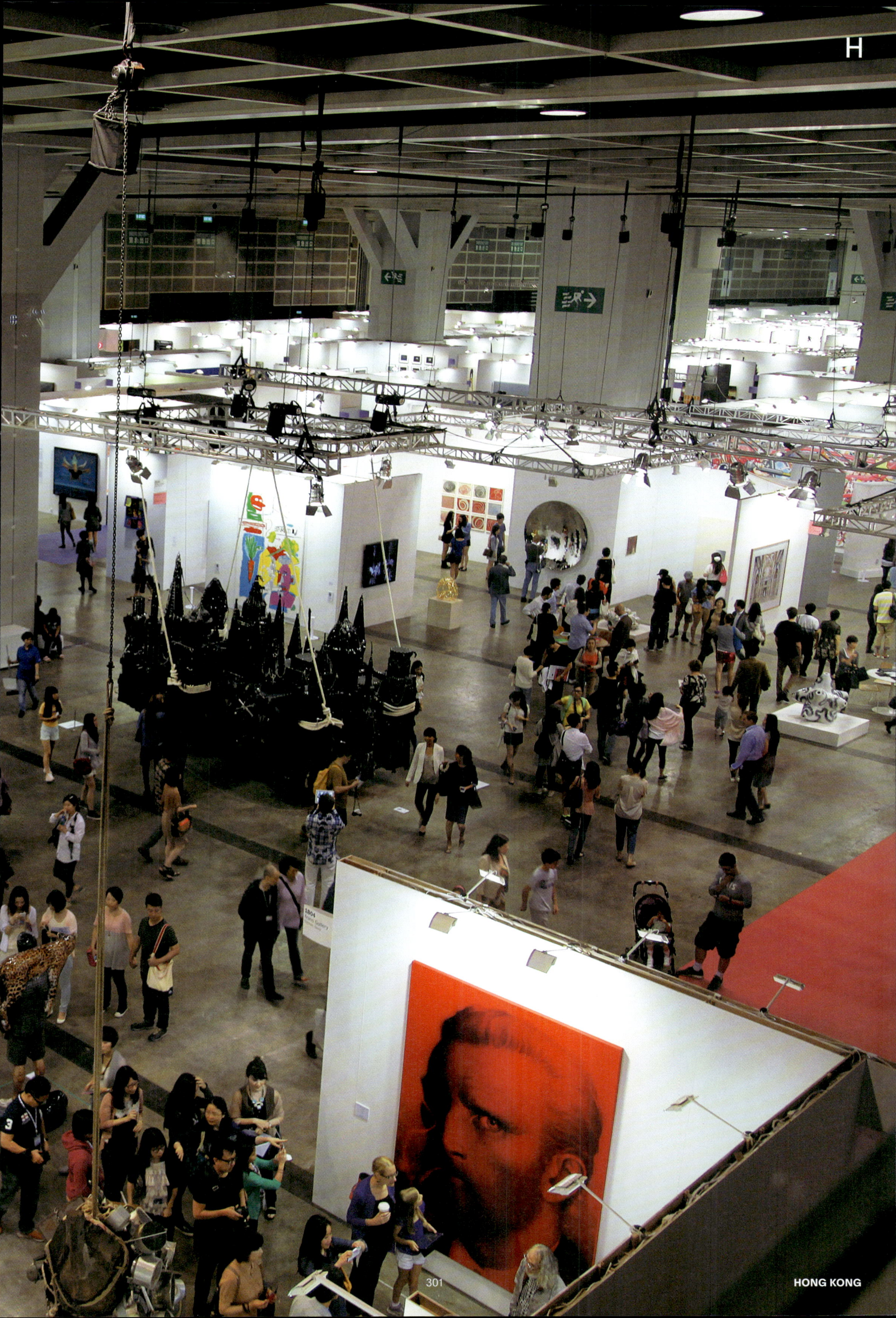

Wako Works of Art

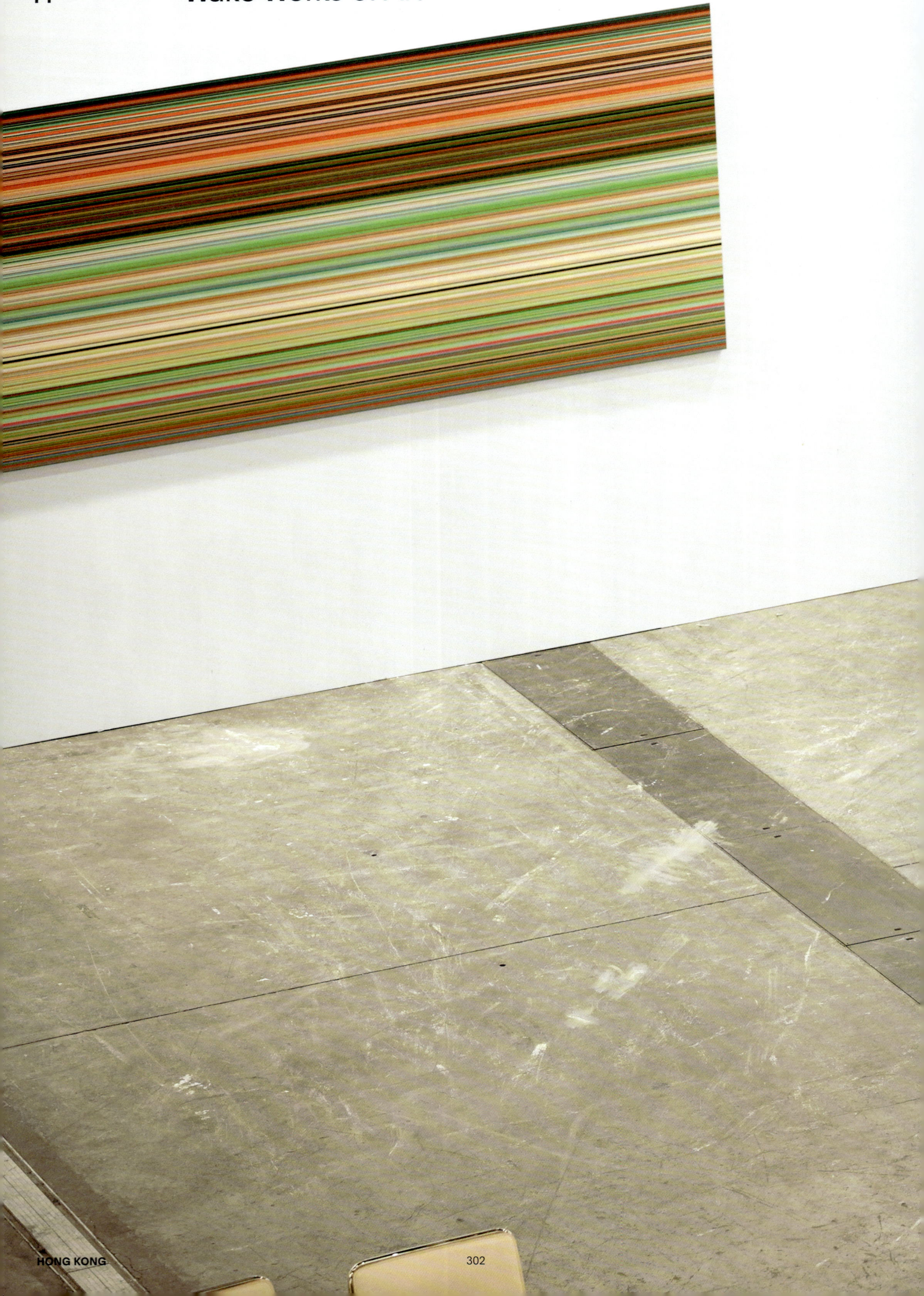

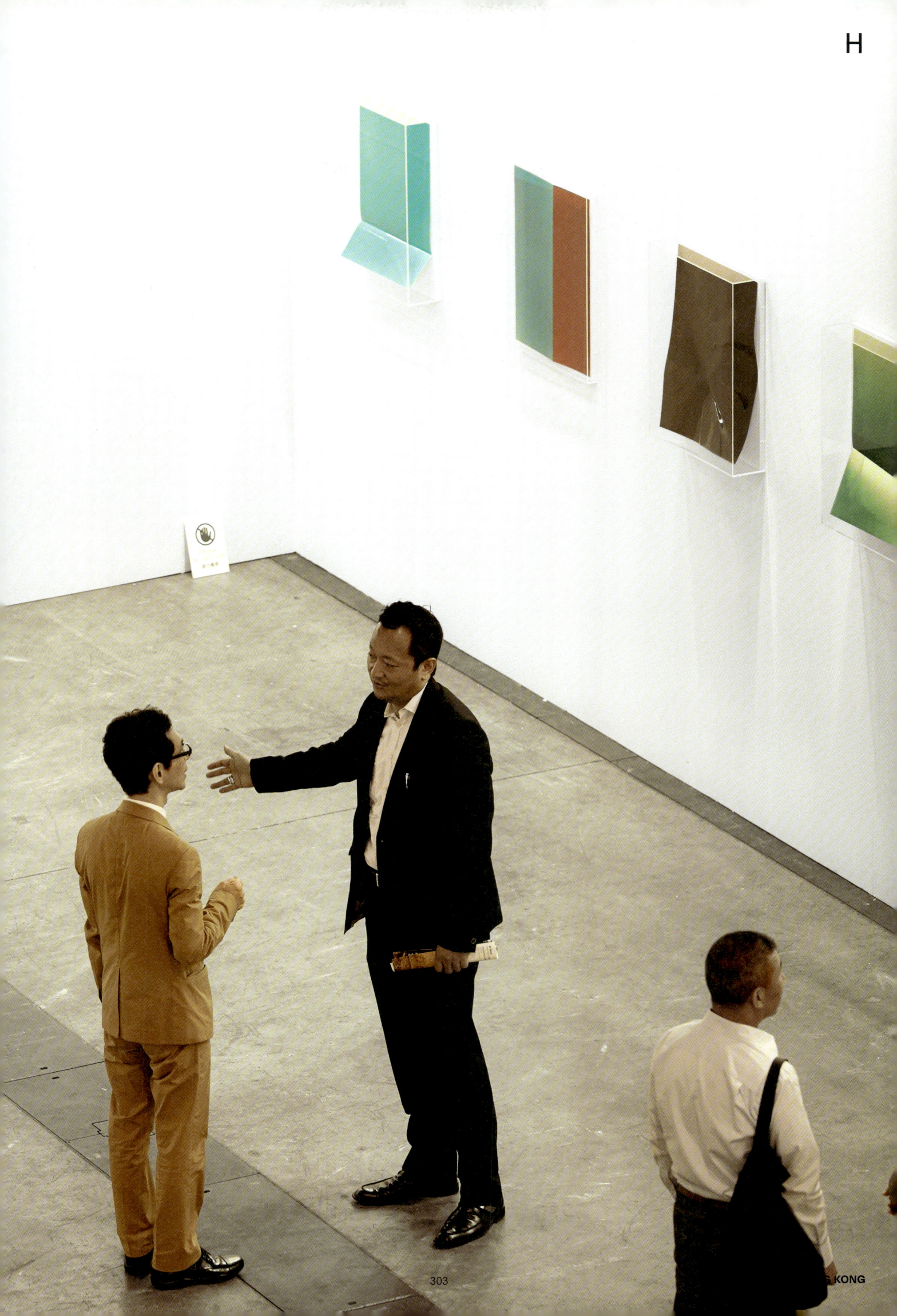

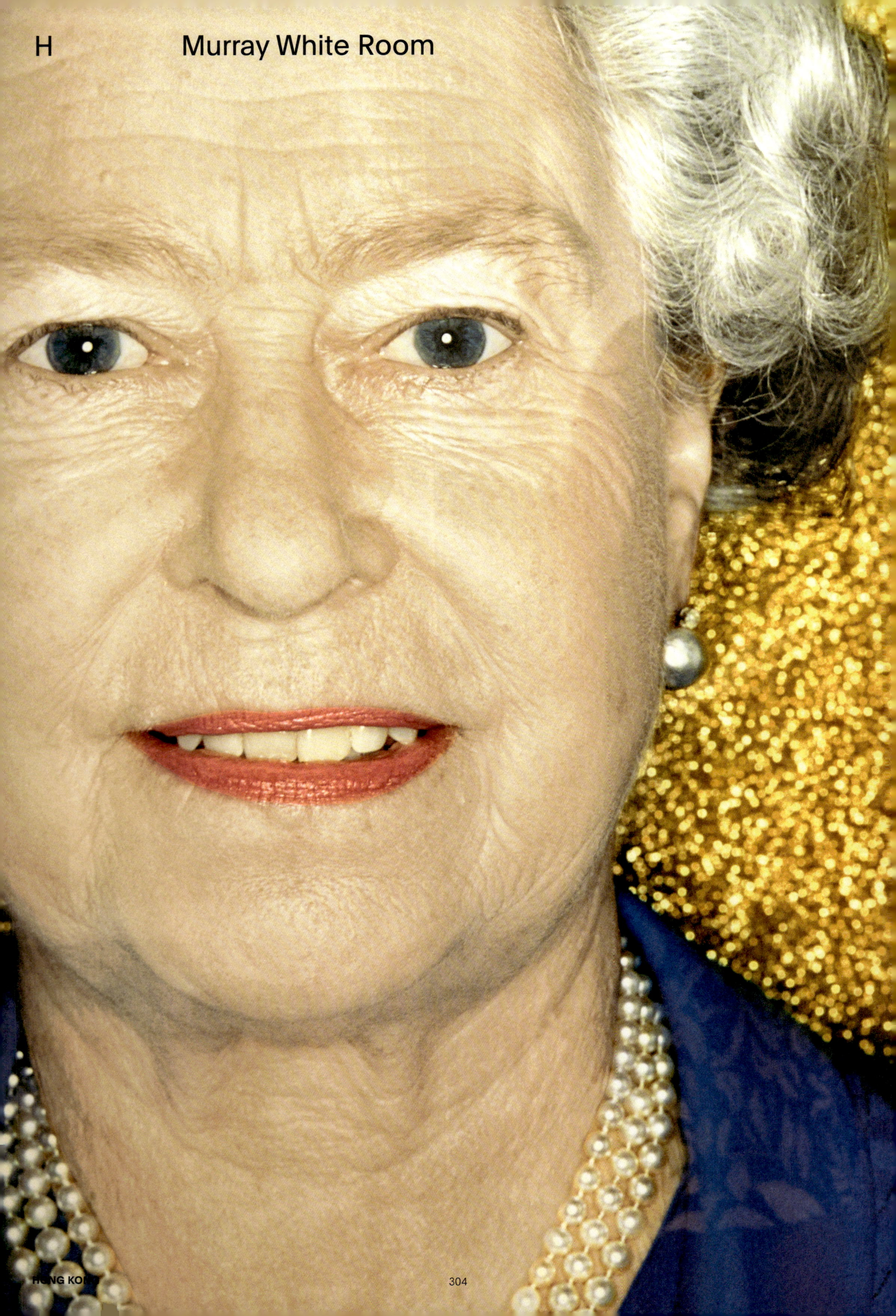

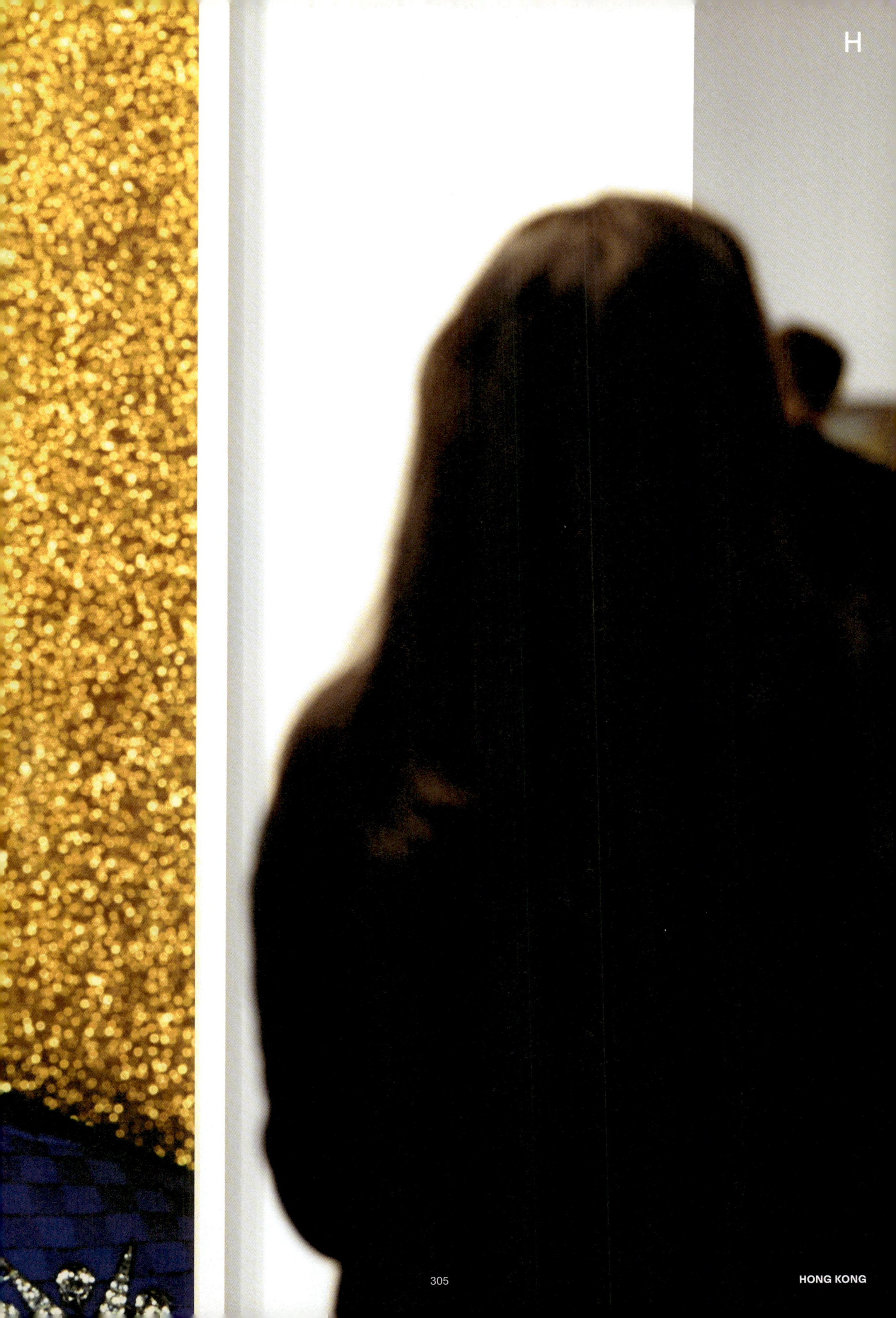

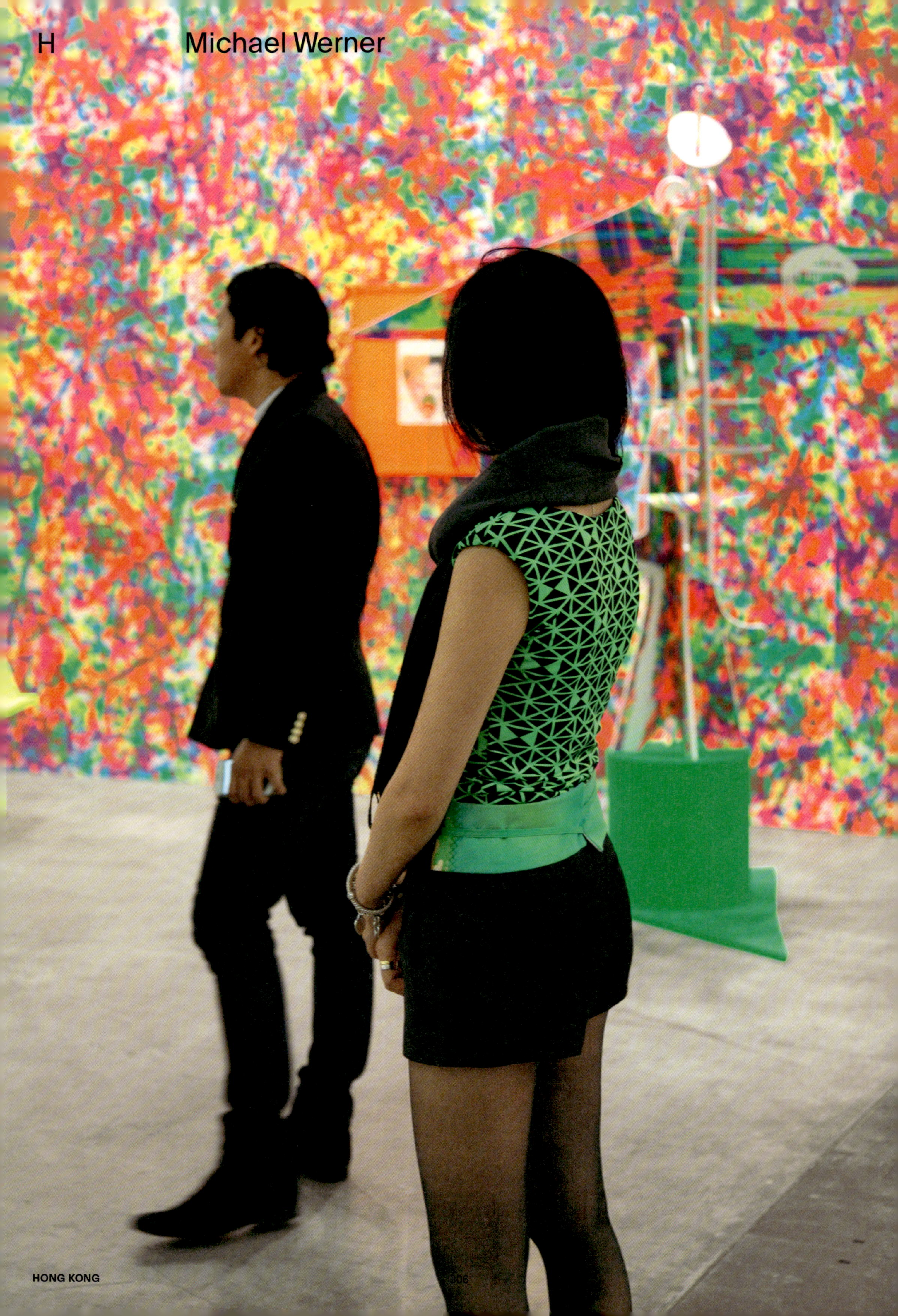

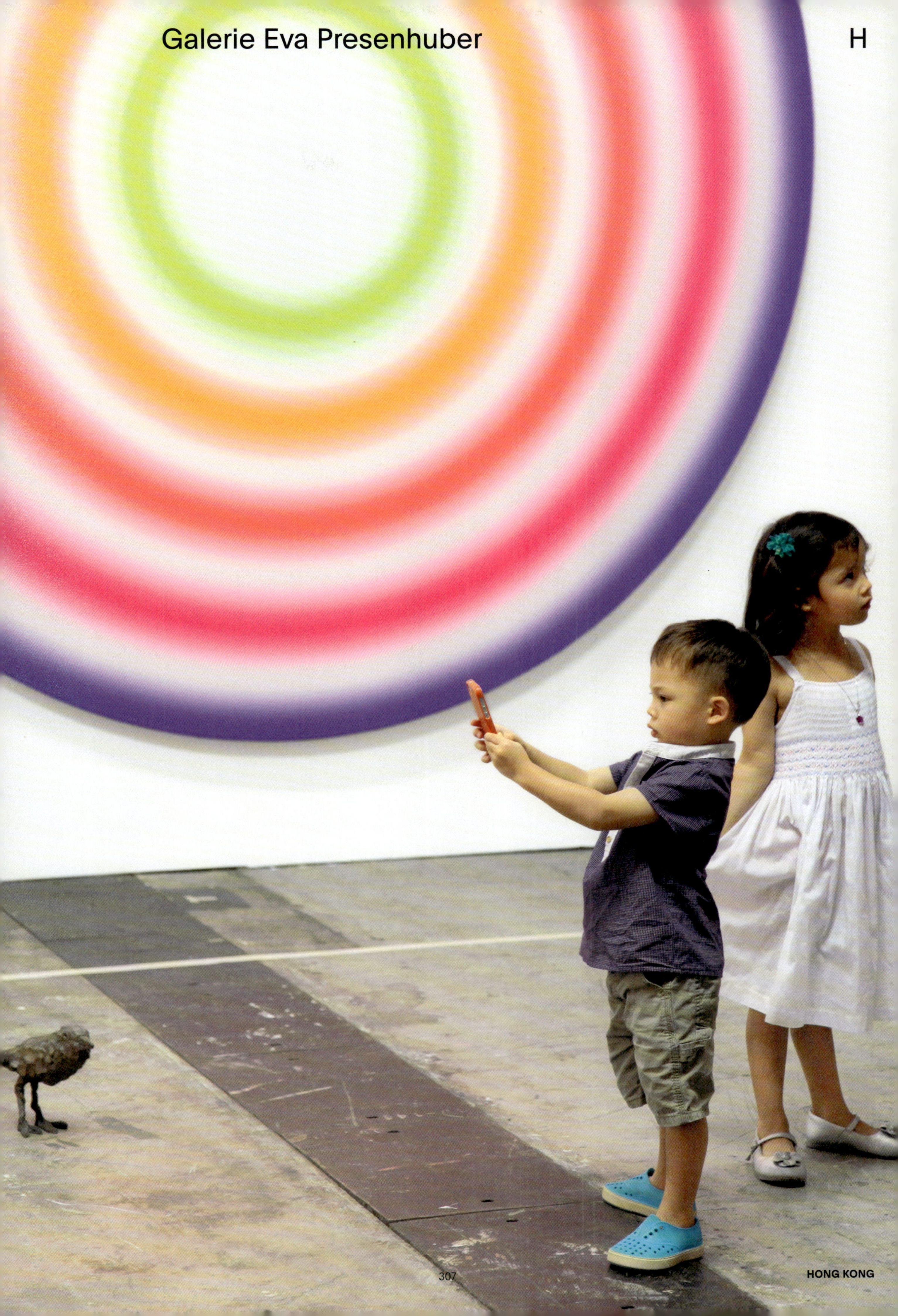

Victoria Miro/Ota Fine Arts

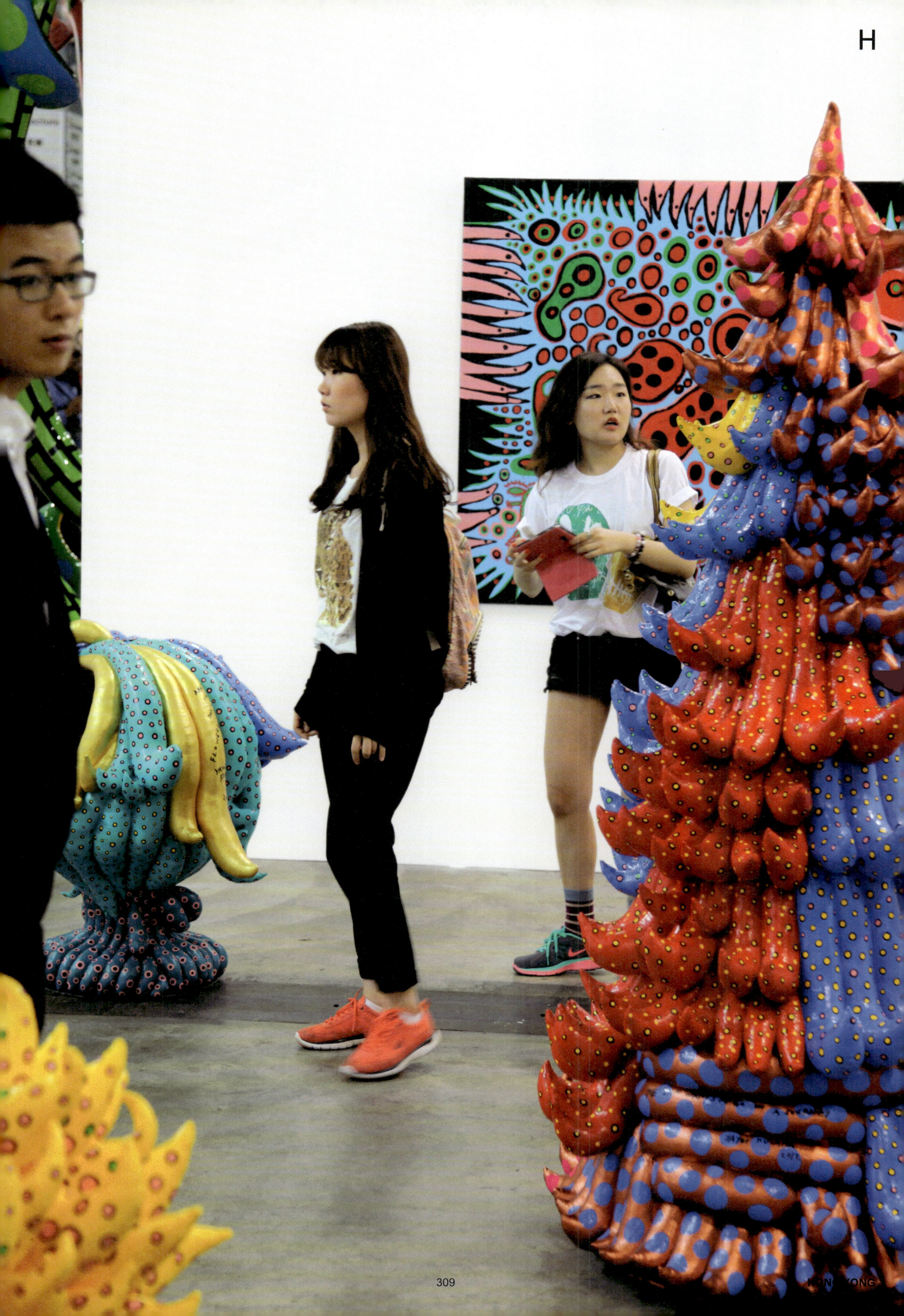

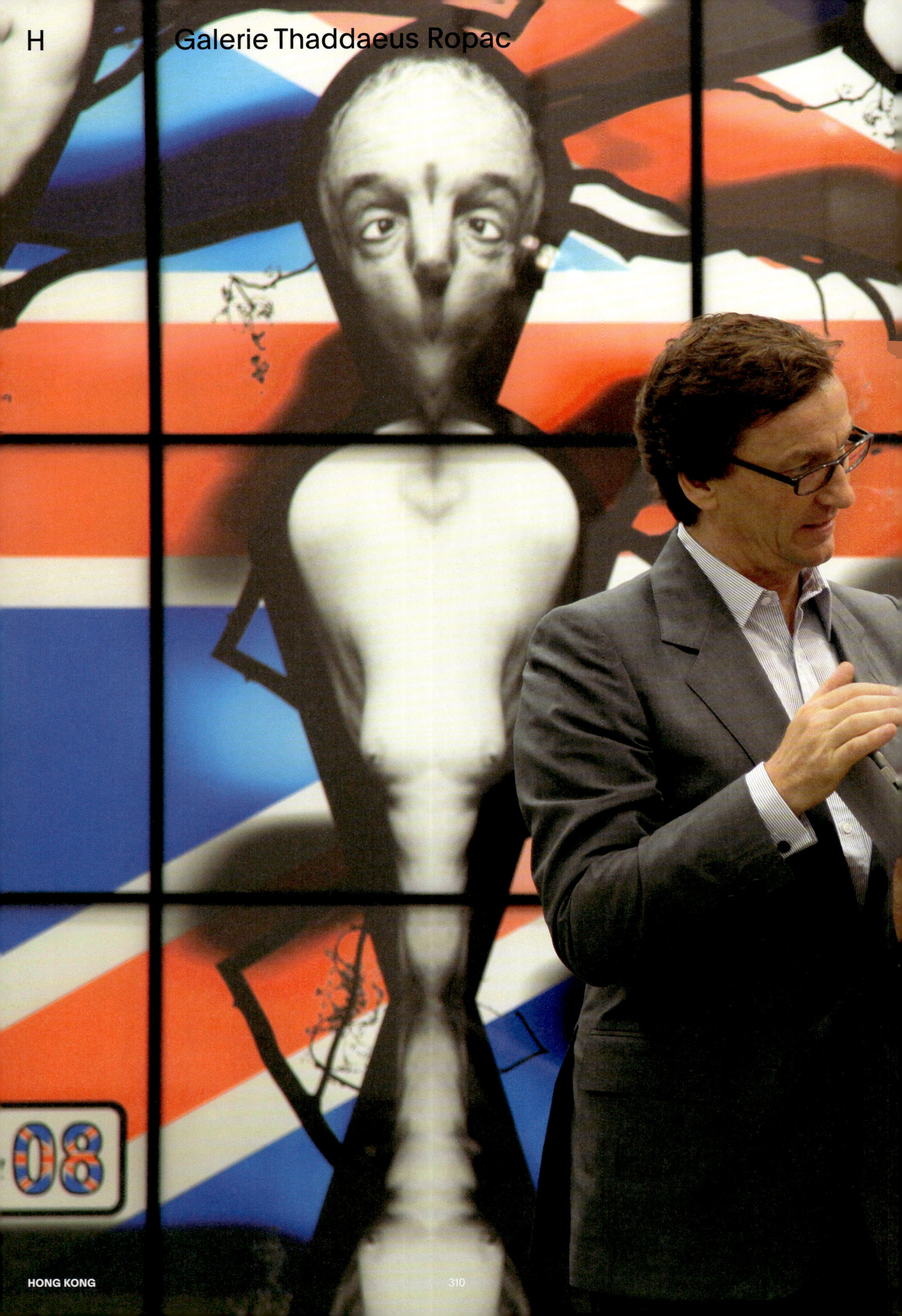
08

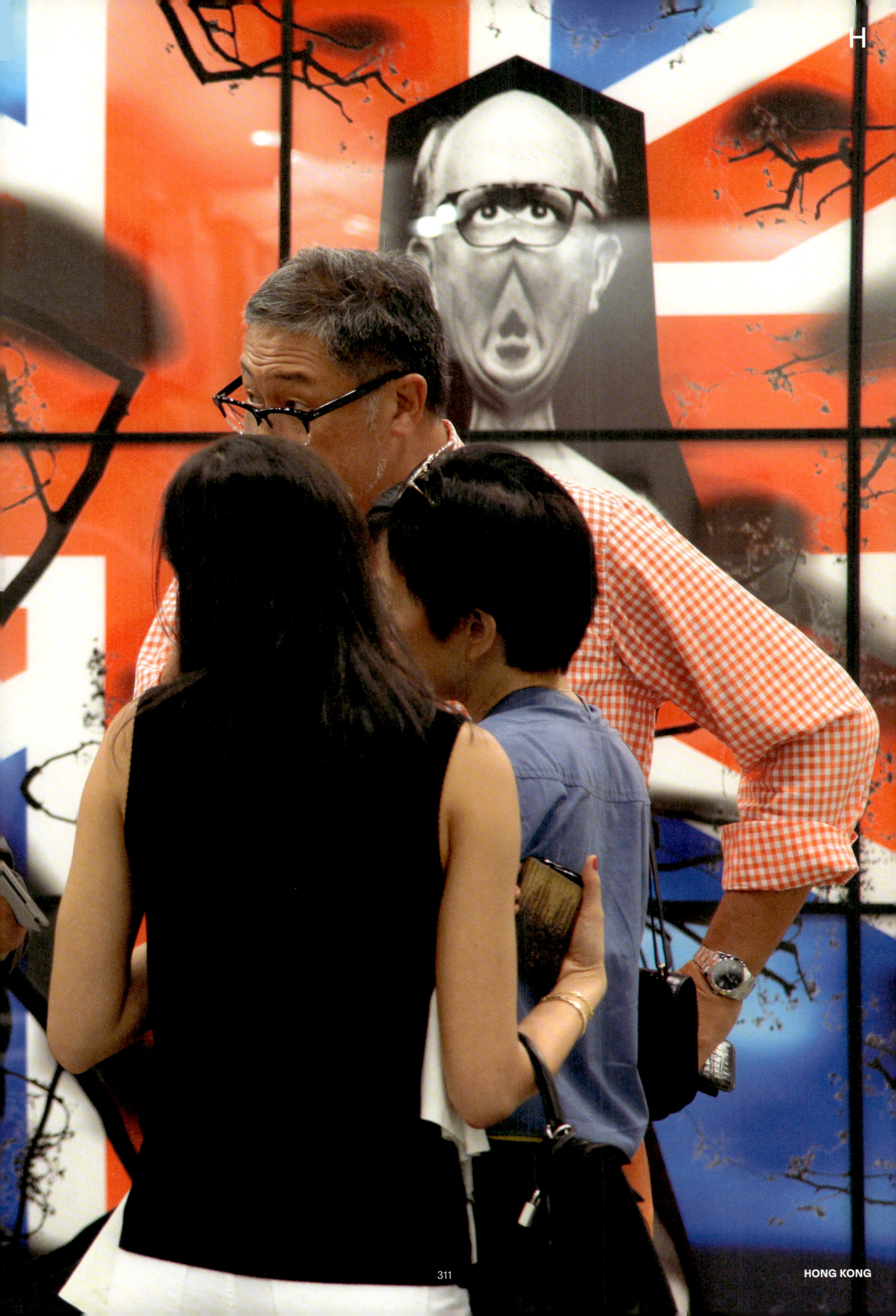

Sies + Höke

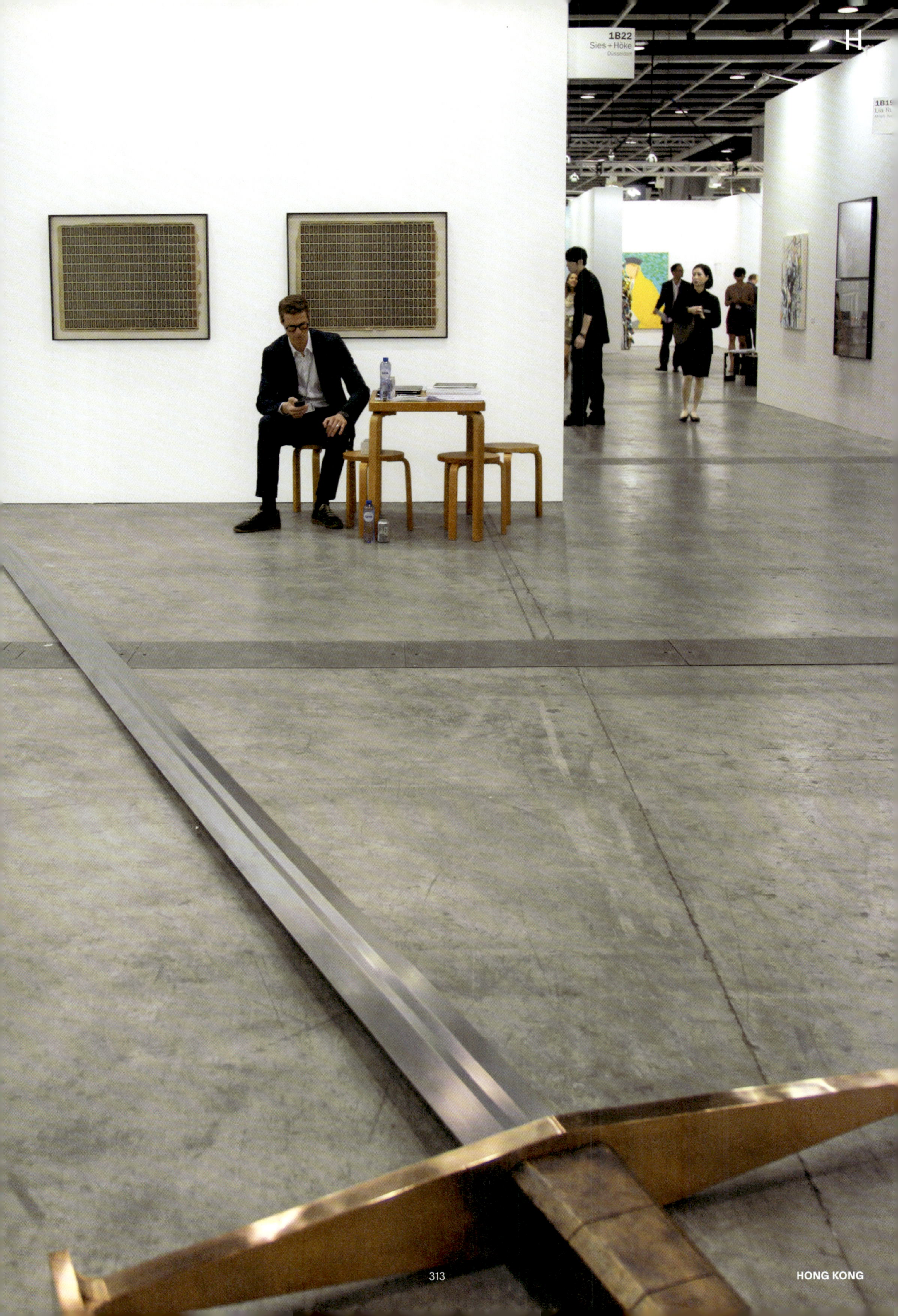
1B22
Sies + Höke
Düsseldorf

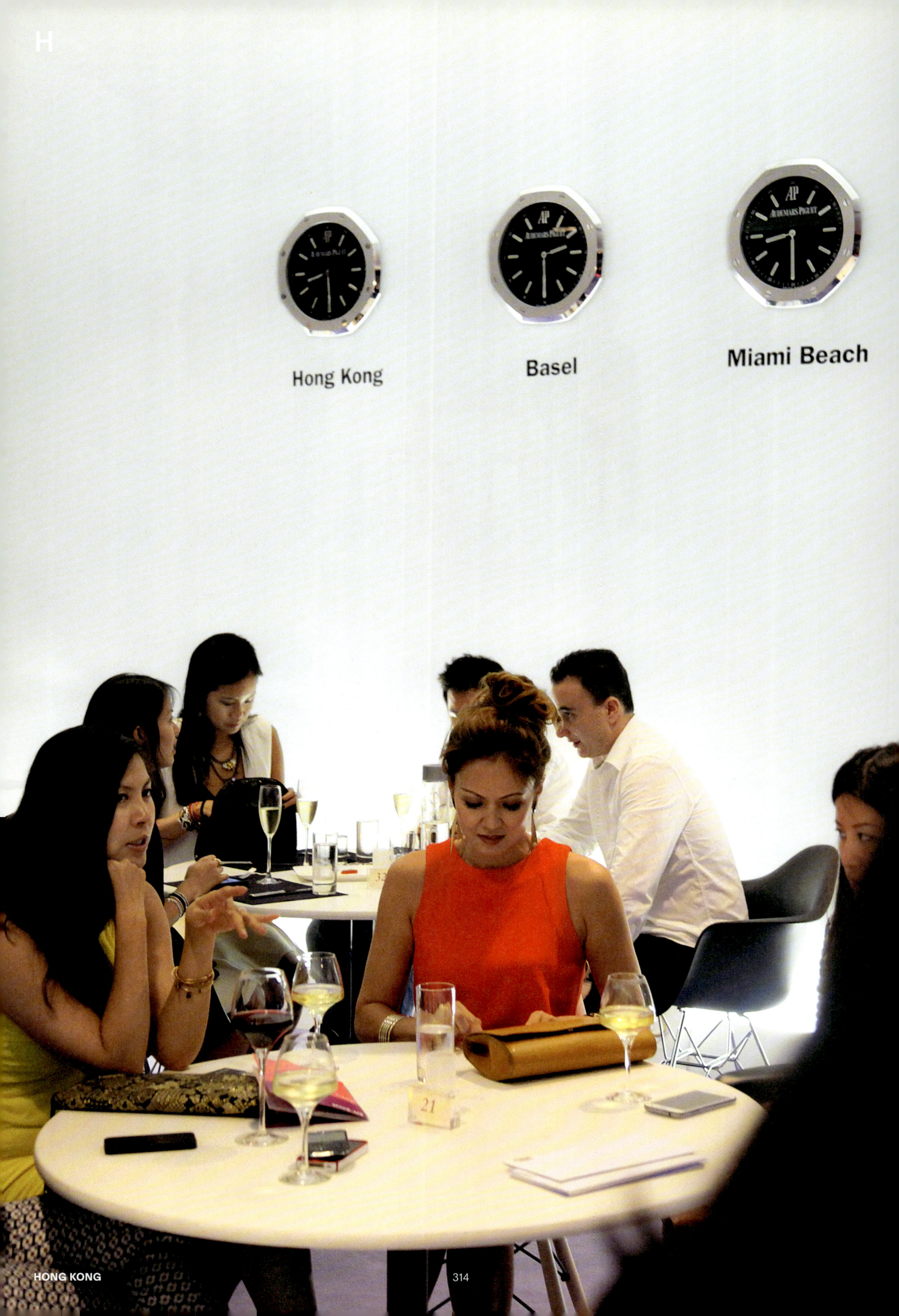
Hong Kong
Basel
Miami Beach

HOME GROWN

Talent

Hong Kong: Homegrown Talent
Chow Chun Fai, Linda Lai, Ho Sin Tung, Adrian Wong, and Pauline J. Yao

Conversations
Homegrown Talent

Art Basel in Hong Kong
May 19, 2013

Chow Chun Fai, Artist, Hong Kong

Linda Lai, Artist & Associate Professor, School of Creative Media, City University, Hong Kong

Ho Sin Tung, Artist, Hong Kong

Adrian Wong, Artist, Hong Kong

Moderator: Pauline J. Yao, Curator, M+, Hong Kong

A complete version of the conversation is available at www.artbasel.com

PAULINE J. YAO It's often said that there is an absence of value attached to specific places in contemporary cultural life, and this might be especially true in the art world, which is often viewed as global, increasingly virtual, or even placeless. The *début* of Art Basel in Hong Kong is but one example of the global reach of today's art world. And yet I have to think that Art Basel in Hong Kong forces a confrontation with its locals in ways that differ from Art Basel in Miami Beach perhaps, or even Art Basel. It certainly stems from an appreciation of difference and a desire to recognize that Hong Kong has its own legacy of artistic production. It might also have to do with a Hong Kong sort of "topophilia," a strong sense of place (or even of love for place), which overwhelmingly becomes mixed with a sense of cultural identity. So, even if we admit that generally the power of place is increasingly diminished, and occasionally lost, here it certainly thrives with implications that are quite complex, if only because this city is a space of transit that has become a permanent home for many.

This topic and its subtext of locality and specificity can be approached with two kinds of perspectives and interpretations. The first relates to the individual: the person, the producer in this case, or artist, as someone being deemed homegrown because of the nature of his/her upbringing or background. The other might be "homegrown" in terms of process: something owing to the space in which it's produced. My interest is to focus on the latter.

Place is both temporal and spatial, personal and political, and comes layered with histories and memories that run wide and deep. In all discussions of place, it is a question of abstraction and specifics; if art is defined as universal, or form is valued over content, then artists might be encouraged to transcend their local, or shed their locality. If we look at it as content, prime material, then certainly this notion of regionalism, or localism, wouldn't be seen as a limitation, but as an advantage.

So, what I wanted to do today is to explore the ways in which ideas that originate in this place are materialized in this place, and to what extent these artists and others evaluate aspects of their working practice, their chosen medium, their relationship to material, and ultimately, by extension, their roles as artist in this place.

Chow Chun Fai is a Fine Arts graduate from the Chinese University of Hong Kong. Chow is an active member of the Fotanian Art Village (www.fotanian.org), a visiting lecturer at several different universities, and is best known for his paintings of street scenes. Chow Chun has also been involved in a variety of projects, one of which is *Painting On and On*, an artist-initiated project looking at evolving local artists, and in organizing group exhibitions, seminars, and publications.

Linda Lai has a PhD in Cinema Studies from NYU, and is now a professor in the school of Creative Media in Hong Kong, as a historian and multidisciplinary artist. Her experimental videos and digital installations are often made from found footage, and involve notions of historiography, auto-ethnography, urban studies, and archiving.

Ho Sin Tung, born here in Hong Kong, has also graduated from the Chinese University Fine Arts Department. Her work consists predominantly of drawings, using found and readymade images, maps, charts, and timelines, and involves a combination of imagined and real places.

Adrian Wong was born in Chicago, graduated from Stanford University, and studied sculpture at Yale University. He is best known for installations, sculptures, and videos that uncover lost or hidden histories, and examine the vibe between reality and myth. Interested in modes of narrative and story telling, Wong's background draws him to performed acts of excavation, narration, and flirtation with the unknown. He will be hosting the *Wun Dun* bar during this week of the fair.

I would like to ask each of you to say something about the working methods that you think define your own practice and how they relate to where you live. And in particular, is your practice studio-based, non studio-based? Are you working independently or do you work with others, and in what kind of ways?

CHOW CHUN FAI I will use only four minutes to tell four stories. The first one is that I was a taxi driver. Owning a taxi license in Hong Kong is crazy. Today, if you were to buy one it would be about seven billion Hong Kong dollars! This experience taught me a lot about how to run a business, how to communicate with others, and how to face the reality of the city.

The second is that I have a studio in Fo Tan, an industrial area in the new territories. This is quite significant because you can tell from the local art history that in the 1990s not many artists had a studio. All you could see in the art scene were installations, performances—because there weren't spaces to produce works. You had to install the things at a venue and then you just threw them away after the show. Of course, before us, there were artists working in factories, but maybe we are the first group loud enough to organize some open studios events, so now even the general public recognize us as the Fotanian—as a group of artists working in former factories.

The third story: I am said to be part of the first generation who can be full-time artists in Hong Kong. This is horrible. The debate was that if you want to be professional then you have to be a full-time artist. I don't think this is a very good measure to decide who is an artist. I wanted to tell this story because the art fair is coming here, and working with galleries now has become a common phenomenon in Hong Kong.

The fourth story: I ran the election for the Hong Kong Legislative Council. When I ran the election—well, I gave up all my work last year, and spent the whole year running the election, I didn't declare that this was an art piece, because if I declared that this was some kind of performance, all the audience would just watch it as a performance, and not as a serious election. For me it was also a very local experience, because when you talk about politics, it *has* to be local.

LINDA LAI I think I'm a very typical homegrown Hong Kong person, in the sense that I have done all those typical things that the Hong Kong kids who might have a flair for art would do: I joined a studio, I learned painting, and would do teacher-student exhibitions, I trained in music, joined a choir, and was very into theater when I was an undergraduate student. But in fact, one or two semesters of oil painting really put me off, and something else took me away from theater.

There's a 20-year gap between those days and when I started self-consciously working on artworks

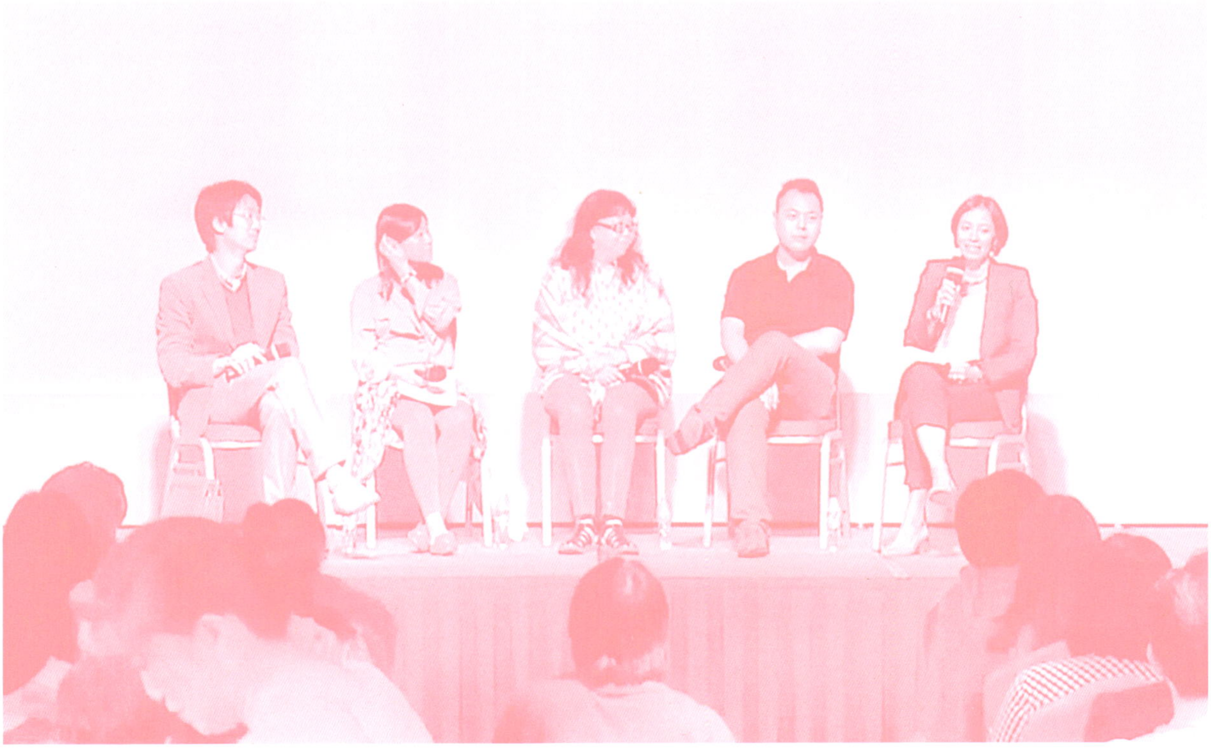

From left to right: Adrian Wong, Ho Sin Tung, Linda Lai, Chow Chun Fai, Pauline J. Yao

H

and felt I was an artist. I was hired to teach creative writing at the School of Creative Media. And something happened. I had to criticize my students' works day and night, and suddenly I felt: "It seems I have all the ideas and principles to make them artists and I'm not making anything."

The first thought that came to my mind was to make a movie. I wanted to do something about my grandmother. I always carried a camera, all those years, so, when I started to think of this in 2002, I already had ten years of video footage with me. Video diaries made without any purpose most of the time. So I started to look at these images as a stranger. Wonderful things came up. I felt I was studying another person's life.

I don't work in a studio: I collect things. I'm like a gleaner of my own images in everyday life. Gleaner of found footage—I love Hong Kong movies although they are banal, disgusting, sometimes really horrible, but I love looking at them. That gives me a lot of material to hand. I cut out all these locations shots, and save them.

It might have to do with a Hong Kong sort of "topophilia," a strong sense of place (or even of love for place), which overwhelmingly becomes mixed with a sense of cultural identity. — Pauline J. Yao

This is how I get the chance to look at Hong Kong in the past and the swift changes that take place every day in the city space. I hope this portrays the kind of ecology that I wanted to suggest about what is homegrown and how to respond to what you have. I think that when I didn't try very hard to be a good artist, I became a better artist.

HO SIN TUNG I want to begin with how I started painting in the first place. I was three years old and I had just decided to learn painting … All the kids were going to painting classes in their neighborhoods. And, just downstairs from my house there was a painting studio organized by a quite established painter. Of course, my parents and I didn't know him. That was simply the closest painting studio to my house. It offered me quite a different education from the classic

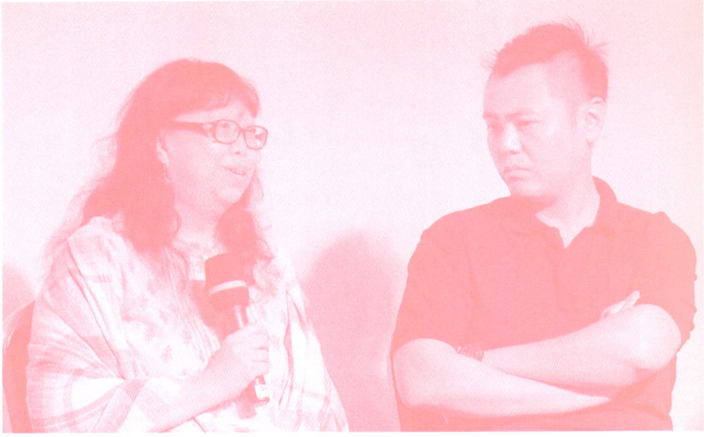

Linda Lai and Chow Chun Fai

Hong Kong one. Already as a kid, they gave me a big canvas to work on without any specific topic, so you had to think of who you are, what you want to say, and what are you trying to do with your own little space and your own little world. I never had any intention to use Hong Kong as a subject of my work. I think this is just the result of being an artist: I simply capture things that seem strong to me. Many of my references are Western literature and Western movies. I never consider myself typical Hong Kong. But when I was around ten years old, my family moved to Sheung Shui, the most northern part of Hong Kong, very very close to China. I still live there now. My house is far away from everything in Hong Kong; going to China is closer for me than to go to the center of the city. Living there is an interesting experience because you know a lot of mainland people coming to Hong Kong and this experience got into me. You have a strong feeling that your home and the things around you keep changing, not according to your needs but to other people's needs, the mainland and urban planning. You get the feeling that the place you are in, the place you have memory in, keeps disappearing. You have a fear of losing your own language, and the fear of losing your memory and place. This is one of the reasons why I started doing maps in the first place.

ADRIAN WONG I'm not from here. I grew up in Chicago, and came here on vacation in 2005 and I've been here for eight years. I found a haunted studio at 50% off and signed a two-year lease, thinking that I could just walk away. The first thing that really made me fall in love with Hong Kong is its inexpensive wood. In the States, wood costs were really escalating, and as a sculptor who works quite large, this was a big issue! So, I was really kind of in hog heaven …

I'm quite transient: I travel a lot, I teach in the United States, but I keep coming back because I started to glean bits of the culture. I am ethnically Chinese, my mother and my father were born in Hong Kong, but were both estranged from their families, so I used that as an excuse to dig into my own genealogy and absorb a culture that I had no real access to. I am fascinated by the place, but I don't entertain any sort of fantasy that this is who I am.

PJY One thing I wanted to discuss, and, Adrian, you mentioned it very practically, is the materials and access to them. I realized when putting this group of people together, that we have Adrian who works primarily in sculpture, Ho Sin Tung doing primarily drawings, Linda predominantly working in video, and Chow Chun working primarily in painting. So we have a kind of representation of all these different media, but at the same time all of you have not only done things that are outside that comfort zone, but in some cases combined and worked across media.

Chow Chun Fai, I think of your paintings and how they are embedded with film. And Adrian, some of your sculptural works involve some kind of theatrical and performative parts. There's a kind of crossing over, and a kind of "intermedia" maybe, but not so much in the sense of being new media as much as it is crossing these disciplines or areas. How have you settled on a particular media that you work in? And when you're coming up with certain concepts, ideas, what is the chosen avenue for that sort of manifestation?

AW I was originally trained as a social scientist. I left a psychology program to become a sculptor. The initial outlet for a lot of my projects has been theater, but I became more and more interested in reality. For example, for the bar that I'm producing with Absolut Art Bureau, I thought initially to stage the entire thing as a theatrical production. We were hiring professional actors and singers to portray characters that I found to be emblematic of this city. For budgetary reasons and difficulties in managing such a large cast, I decided to actually cast people in the bar … as themselves. So now, our bathroom attendant is the security guard from my apartment complex and the maître d' is the captain of the Star Ferry that goes across the harbor. I was looking for an awkward waiter and we were auditioning to find somebody who could play a sort of mix between Buster Keaton and Goofy the dog, but we thought, "well, we want a goofy waiter, let's go to some restaurant and find one!" I think a lot of the things about bridging boundaries allows me to approach these projects through the techniques of research that I've learned in a different field, as a psychologist, to plum out the little nugget of interests that I'm stopping at as I just go through my daily life.

I am fascinated by the place, but I don't entertain any sort of fantasy that this is who I am. — Adrian Wong

CCF Two things are affecting my choice of media. The first one is my training. I studied at the Chinese University in Hong Kong, which is not like in the Central Academy in China: we learn everything, from brush and ink to landscape, and then two hours later we do installation, then oil painting. So, when I pick up the brush, I always ask myself why should I pick up oil as a medium? I could always do something else. The other thing is space. Even though I now have my own studio, and many artists have a shared studio in the industrial area, space is still very limited. Space is always the biggest issue in Hong Kong. Not only because of the cost but also because of who owns it. Space is something that affects our working process and even our practice.

HST I do videos and sometimes installations, drawings, and I also have a column in the newspaper. I never really use a medium to set boundaries to myself, but when people introduce me, they need this kind of label. Usually I am described as a painter who uses pencil, and that's sort of true, because I mostly use pencil as my medium. I think pencil offers a very intimate relationship with the material. When I use pencil, I feel like I am at a desk, writing something. When I first started making my artwork, I never considered anything like an audience. So it's like the relationship of writing a letter to someone, and the audience is sort of an extra to me.

LL I consider myself an intermedia artist, and intermedia is actually a very important principle in my work. I guess that for the sake of communicating myself to others, I would say that I'm primarily a montage artist, working with moving images. One test for each work I make is always where it goes. The works I like the best are those that happen to be accepted in different places. For example, a film I made was accepted as an experimental film in an experimental film festival, but has also been accepted as a documentary in a documentary film festival. In editing my videos, I often bring in things from other disciplines, from ethnography for instance, or from generative art, calculation, formalism.

Things need to gestate; sometimes they match together and evolve in different things. It's exciting to work together artistically to spring forth out of that and to kind of dump things into the world that maybe won't necessarily come from a particular category.

AUDIENCE I'm from Switzerland where young artists often start their practice by forming groups, even running a space together. Additionally, they travel constantly, creating new relations between these groups. I wonder if you do the same, and if you travel, where do you go? Are there a lot of collective practices, collaborations between young artists?

CCF I used to have a studio in Beijing. I rented it for three years and then they wanted to clear the artists out in 2010, so I moved back to Hong Kong. I saw the differences, too. When I dropped into my friends' studios in Beijing, sometimes I saw ten assistants mixing the paint, and the other ten assistants doing the ceramics, while in Hong Kong there isn't the space. Instead, you would cooperate with a partner, a contractor for instance.

Adrian Wong

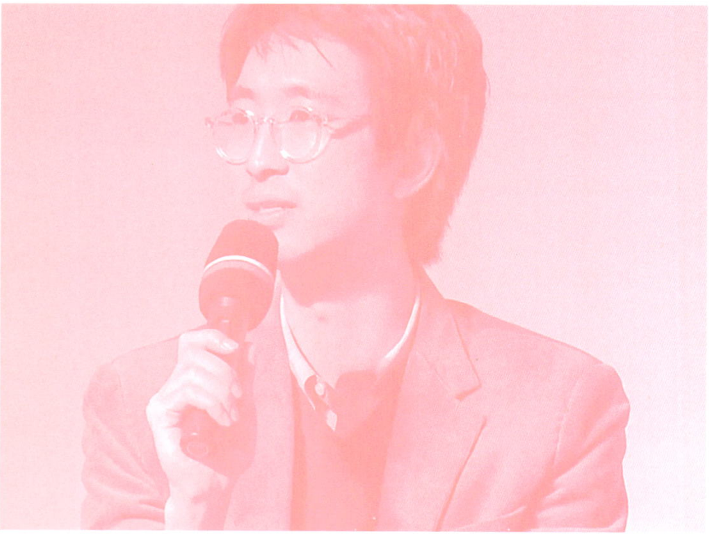

AW There's a sense of community today. I think Fotan has a strong art scene. It allows emerging artists, mid-career artists, late-career artists to have a space to meet, to interact. Its open studios bring the whole city together once a year. There's also the Foo Tak building in Wan Chai district. There are some very strong communities that are forming, some around galleries' programs. Until recently, Hong Kong has not been a place that offered a large enough community or a large enough flow of international artists to stay here and remain engaged and excited as an artist. But we are bouncing around; there's a fair amount of back and forth between here and, say, Singapore, Tokyo, Bangkok, Taipei, and obviously Beijing, Shanghai.

LL I just noticed that in the past few years most of my media art students who graduate form groups. This might be a trend that will continue. There are more and more new festivals, grants available, and actually in terms of resources this might be the best time I have seen so far in Hong Kong! Still, students like to go overseas: they are not only aiming to show their works locally—also because all the major media art festivals are outside Hong Kong. To begin with Asian soil: South Korea, Singapore, Taiwan—these are places we all want to go to.

AUDIENCE I have a question about censorship. What do you think about this as an issue for your work to be displayed in Hong Kong or China?

CCF I play with that. I always say I'm doing experiments to test censorship. I just did a work about the Tiananmen incident. I cannot show that work in China. But I wanted to test what would happen in Hong Kong, so I tried to apply that painting to different occasions. It was accepted by a gallery, but it was rejected by the Hong Kong Biennale. I tried to show it at the University, and finally it sold to Switzerland. For me, the work could be considered finished when it is exhibited on the mainland. When reporters ask for images, I try to send this painting. I tried to send it to a mainland magazine, but of course it was censored. I then sent a portrait of me with the painting in the background. The work just hides in my back, so it finally became public on the mainland. But somehow this is also due to self-censorship, hiding the work in my back …

HST Usually my work is not so political, but I had a show right after Ai Weiwei was taken away, so I did a picture of him and also a picture of the Hong Kong government. The art space didn't censor the Ai Weiwei work, but they did try to censor the Hong Kong government painting, because they said it's not very appropriate to have a show here and criticize the government. They wanted to take the painting away, and of course I refused. The owner of the space sent the image to a lot of different organizations in Hong Kong and asked people, "How do you feel as a Hong Kong person looking at a painting that criticizes the Hong Kong government?" and actually a lot of people said, "We feel very pleased that people criticize their own government, we are very happy to see that." So they finally showed the painting. I don't consider my paintings to be political, but I use some materials from Chinese news and it actually got shown in China without problems. I think they didn't have time to really look at the painting and just visually it seems okay, so it gets through each time.

LL I normally like to play within safe constraints. I have very strong political opinions, but I try not to make them too explicit. For a recent work, I did a lot of research on the postwar history of Hong Kong and I turned that into numbers, into how much people had spent, in money but also in purchasing materials, to send back to mainland China. It's ironic, about the position of Hong Kong regarding the whole story of the Cultural Revolution, as it shows how actually it is us, our energy, our money, and our time, especially by women in a domestic space, who sustained the spirit of people in mainland China.

I was very pleased that a lot of older people liked the work, while younger people didn't know that I was criticizing anything ... The most recent censorship I encountered was with the 19th Hong Kong experimental film and video festival: everything was planned, a catalogue was produced, and at the last minute the whole festival was scrapped. The organizers got a series of phone calls from people who were participating who withdrew from the event. So there was not a trace of evidence that it had been censored, but it was. We didn't know what was going on, except that it was somehow related to Ai Weiwei. Ai Weiwei's work made the authorities realize that all independent work can be subversive.

It's ironic, about the position of Hong Kong regarding the whole story of the Cultural Revolution, as it shows how actually it is us, our energy, our money, and our time, especially by women in a domestic space, who sustained the spirit of people in mainland China.
— Linda Lai

I

- Hong Kong
- Basel
- Miami Beach

i8

Reykjavik

Galleries

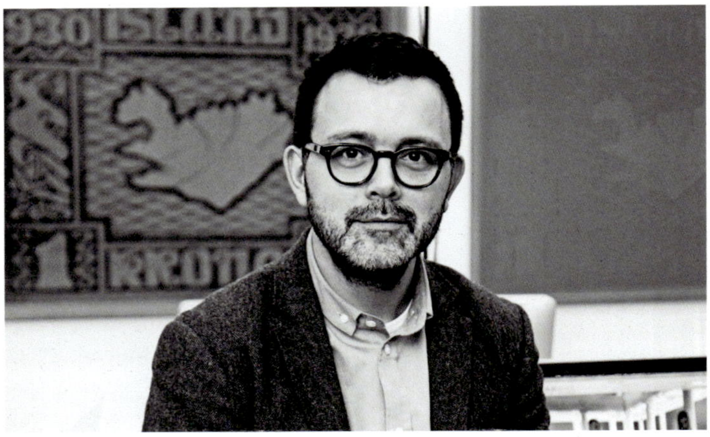

What first compelled you to open a gallery?
When we first opened the gallery in 1995, there were no commercial contemporary art galleries in Reykjavik. Edda, an artist at the time, had become increasingly interested in showing international artists in Reykjavik, and for the first years this was i8's main focus. Gradually, as the gallery grew, i8 began to bring Icelandic artists to the international stage as well. More than half of the artists we represent today have been with the gallery from the start.

When did you first participate in Art Basel and what was most memorable about that show?
Our first participation in Art Basel was in 2004. We had artists in both Statements and Unlimited sectors. We had great success with one and the other was a complete disaster.

- **Contact** — i8 Gallery
Audur Jorundsdottir
audur@i8.is
info@i8.is
- **Established** — 1995
- **Owner(s) / Partner(s)** — Borkur Arnarson (Owner & Director)
Sigurdur Gisli Palmason (Partner)
Edda Jonsdottir (Partner & Founder)
- **Team** — 6
- **Space(s)** — 250 m²
- **Artists at Art Basel** — Birgir Andresson
Ingolfur Arnarsson
Margrét H. Blöndal
Olafur Eliasson
Janice Kerbel
Ragnar Kjartansson
Ernesto Neto
- **Further artists represented** — Hreinn Fridfinnsson
Kristjan Gudmundsson
Sigurdur Gudmundsson
Elin Hansdottir
Roni Horn
Eggert Petursson
Finnbogi Petursson
Ragna Robertsdottir
Egill Sæbjörnsson
Karin Sander
Hrafnkell Sigurdsson
Ignacio Uriarte
Ivar Valgardsson
Thor Vigfusson
Lawrence Weiner

Ibid

London

Galleries

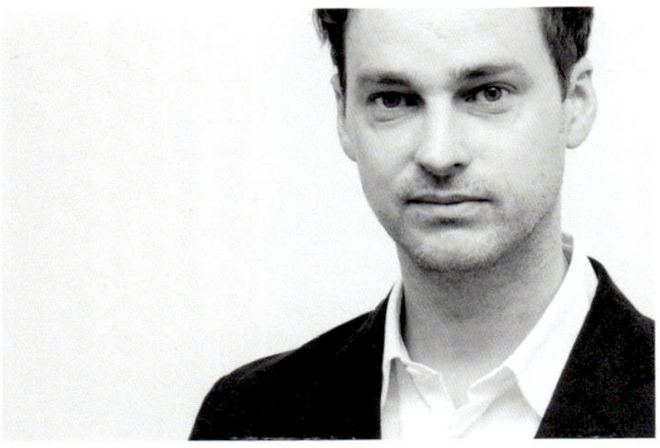

What first compelled you to open a gallery?
Ibid. started while I was still studying at Royal College of Art and it was conceived to seek out artists and positions that had previously not been shown in London or that where under-represented, at the time preliminary artists from Eastern Europe.

Who is the first artist you showed and what was most memorable about that show?
Dan Perjovschi and Nathaniel Mellors, with Perjovschi using the entire gallery as backdrop for his drawings, including floor, ceilings and walls; his hundreds of scribbles and cartoon-like drawings became a diaristic record of the gallery's young history.

When did you first participate in Art Basel and what was most memorable about that show?
It was in the Art Positions sector, a shipping container on the beach at Art Basel in Miami Beach in 2003. It was the gallery's second ever art fair and an interesting experience that suggested that art fairs do not only have to be hosted in corporate convention centers, but that there was room for experimentation to the art fair format.

- **Contact** — Ibid
Magnus Edensvard
magnus@ibidprojects.com
info@ibidprojects.com
- **Established** — 2002
- **Owner(s) / Partner(s)** — Magnus Edensvard
- **Team** — 4
- **Space(s)** — 65 m²
- **Artists at Art Basel** — Chris Burden
Louise Despont
William Hunt
Amir Mogharabi
Carsten Nicolai
Christopher Orr
Michael Part
Christoph Weber
- **Further artists represented** — David Adamo
Jānis Avotiņš
Ross Chisholm
Rallou Panagiotou
Michael Portnoy
Olivier Richon

ifa

Brussels
Shanghai

Insights

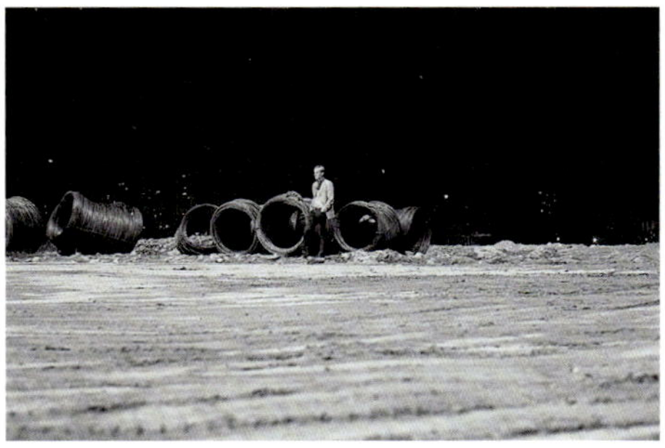

What first compelled you to open a gallery?
I had already been living in China for three years. The art scene was developing at a fast pace,

but very few galleries there had a clear artistic direction. Many artists with talent came to the scene; it was a chance for me to collaborate with them and vice versa. After more than six years in Shanghai, I decided to exhibit them in Europe with a new gallery in Brussels.

Who is the first artist you showed and what was most memorable about that show?
Park Sung Tae, an artist from South Korea. Park has an amazing technique of making sculptures and installation with aluminum screening. We created a huge dark exhibition room with negative lights. Visitors entered in a fantastic world where the sculptures looked like colorful floating ghosts.

When did you first participate in Art Basel and what was most memorable about that show?
At ART HK in 2012 (produced by Art Basel). The fair became a part of Art Basel for the first time. Although the name of the fair did not change for this edition, the entire show was produced by Art Basel, with many changes in the program, new galleries, and important collectors coming from all over the globe. ifa gallery presented a solo show by Dai Guangyu, an exceptional conceptual Chinese artist originally from Sichuan, with paintings, photography of Land art, and a progressive installation that was finalized on the last day with a performance.

• **Contact**	ifa gallery Alexis Kouzmine-Karavaieff alexis@ifa-gallery.com contact@ifa-gallery.com
• **Established**	2006–2007
• **Owner(s) / Partner(s)**	Alexis Kouzmine-Karavaïeff
• **Team**	4
• **Space(s)**	120 m² (Brussels) 50 m² (Shanghai)
• **Artists at Art Basel**	Dai Guangyu Gao Brothers Zhang Dali
• **Further artists represented**	Christophe Demaitre Fan Jiupeng Li Rui Liu Bolin Zane Mellupe Wu Junyong

Ihn

Seoul ● Galleries

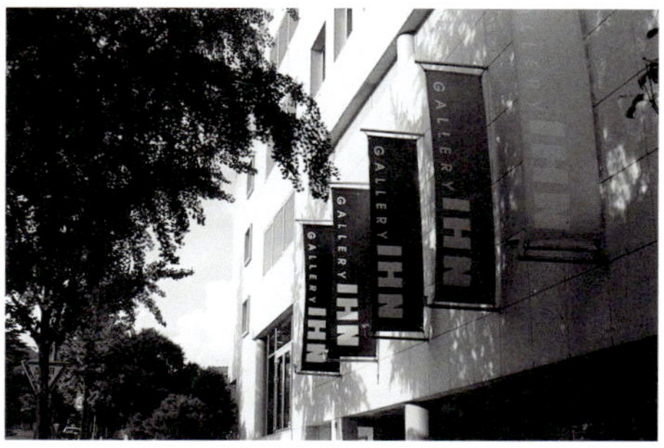

What first compelled you to open a gallery?
Even though the Korean art market in the 1980s and 1990s was small, Yang's mother started to collect well known and emerging artists' work, which inspired Yang to study sculpture at university. Yang always felt that there weren't enough exhibition spaces for artists in Korea and she also wanted to introduce international artworks to Korean audiences.

Who is the first artist you showed and what was most memorable about that show?
Ryoo Byung Yup. He is considered one of the most important artists in Korea and it was a sensational exhibition that attracted many visitors. It was interesting to see people interacting with the artworks.

When did you first participate in Art Basel and what was most memorable about that show?
Hong Kong in 2013 was our first participation in Art Basel. It was a great experience for us; we met a wide range of collectors from all over the world. Our Korean clients had the chance to build an ongoing relationship with our international clients.

• **Contact**	Gallery Ihn Jini Yang jiniyang@gmail.com ihn@galleryihn.com
• **Established**	1989
• **Owner(s) / Partner(s)**	Ihn Yang
• **Team**	7
• **Space(s)**	600 m²
• **Artists at Art Basel**	Bae Joonsung Bahk Seon Ghi Unsung Han Eddie Kang Whang Inkie
• **Further artists represented**	James Casebere Kwang-Yup Cheon Teo Gonzalez Ha Sang-Rim Hong Sung-Chul Hong Sung-Do Jeong Bo-Young Jeong Dae-Hyun Joo Myung-Duck Camill Leberer William Steiger Yoo Hyun-Mi

Ingleby

Edinburgh ● Galleries ● Galleries

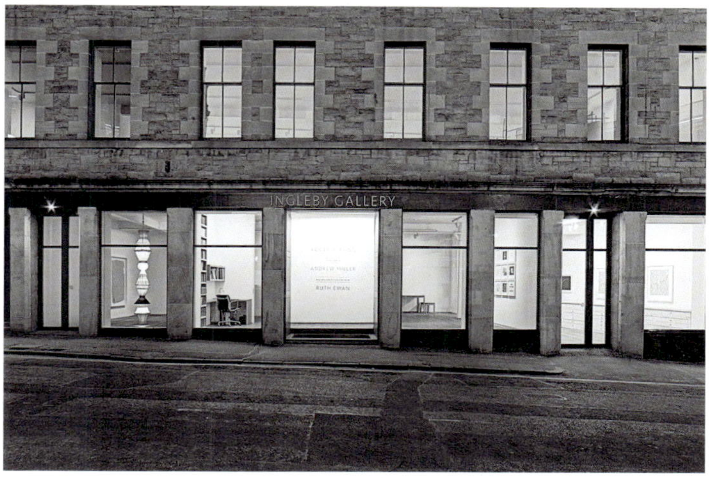

What first compelled you to open a gallery?
A belief that from time to time it is possible to achieve something that makes the world more interesting.

Who is the first artist you showed and what was most memorable about that show?
Howard Hodgkin—it was memorable for the fact that Howard agreed to it.

When did you first participate in Art Basel and what was most memorable about that show?
Art Basel, in the Statements sector in 2007 with the artist Peter Liversidge. He wrote *135 Proposals for the city of Basel*, many of which we realized. There were many memorable moments, not least dodging the police outside the Kunsthalle in the middle of the night while installing owl boxes on lampposts.

• **Contact**	Ingleby Gallery Dan Smernicki dan@inglebygallery.com info@inglebygallery.com
• **Established**	1998
• **Owner(s) / Partner(s)**	Richard Ingleby Florence Ingleby
• **Team**	8
• **Space(s)**	2,000 m²
• **Artists at Art Basel**	David Austen Iran do Espírito Santo Richard Forster James Hugonin Callum Innes Peter Liversidge Garry Fabian Miller Harland Miller Katie Paterson Frank Walter

- **Further artists represented**
  Roger Ackling
  David Batchelor
  Thomas Joshua Cooper
  Ian Davenport
  Susan Derges
  Ian Hamilton Finlay
  Tommy Grace
  Howard Hodgkin
  Jeremy Millar
  Jonathan Owen
  Winston Roeth
  Kay Rosen
  Jon Schueler
  Sean Scully
  Alison Watt

Invernizzi

Milan ● Galleries

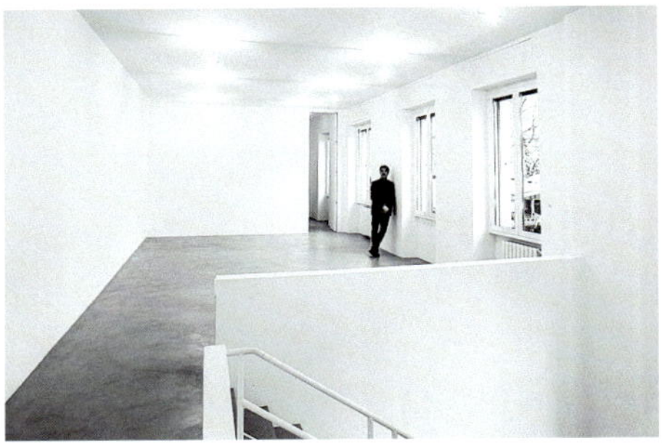

What first compelled you to open a gallery?
I opened my gallery because I have always been fascinated by the magic of art. With my father since I was a child, I have always visited exhibitions of contemporary art and artists' studios such as those of Gianni Colombo, Carlo Ciussi, Mario Nigro, Rodolfo Aricò, Dadamaino.

Who is the first artist you showed and what was most memorable about that show?
The first exhibition was with Dadamaino, François Morellet, and Günther Uecker. I remember the presence of the artists at the opening and their great enthusiasm. You could not move in the gallery and people came from all over Italy and from Europe: it was a period of crisis and opening a gallery was a great challenge.

When did you first participate in Art Basel and what was most memorable about that show?
My first participation at Art Basel dates back to 1995, and I remember the great interest that the booth generated; I exhibited representative works of Italian artists in dialogue with works of European artists.

- **Contact**: A arte Invernizzi
  Tiziana Invernizzi
  epicarmo@aarteinvernizzi.it
  info@aarteinvernizzi.it
- **Established**: 1994
- **Owner(s) / Partner(s)**: Epicarmo Invernizzi
- **Team**: 7
- **Space(s)**: 400 m²
- **Artists at Art Basel**: Dadamaino
  Niele Toroni
- **Further artists represented**: Rodolfo Aricò
  Francesco Candeloro
  Nicola Carrino
  Alan Charlton
  Carlo Ciussi
  Gianni Colombo
  Riccardo De Marchi
  Lesley Foxcroft
  Igino Legnaghi
  John McCracken
  François Morellet
  Mario Nigro
  Pino Pinelli
  Bruno Querci
  Ulrich Rückriem
  Nelio Sonego
  Mauro Staccioli
  David Tremlett
  Günter Umberg
  Michel Verjux
  Rudi Wach

Ishii

Tokyo ● Galleries ● Galleries Unlimited

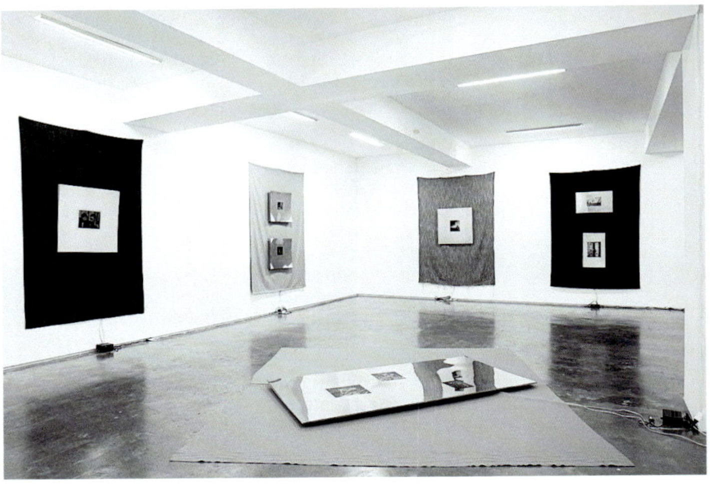

What first compelled you to open a gallery?
Before I came back to Japan, I began working as an art dealer. At the time, there were not many international contemporary art galleries so I decided to open a space in 1994.

Who is the first artist you showed and what was most memorable about that show?
The first artist I showed was Larry Clark. I saw his works for the first time at Temporary Contemporary in LA MOCA in the mid-1980s. His works impressed me so much that it was memorable for me to be able to show his *Tulsa* and *Teenage Lust* series. Publishing the Japanese version of *Tulsa* was also very special.

When did you first participate in Art Basel and what was most memorable about that show?
Ten years ago. Gallery artist Kyoko Murase made a wall drawing installation at our booth.

- **Contact**: Taka Ishii Gallery
  Elisa Uematsu
  elisa@takaishiigallery.com
  tig@takaishiigallery.com
- **Established**: 1994
- **Owner(s) / Partner(s)**: Takayuki Ishii
- **Team**: 8
- **Space(s)**: 330 m²
- **Artists at Art Basel**: Ei Arakawa
  Nobuyoshi Araki
  Koji Enokura
  Hideko Fukushima
  Mario Garcia Torres
  Takashi Ishida
  Zon Ito
  Yuki Kimura
  Kiyoji Otsuji
  Sterling Ruby
- **Further artists represented**: Amy Adler
  Thomas Demand
  Michael Elmgreen & Ingar Dragset
  Luke Fowler
  Tomoo Gokita
  Dan Graham
  Naoya Hatakeyama
  Nobuya Hoki
  Naoto Kawahara
  Annette Kelm
  Sean Landers
  Lisa Lapinski
  Yukinori Maeda
  Helen Mirra
  Daido Moriyama
  Kyoko Murase
  Silke Otto-Knapp
  Hiroe Saeki
  Taro Shinoda
  Kei Takemura
  Marijke van Warmerdam
  Christopher Wool
  Cerith Wyn Evans

A arte Invernizzi
Three Questions for Epicarmo Invernizzi

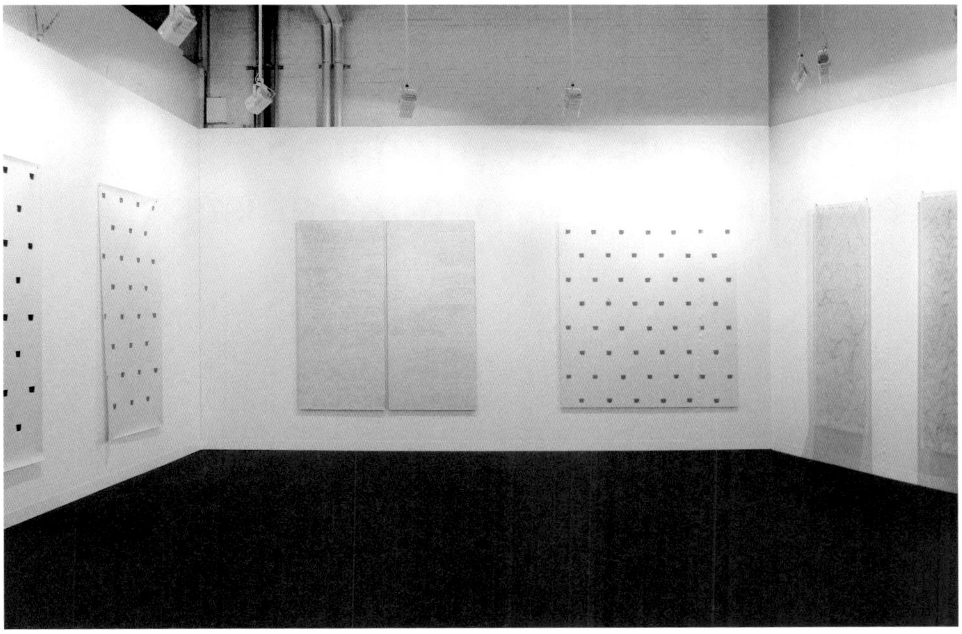

Art Basel in Basel, 2013

Founded in 1994 with an exhibition of works by Dadamaino, François Morellet, and Günther Uecker, the philosophy of your gallery is firmly contemporary. Could you please present your program and policy to us?

The gallery joins the international contemporary artistic debate, presenting artists of different generations, alternating Italians and other Europeans, in order to both create a dialogue and allow comparisons. The philosophy of the gallery is that what exists in the present will be memory in the future: fresh, cognitive possibilities are made perceptible, giving rise to new openings.

The exhibitions are conceived directly by the artists in close relationship with the gallery space. The gallery develops a first market activity presenting a generation of artists who elaborate their own language, but we also represent the estate of Mario Nigro (1917–1992)—whose catalogue raisonné was curated by Prof. Germano Celant (Skira Editore, 2009)—and the estates of Rodolfo Aricò and Carlo Ciussi, two protagonists of Italian contemporary art who participated many times in the Venice Biennale with solo shows. On the occasion of each exhibition a bilingual catalogue is published with a critical essay from a renowned scholar, illustrations of the works displayed in the gallery, and a bio-bibliography.

Furthermore, the gallery is invited by museums, foundations, and public institutions, both in Italy and abroad, to cooperate in the realization of monographic or group exhibitions, as a point of reference for directors and curators of museums and scholars. The gallery also organizes lectures of the most important contemporary Italian philosophers and poets in order to create a discussion concerning the arts. For instance, we are collaborating on the project *Natura Poesia Arte* at the outdoor Museum of Contemporary Art of Morterone, where more than 30 works by international artists are installed, artists that include Nicola Carrino, Gianni Colombo, François Morellet, Ulrich Rückriem, Mauro Staccioli, David Tremlett, Grazia Varisco, Michel Verjux, etc. The gallery is also working on the exhibition *Arte Contemporanea a Villa Pisani*, an integration of contemporary art in dialogue with the Villa, which is a work by the Renaissance architect Andrea Palladio.

At Art Basel in 2013 you presented a two-person exhibition with Niele Toroni and Dadamaino: Toroni is viewed as an historical artist of the 1960s avant-gardes, while Dadamaino currently benefits from growing attention. Why this choice for your booth?

The exhibition project does not limit itself to show the formal results achieved by the two artists. It wants to endorse a significant reflection upon the value of the gesture and the sign, which characterize both artists and are "declined" by them according to different modalities. Their unique languages investigate forms that give rise to images of a new amazement.

The works by Niele Toroni—characterized by sequences of marks made by a no. 50 brush at a distance of 30 cm from each other and left on different types of surfaces—with their constant and faithful rhythm, present a possible path, a succession of hypothetical passes that can be crossed: through their physical existence they describe an elementary and physiological relationship with the world, at the same time as sounding its space in order to discover its essence. In the same way the intermittence of the signs drawn out by Dadamaino, purposely fragmentary and discontinuous, opens a complex dialogue with existence itself, which is announced as being potentially infinite and changeable as is the very essence of life, which is subject to the rhythm of time, and yet belongs to the inexhaustible movement of the universe in its becoming.

You have participated consistently in the fair almost since the opening of the gallery. How do you think this platform evolved?

In the first few years everyone worked intensely because the fair was becoming a catalyzing moment of art at an international level, despite being the fair "par excellence." I remember the excitement of those years, which have resulted in the success of Art Basel worldwide.

I

Insights hosted projects developed specifically for the Hong Kong show. Participating galleries must be based in Asia, the Middle East, or the Asia-Pacific region and exclusively present works by artists from that region. The sector featured a select range of solo shows, exceptional art-historical material, and thematic exhibitions of two or more artists.

2013 participants

A Thousand Plateaus
People's Park Project

Arataniurano
Tatzu Nishi
Takahiro Iwasaki

Art:1
Ichwan Noor

Artcourt
Nomura Hitoshi

Artinformal
Pam Yan-Santos
Marina Cruz

Blindspot
anothermountainman
(aka Stanley Wong)

CAIS
Seoung Won Won

Canna
Entang Wiharso

Cda-Projects
Zeren Göktan
Nazli Eda Noyan
Ipek Duben

Chambers
Zhao Zhao

Chan Hampe
Dawn Ng

Cheng
Wang Gongxin
Li Yongbin

Chiba
Yuken Teruya

de Montferrand
Liu XiaoDong
Ding Yi
Zao WouKi
Chu Teh-Chun
Liu Wei
Sui JianGuo
Guo Wei
Huang Rui
Mao Yan
Zeng Hao
Wang Du
Tang Haiwen

Edwin's
Heri Dono
Jumaldi Alfi

EM
Jae Yong Rhee

Exhibit320
Nandan Ghiya

Feast
T'ang Haywen

Fine Arts Literature
Shi Jingsong and
Zhang Quan

ifa
Dai Guangyu
Gao brothers
Zhang Dali
Gao Xingjian

Magician Space
Guan Yong
Jiang Zhi
Liu Zhuoquan
Zhuang Hui
Dan'er

Malingue
Cui Xin Ming

Manila Contemporary
Winner Jumalon

Mirchandani + Steinruecke
Manish Nai

313 Art Project
Insook Kim

Neon Parc
Katherine Huang

Ora-Ora
Halley Chang

Park Ryu Sook
Kang Kang Hoon

Pi
Mehmet Ali Uysal

Renshaw
Rodney Glick
Peter Madden

Schoeni
Hung Keung

Semarang
EddiE HaRa

Shin
Shimizu Jio
Tomatsu Shomei

Side 2
Udomsak Krisanamis
Takeo Hanazawa
Yusuke Saito

Sin Sin
Muhamad Irfan
Andy Dewantoro

Standing Pine
Shinji Ogawa

Star
Chen Ke

Sullivan+Strumpf
Penny Byrne

tanzer
Juan Ford

Tolarno
Martin Bell
Brendan Huntley

Tsuruno
Yuichiro Tamura

Wei-Ling
Ivan Lam

x-ist
Ceren Oykut
Nuri Kuzucan

XVA
Imran Channa

Y++ Wada
Tetsuya Ishida

Yamaki
Susumu Koshimizu

Yang
Yan Bing

Art:1 by Mondecor Gallery
Ichwan Noor

I

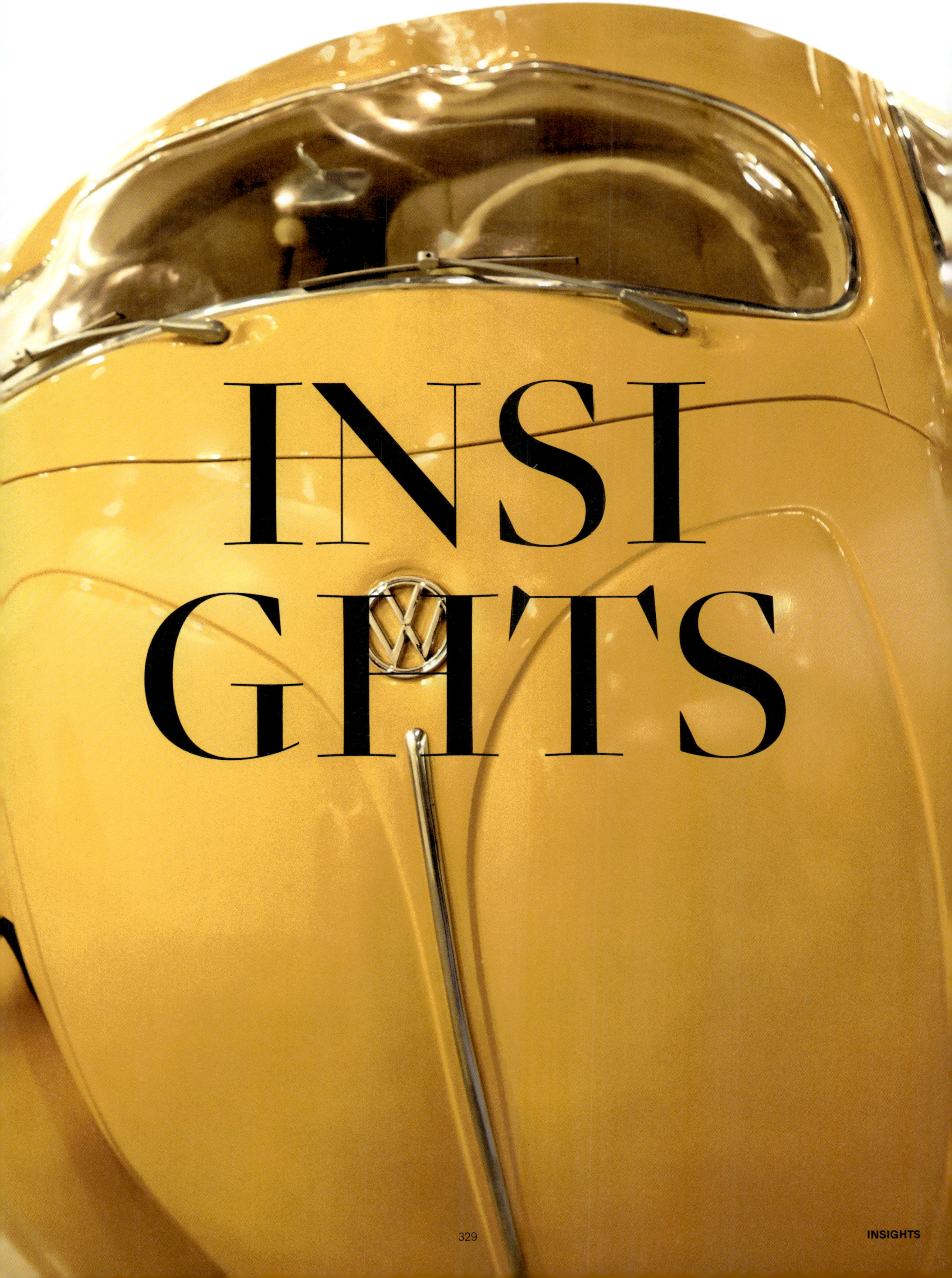

INSI GHTS

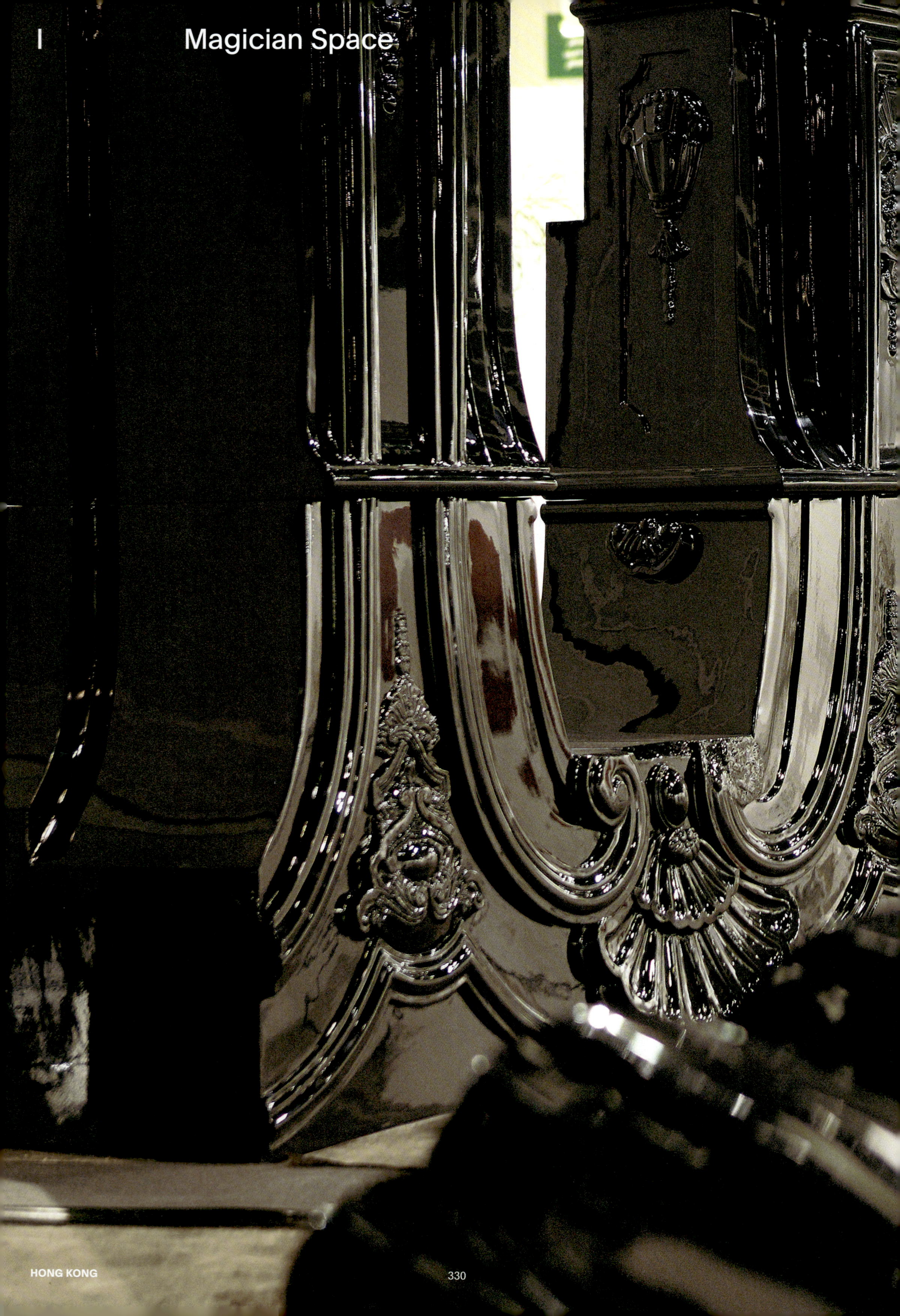

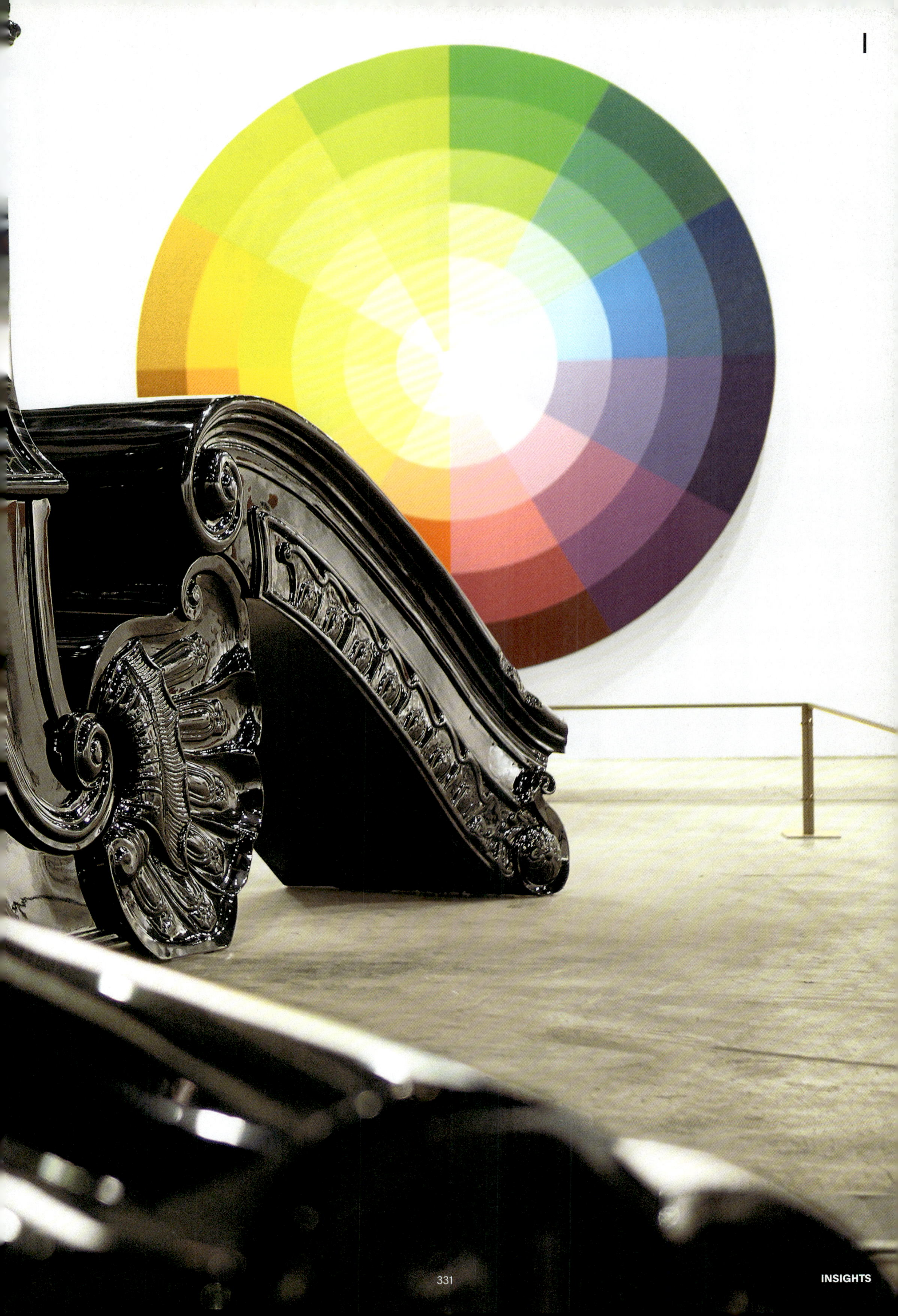

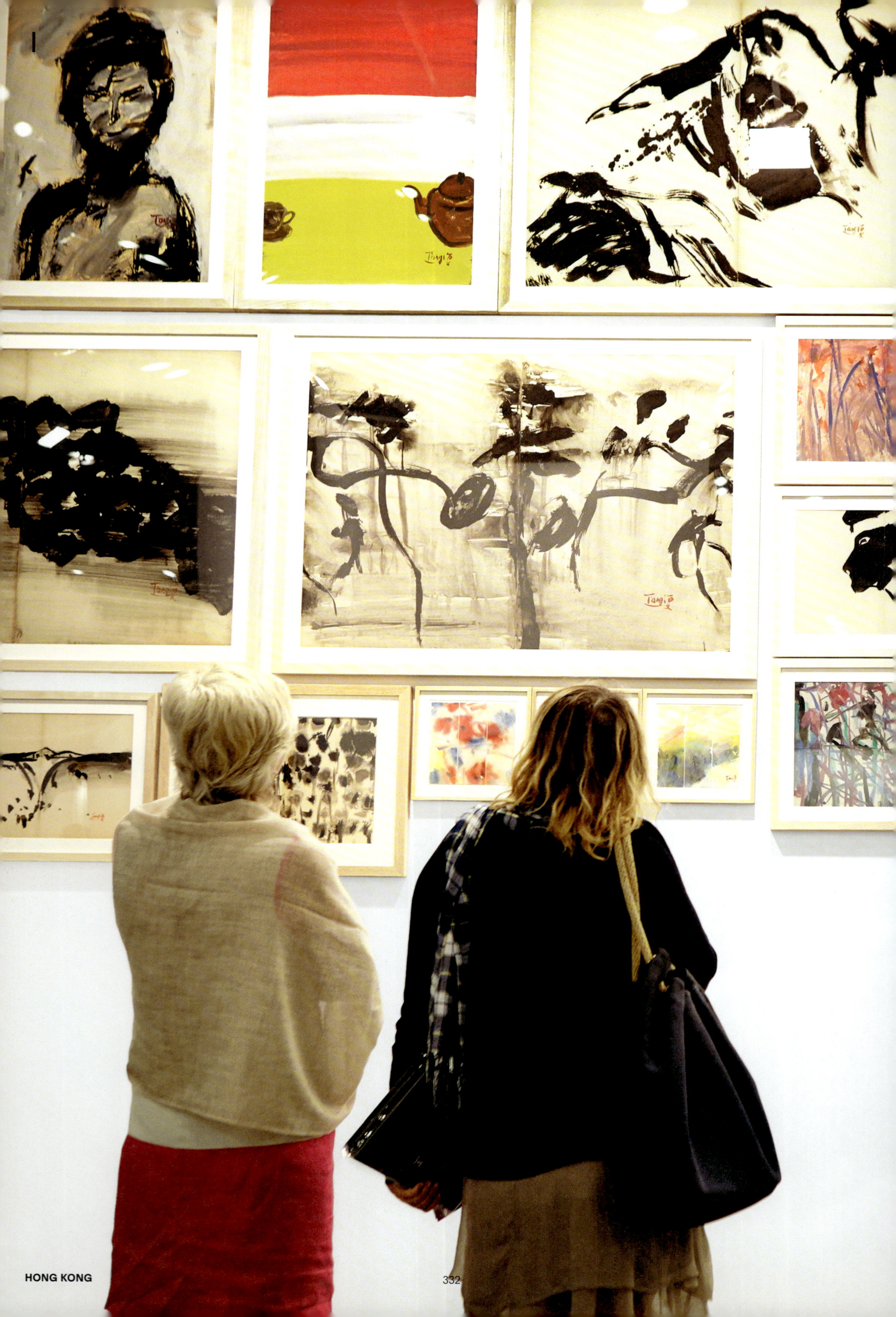

Feast Projects
T'ang Haywen

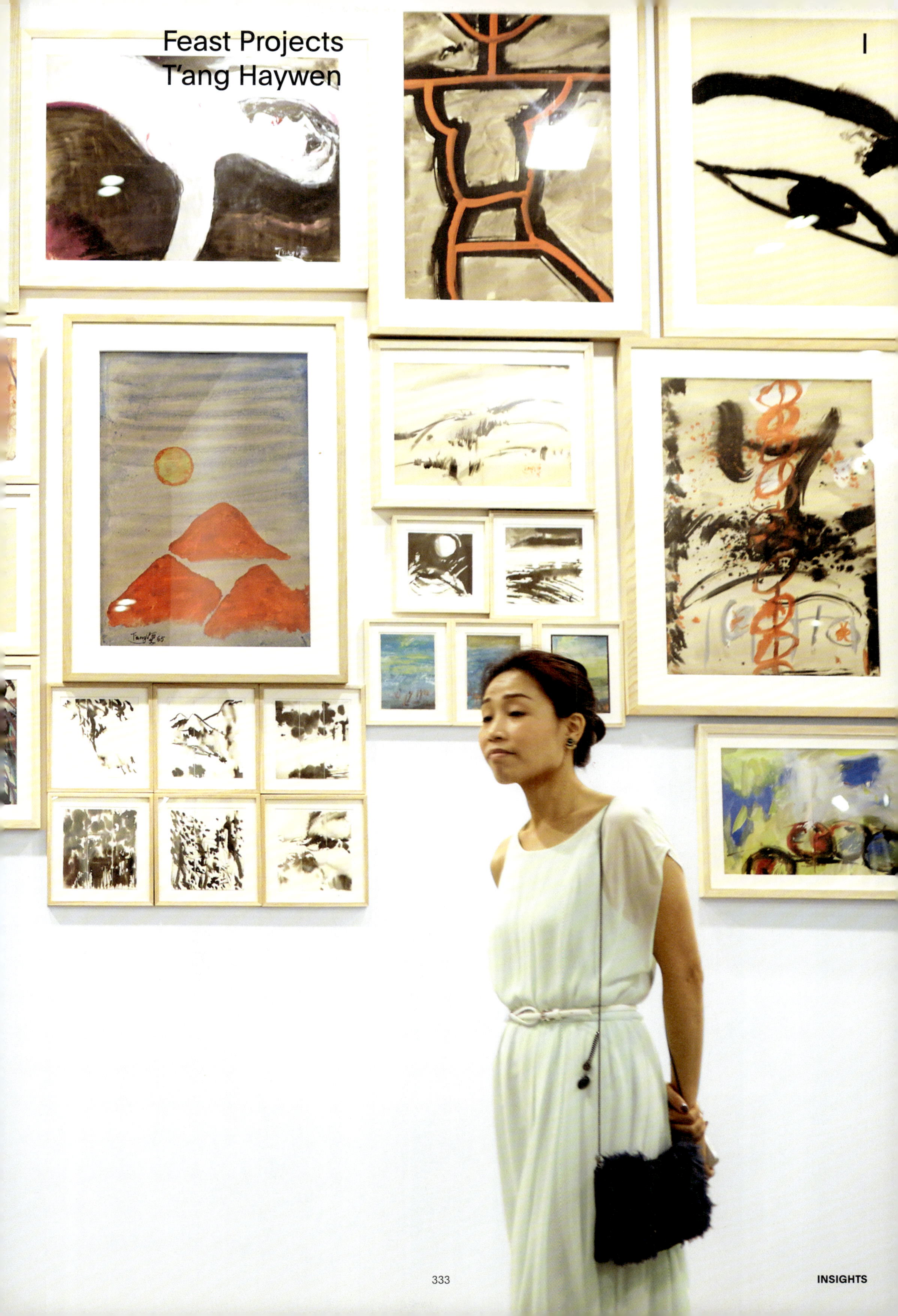

I

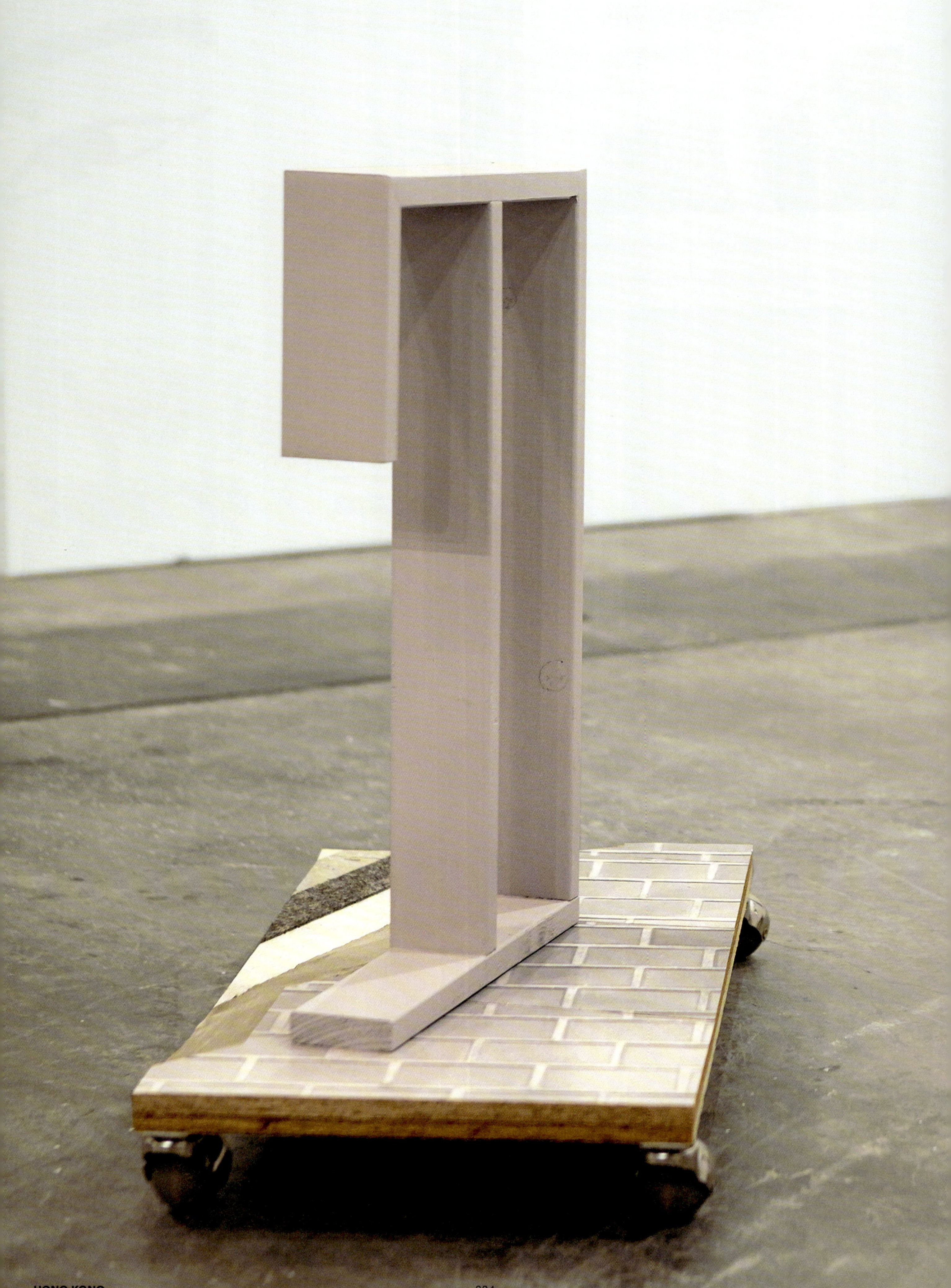

Gallery Side 2
Yusuke Saito

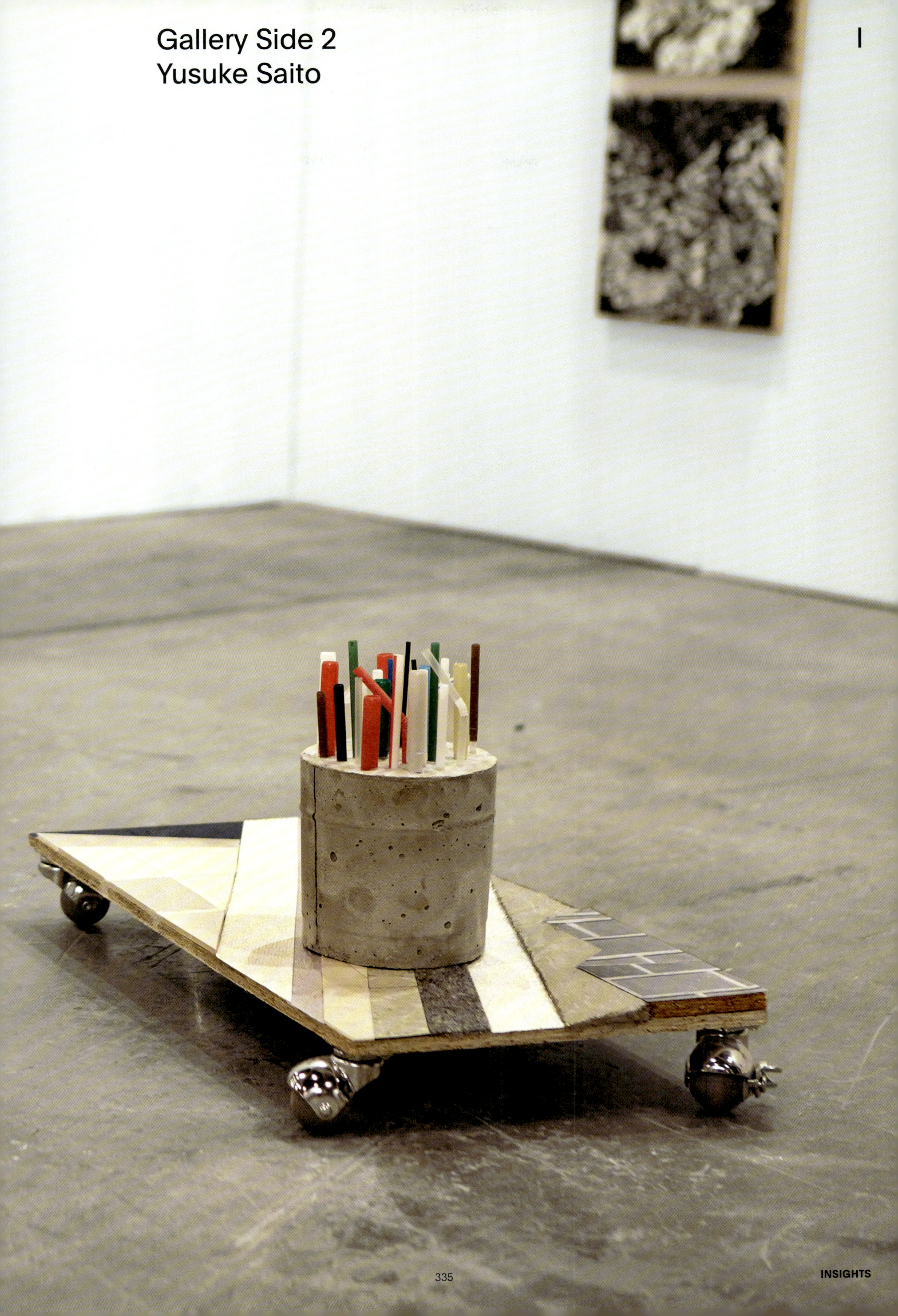

J

J

Hong Kong
Basel
Miami Beach

Jablonka

Cologne — Galleries

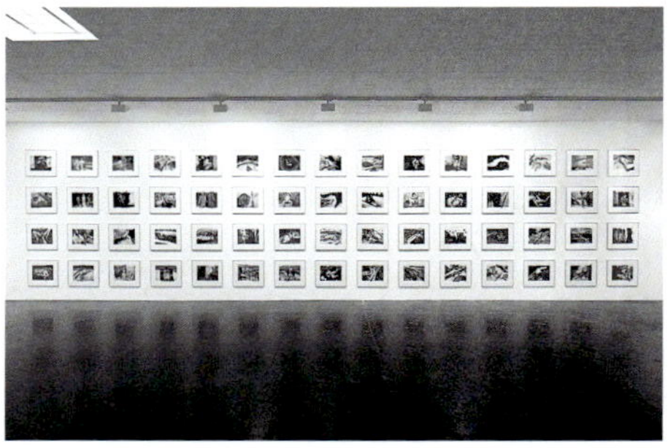

What first compelled you to open a gallery?
Passion for art.

When did you first participate in Art Basel and what was most memorable about that show?
In 1989. The most memorable booths were Katharina Fritsch in my stand, and Philip Taaffe at Galerie Crone.

- **Contact**: Jablonka Galerie
  Viola Oberle
  viola@jablonka.net
  info@jablonkagalerie.com
- **Established**: 1988
- **Owner(s) / Partner(s)**: Rafael Jablonka
- **Team**: 3
- **Space(s)**: 350 m²
- **Artists at Art Basel**: Nobuyoshi Araki
  Miquel Barceló
  Francesco Clemente
  Eric Fischl
  Alex Katz
  Mike Kelley
  Sherrie Levine
  Andreas Slominski
  Philip Taaffe
  Andy Warhol
  Terry Winters

Jacobson

London — Galleries
New York — Galleries

- **Contact**: Bernard Jacobson Gallery
  mail@jacobsongallery.com
- **Established**: 1969
- **Owner(s) / Partner(s)**: Bernard Jacobson
- **Artists at Art Basel**: Larry Bell
  Bram Bogart
  Sam Francis
  Helen Frankenthaler
  Pia Fries
  Karl Hyde
  Shirley Kaneda
  Bruce McLean
  Robert Motherwell
  Ben Nicholson
  Kurt Schwitters
  Pierre Soulages
  Frank Stella

Graham Sutherland
William Tillyer
Marc Vaux
Tom Wesselmann

Jacques

London — Galleries, Unlimited; Galleries

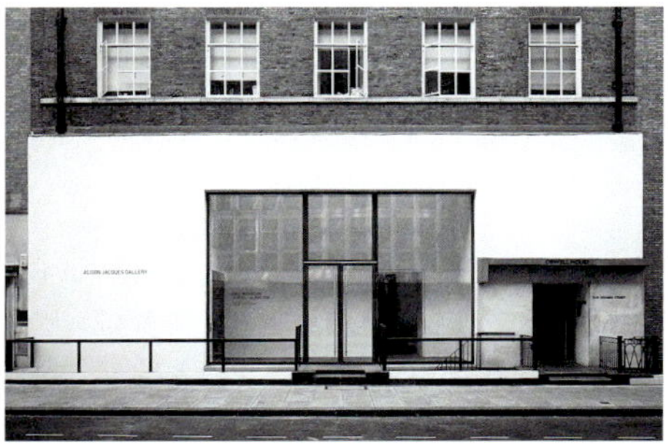

What first compelled you to open a gallery?
I came from a curatorial background but felt restricted by the rules and regulations of institutions. I wanted to do my own thing without red tape and memos, without having to ask anyone's permission; the freedom to see a great artist and offer him/her a space to show his/her work.

Who is the first artist you showed and what was most memorable about that show?
I was lucky enough to already represent the Mapplethorpe Estate in the UK by the time I opened my own gallery, and the first show I did was Mapplethorpe, curated by David Hockney. It was incredible to see the eye of a great artist through the eye of another great artist. David was incredibly dedicated to the project. After the show opened, he kindly invited me to visit him in Los Angeles so I got to swim in the pool, it felt like being in one of his paintings.

When did you first participate in Art Basel and what was most memorable about that show?
I first showed at Art Basel in the Statements sector in 2004 with Ian Kiaer. It was the first year of the gallery and I wanted to showcase the work of a younger artist such as Ian. So many museum shows for him stemmed from meetings at that fair, not to mention sales to new collectors I met there.

- **Contact**: Alison Jacques Gallery
  Roger Tatley
  info@alisonjacquesgallery.com
- **Established**: 2004
- **Owner(s) / Partner(s)**: Alison Jacques
- **Team**: 10
- **Space(s)**: 113.5 m²
- **Artists at Art Basel**: Michael Bauer
  Lygia Clark
  Tomory Dodge
  Dan Fischer
  Saul Fletcher
  Fernanda Gomes
  Sheila Hicks
  Matt Johnson
  Birgit Jürgenssen
  Ian Kiaer
  Klara Kristalova
  Graham Little
  Antonio Manuel
  Robert Mapplethorpe
  Ryan McGinley
  Ana Mendieta
  Paul Morrison
  Ryan Mosley
  Hélio Oiticica
  Alessandro Raho
  Dorothea Tanning
  Mathew Weir
  Hannah Wilke
  Catherine Yass
  Thomas Zipp
- **Further artists represented**: Haluk Akakçe
  Alessandro Raho
  Bernd Ribbeck
  Michael van Ofen

Janda

Vienna

- Galleries
- Galleries

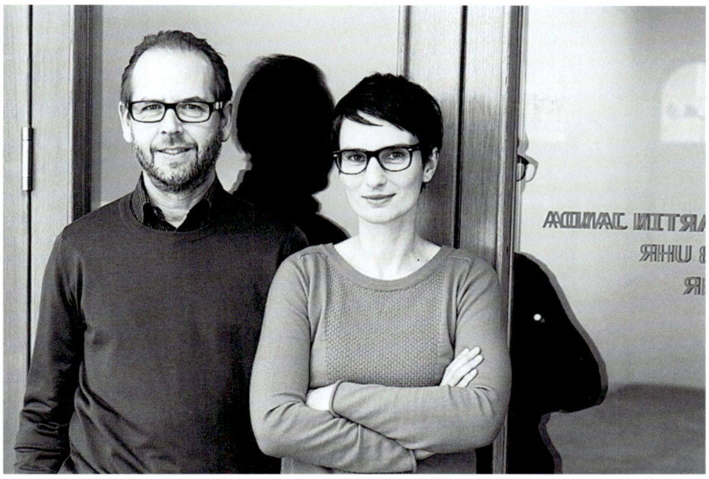

What first compelled you to open a gallery?
Having been a curator beforehand, it was the idea of being free in my decisions to do shows and work with artists.

Who is the first artist you showed and what was most memorable about that show?
Raoul De Keyser, in 1992. I remember we spent hours and hours to hang a few paintings, and the precision and accuracy we devoted to the installation.

When did you first participate in Art Basel and what was most memorable about that show?
At Art Basel in the Statements sector with Gregor Zivic in 2000. I especially recall seeing a wonderful sculpture by Alighiero Boetti at the show.

- **Contact** Galerie Martin Janda
Elisabeth Konrath
elisabeth.konrath@martinjanda.at
galerie@martinjanda.at
- **Established** 1992
- **Owner(s) / Partner(s)** Martin Janda
- **Team** 10
- **Space(s)** 230 m² (gallery)
270 m² (showroom)
- **Artists at Art Basel** Martin Arnold
Alessandro Balteo Yazbeck
Benjamin Butler
Adriana Czernin
Raoul De Keyser
Svenja Deininger
Milena Dragicevic
Werner Feiersinger
Giuseppe Gabellone
Nilbar Güres
Christine & Irene Hohenbüchler
Christian Hutzinger
Jakob Kolding
Július Koller
Jan Merta
Roman Ondák
Peter Pommerer
Allen Ruppersberg
Joe Scanlan
Ene-Liis Semper
Gabriel Sierra
Roman Signer
Mladen Stilinovic
Adrien Tirtiaux
Johannes Vogl
Maja Vukoje
Corinne Wasmuht
Donelle Woolford
Sharon Ya'ari
Jun Yang
Jakub Julian Ziolkowski

Janssen

Brussels

- Galleries

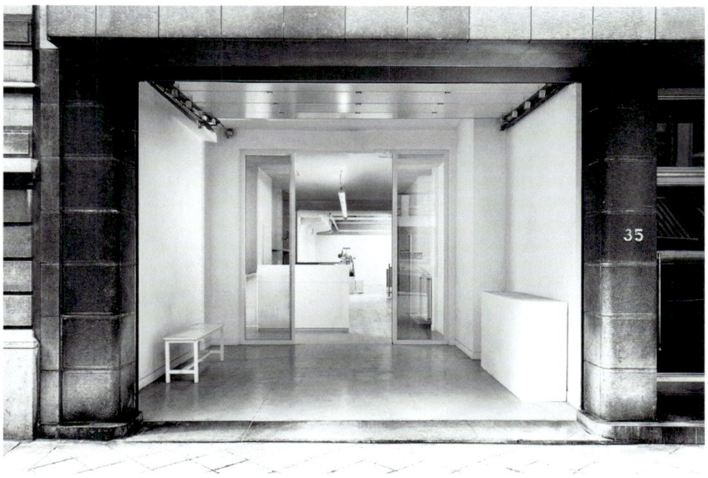

What first compelled you to open a gallery?
1991 was the financial and art market crisis and I thought it was a good opportunity to begin a gallery.

Who is the first artist you showed and what was most memorable about that show?
The first artist I showed was Lynne Cohen, and I'll always remember that the first work I sold was to the Museum of Photography in Antwerp.

When did you first participate in Art Basel and what was most memorable about that show?
My first participation at Art Basel was in 1992 and I discovered you could meet the art people and collectors at the Bratwurst bar.

- **Contact** Galerie Rodolphe Janssen
Sybille du Roy
sybille@galerierodolphejanssen.com
info@galerierodolphejanssen.com
- **Established** 1991
- **Owner(s) / Partner(s)** Rodolphe Janssen
- **Team** 8
- **Space(s)** 500 m²
- **Artists at Art Basel** David Adamo
Davide Balula
Walead Beshty
Elaine Cameron-Weir
Thomas Lerooy
Justin Lieberman
Sam Moyer
Gert & Uwe Tobias
- **Further artists represented** Wim Delvoye
Jürgen Drescher
Kendell Geers
Sean Landers
Esko Männikkö
Chris Martin
Adam McEwen
Jean-Luc Moerman
Farhad Moshiri
David Ratcliff
Torbjørn Rødland
Sam Samore
Stephen Shore
Betty Tompkins
Banks Violette

Jeffries

Vancouver

Galleries

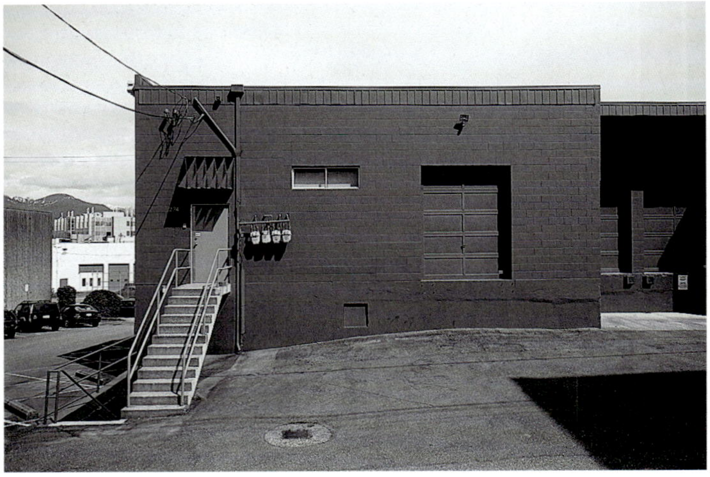

What first compelled you to open a gallery?
In the mid-1980s I became very interested in cultural systems internationally contributing to society, and shifted my university studies to art history. The gallery emerged out of such thinking and research. The exhibition made a position and statement about the gallery's interest in the conceptual histories that emerged from Vancouver in the late 1960s–1970s, and from my intentions to explore these histories and establish trajectories moving forward.

Who is the first artist you showed and what was most memorable about that show?
The first exhibition was a group show in 1994, with Ian Wallace, Marian Penner Bancroft, and Christos Dikeakos.

When did you first participate in Art Basel and what was most memorable about that show?
Our first exhibition at Art Basel was in 2008. The booth design was by artist/architect Robert Kleyn.

- **Contact** — Catriona Jeffries Gallery
  Catriona Jeffries
  catriona@catrionajeffries.com
  gallery@catrionajeffries.com
- **Established** — 1994
- **Owner(s) / Partner(s)** — Catriona Jeffries
- **Team** — 6
- **Space(s)** — 604 m²
- **Artists at Art Basel** — Raymond Boisjoly
  Geoffrey Farmer
  Julia Feyrer
  Brian Jungen
  Janice Kerbel
  Christina Mackie
  Liz Magor
  Gareth Moore
  Damian Moppett
  Judy Radul
  Ian Wallace
- **Further artists represented** — Arabella Campbell
  Christos Dikeakos
  Sam Durant
  Myfanwy MacLeod
  Alex Morrison
  Isabelle Pauwels
  Jerry Pethick
  Kevin Schmidt
  Ron Terada
  Jin-me Yoon

Jensen

Sydney
Auckland

Galleries

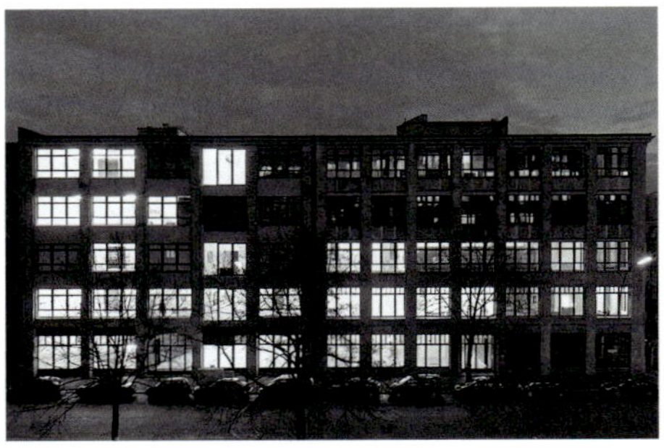

What first compelled you to open a gallery?
While studying law at University I took minor in art history. The faculty shared its building with the Fine Arts School and, quite frankly, what was happening there seemed vital and compelling and I wanted to be involved somehow, if not in the "making" of, then in the advocacy and mediation of art.

Who is the first artist you showed and what was most memorable about that show?
A local painter Linda James, whose work drew its inspiration from Giotto's depiction of ten dancing women. I recall the warmth of the reception of her work, the enthusiasm for a new gallery in a small city that had only a handful of venues. Immediately it felt as if the gallery had a mandate.

When did you first participate in Art Basel and what was most memorable about that show?
In 2012 in Hong Kong.

- **Contact** — Jensen Gallery
  Andrew Jensen
  andrew@jensengallery.com.au
  gallery@jensengallery.com.au
- **Established** — 1988
- **Owner(s) / Partner(s)** — Andrew Jensen (Director)
  Emman Fox (Director)
- **Team** — 4
- **Space(s)** — 700 m²
- **Artists at Art Basel** — Helmut Federle
  Sam Harrison
  Imi Knoebel
  Tomislav Nikolic
  Tony Cursler
  Jude Rae
  Winston Roeth
  Fred Sandback
  Günter Umberg
  Judith Wright
- **Further artists represented** — James Casebere
  Melissa Coote
  Lisa Crowley
  Eric Fischl
  Jacqueline Humphries
  Callum Innes
  Leigh Martin
  Geoff Thornley
  Elisabeth Vary

Johnen

Berlin

- Galleries
- Galleries

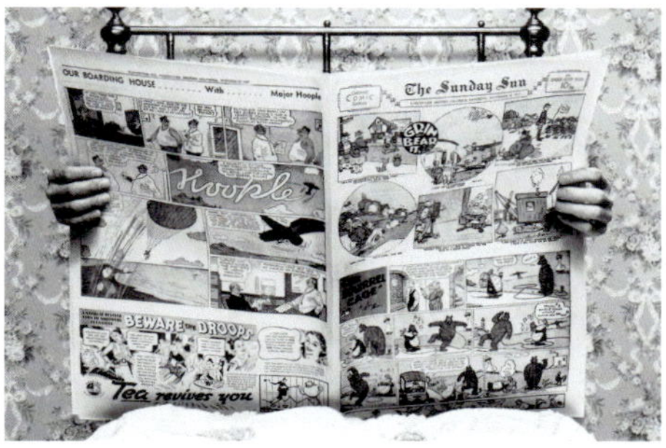

What first compelled you to open a gallery?
Jörg Johnen: To bring culture out of the private sphere's and museum's exile and create an environment and symbols in which the individual can mirror and find oneself again (original quote in German, from my essay in "Goldener Oktober," *Kunstforum* 9/1983).

Who is the first artist you showed and what was most memorable about that show?
Thomas Schütte and Aldo Rossi. No one was interested to buy—hard to imagine nowadays.

When did you first participate in Art Basel and what was most memorable about that show?
In 1986, as Johnen + Schöttle. It was so much more relaxed back then. I was the only one from the gallery and could bring my lover as assistant, and we managed just fine!

- **Contact** Johnen Galerie
  Cornelia Tischmacher
  tischmacher@johnengalerie.de
  mail@johnengalerie.de
- **Established** 1984 (Johnen + Schöttle)
  2004 (Johnen Galerie)
- **Owner(s) / Partner(s)** Jörg Johnen (Owner)
  Cornelia Tischmacher (Senior Director)
- **Team** 7
- **Space(s)** 400 m²
- **Artists at Art Basel** Stephan Balkenhol
  Martin Creed
  Hans-Peter Feldmann
  Ryan Gander
  Rodney Graham
  Andrew Grassie
  Candida Höfer
  Martin Honert
  Liu Ye
  Yoshitomo Nara
  Thomas Ruff
  Wilhelm Sasnal
- **Further artists represented** Jānis Avotiņš
  Stefan Bertalan
  Martin Boyce
  Michał Budny
  Rafał Bujnowski
  David Claerbout
  James Coleman
  Slawomir Elsner
  Elger Esser
  Francesco Gennari
  Dan Graham
  David Hahlbrock
  Olaf Holzapfel
  Raimer Jochims
  Robert Kuśmirowski
  Tim Lee
  Jan Merta
  Florin Mitroi
  Roman Ondák
  Pietro Roccasalva
  Anri Sala
  Tino Sehgal
  Wiebke Siem
  Helmut Stallaerts
  Michael van Ofen
  Jeff Wall

Jongma

Amsterdam

- Discoveries

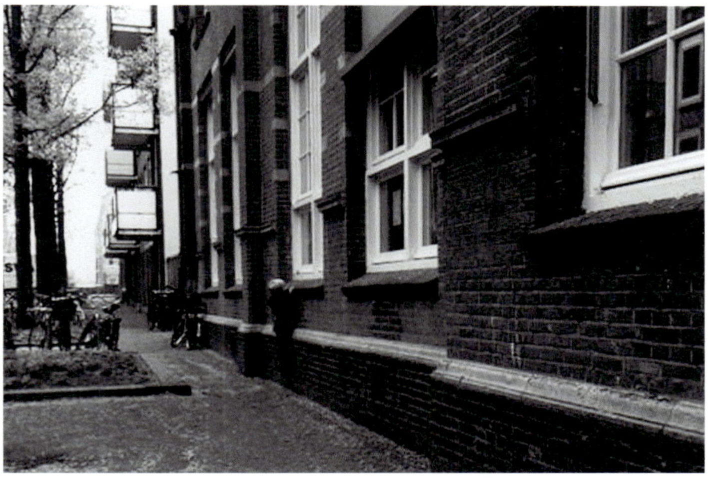

What first compelled you to open a gallery?
Sheer ambition.

Who is the first artist you showed and what was most memorable about that show?
Arjan van Helmond. The gallery space was 15 m² and we pushed-pinned drawings on the wall.

When did you first participate in Art Basel and what was most memorable about that show?
In 2009, with a memorable piece by Guido van der Werve and a chess match performance and a chess piano built by the artist.

- **Contact** Galerie Juliètte Jongma
  Sanne Luteijn
  info@juliettejongma.com
- **Established** 2004
- **Owner(s) / Partner(s)** Juliette Jongma
- **Team** 2
- **Space(s)** 180 m²
- **Artists at Art Basel** Donna Huddleston
  Nina Yuen
- **Further artists represented** Tim Braden
  Misha de Ridder
  Chris Evans
  Melissa Gordon
  Frank Hannon
  Ursula Mayer
  Lisa Oppenheim
  Pablo Pijnappel
  Karen Sargsyan
  Guido van der Werve
  Arjan van Helmond

Juda

London

- Galleries
- Galleries
- Galleries

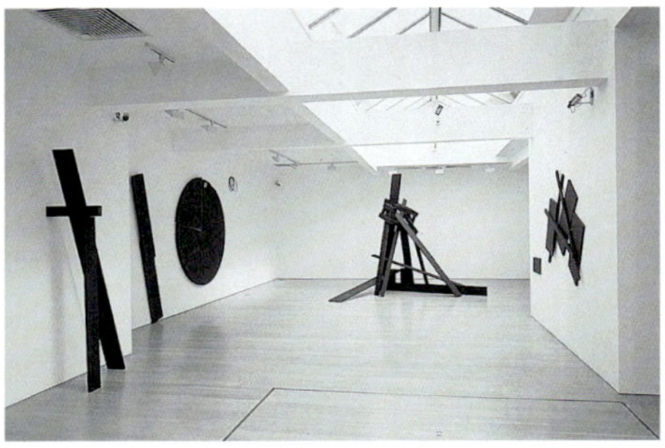

What first compelled you to open a gallery?
David Juda: My mother had the gallery and her mother was an artist.

Who is the first artist you showed and what was most memorable about that show?
My first contribution to the gallery was Christo.

When did you first participate in Art Basel and what was most memorable about that show?
My first Art Basel was the first one in 1970. It was much more like a car boot sale, not so chic as now and probably greater works of art.

- **Contact** Annely Juda Fine Art
  Nina Fellmann
  nina@annelyjudafineart.co.uk
  ajfa@annelyjudafineart.co.uk
- **Established** 1960
- **Owner(s) / Partner(s)** David Juda
- **Team** 10
- **Space(s)** 650 m²
- **Artists at Art Basel** Roger Ackling
  Max Bill
  Anthony Caro
  Alan Charlton
  Christo
  Prunella Clough
  Gloria Friedmann
  Katsura Funakoshi
  Naum Gabo
  Philipp Goldbach
  Alan Green
  Nigel Hall
  Werner Haypeter
  David Hockney
  Sigrid Holmwood
  Peter Kalkhof
  Tadashi Kawamata
  Leon Kossoff
  Darren Lago
  Edwina Leapman
  Kasimir Malevich
  Kenneth Martin
  Mary Martin
  Michael Michaeledes
  László Moholy-Nagy
  François Morellet
  David Nash
  Ben Nicholson
  Sarah Oppenheimer
  Liubov Popova
  Edda Renouf
  Alexander Rodchenko
  Kazuo Shiraga
  Yuko Shiraishi
  Suzanne Treister
  Georges Vantongerloo
  Friedrich Vordemberge-Gildewart
  Graham Williams
- **Further artists represented** Duan Jianyu
  Catherine Lee
  Kenneth & Mary Martin
  Alan Reynolds
  Yoshishige Saito

Catriona Jeffries Gallery

Interview with Catriona Jeffries

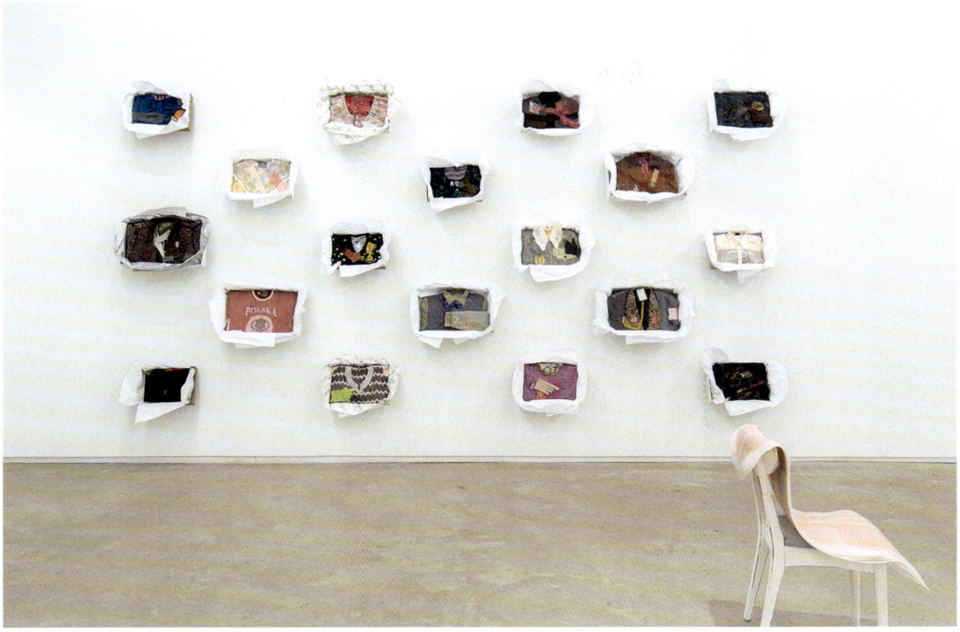

Art Basel in Basel, 2013

Since 1994, your gallery has been one of the most important ambassadors of Canadian art and especially of Vancouver's conceptual art scene. Tell us about your program and how it has developed over the course of 20 years.

The gallery was born from Vancouver's artistic community, which continues to change since its earliest experimental days in the late 1960s. The gallery's program represents seminal shifts and contributions to art history that have emerged in Vancouver. Our early work with Roy Kiyooka and N.E. Thing Co. (Iain and Ingrid Baxter) were central to the historicization of the avant-garde in Vancouver. Photoconceptualism has left an indelible mark on Vancouver's artists—it established a rigorous theoretical approach in the intellectual production of art and also, in its larger reach, in writing and exhibitions which established relationships with Europe and worldwide.

Ian Wallace's work, among that of other senior artists such as Liz Magor whom I have recently brought into the program, helps galvanize a next generation of practices such as Geoffrey Farmer, Brian Jungen, Judy Radul, and later, Gareth Moore, Julia Feyrer, and Raymond Boisjoly, whose careers have grown together with the gallery. As these practices transform, the idea of Vancouver opens up. At its heart lies a rigor that is tempered with a spirit of experimentalism, and the gallery has always sought to reflect this, as well as paying attention to the shifts and lineages which emerge from Vancouver while being very conscious and committed to the international context—we elaborate relationships with artists outside Vancouver such as Christina Mackie and Janice Kerbel.

How does your booth at Art Basel 2013 reflect your program, and how did you conceive it?

Generally our booth at Art Basel is built around the works produced by our artists at that moment, coming out of major international exhibitions or new bodies of work. Given our work with figures such as Ian Wallace, Liz Magor, and Jerry Pethick, we also present key historical works from the 1970s and 1980s by these artists. We always seek to install works thoughtfully in space and find subtle relationships between them, sometimes historical and in other instances more intuitive.

This year a portion of our booth was given over to a large sculptural work by Gareth Moore, which came out of his major documenta 13 installation, *a place – near the buried canal*. It was installed with a series of new works by Liz Magor, which were part of her exhibition *I Is Being This* at the gallery in 2012. Magor is a very influential senior artist in Vancouver and her work bears material concerns similar to that of Moore's, while also having a more subtle relationship to the paintings of Rebecca Brewer—a very young painter from Vancouver who studied in New York—whom we also presented. In addition we showed the original photographs from Ian Wallace's significant 1980s body of work *Poverty*. This work marks a turning point within Wallace's practice, and in a wider context, for the status of photography at the time. Most often, what is shown in our booth reflects our gallery's explorations at the time of the fair.

You give major importance to curatorial activities that Catriona Jeffries Gallery organizes (the creation of CJ Press, the implementation of external projects, etc.). How would you define the role of galleries now?

My thinking and way of directing the gallery, as well as its continual evolution, is lead by artists' practices at the gallery. Our relationships with our artists are the bedrock on which all work is built, and the gallery's curatorial projects reflect our own desire and curiosity to analyze and produce a context for the work of our artists. As such, the curatorial practices that can expand meaning and dialogue within the contemporary art history context have always been central to our work—this is the reason why we also work closely with museums. Since the late 1990s, the gallery has published writing concurrent to exhibitions, in a commitment to bringing writers and artists together. CJ Press was formed in 2006; they publish anthologies of exhibition essays every two years or so.

The role of the gallery today is a complicated question to answer as we are in the middle of massive transformations of the global gallery system. The large mega galleries modeling themselves on multinational corporate structures are creating a new monolith. In this context, it becomes an imperative, or opportunity, to define the committed rigor and intentions of our work as a gallery. A gallery is relevant through its work with artists, in representing them and placing their practices within the contemporary discourse, and in disseminating those ideas/works through relationships with museums, private collections, patrons, critical writing, and the ecosystem of contemporary art.

Four Decades at Art Basel: A Retrospective Conversation

DAVID JUDA

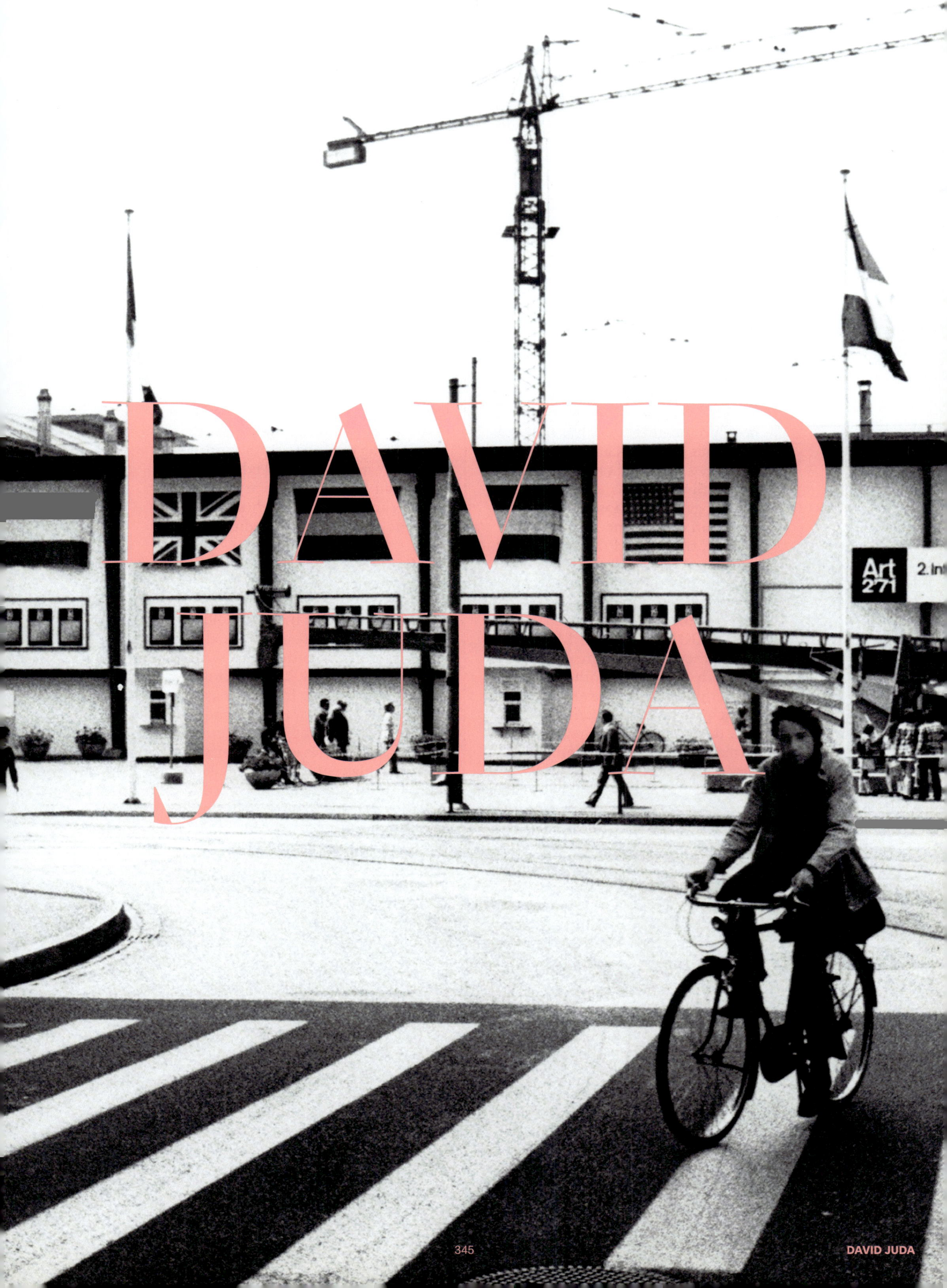

J

David Juda, Owner and Director, Annely Juda Fine Art, London

A conversation about the fair's beginnings, how to hang works, and major changes over the past 40 years, illustrated by Kurt Wyss

All photographs by Kurt Wyss, Basel, with the exception of Annely and David Juda portraits

CLÉMENT DIRIÉ Annely Juda Fine Art has been part of Art Basel since the beginning and your mother, Annely Juda, who died in 2006, was one of its first board members. Do you remember the atmosphere and the audience during the first years of your participation in the 1970s?

DAVID JUDA The first two or three fairs were not held in the same halls as today, but where the Swisshotel is now. I remember there was only one floor, but there was a mezzanine, and this mezzanine had only one gallery, the Marlborough Gallery. It was the biggest gallery in those days, the Gagosian of the time. I remember Gilbert, the son of Frank Lloyd, the founder of the Marlborough Gallery, came to talk to my mother, because they wanted to put a sign, 30 meters long, on the mezzanine wall: "MARLBOROUGH GALLERY," and my mother said: "It's great if it's cigarette advertising, but otherwise … "

I think we were very excited to participate in Basel, because we had only done one or two fairs before. In terms of general atmosphere, it was very conventional-looking, with floor to ceiling pictures—even on the floor! Once a visitor came in with a dog who peed on one of our paintings lying on the floor, and was upset that I took the dog away, asking me if I would like it if I was pushed away from the toilets … If the hanging was not that aesthetic, there was probably better art, just badly hung—whereas now there is a lot of bad art very well hung … Certainly things have improved enormously, but there was a certain charm to this salon style. Galerie 1900–2000 from Paris actually makes an issue of doing it a bit the way it used to be—except it was rougher!

In 1970 we were quite naive about everything: we didn't know how many works to hang, where to hang them, and how to do it. Our "official" shipper stuck all our works on a truck with toilet paper … We weren't very successful. 1971 was quite important because we were probably the first gallery who did a one-person show—a Christo show—and that year we really didn't have the money to do the fair. But right before going to Basel we sold a picture, gave the fair the money, got in the car, and drove to Basel. We couldn't pay for the hotel, but then the booth sold out! It had a wonderful feeling and nice atmosphere to it with the Christo collages.

For the first ten, 15 years, we would bring our own carpets and lights. My mother unpacked the pictures, and I would bring carpet squares and install the lights that we brought directly from London.

CD So the gallery in London was closed when you were at the fair?

DJ No, it wouldn't be closed, but it would be very dimmed! It looked like the Winter of Discontent that we had in Britain in the 1980s. But that was how people worked. It was not as professional, but it was quite good.

At the beginning, the director of the Swiss fairs (Messe Schweiz) was always saying that they were loosing money on the art fair, and I think it was the case. It was more about prestige than a source of revenue. The Swiss fairs made the money on the watches, and then they could spend a bit on the art.

CD Was the fair immediately important and successful for the art dealers?

DJ The fair was always pretty important. Then there were years when it went down a bit, and that's when they changed the whole system, because the most important fair, or the best fair for a while was Art Chicago. Cologne was a very important city, but Chicago was the most exciting fair in the late 1970s, early 1980s. But, through bad management, Chicago's fair went down, and through really good management, Basel went up. The Basel management is pretty efficient.

In the first years the audience was mainly composed of collectors, and I think the reason why the fair was such an immediate success was because of its location. Particularly at the time when Switzerland was a country where wealthy people would go and spend money, come on vacation or for business. It's at the corner of France, Germany, and not so far from the Benelux countries. It was also a city that wasn't Paris, London, or New York: I believe the best fairs are outside the main capitals: people come to Basel especially for the art, they are thus more concentrated.

For the first ten, 15 years, we would bring our own carpets and lights. My mother unpacked the pictures, and I would bring carpet squares and install the lights that we brought directly from London. — David Juda

My mother was on the committee when it started. The committees were composed of ambassadors from each country—she was representing Britain, and later I did it. About 1980 this stopped, and they started a committee of three and pushed out galleries who where not so good, replacing them with new galleries. In retrospect, it was really necessary.

I was on the committee for about 12 years in Basel, and a few years in Miami Beach. We were going to start the fair in Miami Beach, and then there was that terrible sarin attack and 9/11. I remember we came here, to Miami Beach, Sam Keller, myself, and a few other people, to talk to the collectors who'd been supporting the fair, and in the end we made the decision not to do the fair. I think it was the right decision.

CD How has the fair evolved since the 1970s, especially in terms of the addition of new sectors?

DJ There were no real sectors at the beginning; everything was mixed up. Print galleries were much more important in those days. People would very often start to be print collectors or drawing collectors. They were a lot of good print galleries; now there are only really a few.

In 1973 they started a series of special exhibitions, in which one country was invited each year to do an exhibition. After Germany and Switzerland, we did it for the United Kingdom in 1975. We were a committee of three people. We decided to show 50 artists. Once the decision was made, we managed to get some money from the British Council to do it. It was all done very modestly. The fair organizers gave us a space, the walls, and lights. It was upstairs in the main hall, where the print galleries are now. This show—including Bacon, Hockney, and every major British artist of the time—was brilliant. We went to all the galleries we had taken artworks from for the exhibition and persuaded them to advertise in a catalogue. We printed about 10,000 copies, with a Union Jack in the wrong colors on the cover. It was all done very professionally actually (we even had people to explain the project to the public), but in a rather amateurish way. This series stopped a few years after because there weren't that many countries that could afford to do it.

At the beginning galleries attending the fair used to get financial support from what was called in England the Fine Art and Antiques Export Committee of the Department of Trade and Industry: they would give around £2,000 to travel, ship things, etc. In 1971, £2,000 was enough to rent a booth, get in a car, and drive to Basel with works to sell. Today I'm afraid that with $3,000 I won't even get a meter of wall! The market has changed. In 1993, during the oil crisis, I remember my mother saying: "It's a disaster, we're not going to sell anything: none of the three collectors we have will buy anything." Today there are thousands of collectors from all over the world.

David Juda,
Miami Beach, 2013

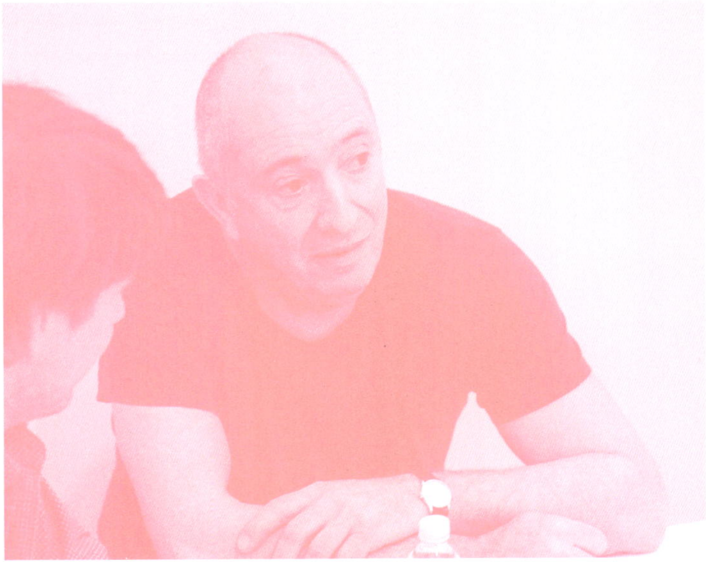

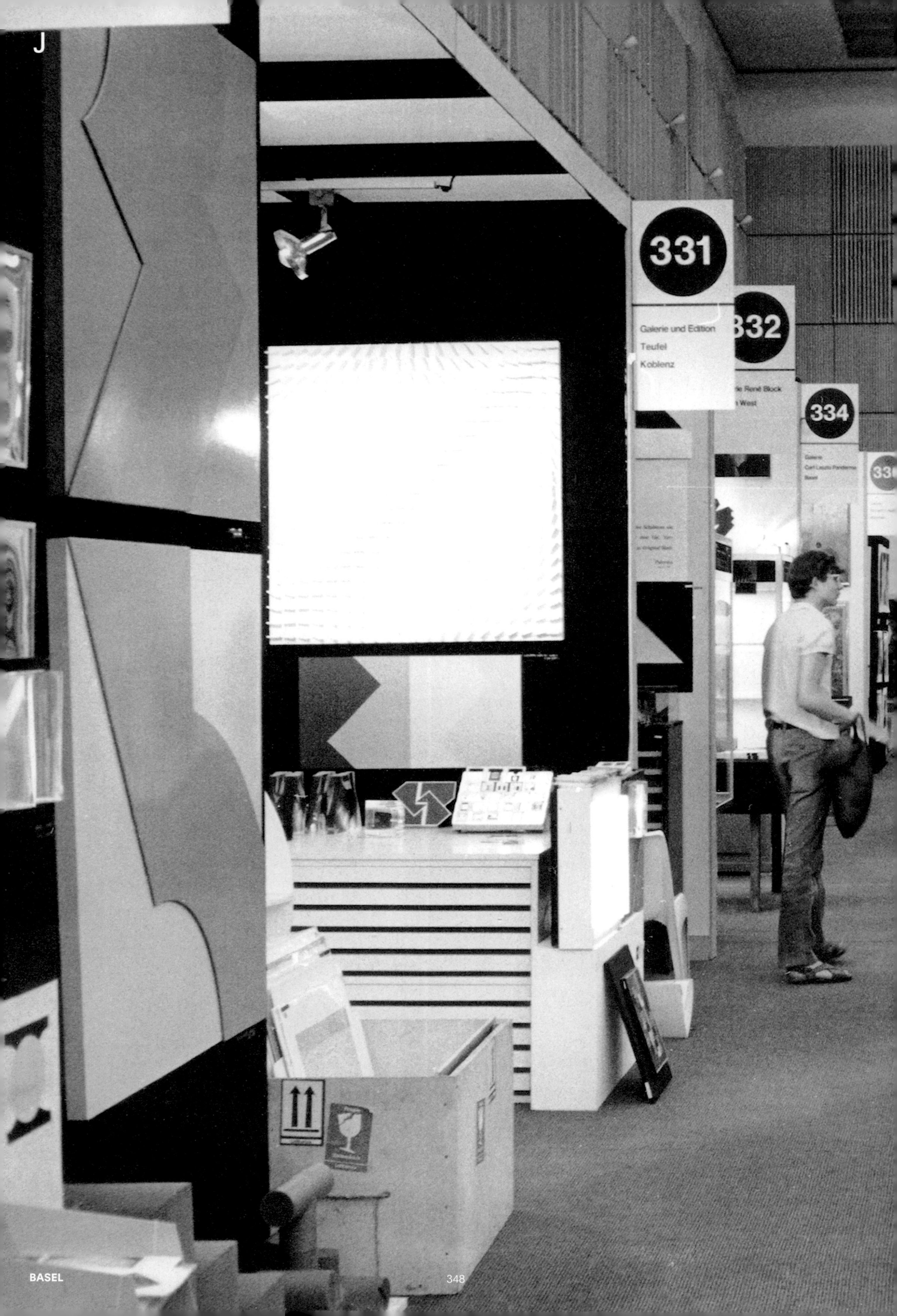
331
Galerie und Edition
Teufel
Koblenz
332
334

Art 01 Basel 1970

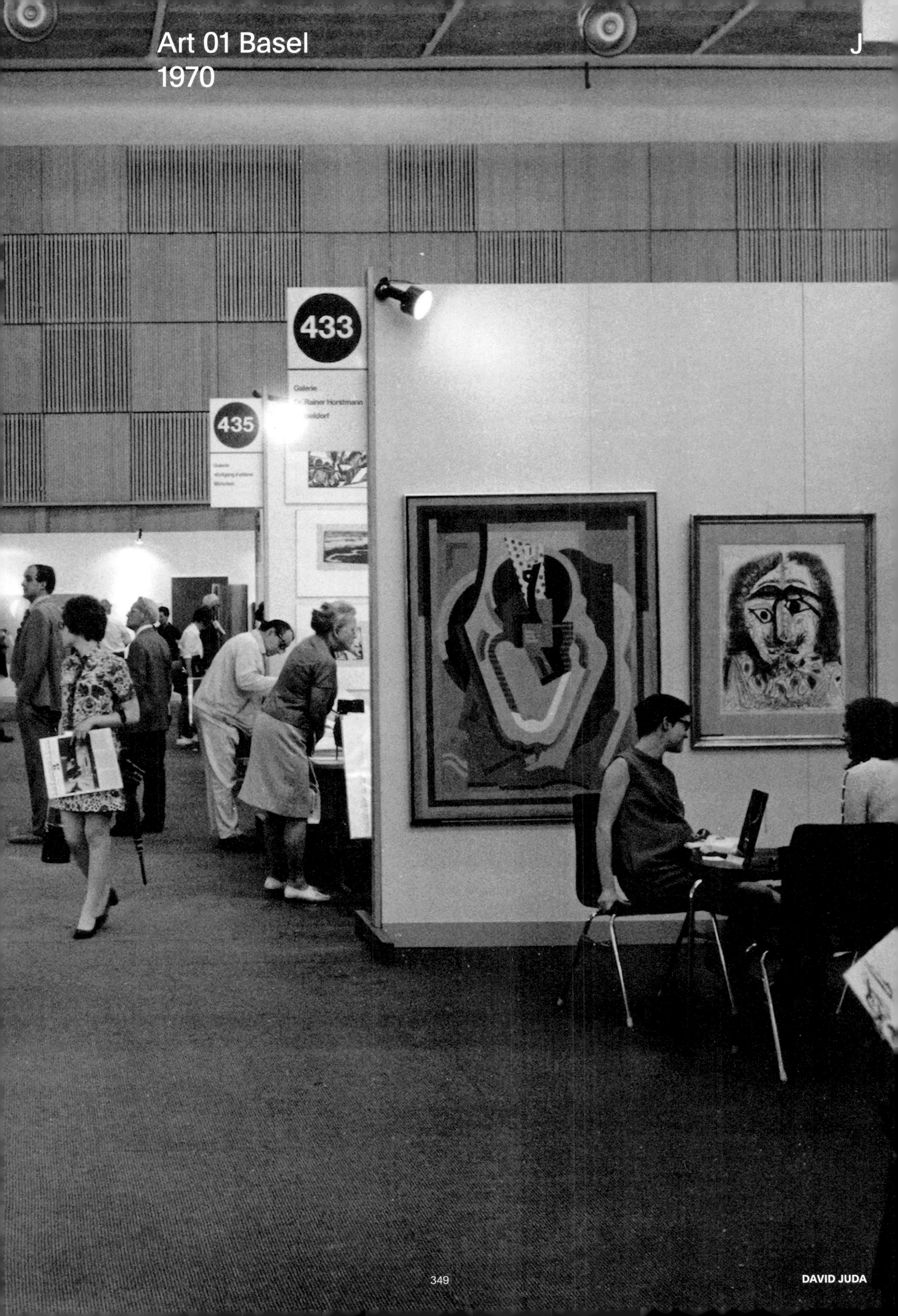

J

Treadwell Gallery
Art 06 Basel
1975

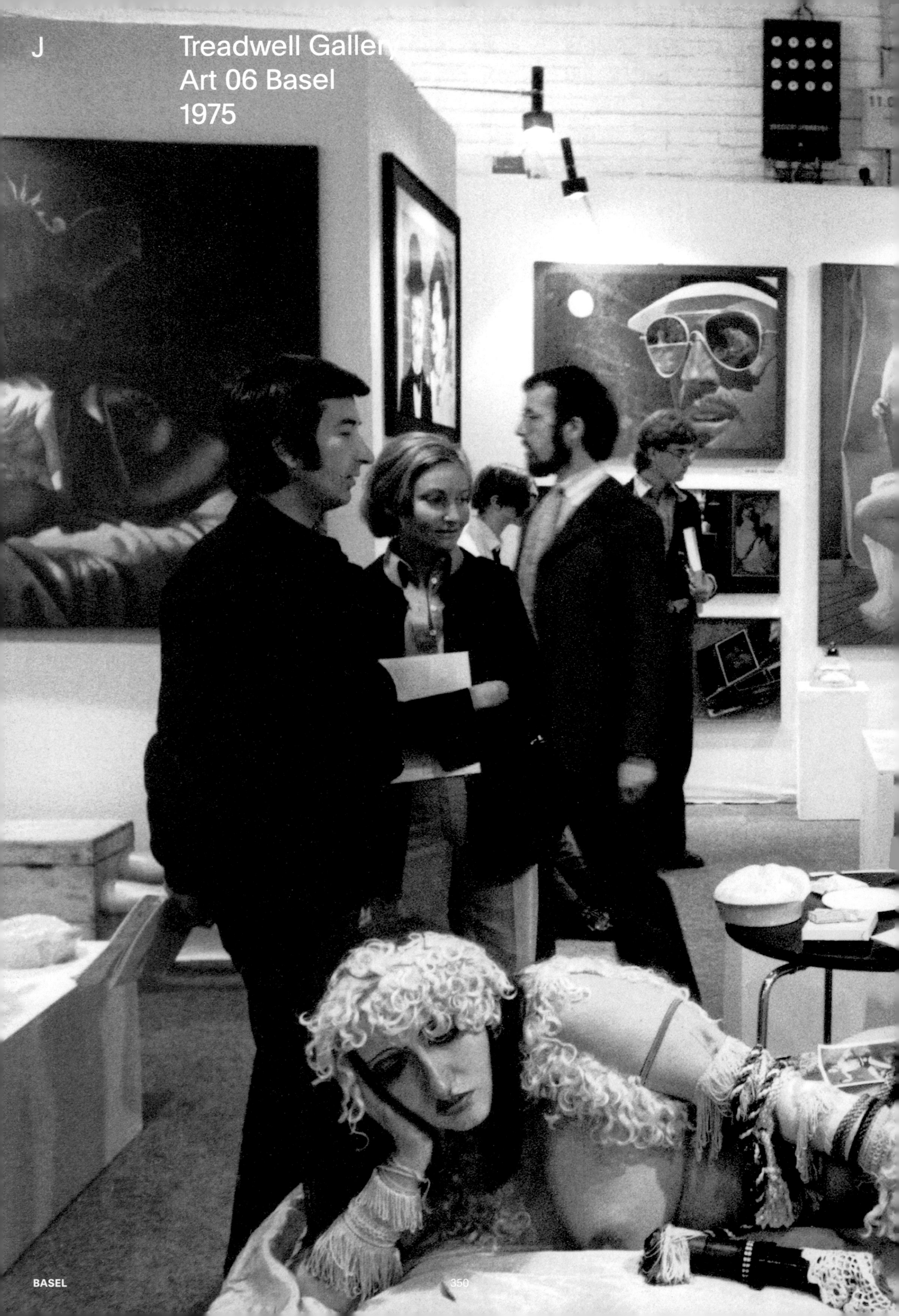

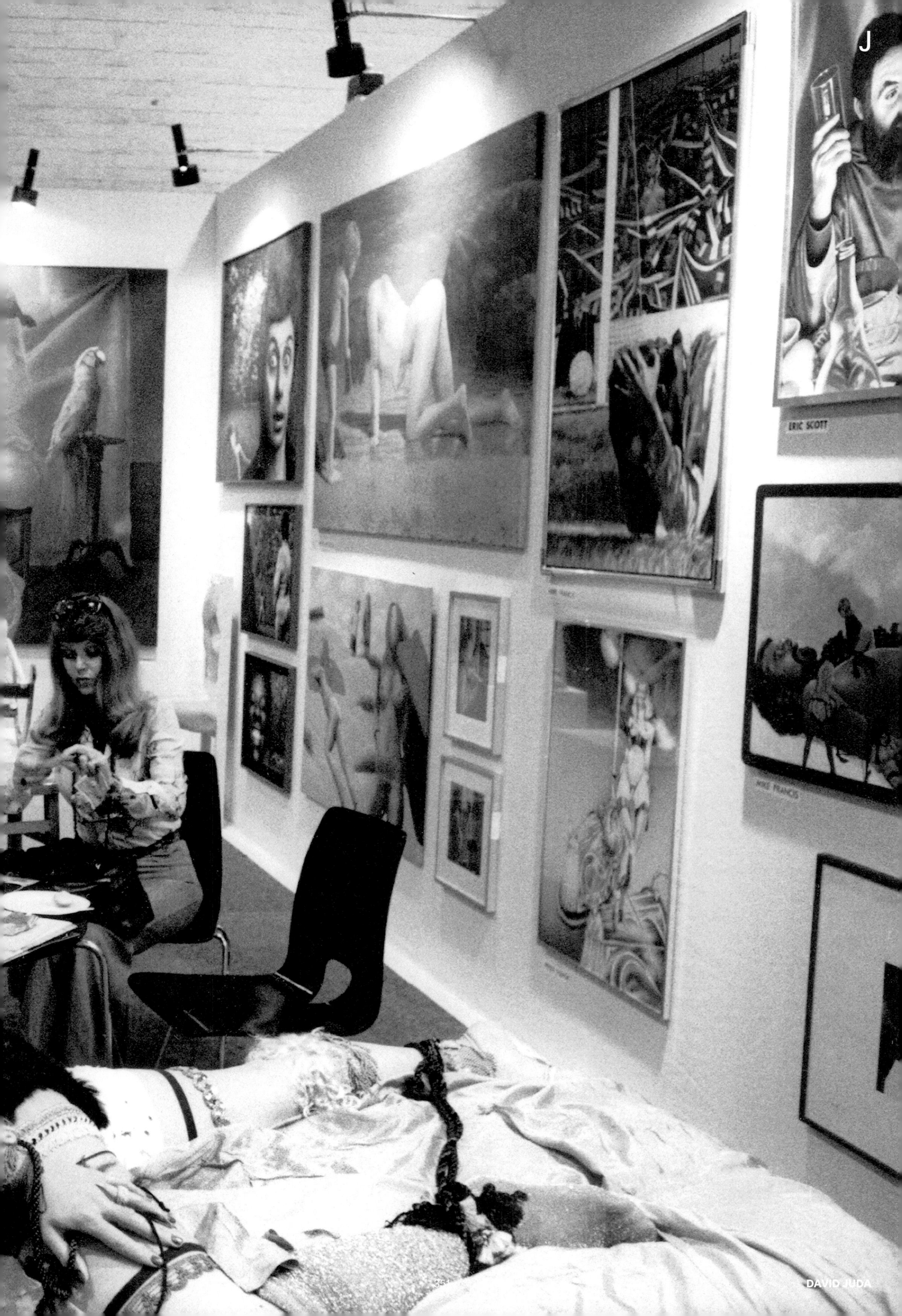

DAVID JUDA

Daniel Keel
Art 04 Basel
1973

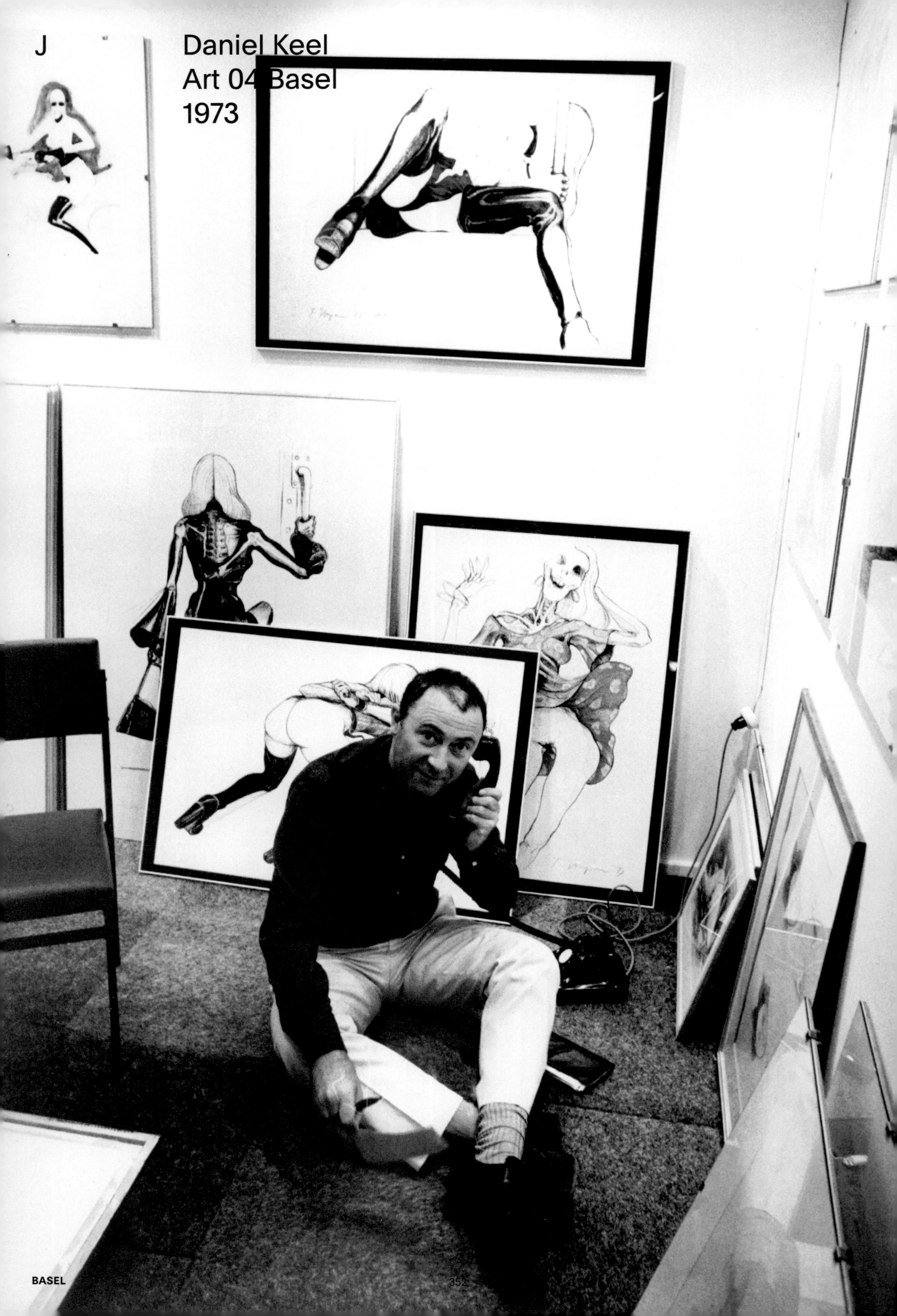

LIONEL BOVIER Over the years, the fair has made considerable efforts to *curate* itself, for example with the creation of film/video sector, the Unlimited and Public projects, and so on ...

DJ This all came with Lorenzo Rudolf, director of the fair in the 1990s. Beforehand, directors were really good "Messe" organizers, but they were not creative people. Lorenzo Rudolf started this whole thing, and Sam Keller furthered it. It can be a danger to make the fair too curated—the fair should remain a fair, a place for trade, but I think the current directors are getting the balance right.

CD Could you recount some anecdotes about the founders of the fair, Ernst Beyeler, Trudi Bruckner, and Balz Hilt?

DJ Beyeler was the biggest dealer in the world. He ran an extremely professional small business, with mammoth figures for those days. The fair would open around 10 or 11 am, and you would go to Beyeler in the morning and have an audience. You could look at his stock, where he had wonderful things. His stock would be selling like hotcakes between 8 and 11 am. At the time, there were a lot more dealers who would buy from dealers. The stock was actually much more often owned than today. The fair used to end on the Monday evening, and the reason for that was that Monday was really the day when dealers would go around and, if they'd made some money, buy something. This has changed a lot.

CD Could you tell us about the history of the Annely Juda gallery?

DJ Its history starts with my mother and father's divorce in 1955, when I was a child. My mother, who had lived in England during the war (both my parents were German), went back to live in Germany for four or five years between 1950 and 1955, and then came back to London after the divorce. She had three children, and got difficult jobs before eventually starting to work as a secretary for the collector Eric Estorick. She learned a lot there, though he was a very difficult person.

She then found a job in a gallery, and in 1960 she set up her own gallery with a backer—the Molton Gallery. In 1963 she opened Hamilton Galleries, again with a backer. The collectors who backed the gallery were not very pleased because it wasn't making any money. My mother put on a lot of very contemporary exhibitions that didn't sell. So in November 1967 she had to close, and I, who was at the time in the Merchant Navy, rang her. She was very upset by the gallery closing so I left the Navy and gave her a hand.

I didn't know much about galleries, but I'd been brought up in the art world, and I was quite good with figures. We then worked from home, and with £1,000 that a collector gave us we opened in a small space near Charlotte Street, which was not an area for art galleries in those days. It was an old warehouse, which we converted into a room. Our rent was, I think, £4,000 per year! Then we got another room, and another room.

We didn't have any money, but my mother had a very good reputation. She knew a lot of people, she could go to people like Ernst Beyeler and they would lend her pictures. She had a quite good group of young artists—we always, right from the very beginning, wanted to show contemporary and mid-career artists, as well as mount historical exhibitions.

In the 1970s we started being very involved in Russian art, which interested us, and we did a series of exhibitions that became quite important. It was mainly Russian art, but also De Stijl, Bauhaus, and so on. Some of the exhibitions were the most important at the time in London—people would come to London in the summer then, something else that has changed. One of the first shows my mother did was called *Modern Images in Ancient Times* (1969), which mixed contemporary artworks like a Giacometti with antiquities such as Persian pieces. At that time, this sort of mix was new. We were also one of the few galleries in Britain at that time that was showing quite a few foreign artists. My mother showed quite a lot of artists from France in the early 1960s.

I started in 1967, became a partner in the late 1970s, and officially took over the gallery in 1988. My mother continued to work and was part of the gallery right up until she died. She was at Art Basel when she was 90, standing there. She came to Basel until 2004, and died in 2006. So we worked together for a long time, which has its advantages and disadvantages. But the disadvantages are outweighed, because when you work with somebody in the family you understand each other's thinking. We would go to a collector, see an image,

J

Galerie Schmela
Art 05 Basel
1974

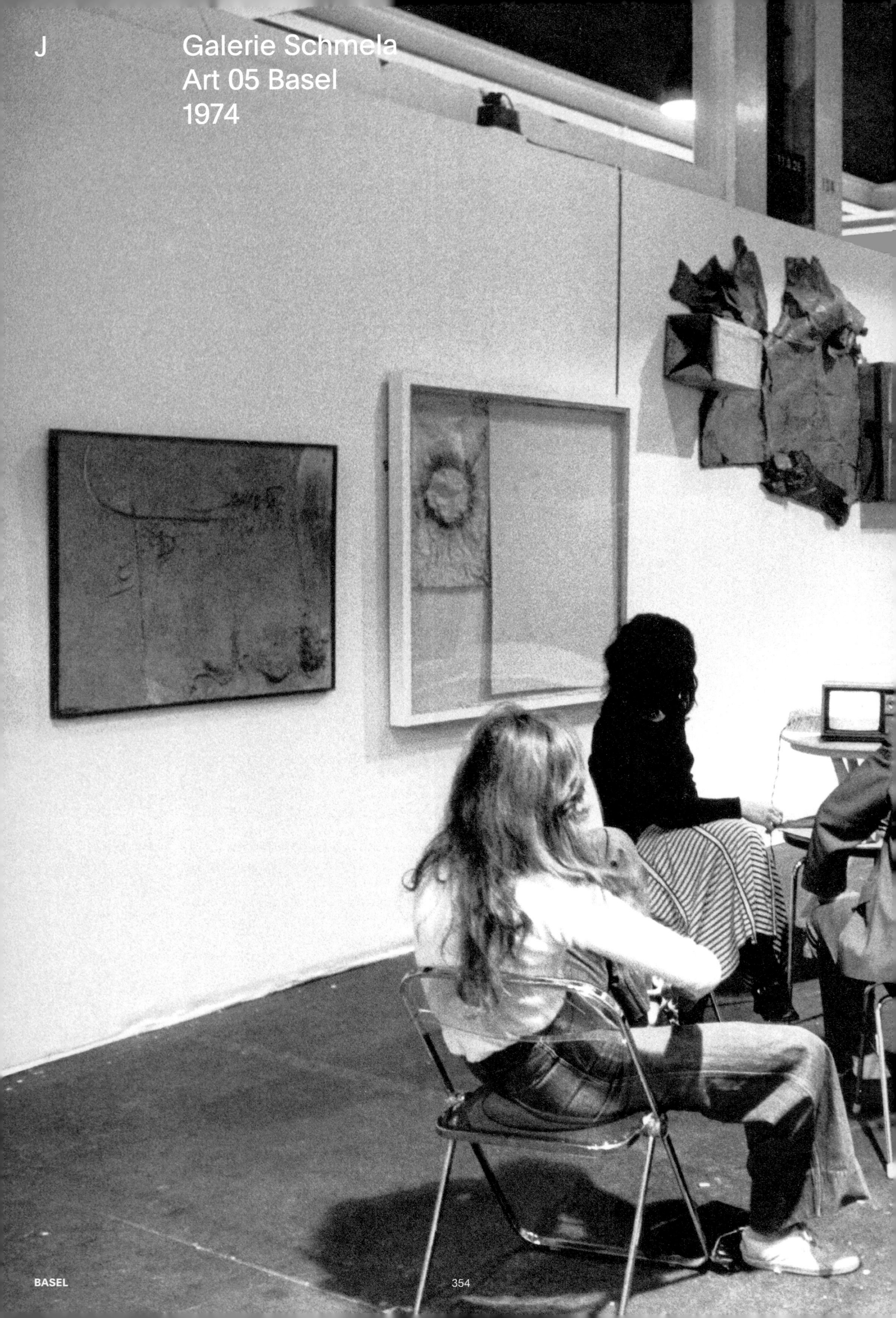

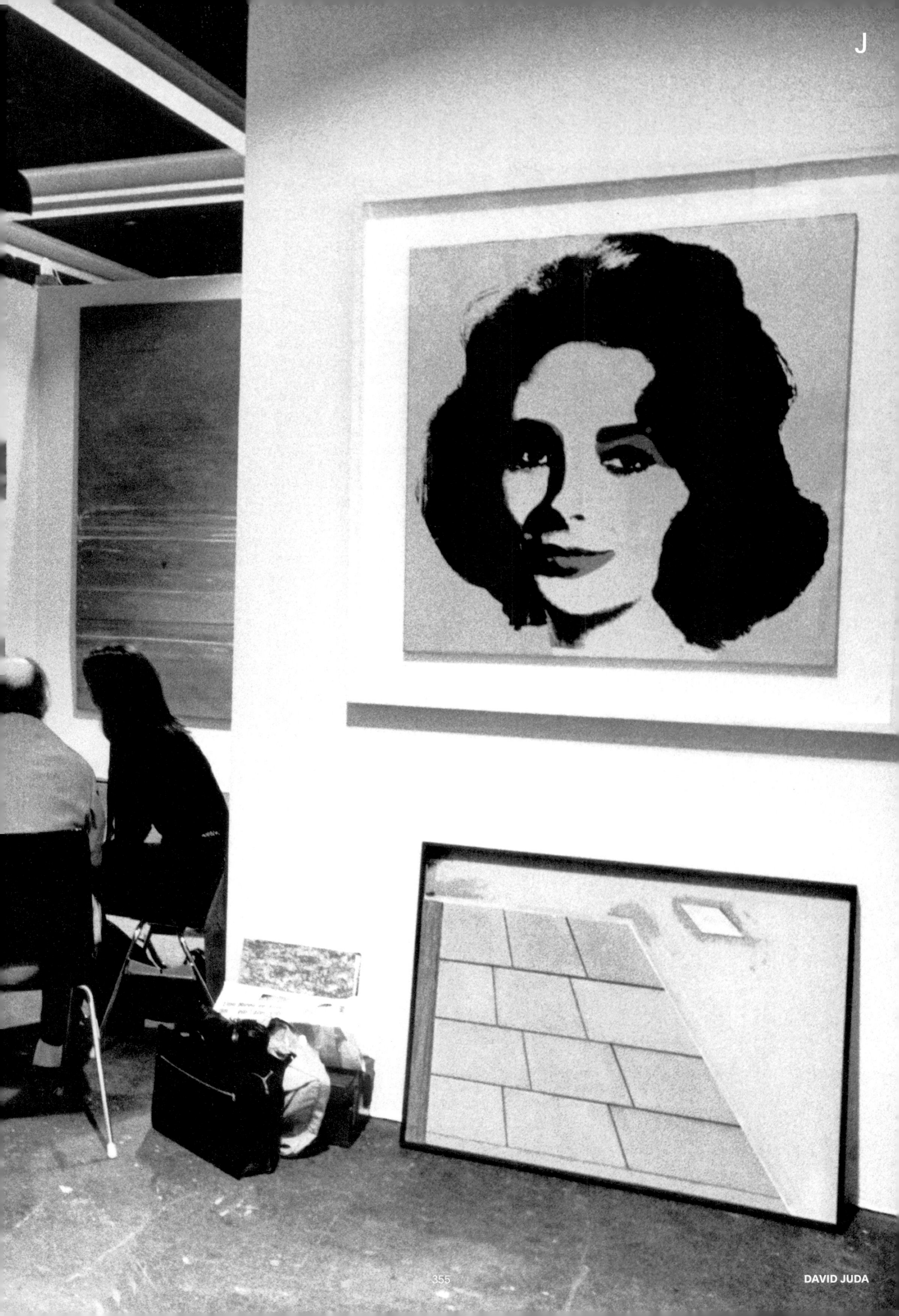

J

and know immediately what we would like to do. Except toward the end, when my choices became maybe too contemporary for her, we had very similar taste.

CD You were also present at the beginning of Art Basel in Miami Beach, and you participated in Art Basel in Hong Kong's first edition in May 2013. How do you approach each fair and each audience?

DJ Probably the easiest for us is Art Basel, because we are very European in our outlook. It's the most successful fair for us, and the one at which the collectors understand what we are showing the best. Miami Beach is more difficult because we don't have a lot of American artists. Even artists like David Hockney or Leon Kossoff are in a way not so popular in Miami Beach. Hong Kong, on the other hand, is much easier for us because my mother sold works in Japan since the early 1960s. I started going to Japan and building connections with the Far East in 1970. Later on, in the late 1970s, I married a Japanese woman, and I've been doing business since the early 1980s with Korea. Not so much in mainland China, but in Hong Kong, Singapore, Malaysia, so we have quite a lot of connections and we have the sort of art they are interested in.

CD Did artists used to come to the fair at the beginning?

DJ Not so much, because they thought it wasn't their place, and also it was much more like a trade fair. The business between the gallerists was what was the most important.

LB Regarding the relationship to institutions, was it more important in terms of business at the time?

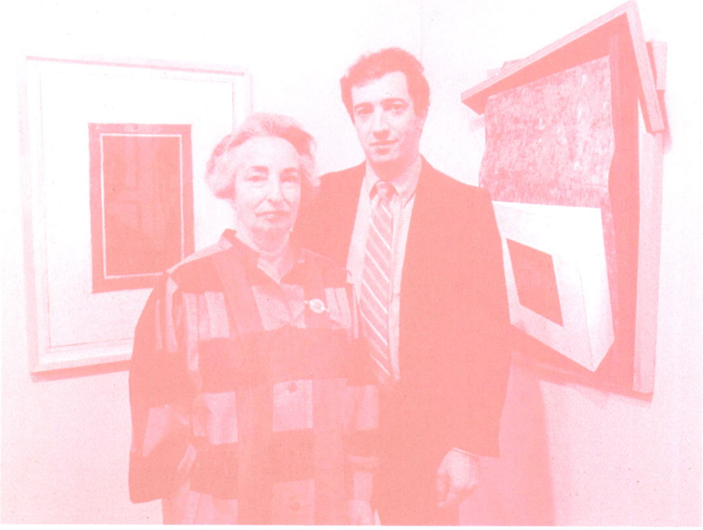

Annely & David Juda, 1985

There are a lot of people involved in the arts now who are probably extremely professional and very good, but not so intensely involved. — David Juda

DJ Yes, there were very important museum directors who came, and I'm sure it is still the case today, but institutions don't come so much anymore to make acquisitions. There's a lot of manipulation now. When there are pictures being sold at a price higher than one's country's GDP, put that into perspective! It was also not such a mass of money, and not so serious. I would go out all night and turn up at the fair looking like shit, and it was OK. The whole art business has changed a lot: if you make a mistake now on a price, you can be in deep trouble.

There are a lot of people involved in the arts now who are probably extremely professional and very good, but not so intensely involved. I'm not simply being nostalgic, it's true. There is a side of the art business that is very beautiful, but there's also a side that's a bit depressing.

LB What is the level of preparation that you do now compared to those first years? When you organize a booth at the fair, do you send documentation to your collectors, starting months in advance?

DJ Yes. Things have also changed in the sense that if you would ask me what percentage of my business is art-fair involved, even seven or eight years ago, I would have said between 5 or 10 percent maximum. Now it could be 30 percent. It's a lot. And for some galleries this is 80 or 90 percent.

Most of my time I spend organizing exhibitions, making catalogues, and doing things in the gallery, but the gallery is becoming less and less involved. People are not coming to the galleries as much. We have people coming to our David Hockney show, of course, but if I take one of my "normal" artists, it can be very quiet at the gallery sometimes, which is quite depressing because that's the core. I'm not a nomad that goes from fair to fair. In a way I would prefer not to do as many fairs as I'm doing.

Ernst Beyeler
Art 07 Basel
1976

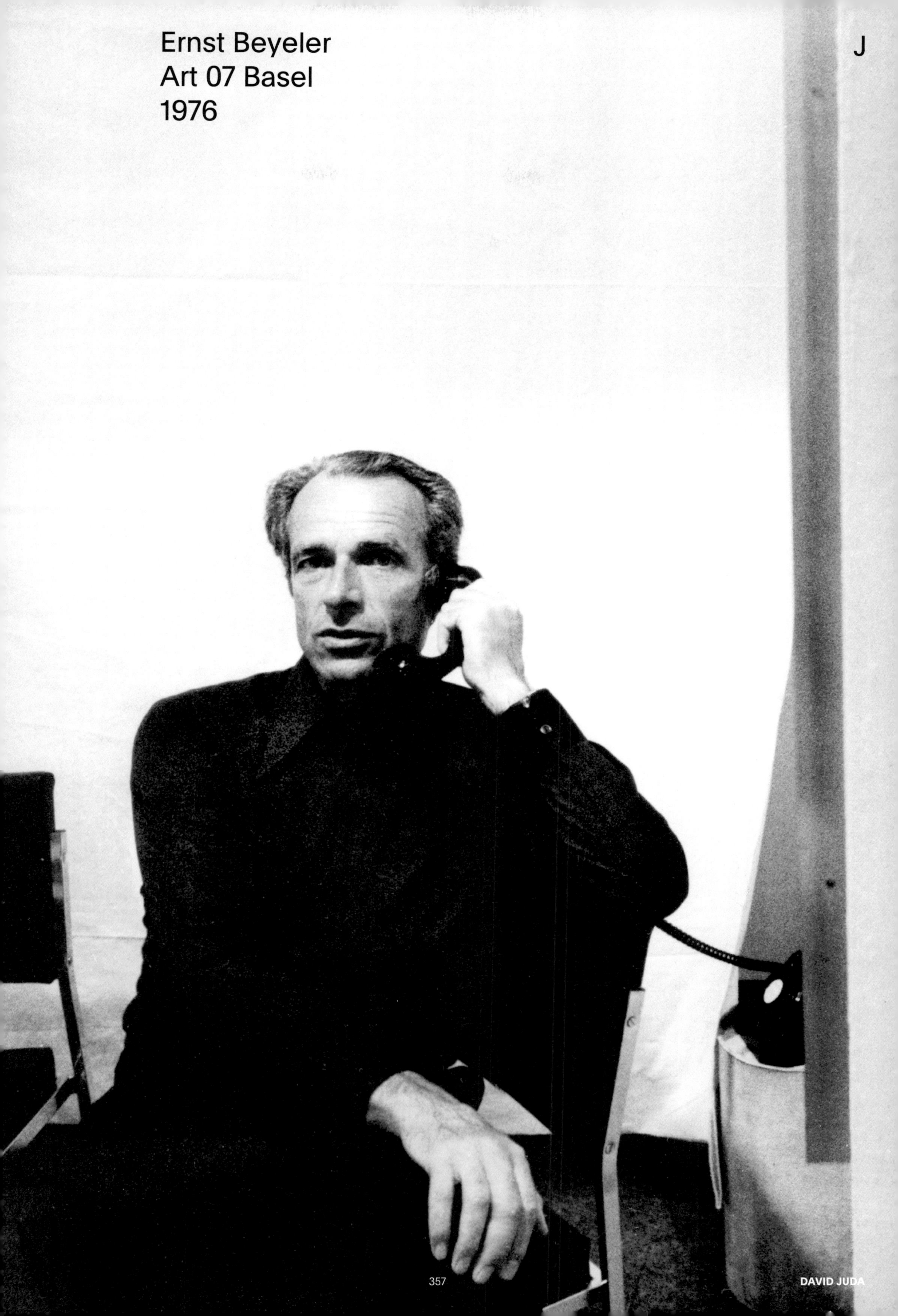

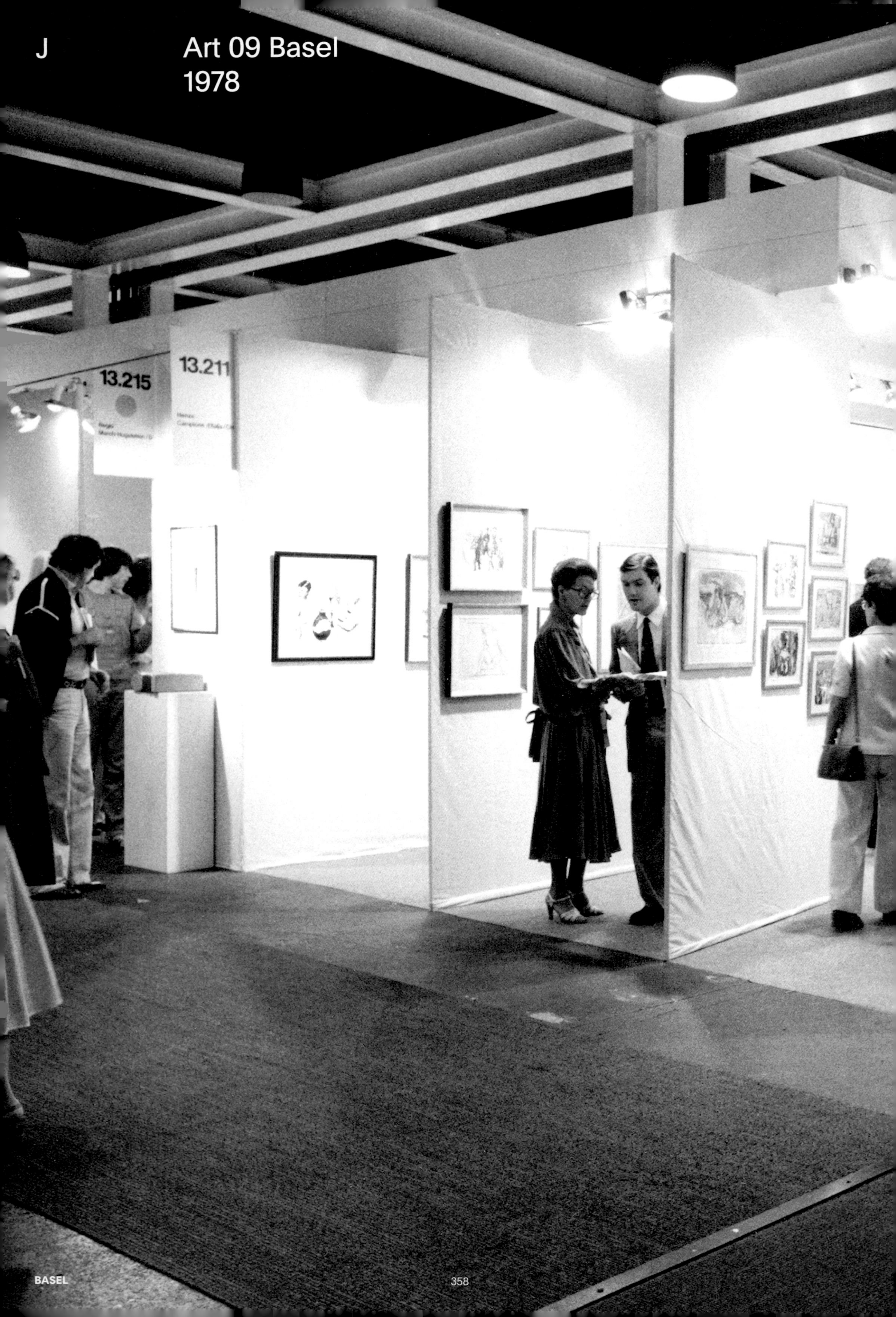

Art 09 Basel
1978

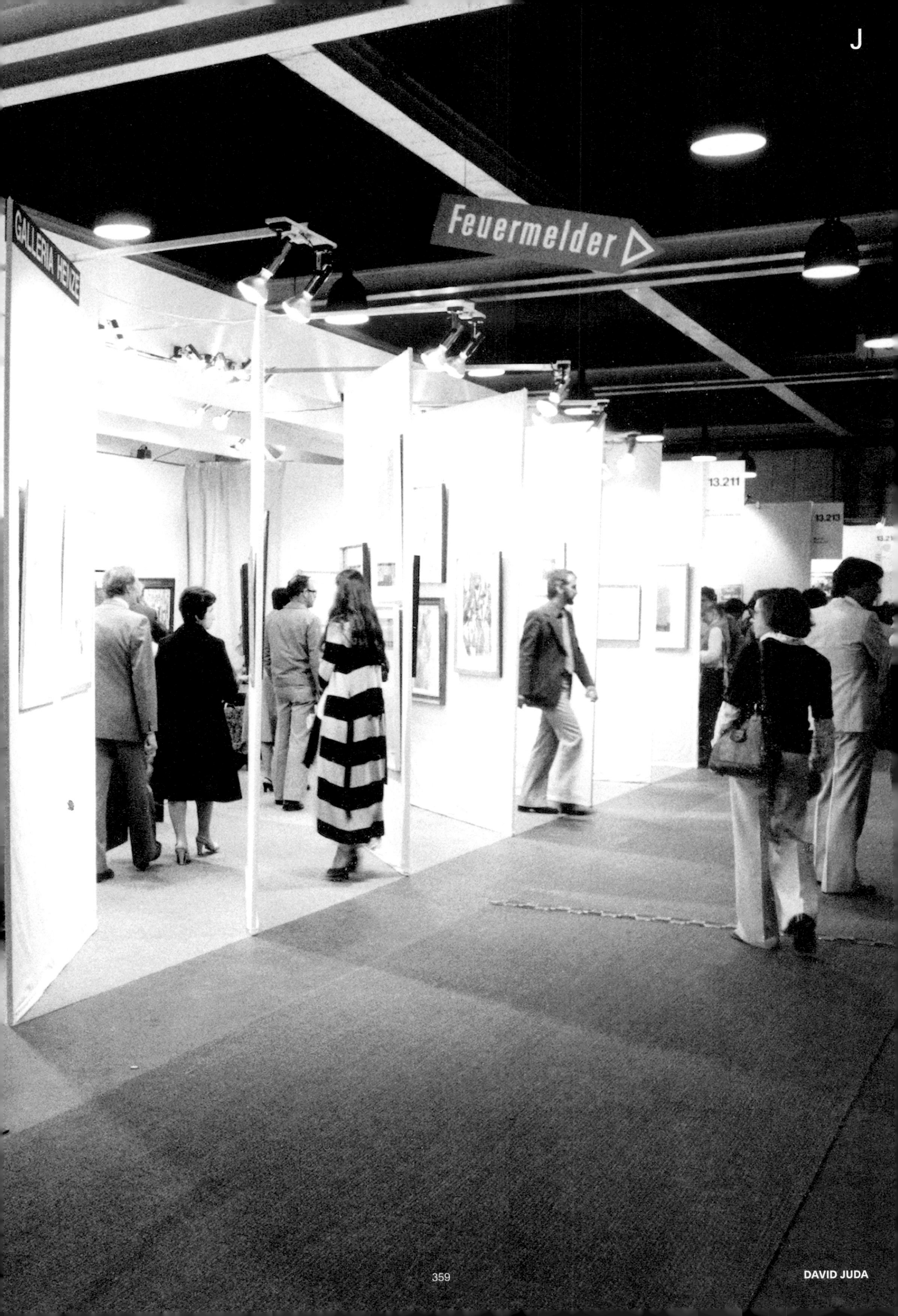
Feuermelder
GALLERIA HENZE
13.211
13.213

K

- Hong Kong
- Basel
- Miami Beach

Kaikai Kiki

Tokyo
Taipei

Galleries

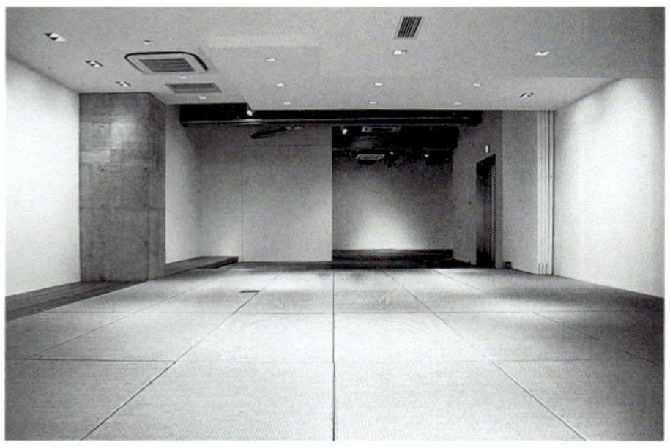

What first compelled you to open a gallery?
As an artist, I often observed the gallerists I deal with and was envious of the joy which they seemed to bring to their work. Specifically: 1. They deal with the artists of their age in real time. 2. To deal directly with clients gives one a real sense of the present state of the art world. 3. They are able to present to an audience artists and works that they admire and have those audience members like them.

Who is the first artist you showed and what was most memorable about that show?
The first show was a group exhibition featuring Chiho Aoshima, Chinatsu Ban, Mark Grotjahn, Seonna Hong, Akane Koide, Matthew Monahan, Mr., Takashi Murakami, Rei Sato, and Aya Takano. In other words, it was the first time that the artists whose careers I had helped cultivate were exhibited alongside my own work.

When did you first participate in Art Basel and what was most memorable about that show?
Our first participation at an Art Basel fair was in Hong Kong in 2013. We were blown away by the energy, the quality of the galleries on view, and the mentality of the collectors. It was a great reminder of the current vitality of the Asian market. We hope to participate to the fair in Basel at some point in the future.

- **Contact** Kaikai Kiki Gallery
  Brad Plumb
  brad@kaikaikikiny.net
  info@kaikaikikiny.net
- **Established** 2008
- **Owner(s) / Partner(s)** Takashi Murakami
- **Team** 7
- **Space(s)** 160 m²
- **Artists at Art Basel** JNTHED
  Friedrich Kunath
  Haruka Makita
  Matthew Monahan
  ob
  Oguchi
  Anselm Reyle
  Anri Sala

Kalfayan

Athens
Thessaloniki

Discoveries
Positions

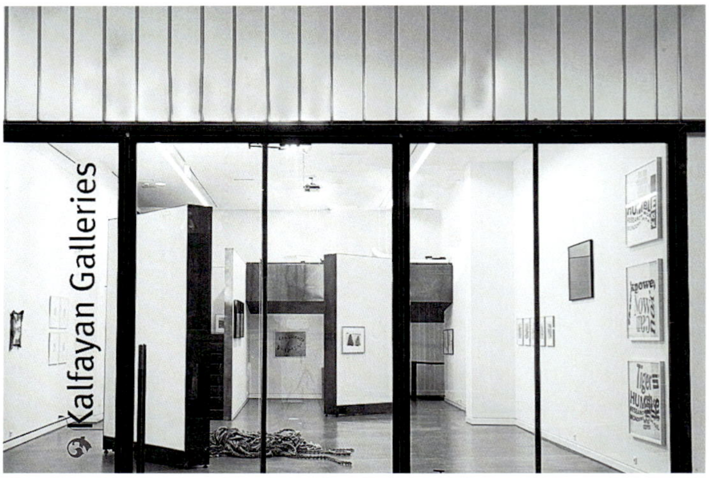

What first compelled you to open a gallery?
The wish to promote the work of Greek artists internationally, and at the same time to create a dynamic platform which would act as a bridge between Eastern and Western visual cultures.

Who is the first artist you showed and what was most memorable about that show?
The first gallery show was with Nikos Navridis and it was also his first solo show. Photographs from 18 years ago reveal the glamour and formal character of gallery openings as social events, where people would come in their Sunday best. In today's world of crisis and collapse of the old order, these events are accompanied by a more "casual" attitude, at least in Greece.

When did you first participate in Art Basel and what was most memorable about that show?
The first participation was Art Basel in Hong Kong in 2013, with a curated show featuring photographs from Hrair Sarkissian's *Istory* (2011) series and porcelain works from Raed Yassin's *Yassin Dynasty* (2013). A Greek gallery exhibiting Middle Eastern artists in Asia proved a unique and successful blending of cultures!

- **Contact** Kalfayan Galleries
  Yuli Karatsiki
  yuli@kalfayangalleries.com
  info@kalfayangalleries.com
- **Established** 1995
- **Owner(s) / Partner(s)** Arsen Kalfayan
  Roupen Kalfayan
- **Team** 8
- **Space(s)** 400 m²
- **Artists at Art Basel** Hrair Sarkissian
  Stefanos Tsivopoulos
  Raed Yassin
- **Further artists represented** Alexis Akrithakis
  Stephen Antonakos
  Vartan Avakian
  Bill Balaskas
  Breda Beban
  Rania Bellou
  Emmanouil Bitsakis
  Vlassis Caniaris
  Ala Dehghan
  Diohandi
  Aikaterini Gegisian
  Stratos Kalafatis
  Maria Loizidou
  Adrian Paci
  Nina Papaconstantinou
  Sister Corita
  Dimitris Tataris
  Panos Tsagaris
  Constantin Xenakis

Kamm

Berlin • Galleries

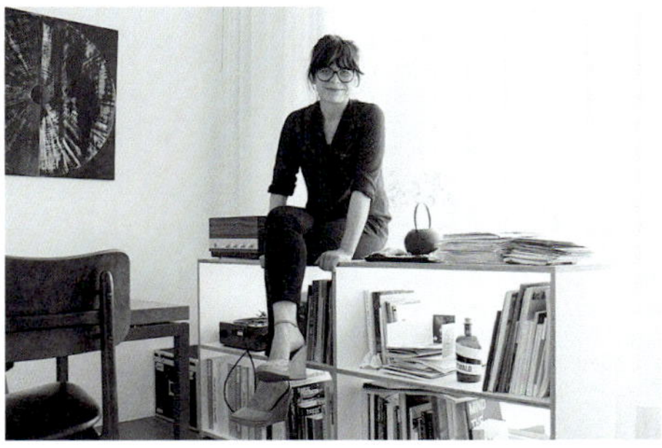

What first compelled you to open a gallery?
To work together with a small group of artists, to grow together with them, to dip deep into their imagination.

Who is the first artist you showed and what was most memorable about that show?
Albrecht Schäfer had the first show in the gallery, the title was *Berlin Alexanderplatz*. Based on the notion that the history of Alexanderplatz isn't only what was actually constructed, but also of the many proposals by architects and political organizations that were never realized, the artist developed a number of scenarios that integrate historical facts with historical possibilities. It was in 2001 when the discussion about Alexanderplatz was a big social topic. We got tons of reviews and we had 100 visitors on one day. I had never worked in a gallery before and thought that it will always be like that.

When did you first participate in Art Basel and what was most memorable about that show?
My first participation was in 2006 in the Statements sector. We showed Simon Dybbroe Møller with his project *All yesterday's parties*. The project was about the quality of decay and disappearance as a chance to create something new, and this reflected a new chapter in the history of the gallery that started at this time. There was an incredible intensity in both.

- **Contact** — Galerie Kamm, Joanna Kamm, joanna@galeriekamm.de, info@galeriekamm.de
- **Established** — 2001
- **Owner(s) / Partner(s)** — Joanna Kamm
- **Team** — 4
- **Space(s)** — 214 m²
- **Artists at Art Basel** — Kate Davis, Michele Di Menna, Simon Dybbroe Møller, Charlie Hammond, Christoph Meier, Albrecht Schäfer, Claudia Wieser
- **Further artists represented** — Agnieszka Brzezanska, Amy Granat, Katharina Jahnke, Annette Kisling, Lorna Macintyre, Pavel Pepperstein, Bernd Ribbeck, Annette Ruenzler, Kathrin Sonntag

Kaplan

New York • Galleries • Galleries

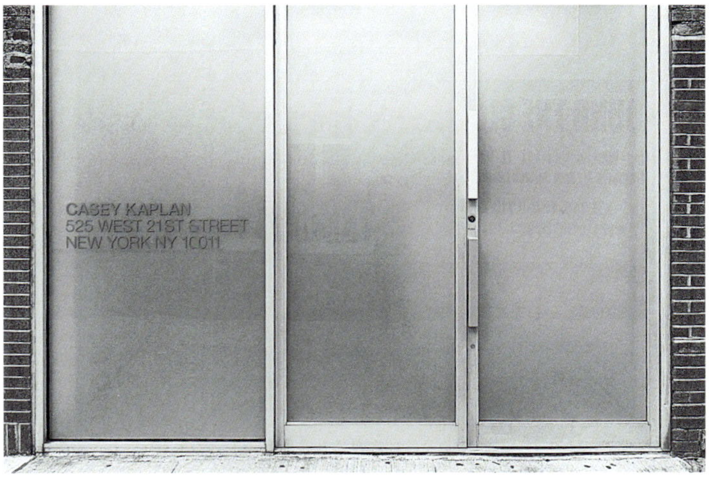

What first compelled you to open a gallery?
Growing up in Manhattan, I spent a large part of my childhood being taken by family members to museums and galleries. In my immediate family no one was a true collector, but their access to and knowledge of the art of their time was very much informed by my grandmother's sister, the collector Ethel Scull. These influences pushed me toward the study of art history. I soon realized that my calling was not in darkened lecture halls viewing slides of projected artworks, but rather with my deep desire to be around artists. During the summer breaks at university, I began working at art galleries uptown and in SoHo, and upon graduation I started an internship at Paula Cooper. I was soon hired to work at the front desk and as an archivist at Pace Gallery at their Greene Street location, where I had the chance to witness exhibitions by Robert Irwin, Donald Judd, Dan Flavin, Robert Ryman, and many others. After two years I left in order to begin collaborations with artists of my own generation, and opened a space where I could create my own program.

Who is the first artist you showed and what was most memorable about that show?
It was in 1995, in a single room on an upper floor of a cast iron building in SoHo on Broadway between Houston and Prince Streets, with a solo show by artist Jane Fine.

- **Contact** — Casey Kaplan, Alice Conconi, alice@caseykaplangallery.com, info@caseykaplangallery.com
- **Established** — 1995
- **Owner(s) / Partner(s)** — Casey Kaplan
- **Team** — 7
- **Space(s)** — 465 m²
- **Artists at Art Basel** — Henning Bohl, Matthew Brannon, Jeff Burton, Nathan Carter, Jason Dodge, Trisha Donnelly, Geoffrey Farmer, Liam Gillick, Giorgio Griffa, Brian Jungen, Sanya Kantarovsky, Jonathan Monk, Marlo Pascual, Diego Perrone, Pietro Roccasalva, Julia Schmidt, Simon Starling, David Thorpe, Annika von Hausswolff, Gabriel Vormstein, Garth Weiser, Johannes Wohnseifer

Kargl

Vienna — Galleries

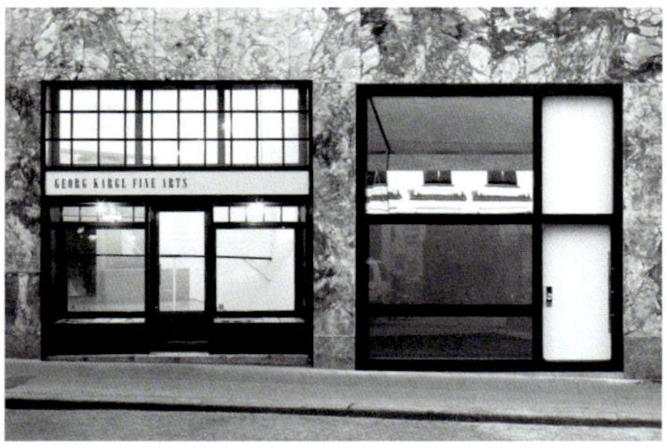

What first compelled you to open a gallery?
The change from Art Nouveau to contemporary art and the ever persisting interest in contemporary art since 1971.

Who is the first artist you showed and what was most memorable about that show?
Chuck Close—the possibility to show such a grandmaster in an almost new gallery in "little" Vienna.

When did you first participate in Art Basel and what was most memorable about that show?
In 2000, in the Statements sector, and since 2001 we participate annually in Art Basel. Best art fair "as always as ever" (Stan Laurel).

- **Contact** Georg Kargl Fine Arts
  Fiona Liewehr
  georg.kargl@georgkargl.com
- **Established** 1990 (Galerie Metropol)/1998
- **Owner(s) / Partner(s)** Georg Kargl
- **Team** 8
- **Space(s)** 350 m² (gallery)
  30 m² ("BOX")
  30 m² ("Permanent")
- **Artists at Art Basel** Clegg & Guttmann
  Mark Dion
  Andreas Fogarasi
  Herbert Hinteregger
  Bernhard Leitner
  Thomas Locher
  Inés Lombardi
  David Maljkovic
  Matt Mullican
  Muntean/Rosenblum
  Gerwald Rockenschaub
  Nedko Solakov
  Erwin Thorn
  Marcel van Eeden
  Nadim Vardag
- **Further artists represented** Richard Artschwager
  Matthias Bitzer
  Carter
  Martin Dammann
  Koenraad Dedobbeleer
  Agnes Fuchs
  Franz Graf
  Michael Gumhold
  Jitka Hanzlová
  Chris Johanson
  Björn Kämmerer
  Sanna Kannisto
  Herwig Kempinger
  Harald Klingelhöller
  Yves Mettler
  Christian Philipp Müller
  Max Peintner
  Raymond Pettibon
  Wolfgang Plöger
  Agnieszka Polska
  Liddy Scheffknecht
  Gabi Trinkaus
  Rosemarie Trockel
  Marijke van Warmerdam
  Costa Vece
  Ina Weber
  Nicole Wermers
  Cerith Wyn Evans
  Richard Zeiss

Karma International

Zurich — Discoveries, Nova

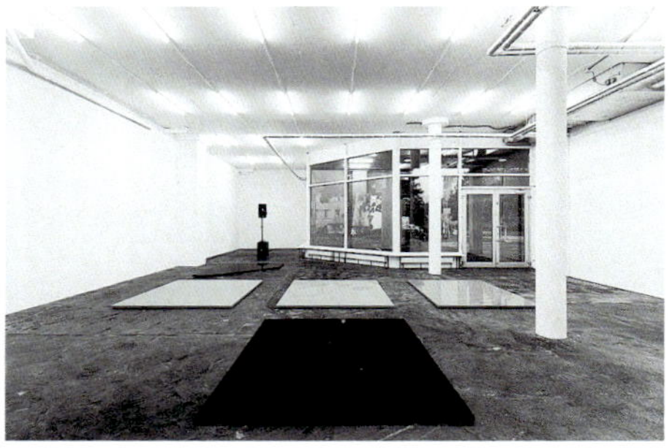

What first compelled you to open a gallery?
We met during our studies in art history at Zurich University. We were both strongly interested in contemporary art. Marina worked in galleries and institutions to support her studies, Karolina as an art critic, so our paths would often cross. Around that time we decided to curate a show together. It took place in a huge empty attic space in the flat share where Karolina lived. We did not have a lot of money so each of us chipped in 300 CHF. That was all we needed and the project took on its own dynamic right away. We created a website, a publication, and an edition. An artist friend suggested the name "Karma International" by text message; we loved it. From that time on we curated shows in different places, such as Zurich, Warsaw, New York, and Los Angeles. After two years we grew close to our artists, and followed the development of their careers. Together with the artists we decided it made sense to grow and develop together from a not-for-profit curatorial project into a commercial gallery.

- **Contact** Karma International
  Victoria Gaemperli
  victoria@karmainternational.org
  info@karmainternational.org
- **Established** 2008
- **Owner(s) / Partner(s)** Karolina Dankow
  Marina Leuenberger
- **Team** 5
- **Space(s)** 160 m²
- **Artists at Art Basel** Ida Ekblad
  Pamela Rosenkranz
  Thomas Sauter
  Keiichi Tanaami
- **Further artists represented** Agnieszka Brzezanska
  Kim Seob Boninsegni
  David Hominal
  Thomas Julier
  Tobias Madison
  Carissa Rodriguez
  Emanuel Rossetti
  Martin Soto Climent
  Sergei Tcherepnin

Kasmin

New York — Galleries, Galleries

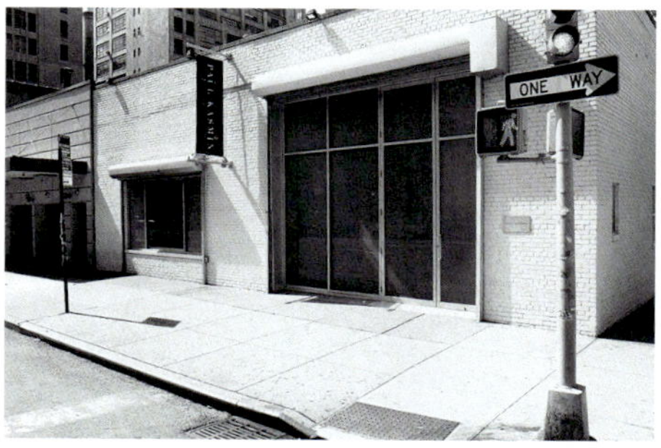

What first compelled you to open a gallery?
After a number of years dealing privately, I felt a need to open a space and exhibit what interested me. Soon thereafter I started representing contemporary artists; and this is what

gives me the most pleasure in life.

Who is the first artist you showed and what was most memorable about that show?

My first exhibition was a selection of Brancusi's photographs, an excellent medium for the artist as it was of utmost importance to him that the viewer see his sculptures as he saw them. In a minuscule gallery space on Broadway in SoHo I opened my doors with this exhibition, and the response was tremendously positive. Now it is a great privilege to revisit this artist with an exhibition celebrating the centennial anniversary of the 1913 Armory Show, in which Brancusi showed five sculptures that directed modern sculpture onto a radical new path.

When did you first participate in Art Basel and what was most memorable about that show?

Paul Kasmin Gallery exhibited in the inaugural edition of Art Basel in Miami Beach. We brought a broad mix of artists and estates we represented, and it was an extraordinary success. I was immediately impressed by the organization of the fair, and how it was unlike any other art fair in America.

- **Contact** — Paul Kasmin Gallery
Clara Ha
claraha@paulkasmingallery.com
info@paulkasmingallery.com
- **Established** — 1989
- **Owner(s) / Partner(s)** — Paul Kasmin
- **Team** — 25
- **Space(s)** — 1,700 m²
- **Artists at Art Basel** — Arman
Mattia Bonetti
Taner Ceylan
Saint Clair Cemin
Ian Davenport
Barry Flanagan
Caio Fonseca
Walton Ford
Simon Hantaï
Nir Hod
Robert Indiana
Deborah Kass
David LaChapelle
Claude & François-Xavier Lalanne
Morris Louis
Nyoman Masriadi
Santi Moix
William N. Copley
James Nares
Iván Navarro
Erik Parker
Elliott Puckette
Nancy Rubins
Mark Ryden
Will Ryman
Makoto Saito
Kenny Scharf
Tseng Kwong Chi
Andy Warhol

kaufmann repetto

Milan
New York (temporary)

Galleries
Unlimited
Galleries

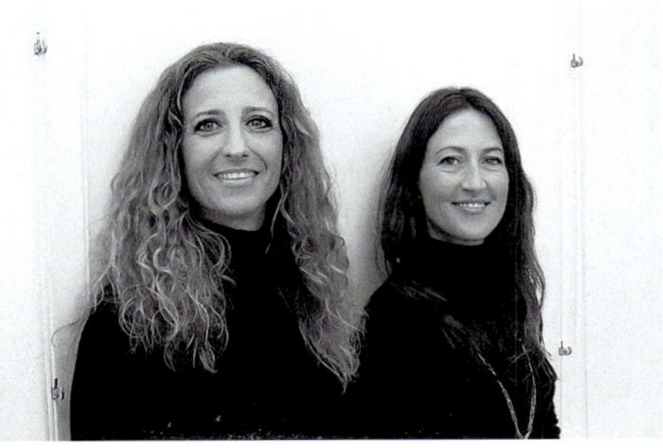

What first compelled you to open a gallery?

The will to work side by side with artists and to actively share their vision.

Who is the first artist you showed and what was most memorable about that show?

Candice Breitz opened our gallery with a blasting multi-channel video installation entitled *Babel Series*. The Milanese public was shocked. The general feeling was "Francesca is a kamikaze." Within the next two years, the work was shown in the greatest international museums.

When did you first participate in Art Basel and what was most memorable about that show?

In 2004, in the Statements sector with Pierpaolo Campanini. It was really exciting for a young dealer to be part of such a legendary sector of the most established art fair in the world.

- **Contact** — kaufmann repetto
Maria Acciaro
info@kaufmannrepetto.com
- **Established** — 2000
- **Owner(s) / Partner(s)** — Francesca Kaufmann
Chiara Repetto
- **Team** — 6
- **Space(s)** — 320 m² + 50 m² (courtyard)
- **Artists at Art Basel** — Andrea Bowers
Pierpaolo Campanini
Gianni Caravaggio
Thea Djordjadze
Shannon Ebner
Latifa Echakhch
Judith Hopf
Nicola Martini
Carlo Mollino
Adrian Paci
Matt Sheridan Smith
Pae White
- **Further artists represented** — Candice Breitz
Maggie Cardelús
Talia Chetrit
Edi Hila
Yoshua Okón
Dan Perjovschi
Eva Rothschild
Aïda Ruilova
Billy Sullivan
Lily van der Stokker
Thomas Zipp

Kelly

New York

Galleries
Galleries
Unlimited
Galleries

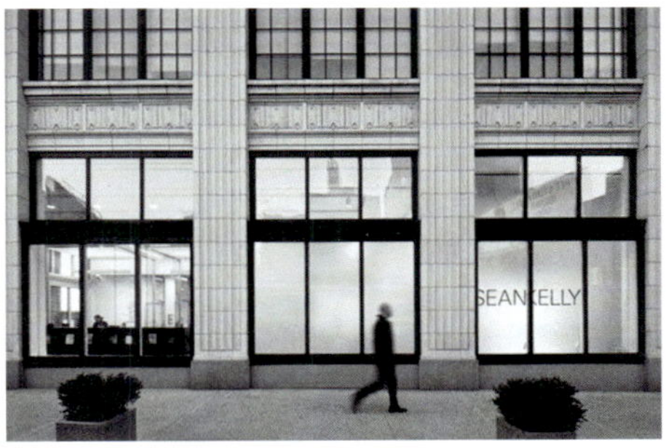

What first compelled you to open a gallery?

I am originally from the curatorial side of the art world—I was the Visual Arts Director of the Bath International Art Festival in the 1980s. I came to New York in the early 1990s to develop my commercial presence in the industry—in one of the most important and vibrant arts centers in the world. From the beginning it was my mission to establish a reputation for a diverse, intellectually driven, unconventional exhibition program and to represent artists that exemplify the gallery's commitment to exhibiting important, challenging contemporary art.

Who is the first artist you showed and what was most memorable about that show?

An early memorable exhibition was Marina Abramović in 1995. It opened with a one-evening performance, the artist's first performance in more than ten years in New York.

When did you first participate in Art Basel and what was most memorable about that show?

Our first participation was in 2001 in Basel, and 2002 in Miami Beach. It was wonderful to receive such an enthusiastic response to our inaugural participation.

- **Contact** Sean Kelly Gallery
Thomas Kelly
thomas@skny.com
info@skny.com
- **Established** 1995
- **Owner(s) / Partner(s)** Sean Kelly
- **Team** 15
- **Space(s)** 2,043 m²
- **Artists at Art Basel** Marina Abramović
Los Carpinteros
James Casebere
Iran do Espírito Santo
Leandro Erlich
Antony Gormley
Laurent Grasso
Johan Grimonprez
Rebecca Horn
Tehching Hsieh
Callum Innes
Idris Khan
Terence Koh
Joseph Kosuth
Peter Liversidge
Nathan Mabry
Robert Mapplethorpe
Anthony McCall
Julião Sarmento
Alec Soth
Frank Thiel
Kehinde Wiley

Keng

Taipei
Beijing

● Galleries

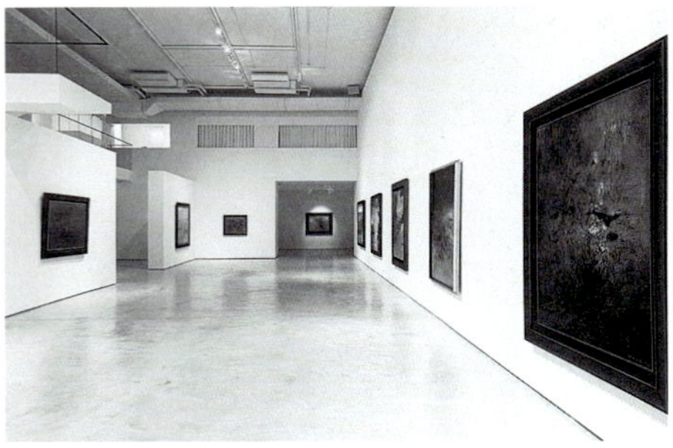

What first compelled you to open a gallery?
To support visionary Asian artists and to build bridges with international institutions, collections, and connoisseurs of Asian modern art to promote these artists.

Who is the first artist you showed and what was most memorable about that show?
The first solo exhibition we presented was of Sanyu. In general, audiences were amazed by his art, as it was very different from the trends of the time. One unforgettable response of a client was that he thought it was too simple, he believed his child could paint just as well.

When did you first participate in Art Basel and what was most memorable about that show?
In 2013. It was really the best and most international fair of all times. We saw the best galleries, collectors, and institutions. And the Basel team was very professional!

- **Contact** Tina Keng Gallery
Chih-Ting Lee
info@tinakenggallery.com
- **Established** 1992
- **Owner(s) / Partner(s)** Tina Keng
- **Team** 12
- **Space(s)** 470 m²
- **Artists at Art Basel** Sanyu
Xu Jiang
Yun Gee
Zao Wou-Ki
- **Further artists represented** George Chann
Chen Chun-Hao
Chu Shu-Hsien
Guan Liang
Hou I-Ting
Hsu Yunghsu
Hung Ying
Kao Chung-Li
Li-lan
Lin Fengmian
Lin Ju
Peng Wei
Su Meng-Hung
Tu Wei-Cheng
Wang Huaiqing
Tony Wong
Wu Dayu
Wu Tien-Chang
Xiaobai Su
Yang Mao-Lin
Yao Jui-chung
Zhang Hongtu

Kerlin

Dublin

● Galleries Encounters
● Galleries Unlimited

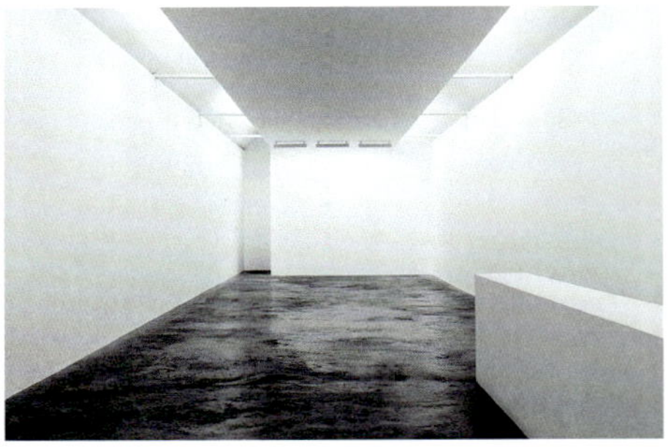

What first compelled you to open a gallery?
To initiate a cultural exchange between contemporary Irish art and the rest of the world. Before Kerlin Gallery this was non-existent.

Who is the first artist you showed and what was most memorable about that show?
David Fitzgerald. He then gave up painting and became a Partner of the gallery.

When did you first participate in Art Basel and what was most memorable about that show?
In 1995. The thrill of participating on the highest level.

- **Contact** Kerlin Gallery
John Kennedy
jken@kerlin.ie
gallery@kerlin.ie
- **Established** 1988
- **Owner(s) / Partner(s)** David Fitzgerald
Darragh Hogan
John Kennedy
Patrick McKillen
- **Space(s)** 290 m²
- **Artists at Art Basel** Phillip Allen
Phil Collins
Dorothy Cross
Willie Doherty
Aleana Egan
Mark Francis
Maureen Gallace
Mark Garry
Liam Gillick
David Godbold
Siobhán Hapaska
Callum Innes
Jaki Irvine
Merlin James
Sam Keogh
Elizabeth Magill
Eoin Mc Hugh
Stephen McKenna
Isabel Nolan
Kathy Prendergast
Norbert Schwontkowski
Sean Scully
Paul Seawright
Paul Winstanley

Kern

New York

- Galleries Parcours
- Galleries Public

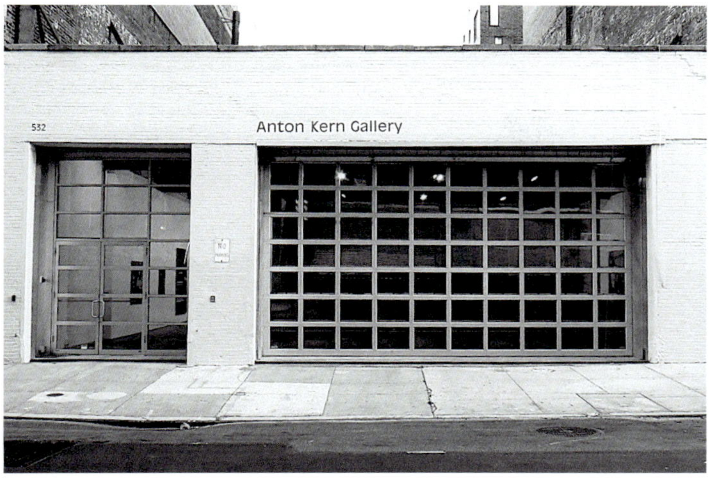

What first compelled you to open a gallery?
I primarily wanted to provide a platform for European artists to show in New York, and introduce them to an American audience.

Who is the first artist you showed and what was most memorable about that show?
My first show was a two-person exhibition with Angus Fairhurst and Lothar Hempel. Angus presented a musical performance, and Lothar made a sculpture of the now destroyed parking garage across the street from the gallery.

When did you first participate in Art Basel and what was most memorable about that show?
Our first participation was with Lothar Hempel in the Statements sector of Art Basel. One single sculpture, sort of like a stage set.

- **Contact** Anton Kern Gallery
Nahna Kim
nahna@antonkerngallery.com
info@antonkerngallery.com
- **Established** 1996
- **Owner(s) / Partner(s)** Anton Kern
- **Team** 9
- **Space(s)** 350 m²
- **Artists at Art Basel** Nobuyoshi Araki
Ellen Berkenblit
John Bock
Brian Calvin
Anne Collier
Saul Fletcher
Mark Grotjahn
Bendix Harms
Eberhard Havekost
Lothar Hempel
Richard Hughes
Sergej Jensen
Sarah Jones
Shio Kusaka
Jim Lambie
Marepe
Dan McCarthy
Matthew Monahan
Marcel Odenbach
Manfred Pernice
Alessandro Pessoli
Wilhelm Sasnal
Lara Schnitger
David Shrigley
Francis Upritchard
Andy Warhol
Jonas Wood

Kewenig

Berlin
Palma de Mallorca

- Galleries
- Galleries

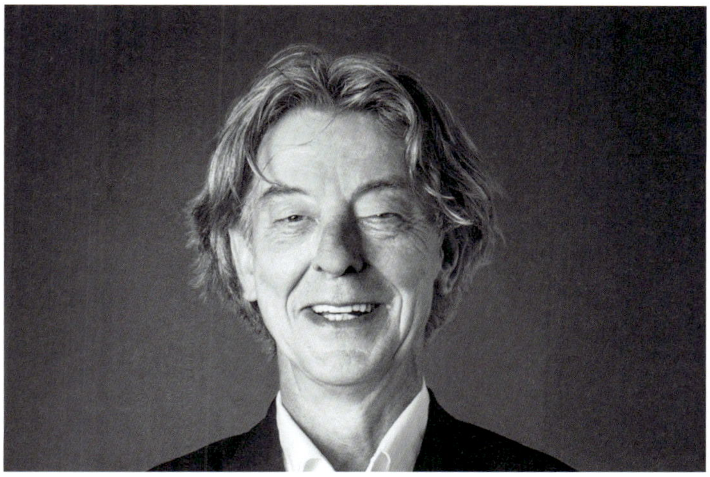

What first compelled you to open a gallery?
The close friendship with renowned artists of the time such as Marcel Broodthaers, James Lee Byars, Hanne Darboven, Christian Boltanski, Mario Merz, et al.

Who is the first artist you showed and what was most memorable about that show?
We opened the gallery with Hendrik Krawen. If you look back at more than 100 exhibitions, you sometimes cannot recall the exact month and year of a specific show, but you will always remember perfectly the very first exhibition you did!

When did you first participate in Art Basel and what was most memorable about that show?
We participated for the first time in Art Basel in the late 1990s. It felt like an honor.

- **Contact** Kewenig Galerie
Anna Duque y González
adyg@kewenig.com
gallery@kewenig.com
- **Established** 1986
- **Owner(s) / Partner(s)** Jule Kewenig
Michael O. Kewenig
- **Team** 6
- **Space(s)** 1,000 m²
- **Artists at Art Basel** Christian Boltanski
Marcel Broodthaers
Elger Esser
Ilya & Emilia Kabakov
Seydou Keïta
Kimsooja
Anselm Kiefer
Imi Knoebel
Jannis Kounellis
Bertrand Lavier
James Lee Byars
Mario Merz
Pavel Pepperstein
Miroslav Tichý
Sandra Vásquez de la Horra
Marcelo Viquez
Ralf Ziervogel
- **Further artists represented** Ivan Bazak
Frédéric Bruly Bouabré
Hanne Darboven
Bert de Beul
Ian Hamilton Finlay
Bernd Koberling
Hendrik Krawen
Viktor Pivovarov
Niele Toroni
Peter Wüthrich

Kicken

Berlin

- Galleries
- Galleries Kabinett

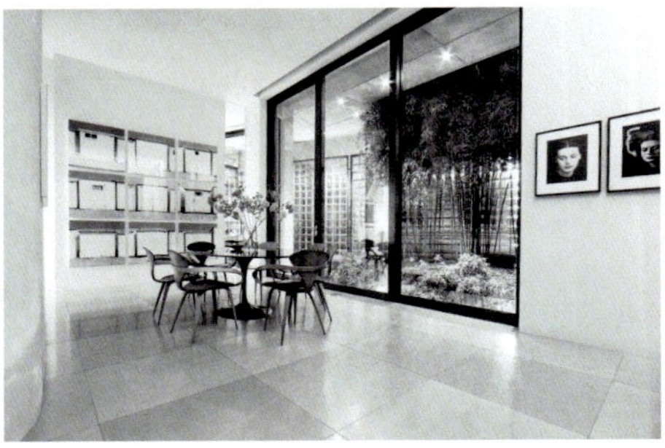

What first compelled you to open a gallery?
It was the urgent desire to promote in the art market photography as an art form, which practically did not exist in Europe in the early 1970s. I was hooked when I visited the Visual Studies Workshop at George Eastman House, Rochester, with its marvelous collections. Then the example of extraordinary galleries such as Light Gallery in New York City and Die Brücke in Vienna, Austria, showed me the way.

Who is the first artist you showed and what was most memorable about that show?
I started with the people on my doorstep in Aachen, and showed local contemporary photographers. I was so proud to sell prints to the Stedelijk Museum Amsterdam! Photography is such a rich medium, and I wanted to show my personal choice of the most important modernist and contemporary photographers, so from January to December 1974 I presented (in chronological order): André Gelpke, Michael Spencer, André Kertész, Paul Strand, Wynn Bullock, Harry Callahan, Alex Kayser, and Emmet Gowin.

When did you first participate in Art Basel and what was most memorable about that show?
We first participated in the fair around 1975, and I remember well our sensational sales this first time—we were more than positively surprised by this success!—despite the fact we had to wait for payment of US$ 300 from a well-known (and well-to-do) US dealer for a whole year …

- **Contact** Kicken Berlin
Petra Helck
phelck@kicken-gallery.com
kicken@kicken-gallery.com
- **Established** 1974 (Aachen, as Galerie Lichttropfen)
- **Owner(s) / Partner(s)** Rudolf Kicken
Annette Kicken
- **Team** 8
- **Space(s)** 150 m²
- **Artists at Art Basel** Dieter Appelt
Bauhaus
Bernd & Hilla Becher
Anna & Bernhard Blume
Erwin Blumenfeld
Rudolf Bonvie
Constantin Brancusi
Joachim Brohm
Harry Callahan
Götz Diergarten
František Drtikol
fotoform
Charles Fréger
Jaromír Funke
Heinz Hajek-Halke
Jitka Hanzlová
Fritz Henle
Peter Keetman
André Kertész
Rudolf Koppitz
Helmar Lerski
El Lissitzky
Werner Mantz
László Moholy-Nagy
Arnold Newman
Helmut Newton
Kiyoshi Niiyama
Richard Pare
Man Ray
Albert Renger-Patzsch
Alexander Rodchenko
Jaroslav Rössler
August Sander
Hans-Christian Schink
Alfred Seiland
Aaron Siskind
Otto Steinert
Christer Strömholm
Josef Sudek
Ed van der Elsken
Ludwig Windstosser
- **Further artists represented** Sibylle Bergemann
Karl Blossfeldt
Hugo Erfurth
Alfred Erhardt
Arno Fischer
Lee Friedlander
Ernst Fuhrmann
F.C. Gundlach
Klaus Kinold
Heinrich Kühn
Helga Paris
Walter Peterhans
Heinrich Riebesehl
Karl-Hugo Schmölz
Wilhelm Schürmann
Anton Josef Trcka
Umbo (Otto Umbehr)
Dr. Paul Wolff

Kilchmann

Zurich

- Galleries Unlimited Parcours
- Galleries

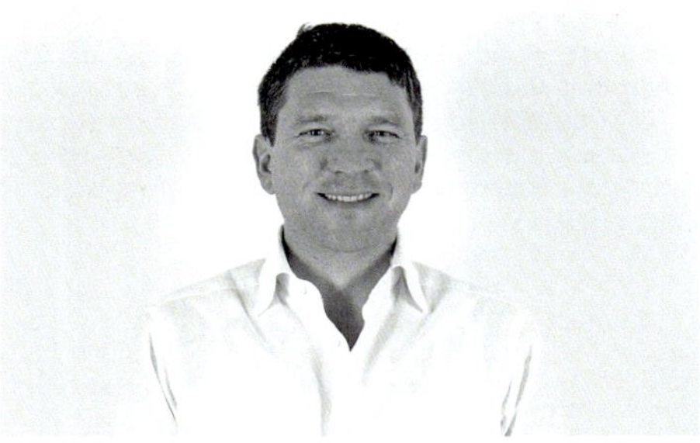

What first compelled you to open a gallery?
I've always been fascinated by the profession of the gallerist, a profession that combines many aspects of my personal interest, such as how to communicate art, meet interesting collectors, curators, and critics, and not least, to deal with artists and grow with them.

Who is the first artist you showed and what was most memorable about that show?
The first exhibition was with Willie Doherty, an artist we are still working with. What I will always remember is the reserved attitude of the visitors, because back then, in 1992, photography was not yet fully accepted as an art form.

When did you first participate in Art Basel and what was most memorable about that show?
That was in 1995 or 1996. I keep as a good memory one of the few sales to a then unknown collector, with whom I kept good contact to the present day.

- **Contact** Galerie Peter Kilchmann
Sabine Leuzinger
s.leuzinger@peterkilchmann.com
info@peterkilchmann.com
- **Established** 1992
- **Owner(s) / Partner(s)** Peter Kilchmann
- **Team** 8
- **Space(s)** 550 m²
- **Artists at Art Basel** Francis Alÿs
Hernan Bas
Michael Bauer
Armin Boehm
Los Carpinteros
Willie Doherty
Valérie Favre
Raffi Kalenderian
Tobias Kaspar
Zilla Leutenegger
Jorge Macchi

Teresa Margolles
Fabian Marti
David Renggli
Melanie Smith
Javier Téllez
Tercerunquinto
Erika Verzutti

- **Further artists represented** Maja Bajevic
Marc-Antoine Fehr
Bruno Jakob
Claudia & Julia Müller
Adrian Paci
Bernd Ribbeck
Artur Żmijewski

Klosterfelde

Berlin — Galleries, Unlimited, Parcours

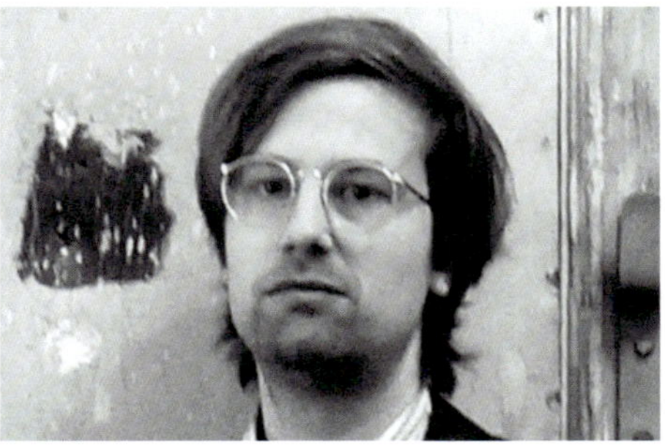

- **Contact** Klosterfelde
office@klosterfelde.de
- **Established** 1996
- **Owner(s) / Partner(s)** Lena Kiessler
- **Artists at Art Basel** Nader Ahriman
Matthew Antezzo
John Bock
Tobias Buche
Hanne Darboven
Jürgen Drescher
Lara Favaretto
Ulrike Heise
Christian Jankowski
Edward Krasinski
Ulrike Kuschel
Armin Linke
Jonas Lipps
Matt Mullican
Lisa Oppenheim
Dan Peterman
Steven Pippin
Kay Rosen
Michael Snow
Vibeke Tandberg
Jorinde Voigt

Klosterfelde Edition

Berlin, Hamburg — Edition

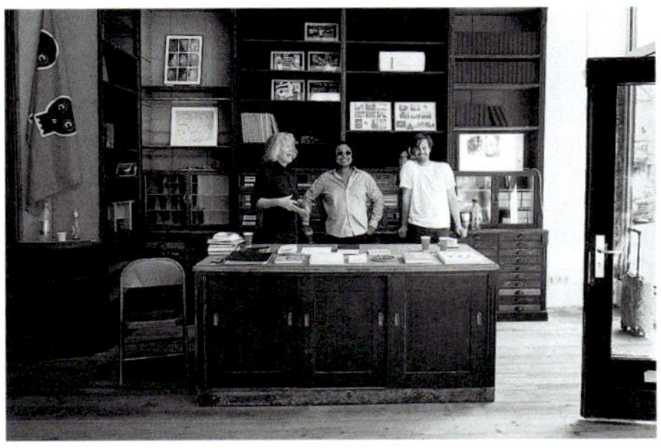

What first compelled you to open a gallery?
Helga Maria Klosterfelde supported the foundation of the Deichtorhallen in Hamburg by publishing editions with Donald Baechler, Hanne Darboven, Rosemarie Trockel, and Lawrence Weiner, in 1990. This initiated the establishment of the gallery.

Who is the first artist you showed and what was most memorable about that show?
The inaugural show at the gallery was with Hanne Darboven. This led to a deep and rewarding relationship.

When did you first participate in Art Basel and what was most memorable about that show?
Helga Maria Klosterfelde first participated at Art Basel in 1990. We were immediately overwhelmed by the genuine interest in our editions and multiples.

- **Contact** Helga Maria Klosterfelde Edition
Alfons Klosterfelde
office@helgamariaklosterfelde.de
- **Established** 1990
- **Owner(s) / Partner(s)** Helga Maria
Alfons Klosterfelde
- **Team** 2
- **Space(s)** 90 m²
- **Artists at Art Basel** Donald Baechler
John Bock
Tobias Buche
Werner Büttner
Hanne Darboven
General Idea
Ulrike Heise
Christian Jankowski
Joseph Kosuth
Jonas Lipps
Matt Mullican
Henrik Olesen
Dan Peterman
Steven Pippin
Kay Rosen
Haim Steinbach
Fiete Stolte
Rirkrit Tiravanija
Rosemarie Trockel
Rosemarie Trockel/Carsten Höller
Lily van der Stokker
Jorinde Voigt
Lawrence Weiner

Klüser

Munich — Galleries

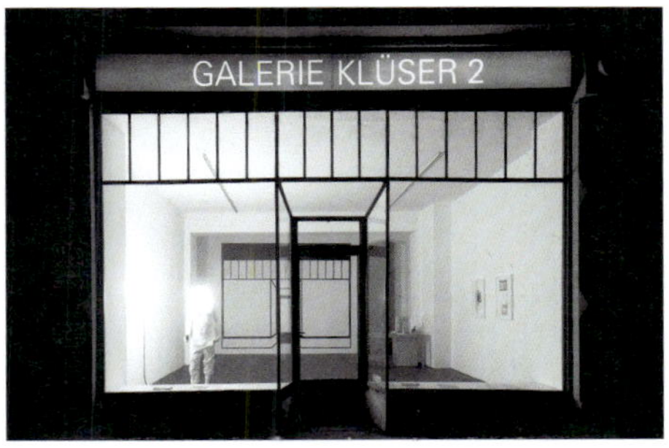

What first compelled you to open a gallery?
The close cooperation with Joseph Beuys was the starting point of Bernd Klüser's gallery and publishing activity.

Who is the first artist you showed and what was most memorable about that show?
Robert Mangold, in 1978. The most memorable thing about that show was the amazing number of visitors, including museum people from all over Europe.

When did you first participate in Art Basel and what was most memorable about that show?
In 1978 with our gallery, in 1975 with the Edition Schellmann & Klüser. The most memorable about that show was, besides the high appreciation of our program, the friendly and supportive cooperation between the exhibiting galleries.

- **Contact** Galerie Klüser
Julia Klüser
julia@galerieklueser.com
info@galerieklueser.com
- **Established** 1978
- **Owner(s) / Partner(s)** Julia Klüser
Bernd Klüser
- **Team** 5
- **Space(s)** 320 m²

- **Artists at Art Basel**
  Joseph Beuys
  Tony Cragg
  Jan Fabre
  Alex Katz
  Mimmo Paladino
  Sean Scully
  Andy Warhol
- **Further artists represented**
  Donald Baechler
  Christian Boltanski
  Enzo Cucchi
  David Godbold
  Isca Greenfield-Sanders
  Clemens Hollerer
  Rita McBride
  Olaf Metzel
  Bernardí Roig
  Julião Sarmento
  Conrad Shawcross
  Jorinde Voigt

Knust

Munich

● Edition
● Edition

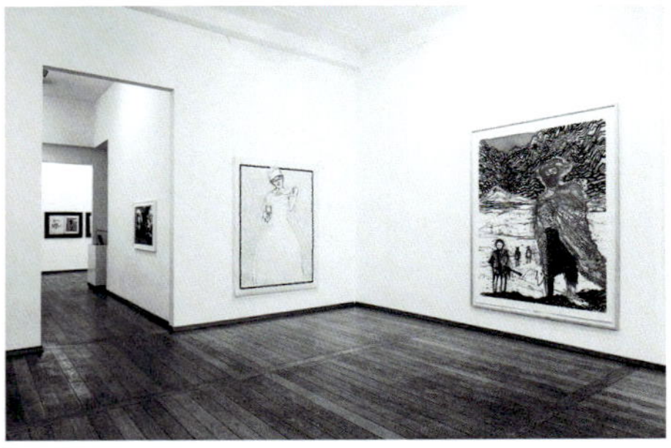

What first compelled you to open a gallery?
Sabine Knust began working as a publisher of prints and editions and an organizer of exhibitions by artists such as Georg Baselitz, Dan Flavin, Imi Knoebel, Blinky Palermo, Sigmar Polke, Gerhard Richter, and Fred Sandback at the Galerie Heiner Friedrich in Munich. In 1982 she opened her own gallery on the Maximilianstrasse, and her work as both a publisher and an art dealer steadily intensified. The gallery moved to its current premises at Ludwigstrasse 7, near Odeonsplatz, in 2004.

Who is the first artist you showed and what was most memorable about that show?
The three portfolios entitled *1.Konzentration*, with prints by the following artists: Georg Baselitz, Antonius Höckelmann, Jörg Immendorff, Per Kirkeby, Markus Lüpertz, A.R. Penck.

When did you first participate in Art Basel and what was most memorable about that show?
In 1981. It was important to me to show the recently published portfolios *1.Konzentration* to emphasize the significance of print work by these artists.

- **Contact**
  Sabine Knust
  Matthias Kunz
  kunz@sabineknust.com
  mail@sabineknust.com
- **Established** 1982
- **Owner(s) / Partner(s)**
  Sabine Knust
  Matthias Kunz
- **Team** 4
- **Space(s)** 160 m²
- **Artists at Art Basel**
  Georg Baselitz
  Marc Brandenburg
  Günther Förg
  Eberhard Havekost
  Per Kirkeby
  Imi Knoebel
  Markus Lüpertz
  Paul Morrison
  Jorge Pardo
  Lari Pittman
  Richard Prince
  Daniel Richter
  Katharina Sieverding
  Gert & Uwe Tobias
- **Further artists represented**
  John M Armleder
  John Baldessari
  Michael Elmgreen & Ingar Dragset
  Matias Faldbakken
  Helmut Federle
  Liam Gillick
  Mark Grotjahn
  Olaf Holzapfel
  Jenny Holzer
  Andy Hope 1930
  Jörg Immendorff
  Alex Katz
  Sandra Kranich
  Michael Landy
  Jonathan Lasker
  Fabian Marcaccio
  Jonathan Meese
  Olaf Nicolai
  A.R. Penck
  Jack Pierson
  Tal R
  Arnulf Rainer
  Anselm Reyle
  Thomas Scheibitz
  Thomas Schütte
  Ena Swansea
  Franz West
  Christopher Wool
  Thomas Zipp

Koenig & Clinton

New York

● Nova

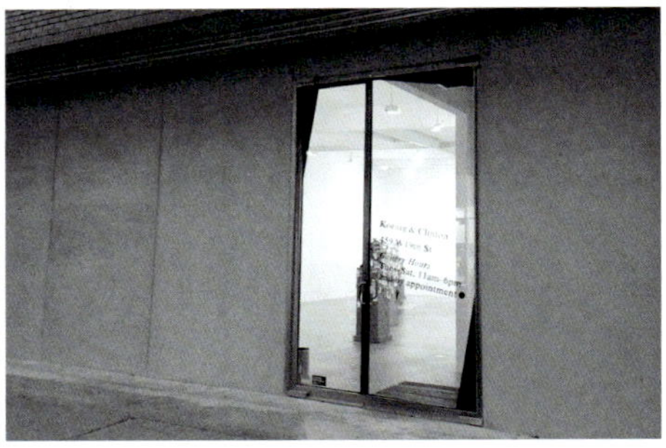

What first compelled you to open a gallery?
Leo Koenig: The scene in late 1990s New York was exciting and full of optimism. A new art neighborhood was forming in Williamsburg and pockets of creativity were everywhere—a beautiful time to start an experimental space. The idea of becoming a commercial gallery only formed after we started to sell works somewhat unexpectedly.
Maggie Clinton: While taking a break from a Ph.D. program, I began working with a Lower East Side gallery and ended up remaining there. At that time, it felt as though paradigms were shifting. Alternative models formed in response to the dominant commercial gallery system of the early 2000s. With a desire to nourish a local arts community, we screened films, hosted lectures, book launches, musical events, and collaborated with curators. A gallery grants me flexibility in supporting the arts through commercial and non-commercial activity.

Who is the first artist you showed and what was most memorable about that show?
At Leo Koenig Inc., it was Aidas Barekis: *Embarkation for Cythere*. As there were no funds available, besides payment for the first months rent, to put up this exhibition we transported the entire show on our bicycles from the studio to the space. I remember getting hit by a car, but was so excited about the installation I simply left the bike and walked, giant garbage bags full of art in hand, the rest of the way to the gallery. At Koenig & Clinton: Paul Ramírez Jonas, *Aggregate*, the first one-person exhibition in our new space.

- **Contact**
  Koenig & Clinton
  Margaret Clinton
  mc@koenigandclinton.com
  info@koenigandclinton.com
- **Established**
  1999 (Leo Koenig Inc.)
  2013 (Koenig & Clinton)
- **Owner(s) / Partner(s)**
  Leo Koenig
  Margaret Liu Clinton
- **Space(s)** 120 m²
- **Artists at Art Basel**
  Nicole Eisenman
  Tony Matelli
- **Further artists represented**
  Norbert Bisky
  Greg Bogin
  Anoka Faruqee

Ridley Howard
Brandon Lattu
Olivier Mosset
Frank Nitsche
Sigmar Polke
Paul Ramírez Jonas
Miljohn Ruperto
Lily van der Stokker

Kohn

Los Angeles ● Galleries

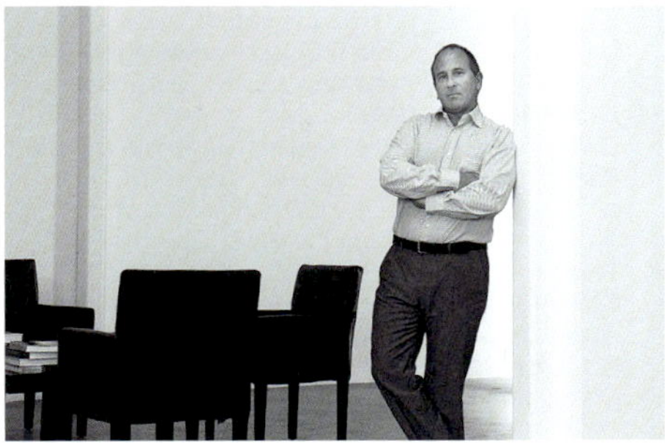

What first compelled you to open a gallery?

I have a Master's degree in Art History from NYU, and while pursuing my studies in New York I became an art critic. During the early 1980s I was a Teaching Assistant at NYU, an intern at the Guggenheim Museum, US Editor of *Flash Art* magazine, contemporary art correspondent for *Art & Auction*, and East Village gallery owner. It was a natural progression from academic pursuits to business that brought me to contemporary gallery owner.

Who is the first artist you showed and what was most memorable about that show?

The first show was a group exhibition, titled *New York's Finest*, which is what the NYPD is called. It included works by Kenny Scharf, Jon Kessler, Mark Innerst, Futura 2000, among others. Since I had spent the previous five years in NYC the show was centered upon New York-based artists. It was an energetic show, and the gallery had black shag carpeting because I could not afford to change the flooring before I opened in 1985!

When did you first participate in Art Basel and what was most memorable about that show?

We participated in the very first Art Basel in Miami Beach, which was amazing from the very start. It was, of course, smaller then, without the other city wide fairs. And the hotel rooms were a lot cheaper! Then at my first Art Basel in Switzerland, around 2007, I mounted a one-person show of works by Bruce Conner in the booth, and showed his film *THREE SCREEN RAY* (2006) in the Unlimited sector.

- **Contact** Michael Kohn Gallery
  Laura Sumser
  laura@kohngallery.com
  samantha@kohngallery.com
- **Established** 1985
- **Owner(s) / Partner(s)** Michael Kohn
- **Team** 6
- **Space(s)** 1,115 m²
- **Artists at Art Basel** Wallace Berman
  Bruce Conner
  Camille Rose Garcia
  Joe Goode
  Dennis Hollingsworth
  Rosa Loy
  Eddie Martinez
  Ryan McGinness
  Retna
  Mark Ryden
  Simmons & Burke
  Cristof Yvoré
- **Further artists represented** Charles Brittin
  Will Cotton
  James Nares
  Joan Nelson

König

Berlin ● Galleries Unlimited ● Galleries Public

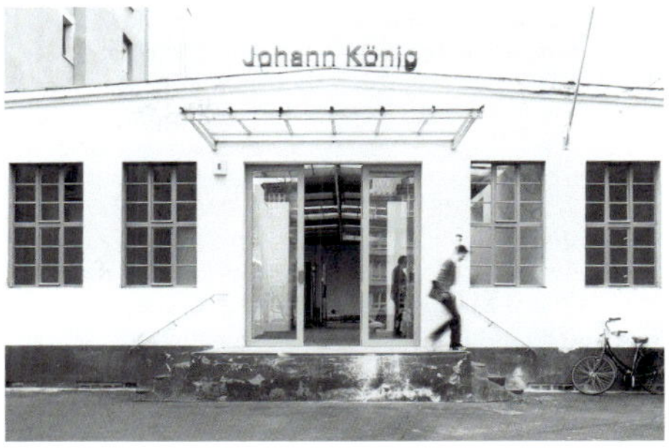

Who is the first artist you showed and what was most memorable about that show?

It was Michaela Meise.

When did you first participate in Art Basel and what was most memorable about that show?

In 2006.

- **Contact** Johann König
  Aurélien Calpas
  aurelien@johannkoenig.de
  info@johannkoenig.de
- **Established** 2002
- **Owner(s) / Partner(s)** Johann König
- **Team** 9
- **Space(s)** 1 400 m²
- **Artists at Art Basel** Micol Assaël
  Henning Bohl
  Monica Bonvicini
  Andreas Fischer
  Tue Greenfort
  Katharina Grosse
  Jeppe Hein
  Nathan Hylden
  Annette Kelm
  Kiki Kogelnik
  Manfred Kuttner
  Alicja Kwade
  Lisa Lapinski
  Helen Marten
  Justin Matherly
  Michaela Meise
  Amalia Pica
  Natascha Sadr Haghighian
  Michael Sailstorfer
  Jeremy Shaw
  Tatiana Trouvé
  Corinne Wasmuht
  Johannes Wohnseifer
  Jordan Wolfson
  David Zink Yi

Kordansky

Los Angeles ● Galleries ● Galleries Public

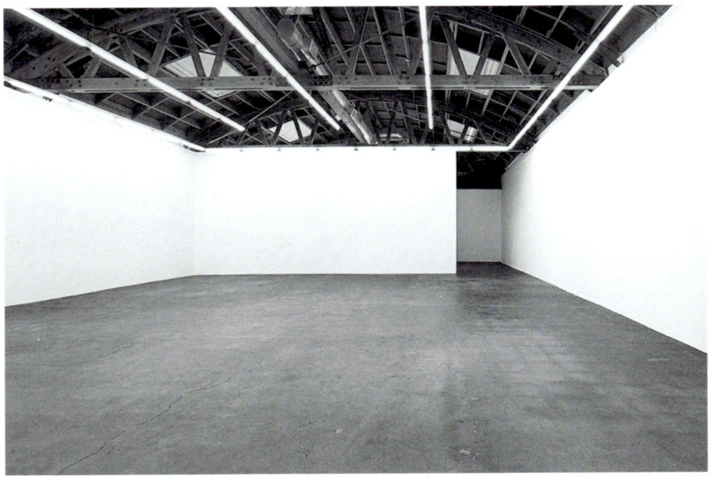

What first compelled you to open a gallery?

I moved to Los Angeles in 2000 to attend CalArts and I was blown away by the work of some of my peers. I decided that opening a gallery would be the best way to continue the work we were all doing, and to draw attention to the great young artists who were making Los Angeles one of the best places in the world for contemporary art.

Who is the first artist you showed and what was most memorable about that show?

The first exhibition at the gallery was a group show. It featured a number of artists who continue to be important parts of the gallery's program. It really was a celebration of the initial energies that led to the formation of the gallery, and also of the incredible, youthful energy that was coursing through Los Angeles at that time. The gallery was located in Chinatown, which was a strong community of artists and galleries.

When did you first participate in Art Basel and what was most memorable about that show?

Our first participation was in 2006 in the Statements sector of Art Basel, with Matthew Brannon. It was an honor to see Matthew's presentation in conversation with the work of artists exhibited by such a critically sharp range of galleries also participating in the fair. The community we were trying to exemplify in Los Angeles was now open to other communities of its kind around the world.

- **Contact** David Kordansky Gallery
Alexis Kerin
alexis@davidkordanskygallery.com
- **Established** 2003
- **Owner(s) / Partner(s)** David Kordansky
- **Team** 12
- **Space(s)** 600 m²
- **Artists at Art Basel** Valentin Carron
Aaron Curry
Sam Gilliam
Rashid Johnson
Elad Lassry
John Mason
Scott Myles
Mai-Thu Perret
Jon Pestoni
Pietro Roccasalva
Lesley Vance
John Wesley
- **Further artists represented** Markus Amm
Kathryn Andrews
Amy Bessone
Matthew Brannon
Steven Claydon
Heather Cook
Andrew Dadson
Will Fowler
Patrick Hill
Richard Jackson
Larry Johnson
William E. Jones
Thomas Lawson
Alan Michael
Ruby Neri
David Noonan
Anthony Pearson
Mary Weatherford
Jonas Wood

Koyama

Tokyo ● Galleries
Singapore ● Galleries
● Galleries

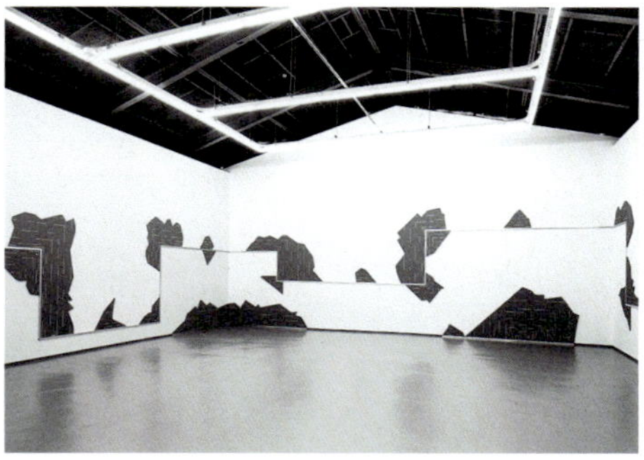

What first compelled you to open a gallery?

I wanted to present the Japanese artists of my generation to the world.

Who is the first artist you showed and what was most memorable about that show?

Japanese artist Chiezo Taro.

When did you first participate in Art Basel and what was most memorable about that show?

In 2001. The most memorable thing was that Richard Prince came to my booth, and he praised Yoshitomo Nara's dish-shaped paintings.

- **Contact** Tomio Koyama Gallery
Tetsuya Kamimura
kamimura@tomiokoyamagallery.com
info@tomiokoyamagallery.com
- **Established** 1996
- **Owner(s) / Partner(s)** Tomio Koyama (Owner & Director)
Yuko Nagase (Director)
Kosaku Kanechika (Director)
Futaba Fujikawa (Director)
- **Team** 15
- **Space(s)** 278 m²
- **Artists at Art Basel** Katsuyo Aoki
Varda Caivano
Nobuhiro Fukui
Atsushi Fukui
Daisuke Fukunaga
Nana Funo
Satoshi Hirose
Hideaki Kawashima
Naoki Koide
Makiko Kudo
Masahiko Kuwahara
Toru Kuwakubo
Takuro Kuwata
Shintaro Miyake
Mika Ninagawa
Satoshi Ohno
Rieko Otake
Makoto Saito
Diego Singh
Yuko Someya
Kishio Suga
Hiroshi Sugito
Richard Tuttle
Zhao Xuebing
- **Further artists represented** Franz Ackermann
Masako Ando
Ryota Aoki
Stephan Balkenhol
Benjamin Butler
Jeremy Dickinson
Inka Essenhigh
Tom Friedman
Gelitin
Rieko Hidaka
Tamami Hitsuda
Dennis Hollingsworth
Aya Ito
Yuka Kashihara
Mika Kato
Yoshino Masui
Ryan McGinley
Satoko Nachi
Tomoko Nagai
Ernesto Neto
Tam Ochiai
Yoko Ono
Jonathan Pylypchuk
Tal R
David Ratcliff
Mark Ryden
Tom Sachs
Midori Sato
Adam Silverman
Laurie Simmons
Vibeke Tandberg
Jason Teraoka
Gert & Uwe Tobias
Kumie Tsuda
Naoyuki Tsuji
Mamoru Tsukada
Yutaka Watanabe
Jenny Watson
Terry Winters
Erwin Wurm
Wang Yahui
Keisuke Yamamoto
Lee Youngbin

Koyanagi

Tokyo

- Galleries
- Galleries

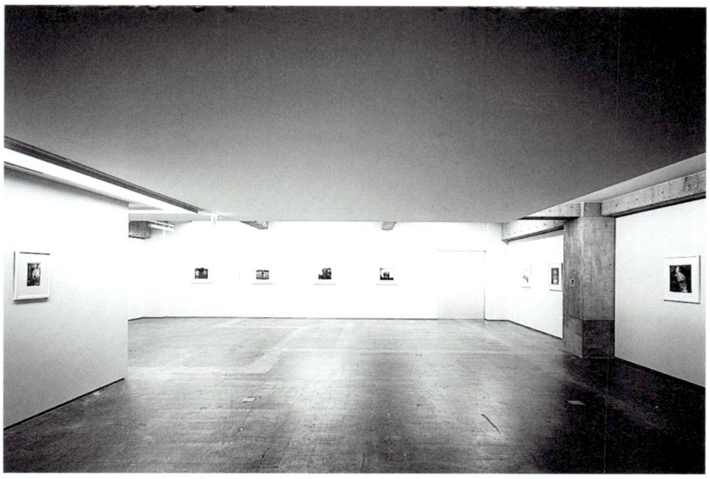

What first compelled you to open a gallery?
I was interested in working directly with artists as a primary gallery.

Who is the first artist you showed and what was most memorable about that show?
We first showed Hiroshi Sugimoto and I recall that we sold much less than expected.

When did you first participate in Art Basel and what was most memorable about that show?
We first participated at Art Basel in 2000 in the Statements sector with Yoshihiro Suda, and I recall that we sold much more than expected.

- **Contact** Gallery Koyanagi
  Sho Kuwajima
  kuwajima@gallerykoyanagi.com
  mail@gallerykoyanagi.com
- **Established** 1995
- **Owner(s) / Partner(s)** Atsuko Koyanagi
- **Team** 6
- **Space(s)** 210 m²
- **Artists at Art Basel** Michaël Borremans
  Marlene Dumas
  Olafur Eliasson
  Yoon Heechang
  Federico Herrero
  Kengo Kito
  Kae Masuda
  Rei Naito
  Ataru Sato
  Yoshihiro Suda
  Hiroshi Sugimoto
  Risaku Suzuki
  Tabaimo
  Kouichi Tabata
  Yuriko Terazaki
- **Further artists represented** Sophie Calle
  Janet Cardiff
  & George Bures Miller
  Yuumi Domoto
  Dominique Gonzalez-Foerster
  Hanayo
  Ryoji Ikeda
  Junya Ishigami
  Luisa Lambri
  Christian Marclay
  Tetsuya Nakamura
  Robert Platt
  Noguchi Rika
  Thomas Ruff
  Hellen van Meene
  Bill Viola
  Tomoko Yamaguchi

Kreps

New York

- Galleries
- Galleries

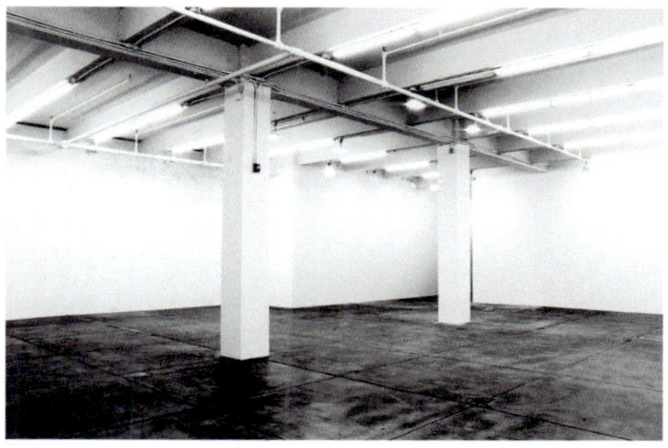

What first compelled you to open a gallery?
I wanted to work with artists.

Who is the first artist you showed and what was most memorable about that show?
A group show with Lawrence Seward, Meredith Danluck, Jonah Freeman, and Rick Prol.

When did you first participate in Art Basel and what was most memorable about that show?
It was in 2000.

- **Contact** Andrew Kreps Gallery
  Colleen Grennan
  colleen@andrewkreps.com
  contact@andrewkreps.com
- **Established** 1996
- **Owner(s) / Partner(s)** Andrew Kreps (Owner)
  Liz Mulholland (Partner)
- **Team** 8
- **Space(s)** 7,000 m²
- **Artists at Art Basel** Ricci Albenda
  Darren Bader
  Martin Barré
  Frank Benson
  Andrea Bowers
  Marc Camille Chaimowicz
  Roe Ethridge
  Uwe Henneken
  Christian Holstad
  Jamie Isenstein
  Annette Kelm
  Maria Loboda
  Goshka Macuga
  Ján Mančuška
  Robert Melee
  Robert Overby
  Peter Piller
  Ruth Root
  Cheyney Thompson
  Pádraig Timoney
  Hayley Tompkins
  Fredrik Værslev
  Klaus Weber

Krinzinger

Vienna

- Galleries
- Galleries
  Unlimited
  Parcours
- Galleries
  Kabinett

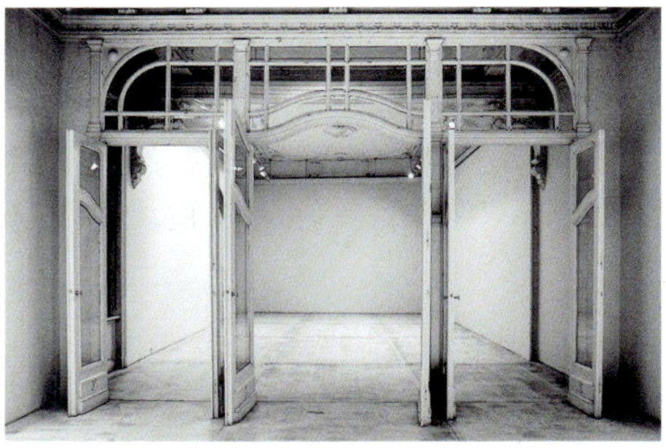

What first compelled you to open a gallery?
As an art historian my greatest interest was always contemporary art and I absolutely wanted to work on a free basis to realize exhibition concepts together with contemporary artists and this consequently led to the foundation of a contemporary gallery.

Who is the first artist you showed and what was most memorable about that show?
It was a thematic show including mainly Austrian artists who are still working internationally, such as Gottfried Bechtold, Bruno Gironcoli, Maria Lassnig, Arnulf Rainer. Immediately after, the gallery program started to focus on Austrian Actionism and to position it in an international context. A very important event for the life of the gallery happened during the first exhibition: a friendly but very special guy with a beard entered the gallery space and had a long dialogue with me about contemporary art and the works exhibited; it was Harald Szeemann, who consequently invited one of my artists to documenta; until his death Szeemann remained interested in the gallery program and became a very close friend supporting the gallery.

When did you first participate in Art Basel and what was most memorable about that show?
In 1972. It was an incredible pioneering and most exciting time where most of the gallerists, out of passion, transported the works of the artists themselves. In addition, the artists also helped to build the booths with great excitement. It was a time when nobody could imagine—we were working from a very idealistic background—that the art market (especially because of the fairs) would develop as far and as professionally as it has today.

- **Contact** Galerie Krinzinger
Emilie Kiefhaber
emilie.kiefhaber@galerie-krinzinger.at
galeriekrinzinger@chello.at
- **Established** 1971
- **Owner(s) / Partner(s)** Ursula Krinzinger
- **Space(s)** 1,500 m² (gallery + project space)
- **Artists at Art Basel** Marina Abramović
Nader Ahriman
Kader Attia
Gottfried Bechtold
Günter Brus
Chris Burden
Angela de la Cruz
Vladimir Dubossarsky & Alexander Vinogradov
Franz Graf
Sakshi Gupta
Secundino Hernández
Jonathan Hernández
Ken Kagami
Waqas Khan
Zenita Komad
Valery Koshlyakov
Angelika Krinzinger
Oleg Kulik
Ulrike Lienbacher
Jonathan Meese
Bjarne Melgaard
Shintaro Miyake
Otto Muehl
Hermann Nitsch
Hans Op de Beeck
Meret Oppenheim
Goran Petercol
Werner Reiterer
Eva Schlegel
Erik Schmidt
Rudolf Schwarzkogler
Christian Schwarzwald
Mithu Sen
Sudarshan Shetty
Eliezer Sonnenschein
Daniel Spoerri
Frank Thiel
Gavin Turk
Atelier Van Lieshout
Erik van Lieshout
Jannis Varelas
Martin Walde
Mark Wallinger
Zhang Ding
Thomas Zipp

Krobath

Vienna
Berlin

Statements

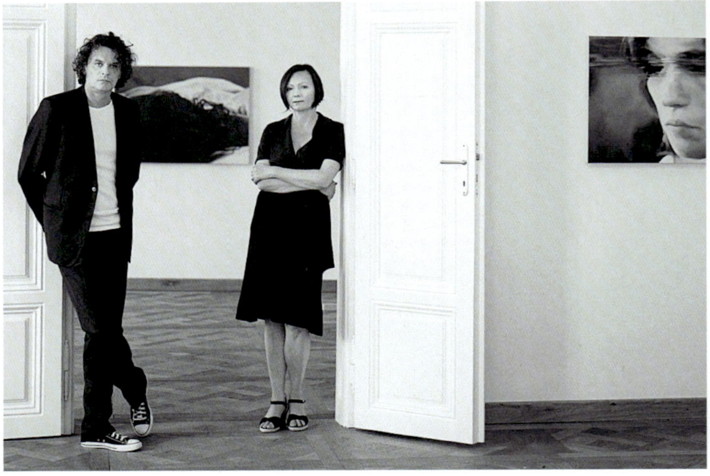

What first compelled you to open a gallery?
It came out of having contacts with artists in Vienna.

Who is the first artist you showed and what was most memorable about that show?
Rudi Molacek. The most memorable thing was to see that after the crises in 1993, collectors were still interested in buying art.

When did you first participate in Art Basel and what was most memorable about that show?
In 2003. In the Statements sector, with Florian Pumhösl; it was the start of his international career.

- **Contact** Krobath
Gabriela Gutmann
office@galeriekrobath.at
- **Established** 1996
- **Owner(s) / Partner(s)** Helga Krobath
Peter Krobath
- **Team** 4
- **Space(s)** 300 m²
- **Artists at Art Basel** Jenni Tischer
- **Further artists represented** Michael Bauch
Thomas Baumann
Hannes Böck
Katrina Daschner
Judith Eisler
Berta Fischer
Max Frey
Andreas Golinski
Maria Hahnenkamp
Isabell Heimerdinger
Šejla Kameric
Jirí Kolár
Bela Kolárová
Jirí Kovanda
Brigitte Kowanz
Dominik Lang
Dorit Margreiter
Ursula Mayer
Anna Meyer
Gerold Miller
Julian Opie
Fritz Panzer
Florian Pumhösl
Ugo Rondinone
Esther Stocker
Despina Stokou
Sofie Thorsen
Otto Zitko

Krupp

Basel — Galleries

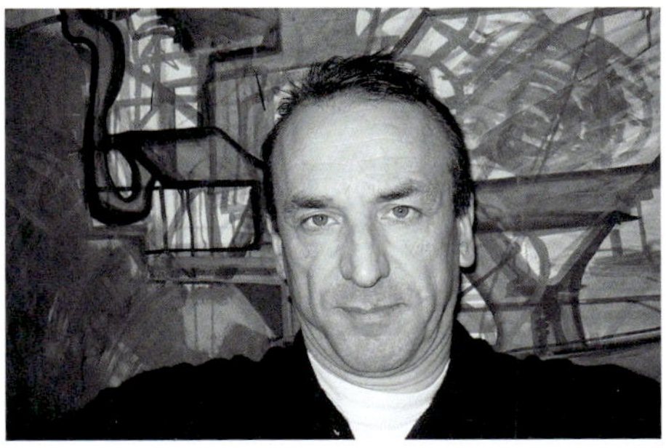

What first compelled you to open a gallery?
There is no other profession I could practice with the same enthusiasm.

Who is the first artist you showed and what was most memorable about that show?
Forty Acres and a Mule (2001) by Peter Friedl, with a living mule in the gallery space during the opening.

When did you first participate in Art Basel and what was most memorable about that show?
In 2008, a Statements booth with Emil Michael Klein, and at the same time *Wak* by Thomas Baumann, a public art project in the Messeplatz fountain which required a huge effort.

- **Contact** Nicolas Krupp
nic@nicolaskrupp.com
gallery@nicolaskrupp.com
- **Established** 2000
- **Owner(s) / Partner(s)** Nicolas Krupp
- **Team** 2.5
- **Space(s)** 400 m²
- **Artists at Art Basel** Thomas Baumann
Angela de la Cruz
Peter Friedl
Joanne Greenbaum
Lone Haugaard Madsen
Dani Jakob
Piotr Janas
Michael Kunze
Atta Kwami
Claudio Moser
Markus Müller
Markéta Othová
Marjetica Potrč
Werner Reiterer
Rico Scagliola & Michael Meier
Dominik Sittig
Studer/van den Berg
Walter Swennen
Heimo Zobernig
- **Further artists represented** Tobias Madison
Kaspar Müller

Kukje/Kim

Seoul
New York

Galleries
Encounters
Galleries
Unlimited
Galleries

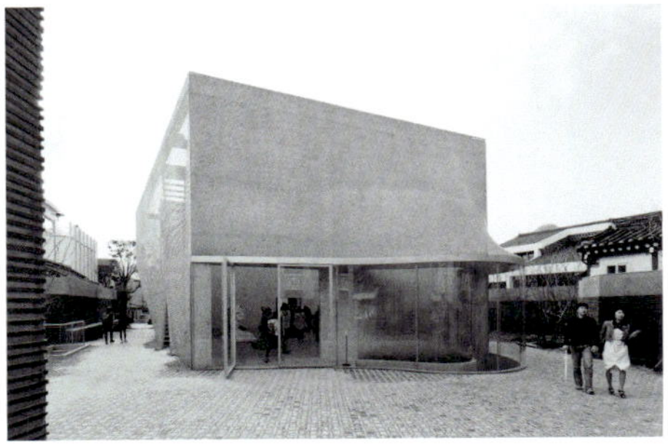

What first compelled you to open a gallery?
Hyun-Sook Lee was first an avid collector, focusing both on Korean artists and international masters. As she developed, her eye and her passion for art grew and she began to think seriously about opening a gallery. She was very forward-thinking and was one of the first to show international artists in Korea, opening Kukje Gallery in 1982. The gallery started as a small space where she organized special exhibitions with artists she collected. Later she expanded her program to include Korean artists, taking special pride in promoting them abroad. This balance of international and domestic artists is the foundation of our success.

Who is the first artist you showed and what was most memorable about that show?
The first exhibition presented works from Hyun-Sook Lee's collection. There was a diversity of international and domestic artists. A number of them were present to celebrate the opening of this dynamic space in Seoul.

- **Contact** Kukje Gallery/Tina Kim Gallery
Eliza Ravelle-Chapuis
eliza@tinakimgallery.com
kukje@kukjegallery.com
- **Established** 1982
- **Owner(s) / Partner(s)** Hyun-Sook Lee
Tina Kim
Suzie Kim
Charles Kim
- **Team** 20
- **Space(s)** 980 m²
- **Artists at Art Basel** Ghada Amer & Reza Farkhondeh
Jean-Michel Basquiat
Louise Bourgeois
Cecily Brown
Alexander Calder
John Chamberlain
Willem de Kooning
Gimhongsok
Candida Höfer
Jenny Holzer
Roni Horn
Michael Joo
Donald Judd
Anish Kapoor
Bharti Kher
Sora Kim
Kimsooja
Joan Mitchell
Julian Opie
Jean-Michel Othoniel
Seo-Bo Park
Anselm Reyle
Kibong Rhee
Lee Ufan
Bill Viola
Andy Warhol
Haegue Yang
Yeesookyung
Aaron Young
- **Further artists represented** Anthony Caro
Jae-Eun Choi
Sen Chung
Gimhongsok
Eva Hesse
Damien Hirst
Candida Höfer
Kim Hong Joo
Seung-Hye Hong
Duck Hyun Cho
Yeondoo Jung
Eemyun Kang
Anselm Kiefer
Hong-Joo Kim
Kira Kim
Bohnchang Koo
Joris Laarman
Kwang-Ho Lee
Richard Long
Paul McCarthy
Sungsic Moon
David Nash
Hein-Kuhn Oh
MeeNa Park
Jack Pierson
Choong-Hyun Roh
Sterling Ruby
Ed Ruscha
Sasa[44]
Frank Stella
U Sunok
Lin Tianmiao
Jeff Wall

kurimanzutto

Mexico D.F.

Galleries
Galleries

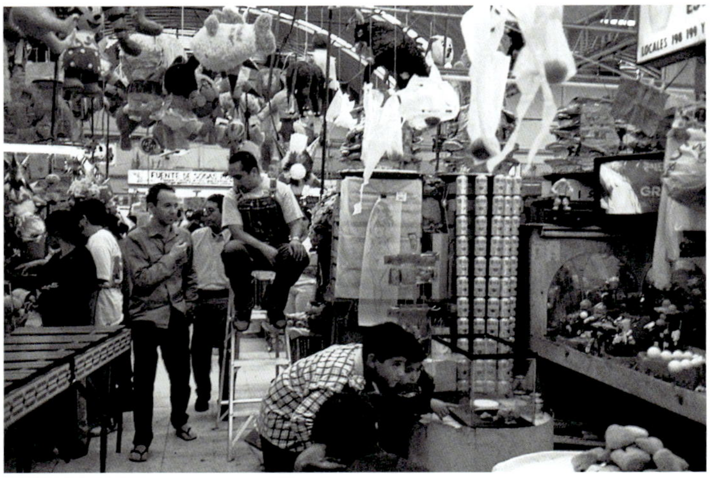

What first compelled you to open a gallery?

We started working as a gallery in 1999, attracted by a fascinating generation of Mexican artists that did not have a hub in the city. The necessity for a gallery in Mexico drew us to it; also Gabriel Orozco wanted to return to Mexico and proposed the idea. There had been a generational change, but at the time, this generation we worked with had no response from institutions or galleries in Mexico City, or were not given a true commitment to help develop their careers. We were in the backwash of a painting boom, not only in Mexico, but in the world, where artists hardly found any accomplices for their work and ideas. The participating artists were: Eduardo Abaroa, Minerva Cuevas, Gabriel Orozco, Abraham Cruzvillegas, Damián Ortega, Sofía Táboas, Gabriel Kuri, Daniel Guzmán, Jonathan Hernández, Fernando Ortega, Luis Felipe Ortega, Dr. Lakra, and Rirkrit Tiravanija.

Who is the first artist you showed and what was most memorable about that show?

For approximately the first nine years of the gallery we worked without a defined space. Our first show was staged at a street food market, the Medellin Market, in Mexico City in August of 1999. We rented two of the market's spaces and the participating artists made work to be exhibited and sold within that context and at market prices. The market was our first space.

- **Contact** kurimanzutto
  Michele Fiedler
  michele@kurimanzutto.com
  info@kurimanzutto.com
- **Established** 1999
- **Owner(s) / Partner(s)** Monica Manzutto
  Jose Kuri
- **Team** 14
- **Artists at Art Basel** Eduardo Abaroa
  Allora & Calzadilla
  Carlos Amorales
  Miguel Calderón
  Abraham Cruzvillegas
  Minerva Cuevas
  Jimmie Durham
  Daniel Guzmán
  Jonathan Hernández
  Gabriel Kuri
  Dr. Lakra
  Sarah Lucas
  Wilfredo Prieto
  Roman Ondák
  Gabriel Orozco
  Damián Ortega
  Fernando Ortega
  Anri Sala
  Gabriel Sierra
  Monika Sosnowska
  Sofía Táboas
  Rirkrit Tiravanija
  Adrián Villar Rojas
  Apichatpong Weerasethakul
  Akram Zaatari

Kaikai Kiki Gallery

Three Questions for Takashi Murakami

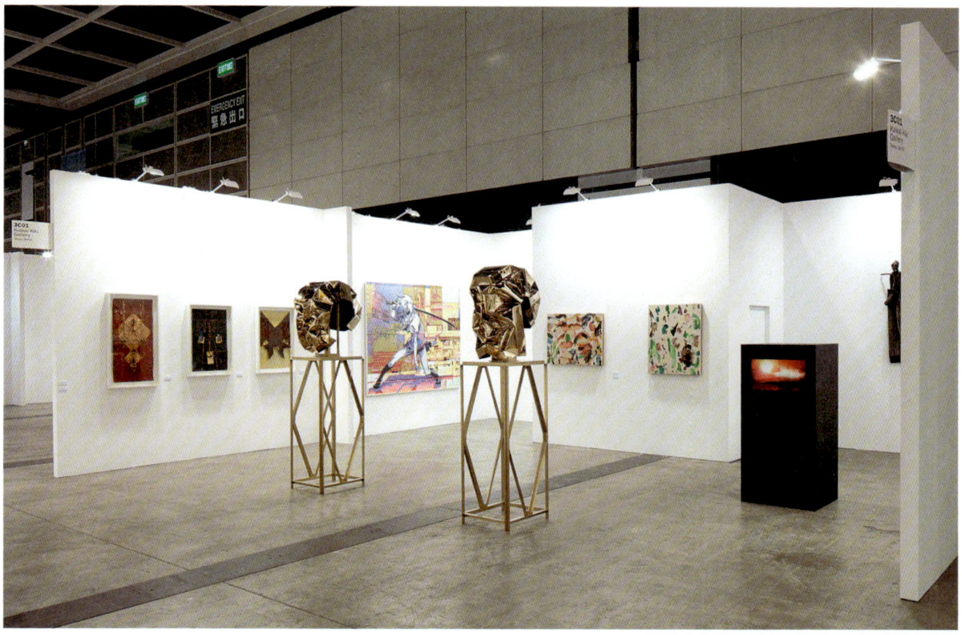

Art Basel in Hong Kong, 2013

Kaikai Kiki Gallery enjoys a distinctive identity: it's both an exhibition space for international artists and the extension of Kaikai Kiki, the art production company founded by Takashi Murakami in 1996 (first called Hiropon Factory). Could you please tell us about Kaikai Kiki's history, its program, and its singularity in the Japanese art world?

The name Kaikai Kiki is taken from a term used in the art history/criticism book *Honchō Gashi* by Kanō Einō. Kanō Einō was a third generation member of the Kanō School, a painting production syndicate that, starting 600 years ago, managed to uphold its artistic heritage for over 400 years in Japan. The term "kaikai kiki" means "grotesque yet alluring," and was used to describe the work of painter Kanō Eitoku. The Kanō School is considered the greatest line in all of Japanese painting history. From the 15th to the 19th centuries they worked as artisans in every painting genre imaginable, always occupying the center of the era's artistic movements, while serving leaders such as Oda Nobunaga, Toyotomi Hideyoshi, and the Tokugawa Shogunate. Besides the Kanō School, Japanese art history contains many examples of artistic families and collectives, such as the studio of Honami Kōetsu, which produced tea ceremony equipment and the decorative elements for Samurai swords, as well as the Kei School, which, through its structured system of masters and pupils, produced Buddhist statues over several generations.

In other words, the key to artistic achievement throughout Japanese art history has always been to act creatively as a group, rather than individually, and to maintain a natural connection to commerce. However, in the almost 146 years since the Meiji restoration and the wave of Westernization that swept over the nation, there has been an over-emphasis on the superiority of individualism. In addition, with Japan's defeat in the Pacific War, the Japanese have lost confidence in their own art. The Japanese style of collective artistic production has thus come to be undervalued.

I began my career as an artist in the aftermath of the collapse of the bubble economy. There was no environment in the Japanese art scene that could offer me any support. While groping around in the dark I began exploring the concept of what defines Japanese originality, and in the process I discovered that it is natural to focus not just on the production of artworks but also on their sale, distribution, and continued care into the future. I have proceeded vigorously down that road ever since. So while an artist running a gallery and selling artwork may seem strange in the eyes of the Western art community, in the context of Japanese art history, I believe it to be a perfectly normal act.

How does your booth at Art Basel in Hong Kong reflect the gallery's distinctive position within the art world?

Perhaps we are unique in that we cover everything from the production and sale of artworks to managing artists, while still staying true to the ways of Japanese artistic tradition. I believe this could not have manifested itself in the West; it is because we are in Asia that this has become a reality.

Case in point: though we have applied for five years running, our gallery has never been permitted to have a booth at Art Basel in Switzerland. I think this fact embodies the different realities of the art scenes surrounding the West and the East.

As a longtime active and dynamic actor in the Asian-Pacific scene, what is your perception of the structure and of the current growth and organization of the art world and its market in this specific geographical zone?

During the bubble years, Japanese galleries would show up at auctions in London and New York with bags full of money that they used to buy up Western masterpieces at record-breaking prices. Domestically, too, with "art patronage" as their catchphrase, they bought into the idea that contemporary art is defined by primitive expressions that defy understanding, and spent gobs of cash on works that stylistically were merely copies of Jean-Michel Basquiat and other artists in the New York scene of the time. Works suited to the tastes of these movers and shakers proliferated, sucking up all the bubble-fed cash available, and when the bubble burst, contemporary art had left nothing of substance in its wake.

I began my career at the very moment that this crazed bubble economy crashed, and as the euphoria began to fade, the whole of Japanese society was overcome with the feeling that art was nothing but a con game. Since that moment, until now, the Japanese art scene has not seen any improvements, becoming lost in a negative spiral of reduced reproduction. Art exhibitions and performances now exist mainly to fill the yearly program requirements of the many museums built around the country during the bubble economy; artists get by on the minor financial support these institutions provide as the economy recovers incrementally. It is difficult to create new movements in this context, however, and those events and exhibitions that are carried out are still heavily influenced by the remaining arbitrators of the bubble period.

In addition, postwar Japanese society, particularly in the aftermath of the bubble, has become victim of a mentality in which buying art is seen as a frivolous act by people putting on airs.

In order to free artists from the restraints imposed by the tastes of small groups of decision-makers, I created GEISAI. Realizing that I could not rely on anyone else and that I would have to forge my own independent art market, I created the commercial art firm Kaikai Kiki, a company that carries the regrets of the bubble period's aftermath in its DNA. Despite all this, the goals that I have set for myself have been focused outside of Japan, rather than trying to cultivate demand domestically.

For the Kabinett sector in Miami Beach, Galleries sector participants were chosen to present curated exhibitions in a separately delineated space within their booths. The concepts within Kabinett are diverse, including thematic group shows, art-historical showcases, and solo exhibitions for rising stars.

KABI NETT

2013 participants

A Gentil Carioca
José Bento
Raymundo Colares

Art : Concept
Richard Fauguet

Borch Jensen
Al Taylor

Brito
Marina Abramović

Carberry
Leon Polk Smith

Chouakri
Gerold Miller

Faria
Yeni & Nan

Gmurzynska
Richard Meier

Alexander Gray
Luis Camnitzer

Gupta
Theaster Gates

Hirschl & Adler
James Edward Deeds

Hoffman
Luis Gispert

Kicken
Götz Diergarten
Jitka Hanzlová
Maurice Loewy &
Pierre Puiseux
László Moholy-Nagy
Kiyoshi Niiyama
Heinrich Riebesehl
Hans Christian Schink
Alfred Seiland
Otto Steinbert
Christer Strömholm
Ed van der Elsken

Krinzinger
Jude Anogwih
Johanna Calle
Adriano Costa
Istvan Csákány
Zhang Ding
Inci Furni
Markus Hanakam &
Roswitha Schuller
Jonathan Hernández
Tamás Kaszás
Waqas Khan
Jarbas Lopes
Mithu Sen

Lambert
Damir Očko

Lehmann Maupin
Tracey Emin

Lelong
Sean Scully

Meile
Hu Qingyan

Metro Pictures
Claire Fontaine

Galerie 1900-2000
Marius de Zayas

Naumann
Man Ray

Nolan
Mel Kendrick

Obadia
Martin Barré

Schulte
Danilo Dueñas

Van Doren Waxter
Sam Francis

Kavi Gupta Gallery
Theaster Gates

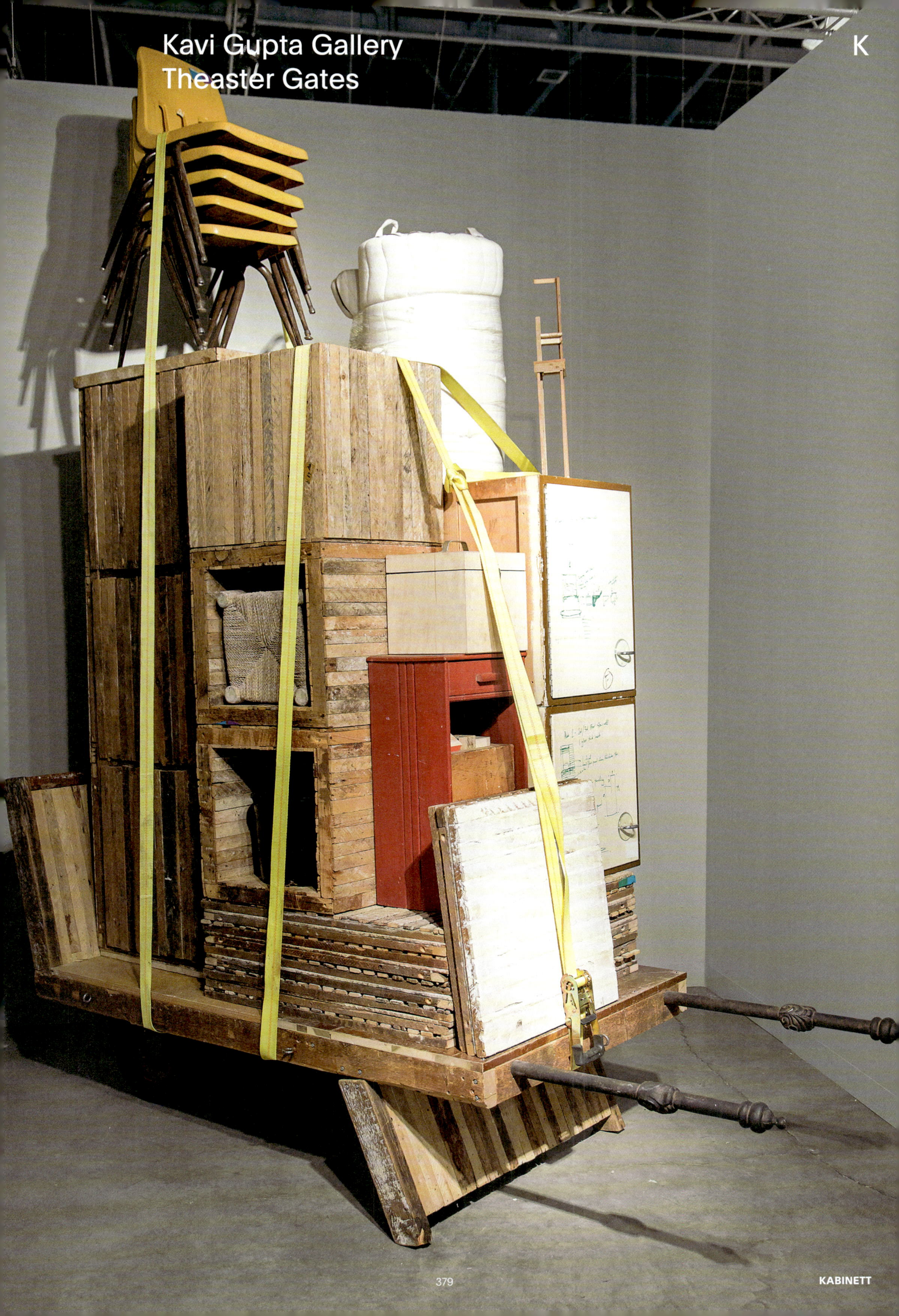

K

A Gentil Carioca
José Bento/Raymundo Colares

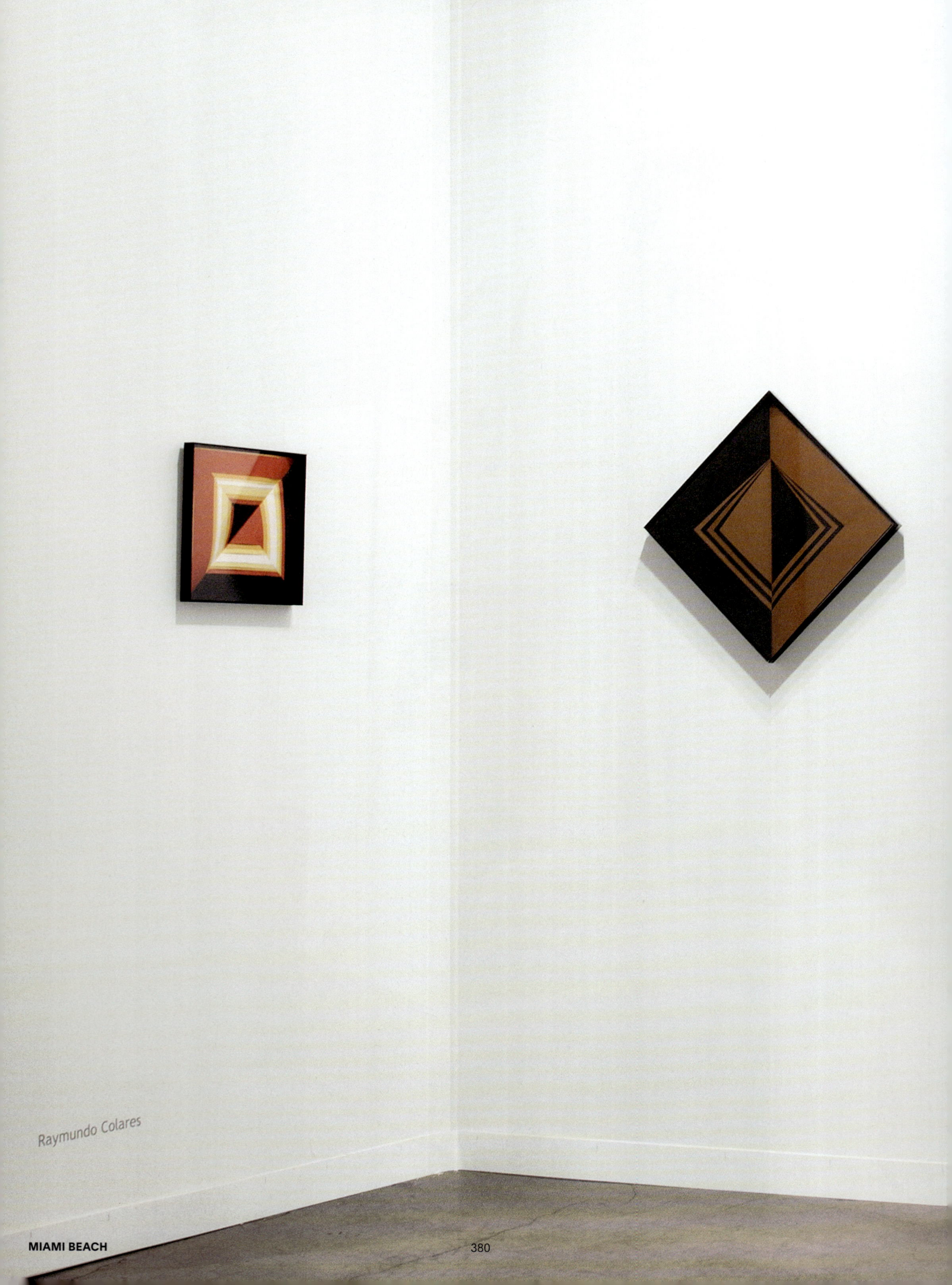

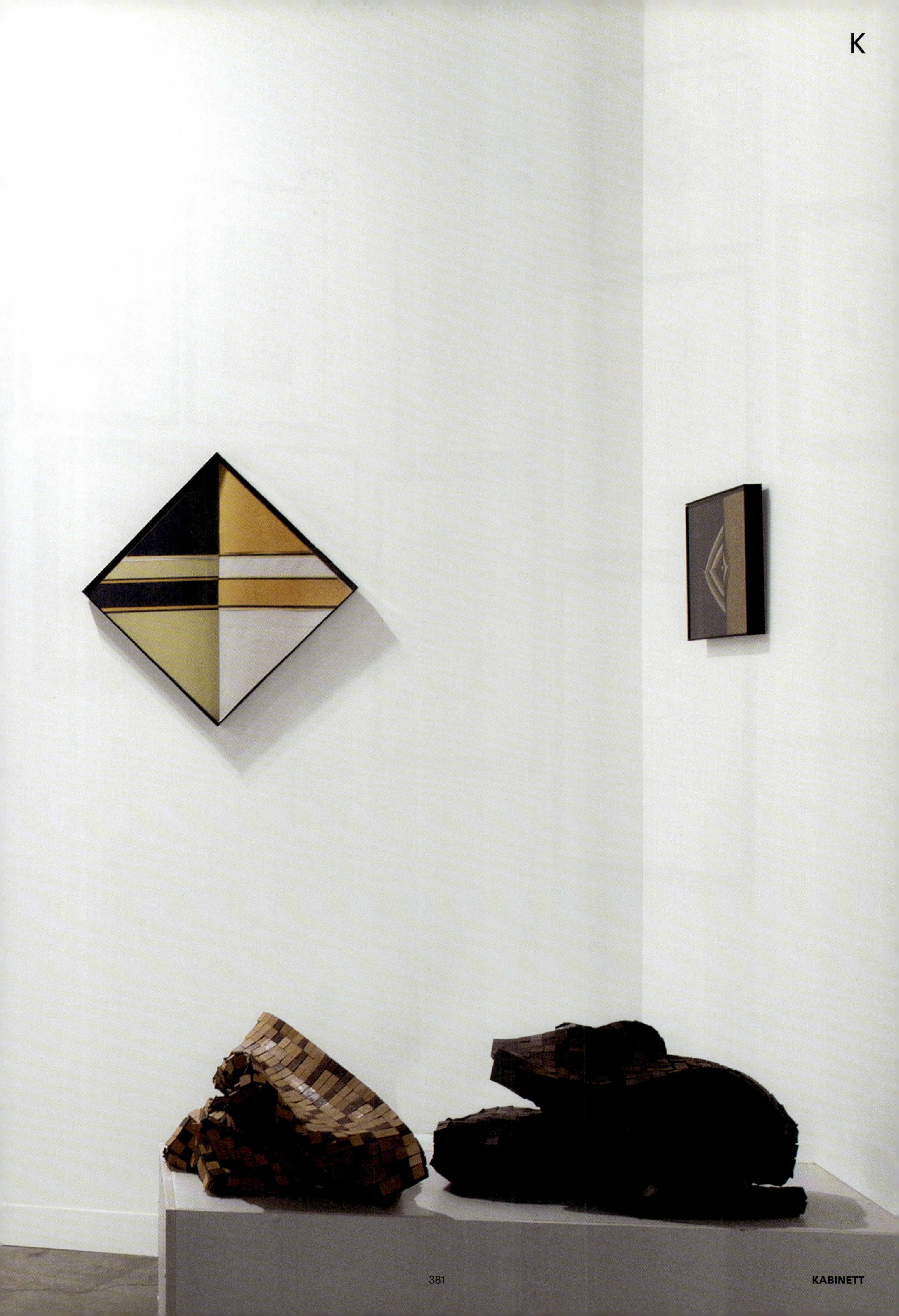

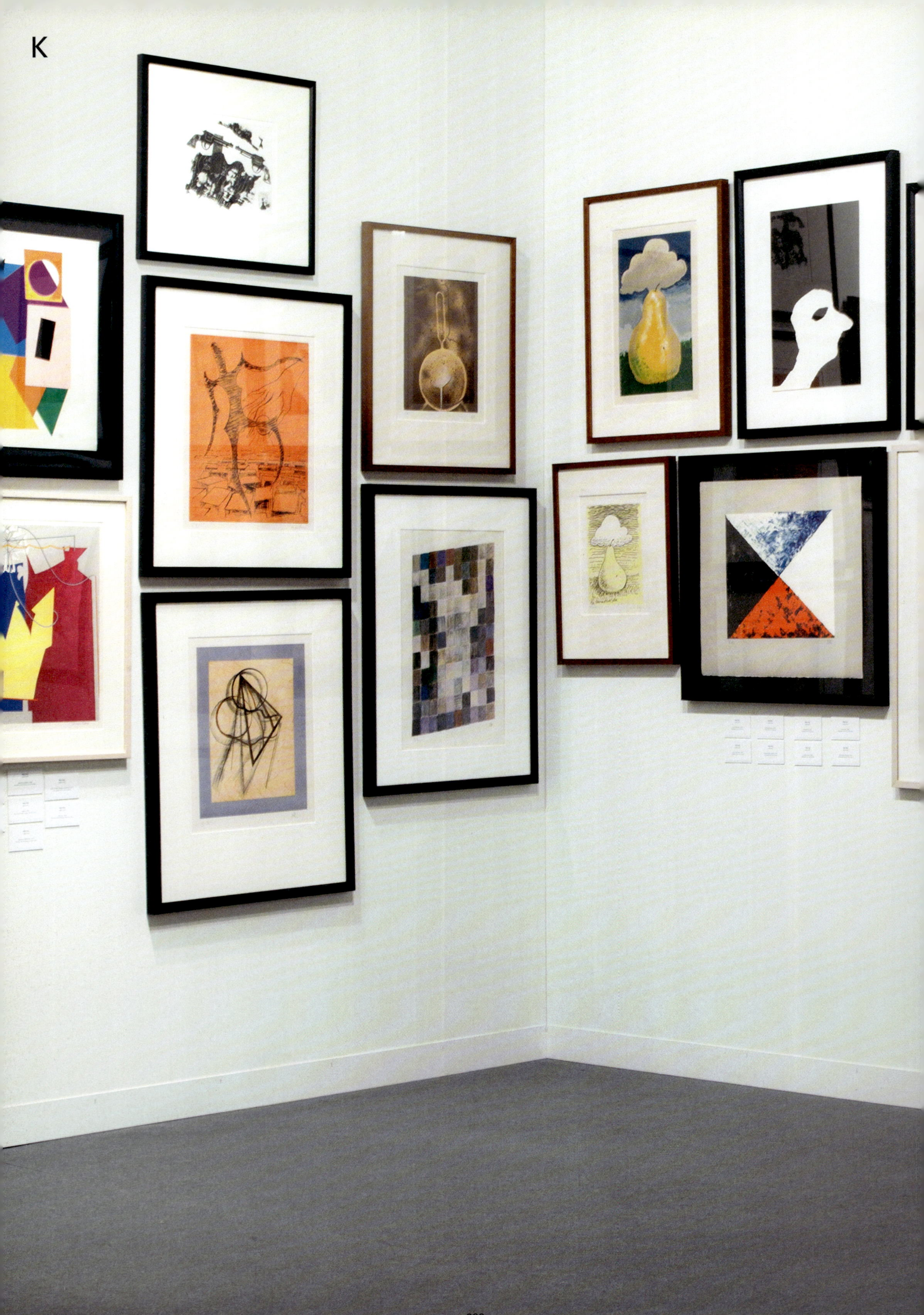

Francis M. Naumann Fine Art
Man Ray

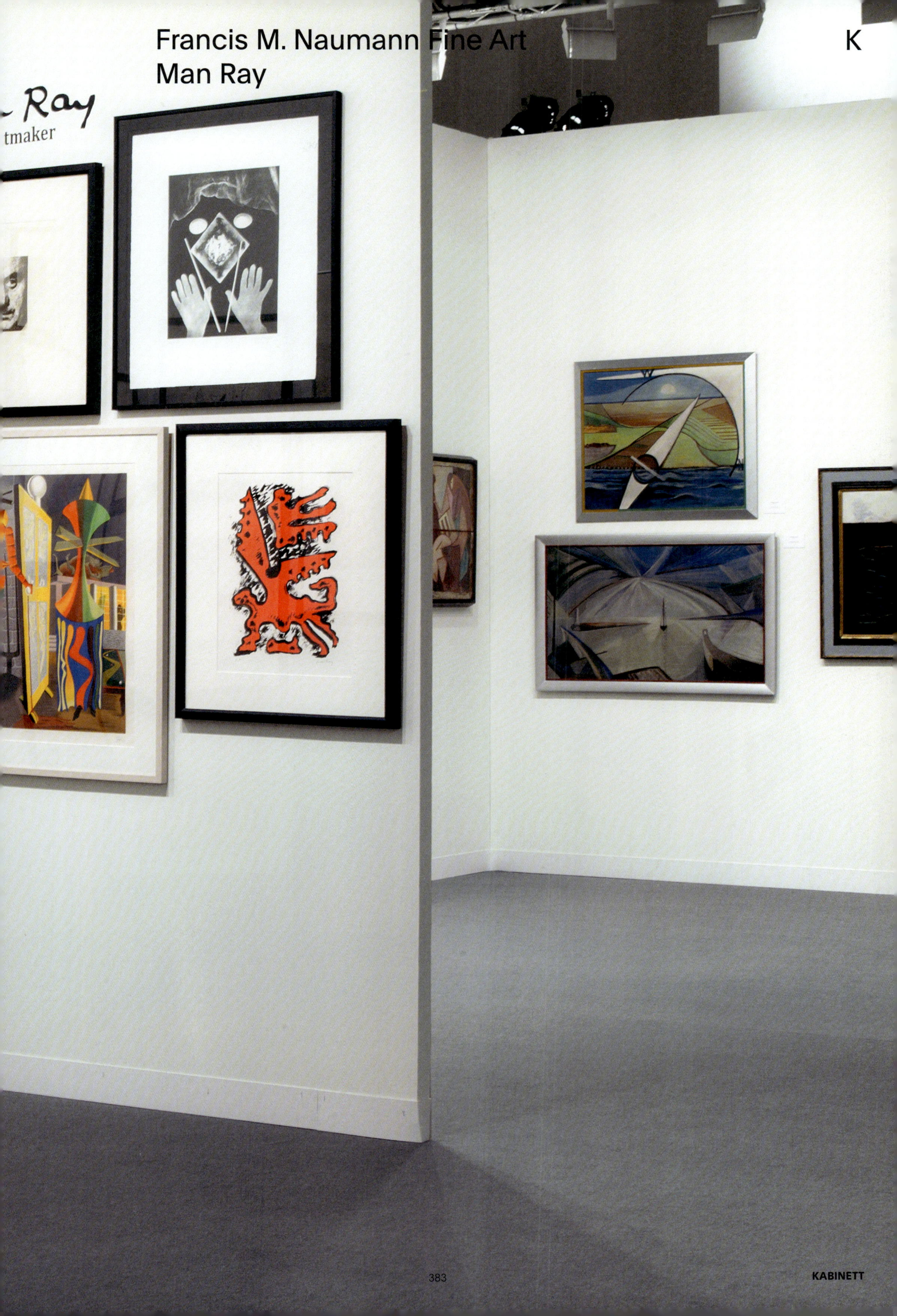

K

Valerie Carberry Gallery
Leon Polk Smith

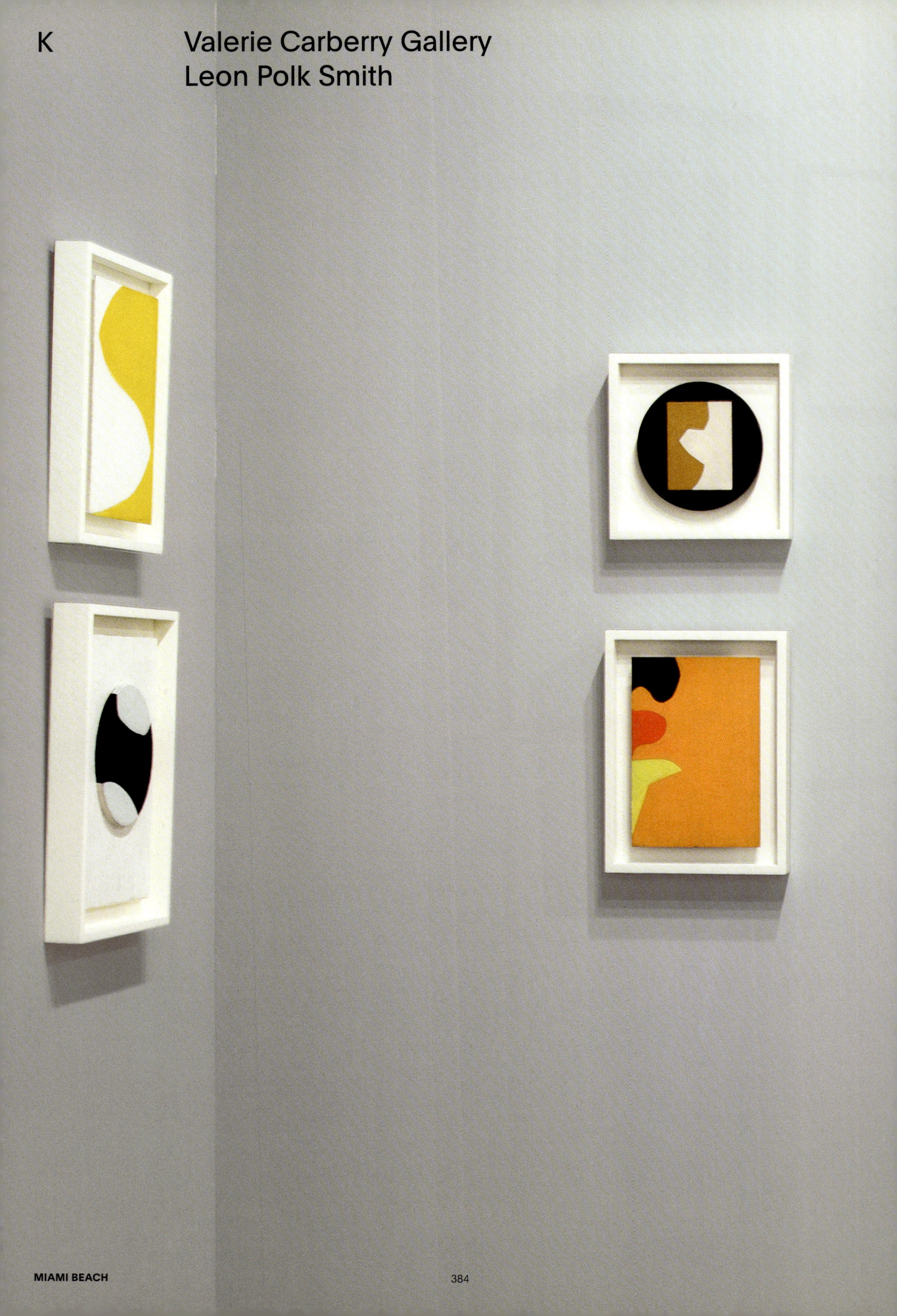

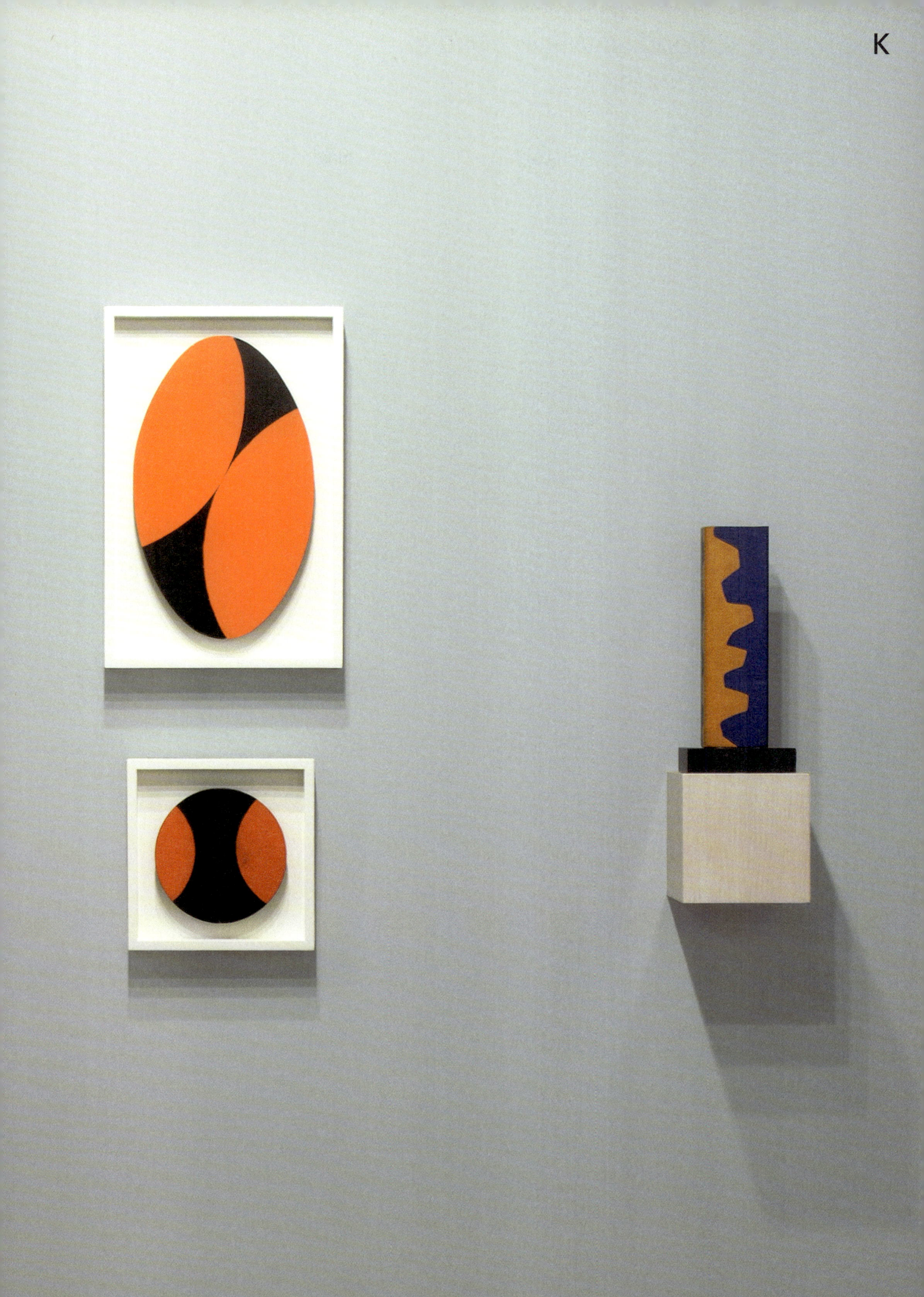

Galerie Nathalie Obadia
Martin Barré

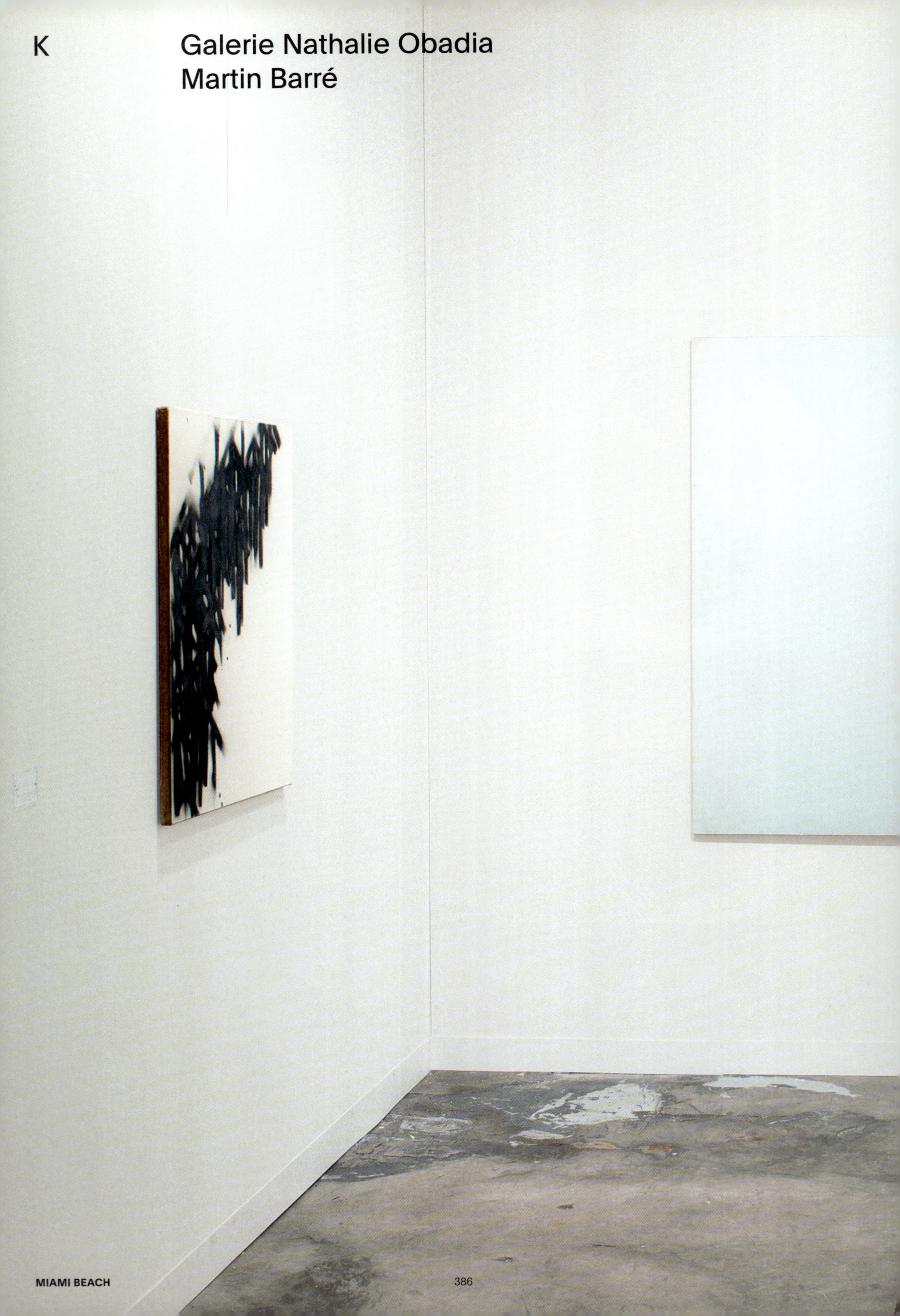

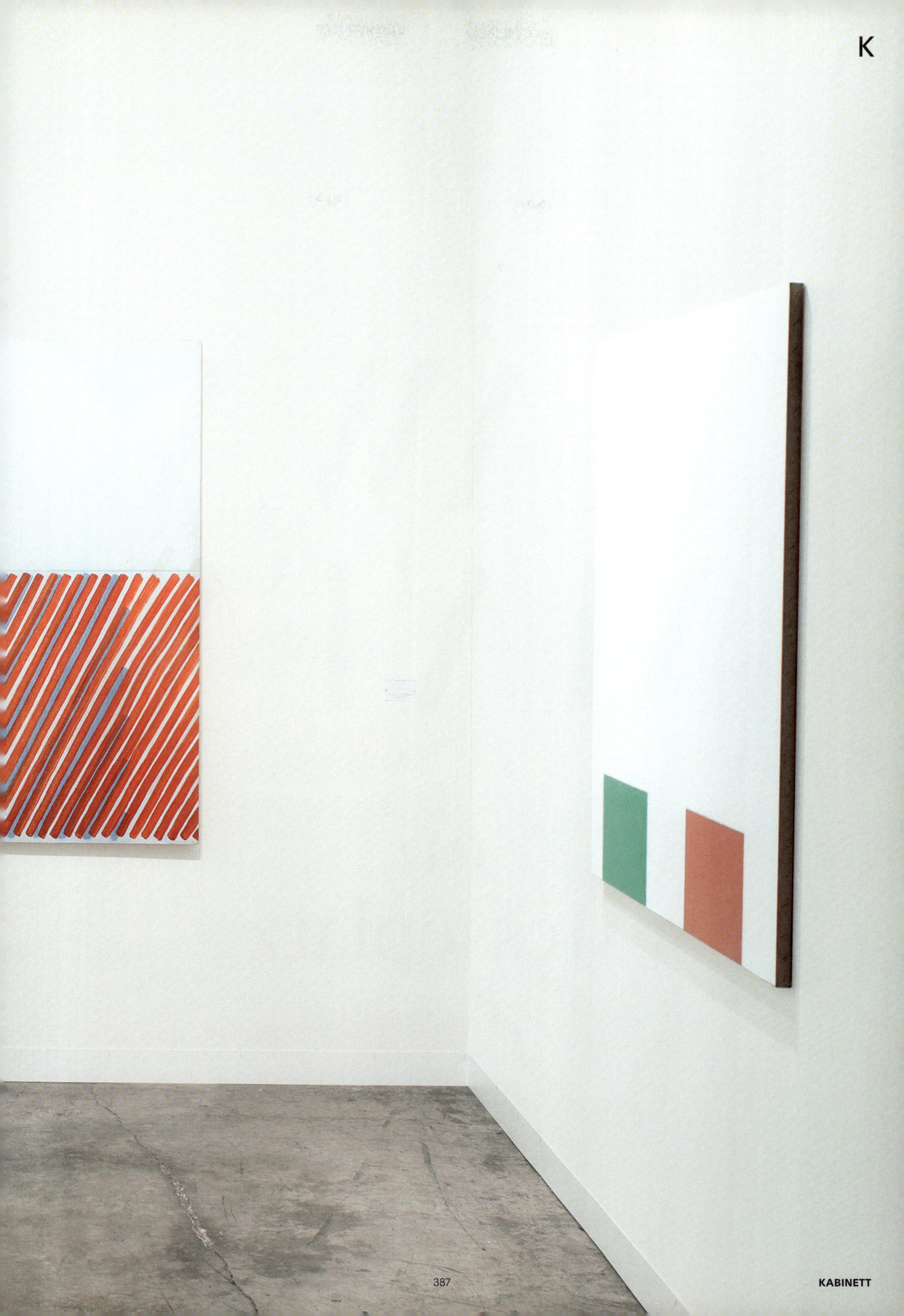

KAWA MATA

on Messeplatz

Tadashi Kawamata
Favela Café
2013

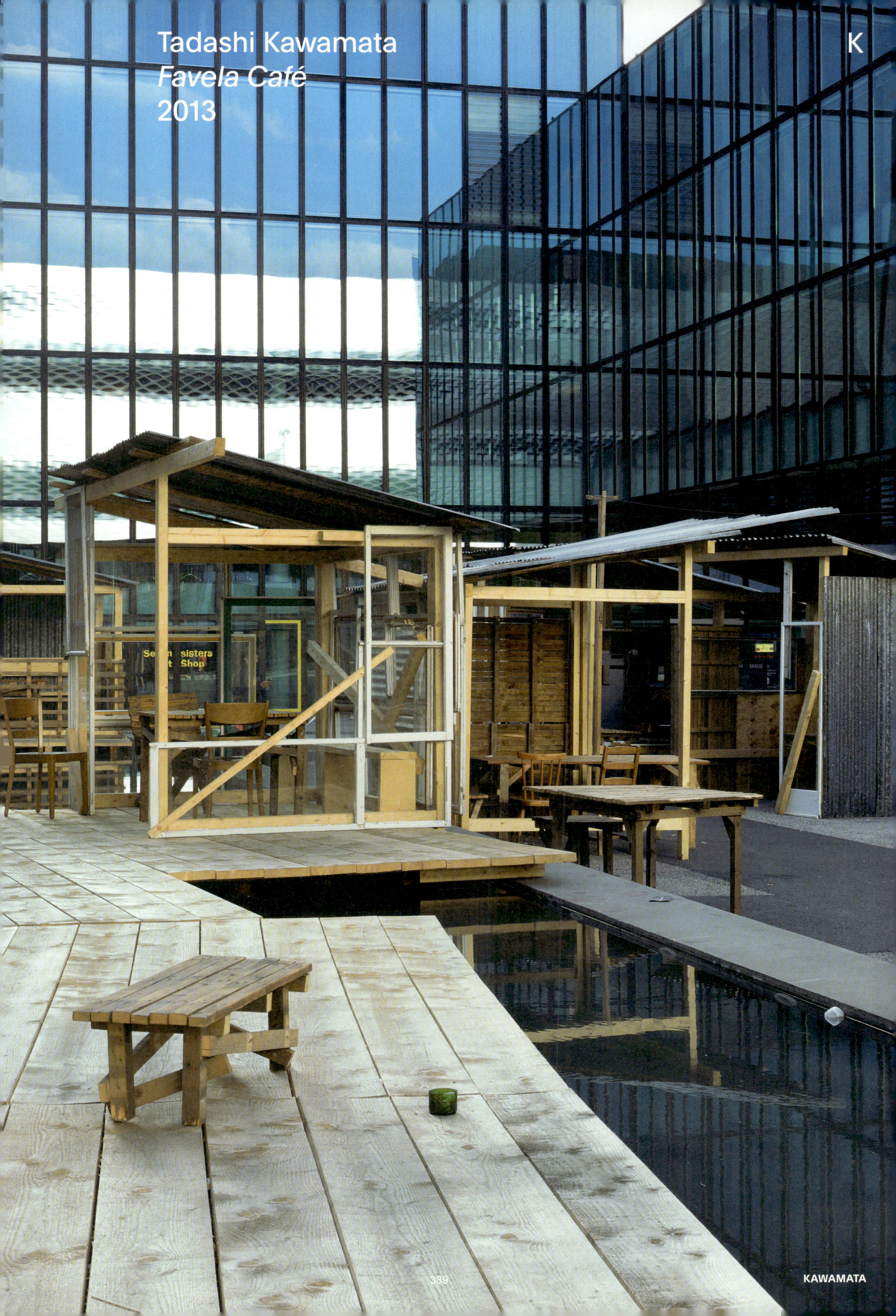

K

Tadashi Kawamata
Favela Café
2013

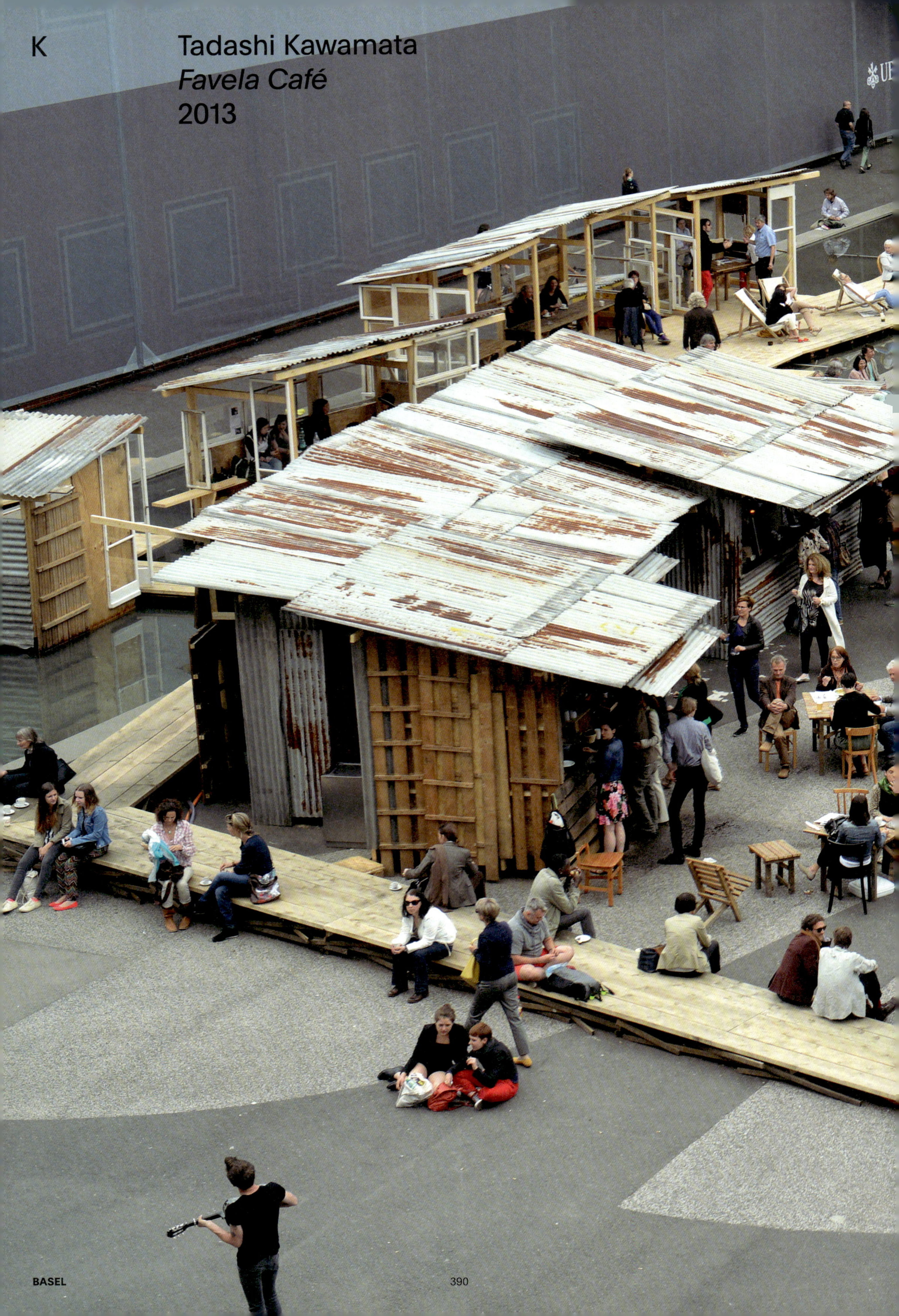

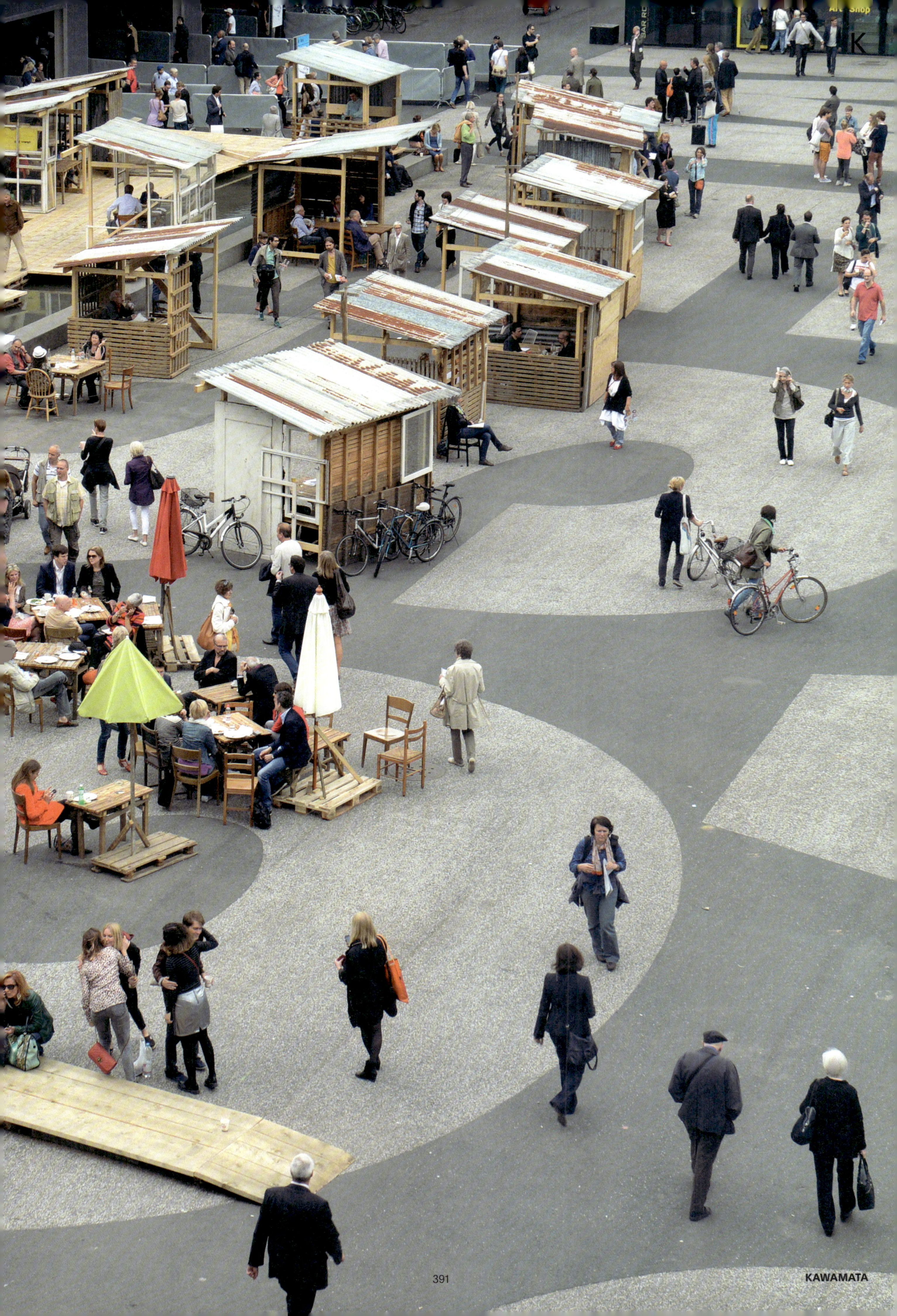

K

Tadashi Kawamata
Favela Café
2013

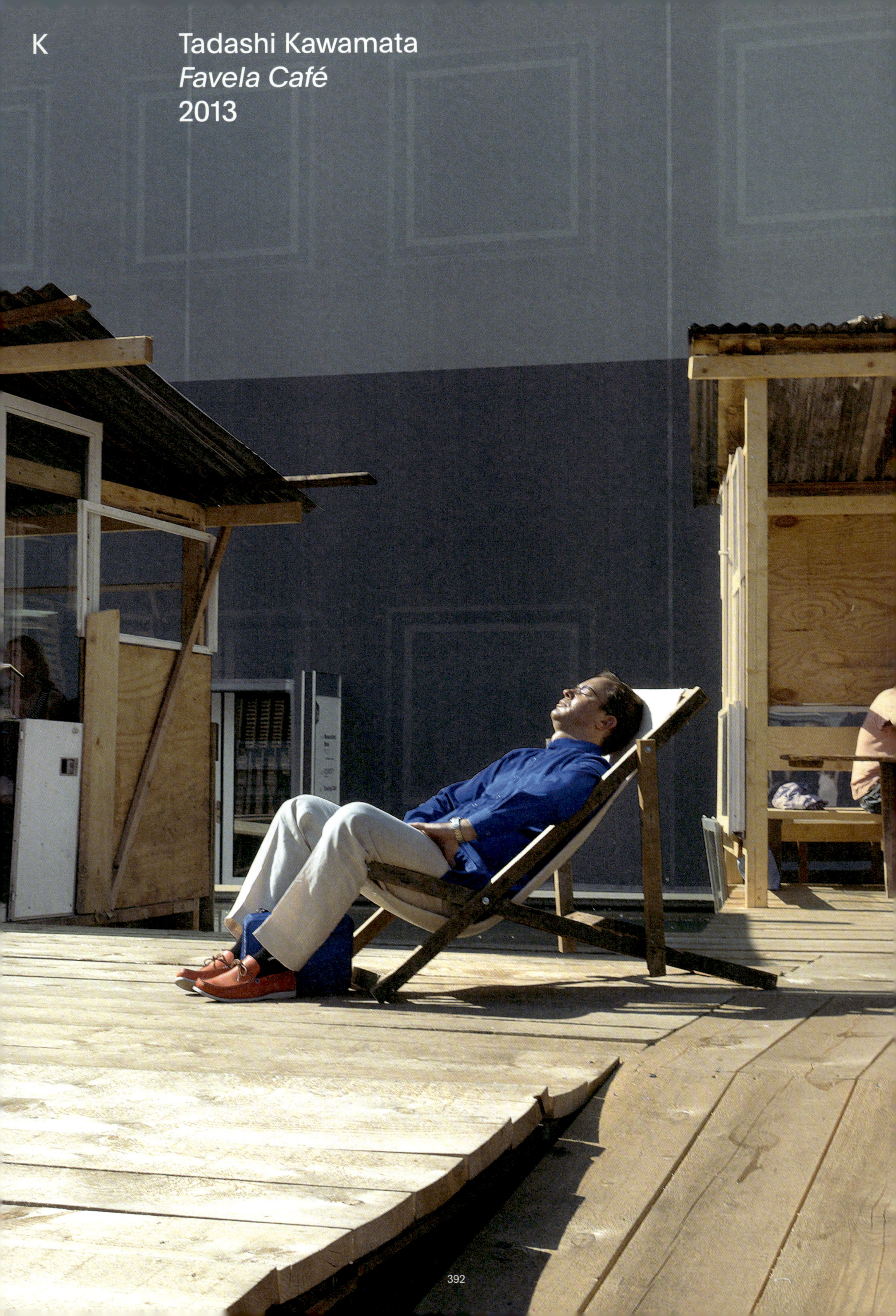

Tadashi Kawamata's *Favela Café*
A Resting Place for Travelers
By Philipp Meier

Text by Philipp Meier

Originally published in *Neue Zürcher Zeitung*, Monday June 10, 2013.

Messeplatz in Basel is unrecognizable. Town planning development has resulted in a lot of building in this area, important for this city on the Rhine. A monumental wall woven from silver yarn has extended diagonally across the square and transformed the area that used to be open to the city center into a closed court. This is now lined by the Hofmann-Rundhalle, the Messeturm, the multi-story car park—and just recently, the complex of halls by Herzog & de Meuron. Anyone paying a visit to Art Basel this year could therefore initially be puzzled by the changed spatial situation they encounter at the gates of the fair. However, our perception is challenged not only by the new group of buildings, but still more by a handful of corrugated iron and wood shacks scattered along the facade of the Hofmann-Rundhalle near the large fountain. Where visitors used previously to be received on the spacious square by large sculptures from international artists, a small favela village has now lodged itself among the distinctive exhibition buildings at the edge of the remaining square.

Our perception is challenged not only by the new group of buildings, but still more by a handful of corrugated iron and wood shacks scattered along the facade of the Hofmann-Rundhalle near the large fountain.
— Philipp Meier

A TEMPORARY COMMUNITY

The signature of these wooden and corrugated sheds with a wooden catwalk meandering through them can be recognized at second glance. The Japanese architectural poet Tadashi Kawamata has been at work here. Famous worldwide for decades for his architectonic interventions involving wooden constructions lashed together in a makeshift way in public space, here he has taken on a commission from the exhibition organizers and created *Favela Café* for Art Basel. As they busily come and go, visitors to the fair can take a break here, give their tired legs a rest, get something to eat, and find shade from the sun or protection from the wind and weather in one of the shelters. Not very different from all the gallery booths in the exhibition halls, these stalls have been set up only temporarily. Kawamata's work will disappear again, just like all the rest of the art fair bustle. This is no longer unusual, for most of Kawamata's artworks are only temporary phenomena.

During construction of the piece the tall and powerful-looking artist, now a good 60 years old, could be met in person with a drill in hand on his building site. In reply to the question as to whether his *Favela Café* is art or architecture, he modestly says: "Neither, more of a construction." Kawamata is not the kind of artist to put on airs. Featuring himself along with his art is not his thing. And anyway his Basel favela, like so many of his earlier works, is a communal enterprise. He has developed the village of huts together with volunteers from Basel's Landestelle (Pier) association. The material—old boards, corrugated iron, and scrap windowpanes—was procured from the port of Basel by the Basel architect Christophe Scheidegger, who has collaborated with Kawamata since 1998. The wooden booths will go back there again after Art Basel. In return

K

for their help in the construction, Kawamata is leaving his sheds to the people who run Landestelle; under this name, by way of an interim land use, they will run a bar and a restaurant on wasteland at the port of Basel for five years. During the three-week development, Kawamata formed a quite strange community with the young people so to speak—not so very different from the residents of favelas in South American cities, as the artist says.

Kawamata's favelas can be perceived as metaphors for the urban changes taking place in the course of daily life, opposing all urban planning.
— Philipp Meier

For he has already created favela projects before, in 1991 in Houston, in 1992 at documenta in Kassel, and last summer during the TRACK art festival in Ghent in Belgium. Kawamata does not take pleasure in the simulated or imitated wretchedness of poor South American districts. His interest is directed rather at the mostly illegally erected and generally temporary substructures, and how they fit into official urban structures in the form of shantytowns. Favelas, shantytowns, or slum villages come into being between rows of houses, in urban interstices, and take over empty city sites and gaps. Such anarchically proliferating alternative housing developments, cleared away by the authorities from time to time, and rebuilt again and again by a subculture, represent not least a striking counter-image to the cool architectural icons of modern megalopolises, built to last for ever, as it were.

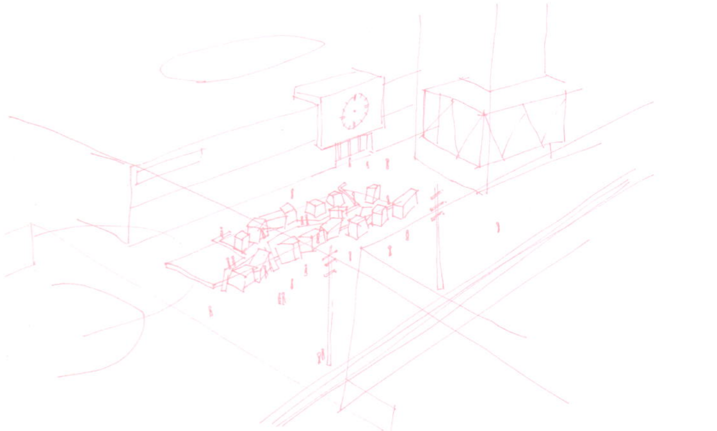

THE WORLD AS A PROVISIONAL ABODE

Kawamata's favelas can be perceived as metaphors for the urban changes taking place in the course of daily life, opposing all urban planning. The Basel *Favela Café*, with the special conditions of its site on Messeplatz, interacts in this way: for ultimately, its reconfiguration—already long regarded as unsuccessful town planning in the eyes of many—is due to the changing requirements of Basel as an exhibition venue.

Furthermore, for Kawamata as a Japanese and a Buddhist, it is not unusual for the images of cities to change. In Japan old houses are regularly demolished, natural catastrophes destroy villages or whole towns from time to time, and the wooden Shinto shrine at Ise, for instance, Japan's supreme Shinto sanctuary, is rebuilt from scratch every 20 years.

Kawamata's temporary art to some extent reflects the Buddhist concept of the "Kari no Yado," the "temporary abode." According to this concept, the world is only a temporary dwelling for human beings who are perceived as passing travelers on their life's path. So Kawamata's wooden sheds do not appear very different from those roadside refuges that in the olden days in Japan served travelers both as a resting place and a shelter.

Tadashi Kawamata and Christophe Scheidegger, sketch for *Favela Café*, Messeplatz, Basel, 2013

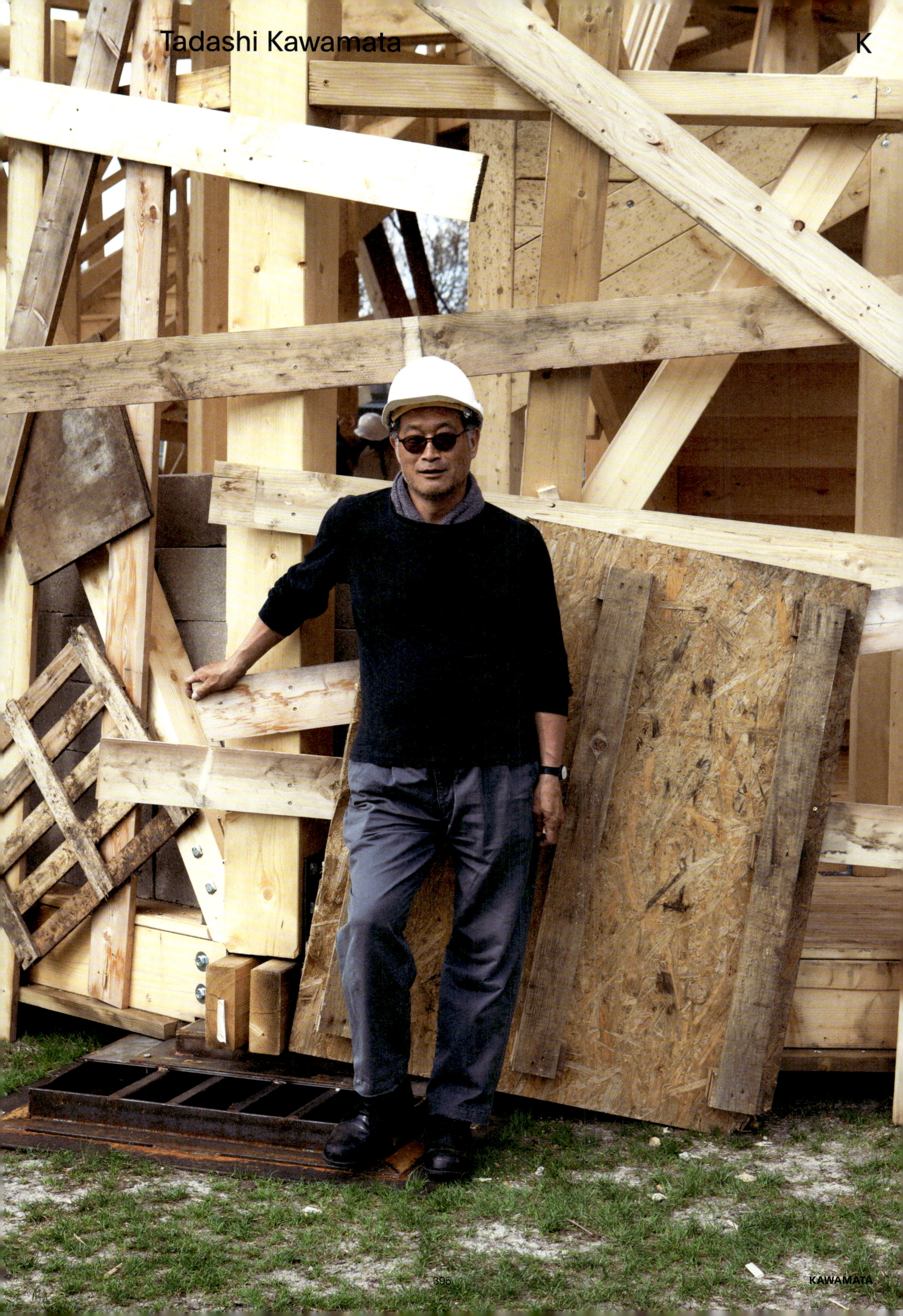

L

- Hong Kong
- Basel
- Miami Beach

La Central

Bogotá — Positions

- **Contact** — La Central, info@lacentral.com.co
- **Established** — 2009
- **Owner(s) / Partner(s)** — Beatriz Lopez, Katy Hernandez
- **Artists at Art Basel** — Nicolás Consuegra
- **Further artists represented** — Felipe Arturo, Otto Berchem, Pia Camil, Carolina Caycedo, Sebastián Fierro, Juan David Laserna, Alberto Lezaca, Miltos Manetas, Ana Roldán, Daniel Santiago Salguero, Manuela Viera Gallo

Labor

Mexico D.F. — Nova

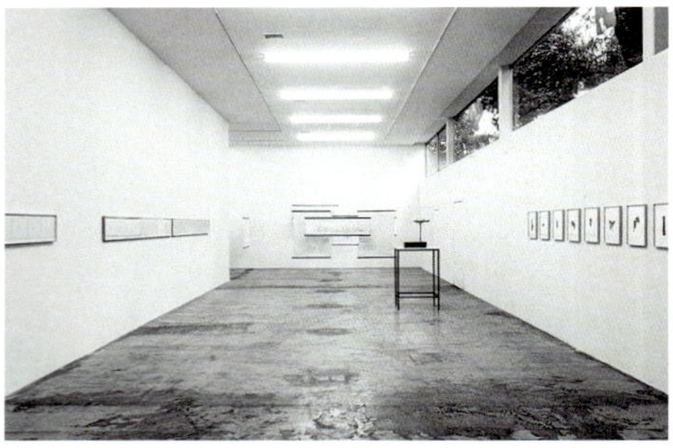

What first compelled you to open a gallery?
Freedom. I used to be a curator in a couple of museums in Mexico. To have a gallery you have to use the same talents but you don't have to keep anyone else happy but yourself and the artists.

Who is the first artist you showed and what was most memorable about that show?
It was a group show with all the artists. The whole day was memorable.

When did you first participate in Art Basel and what was most memorable about that show?
We did Art Basel in Miami Beach in 2010.

- **Contact** — Labor, Rodrigo Feliz, rodrigo@labor.org.mx, info@labor.org.mx
- **Established** — 2009
- **Owner(s) / Partner(s)** — Pamela Echeverría
- **Team** — 3
- **Space(s)** — 120 m²
- **Artists at Art Basel** — Jill Magid, Teresa Margolles, Pedro Reyes
- **Further artists represented** — Erick Beltrán, Etienne Chambaud, Santiago Cucullu, Terence Gower, Irene Kopelman, Nicholas Mangan, Raphael Montañez Ortiz, Jorge Satorre, Pablo Vargas Lugo, Antonio Vega Macotela, Héctor Zamora

Lahumière

Paris — Galleries

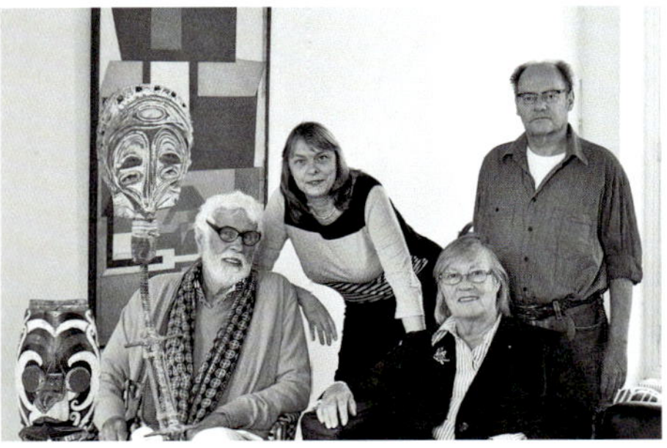

What first compelled you to open a gallery?
My husband and I had been working both in the cultural field, he was for several years the assistant of Dorothea Speyer, Head of the American Cultural section at the Embassy in Paris, and I had been working for six years with a gallery of modern art in Paris. When the Embassy closed the section, we opened our own space.

Who is the first artist you showed and what was most memorable about that show?
It was a sculpture show, in which we tried to present a relatively complete view of the "contemporary" sculpture of the moment in the 1960s. Being a young gallery it was very easy to borrow works of art from older colleagues and private collectors. We presented 32 pieces, borrowing a Giacometti from Claude Bernard, and a Picasso from Kahnweiler, Jean Arp, Edgar Degas, Henri Laurens, Germaine Richier, and others, but we also had an unpublished plaster from Rodin from a private collection, and Henri Moore sent a piece from London, which I picked up myself at Le Bourget airport, laughing at the custom officers.

When did you first participate in Art Basel and what was most memorable about that show?
We participated in the very first Art Basel show, that was held in a building now destroyed. You could walk outside onto the street, nobody would ask you anything. Most memorable about that show was that my husband decided he could build the booth—we had published a series of works by Jean Dewasne and our booth was not long enough. We were still hammering and working on it the evening of the opening … The next day Harald Szeemann visited the booth; he admired the pieces I showed, and brought a number of buyers—I was delighted!

- **Contact** — Galerie Lahumière, Diane Lahumière, diane@lahumiere.com, galerie@lahumiere.com
- **Established** — 1963
- **Owner(s) / Partner(s)** — Jean-Claude Lahumière, Anne Lahumière, Diane Lahumière
- **Space(s)** — 120 m²
- **Artists at Art Basel** — Jean Arp, Etienne Béothy, Pol Bury, Jean-Gabriel Coignet, Jo Delahaut, Jean Dewasne, Naum Gabo, Emile Gilioli, Jean Gorin, Gottfried Honegger, Robert Jacobsen, Piotr Kowalski, François Morellet, Antoine Perrot, Denis Pondruel, Sigurd Rompza, André Stempfel

- **Further artists represented** Bauduin
Charles Bézie
Nicholas Bodde
Andreas Brandt
Marcelle Cahn
Nathalie Delasalle
Jean-François Dubreuil
Jean-Michel Gasquet
Hans-Jörg Glattfelder
Auguste Herbin
Renaud Jacquier Stajnowicz
Jean Legros
Jean Leppien
Alberto Magnelli
Yves Popet
Henri Prosi
Moon-Pil Shim
Victor Vasarely

Lam

Hong Kong
Shanghai
Singapore

Galleries

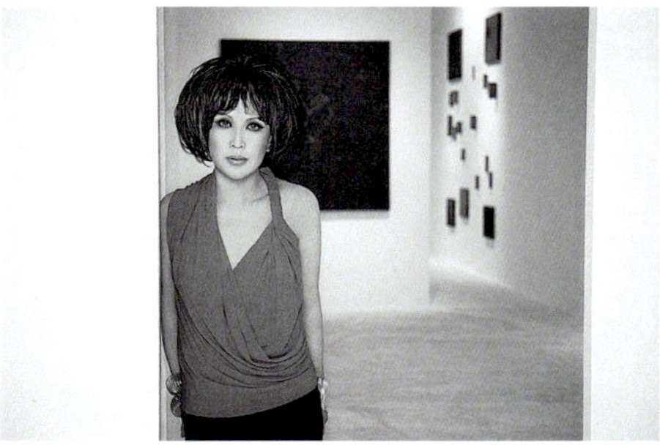

What first compelled you to open a gallery?

I grew up with traditionally-minded parents for whom art was a hobby and not a career. My education in the West was really where my interest in art began. I dreamed of being involved in art, even though I did not really know what that would entail. I managed to negotiate the possibility of doing some pop-up shows in Hong Kong, and that's where it all started. I became a collector, sponsored museum shows, and started organizing exhibitions. It was only in 2006 that I started to have a physical space in Shanghai to show Chinese art other than what was mainstream, which was defined by political Pop. I also opened a design gallery where I invite international designers to experience and get inspiration from 5,000 years of Chinese traditions.

When did you first participate in Art Basel and what was most memorable about that show?

In Hong Kong in 2013. Art Basel really put Hong Kong on the international art map and changed the cultural landscape of the city. Despite the sophistication of the place, Hong Kong's culture has always been about money, which is not enough. My generation was educated abroad and we've all brought something back. Art Basel has pulled everybody together, and is now a key event on the international art calendar.

- **Contact** Pearl Lam Galleries
Harriet Onslow
harriet@pearllamfineart.com
info@pearllamgalleries.com
- **Established** 2002
- **Owner(s) / Partner(s)** Pearl Lam
- **Team** 72
- **Space(s)** 2,600 m²
- **Artists at Art Basel** Jenny Holzer
Hu Jun Jun
Li Huasheng
Li Xiaojing
Jason Martin
Su Xiaobai
Suraji
Tsang Kin-Wah
Entang Wiharso
Yinghua
Zhu Jinshi
- **Further artists represented** Golnaz Fathi
Jim Lambie
Lan Zhenghui
Lei Hong
Li Tianbing
Qiu Zhenzhong
Yinka Shonibare
Sun Juju
Wang Dongling
Michael Wilkinson
Yan Binghui
Jonathan Yeo
Zhang Huan
Zhang Yu
Zheng Chongbin
Zhou Yi

Lambert

Paris

Galleries
Galleries Unlimited
Parcours
Galleries Kabinett

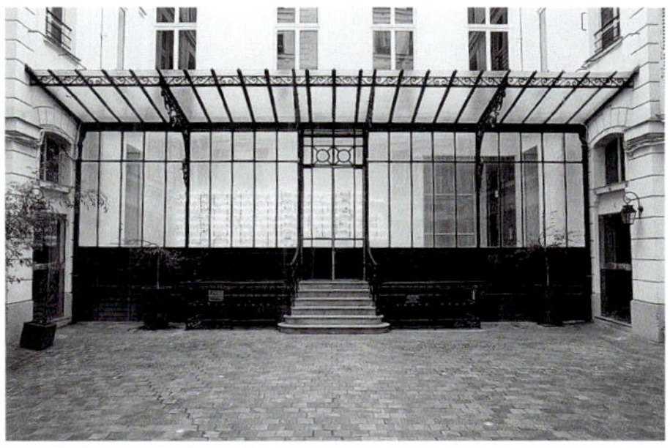

Who is the first artist you showed and what was most memorable about that show?

Yvon Lambert opened his Parisian gallery with a Phillip King show in which only two monumental sculptures were presented. At the end of the exhibition, one of those works was sold to the Centre Pompidou Collection.

- **Contact** Yvon Lambert
Mathieu Cénac
mathieu@yvon-lambert.com
paris@yvon-lambert.com
- **Established** 1966
- **Owner(s) / Partner(s)** Yvon Lambert
- **Team** 17
- **Space(s)** 620 m²
- **Artists at Art Basel** Carlos Amorales
Mircea Cantor
Mounir Fatmi
Douglas Gordon
Loris Gréaud
Karl Haendel
Candida Höfer
Jenny Holzer
Zilvinas Kempinas
Bertrand Lavier
Damir Očko
Andres Serrano
Mario Testino
Niele Toroni
Nick van Woert
Francesco Vezzoli
Lawrence Weiner
Cerith Wyn Evans
- **Further artists represented** Carl Andre
Robert Barry
Stefan Brüggemann
Mircea Cantor
David Claerbout
Jason Dodge
Gardar Eide Einarsson
Spencer Finch
Vincent Ganivet
Anna Gaskell
Kendell Geers
Shilpa Gupta
Koo Jeong-A
Joan Jonas
On Kawara
Idris Khan
Anselm Kiefer
Barbara Kruger
Louise Lawler
Sol LeWitt
Jill Magid

Jonathan Monk
Roman Opalka
Giulio Paolini
Diogo Pimentão
Charles Sandison
Markus Schinwald
Ariel Schlesinger
David Shrigley
Shinique Smith
Salla Tykkä
Ian Wallace

Landau

Montreal — Galleries
Meggen (Lucerne) — Galleries

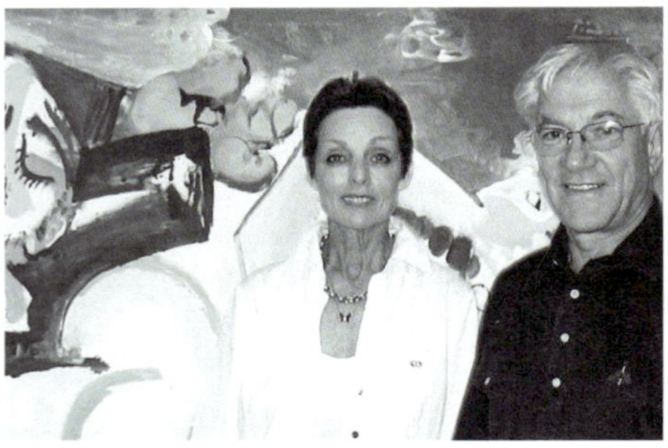

Who is the first artist you showed and what was most memorable about that show?
Jean Dubuffet.

When did you first participate in Art Basel and what was most memorable about that show?
In the early 1990s.

- **Contact** Landau Fine Art, Inc.
  Nissa Khan
  nkhan@landaufineart.ca
  landau@landaufineart.ca
- **Established** 1987
- **Owner(s) / Partner(s)** Robert Landau
  Alice Landau
- **Team** 7
- **Space(s)** 1,860 m²
- **Artists at Art Basel** Josef Albers
  Louis Anquetin
  Karel Appel
  Alexander Archipenko
  Jean Arp
  Victor Brauner
  Heinrich Campendonk
  Massimo Campigli
  Lynn Chadwick
  Marc Chagall
  Kwang Young Chun
  Le Corbusier
  Giorgio de Chirico
  Edgar Degas
  André Derain
  Jean Dubuffet
  Max Ernst
  Lyonel Feininger
  Alberto Giacometti
  Juan Gris
  Hans Hofmann
  Wassily Kandinsky
  Christoph Kiefhaber
  Paul Klee
  Sara Landau
  Henri Laurens
  Fernand Léger
  Jacques Lipchitz
  René Magritte
  Marino Marini
  Henri Matisse
  Joan Miró
  Amedeo Modigliani
  Henry Moore
  Giorgio Morandi
  Emil Nolde
  Pablo Picasso
  Georges Rouault
  Yves Tanguy
  Georges Valmier
  Kees van Dongen
  Alexej von Jawlensky

Langgeng

Magelang — Galleries

- **Contact** Langgeng Gallery
  deddy@langgeng.net
- **Established** 2002
- **Owner(s) / Partner(s)** Deddy Irianto
- **Artists at Art Basel** Christine Ay Tjoe
  Arin Dwihartanto
  FX Harsono
  Guerlillas Indie
  J. Ariadhitya Pramuhendra
  Yuli Prayitno
  Filippo Sciascia
  Handoko Uji Hahan
- **Further artists represented** Dadang Christanto
  Heri Dono
  Eddie Hara
  Geraldine Javier
  Irfan Mohamad
  Jasmine Sison
  Agus Suwage

Layr

Vienna — Nova

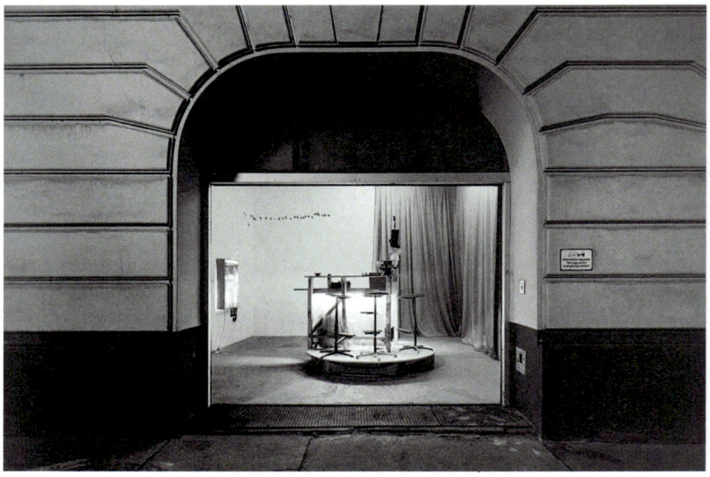

What first compelled you to open a gallery?
The belief in the necessity of art. Passion and interest for all the steps involved in the production of art works and exhibitions.

Who is the first artist you showed and what was most memorable about that show?
It was a show by Tillman Kaiser. At the time we didn't have our own gallery space. It was in an amazing place: a former coffee house from the turn of the century in the middle of Vienna's city center. The space was approximately ten times bigger than the space we rented afterward.

When did you first participate in Art Basel and what was most memorable about that show?
In 2013.

- **Contact** Galerie Emanuel Layr
  Emanuel Layr
  layr@emanuellayr.com
  gallery@emanuellayr.com
- **Established** 2005/2011
- **Owner(s) / Partner(s)** Emanuel Layr
- **Team** 2
- **Space(s)** 180 m²
- **Artists at Art Basel** Plamen Dejanoff
  Lisa Holzer
- **Further artists represented** Franz Amann
  Julien Bismuth
  Marius Engh
  Stano Filko
  Benjamin Hirte
  Tillman Kaiser
  Mahony
  Nick Oberthaler
  Fabian Seiz

Lee

London
Hong Kong

- Galleries Encounters
- Galleries Unlimited Parcours
- Galleries Public

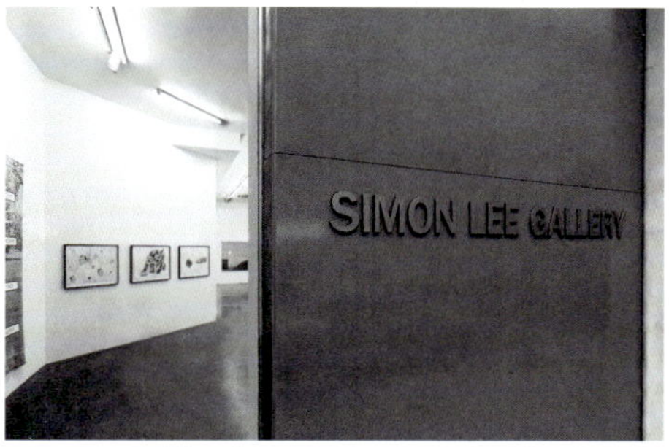

What first compelled you to open a gallery?
God knows!

Who is the first artist you showed and what was most memorable about that show?
Raymond Pettibon and how many incredible works we brought together for the show and sold.

When did you first participate in Art Basel and what was most memorable about that show?
In 2004.

- **Contact** Simon Lee Gallery
  Amy Facey
  amy@simonleegallery.com
  info@simonleegallery.com
- **Established** 2002
- **Owner(s) / Partner(s)** Simon Lee
- **Team** 21
- **Artists at Art Basel** Mel Bochner
  Alighiero e Boetti
  Angela Bulloch
  Merlin Carpenter
  Larry Clark
  James Coleman
  George Condo
  Jeff Elrod
  Matias Faldbakken
  Hans-Peter Feldmann
  Bernard Frize
  Ran Huang
  Alex Hubbard
  Donald Judd
  Sherrie Levine
  Paulina Olowska
  David Ostrowski
  Claudio Parmiggiani
  João Penalva
  Michelangelo Pistoletto
  Josephine Pryde
  Jim Shaw
  Gary Simmons
  Valerie Snobeck
  Marnie Weber
  Christopher Wool
  Toby Ziegler
  Heimo Zobernig

Lehmann

Dresden
Berlin

- Galleries
- Galleries Parcours

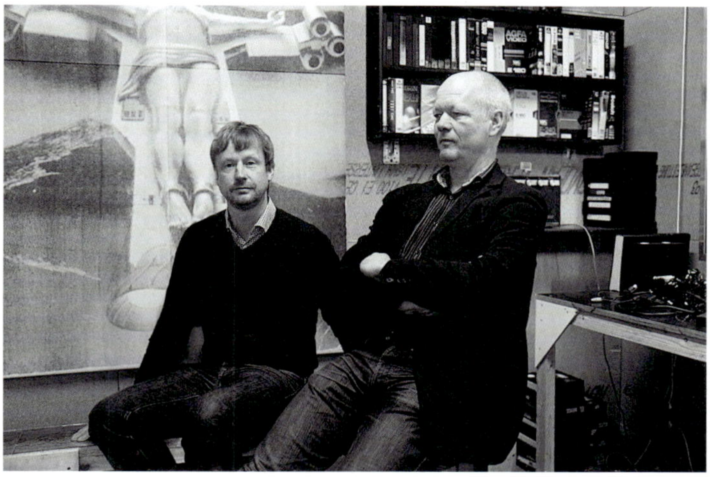

What first compelled you to open a gallery?
In January 1988 Frank and Ralf Lehmann launched a project room in their joint apartment in Dresden, in what was then the German Democratic Republic (East Germany). From this project arose the Galerie Gebr. Lehmann in 1992.

Who is the first artist you showed and what was most memorable about that show?
It was the artist called Hirschvogel (Robert Makolies). He brought his paintings, unwrapped, in an old rented truck half an hour before the exhibition was to begin. That is the most memorable.

When did you first participate in Art Basel and what was most memorable about that show?
In 1999, in the Statements sector in Art Basel, with the artist Eberhard Havekost. An incredible number of American collectors were there. Havekost immediately sold out, even to the most important institutions. That was not to be expected for a first participation.

- **Contact** Galerie Gebr. Lehmann
  Jörg Goedecke
  joerg@g-gl.de
  info@galerie-gebr-lehmann.de
- **Established** 1992
- **Owner(s) / Partner(s)** Ralf Lehmann
  Frank Lehmann
- **Team** 6
- **Space(s)** 200 m²
- **Artists at Art Basel** Tatjana Doll
  Slawomir Elsner
  Eberhard Havekost
  Olaf Holzapfel
  Martin Honert
  Tilman Hornig
  Thoralf Knobloch
  Frank Nitsche
  Keiichi Tanaami
  Joep van Liefland
- **Further artists represented** Ellen Harvey
  Hirschvogel
  Herbert Hoffmann
  Yeondoo Jung
  Martin Mannig
  Dan McCarthy
  Lara Schnitger
  Daniel Schubert
  Kohei Yoshiyuki

Lehmann Maupin

New York
Hong Kong

- Galleries
- Galleries Unlimited
- Galleries Kabinett

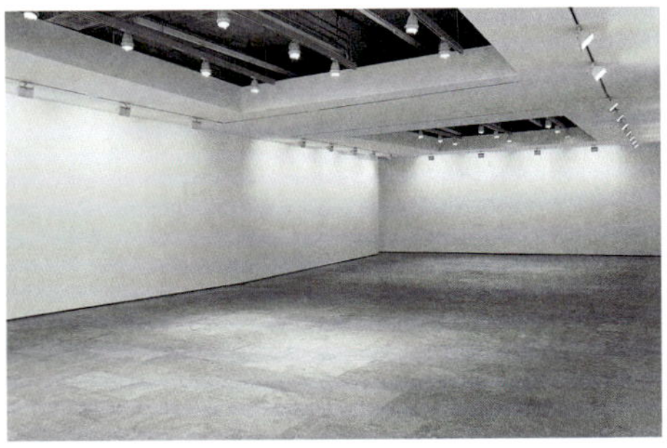

What first compelled you to open a gallery?
Rachel Lehmann and David Maupin met in Italy in 1991 and, in 1993, in collaboration with Janelle Reiring and Helene Winer of Metro Pictures, they established Offshore Gallery in East Hampton, where for two years artists such as Richard Prince, David Salle, and Ross Bleckner were exhibited. Three years later, Lehmann Maupin Gallery opened in New York's SoHo neighborhood, designed by the Dutch architect Rem Koolhaas. The gallery moved to its present location in Chelsea in 2002. A second New York gallery was established in 2007 on the Lower East Side, Manhattan's new cultural hub, and Lehmann Maupin inaugurated its first international gallery space in the historic Pedder Building in Central, Hong Kong, in 2013.

When did you first participate in Art Basel and what was most memorable about that show?
In 2006. We dedicated a part of the booth to the work of Do Ho Suh as it was an important opportunity to exhibit Suh's work in an international setting; a room up the stairway was created to show an installation video projection by Jennifer Steinkamp.

- **Contact** Lehmann Maupin
Drew Moody
drew@lehmannmaupin.com
newyork@lehmannmaupin.com
- **Established** 1996
- **Owner(s) / Partner(s)** David Maupin (Owner)
Rachel Lehmann (Owner)
Stephanie Smith (Partner)
Carla Camacho (Partner)
- **Team** 30
- **Space(s)** 1,000 m²
- **Artists at Art Basel** Stefano Arienti
Hernan Bas
Ashley Bickerton
Ross Bleckner
Billy Childish
Mary Corse
Tracey Emin
Teresita Fernández
Anya Gallaccio
Gilbert & George
Sonia Gomes
Shirazeh Houshiary
Klara Kristalova
Lee Bul
Liu Wei
Mr.
Jun Nguyen-Hatsushiba
Os Gêmeos
Angel Otero
Tony Oursler
Alex Prager
Robin Rhode
Tim Rollins and K.O.S.
Rei Sato
Jennifer Steinkamp
Do Ho Suh
Juergen Teller
Mickalene Thomas
Adriana Varejão
Suling Wang
Nari Ward
Erwin Wurm
Mario Ybarra, Jr.

Leighton

Berlin

- Nova

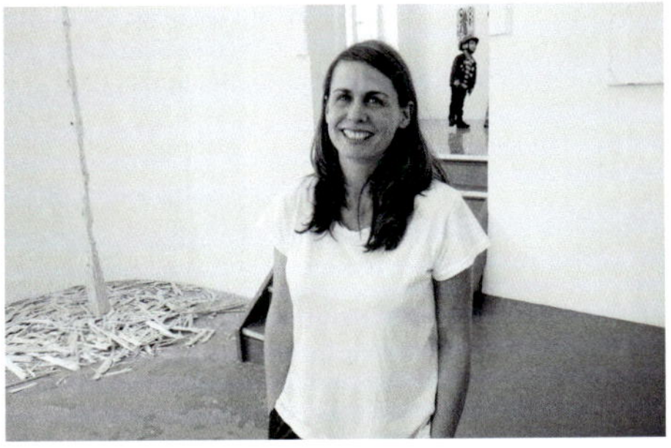

Who is the first artist you showed and what was most memorable about that show?
Sharon Hayes.

When did you first participate in Art Basel and what was most memorable about that show?
John Smith at Art Basel in the Features sector in 2011.

- **Contact** Tanya Leighton
Sonya Merutka
sonya@tanyaleighton.com
info@tanyaleighton.com
- **Established** 2008
- **Owner(s) / Partner(s)** Tanya Leighton
- **Team** 4
- **Space(s)** 160 m²
- **Artists at Art Basel** Aleksandra Domanovic
Oliver Laric
- **Further artists represented** Ayreen Anastas
Pave Büchler
Alejandro Cesarco
David Diao
Sean Edwards
Rene Gabri
Aurélien Gamboni
Sharon Hayes
Sanya Kantarovsky
Enzo Mari
Bruce McLean
Lucas Ospina
Dan Rees
John Smith

Lelong

Paris
New York

- Galleries
- Galleries Unlimited
- Galleries Kabinett Public

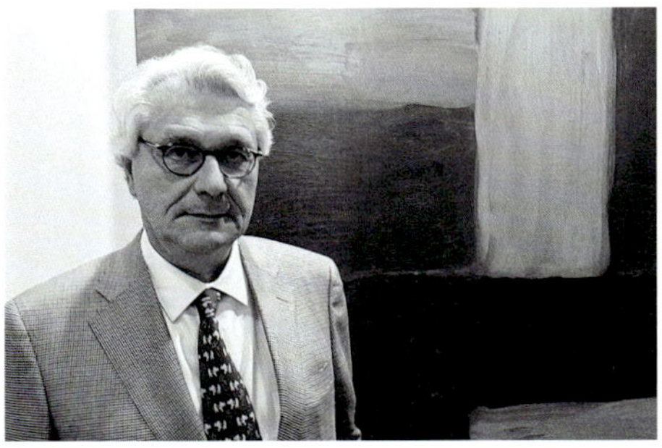

What first compelled you to open a gallery?
Jacques Dupin, Daniel Lelong, and Jean Frémon were associates of Aimé Maeght, who opened the gallery in Paris in 1945, 13 rue de Téhéran, and in New York in 1978; Dupin, Lelong, and Frémon took over after his death.

Who is the first artist you showed and what was most memorable about that show?
We invited Henry Moore and Francis Bacon to join the gallery right after Aimé Maeght's death. Their shows were strong events and significant signs of confidence in the new owners of the gallery.

When did you first participate in Art Basel and what was most memorable about that show?
Early in the 1970s Art Basel was a lively and stimulating meeting place for collectors and dealers before the summer break. We used to show huge paintings and sculptures by Miró, Tàpies, and Chillida, which were often purchased by Swiss and German museums.

- **Contact** Galerie Lelong
  Patrice Cotensin
  cotensin@galerie-lelong.com
  info@galerie-lelong.com
- **Established** 1981
- **Owner(s) / Partner(s)** Paris: Jean Frémon (Partner and President)
  Daniel Lelong (Partner and Managing Director)
  Patrice Cotensin (Director)
  New York: Jean Frémon (Partner and President)
  Daniel Lelong (Partner and VP)
  Mary Sabbatino (Partner and VP)
- **Space(s)** 3,000 m² (Paris, including showroom and storage)
  500 m² (New York)
- **Artists at Art Basel** Sarah Cain
  Petah Coyne
  Angelo Filomeno
  Günther Förg
  Andy Goldsworthy
  Wang Gongxin
  David Hockney
  Alfredo Jaar
  Konrad Klapheck
  Jannis Kounellis
  Rosemary Laing
  Cildo Meireles
  Ana Mendieta
  Joan Miró
  David Nash
  Hélio Oiticica
  Yoko Ono
  Emilio Perez
  Jaume Plensa
  Zilia Sánchez
  Sean Scully
  Kiki Smith
  Ettore Spalletti
  Nancy Spero
  Antoni Tàpies
  Lin Tianmiao
  Juan Uslé
- **Further artists represented** Pierre Alechinsky
  Eduardo Chillida
  Nicola De Maria
  Barry Flanagan
  Leon Golub
  Jane Hammond
  Rebecca Horn
  Jiri Kolár
  Leon Kossoff
  Wolfgang Laib
  Catherine Lee
  Urs Lüthi
  Nalini Malani
  Robert Motherwell
  Arnulf Rainer
  Antonio Saura
  Kate Shepherd
  Barthélémy Toguo
  Ursula von Rydingsvard
  Krzysztof Wodiczko
  Catherine Yass

Lelong Editions

Paris ● Edition

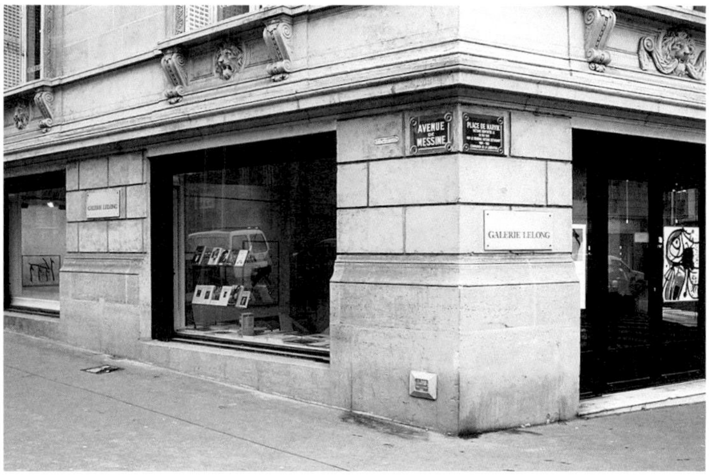

Who is the first artist you showed and what was most memorable about that show?
Our first publication as Lelong Editions was a set of 12 large lithographs by Marc Chagall, the largest he ever made.

When did you first participate in Art Basel and what was most memorable about that show?
Our first participation was when the Edition sector was created, in 1991. We showed *Quarantania*, a series of prints by Louise Bourgeois that we had just published, as well as her famous etching *Femme Maison*.

- **Contact** Lelong Editions
  Francois Dournes
  dournes@galerie-lelong.com
  art@galerielelong.com
- **Established** 1981
- **Owner(s) / Partner(s)** Jean Frémon (Partner and President)
  Daniel Lelong (Partner and Managing Director)
  Patrice Cotensin (Director)
  Serge Béreau (Head of Prints Department)
- **Team** 18
- **Space(s)** 60 m²
- **Artists at Art Basel** Pierre Alechinsky
  Eduardo Chillida
  Barry Flanagan
  Joan Miró
  Robert Motherwell
  David Nash
  Jaume Plensa
  Sean Scully
  Kiki Smith
  Antoni Tàpies
  Barthélémy Toguo
- **Further artists represented** Francis Bacon
  Louise Bourgeois
  Alexander Calder
  Nicola De Maria
  Günther Förg
  Andy Goldsworthy
  David Hockney
  Ellsworth Kelly
  Konrad Klapheck
  Jiri Kolár
  Jannis Kounellis
  Nalini Malani
  Pablo Palazuelo
  Ernest Pignon-Ernest
  Arnulf Rainer
  Antonio Saura
  Kate Shepherd
  Nancy Spero
  Juan Uslé
  Jan Voss

Leme

São Paulo ● Nova

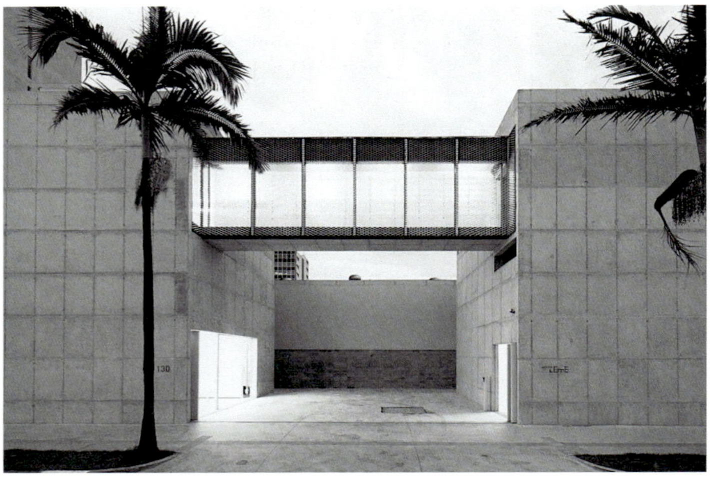

What first compelled you to open a gallery?
I was a collector, and my passion for art turned me into an art dealer.

Who is the first artist you showed and what was most memorable about that show?
The gallery's first show was a group show and for me what was most memorable about it was the great response I had from the audience at the opening, as the gallery was completely packed with artists, friends, and collectors .

When did you first participate in Art Basel and what was most memorable about that show?
It was in 2007 in Miami Beach. To be accepted at an important art fair like Art Basel was really fantastic! It felt great to be accepted in a group of galleries that I really admire and respect.

- **Contact** Galeria Leme
Camila Siqueira
camila@galerialeme.com
info@galerialeme.com
- **Established** 2004
- **Owner(s) / Partner(s)** Eduardo Leme
- **Team** 7
- **Space(s)** 600 m² (gallery) + 150 m² (storage)
- **Artists at Art Basel** Sandra Gamarra
Mariana Mauricio
Mauro Piva
- **Further artists represented** Gabriel Acevedo Velarde
Paulo Almeida
AVPD (Aslak Vibæk and Peter Dossing)
David Batchelor
Luiz Braga
Sebastiaan Bremer
Felipe Cama
Paulo Climachauska
Marcia de Moraes
Ana Elisa Egreja
Richard Galpin
Neil Hamon
Candida Höfer
Zilvinas Kempinas
Henry Krokatsis
Mariana Manhães
Milton Marques
José Carlos Martinat
Jessica Mein
Flavia Metzler
Marcelo Moscheta
Patricia Osses
Nina Pandolfo
Frank Thiel
João Pedro Vale
Gustavo Von Ha

Lévy

New York ● Galleries ● Galleries ● Galleries

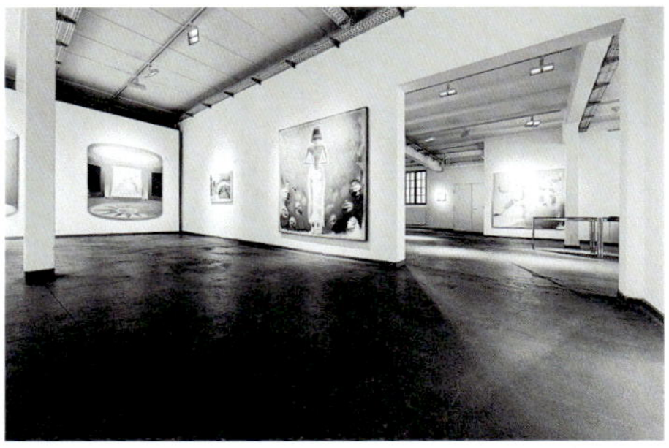

What first compelled you to open a gallery?
I grew up in Geneva and was fortunate enough to be surrounded by great men and women such as the young Jan Krugier and Alice Pauli. The passion for art had always been there, but meeting them was inspiring and decisive.

Who is the first artist you showed and what was most memorable about that show?
My first show was with young Swiss artists in their late teens in an 18th-century house in Geneva. I had just turned 18 years old. The most memorable aspect of this experience was the togetherness, the sense of community, and the excitement of showing the art and observing people looking at it.

When did you first participate in Art Basel and what was most memorable about that show?
I attended Art Basel as a child, as an adolescent, and as an adult many times. The most memorable aspect is perhaps the evolution over the years of my eye and the refinement of my taste; how seeing the art in that context constantly forced me to question all preconceived opinions and ideas about what art is and should be.

- **Contact** Dominique Lévy Gallery
Begum Yasar
begum@dominique-levy.com
info@dominique-levy.com
- **Established** 1999
- **Owner(s) / Partner(s)** Dominique Lévy
- **Team** 11
- **Space(s)** 292 m²
- **Artists at Art Basel** Jean-Michel Basquiat
Louise Bourgeois
Alberto Burri
Alexander Calder
John Chamberlain
Willem de Kooning
Jean Dubuffet
Max Ernst
Eric Fischl
Dan Flavin
Lucio Fontana
Lucian Freud
David Hammons
Damien Hirst
Donald Judd
Ellsworth Kelly
Yves Klein
Franz Kline
Jeff Koons
Roy Lichtenstein
Piero Manzoni
Brice Marden
Agnes Martin
Barnett Newman
Pablo Picasso
Germaine Richier
Gerhard Richter
Mark Rothko
Ed Ruscha
Robert Ryman
David Smith
Pierre Soulages
Frank Stella
Yves Tanguy
Cy Twombly
Günther Uecker
Andy Warhol

Lin & Lin

Taipei
Beijing

Galleries

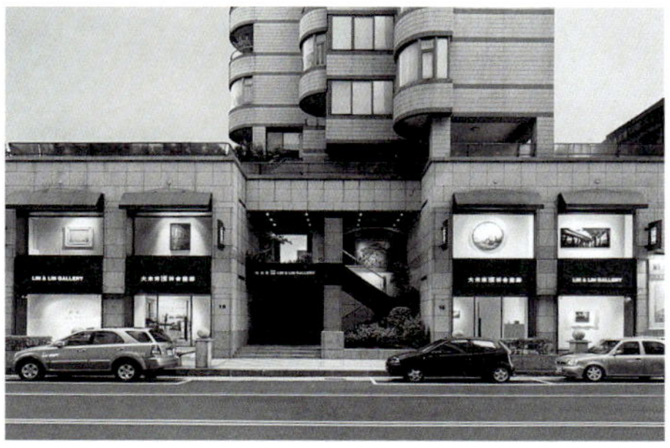

What first compelled you to open a gallery?
To introduce Asian artists to the world, Lin and Lin Gallery tried to construct a complete and diverse program from early modern Chinese art of the 20th century to contemporary art. We would also like to develop cultural exchange with others.

Who is the first artist you showed and what was most memorable about that show?
The first artist we exhibited was Sanyu. At that time not many people grasped the beauty of his works, which are often like classical academic paintings. But after our continuous promotion, people began to understand and started to adore Sanyu's works.

When did you first participate in Art Basel and what was most memorable about that show?
The first time we participated at Art Basel was in 2013. We aim to promote Asian art to the world, so we exhibited the work of Chen Chieh-Jen and Liu Wei. Most memorable was to realize that not only the Asian, but also the Western audience like their works, and wanted to know more about them.

- **Contact** Lin & Lin Gallery
  Muo Zheng
  linlingallery@gmail.com
- **Established** 1984
- **Owner(s) / Partner(s)** Tien-Min Lin (David Lin)
- **Team** 10
- **Space(s)** 2,000 m²
- **Artists at Art Basel** Chen Chieh-jen
  Liu Wie
- **Further artists represented** George Chann
  Chiu Chien-Jen
  Guan Liang
  Hsiao Chin
  Huang Chia-Ning
  Hung Tung-Lu
  Kuo Wei-Kuo
  Lai Chiu-Chen
  Leng Bingchuan
  Liu Shih-Tung
  Lu Hsien-Ming
  Mao Yan
  Sanyu
  Wang Huai Qing
  Wu Da-Yu
  Xia Yang
  Xu Jiang
  Ye Nan
  Yin Zhaoyang
  Yun Gee
  Zao Wou-Ki
  Zhao Gang

Linder

Basel

Galleries

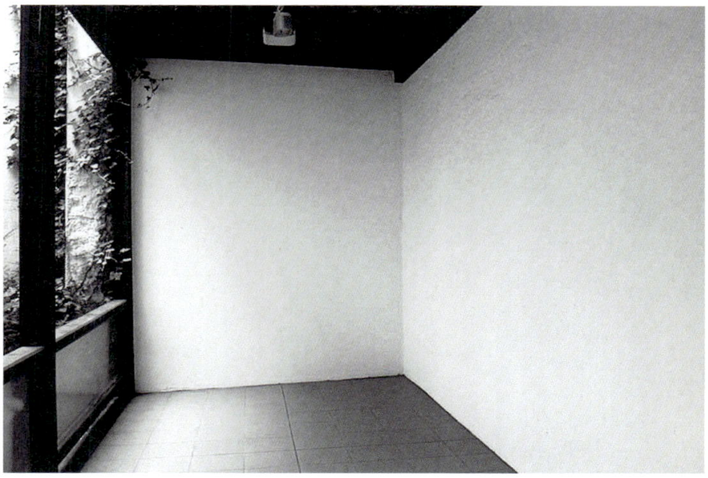

What first compelled you to open a gallery?
Love of art!

Who is the first artist you showed and what was most memorable about that show?
Daniel Gaemperle. I was proud that my father could see the gallery before he died.

When did you first participate in Art Basel and what was most memorable about that show?
In 1987.

- **Contact** Galerie Gisèle Linder
  Harrant Frederike
  frederike.harrant@googlemail.com
  glinder@tiscalinet.ch
- **Established** 1984
- **Owner(s) / Partner(s)** Gisèle Linder
- **Team** 1
- **Space(s)** 100 m²
- **Artists at Art Basel** Roger Ackling
  John Beech
  Renate Buser
  Philipp Goldbach
  Serge Hasenböhler
  Luzia Hürzeler
  Clare Kenny
  Kathrin Kunz
  Luo Mingjun
  Ingeborg Lüscher
  François Morellet
  Ursula Mumenthaler
  Carmen Perrin
  Andrei Roiter
  Yuko Shiraishi
  Werner von Mutzenbecher
  Andrea Wolfensberger
- **Further artists represented** Alan Ebnother
  Alfonso Fratteggiani Bianchi
  Maria Elena González
  Julije Knifer
  Marta Kolendo
  John Meyer
  Michael Rouillard
  Anne Sauser-Hall
  Jordan Tinker
  Peter Willen

Liprandi

Buenos Aires

Positions

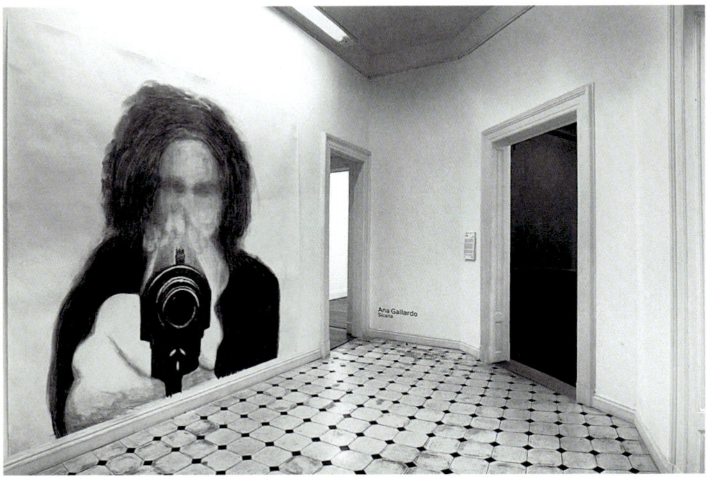

What first compelled you to open a gallery?
Ignacio Liprandi Arte Contemporáneo is a space dedicated to the exhibition and diffusion of international contemporary art. Founded by Ignacio Liprandi in 2009, it is characterized by a curatorial proposal that articulates a program of exhibitions, participation in international fairs, and the development of a network of curators, galleries, and institutions to allow the insertion of its artists onto the international circuit.

Who is the first artist you showed and what was most memorable about that show?
The first artist we featured was Fabián Bercic. One important aspect of his work is the intimate relationship that he establishes between his creative process and the development of the research on which his work is based. His working method is based on a thorough compilation of images taken from distinct cultures and disciplines, whose essence he seeks to understand. His pieces, which demand hard work and long periods of production, reflect a marked interest in soft textures, bright colors, and equilibrium of form. The result is that the pieces of art he creates look like commercial products, but carry the stamp of arduous manual work: a kind of "imperfect perfection."

When did you first participate in Art Basel and what was most memorable about that show?
It was in 2012. True to our mission of promoting international contemporary artists, that year we presented three talented artists from three different parts of the globe.

- **Contact** — Ignacio Liprandi Arte Contemporáneo
  Denise Obrador
  denise@ignacioliprandi.com
  info@ignacioliprandi.com
- **Established** — 2009
- **Owner(s) / Partner(s)** — Ignacio Liprandi
- **Artists at Art Basel** — Vijai Patchineelam
- **Further artists represented** — Pablo Accinelli
  Fabián Bercic
  Adriana Bustos
  Alejandro Cesarco
  Tomás Espina
  Claudia Fontes
  Ana Gallardo
  Magdalena Jitrik
  David Lamelas
  Mauricio Lupini
  Mathieu Mercier
  Eduardo Navarro
  Jorge Pedro Nuñez
  Cristina Piffer
  Rita Ponce de León
  José Alejandro Restrepo
  Leandro Tartaglia

Lisson

London
Milan

Galleries
Galleries
Unlimited
Parcours
Galleries

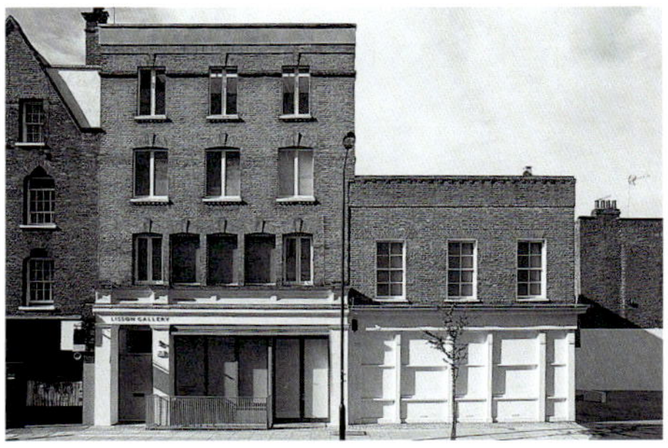

What first compelled you to open a gallery?
In a way it was a mistake: it was only intended to be for one show and in the third week of its run, I was expelled from the Slade School of Art. Although I didn't know it at the time, it was the best thing that could have happened to me. I wanted to do something different in a different way and believed I could change the landscape of the London art world. It was not strategic in any way, but an experiment, opening up an empty shop and a basement to make the infrastructure in which to show the work of fellow students.

Who is the first artist you showed and what was most memorable about that show?
The first show was a group of students including Derek Jarman, and in the first year we showed Mira Schendel and Yoko Ono too. It attracted so much attention that I met most of the contemporary art world at the time, including early supporters of the gallery such as Guy Brett and Nicholas Serota.

When did you first participate in Art Basel and what was most memorable about that show?
It was Art Basel's second edition, it was relatively inexpensive and we covered our costs with sales of about £3,000. This was before they segmented the galleries into two floors. Ironically, we now find ourselves going back downstairs to almost the same spot we were in in 1971.

- **Contact** — Lisson Gallery
  Ossian Ward
  ossian@lissongallery.com
  contact@lissongallery.com
- **Established** — 1967
- **Owner(s) / Partner(s)** — Nicholas Logsdail
- **Team** — 50
- **Space(s)** — 1,500 m² (including office space)
- **Artists at Art Basel** — Marina Abramović
  Ai Weiwei
  Allora & Calzadilla
  Cory Arcangel
  James Casebere
  Tony Cragg
  Richard Deacon
  Nathalie Djurberg & Hans Berg
  Spencer Finch
  Ryan Gander
  Rodney Graham
  Carmen Herrera
  Anish Kapoor
  Liu Xiaodong
  Richard Long
  Jason Martin
  Haroon Mirza
  Tatsuo Miyajima
  Julian Opie
  Pedro Reyes
  Lawrence Weiner
  Richard Wentworth
- **Further artists represented** — Art & Language
  Daniel Buren
  Gerard Byrne
  Angela de la Cruz
  Spencer Finch
  Ceal Floyer
  Dan Graham
  Shirazeh Houshiary
  Christian Jankowksi
  Peter Joseph
  John Latham

Tim Lee
Sol LeWitt
Robert Mangold
Jonathan Monk
Tony Oursler
Giulio Paolini
Florian Pumhösl
Rashid Rana
Santiago Sierra
Sean Snyder
Lee Ufan

Löhrl

Mönchengladbach ● Galleries

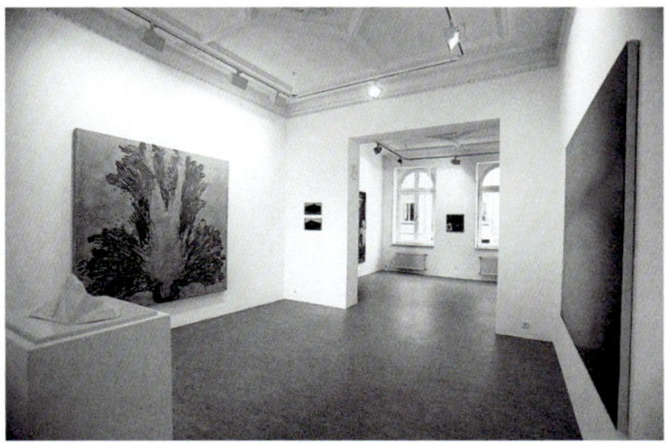

What first compelled you to open a gallery?
To present contemporary art to the public. Hoping that many people be convinced and start collecting.

Who is the first artist you showed and what was most memorable about that show?
Otto Piene, with a documentation of the process of his *Fire Paintings* in a series of photos, and presenting his technique, which was new to most of the visitors, with original fire paintings.

When did you first participate in Art Basel and what was most memorable about that show?
It was probably in 1981, with a one man show by Stephan Balkenhol. We designed a booth of 24 m² (6 × 4 m), the smallest booth at the Art Basel that year, with only one entrance of a meter in the middle, without any additional light. The artist was able to realize his idea of an unusual installation of his new wooden sculptures (it was impossible to place anything else in the booth, not even a table or chair, so we had to sit outside in the corridor).

- **Contact** — Galerie Löhrl
  Dietmar Löhrl
  info@galerieloehrl.de
- **Established** — 1975
- **Owner(s) / Partner(s)** — Christa Löhrl
  Dietmar Lhörl
  Christian Löhrl
- **Team** — 7
- **Space(s)** — 500 m² (gallery)
  100 m² (office)
  450 m² (storage)
- **Artists at Art Basel** — Terry Fox
- **Further artists represented** — Amador
  Stephan Balkenhol
  Joseph Beuys
  Henri Cartier-Bresson
  Fabian Chiquet
  Ulrich Erben
  Jochen Gerz
  Angela Glajcar
  Christof Klute
  Roman Kochanski
  Heinz Mack
  Blinky Palermo
  Otto Piene
  Sigmar Polke
  Gerhard Richter
  Julia Rothmund
  Ulrich Rückriem
  Gregor Schneider
  Gil Shachar
  Anett Stuth
  Günther Uecker
  Keiji Uematsu
  Thomas Virnich
  Franz Erhard Walther

Lombard Freid

New York ● Galleries

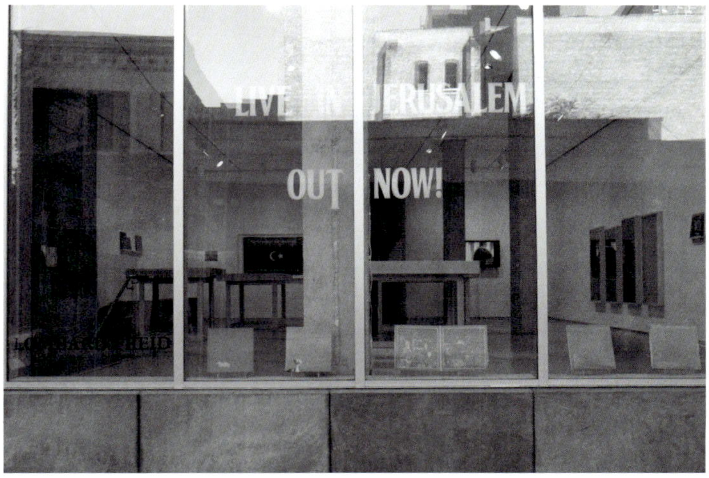

What first compelled you to open a gallery?
We had both been working and traveling internationally for most of our careers, Jane as an avid art collector, Lea as an arts administrator. We met while working at an international organization managing cultural diplomacy arts funding projects in emerging independent countries of the USSR and Eastern Block. The tremendous upheaval happening in the cultural sectors was a revelation to both of us—boundaries were being broken, political and social systems being tested. We were inspired by the innovative work we saw and risks being taken, and decided to open a commercial gallery that would introduce New York audiences to more socially engaged artists emerging from truly global contexts, such as China and Cuba. This work was not being seen, discussed. or part of the art market at the time. We continue to be pioneers and incubators for emerging artists and markets most recently in South-East Asia and the Middle East. Along with Carlos Garaicoa, Cao Fei, Lee Kit, Lee Mingwei, Eko Nugroho, and Dan Perjovschi, the gallery also introduced such notable American artists as Mark Bradford, Michael Rakowitz, and Tala Madani.

- **Contact** — Lombard Freid Gallery
  Alia Fattouh
  alia@lombardfreid.com
  info@lombardfreid.com
- **Established** — 1995
- **Owner(s) / Partner(s)** — Jane Lombard
  Lea Checroni-Freid
- **Team** — 6
- **Space(s)** — 50 m²
- **Artists at Art Basel** — Cao Fei
  William Earl Kofmehl III
  Lee Kit
  Lee Mingwei
  Eko Nugroho
  Ana Prvacki
  Pascale Marthine Tayou
- **Further artists represented** — Haig Aivazian
  Motoyuki Daifu
  Mounir Fatmi
  Claire Harvey
  Ulrich Lamsfuss
  Tameka Norris
  Dan Perjovschi
  Michael Rakowitz
  Mona Vatamanu/Florin Tudor
  Kemang Wa Lehulere
  Nina Yuen

Long March

Beijing

- Galleries Encounters
- Galleries Unlimited
- Galleries

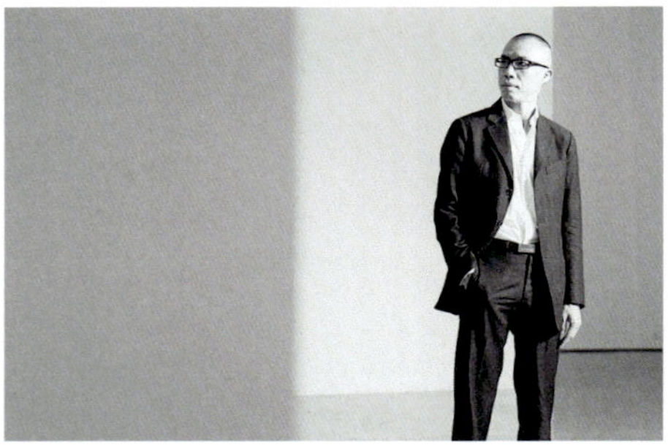

What first compelled you to open a gallery?
When I decided to open Long March Space in 2002, the primary concern was with the landscape of the Beijing art world and art community at the time, which is very different to now: there was a severe lack of support mechanisms for artists, or agencies to help archive, promote, and distribute their works systematically and strategically, and to develop their careers on a long-term basis.

Who is the first artist you showed and what was most memorable about that show?
Wang Jinsong. It was a 14-meter mural ink painting installation. The exhibition set out to rethink the heritage of Chinese ink painting. The format, framework, and context challenged the literati tradition of ink painting. The artist focused on the subject matter of the civil war in China in the 1940s, creating a piece that was based on a crucial political event in China's modern history. Ink painting was once again directly engaged with the political, social, and cultural spheres of contemporary lives.

When did you first participate in Art Basel and what was most memorable about that show?
It was in 2009, with a solo presentation of a female artist, Guo Fengyi. Guo is very significant in Long March's history. She joined us during an ongoing curatorial endeavor, and her work has always provided food for thought for me. In 2013 Guo was included in the Venice Biennale, as well as the Carnegie International, which only makes the success we had at Art Basel in 2009 more pivotal and significant.

• **Contact**	Long March Space Theresa Liang theresa@longmarchspace.com lm@longmarchspace.com
• **Established**	2002
• **Owner(s) / Partner(s)**	Lu Jie
• **Team**	15
• **Space(s)**	2,500 m²
• **Artists at Art Basel**	Chen Chieh-Jen Guo Fengyi Hu Xiangqian Ran Huang Li Tianbing Liu Wei MadeIn Company Wang Jianwei Wang Sishun Wu Shanzhuan Wu Shanzhuan & Inga Svala Thorsdottir Xu Zhen Yang Shaobin Yu Hong Zhan Wang Zhang Hui Zhou Xiaohu Zhu Yu

Luhring Augustine

New York

- Galleries Unlimited
- Galleries Public

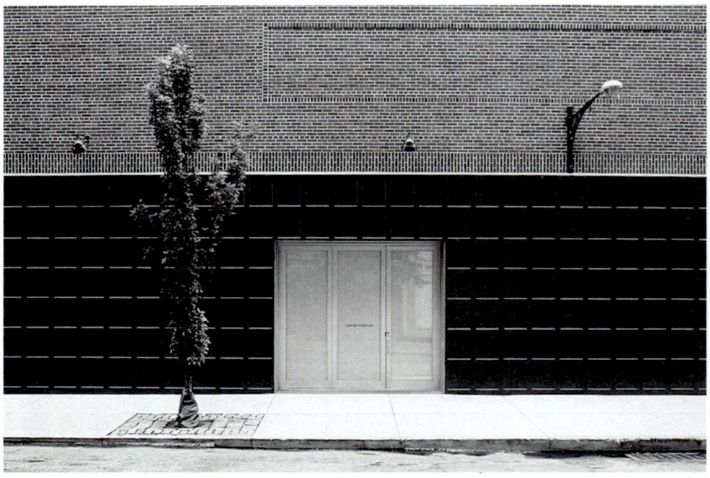

What first compelled you to open a gallery?
A desire to work closely with and represent artists.

Who is the first artist you showed and what was most memorable about that show?
Christopher Wool was among the first artists we showed. I can still remember the precise hanging location of every painting in the show.

When did you first participate in Art Basel and what was most memorable about that show?
I believe Luhring Augustine first shared a booth in the Edition sector, with Gisela Capitain, in 1990 or 1991.

• **Contact**	Luhring Augustine Caroline Burghardt caroline@luhringaugustine.com info@luhringaugustine.com
• **Established**	1985
• **Owner(s) / Partner(s)**	Roland Augustine Lawrence Luhring
• **Team**	23
• **Space(s)**	610 m² (Manhattan) 760 m² (Brooklyn)
• **Artists at Art Basel**	Janine Antoni Charles Atlas Janet Cardiff & George Bures Miller Larry Clark William Daniels Jeff Elrod Tom Friedman Zarina Hashmi Roger Hiorns Johannes Kahrs Ragnar Kjartansson Luisa Lambri Glenn Ligon Yasumasa Morimura Daido Moriyama Reinhard Mucha David Musgrave Michelangelo Pistoletto Pipilotti Rist Josh Smith Joel Sternfeld Philip Taaffe Tunga Guido van der Werve Rachel Whiteread Steve Wolfe Christopher Wool

Galerie Gisèle Linder

Two Questions for Gisèle Linder

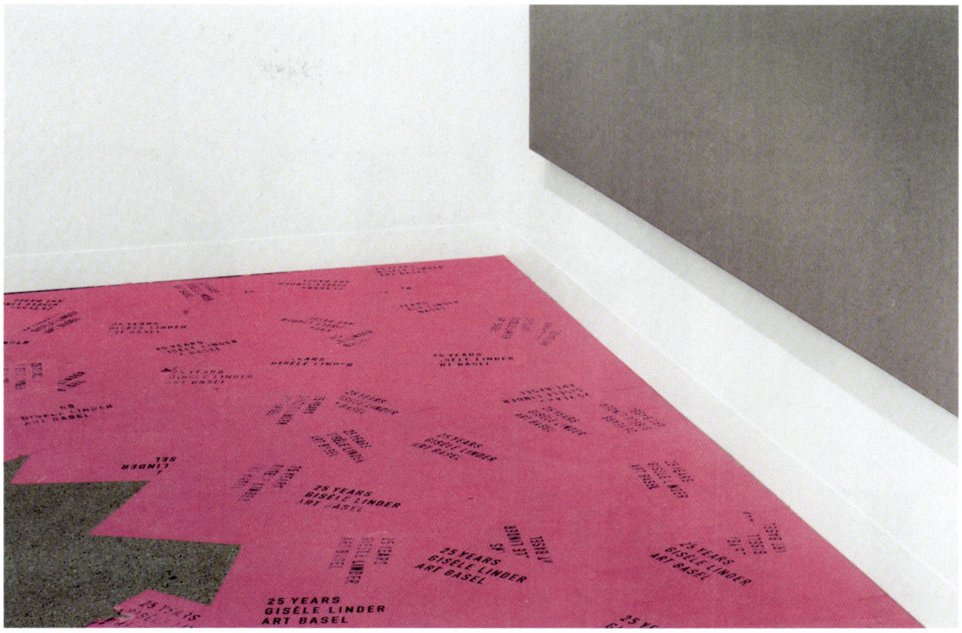

Art Basel in Basel, 2013

This year, you celebrated 25 years of participation in Art Basel. How did you celebrate this birthday?

2013 was my 25th show at Art Basel! A special year! One of our artists, Luo Mingjun, designed a special floor for Art Basel 2013, covered with pink paper—we had a fantastic booth.

I still remember the first years of Art Basel. The fair was always unique and innovative. The first years were especially exciting, everything was new, the atmosphere informal, everybody knew each other; after business we partied together. After so many years Art Basel has changed a lot. Now more than 300 galleries exhibit, it has become a mega-event for the art world and for Basel. The fair has to deal with other competitive fairs all over the world, the art market has grown a lot and became global. The atmosphere as well as the focus has therefore taken on a broader direction.

You founded the gallery in 1984, 29 years ago—only four years before your first participation in the fair. What are the fundamental ideas of your gallery and its program? What do you support, and which artists?

I started my gallery activities in my living room—I organized small exhibitions with editions and prints. But when I found the space in Elisabethenstrasse 54 in Basel I quit my job and opened Galerie Gisèle Linder, and my big adventure began. I started presenting Concrete art, but over the years I gradually opened my program to sculptural and figurative art as well. The exhibitions, taking place and organized at the gallery six to seven times a year, include both monochrome painting and constructive works by internationally known artists, as well as photographs and new art forms. In addition to solo shows of different contemporary artists the gallery also curates exhibitions on specific topics—for example, the exhibition *La magie des années 1960 – Art & Design* (2011) presented art and design of the 1960s, and in *Chromie* (2010) the gallery focused on various monochromatic paintings by different artists. To me the collaboration with the artists has been always very important; most of them have been with me since the very beginning.

ARTO LIND SAY'S

Paper Rain Parade

Arto Lindsay
Paper Rain Parade

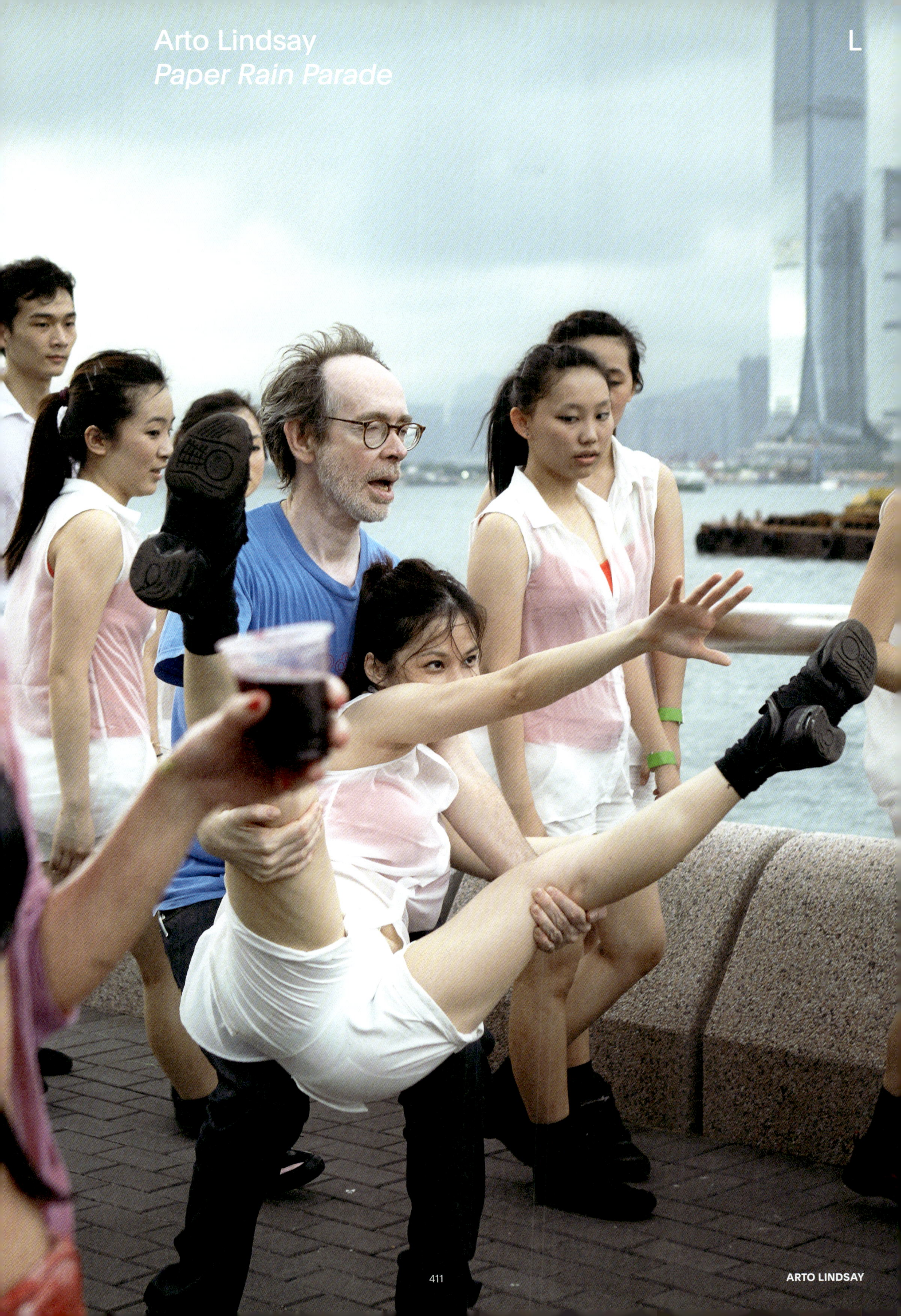

L

Arto Lindsay
Paper Rain Parade
Nadim Abbas

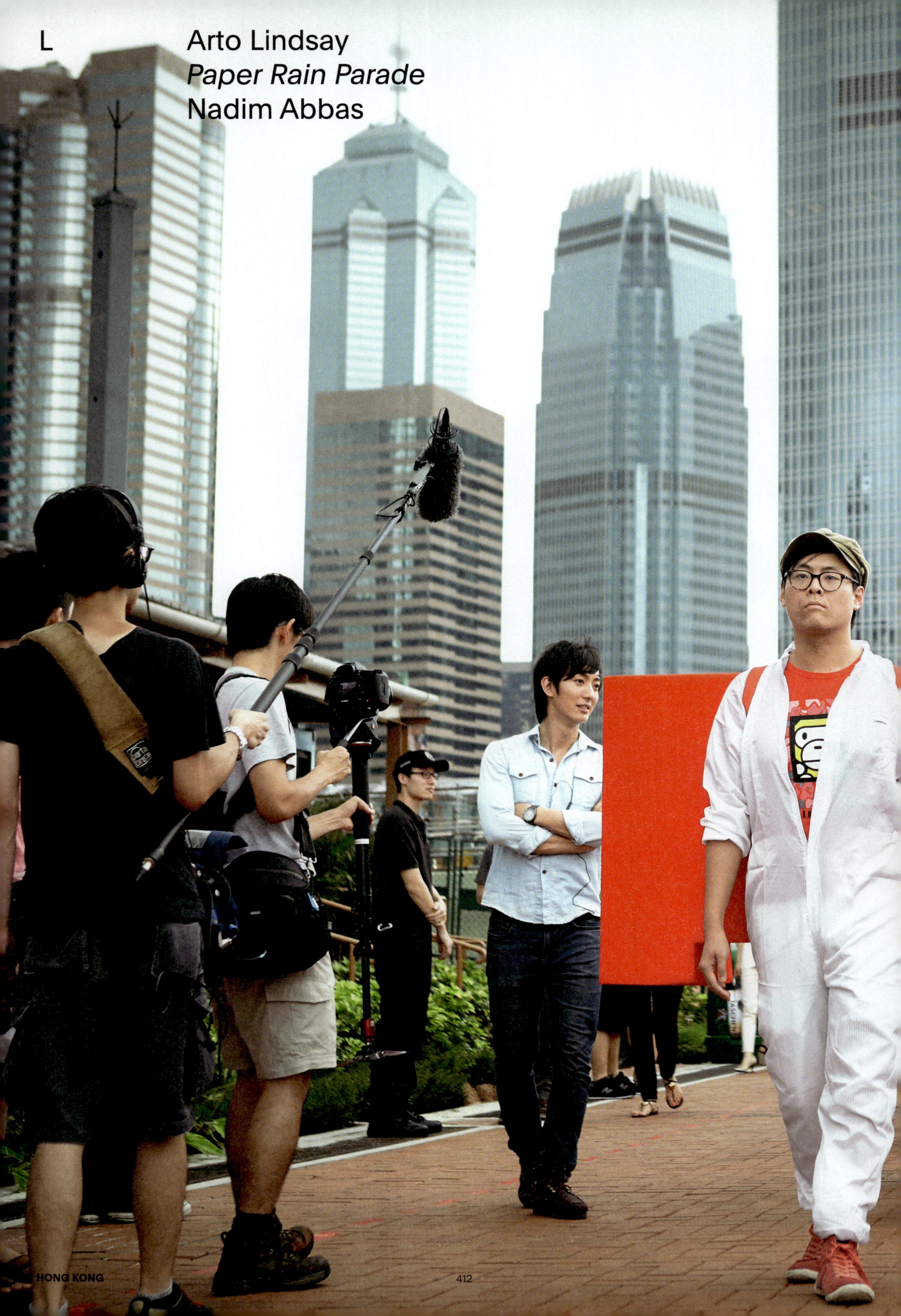

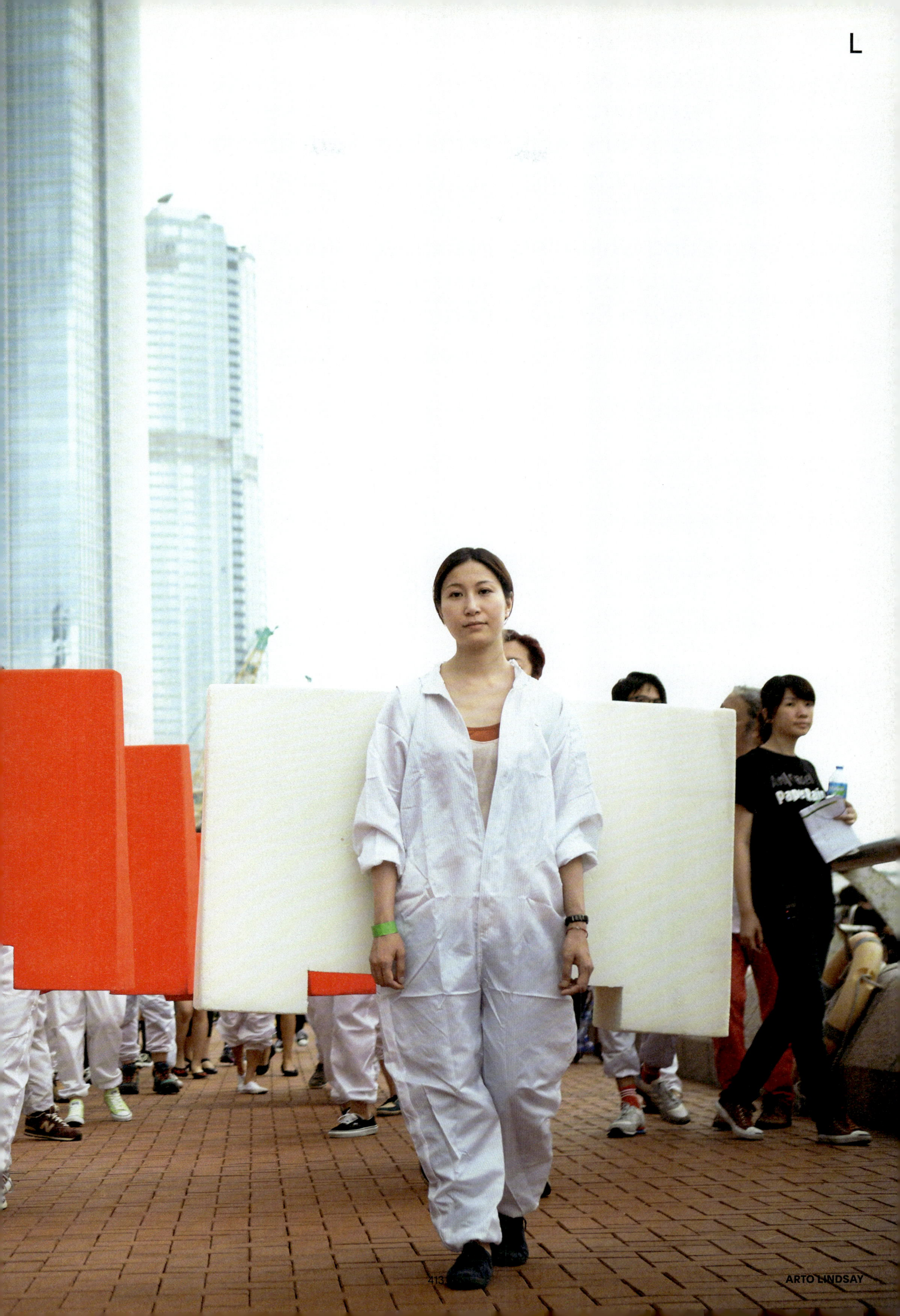

Hans Ulrich Obrist talks to Arto Lindsay about *Paper Rain Parade*

Featuring contributions from artists, actors, musicians, and filmmakers from across Asia, including Nadim Abbas, Shane Aspegren, Enoch Cheng, Haegue Yang, Kung Chi Shing, João Vasco Paiva, Korakrit Arunanondchai, Alice Ma, Cédric Maridet, Angela Su, and Otomo Yoshihide.

Hong Kong
Paper Rain Parade

May 23, 2013
Central Pier No. 10–
Victoria Harbourfront

Hans Ulrich Obrist interviewed Arto Lindsay on May 24, 2013, at the Mandarin Oriental, Hong Kong

HANS ULRICH OBRIST Before we talk about *Paper Rain*, how did your parade projects start?

ARTO LINDSAY As we say in Portuguese, when I was a teenager in Brazil, I "played Carnival," and I was always fascinated by the visual and musical side of the Rio Carnival and the Carnival in Recife, where I grew up. I performed in them and was really involved in the Carnival of Bahia for many years. There's a whole group of people who are like amateur historians of this carnival because it reflects so much about the city, about the African influence, racism, and resistance: people like Carlinhos Brown, Cateano Veloso, etc. In the 1960s, white and black people had their respective carnival. While the black people's carnival was very connected to religion, it was also a kind of parody of the white carnival groups. In the 1970s and 1980s there were several groups inspired by African liberation and the American civil rights movements. Their music was very different. The white carnival groups changed their music, started to use big trucks, and the musicians would parade on top of them, with a loud sound system. Eventually those musicians started to pick up on the rhythms from the street groups, from the black groups. So parades can be political, religious, or fun, and all this at the same time … A parade is by definition political because it implies a *mass* of people, so it's got to be controlled by the state. It's a kind of statement about freedom to assemble, or resistance against control. And as an art form it's like a social sculpture. It's also like a film, because it unspools in front of you, scene after scene.

HUO Can one say that it's a *Gesamtkunstwerk?* There are different notions of *Gesamtkunstwerk*: the early Wagnerian notion is more participatory, and the late Wagnerian one is more oppressive. I would say your work has more to do with that participatory *Gesamtkunstwerk.*

AL Anybody can enjoy a parade and you don't really need to rehearse to participate in it. You just walk, you show off, it's about display. One of the reasons why I like to do these parades in an art context is because people bring a kind of critical thought to them. In the music world, you have the immediate response of the audience, but a critical response is lacking.

HUO With your parades you bring something from the music world to the art world. Your first parade was with Matthew Barney, and it really was this "1 + 1 = 1" situation.

AL Exactly. We did our collaboration in the context of the Salvador Carnival, which is porous enough to admit something as outrageous as our parade: Matthew had a huge mining vehicle with these big claw arms and with a real tree on it; he had a woman climbing in the tree, he had a guy masturbating against the drive shaft and another vehicle that was a shipping container covered with mud; and the band was on top of that. Matthew and I wanted to collaborate for some time and, at his retrospective in Rotterdam, he did a parade of his characters. At that time I was starting to get really involved in carnival in Brazil, and I brought him articles; we somehow ended up doing our project in Salvador. That was the first one. Then I was asked to do one in Paris at the Pompidou, but they didn't have enough money. I nevertheless came up with a lot of ideas for that one, and we ended up doing it in Frankfurt, for some festival. One of the ideas was a parade that tries to impede its own progress. So part of the parade would stop and the rest would have to burst through. I also had an idea for using these recently obsolete robot dogs, the Aibos: I had envisioned that each robot—there would be 24—would have a loudspeaker with one track and, when they spread out, the sound would come apart. One would have the vocals, one would have the snare drum, one the base drum, etc. All the pieces of a pop song would wander off in different directions. [In the end, that part was unrealized.]

For the *Paper Rain Parade* I asked a young artist from Hong Kong, Nadim Abbas, to do the obstacles and he did a beautiful job: he made these sculptures based on the red and white road barriers that you see all over the city. I also invited Haegue Yang, and she made bell sculptures, and we got a group of high school kids from a local school to take part in the parade. And then, there were posters by Korakrit Arunanondchai, musicians, dancers, etc.

HUO You called your parade *Paper Rain*, and that obviously refers to *Purple Rain* (Prince) and to what they call "Black Rain" here, the heavy tropical rain.

It's a kind of a political parade, without any political content. It was like the form, the husk, the skin that has been shed by whatever insect.
— Arto Lindsay

AL I don't know why but I've been listening a lot to the soundtrack to *Under the Cherry Moon* (1986), which is a tacky but wonderful Prince movie. It was actually written by Becky Johnston who was one of the No Wave cinema people from New York. Prince is a great musician. He really manages to blend everything and come up with something original. He's sonically innovative, he's sexually indecipherable—which I think are two primary functions of popular music.

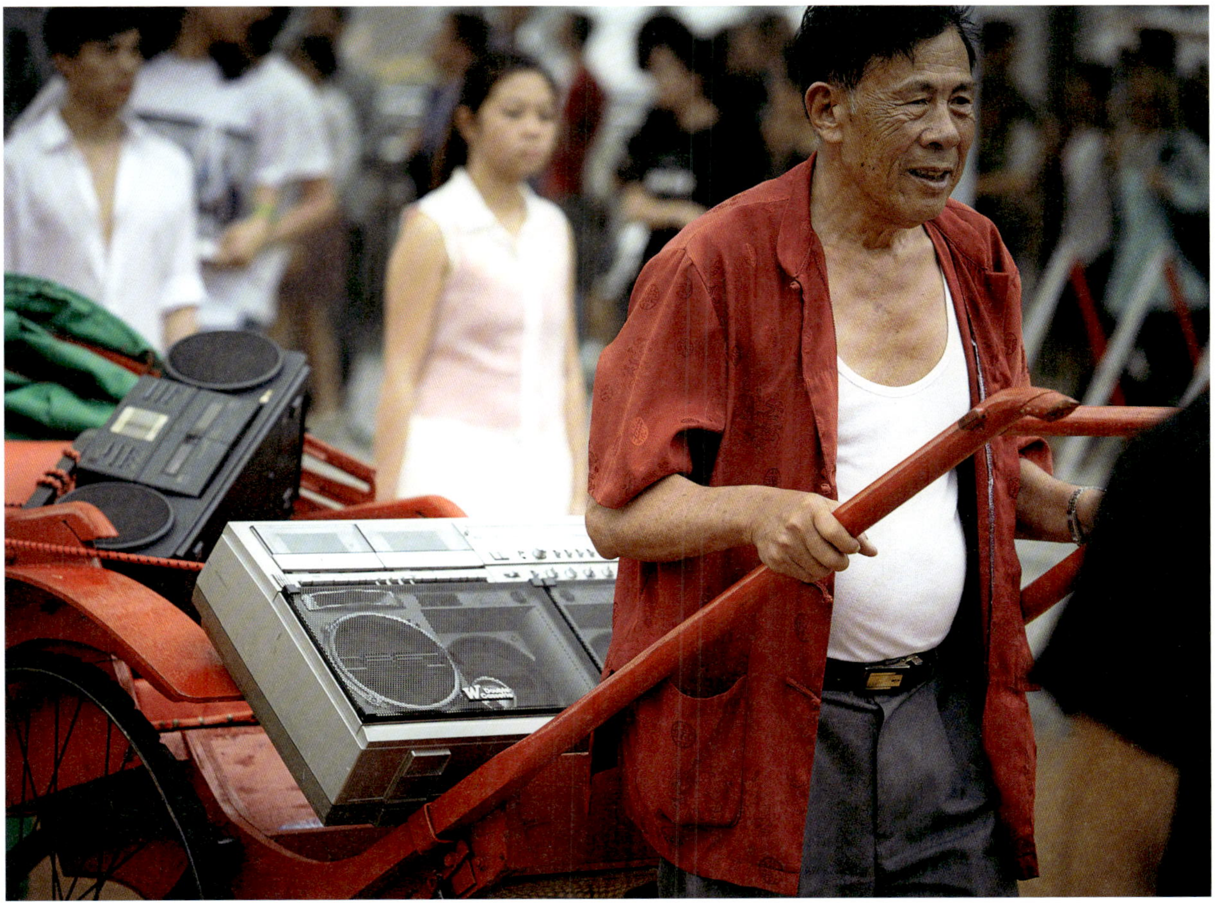

Arto Lindsay, *Paper Rain Parade*, Hong Kong, May 23, 2013

One idea I always had was to shoot a film in a carnival. The entire film would take place outdoors, in the crowd. You would have a kind of conventional story but you would never go indoors. Like: boy meets girl, they fuck, then, somehow, they get lost in the crowd, and he sees her with another guy, etc. I tried to find a young filmmaker to make a film of the parade and I asked Apichatpong Weerasethakul to shoot it.

HUO So, it's very much about the parade within the parade, the film within the film, a kind of *mise en abyme*. Do you have many unrealized parades?

AL I do have a parade that is so far unrealized: I'd like to make a parade in São Paulo about Maria Martinez and Marcel Duchamp, and about molding. Because so much of Duchamp was literally molded on her body, her pussy, her tits, and then the *Etant donnés* is like half a mold of Maria Martinez's body and half a mold of Teeny's body, since he got married to Teeny in the middle of the process of the piece's realization. He never depicted, he literally molded. I'd like to figure out what that means musically. How would you mold one element on another? I'd like to do this in São Paulo, Avenida de Paulista, which runs through the middle of the city, because that's another intense valley …

HUO Ackbar Abbas wrote that great book about Hong Kong as the city of disappearance (*Hong Kong: Culture and the Politics of Disappearance*, 1997). I was wondering to what extent Hong Kong changed the way you make a parade.

AL I feel something here that's similar to Berlin before the Wall came down. It's an isolated city and it's a city where there's something very uncertain about life; nobody knows what's going to happen. The parade in Hong Kong had a very tenuous feel to it and I think I allowed it to be even more fragile than usual to reflect that maybe. I was trying to indicate some of the anguish that I feel here, in the city. We did the parade exactly where all the big demonstrations take place, in front of where the British Naval Yard used to be, in an area where the PLA wants to put a naval base. It's a kind of a political parade, without any political content. It was like the form, the husk, the skin that has been shed by whatever insect.

Arto Lindsay
Paper Rain Parade

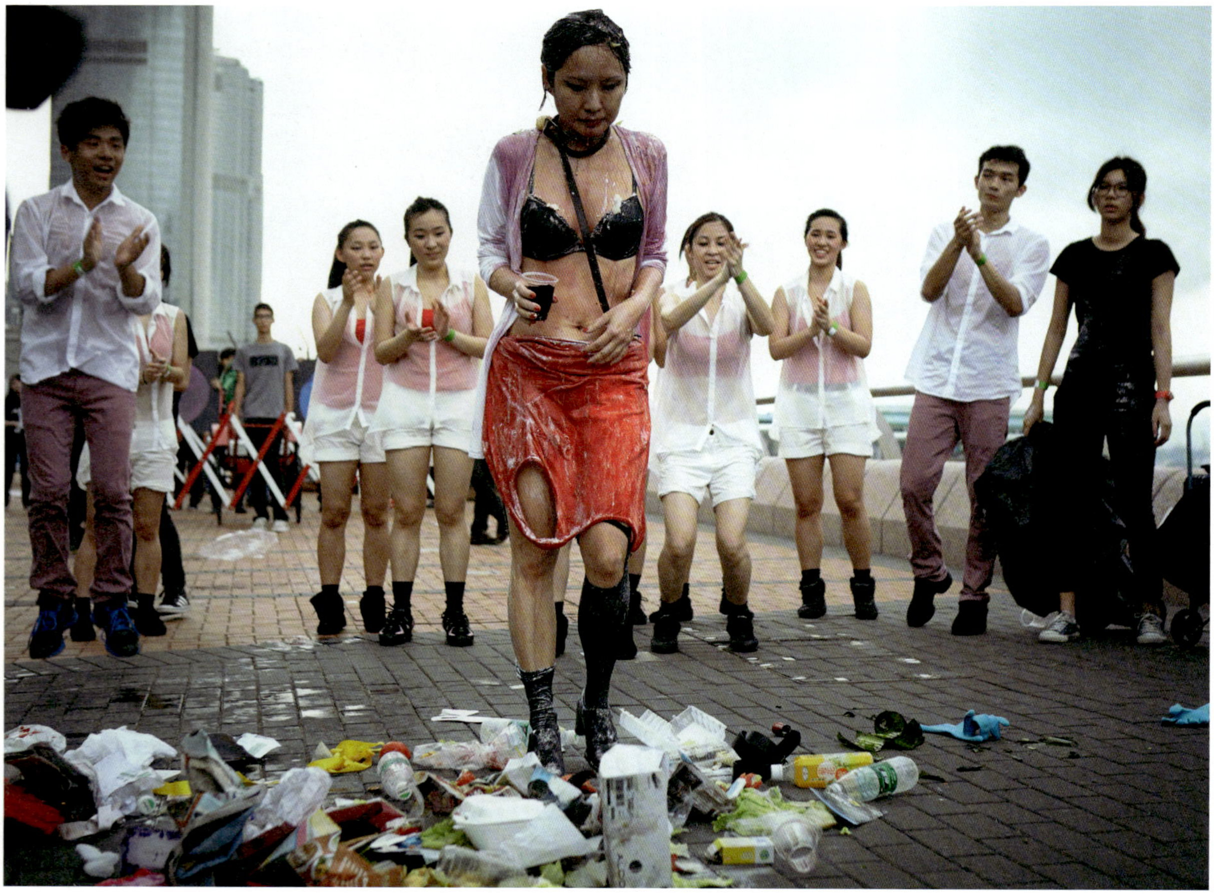

Arto Lindsay
Paper Rain Parade

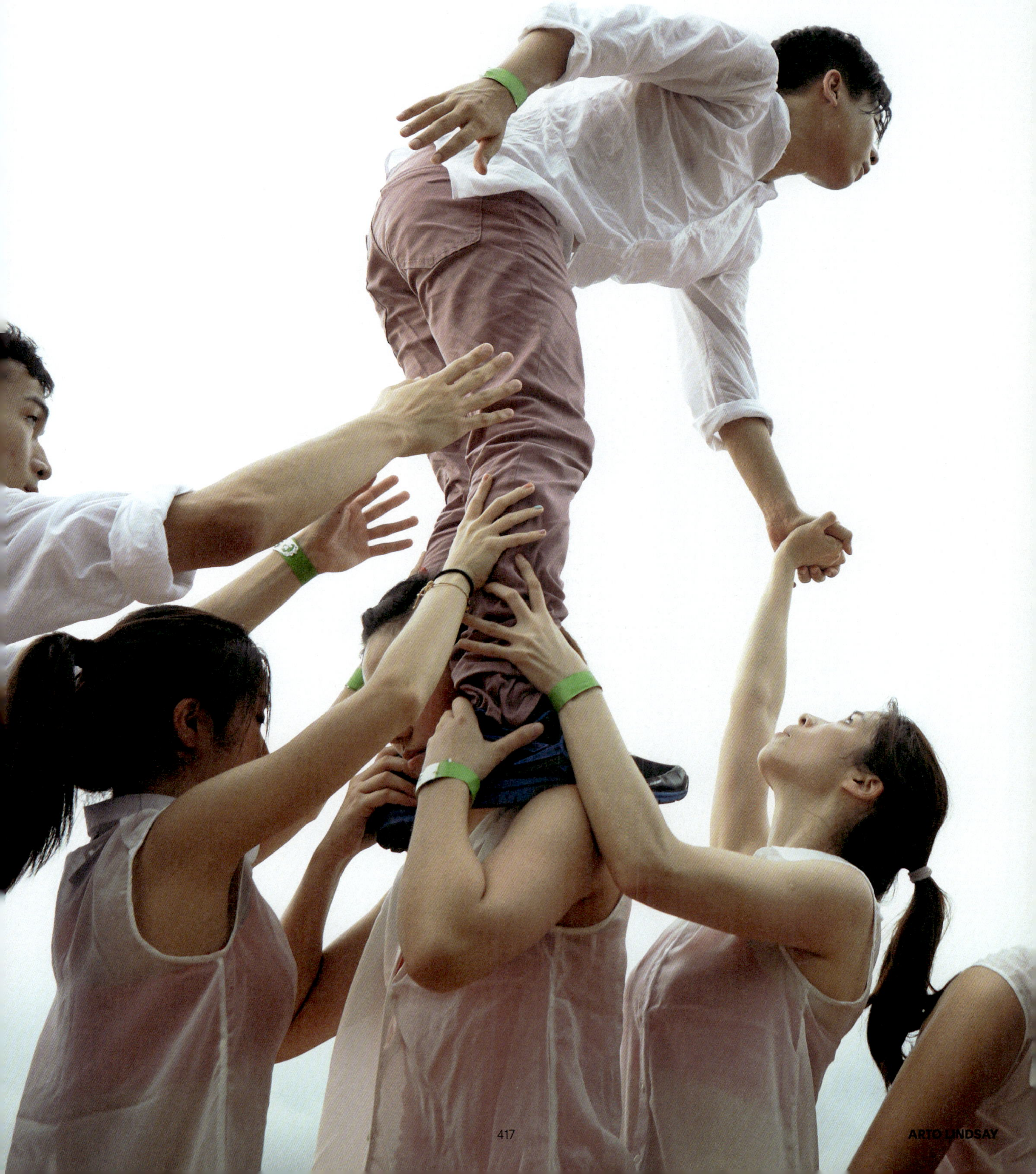

Hans Ulrich Obrist

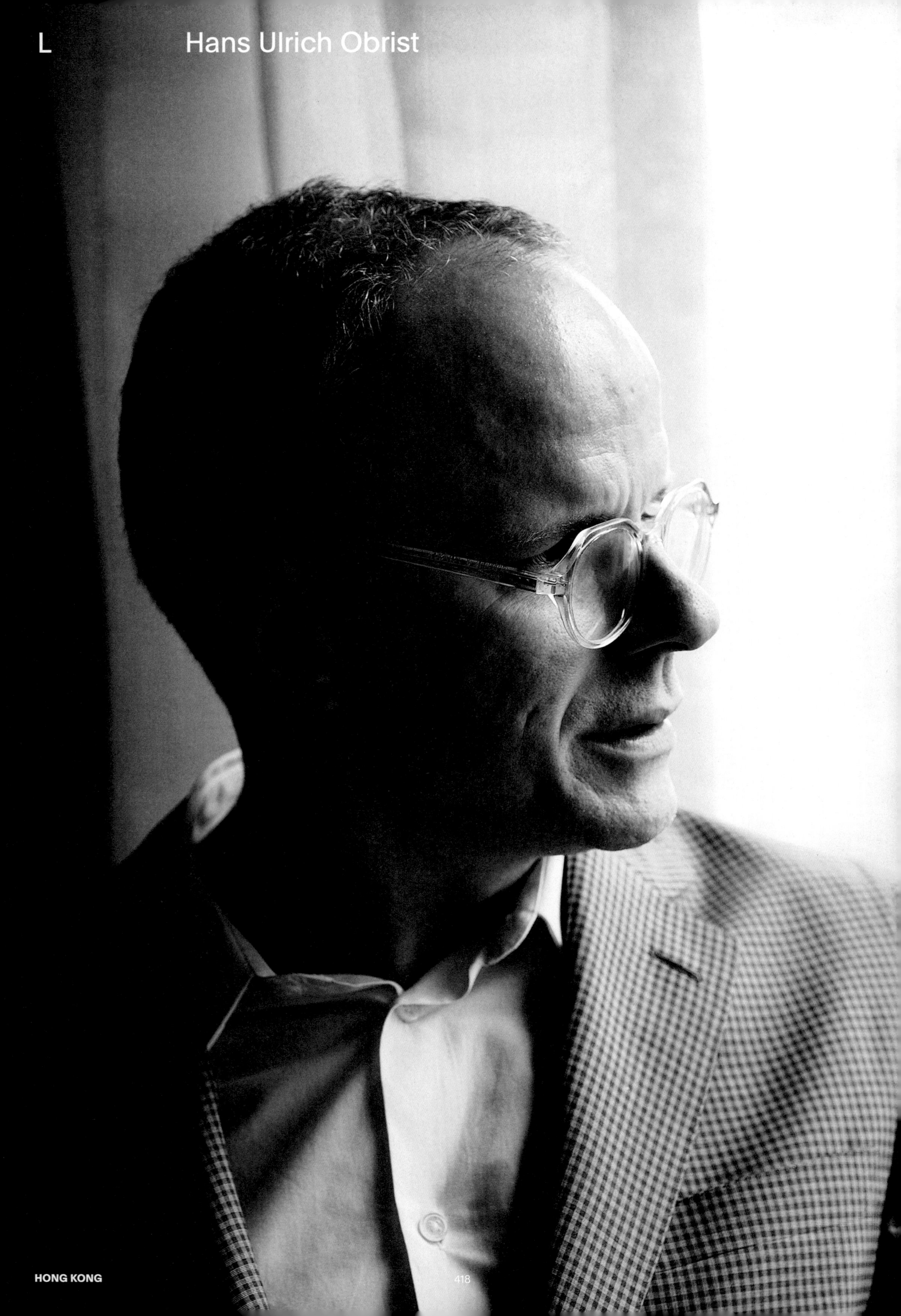

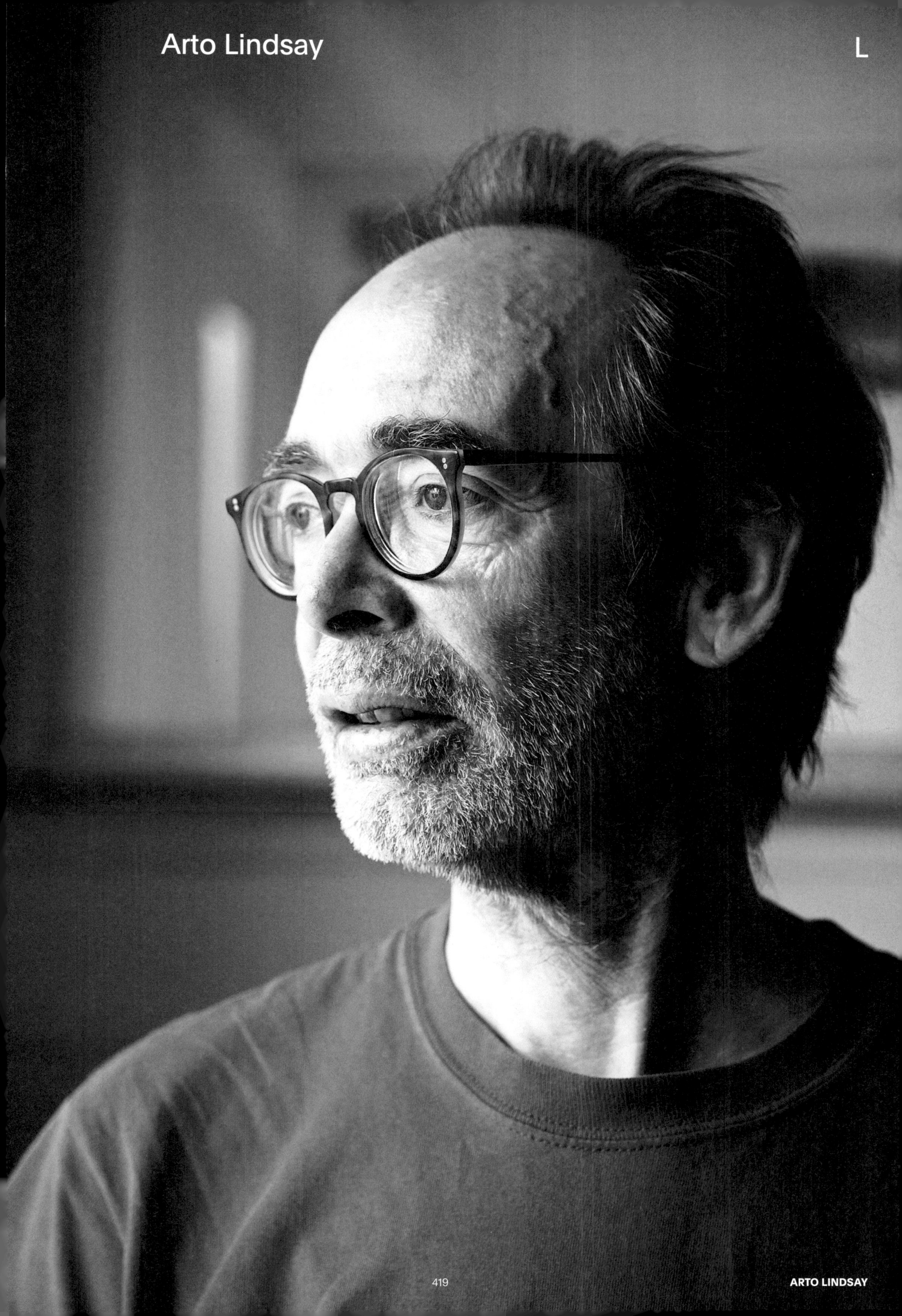

M

- **Further artists represented**
  Peter Wegner
  Sybille Berger
  Paco Fernández
  Claus Goedicke
  Carla Guagliardi
  Marta Guisande
  Barbara Köhler
  Norbert Kricke
  Kenneth Martin
  Tanya Poole
  David Rabinowitch
  Dirk Reinartz
  Giuseppe Spagnulo
  Boris Savelev
  Apolonija Šušteršic
  Ger van Elk

m Bochum

Bochum — Galleries

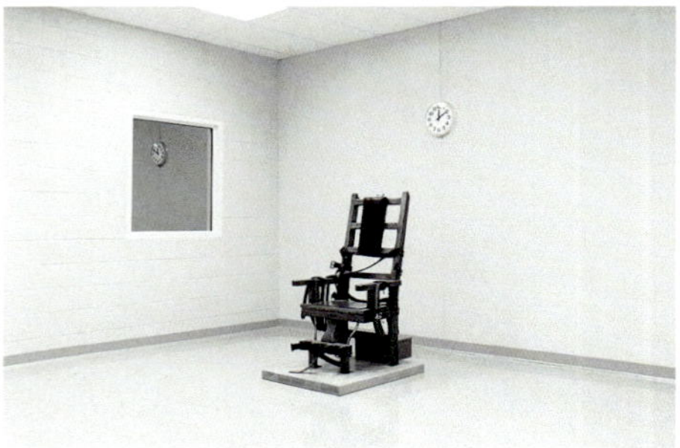

What first compelled you to open a gallery?
I took over the Galerie m Bochum in 2003 after working there since 1985. Once I met the artists and tasted the conversations with them, the atmosphere of the gallery, the set-up of the exhibitions, I knew that this was what I wanted to do: be part of the art world and develop lasting collaborations with artists to accompany them on their way to achieving recognition for their work and outstanding talent.

Who is the first artist you showed and what was most memorable about that show?
I showed Lucinda Devlin's series *The Omega Suites* in 1998. If you look at these color photographs of American death chambers, you can imagine what was memorable about that show.

When did you first participate in Art Basel and what was most memorable about that show?
Looking back at my first time at the fair, in 1987, I remember that Art Basel had a calm and concentrated atmosphere then that is inconceivable nowadays. Everybody seemed to have an inexhaustible amount of time to devote to the artworks and to conversations about them. I really miss those days.

- **Contact**
  Galerie m Bochum
  Carina Berndt
  galerie@m-bochum.com
- **Established** 1969
- **Owner(s) / Partner(s)** Susanne Breidenbach
- **Team** 4
- **Space(s)** 250 m²
- **Artists at Art Basel**
  Evelina Cajacob
  Lucinda Devlin
  Antje Dorn
  Thomas Florschuetz
  Gotthard Graubner
  Evelyn Hofer
  Aino Kannisto
  Lee Ufan
  Laura Letinsky
  Melanie Manchot
  François Morellet
  Simone Nieweg
  François Perrodin
  Alfredo Álvarez Plágaro
  Qiu Shihua
  Arnulf Rainer
  Jan J. Schoonhoven
  Richard Serra
  Elisabeth Vary
  Caroline von Grone
  Jan Wawrzyniak

Maass

Berlin — Galleries

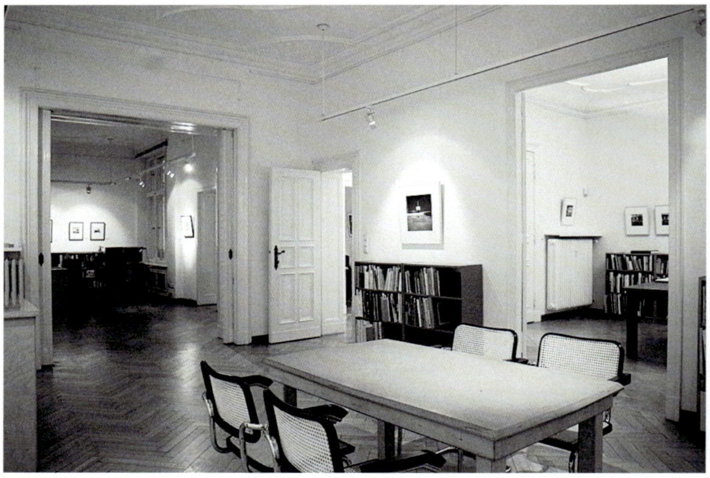

What first compelled you to open a gallery?
I wanted to see the works hanging on the walls in a context, combined in groups that make sense.

Who is the first artist you showed and what was most memorable about that show?
Max Beckmann. The opening was so crowded, we could not move, and it went until midnight.

When did you first participate in Art Basel and what was most memorable about that show?
In 2005.

- **Contact**
  Jörg Maass Kunsthandel
  Jörg Maaß
  joerg@kunsthandel-maass.de
  kontakt@kunsthandel-maass.de
- **Established** 1987
- **Owner(s) / Partner(s)** Jörg Maaß
- **Team** 4
- **Space(s)** 230 m²
- **Artists at Art Basel**
  Max Beckmann
  Otto Dix
  Lyonel Feininger
  Conrad Felixmüller
  George Grosz
  Erich Heckel
  Ernst Ludwig Kirchner
  Paul Klee
  Otto Mueller
  Emil Nolde
  Hermann Max Pechstein
  Christian Rohlfs
  Karl Schmidt-Rottluff
- **Further artists represented**
  Robert Adams
  Willi Baumeister
  Harry Callahan
  William Eggleston
  Robert Frank
  Gerhard Hoehme
  Karl Hubbuch
  Wassily Kandinsky
  Max Kaus
  Käthe Kollwitz
  Ludwig Meidner
  Rolf Nesch
  Pablo Picasso
  Sigmar Polke
  Gerhard Richter

Jorge Peris
Alessandro Piangiamore
Daniele Puppi
Serge Spitzer
Ouattara Watts

Maccarone

New York

Galleries Unlimited

- **Contact** Maccarone
kitchen@maccarone.net
- **Established** 2001
- **Owner(s) / Partner(s)** Michele Maccarone
Ellen Langan
- **Artists at Art Basel** Carol Bove
Ann Craven
Alex Hubbard
David Lamelas
Paul Lee
Nate Lowman
Rodney McMillian
Ryan Sullivan
Oscar Tuazon
- **Further artists represented** Chivas Clem
Eli Hansen
Hanna Liden
Corey McCorkle
Otto Muehl
Claudia & Julia Müller
Daniel Roth

Magazzino

Rome

Galleries
Galleries

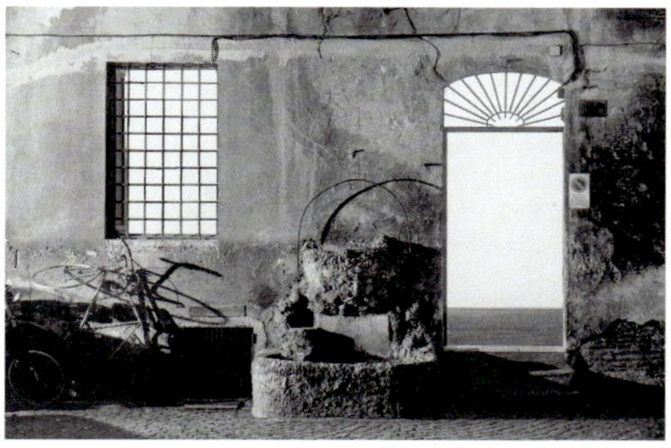

Who is the first artist you showed and what was most memorable about that show?
The first exhibition featured works by Ouattara Watts. Apart from the special relation I have with Ouattara, memorable things from that opening was the official visit of the Ivory Coast ambassador, with all the diplomatic staff, and Ouattara himself dancing at the opening party until 5 am.

When did you first participate in Art Basel and what was most memorable about that show?
My first participation to Art Basel dates back to 2006. You can imagine the expectation for a gallery running for eight years, to be part of it. So I asked Massimo Bartolini (the gallery artist who had a strong relation to space and architecture) to design the booth, and tried to include pieces by all the artists I was working with in that period; it looked like a Salon, quite clumsy. I was afraid I blew it. Nevertheless, after the fair ended I sold many of the works on display, to my great satisfaction.

- **Contact** Magazzino
Gabriele Gaspari
gabriele@magazzinoartemoderna.com
info@magazzinoartemoderna.com
- **Established** 1997
- **Owner(s) /** Mauro Nicoletti
- **Team** 3
- **Space(s)** 120 m²
- **Artists at Art Basel** Massimo Bartolini
Elisabetta Benassi
Antonio Biasiucci
Pedro Cabrita Reis
Mircea Cantor
Jonas Dahlberg
Jan Fabre
Alberto Garutti
Gianluca Malgeri
Domenico Mangano
Aleksandra Mir
Jeannette Montgomery Barron

Maggiore

Bologna
Paris

Galleries

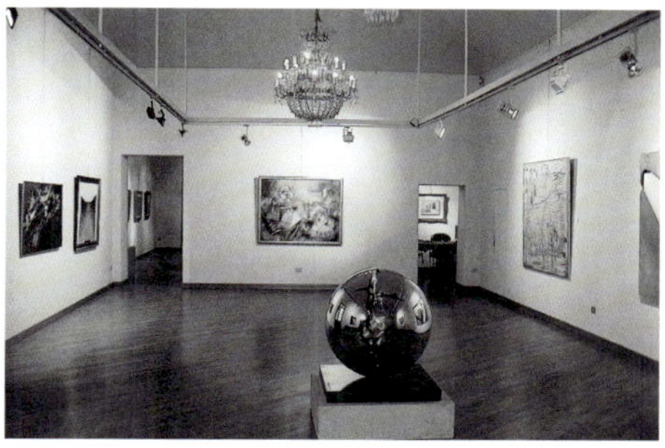

What first compelled you to open a gallery?
My wife, Roberta, and I founded the gallery at the end of the 1970s, after having gained experience in the art field at a moment when there was a renewed interest from modern institutions for the cultural events. Responding to the absence of a proper mediator in Italy between the cultural proposals and the passionate people who started to approach art in those years and who would have soon became collectors, our gallery aimed to be a meeting and mediation point between collectors, critics, and artists. Gradually becoming a place of culture, with collaborations with some of the most important public institutions in the world and academics, the gallery contributes to find authentic values. We also realize exhibitions outside our gallery space—these collaborations characterize our activity.

Who is the first artist you showed and what was most memorable about that show?
From the very beginning the gallery specialized in the work of Giorgio Morandi. Nevertheless, among the first exhibitions we had a major retrospective dedicated to Gino Severini. The most peculiar aspect of the show was to reconstruct full-size, in the gallery's main exhibition area, the room that Severini had frescoed inside the Castle of Montegufoni (Arezzo). It was like entering another dimension. The audience really enjoyed that particular set-up.

- **Contact** Galleria d'Arte Maggiore G.A.M.
Alessia Calarota
info@maggioregam.com
- **Established** 1978
- **Owner(s) / Partner(s)** Franco Calarota
Roberta Calarota (Founders)
Franco Calarota (Chairman)
Alessia Calarota (Director)
- **Space(s)** 400 m²
- **Artists at Art Basel** Giorgio Morandi
Mimmo Paladino
- **Further artists represented** Arman
Giacomo Balla
Georges Braque
Alberto Burri
Sandro Chia
Antoni Clavé
Giorgio de Chirico
Paul Delvaux
Max Ernst
Lucio Fontana
Sam Francis
Robert Indiana
Allen Jones
Wassily Kandinsky
Paul Klee
Franz Kline
Joseph Kosuth
Wifredo Lam
Fernand Léger
Leoncillo
René Magritte
Marino Marini

Roberto Sebastian Matta
Joan Miró
Mattia Moreni
Louise Nevelson
Pablo Picasso
Serge Poliakoff
Arnaldo Pomodoro
Mel Ramos
Gino Severini
Andy Warhol

Magician Space

Beijing

- Insights
- Encounters

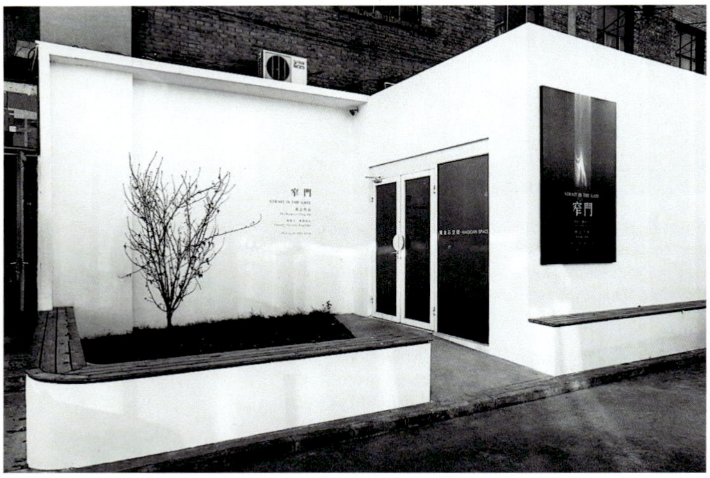

What first compelled you to open a gallery?
Very early we observed a gap that was overlooked by the commercial radar in the Chinese art world. We have been supporting artists at a formative time in their career with important first solo exhibitions and have been working with successive generations of artists who have challenged the specificity of their medium.

Who is the first artist you showed and what was most memorable about that show?
It was a two-person show with artists Liu Zhuoquan and Lian Dongya. It was during the build up to the Beijing Olympics and the show directly challenged the hyperactivity of the State and the structures that were unfolding around the entire city at the time.

When did you first participate in Art Basel and what was most memorable about that show?
Our first participation was in 2013 at Art Basel in Hong Kong. It was inspiring to have a large-scale work by the artists Zhuang Hui and Dan'er selected by Yuko Hasegawa for the Encounters section. There was a beautiful balance of art across Asia, which shared a truly equal platform with our Western counterparts on a global stage.

- **Contact** Magician Space
  Billy Tang
  billytang@magician-space.com
  info@magician-space.com
- **Established** 2008
- **Owner(s) / Partner(s)** Qu Kejie
  Pan Baohui
- **Team** 5
- **Space(s)** 100 m²
- **Artists at Art Basel** Guan Yong
  Jiang Zhi
  Liu Zhuoquan
  Zhuang Hui/Dan'er
- **Further artists represented** Bai Yiluo
  Gao Weigang
  Guan Xiao
  He An
  Hu Liu
  Hu Youchen/Pan Honggang
  Hu Yun
  Li Ran
  Lian Dongya
  Qin Jin
  Wang Wei
  Wang Zhongjie
  Wu Xiaojun
  Yu Bogong

Mai 36

Zurich

- Galleries Unlimited
- Galleries

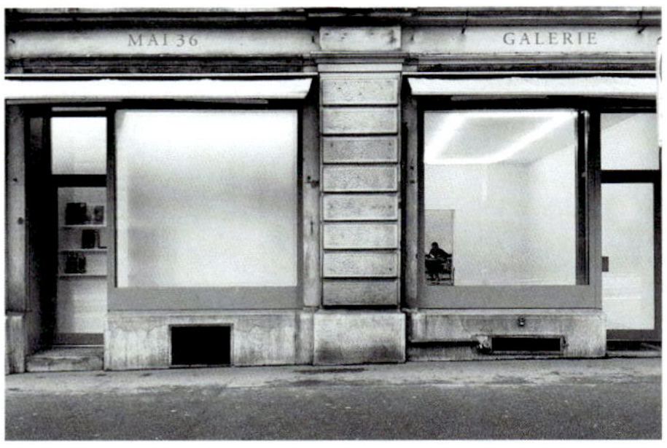

What first compelled you to open a gallery?
When standing in front of the painting *La nuit espagnole* by Picabia in the Ludwig Museum Cologne in the early 1980s, I felt heavily seduced and attracted to the idea to find a way to engage myself with artistic productions, images, and ideas. A few years later I was faced with the request by a real estate owner to come up with some ideas for an industrial building in the city of Lucerne. I dreamed of an ideal gallery space; I took over the idea for myself and started planning the artistic program and gallery model.

Who is the first artist you showed and what was most memorable about that show?
Mai 36 opened its doors with *Media Project and Public Advertisements* by American media artist Les Levine, following his media project for documenta 8. Television and newspaper coverage were memorable, as well as some reported viewers' irritation from the artist's billboard *Consume Yourself* in the city of Lucerne.

When did you first participate in Art Basel and what was most memorable about that show?
We first participated at Art Basel in 1990. Our booth featured contemporary legendary large-scale portraits by German photographer Thomas Ruff. Everything was new to us and the fair was an amazing start to connect with the art world outside our local and national context.

- **Contact** Mai 36 Galerie
  Victor Gisler
  victor.gisler@mai36.com
  mail@mai36.com
- **Established** 1987–1988
- **Owner(s) / Partner(s)** Victor Gisler
- **Team** 5
- **Space(s)** 223 m²
- **Artists at Art Basel** Franz Ackermann
  Ian Anüll
  John Baldessari
  Stephan Balkenhol
  Troy Brauntuch
  Pedro Cabrita Reis
  Ernst Caramelle
  Raúl Cordero
  Koenraad Dedobbeleer
  Jürgen Drescher
  Roe Ethridge
  Pia Fries
  Flavio Garciandía
  General Idea
  Luigi Ghirri
  Jitka Hanzlová
  Robert Mapplethorpe
  Rita McBride
  Harald F. Müller
  Matt Mullican
  Michel Pérez El Pollo
  Manfred Pernice
  Magnus Plessen
  Glenn Rubsamen
  Thomas Ruff
  Christoph Rütimann
  Paul Thek
  Stefan Thiel
  Daan van Golden
  Lawrence Weiner
  Rémy Zaugg
- **Further artists represented** Matthew Benedict
  Matthias Zinn

Maisterravalbuena

Madrid ● Nova

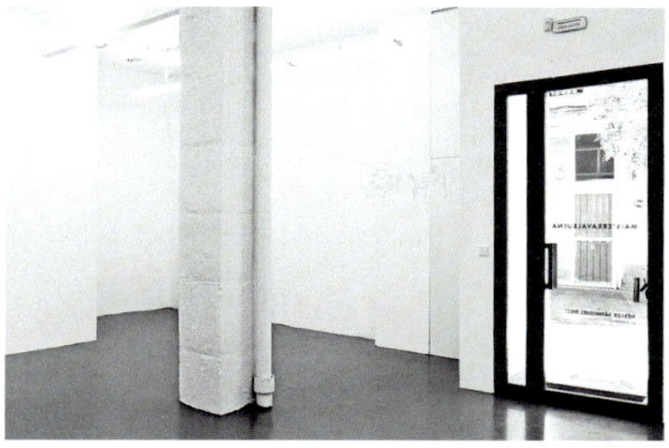

What first compelled you to open a gallery?
The desire to promote and show artists we believed in; the ambition to have our own space and make people interested in them. We also wanted to travel to fairs to present quality artists to collectors. We are very proud of the friendships we have built with the artists we work with and the collectors we got to know.

Who is the first artist you showed and what was most memorable about that show?
It was a solo show by Patricia Esquivias. A difficult first show as it was a video installation, which was not so easy for everyone to approach. We installed the show in one night as the works in the space had only finished the day before. It was very intense, but we were very happy with that show.

When did you first participate in Art Basel and what was most memorable about that show?
It was in 2009, and we have been here since then. We had a solo show by Karmelo Bermejo in Art Positions with golden I-shaped hooks hidden by 18th-century engraving. The booth looked really out of place as you could only see the old engravings, but it was a very good project, which is still ongoing. We also did a project with the same artist for the closing ceremony of Art Basel Miami Beach in 2009: a firework installation writing the word "Recession," which was lit at closing time. It was amazing to see those fireworks on the beach, at night.

- **Contact** Maisterravalbuena, Belen Valbuena, belen@maisterravalbuena.com, galeria@maisterravalbuena.com
- **Established** 2007
- **Owner(s) / Partner(s)** Pedro Maisterra, Belen Valbuena
- **Team** 3
- **Space(s)** 170 m²
- **Artists at Art Basel** Daniel Jacoby, Néstor Sanmiguel Diest
- **Further artists represented** A Kassen, Antonio Ballester Moreno, Karmelo Bermejo, Ana Cardoso, Regina De Miguel, Kate Gilmore, Claire Harvey, Maria Loboda, Erlea Maneros Zabala, Hiraki Sawa, Dan Shaw-Town, Cristián Silva

Malingue

Hong Kong ● Insights, Encounters

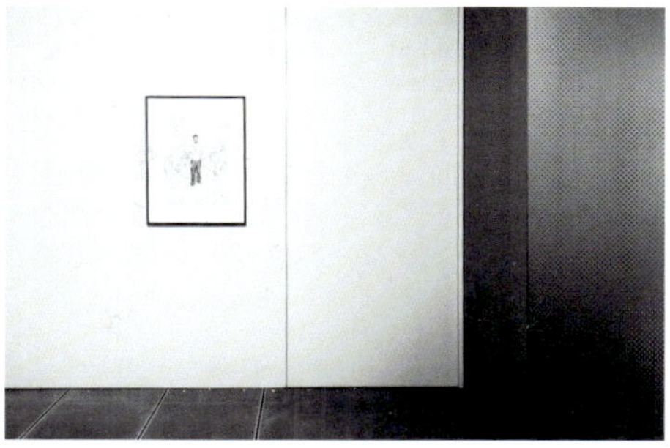

What first compelled you to open a gallery?
To work with Asian artists as well as to promote international artists, and to help create a culture for art appreciation.

Who is the first artist you showed and what was most memorable about that show?
Picasso—it was the largest exhibition of the artist held in Hong Kong. We received front-page coverage in the local newspaper *South China Morning Post*.

When did you first participate in Art Basel and what was most memorable about that show?
In 2012.

- **Contact** Edouard Malingue Gallery, Lorraine Malingue, lorraine@edouardmalingue.com, mail@edouardmalingue.com
- **Established** 2010
- **Owner(s) /** Edouard Malingue, Lorraine Malingue
- **Team** 4
- **Space(s)** 180 m²
- **Artists at Art Basel** Cui Xinming
- **Further artists represented** Laurent Grasso, Callum Innes, Nuri Kuzucan, Lee Kit, Liu Weijian, Los Carpinteros, Fabien Mérelle, João Vasco Paiva, Song Hyun-Sook, Sun Xun, Wang Zhibo, Yuan Yuan

Manila Contemporary

Manila ● Insights

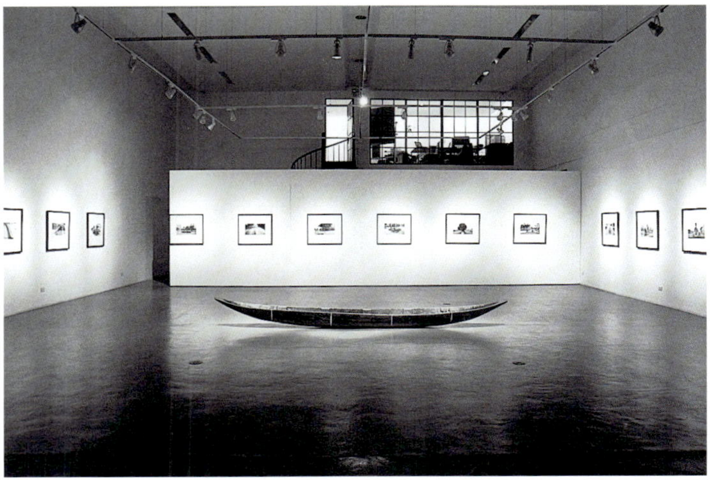

What first compelled you to open a gallery?
To promote South-East Asian and contemporary Filipino art.

Who is the first artist you showed and what was most memorable about that show?
A group show of 26 Filipino artists featuring works by Louie Cordero, MM Yu, Geraldine Javier, Alvin Villaruel, and many more.

When did you first participate in Art Basel and what was most memorable about that show?
In 2013 in Hong Kong. We were thrilled to see the largest works ever made by our exhibiting artist Winner Jumalon.

- **Contact** Manila Contemporary
  Eva McGovern
  mcgovern.eva@gmail.com
  info@manilacontemporary.com
- **Established** 2008
- **Owner(s) / Partner(s)** Valentine Willie
- **Team** 4
- **Space(s)** 300 m²
- **Artists at Art Basel** Winner Jumalon

Mara La Ruche

Buenos Aires

Galleries
Galleries

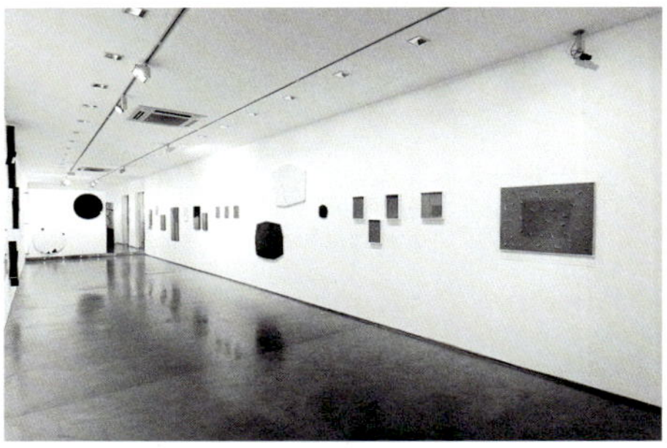

What first compelled you to open a gallery?
The love of art.

Who is the first artist you showed and what was most memorable about that show?
We opened the gallery with a magnificent Marc Chagall exhibition. It was very successful.

When did you first participate in Art Basel and what was most memorable about that show?
We showed at Art Basel in Miami Beach for the first time in 2010. We sold works to top Museums (MoMA, Met) and important collections in Latin America and the US. We were very pleased with the results.

- **Contact** Jorge Mara - La Ruche
  Stella Maris Estevez
  stellamaris@jorgemaralaruche.com.ar
  info@jorgemaralaruche.com.ar
- **Established** 1985
- **Owner(s) / Partner(s)** Nelly Corral
  Jorge Mara
- **Space(s)** 300 m²
- **Artists at Art Basel** Carlos Arnaiz
  Carmelo Arden-Quin
  Horacio Coppola
  León Ferrari
  Sarah Grilo
  Alfredo Hlito
  Kirin
  Macaparana
  Kveta Pacovská
  Ana Sacerdote
  Eduardo Stupía
- **Further artists represented** Natalia Abot Glenz
  Marcolina Dipierro
  Adolfo Estrada
  José Antonio Fernández-Muro
  Juan Lecuona
  Fabio Miniotti
  Amalia Nieto
  Fidel Sclavo
  Grete Stern

Marconi

Milan

Galleries

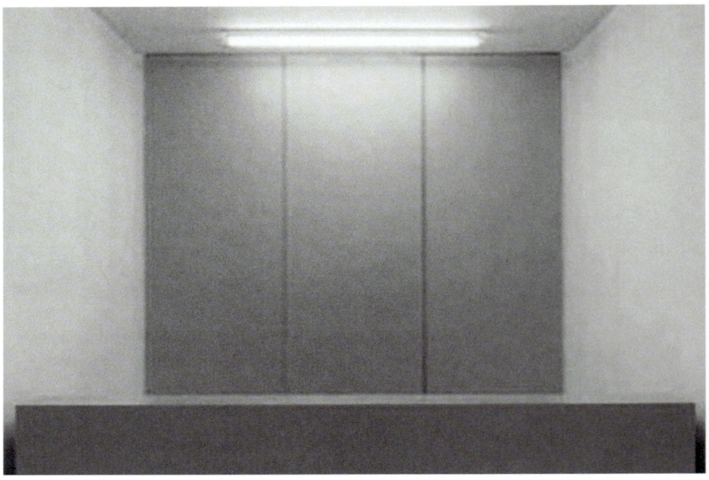

What first compelled you to open a gallery?
Since I was a child I was surrounded by art. I grew up between artworks and artists—it has always been part of my life. My grandfather was a framer and my father, after having first worked with my grandfather, decided in the 1960s to follow his passion and open a gallery. I worked with my father too for many years, sharing some projects and directing other ones by myself. In 1990 I founded my own gallery.

Who is the first artist you showed and what was most memorable about that show?
One of the first shows was with Martin Kippenberger; we immediately realized there weren't enough works for the space so we started to look for objects all over the city (plinths, letterheads, shoes …), in order to be able to create installations to fill the rooms.

When did you first participate in Art Basel and what was most memorable about that show?
My first participation at Art Basel was in 2002, in the Art Statements sector, with a Francesco Vezzoli solo presentation. The show was a big success and I still remember the excitement of being able to participate at the greatest art fair in the world for the very first time.

- **Contact** Gió Marconi
  Teresa Bovi
  teresa@giomarconi.com
  info@giomarconi.com
- **Owner(s) / Partner(s)** Gió Marconi
- **Team** 5
- **Space(s)** 400 m²
- **Artists at Art Basel** Franz Ackermann
  Atelier Van Lieshout
  Enrico Baj
  Rosa Barba
  Will Benedict
  John Bock
  Matthew Brannon
  Kerstin Brätsch
  André Butzer
  Nathalie Djurberg
  Günther Förg
  Simon Fujiwara
  Nikolas Gambaroff
  Wade Guyton
  Annette Kelm
  Sharon Lockhart
  David Noonan
  Jorge Pardo
  Tobias Rehberger
  Markus Schinwald
  Dasha Shishkin
  Lucie Stahl
  Catherine Sullivan
  Grazia Toderi
  Francesco Vezzoli

Marks

New York
Los Angeles

- Galleries
- Unlimited
- Galleries

- **Contact** Matthew Marks Gallery
info@matthewmarks.com
- **Established** 1991
- **Owner(s) / Partner(s)** Jeffrey Peabody
Stephanie Dorsey
Jacqueline Tran
Adrian Rosenfeld
- **Artists at Art Basel** Robert Adams
Darren Almond
Nayland Blake
Peter Cain
Thomas Demand
Vincent Fecteau
Peter Fischli/David Weiss
Lucian Freud
Katharina Fritsch
Luigi Ghirri
Robert Gober
Nan Goldin
Martin Honert
Peter Hujar
Gary Hume
Jasper Johns
Ellsworth Kelly
Brice Marden
Ken Price
Martin Puryear
Charles Ray
Paul Sietsema
Tony Smith
Anne Truitt
Rebecca Warren
Terry Winters

Marlborough

London
Madrid
Monte-Carlo
New York

- Galleries
- Galleries
- Unlimited
- Galleries

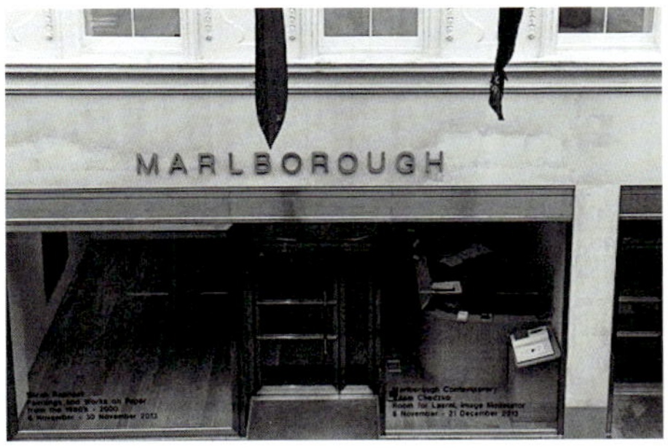

What first compelled you to open a gallery?
After leaving the British Army, Frank Lloyd foresaw the enormous potential in the art world. Initially, Lloyd dealt in old masters, Impressionist, and 19th-century art. He subsequently branched out into 20th-century art and started representing leading artists.

Who is the first artist you showed and what was most memorable about that show?
Between 1946 and 1961, many exhibitions were held including Henri de Toulouse-Lautrec, André Dunoyer de Segonzac, Auguste Renoir, Théodore Géricault, Gustave Courbet, Mary Cassatt, Pablo Picasso, Fernand Léger, Henri Laurens, and Juan Gris. To celebrate the opening of the new premises at 39 Old Bond Street, London W1, a *Van Gogh Self-Portrait* exhibition was organized in 1960 with the cooperation of Van Gogh's nephew, and included 29 self-portraits. It was a sensation; there was a queue around the block, even in the pouring rain. All these exhibitions were of museum quality and groundbreaking for the international art world at the time.

When did you first participate in Art Basel and what was most memorable about that show?
Our first participation in Art Basel was in 1970. We showed a cross-section of gallery artists including several works by Francis Bacon, Henry Moore, Ben Nicholson, and Graham Sutherland. What was memorable about the first Art Basel was the participating dealers' pioneering spirit that was in the air, and Ernst Beyeler's enormous drive in launching this art fair, which was to become the most important in the world.

- **Contact** Marlborough Fine Art (London) Ltd
Mark Hamment
mhamment
@marlboroughfineart.com
mfa@marlboroughfineart.com
- **Established** 1946
- **Owner(s) / Partner(s)** The heirs of Frank Lloyd
- **Team** 17
- **Space(s)** 285 m²
- **Artists at Art Basel** Magdalena Abakanowicz
Avigdor Arikha
Frank Auerbach
Francis Bacon
Fernando Botero
Claudio Bravo
Jason Brooks
David Rodríguez Caballero
Santiago Calatrava
Michele Oka Doner
Richard Estes
Juan Genovés
Karl Gerstner
Red Grooms
Stephen Hannock
R.B. Kitaj
Robert Lazzarini
Jacques Lipchitz
Henry Moore
Rashaad Newsome
Tom Otterness
Beverly Pepper
Paula Rego
George Rickey
Kenneth Snelson
Chu Teh-Chun
Joe Tilson
Manolo Valdés
Zao Wou-Ki
Chen Yifei
- **Further artists represented** L.C. Armstrong
Grisha Bruskin
Dale Chihuly
Vincent Desiderio
Thierry W. Despont
Israel Hershberg
Bill Jacklin
Kcho
Julio Larraz
Ricardo Maffei
Clement Meadmore
Arnaldo Pomodoro
Tomás Sánchez
Steven Siegel
Hunt Slonem
Clive Smith
Robert Weingarten

Martin

New York

- Galleries

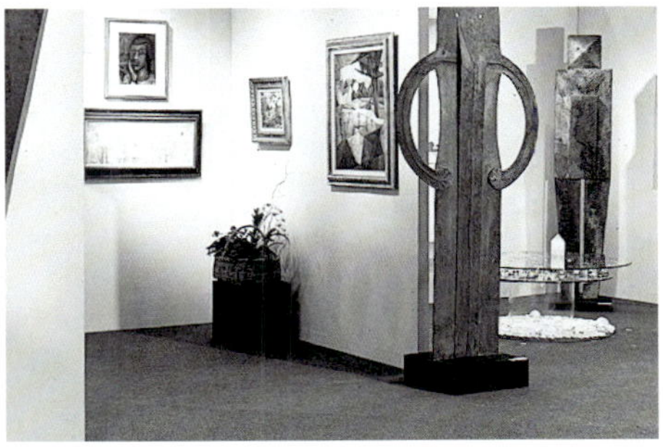

What first compelled you to open a gallery?
I was the founder of the Latin American Department at Sotheby's auction house. I decided to leave the auction firm and start a gallery that would be specialized in Mexican and Latin American art, as there were no galleries in this field in New York City at that time.

Who is the first artist you showed and what was most memorable about that show?

The first artist I showed in New York was the renowned abstract and Surrealist painter, Gunther Gerzso from Mexico. We did not sell a single work.

When did you first participate in Art Basel and what was most memorable about that show?
I was accepted for the first year in Miami Beach in 2001, but the fair was cancelled because of the 9/11 attack on the World Trade Center. The Art Basel in Miami Beach catalogue had already been published and this was very useful in convincing important galleries to apply for 2002, which was a great success.

- **Contact** Mary-Anne Martin / Fine Art
Mary-Anne Martin
mamartin@mamfa.com
mail@mamfa.com
- **Established** 1982
- **Owner(s) / Partner(s)** Mary-Anne Martin
- **Team** 5
- **Space(s)** 200 m²
- **Artists at Art Basel** Fernando Botero
Claudio Bravo
Leonora Carrington
Alfredo Castañeda
Elena Climent
Miguel Covarrubias
Isabel De Obaldía
Gunther Gerzso
Mathias Goeritz
Maria Izquierdo
Frida Kahlo
Wifredo Lam
Roberto Matta
Carlos Mérida
José Clemente Orozco
Carlos Orozco Romero
Wolfgang Paalen
Alice Rahon
Diego Rivera
David Alfaro Siqueiros
Rufino Tamayo
Francisco Toledo
Joaquín Torres-García
Alejandro Xul Solar

Mathes

New York

Galleries
Galleries

What first compelled you to open a gallery?
I was an art historian and wanted to have direct contact with art.

Who is the first artist you showed and what was most memorable about that show?
Early 20th-century artist, Oscar Bluemner, who was a member of the Stieglitz circle and had been largely overlooked. My exhibition re-examined his importance and created a market for his work.

When did you first participate in Art Basel and what was most memorable about that show?
Approximately 30 years ago. I was thrilled to be participating in the best contemporary art fair in the world and to be surrounded by the most important international dealers of the time.

- **Contact** Barbara Mathes Gallery
Jill Bishins
jill@barbaramathesgallery.com
- **Established** 1978
- **Owner(s) / Partner(s)** Barbara Mathes
- **Team** 5
- **Space(s)** 110 m²
- **Artists at Art Basel** Peter Alexander
John Baldessari
Agostino Bonalumi
Lee Bontecou
Louise Bourgeois
Alexander Calder
Pier Paolo Calzolari
Enrico Castellani
John Chamberlain
George Condo
Joseph Cornell
Mary Corse
Allan D'Arcangelo
Dadamaino
Jan Dibbets
Lucio Fontana
Joe Goode
Al Hansen
Neil Jenney
Jasper Johns
Ellsworth Kelly
Anslem Kiefer
Karen Kilimnik
Jeff Koons
Yayoi Kusama
Louise Lawler
Sol LeWitt
Roy Lichtenstein
Robert Mangold
John McLaughlin
Fausto Melotti
Joan Mitchell
Claes Oldenburg
Jack Pierson
Michelangelo Pistoletto
Martin Puryear
Robert Rauschenberg
Gerhard Richter
Ugo Rondinone
Ed Ruscha
Robert Ryman
Lucas Samaras
Paolo Scheggi
Cy Twombly
Andy Warhol
De Wain Valentine
Tom Wesselmann
- **Further artists represented** Carla Accardi
Billy Al Bengston
Ron Davis
Frederick Hammersley
Damien Hirst
Karin Kneffel
Piero Pizzi Cannella
Ad Reinhardt
Serse
David Smith
Philip Taaffe
Lee Ufan

Mayer

Düsseldorf

Galleries
Galleries
Galleries

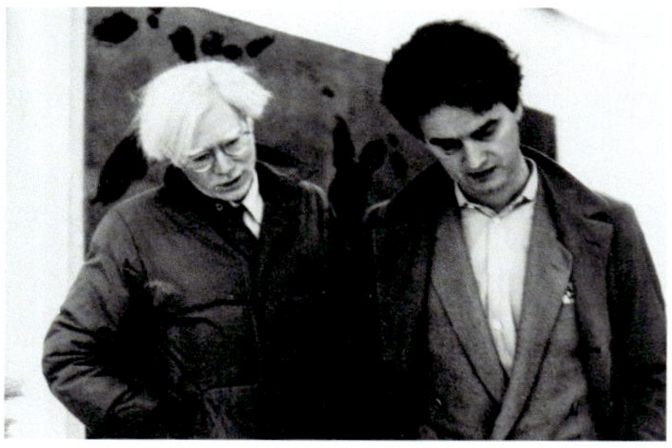

What first compelled you to open a gallery?
As I was born in Ulm, a town where the the Hochschule für Gestaltung—founded by Bauhaus members—was located, I have been deeply influenced by its program in general and by some of its professors and students, such as Max Bill and Almir Mavignier. They convinced me to follow my deep conviction in art by opening a gallery.

Who is the first artist you showed and what was most memorable about that show?
My first gallery, the (op)art Galerie, opened in a small town in South Germany, Esslingen, in 1965. I was really lucky not only to show a group of fantastic Josef Albers paintings, but also to have Irmin Schmidt (the later founder of the band Can) and Dieter Schönbach to play John Cages' famous *Pieces for Prepared Piano*, a composition of 1938: a truly fantastic vernissage!

When did you first participate in Art Basel and what was most memorable about that show?
I have participated at Art Basel from 1970 until today without any interruption. I had a booth together with Denise René and we showed a big, beautiful painting by Robert Delaunay.

- **Contact** Galerie Hans Mayer
  Assunta Huyn
  galerie@galeriehansmayer.de
- **Established** 1965
- **Owner(s) / Partner(s)** Hans Mayer
- **Team** 9
- **Space(s)** 220 m²
- **Artists at Art Basel** Bill Beckley
  Joseph Beuys
  David Bill
  Werner Büttner
  William N. Copley
  Liam Gillick
  Peter Halley
  Keith Haring
  Hans Hofmann
  Dennis Hopper
  Jürgen Klauke
  Imi Knoebel
  Peter Lindbergh
  Robert Longo
  Markus Oehlen
  Claes Oldenburg
  Tony Oursler
  C.O. Paeffgen
  Nam June Paik
  Robert Rauschenberg
  Hans Peter Reuter
  Kenny Scharf
  Jesús Rafael Soto
  Frank Stella
  Jean Tinguely
  Andy Warhol
  Tom Wesselmann
  Ben Willikens
  Jean-Pierre Yvaral

Mayor

London ● Galleries

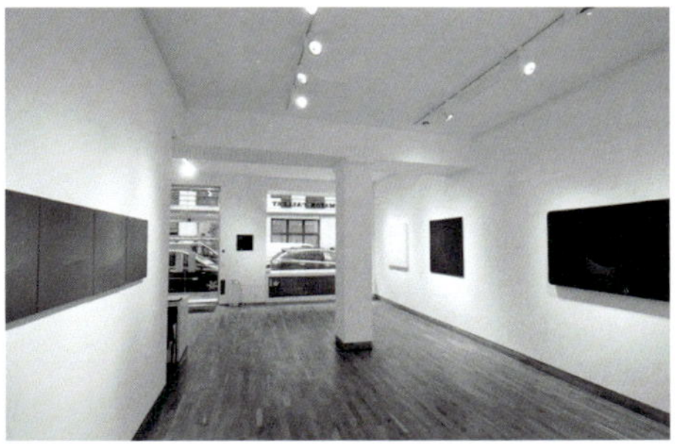

What first compelled you to open a gallery?
James Mayor took over his father's avant-garde gallery in 1973, after his death.

Who is the first artist you showed and what was most memorable about that show?
In 1925, a group of six male artists, and when James took over his father, he started with Andy Warhol in 1973.

When did you first participate in Art Basel and what was most memorable about that show?
In 1974, it was a solo show of Agnes Martin, the first commercial show in Europe of this American artist.

- **Contact** The Mayor Gallery
  Christine Hourde
  christine@mayorgallery.com
- **Established** 1925
- **Owner(s) / Partner(s)** James Mayor
  John Austin
- **Team** 4
- **Space(s)** 90 m²
- **Artists at Art Basel** Billy Apple
  Armando
  Bernard Aubertin
  Enrico Castellani
  Gianni Colombo
  Carlos Cruz-Díez
  Dadamaino
  Lucio Fontana
  Walter Leblanc
  Robert Mallary
  Piero Manzoni
  Agnes Martin
  Christian Megert
  François Morellet
  Otto Piene
  Jan Schoonhoven
  Turi Simeti
  Jesús Rafael Soto
  Vassilakis Takis
  Luis Tomasello
  Günther Uecker
  Gerhard von Graevenitz

Mayoral

Barcelona ● Galleries

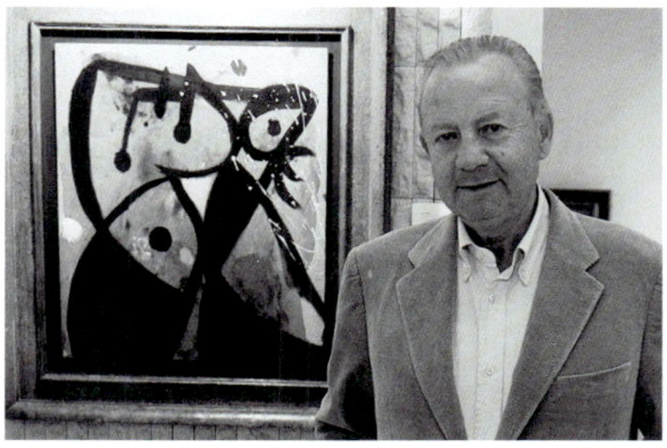

What first compelled you to open a gallery?
Passion for art.

Who is the first artist you showed and what was most memorable about that show?
The first artist to be exhibited was Salvador Dalí, and the most memorable show was 35 Picassos, in 2008.

When did you first participate in Art Basel and what was most memorable about that show?
In 2013 in Hong Kong with a solo show of Miró. It was great to see the Asian collectors excited; they understood and enjoyed the works of Miró as the Catalans do, as one of the great artists of our history. As the artist said, it shows that the best way to be global is to be local.

- **Contact** Mayoral Galeria d'Art
  Jordi Mayoral
  jordi@galeriamayoral.com
  info@galeriamayoral.com
- **Established** 1989
- **Owner(s) / Partner(s)** Manel Mayoral (President)
  Jordi Mayoral (Co-Director)
  Eduard Mayoral (Co-Director)
- **Team** 5
- **Space(s)** 200 m²
- **Artists at Art Basel** Joan Miró

McCaffrey

New York ● Galleries
● Galleries Unlimited
● Galleries

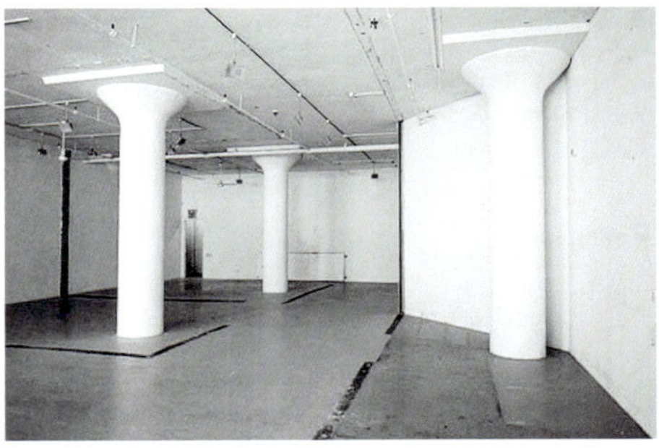

What first compelled you to open a gallery?
It was always an ambition of mine.

Who is the first artist you showed and what was most memorable about that show?
The first exhibition we made at our gallery in 2006 was the first solo exhibition of Hitoshi Nomura in the US. What was so memorable about that was the support from institutions and major collectors for a previously unknown artist. It was most gratifying.

When did you first participate in Art Basel and what was most memorable about that show?
Our first Basel event was Art Basel in Miami Beach in 2011. It was a solo exhibition of the work of Sadamasa Motonaga, who had sadly passed away six weeks before the fair opened. The response to the work was remarkable, and I only wish that Motonaga-san was alive so that I could tell him about how much people loved his work.

- **Contact** McCaffrey Fine Art
  Kevin Lay
  kevin@mccaffreyfineart.com
  lisa@mccaffreyfineart.com
- **Established** 2006
- **Owner(s) / Partner(s)** Fergus McCaffrey
- **Team** 5
- **Space(s)** 1,000 m² (two spaces)
- **Artists at Art Basel** Birgit Jürgenssen
  Sadamasa Motonaga
  Hitoshi Nomura
  Sigmar Polke
  William Scott
- **Further artists represented** Jack Early
  Koji Enokura
  Meschac Gaba
  Noriyuki Haraguchi
  Saburo Murakami
  Tomoharu Murakami
  Natsuyuki Nakanishi
  Hitoshi Nomura
  Richard Nonas
  Gary Rough
  Fujiko Shiraga
  Kazuo Shiraga
  Jiro Takamatsu
  Atsuko Tanaka
  Andy Warhol
  Yukinori Yanagi

McKee

New York • Galleries

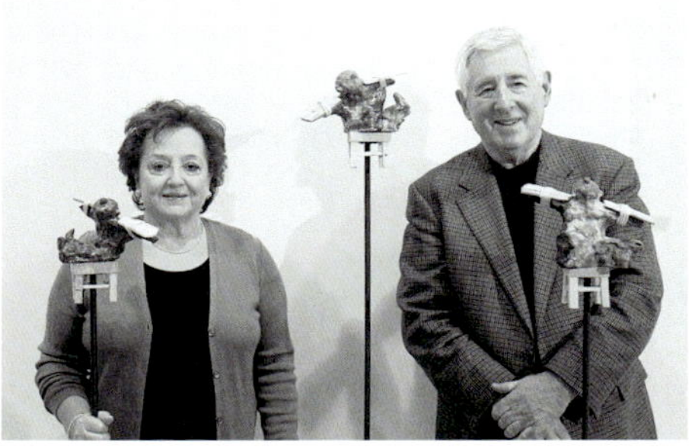

What first compelled you to open a gallery?
To show contemporary painters and sculptors in whom we personally believe.

Who is the first artist you showed and what was most memorable about that show?
Philip Guston, *New Paintings*, in 1974. Most memorable is Guston's late work influencing a new generation of painters.

When did you first participate in Art Basel and what was most memorable about that show?
In 1995.

- **Contact** McKee Gallery
  Anders Bergstrom
  anders@mckeegallery.com
  info@mckeegallery.com
- **Owner(s) / Partner(s)** David McKee
  Renee Conforte McKee
- **Team** 9
- **Space(s)** 850 m²
- **Artists at Art Basel** Vija Celmins
  Philip Guston
  Franz Kline
  Richard Learoyd
  Leonid Lerman
  Loren Madsen
  Martin Puryear
  Harvey Quaytman
  Kit Rank
  Jeanne Silverthorne
  William Tucker
  Lucy Williams
  Daisy Youngblood

Meert

Brussels • Galleries

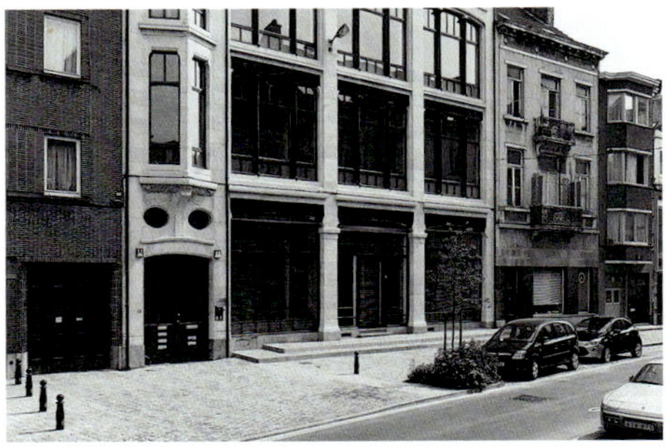

What first compelled you to open a gallery?
I have been involved in the art world since the late 1970s, visiting all the major international shows like Kassel, *Westkunst*. I was also already buying art, by Gerhard Richter, Robert Ryman, without thinking I was collecting. Opening a gallery was a dream to be close to the artists, and to have a space, where I could curate, and show the artists I admired.

Who is the first artist you showed and what was most memorable about that show?
The first artist we showed in the gallery was the young Thomas Struth. It was his first gallery show outside Germany.

When did you first participate in Art Basel and what was most memorable about that show?
My first participation in Basel was in 1993. The biggest emotion was to participate in the Basel art fair, which I had visited for years, every year. I was very proud of my booth, and showed marvelous artists, such as Enrico Castellani, Robert Mangold, Richard Tuttle, all the artists I had showed in the first years of the gallery's existence.

- **Contact** Galerie Greta Meert
  Tanja Boon
  info@galeriegretameert.com
- **Established** 1988
- **Owner(s) / Partner(s)** Greta Meert
- **Space(s)** 750 m² (three spaces)
- **Artists at Art Basel** Carl Andre
  John Baldessari
  Robert Barry
  Gianfranco Baruchello
  Enrico Castellani
  Hanne Darboven
  Johannes Döring
  Peter Joseph
  Valerie Krause
  Louise Lawler
  Jean-Luc Moulène
  Sophie Nys
  Tobias Putrih
  Niele Toroni
  Koen van den Broek
  Didier Vermeiren
  Johannes Wald
  Ian Wallace
- **Further artists represented** Carla Accardi
  Dennis Adams
  Robert Adams
  Mario Airò
  Eric Baudelaire
  Iñaki Bonillas
  Maria-Anna Dewes
  Paul Drissen
  Sylvie Eyberg
  Isa Genzken
  Jef Geys
  Robert Grosvenor
  Shirley Jaffe
  Mimmo Jodice
  Donald Judd
  Brandt Junceau
  Melissa Kretschmer
  Sherrie Levine
  Sol LeWitt
  Francesco Lo Savio
  Ken Lum

Robert Mangold
Eva Marisaldi
Liliana Moro
Fred Sandback
Thomas Struth
Walter Swennen
Grazia Toderi
Richard Tuttle
Catharina van Eetvelde
Michael Venezia
Jeff Wall

Meessen De Clercq

Brussels — Statements, Unlimited, Parcours; Nova, Public

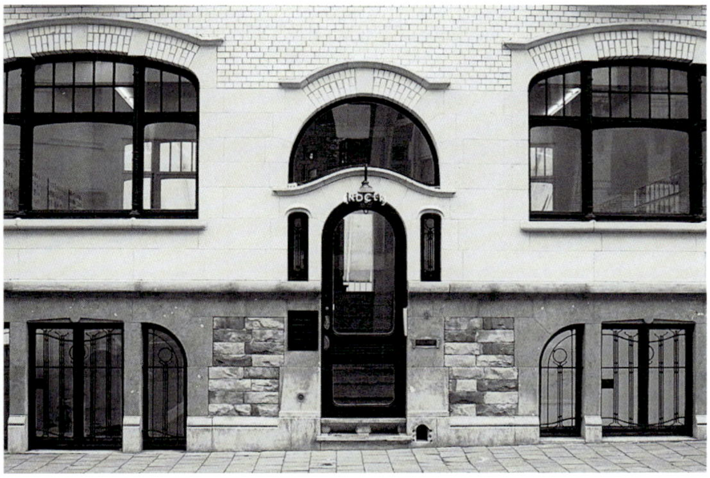

What first compelled you to open a gallery?
The passionate need to enable and bring essential projects to life.

Who is the first artist you showed and what was most memorable about that show?
Spanish artist Ignasi Aballí. The most memorable: the monster attendance that made us fear for the building.

When did you first participate in Art Basel and what was most memorable about that show?
Art Basel in Miami Beach in 2010, with a project by Mexican artist Jorge Méndez Blake. Most memorable was the insurance and logistical nightmare to get an amazing floating sculpture installed in the pool of the Sagamore hotel. But what satisfaction once it was realized!

- **Contact** Meessen De Clercq
  Stéphanie Roisin
  info@meessendeclercq.be
- **Established** 2008
- **Owner(s) / Partner(s)** Olivier Meessen
  Jan De Clercq
- **Team** 5
- **Space(s)** 400 m²
- **Artists at Art Basel** Thu Van Tran
  Susan Collis
  Ellen Harvey
  Evariste Richer
- **Further artists represented** Ignasi Aballí
  Sarah Bostwick
  Jordi Colomer
  Lieven De Boeck
  Hreinn Fridfinnsson
  Adam Henry
  Rinko Kawauchi
  Jorge Méndez Blake
  Claudio Parmiggiani
  Bruno Perramant
  Sarah Pickering
  Fabrice Samyn
  Kelly Schacht
  José María Sicilia
  Katrín Sigurdardóttir
  Maarten Vanden Eynde
  Leon Vranken

Meier

San Francisco — Galleries; Galleries

- **Contact** Anthony Meier Fine Arts
  gallery@anthonymeierfinearts.com
- **Established** 1984
- **Owner(s) / Partner(s)** Rebecca Camacho
  Megan McConnell
  Lauren Ryan
- **Artists at Art Basel** Hurvin Anderson
  Janine Antoni
  Nicholas Byrne
  Sarah Cain
  Rosana Castrillo Diaz
  John Chamberlain
  Jeremy Dickinson
  Leonardo Drew
  Cecilia Edefalk
  Tony Feher
  Teresita Fernández
  Barnaby Furnas
  Robert Gober
  Gonkar Gyatso
  Richard Hoblock
  Jim Hodges
  Donald Judd
  Agnes Martin
  Roy McMakin
  Donald Moffett
  Kristen Morgin
  Dave Muller
  Jockum Nordström
  Sigmar Polke
  Rob Reynolds
  Gerhard Richter
  Robert Ryman
  Kate Shepherd
  Jasmin Sian
  Gary Simmons
  Tavares Strachan
  Caragh Thuring
  Tam Van Tran
  Yuh-Shioh Wong

Meile

Lucerne — Galleries
Beijing — Galleries, Unlimited; Galleries, Kabinett

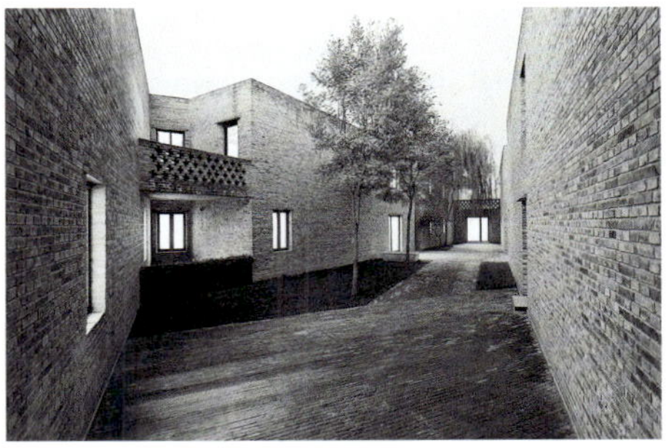

What first compelled you to open a gallery?
Already during my days as an auctioneer and later on as a paper restorer, I always collected contemporary art. In 1992 I decided to turn my passion into a career.

Who is the first artist you showed and what was most memorable about that show?
The first artist shown was Annelies Strba. Contrary to my expectations, it all went smoothly.

When did you first participate in Art Basel and what was most memorable about that show?
In 1998.

- **Contact** Galerie Urs Meile, Beijing-Lucerne
  Elena Federici
  elenafederici@galerieursmeile.com
  galerie@galerieursmeile.com
- **Established** 1992
- **Owner(s) / Partner(s)** Urs Meile
- **Space(s)** 167 m² (Lucerne)
  435 m² (Beijing)

- **Artists at Art Basel** Ai Weiwei, Cheng Ran, Brendan Earley, Andreas Golder, Hu Qingyan, Li Gang, Not Vital, Qiu Shihua, Christian Schoeler, Shao Fan, Anatoly Shuravlev, Julia Steiner, Wang Xingwei, Xia Xiaowan, Xie Nanxing, Yan Xing
- **Further artists represented** Chen Hui, Wim Delvoye, L/B, Li Dafang, Li Zhanyang, Liu Ding, Meng Huang

Melas Papadopoulos

Athens — Statements

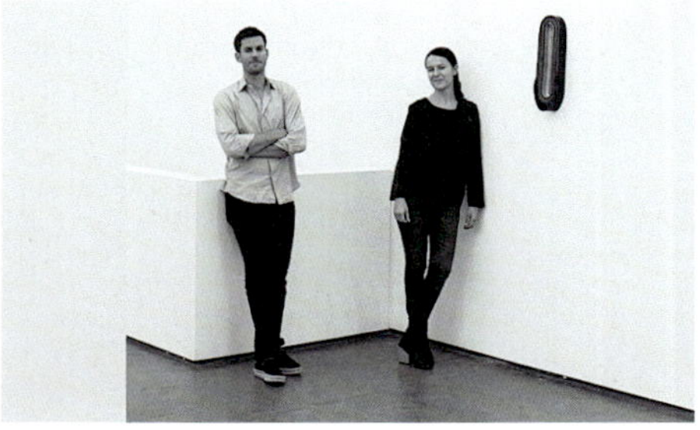

What first compelled you to open a gallery?

Helena: The desire to work closely with artists and see aesthetic ideas materialize in an environment of complete freedom.

Andreas: There was a gap that needed to be filled in Athens, so opening a gallery felt natural.

Who is the first artist you showed and what was most memorable about that show?

Andreas: The first artist we showed together was Michele Abeles. Every show is memorable one way or another.

Helena: Michele's show was fantastic. But I consider Claire Fontaine as the first exhibition in the Athens gallery—that was before our formal collaboration with Andreas. It included an installation that consisted of 80,000 matchsticks; it took a team of nine people and six days to put it together. I will never forget how hard we all worked, Fulvia Carnevale, James Thornhill, and all our artist and curator friends who did this for free.

When did you first participate in Art Basel and what was most memorable about that show?

It was in 2013, in the Statements sector with Kostas Sahpazis.

Helena: I have been visiting Art Basel since 1991 but this was the first time I saw it from the other side. I really enjoyed the installation, the town was so empty. I loved how the Messe gradually came to life.

Andreas: Being part of such a complex network felt exhilarating.

- **Contact** Melas Papadopoulos, Helena Papadopoulos, helena@melaspapadopoulos.com
- **Established** 2010
- **Owner(s) / Partner(s)** Helena Papadopoulos, Andreas Melas
- **Space(s)** 400 m²
- **Artists at Art Basel** Kostas Sahpazis
- **Further artists represented** Michele Abeles, Erica Baum, Dirk Bell, Sarah Crowner, Liz Deschenes, Claire Fontaine, Rallou Panagiotou, Georgia Sagri

Mendes Wood

São Paulo — Discoveries, Feature, Unlimited, Parcours, Nova

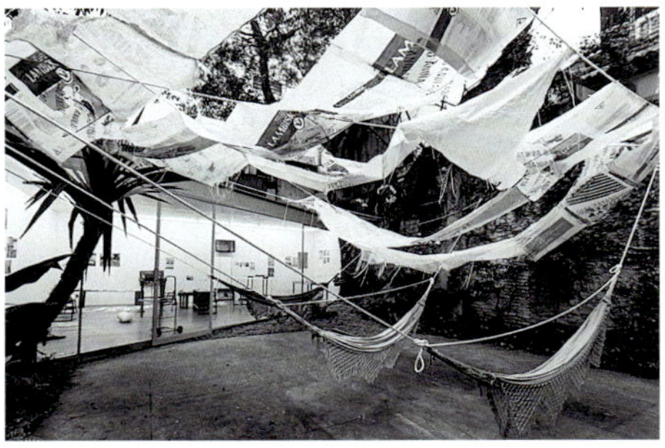

What first compelled you to open a gallery?

Matthew Wood: Pedro Mendes and I have a background in philosophy and prior to opening the gallery founded a not-for-profit artists' residence in Belo Horizonte which focused on promoting conversations between Brazilian and international artists. Moving to São Paulo in 2009 we met Felipe Dmab, who was running an alternative artist's space also centered on encounters between artists and the exchange of ideas. When we opened the gallery as partners in 2010 it was very much along the lines of harmonizing our conception of an open space for cross-pollination and dialogue—and especially one which sought to connect an extremely dynamic and rich but often very insular Brazilian scene to the rest of the world.

Who is the first artist you showed and what was most memorable about that show?

The first artist we showed—prior even to the gallery's formalization as a company—was Lucas Arruda, whose intimate show of small paintings in the tradition of Volpi and Modernist Brazilian compositions drew an enormous response from collectors and curators. It was both Arruda's first show in an art gallery and our own, and I vividly recall exchanging quizzical looks with him and my partners, as if to affirm: that's how it's done? What also really stands out in my memory is the tremendous feeling of support that the city gave us in our undertaking.

- **Contact** Mendes Wood, Matthew Wood, matthew@mendeswood.com, info@mendeswood.com
- **Established** 2010
- **Owner(s) / Partner(s)** Felipe Dmab, Matthew Wood, Patricia Fainziliber, Pedro Mendes
- **Team** 13
- **Space(s)** 1,000 m² (2 locations, 3 exhibition spaces, and a garden)
- **Artists at Art Basel** Lucas Arruda, Deyson Gilbert, Sonia Gomes, Marina Simão
- **Further artists represented** Adriano Costa, Theo Craveiro, Jen DeNike, Ana Dias Batista, Kota Ezawa, Kevin Francis Gray, Runo Lagomarsino, Patricia Leite, f. marquespenteado, Thiago Martins de Melo, Paulo Nazareth, Paulo Nimer Pjota, Leticia Ramos, Matheus Rocha Pitta, Daniel Steegmann Mangrané, Tunga, Roberto Winter

mennour

Paris

- Galleries Unlimited
- Galleries Public

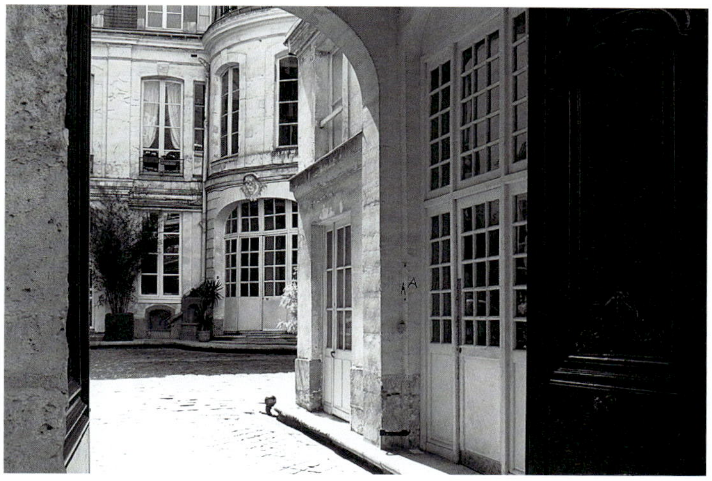

What first compelled you to open a gallery?
While I was visiting museums and galleries, I was magnetized by this world. Taken by this force, a vocation was born: I wanted to be a gallerist.

Who is the first artist you showed and what was most memorable about that show?
Pierre Molinier, in my first 80 m2 space. The pictures were so strong that we were compelled to obscure the windows. We published a book on this occasion, *Pierre Molinier: A Retrospective*, which is now a reference, which carries the trace of this first experience.

When did you first participate in Art Basel and what was most memorable about that show?
In 2003, in the Statements sector of Art Basel, with Kader Attia. We were there (!), but we realized all the work that remained to be done.

- **Contact** kamel mennour
Marie-Sophie Eiché
mariesophie@kamelmennour.com
galerie@kamelmennour.com
- **Established** 1999
- **Owner(s) / Partner(s)** Kamel Mennour
- **Team** 19
- **Space(s)** 750 m²
- **Artists at Art Basel** Mohamed Bourouissa
Marie Bovo
Daniel Buren
Pier Paolo Calzolari
Latifa Echakhch
Dario Escobar
Michel François
Yona Friedman
Alberto Garcia-Alix
Johan Grimonprez
Camille Henrot
David Hominal
Huang Yong Ping
Alfredo Jaar
Ann Veronica Janssens
Anish Kapoor
Tadashi Kawamata
Alicja Kwade
Sigalit Landau
Lee Ufan
Claude Lévêque
François Morellet
Gina Pane
Martial Raysse
Zineb Sedira
Miri Segal
Shen Yuan

Metro Pictures

New York

- Galleries Parcours
- Galleries Kabinett Public

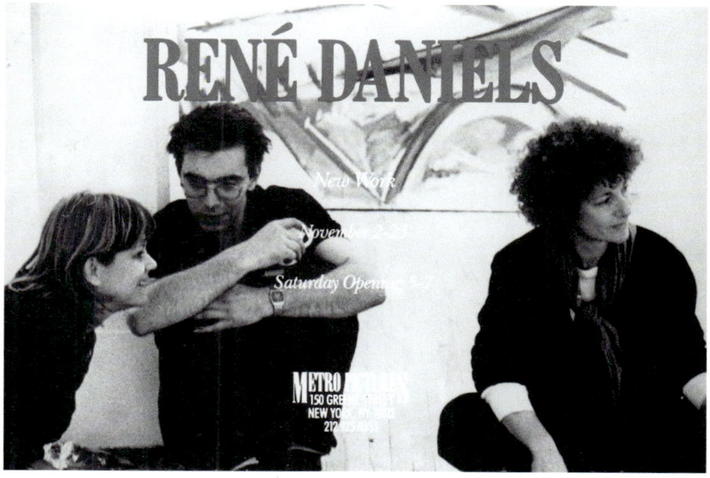

What first compelled you to open a gallery?
The then young artists we knew did not have gallery representation, or interesting possibilities at that time, and the idea of opening gallery grew from a casual concept to a serious gallery in response to what the artists wanted.

Who is the first artist you showed and what was most memorable about that show?
We opened with a group exhibition of the artists we represented, and who had shows in our first year. Beginning with Jack Goldstein, Cindy Sherman, Robert Longo, Richard Prince, Sherrie Levine, James Welling, and Troy Brauntuch.

When did you first participate in Art Basel and what was most memorable about that show?
Our first participation is memorable because we wanted to make a good impression, so we brought the most important pieces possible, a Martin Kippenberger painting, a Mike Kelley blanket piece, Cindy Sherman larger format film stills, an iconic Louise Lawler image with Koons basketball *Tank*, and an early Longo *Men in the Cities* drawing.

- **Contact** Metro Pictures
Helene Winer
helene@metropictures.com
gallery@metropictures.com
- **Established** 1980
- **Owner(s) / Partner(s)** Helene Winer
Janelle Reiring
- **Space(s)** 372 m²
- **Artists at Art Basel** Olaf Breuning
André Butzer
Claire Fontaine
Andy Hope 1930
Isaac Julien
Louise Lawler
Robert Longo
David Maljkovic
John Miller
Paulina Olowska
Tony Oursler
Trevor Paglen
Stephen G. Rhodes
Jim Shaw
Cindy Sherman
Gary Simmons
Alexandre Singh
Andreas Slominski
Catherine Sullivan
Sara VanDerBeek
Tris Vonna-Michell
T.J. Wilcox
B. Wurtz

City population
93,271
(Miami Metropolitan Area: 5,564,635)

Population density
6,620 inhabitants per square kilometer

Fair founded in
2001 but postponed to 2002 due to 9/11 attacks

Visitors in 2013
75,000

Number of exhibitors in 2013
259

Number of artists exhibited in 2013
over 4,000

MIAMI BEACH

Exhibition Partners: Museums & Cultural Institutions Miami Beach

Art and Culture Center of Hollywood
Francie Bishop Good: *Not on Allen St*; Charles LaBelle: *Selections from the Dwelling Archive*; Sarah Michelle Rupert: *In Search of Ever After*

Art Center/South Florida
Juan López: *Between Walls*

Bass Museum
Piotr Uklański: *ESL*

Boca Raton Museum of Art
Southwestern Allure: The Art of the Santa Fe Art Colony; Nancy Davidson: *Let'er Buck*

CasaLin
HotBed: *Reverence*

Fairchild Tropical Botanic Garden
Design at Fairchild, featuring Hugo França

The Patricia & Phillip Frost Art Museum
Manuel Mendive: *Things that Cannot be Seen Any Other Way*; Humberto Castro: *Tracing Antilles*; 'Javier Velasco: *Deep Blue*

Jewish Museum of Florida
Graphic Details: Confessional Comics by Jewish Women

Locust Projects
Nicholas Hlobo: *Intethe*; Frances Trombly: *Over and Under*; Bus Shelter Project: *Angel Otero*

Lowe Art Museum
Beauty Beyond Nature: The Glass Art of Paul Stankard; ?#@*$%! The Mainstream: The Art of DIY Self Expression, Zines from Special Collections, University of Miami Libraries

MDC Museum & Galleries of Art + Design
Cristina García Rodero; *Rituales en Haití*

Pérez Art Museum Miami
Ai Weiwei: *According to What?*; Commissioned projects by Yael Bartana, Bouchra Khalili, Hew Locke, and Monika Sosnowska

Miami Children's Museum
Dino Island

Museum of Art, Fort Lauderdale
Spirit of Cobra

Museum of Contemporary Art
Tracey Emin: *Angel Without You*

Norton Museum of Art
Third Annual Recognition of Art by Women exhibition (RAW); Phyllida Barlow: *Hoard*; Mickalene Thomas: Museum lobby installation

University Galleries, Florida Atlantic University
2013 Biennial Faculty Art Exhibition; SouthXeast: Contemporary Southeastern Art

Vizcaya Museum & Gardens
The Academic and the Avant-Garde: Artists of the 1913 Armory Show at Vizcaya

Wolfsonian-Florida International University
Rebirth of Rome

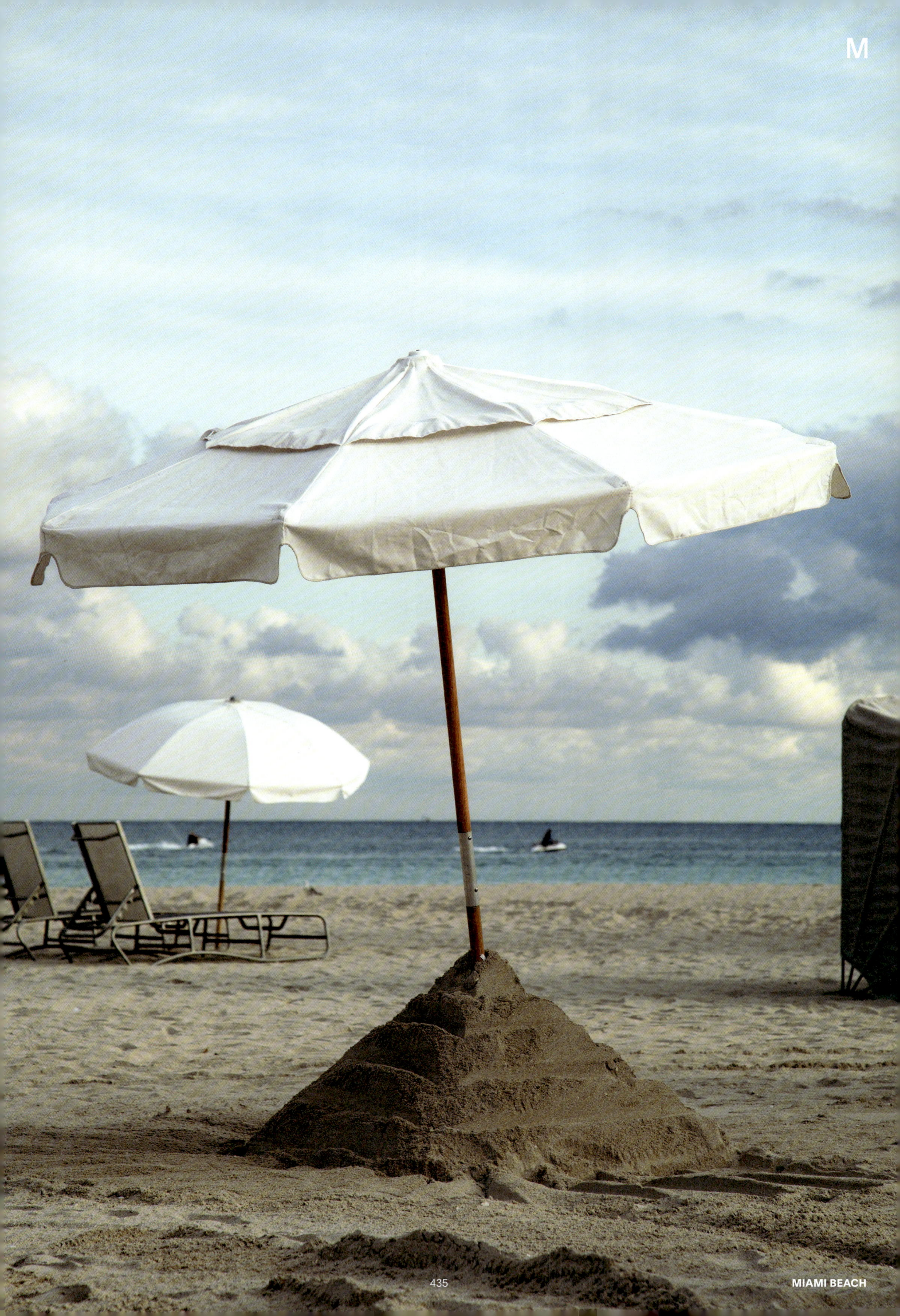

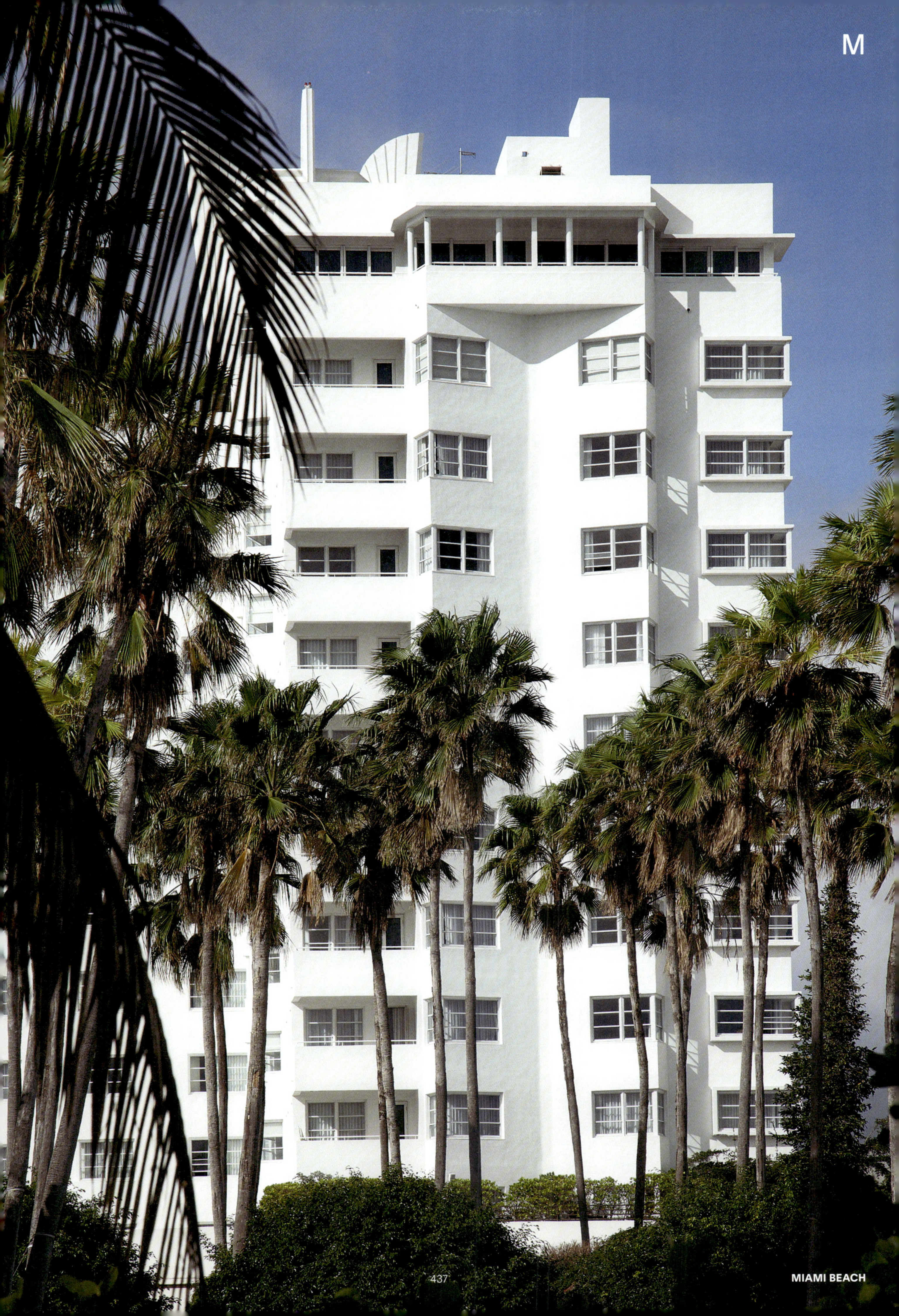

M

Keith Haring
Untitled (Car)
1986

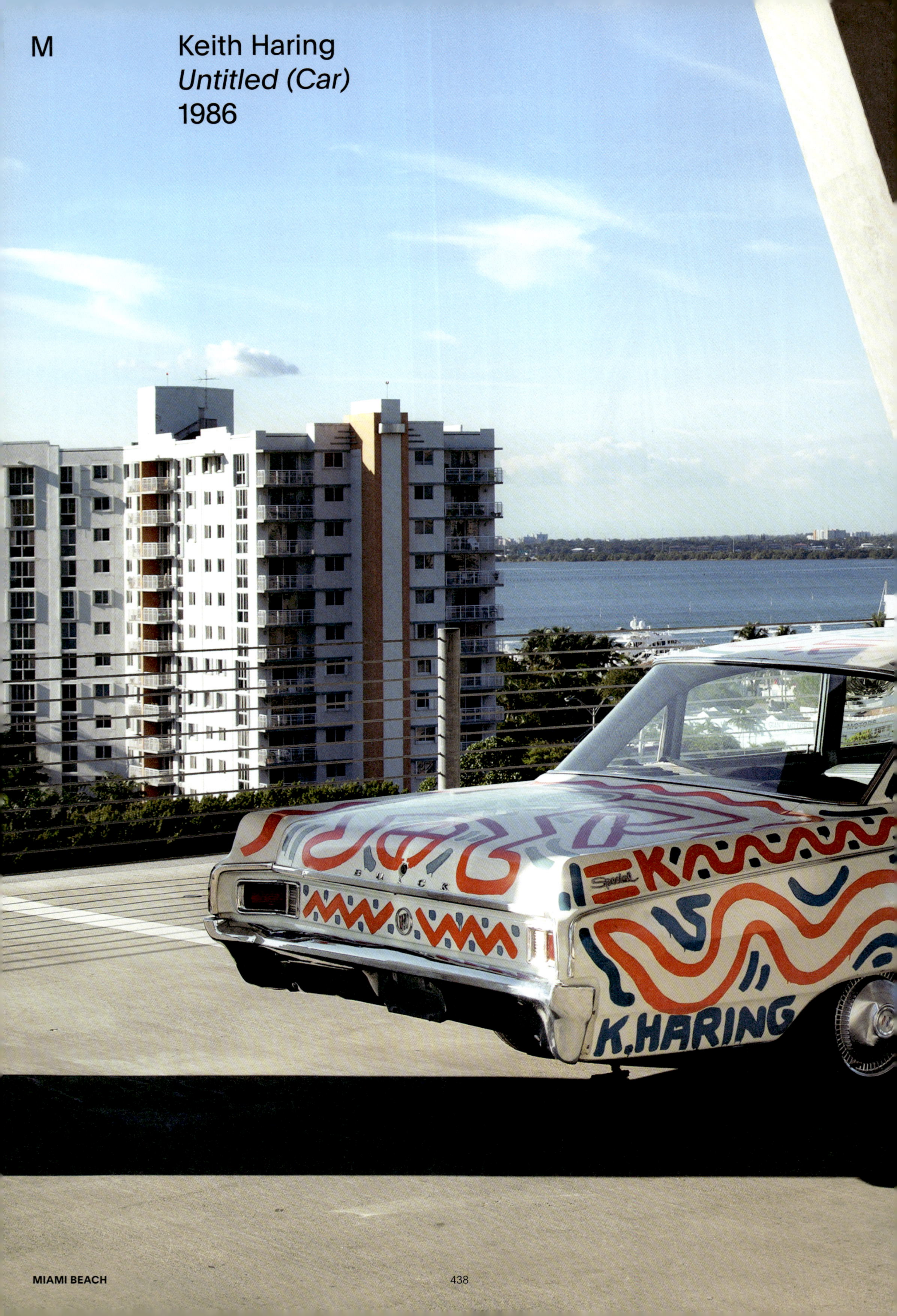

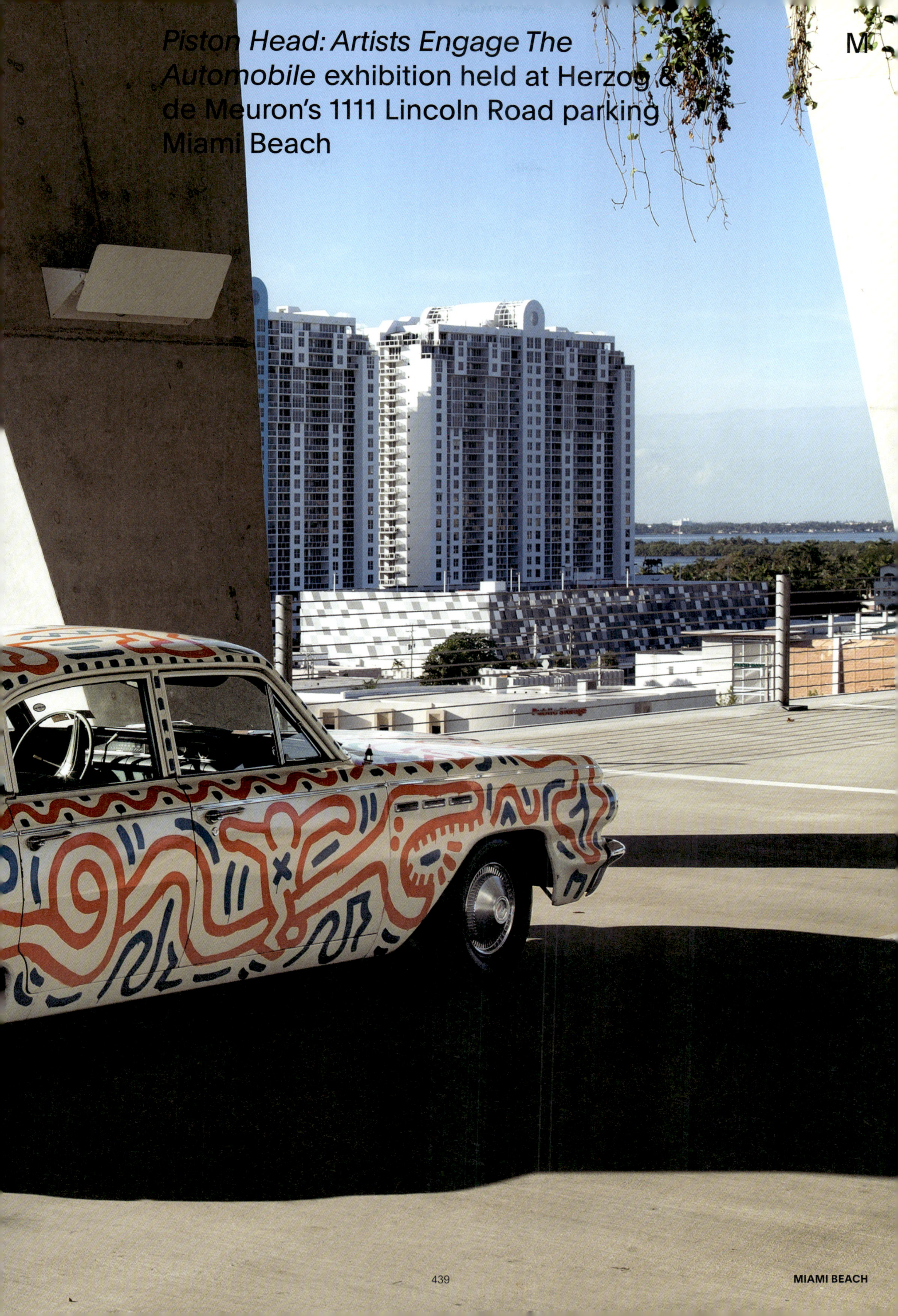

Piston Head: Artists Engage The Automobile exhibition held at Herzog & de Meuron's 1111 Lincoln Road parking Miami Beach

Miami Marine Stadium with Kolkoz's *Curiosity* presented by Audemars Piguet and Galerie Perrotin Virginia Key

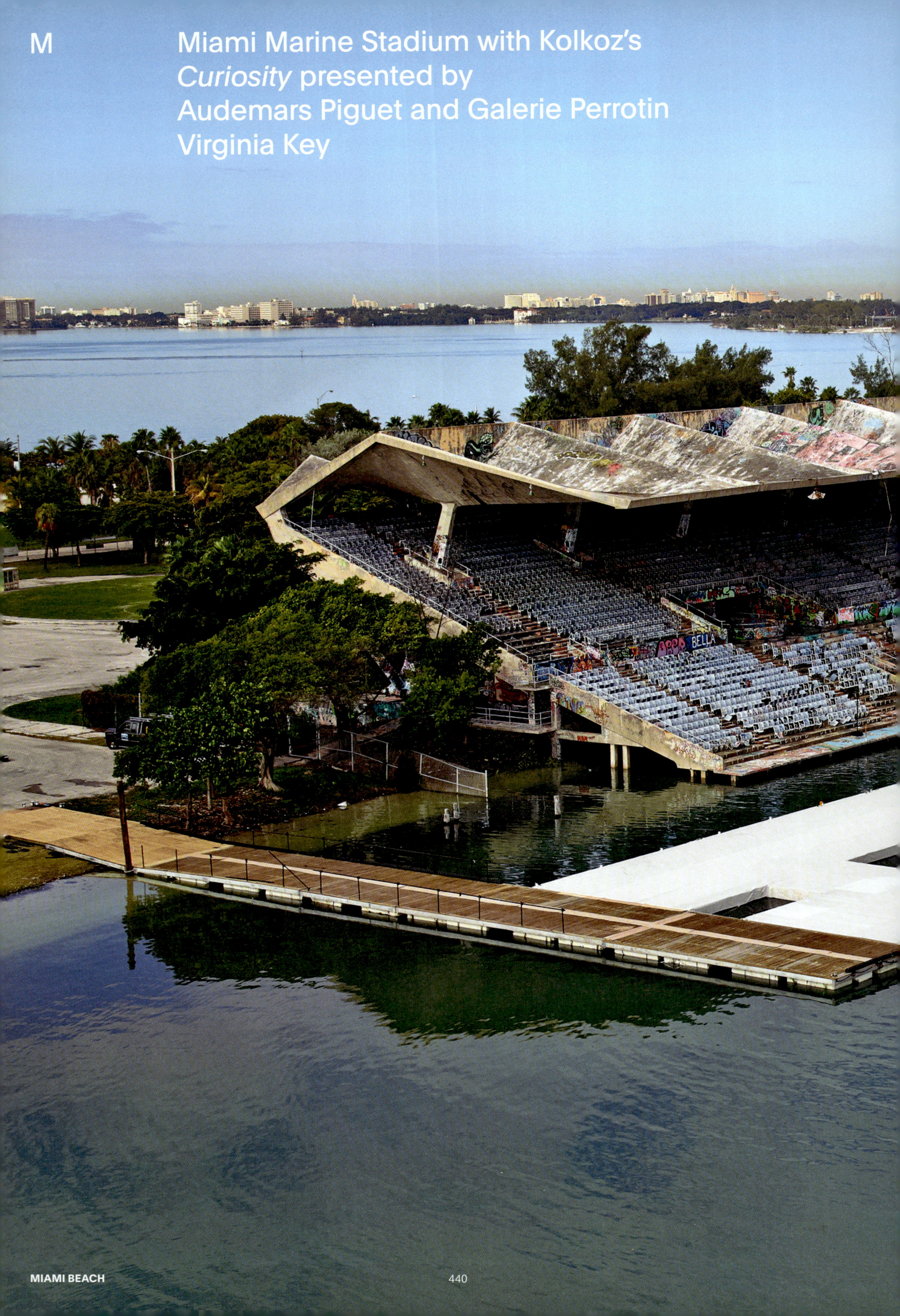

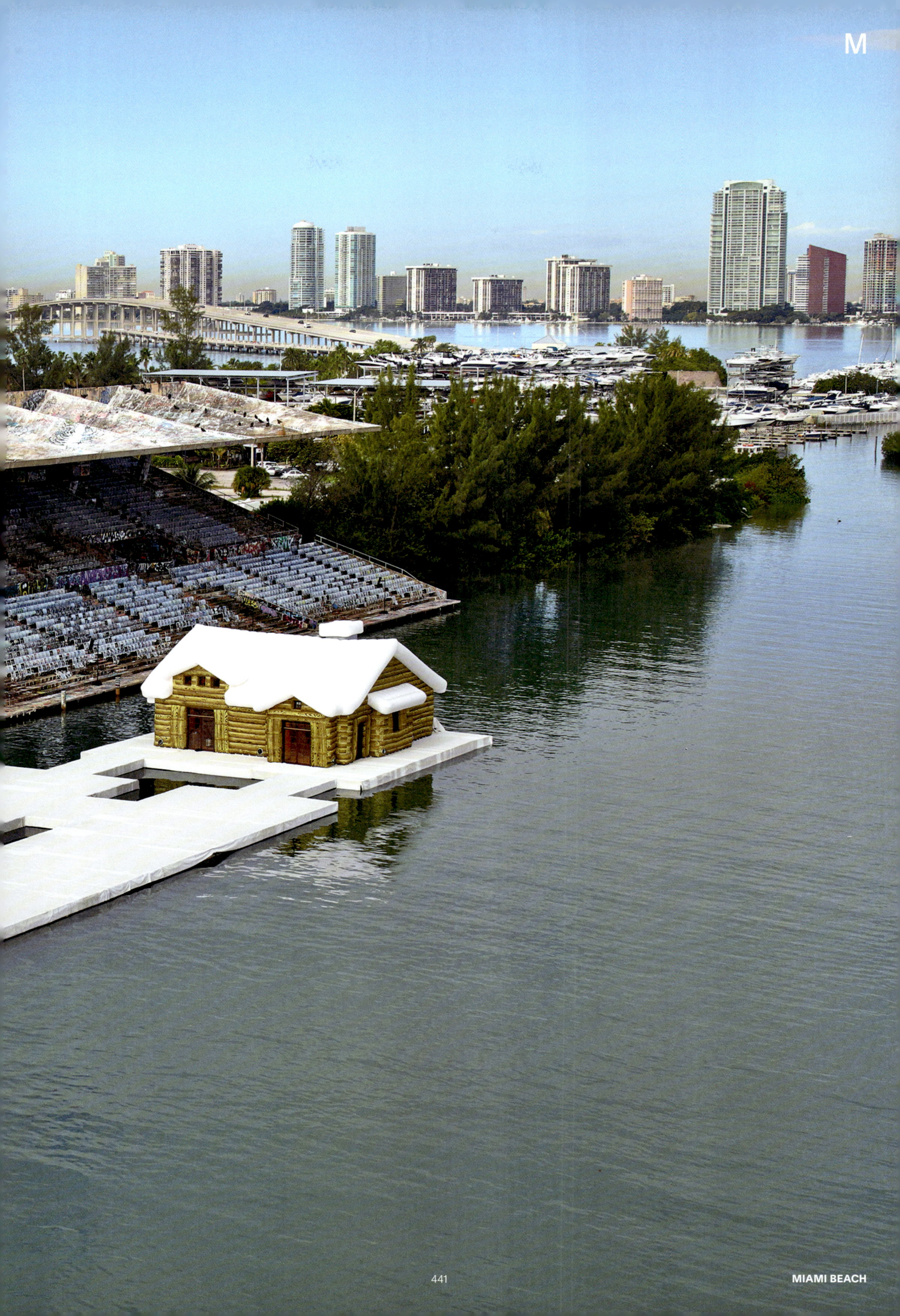

Miami Beach Convention Center

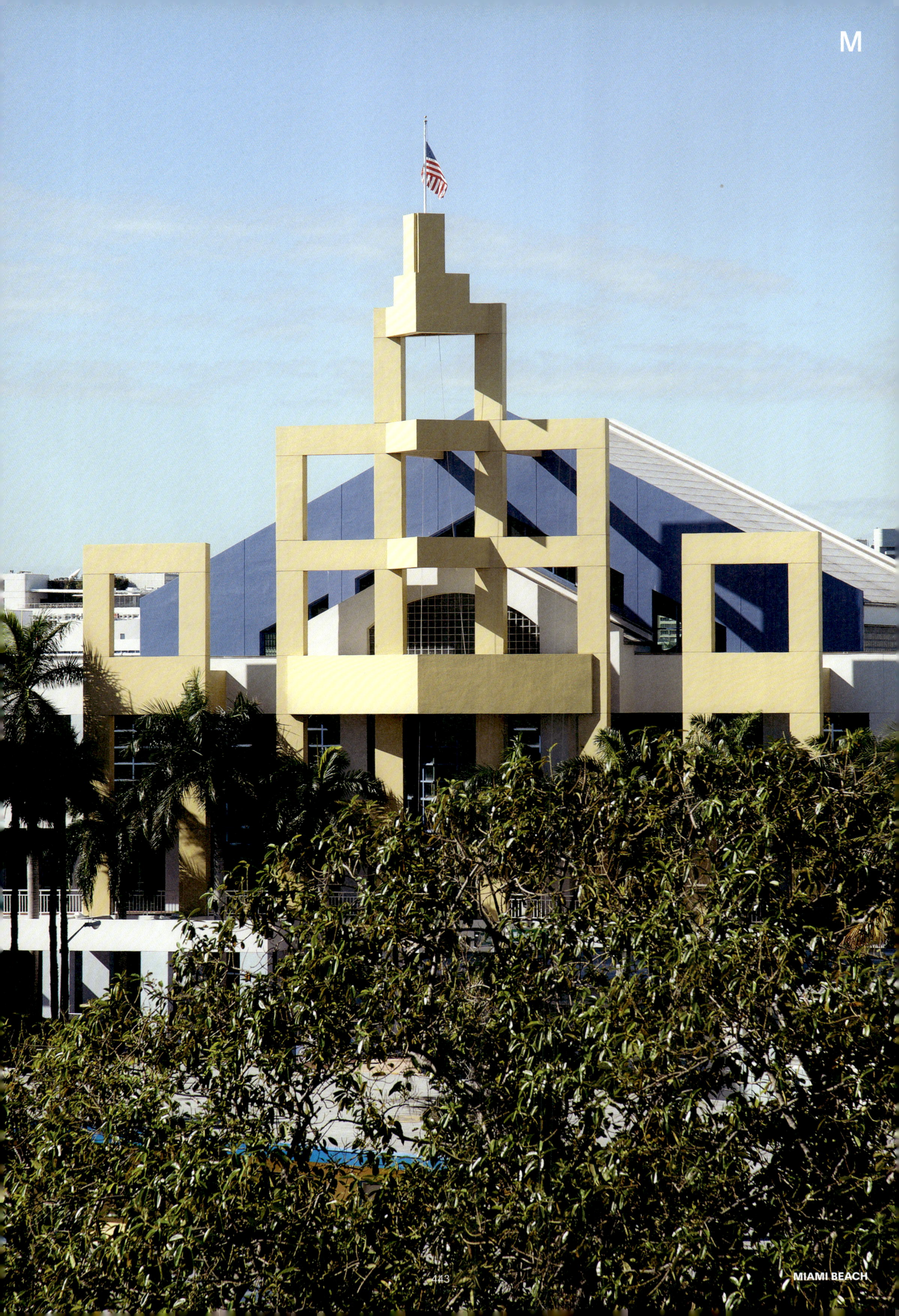

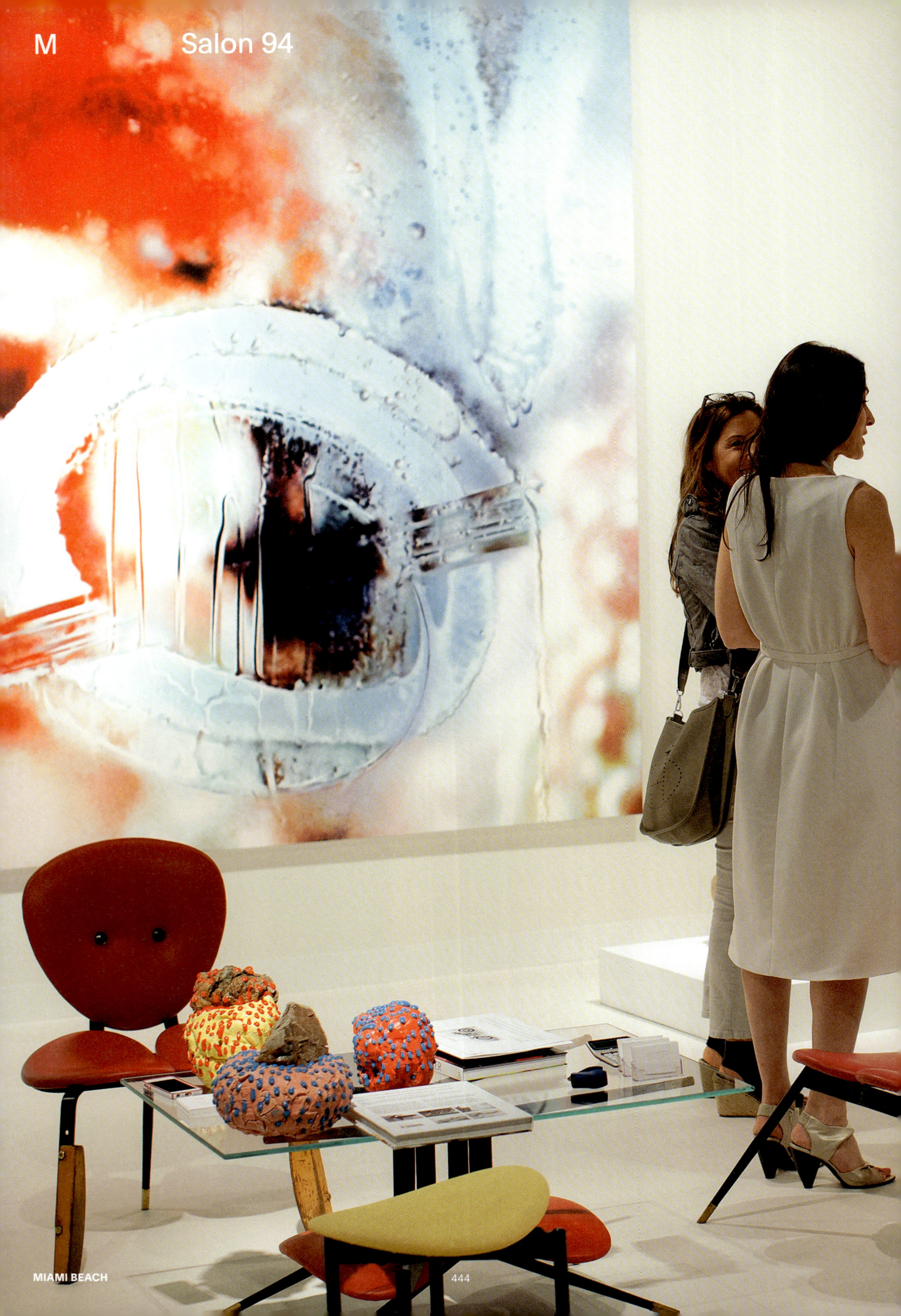

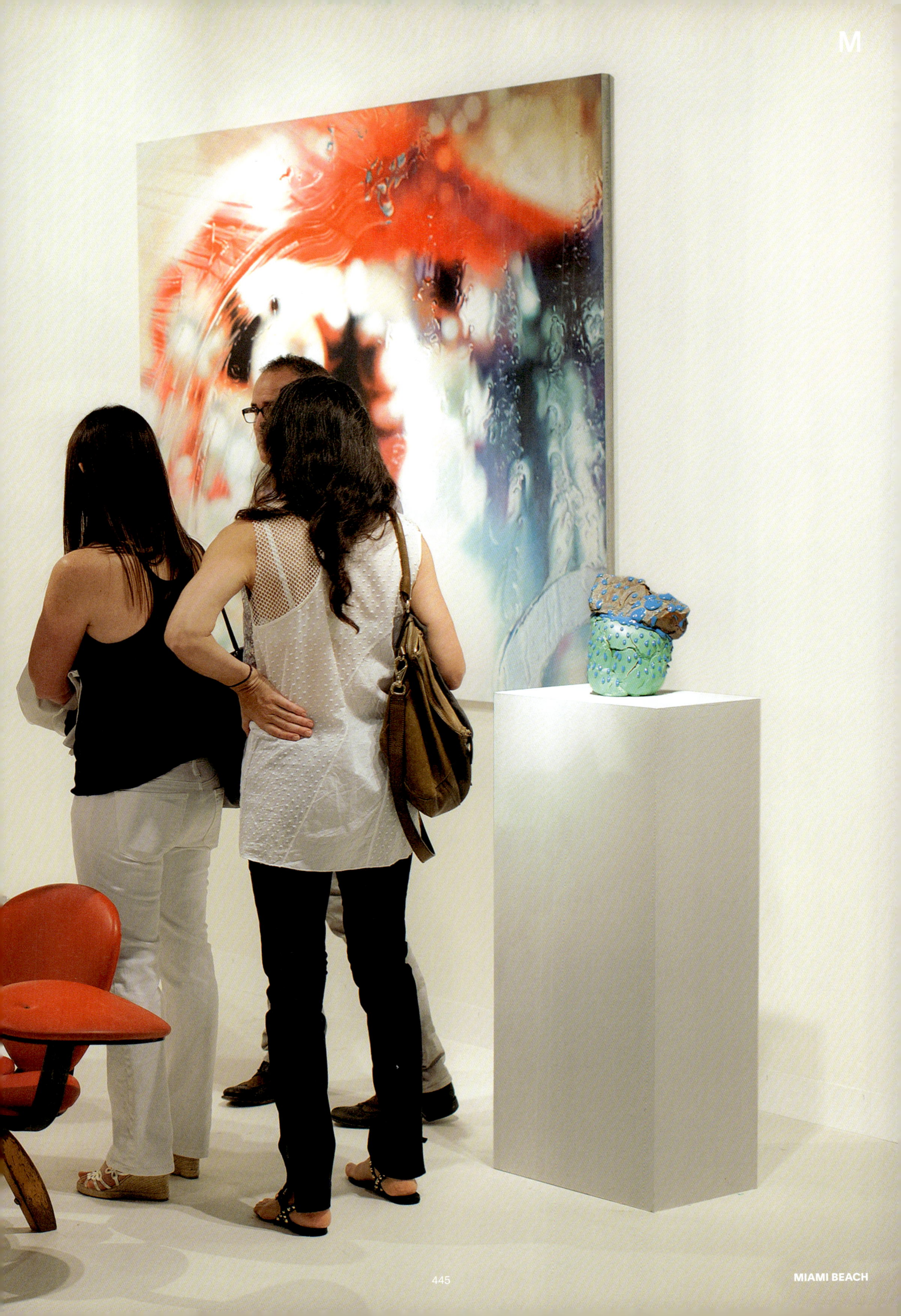

neugerriemschneider
Jorge Pardo

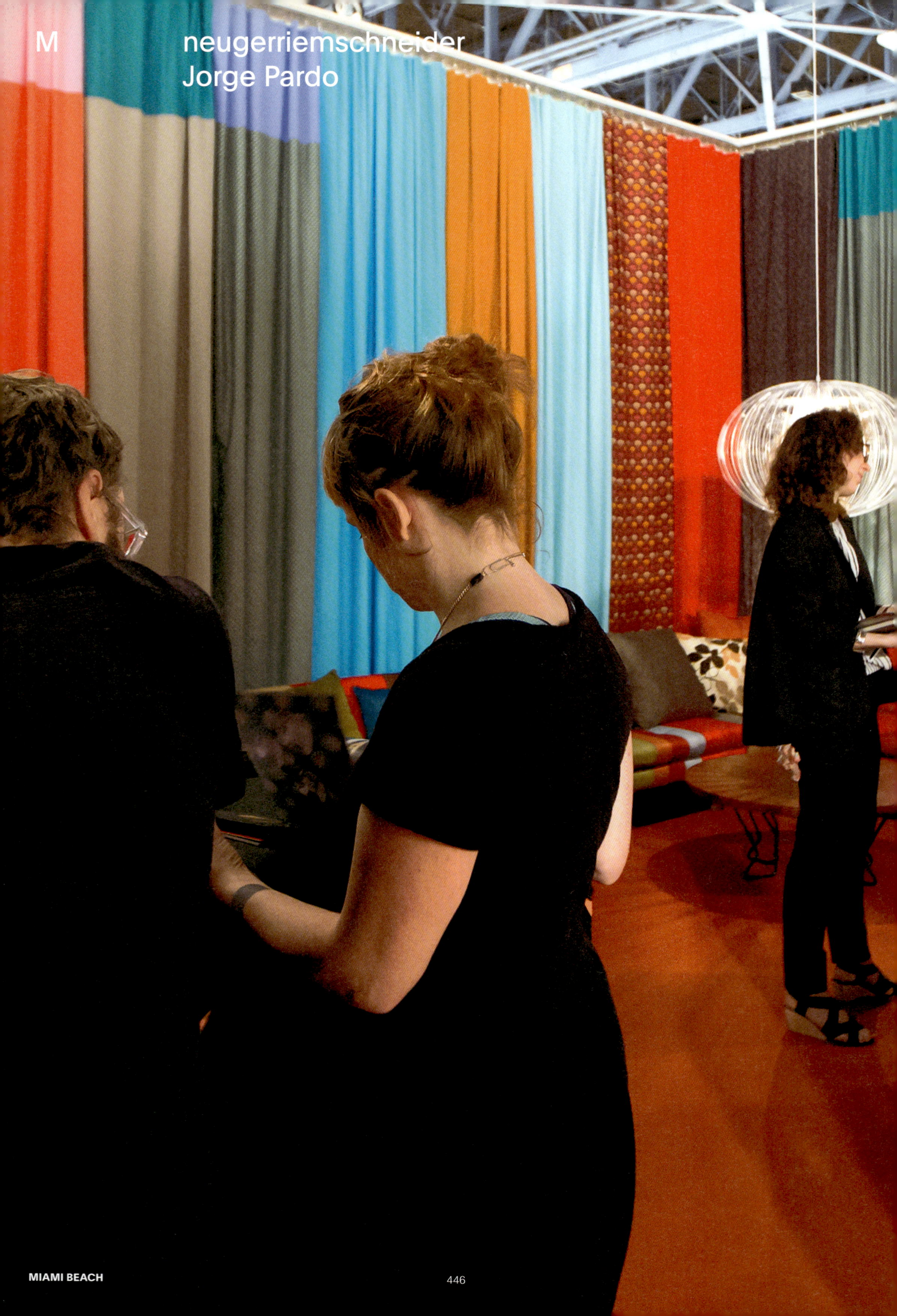

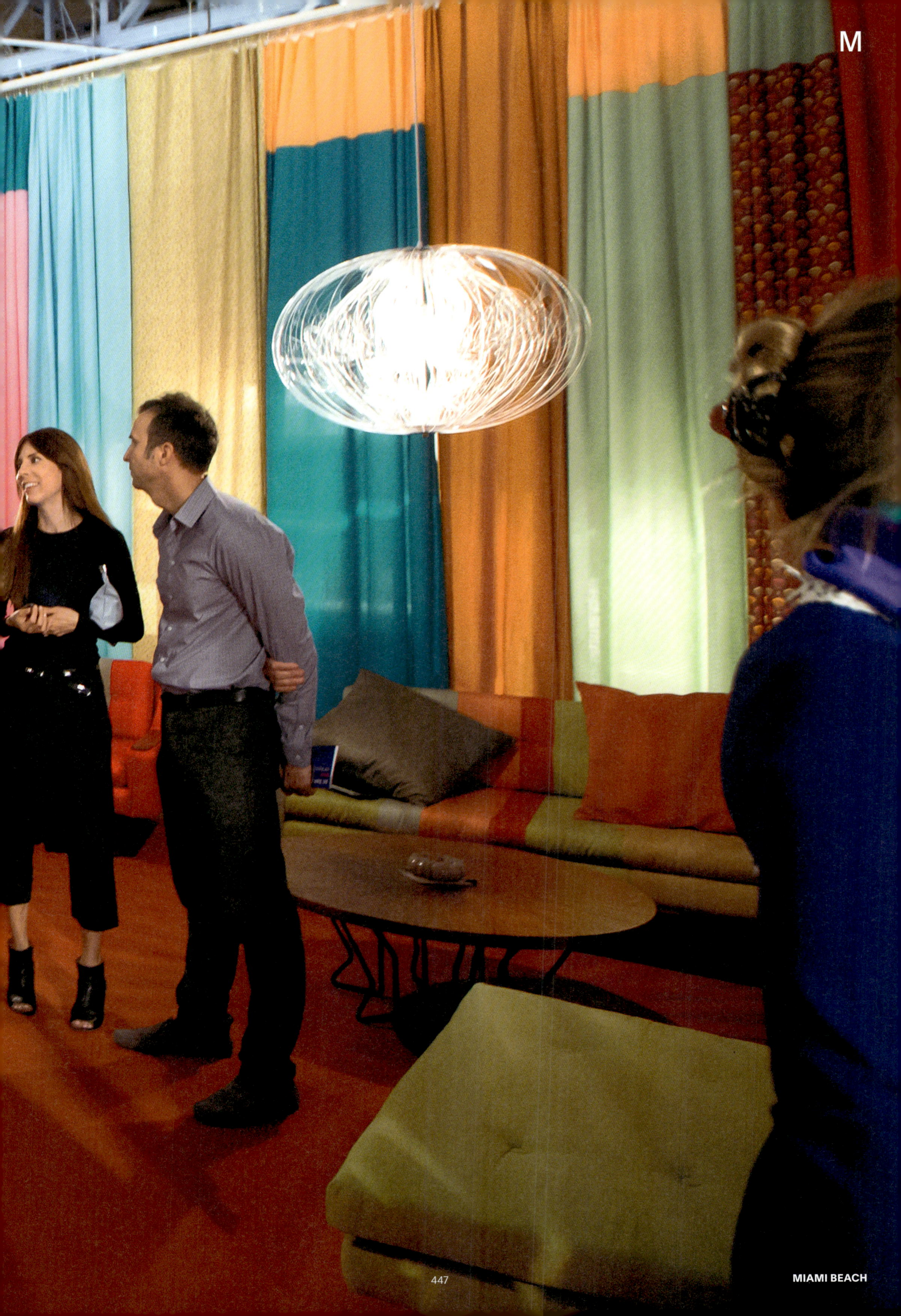

Massimo De Carlo
booth design by John M Armleder

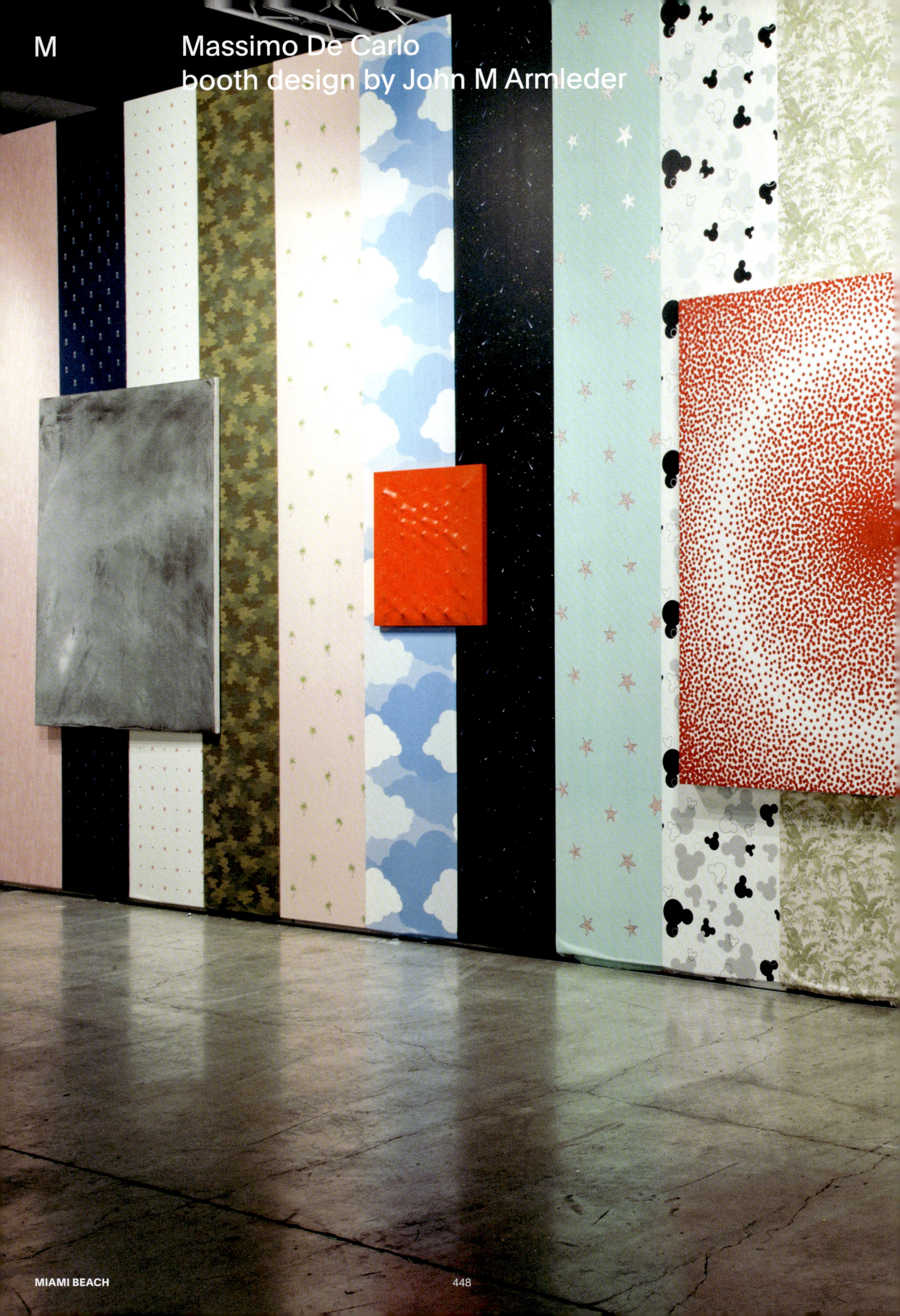

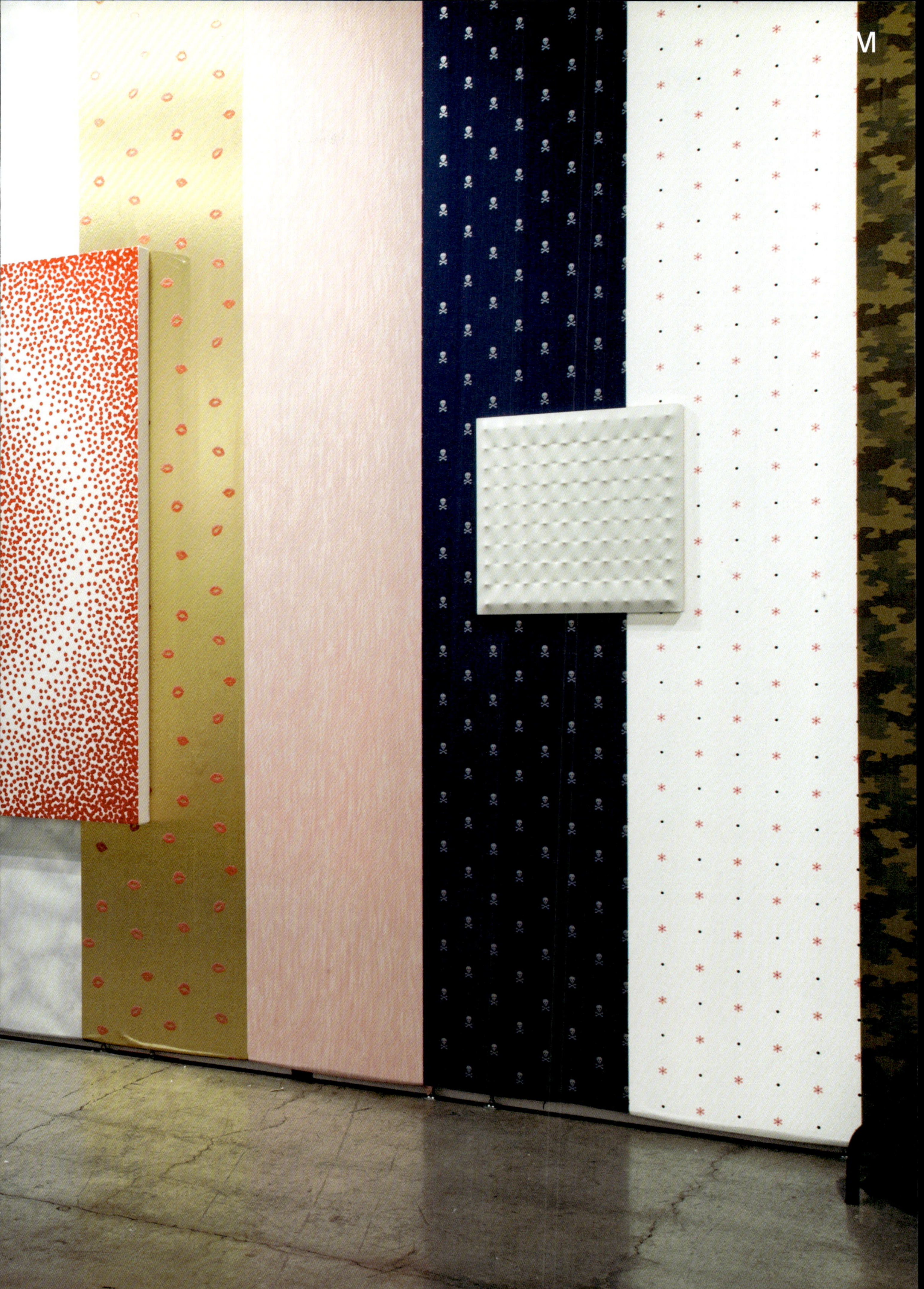

Greene Naftali Gallery
Guyton\Walker

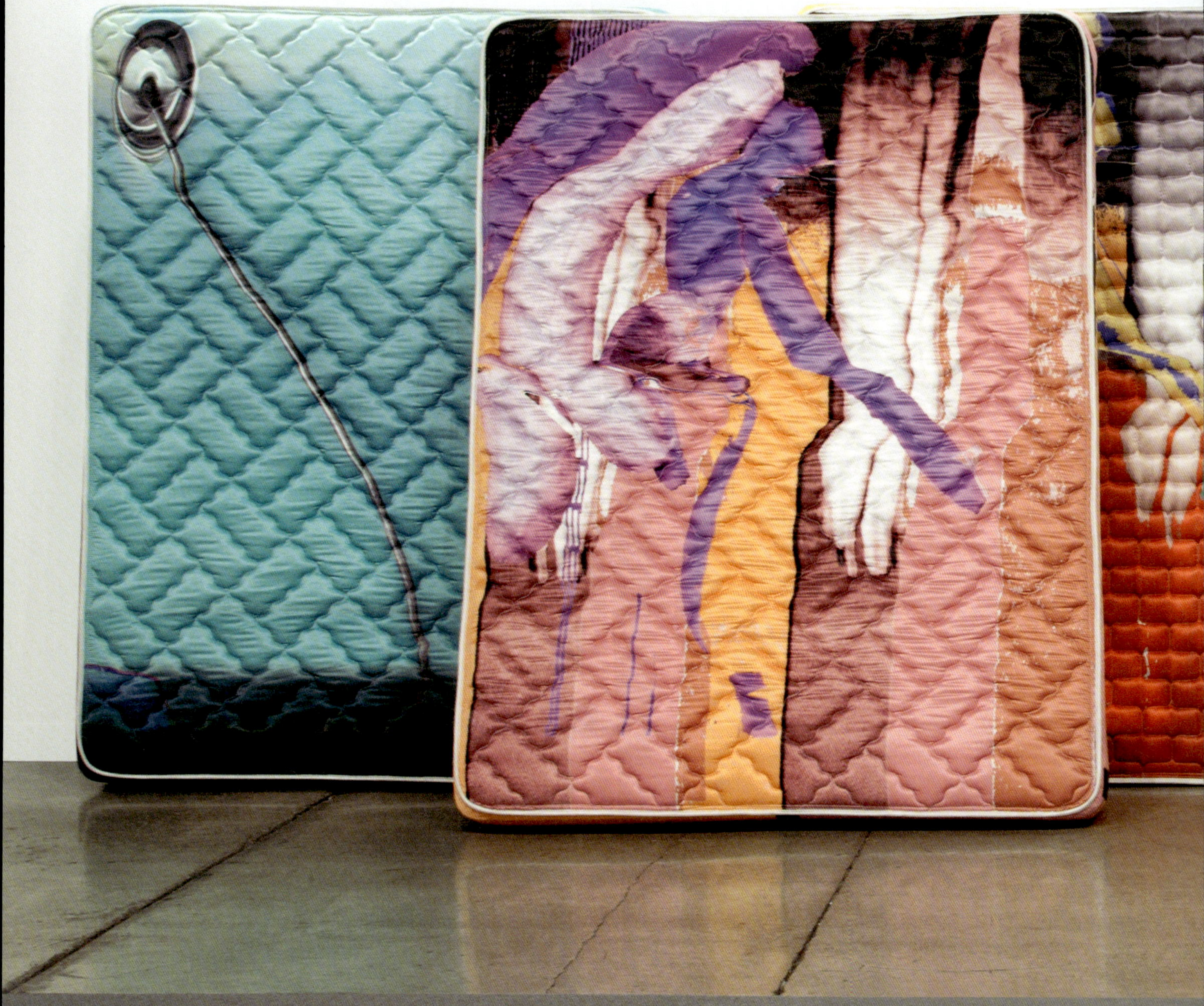

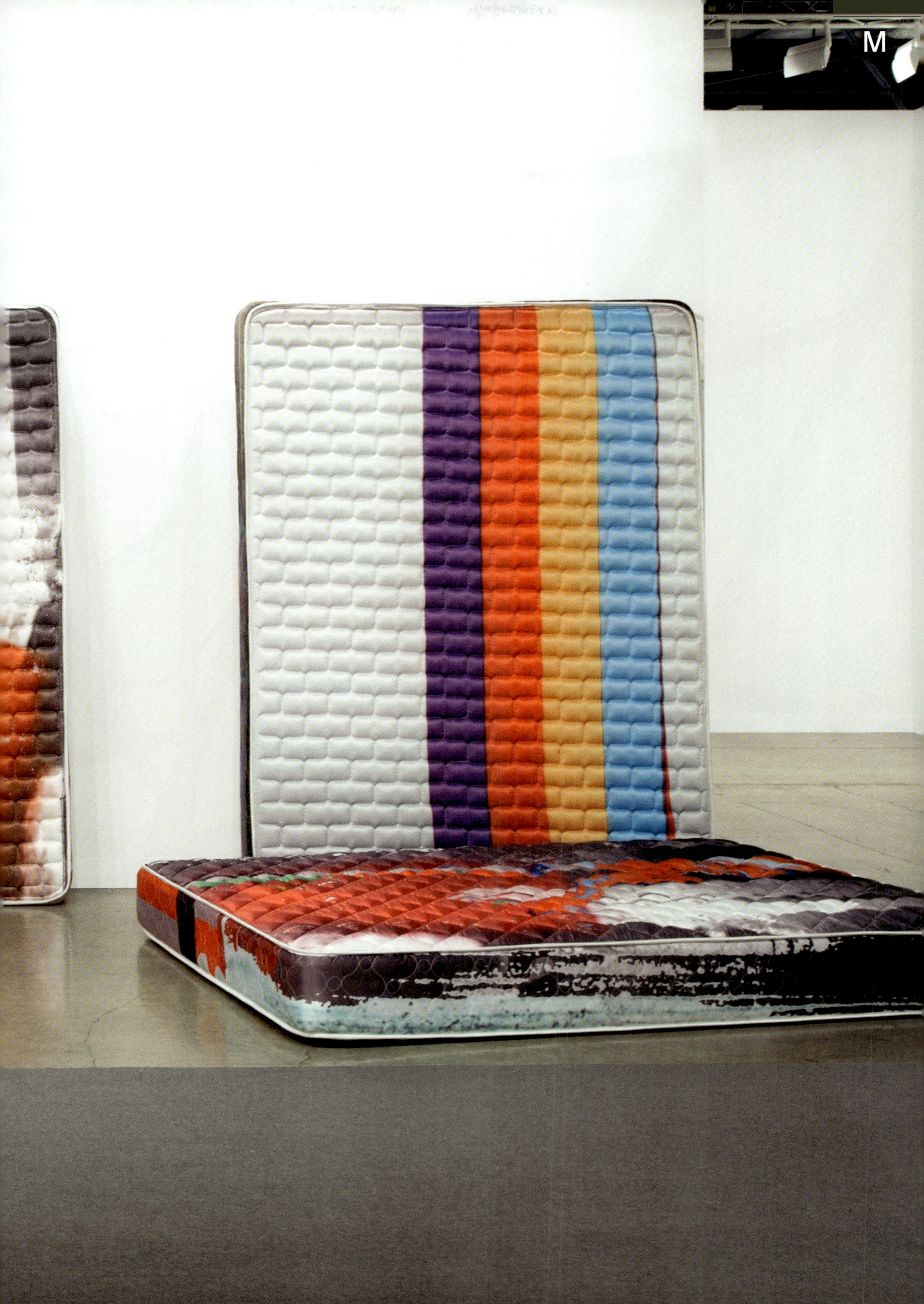

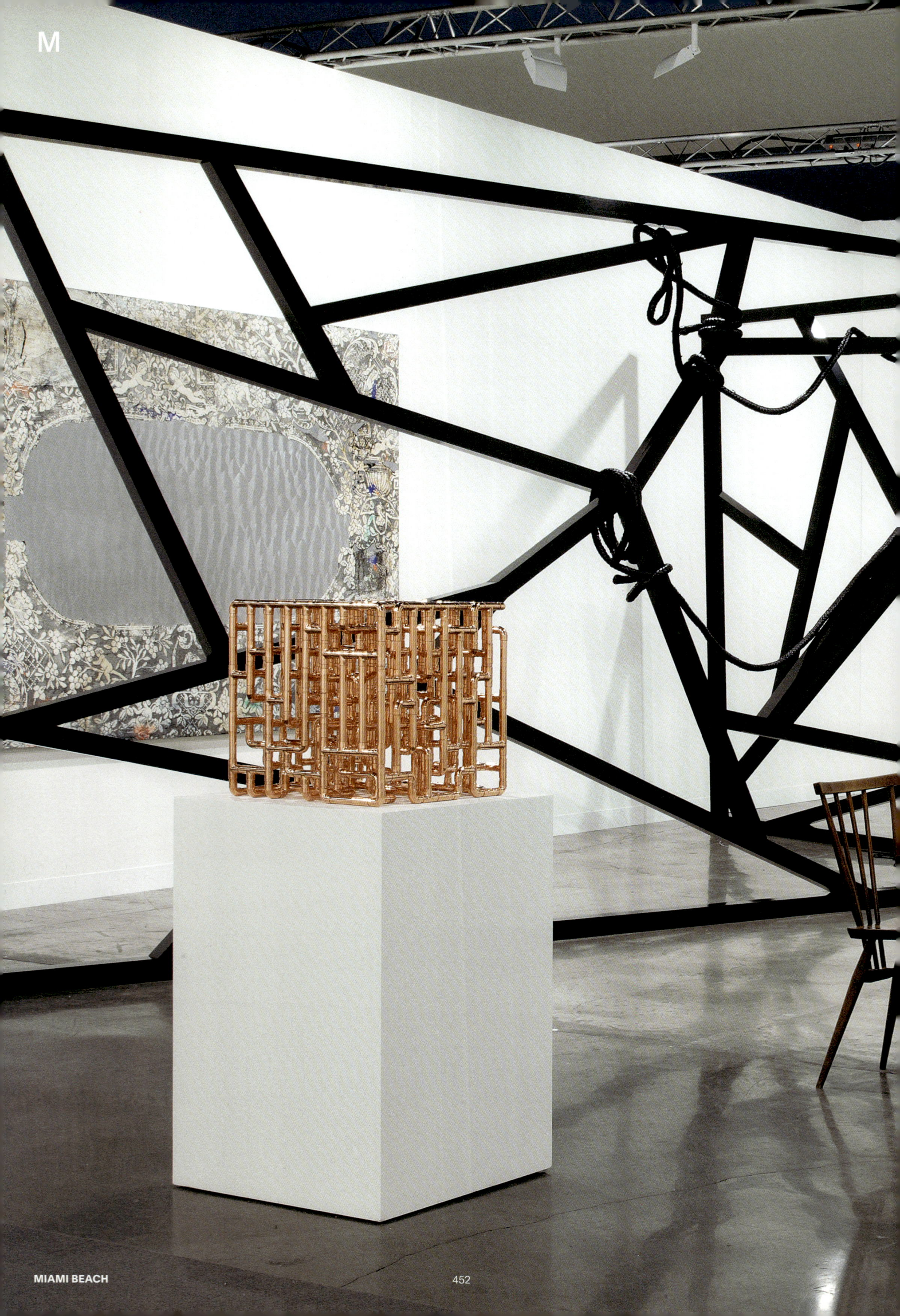

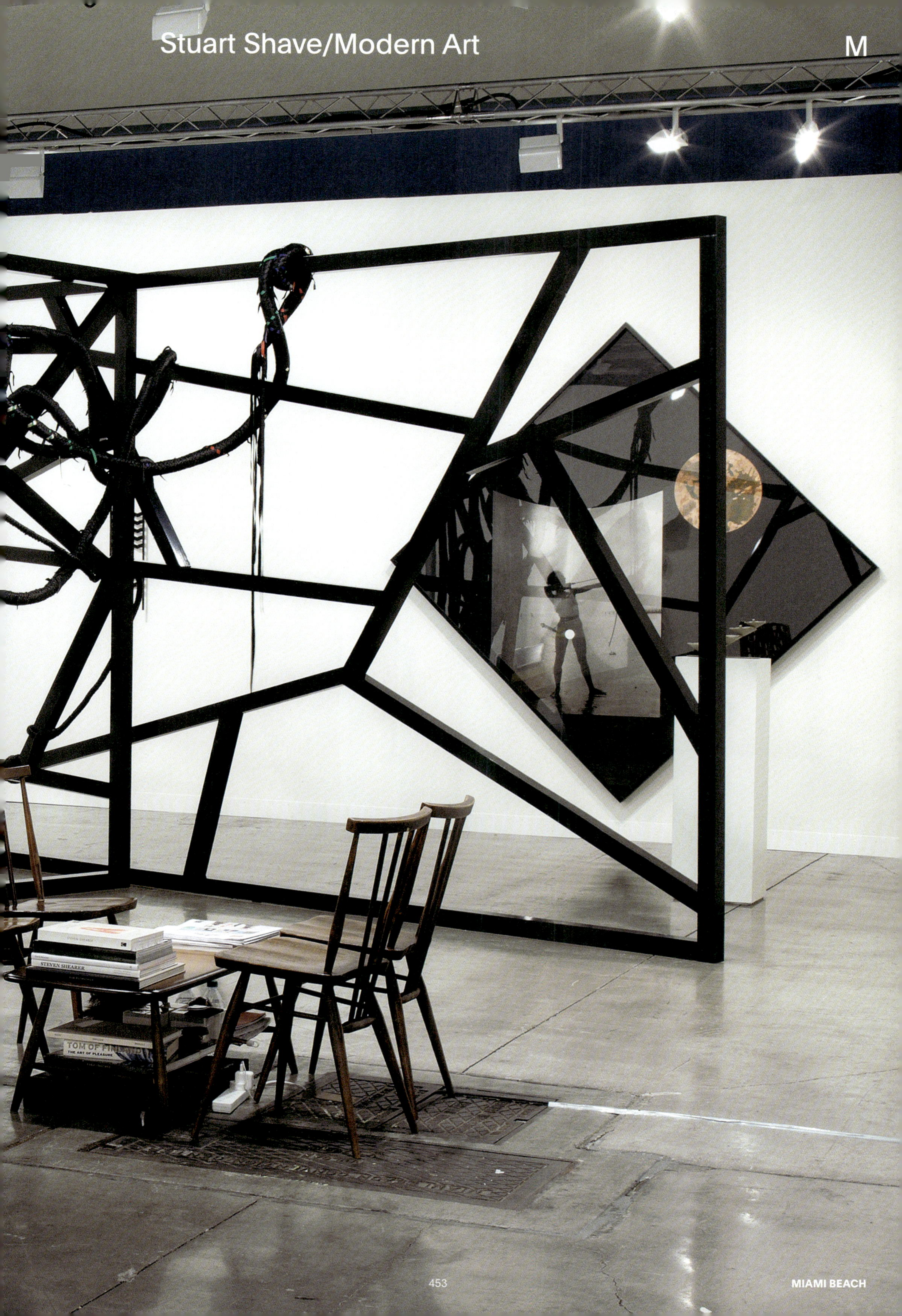
STEVEN SHEARER
TOM OF FINLAND
THE ART OF PLEASURE

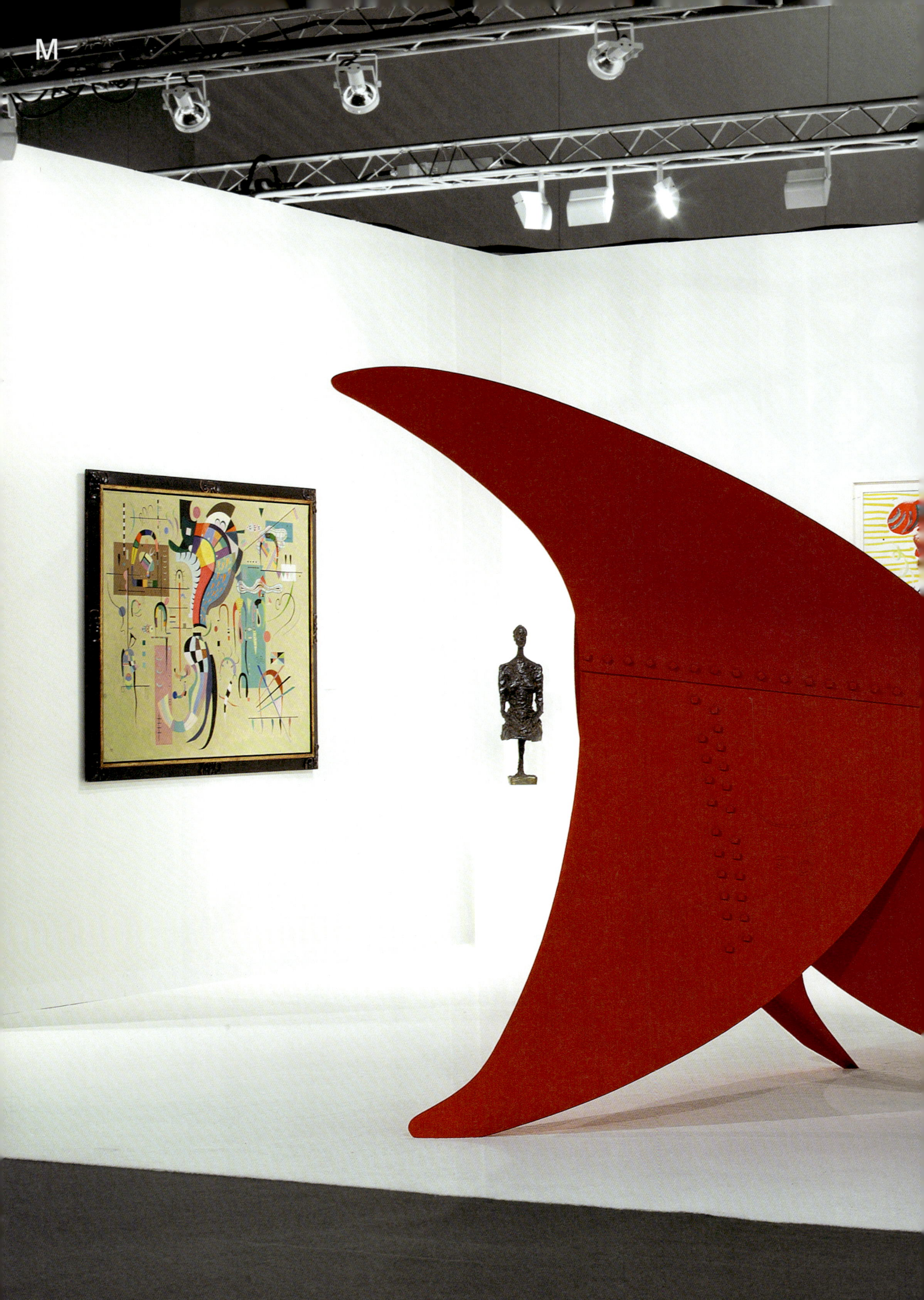

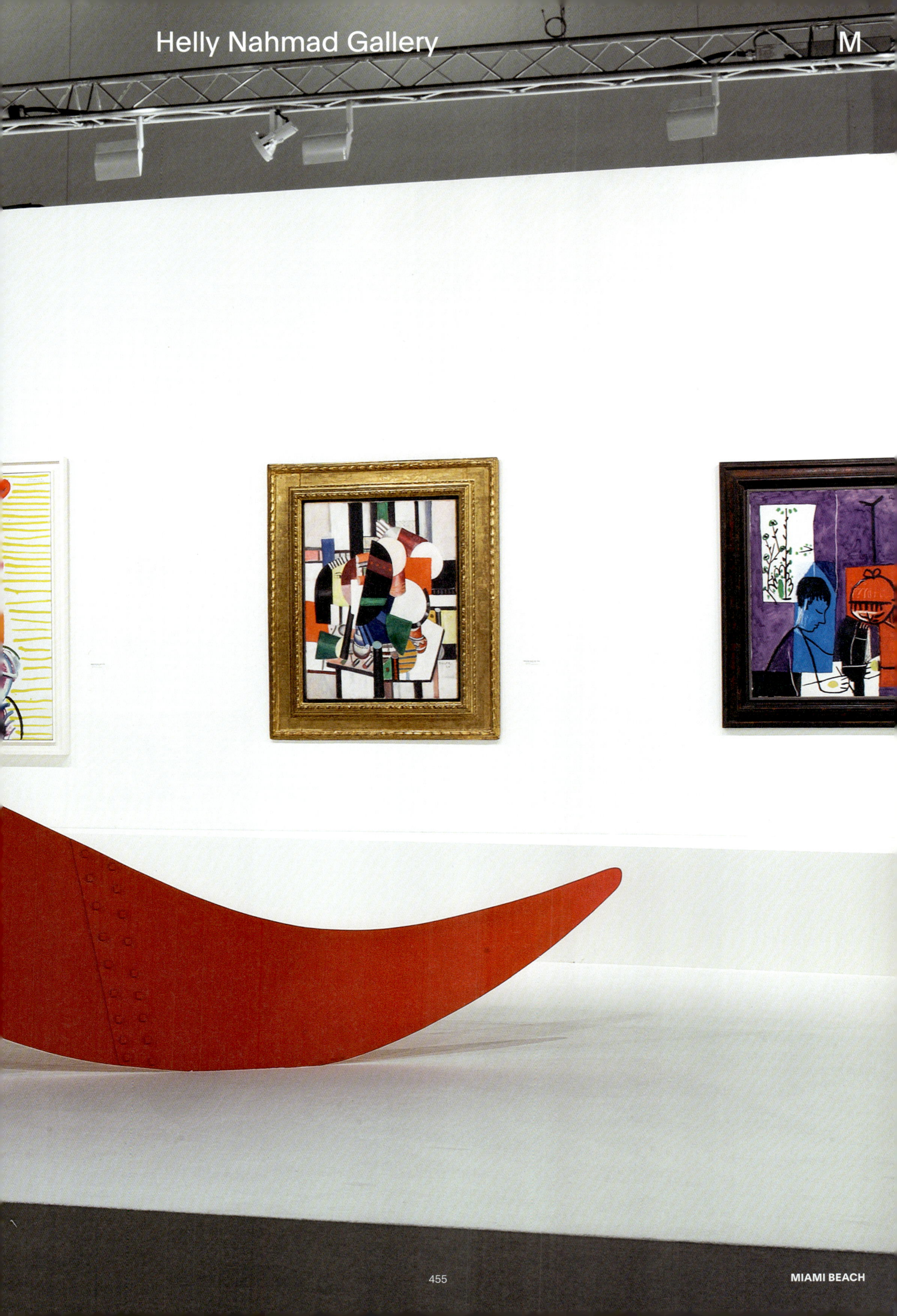

Paul Kasmin Gallery

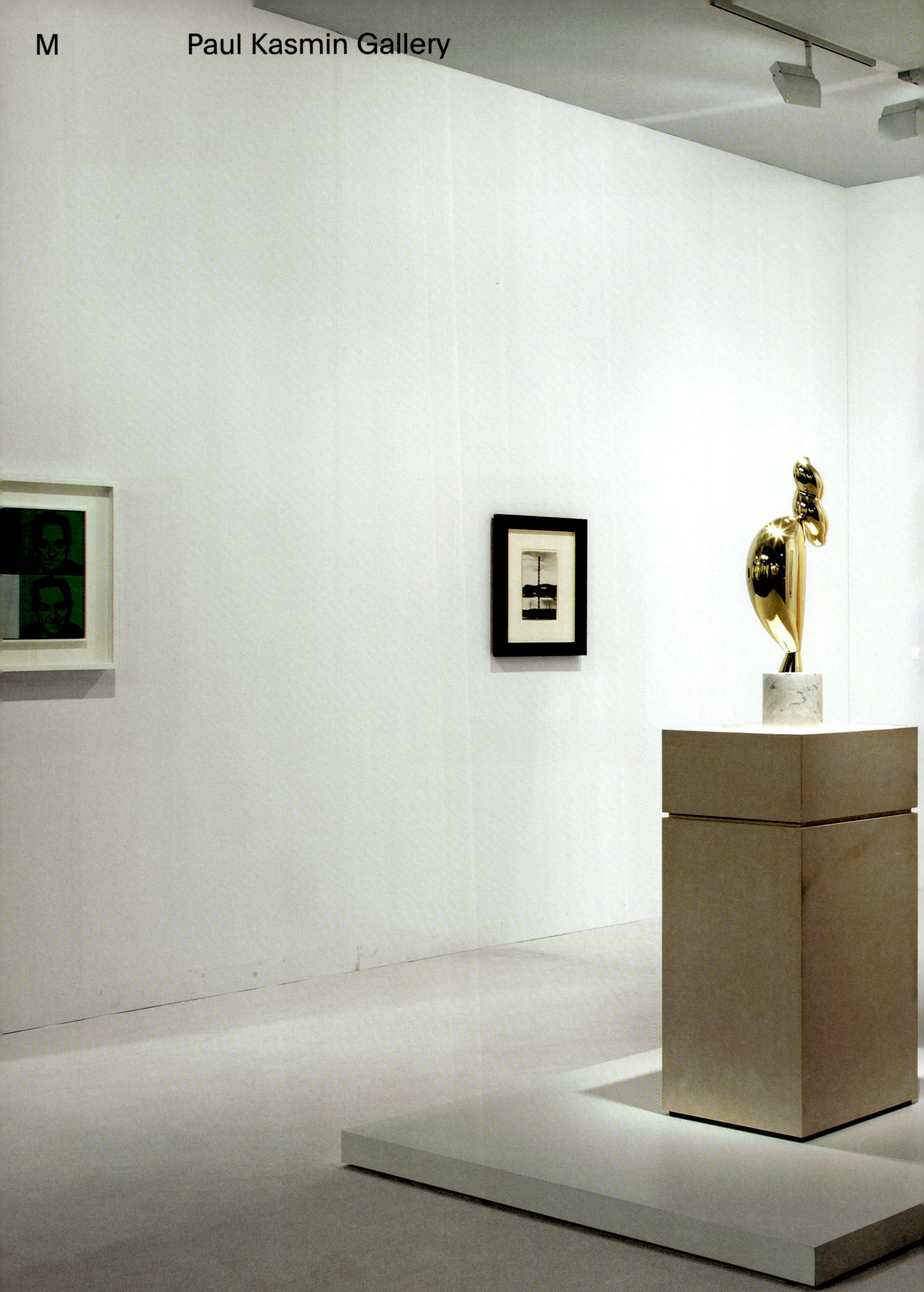

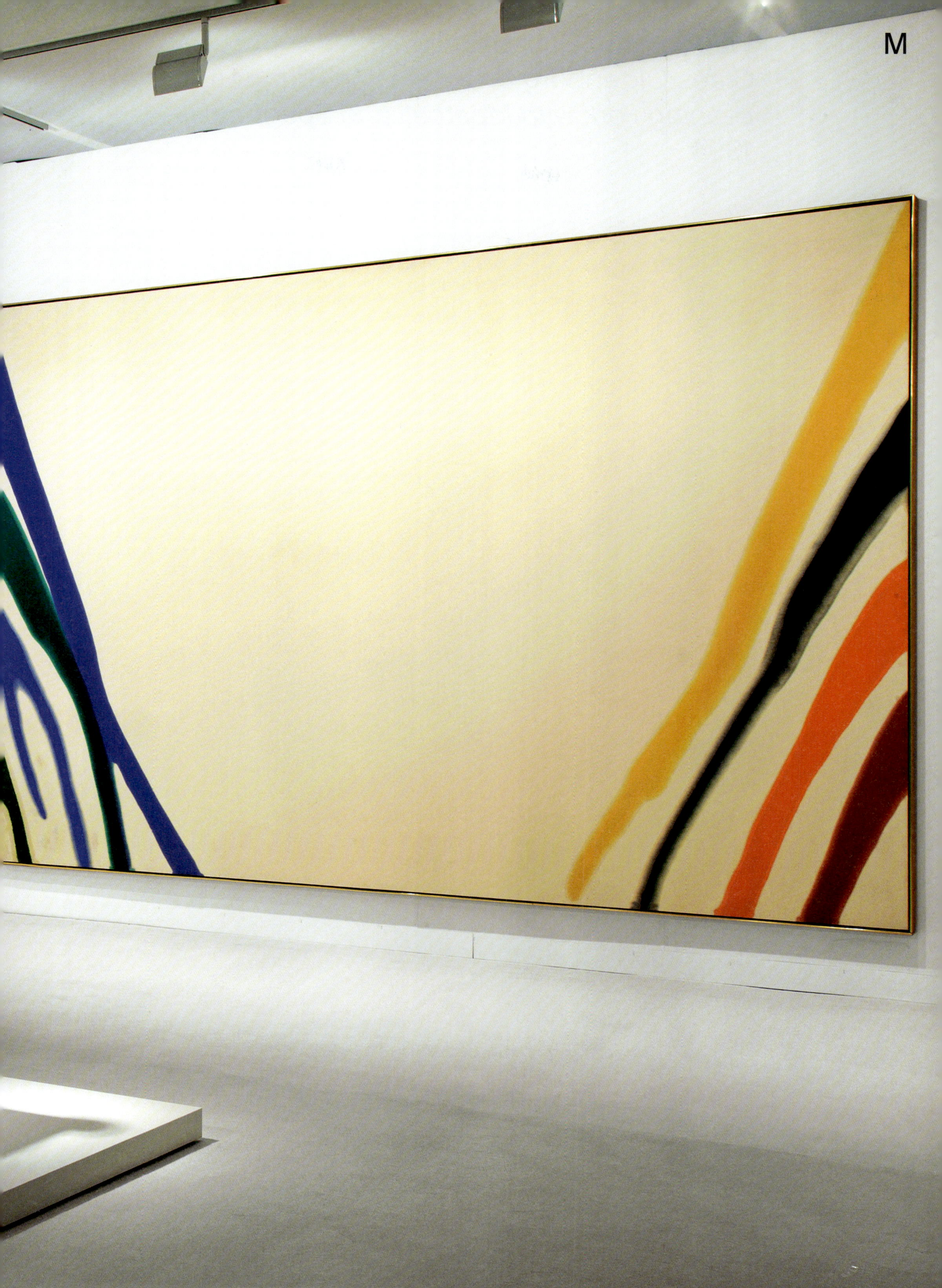

Waddington Custot Galleries
Claes Oldenburg & Coosje van Bruggen
Leaning Fork with Meatball and Spaghetti III
1994

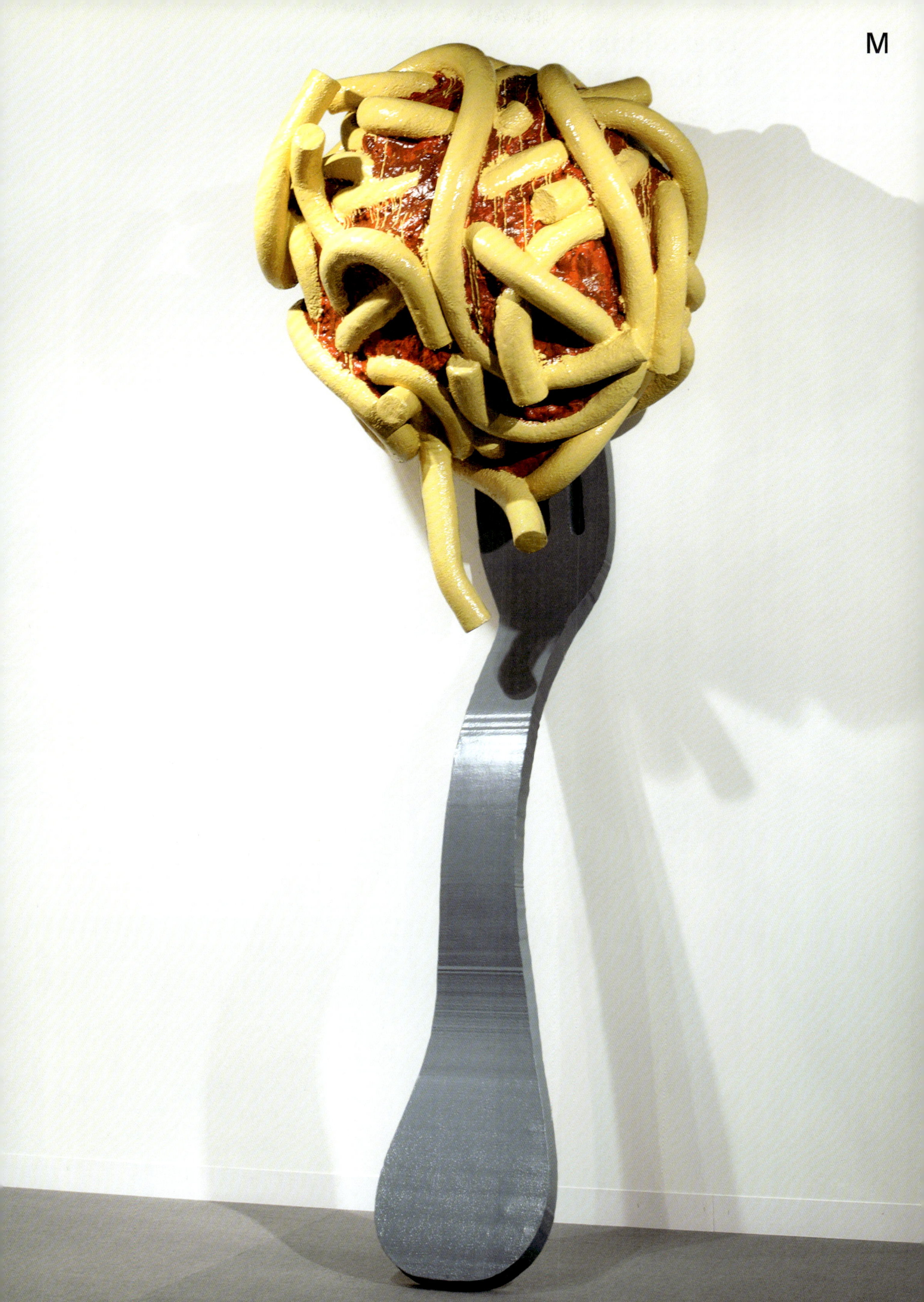

M

Leslie Tonkonow Artworks + Projects
Robert Watts
The American Supermarket
1962–2002

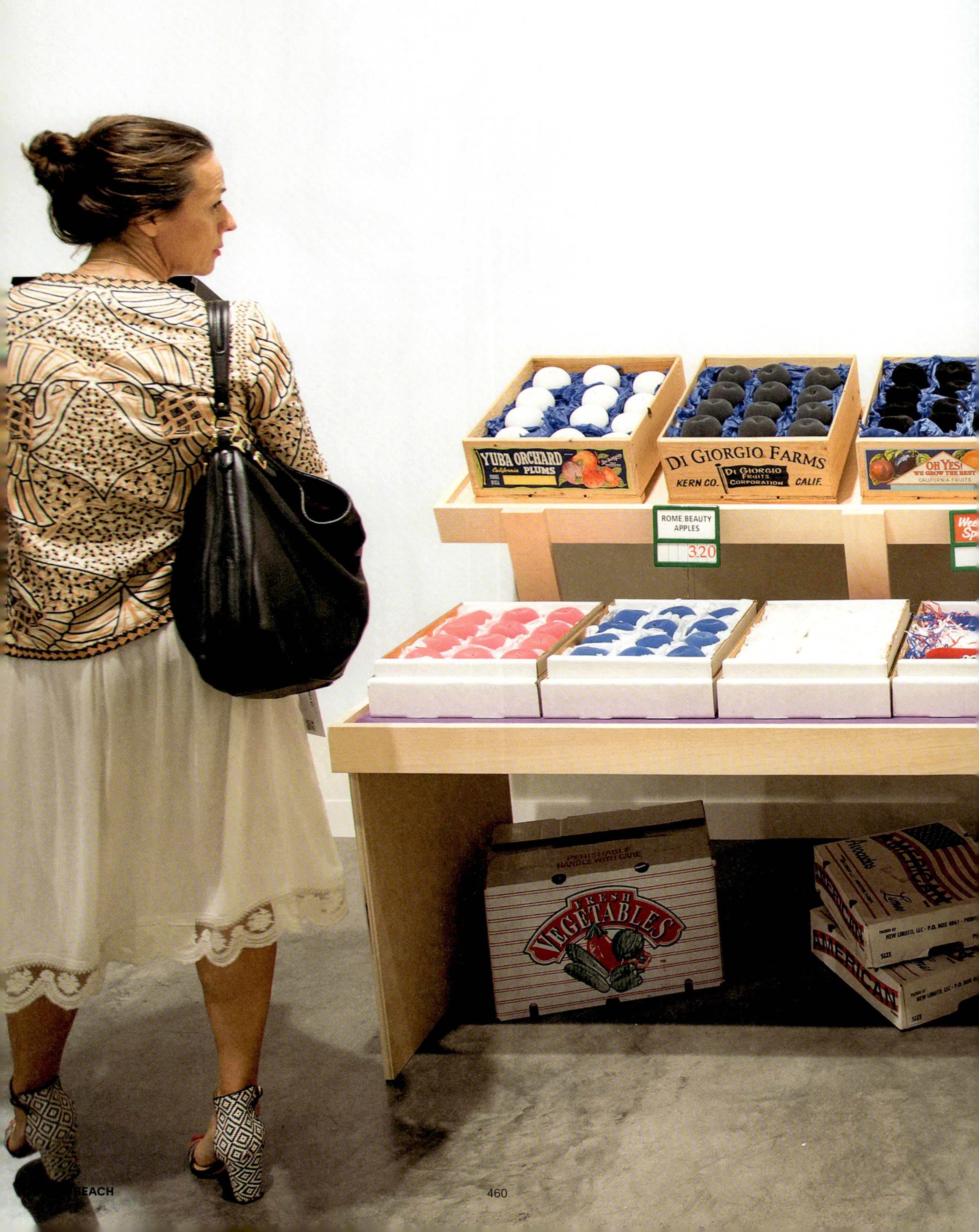

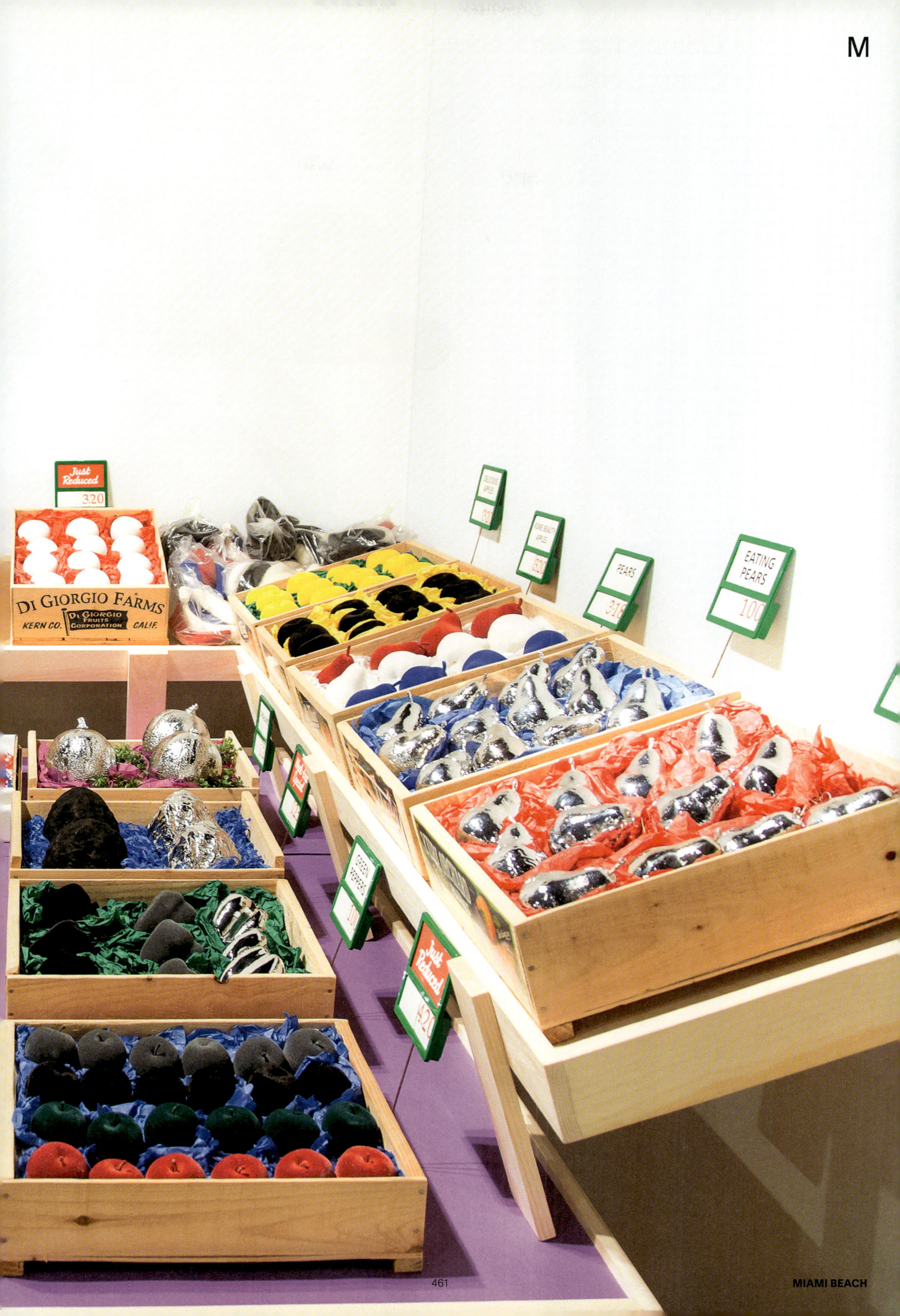
Just Reduced
320
DI GIORGIO FARMS
DI GIORGIO FRUITS CORPORATION
KERN CO.
CALIF.
PEARS
318
EATING PEARS
100
GREEN PEPPERS
Just Reduced

Galeria Nara Roesler
Carlo Carvalhosa

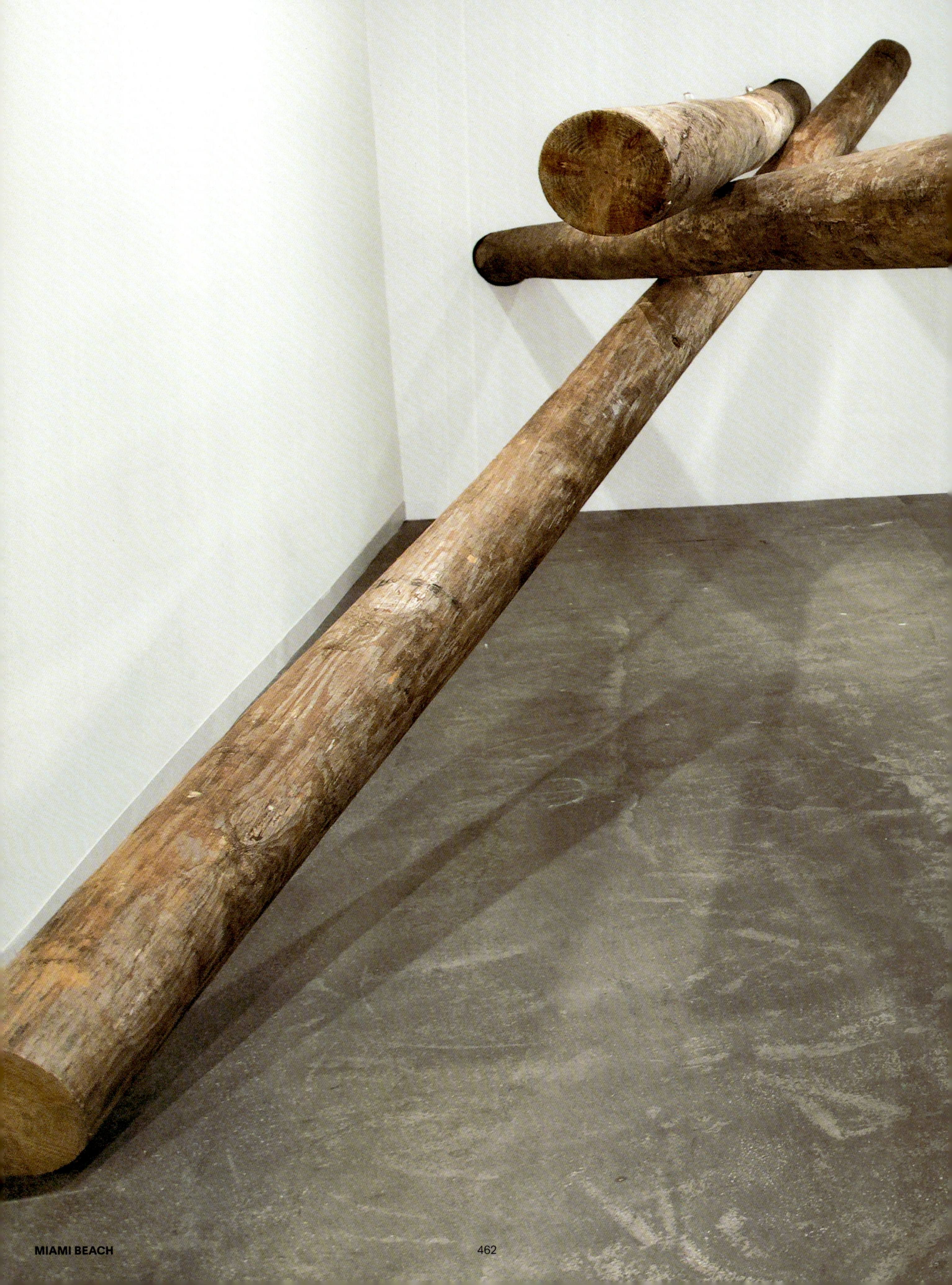

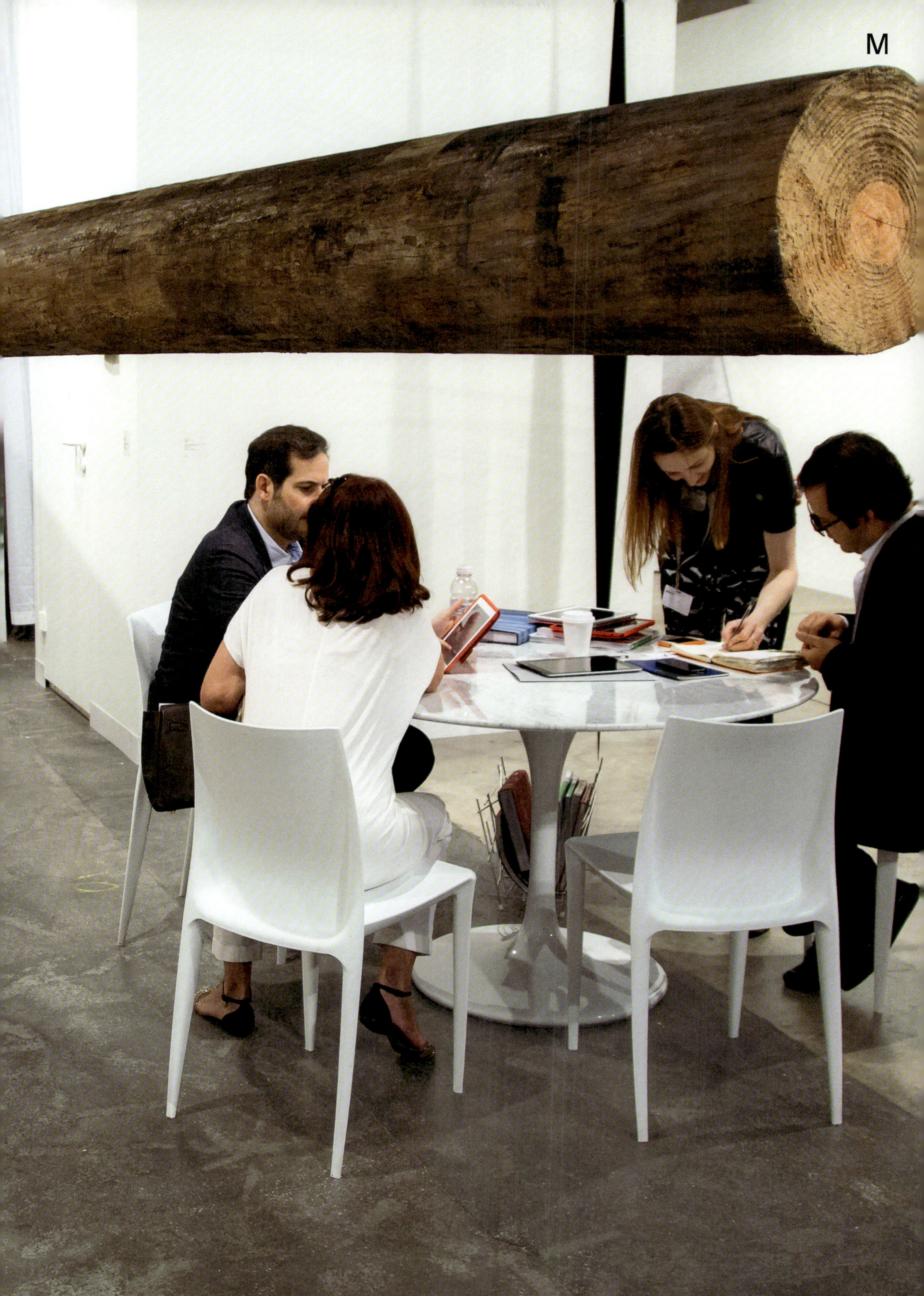

M

Nova Bar
Naomi Fisher & Jim Drain

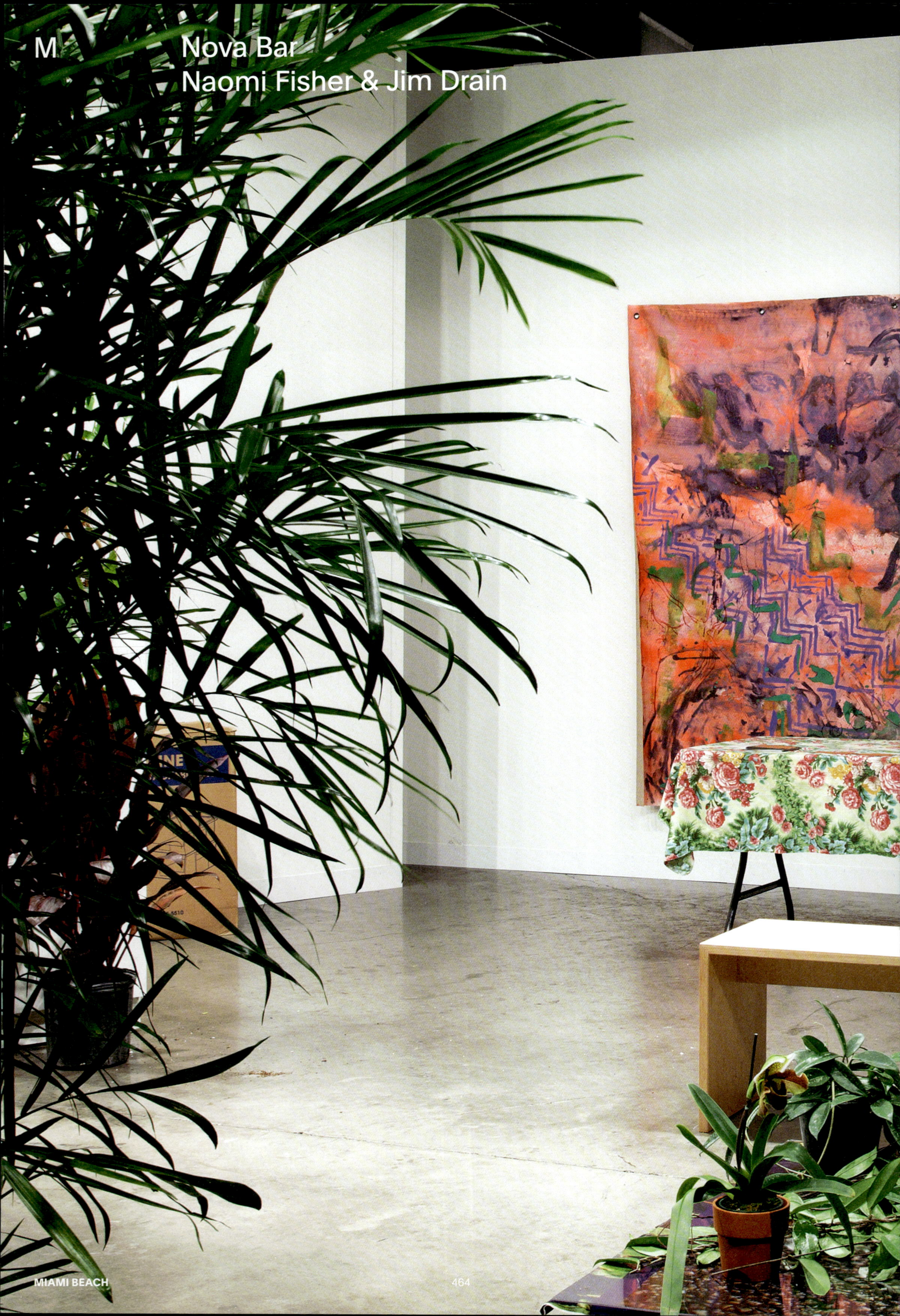

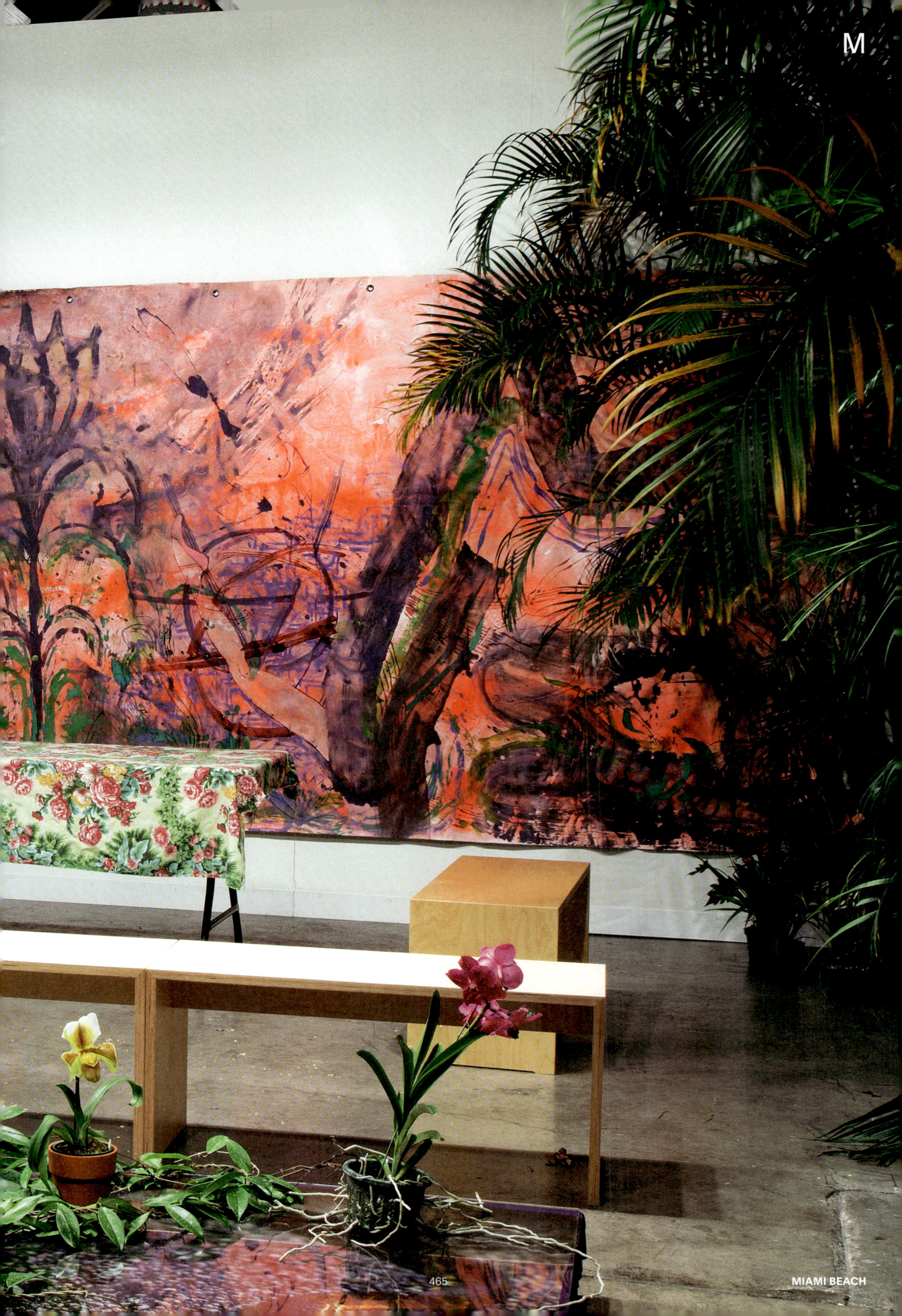

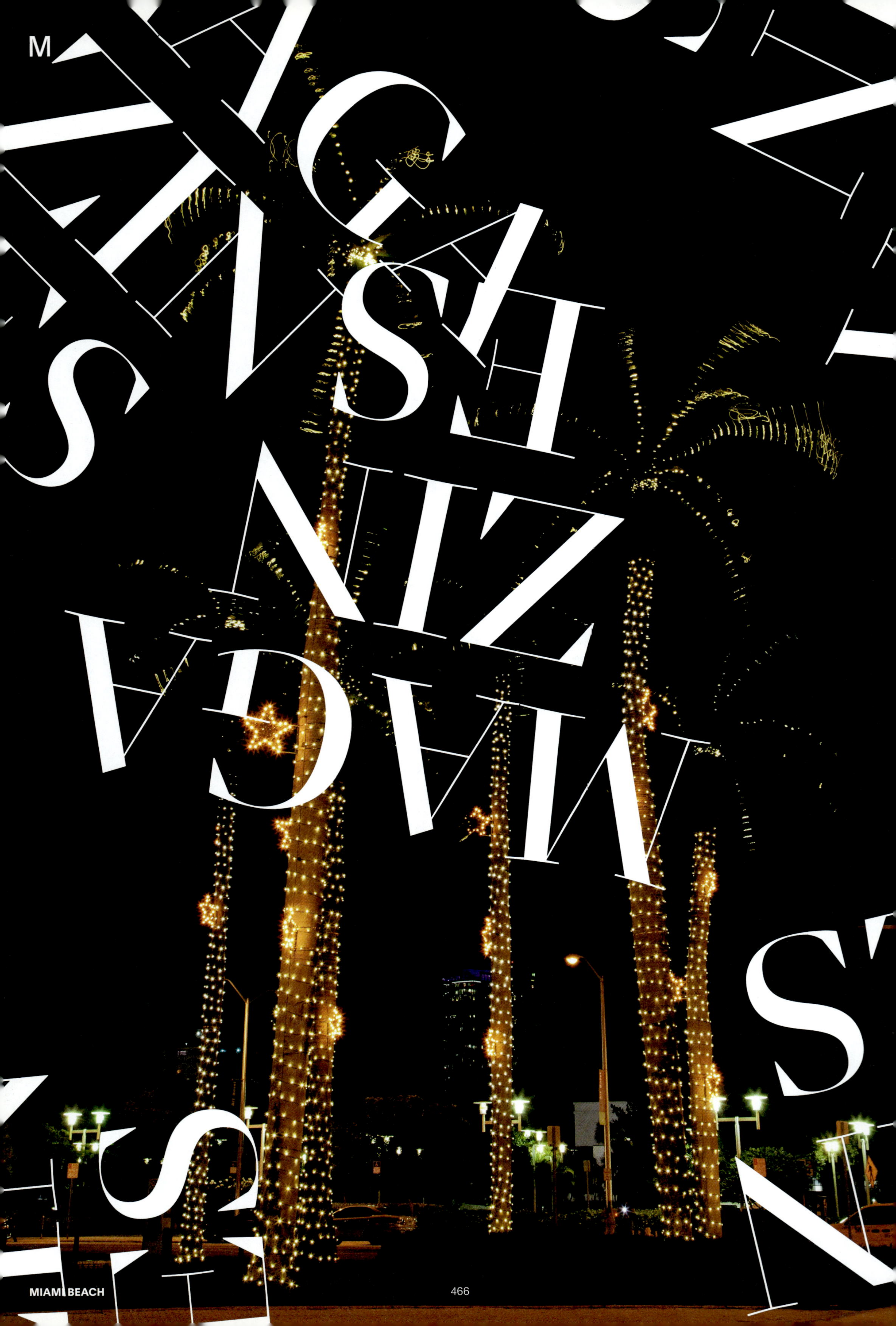

MAGAZINES

M

The Magazines sector, present at all three Art Basel exhibitions, features a selective range of premier publications. Visitors can explore both the art world's major internationally active publications as well as those that cover regional art scenes in greater detail and depth. Each year several publishers also offer limited-edition artworks created in direct collaboration with artists.

A

Adventice
Lausanne
adventice-editions.com

Aesthetica Magazine
York
aestheticamagazine.com

Afterall Journal
London
afterall.org

Aperture
New York
aperture.org

Art - Das Kunstmagazin
Hamburg
art-magazin.de

Art & Deal Magazine
New Delhi
artanddealmagazine.com

Art + Auction
New York
artinfo.com

Art.Investment
Taipei
arttouch.com/investment

Art Bank Magazine
Beijing
artbank.net.cn

Art Collector (Australian)
Ultimo
artcollector.net.au

Art Gallery Magazine
Guangzhou
53-gallery.com

Art in America
New York
artinamericamagazine.com

art in ASIA
Seoul
artinasia.kr

art ltd. magazine
Woodland Hills
artltdmag.com

Art Map
Hong Kong
artmap.com.hk

Art Metropole
Toronto
artmetropole.com

Art Papers
Atlanta
artpapers.org

art press
Paris
artpress.fr

art.es
Madrid
art-es.es

Artam Global Art & Design
Macka - Istanbul
artam.com

ArtAsiaPacific
Hong Kong
artasiapacific.com

ArtChronika Magazine
Moscow
artchronika.ru

Artco Monthly
Taipei
artouch.com/artco

ARTcollectors'
Tokyo
tomosha.com

Arte
Milano
cairoeditore.it

ARTE AL DIA International
Miami
artealdia.com

Arte al Limite
Santiago de Chile
arteallimite.com

Arte e Critica
Roma
arteecritica.it

Arte por Excelencias
La Habana
arteporexcelencis.com

Arte y Parte
Santander
arteyparte.com

Arte!Brasileiros
São Paulo
artebrasileiros.com.br

ARTEiN International Art Magazine
Venezia Mestre
artein.it

Artfacts.Net Ltd.
London
artfacts.net

ARTFORUM International Magazine
New York
artforum.com

Artitude Monthly
Taipei
yamore.com.tw

ArtNexus
Miami
artnexus.com

artports.com
Karlsruhe
artports.com

ArtPremium
Paris
artpremium.com

ArtPULSE
Miami
artpulsemagazine.com

ArtReview
London
artreview.com

Artron.net
Beijing
artron.net

B

Baku
London
baku-magazine.com

Beaux Arts magazine
Issy-les-Moulineaux
beauxartsmagazine.com

Bijutsu Techo - BT
Tokyo
bijutsu.co.jp/bt

Blouinartinfo.com Asia
New York
artinfo.com

Border Crossings
Winnipeg
bordercrossingsmag.com

Brownbook Magazine
Dubai
brownbook.me

C

Camera Austria International
Graz
camera-austria.at

Canvas
Dubai
canvasonline.com

Carrier Pigeon
New York
carrierpigeonmag.com

Carte d'Arte Magazine
Messina
cartedartemagazine.it

Chinese Contemporary Art News
Beijing
canart.com.tw

Contemporary Art Philippines
Pasig City
contemporaryartphilippines.com

Contemporary Artists
Chong Qing
artistchina.org

Cura.Magazine
Roma
curamagazine.com

D

Dardo Magazine
Santiago de Compostela
dardomagazine.com

DASartes
Rio de Janeiro
dasartes.com

Dear Dave Magazine
New York
deardavemagazine.com

DROME magazine
Brussels
dromemagazine.com

E

Elephant Magazine
Amsterdam
frameweb.com/elephant

esse arts + opinions
Montréal
esse.ca

ETC
Prevost
etcmontreal.com

Eyeline
Brisbane
eyelinepublishing.com

F

Fine Arts Literature
Wuhan
meishuwenxian.com

Fisheye magazine
Poggibonsi (Siena)
carlocambieditore.it

Flash Art
Milano
flashartonline.com

frieze
London
frieze.com

frieze d/e
Berlin
frieze-magazin.de

FUTURO contemporaryart
Meisterschwanden
futuro-magazin.ch

G

g&e
Madrid
grabadoyedicion.com

Gallery.spb
Saint-Petersburg
spb-gallery.info

H

Harper's Bazaar Art Arabia
Dubai
itp.com

Harper's Bazaar Art Brasil
São Paulo
harpersbazaar.com.br

Harper's Bazaar Art China
Beijing
bazaarart.com.cn

Harper's Bazaar Art Hong Kong
Hong Kong
scmpgroup.com

Harper's Bazaar Art Indonesia
Jakarta
harpersbazaar.co.id

Harper's Bazaar Art Russia
Moscow
bazaar.ru

Hi Art
Beijing
hiart.cn

I

Iberoamericana Internacional Magazine
Lima
iberointernacional.com

K

Kaleidoscope
Milano
kaleidoscope-press.com

KQ kunstquartal
Ostfildern
kq-daily.de

Kunst-Bulletin
Zürich
kunstbulletin.ch

L

Le Journal des Arts
Paris
lejournaldesarts.fr

Leap Magazine
Beijing
leapleapleap.com

LLEI D'ART
Alpicat - Lleida
lleidart.com

L'oeil
Paris
loeil.fr

L'OFFICIEL Art
Beijing
lofficielart.cn

M

Masdearte.com
Madrid
masdearte.com

Modern Painters
New York
artinfo.com

Monopol
Berlin
monopol-magazin.de

Mousse Magazine
Milano
moussemagazine.it

Mutualart.com
Brooklyn, NY
mutualart.com

99ArtWeb
Beijing
99ys.com

#

[Crudelia?]
Roma
crudeliartmagazine.com

N

NERO
Roma
neromagazine.it

Next Level
London
nextleveluk.com

P

Parkett
Zürich
parkettart.com

Parnass
Wien
parnass.at

photography-now.com
Berlin
photography-now.com

Pipeline Magazine
Sheung Wan, Hong Kong
pipelinemag.com

Prefix Photo Magazine
Toronto
prefix.ca

Printed Matter, Inc
New York
printedmatter.org

R

Res Art World / World Art
Istanbul
resartworld.com

Rooms Magazine
London
roomsmagazine.com

S

Sculpture
Hamilton
sculpture.org

Segno
Pescara
rivistasegno.eu

sleek magazine
Berlin
sleekmag.com

Some/Things Magazine
Paris
someslashthings.com

Spike Art Quarterly
Wien
spikeart.at

springerin
Wien
springerin.at

T

Tagboat/ TOKYO ART GUIDE
Tokyo
tagboat.com/artguide

Take on Art
New Delhi
takeonart.wordpress.com

Tar Mag
Firenze
tar-mag.com

tasj
New York
tasjmagazine.com

Texte zur Kunst
Berlin
textezurkunst.de

THAT Magazine
Istanbul

The Art Newspaper
London
theartnewspaper.com

The Pocket Arts Guide
Hong Kong
thepocketartsguide.com

The Wall
Gurgaon
thewallartmag.com

V

Vellum
Brooklyn, NY
vellumonline.com

W

Weltkunst
Hamburg
zeitkunstverlag.de

White Zinfandel
New York
whitezinf.org

Y

Yishu - Journal of Contemporary Chinese Art
Vancouver
yishu-online.com

Meyer Riegger

Berlin — Galleries Unlimited
Karlsruhe — Galleries

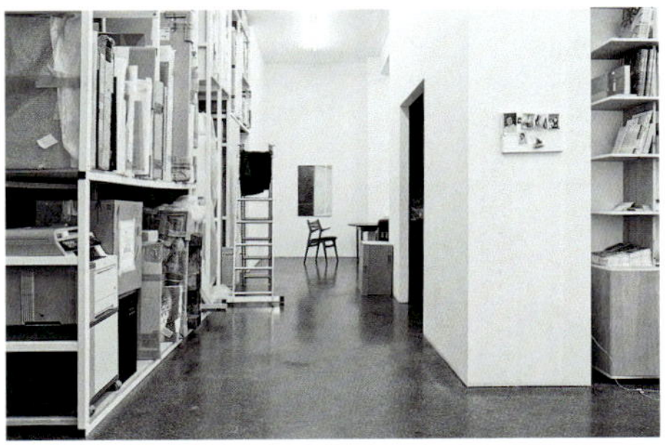

What first compelled you to open a gallery?
We started without any commercial intentions. Our impulse to engage in the field of contemporary art was the versatile art practice we experienced during our studies in Karlsruhe. First of all we were keen to create a platform for the art we were interested in, to force a public notion of the potential of these young artists from the Art Academy in Karlsruhe. We were invited by Liste to participate at their art fair in Basel already from our first year. That was the moment when we decided to become a commercial gallery. With our program we focus on conceptual positions that emphasize the emancipatory potential of art as well as underlining the transcendent capacity of its existence, while always remaining aware that art, as a product of human labor, also reflects society's condition of dependency.

Who is the first artist you showed and what was most memorable about that show?
We opened the gallery with the group show *And then there were none*, which showed pieces from the Marzona Collection, including the following artists: Stanley Brouwn, Jan Dibbets, Hans Haacke, Stephen Kaltenbach, On Kawara, Gordon Matta-Clark, Robert Morris, Gerry Schum, Robert Smithson, and Lawrence Weiner. That exhibition was thought as a reference to a certain era, and simultaneously was a benchmark for the following gallery program, in which we have tried to use the political and aesthetic potential of those positions as a link to the present.

- **Contact**: Meyer Riegger
  Eva Scherr
  eva@meyer-riegger.de
- **Established**: 1997
- **Owner(s) / Partner(s)**: Jochen Meyer
  Thomas Riegger
- **Space(s)**: 560 m² (two galleries)
- **Artists at Art Basel**: Franz Ackermann
  Katinka Bock
  Armin Boehm
  Björn Braun
  Miriam Cahn
  Henrik Håkansson
  Jamie Isenstein
  Eva Kotátková
  Ján Mancuška
  Meuser
  John Miller
  Helen Mirra
  Jonathan Monk
  Melvin Moti
  Scott Myles
  Paulo Nazareth
  Daniel Roth
  Julia Schmidt
  David Thorpe
  Tunga
  Gabriel Vormstein
  Waldemar Zimbelmann
- **Further artists represented**: Heike Aumüller
  Jeanne Faust
  Sebastian Hammwöhner
  Uwe Henneken
  Anna Lea Hucht
  Jamie Isenstein
  Korpys/Löffler
  Kalin Lindena
  Silke Schatz

Mezzanin

Vienna — Galleries, Feature, Galleries

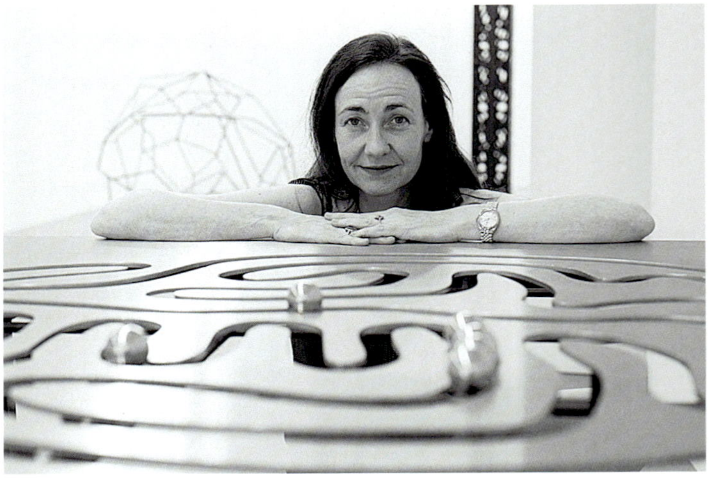

What first compelled you to open a gallery?
Gallery Mezzanin emerged from a non-commercial exhibition space that I had started in an untenanted flat in my mid-20s. After five years of running it I had to make a decision about the future of my growing network of artists with whom I worked closely. I decided to put my entire focus on the support and growth of artists by opening Galerie Mezzanin. The name of the gallery is a reminder of its roots, as the early exhibition space was located in a mezzanine.

Who is the first artist you showed and what was most memorable about that show?
The first show in the non-commercial exhibition space Mezzanin was a group show of students of the Academy of Fine Arts of Vienna. In the first year as a commercial gallery, in 2002, I had shows with Alexander Wolff, Sturtevant, Katrin Plavcak, Lisa Lapinski, and Catherine Sullivan among others. The excitement and special atmosphere of starting something new in those early days are very memorable even now.

When did you first participate in Art Basel and what was most memorable about that show?
The first participation of Mezzanin at Art Basel was in 2005 in the Statements sector, with a presentation of Alexander Wolff. At that point I had already worked closely with the artist for a number of years. It was special to have come such a long way together; from the early days of the exhibition space to finally present him at the most important art fair in the world.

- **Contact**: Galerie Mezzanin
  Karin Handlbauer
  office@galeriemezzanin.com
- **Established**: 2002
- **Owner(s) / Partner(s)**: Karin Handlbauer
- **Team**: 3
- **Space(s)**: 120 m²
- **Artists at Art Basel**: Etti Abergel
  Thomas Bayrle
  Marino Formenti
  Bernhard Frue
  Christian Mayer
  Marzena Nowak
  Stephen Prina
  Mandla Reuter
  Christina Zurfluh
- **Further artists represented**: Gerald Domenig
  Michael Hakimi
  Peter Kogler
  Lisa Lapinski
  Michelangelo Pistoletto
  Katrin Plavcak
  Santos R. Vasquez
  Sturtevant
  Alexander Wolff

Millan

São Paulo ● Galleries

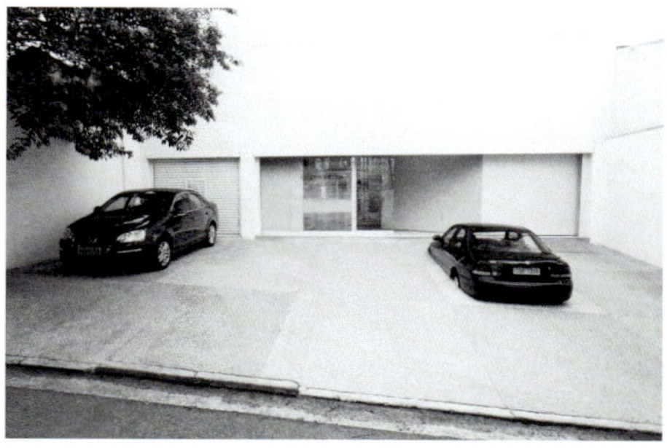

What first compelled you to open a gallery?
I majored in History and specialized in Art History, and my father already worked as a dealer, therefore I had developed an interest in art since I was young.

Who is the first artist you showed and what was most memorable about that show?
The first artist was Tunga, and the most memorable thing about the show was the quality of his works, both sculpture and drawing.

When did you first participate in Art Basel and what was most memorable about that show?
The first time we participated to Art Basel was in 2003. We were proud to be part of the greatest international art fair. I saw it as an acknowledgment of the hard work we had done, developing as an art gallery over the years.

- **Contact** Galeria Millan
Cristiane Komesu
cris@galeriamillan.com.br
galeria@galeriamillan.com.br
- **Established** 1986
- **Owner(s) / Partner(s)** André Millan (Founder and Partner-Owner)
Socorro de Andrade Lima (Partner-Owner)
- **Team** 13
- **Space(s)** 370 m²
- **Artists at Art Basel** Rodrigo Andrade
Artur Barrio
Rodrigo Bivar
Tatiana Blass
Sofia Borges
Felipe Cohen
Lenora de Barros
Nelson Felix
Dudi Maia Rosa
Anna Maria Maiolino
Rubens Mano
Emmanuel Nassar
Henrique Oliveira
Paulo Pasta
Ana Prata
Berna Reale
Miguel Rio Branco
Thiago Rocha Pitta
Otavio Schipper
Bob Wolfenson

Miller

New York ● Galleries

- **Contact** Robert Miller Gallery
rmg@robertmillergallery.com
- **Established** 1977
- **Owner(s) / Partner(s)** Betsy Wittenborn Miller
- **Artists at Art Basel** Diane Arbus
Louise Bourgeois
Eva Hesse
Lee Krasner
Yayoi Kusama
Joan Mitchell
Alice Neel
Patti Smith
- **Further artists represented** Justin Allen
Dirk Braeckman
Robert Greene
Bill Henson
Clarence John Laughlin
Herbert List
Walter Niedermayr
Willem Oorebeek
Hirsch Perlman
George Platt Lynes
Glen Rubsamen
Mayumi Terada

Francesca Minini

Milan ● Discoveries
● Nova

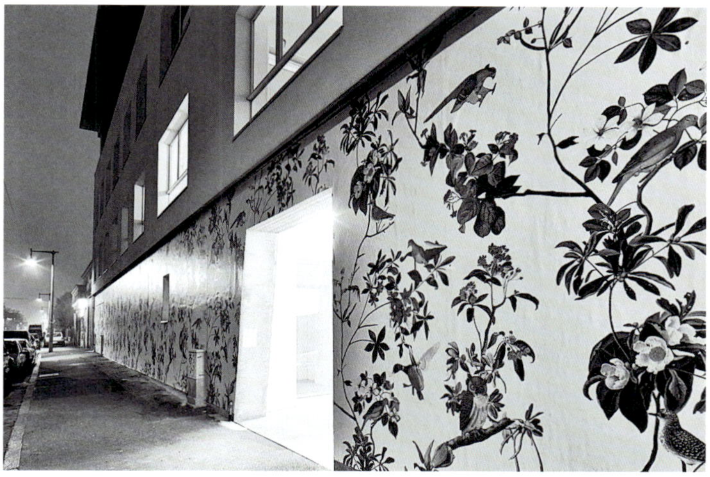

What first compelled you to open a gallery?
I'm the daughter of an incredible gallerist, Massimo Minini. Art and the art world have always been extremely present in our lives. Experiencing all this has naturally brought me to want to be part of it and to create my own history and research with the artists of my generation.

Who is the first artist you showed and what was most memorable about that show?
The first exhibition at the gallery, in 2006, was an impressive show of Riccardo Previdi. The whole project was revolving around a film by Claude Lelouch. It was incredible to witness the positive reaction to the project. The public came *en masse* to the opening and we got a lot of support from collectors, curators, and press. Our history started that night.

When did you first participate in Art Basel and what was most memorable about that show?
The next year (in 2007), we presented a site-specific installation of Riccardo Previdi, a memorable installation that we thought impossible to sell, but which sold immediately to an important museum; the work is still installed in their collection.

- **Contact** Francesca Minini
Anna Abbá
anna@francescaminini.it
info@francescaminini.it
- **Established** 2006
- **Owner(s) / Partner(s)** Francesca Minini
Alessandra Minini
- **Team** 5
- **Space(s)** 200 m²
- **Artists at Art Basel** Becky Beasley
Matthias Bitzer
Francesco Simeti
- **Further artists represented** Ghada Amer
Armin Boehm
Paolo Chiasera
Jan De Cock
Simon Dybbroe Møller
Giulio Frigo
Dan Graham
Ali Kazma
Deborah Ligorio
Gabriele Picco
Riccardo Previdi
Mandla Reuter

Massimo Minini

Brescia • Galleries

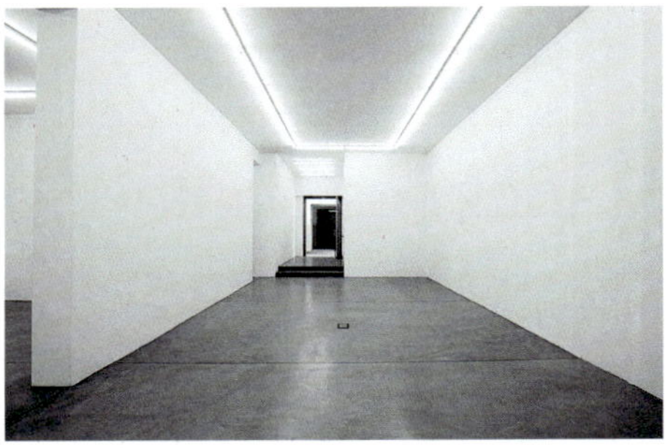

What first compelled you to open a gallery?
After my experience at *Flash Art* from 1971 to 1973, I needed to do something different, so it was logical for me to open my own gallery.

Who is the first artist you showed and what was most memorable about that show?
A group show, with Mel Bochner, Giuseppe Chiari, Hamish Fulton, Marco Gastini, Gilbert & George, Les Levine, Sol LeWitt, Roman Opałka, Ben Vautier, Dorothea Rockburne. Most memorable was the Gilbert & George work.

When did you first participate in Art Basel and what was most memorable about that show?
In 1977. The sale of a big double Boetti to the Hoffmann-La Roche collection made by the director of the Gegenwartskunst Museum in Basel.

- **Contact** Galleria Massimo Minini
  Valentina Costa
  valentina@galleriaminini.it
  info@galleriaminini.it
- **Established** 1973
- **Owner(s) / Partner(s)** Massimo Minini
- **Team** 8
- **Space(s)** 700 m²
- **Further artists represented** Carla Accardi
  Ghada Amer
  Stefano Arienti
  Roger Ballen
  Olivo Barbieri
  Robert Barry
  Gabriele Basilico
  Vanessa Beecroft
  Alighiero Boetti
  Monica Bonvicini
  Daniel Buren
  Letizia Cariello
  Jota Castro
  Elisabetta Catalano
  Paolo Chiasera
  Jan De Cock
  Maurizio Donzelli
  Jan Fabre
  Hans-Peter Feldmann
  Ian Hamilton Finlay
  Yona Friedman
  Alberto Garutti
  Luigi Ghirri
  Paolo Gioli
  Dan Graham
  Peter Halley
  Anish Kapoor
  Bertrand Lavier
  Sol LeWitt
  David Maljkovic
  Eva Marisaldi
  Ryan Mendoza
  Mathieu Mercier
  Sabrina Mezzaqui
  Paul P.
  Giulio Paolini
  Nedko Solakov
  Ettore Spalletti
  Haim Steinbach
  Paul Thorel
  Ian Wilson
  Betty Woodman

Mirchandani + Steinruecke

Mumbai • Insights

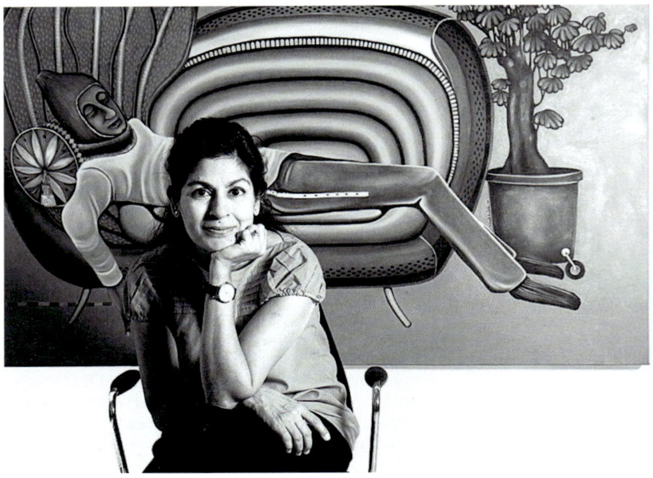

What first compelled you to open a gallery?
Usha Mirchandani had been dealing in Indian modern and contemporary art and worked as a consultant for the Deutsche Bank Art Collection in India. She had also curated a retrospective of Bhupen Khakhar at the National Gallery of Modern Art in Mumbai. Her daughter Ranjana Steinruecke ran a space for contemporary Indian art in Berlin, and when she returned to Mumbai, they decided to launch the gallery Mirchandani + Steinruecke together, to express their vision within the context of emerging art in India.

Who is the first artist you showed and what was most memorable about that show?
Jyothi Basu is the first artist we showed. It resurrected him because he had taken a seven-year hiatus from painting. He made some of the most riveting and memorable paintings for that show.

When did you first participate in Art Basel and what was most memorable about that show?
In 2013 in Hong Kong. It was a marvelous experience to meet Chinese collectors interested in and buying art from India.

- **Contact** Galerie Mirchandani + Steinruecke
  Ranjana Steinruecke
  ranjana@galeriems.com
- **Established** 2006
- **Owner(s) / Partner(s)** Usha Mirchandani (Owner)
  Ranjana Steinruecke (Director)
- **Space(s)** 200 m²
- **Artists at Art Basel** Manish Nai
- **Further artists represented** Vinod Balak
  Jyothi Basu
  Nicola Durvasula
  Tanya Goel
  Sosa Joseph
  Abir Karmakar
  Siji Krishnan
  Sarika Mehta
  Kanishka Raja
  C.K. Rajan
  Ranjith Raman
  Surabhi Saraf
  Varunika Saraf
  Vidha Saumya
  Ratheesh T.
  Parul Thacker
  Aji V.N.

Miro

London

- Galleries
- Galleries Unlimited
- Galleries

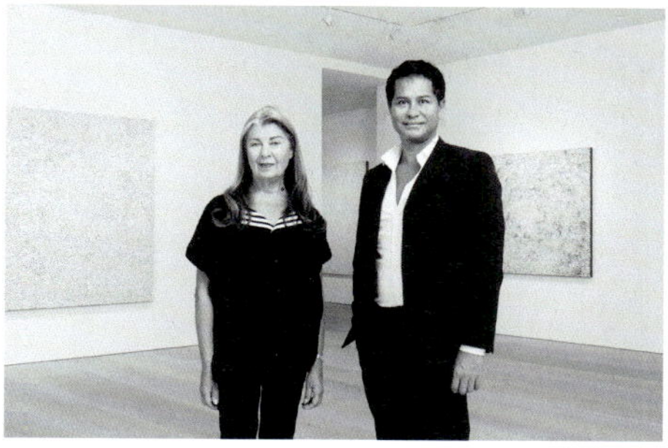

What first compelled you to open a gallery?
A desire to show those whom you really believe in, to give them a platform, and make sure they are seen. What you are trying to do is present the artist in the very best way possible so that other people see in that artist what you see.

Who is the first artist you showed and what was most memorable about that show?
One of the earliest exhibitions was *Marat assassiné* by Ian Hamilton Finlay. The exhibition was very well received, especially by curators (including Richard Morphet from Tate). One of the central works in the exhibition was *Four Guillotine Blades* (1987).

When did you first participate in Art Basel and what was most memorable about that show?
It was in the mid-1990s and I particularly remember bringing a number of wonderful works by Peter Doig and Andreas Gursky. I'm not sure any collectors even asked for prices, they certainly did not sell—how things have changed!

- **Contact** Victoria Miro
  Mary McNicholas
  mary.eleanor@victoria-miro.com
  info@victoria-miro.com
- **Established** 1985
- **Owner(s) / Partner(s)** Victoria Miro
  W. P. Miro
  Glenn Scott Wright
- **Team** 35
- **Space(s)** 1,765 m² (three galleries)
- **Artists at Art Basel** Doug Aitken
  Hernan Bas
  Varda Caivano
  Verne Dawson
  Jules de Balincourt
  Peter Doig
  Stan Douglas
  William Eggleston
  Elmgreen & Dragset
  Inka Essenhigh
  Barnaby Furnas
  Ian Hamilton Finlay
  David Harrison
  NS Harsha
  Alex Hartley
  Christian Holstad
  Chantal Joffe
  Isaac Julien
  Idris Khan
  John Kørner
  Udomsak Krisanamis
  Yayoi Kusama
  Wangechi Mutu
  Alice Neel
  Maria Nepomuceno
  Chris Ofili
  Jacco Olivier
  Grayson Perry
  Tal R
  Conrad Shawcross
  Sarah Sze
  Adriana Varejão
  Suling Wang
  Stephen Willats
  Francesca Woodman

Mitchell-Innes & Nash

New York

- Galleries Unlimited
- Galleries

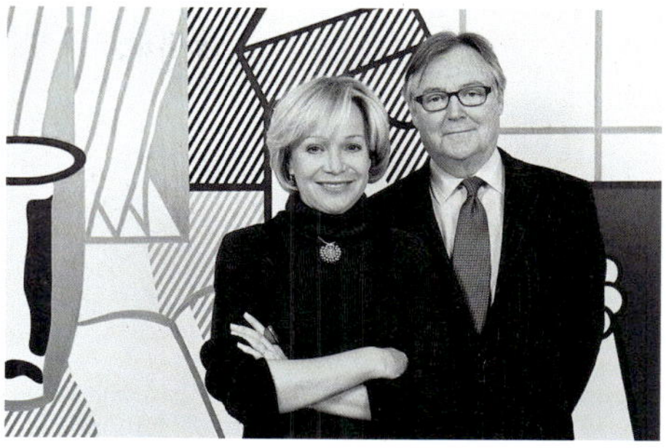

What first compelled you to open a gallery?
Since opening our gallery in 1996, Mitchell-Innes & Nash has sought to place contemporary artists within a historical context, revealing a continuity of ideas and aesthetic concerns from the modern era through the present. Our recent additions to the program are a reflection of this mission, which is presented in exhibitions from prominent estates, 20th-century masters, and by well-established and emerging artists in both our uptown and downtown locations.

Who is the first artist you showed and what was most memorable about that show?
Our first exhibitions focused on modern artists who pushed the evolution of art history forward, but were less known in the US than we felt they deserved to be. In our first years we presented retrospectives of Nicolas de Staël, Georges Braque, Jean Arp, and Edvard Munch in addition to our postwar estates. What became abundantly clear was that there was not only a desire for these shows from the art-appreciating public, but that collectors too were eager to discover or rediscover work by these seminal figures.

When did you first participate in Art Basel and what was most memorable about that show?
Our first participation as an exhibitor at Art Basel was in 1999 and although we had attended the fair in the past as visitors we were memorably taken by the passion and knowledge that the guests to the fair brought with them.

- **Contact** Mitchell-Innes & Nash
  Josephine Nash
  josie@miandn.com
  info@miandn.com
- **Established** 1996
- **Owner(s) / Partner(s)** David Nash
  Lucy Mitchell-Innes
- **Team** 12
- **Space(s)** 464 m²
- **Artists at Art Basel** Jean Arp
  Sarah Braman
  Alberto Burri
  Anthony Caro
  Allan D'Arcangelo
  Jay DeFeo
  Keltie Ferris
  Chris Johanson
  Martin Kersels
  Leon Kossoff
  Justine Kurland
  Daniel Lefcourt
  Alexander Liberman
  Roy Lichtenstein
  Chris Martin
  Christopher Miner
  Kenneth Noland
  Catherine Opie
  Virginia Overton
  William Pope.L
  Martha Rosler
  Amanda Ross-Ho
  Norbert Schwontkowski
  Julian Stanczak
  Jessica Stockholder
  Jack Tworkov
  Paul Winstanley

Mizuma

Tokyo
Singapore
Beijing

Galleries
Encounters

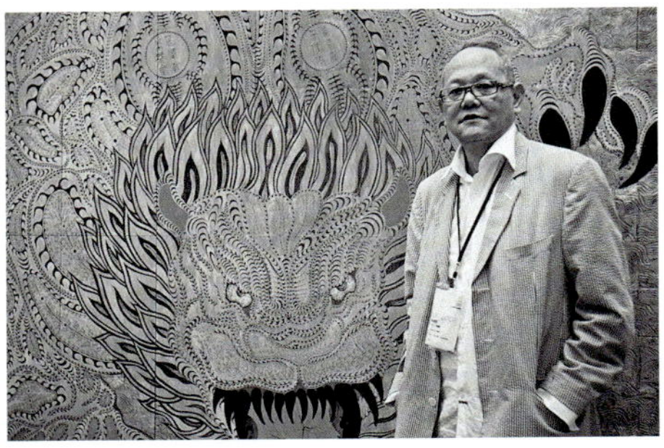

What first compelled you to open a gallery?
I was collecting art and nobody was supporting the young artists that I liked so I decided to open my own gallery.

Who is the first artist you showed and what was most memorable about that show?
Aki Kuroda. He is a Japanese artist who lives in Paris and I learned a lot from him about the international contemporary art scene.

When did you first participate in Art Basel and what was most memorable about that show?
The first time was at Art Basel in Miami Beach back in 2002. I am glad now that an international fair of such a scale has eventually come to Asia.

- **Contact** Mizuma Art Gallery
Antoine Perrin
antoine@mizuma.sg
gallery@mizuma-art.co.jp
- **Established** 1994
- **Owner(s) / Partner(s)** Sueo Mizuma
- **Team** 15
- **Space(s)** 500 m²
- **Artists at Art Basel** Makoto Aida
Yoshitaka Amano
Sai Hashizume
Takashi Hinoda
Toru Ishii
Tomiyuki Kaneko
Hyung Koo Kang
Tomoko Konoike
Mikiko Kumazawa
Jane Lee
Natsunosuke Mise
Aiko Miyanaga
Susan Philipsz
Koji Tanada
teamLab
Hisashi Tenmyouya
Akira Yamaguchi
Taro Yamamoto
Fumio Yamazaki
Zheng Jiang
- **Further artists represented** Satoru Aoyama
Manabu Ikeda
Akino Kondoh
Kun Du
Jin Kurashige
Li Hongbo
Hiroyuki Matsukage
Junichi Mori
Kaoru Motomiya
Jun Nguyen-Hatsushiba
O Jun
Hiroko Okada
Masakatsu Sashie
Shinsuke Tsutsui
Ai Yamaguchi
Masao Yamamoto
Ryuki Yamamoto
Zhao Na

Mnuchin

New York

Galleries
Galleries

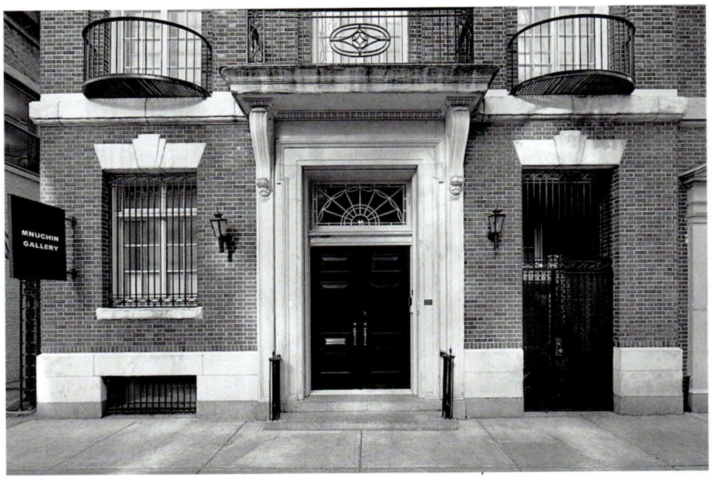

What first compelled you to open a gallery?
Passion and art; this was the way to have it surround your life.

Who is the first artist you showed and what was most memorable about that show?
Willem de Kooning: *Transcending Landscape Paintings 1975–1979*. The show was early recognition of de Kooning's works from the 1970s, which was a truly extraordinary period.

When did you first participate in Art Basel and what was most memorable about that show?
Seventeen years ago. My gallery, C&M Arts at the time, was surrounded by international galleries of stature and great taste. To be amid this extraordinary collection of galleries was truly remarkable.

- **Contact** Mnuchin Gallery
Hudson Nicole
nicole@mnuchingallery.com
contact@mnuchingallery.com
- **Established** 1992
- **Owner(s) / Partner(s)** Robert Mnuchin (Owner)
Sukanya Rajaratnam (Partner)
- **Space(s)** 215 m²
- **Artists at Art Basel** Alexander Calder
John Chamberlain
Joseph Cornell
Willem de Kooning
Richard Diebenkorn
Jean Dubuffet
Lucio Fontana
Sam Francis
Alberto Giacometti
David Hammons
Donald Judd
Ellsworth Kelly
Franz Kline
Jeff Koons
Barbara Kruger
Roy Lichtenstein
Piero Manzoni
Brice Marden
Agnes Martin
Joan Miró
Pablo Picasso
Mark Rothko
Ed Ruscha
Robert Ryman
David Smith
Frank Stella
Cy Twombly
Andy Warhol

Modern Art

London

- Galleries
- Galleries Unlimited Parcours
- Galleries

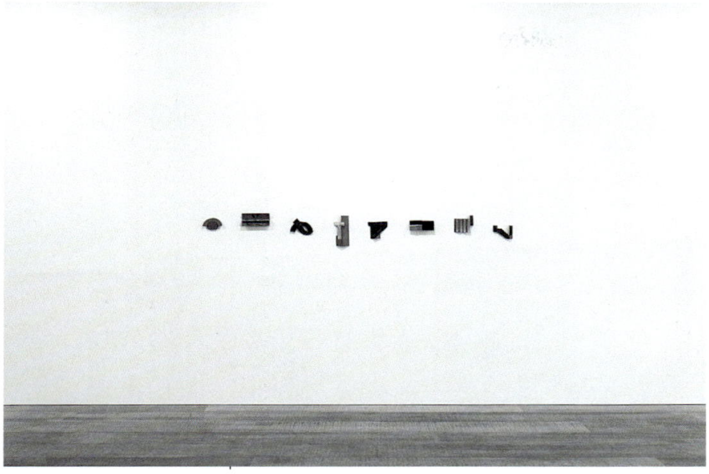

What first compelled you to open a gallery?
The decision to open a gallery was compelled by the lucky coincidences of having a number of artist friends who didn't yet have representation, the enthusiasm of my former business partners Detmar and Isabella Blow to support me in opening a gallery together, and that the landscape in London that could not have been more different in the late 1990s. Fifteen years ago it felt like there was the space for new galleries and artists needed them.

When did you first participate in Art Basel and what was most memorable about that show?
My first participation in Art Basel was a Statements stand with the artist Eva Rothschild in 2003.

• **Contact**	Stuart Shave/Modern Art Ryan Moore ryan@modernart.net info@modernart.net
• **Established**	1998
• **Owner(s) / Partner(s)**	Stuart Shave (Founder and Owner) Jimi Lee (Partner)
• **Team**	7
• **Space(s)**	150 m² (500 m² in 2014)
• **Artists at Art Basel**	David Altmejd Karla Black Tom Burr Nigel Cooke Mark Flood Tim Gardner Lothar Hempel Jacqueline Humphries Ansel Krut Phillip Lai Paul Lee Linder Barry McGee Jonathan Meese Matthew Monahan Katy Moran David Noonan Anna-Bella Papp Eva Rothschild Bojan Šarcevic Lara Schnitger Collier Schorr Steven Shearer Ricky Swallow Richard Tuttle Clare Woods

Modern Institute

Glasgow

- Galleries
- Galleries

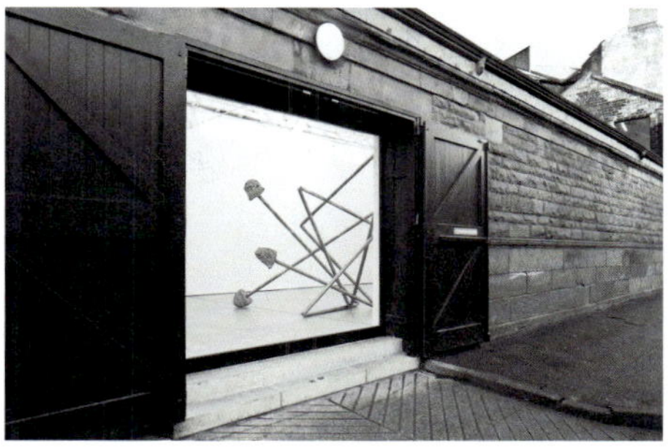

What first compelled you to open a gallery?
I was surrounded by amazing artists who were not represented and starting to look elsewhere for representation. Glasgow needed to have a gallery that worked in the local context.

Who is the first artist you showed and what was most memorable about that show?
Simon Starling, *Le Jardin Suspendu*. All the artists helped build the space—we even sold the work to a museum, which was a good place to start.

When did you first participate in Art Basel and what was most memorable about that show?
2001, Statements, Cathy Wilkes. We'd sold it all in the first hour of Statements and won the Baloise Art Prize. It was really important how seriously people tock the gallery.

• **Contact**	The Modern Institute / Toby Webster Ltd Margot Samel margot@themoderninstitute.com mail@themoderninstitute.com
• **Established**	1998
• **Owner(s) / Partner(s)**	Toby Webster (Owner) Andrew Hamilton (Partner)
• **Team**	15
• **Space(s)**	1,342 m²
• **Artists at Art Basel**	Dirk Bell Martin Boyce Jeremy Deller Alex Dordoy Urs Fischer Kim Fisher Luke Fowler Henrik Håkansson Mark Handforth Thomas Houseago Richard Hughes Chris Johanson William E. Jones Andrew Kerr Jim Lambie Duncan MacQuarrie Adam McEwen Victoria Morton Scott Myles Nicolas Party Toby Paterson Simon Periton Manfred Pernice Mary Redmond Anselm Reyle Eva Rothschild Monika Sosnowska Simon Starling Katja Strunz Tony Swain Spencer Sweeney Joanne Tatham & Tom O'Sullivan Pádraig Timoney Hayley Tompkins Sue Tompkins Cathy Wilkes Michael Wilkinson Gregor Wright Richard Wright

Chaïm Soutine
Kees van Dongen
Vincent van Gogh

Moeller

New York
Berlin

Galleries

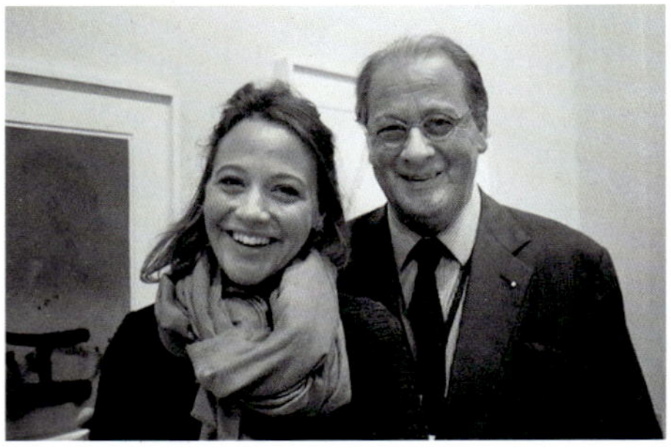

What first compelled you to open a gallery?
Achim Moeller had worked in galleries since 1965 (Cologne, New York), so it was a logical step to open his own gallery, first in 1972 (in London), then with Stephanie Moeller in 2009 (in Berlin).

Who is the first artist you showed and what was most memorable about that show?
A group show with Sisley, Monet, Kandinsky, Klee, Feininger, Max Ernst, Lehmbruck, Kirchner, Masson, Pollock, Tobey, Motherwell, David Smith … Most memorable was its unexpected success in 1972 in London.

When did you first participate in Art Basel and what was most memorable about that show?
In 1970, or 1971 with Marlborough-Gerson, and in the mid-1970s with my gallery (Achim Moeller Ltd). Most memorable is the big difference between Art Basel then and now.

- **Contact** Moeller Fine Art
Patrick Monahan
patrick@moellerfineart.com
mail@moellerfineart.com
- **Established** 1972
- **Owner(s) / Partner(s)** Achim Moeller (CEO & Owner)
Stephanie Moeller (CEO & Partner)
- **Team** 10
- **Space(s)** 450 m²
- **Artists at Art Basel** Karel Appel
Jean Arp
Max Beckmann
Alexander Calder
Christo
Piero Dorazio
Jean Dubuffet
Marcel Duchamp
Lyonel Feininger
George Grosz
Wassily Kandinsky
Ernst Ludwig Kirchner
Ronald B. Kitaj
Paul Klee
Richard Lindner
Heinz Mack
Marino Marini
Henry Moore
Robert Motherwell
Emil Nolde
Pablo Picasso
Otto Piene
Kurt Seligmann
David Smith
Mark Tobey
Alexej von Jawlensky
- **Further artists represented** Giacomo Balla
Georges Braque
Honoré Daumier
Robert Delaunay
Maurice Denis
Lucio Fontana
Paul Gauguin
David Hockney
Alain Jacquet
Yves Klein
Franz Kline
Jacques Lipchitz
Aristide Maillol
Albert Marquet
Henri Matisse
Amedeo Modigliani
Jackson Pollock
Auguste Rodin
Lucas Samaras
Paul Signac

Monclova

Mexico D.F.

Feature
Galleries

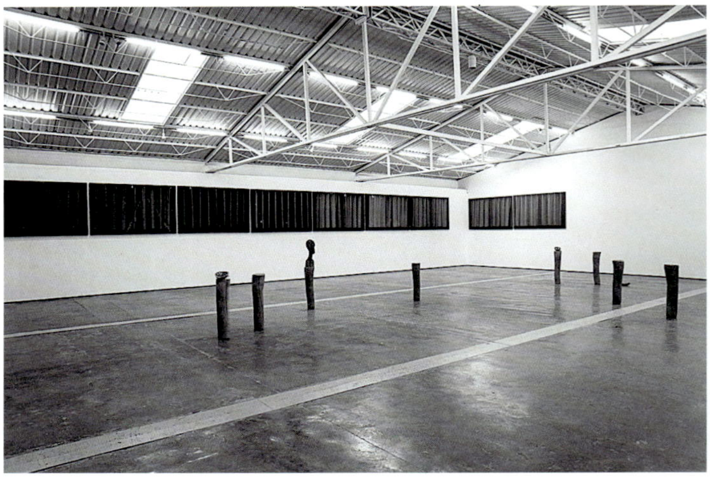

What first compelled you to open a gallery?
At the time (2005) in Mexico City, there were very few contemporary art galleries, most of which had very definite, structured programs; the time was right to open a project space to experiment with making exhibitions that showed young artists without the aim of profit. This was the case until 2008 when we decided to evolve into a commercial space and when we started to formally represent artists, as a result of the natural evolution of the project and as a natural demand of the artists' developing careers.

Who is the first artist you showed and what was most memorable about that show?
The first artist we showed was Todd Cole, an LA-based artist. He was very special for us. I had been collaborating for a long time with Cole in *Celeste* magazine, a publication that I directed, and it was a natural transition to open the space with his work, which was in the limit between the art world and the film world of Hollywood.

When did you first participate in Art Basel and what was most memorable about that show?
Our first participation in Art Basel in Miami Beach was in 2008 with a project for Positions, with works by Mario García Torres and Marco Rountree. It was the last year that the sector had the containers by the beach. We had a lot of fun and we met fantastic people with whom we established long-term relationships.

- **Contact** Proyectos Monclova
José García
jose@proyectosmonclova.com
info@proyectosmonclova.com
- **Established** 2005/2008
- **Owner(s) / Partner(s)** José García
Teofilo Cohen
David Trabulsi
- **Team** 7
- **Space(s)** 1,200 m²
- **Artists at Art Basel** Nina Beier
Simon Fujiwara
Mario Garcia Torres
Eduardo Terrazas
- **Further artists represented** Edgardo Aragón
François Bucher
José León Cerrillo
Tania Pérez Córdova
Christian Jankowski
Marie Lund
Eduardo Sarabia
Tercerunquinto

Monitor

Rome
New York

Discoveries

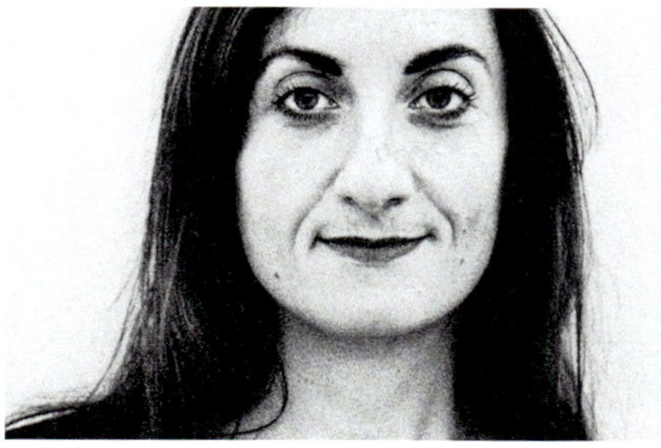

What first compelled you to open a gallery?
I decided to open Monitor during my PhD at Rome University (La Sapienza) when I was 28. I wanted to have my own space, to show the artists I liked without any kind of compromises.

Who is the first artist you showed and what was most memorable about that show?
Rä di Martino. The most memorable thing was that nobody from the art system was there. Nowadays, Ra di Martino shows at Tate Modern, Sandretto Re Rebaudengo, Adelaide International. This is also quite memorable.

When did you first participate in Art Basel and what was most memorable about that show?
In the Statements sector in 2010, with Francesco Arena. The most memorable thing was that we were all standing in an empty booth with just a carved stone in the middle.

- **Contact** Monitor
Manuela Contino
monitor@monitoronline.org
- **Established** 2003
- **Owner(s) / Partner(s)** Paola Capata
- **Team** 4
- **Space(s)** 120 m²
- **Artists at Art Basel** Adam Avikainen
- **Further artists represented** Francesco Arena
Jesse Ash
Peter Linde Busk
Tomaso De Luca
Rä di Martino
Graham Hudson
Ursula Mayer
Nathaniel Mellors
Antonio Rovaldi
Alexandre Singh
Ian Tweedy
Guido van der Werve
Nico Vascellari
Kostis Velonis
ZimmerFrei

mor charpentier

Paris
Bogotá

Nova

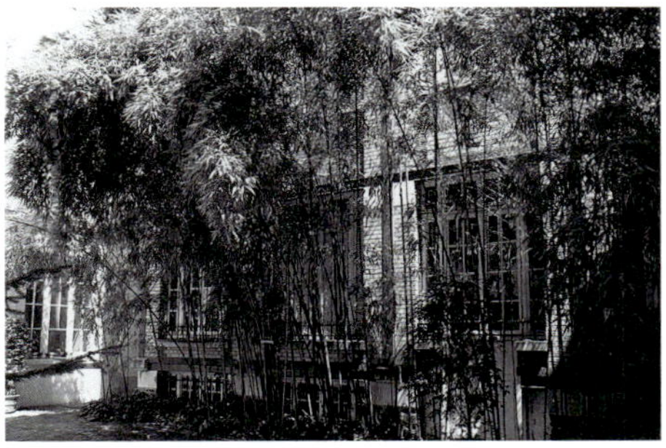

What first compelled you to open a gallery?
Alex Mor: My dad is a collector, it was somehow a romantic childhood dream; nowadays I realize that it was very easy to leave a corporate "safe" life for the uncertainties of the art world.
Philippe Charpentier: Passion!

Who is the first artist you showed and what was most memorable about that show?
Oscar Muñoz, a major Colombian artist. An hour before the opening we had an armada of workers trying to finish the walls and floor on time, and a plumber trying to fix a flood within our video installation! We were so stressed that we don't remember much about the opening, it was great, but we have no clear memories about it.

When did you first participate in Art Basel and what was most memorable about that show?
In 2012, a solo show with Julieta Aranda. Memorable? The fantastic sales!

- **Contact** mor charpentier
Alex Mor
alex@mor-charpentier.com
contact@mor-charpentier.com
- **Established** 2010
- **Owner(s) / Partner(s)** Alex Mor
Philippe Charpentier
- **Space(s)** 135 m² (Paris)
currently 2,000 m² (Bogotá, itinerant gallery)
- **Artists at Art Basel** Julieta Aranda
Voluspa Jarpa
Oscar Muñoz
- **Further artists** Alexander Apóstol
Maria José Arjona
Milena Bonilla
Cevdet Erek
Maria Elvira Escallón
Marcos López
Teresa Margolles
Enzo Mianes
Mohamed Namou
Yoshua Okón
Uriel Orlow
Liliana Porter
Charwei Tsai

Mot

Brussels

Galleries

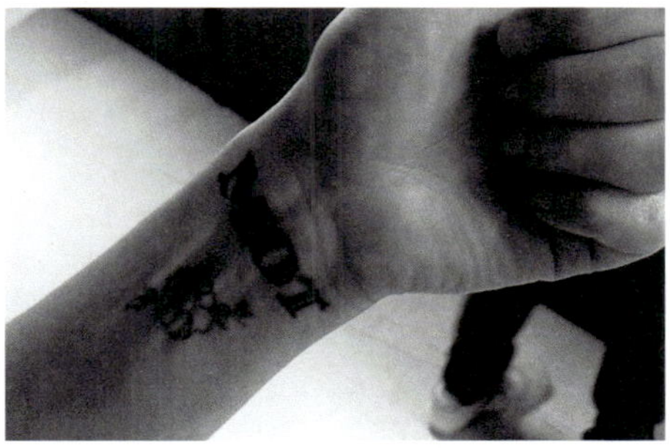

What first compelled you to open a gallery?
Freedom.

Who is the first artist you showed and what was most memorable about that show?
Pierre Bismuth—the quality!

When did you first participate in Art Basel and what was most memorable about that show?
In 1999, with Uri Tzaig. Its poetry.

- **Contact** Jan Mot
office@janmot.com
- **Established** 1996
- **Owner(s) / Partner(s)** Jan Mot
- **Artists at Art Basel** Sven Augustijnen
Pierre Bismuth
Manon de Boer
Rineke Dijkstra
Mario Garcia Torres
Dominique Gonzalez-Foerster
Douglas Gordon
Joachim Koester
David Lamelas
Sharon Lockhart
readymades belong to everyone®
Tino Sehgal
Tris Vonna-Michell
Ian Wilson

M

mother's tankstation

Dublin

- Galleries
- Discoveries
- Statements

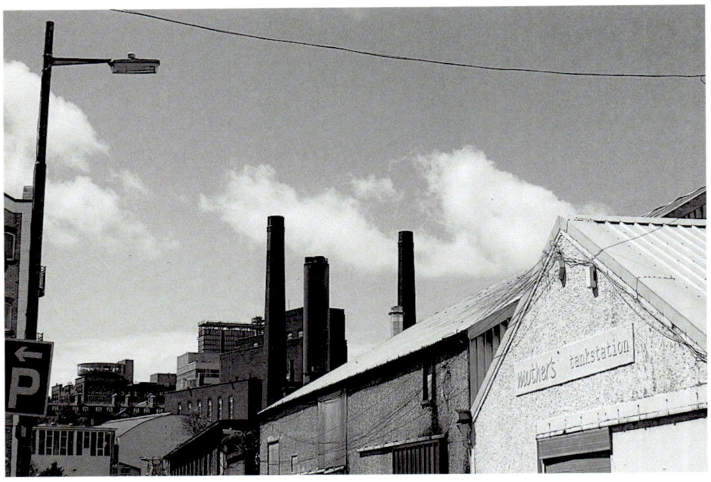

What first compelled you to open a gallery?
When I opened the gallery in 2006, it was for a couple of major reasons. Ostensibly, there appeared to be a significant culture gap in the Irish contemporary art environment that dominantly ignored or seemed to preclude almost a generation of very good artists who were working with more challenging conceptual and structural forms. The existing scene seemed to import more artists than it exported and was poor at providing opportunities for younger practitioners. I wanted the gallery to directly address these problems and to be grounded in a thoughtful, intellectual place that foregrounded experimental, three and four dimensional practices; installation, sculpture, video, sound. Concept must drive form, so this of course, could not exclude any form, but rather focused critical excellence. At the time I was also running an MA course in Dublin that combined curatorial, critical, and practical pathways. Having thought this program for a couple of years, I was hoping that somebody would take what we were preaching and help open up the Irish scene. Frustratingly, this didn't appear to be happening; the best talent, as ever, was filtering away or hitting a wall, so I decided to quit teaching and do it myself. It has had an interesting ripple effect.

Who is the first artist you showed and what was most memorable about that show?
Nina Canell.

When did you first participate in Art Basel and what was most memorable about that show?
Our first participation was in 2008 in Art Statements in Art Basel.

- **Contact** — mother's tankstation
  Finola Jones
  gallery@motherstankstation.com
- **Established** — 2006
- **Owner(s) / Partner(s)** — Finola Jones
- **Team** — 4
- **Space(s)** — 150 m²
- **Artists at Art Basel** — Mairead O'hEocha, Brendan Earley, Uri Aran
- **Further artists represented** — Ian Burns, Nina Canell, Kevin Cosgrove, Fergus Feehily, Atsushi Kaga, Shane McCarthy, Matt Sheridan Smith, David Sherry

Mujin-to

Tokyo

- Discoveries

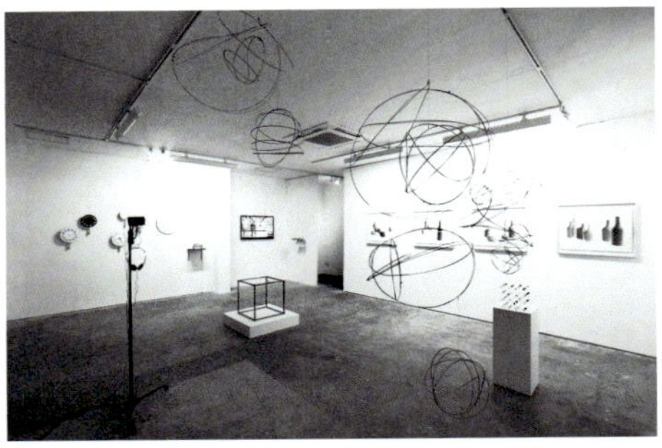

What first compelled you to open a gallery?
I worked for an art gallery in Tokyo for more than ten years, but started to think that there have got to be more ways to promote young and emerging talent, and wanted to experimentally put this into practice. Now that the art methodologies are expanding into different media and execution, I feel that I had some degree of significance in promoting artworks in non-conventional forms, in other words, pieces that are not easy to sell/buy such as video or installation.

Who is the first artist you showed and what was most memorable about that show?
Lyota Yagi.

When did you first participate in Art Basel and what was most memorable about that show?
In Hong Kong in 2013. We had previously participated to ART HK in 2012. We are very satisfied with the fact that we are expanding a new network there, gaining new connections every year. We notice that many collectors come and look at the works very seriously, and we get many questions on the works' themes, materials, etc. We brought woodcut prints by the artist Sachiko Kazama this year in Hong Kong, and we got quite a lot feedback.

- **Contact** — Mujin-to Production
  Rika Fujiki
  r-fujiki@mujin-to.com
  info@mujin-to.com
- **Established** — 2006
- **Owner(s) / Partner(s)** — Rika Fujiki
- **Team** — 4
- **Space(s)** — 68 m²
- **Artists at Art Basel** — Chim↑Pom, Sachiko Kazama
- **Further artists represented** — Yoko Asakai, Kazuhiko Hachiya, Tsubasa Kato, Osamu Matsuda, Yukihiro Taguchi, Ryohei Usui, Lyota Yagi

Müller

Zurich

- Galleries
- Galleries

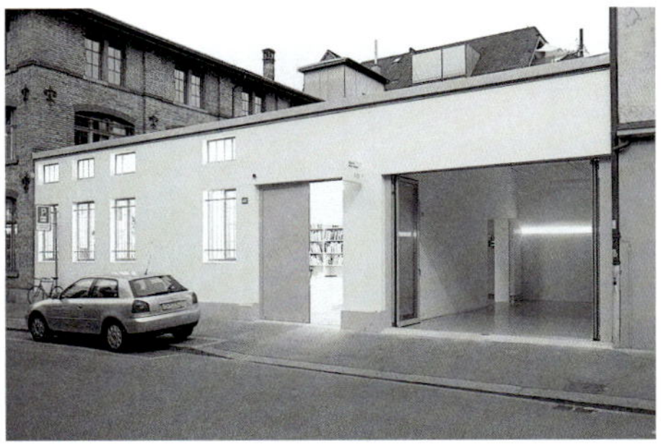

What first compelled you to open a gallery?
To do exhibitions with younger artists from Switzerland, Europe, and the US!

Who is the first artist you showed and what was most memorable about that show?
Markus Weggenmann—we got wonderful reviews, sold all the works and we still work together!

When did you first participate in Art Basel and what was most memorable about that show?
In 1993—I brought new artists to Basel.

- **Contact** Galerie Mark Müller
Mark Müller
mark.mueller@markmueller.ch
mail@markmueller.ch
- **Established** 1990
- **Owner(s) / Partner(s)** Mark Müller
- **Team** 2
- **Space(s)** 220 m²
- **Artists at Art Basel** Joachim Bandau
Reto Boller
Heinz Breloh
Urs Frei
Katharina Grosse
Marcia Hafif
Joseph Marioni
Martín Mele
Judy Millar
François Morellet
Giacomo Santiago Rogado
Christine Streuli
Markus Weggenmann
Duane Zaloudek
- **Further artists represented** Francis Baudevin
Sabina Baumann
Monika Brandmeier
Stefan Gritsch
Dennis Hollingsworth
Axel Lieber
John Nixon
Patrick Rohner
Jürg Stäuble
Michel Verjux
Silvia Bächli
Jean-Marc Bustamante
Helmut Dorner
Günther Förg
Imi Knoebel
Linda McCue
Kohei Nawa
Miwa Ogasawara
Gerwald Rockenschaub
Wawrzyniec Tokarski
Franz Erhard Walther
Maja Weyermann
Paul Winstanley

Munro

Hamburg ● Galleries

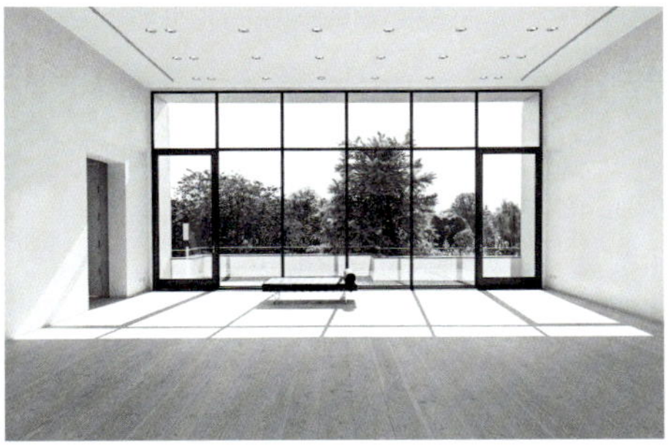

What first compelled you to open a gallery?
Love for art.

Who is the first artist you showed and what was most memorable about that show?
Joseph Beuys. At that time he was the most hated artist. The opening was a tumult. I was the only one who bought anything. Ten years later (!) Andy Warhol purchased the fantastic *Braunkreuz* series from that show.

When did you first participate in Art Basel and what was most memorable about that show?
I opened in April 1977 and went straight to Basel in June with a radical minimalistic booth. I was frightened to death.

- **Contact** Galerie Vera Munro
Tom Reichstein
gallery@veramunro.de
- **Established** 1977
- **Owner(s) / Partner(s)** Vera Munro
- **Team** 6
- **Space(s)** 600 m²
- **Artists at Art Basel** Eriks Apalais
John M Armleder
Janis Avotinš

Murray Guy

New York ● Statements

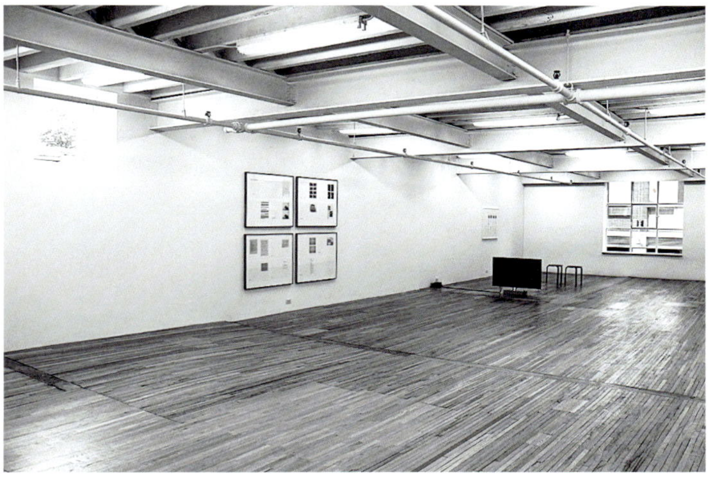

What first compelled you to open a gallery?
To show and promote the work of young, international artists with a distinctive, conceptual practice.

Who is the first artist you showed and what was most memorable about that show?
Matthew Buckingham.

When did you first participate in Art Basel and what was most memorable about that show?
In 2000 in the Statements sector at Art Basel, with Francis Cape.

- **Contact** Murray Guy
Janice Guy
info@murrayguy.com
- **Established** 1998
- **Owner(s) / Partner(s)** Janice Guy
Margaret Murray
- **Team** 6
- **Space(s)** 250 m²
- **Artists at Art Basel** Sergei Tcherepnin
- **Further artists represented** Matthew Buckingham
Francis Cape
Alejandro Cesarco
Moyra Davey
Patricia Esquivias
Kota Ezawa
Matthew Higgs
An-My Lê
Zoe Leonard
Ann Lislegaard
Nashashibi/Skaer
Barbara Probst
Lucy Skaer
Beat Streuli

Galleria Massimo Minini

Pizzini by Massimo Minini

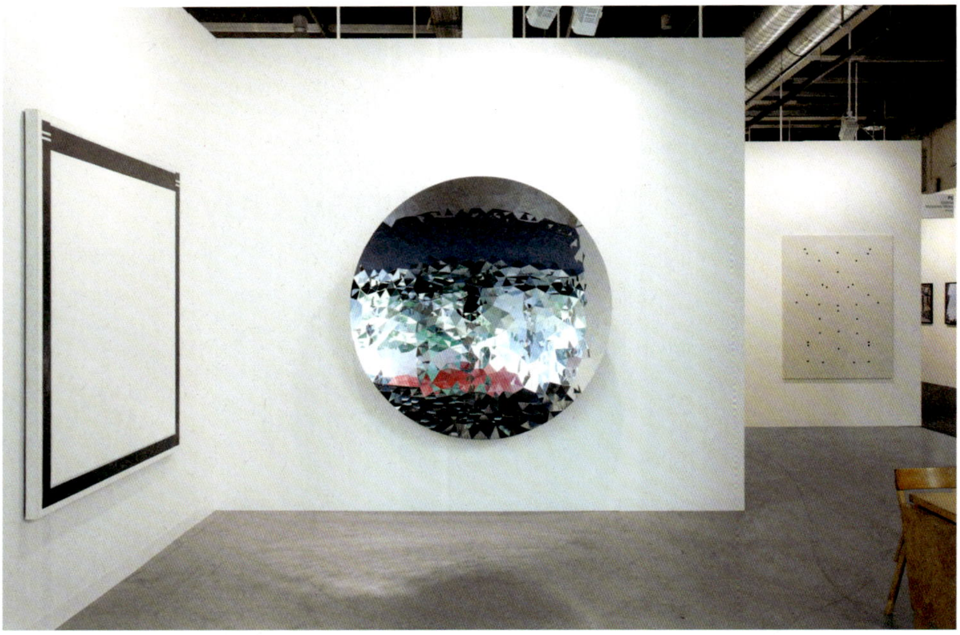

Art Basel in Basel, 2013

Three years after opening the gallery, in 1973, art fairs were springing up and my artists were beginning to show signs of nervosity: they wanted to be in Basel. They pushed me every way they could to apply for this important event and, to my surprise, my application was accepted. (I've been exhibiting at Basel non-stop ever since—for 37 years.) Hey, guys! We're at Basel! We need to get ready, find the cash and the works too, because the artists who want to go do not have great visibility.

Alighiero Boetti submitted two large red Biros (ballpoint pen drawings) for the display—*Mettere Al Mondo Il Mondo* (*Bringing the World into the World*, 1972–1973). Great help. Cadere and Toroni come to the fair. This is where I met Colette, the New York artist, who suggested a performance. Rashly, I agreed, and she took pills and slept on the stand, which in the meantime she had filled with curtains and silks.
Lucio Amelio and Holly Solomon came to me a number of times, bringing collectors and inquisitive people. Lucio screamed like a maniac: "That's what you need to do!"

Holly bought some works. But it wasn't enough to pay for the fair.

Quite incredibly, Franz Meyer, director of the Kunstmuseum, came racing past my stand on the last day. Out of the corner of his eye he spotted the enormous blotch of red of Boetti's diptych, stepped back three paces and asked me how much it cost. "Put the Boetti aside for me. I'll be straight back." He returned with 15 people. They talked among themselves. I don't understand German. Then Franz came to me: "Boetti's ours!" My first Basel art fair was salvaged.

***

Lucio Amelio—him again! One day he quit the Committee for health reasons. Amelio pointed to me as his successor. The post was clearly hereditary, like in the days of kings. Lucio was and always had been a key personality in the fair—very influential. In those days the Committee comprised representatives of every nation. Not so today. So Lucio designated Massimo Minini, and the others in the committee came to see who this Minini was. Bammatter, then Director of the fair, came by to meet me. Everyone was rather astonished. The first Committee was strictly in German. Isy Brachot and I had an interpreter. But Isy, who smoked Cohiba cigars (it was allowed in those days), opened his briefcase, lit a monster and puffed it down the interpreter's throat. The poor thing rushed out in paroxysms and never came back, so I understood nothing of my first committee meeting in Basel … Fortunately, we soon switched to English.

I joined the committee at a time of great changes in the fair, when competitors were breathing down its neck and it was decided to play more tough. New ideas, new sections, new galleries, and space needed to be made for them. Interesting new galleries were trying to enter, but every place was taken. To make the change, many galleries were dropped and new energies entered. For me, a fresh young commissioner, this meant making lots of enemies. But it was an amazing experience.

***

A few years ago I showed Nedko Solakov's *A Beauty* (2000–2009) at Unlimited.

A great white whale covered in immaculate plush. In its belly, like Jonah, was a shiny painted moon, but in order to see it you had to get down on your hands and knees, with your bum in the air. As I write this, Solakov is here with me, and he has something to say. Here it is (this is from Nedko): "While Massimo was writing the previous sentences explaining that I was sitting next to him, I was thinking what exactly does he sell. Here is what he sells, as one of the most important gallerists working nowadays—he sells relations. Relations between the artist, the work of art, and the collector, and, respectively, the viewer, relations of devoted appreciation and love."

Well, thanks Nedko, but let me say that during that week at Basel/Unlimited I saw countless big names kneeling down to see the moon in the belly of your sculpture, and they laughed and were all happy about it. Sometime art makes you laugh or smile, and gives you joy, and all these important people with their bums in the air certainly took any tension out of the world's top art fair.

MU SEUMS MESSE PLATZ

Herzog & de Meuron

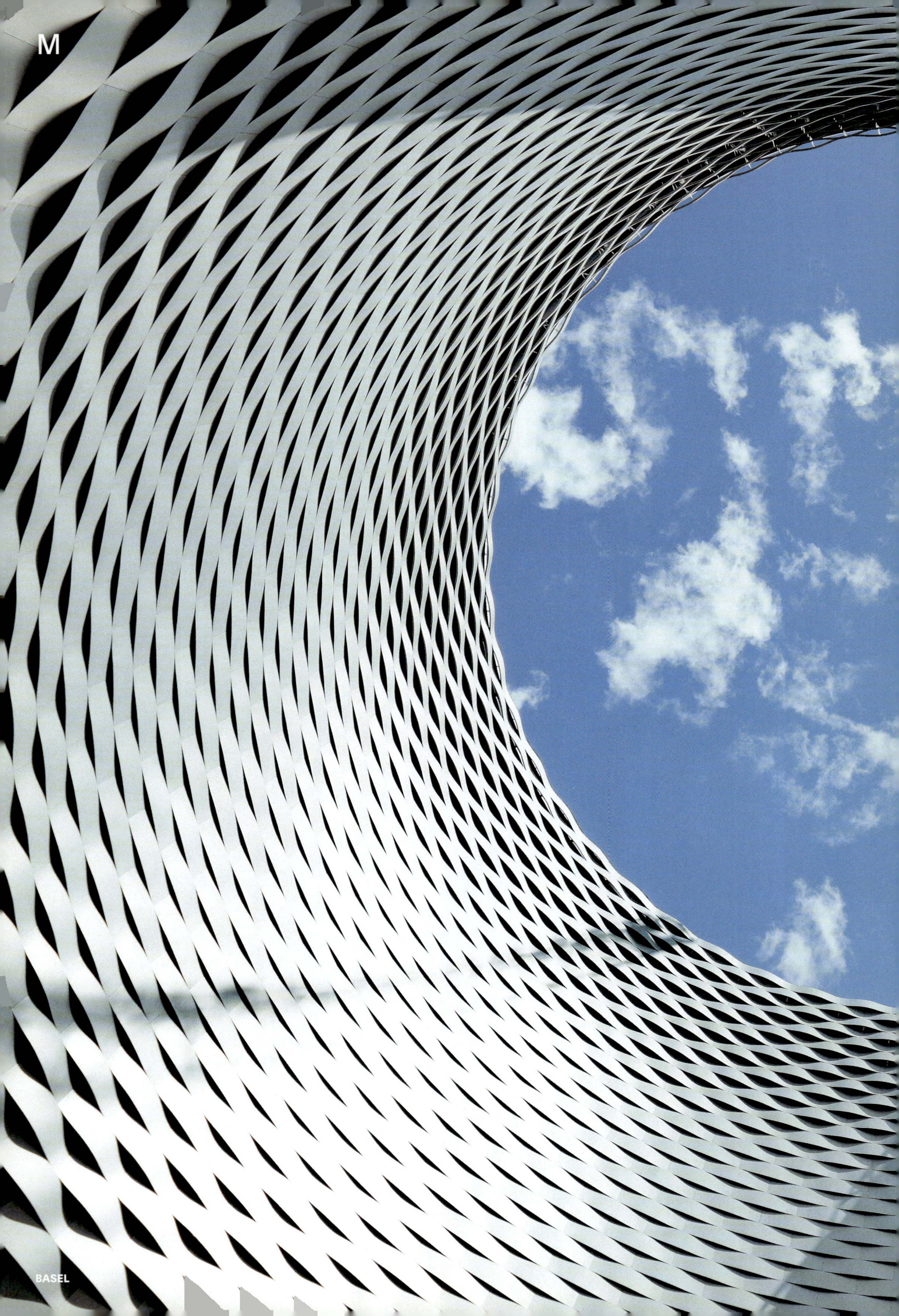
M
BASEL

Herzog & de Meuron
Messe Basel–New Hall

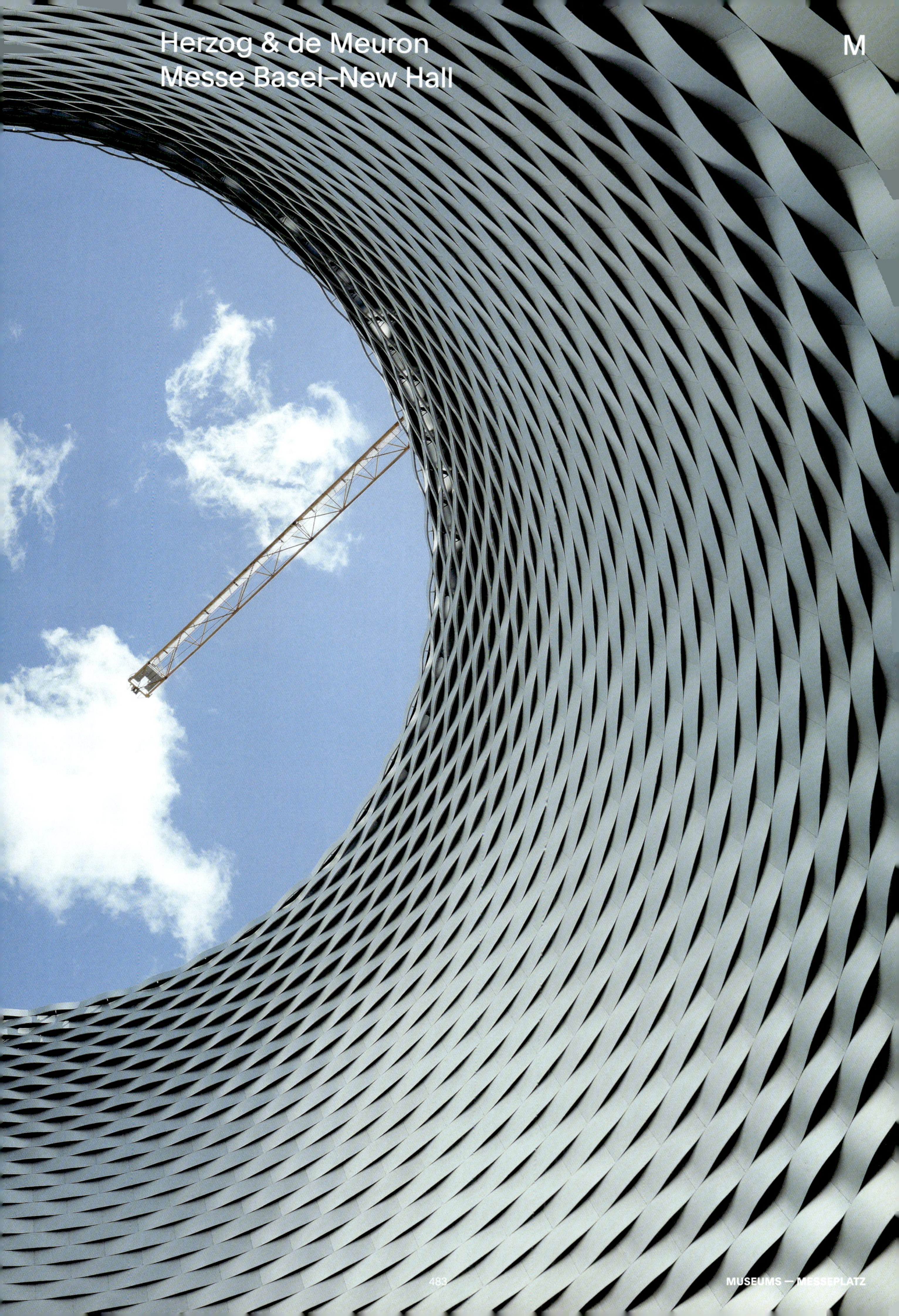

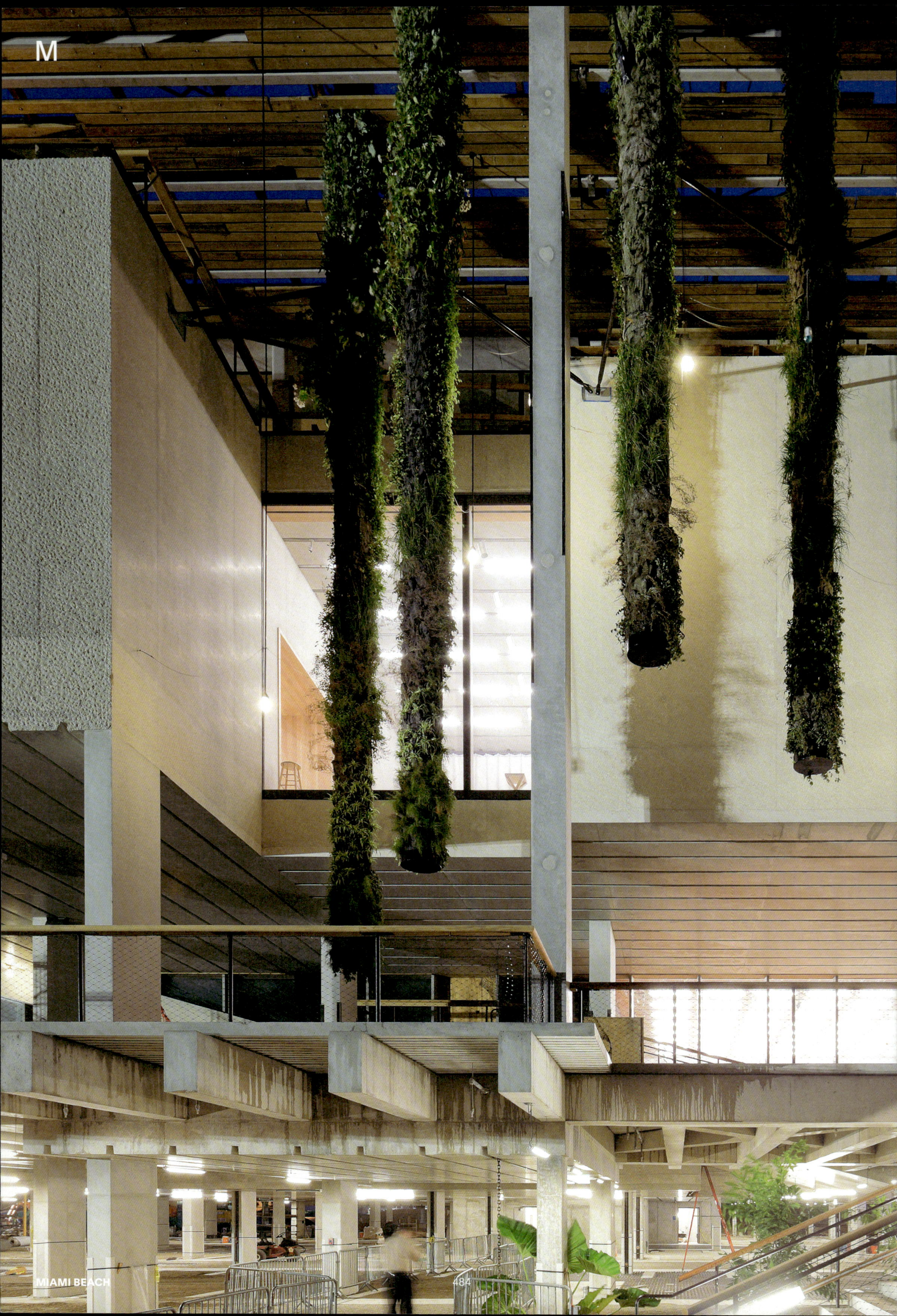

Herzog & de Meuron
Pérez Art Museum Miami

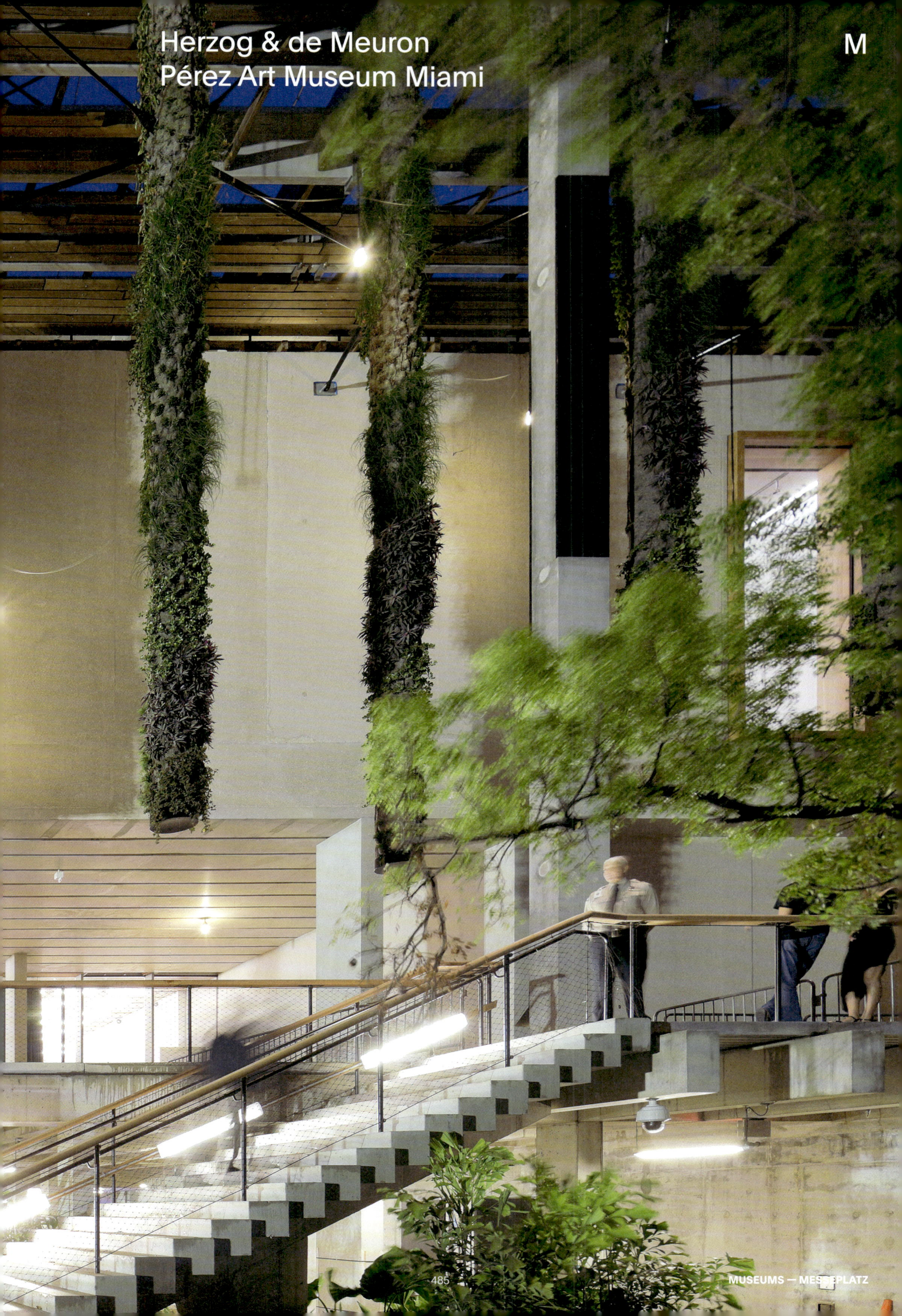

M

Architecture Has to Generate Publicity

Interview with Jacques Herzog on the Messe Basel–New Hall and the projects in Miami and Hong Kong by Philip Ursprung

This conversation was conducted at Herzog & de Meuron's studio in Basel on November 26, 2013

Messe Basel–New Hall, Basel; project 2004–2012, realization 2010–2013

Pérez Art Museum Miami, Miami; project 2006–2010, realization 2010–2013

M+, Hong Kong; competition 2012–2013, project 2013–

PHILIP URSPRUNG Since they first started to practice, Herzog & de Meuron have explored the themes of the museum, of storage, and of memory, from the Ricola Storage Building in Laufen (1987) by way of Tate Modern (2000) to the project in Münchenstein, which will is soon be completed and which includes new spaces for your own archive. The projects focus on the question of how stepping out of the course of time can be represented—thus on something static, on states of affairs. A trade fair has a different function. A trade fair, or any kind of exhibition or market, is about constant, rapid exchange, in conjunction with comings and goings that are not linked to a specific place. This theme makes completely different demands on representation. How have you approached the theme of the trade fair? How do you create enduring architecture for the ephemeral?

JACQUES HERZOG Compared to many other commissions, a trade fair today is a very humdrum affair. The interiors are defined by the prescribed width, height, and load-bearing capacity of the floors. So for the halls of the exhibition buildings we had no kind of latitude—none whatsoever! The location was given too. The citizens of Basel had decided in a plebiscite that the Messe Basel exhibition site should not move out to the airport, but should remain in the city center. The Messe is in fact deeply rooted in Basel's memory. They go back to the "Schweizer Mustermesse," or sample fair, launched in 1917. In the now demolished exhibition building this symbolism was present in the form of the head of Hermes, so in the form of an architectonic ornament. On the front of the exhibition center, which contains the beautiful building by Hans Hofmann with its round center court dating from 1953, the big clock takes on the representation of the theme. This can be understood as naive symbolism, or as analogous,

Herzog & de Meuron
Ricola Storage Building,
Laufen

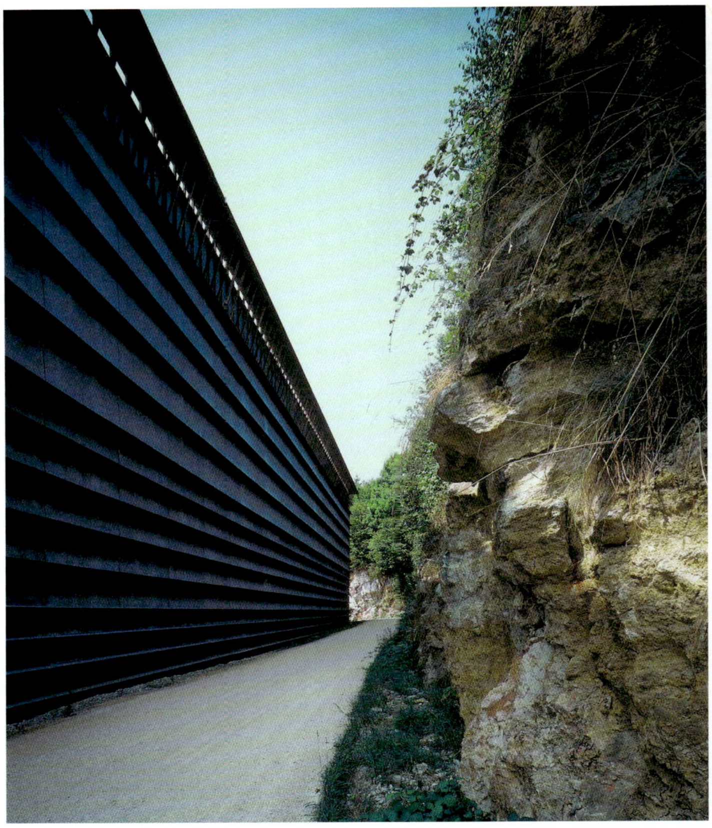

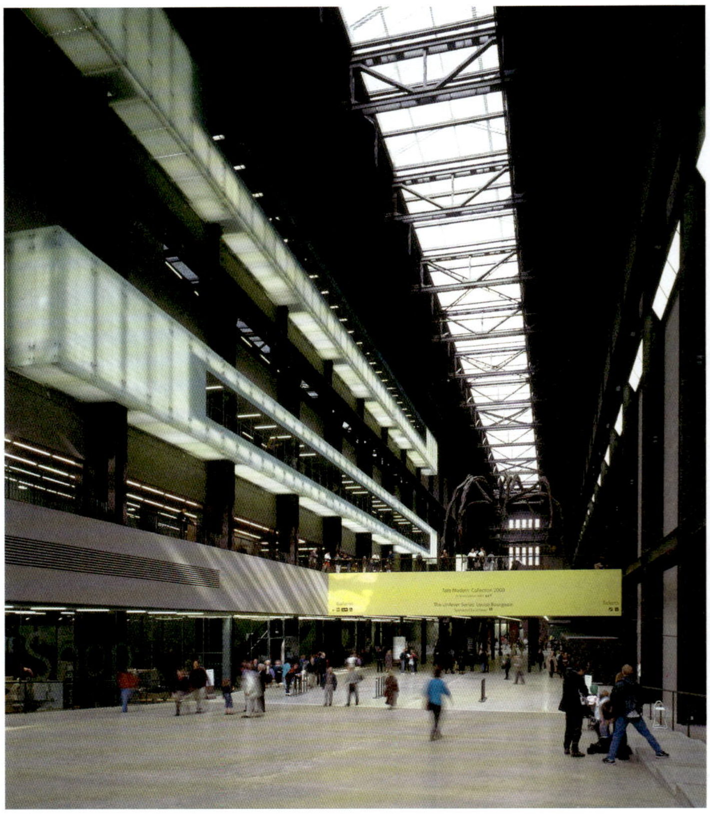

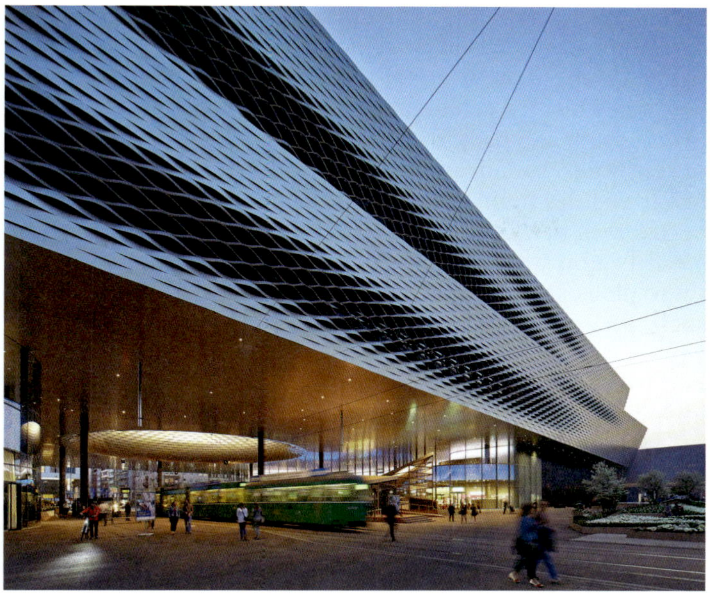

Herzog & de Meuron
Messe Basel–New Hall

narrative architecture from a period when exhibition halls already had to satisfy the requirements for functionality, but not to anything like the extent demanded by present-day globalized exhibition venues. This was our starting point.

PU In the 1950s exhibitions were a manageable size, part of the city, and at the same time a window onto the world. Today they're part of a worldwide network. How have you articulated this altered dimension and given the exhibition site a face?

JH In Hofmann's building the halls are grouped around an internal court. This wasn't an option for us, I mean we had to stack the halls on top of one another. We had to build as an extension to the existing building by Theo Hotz, and—it wasn't our decision—we had to build across the street. But for those very reasons, a space was created there that became the real architectonic event. The intervening space became the architectonic place. As the somewhat questionable name "City Lounge" suggests, it was intended to be more than a covered area, rather a place where people like hanging out and where they can meet. In an almost subversive act—something we often call upon in architecture—we appropriated the open space to invent other, unforeseen programs that can serve the public sphere. Architecture that is so centrally placed, whether it is a museum or an exhibition hall, must necessarily generate publicness.

PU The distinctive feature of the newly developed place is the spectacular, circular opening to the sky. It has become a landmark for people. How did you come up with that idea?

← Herzog & de Meuron
Tate Modern, London

JH We were inspired to use a circular shape by the round internal court of Hofmann's building, which fascinated us even when we were children. That court still works very well today, especially during Art Basel. Roundness is a form of collectivity. Originally we wanted to fit windows into the upper floor of the circle, so that a kind of arcade would have been created, which would have made eye contact possible from the halls to down below. Unfortunately that wasn't given permission. But it would be quite possible to introduce those openings one day, and thereby facilitate a much more genuine spatial connection.

PU The aperture not only defines a place, it also changes our perception. On my first visit I was very surprised. It led to me change my perspective—instead of looking at the ground, as one so often does in Swiss cities, I looked up at the sky.

JH The aperture works almost like an optical instrument, a telescope, a perceptual equipment that directs attention to something that is admittedly always there, but is hardly noticed any more. On the big open square you used to be less aware of seeing the sky than you are now. Now you cut it out as it were, make it into an image where you see clouds traveling past, rain or snow falling. This attentiveness toward everyday things was more important to us than questions of materialization. And it was a decisive element in the design. The circle functions as a joint, a hinge, with the two halls swiveled around it. That's the real architectonic invention.

PU The halls are are almost fanned out …

JH We know of no other exhibition center where the halls are offset in relation to one another. What at first glance looks statically complicated was really not that problematic. It was the only option for getting to grips with the huge volume. We've always been interested in how we can leave each thing with its identity. Of course the Messe Basel is a building, but primarily it's a stack of halls. Two halls are placed on top of one another and are supported over a ground floor. This horizontal layering was the theme. That brings us back to the storage themes mentioned at the beginning. We offset the halls around the joint so that projections and setbacks could be formed, and therefore an in-scale reference to the people and adjacent buildings could come about. Reference points for the human eye are produced at different heights, as used to happen in the history of architecture by means of cornices and pilaster strips. Without this offset, the building would have looked like the retaining wall of a dam, like an enormous bar across the town.

PU The project has been sharply criticized by the local population.

JH The criticism that public space was being built over and taken away from the citizens was very forcefully expressed. Especially in a democracy such as Switzerland, this is a central issue that we took very seriously. We had never intended to take anything away with the building, rather we wanted to create something which wasn't there before, namely this covered place. That was far more important to us than symbolism. To put it simply, it had to do with the question of how a huge volume, that is unquestionably much larger than Hofmann's building, could be designed in an already densely built-up city in such a way that an added value was created for the people. That was the challenge.

PU What is a benefit for passersby with the opening to the sky means a loss of surface area for the client. How were you able to mediate between the interests of the public and the client?

JH That aperture was very controversial, for valuable space is lost in the exhibition hall that can't be rented out. We had to argue for it vehemently. The fairs, particularly Art Basel, are of course much loved by the people of Basel, Art Basel is the city's favorite child. But it has also become a globalized enterprise, just like Roche and Novartis and other companies. Therefore the requirements don't correspond, even if Art Basel is comparatively open to such ideas thanks to its connection with art.

PU In your work you're often dealing with monstrous situations, with structures that go beyond the human dimension. At the Schaulager (2003), for example, communication with the human dimension is effected by means of a small object reminiscent of a house in front of the entrance. I'd like to describe that object as an ornament in the broadest sense of that concept—the roots of the German word for ornament, "Verzierung" go back to, among other things, the meaning "to thread in." It enables human beings to cope better with the jump in scale, to identify a bit with the opposite. Were there plans at the Messe Basel for any such mediating object?

JH No. But we did in fact try to introduce a smaller scale. The first base course is already more than ten meters high, which means there would be room in it for a three-story building. There we wanted to have compartmentalized local uses at the intersection point between the global and the local city. We envisaged offering sorts of micro-shops at very low rents in the three- to four-meter-wide areas between the glass front and the wall of the hall on the ground floor, to local greengrocers or tiny souvenir shops, for example. These micro-shops could have nestled in these recesses like mushrooms on the edge of the forest, or lichen and moss on old trees. We love those kinds of unexpected and really inappropriate uses, the docking of local life on to the smooth shell of global architecture.

PU Today there are two up-market restaurants there. Was there no possibility of making the smaller recesses?

JH It didn't work, at least not in this first phase. But such a building has to live with the city—and vice versa. It has to have the potential for transformation. In the Middle Ages countless stallholders backed onto the huge cathedrals, you can see that at the Stephansdom in Vienna. We're trying to bring that compartmentalization into play architectonically, spatially, and physically. For reasons of cost it was unfortunately not possible to enliven the roof, which towers above the adjacent district. We thought of a bar, a restaurant, or sports grounds, for example for city golf or outdoor volleyball. These programs would have animated the building, virtually crisscrossed it with beaten tracks, connected it and reconciled it with the city. It would have been comparable to a big elephant or a hippopotamus, with smaller animals riding on it and leading parallel lives. For several weeks during the year a building of that kind has a very intensive life, a kind of hyper-life, only to sink back into hibernation again. The program can alter the scale too. It's important to convince the clients that it can be advantageous for them and for the building. Architects can't program such additional uses, but they can think of them. Architecture should facilitate them, not exclude them.

PU The structural engineering would have been adequate for it—the ceilings span gigantic halls in a strongman act. Yet the building doesn't show its muscles.

JH At this site we didn't want to put on a strongman act. But in other projects—for instance the Olympic Stadium in Beijing (2008), Prada Aoyama in Tokyo (2003), 1111 Lincoln Road, Miami (2010), and the new Pérez Art Museum in Miami (2013)—the buildings really do show their strength, they're virtually naked buildings. At the same time we never stage this in the sense of excesses, as is the case in Santiago Calatrava's projects, for example.

PU In this connection do you use concepts such as statics or anatomy?

JH We speak about structure. Basically they all coincide—ornamentation, structure, and space. In these projects we don't talk about a facade, there is none, or it emerges. At the Messe Basel it's a membrane, a sheet-metal skin that continues the visual interplay started in the circle.

PU And how do you understand the concept of ornament, which had an ambivalent history in the 20th century?

JH The concept of ornament as used today by Jean-François Chevrier is a fertile one for us, for it has to do with ornamentation in the sense of a holistic view. Seemingly paradoxically, ornament is what unites the whole within itself and brings everything together. If it reflects or contains the whole idea, it is an ornamental concept. If it doesn't, it's a decorative appendage, and we've always been opposed to the concept of decoration.

PU Does this exhibition building communicate with other buildings from the history of architecture? I'm thinking for example of Peter Eisenman's Greater Columbus Center in Columbus, Ohio (1993), the first large exhibition building where the architect set out to give a countenance to the enormous dimensions of exhibition buildings. Or I'm thinking of Hans Poelzig's brick facades, or the expressionistic metal skin of Hans Scharoun's Berlin Philharmonic building.

In an almost subversive act—something we often call upon in architecture—we appropriated the open space to invent other, unforeseen programs that can serve the public sphere.
— Jacques Herzog

JH We aren't consciously corresponding with those buildings. We proceeded pragmatically, tried out and then rejected many things, but without considering any references. Brick was a theme, as was glass, so materials that already occur on the spot. But a brick building would have become a colossus and would have killed Hofmann's building. Because of the twist as well, neither brick nor glass would have come into consideration. We simulated the twist with soft surfaces, and by that means the slanting deformations came into being. They are reminiscent of pitched roofs, so traditional, protective shapes familiar from farmhouses in the Bern canton, dynamic and at the same time restful. Therefore metal was the only option for achieving this all-over concept. But unlike Frank Gehry, for example, who uses panels, we wanted to break up the large surfaces, and came up with the structure of twisted metal strips.

PU Does that element tie up with the signal boxes swathed in copper strips at the Basel train station that were built in the 1990s?

JH Yes, even then it had to do with the motif of untwisting, the softness and malleability of the material. For the exhibition buildings we carried out lots of tests with different sizes. In doing so we again got back to the fundamental questions of architecture, the way the building relates to the human body. It is always about the same question, whether gigantic volumes scare human beings, or connect with them. We like large scales, but for human beings they are unbearable unless the connection with them is "threaded in" as we were saying before. Otherwise we end up with fascist architecture, or places like Stalinallee.

PU In the M+ in Hong Kong you open a new chapter. You take the subterranean as a theme, as in fact you did before at the Serpentine Gallery Pavilion (2012) with Ai Weiwei in London.

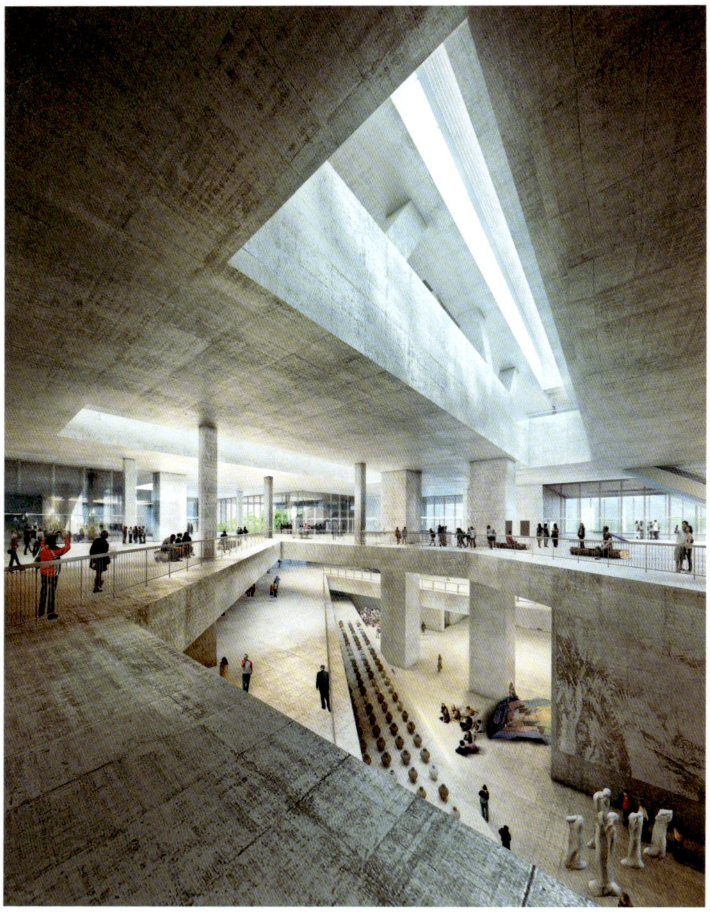

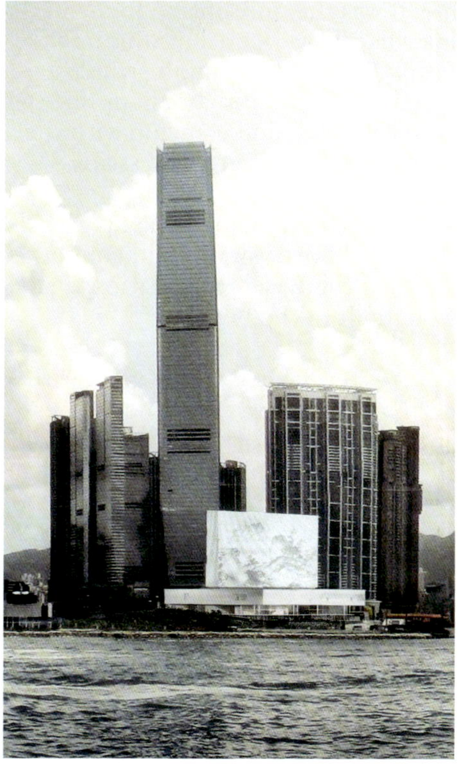

Herzog & de Meuron
M+, Hong Kong

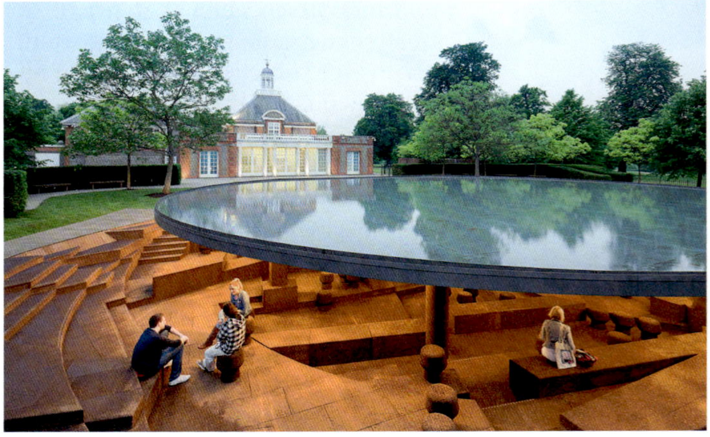

Herzog & de Meuron
and Ai Weiwei
Serpentine Gallery
Pavilion, London

JH It's an archaeological concept that allows the project to be anchored on the site, and a basis to be given to the building that will be constructed on an artificial mound with no history. We welcomed the tunnel lying under it as a stroke of luck—many people had at first regarded it as an obstacle that had to be spanned with complicated static constructions. We perceived it as a treasure that we found already there in the ground. It offers precisely that spatiality which is so sought after today, a "found space," an "industrial space," a "production space," if you want to put it that way. The express rail track to the airport is an element that is characteristic of the dynamism of Hong Kong. We put concrete over the spine of the tunnel and "depict" this space, so to speak. The negative space is the background for the space where the exhibition areas and studios stand.

PU Thus the project relates not to the slow accretion of sediments, as in the case of the Ricola Storage Building, but on the contrary to high speed. This juxtaposition of static architecture and a dynamic transport route produces an anachronism, a meeting of different temporalities. How do these dynamics manifest themselves?

JH Perhaps people sense something of the movement, we don't know. As a situation it would be comparable to the Turbine Hall, where the quiet hum of the substation can in fact always be heard too. And it leads back to our very first project, the redesign for the Marktplatz, the market square in Basel, which we started in 1979 but which has not been realized. There we wanted to produce an acoustic link to the canalized, invisible stream under the square, to bring to mind what was hidden. As in many later projects, we were also concerned with producing a connection with things that can no longer be seen directly, but are still present as traces, real traces on the ground, or mental ones in people's memories.

PU For the Pérez Art Museum Miami you took the vegetation, the climate, "nature," as the starting point for the architecture. But nature is potentially destructive, there are hurricanes and floods in Florida. How do you translate the inhumanity of nature into something that is pleasant for people without lapsing into cliché?

JH The starting point was the criticism of American architecture that excludes nature and uses technology—primarily the technology of the oil industry—to produce machines that provide a constant temperature, irrespective of whether it's hot or cold, wet or dry, outside. We were therefore concerned with developing an architecture that can play on the relationship between interior and exterior in a more varied way than conventional American architecture does, for instance Art Deco architecture which is very prevalent in Miami, consisting of hermetically sealed boxes with air conditioning. The old Miami Art Museum by Philip Johnson has a black glass door intended to keep the sun out. A more powerful contrast than that between the extremely hot forecourt and the icy-cold interior can hardly be imagined. It almost bowls you over as you go in, and experiencing that contrast is very unpleasant. It was was a defining experience for us—the PAMM had to overcome that American convention.

PU Do you use plants as an architectonic material?

JH Architecture has various ways of dealing with climatic conditions; in fact it is there to create comfortable surroundings. Plants and gardens are a good means of doing so, as we know from Arabia, Spain, Latin America, and China. The 1111 Lincoln Road project, which combines a parking garage, commercial premises, and apartments, functions in this way as a building that allows those using it to be out in the open, as a kind of walk-on sculpture. In the newly opened Pérez Art Museum the local vegetation mediates between inside and outside. Originally we wanted to lead visitors even more directly through the plants, as through a buffer formed of coolness and scents, a preparatory space for the transition, as an area that attenuates the contrast. In a museum that's even more important than in a restaurant or an office block. Of course hurricanes can easily destroy these plants, but they can be replaced. The fact that the plants overrun the architecture in places is a precursor of the fate that Miami will suffer one day when nature reclaims the city.

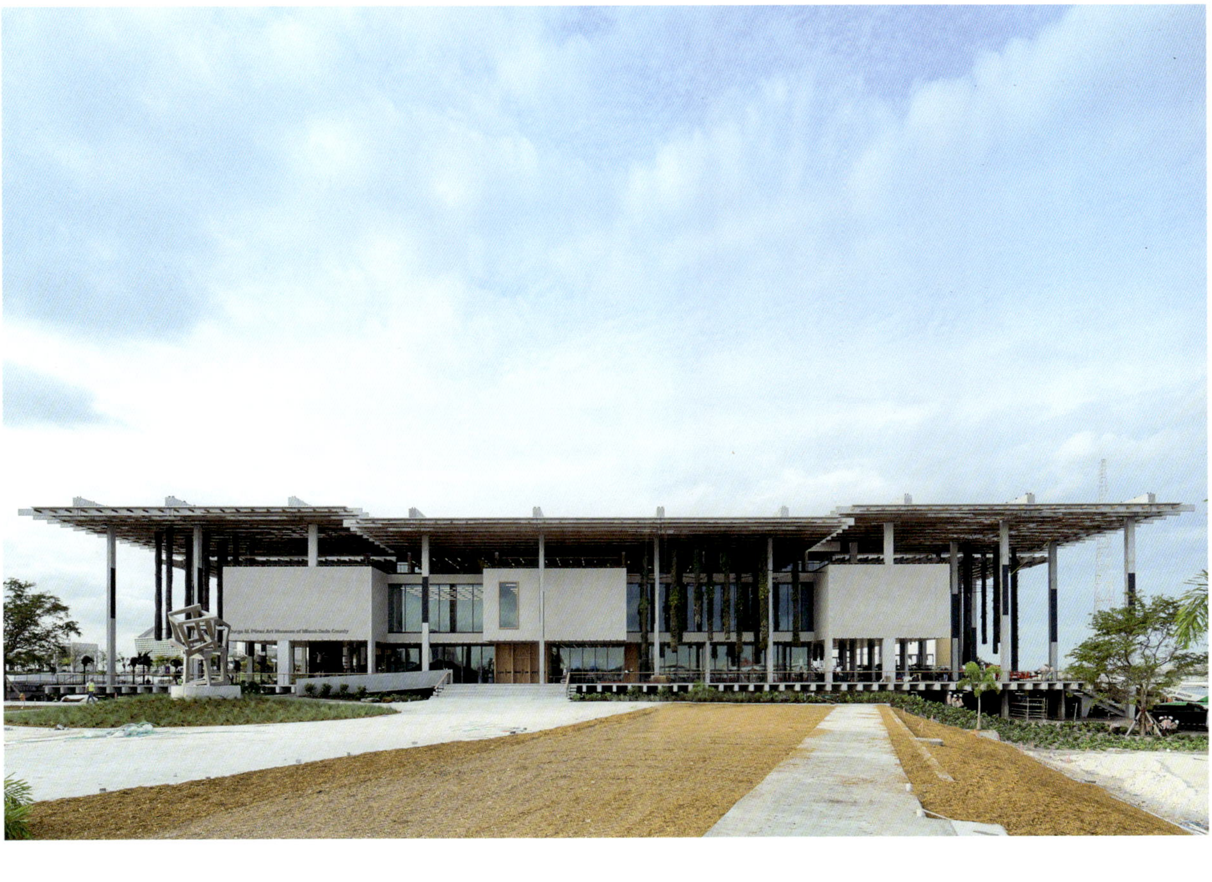

Herzog & de Meuron
Pérez Art Museum
Miami

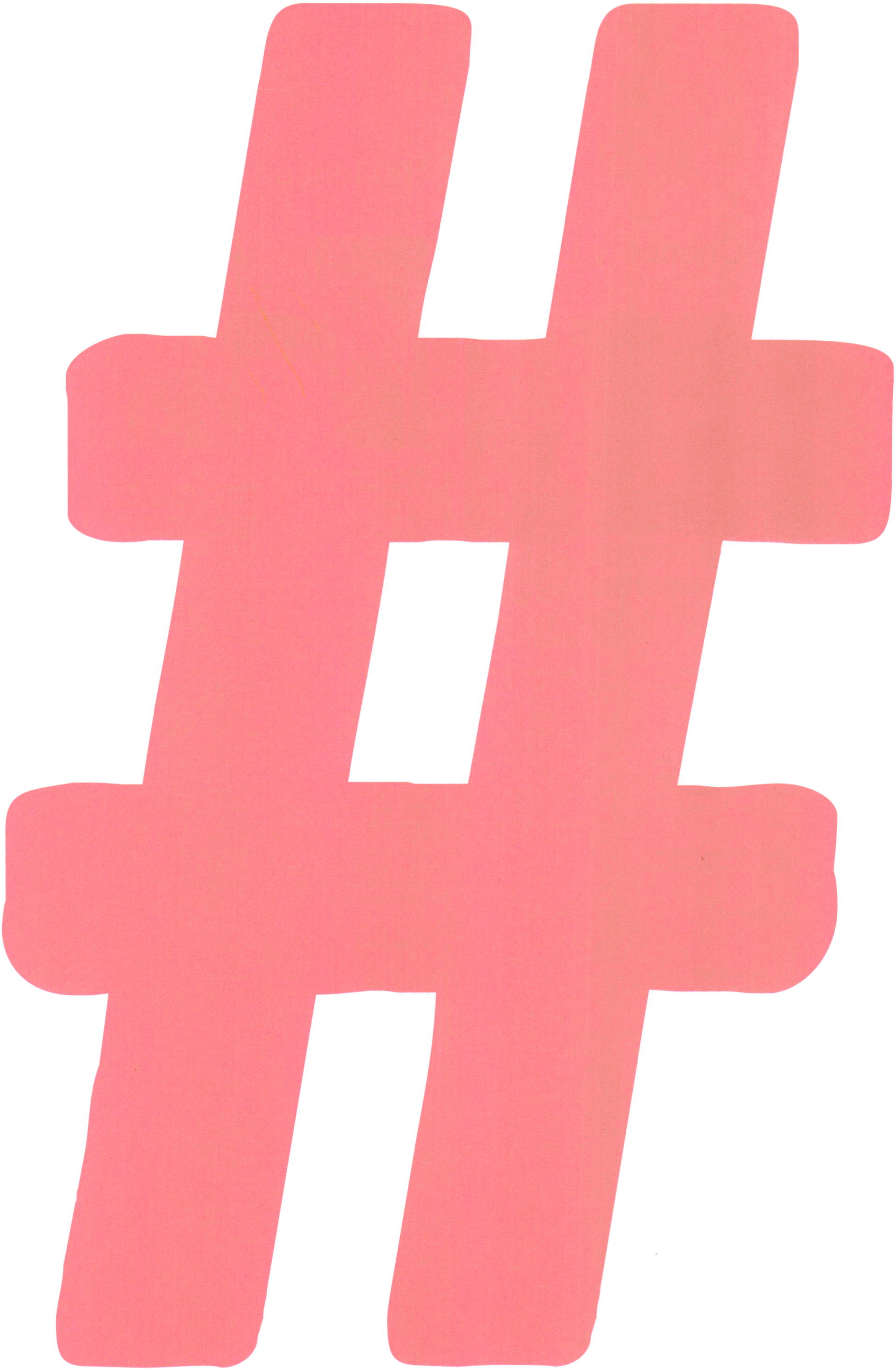

#

- Hong Kong
- Basel
- Miami Beach

Christine Nguyen
Tuan Andrew Nguyen
Pan Jian
Sopheap Pich
Petroc Sesti
Shao Yinong and Muchen
Shi Guorui
The Propeller Group
Xiao Lu
Ai Yamaguchi
Yang Zhichao
John Young

10 Chancery Lane

Hong Kong — Galleries

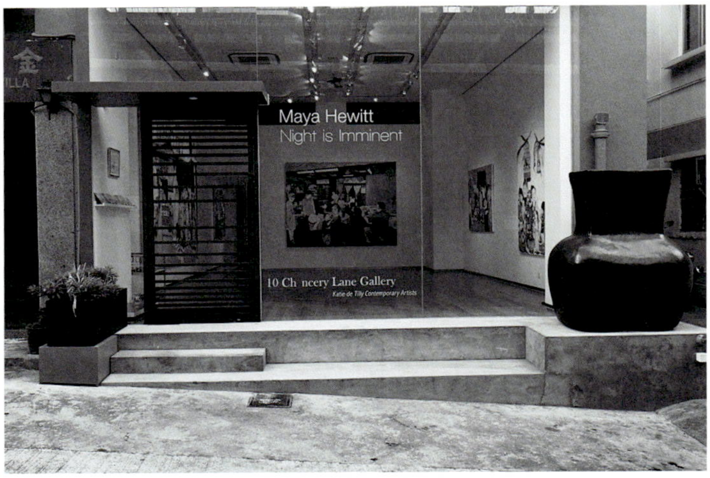

What first compelled you to open a gallery?
Madness, passion, guts, and naïveté.

Who is the first artist you showed and what was most memorable about that show?
Wang Keping. Sold out.

When did you first participate in Art Basel and what was most memorable about that show?
In 2013, it was the first year Art Basel came to Hong Kong. The most memorable aspects were the diversity of collectors and the real interest in the artworks we were showing with many of them not having knowledge of Asian art but loving it.

- **Contact** — 10 Chancery Lane Gallery, Katie de Tilly, katie@10chancerylanegallery.com, info@10chancerylanegallery.com
- **Established** — 2001
- **Owner(s) / Partner(s)** — Katie de Tilly
- **Team** — 6
- **Space(s)** — 120 m² (Central), 300 m² (Chai Wan)
- **Artists at Art Basel** — Bui Cong Khanh, Sutee Kunavichayanont, Tawatchai Puntusawasdi, Michael Shaowanasai, Manit Sriwanichpoom, Nawapol Thamrongrattanarit, Wang Keping
- **Further artists represented** — Hannah Bertram, Cai Yuan and JJ Xi, Atul Dodiya, Nandan Ghiya, Guan Wei, Gonkar Gyatso, Maya Hewitt, Huang Rui, Hung Liu, Dinh Q. Lê, Lindy Lee, Carol Lee Mei Kuen, Winus Lee Yee Mei, Li Wei, Ken Matsubara, Sonia Mehra Chawla

100 Tonson

Bangkok — Galleries

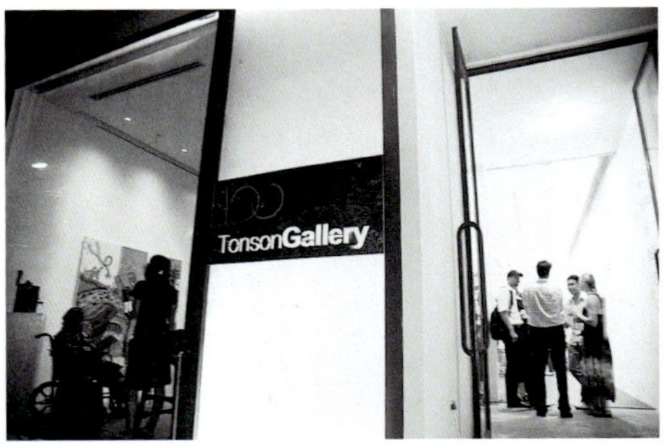

What first compelled you to open a gallery?
Passion for art. Thai contemporary art is unique and Thai artists are very talented, but they need good support. We would like to take this opportunity to do that.

Who is the first artist you showed and what was most memorable about that show?
There are many memorable moments. The exhibitions that drew a lot of viewers, students, curators, and collectors include Araya Rasdjarmrearnsook, Chatchai Puipia, Phaptawan Suwanakudt, Pinaree Sanpitak, Sakarin Krue-On, Pichet Klunchuen, and Rirkrit Tiravanija, among numerous others; they are all memorable shows.

When did you first participate in Art Basel and what was most memorable about that show?
We had the extraordinary honor of participating at Art Basel in 2011 where 100 Tonson Gallery was the first Thailand-based organization to join this distinguished art fair, and the only gallery to be invited from Southeast Asia. We featured Rirkrit Tiravanija's lively, participatory work, *Untitled 2011 (who's afraid of …)*, which was originated and attended by the artist. Nearly 80 visitors contributed to Tiravanija's wall drawings, while more than 1,000 participated in his signature culinary "conversation." All in all, a very successful project!

- **Contact** — 100 Tonson Gallery, Aey Phanachet, aey@100tonsongallery.com, info@100tonsongallery.com
- **Established** — 2003
- **Owner(s) / Partner(s)** — Aey Phanachet
- **Team** — 2
- **Space(s)** — 110 m²
- **Artists at Art Basel** — Yuree Kensaku, Sakarin Krue-on, Chatchai Puipia, Pinaree Sanpitak, Prateep Suthathongthai
- **Further artists represented** — Thanet Awsinsiri, Manut Lao-on, Utai Nopsiri, Wit Pimkanchanapong, Araya Rasdjarmrearnsook, Montri Toemsombat, Peggy Wauters

1301PE

Los Angeles — Galleries

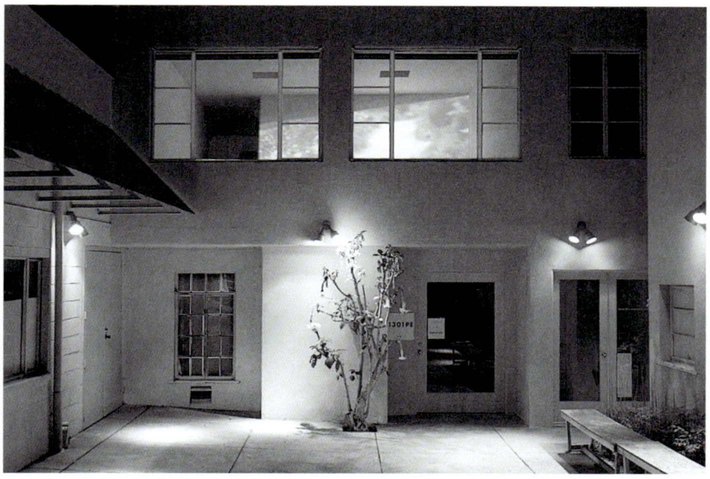

What first compelled you to open a gallery?
The founding principle was to present world class exhibitions of artists primarily based in Los Angeles.

Who is the first artist you showed and what was most memorable about that show?
The first show at 1301 was *Raw Material* (1992) by Kate Ericson and Mel Ziegler, which opened on April 29, 1992, the day the LA Riots started.

When did you first participate in Art Basel and what was most memorable about that show?
Our first participation was in 2005.

- **Contact** 1301PE, Isha Welsh, isha@1301pe.com, info@1301pe.com
- **Established** 1992
- **Owner(s) / Partner(s)** Brian Butler
- **Team** 4
- **Space(s)** 140 m²
- **Artists at Art Basel** Fiona Banner, Kirsten Everberg, Judy Ledgerwood, Jorge Méndez Blake, Rirkrit Tiravanija, Kerry Tribe, Pae White, Paul Winstanley
- **Further artists represented** Uta Barth, Angela Bulloch, Fiona Connor, Jack Goldstein, Ann Veronica Janssen, Jorge Pardo, Philippe Parreno, Blake Rayne, John Reynolds, Jessica Stockholder, SUPERFLEX, Diana Thater, Charline von Heyl

Galerie 1900–2000

Paris — Galleries; Galleries Kabinett

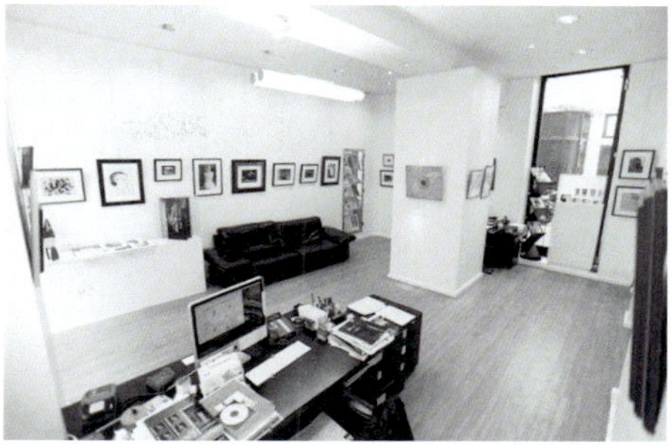

What first compelled you to open a gallery?
It was an idea of Man Ray in 1971: he had no gallery at the time, and suggested I open one.

When did you first participate in Art Basel and what was most memorable about that show?
In 1973, and we sold the whole booth.

- **Contact** Galerie 1900–2000, David Fleiss, info@galerie1900-2000.com
- **Established** 1972 (Galerie des Quatre Mouvements)
- **Owner(s) / Partner(s)** Marcel & David Fleiss
- **Team** 5
- **Space(s)** 120 m²
- **Artists at Art Basel** Carl Andre, Arman, Robert Barry, Hans Bellmer, Ben, Jean Louis Brau, George Brecht, Pol Bury, Guiseppe Chiari, William Copley, Marius de Zayas, Marcel Duchamp, Öyvind Fahlström, Robert Filliou, Pinot Gallizio, Giorgio Griffa, Geoffrey Hendricks, Dick Higgins, Georges Hugnet, Isidore Isou, Ray Johnson, Allan Kaprow, Alison Knowles, Joseph Kosuth, Tetsumi Kudo, Jean-Jacques Lebel, Maurice Lemaître, Jackson Mac Low, Robert Malaval, Roberto Matta, Pierre Molinier, Claes Oldenburg, Giulio Paolini, Francis Picabia, Man Ray, Edda Renouf, Ed Ruscha, Takako Saito, Kurt Seligmann, Dorothea Tanning, Wolf Vostell, James Waring, Robert Watts, Tom Wesselmann, Robert Whitman
- **Further artists represented** Gaston Bertin, Jean Dubuffet, Aube Elléouët, Max Ernst, Xavier Escriba, Natalia Gontcharova, Philippe Jusforgues, Wifredo Lam, Frédéric Léglise, Miguel Rio Branco

Jeppe Hein
Jens Hoffmann
Larry Johnson
Matt Johnson
Jacob Kassay
Karen Kilimnik
Elad Lassry
Florian Maier-Aichen
Nick Mauss
Mike Nelson
Kristin Oppenheim
Eva Rothschild
Collier Schorr
Stephen Shore
Sue Williams
Jane and Louise Wilson

2P

Hong Kong
Sai Ying Pun

● Discoveries

- **Contact** 2P Contemporary Art Gallery
  info@2p-gallery.com
- **Established** 2010
- **Owner(s) / Partner(s)** Pui Pui To
- **Artists at Art Basel** Tang Kwok Hin
- **Further artists represented** Will Kwan
  Chi Wo Warren Leung
  Cedric Maridet
  Yotaro Niwa
  Yuk King Tan
  Morgan Wong
  Wai Yin Wong

303 Gallery

New York

● Galleries
● Galleries Unlimited
● Galleries Public

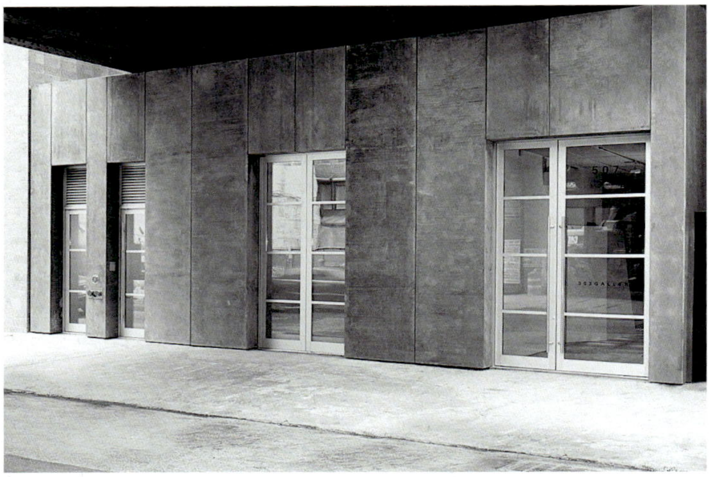

What first compelled you to open a gallery?
I had a lot of friends making work who couldn't show within the traditional gallery or museum system in NYC in the 1980s, and the studio beneath mine was up for rent, so I decided to do a show there.

Who is the first artist you showed and what was most memorable about that show?
The first show at 303 was a two-person exhibition with Richard Prince and David Robbins. The most memorable thing about that show was the magic of it actually happening!

When did you first participate in Art Basel and what was most memorable about that show?
Our first Art Basel was in 2002, and I remember being really amazed and excited by the energy in the room—it felt like a whole new way to look at art and the gallery system.

- **Contact** 303 Gallery
  Erika Weiss
  erika@303gallery.com
  info@303gallery.com
- **Established** 1984
- **Owner(s) / Partner(s)** Lisa Spellman (Owner)
  Kathryn Erdman (Director)
  Cristian Alexa (Director)
  Erika Weiss (Associate Director)
  Thomas Arsac (Artist Manager)
- **Team** 16
- **Artists at Art Basel** Doug Aitken
  Valentin Carron
  Hans-Peter Feldmann
  Ceal Floyer
  Karel Funk
  Maureen Gallace
  Tim Gardner
  Dominique Gonzalez-Foerster
  Rodney Graham
  Mary Heilmann

313 Art Project

Seoul

● Insights

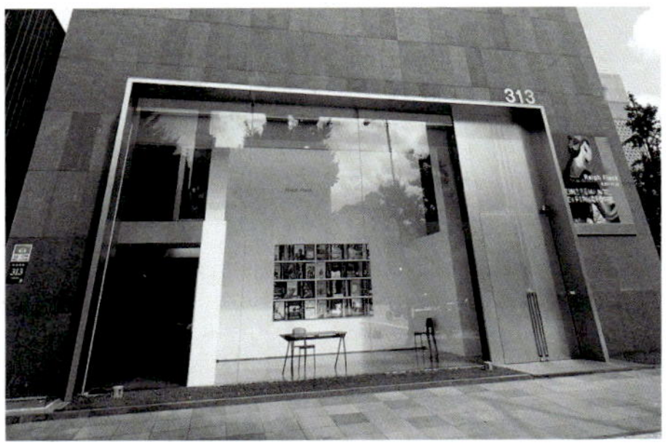

What first compelled you to open a gallery?
313 Art Project intends to support globally acclaimed and distinguished, yet domestically less-known artists with a successful debut in Korea. The primary objective of our space is to exhibit contemporary artists, and introduce their best works with accurate context and explanation. 313 Art Project strives for viewers and collectors to vividly experience the newest trends in contemporary art.

Who is the first artist you showed and what was most memorable about that show?
The first Korean artist we showed was Heryun Kim. German literature major Heryun Kim has represented the beauty and grotesqueness of objects and emotion with a keen sense for almost 20 years, since she studied in Berlin. Although experiments with diverse mediums are prevalent these days, Kim has focused on painting, always questioning the notion of existence through this medium. While her intense colors and vigorous brushstrokes are suggestive of German Neo-Expressionism, the artist has consistently taken note of the history and reality she faces, and above all had a sense of awe toward Korean art's spirituality. In the show, her *Until Peony Blooms* series represented her literary quality and narrative dynamism, visualizing Kim Young-rang's poem with flamboyant, desperate peony.

When did you first participate in Art Basel and what was most memorable about that show?
In 2013 in Hong Kong. Everything was nicely organized and staff was very supportive when we needed.

- **Contact** 313 Art Project
  Bonaventure Kwak
  bkwak313@gmail.com
  313artproject@gmail.com
- **Established** 2010
- **Owner(s) / Partner(s)** Mikeum Lee
- **Team** 7
- **Space(s)** 330 m²
- **Artists at Art Basel** Insook Kim
- **Further artists represented** Ralph Fleck
  Ahreum Han
  Youngjin Jo
  Jon Kessler
  Beum Kim
  Heryun Kim
  Jinhoon Lee
  Tony Oursler
  Ena Swansea
  Xavier Veilhan

47 Canal

New York

Statements
Nova

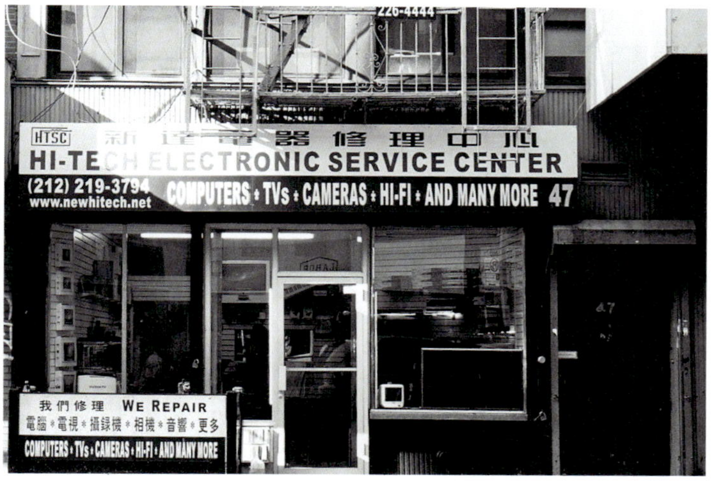

What first compelled you to open a gallery?
Supporting a specific group of artists in New York City.

Who is the first artist you showed and what was most memorable about that show?
The first show at the gallery was also Michele Abeles' first solo exhibition in Manhattan. Photographs included: red, rock, cigarettes, body, wood, lycra, bottle, pitcher, paper, arm, scuba, hand, fly, table, lines, numbers, letters, tape, magenta, veneer, frame, concrete, blue, green, orange, and plant.

When did you first participate in Art Basel and what was most memorable about that show?
We did an Antoine Catala Statements booth at Art Basel in 2013. There was a :)/:(hologram, an inflate/delate sculpture, and a vacuumed latex wall piece.

- **Contact** 47 Canal
Oliver Newton
info@47canalstreet.com
- **Established** 2011
- **Owner(s) / Partner(s)** Oliver Newton
Margaret Lee
- **Team** 1
- **Space(s)** 110 m²
- **Artists at Art Basel** Antoine Catala
Alisa Baremboym
John Finneran
- **Further artists represented** Michele Abeles
Martin Beck
Gregory Edwards
Josh Kline
Amy Lien/Enzo Camacho
Trevor Shimizu
Nolan Simon
Stewart Uoo
Anicka Yi

80m2

Lima

Nova
Public

- **Contact** 80m2 Livia Benavides
galeria@80m2galeria.com
- **Established** 2011
- **Owner(s) / Partner(s)** Livia Benavides
- **Artists at Art Basel** Daniela Ortiz
Rita Ponce de León
David Zink Yi
- **Further artists represented** Iosu Aramburu
Luz Maria Bedoya
Arturo Kameya
Nancy La Rosa
Claudia Martinez
Raura Oblitas
Eliana Otta
Marco Pando
Gianfranco Piazzini
Santiago Roose
Juan Javier Salazar
Juan Diego Tobalina
Adán Vallecillo

Galerie 1900–2000
Interview with David Fleiss

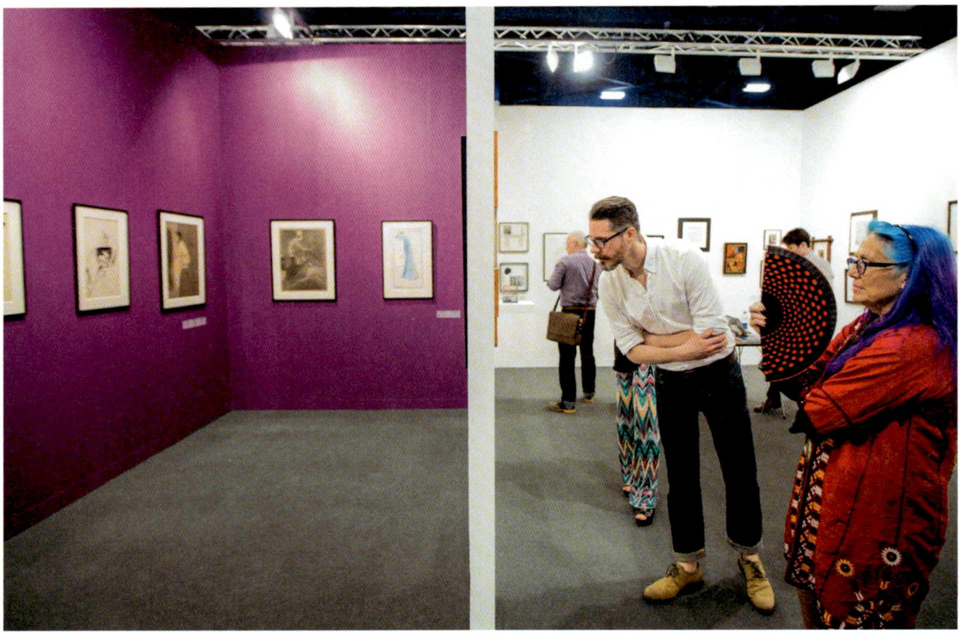

Art Basel in Miami Beach, 2013

Could you sum up the history of your gallery?

My father, Marcel, opened the gallery in 1972. His family was in the fur trade, which in Paris was traditionally based not far from the Drouot auctioneers, in the neighborhood where the antique dealers and auction houses are.

He learned about art just by walking around the neighborhood and going to Drouot every day. In the late 1960s he became friends with Man Ray, who encouraged him to open a gallery in 1972, because he was no longer represented by any gallery in Paris. So the two of them opened the Galerie des Quatre Mouvements, the name referring to Surrealism, Pop art, Dada, and Hyper-Realism. My father closed the gallery when Man Ray died in 1977, then opened the Galerie 1900–2000 in 1981. I began working with him in 1990.

What is the gallery's main focus now?

All the 20th-century avant-garde movements, especially Surrealism.

One thing your gallery is known for is the way you display works at art fairs.

I hang the works on our stands the same way I do at home, the way most people do. Most collectors own numerous works of art and, if they don't leave it up to their decorator to hang them, they display many of them on their walls. That's what many people do. But it's true that the way we display works is specific to us, and a lot of people from the contemporary art world, and artists, like it. However, there are also a lot of collectors who don't visit our stand because they think they won't find any major works in such a display. That doesn't matter; I find it fun. Our stands are very different from today's "curated" stands, but it's a matter of effort and deliberate choice. There are more and more stands following our example at Art Basel and even at other fairs. Actually, the way we display the works is inspired by Surrealist exhibitions. When you look at photographs of Surrealist exhibitions, there's never any wall left bare.

For Art Basel in Miami Beach you have put together a Kabinett devoted to Marius de Zayas. Why this choice and can you say a few words about him?

We recently gained access to a number of works by Marius de Zayas, via a collection that had remained untouched since the 1920s or 1930s. We will be holding an exhibition at the Paris gallery in 2014, so we said to ourselves, "Since we're holding the exhibition, why not feature it at an art fair before the gallery?" Why here? Because we're not far from Mexico, where Marius de Zayas was born, and we hope to attract Mexican collectors. Obviously, since he also co-founded the first modern art gallery in New York, New York collectors are also likely to show an interest.

Marius de Zayas (1880–1961) was a Mexican caricaturist who came to New York in the early 1910s. He was a close friend of Alfred Stieglitz, who co-founded the 291 Gallery with him. Marius de Zayas was the man who first brought French artists like Marcel Duchamp and Francis Picabia and their ilk to New York and organized their first exhibitions. He also kept up his caricature work, providing numerous illustrations for Stieglitz's magazine. He was very good friends with artists we often show and a highly influential figure in the New York art world.

THE MAIN TIPPING POINTS
MOMENTS/EVENTS/SHIF
THAT MARKED THE E
OF THAT PHOENOME
CALL "ART" IN THE
YEARS TODAY, AND IN

24 HRS

#FACTS/
TS/PEOPLE
VOLUTION
NON WE
LAST 40-50
THE FUTURE

2013 participants

Bashar Al Shroogi
Dubai
United Arab Emirates

Tobias Berger
Hong Kong
China

Luca Belgiorno-Nettis
Woolloomooloo
North South Wales
Australia

Hu Bin
Guangzhou
China

Thomas Berghuis
Sydney
Australia

Bonnie Clearwater
North Miami
United States

Joselina Cruz
Manila
Philippines

Marko Daniel
London
United Kingdom

Jeffrey Deitch
Los Angeles
United States

Füsun Eczacibasi
Istanbul
Turkey

Alexie Glass
Melbourne
Australia

Yi Guan
Shanghai
China

Wang Huangsheng
Beijing
China

Agung Hujatnikajennong
Bandung
Indonesia

Farouk Khan
Kuala Lumpur
Malaysia

Sunjung Kim
Seoul
South Korea

Sook-Kyung Lee
London
United Kingdom

Pi Li
Hong Kong
China

Julie Lomax
Sydney
Australia

Xun Lu
Nanjing
China

Daisuke Miyatsu
Tokyo
Japan

Frances Morris
London
United Kingdom

Alexandra Munroe
New York
United States

Lars Nittve
Hong Kong
China

Sabyasachi Mukherjee
Mumbai
India

Hong Djien Oei
Magelang
Indonesia

Philippe Pirotte
Antwerp
Brussels
Belgium

Adriano Pedrosa
Sao Paulo
Brazil

Zhi Bing Qiao
Shanghai
China

Annette Schönholzer
Basel
Switzerland

Gene Sherman
Sydney
Australia

Uli Sigg
Mauensee
Switzerland

Claudia Steinfels
Zurich
Switzerland

Alia Swastika
Jogjakarta
Indonesia

András Szántó
Brooklyn
United States

Philip Tinari
Beijing
China

Rudy Tseng
New Taipei City
Taiwan

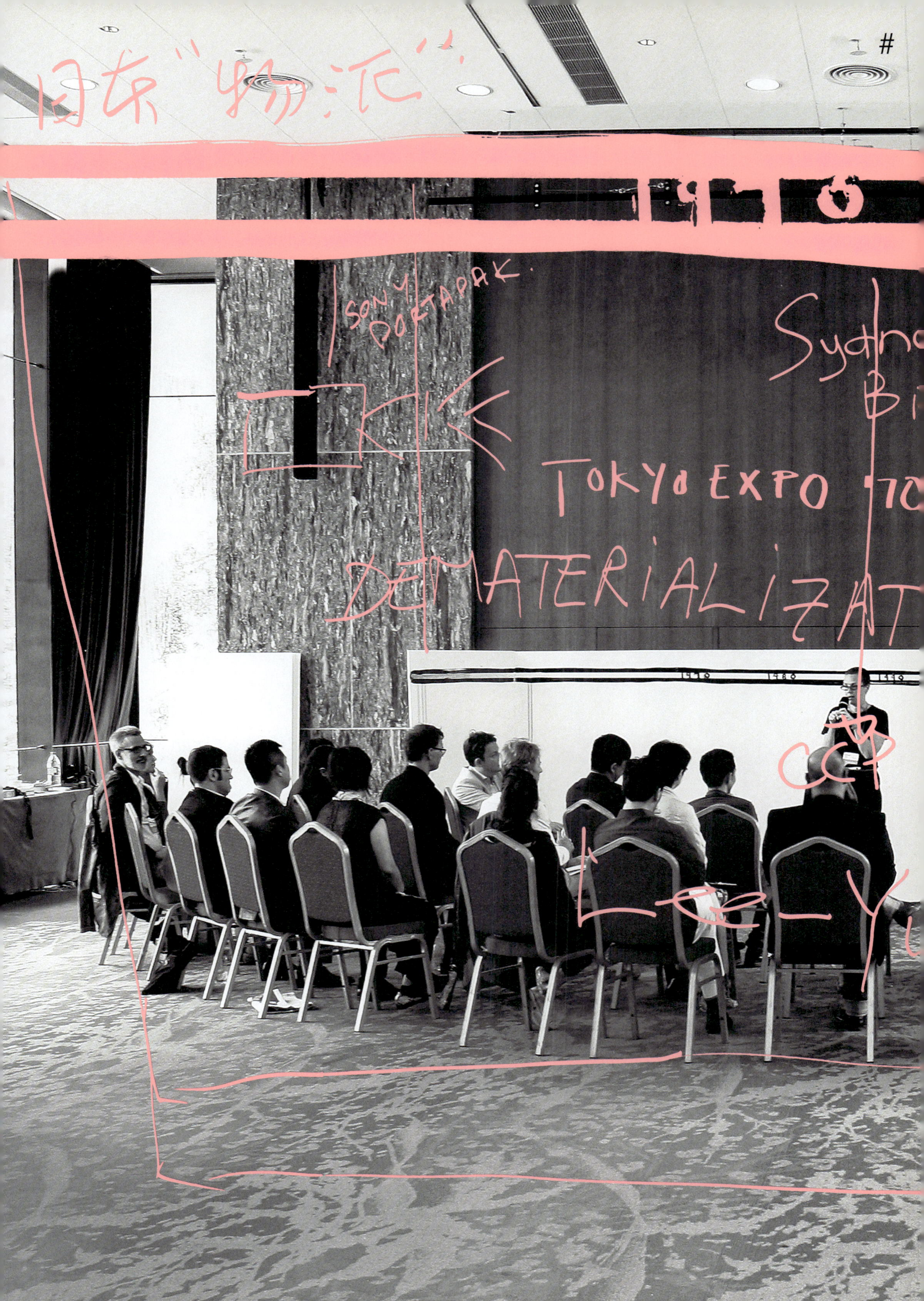
SONY PORTAPAK.
TOKYO EXPO '70
DEMATERIALIZAT

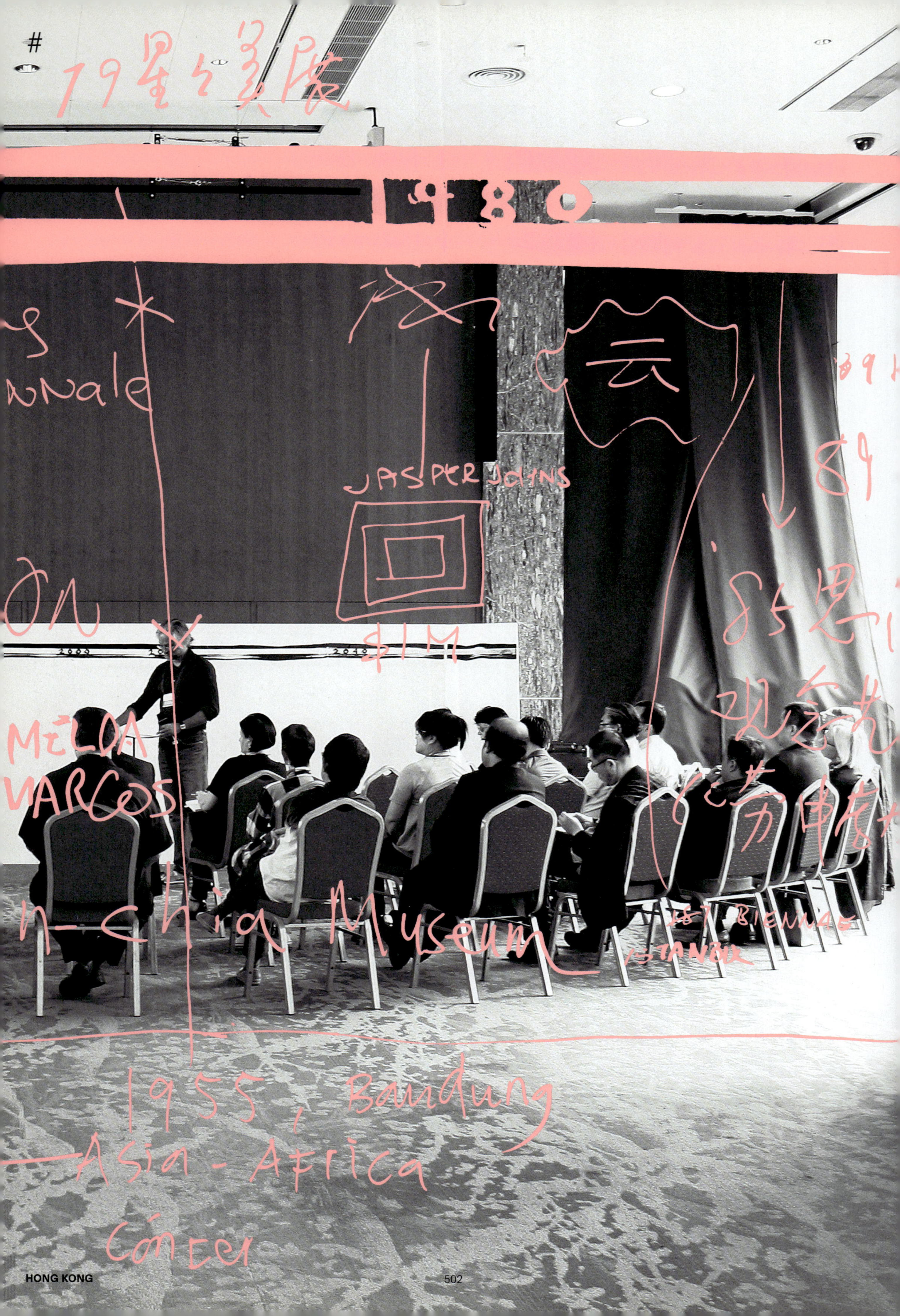
1980
JASPER JOHNS
$1M
Museum
1955, Bandung
Asia - Africa

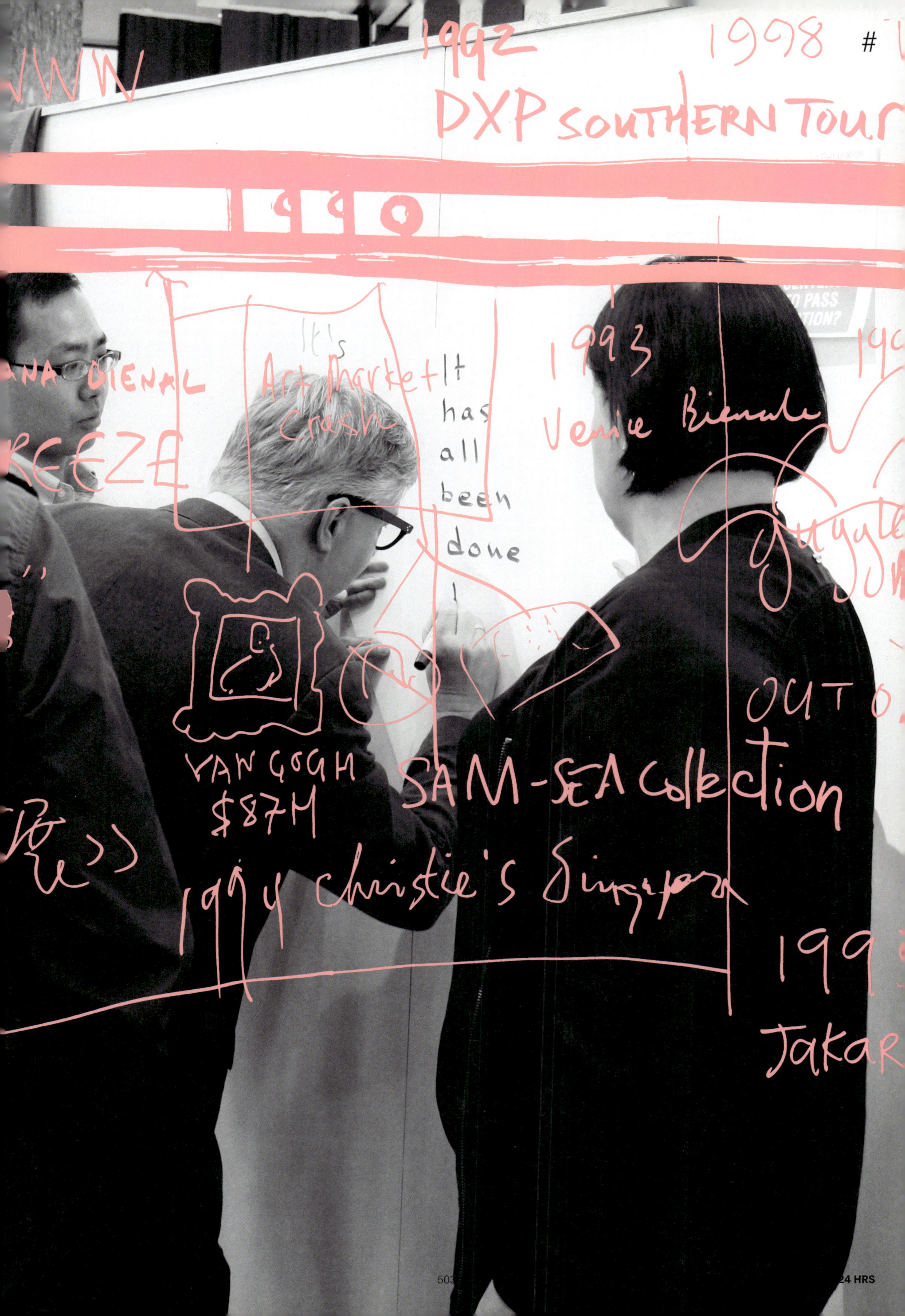
1992
1998
DXP SOUTHERN TOUR
1990
It's Art Market Crash
It has all been done
1993
VAN GOGH $87M
SAM-SEA Collection
1994 christie's Singapore
Jakar

'98 fall of Soeharto/ new order regime

2000 上海双年展 / Fuck U

2002 广州三年展

2000

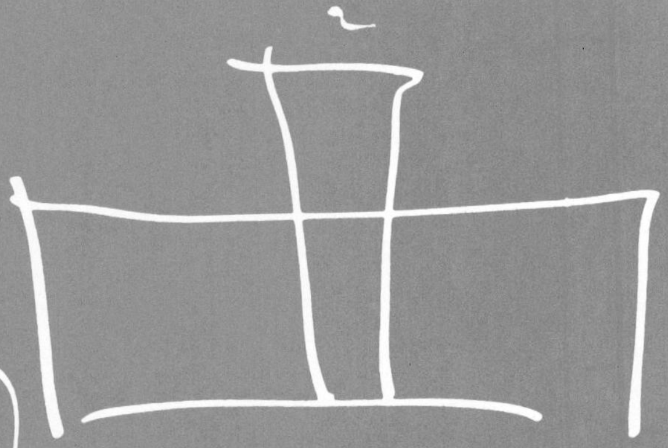

2001 FRIEZE

2010

2002 Pause

2008 金融

SEPT 11

ACTION

, contemporary art from non-aligned countries

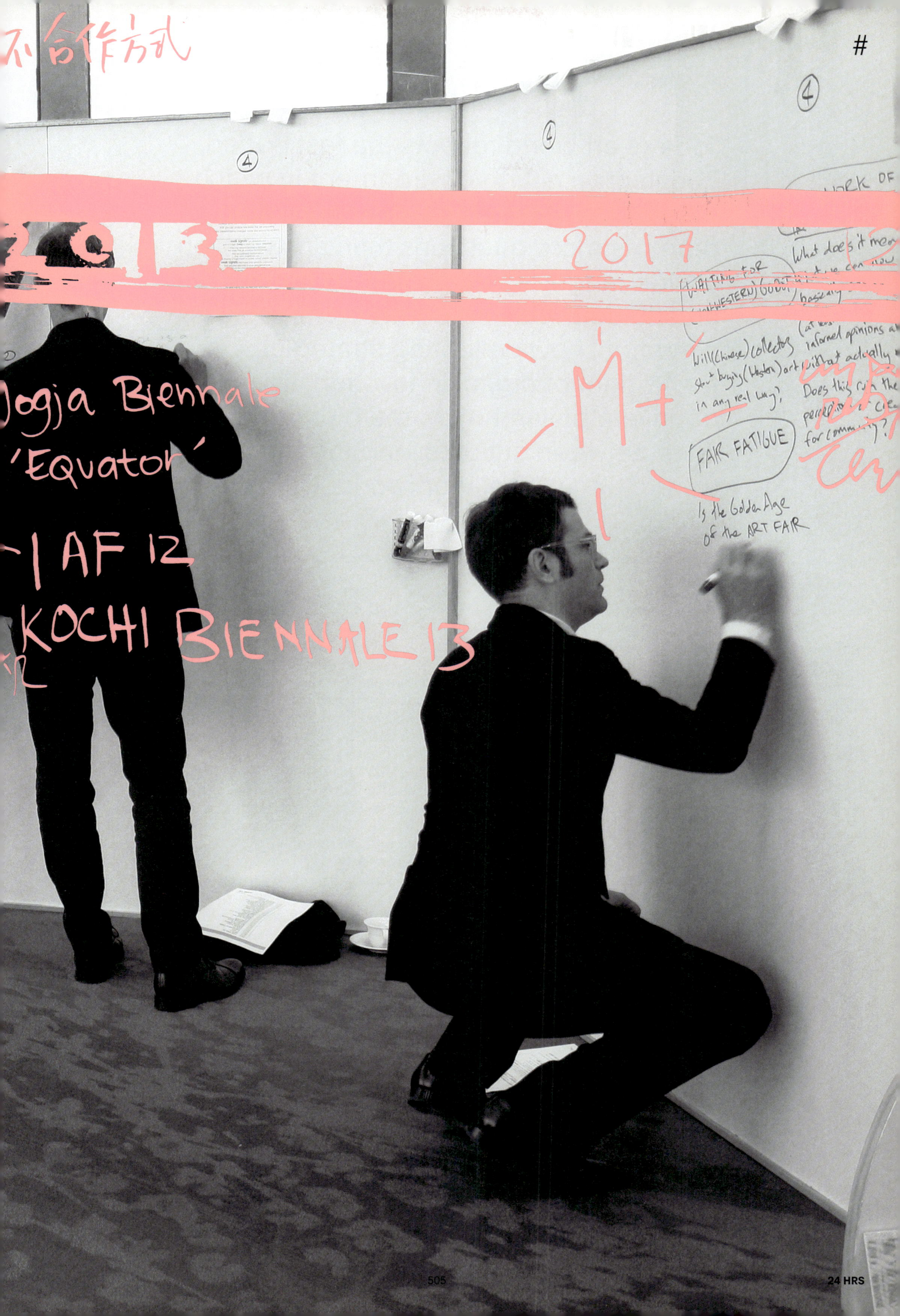
不合作方式
2013
2017
What does it mean
WAITING FOR (WESTERN) GODOT
Will (Chinese) collectors start buying (Western) art in any real way?
informed opinions
Does this
M+
FAIR FATIGUE
Is the Golden Age of the ART FAIR
Jogja Biennale
'Equator'
IAF 12
KOCHI BIENNALE 13

24 HRS

Annette Schönholzer

Today's art world reflects the fast paced, constantly shifting environment in which we live. The emerging landscape often prompts more questions than answers, on a wide range of topics, among them: artistic practice and commercial representation; new collecting strategies; the impact of digital innovation; the role of private philanthropy; the blurring of lines between cultures; and the rapid turn toward a multi-polar art world.

Nominators

Lars Nittve, Executive Director, M+ Museum, Hong Kong

Fumio Nanjo, Director, Mori Art Museum, Tokyo

Uli Sigg, Collector, Mauensee, Switzerland

Chris Dercon, Director, Tate Modern, London

Anne Pasternak, President and Artistic Director, Creative Time, New York

Wang Huangsheng, Director, CAFA Art Museum, Beijing

Patricia Phelps de Cisneros, Fundación Cisneros, Caracas and New York

The individuals at the art world's core come from diverse backgrounds—they are highly influential men and women linked through a shared passion for art. Nonetheless, for such key art world players, opportunities to explore common interests and imperatives with their international peers remain rare.

Convened for the first time in May 2013, on the eve of the inaugural Art Basel show in Hong Kong, 24 HRS is such an opportunity. Nominators have designated a group of globally-active collectors, museum directors, curators, and others active in the art world on a daily basis—people whose perspectives transcend their own regions and official functions, and who command the knowledge, the influence, and the resources to have an impact on our ever-changing cultural environment.

Spanning three world regions—Europe, Asia, and the Americas—Art Basel has always been a connecting point for the art world. Now, going a step further, Art Basel has conceived a singular setting to assess and address some of the most urgent issues confronting the global art community, today and tomorrow. Art Basel, with a committee of art world leaders, has invited a roster of personalities, divided in small groups, to determine the key questions to be considered and discussed by going through a series of off-the-record conversations. 24 HRS had no panels, no lectures, no pre-set themes. It was a day simply devoted to pausing and reflecting upon our shared cultural legacy and responsibility.

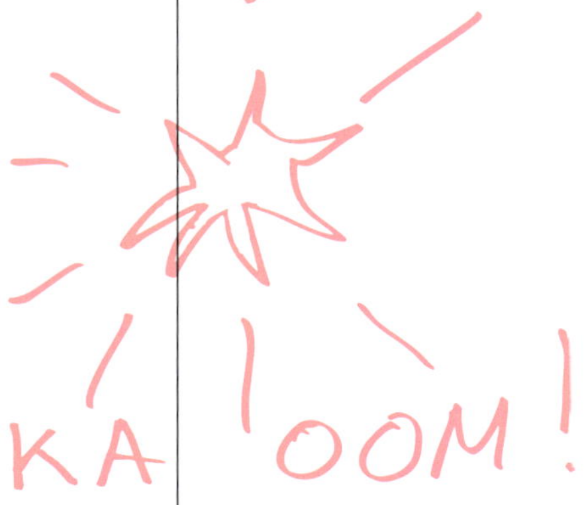

N

- Hong Kong
- Basel
- Miami Beach

nächst St. Stephan

Vienna

- Galleries (Basel)
- Galleries (Miami Beach)

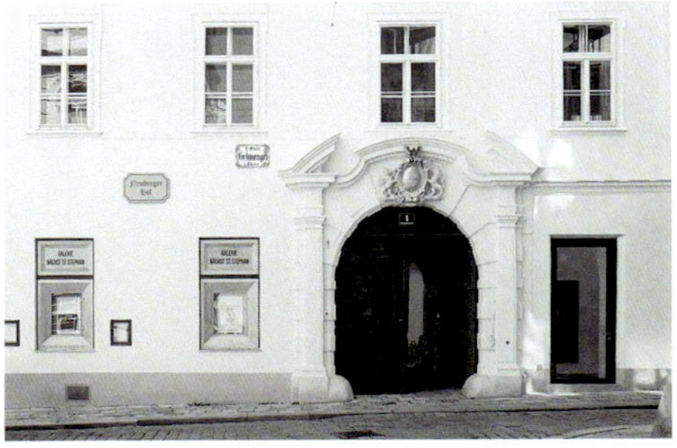

What first compelled you to open a gallery?

After some years as an art journalist—during which I learned a great deal, visited countless exhibitions, got to know many artists, and became familiar with the wide world of art—I decided I wanted to share art in a more direct way and do my own exhibitions. I was convinced that the art scene in Vienna needed to become more international and this was an inspiring vision for my programmatic direction.

Who is the first artist you showed and what was most memorable about that show?

The art scene in Vienna was very provincial at the end of the 1970s. For me, Ernst Caramelle's exhibition (in 1979) was the first major exception. He curated my first exhibition, called *Multiples* (1978), in which I showed young Austrian and international artists, such as Franz Vana, Engratia Mölk, Patrizia Caire, Juan Navarro Baldeweg, Günther Schrom, and others. The minimal effort involved in its production was a rejection of traditional artistic means and conventional media, like painting; it was about having a certain attitude in art—one that was the opposite of the conventional artists represented in the Secession and the Künstlerhaus in Vienna.

When did you first participate in Art Basel and what was most memorable about that show?

I was born and raised in Basel, and even went to school where the exhibition halls now stand. And that was back when they used to have separate classes for boys and girls! As a teenager, the Basel Kunstmuseum was my favorite place to hang out, and its unique collection shaped how I see art today. I moved to Vienna in the 1970s, and the gallery has been to Art Basel every year since 1982. Already in those days Art Basel showed its potential as a strong platform for galleries and collectors, the perfect atmosphere for networking.

- **Contact** Galerie nächst St. Stephan
Rosemarie Schwarzwälder
Elisabeth Madlener
madlener@schwarzwaelder.at
galerie@schwarzwaelder.at
- **Established** 1954 (by Msgr. Otto Mauer)
- **Owner(s) / Partner(s)** Rosemarie Schwarzwälder
- **Team** 9
- **Space(s)** 500 m²
- **Artists at Art Basel** Adam Adach
Polly Apfelbaum
Herbert Brandl
Michał Budny
Ernst Caramelle
Heinrich Dunst
Helmut Federle
Bernard Frize
Katharina Grosse
Luisa Kasalicky
Imi Knoebel
Daniel Knorr
Lee Ufan
Sonia Leimer
Isa Melsheimer
Manfred Pernice
Karin Sander
Jörg Sasse
Adrian Schiess
Jessica Stockholder
Joëlle Tuerlinckx
Günter Umberg
Christoph Weber
James Welling
- **Further artists represented** Sabine Boehl
Rainer Ganahl
Aneta Grzeszykowska
Agnieszka Kalinowska

Nadi

Jakarta

- Galleries (Hong Kong)

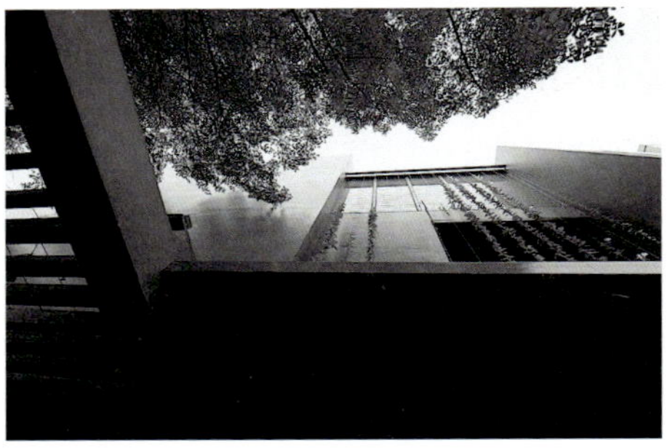

What first compelled you to open a gallery?

My devotion for art and my desire to take part in promoting Indonesian contemporary art. There were so many potential artists in Indonesia that I wanted to introduce to a broader audience; I wanted to provide a space for them to show their qualified works. Also I wanted to try making better and more qualified exhibitions by doing collaborations with guest or independent curators.

Who is the first artist you showed and what was most memorable about that show?

The first artist shown in Nadi Gallery was Heri Dono. What I remember most about that show was that for a newly-opened gallery, it became a very successful one, in terms of its quality and the public's enthusiasm for visiting and collecting the works of the artist. Another important thing was that there were reviews of the show even in the mass media.

When did you first participate in Art Basel and what was most memorable about that show?

Nadi Gallery took part in Art Basel in Hong Kong in 2013. But before that, when the name of the fair was still ART HK, we already had been participating in this event for several years. We haven't had the chance to participate in Art Basel in Basel, though we are looking forward to that. What was most memorable about this year's show was the plurality, quantity, and enthusiasm of the audience. Also the committee had done a very good job in selecting the art fair's participants.

- **Contact** Nadi Gallery
Meli Angkapradipta
nadigallery@gmail.com
- **Established** 2000
- **Owner(s) / Partner(s)** Biantoro Santoso
Meli Angkapradipta
- **Team** 3
- **Space(s)** 250 m²
- **Artists at Art Basel** Jumaldi Alfi
Samsul Arifin
Eddie Hara
Yusra Martunus
Yuli Prayitno
Handiwirman Saputra
Arin Dwihartanto Sunaryo

- **Further artists represented** Heri Dono
  Dadang Rukmana
  Laksmi Shitaresmi
  Agus Suwage

Nagel Draxler

Cologne
Berlin

Galleries

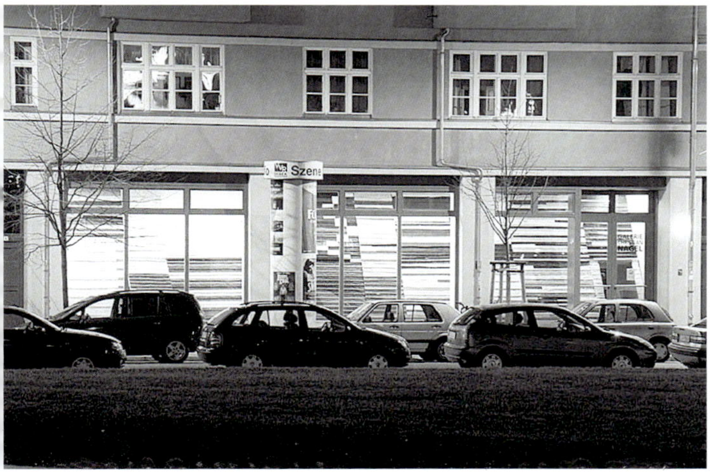

What first compelled you to open a gallery?
As a young art historian I applied for the directorship of the Kunstverein Münster. The artists I proposed were Martin Kippenberger, Richard Prince, Mark Dion, Andrea Fraser, and Michael Krebber. I received a letter saying they rather look for somebody with better knowledge of contemporary art. That was when I realized that the institutional way was not the right way for me and I had to make exhibitions on my own. I became a gallerist.

Who is the first artist you showed and what was most memorable about that show?
Cosima von Bonin. On April 26, 1990, in Cologne, concurrently with Köln-show. Bonin only showed five smaller black and white photographs of an English fishing club, where for once a woman had won the main trophy. This started the career of the artist and also of the gallery, which assumed an important role in the new discourses of contextual art, political correctness, and gender, namely of the new post-avant-garde.

When did you first participate in Art Basel and what was most memorable about that show?
In 1995, with a solo booth of Michael Krebber. Krebber was not necessarily known as an artist with a big production. Nevertheless in Basel he filled the entire big booth with new paintings and drawings, which we sold to important collectors.

- **Contact** Galerie Nagel Draxler
  Saskia Draxler
  saskia.draxler@nagel-draxler.de
  berlin@nagel-draxler.de
- **Established** 1990
- **Owner(s) / Partner(s)** Christian Nagel
  Saskia Draxler
- **Team** 10
- **Space(s)** 350 m²
- **Artists at Art Basel** Kader Attia
  Clegg & Guttmann
  Keren Cytter
  Mark Dion
  Andrea Fraser
  Lone Haugaard Madsen
  Christian Philipp Müller
  Stefan Müller
  Josephine Pryde
  Martha Rosler
  Dominik Sittig
  Joëlle Tuerlinckx
  Luca Vitone
  Stephen Willats
  Heimo Zobernig

Nagy

London

Galleries

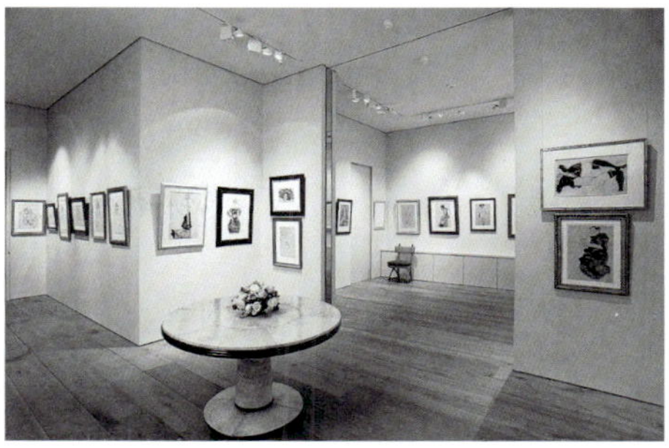

When did you first participate in Art Basel and what was most memorable about that show?
In 2005.

- **Contact** Richard Nagy Ltd.
  Nina Hartl
  info@ichardnagy.com
- **Established** 1980
- **Owner(s) / Partner(s)** Richard Nagy
- **Team** 4
- **Space(s)** 150 m²
- **Artists at Art Basel** Francis Bacon
  Max Beckmann
  Heinrich Campendonk
  Otto Dix
  James Ensor
  Lyonel Charles Feininger
  Lucian Freud
  Alberto Giacometti
  George Grosz
  Erich Heckel
  Karl Hubbuch
  Ernst Ludwig Kirchner
  Gustav Klimt
  Oskar Kokoschka
  Alfred Kubin
  Wilhelm Lehmbruck
  Henri Matisse
  George Minne
  Emil Nolde
  Hermann Max Pechstein
  Anton Peschka
  Pablo Picasso
  Odilon Redon
  Auguste Rodin
  Christian Schad
  Egon Schiele
  Oskar Schlemmer
  Rudolf Schlichter
  Karl Schmidt-Rottluff
  Stanley Spencer

Nahem

New York

Galleries
Galleries

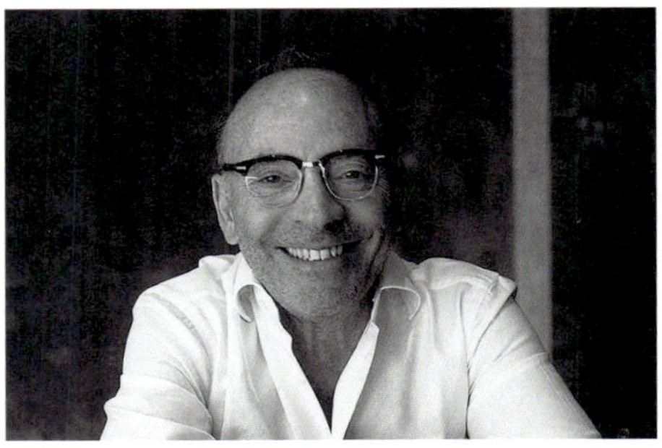

- **Contact** Edward Tyler Nahem Fine Art LLC
  Janis Cecil
  janis@etnahem.com
  info@etnahem.com
- **Established** 1985
- **Owner(s) / Partner(s)** Edward Nahem
- **Team** 7
- **Space(s)** 400 m²

- **Artists at Art Basel** Jean-Michel Basquiat
Alighiero Boetti
Alexander Calder
John Chamberlain
Willem de Kooning
Richard Diebenkorn
Jean Dubuffet
Sam Francis
Alberto Giacometti
Philip Guston
Keith Haring
Ellsworth Kelly
Anselm Kiefer
Franz Kline
Roy Lichtenstein
René Magritte
Joan Miró
Joan Mitchell
Pablo Picasso
Richard Prince
Robert Rauschenberg
Gerhard Richter
Mark Rothko
Ed Ruscha
Frank Stella
Cy Twombly
Andy Warhol
Tom Wesselmann

Nahmad

New York — Galleries
London — Galleries

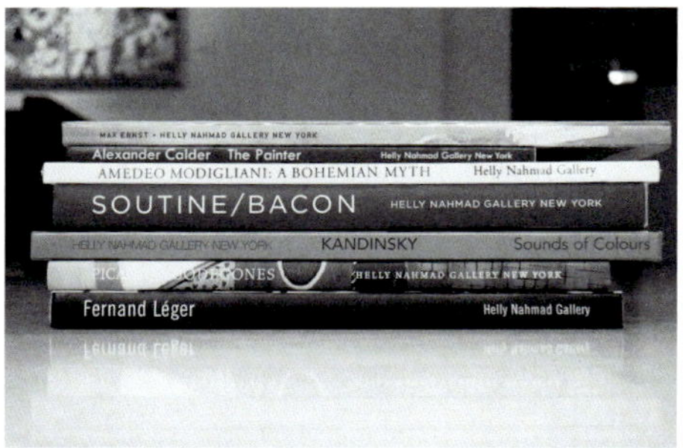

What first compelled you to open a gallery?
Art collecting and art dealing has been a family business, so I was not only exposed to fantastic artworks growing up, but also inspired by some of the best experts in the field: my family members. Opening a gallery was a way to pursue that inherited passion for art and contribute to a legacy of which I am very proud.

Who is the first artist you showed and what was most memorable about that show?
One of the first and most memorable shows we had was a retrospective of Wassily Kandinsky in 2004, called *Sounds of Colours*, which focused on the aesthetic power of music and the profound influence it had on the artist's work.

When did you first participate in Art Basel and what was most memorable about that show?
Our first Art Basel participation was in Switzerland, the fair that has continued to be our favorite ever since, maybe in part due to the continued good company we keep. We are just as excited to see the works other galleries bring as we are to exhibit ourselves.

- **Contact** Helly Nahmad Gallery
Margaret Zuckerman
info@hellynahmadgallery.com
- **Established** 1999
- **Owner(s) / Partner(s)** Helly Nahmad
- **Team** 5
- **Space(s)** 250 m² (New York)
- **Artists at Art Basel** Josef Albers
Arman
Alighiero Boetti
Fernando Botero
Georges Braque
Alberto Burri
Alexander Calder
Marc Chagall
Salvador Dalí
Giorgio de Chirico
Nicolas de Stäel
Edgar Degas
Paul Delvaux
Jean Dubuffet
Max Ernst
Lucio Fontana
Sam Francis
Alberto Giacometti
Juan Gris
Hans Hartung
Damien Hirst
Robert Indiana
Wassily Kandinsky
Paul Klee
Yves Klein
Wifredo Lam
Fernand Léger
René Magritte
Kazimir Malevich
Giacomo Manzù
Marino Marini
André Masson
Henri Matisse
Roberto Matta
Joan Miró
Amedeo Modigliani
Piet Mondrian
Claude Monet
Henry Moore
Giorgio Morandi
Ben Nicholson
Francis Picabia
Pablo Picasso
Camille Pissarro
Serge Poliakoff
Jean-Paul Riopelle
Mark Rothko
Kurt Schwitters
Pierre Soulages
Chaïm Soutine
Yves Tanguy
Antoni Tàpies
Wayne Thiebaud
Cy Twombly
Victor Vasarely
Andy Warhol
- **Further artists represented** Pierre Auguste Renoir
Kees van Dongen

Nanzuka

Tokyo — Galleries
Hong Kong

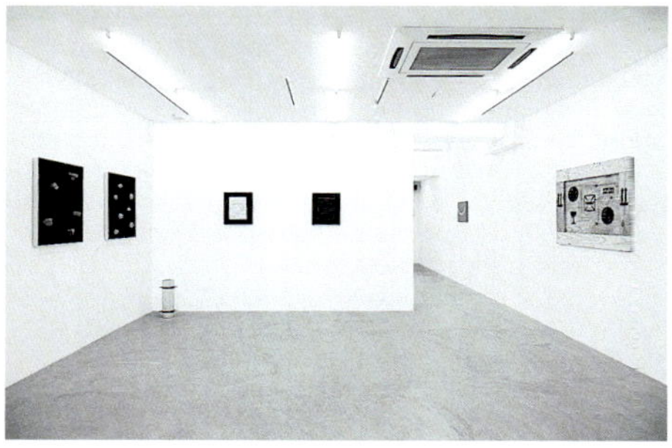

What first compelled you to open a gallery?
Studying art history through BA and MA courses at university made me more curious about the artists working in the present time and the future, rather than the history of the past. After the graduation, I started the business to support the many young and less famous artists who were not yet appreciated.

Who is the first artist you showed and what was most memorable about that show?
The first exhibition was a group show, a tribute to Fishmans—the legendary reggae band from 1990s Japanese music scene. The artists participating included Naohiro Ukawa and some of our represented artists, such as Akiyoshi Mishima.

When did you first participate in Art Basel and what was most memorable about that show?
It was in 2011, we participated in Art Basel with a Feature booth and held a solo exhibition of Keiichi Tanaami. Impressed by the reactions after the fair, I realized that was the influence of Europe's main fair.

- **Contact** Nanzuka
  Yuki Itaya
  itaya@nug.jp
  info@nug.jp
- **Established** 2005
- **Owner(s) / Partner(s)** Shinji Nanzuka
- **Space(s)** 40 m²
- **Artists at Art Basel** Julia Chiang
  Tatjana Doll
  Yuji Honbori
  Todd James
  Saya Kubota
  Tomoki Kurokawa
  Keiichi Tanaami
  Yuichi Yokoyama
- **Further artists represented** Akiyoshi Mishima
  Hajime Sorayama

Nature Morte

New Delhi — Galleries
Berlin — Galleries
Gurgaon — Unlimited

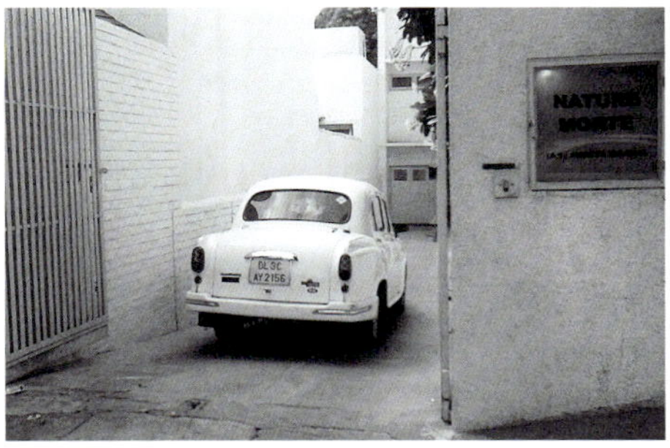

What first compelled you to open a gallery?
The desire to work with artists to mount exhibitions of their work.

Who is the first artist you showed and what was most memorable about that show?
Our first show in India was a group show with four Indian and four international artists. We fabricated a neon piece for Joseph Kosuth in the three languages of Delhi (Hindi, Urdu, Punjabi), but unfortunately Joseph wasn't able to come for the show.

When did you first participate in Art Basel and what was most memorable about that show?
In the Feature sector in 2006. Having visited Art Basel only once previously, we were thrilled to realize that Feature was along the periphery of the main fair. We thought it would be in a separate sector like Statements.

- **Contact** Nature Morte
  Peter Nagy
  naturemorte@hotmail.com
  info@naturemorte.com
- **Established** 1982 (New York)
  1997 (New Delhi)
- **Owner(s) / Partner(s)** Peter Nagy
  Aparajita Jain
- **Team** 21
- **Space(s)** 300 m² (New Delhi)
  200 m² (Berlin)
  100 m² (Gurgaon)
- **Artists at Art Basel** Suhasini Kejriwal
  Mona Rai
  Mithu Sen
  Seher Shah
  Dayanita Singh
  L.N. Tallur
  Hema Upadhyay
- **Further artists represented** Ramakrishna Behera
  Sheba Chhachhi
  Samit Das
  Rohini Devasher
  Anita Dube
  Gauri Gill
  Subodh Gupta
  Arunkumar HG
  Jitish Kallat
  Reena Saini Kallat
  Alexis Kersey
  Bharti Kher
  Pushpamala N.
  Jagannath Panda
  Aditya Pande
  Manisha Parekh
  Josh PS
  Raqs Media Collective
  Bharat Sikka
  Schandra Singh
  Thukral & Tagra
  JJ Valaya

Naumann

New York — Galleries Kabinett

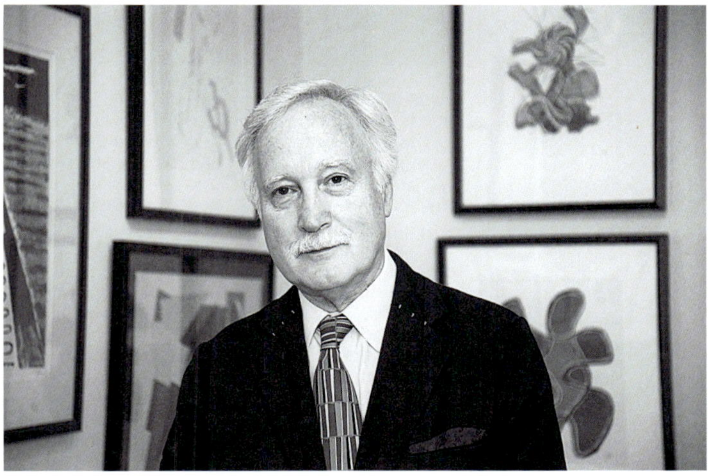

What first compelled you to open a gallery?
Financial (I was a professor of art history, and the salary was not enough to support me and my family).

Who is the first artist you showed and what was most memorable about that show?
Man Ray. The gallery opened in October 2001, one month after 9/11. Although the show was well received by the critics (a half-page article in *The New York Times*), nothing sold for over a year, it was a financial disaster.

When did you first participate in Art Basel and what was most memorable about that show?
In 2007. We presented a "Kabinett" on the subject "Daughters of Dada," which was exceptionally well received.

- **Contact** Francis M. Naumann Fine Art
  Dana Martin
  dana@francisnaumann.com
  LHOOQ@francisnaumann.com
- **Established** 2001
- **Owner(s) / Partner(s)** Francis M. Naumann
- **Team** 2
- **Space(s)** 111.5 m²
- **Artists at Art Basel** Eugene Berman
  Marcel Duchamp
  Suzanne Duchamp
  Arnold Friedman
  Stanley William Hayter
  Marcel Jean
  Leon Kelly
  Man Ray
  Walter Pach
  Larry Rivers
  Kurt Seligman
  Laurence Vail
  Beatrice Wood
- **Further artists represented** Rafael Leonardo Black
  Jean Crotti
  Marius de Zayas
  Katherine Dreier
  Kathleen Gilje
  Don Joint
  Pamela Joseph
  Carlo Maria Mariani
  Sophie Matisse
  Wallace Putnam
  Naomi Savage
  Jacques Villon
  Douglas Vogel
  Elsa von Freytag-Loringhoven
  Tetsuya Yamada

N

Navarro

Madrid

Galleries
Galleries

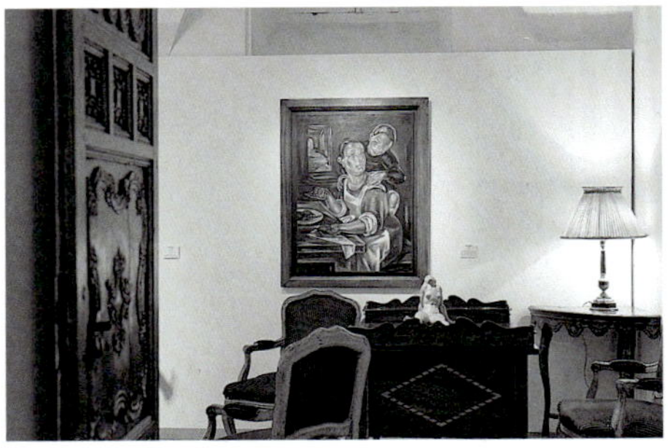

What first compelled you to open a gallery?
The gallery was founded by Leandro Navarro and it is managed by his son, Iñigo. What compelled them in the past, and is still true today, is their dedication to art.

Who is the first artist you showed and what was most memorable about that show?
Óscar Domínguez. It was also the first solo show of Domínguez's work in Madrid. There were works collected from several European collectors and the catalogue was introduced by the painter and art critic Eduardo Westerdahl, who is also a biograher of the artist.

When did you first participate in Art Basel and what was most memorable about that show?
Our first participation was in 2009. Most memorable were the contacts with Latin and North American collectors.

- **Contact** Galeria Leandro Navarro
Iñigo Navarro
galeria@leandro-navarro.com
- **Established** 1978
- **Owner(s) / Partner(s)** Galería Leandro Navarro SL
- **Team** 5
- **Space(s)** 300 m² (gallery)
150 m² (office)
- **Artists at Art Basel** Salvador Dalí
Pablo Gargallo
Juan Gris
Manolo Millares
Joan Miró
Ben Nicholson
Pablo Picasso
Manuel Rivera
Gerardo Rueda
Kurt Schwitters
Antoni Tàpies
Joaquín Torres García
María Helena Vieira da Silva
- **Further artists represented** Juan Barjola
Francisco Bores
Oscar Domínguez
Baltasar Lobo
Giorgio Morandi
Benjamin Palencia
Georges Valmier

Neon Parc

Melbourne

Insights

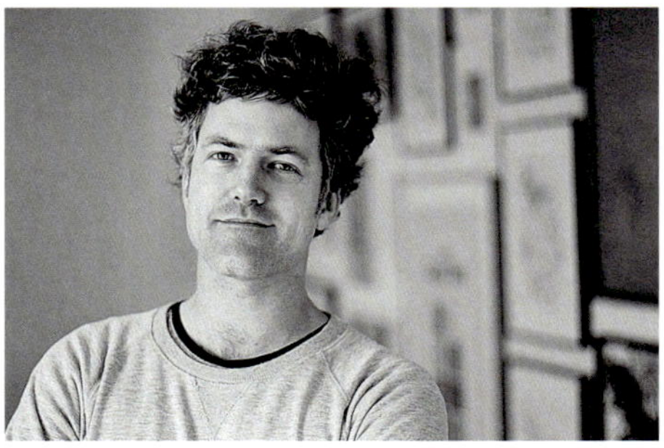

What first compelled you to open a gallery?
To promote Australian contemporary art in an international context.

Who is the first artist you showed and what was most memorable about that show?
Colleen Ahern.

When did you first participate in Art Basel and what was most memorable about that show?
In 2013 in Hong Kong.

- **Contact** Neon Parc
Geoff Newton
geoff@neonparc.com.au
info@neonparc.com.au
- **Established** 2006
- **Owner(s) / Partner(s)** Geoff Newton
- **Team** 5
- **Space(s)** 70 m²
- **Artists at Art Basel** Katherine Huang
- **Further artists represented** Colleen Ahern
Dan Arps
Janet Beckhouse
Damiano Bertoli
Trevelyan Clay
Julian Dashper
Irene Hanenbergh
Josey Kidd-Crowe
Paul Knight
James Lynch
Rob McLeish
Viv Miller
Elizabeth Newman
Elizabeth Pulie
Noël Skrzypczak
John Spiteri
The Kingpins

Neu

Berlin

Galleries

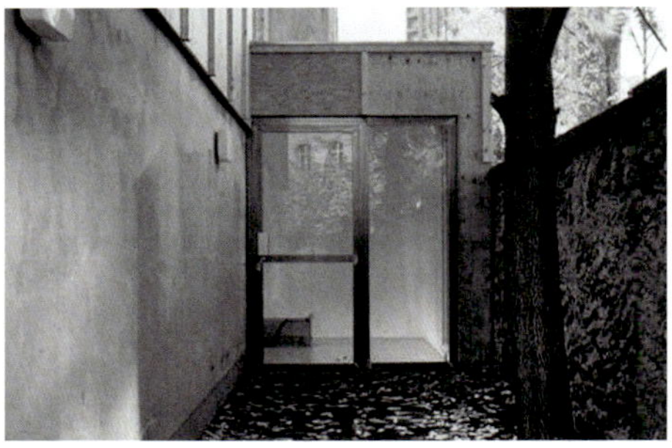

Who is the first artist you showed and what was most memorable about that show?
Andreas Slominski. The exhibition was called: *The Artist in the Transportkiste.*

When did you first participate in Art Basel and what was most memorable about that show?
The first participation was in 1998 at Art Basel.

- **Contact** Galerie Neu
Marta Fontolan
mail@galerieneu.com
- **Established** 1994
- **Owner(s) / Partner(s)** Alexander Schröder
Thilo Wermke
- **Team** 5
- **Space(s)** 200 m²
- **Artists at Art Basel** Bernadette Corporation
Tom Burr
Claire Fontaine
Sergej Jensen
Kitty Kraus
Klara Lidén
Nick Mauss
Manfred Pernice
Josephine Pryde
Gedi Sibony
Andreas Slominski
Sean Snyder
Katharina Wulff
Cerith Wyn Evans

- **Further artists represented**
  Kai Althoff
  Keith Farquhar
  Christian Flamm
  Saul Fletcher
  Florian Hecker
  Ull Hohn
  Hilary Lloyd
  Birgit Megerle
  Daniel Pflumm
  Francesco Vezzoli
  Cosima vonBonin

neugeriemschneider

Berlin

- Galleries
- Galleries Unlimited
- Galleries

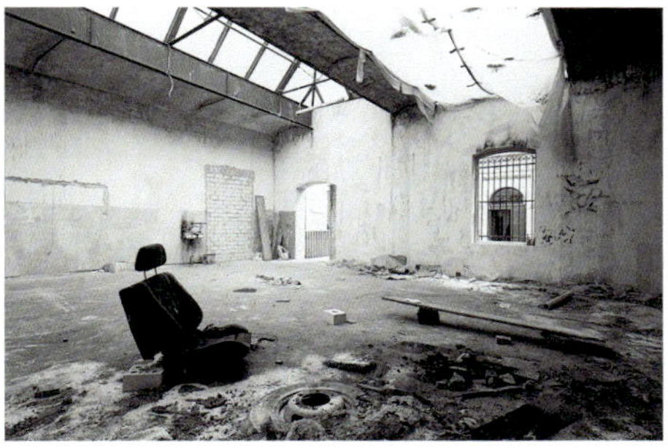

Who is the first artist you showed and what was most memorable about that show?

Many wonderful artists joined our gallery over the last 20 years, but those we showed in our first two years still remain central to the gallery program until today. In 1994, we opened the gallery with an exhibition of works by Jorge Pardo, followed by shows with Franz Ackermann, Sharon Lockhart, Rirkrit Tiravanija, Michael Majerus, Tobias Rehberger, Elizabeth Peyton and Olafur Eliasson. We still work very closely with all of these artists and—knocking on wood—have never lost any of them. Today we represent 21 artists.

When did you first participate in Art Basel and what was most memorable about that show?

It was in 1997, with Jorge Pardo in the Statements secor. Already Back then we faced the challenge to develop exhibitions for Art Basel with exactly the same approach and impact as those in our gallery space over the years. Until today it is out absolute focus never to compromise on the presentation of the works by our artists and to keep questioning the conventions of our profession. After all: without our artists we would be nothing.

- **Contact**
  neugerriemschneider
  mail@neugerriemschneider.com
- **Established** 1994
- **Owner(s) / Partner(s)**
  Tim Neuger
  Burkhard Riemschneider
- **Team** 21
- **Space(s)** 98 m²
- **Artists at Art Basel**
  Franz Ackermann
  Ai Weiwei
  Pawel Althamer
  James Benning
  Billy Childish
  Keith Edmier
  Olafur Eliasson
  Noa Eshkol
  Isa Genzken
  Sharon Lockhart
  Renata Lucas
  Michel Majerus
  Antje Majewski
  Mike Nelson
  Jorge Pardo
  Elizabeth Peyton
  Tobias Rehberger
  Simon Starling
  Thaddeus Strode
  Rirkrit Tiravanija
  Pae White

New Art Centre

Salisbury

- Galleries Parcours

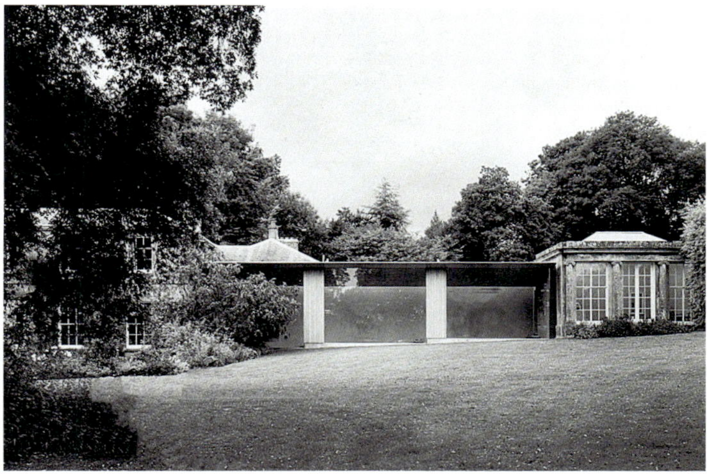

What first compelled you to open a gallery?

To give new and emerging artists the chance to exhibit and sell their work in London, at a time when opportunities were actually very rare.

Who is the first artist you showed and what was most memorable about that show?

The work of a then new artist called Ian Stephenson. It was a show that was universally acclaimed and work was acquired by the Tate Gallery, the Arts Council, and many important private collectors.

When did you first participate in Art Basel and what was most memorable about that show?

In 1973. It was our first opportunity to see the work of a large number of young artists from all over Europe, since people traveled less then. Also an exhibition at the Beyeler gallery of the English artist Ben Nicholson.

- **Contact**
  New Art Centre
  Stephen Feeke
  stephen@sculpture.uk.com
  nac@sculpture.uk.com
- **Established** 1958
- **Owner(s) / Partner(s)**
  Madeleine Bessborough
  Stephen Feeke
- **Team** 9
- **Space(s)**
  200 m² (gallery)
  25 hectares (sculpture park)
- **Artists at Art Basel**
  David Batchelor
  Anthony Caro
  Keith Coventry
  Michael Craig-Martin
  Edmund de Waal
  Richard Deacon
  Ian Hamilton Finlay
  Barbara Hepworth
  Des Hughes
  Henry Moore
  Nicholas Pope
  David Tremlett
  Clare Woods
- **Further artists represented**
  Phyllida Barlow
  Fernando Casasempere
  Barry Flanagan
  Laura Ford
  Antony Gormley
  Christopher Le Brun
  Richard Long
  Camilla Löw
  Paul Morrison
  Julian Opie
  Vicken Parsons
  Simon Periton
  Sarah Pickstone
  Eva Rothschild
  Nina Saunders
  Alison Wilding
  Bill Woodrow

Richard Dupont
Simryn Gill
Robert Gober
Paula Hayes
Jenny Holzer
Donald Judd
Martin Kippenberger
Sherrie Levine
Vera Lutter
Marilyn Minter
Bruce Nauman
Olaf Nicolai
Richard Prince
Thomas Schütte
Cindy Sherman
Ranjani Shettar
Alyson Shotz
Hiroshi Sugimoto
Sarah Sze
Jeff Wall
Matthew Weinstein
Christopher Wool

Ning

Hong Kong

Galleries

What first compelled you to open a gallery?

My passion for art led me to establish Anna Ning Fine Art in 2005. I had previously worked in the contemporary art world and felt the time was right to open my own gallery. My aim was to introduce the best Chinese artists to top international collectors. At the same time, I wanted to bring the attention of collectors to some exciting upcoming Chinese artists.

Who is the first artist you showed and what was most memorable about that show?

The first artist I exhibited was Luo Zhongli (b. 1948). One of the leading realist painters in China, he has been lauded for his arresting portraits of the people of southwest China. He gained international acclaim when his 1980 portrait Father was awarded 1st Prize at the 2nd China Youth Art Exhibition. His haunting compositions are marked by meticulous attention to detail and a remarkable ability to capture and evoke powerful emotion through the canvas.

When did you first participate in Art Basel and what was most memorable about that show?

I have participated in ART HK, now Art Basel, from the inaugural fair in 2008 until now. From the first show I remember feeling that it was so good to see Hong Kong as a major platform to showcase so many international artists' works.

Contact	Anna Ning Fine Art Anna Ning info@annaningfineart.com
Established	2005
Owner	Anna Ning
Team	2
Space(s)	100 m²
Artists at Art Basel	Ai Xuan Chiu Yatsai Luo Zhongli Pan Yuliang San Yu Wu Guanzhong Zao Wouki
Further artists represented	He Duoling Jing Kewen Wang Yidong

Nitsch

New York

Edition
Edition

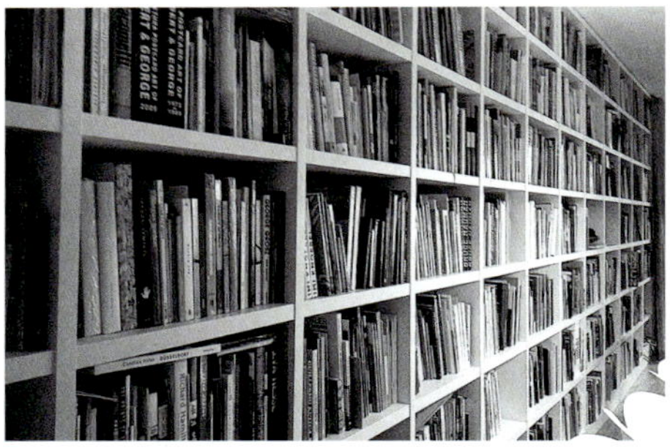

What first compelled you to open a gallery?

I always knew I would be a gallerist. I grew up surrounded by art and started collecting when in high school.

Who is the first artist you showed and what was most memorable about that show?

Louise Bourgeois.

Contact	Carolina Nitsch Brian Rumbolo brian@carolinanitsch.com
Established	2000
Owner(s) / Partner(s)	Carolina Nitsch
Team	3
Space(s)	279 m² (two spaces)
Artists at Art Basel	Ai Weiwei Richard Artschwager Tauba Auerbach Louise Bourgeois

Noero

Turin

Galleries
Unlimited
Galleries

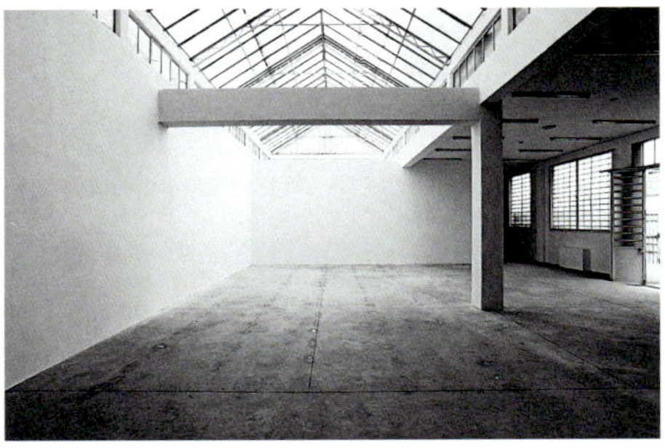

What first compelled you to open a gallery?

Franco Noero: The urgent need to start working with some young artists, my peers, who I used to frequent and with whom I began to collaborate. A good example is Francesco Vezzoli, as at a certain point it became necessary to follow him differently and more effectively.

Who is the first artist you showed and what was most memorable about that show?

It is again Francesco Vezzoli, with whom I was collaborating and who I was showing already before the gallery was opened.

Contact	Galleria Franco Noero Elisa Facchin elisa@franconoero.com
Established	1999
Owner(s) / Partner(s)	Franco Noero Pierpaolo Falone
Team	8
Space(s)	600 m² (+ a courtyard)
Artists at Art Basel	Darren Bader Pablo Bronstein Tom Burr Jeff Burton Neil Campbell Andrew Dadson Jason Dodge Lara Favaretto Martino Gamper Henrik Håkansson Mark Handforth Arturo Herrera Gabriel Kuri Phillip Lai Jim Lambie Robert Mapplethorpe Paulo Nazareth Mike Nelson Henrik Olesen João Onofre Kirsten Pieroth Steven Shearer Simon Starling Tunga Costa Vece Francesco Vezzoli

NoguerasBlanchard

Barcelona
Madrid

● Positions

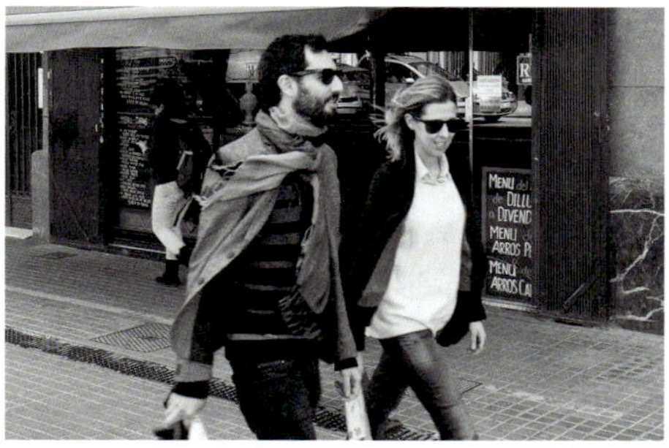

What first compelled you to open a gallery?
We had artist friends who encouraged us to open a gallery. We met working together in a gallery and shared same ideas and positions.

Who is the first artist you showed and what was most memorable about that show?
Haluk Akakçe. The construction work on the gallery wasn't finished in time, there were no walls or ceiling and they were still bringing in the stairs on the afternoon of the opening. Thankfully it was video and it looked great!

When did you first participate in Art Basel and what was most memorable about that show?
In Art Basel in the Statements sector in 2008, with Cuban artist Wilfredo Prieto. What we remember most was shipping 28 million fake diamonds from China for his piece *One*.

- **Contact**: NoguerasBlanchard
  Rebeca Blanchard
  rebeca@noguerasblanchard.com
  info@noguerasblanchard.com
- **Established**: 2004
- **Owner(s) / Partner(s)**: Rebeca Blanchard
  Alex Nogueras
- **Team**: 4
- **Space(s)**: 150 m² (Barcelona)
  150 m² (Madrid)
- **Artists at Art Basel**: Juan López
- **Further artists represented**: Rafel G. Bianchi
  Anne-Lise Coste
  Leandro Erlich
  Rubén Grilo
  Marine Hugonnier
  Michael Lin
  David Maljkovic
  Fran Meana
  Ester Partegàs
  Wilfredo Prieto
  Shimabuku
  Ignacio Uriarte

Nolan

New York

● Galleries
● Galleries Kabinett

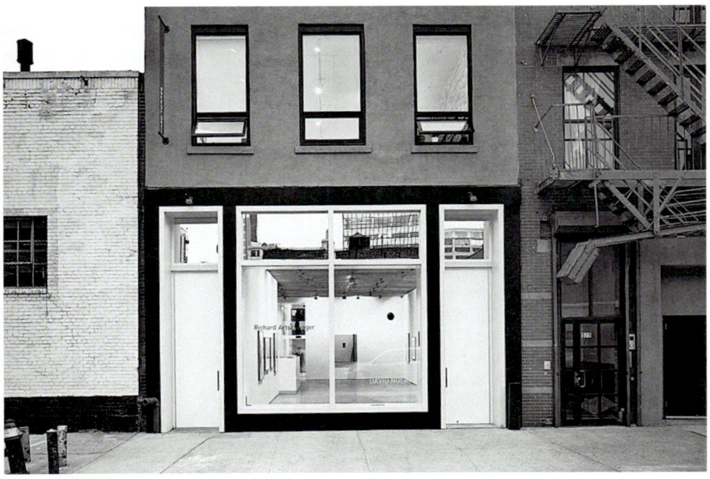

What first compelled you to open a gallery?
I believed there was a void in the contemporary art scene for a gallery specialized in works on paper and European art.

Who is the first artist you showed and what was most memorable about that show?
The first one-person show was of Sigmar Polke, drawings from the 1960s, with a catalogue.

When did you first participate in Art Basel and what was most memorable about that show?
My first participation was with a solo presentation of paintings and drawings by William Copley, which sold out.

- **Contact**: David Nolan Gallery
  David Nolan
  david@davidnolangallery.com
  info@davidnolangallery.com
- **Established**: 1987
- **Owner(s) / Partner(s)**: David Nolan
- **Team**: 6
- **Space(s)**: 260 m²
- **Artists at Art Basel**: Richard Artschwager
  Dylan Bailey
  Georg Baselitz
  Carroll Dunham
  Neil Gall
  George Grosz
  David Hartt
  Mel Kendrick
  Martin Kippenberger
  Barry Le Va
  Jim Nutt
  Alexander Ross
  Eugen Schönebeck
  Gavin Turk
  Sandra Vásquez de la Horra
  Jorinde Voigt
- **Further artists represented**: Steve DiBenedetto
  Ian Hamilton Finlay
  Victoria Gitman
  Alice Maher
  Ciprian Muresan
  Serban Savu

NON

Istanbul

● Nova

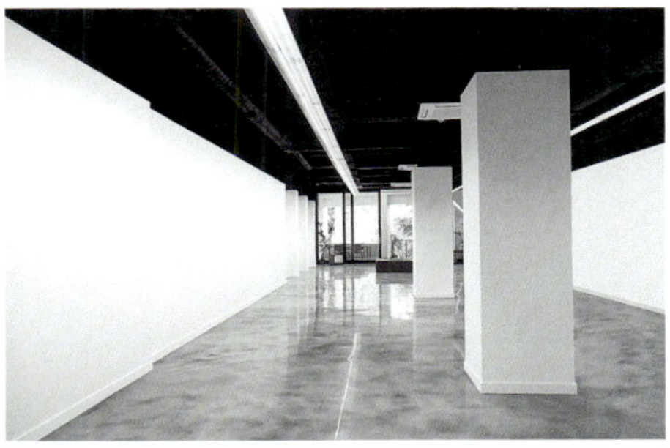

What first compelled you to open a gallery?
I used to work at a contemporary art center and simultaneously I was curating exhibitions and performances independently. It was then that I realized that being a gallerist is the only profession that allows you to be in close contact with both the artists and their work, to be immediately involved in the artists' creative production process, and continuously bound up in the development of their career. At the time, none of the galleries in Istanbul represented these artists and consequently I established Galeri NON.

Who is the first artist you showed and what was most memorable about that show?
The first solo exhibition at NON was the research project *Studio Osep* by Tayfun Serttaş. For this exhibition, Serttaş focused on the life story and career of the then 80-year old Osep Minasoğlu, one of Istanbul's oldest living studio and set photographers.

When did you first participate in Art Basel and what was most memorable about that show?
The first time we attended Art Basel was in the Positions sector of Art Basel in Miami Beach, with Aslı Çavuşoğlu, in 2012.

- **Contact** Galeri NON
Derya Demir
derya@galerinon.com
info@galerinon.com
- **Established** 2009
- **Owner(s) / Partner(s)** Derya Demir
- **Team** 3
- **Space(s)** 200 m²
- **Artists at Art Basel** Meriç Algün Ringborg
Erdem Tasdelen

Nordenhake

Berlin
Stockholm

Galleries
Unlimited
Galleries

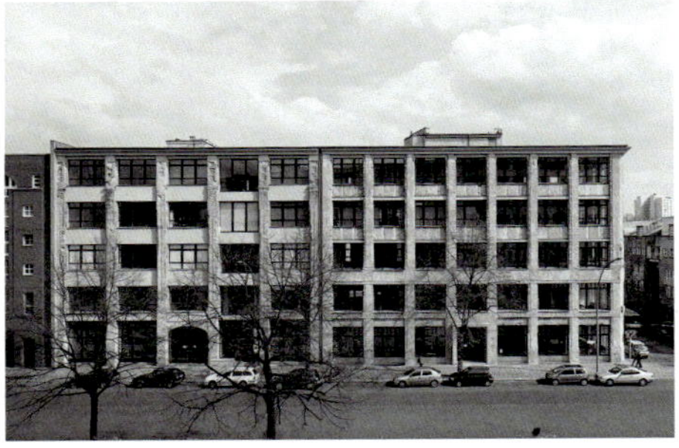

What first compelled you to open a gallery?
Academic failure.

Who is the first artist you showed and what was most memorable about that show?
Olle Baertling, who is still in the gallery's program.

When did you first participate in Art Basel and what was most memorable about that show?
In 1978.

- **Contact** Galerie Nordenhake
Isabelle Köhncke
isabelle@nordenhake.com
berlin@nordenhake.com
- **Established** 1976
- **Owner(s) / Partner(s)** Claes Nordenhake
- **Team** 10
- **Space(s)** 200 m² (Berlin)
148 m² (Stockholm)
- **Artists at Art Basel** Christian Andersson
Olle Baertling
Mirosław Bałka
Iñaki Bonillas
Gerard Byrne
John Coplans
Sarah Crowner
Ann Edholm
Paul Fägerskiöld
Spencer Finch
Hreinn Fridfinnsson
Franka Hörnschemeyer
Sofia Hultén
Gunilla Klingberg
Eva Löfdahl
Esko Männikkö
Meuser
Helen Mirra
Sirous Namazi
Walter Niedermayr
Scott Olson
Marjetica Potrč
Håkan Rehnberg
Michael Schmidt
Florian Slotawa
Johan Thurfjell
Alan Uglow
Günter Umberg
Not Vital
Magnus Wallin
Stanley Whitney
Rémy Zaugg
John Zurier
- **Further artists represented** Meriç Algun Ringborg
Anna Barham
Ann Böttcher
Jonas Dahlberg
Felix Gmelin
Karl Larsson
Mikael Olsson
Ulrich Rückriem
Leon Tarasewicz

Nothelfer

Berlin

Galleries

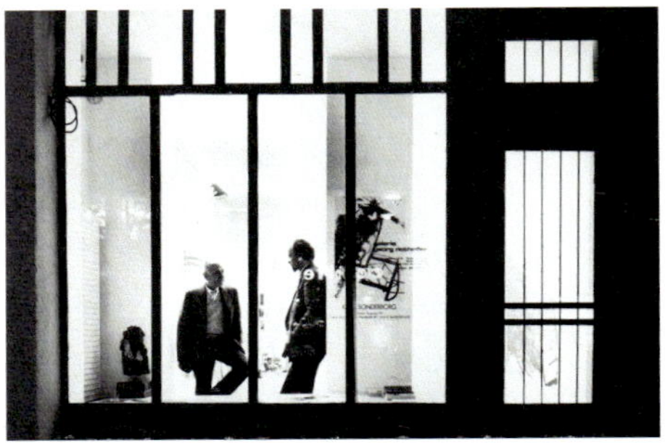

What first compelled you to open a gallery?
The passion for art.

Who is the first artist you showed and what was most memorable about that show?
Cy Twombly. Visitors insulted Georg Nothelfer for exhibiting scratches as art.

When did you first participate in Art Basel and what was most memorable about that show?
The first participation was in 1972. Unfortunately the art works were shipped to Amsterdam instead of Basel. Some of the artists represented by the gallery and present at the fair instead drew and painted works for the opening of the exhibition.

- **Contact** Galerie Georg Nothelfer
Vera Ehe
nothelfer@galerie-nothelfer.de
- **Established** 1971
- **Owner** Georg Nothelfer
- **Team** 5
- **Space(s)** 270 m² (Tiergarten)
60 m² (Charlottenburg)
- **Artists at Art Basel** Christo & Jeanne-Claude
Madeleine Dietz
Christoph M. Gais
K.O. Götz
Thomas Hartmann
Gerhard Hoehme
László Lakner
Henri Michaux
Herta Müller
Georges Noël
Robert Schad
Emil Schumacher
Kazuo Shiraga
K.R.H. Sonderborg
Walter Stöhrer
Fred Thieler
Jan Voss
- **Further artists represented** Adochi
Pierre Alechinsky
Shusuka Arakawa
Armando
Peter Brüning
Michael Buthe
Ouhi Cha
Eduardo Chillida
K.F. Dahmen
Dieter Finke
Lothar Fischer
Manfred Hamm
Edgar Hofschen
Rolf Iseli
Asger Jorn
Michel Macréau
Walter Menne
Jürgen Messensee
Robert Motherwell
Max Neumann
Dieter Roth
Arno C. Schmetjen
Bernard Schultze
Richard Serra
Daniel Spoerri
Helmut Sturm
Antoni Tàpies
Wolfgang Troschke
Cy Twombly

David Nolan Gallery

A Question for David Nolan

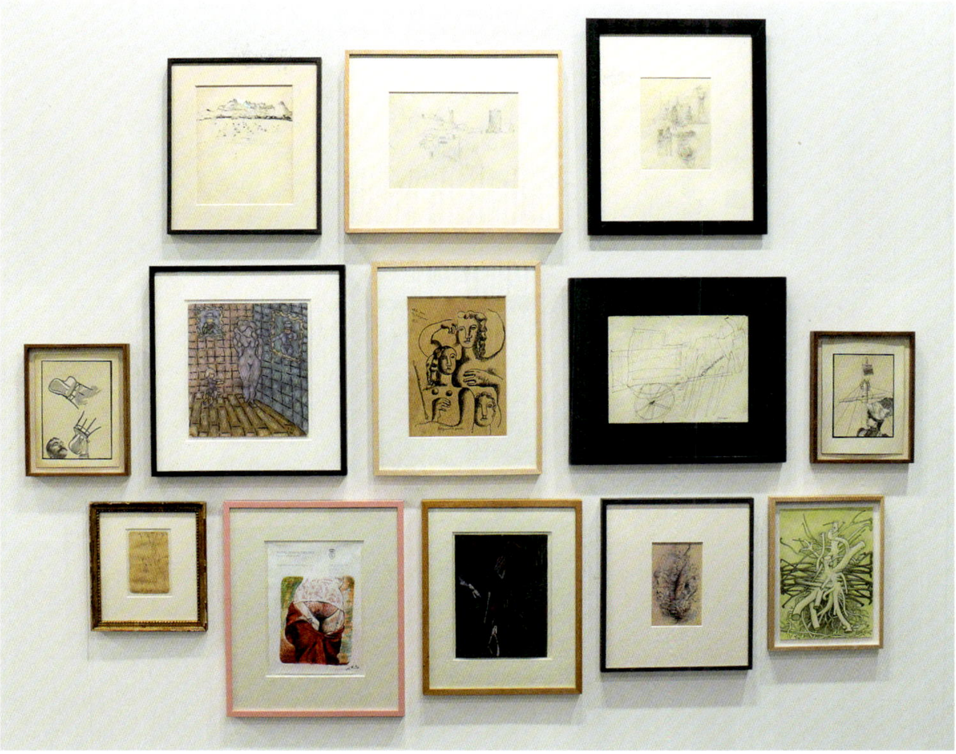

Art Basel in Basel, 2013

For the 2013 edition of Art Basel you presented an historical and contemporary display of drawings covering over 12 decades. Could you please tell us about the origins of this display and the reasons for this choice? How did the display reflect the gallery's general program?

Since the beginning of my participation in Art Basel I have always brought a particularly serious amount of modern and contemporary drawing (in addition to painting and sculpture) to the fair. One of my basic interests in having a gallery is to make connections between American and European thought in art, today and in the past. This particular display was very focused, with tight connections, beginning with a drawing by Cezanne that shows his interest in landscape, complex composition, and the influence of his immediate surroundings. This was juxtaposed against an early landscape drawing by Louis Kahn, whose travels around the world strongly influenced his architecture.

Hans Bellmer, on the other hand, fetishizes his buildings and what occurs within and around them. His interest in Renaissance drawing is what links him to Cézanne, and this influence leads on to Léger, Copley, and Cornell. A more Surrealist line can be detected in Dubuffet's drawings while he lived in the south of France. The "surreal" drawings of Alexander Ross and Carroll Dunham are clearly inspired by Wols, Copley, and Bellmer, particularly in their sexual content—and we see this imagery carried on through a provocative colored drawing by Martin Kippenberger on hotel paper.

These connections are what the gallery stands for, and in our program we have mounted many shows specifically of German artists from the last 100 years with George Grosz, Hans Bellmer, Eugen Schönebeck, Georg Baselitz, Gerhard Richter, Sigmar Polke, Martin Kippenberger, Albert Oehlen, and Jorinde Voigt. Exhibitions of British artists include the sculptor and philosopher Ian Hamilton Finlay, Neil Gall, and Gavin Turk. The gallery has also shown American artists such as Richard Artschwager, William Copley, Barry Le Va, Mel Bochner, Peter Saul, Jim Nutt, Carroll Dunham, and Alexander Ross, as well as younger artists such as David Hartt and Dylan Bailey.

Over the years Basel has become a place where I experiment with the architectural design of the booth in order to move away from the classic rectangular designs of the past. The richness and breadth of serious collectors and curators make Basel one of the best fairs in the world, where thoughtful and well-considered experimentation is well received.

WHAT THE THREE

you are looking

ARE

NEXT

THINGS

forward to in 2014?

Daniel Birnbaum

Director, Moderna Museet, Stockholm

1 Kim Gordon, *Is It My Body? Selected Texts*, Sternberg Press

No other major rock star, not even David Bowie, writes critical essays like this. Edited by Branden W. Joseph, one of today's most visionary art historians, these writings chart Gordon's trajectory from emerging artist to member of the influential rock group Sonic Youth. Interior design, conceptual art, rock 'n' roll come together in a way we haven't experienced since Dan Graham's *Rock My Religion*, 30 years ago.

2 Martin Heidegger, *Die Schwarzen Hefte (The Black Notebooks)*, Vittorio Klostermann Verlag

Without Heidegger there would be no Jacques Derrida, no Jacques Lacan, and no Michel Foucault. The appearance of brutally anti-Semitic writings by the most influential thinker of the 20th century is not good news for Continental philosophy even if it comes as no surprise to some of us. The writings have not been published yet, but already the rumor of their existence is creating turmoil in intellectual circles from Freiburg to Paris. Fasten your seatbelt, there is turbulence ahead.

3 *Fundamentals*, the 14th Architecture Venice Biennale, June 7–November 23, 2014

Says curator Rem Koolhaas: "*Fundamentals* will be a Biennale about architecture, not architects." It opens in June. Can't wait to see it!

Suzanne Cotter

Director, Serralves Museum, Porto

1 The European premiere of Matthew Barney's *River of Fundament*, March 17–August 17, 2014

Curated by Okwui Enwezor at Haus der Kunst and Bayerische Staatsoper, Munich.

2 *Fundamentals*, the 14th Architecture Venice Biennale, June 7–November 23, 2014

Under the artistic directorship of Rem Koolhaas.

3 The 31st São Paulo Biennale, September 2–December 7, 2014

Curated by Charles Esche, Galit Eilat, Nuria Enguita Mayo, Pablo Lafuente, and Oren Sagiv.

Bice Curiger

Co-founder of *Parkett*, and Director, Fondation Vincent van Gogh Arles, Arles

1 The inauguration of the Fondation Vincent van Gogh Arles

In the South of France, a new institution that I am heading confronts Vincent van Gogh with Thomas Hirschhorn, Elizabeth Peyton, Bertrand Lavier, Bethan Huws, Raphael Hefti, Guillaume Bruère, Camille Henrot, and Fritz Hauser. The building is splendid and the city is a sleeping beauty with enormous potential for a culturally radiating future, considering also the ambitious plans by the Luma Foundation for a big cultural center to be built by Frank Gehry.

2 *Alibis: Sigmar Polke 1963–2010*, The Museum of Modern Art, New York, April 19–August 3, 2014

I am convinced that he is an artist whose œuvre still offers a multitude of undiscovered aspects.

3 *Fundamentals*, the 14th Architecture Venice Biennale, June 7–November 23, 2014

Curated by Rem Koolhaas, of whom I am a fan of since I read his *Delirious New York* in the early 1980s.

Massimiliano Gioni

Associate Director and Director of Exhibitions, New Museum, New York, and Curator, 55th Venice Biennale, 2013

1 *Fundamentals*, the 14th Architecture Venice Biennale, June 7–November 23, 2014

Curated by Rem Koolhaas.

2 *Manifesta 10*, Hermitage, St. Petersburg, June 28–October 31, 2014

It's the 20th anniversary of *Manifesta*, an exhibition I love and that I had the honor of curating in 2004. This time it will be curated by Kasper König, so there are great expectations to see if the King will pull this one off or if the Winter Palace will bring bad luck to the Tzar …

3 Charles Ray, Kunstmuseum, Basel, June 15–September 28, 2014

For this explorer of ontology there is no better place than the Kunstmuseum, where Ray's creatures will live a few meters away from Rodin's *Bourgeois of Calais* and Holbein's *Christ*.

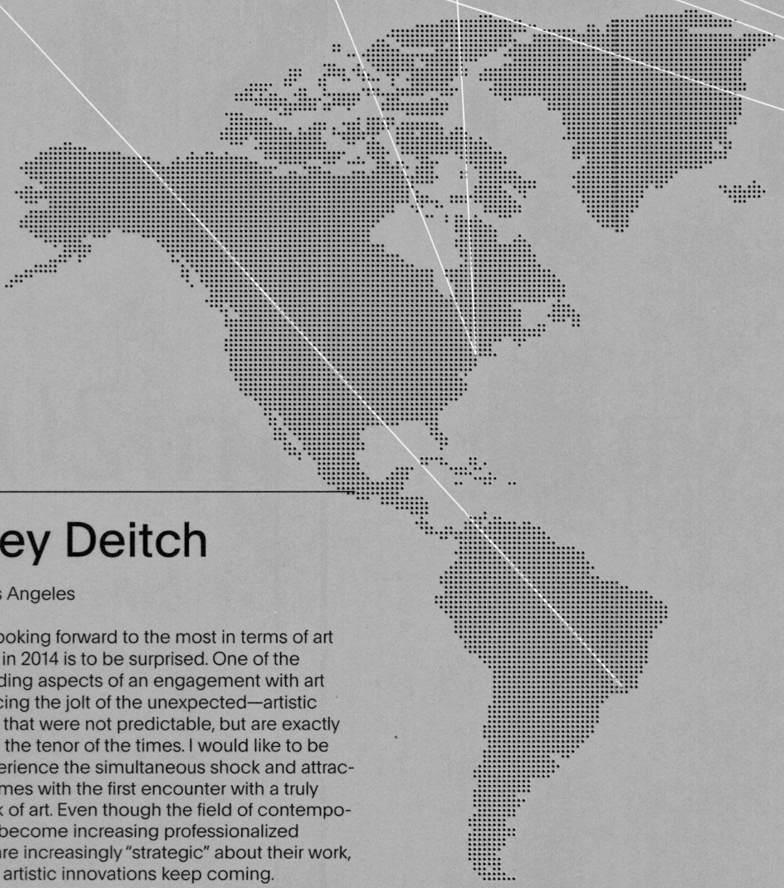

Jeffrey Deitch

Curator, Los Angeles

What I am looking forward to the most in terms of art and culture in 2014 is to be surprised. One of the most rewarding aspects of an engagement with art is experiencing the jolt of the unexpected—artistic innovations that were not predictable, but are exactly in sync with the tenor of the times. I would like to be able to experience the simultaneous shock and attraction that comes with the first encounter with a truly radical work of art. Even though the field of contemporary art has become increasing professionalized and artists are increasingly "strategic" about their work, astonishing artistic innovations keep coming.

Maria Baibakova

Founder & Director, Baibakov Arts Projects, Moscow/ New York

1 Marker at Art Dubai, March 2014

I have been on the Board of Patrons of Art Dubai for years, and the Marker exhibition has always been a highlight of my experience at the fair because it has allowed me to discover the art scenes of many off-the-beaten-path geographies. This year, Marker is curated by the incredible artists Slavs and Tatars with a focus on the Caucuses and Central Asia; I am particularly excited to learn more about art from this region because my family is from there, and although I recently traveled to Yerevan, Tbilisi, and Baku, I have so much left to learn about the contemporary art scene there.

2 *Manifesta 10*, Hermitage, St. Petersburg, June 28–October 31, 2014

St. Petersburg has always been a city close to any Russian's heart, so I was thrilled to hear that *Manifesta* would follow up its 2012 stint in a Belgian coal mine with a sojourn in the halls of the Hermitage. While the decision may have first been met with protest, curator Kaspar König has handled the criticisms with aplomb, selecting artists from Louise Bourgeois and Maria Lassnig to Timur Novikov and Vlad Mamyshev-Monroe, late heroes of Petersburg's New Academy scene, a movement which offered an openly homoerotic spin on the classics. I will be particularly intrigued to see the Ilya Kabakov works, having written my masters' thesis on the artist's early albums.

3 Kochi-Muziris Biennale, Kerala, December 12, 2014–March 29, 2015

I visited India for the first time with the Guggenheim Museum in Spring 2008, which basically provided a crash course to the current scene, and most recently last year—it's fascinating to see how quickly the art world is evolving there. It's even more amazing to think that India only got its first biennale in 2010. But what a kick-off! Despite some slight controversy over funding and censorship concerns, the biennale received rave reviews and drew the kind of audience other biennales can only dream of (one quote estimated an average 1,000 visitors a day!). The second edition of Kochi-Muziris Biennale should be no less spectacular, curated by artist Jitish Kallat.

Shwetal Patel & Riyas Komu

Executive Officer of the Kochi-Muziris Biennale, Fort Kochi, Kerala [Patel]
Multi-media artist, co-founder of the Kochi-Muziris Biennale Foundation, Director of Programs of the Kochi-Muziris Biennale, Mumbai & Kerala [Komu]

1 The Companies Bill, August 2013

This bill has introduced the concept of "Corporate Social Responsibility" (CSR) into Indian company law. We are glad that there seems to be a greater commitment by businesses to behave ethically, and to contribute to economic development while improving the quality of life of the local community and society at large. Some of these CSR budgets may help benefit art, culture, and education, which could be very crucial for India's development model.

2 *Fundamentals*, the 14th Architecture Venice Biennale, June 7–November 23, 2014

Rem Koolhaas' *Fundamentals* will focus on histories, and in his text for the exhibition he talks about how perhaps "national identity has seemingly been sacrificed to modernity." This has also been a debate on the subcontinent since independence, and has accelerated due to economic liberalization policies of the early 1990s. By attempting to tell the history of architecture over the last 100 years, the International Architecture Exhibition hopes to uncover some of the "unique national features and mentalities that continue to exist and flourish" within globalization. It will be interesting to see how Indian practitioners and intellectuals will respond to this idea and exhibition.

3 Kochi-Muziris Biennale, December 12, 2014–March 29, 2015

It is of course something we are working hard toward. Artist Jitish Kallat has been appointed as the new Artistic Director and will be responsible for curating the main exhibition.

Philippe Vergne

Director, MOCA, Los Angeles, and former Director, Dia Art Foundation, New York

1 Less oil.
2 More time.
3 True free will.

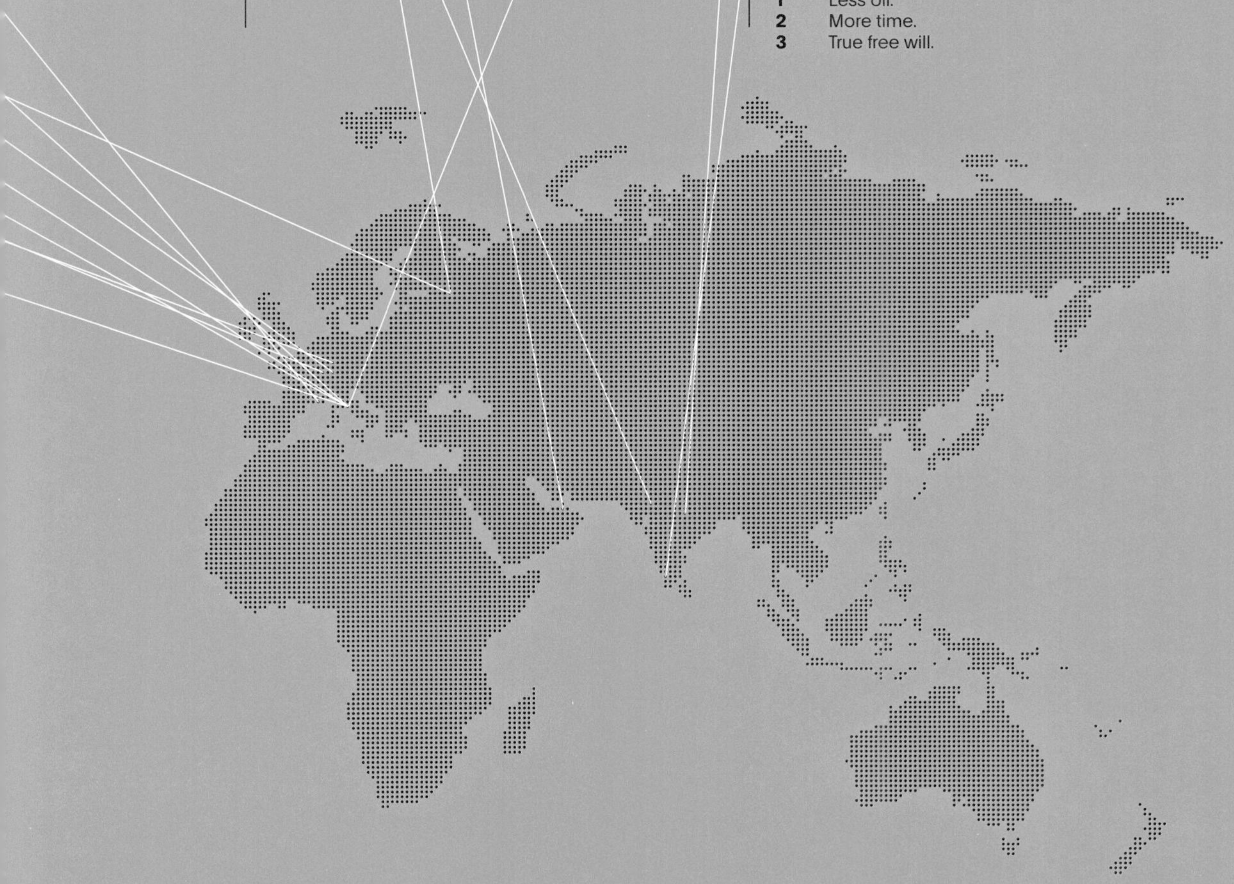

N

Designed for galleries to present one, two, or three artists showing works created within the last three years, the Nova sector in Miami Beach is a site of discovery, featuring dozens of never-before-seen pieces direct from the artist's studio.

2013 participants

Altman Siegel
Shannon Ebner
Chris Johanson

Casas Riegner
José Antonio Suárez Londoño
Johanna Calle

Cherry and Martin
Matt Connors
Bernard Piffaretti

elbaz
Blair Thurman
Mungo Thomson
Davide Balula

Karma International
Pamela Rosenkranz
Keiichi Tanaami

Koenig & Clinton
Nicole Eisenman
Tony Matelli

Labor
Teresa Margolles
Pedro Reyes
Jill Magid

Layr
Plamen Dejanoff
Lisa Holzer

Leighton
Aleksandra Domanović
Oliver Laric

Leme
Mariana Mauricio
Mauro Piva
Sandra Gamarra

Maisterravalbuena
Daniel Jacoby
Néstor Sanmiguel Diest

Meessen De Clercq
Susan Collis
Ellen Harvey
Evariste Richer

Mendes Wood
Deyson Gilbert
Marina Simão

Francesca Minini
Matthias Bitzer
Francesco Simeti

mor charpentier
Oscar Muñoz
Julieta Aranda
Voluspa Jarpa

80m2
Daniela Ortiz
Rita Ponce de León
David Zink Yi

47 Canal
John Finneran
Alisa Baremboym

NON
Meriç Algün Ringborg
Erdem Taşdelen

Office Baroque
Aaron Bobrow
David Diao

Overduin and Kite
Nick Relph
Math Bass

Peres Projects
David Ostrowski

Preston
Hans Schabus
Josh Tonsfeldt

RaebervonStenglin
Saâdane Afif
Karsten Födinger

Revolver
Giancarlo Scaglia
Jerry B. Martin
José Carlos Martinat

Schubert
Lydia Gifford
Sue Tompkins

Schwartz
Abraham Palatnik
Antonio Manuel
Carla Guagliarci

SKE
Bharti Kher
Sheela Gowda
Prabhavathi Meppayil

Spinello
Agustina Woodgate
Naama Tsabar
Sinisa Kukec

T293
Sam Falls
Wyatt Kahn

Travesía Cuatro
Gonzalo Lebrija
Jorge Méndez Blake

Untitled
Matthew Chambers
Phil Wagner

Vilma Gold
Charles Atlas

Wallspace
John Divola
Gaylen Gerber

Wigram
Jose Dávila

Revolver Galería

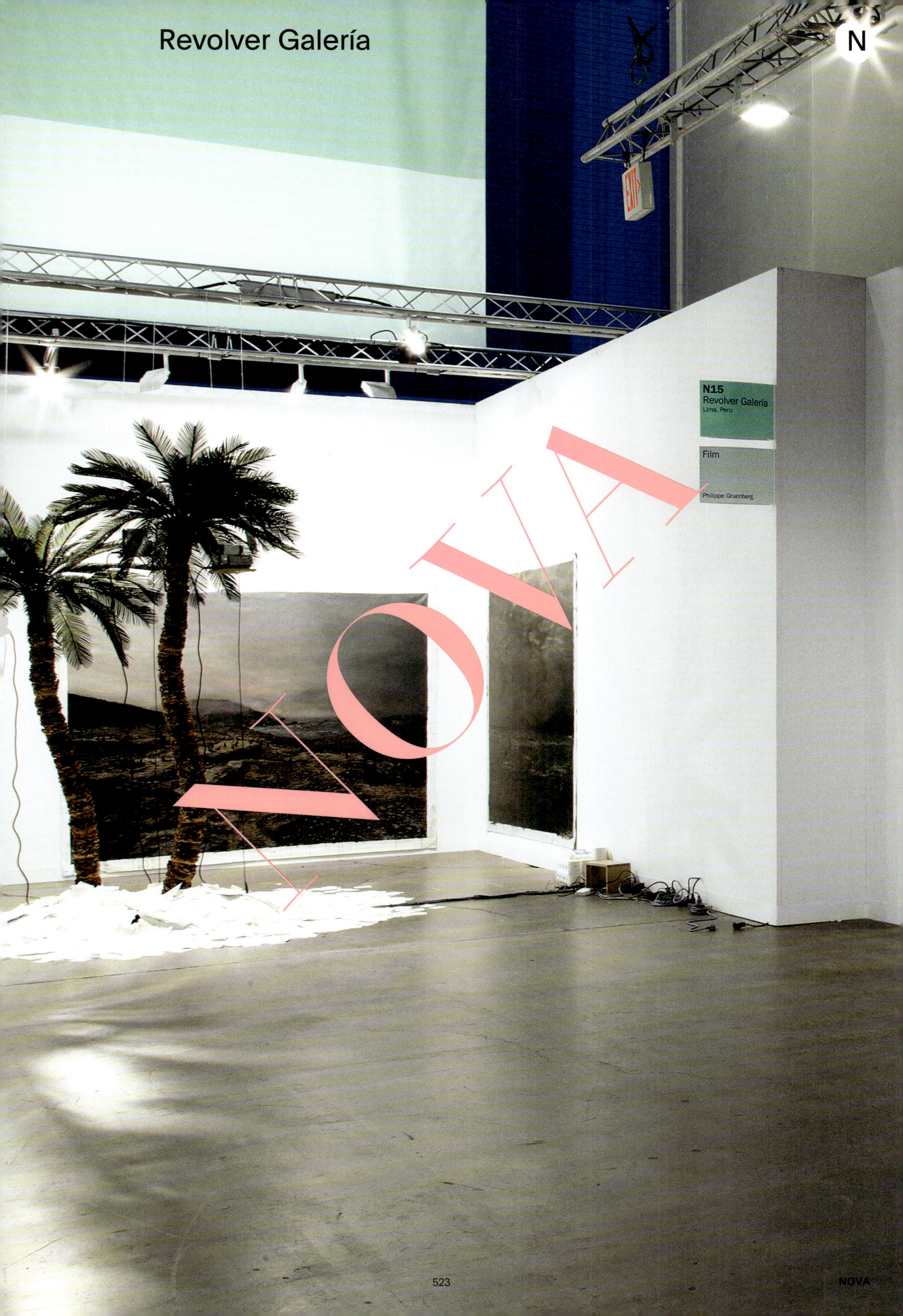

Tanya Leighton

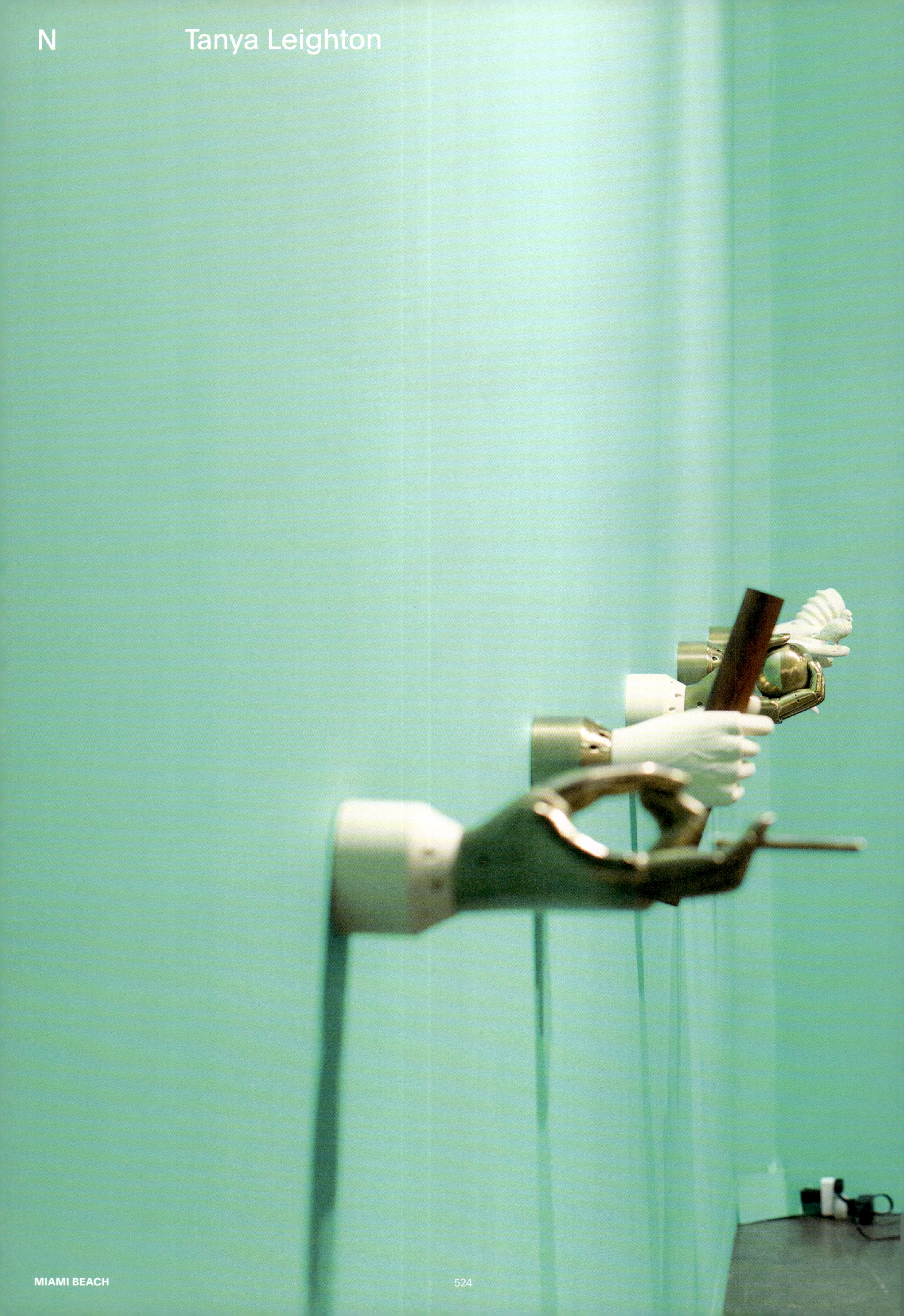

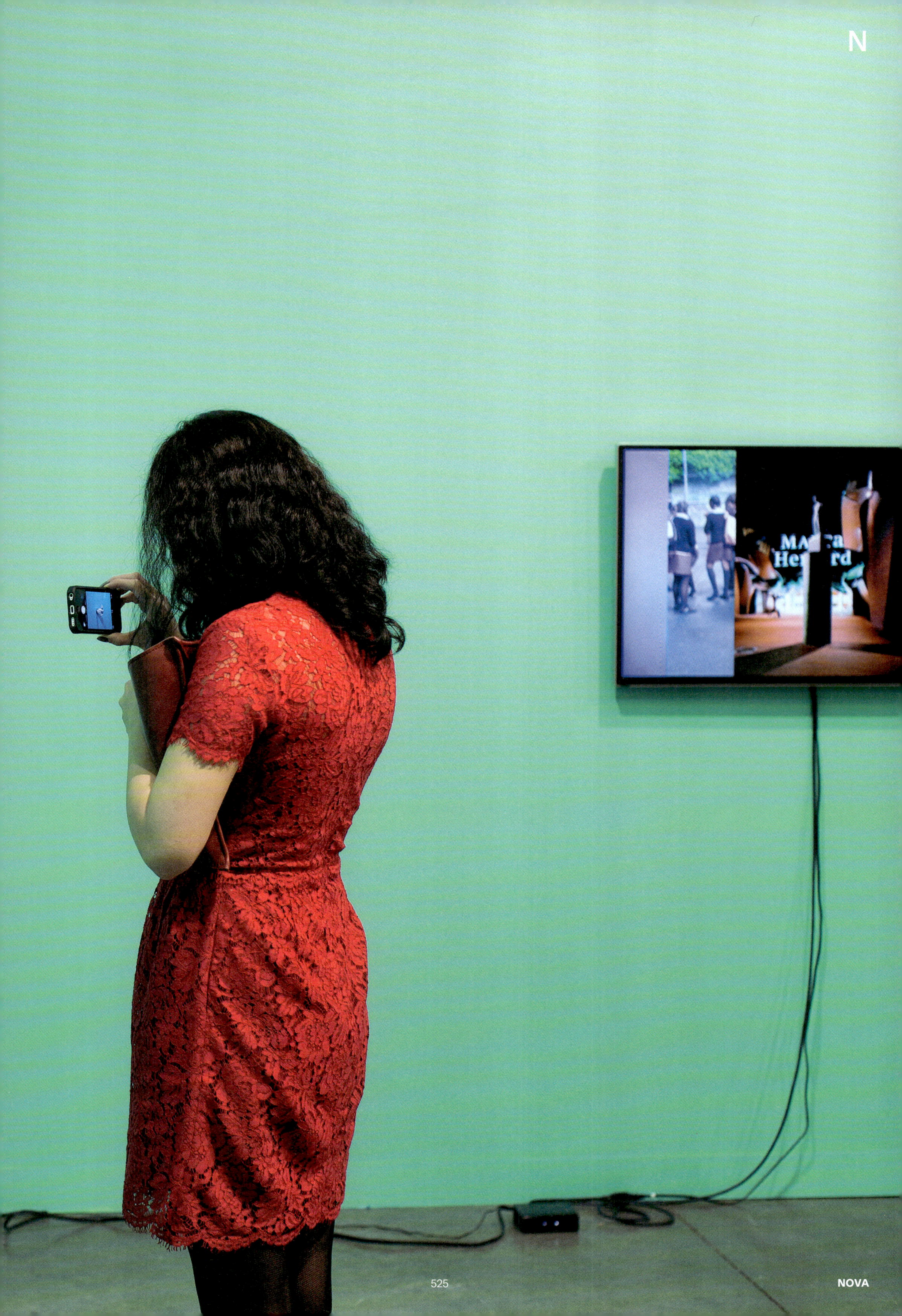

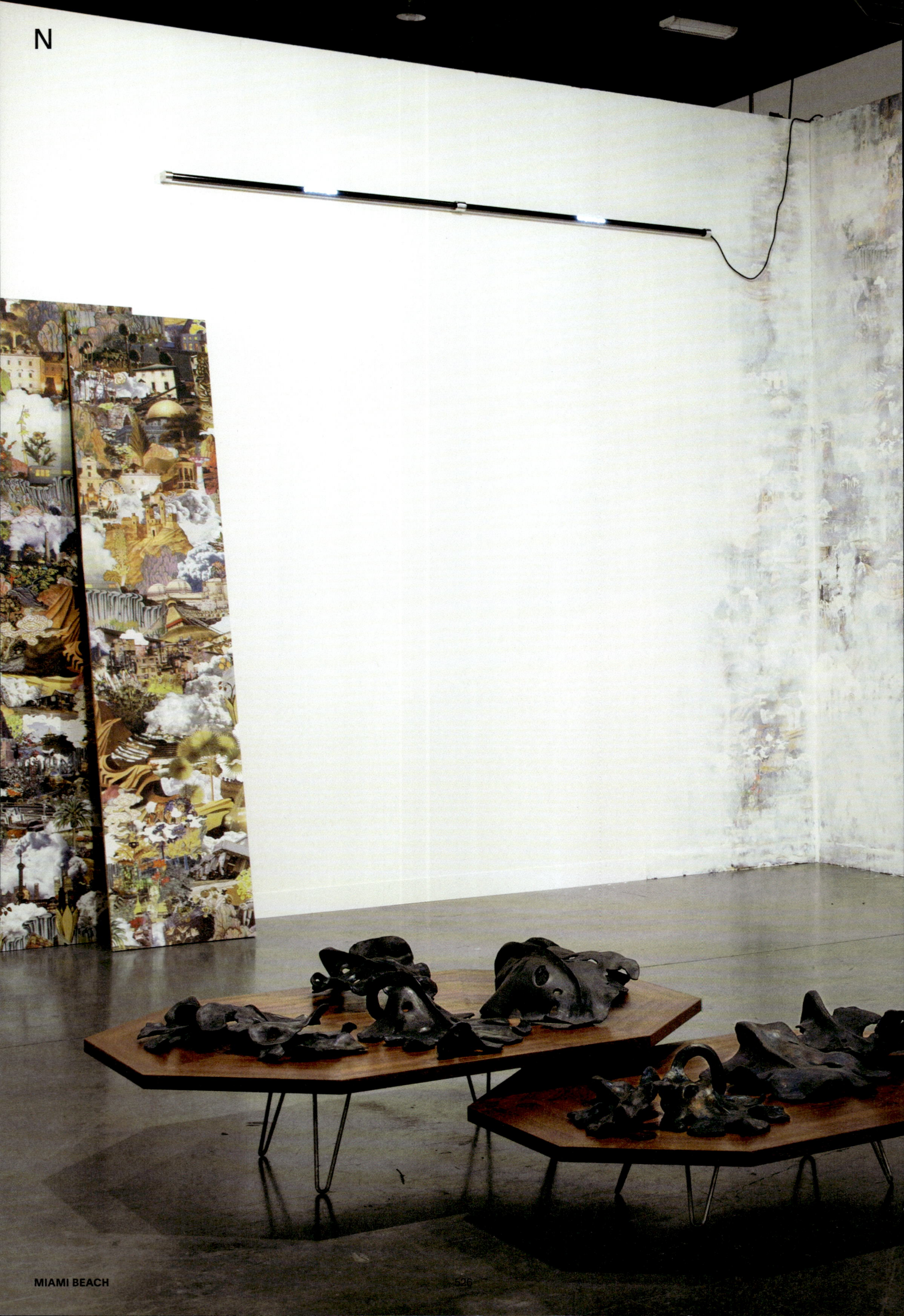

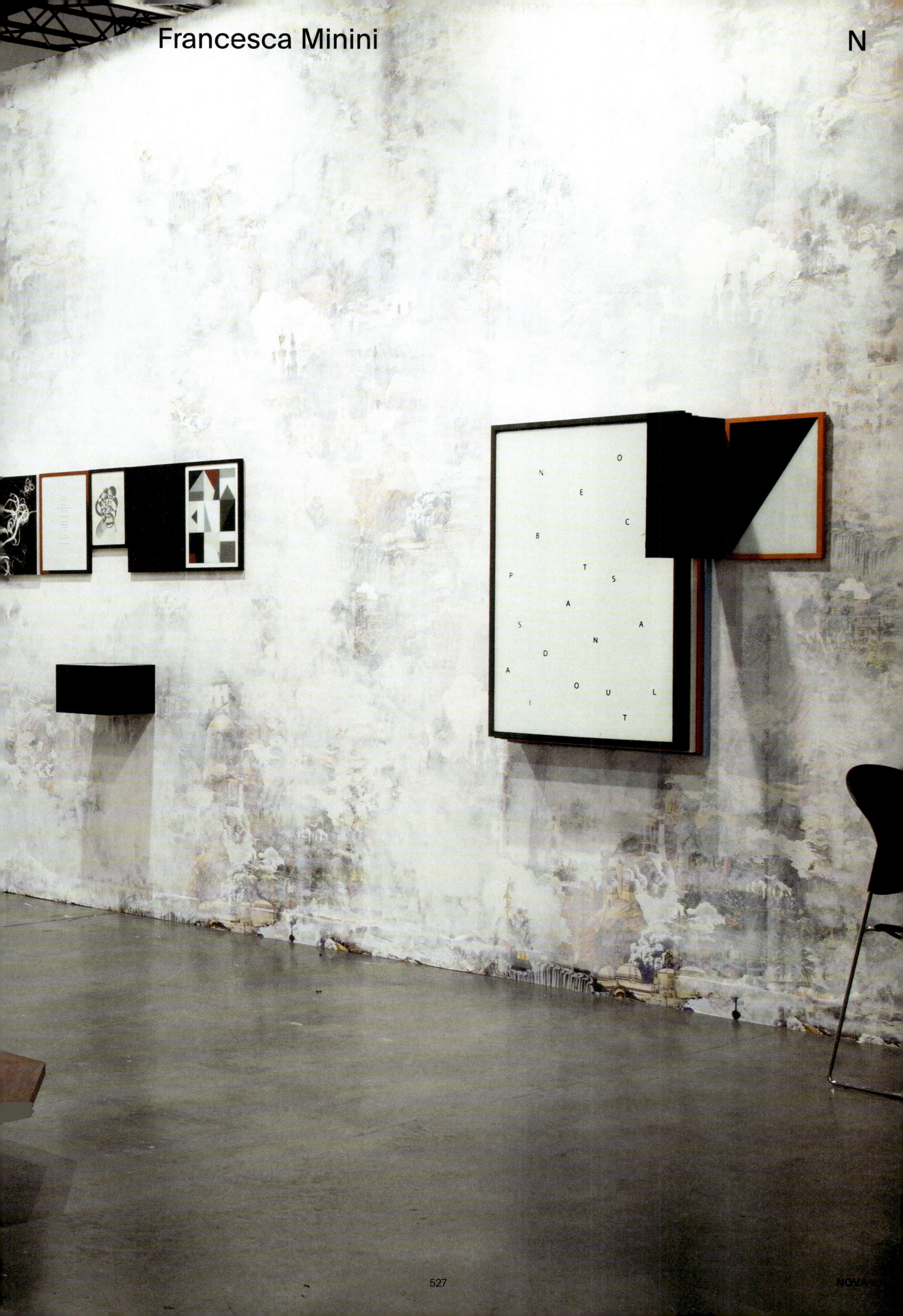

Karma International

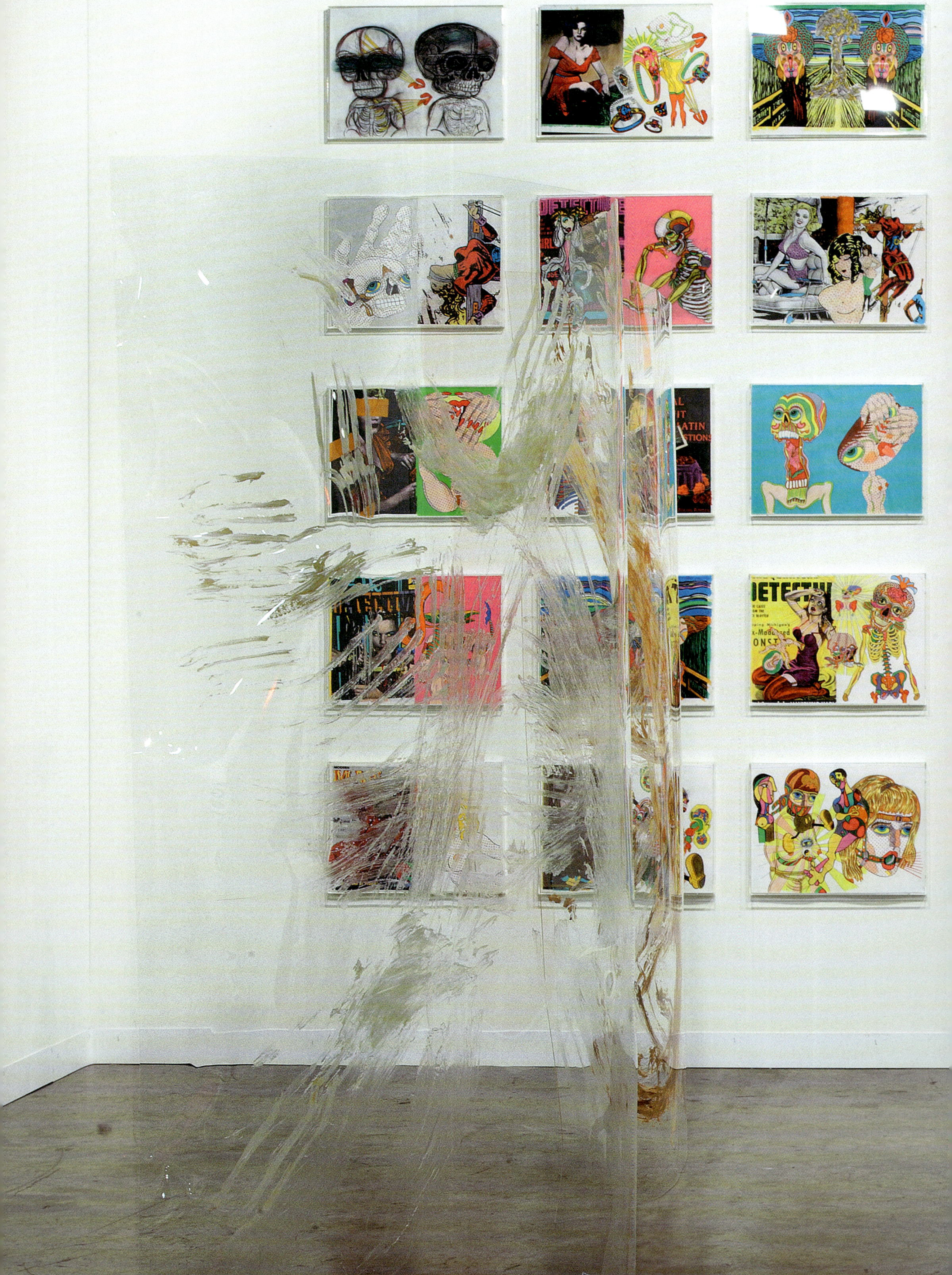

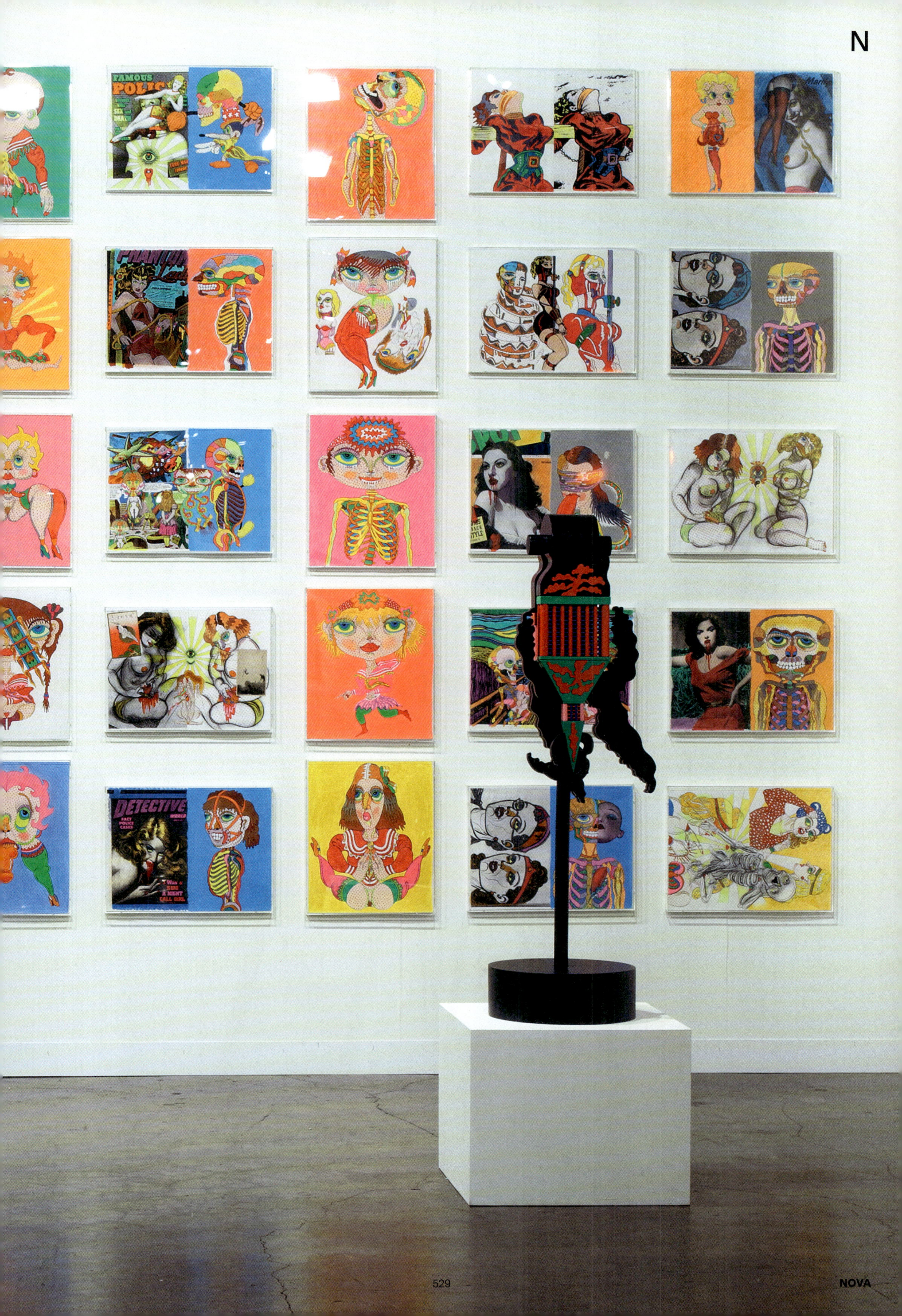
FAMOUS
DETECTIVE

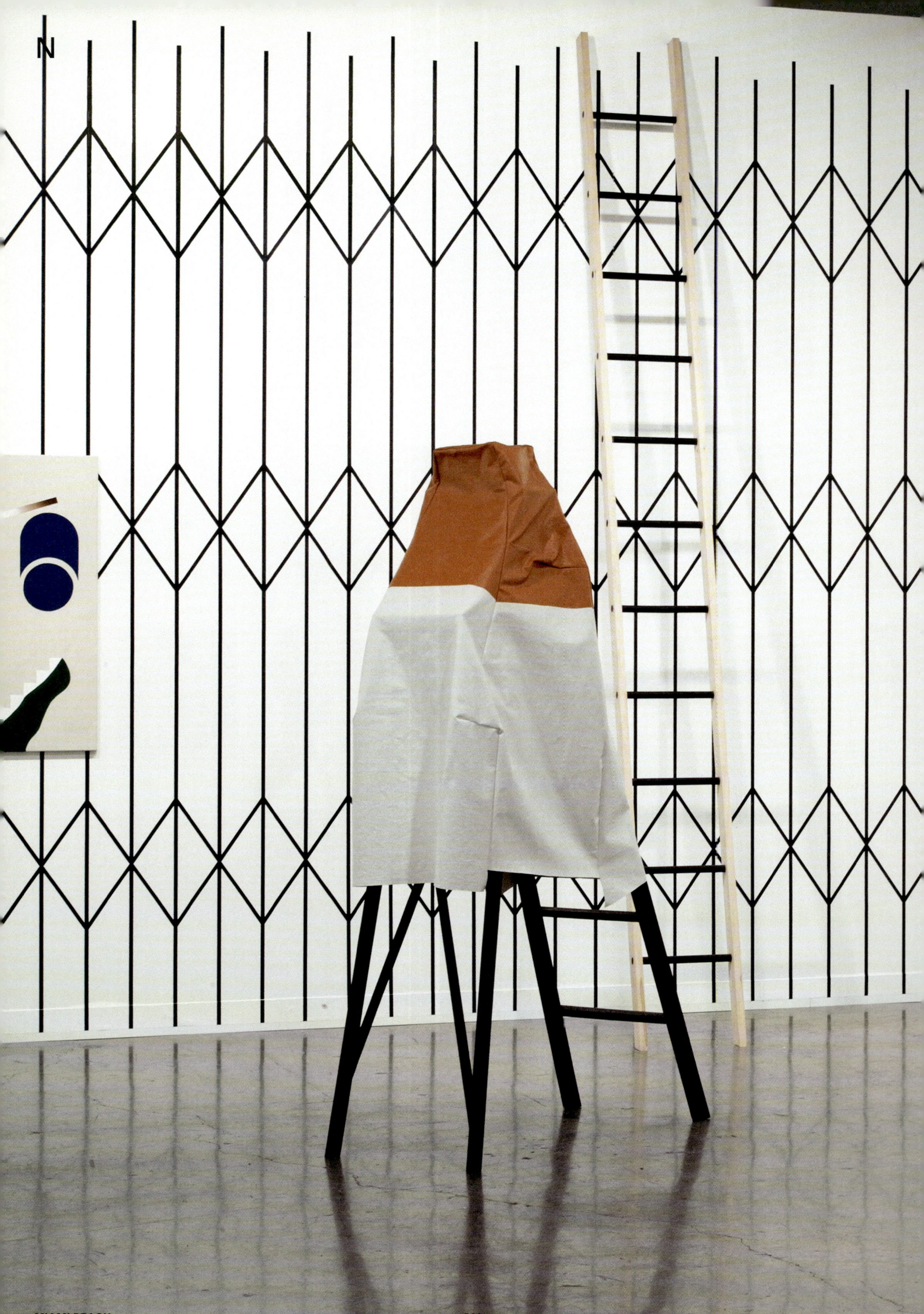

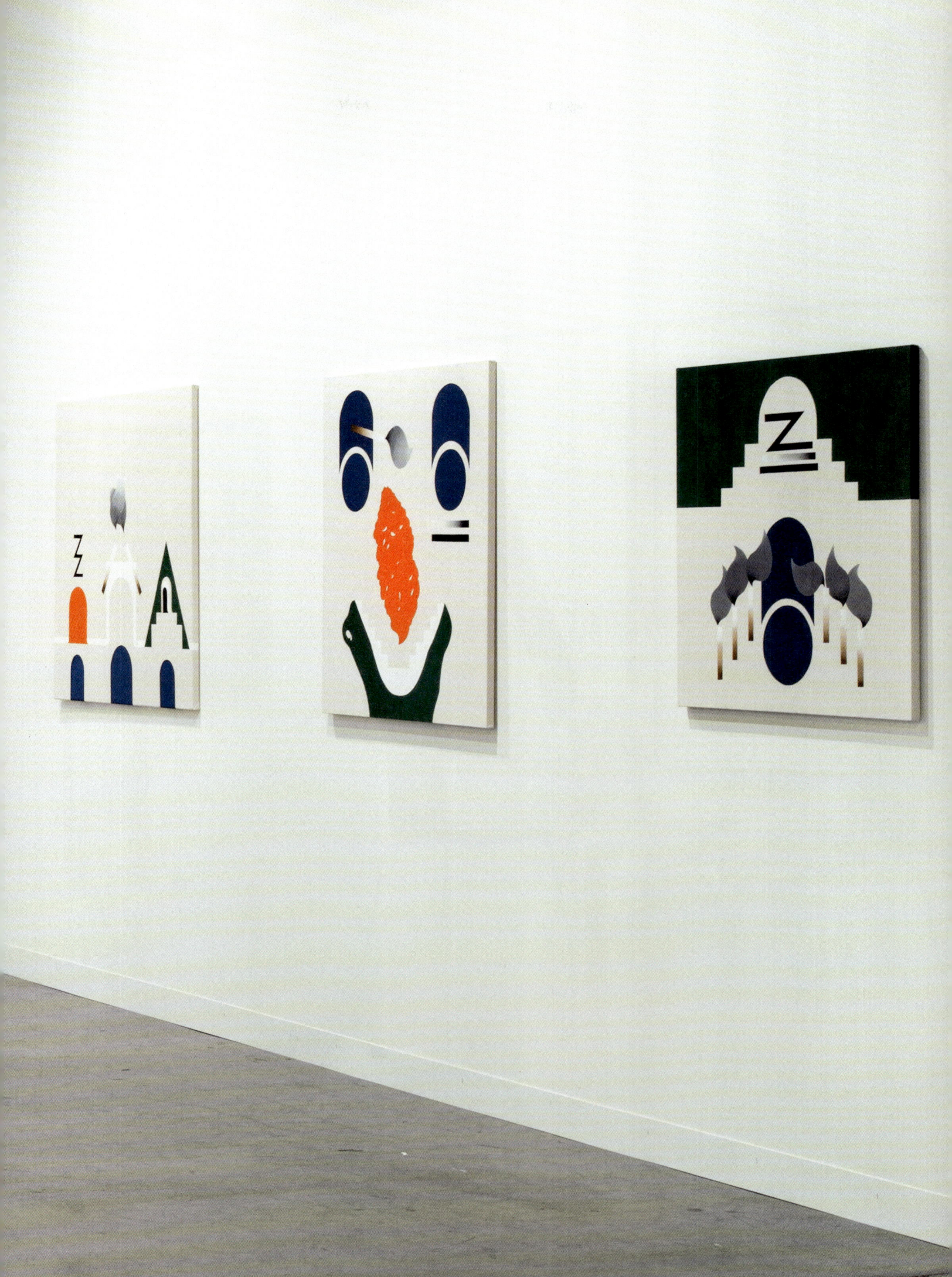

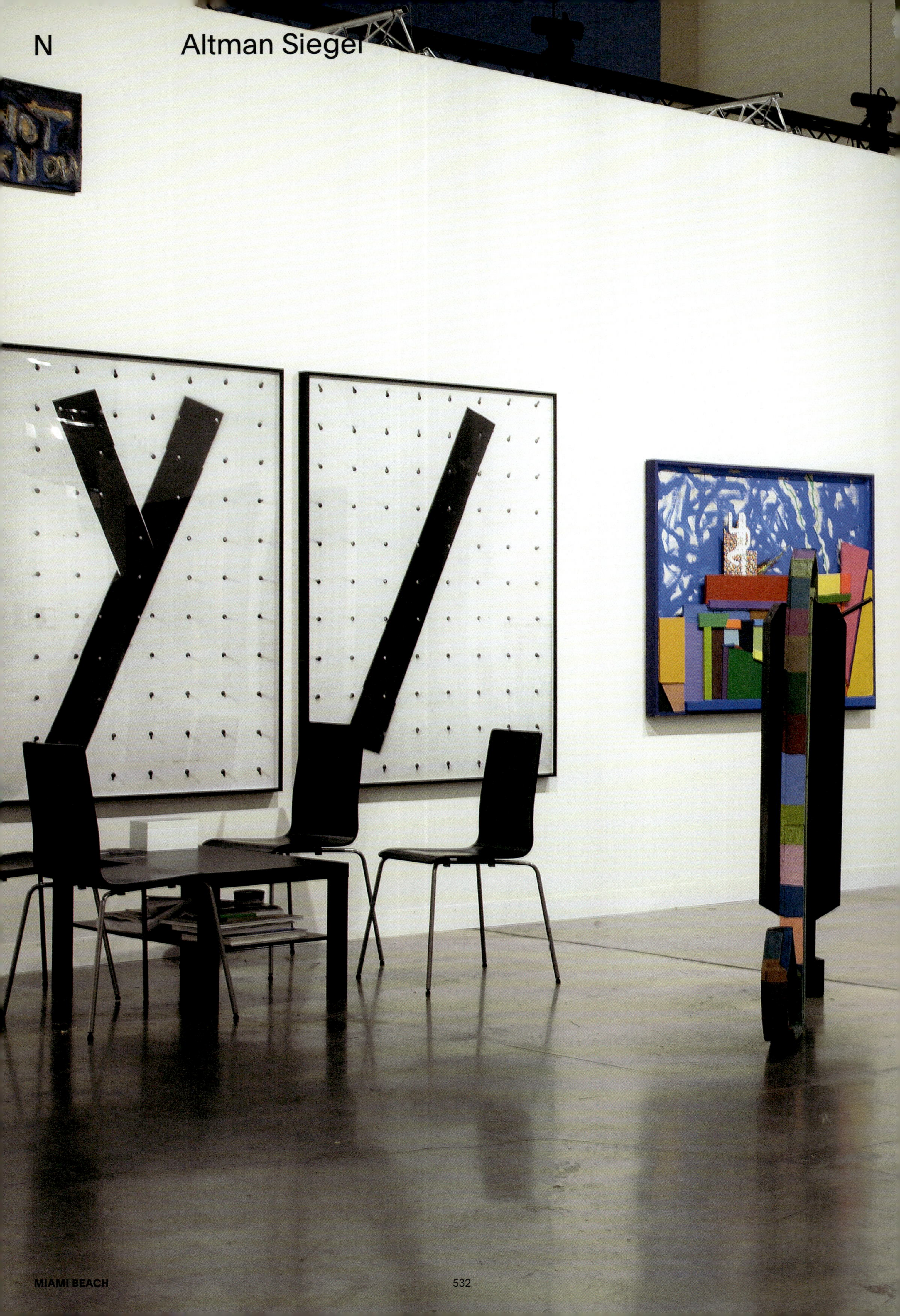

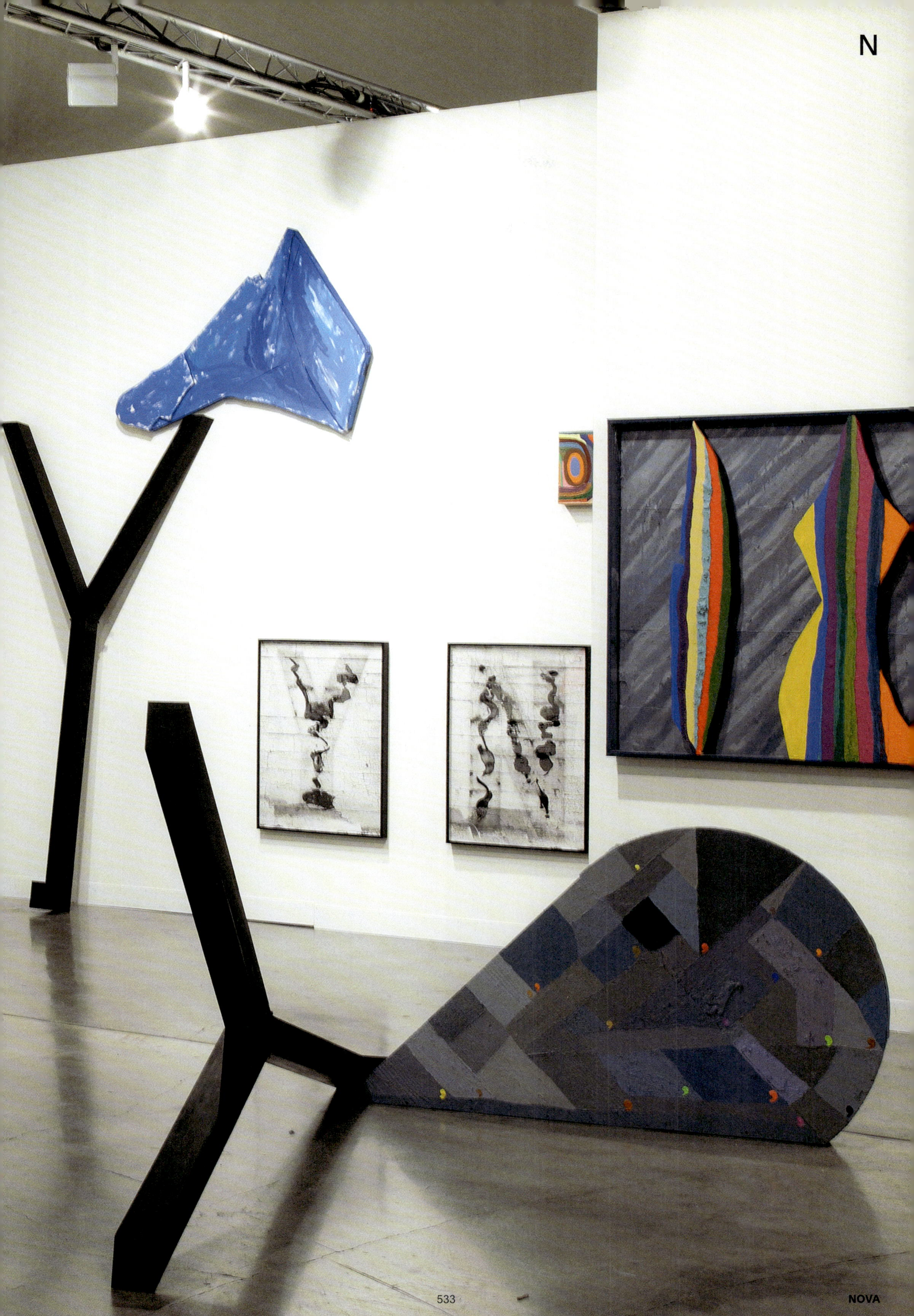

0

O

- Hong Kong
- Basel
- Miami Beach

O

O'Neill

Rome — Galleries

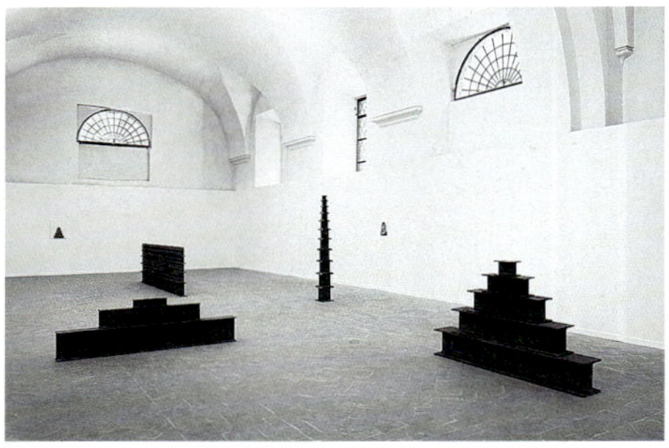

What first compelled you to open a gallery?
I'd worked in the art world since a I was teen-ager—first at the Fogg Museum in Cambridge (MT), then at the Barbara Krakow Gallery (Boston), and later at the d'Offay Gallery (London)—opening a gallery myself was a natural next step.

Who is the first artist you showed and what was most memorable about that show?
Richard Long did the first exhibition in the gallery in Rome, and he used mud from the Tiber, which had flooded that week, to make new work. We also did the first exhibition of a young Italian painter, Manfredi Beninati, who then went on to be in the following two Venice Biennales.

When did you first participate in Art Basel and what was most memorable about that show?
We did Art Basel in Hong Kong in 2013 and it was very eye-opening: the energy in Hong Kong, the sense that young and well-educated people (they do architecture, banking, trading, hotel management, and so on) from around the world consider it a place to live.

- **Contact** — Galleria Lorcan O'Neill Roma; Serena Basso; serena@lorcanoneill.com
- **Established** — 2003
- **Owner(s) / Partner(s)** — Lorcan O'Neill
- **Team** — 10
- **Space(s)** — 325 m² (three spaces)
- **Artists at Art Basel** — Manfredi Beninati; Eddie Peake; Pietro Ruffo; Kiki Smith; Jeff Wall; Rachel Whiteread
- **Further artists represented** — Don Brown; Juliana Cerqueira-Leite; Francesco Clemente; Martin Creed; Tracey Emin; Gary Hume; Anselm Kiefer; Matvey Levenstein; Richard Long; MASBEDO; Carsten Nicolai; Luigi Ontani; Simon Popper; Emilio Prini; Max Renkel; Prem Sahib; Sam Taylor-Johnson; Cerith Wyn Evans

Obadia

Paris — Galleries
Brussels — Galleries Unlimited; Galleries Kabinett

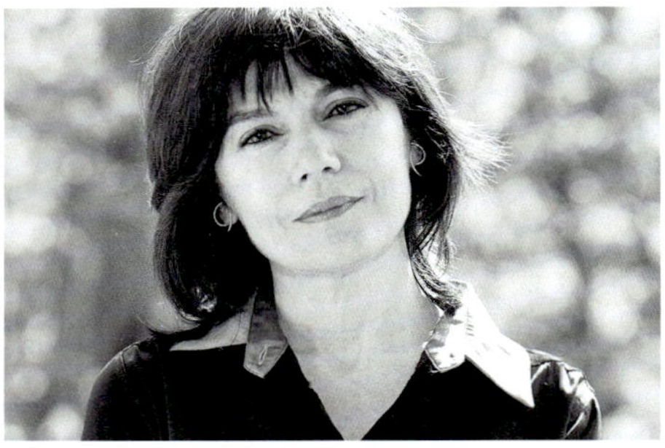

What first compelled you to open a gallery?
Passion since adolescence thanks to parents who were collectors and took me to museums and galleries all around Europe.

Who is the first artist you showed and what was most memorable about that show?
Pascal Pinaud was the first artist I showed. Although we were, in 1993, in the middle of the crisis, we immediately sold to private collectors as well as to public institutions!

When did you first participate in Art Basel and what was most memorable about that show?
We first participated at Art Basel in 1996 with a show of Valérie Favre. Most memorable about this show? The pride in being at Art Basel!

- **Contact** — Galerie Nathalie Obadia; Bianca Duclert; bianca.duclert@galerie-obadia.com; info@galerie-obadia.com
- **Established** — 1993
- **Owner(s) / Partner(s)** — Nathalie Obadia (Owner); Rachel Rechner (Paris Director); Constance Dumas (Brussels Director); Anne-Laure Buffard (Associate Director)
- **Space(s)** — 1,200 m² (two galleries in Paris, one in Brussels)
- **Artists at Art Basel** — Rina Banerjee; Martin Barré; Huma Bhabha; MadeIn Company; Michael DeLucia; Rokni Haerizadeh; Manuel Ocampo; Jorge Queiroz; Fiona Rae; Sarkis; Mithu Sen; Lorna Simpson; Jessica Stockholder; Joana Vasconcelos
- **Further artists represented** — Mequitta Ahuja; Brook Andrew; Barry X Ball; Carole Benzaken; Guillaume Bresson; Rosson Crow; Luc Delahaye; Patrick Faigenbaum; Roland Flexner; Ramin Haerizadeh; Shirley Jaffe; Thomas Lerooy; Meuser; Youssef Nabil; Frank Nitsche; Enoc Perez; Chloe Piene; Pascal Pinaud; Pieter Schoolwerth; Andres Serrano; Mickalene Thomas; Nicola Tyson; Joris van de Moortel; Agnès Varda; Xu Zhen (MadeIn Company); Brenna Youngblood

Office Baroque

Brussels — Nova

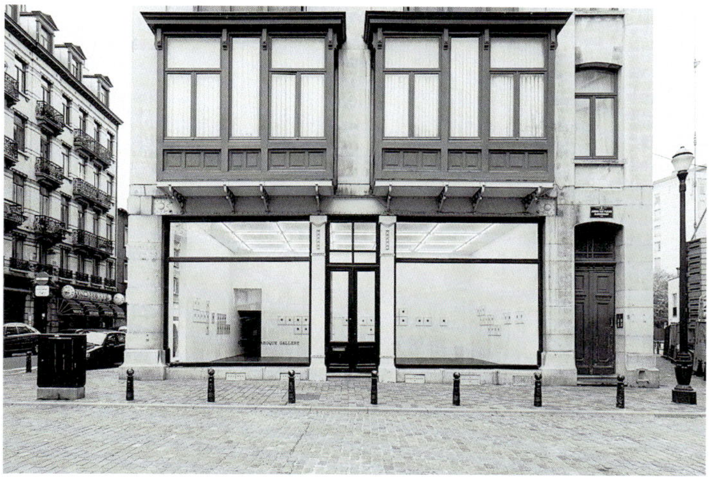

What first compelled you to open a gallery?
Coming from the large Antwerp not-for-profit Extra City, we wanted to start our own business. The format of a commercial gallery allowed us to be closer to a group of artists and to have full curatorial independence. Working within the scale of the gallery also gave us more flexibility and allowed us to be more specific in terms of programming.

Who is the first artist you showed and what was most memorable about that show?
Our first show entitled *On the Marriage Broker Show* featured works by Robert Beck, Matthew Brannon, Mathew Cerletty, Keren Cytter, Armen Eloyan, and Owen Land. That show is still a milestone for us as it took place in our private apartment where the gallery was originally located and we were closely engaged with the works of the presented artists for a period of time. The show also marked the strong curatorial ambitions of the gallery that still determine the program, as well as our participation at Art Basel in Miami Beach.

When did you first participate in Art Basel and what was most memorable about that show?
Art Basel in Miami Beach in 2013 was our first participation.

- **Contact** — Office Baroque Gallery, Louis-Philippe Van Eeckhoutte, louis-philippe@ officebaroque.com, info@officebaroque.com
- **Established** — 2007
- **Owner(s) / Partner(s)** — Marie Denkens, Wim Peeters, Louis-Philippe Van Eeckhoutte (Associate Director)
- **Team** — 5
- **Space(s)** — 200 m²
- **Artists Art Basel** — Aaron Bobrow, David Diao
- **Further artists represented** — Michel Auder, Matthew Brannon, Neil Campbell, Mathew Cerletty, Tamar Halpern, Owen Land, Leigh Ledare, Kirsten Pieroth, Davis Rhodes, Margaret Salmon, Daniel Sinsel, B. Wurtz

OMR

Mexico D.F. — Galleries, Galleries, Galleries

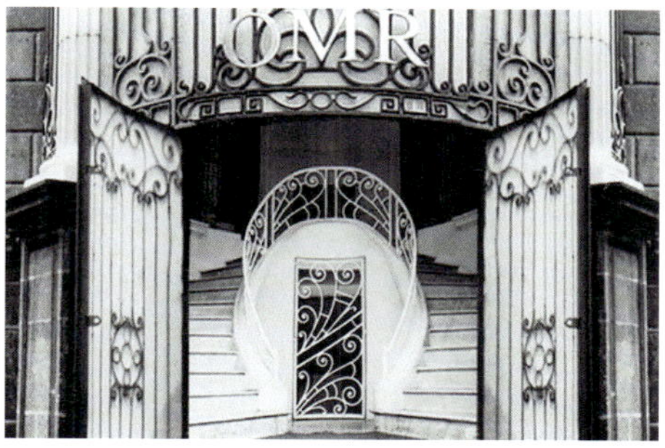

What first compelled you to open a gallery?
In the early 1980s there was a need for galleries in Mexico to represent the new generation of artists.

Who is the first artist you showed and what was most memorable about that show?
We started by doing a photography group show that included artists from several generations, from Manuel Álvarez Bravo, arguably Mexico's most famous photographer, to the very young artists that were just starting out. The show was a complete success with over 350 people at the opening, and it sold out. It was clear that the need for new and daring galleries was indeed a reality.

When did you first participate in Art Basel and what was most memorable about that show?
We first participated in 2001. It was an exciting experience, because although we had been doing international art fairs since 1992, Basel was the entry to important European collections and institutions, such as Daros in Zurich, SMAK in Belgium, and KIASMA in Helsinki. It was also the beginning of long standing friendships and collaborations with galleries from different parts of the world. At the time there was very little participation of galleries from Latin America and we were the first Mexican gallery to attend the fair.

- **Contact** — Galería OMR, Patricia Ortiz Monasterio, galomr@mac.com, info@galeriaomr.com
- **Established** — 1983
- **Owner(s) / Partner(s)** — Jaime Riestra (Member of the Board, Owner), Patricia Ortiz Monasterio (Member of the Board, Owner), Cristobal Riestra (Member of the Board, CEO)
- **Team** — 13
- **Space(s)** — 800 m² (two spaces + office and storage)
- **Artists at Art Basel** — Julieta Aranda, José Arnaud-Bello, Iñaki Bonillas, Sofia Borges, Ryan Brown, Pia Camil, Aldo Chaparro, Félix Curto, Jose Dávila, Gabriel de la Mora, Alberto García-Alix, Candida Höfer, Artur Lescher, Rafael Lozano-Hemmer, Jorge Méndez Blake, Theo Michael, David Moreno, Rubén Ortiz Torres, Pablo Rasgado, Daniel Silver, Troika
- **Further artists represented** — Raúl Cárdenas – Torolab, Yishai Jusidman, Adolfo Riestra, Maruch Sántiz Gómez, Bonnie Seeman, Laureana Toledo, Atelier Van Lieshout

One and J.

Seoul

- Galleries
- Encounters
- Statements
- Positions

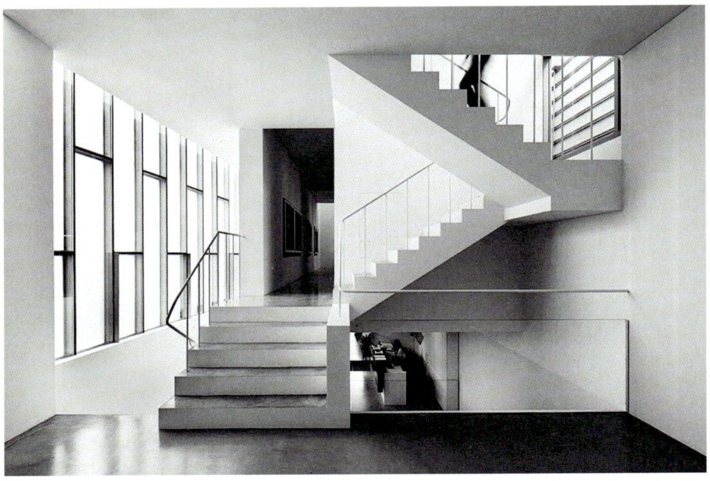

What first compelled you to open a gallery?
Won Jae Park, a graduate of the Rhode Island School of Design (RISD), knew many young Korean artists and musicians, and at the time there were only a few viable outlets to show works in a professional manner within a gallery setting. The idea was to create a platform to showcase these talented artists to a global audience.

Who is the first artist you showed and what was most memorable about that show?
MeeNa Park was the first show we had. The entire first year was memorable as the lineup of artists was strong and had a very good energy. Very few primary galleries representing young Korean artists existed at the time. It's been almost eight years, but that raw energy is something that we remember fondly.

When did you first participate in Art Basel and what was most memorable about that show?
We have participated in Art Basel in Hong Kong since it existed as ART HK. To see that fair grow over the years and to be a part of that history is a nice thing. The first time we participated in Art Basel in Switzerland was in 2013 in the Statements sector. Of course, to be able to participate on that stage was a huge validation for our program. The diverse group of visitors to the fair was memorable. Our first participation in Art Basel in Miami Beach was also in 2013; we were very much looking forward to it and to representing interesting works from Korea.

- **Contact** One and J. Gallery
  Patrick Lee
  pat@oneandj.com
  info@oneandj.com
- **Established** 2005
- **Owner(s) / Partner(s)** Won Jae Park
  Patrick Lee
- **Team** 3
- **Artists at Art Basel** Honggoo Kang
  Chosil Kil
  Yunho Kim
  Jung Lee
  Seung Yul Oh
  Jina Park
- **Further artists represented** Minseung Jang
  Jongku Kim
  Suyoung Kim
  Kyunghwan Kwon
  Nikki S. Lee
  Quirarte + Ornelas
  Dongwook Suh
  Joongho Yum

Ora-Ora

Hong Kong

- Insights

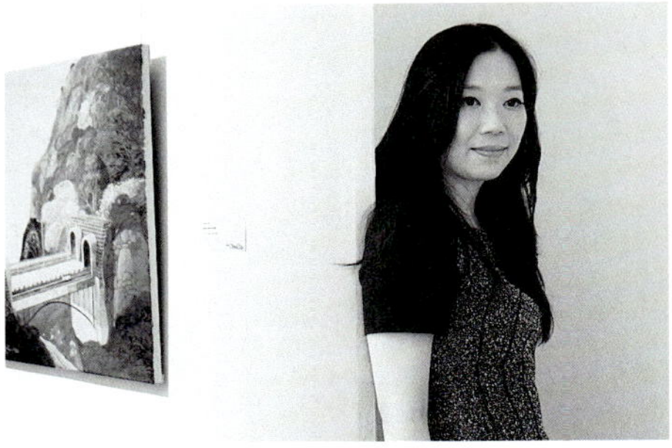

What first compelled you to open a gallery?
Passionate about art from an early age, Henrietta Tsui originally wanted to become an artist. However her education took her on a different path and she worked in banking for over 11 years. Through the coursework of an MBA she began developing ideas for an art gallery business, encouraged by her professors. Tsui understood that in order to become a successful entrepreneur, it must be within an industry she loved, and naturally she chose art. Even if unsuccessful at first in terms of profit, the process and experience alone would be a valuable achievement.

Who is the first artist you showed and what was most memorable about that show?
The first artist Ora-Ora showed was Spanish artist Josep Maria Subirachs. To have the opportunity to work with an internationally renowned artist for a first gallery show was a very rewarding experience. We were a young gallery with limited resources but even using minimal means we put together a quality show. We garnered trust from Subirachs, support from his team, and noteworthy response from our audience, which further validated our decision to open the gallery.

When did you first participate in Art Basel and what was most memorable about that show?
Our first participation in Art Basel was in 2013 in Hong Kong, with a solo exhibition by Halley Cheng.

- **Contact** Galerie Ora-Ora
  Odetti Tse
  odetti@ora-ora.com
  info@ora-ora.com
- **Established** 2006
- **Owner(s) / Partner(s)** Henrietta Tsui (Founder and CEO)
  Alfred Leung (Founder)
- **Team** 8
- **Space(s)** 400 m²
- **Artists at Art Basel** Halley Cheng
- **Further artists represented** Will Clift
  Guan Qijun
  Hao Jiantao
  Hao Liang
  Huang Haifei
  Huang Yongyu
  Jun June Mo
  Kum Chi Keung
  Lai Jing
  Li Pang
  Li Zhijian
  Liu Dewei
  Man Fung-yi
  Mok Yat-san
  Joe Joe Ngai
  Peng Jian
  Joseph Maria Subirachs
  Sun Wen
  Joseph Vernis
  Wang Yongcheng
  Stephen Wong
  Xiao Xu
  Xu Hongfei
  Xu Maoping
  Yolanda Yeung
  Yu Hongbo
  Zeng Guoqing

Osage

Hong Kong
Shanghai (in 2014)

Galleries
Encounters

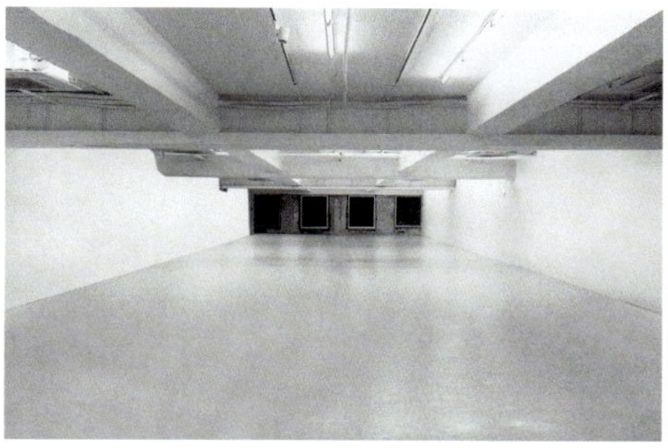

What first compelled you to open a gallery?
A need to build knowledge for the understanding of the art of our region and promote underrepresented emerging and mid-career artists to the rest of the world.

Who is the first artist you showed and what was most memorable about that show?
It was the Chinese artist Chan Sicpo from Madagascar. The exhibition, *Une Ode de Madagascar*, was shown at the National Art Museum of China in Beijing—how can that not be memorable!

When did you first participate in Art Basel and what was most memorable about that show?
The first participation was in Art Basel's Statements sector in 2011. Memorable: being the first gallery with the first Hong Kong artist (Lee Kit) to participate in Art Basel in Basel.

- **Contact** Osage Gallery
  Ginie Shi-Collins
  ginieshicollins@osagegallery.com
  info@osagegallery.com
- **Established** 2004
- **Owner(s) / Partner(s)** Agnes Lin (Director)
- **Team** 10
- **Space(s)** 1,500 m² (indoor)
  500 m² (outdoor)
- **Artists at Art Basel** Au Hoi Lam
  Bea Camacho
  Roberto Chabet
  Louie Cordero
  Robert Gutierrez
  Liang Quan
  Lim Tzay Chuen
  Lui Chun Kwong
  Ng Joon Kiat
  Kingsley Ng
  Wilson Shieh
  Maria Taniguchi
  Tintin Wulia
  MM Yu
- **Further artists represented** Li Xinping
  Sun Yuan & Peng Yu
  Min Thein Sung

Ota

Tokyo
Singapore

Galleries

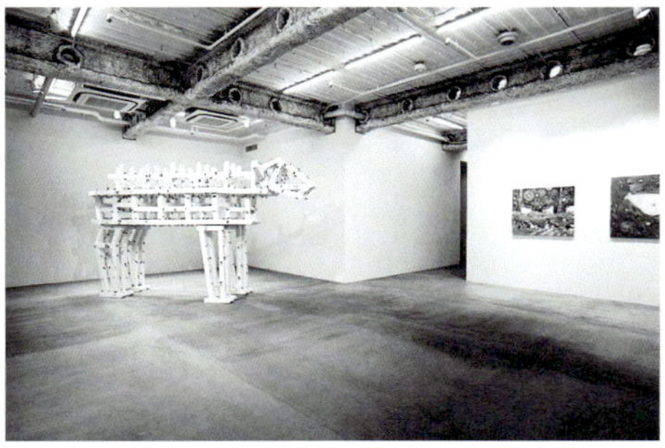

What first compelled you to open a gallery?
As Tokyo was facing an excess of imported art and the majority of galleries were in the secondary market in early 1990s, opening a primary market gallery that manages only its represented artists was high risk and very challenging. We wanted to give it a try.

Who is the first artist you showed and what was most memorable about that show?
The first artist we showed was Yuji Akatsuka. The exhibition showed only litographs—the market for young artists was so small that we could only sell reasonably priced editioned works.

When did you first participate in Art Basel and what was most memorable about that show?
We have been participating in ART HK since the first edition, however this year was the first time we participated in Art Basel. The collaboration with Victoria Miro this year is the most memorable work we have ever done.

- **Contact** Ota Fine Arts
  Yoshiko Kogi
  kogi@otafinearts.com
  sg@otafinearts.com
- **Established** 1994
- **Owner(s) / Partner(s)** Hidenori Ota (Owner)
  Yoriko Tsuruta (Partner)
  Yasuko Kaneko
  (Director of Singapore)
- **Team** 5
- **Space(s)** 181 m² (Tokyo)
  108 m² (Singapore)
- **Artists at Art Basel** Yayoi Kusama
- **Further artists represented** Akira the Hustler
  Christine Ay Tjoe
  BuBu de la Madeleine
  Monir Shahroudy Farmanfarmaian
  Masanori Handa
  Tomoko Kashiki
  Manami Koike
  Firoz Mahmud
  Takao Minami
  Masayasu Mitsuke
  Hiraki Sawa
  Yoshiko Shimada
  SHINCHIKA
  Nobuaki Takekawa
  Yuken Teruya
  Jay Flores Ticar
  Tetsuya Umeda
  Yeesookyung

Overduin and Kite

Los Angeles

Statements
Nova

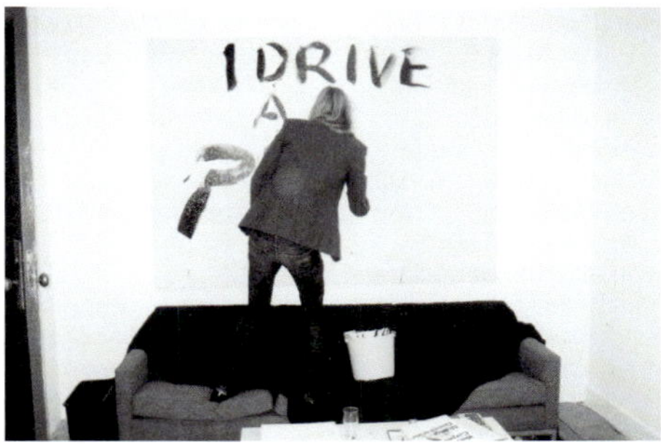

What first compelled you to open a gallery?
We wanted to create a program that included multiple generations of artists as well as historical shows as context for younger artists. This was not really being done at the time, especially not in LA.

Who is the first artist you showed and what was most memorable about that show?
Tony Conrad. We showed a film Tony made starring Mike Kelley and Tony Oursler. The audience had to be photographed for military badges required to enter the exhibition space. They had to choose if they wanted to be civilian or military.

When did you first participate in Art Basel and what was most memorable about that show?
For our first participation in Art Basel we showed Kaari Upson. Kaari made a large scale installation of abstracted architectural fragments and video projection. She also included latex soft sculptures. It was a striking, immersive installation.

- **Contact** Overduin and Kite
  Lisa Overduin
  lisa@overduinandkite.com
  info@overduinandkite.com
- **Established** 2007
- **Owner(s) / Partner(s)** Lisa Overduin
  Kristina Kite
- **Team** 9
- **Space(s)** 375 m²
- **Artists at Art Basel** Math Bass
  Nick Relph
  Erika Vogt
- **Further artists represented** Ei Arakawa
  Frank Benson
  Merlin Carpenter
  Marc Camille Chaimowicz
  Maureen Gallace
  Nikolas Gambaroff
  Barry Johnston
  Dianna Molzan
  Scott Olson
  Silke Otto-Knapp
  Eileen Quinlan
  Stephen G. Rhodes
  Haim Steinbach
  Cheyney Thompson
  Kaari Upson
  Tris Vonna-Michell

Oxley9

Sydney ● Galleries

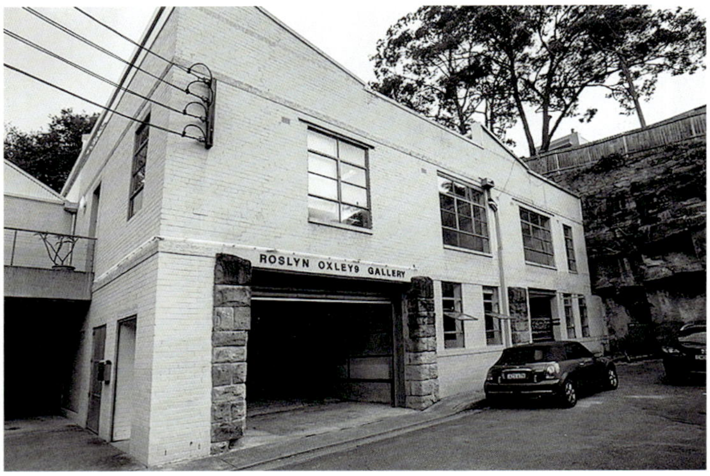

What first compelled you to open a gallery?
After 20 years working with major architectural firms as an interior designer in Melbourne, Sydney, and New York, it seemed the logical step in my career. Having worked so closely with artists, designers, and corporate collections, opening a gallery was a natural progression for me. Tony and I opened Roslyn Oxley9 Gallery in Sydney in March 1982.

Who is the first artist you showed and what was most memorable about that show?
The first artist we showed was Gareth Sansom in March 1982. The first year the gallery was open was exceptional. All the artists were young and new to Sydney and we had opened the largest commercial exhibition space in the city.

When did you first participate in Art Basel and what was most memorable about that show?
1996 was the first year we exhibited at Art Basel. The most memorable thing for me was how completely excited I was to be a part of the fair, a fair I had wanted to participate in since attending the very first Art Basel in 1970.

- **Contact** Roslyn Oxley9 Gallery
  Roslyn Oxley
  roslyn@roslynoxley9.com.au
  oxley9@roslynoxley9.com.au
- **Established** 1982
- **Owner(s) / Partner(s)** Roslyn & Tony Oxley
- **Team** 10
- **Space(s)** 700 m²
- **Artists at Art Basel** Hany Armanious
  Mikala Dwyer
  Newell Harry
  Tracey Moffatt
  David Noonan
- **Further artists represented** James Angus
  Del Kathryn Barton
  Daniel Boyd
  Tony Clark
  Bill Culbert
  Marley Dawson
  Destiny Deacon
  Wim Delvoye
  Dale Frank
  Jacqueline Fraser
  Rosalie Gascoigne
  David Griggs
  Fiona Hall
  Louise Hearman
  Bill Henson
  Isaac Julien
  Teppei Kaneuji
  Yayoi Kusama
  Lindy Lee
  Linda Marrinon
  TV Moore
  Callum Morton
  Nell
  Michael Parekowhai
  Patricia Piccinini
  Julie Rrap
  Gareth Sansom
  Glenn Sorensen
  Kathy Temin
  Imants Tillers
  Jenny Watson
  Rohan Wealleans
  John Wolseley
  Nyapanyapa Yunupingu

Roslyn Oxley9 Gallery

Interview with Roslyn and Tony Oxley

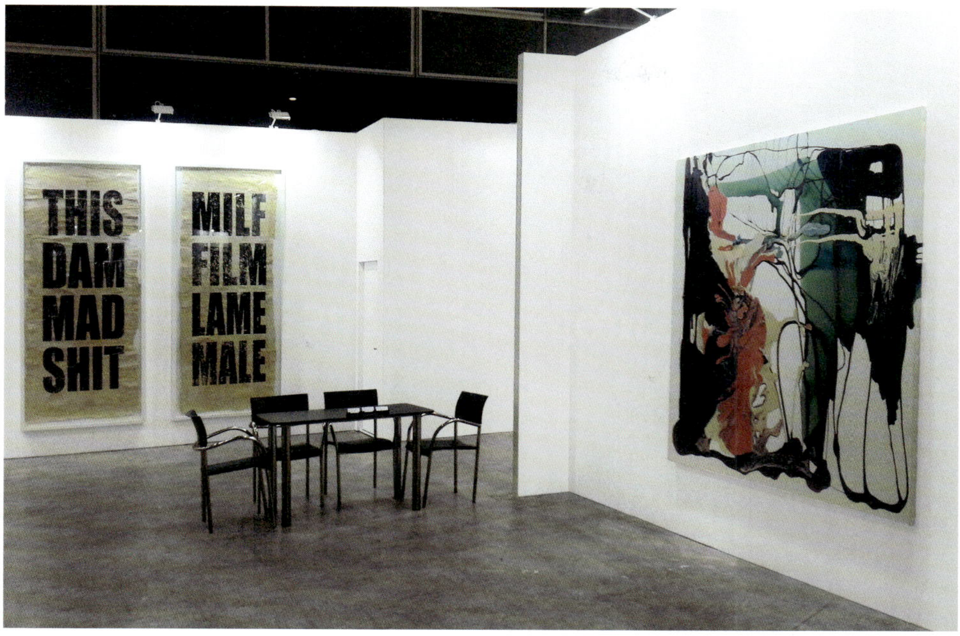

Art Basel in Hong Kong, 2013

You have been active since 1982, and are a pioneer in the Asia-Pacific region. How has your program developed over 30 years? How do you think the regional scene has evolved, especially within the broader context of the international art scene?

When we opened our gallery in 1982, it was the largest commercial space for art in Sydney. Right from the beginning we wanted to show cutting-edge contemporary art, but with a particular focus on Australian artists and the art of our region. We also felt it was important to bring international artists to Australia in order to open up a dialogue between Europe, America, and the Asia-Pacific region.

Our involvement with the Asian contemporary art scene really began in 1986 when a group of Japanese curators including Akira Tatehata visited Australia in preparation for the exhibition *Edge to Edge: Australian Contemporary Art to Japan* (1988). They selected a number of our artists for the show and we were excited by a new sense of interaction between Japan and Australia. Then in 1991, Judy Annear curated one of the first museum survey exhibitions of Japanese contemporary art ever held outside of Japan at the Museum of Contemporary Art in Sydney. Exhibitions such as these established a dialogue between the Australian and Asian contemporary art scenes. Government initiatives have since continued to foster the cultural exchange between our regions.

In the 1990s and 2000s there was an influx of Asian curators visiting Australia and further regional survey exhibitions were mounted. Their influence has been widespread, even extending to Europe. Indeed, it was a result of the exhibition *Edge to Edge: Australian Contemporary Art to Japan* that we began to work with the artist Yayoi Kusama. We were in Tokyo for the opening celebrations of this exhibition and we were very impressed by a large show of Kusama's work at the Fuji Television Gallery. We soon began exhibiting her recent work at European art fairs, including Art Basel from 1996 onward. Since then we have continued to maintain a focus on including Asian artists in our program. In addition to Yayoi Kusama, we have held exhibitions by Mariko Mori, Tatzu Nishi, Issey Miyake, and Teppei Kaneuji.

According to you, what does the introduction of Art Basel in the Asia-Pacific region represent, and how did you experience this first edition of Art Basel in Hong Kong? You had already participated in the 2012, 2011, and 2010 editions of the Hong Kong Art Fair.

For a long time we felt that our main international platforms for art fairs were Europe (Basel) and America (New York). In the last ten years, however, this has shifted to Asia, and more particularly to Hong Kong, which has become very relevant to Australia and the rest of the world as a major art center. We began exhibiting at ART HK in 2010, and since then we have noticed a steady increase in the knowledge and sophistication of collectors in the region. We were very pleased when Art Basel took over the fair in 2013, as the Basel brand has given recognition to the growing importance of the region. The Art Basel name carries influence in Asia and we felt that this probably encouraged a wider range of collectors and attending galleries, which can only help to increase the diversity and dynamism of the contemporary art scene in Asia. Compared with previous years, the first edition of Art Basel in Hong Kong featured a much-improved general presentation. Of particular note was the stand layout featuring wider and better-defined passageways. The democratic distribution of the variety of different gallery types over the stand spaces on each level was another conspicuous improvement.

How did you conceive your Art Basel in Hong Kong booth and how did it reflect your general gallery program?

For our first booth at Art Basel in Hong Kong we decided to present a curated exhibition of work by leading Australian artists. We selected artists who had recently exhibited at international venues, such as Hany Armanious who represented Australia at the Venice Biennale, and Tracey Moffatt who had recently shown her video works at MoMA in New York. We also included Newell Harry, a younger artist whose work is heavily influenced by his travels in the Asia-Pacific region. For Art Basel in Hong Kong Harry made bold text works printed on Tongan bark cloth. All of the selected artists have been an integral part of the gallery's exhibition program in the preceding years.

O

Richard Artschwager
1923–2013

Gabriele Basilico
1944–2013

Anthony Caro
1924–2013

Sarah Charlesworth
1947–2013

Arthur C. Danto
1924–2013

León Ferrari
1920–2013

Günther Förg
1952–2013

Roberto Gutiérrez
1939–2011

Channa Horwitz
1932–2013

Mike Kelley
1954–2013

Steven Leiber
1957–2012

Walter De Maria
1935–2013

Thomas McEvilley
1939–2013

Otto Mühl
1925–2013

Jonathan Napack
1967–2007

Jean-Louis Pradel
1946–2013

Kenneth Price
1935–2012

Lou Reed
1942–2013

Pierre Schneider
1925–2013

Allan Sekula
1951–2013

Seth Siegelaub
1941–2013

Dorothea Tanning
1910–2012

Zao Wou-Ki
1920–2013

OVA TIONS

O

Totentanz

Harry Bellet

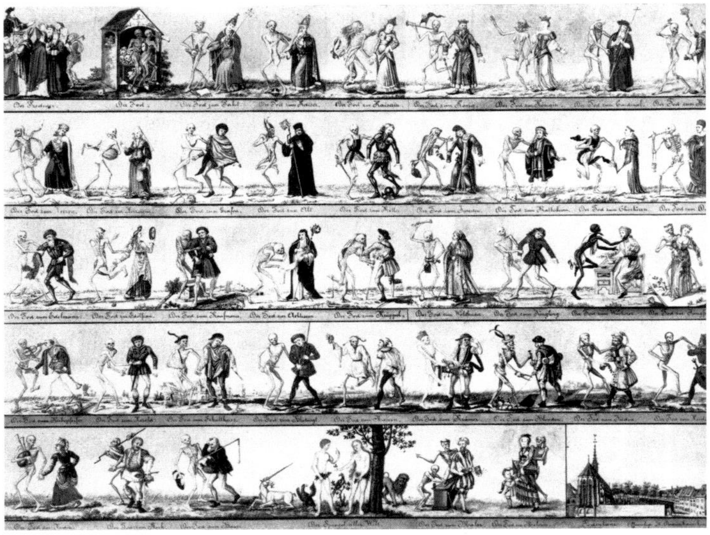

Johann Rudolf Feyerabend, *Basler Totentanz*, 1806, copy after Matthaus Merian (1621) of the *Totentanz* fresco paintings located at the monastery of the Dominican Order of Preachers, c. 1440–1450 Historisches Museum, Basel

I don't know if the people of Basel like death, but for a long time they have stared it in the face. Hans Holbein drew his famous "Alphabet" there against a background of dancing skeletons, as well as a series of vignettes showing Death interrupting men of every condition as they go about the tasks of daily life, even helping a ploughman to whip his horse so that he can get his furrow finished more quickly, and at last find rest. "Totentanz" (Dance of Death) fresco paintings adorned the walls of the Klingenthal Convent of the Augustinian Sisters, and the monastery of the Dominican Order of Preachers on the opposite bank of the Rhine. They have been destroyed—works are not everlasting either—even if fragments of the latter, believed to have been painted by Konrad Witz, survive at the Historisches Museum in Basel. One of them depicted Death seizing hold of the painter, with a second skeleton even playing at being an apprentice by grinding pigments. For artists die too. I have been assigned to celebrate those dearly departed in 2013. But as I write, I realize I see it differently. Because deaths, like lives, are somehow inextricably intertwined.

The two years that have just gone by have been cruel for the community: a community, for artists have their remoras, just like sharks—critics for example.

The American Arthur Coleman Danto (1924–2013) was undoubtedly one of the best known. A philosopher and art critic, he experienced a form of revelation at an exhibition of Andy Warhol at Stable Gallery in New York in 1964. Warhol was showing identical reproductions of boxes of Brillo scouring pads, presented as sculptures. Why is it art? Danto wondered. His answer was simple: because it is presented in an art gallery. Because a community composed of artists, critics, art historians, museum curators, dealers, and collectors, who constitute the "art world," recognize it as such. The difference between boxes of Brillo pads and a work of art consisting of reproductions of boxes of Brillo pads is therefore "a certain theory of art: it is the theory that takes it up into the world of art and keeps it from collapsing into the real object which it is." Art is profoundly bound up with interpretation. It is that which transforms the object into art, and therefore constitutes art—a distant echo of Marcel Duchamp's "The viewer completes the work of art." Pop, Danto said, had rescued aesthetic philosophy from boredom. He remains a rare example of a philosopher seeking to define art on the basis of the art of his period, by visiting it, liking it, and championing it.

His fellow countrymen Thomas McEvilley (1939–2013) and Pierre Schneider (1925–2013)—even though he spent the greater part of his life in Paris and published in French, Schneider was an American—were perhaps less theorists than lovers of works of art and words. Certainly the former did not lack university qualifications: the fact that a critic knows Latin may not be remarkable, but he was conversant with Ancient Greek too, and even with Sanskrit! These openings to the world sometimes made him a formidable polemicist: Holland Cotter recalled in the *New*

York Times that McEvilley's review in the magazine *Artforum*, which he worked for regularly, had seriously undermined the assumptions that had governed the exhibition *Primitivism in 20th Century Art: Affinity of the Tribal and the Modern*, organized by The Museum of Modern Art in New York in 1984, for all that it was the brainchild of two big names in the profession, William Rubin and Kirk Varnedoe. McEvilley's vision of multiculturalism inspired Jean-Hubert Martin in creating another now legendary exhibition, *Les Magiciens de la terre*, in Paris in 1989; and no doubt echoes of it can still be found in the Pompidou Center's exhibition *Modernités plurielles* (2013–2015) showing the history of 20th-century art on a worldwide scale, as happens in the majority of biennials of contemporary art: it is no longer possible today to think of art solely through the Western prism.

Pierre Schneider had devoted himself to a different form of evangelism, which at the time verged on a vocation: introducing American abstract art, that of his friends Sam Francis and Jean-Paul Riopelle, to the French of the 1950s, and getting them to like it. But also, and very paradoxically, the art of Henri Matisse, then much more widely known and appreciated in the United States than in France. His book on Matisse, published in 1984, is still recommended reading. A monumental work (752 pages!), and one of the very first art publishing bestsellers. I can, I regret to say, vouch for the fact that all students of art history at the time bankrupted themselves to buy it. Thirty years on, it is still in my bookcase, within easy reach, alongside another of his books, the commercial and critical failure of which darkened the last years of his life, all the more so as it was unmerited. *Petite histoire de l'infini en peinture* (2001) is a great book, and Schneider was a great man.

It is again with sadness that I pay tribute to the memory of my friend, Jean-Louis Pradel (1946–2013), who was a fellow traveler in the French "Figuration narrative" movement, but also contributed toward discovering Julio Le Parc. Le Parc has been more or less forgotten, though he had won the prize for painting at the 1966 Venice Biennale. Pradel's funeral at Père-Lachaise cemetery in Paris took place at exactly the same time as the preview of the Foire internationale d'art contemporain: guess where the artists he had championed chose to be? Round the coffin. We don't know whether, as Marc Spiegler once wrote, critics are still of any use ("Do Art Critics Still Matter?" *The Art Newspaper*, April 2005); in any case, between saying hello to a collector and goodbye to a friend, artists knew which choice to make.

But there are other intermediaries. Dealers, for example. They don't all own enormous galleries with branches right across the world that they can travel to on the spur of the moment in their private jets. Steven Leiber (1957–2012), for instance, used to work in his grandmother's cellar in San Francisco. Which didn't stop him from accumulating works by almost a thousand artists! However, nothing monumental: Leiber specialized in "ephemera," tracts, mailings, posters, invitation cards to exhibitions, brochures, a collection he had started with items from the Fluxus movement and works by concrete poets and the Beat Generation. He had also accumulated major archival collections on artists such as Claes Oldenburg, Allan Kaprow, and the journal *Avalanche* from the 1970s, as well as a fair quantity of documentation on movements as diverse as Minimalism, Conceptual art, video, performance, and mail art. He was not satisfied with just dealing in it, but also passed on his passion to his students at the California College of Arts in San Francisco, and visitors to the exhibitions he organized in 1995 at the National Gallery of Art in Ottawa and the Institute of Contemporary Arts in London. His sales catalogues were famous too for their inventive forms: some inspired by boxes for rolls of film, others by cardboard boxes of baseball cards to collect, and even a series of postcards dispatched daily over the course of a month.

Steven Leiber
1957–2012

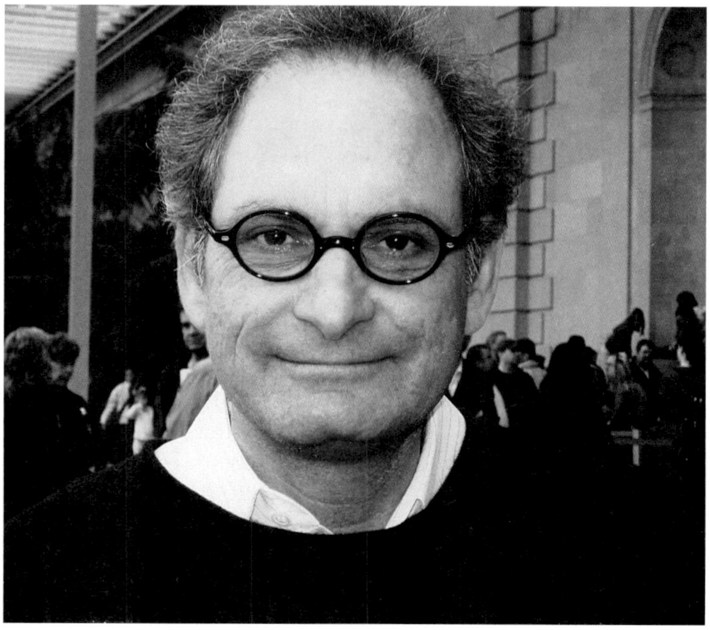

O

A type of formal poetry reminiscent of that of Roberto Gutiérrez (1939–2011), the co-founder and driving force behind the journal *Plages*, which featured artists as diverse as Joseph Beuys, Bram Bogart, Corneille, Ernest Pignon-Ernest, and Wolf Vostell, among hundreds of others, less well known. They gave each issue a new form, depending on the chosen theme: in the one devoted to "the sea," for example, packaged in a net, there was a tin of sardines among other things, while the one concentrating on "love" included a little box in the shape of a heart. Roberto was as much a militant as an artist, and full credit goes to Art Basel for having always kept a stand for him, for all that he was as poor as a church mouse. He died at Roissy airport in France, on his way back from Art Basel in Miami Beach, which he loved so much.

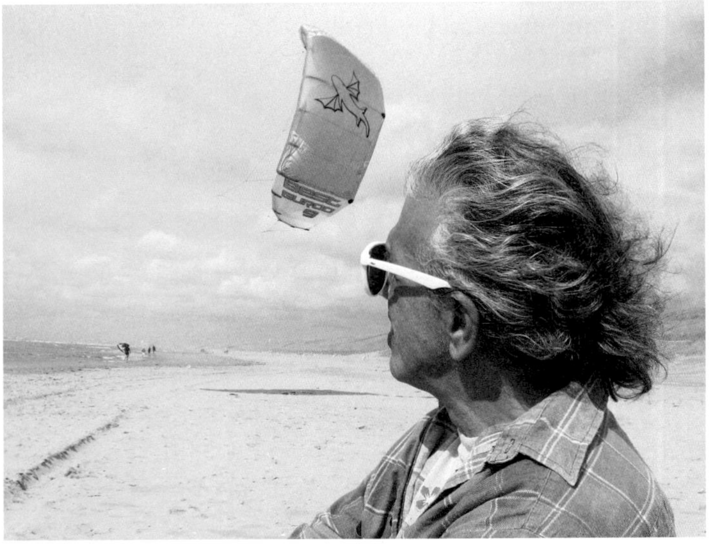

Seth Siegelaub
1941–2013

Seth Siegelaub (1941–2013), who died in Basel, was the same kind of guerillero. He saw his artist's books as an alternative to private galleries, or even museums, the object itself becoming the exhibition and its own documentation, as was the case with his catalogue *Douglas Huebler—November 1968*, the first of its kind. The following year he repeated the venture with *July, August, September 1969,* a catalogue grouping together Carl Andre, Robert Barry, Daniel Buren, Jan Dibbets, Douglas Huebler, Joseph Kosuth, Sol LeWitt, Richard Long, N.E. Thing Co. Ltd., Robert Smithson, and Lawrence Weiner, for an exhibition held simultaneously in eleven different cities throughout the world. He also came up with *The Xerox Book* (1968) in which seven artists (Carl Andre, Robert Barry, Douglas Huebler, Josef Kosuth, Sol LeWitt, Robert Morris, and Lawrence Weiner) used reprography to appropriate the 25 pages offered to them by the publisher; these were then reproduced by offset printing, and distributed. His role in Conceptual art was low-key (after 1980 he preferred to work on a history of textiles), but crucial.

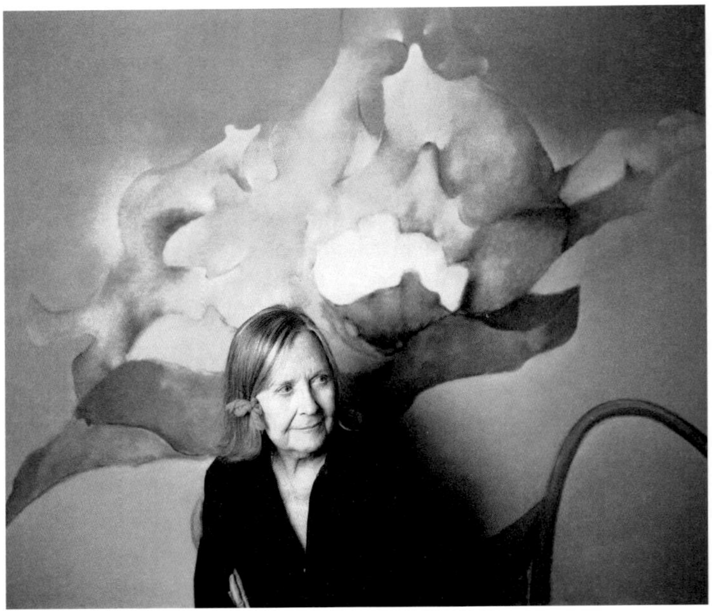

Dorothea Tanning
1910–2012

Sad to say, it would also almost be possible to write a history of 20th-century art based on the artists who have died recently. Starting with Surrealism, there is Dorothea Tanning (1910–2012), who discovered the movement as far back as 1936 on visiting the exhibition *Fantastic Art, Dada, Surrealism* presented by The Museum of Modern Art in New York, a pioneer as so often. In 1942, taking advantage of André Breton's presence in the United States as a refugee, she joined the group, exhibiting at the Julien Levy gallery and meeting Max Ernst, who came to her house to select paintings for an exhibition being prepared by his then wife, Peggy Guggenheim, under the title *Thirty Women*. Ernst left Peggy and married Dorothea in 1946, which apparently prompted Peggy to say that of those "thirty women," there had been one too many ... But it would be wrong to think of her only as "the wife of." In a movement, which, by and large, tended to be macho, she was the first to dare to paint female phantasms. And not just to paint them. As a result of the retrospective of her work organized by Pontus Hultén in 1974 at the Centre national d'Art contemporain, the Pompidou Center in Paris still has an extraordinary installation she made, *Chambre 202, Hôtel du Pavot* (1970), a full-size reconstruction of a room from the walls of which naked bodies emerge, pink flesh bursting through the wallpaper. She had also illustrated collections of poetry, from the work of René Crevel to that of André Pieyre de Mandiargues, as well as writing poems which she regularly published in the *New Yorker* at the age of 100, a magazine not known for publishing anything mediocre.

And then there is Kenneth Price (1935–2012). Why talk about him just after Dorothea Tanning, when he is a generation younger and never laid claim to anything surrealist at all? Simply because I don't know where to put him! It isn't given to all creative artists to defy categorization, and since my respected colleague Jerry Saltz regards him as "one of America's greatest sculptors," I hope that it will not be held against me if I associate him with the extraordinary woman Tanning was. Especially as he didn't conceal his admiration for Joan Miró and Joseph Cornell, in works Holland Cotter described as "genetic accidents." The thing is that Price, regarded when he was very young (as early as 1964) by *Artforum* as one of the two most important artists in Los Angeles (the other being Robert Irwin), stubbornly persisted in working in ceramics, and had no scruples about producing cups or bowls and deriving inspiration from the work of Mexican potters. "Art or craft?" his contemporaries wondered: both, he might have replied, even if merely abandoning the traditional glazing of earthenware in 1983 in favor thereafter of the exclusive use of acrylic paint (sometimes more than 70 layers, rubbed down over and over again) finally allowed them to stand out. But at the same time this does not explain the strange fascination that his sometimes quite small sculptures continue to exert—in Saltz's words a "combination of sexual, sensual, and excremental."

Kenneth Price
1935–2012

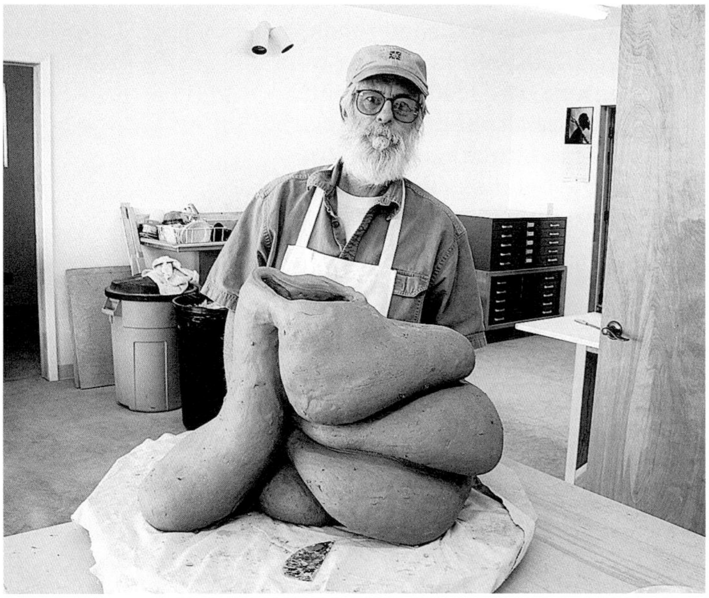

After Surrealism and its probable derivatives, Abstraction. Rightly or wrongly, it is into that movement, in its lyrical or *informel* version, that Zao Wou-Ki (1920–2013) was assimilated. Wrongly, because the space in his pictures is inspired by atmospheric

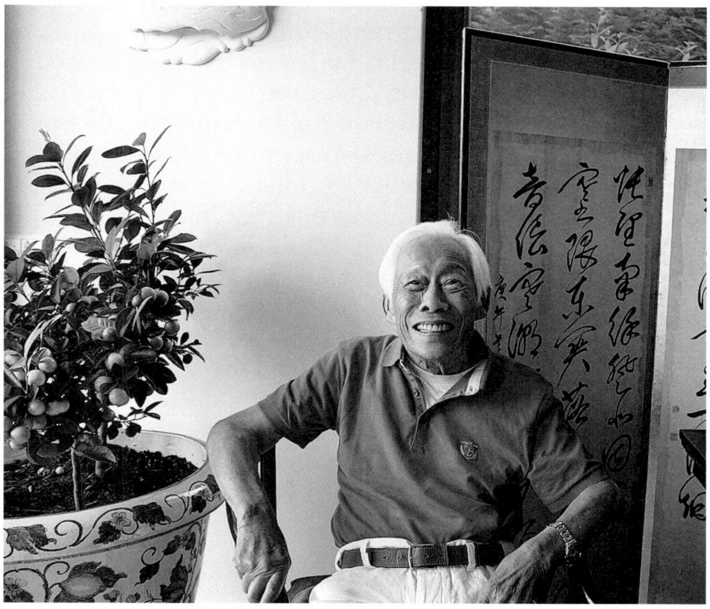

Zao Wou-Ki
1920–2013

perspective as it has been represented by the Chinese for millennia; he had studied this at the Academy of Art in Hangzhou. Rightly, because it was in Paris—where he arrived in 1948 at the height of the gestural art craze, championed in particular by the magazine *Cimaise*, but also by the powerful Galerie de France—that he experienced his first successes, got to know his first friends, the poet and painter Henri Michaux in particular, and was exposed to his first Western influences, such as Paul Klee, who for a long time was his lodestar. At the time the Galerie de France represented Pierre Soulages, and Zao Wou-Ki joined it in his turn. In 1983 he was invited to return to China, after nearly 30 years of voluntary exile, for two major exhibitions in Beijing and Hangzhou. Up until then his fame had mainly been Western, but in Asia it spread from Singapore, where he worked with the architect Ieoh Ming Pei, to South Korea, from Taiwan to Japan. But it is due to the country of his birth that he has today reached the heights of the art market.

His near contemporary, the British artist Sir Anthony Caro (1924–2013)—he was knighted in 1987—was also long considered a representative of Abstract Expressionism, insofar as that notion has any meaning in sculpture. Doubtless because one of the first critics as far back as 1959 to notice a man who was then just an assistant to Henry Moore was the American art critic Clement

Greenberg. Caro spent time in the United States where he was influenced by the work of David Smith, but above all by the spirit of freedom then prevailing in the arts: “America made me see that there are no barriers and no regulations,” he confided to the critic Lawrence Alloway a short time later. That country also did a lot for his career since he was honored by a retrospective organized by William Rubin in 1975. At the time, and for 15 years prior, he was producing abstract polychrome sculpture, sometimes mixing ceramic, bronze, and steel. It took a few decades for his other approach, based on modeling, to be discovered, an approach that didn’t prohibit him from flirting with figures. A mixing of genres that is now commonplace—Hans Richter has caused it to be accepted as possible by the whole world—but in those heroic days it had to be carried out almost in secret.

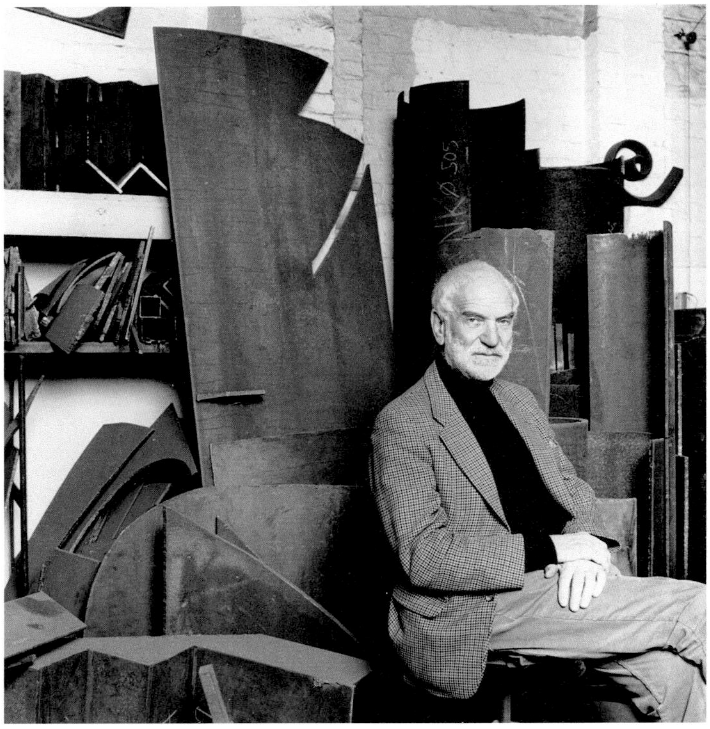

Sir Anthony Caro
1924–2013

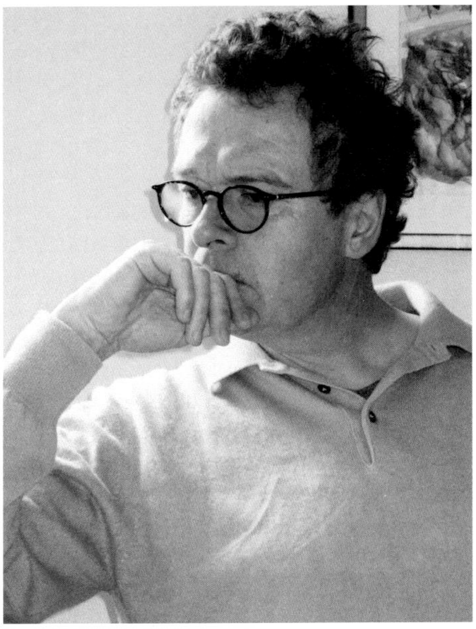

Günther Förg
1952–2013

Richard Artschwager (1923–2013) was cast in the same mold, even if his path was more chaotic. We will skip over his more than romantic youth (apparently he worked for American counter-espionage in Vienna in the immediate postwar period) and his short career as a photographer of babies: he found his direction, if we discount some time spent in the studio of the “purist” painter Amédée Ozenfant, by way of a far from common roundabout route—as a furniture manufacturer. Simple, functional objects, often constructed from Formica, a material that was modern at the time. It was from that mingling of art and craftsmanship that his work derived a large part of its originality, and it did not fail to attract the attention of Donald Judd. Working with wood and Formica, Artschwager dreamt up volumes with a complex geometry, the surfaces of which present combinations of figures of different colors to our view, fitting into one another like elements of marquetry. A first solo exhibition at the Leo Castelli gallery in 1965 revealed his work, which is affiliated as much to Pop art as to Minimalism in that the shapes and materials of the present-day world are captured, misappropriated, and refined in it. In 1968 he came up with the *BLPs*—pronounced “blips”: simple black shapes inspired by punctuation marks that he placed at varying heights, in such a way as to show off the structures of the architecture, that of the Konrad Fischer gallery in Düsseldorf where he presented them for the first time in 1968, and the Whitney Museum, in the same year. The New York museum devoted two retrospectives to him in 1988 and 2013.

Like Artschwager, Günther Förg (1952–2013) employed sometimes exotic materials, not hesitating to mix wood, bronze, and lead with paint. For him it was all about revisiting the history of modern art (so he photographed the buildings designed by the Bauhaus architects and how they had aged, as well as fascist Italian ones), and he had no qualms about following on in the tradition of Barnett Newman, Clyfford Still, and Willem de Kooning, or of the artists of the next generation, such as Cy Twombly and Ellsworth Kelly, and reinterpreting them in his own way, in often gigantic formats. A body of work that is part appropriation, part homage, sustained by a very German view of the aesthetics of the sublime, which was not satisfied with quoting, but really reanimated what it borrowed.

While Channa Horwitz (1932–2013) also liked to explore all the possibilities of a form (her "Sonakinatography" series extended over 36 years!), she did this mainly through drawing, for which she used graph paper divided into squares based on the number eight and its multiples. So it might be imagined that she was close to geometric abstraction, Minimalism, and Op art. However, her work was derived, according to what she said, from sound, movement, and notation, which moreover meant that it could be read as a score, "played" by means of percussion instruments, or even danced. Her first appearance on the scene involved participation in the *Art and Technology* exhibition at the Los Angeles County Museum of Art, where her work was so badly presented that it provoked protests from feminist movements. Her career was extremely unassuming until her recent rediscovery: major exhibitions at the New Museum in New York and the ZKM in Karlsruhe, as well as participation in the 2013 Venice Biennale, have made it possible, too belatedly unfortunately, to make a proper assessment of her work.

Channa Horwitz
1932–2013

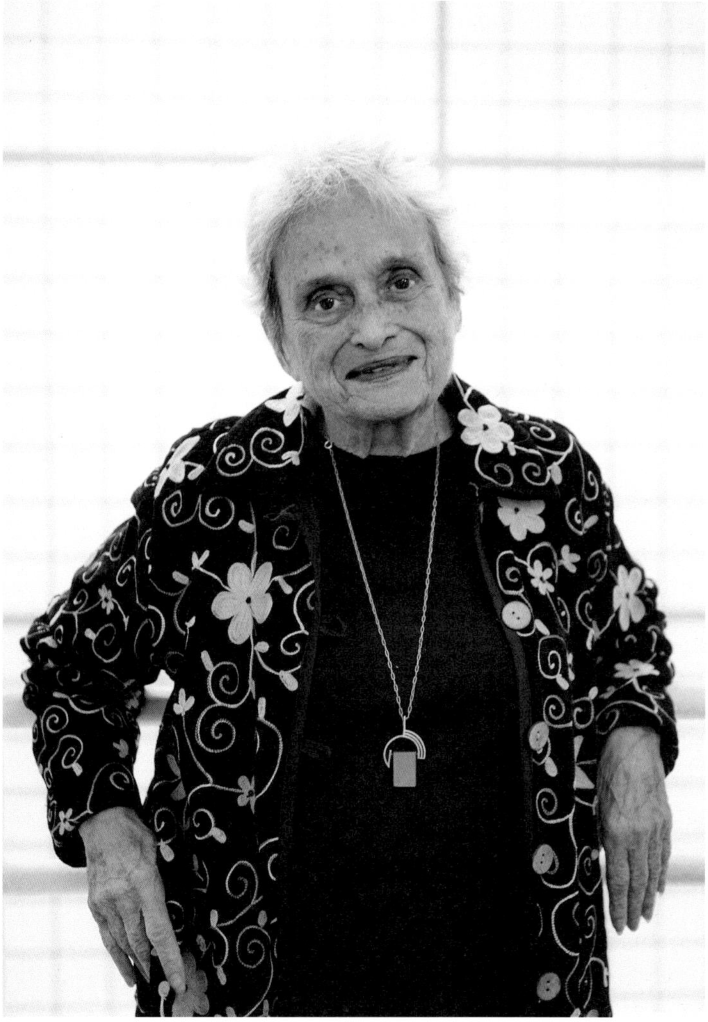

Another Minimalist, but also one of the foremost representatives of Land art, Walter De Maria (1935–2013) had continued to have a keen interest in Dada since his youth, which gave some of his works more than a touch of poetry and sometimes of irony. So for his participation in the legendary exhibition organized in Bern by Harald Szeemann in 1969, *When Attitudes Become Form*, he had installed a simple telephone with a panel inviting visitors to pick it up if it rang, and say "Walter De Maria is on the line and would like to talk to you." But his most famous work is undoubtedly *Lightning Field,* made in 1977 thanks to funding from the DIA Foundation, established in 1974 by Philippa de Menil, Heiner Friedrich, and Helen Winkler to produce radical works of art: 400 pointed stainless steel posts planted in a rectangle one kilometer wide by one mile long, intended to attract thunder onto a plain in New Mexico. Again in 1977, at documenta in Kassel, he exhibited *The Vertical Earth Kilometer,* a bar five centimeters in diameter and a thousand meters long, gradually rammed into the ground until only the tip of it showed on the surface. This work was answered in 1979 by *The Broken Kilometer*, installed in SoHo, New York: a bar of the same type, but cut into 500 sections each two meters long, installed in five parallel rows. An admirer of John Cage, to whom he had dedicated a work in the form of a cage, and close to La Monte Young, with whom he had carried out performances, De Maria had also tried out music, as a drummer. In this role he had played with Lou Reed (1942–2013) in the group known as The Primitives, before the creation of Velvet Underground. Let us dream of that incredible time when artists and musicians were reinventing the New York scene, and the Velvet Underground was playing behind a screen on which the avant-garde films of Jonas Mekas' Cinematheque were projected, a process adopted by Warhol, but with his own films, when he took charge of the group's destiny. And let us remember that Lou Reed was also a photographer: he published two books, *Emotion in Action* in 2003 and *Rimes Rhymes* in 2012.

There were also performances in Europe, and extremely radical ones, such as those staged by the Viennese Actionists. Otto Mühl (1925–2013) was one of the movement's co-founders, along with Adolf Frohner and Hermann Nitsch. Their first "Aktion" took place in Mühl's studio in June 1962: *Die Blutorgel* (*The Blood Organ*) serves as a manifesto for the use of the body in performance; it was followed a year later by the "Fest des psycho-physischen Naturalismus" (Festival of Psycho-Physical Naturalism), regarded as the first public demonstration of Actionism.

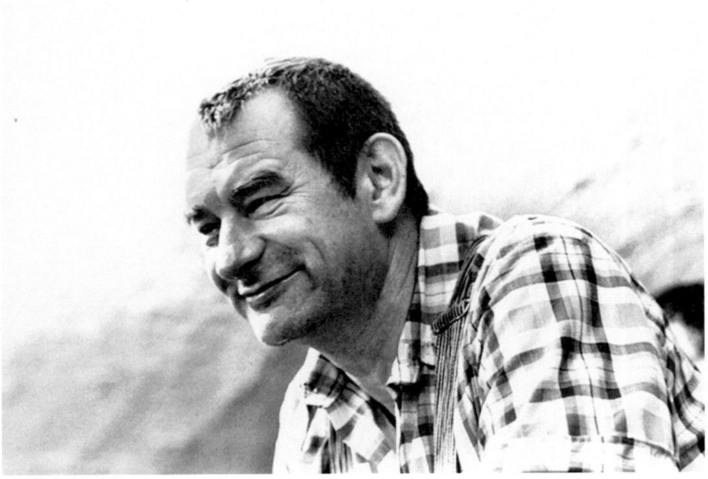

Otto Mühl
1925–2013

"What is Actionism?" you ask. We find a description of it, at least that of a performance staged in 1968 by his friend Günter Brus, in a book by Mühl, *Lettres à Erika* (Presses du réel, Dijon): "Brus was naked. During the Austrian national anthem he slashed his whole body with a razor blade, causing a pattern of red blood and white skin to appear. Red-white-red (the Austrian flag). He then defecated onto his right hand and smeared himself with feces." Performed in public at Vienna University, the action caused a scandal, and Mühl was sentenced to two months in prison. Of course we have to consider this type of activity in the seething context of 1968, when young people throughout the West were trying to burst the seams of the old world. It is also against this yardstick that the "Friedrichshof Commune" experiment embarked on in 1972 has to be viewed: a community—it would have up to 700 members—founded by Mühl, which advocated sexual freedom and the communal upbringing of children. The experiment came to an abrupt end in 1991 when Mühl, regarded by Austrian justice as the founder of a sect, was sentenced to seven years in prison for the "psychological manipulation" of his flock. Of his contribution to the art of the last century, it is better to remember his participation in documenta V, organized by Harald Szeemann in Kassel in 1972, which is still legendary, and his collaboration in 2000 and 2001 in the exhibitions organized at the Louvre by Régis Michel, *Posséder et détruire, stratégies sexuelles dans l'art d'Occident* (Possession and destruction, sexual strategies in Western art), followed by *La Peinture comme crime, ou la part maudite de la modernité* (Painting as a crime, or the curse of modernity).

While Otto Mühl had to endure the wrath of the law, León Ferrari (1920–2013) has the rare distinction among contemporary artists of having attracted the wrath of the Pope. It is true that Jorge Mario Bergoglio, now Pope Francis, was only Archbishop of Buenos Aires at the time. He reacted to an exhibition at which the artist had shoved the Virgin Mary into a mixer, and Christ into a toaster. At the 2007 Venice Biennale, which had awarded him a Golden Lion, he had crucified Jesus on the wings of a fighter plane—an American one, needless to say. Ferrari liked neither religion (he had created an association, or rather a club, to bring together "Impious, Heretics, Apostates, Blasphemers, Atheists, Pagans, Agnostics, and Infidels") nor the military institution (his son was arrested during the dictatorship of the Argentinean army rabble, and is presumed dead). Because of this, the artist is regarded as a hero by the "grandmothers of the Plaza de Majo," who continue to raise questions regarding the fate of the young "disappeared": well worth a few disputes with a Pope.

For when artists get involved in politics, they generally strike where it hurts. I remember Allan Sekula (1951–2013) generously offering to compose a double page for me specifically for the catalogue of the exhibition *Face à l'histoire* (Facing history, Centre Pompidou, 1996), devised by Jean-Paul Ameline; Chris Dercon was in charge of the contemporary section, and I was looking after the edi-

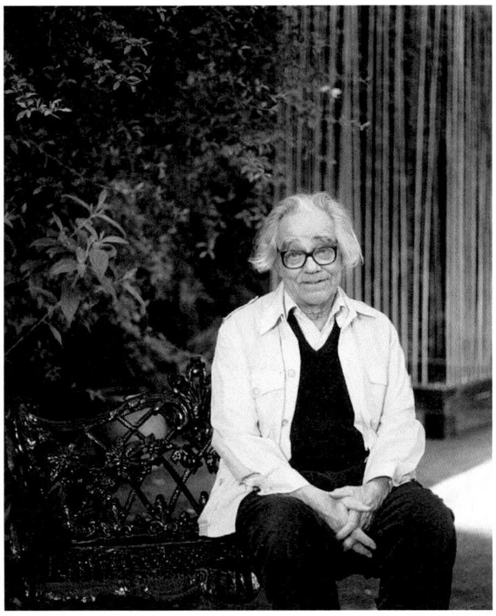

León Ferrari
1925–2013

torial side. The work is entitled *War Without Bodies*. I have it in front of me: young people are poking their fingers into the barrels of a helicopter's heavy machine-gun, including even a fair-haired chubby baby who is visibly finding the experience hilarious. The photographs had been taken at an air show celebrating victory in the Gulf War, at the El Toro Marine Corps Air Station at Santa Ana in California, on April 28, 1991. What is terrifying in these images is not the confrontation between youngsters and one of most murderous weapons in existence, it is the sky behind them, of an almost absolute blue. Before that, at the height of the Vietnam War, he had filmed workmen coming out of a weapons factory, in the style used by the Lumières brothers in one of the very first films in the history of cinematography. In recent years he had a passion for sea workers. Not the romantic ones Victor Hugo wrote about, but real present-day ones—from the fish market in Tokyo to the interchangeable, international workers on factory ships or in container ports. For him they were the last true slaves of the modern world.

Mike Kelley (1954–2012) did not separate art from politics either. He explained this in an interview in the *Le Monde* (June 19, 2006): "Coming from a New Left background, I was very soon confronted with a choice: am I going to become a terrorist or an artist? I decided not to get into trouble, and be socially destructive. But like feminists, I believe that all art is political, in the sense that all reality is the product of social conditioning. Art must be its revealer, by analyzing the language of the visual, by highlighting the fact that everything we see is constructed by someone." This particular someone availed himself of every means, using every possible element, from music (tending to be punk, he had a group in his native city of Detroit called Destroy all Monsters) to the visual arts, where he exploited every conceivable material, with a fine, militant indifference for the distinction between "high" and "low." That is how he came to work a lot with soft toys, "a popular form that nobody thinks of considering in terms of an author," or to reuse doodles drawn by office workers to overcome the boredom of their work, "the by-product of a class system."

Without being as explicitly politically committed, in a 40-year career embarked on after studying architecture, the photographer Gabriele Basilico (1944–2013) looked at the city with new eyes. New, but pessimistic: "Architects and decision-makers are incapable of managing urban development. In town after town I note the scale of the disaster. The works of great architects, good or bad, are the result of a defeat, that of making the city into a utopia of collective living. They are proof that nobody is thinking of town planning in its totality. We are losing the sense of a shared history." He had tried to reconstitute that history right from the start, in a mission organized in 1985 by the Délégation à l'aménagement du territoire régional (Datar; Delegation for the organization of regional territory), a French government body that had commissioned some 30 photographers to produce a geographical and social "portrait" of the country's landscape. Basilico had chosen *Bord de mer* [Seaside] (he published a book under that title in 1990), the English Channel coastline, which he photographed from the Belgian frontier to Mont-Saint-Michel. Frontal, black and white images voided of human beings in favor of what they have constructed, and showing the links between the different elements of the landscape, the framework of multiple superimposed epochs and natural landscapes.

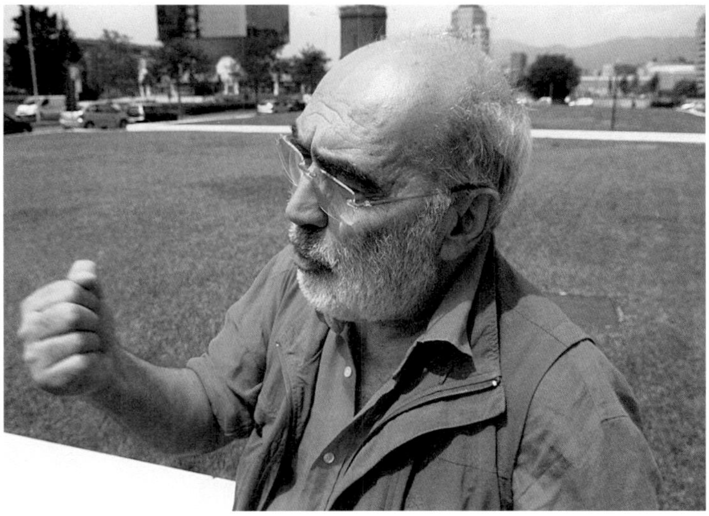

Gabriele Basilico
1944–2013

Sarah Charlesworth (1947–2013) was another person who had an original approach to photography, looking at it from both a sociological and an artistic point of view, if we are to believe this declaration made at the feminist center at the Brooklyn Museum: "I have, through my various series, examined the role of photography within popular culture as it serves to articulate models of sexuality, gender, and political perspective." For all that she had studied the use of this medium with Lisette Model, she was more interested in its perception

O

than in its use as a technique. She was close to the Pictures Generation, a group of artists active in New York in the late 1970s, which pondered the reception of the image and the way it influenced everyday life. In 1975, along with Joseph Kosuth, she created the magazine *The Fox*, and also acknowledged her debt to Seth Siegelaub's *The Xerox Book*. This led to works like *Modern History* (1977–1979), in which she re-photographed 45 front pages from newspapers that had published a portrait of the Italian politician Aldo Moro, sent to the press by the Red Brigades who had kidnapped him, but eliminating all written text, except for the name of the newspaper in question, so highlighting the importance each of the editorial teams accorded to the subject, simply through demonstrating the varying scale accorded to the photograph. From being an illustration, the image became a problem. And that was what fired her passion, as she confided in 1990 to the magazine *Bomb* (which she also co-founded): "I've engaged questions regarding photography's role in culture for 12 years now, but it is an engagement with a problem rather than a medium."

An engagement with a problem: that could sum up all the art of the past century.

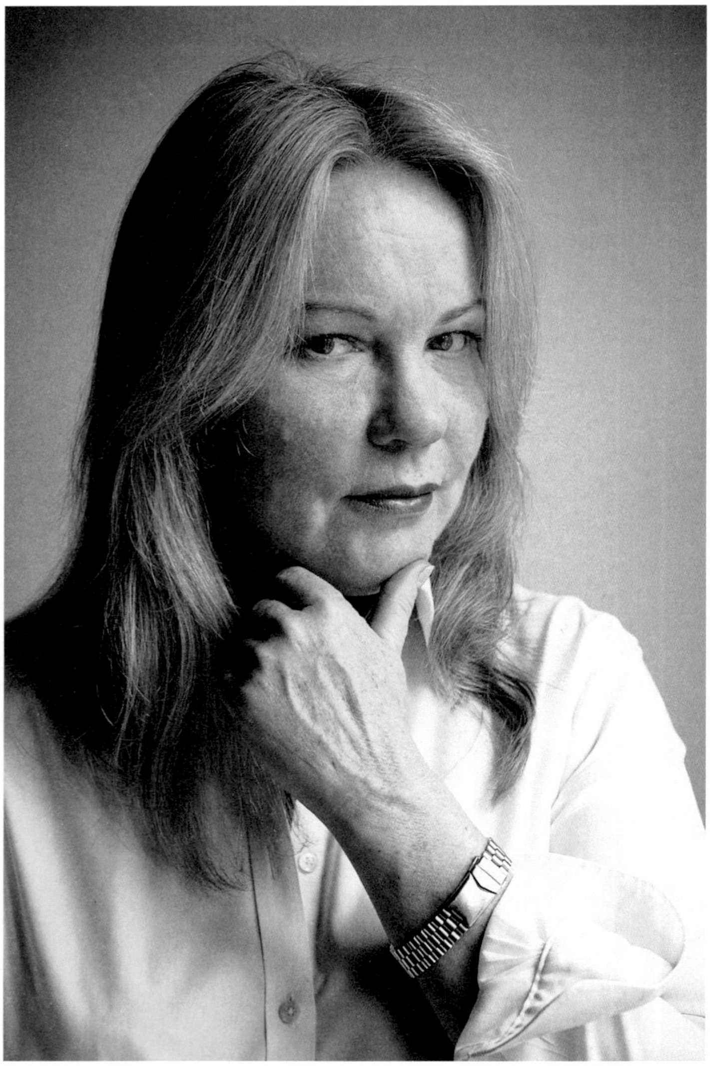

Sarah Charlesworth
1947–2013

Jonathan Napack (1967–2007)

by Philip Tinari

This eulogy was given by Philip Tinari on May 19, 2013, as an introduction to the "Homegrown Talent" conversation held at Art Basel in Hong Kong. A complete version of the conversation is available on the Art Basel website.

I first met Jonathan Napack in March 2003. He had moved to Hong Kong from New York in 1997, and he had come to Beijing to speak on a panel accompanying the opening of an exhibition called *Chinese Maximalism* curated by Gao Minglu. At the end of a heated conversation about contemporary Chinese art and its future, he made his comments. The subject turned to the 1999 Venice Biennale, which was curated by Harald Szeemann, included nearly 20 Chinese artists, and was seen internationally as a sort of coming out party for the contemporary Chinese scene. Jonathan made one of those offhand comments, thickly laced with references, something like: "Well everyone knows that Szeemann's decision to include so many Chinese artists was really just a plea for relevance and novelty by a curator at the end of his career." I was fresh out of college and didn't yet know who Harald Szeemann even was; I decided I needed to become friends with this guy.

Jonathan roamed Asia with confidence and cosmopolitanism, passing out his silver Art Basel "Asia Advisor" name cards through the most obscure reaches of the continent, and coming back to his apartment in Kau U Fong to distill the information he had collected into articles for the *IHT* and dispatches back to the Messeplatz. He had come from a legendary journalistic background, part of the cohort behind the short-lived magazine *SPY* in the early 1990s, and wrote major investigative pieces on things like Mel Bochner's fame, or the dealings of the Wildenstein family. After a few years of that he got bored and decided to move, not to where the action was, but to where it might one day be.

When I decided to settle permanently in Beijing in 2006, one of the first orders of business was to work with him on putting together a delegation of Chinese collectors to be invited at Art Basel's expense to see the fair. We actually spent a lot of time explaining to people what Art Basel was and why they should go, and many of them actually stood us up. (Sorry everyone, that doesn't happen anymore.) Later that year I helped him plan a pop-up session of Art Basel Conversations at the National Art Museum of China, where Ai Weiwei sat side by side with Fan Di'an and others. (Sorry, neither does that.) During that long summer of 2006 I spent a lot of time in Hong Kong writing anonymous essays for Sotheby's, and hanging out with Jonathan was a near nightly occurrence. Among our recurring topics of conversation was the one that he dreamed about most: establishing of a real center of art world gravity somewhere in Asia, which for him meant Hong Kong.

The last time I saw him was over bagels on Collins Avenue on the Monday after Art Basel Miami Beach 2006. We had another variation of this same conversation and then flew off. After his passing the following month, I picked up many of his duties—from freelance assignments that had been in progress to reporting for Art Basel on the situation in China.

It's amazing to think that he did not even live to see the first edition of ART HK in 2008, and more amazing that the fair's gradual, then meteoric growth, followed by its full incorporation into the Art Basel brand—which we celebrate today and this week—played out more or less according to his grand plan.

And so even if he was not ultimately able to participate in this great day, his influence lingers. If you walk up the terraced pathway of Kau U Fong, in the western reaches of Central, you may notice a second floor window that looks a bit different from the others. It features a rounded chrome frame that Jonathan had custom fabricated in Shenzhen, a single pane of glass, and a spotlight, attached to the side of the building, that he could flip on from his writing desk.

P

- Hong Kong
- Basel
- Miami Beach

P.P.O.W

New York — Galleries

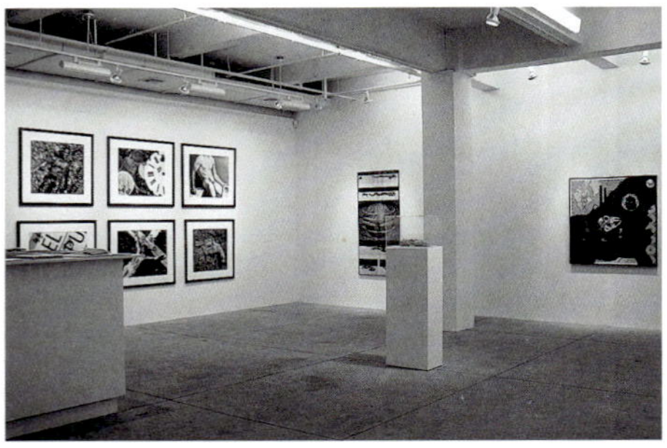

What first compelled you to open a gallery?
We opened P.P.O.W in the East Village in 1983. We had both been working for other dealers and felt we wanted to work on our own with artists of our own generation. The low rents and small but burgeoning community in this area allowed us to open a gallery when we were 27 years old.

Who is the first artist you showed and what was most memorable about that show?
Our first show was the work of Sue Coe. The work was extremely political and we thought we would have rocks thrown through the gallery windows. Instead we sold out the show and got reviewed in *Artforum*. It was a great show and works from it are now in museum collections like The Museum of Modern Art in New York.

When did you first participate in Art Basel and what was most memorable about that show?
P.P.O.W first showed in Art Basel in the early 1990s. Business was tough in those years, but we persevered. Most importantly we made friends with dealers in Europe with whom we have had lifelong relationships.

- **Contact** P.P.O.W
  Kelly Freeman
  kelly@ppowgallery.com
  info@ppowgallery.com
- **Established** 1983
- **Owner(s) / Partner(s)** Penny Pilkington
  Wendy Olsoff
- **Team** 6
- **Space(s)** 325 m²
- **Artists at Art Basel** Carolee Schneemann
- **Further artists represented** Dotty Attie
  Bo Bartlett
  Sandow Birk
  Melanie Bonajo
  George Boorujy
  Dinh Q. Lê
  Judy Fox
  Julie Heffernan
  Timothy Horn
  Ellen Kooi
  Katharine Kuharic
  Walter Martin & Paloma Muñoz
  Portia Munson
  Sarah Oppenheimer
  Adam Putnam
  Hunter Reynolds
  Suzanne Treister
  Martha Wilson
  David Wojnarowicz
  Martin Wong

Pace

New York — Galleries
London — Galleries
Beijing — Galleries

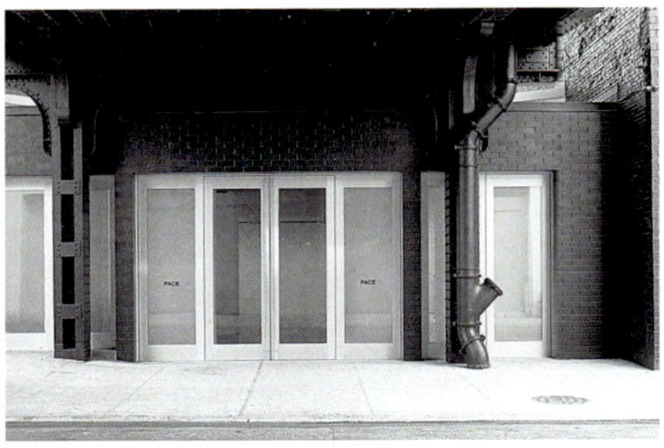

What first compelled you to open a gallery?
I founded Pace Gallery in 1960 on Newbury Street in Boston with my wife Milly. As a former art student, I was compelled to become a dealer to live a life in art and get as close to the creative process as the artists would allow. I wanted to champion artists who I believed were the greatest of our time, and who in turn, shaped Pace Gallery into what is today. These artists include Chuck Close, Jean Dubuffet, Robert Irwin, Agnes Martin, Louise Nevelson, and Lucas Samaras.

Who is the first artist you showed and what was most memorable about that show?
Our first major show in Boston was in 1962 and was a survey of Pop art, including Claes Oldenburg, Andy Warhol, Marisol, Robert Indiana, George Segal, and Tom Wesselmann. Many of these artists came up to Boston for the December opening despite the cold. Major paintings such as Warhol's *Coke Bottles* (1962) and Oldenburg's *Lunchroom Pastries* (1961–1962) were sold for a few hundred dollars. It was a miracle in those days.

When did you first participate in Art Basel and what was most memorable about that show?
Pace participated in Art Basel within the first year of its inception.

- **Contact** Pace Gallery
  Concetta Duncan
  cduncan@pacegallery.com
- **Established** 1960
- **Owner(s) / Partner(s)** Arne Glimcher
  (Founder and Chairman)
  Marc Glimcher (CEO)
- **Space(s)** 3,530 m²
- **Artists at Art Basel** Josef Albers
  Yto Barrada
  Alexander Calder
  Brian Clarke
  Chuck Close
  Keith Coventry
  Willem de Kooning
  Jim Dine
  Tara Donovan
  Jean Dubuffet
  Tim Eitel
  Kevin Francis Gray
  Lee Friedlander
  Adrian Ghenie
  Adolph Gottlieb
  Paul Graham
  Loris Gréaud
  Hai Bo
  Tim Hawkinson
  Barbara Hepworth
  David Hockney
  Hong Hao
  Robert Irwin
  Alfred Jensen
  Donald Judd
  Ilya & Emilia Kabakov
  Lee Tzu-hsun
  Lee Ufan
  Sol LeWitt
  Li Songsong
  Maya Lin
  Liu Jianhua
  Robert Mangold
  Agnes Martin
  Roberto Matta
  Elizabeth Murray
  Yoshitomo Nara

Louise Nevelson
Carsten Nicolai
Isamu Noguchi
Thomas Nozkowski
Claes Oldenburg
Adam Pendleton
Pablo Picasso
Richard Pousette-Dart
Fiona Rae
Robert Rauschenberg
Ad Reinhardt
Bridget Riley
Mark Rothko
Michal Rovner
Robert Ryman
Lucas Samaras
Joel Shapiro
Raqib Shaw
James Siena
Kiki Smith
Bosco Sodi
Song Dong
Keith Sonnier
Saul Steinberg
Hiroshi Sugimoto
Sui Jianguo
Antoni Tàpies
James Turrell
Richard Tuttle
Keith Tyson
Coosje van Bruggen
Corban Walker
Robert Whitman
Fred Wilson
Yin Xiuzhen
Yue Minjun
Zhang Huan
Zhang Xiaogang
Zhao Yao

Pace Prints

New York

- Galleries
- Edition
- Edition

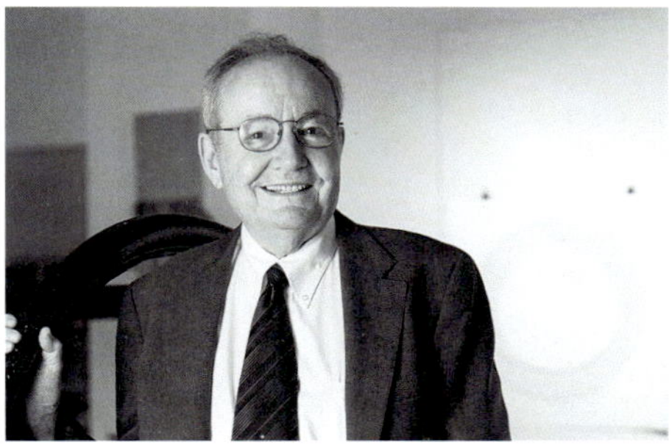

What first compelled you to open a gallery?
Originally the concept was to publish prints by artists represented by Pace Gallery; now, over 40 years later, we have published prints by approximately 150 different artists, with only a small percentage ever represented by Pace.

Who is the first artist you showed and what was most memorable about that show?
The first work that we published was a *Book* by Lucas Samaras, in 1968. It was a very complex multi-media, die-cut, stand-alone accordion object that cost $35,000, which was a lot of money in those days.

When did you first participate in Art Basel and what was most memorable about that show?
I do not remember exactly, but it was in the very early days, and we took a hiatus for several years before we returned on a steady basis.

- **Contact** — Pace Prints
Richard Solomon
dick@paceprints.com
kristin@paceprints.com
- **Established** — 1968
- **Owner(s) / Partner(s)** — Richard Solomon (President)
- **Space(s)** — 1,394 m² (four spaces)
- **Artists at Art Basel** — Ghada Amer & Reza Farkhondeh
Donald Baechler
Rina Banerjee
Francesco Clemente
Chuck Close
Will Cotton
Jim Dine
Leonardo Drew
Inka Essenhigh
Shepard Fairey
Fang Lijun
Helen Frankenthaler
Barnaby Furnas
Anne-Karin Furunes
Peter Halley
Keith Haring
Mary Heilmann
Arturo Herrera
How & Nosm
KAWS
SeaHyun Lee
Lee Ufan
Sol LeWitt
Ling Jian
Nicola Lopez
Robert Mangold
Ryan McGinness
Santi Moix
Paul Morrison
Wangechi Mutu
Yoshitomo Nara
Kenneth Noland
Erik Parker
Peng Wei
Emilio Perez
Qi Zhilong
Qin Feng
Kenny Scharf
James Turrell
Yue Minjun
Zhang Huan
Zhang Jian-Jun
- **Further artists represented** — Ellen Berkenblit
Ingrid Calame
Tara Donovan
Jean Dubuffet
April Gornik
Jane Hammond
Wolf Kahn
Jon Kessler
Louise Nevelson
Don Nice
Claes Oldenburg
Robert Ryman
Julian Schnabel
Yasu Shibata
James Siena
Kiki Smith
Pat Steir
Dan Walsh
Zhang Dali
Zhang Xiaogang

Pace/MacGill

New York
London
Beijing

- Galleries

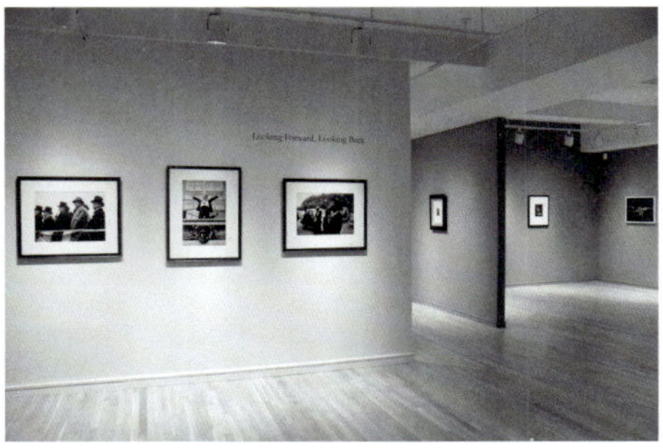

What first compelled you to open a gallery?
I had been the director of Light Gallery in the late 1970s and a number of the artists I worked with there wanted a place to show.

Who is the first artist you showed and what was most memorable about that show?
Our first show at Pace/MacGill Gallery was André Kertész's *Distortions*. André visited everyday to greet people and nap!

When did you first participate in Art Basel and what was most memorable about that show?
In 2013 in Miami Beach, and we just loved being there. It was good for our artists to be

exposed to the enormous and enormously diverse crowd. We enjoyed seeing many old friends and meeting a lot of new collectors and curators.

- **Contact** Pace/MacGill Gallery
  Cassidy Petrazzi
  cassidy@pacemacgill.com
  info@pacemacgill.com
- **Established** 1983
- **Owner(s) / Partner(s)** Peter MacGill
  Arne Glimcher
  Richard Solomon
- **Team** 13
- **Space(s)** 394 m²
- **Artists at Art Basel** Richard Avedon
  Hai Bo
  Harry Callahan
  William Christenberry
  Chuck Close
  William Eggleston
  Robert Frank
  Lee Friedlander
  Emmet Gowin
  Paul Graham
  Hiro
  Peter Hujar
  Richard Misrach
  Irving Penn
  Robert Rauschenberg
  Paolo Roversi
  Frederick Sommer
  Hiroshi Sugimoto
  Andy Warhol
  Henry Wessel
  Garry Winogrand
- **Further artists represented** Adou
  Richard Benson
  David Byrne
  Jim Goldberg
  Mark Klett
  Josef Koudelka
  Jocelyn Lee
  Boris Mikhailov
  Nicholas Nixon
  Tod Papageorge
  Judith Joy Ross
  Michal Rovner
  Lucas Samaras
  Fazal Sheikh
  Kiki Smith
  John Szarkowski
  JoAnn Verburg
  William Wegman

Paley

London ● Galleries

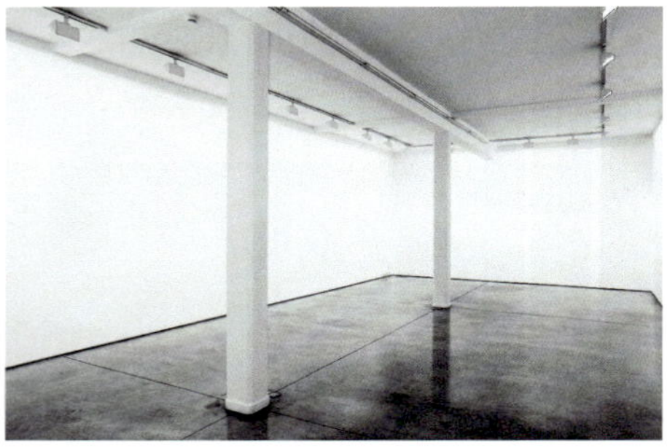

What first compelled you to open a gallery?
My curatorial interest in art and bringing new work from abroad to be seen in London.

Who is the first artist you showed and what was most memorable about that show?
Hannah Collins was the first solo show I presented at the gallery and I was pleased her work combined imagery with text and sound elements.

When did you first participate in Art Basel and what was most memorable about that show?
Having been part of the founding committee at Liste, I was impressed by the sheer scale of Art Basel and the range of art history covered by the galleries showing downstairs in relation to those upstairs.

- **Contact** Maureen Paley
  Oliver Evans
  oliver@maureenpaley.com
  info@maureenpaley.com
- **Established** 1984
- **Owner(s) / Partner(s)** Maureen Paley (Founding Director)
- **Team** 10
- **Space(s)** 180 m²
- **Artists at Art Basel** Keith Arnatt
  Kaye Donachie
  Thomas Eggerer
  Gardar Eide Einarsson
  Morgan Fisher
  Hamish Fulton
  Maureen Gallace
  Liam Gillick
  Andrew Grassie
  Anne Hardy
  Sarah Jones
  Michael Krebber
  Lars Laumann
  Daria Martin
  Saskia Olde Wolbers
  Paul P.
  Stephen Prina
  James Pyman
  Tim Rollins and K.O.S.
  David Salle
  Maaike Schoorel
  Hannah Starkey
  Dirk Stewen
  David Thorpe
  Wolfgang Tillmans
  Gert & Uwe Tobias
  Donald Urquhart
  Erik van Lieshout
  Banks Violette
  Rebecca Warren
  Gillian Wearing
  James Welling

Paradise Row

London ● Discoveries

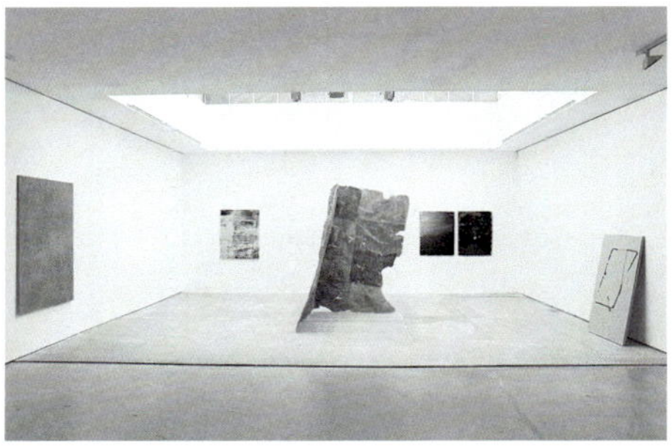

What first compelled you to open a gallery?
"I used to be an art critic and shared a house with artists, so showing their works seemed to be a natural extension of what I was doing. Paradise Row was born," says Nick Hackworth.

Who is the first artist you showed and what was most memorable about that show?
Paradise Row started in artist Shezad Dawood's house in East London on a road called Paradise Row in Bethnal Green. It was memorable as we were experimenting with the idea of the gallery, in this case a space situated in the artist's house-cum-studio.

When did you first participate in Art Basel and what was most memorable about that show?
We first participated to Art Basel in Hong Kong in 2013 where we showed a work by Shezad Dawood—a stunning 15-minute alternative version of his feature film *Piercing Brightness* (2011), an investigation of migration and national identity through the lens of mainstream science fiction.

- **Contact** Paradise Row
  info@paradiserow.com
- **Established** 2006
- **Owner(s) / Partner(s)** Nick Hackworth (Director)
- **Team** 4
- **Space(s)** 279 m²
- **Artists at Art Basel** Shezad Dawood

- **Further artists represented** Anna Bjerger
Adam Broomberg & Oliver Chanarin
Mounir Fatmi
Tom Gidley
Margarita Gluzberg
Kirk Palmer
Barry Reigate
Douglas White

Paragon

London

- Galleries
- Edition
- Edition

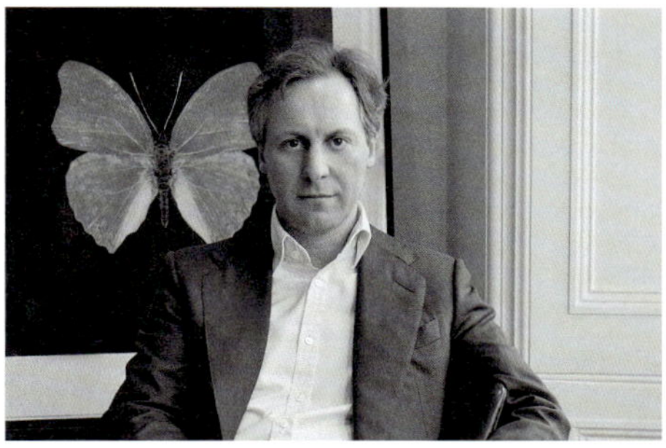

What first compelled you to open a gallery?
I wanted to work with living artists to commission significant works of art, primarily in the medium of print. I was attracted by the direct engagement in the creative process with artists that publishing offered.

Who is the first artist you showed and what was most memorable about that show?
My first project was the *Scottish Bestiary*, a group portfolio with seven Scottish artists, including Bruce McLean and Stephen Campbell, while I was still a student at Edinburgh University. The commitment given to me by these artists when I was still very young was the most memorable and encouraging experience.

When did you first participate in Art Basel and what was most memorable about that show?
I shared a stand with Crown Point Press in 1991 and then a few years later (I believe in 1996) I returned with a stand of my own. There were very few of us from my generation at that stage exhibiting in Basel, and it was a great professional leap to participate.

- **Contact** Paragon
Florian Simm
florian@paragonpress.co.uk
info@paragonpress.co.uk
- **Established** 1986
- **Owner(s) / Partner(s)** Charles Booth-Clibborn
Florian Simm
- **Team** 4
- **Space(s)** 150 m²
- **Artists at Art Basel** Jake & Dinos Chapman
Gillian Carnegie
Leda Catunda
Jake Chapman
Richard Deacon
Tracey Emin
Damien Hirst
Gary Hume
Anish Kapoor
Sarah Morris
Chris Ofili
Grayson Perry
Jonathan Yeo
- **Further artists represented** Kai Althoff
Hurvin Anderson
Georg Baselitz
Peter Doig
Eberhard Havekost
Michael Landy
Christopher Le Brun
Elizabeth Magill
Paul Morrison
Ged Quinn
Marc Quinn
George Shaw
Corinne Wasmuht
Richard Wathen
Rachel Whiteread
Thomas Zipp

Park Ryu Sook

Seoul

- Insights

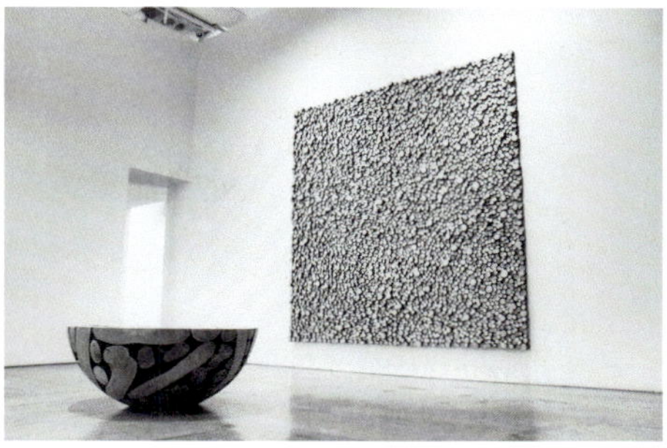

What first compelled you to open a gallery?
For more than 30 years, Park Ryu Sook Gallery has been committed to introducing progressive contemporary art to both domestic and international market. Founded in 1983 by the eponymous art dealer, Park Ryu Sook Gallery is recognized as the pioneer of what is now a vibrant contemporary art scene in the Gangnam area of Seoul. The gallery has contributed to establishing the careers of some of Korea's most important artists, from the first generation of Korean modern/contemporary artists including Kim Tschang Yeul, Park Seo Bo, Chun Kwang Young, and Kim Chong Hak, to today's most promising artists including Kwon Kisoo, Lee Lee Nam, Lee Hun Chung, and Kang Kang Hoon.

Who is the first artist you showed and what was most memorable about that show?
Kang Kang Hoon's large-scaled hyper realistic portraits astonished viewers with their powerful composition and meticulous details. Though young, Kang's solo presentations at Art Basel in Hong Kong in the past two years have enabled him to establish an international reputation, and he is undeniably at the forefront of the current generation of the Korean Hyper Realism movement.

When did you first participate in Art Basel and what was most memorable about that show?
As Art Basel in Hong Kong has become very established, we see a greater participation by "Western" galleries and artists. Needless to say the ultimate quality and originality of art do not depend on the nationality of the artist. However, we believe it is very important to maintain our identity as a Korean gallery and continue promoting exceptional Korean artists to international audiences, especially those from Asia. Park Ryu Sook Gallery is the first Korean gallery to participate in the Art Basel fair since 2007.

- **Contact** Park Ryu Sook Gallery
Soo Choi
choisooyeon@gmail.com
info@parkryusookgallery.com
- **Established** 1983
- **Owner(s) / Partner(s)** Park Ryu Sook (President)
- **Team** 10
- **Space(s)** 450 m²
- **Artists at Art Basel** Kang Kang Hoon
- **Further artists represented** Bill Beckley
Christo
Nathalia Edenmont
Nigel Hall
Damien Hirst
Patrick Hughes
Kim Chong Hak
Kim Kang Yong
Kim Tschang Yeul
Koo Sung Soo
Kubach-Wilmsen
Kwon Ki-soo
Lee Hun Chung
Lee Lee Nam
Nam June Paik
Park Eun Sun
Gavin Turk
Yim Man Hyeok

Parra & Romero

Madrid
Ibiza

● Feature
● Positions

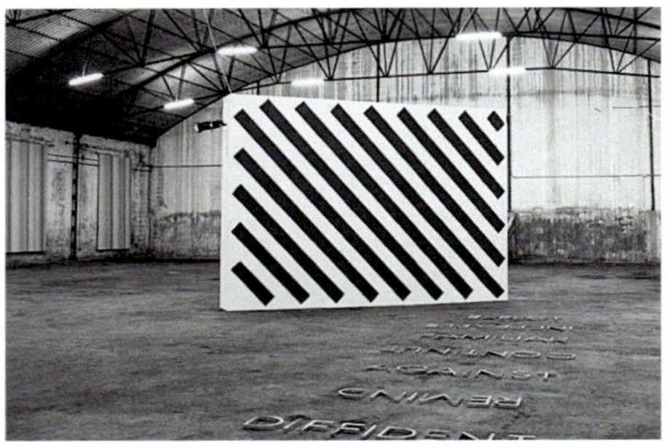

What first compelled you to open a gallery?
Although it was completely vocational for me, meeting Felix Gonzalez-Torres had a great impact; at that time I also saw the gallery as a way to make my life interesting.

Who is the first artist you showed and what was most memorable about that show?
It was a group show of conceptual artists; the most memorable was the illusion of the start and the miracle of sales.

When did you first participate in Art Basel and what was most memorable about that show?
2013 was my first time at Art Basel. I've been coming to Basel since I was 16, which is already 15 years ago, without missing one edition, and what I really enjoyed this time was to see and live from inside the process of the setup of the booths, as well as the Unlimited sector; to see their evolution, and finish before anyone else. That was a privilege.

- **Contact** Parra & Romero
  Guillermo Romero Parra
  guillermo@parra-romero.com
  info@parra-romero.com
- **Established** 2004
- **Owner(s) / Partner(s)** Guillermo Romero Parra
- **Team** 6
- **Space(s)** 1,500 m²
- **Artists at Art Basel** Luis Camnitzer
  Oriol Vilanova
- **Further artists represented** Lara Almarcegui
  Stefan Brüggemann
  Alejandro Cesarco
  Kajsa Dahlberg
  Philippe Decrauzat
  Germaine Kruip
  David Lamelas
  Paloma Polo
  Diego Santomé
  Thomas Scheibitz
  Conrad Shawcross

Parrasch

New York

● Galleries

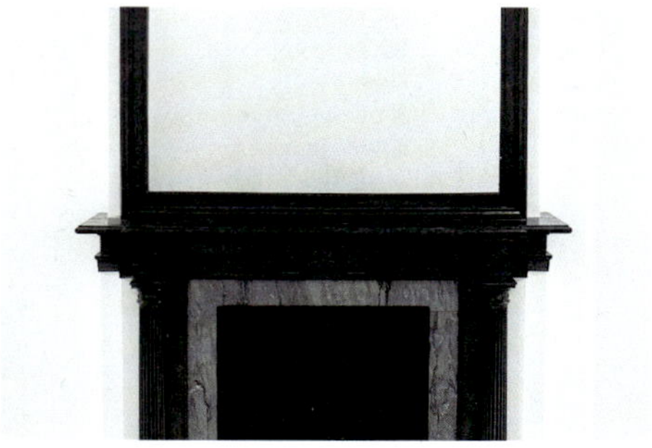

What first compelled you to open a gallery?
The idea for starting a gallery first struck me in graduate school at the Rhode Island School for Design (RISD) in 1985 when I saw a show of what I initially believed was installation art. It was a thesis show by a graduate student in the Furniture Department at RISD and the works were not installation art, but sculptural, oddly functional, pieces of furniture. I became both intrigued and obsessed with this idiom, which I perceived as a direct outgrowth of the installation art movement of that period. I opened the gallery in 1986 in Washington, DC, responding to an ad for a gallery space in trade for management of the building. The focus of this first space was furniture made by artists, and the orientation of the program remained in the context of installation work.

Who is the first artist you showed and what was most memorable about that show?
The show we opened with was, of course, the same RISD grad student whose work inspired the gallery in the first place, Jonathan Benson. I wanted the show to reflect the same experience as the RISD museum show, to connect with viewers on a visual, tactile, and kinetic level. The installation and room were perfect for what I wanted: an environment that questioned function and interaction, space, and physical orientation, though it was quite different than the RISD installation.

When did you first participate in Art Basel and what was most memorable about that show?
Art Basel in Miami Beach in 2010. We created an elaborate installation in tribute to the eponymous Nicholas Wilder Gallery of Los Angeles (which operated from 1965–1979).

- **Contact** Franklin Parrasch Gallery
  Truman Lahr
  info@franklinparrasch.com
- **Established** 1986
- **Owner(s) / Partner(s)** Franklin Parrasch (President)
- **Team** 5
- **Space(s)** 270 m²
- **Artists at Art Basel** Billy Al Bengston
  Mary Corse
  Joe Goode
  Marcia Hafif
  Craig Kauffman
  Agnes Martin
  John McLaughlin
  Ken Price
  Ed Ruscha

Pauli

Lausanne

● Galleries

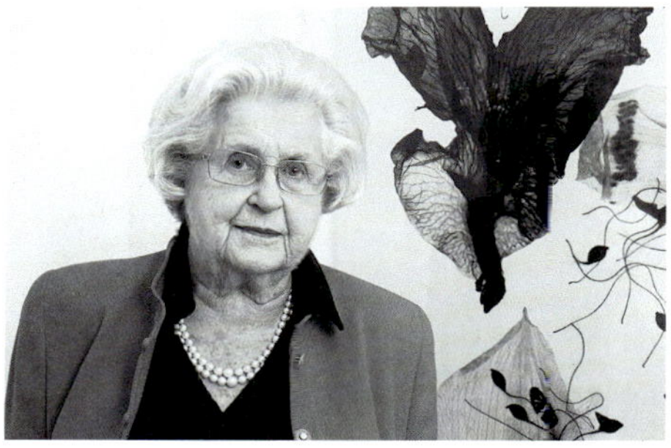

What first compelled you to open a gallery?
Art has always been my passion, and I wanted to share it with artists and collectors.

Who is the first artist you showed and what was most memorable about that show?
Sam Francis. He was totally unknown and the show was an important event.

When did you first participate in Art Basel and what was most memorable about that show?
In 1971. Discovering other galleries and meeting many new international collectors.

- **Contact** Galerie Alice Pauli
  Alice Pauli
  info@galeriealicepauli.ch
- **Established** 1962
- **Owner(s) / Partner(s)** Alice Pauli
- **Space(s)** 400 m²
- **Artists at Art Basel** Julius Bissier
  Philippe Cognée
  Stéphane Guiran
  Rebecca Horn
  Christian Lapie
  Nunzio

	Mimmo Paladino Giuseppe Penone Jaume Plensa Anne & Patrick Poirier Pierre Soulages Peter Wüthrich
• **Further artists represented**	Arcangelo Geneviève Asse Raphaël Benazzi Domenico Bianchi Jean Dubuffet Monique Frydman Peter Haff Rolf Iseli Loïc Le Groumellec Zbigniew Makowski Flavio Paolucci Alicia Penalba Jean-Pierre Pincemin Emil Schumacher Louis Soutter Fabienne Verdier Elena Vieira da Silva

Pékin

Beijing
Hong Kong

Galleries

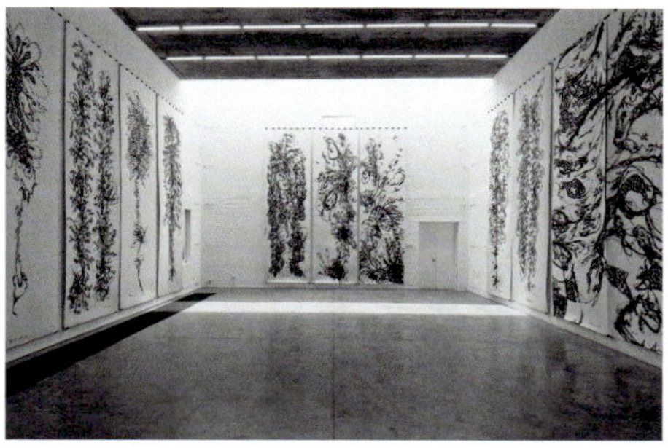

What first compelled you to open a gallery?
This is the second gallery I have opened in Beijing. The first was in 1997 with a group of investors, called CourtYard. I opened Pékin Fine Arts in 2005. There have been many memorable exhibits, including Chen Shaoxiong, Huang Zhiyang, Cao Fei, Lin Tianmiao, Nashunbatu, Liu Ding, Wang Luyan, and others. I am also particularly proud of bringing some overseas artists to Beijng and exhibiting their work for the first time in China, including Japanese artists Aida Makoto and Kohei Nawa, Korean artist Choi Jeong Hwa, Indonesian artist Eko Nugroho.

Who is the first artist you showed and what was most memorable about that show?
The first were Sichuan artist Yang Mian and Beijing artist Zhao Gang. These were shows I inherited from departing gallery managers. I felt that I had to honor the gallery commitment to these artists despite the change in staff. I later started selecting artists such as Lin Tianmiao, Guo Wei, Guo Jin, Li Jin, Liu Xiaodong, Yu Hong, Cao Fei, Liu Wei, Wang Gongxin, Wang Qingsong, Huang Zhiyang, Liu Ding, Wang Chuan, and others.

When did you first participate in Art Basel and what was most memorable about that show?
I have participated at Art Basel in Hong Kong since its inception. It has always been exciting, watching this fair grow from the grass roots and build excitement, local and regional attention, and now world-wide recognition. I feel proud to be part of the original team that built the fair into an attractive acquisition target for Basel.

• **Contact**	Pékin Fine Arts Meg Maggio meg@pekinfinearts.com
• **Established**	2005
• **Owner(s) / Partner(s)**	Meg Maggio (Director)
• **Space(s)**	600 m² (Beijing) 100 m² (Hong Kong)
• **Artists at Art Basel**	Aniwar Chen Shaoxiong John Clang Fang Lu Kata Legrady Liu Di Liu Ding Luo Mingjun Nashunbatu Martin Parr Wang Luyan Yan Lei

Peres Projects

Berlin

Galleries
Nova

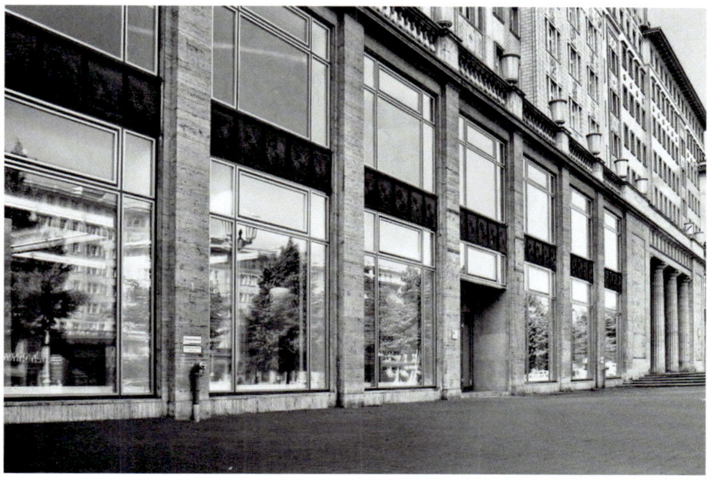

What first compelled you to open a gallery?
Seeing the Eva Hesse exhibition at SFMoMA made me think that I should and could have a gallery. So I would say, Eva Hesse compelled me.

Who is the first artist you showed and what was most memorable about that show?
I opened both my LA and my Berlin gallery with Terence Koh. Terence was for me an important part of my early years as a dealer and I think he was a seminal artist of that time. Working with him at that time was amazing, I learned a lot about myself and it also, in some ways, paved the way for my role as a gallerist who is very active with his artists and involved with all aspects of the artistic process. These days, I am the opposite, or at least I like to think so, and strive to focus on my activities in dealing more than anything.

When did you first participate in Art Basel and what was most memorable about that show?
My first Art Basel fair was in Miami Beach in 2004. I exhibited some great works; the one that really still stands out for me is the Dan Colen's candle painting. This was inside the containers on the beach.

• **Contact**	Peres Projects Nick Koenigsknecht nick@peresprojects.com berlin@peresprojects.com
• **Established**	2002 (San Francisco) 2003 (Los Angeles) 2005 (Berlin)
• **Owner(s) / Partner(s)**	Javier Peres
• **Space(s)**	500 m² (gallery) 1,000 m² (office and showroom)
• **Artists at Art Basel**	Mark Flood Alex Israel David Ostrowski
• **Further artists represented**	assume vivid astro focus Dan Attoe Antonio Ballester Moreno Joe Bradley Kaye Donachie Jeff Elrod Leo Gabin Dorothy Iannone Bruce LaBruce Eddie Martinez Eddie Peake Kirstine Roepstorff Dean Sameshima Marinella Senatore Dash Snow Mark Titchner Brent Wadden

P

Perrotin

Paris
Hong Kong
New York

Galleries
Galleries
Unlimited
Galleries

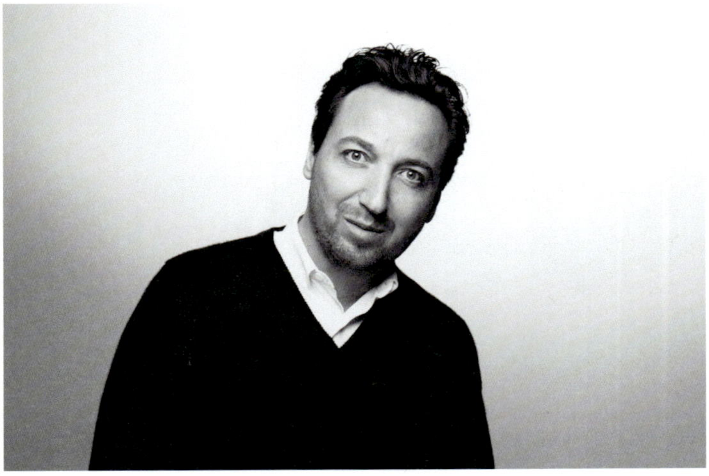

When did you first participate in Art Basel and what was most memorable about that show?
In 1993.

- **Contact** Galerie Perrotin
Stephanie Vaillant
stephanie@perrotin.com
info@perrotin.com
- **Established** 1990
- **Owner(s) / Partner(s)** Emmanuel Perrotin (Owner)
Alice Lung (Co-Director)
Etsuko Nakajima (Co-Director)
- **Team** 8
- **Space(s)** 800 m²
- **Artists at Art Basel** Ivan Argote
Daniel Arsham
Hernan Bas
Sophie Calle
Maurizio Cattelan
Johan Creten
Wim Delvoye
Elmgreen & Dragset
Lionel Estève
Daniel Firman
Bernard Frize
Giuseppe Gabellone
Gelitin
Duane Hanson
John Henderson
Gregor Hildebrandt
JR
Jesper Just
Kaws
Bharti Kher
Kolkoz
Klara Kristalova
Guy Limone
Ryan McGinley
Jin Meyerson
Farhad Moshiri
Gianni Motti
Mr.
Takashi Murakami
Kaz Oshiro
Jean-Michel Othoniel
Paola Pivi
J. Ariadhitya Pramuhendra
Germaine Richier
Claude Rutault
Michael Sailstorfer
Pierre Soulages
Aya Takano
Tatiana Trouvé
Xavier Veilhan
Ronald Ventura
Pieter Vermeersch
Peter Zimmermann

Petzel

New York

Galleries
Unlimited
Galleries

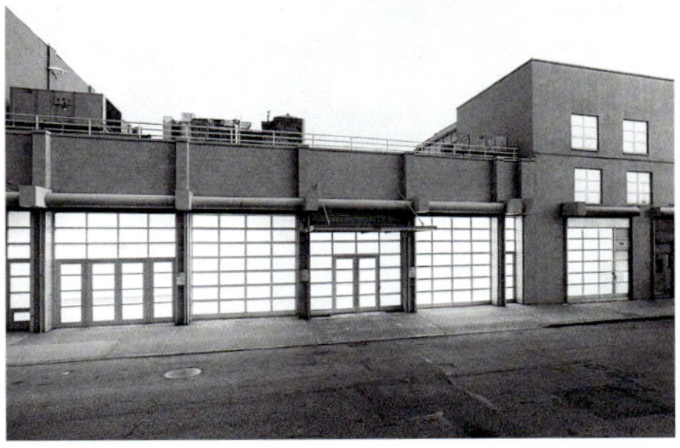

What first compelled you to open a gallery?
I had a talk at a gallery opening in New York with a young artist named Jorge Pardo. He was so argumentative and I became fascinated with his views on what constitutes an exhibition, what artworks "do" and "do not do." I had never seen a work by him but the discussion kept me on my toes and I informed Helene and Janelle at Metro Pictures about this gentleman from Los Angeles. After some visits to California it became clear that he is an exceptional artist and Helene said that if I don't open a gallery myself, they would start showing him. Three sleepless weeks later, I decided to go ahead. In September 1993 I founded my "loft gallery" at home, but continued to work for Metro Pictures for another half year or so. Around that time, several galleries closed in SoHo as a result of the recession. We were mad and lucky at the same time.

When did you first participate in Art Basel and what was most memorable about that show?
I believe in 1996 or 1997. I was told that a new sector in Basel was to be established: the Statements sector. I chose Nicola Tyson with three paintings and 22 charcoal drawings, but I couldn't afford the CHF7,000, so I borrowed the money from my parents and came back to New York with the gross sales result of $184,000. I will never forget that fair! I paid my parents back with one of the charcoal drawings.

- **Contact** Friedrich Petzel Gallery
Laura Higgins
laura@petzel.com
info@petzel.com
- **Established** 1993
- **Owner(s) / Partner(s)** Friedrich Petzel (Owner)
Andrea Teschke
Sam Tsao
- **Team** 16
- **Space(s)** 900 m²
- **Artists at Art Basel** Yael Bartana
Troy Brauntuch
Willem de Rooij
Simon Denny
Keith Edmier
Thomas Eggerer
Wade Guyton
Robert Heinecken
Georg Herold
Dana Hoey
Christian Jankowski
Sean Landers
Maria Lassnig
Allan McCollum
Sarah Morris
Jorge Pardo
Philippe Parreno
Joyce Pensato
Seth Price
Stephen Prina
Jon Pylypchuk
Dana Schutz
Dirk Skreber
John Stezaker
Nicola Tyson
Rezi van Lankveld
Cosima von Bonin
Charline von Heyl
Corinne Wasmuht
Heimo Zobernig

Pi

Istanbul
London

Insights

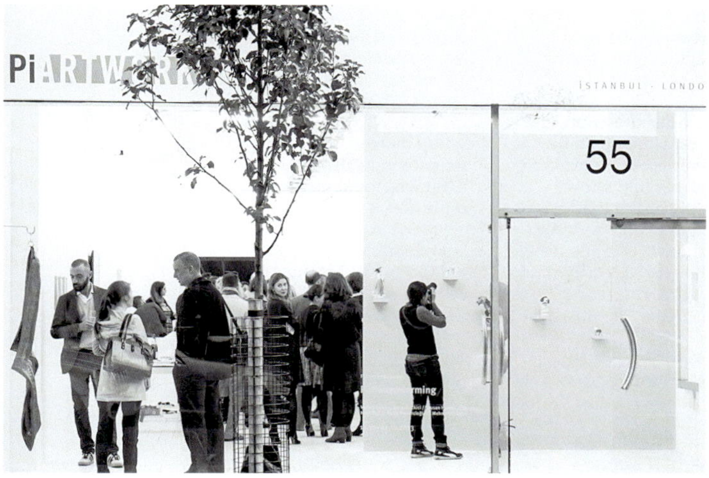

What first compelled you to open a gallery?
It was 1998, I had recently returned to Istanbul after my studies, and the arts scene was in its nascent stages where contemporary art galleries were concerned. It felt like the right time to do something. Fast forward and we have recently opened a second space, in London.

Who is the first artist you showed and what was most memorable about that show?
I actually started with a non-selling exhibition of works by Salvador Dalí. I brought together paintings, sketches, film screenings—I felt it was important to showcase an international artist, and especially one of that caliber, to the Turkish audience—nothing had really been done on that scale before. We received a staggering 8,500 visitors in the course of the show's ten-day run and it really encouraged me to establish a gallery as it proved that audiences were hungry for good quality art.

When did you first participate in Art Basel and what was most memorable about that show?
Last year, at Art Basel in Hong Kong. I was most impressed by the wonderful and warm response from the audience, and it was such a great opportunity to introduce Turkish contemporary art to a different audience.

- **Contact**: Pi Artworks
Anna Wallace-Thompson
awt@piartworks.com
info@piartworks.com
- **Established**: 1998
- **Owner(s) / Partner(s)**: Yesim Turanli (Founding Director)
- **Space(s)**: 150 m² (Istanbul)
200 m² (London)
- **Artists at Art Basel**: Mehmet Ali Uysal
- **Further artists represented**: Turan Aksoy
Volkan Aslan
Nancy Atakan
Juan Botella Lucas
Nezaket Ekici
Cinar Eslek
Jean-Paul Guiragossian
Susan Hefuna
Horasan
Irfan Onurmen
Nejat Sati
Gulay Semercioglu
Ayten Turanli
Ummuhan Yoruk

Pia

Zurich

Galleries
Unlimited

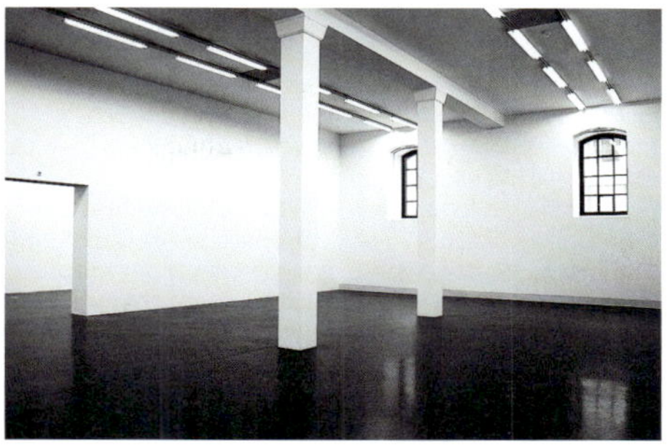

What first compelled you to open a gallery?
Having worked in an English gallery in Zurich and having always been friends with artists and collectors who encouraged me in the project, I decided to open my own space in Bern.

Who is the first artist you showed and what was most memorable about that show?
It was Terry Fox, but I made a first exhibition with Betty Woodman, because Fox was delayed. It got great attention and I felt very encouraged in my work.

When did you first participate in Art Basel and what was most memorable about that show?
In 2004, with Mai-Thu Perret in the Statements sector. Her papier-mâché puppets are unique pieces; I got to know interesting curators and was happy to sell them to an important collection.

- **Contact**: Galerie Francesca Pia
Patricia Hartmann
p.hartmann@francescapia.com
info@francescapia.com
- **Established**: 1990 (Bern)
- **Owner(s) / Partner(s)**: Francesca Pia
- **Space(s)**: 400 m²
- **Artists at Art Basel**: Thomas Bayrle
Isabelle Cornaro
Stéphane Dafflon
Philippe Decrauzat
Hans-Peter Feldmann
Vidya Gastaldon
Elsi Giauque
Aloïs Godinat
Joseph Grigely
Wade Guyton
Fabrice Gygi
Jutta Koether
Elad Lassry
Kaspar Müller
Mai-Thu Perret
Marta Riniker-Radich
Bruno Serralongue
David Shrigley
Josef Strau
Joanne Tatham & Tom O'Sullivan
John Tremblay
Betty Woodman

PKM

Seoul

Galleries
Galleries

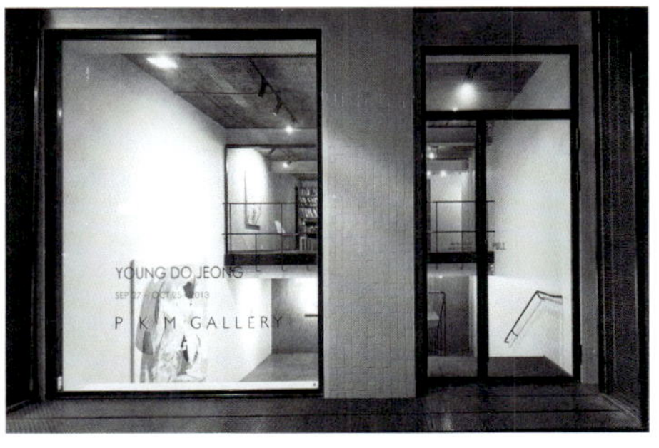

What first compelled you to open a gallery?
PKM Gallery opened in 2001 to represent prominent Korean and international artists in the global context of contemporary art, through a creative program. Since its foundation, the gallery has successfully grown in stature with its various exhibitions, while actively promoting Korean emerging talents on the international stage. Furthermore, the gallery presents selected artworks to provide sophisticated aesthetic experiences to a wide audience.

Who is the first artist you showed and what was most memorable about that show?
Stephen Prina.

When did you first participate in Art Basel and what was most memorable about that show?
It was in 2007.

- **Contact** PKM Gallery, Jiyoung Lee, jylee@pkmgallery.com, info@pkmgallery.com
- **Established** 2001
- **Owner(s) / Partner(s)** Park Kyung-mee
- **Team** 8
- **Space(s)** 500 m²
- **Artists at Art Basel** Bae Young-whan, Hernan Bas, Cho Duck Hyun, Thomas Demand, Olafur Eliasson, Ham Jin, Donghee Koo, Lee Bul, Minouk Lim, Gabriel Orozco
- **Further artists represented** Darren Almond, Cody Choi, Michael Craig-Martin, Jonas Dahlberg, Sangbin IM, Byron Kim, Jiwon Kim, Sanggil Kim, Kangso Lee, Noori Lee, Sang Nam Lee, Claes Oldenburg & Coosje van Bruggen, Jorge Pardo, Park Chan-Kyong, Katie Paterson

Plan B

Cluj
Berlin

● Discoveries
● Feature

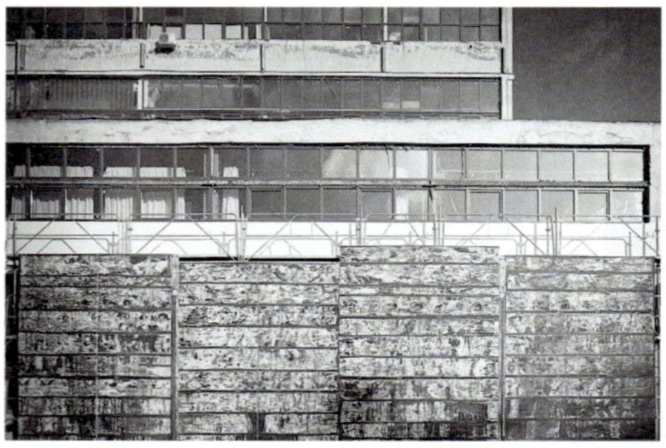

What first compelled you to open a gallery?
Plan B opened in 2005 in Cluj, Romania. Initiated by Mihai Pop and the artist Adrian Ghenie, Plan B has functioned ever since as a production and exhibition space; at the same time it is a documentation center focusing on Romanian art of the last 50 years, by revealing works of remarkable artists without previous international exposure. The emergence of the gallery was determined by the discontent felt in regard to the general situation of art spaces in Romania; as these art spaces depend mostly on insufficient public resources, the "plan B" fallback is animated by individual involvement, a different understanding of the institutional, and a coherent managerial policy. In order to join a larger contemporary art scene, in 2008 Plan B opened a permanent exhibition space in Berlin, which is a project conceived by Mihai Pop and Mihaela Lutea. In 2009, Plan B was one of the initiators of The Paintbrush Factory in Cluj, a collective, independent project, regarded internationally as one of the most compelling and dynamic Eastern European cultural centers.

Who is the first artist you showed and what was most memorable about that show?
The first exhibition was Victor Man's solo show in Cluj. The exhibition had a strong impact on the Cluj (and by extension the Romanian) art scene at that time, questioning the dominant academic thinking trends. The exhibition pointed to another way of working with figurative painting (which at that time was considered by young artists as obsolete), providing a solid trust in its new means and expression.

When did you first participate in Art Basel and what was most memorable about that show?
It was in the Art Basel Feature sector in 2012 with a solo presentation by the Iranian born Dutch artist Navid Nuur

- **Contact** Galeria Plan B, Mihaela Lutea, contact@plan-b.ro
- **Established** 2005
- **Owner(s) / Partner(s)** Mihai Pop, Mihaela Lutea
- **Team** 7
- **Space(s)** 300 m²
- **Artists at Art Basel** Adrian Ghenie, Ciprian Muresan, Navid Nuur
- **Further artists represented** Ioana Batranu, Rudolf Bone, Alexandra Croitoru, Belu-Simion Fainaru, Gheorghe Ilea, Istvan Laszlo, Victor Man, Miklos Onucsan, Cristi Pogacean, Cristian Rusu, Serban Savu, Gabriela Vanga

Platform

Beijing
Hong Kong

● Galleries

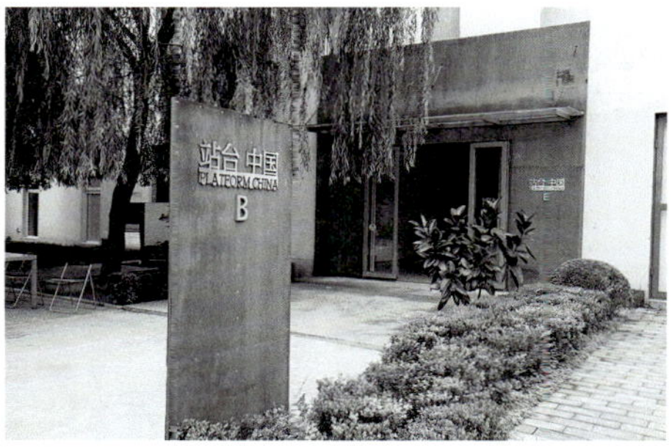

What first compelled you to open a gallery?
The desire to create and provide a platform for young artists to exhibit, present, and explore their practices led us to open the gallery in 2005. Platform China has two main exhibition halls in Beijing. The Hong Kong gallery (since 2012) is a project space in the likeness of an art salon.

Who is the first artist you showed and what was most memorable about that show?
The very first show we presented was a self-curated exhibition featuring several artists. What was most memorable about it was the way this first show came together, its unpredictable yet predictable magic.

- **Contact** Platform China, Claudia Albertini, claudia@platformchina.org, platformchina@gmail.com
- **Established** 2005
- **Owner(s) / Partner(s)** Sun Ning (Owner and Director), Chen Haitao (Owner and Director), Claudia Albertini (Director gallery)
- **Team** 3
- **Space(s)** 1,500 m² (Beijing), 100 m² (Hong Kong)

- **Artists at Art Basel** — Gao Weigang, Jia Aili, Ma Ke, Qin Qi, Wang Yin, Zhou Yilun
- **Further artists represented** — Aniwar, Bi Jianye, Huang Liang, Jin Shan, Li Ming, Shi Jinsong, Song Yuanyuan, Sun Xun, Wang Gongxin, Xiao Bo, Xu Ruotao, Zhao Zhao

Podnar

Berlin
Ljubljana

Galleries

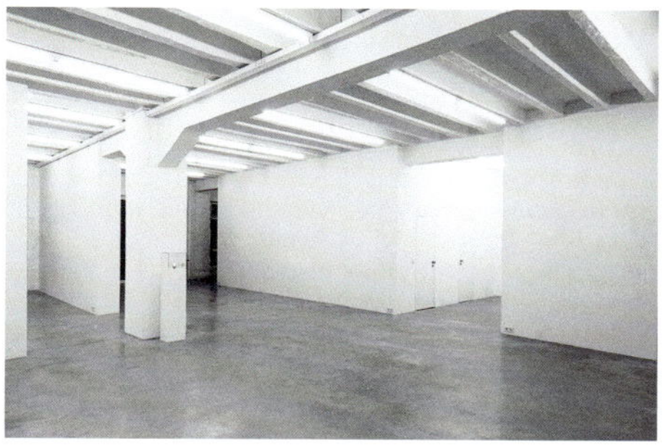

What first compelled you to open a gallery?
Gregor Podnar wanted to run a production center, which would collaborate with galleries and institutions in Europe and abroad. Today the gallery represents internationally renowned and established artists mostly from Eastern European centers, such as Ion Grigorescu, Irwin, Yuri Leiderman, Goran Trbuljak, Dan Perjovschi, and Attila Csörgő. With an emphasis on the heritage of conceptual movements, the gallery has developed toward a wider context, with artists like Alexander Gutke, Tobias Putrih, Ariel Schlesinger, and B. Wurtz.

Who is the first artist you showed and what was most memorable about that show?
Galerija Gregor Podnar opened its premises in the first project space, located in Kranj, with the group exhibition *Venture* (2004), featuring the artists Attila Csörgő, Vadim Fiškin, Alexander Gutke, Irwin, Magnus Larsson, Yuri Leiderman, Kazimir Malevich, Goran Petercol, Marjetica Potrč, Tobias Putrih, Tadej Pogačar, Guia Rigvava.

When did you first participate in Art Basel and what was most memorable about that show?
In 2006, with works by Attila Csörgő, Alexander Gutke, Irwin, Goran Petercol, and Tobias Putrih in the Premiere sector of Art Basel.

- **Contact** — Galerija Gregor Podnar, Nicola Mafessoni, nicola@gregorpodnar.com, berlin@gregorpodnar.com
- **Established** — 2003 (Kranj), 2005 (Ljubljana), 2007 (Berlin)
- **Owner(s) / Partner(s)** — Gregor Podnar
- **Team** — 5
- **Space(s)** — 136 m²
- **Artists at Art Basel** — Attila Csörgö, Vadim Fiškin, Ion Grigorescu, Yuri Leiderman, Marzena Nowak, Tobias Putrih, Goran Trbuljak, B. Wurtz
- **Further artists represented** — Alexander Gutke, Irwin, Anne Neukamp, Dan Perjovschi, Goran Petercol, Ariel Schlesinger, Francisco Tropa

Polígrafa

Barcelona

Galleries
Edition
Edition

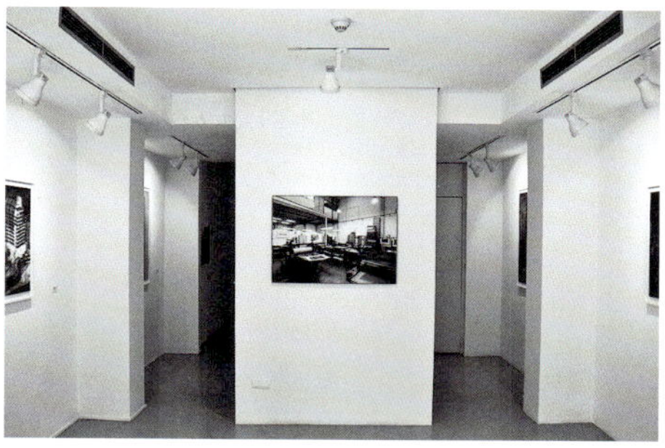

What first compelled you to open a gallery?
The books of our sister company Ediciones Polígrafa gave us the idea of producing graphic works.

Who is the first artist you showed and what was most memorable about that show?
Antoni Tàpies.

When did you first participate in Art Basel and what was most memorable about that show?
In 1970.

- **Contact** — Polígrafa Obra Gráfica, S.L., José Aloy, aloy@poligrafa.net
- **Established** — 1961
- **Owner(s) / Partner(s)** — Juan de Muga, José Aloy, Alvaro Puigdengolas
- **Team** — 11
- **Space(s)** — 120 m²
- **Artists at Art Basel** — El Anatsui, Antonio Asis, Massimo Bartolini, Christo, Michael Craig-Martin, Carlos Cruz-Diez, Claire Fontaine, Patrick Hamilton, Leiko Ikemura, Atsushi Kaga, Jacob Kassay, Nelson Leirner, Mateo López, Ryan McGinness, Joan Miró, Yuko Murata, Enoc Perez, Adrian Piper, Marjetica Potrc, David Salle, Daniel Senise, Gary Simmons, Su Xiaobai, Antoni Tàpies, Luis Tomasello, Bernar Venet, Wang Huai Qing, Garth Weiser, Xingjian Gao, Zao Wou-Ki
- **Further artists represented** — Carlos Amorales, Francis Bacon, Donald Baechler, José Bedia, Lynda Benglis, Olaf Breuning, Stefan Brüggemann, Fernando Bryce, Eduardo Chillida, Saint Clair Cemin, George Condo, León Ferrari, Eric Fischl, Helen Frankenthaler, Liam Gillick, Luis Gordillo, April Gornik, Ilya Kabakov, André Komatsu, Guillermo Kuitca, Wifredo Lam, Julio Larraz, Glenn Ligon, Robert Longo

Jorge Macchi
Enrique Martínez-Celaya
Roberto Matta
Robert Motherwell
Matt Mullican
Carsten Nicolai
Tony Oursler
Paul P.
Jorge Pardo
Nicolás Paris
Dan Perjovschi
Jaume Plensa
Liliana Porter
Tobias Putrih
David Ratcliff
Ed Ruscha
Julião Sarmento
George Segal
James Siena
Regina Silveira
Nedko Solakov
Donald Sultan
Rufino Tamayo
Francisco Toledo
Scott Treleaven
Adrián Villar Rojas

Prats

Barcelona

- Galleries
- Galleries

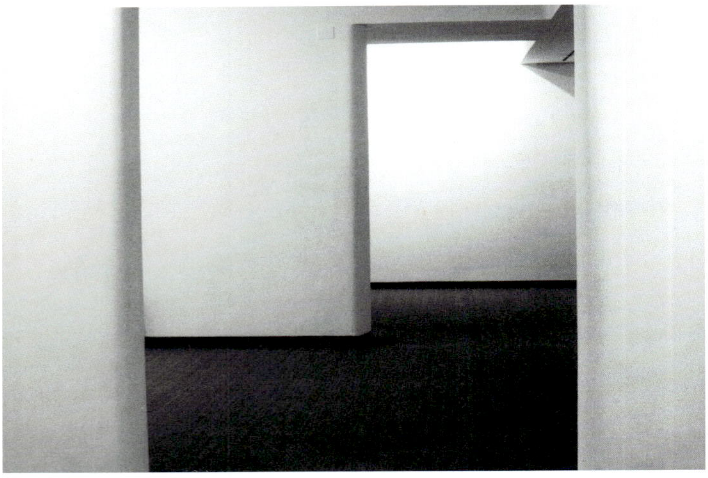

What first compelled you to open a gallery?
The passion for contemporary art.

Who is the first artist you showed and what was most memorable about that show?
The first artist was Alexander Calder. Most memorable was the audience.

When did you first participate in Art Basel and what was most memorable about that show?
In 1976.

- **Contact**: Galeria Joan Prats
Gloria Perez
gloriaperez@galeriajoanprats.com
galeria@galeriajoanprats.com
- **Established**: 1976
- **Owner(s) / Partner(s)**: Juan de Muga
Gloria Perez
- **Team**: 8
- **Space(s)**: 140 m²
- **Artists at Art Basel**: Knut Åsdam
Erick Beltrán
Fernando Bryce
Christo
Hannah Collins
Fabian Marcaccio
Enrique Martínez Celaya
Aleksandra Mir
Antoni Muntadas
Caio Reisewitz
Julião Sarmento
Juan Uslé
Eulàlia Valldosera
Alejandro Vidal
- **Further artists represented**: Perejaume

Presenhuber

Zurich

- Galleries
- Galleries Unlimited
- Galleries Public

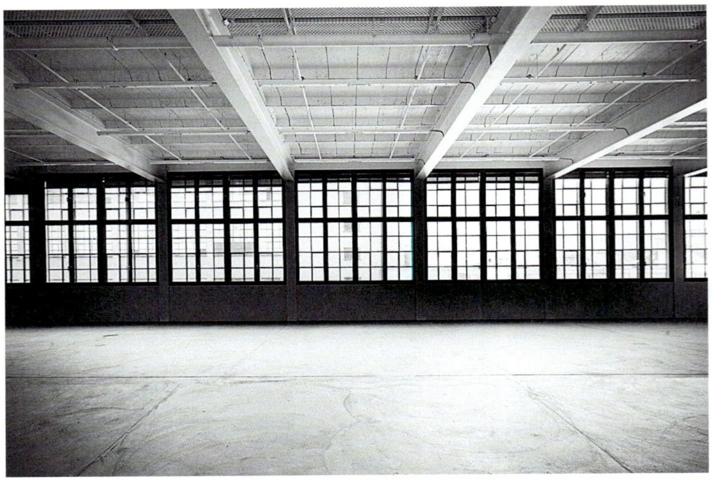

What first compelled you to open a gallery?
I studied art, but thought I would be more efficient in creating a program with artists within a gallery, rather than doing art myself.

Who is the first artist you showed and what was most memorable about that show?
The first show was in October 1989, with Marcus Geiger, a Swiss artist who lived in Vienna, where I come from. He was very rigorous and I liked that.

When did you first participate in Art Basel and what was most memorable about that show?
My first participation at Art Basel was in 1996 as a director of Walcheturm gallery, and with Galerie Eva Presenhuber it was in 2002.

- **Contact**: Galerie Eva Presenhuber
Bjorn Alfers
b.alfers@presenhuber.com
info@presenhuber.com
- **Established**: 2002
- **Owner(s) / Partner(s)**: Eva Presenhuber
- **Team**: 15
- **Space(s)**: 929 m²
- **Artists at Art Basel**: Doug Aitken
Emmanuelle Antille
Martin Boyce
Joe Bradley
Angela Bulloch
Valentin Carron
Verne Dawson
Jay DeFeo
Trisha Donnelly
Carroll Dunham
Latifa Echakhch
Maria Eichhorn
Matias Faldbakken
Sam Falls
Urs Fischer
Peter Fischli/David Weiss
Sylvie Fleury
Liam Gillick
Douglas Gordon
Amy Granat
Mark Handforth
Candida Höfer
Alex Hubbard
Karen Kilimnik
Andrew Lord
Richard Prince
Gerwald Rockenschaub
Tim Rollins and K.O.S.
Ugo Rondinone
Dieter Roth
Eva Rothschild
Jean-Frédéric Schnyder
Steven Shearer
Josh Smith
Beat Streuli
Oscar Tuazon
Franz West
Sue Williams

Preston

New York

Nova
Public

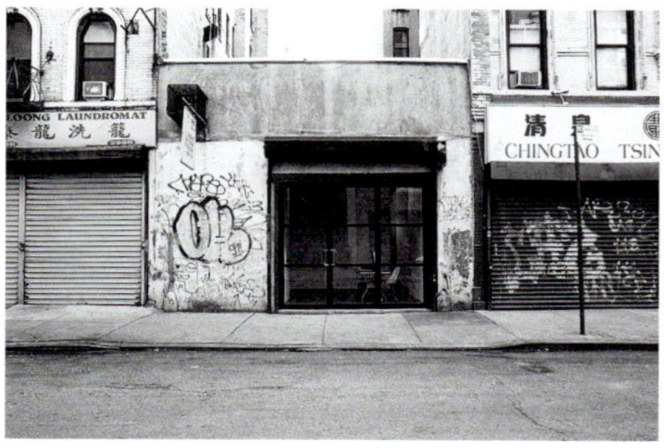

What first compelled you to open a gallery?
The imperative to build a program of challenging exhibitions with exceptional inter-generational artists.

Who is the first artist you showed and what was most memorable about that show?
Daniel Joseph Martinez, Mary Kelly, General Idea, Touhami Ennadre, and Michelle Lopez. Daniel Joseph Martinez created a formidable animatronic sculpture that violently targeted the walls and floor of the gallery shooting pools of theatrical blood from a taxidermied, fisted rabbit.

When did you first participate in Art Basel and what was most memorable about that show?
In Basel in the Positions sector in 2010, with a solo project by Kara Tanaka, titled *Crushed by the Hammer of the Sun* (2008), a mechanical whirling dervish.

- **Contact** — Simon Preston, simon@simonprestongallery.com, office@simonprestongallery.com
- **Established** — 2008
- **Owner(s) / Partner(s)** — Simon Preston
- **Team** — 3
- **Space(s)** — 185 m²
- **Artists at Art Basel** — Hans Schabus, Josh Tonsfeldt
- **Further artists represented** — Carlos Bevilacqua, John Gerrard, Nick Goss, Michelle Lopez, Daniel Joseph Martinez, Jessica Mein, Jenny Perlin, Marco Rios, Kara Tanaka, Caragh Thuring

Project 88

Mumbai

Galleries
Encounters

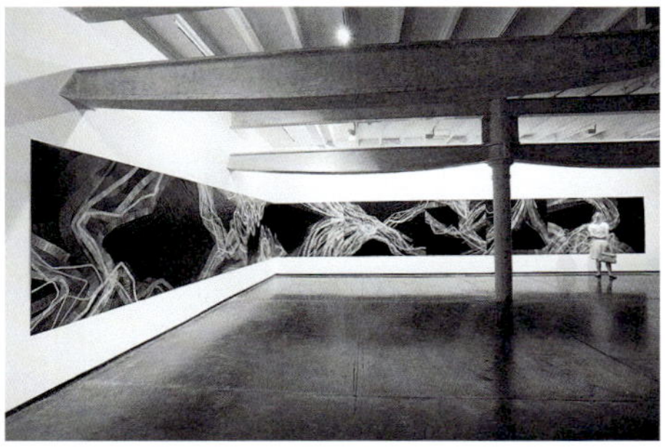

What first compelled you to open a gallery?
I am a second generation gallerist. My mother has run a gallery in Kolkota since 1988 (Galerie 88). While Galerie 88 deals with Indian moderns, Project 88 has a contemporary program.

Who is the first artist you showed and what was most memorable about that show?
Bharti Kher. It put us on the international map from the first exhibition on.

When did you first participate in Art Basel and what was most memorable about that show?
Though we've been at ART HK from the inception, technically Art Basel in Hong Kong in 2013 would be our first participation with the Basel group. The fair was better laid out, and there was an increased presence of notable international collectors.

- **Contact** — Project 88, Zakia Basrai, contact@project88.in, sree@project88.in
- **Established** — 2006
- **Owner(s) / Partner(s)** — Sree Goswami
- **Team** — 5
- **Space(s)** — 360 m²
- **Artists at Art Basel** — Sarnath Banerjee, Neha Choksi, Sandeep Mukherjee, Risham Syed, The Otolith Group
- **Further artists represented** — Mahesh Baliga, Hemali Bhuta, Chirodeep Chaudhuri, Baptist Coelho, Desire Machine Collective, Rohini Devasher, Shreyas Karle, Monali Meher, Huma Mulji, Asma Mundrawala, Tejal Shah

ProjecteSD

Barcelona

Galleries

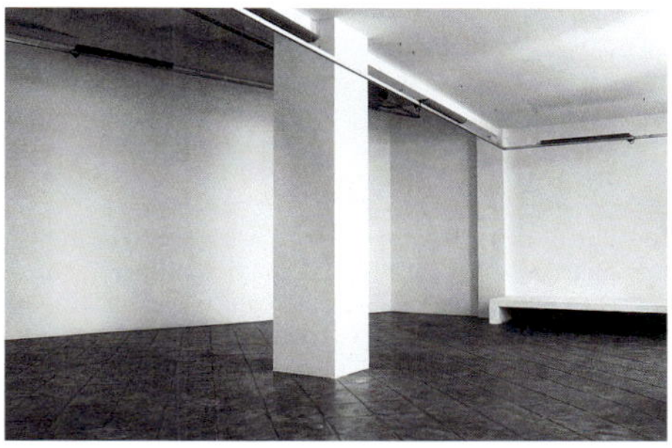

What first compelled you to open a gallery?
My passion for art, my admiration for the work of the gallerists, and the idea that I could start a kind of gallery that does not exist yet in my context, in my city and country. There was an empty space that I thought I could fill in with an interesting proposal.

Who is the first artist you showed and what was most memorable about that show?
German artist Jochen Lempert was my first solo show. Its uniqueness, its freshness and quality, and the satisfaction that, despite showing an artist totally unknown in my context, there was an extremely positive reaction. The show was successful.

When did you first participate in Art Basel and what was most memorable about that show?
I participated in Art Basel within the Statements sector in 2009, showing young Spanish artist Patricia Dauder. A great exposure to a highly professional audience.

- **Contact** — ProjecteSD, María Pose, mp@projectesd.com, info@projectesd.com
- **Established** — 2003
- **Owner(s) / Partner(s)** — Silvia Dauder
- **Team** — 3
- **Space(s)** — 200 m² (including office)
- **Artists at Art Basel** — Iñaki Bonillas, Patricia Dauder, Koenraad Dedobbeleer, Dora García, Guillaume Leblon, Jochen Lempert, Asier Mendizabal

- **Further artists represented**
  Pieter Vermeersch
  Christoph Weber
  Raimond Chaves
  Hans-Peter Feldmann
  Matt Mullican
  Marc Nagtzaam
  Peter Piller
  Xavier Ribas

PSM

Berlin ● Positions

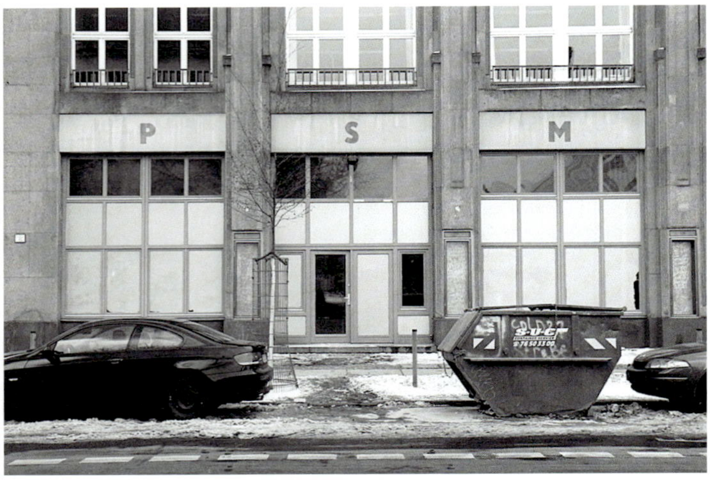

What first compelled you to open a gallery?
Although my first job in the art world was in a gallery, I was dreaming of an institutional career. Nevertheless, as I finally worked in an institution, I realized I was missing the long-term relationship with artists and the day-to-day business of a gallery. Most importantly, I liked the direct financial support of projects through the art market.

Who is the first artist you showed and what was most memorable about that show?
In my first gallery exhibition I showed a sound installation by Ujino Muneteru. Since the piece was pretty loud, the police ended the first opening reception way too early. *FAZ* wrote the next morning: "Better than the police allows."

When did you first participate in Art Basel and what was most memorable about that show?
My first participation in Art Basel was in 2011 with a Statements booth by Daniel Jackson. I will never forget the moment we entered the fair building: the first time under our own name, our own responsibility—Jackson and me, a former gallery technician and a former gallery assistant. The grand moment asked for a grounded gesture: two cans of beer from the little kiosk in the sun outside of the building.

- **Contact**
  PSM
  Sabine Schmidt
  office@psm-gallery.com
- **Established** 2008
- **Owner(s) / Partner(s)** Sabine Schmidt
- **Team** 3
- **Space(s)** 220 m²
- **Artists at Art Basel** Nadira Husain
- **Further artists represented**
  Øystein Aasan
  Eduardo T. Basualdo
  Thomas Chapman
  Paolo Chiasera
  Pauline Curnier Jardin
  Sophie Erlund
  Christian Falsnaes
  Daniel Jackson
  Anca Munteanu Rimnic
  Nathan Peter
  Ariel Reichman
  Ujino Muneteru

Peres Projects
Interview with Javier Peres

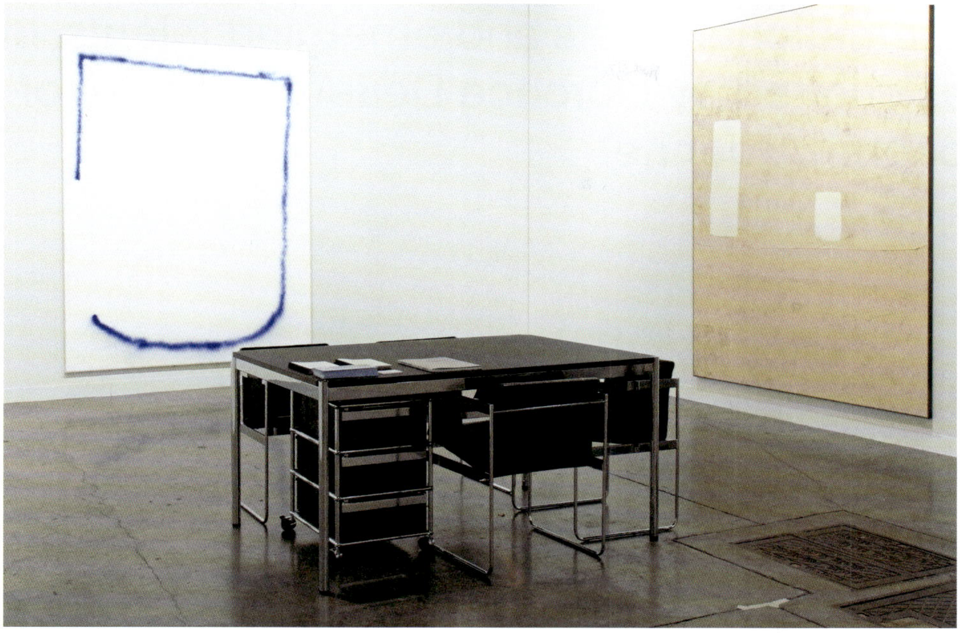

Art Basel in Miami Beach, Nova, 2013

When did you start the gallery?

I originally started the gallery in San Francisco in 2002. I was there for a very short time and moved almsot immediately to Los Angeles where I really founded it in 2003. In 2005 I started a new space in Berlin. I opened a second space in Berlin in 2010 and closed in Los Angeles.

Why?

The commute. I also always found Europe more interesting than the US in terms of mobility and what is happening in the art field, as well as just in terms of quality of life.

Was this choice also related to the artists you represent?

When we opened the first gallery in Berlin, I think the main reason was that I was showing artists who were getting a lot of attention internationally and I wanted to show them in Europe. My long-term plan was to move to Europe anyhow and Berlin was the perfect place to do that. As I did it I decided actually Berlin makes more sense. Period. We already did fairs so it didn't make sense to have multiple locations for me.

At Art Basel in Miami Beach you presented a solo show by David Ostrowski. Could you tell us more about the artist and his project? You showed different paintings every day ...

David Ostrowski's paintings are always very minimal and abstract. While discussing how to present the work in Miami Beach with him—his works are always very large in scale—the idea came that we could rehang each day, so that each day it would really feel and look like a single room in a gallery or a museum, and as the installation unfolded the public could see everything that it was about. Miami Beach gets 40,000–50,000 visitors. How many visitors does a gallery get? So this seemed like a great opportunity. We also decided to publish a book (I used to make my own in-house magazine called *Daddy*) that would show all the paintings and other recent ones too.

We often do solo presentation or curated shows at fairs, so we liked the idea of doing this rotation. It had really great response, people were coming back. There's a lot of interest in David's work right now. Just as it did with me, it really sparked the imagination of the public. We showed him in Art Basel in Hong Kong, at Liste in Basel in June 2013, and we would like to show him again; there's still a lot of work to be done with him, because David is at that point where he has been out of school now for about five years (he studied in Düsseldorf with Albert Oehlen), and where his confidence is really there to make the kind of work that he wants. His work could be said to be about failure: the inherent failure in making a painting, failure of being a studio painter, this practice enclosed in the studio ... He has developed in such a way now that he is constantly taking different risks, he's constantly making bold moves, and sometimes that means having only a footprint on a raw canvas or having an all-white canvas. There's so much to see and experience and it's our goal when we do an art fair to reflect that. The commercial aspect of it is a given. I'm not museum.

This year you participated in Art Basel in Hong Kong and in Miami Beach. What is your approach to each fair, and how the two fairs are different from one another?

I love Hong Kong and Art Basel in Hong Kong was special for us as we decided to do something we normally don't do: to show something from every artist and to focus on super-high quality works, such as exceptional secondary-market works by Joe Bradley. We also showed David of course, and Mark Flood, a very seminal artist in my program, mixed up with a huge painting by Alex Israel, we had an amazing Dash Snow collage, etc. We focused on highlighting the best of the gallery program. The response was incredible, and we're definitely going back, and probably taking a booth twice the size!

P

Parcours engages Basel's historical neighborhoods with site-specific sculptures, interventions, and performances by renowned international artists and emerging talents. In 2013 Parcours was curated by Florence Derieux, Director of the Frac Champagne-Ardenne.

PAR COURS

2013 participants

Marina Abramović
Lisson

Marc Bauer
Freymond-Guth

Olaf Breuning
Metro Pictures

Tom Burr
Bortolami

Michael Craig-Martin
Gagosian
New Art Centre

Lothar Hempel
Kern
Modern Art

Joep van Liefland
Lehmann

Jill Magid
Lambert
RaebervonStenglin

Lisa Oppenheim
Klosterfelde

Evariste Richer
Approach
Meessen De Clercq

Sterling Ruby
Hauser & Wirth
Hufkens

Michael Smith and Joshua White
Greene Naftali

Valerie Snobeck
Lee

Daniel Steegmann Mangrané
Mendes Wood

Danh Vo
Buchholz
Bortolozzi
Crousel
Marian Goodman

Martin Walde
Krinzinger

Artur Żmijewski
Kilchmann
Foksal

Tom Burr
Dressage
Kasernenplatz

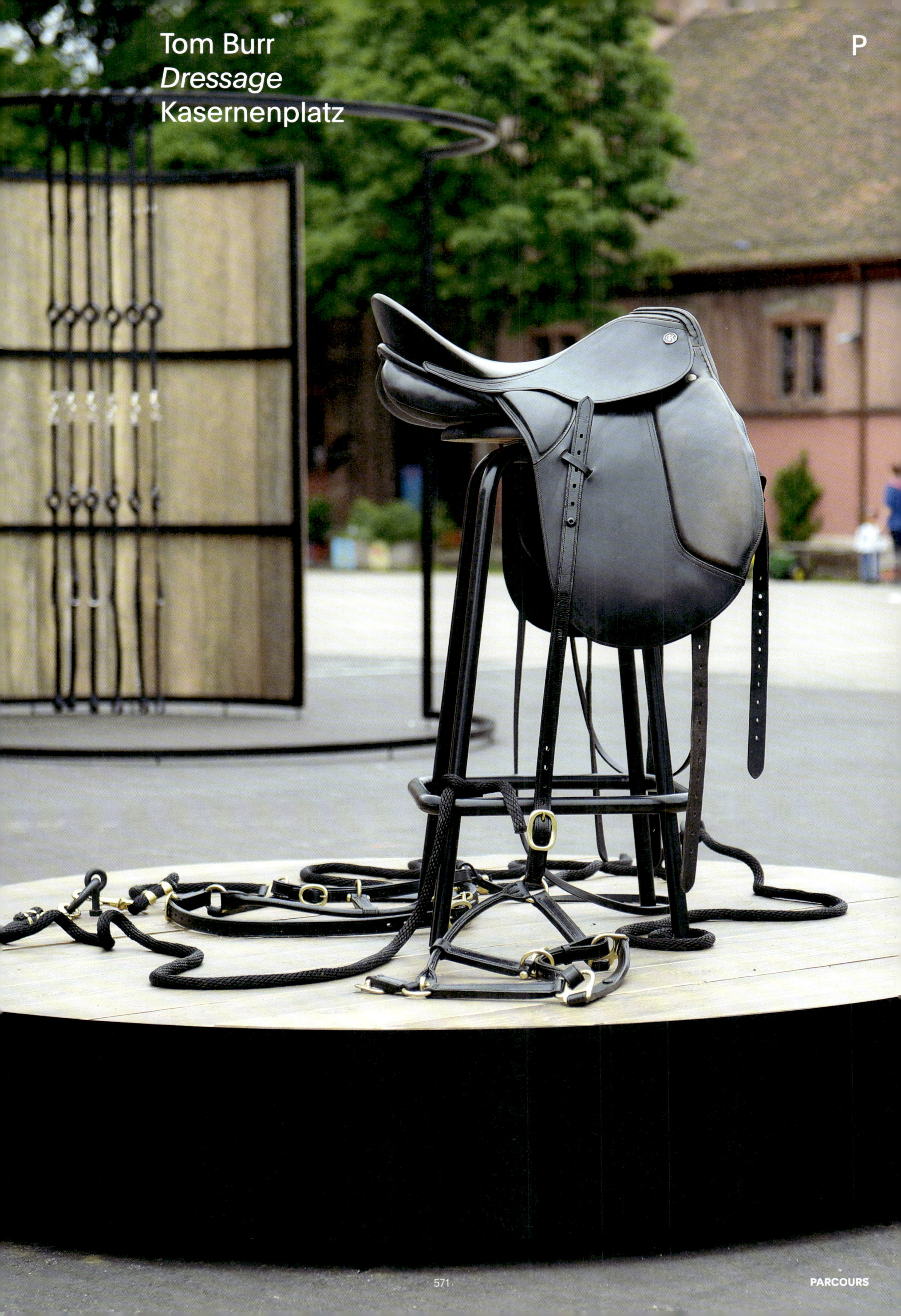

P

Florence Derieux talks to artists Tom Burr and Valerie Snobeck about Parcours

Conversations
Parcours 2013

Basel
June 13, 2013

Tom Burr, Artist, New York

Valerie Snobeck, Artist, New York

Florence Derieux, 2013 Parcours Curator and Director of FRAC Champagne-Ardenne (Reims, France)

A complete version of the conversation is available at www.artbasel.com

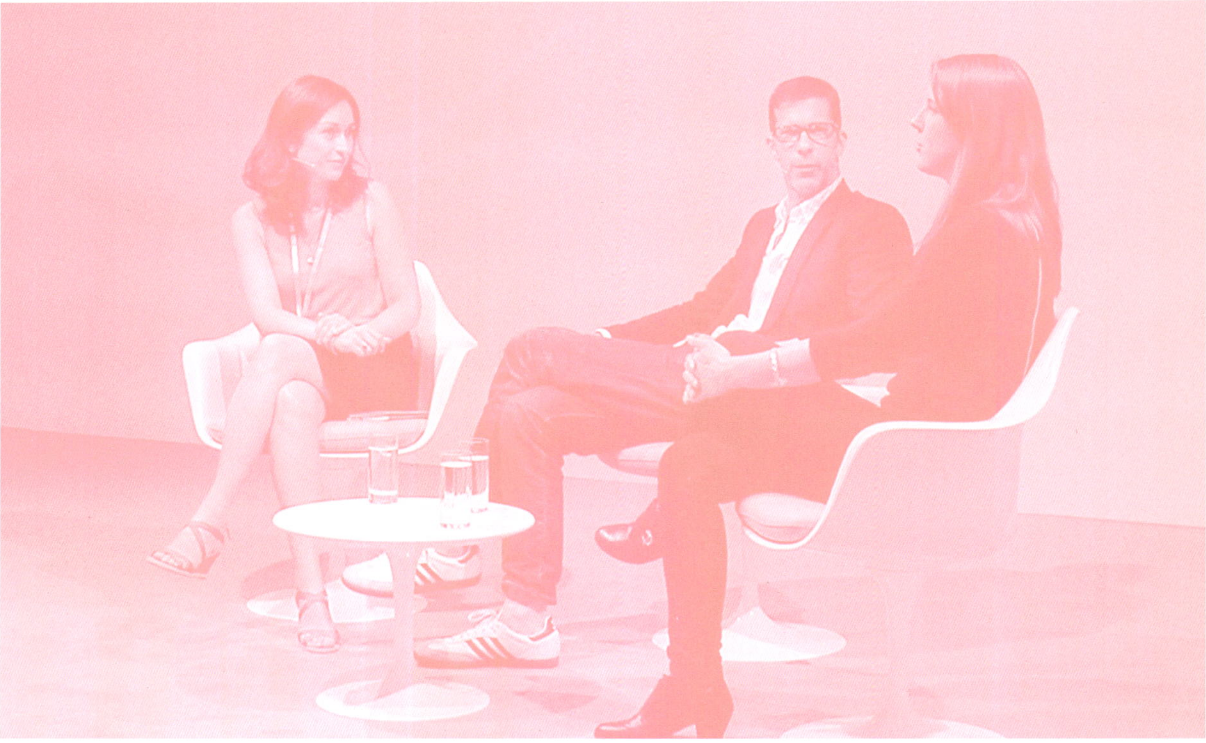

From left to right: Florence Derieux, Tom Burr, Valerie Snobeck

FLORENCE DERIEUX Parcours was created by Art Basel in 2009 to engage the art with the city, to create strong and ongoing links with the inhabitants and the visitors. Jens Hoffmann was the curator for the past three years. Every year, a new area of the city is chosen for this event. This year, it was Klingental, close to the Messeplatz, and condensed around the former military Kaserne, the school of fashion design, and the artists' studios around this plaza. Klingental is a lively area where the cultural mix is strong, and where many individuals and structures, institutions, businesses already dealing with culture, are located. My idea was to meet as many of these protagonists as possible, to understand how the people in the area are actually living in and developing it on an everyday basis. In developing projects with the artists in relation to the venues, each of them responded in a different way to this idea of site-specificity.

TOM BURR Parcours is interesting because it is both inside and outside the parameters of the fair. There's a push-and-pull between the temporary nature of the exhibition and the commitment to particular sites. We are creating an ambitious museum-like project within and for a very brief period of time.

FD Parcours comprises 17 projects, and the idea was to avoid "pasting"—i.e. to paste existing artworks onto available venues—but rather to develop the project in close relationship with the artists. Twelve artists out of 17 were actually present before the fair and installed their works themselves. When I was invited to curate Parcours, my initial thoughts went to Tom's first works that focus on this notion of site-specificity. I've almost never requested such a precise thing from artists, but I asked Tom if he could develop a project on the main plaza, outdoors. I had in mind Tom's sculpture called *Deep Purple* (2000), a reproduction 2:3 scale of *Tilted Arc* by Richard Serra, which was installed on Federal Plaza in New York and then removed.

TB I have grappled with the notion of large-scale site-specific sculptures. Now, for a lot of artists, site is yet another material. The notion of site has evolved: it became a production site as well as simply a location where the artwork exists.

VALERIE SNOBECK Yes, a location is like a material, or something that you can use to add onto ideas and materials you are already working with.

TB Working on sites like these has something to do with the encounter of "ghosts." During the installation we talked about nostalgia, but it's not nostalgia, it's about being confronted with some kind of architectural, historical, or physical ghosts, and incorporating them into the works. Sometimes those "ghosts"—I'm using that term in a provocative way—can be of one's own work, revisiting images and forms used before, or revisiting the conditions and different lives of a site, its many layers. As opposed to many international exhibitions that are spread out throughout the city in quite disparate locations, here it's as if there's an invisible glass wall around Klingental, and that becomes a lens through which to look at some pieces.

FD For Parcours, my role was to select from proposals made by artists and galleries. My job consisted in trying to find the best possible location to exhibit these works. I worked very differently depending on each project. Danh Vo was following a residency in Basel and he had already developed a strong relationship with the city. Artur Żmijewski's video *My Neighbours* [2009] was shot when he was in Israel, precisely at the moment when the war started in Gaza. I was really taken by this work and convinced that it had to be shown, and then the possibility to use a classroom within the school of fashion and design—a platform for learning in an enclosed space, very secure, very protected—came up. It isolated the piece in a perfect way. It created a very particular context in which to experience the work. The same is true for Lisa Oppenheim's work: to hear sounds within a wooden attic as if you were outside is a unique experience. We also developed several projects in collaboration with protagonists of this area, one with Olaf Breuning at the school, another with the Kaserne Basel, a venue for theater and dance. We talked about art and dance and outlined a program together, inviting Benjamin Millepied and his LA Dance Project. Jill Magid's piece is directly linked to the city of Basel: a few months before coming to here, she was in Mexico and became completely fascinated by the work of the Mexican architect Luis Barragán, whose archive is here in Basel. She's using Parcours as a platform to announce a project she would like to realize, probably within the environment of an institution. That's something that pretty much turns the initial purpose of a project like this one upside down, which I think also makes it interesting. It was, all in all, a really nice experiment to build, one day after the other, project by project, over three exciting months.

I have grappled with the notion of large-scale site-specific sculptures. Now, for a lot of artists, site is yet another material.
—Tom Burr

Valerie Snobeck, *Mechanic of Fluid*, Obst & Gemüse

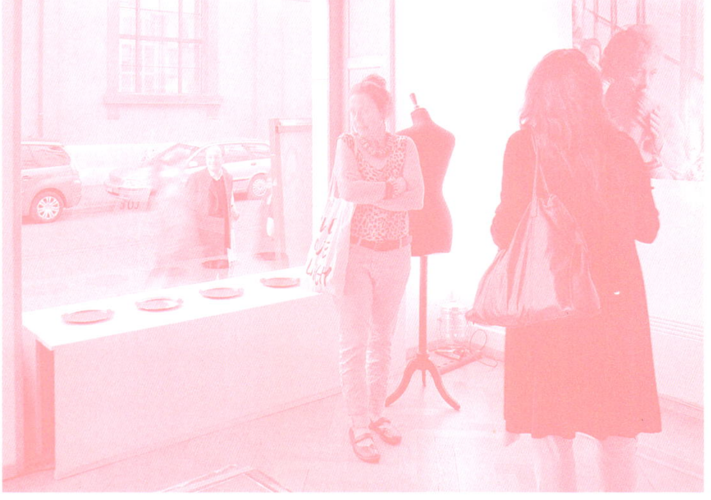

P

Sterling Ruby
Stove
Kasernenplatz

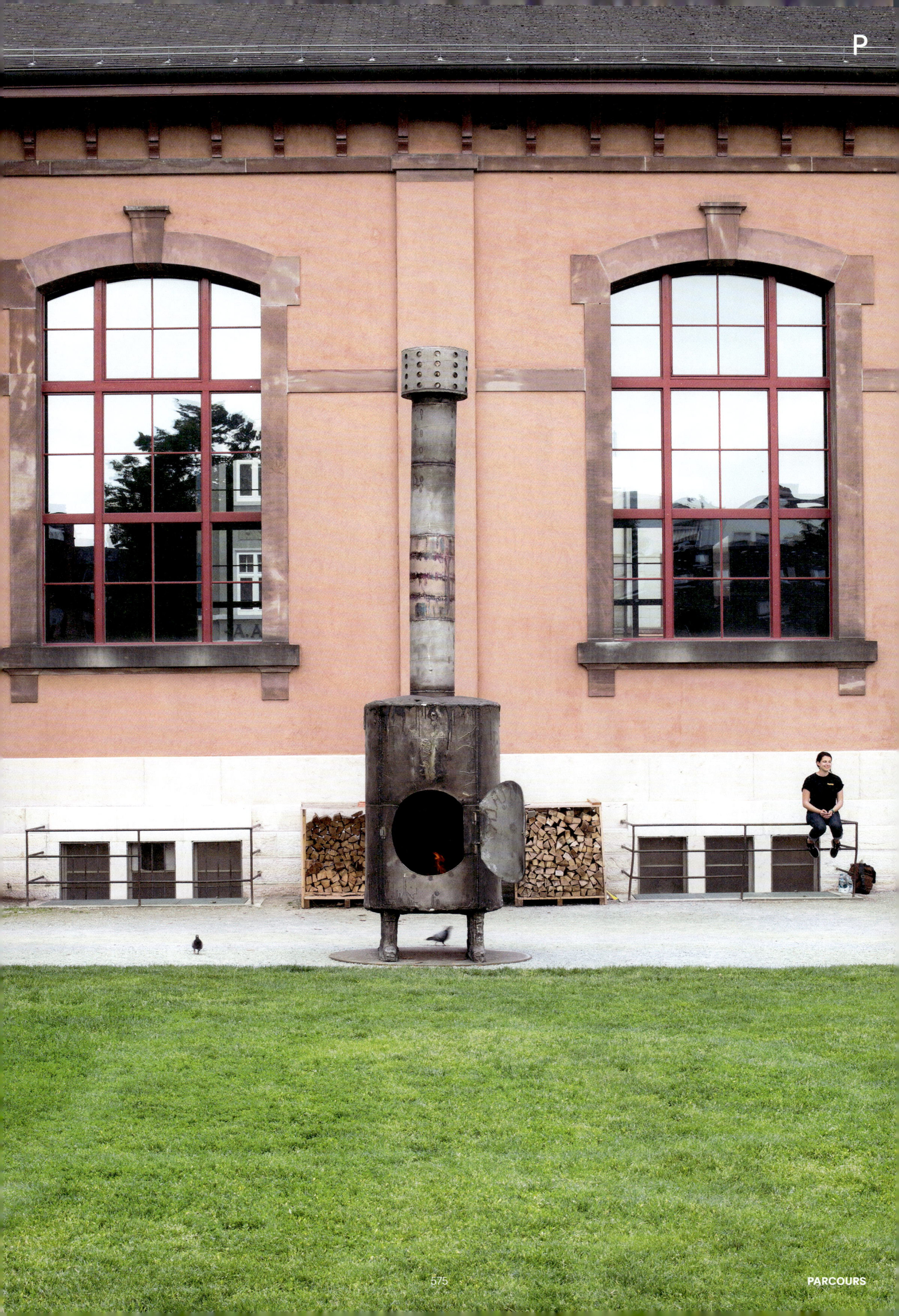

P

Danh Vo
Gustav's Wing
Museum Kleines Klingental
Färberhaus

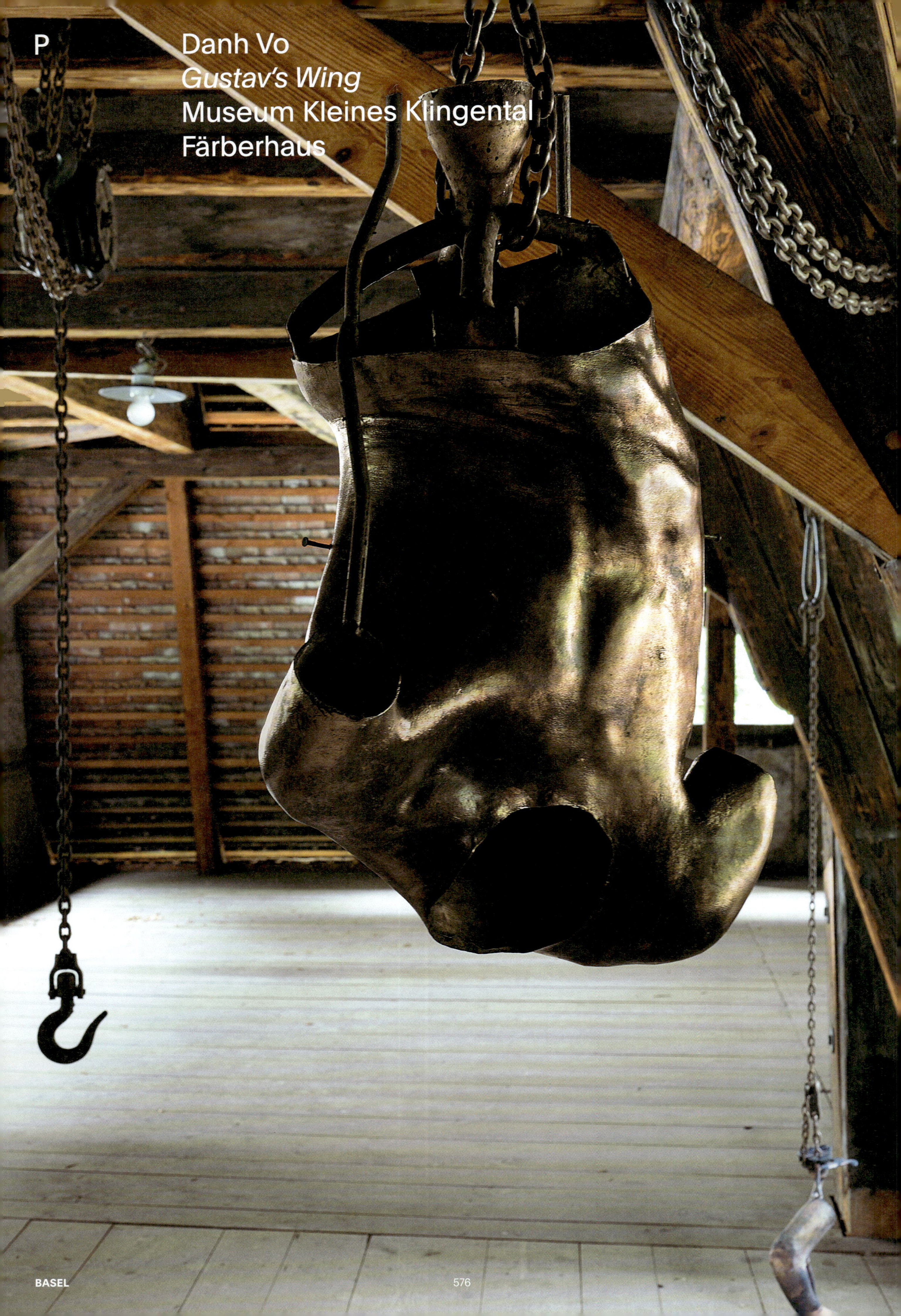

Benjamin Millepied & L.A. Dance Project

Moving Parts

performance during Parcours night

Reithalle Kaserne

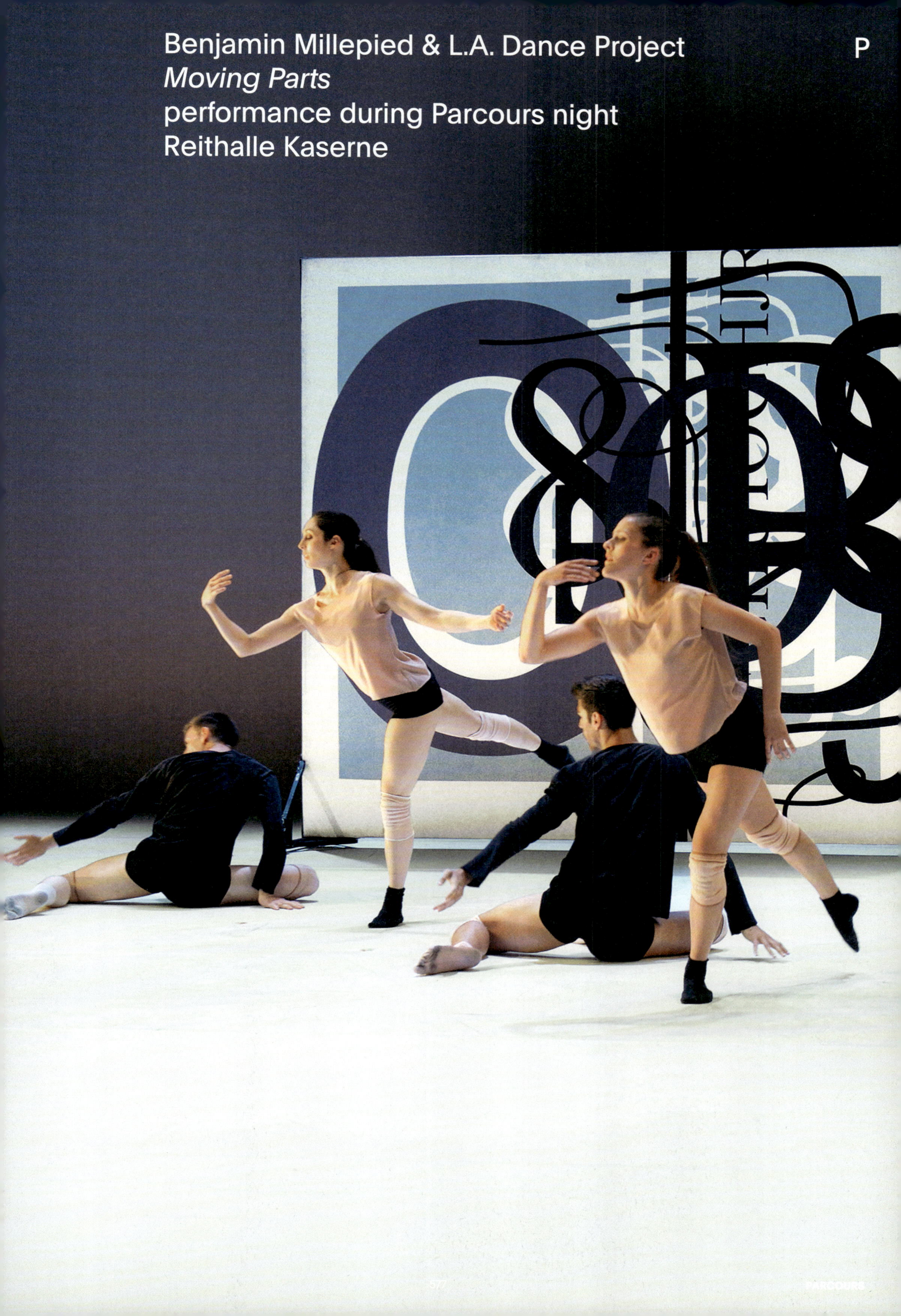

P

Lisa Oppenheim
Smoke
Ateliergenossenschaft Kaserne

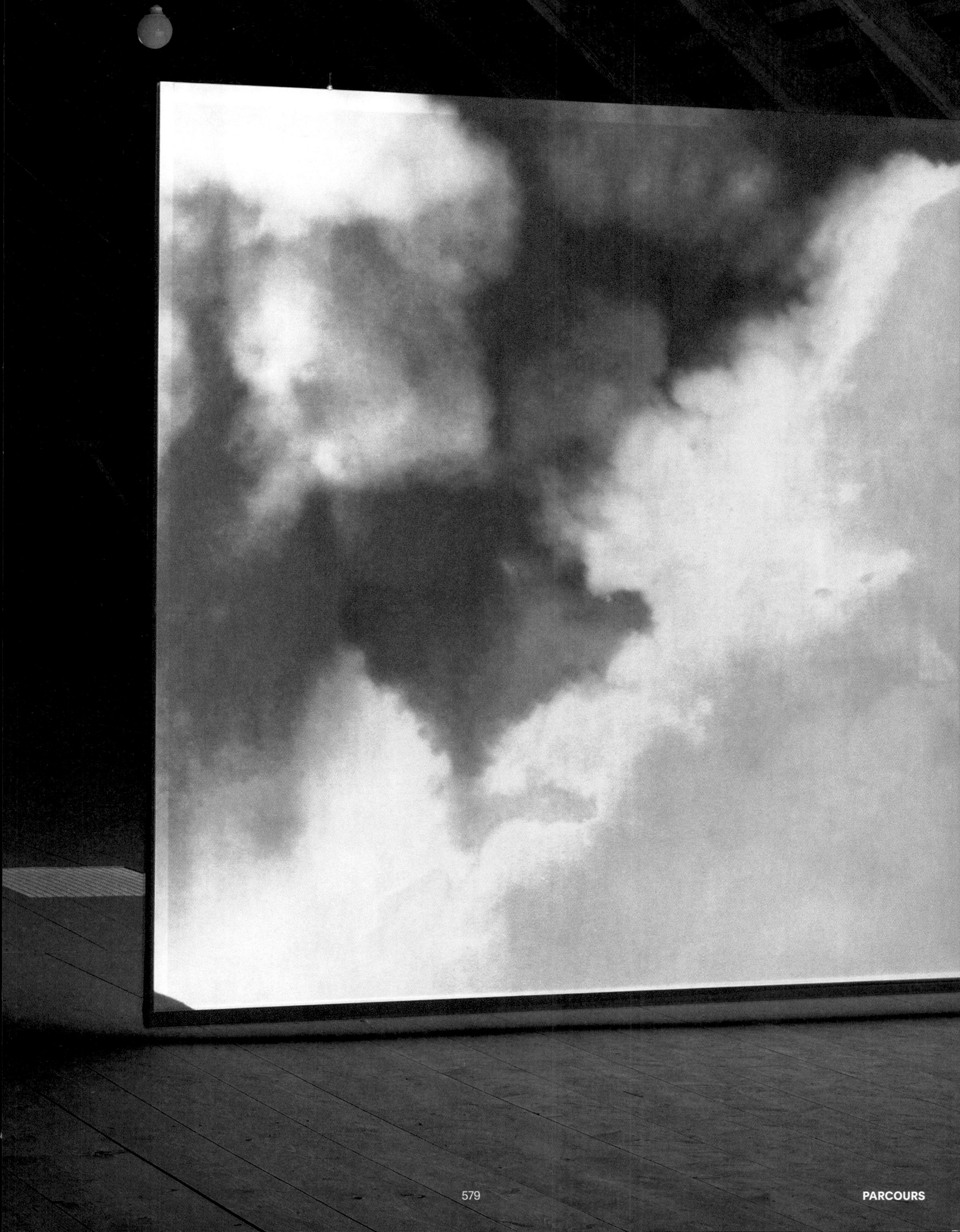

P

Michael Smith
Avuncular Quest
performance during Parcours night
Spielestrich Kaserne

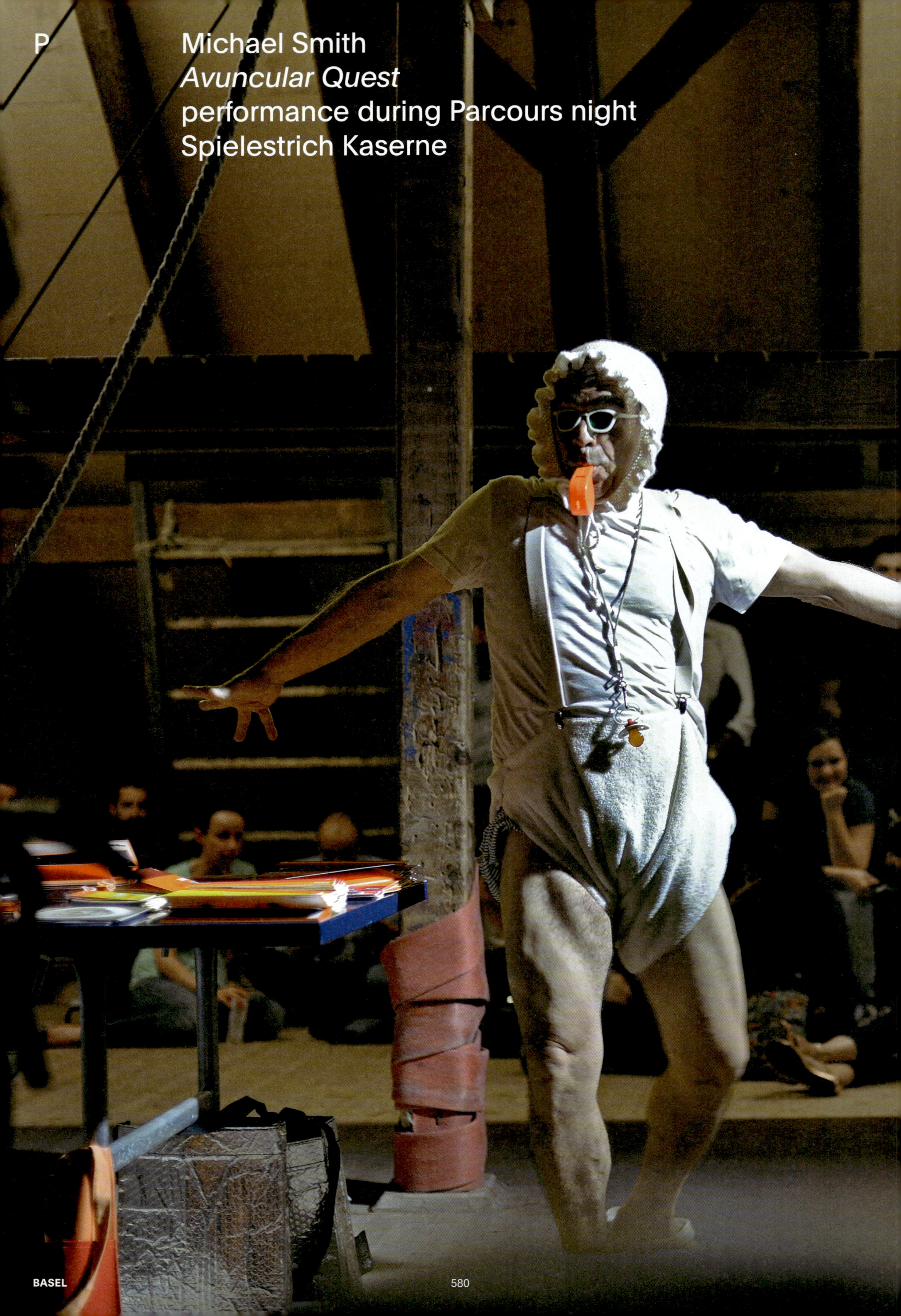

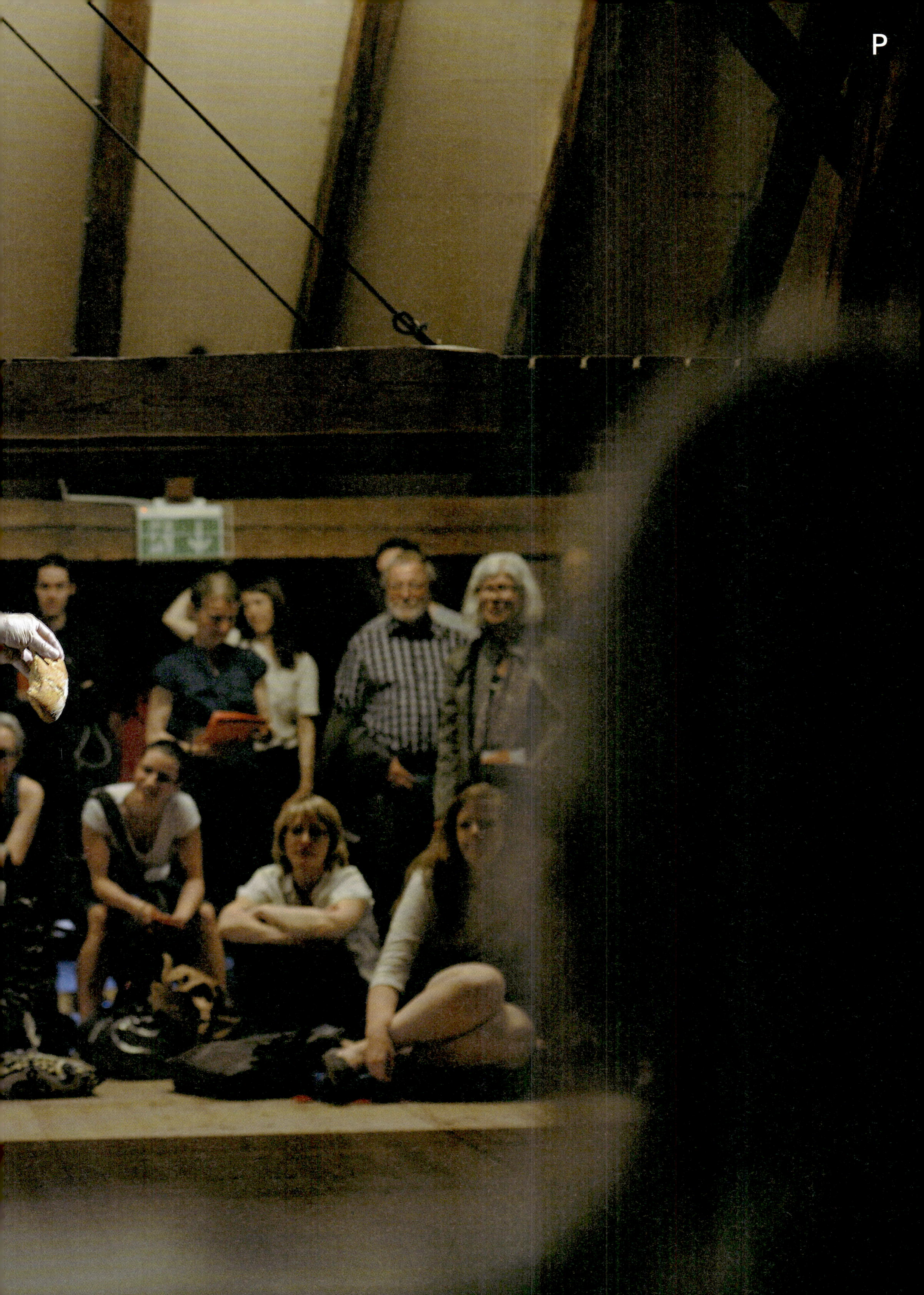

P

Marc Bauer & Kafka
The Architect
2013
performance during Parcours night
Reithalle Kaserne

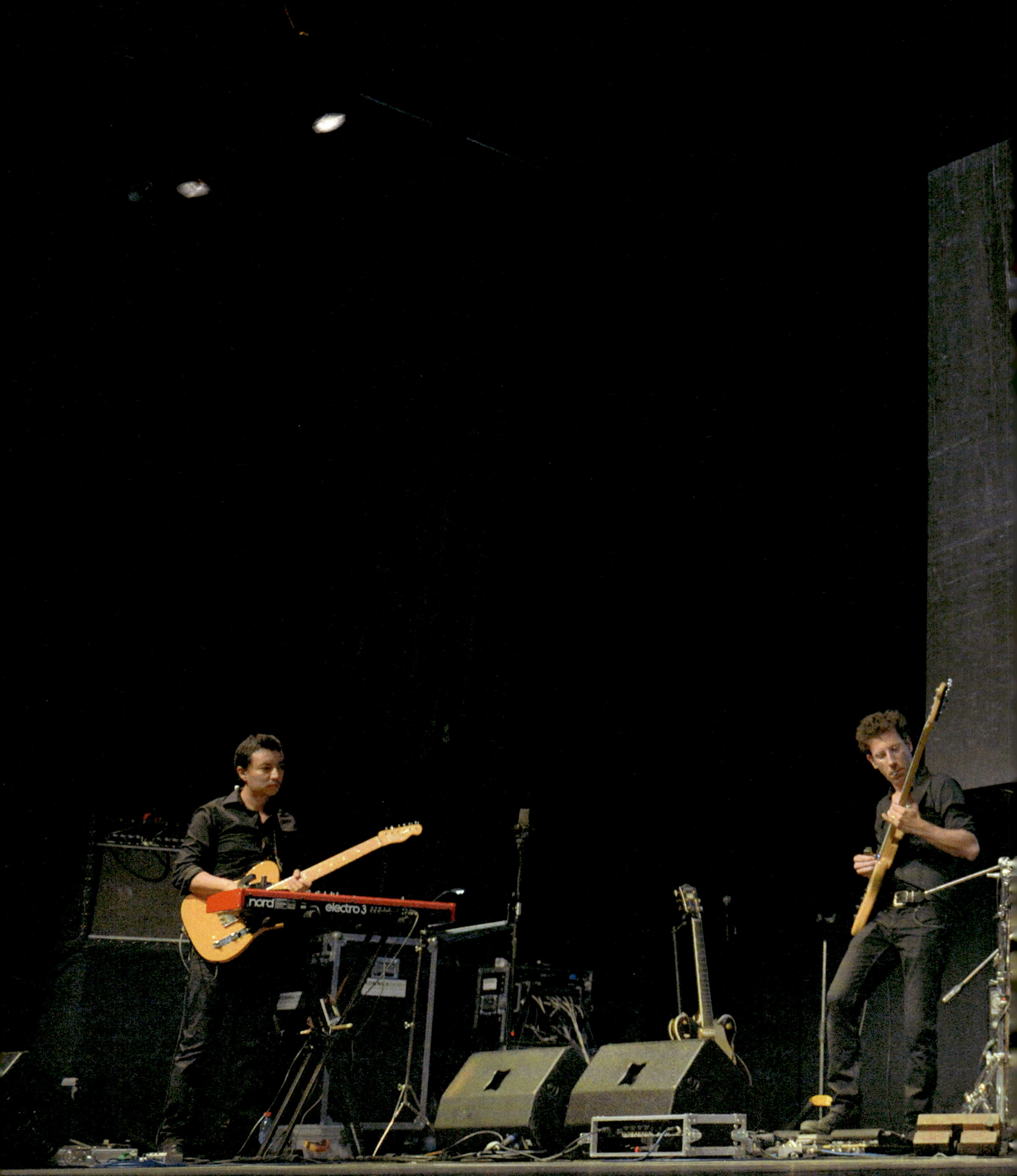

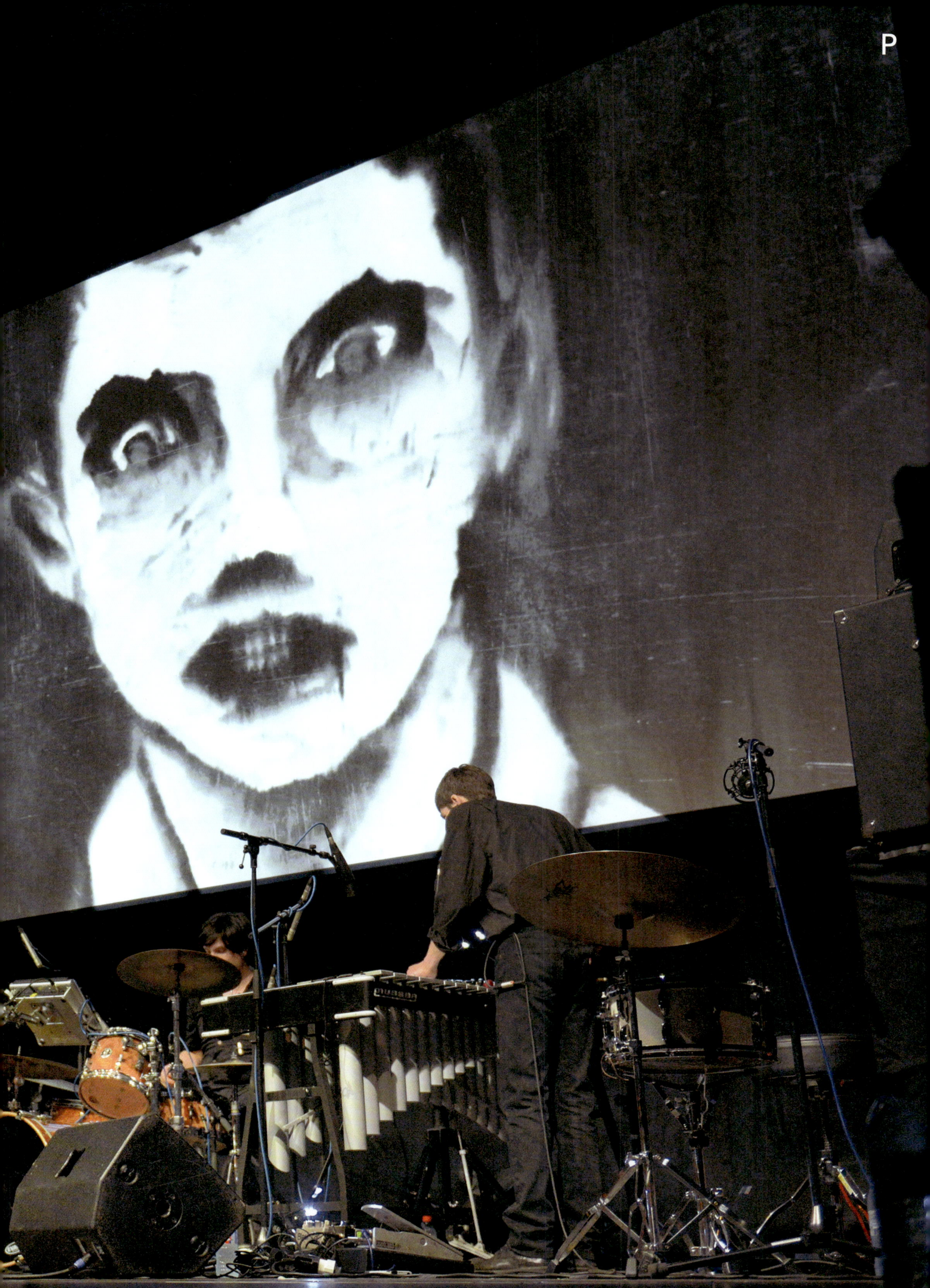

P

Giving curators, critics, and collectors the opportunity to experience ambitious new talents from all over the globe, the Positions sector in Miami Beach offers a platform for a single artist to present one major project.

POSITIONS

2013 participants

Andersen's
Ulrik Heltoft

Arratia Beer
Gabriel Acevedo Velarde

Baró
Lourival Cuquinha

Bureau
Tom Holmes

Cintra + Box 4
Laercio Redondo

Crèvecoeur
Jorge Pedro Nuñez

Gaudel de Stampa
Dove Allouche

Kalfayan
Stefanos Tsivopoulos

La Central
Nicolás Consuegra

Liprandi
Vijai Patchineelam

NoguerasBlanchard
Juan López

One and J.
Seung Yul Oh

Parra & Romero
Oriol Vilanova

PSM
Nadira Husain

Real Fine Arts
Mathieu Malouf

Tang
Wang Yuyang

Crèvecoeur
Jorge Pedro Nuñez

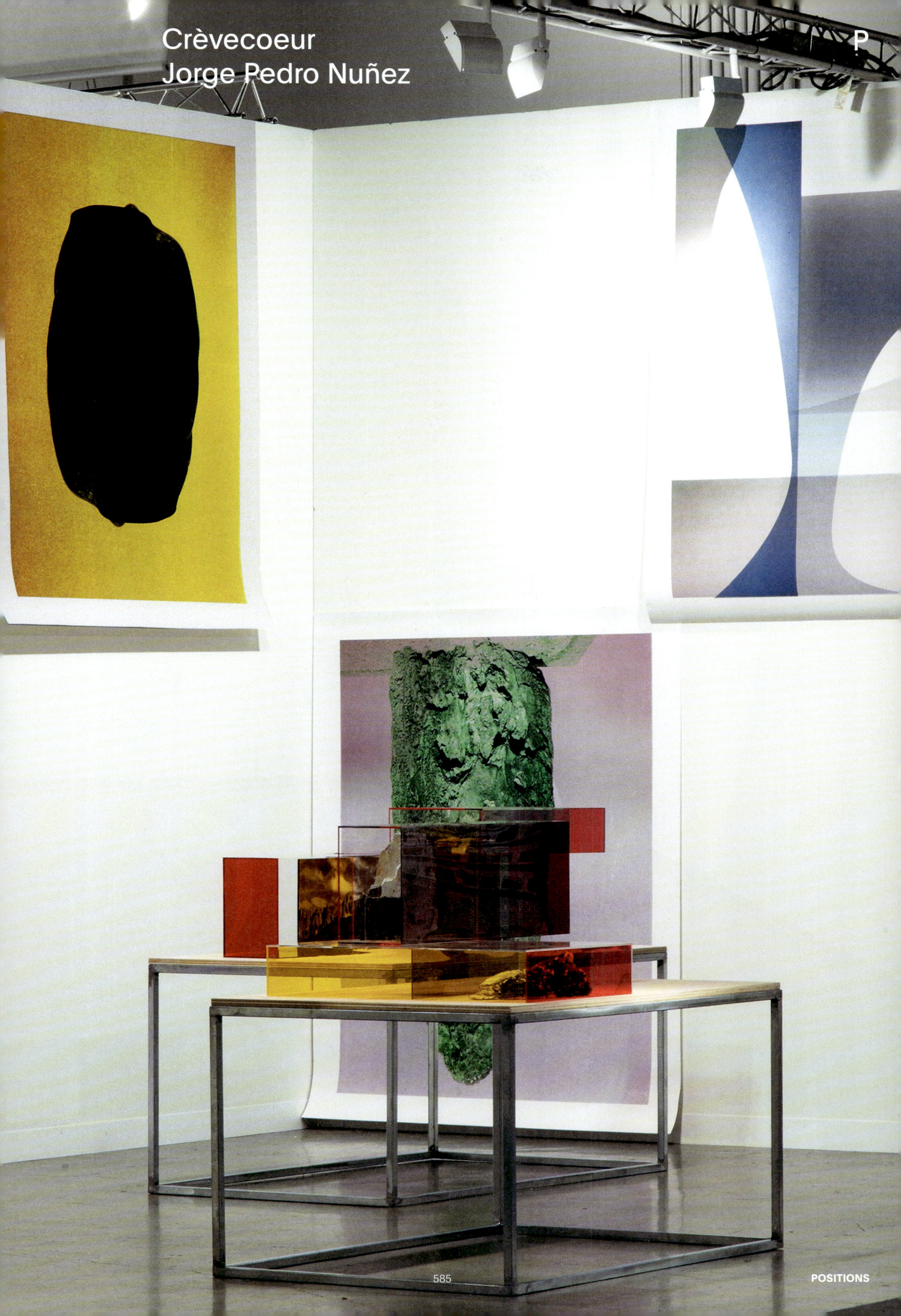

Bureau
Tom Holmes

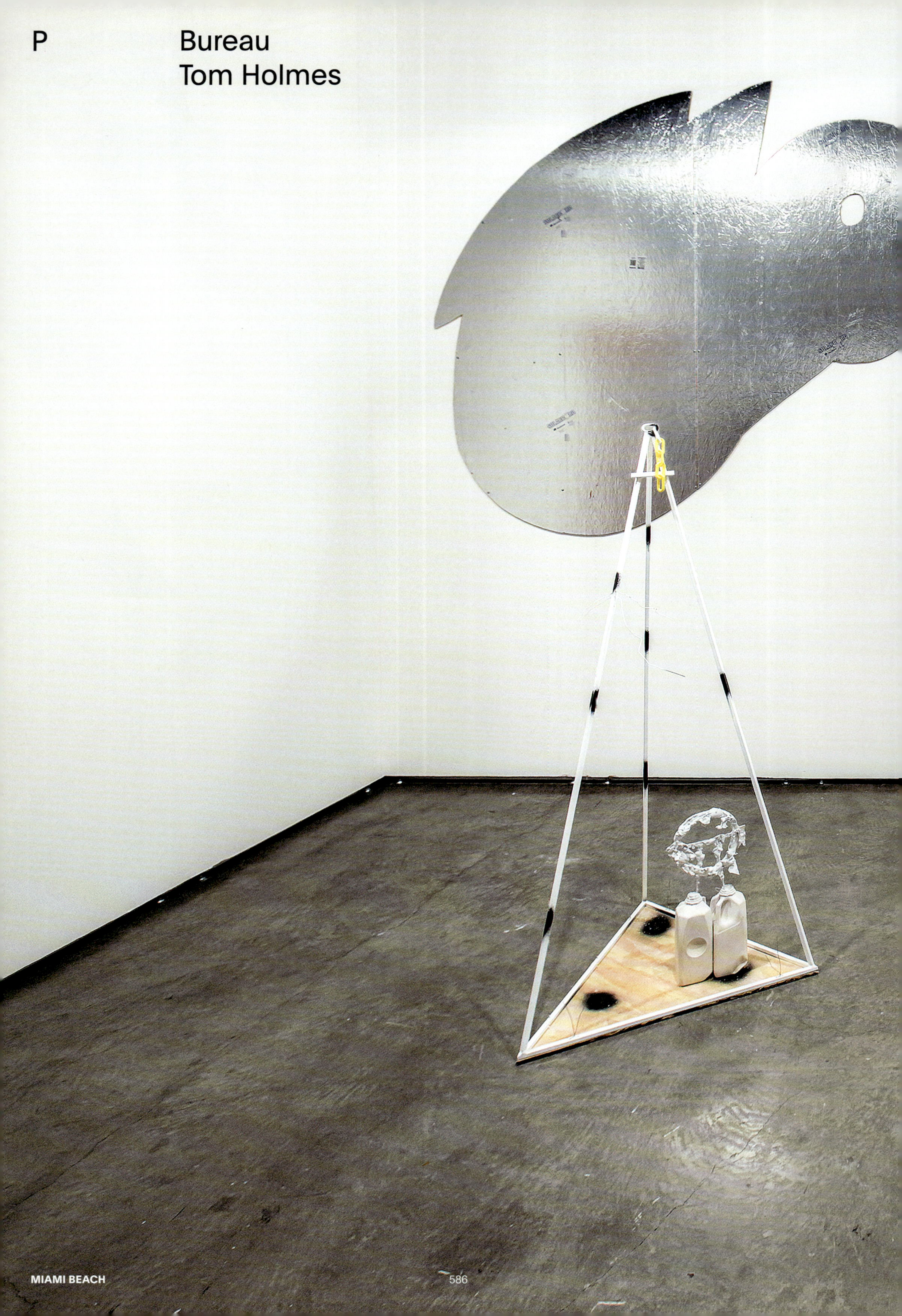

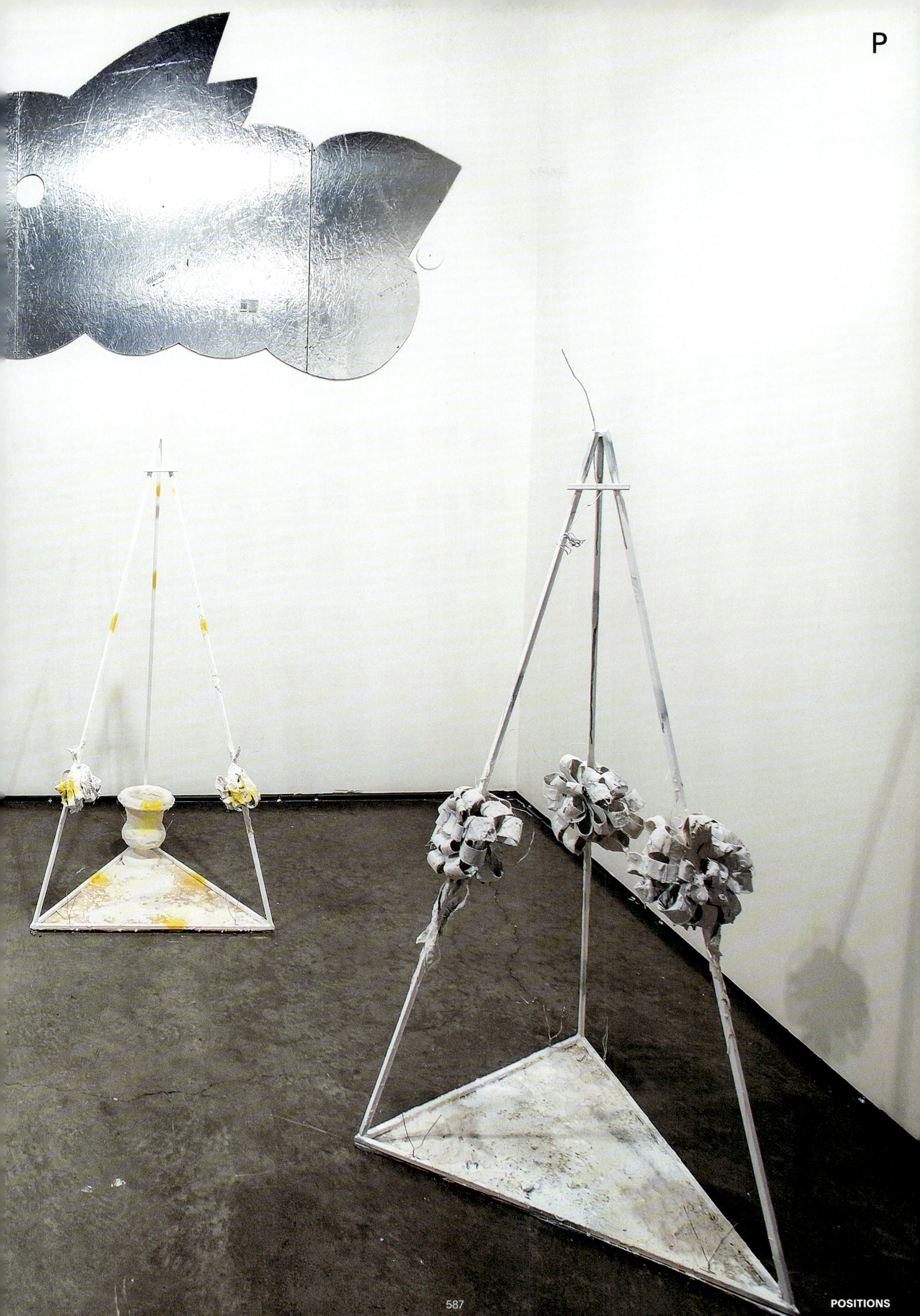

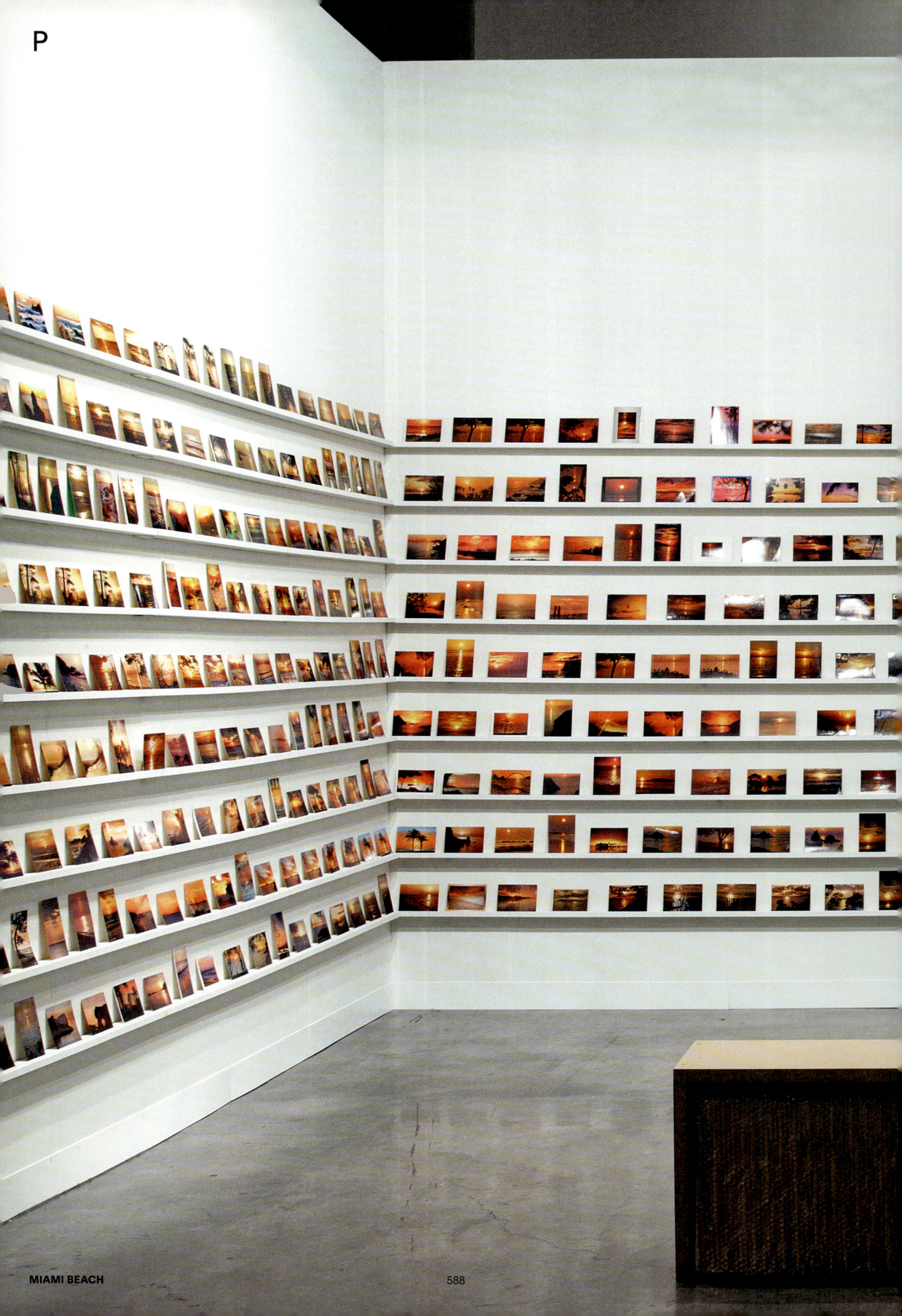

Parra & Romero
Oriol Vilanova
Sunset from …
2013

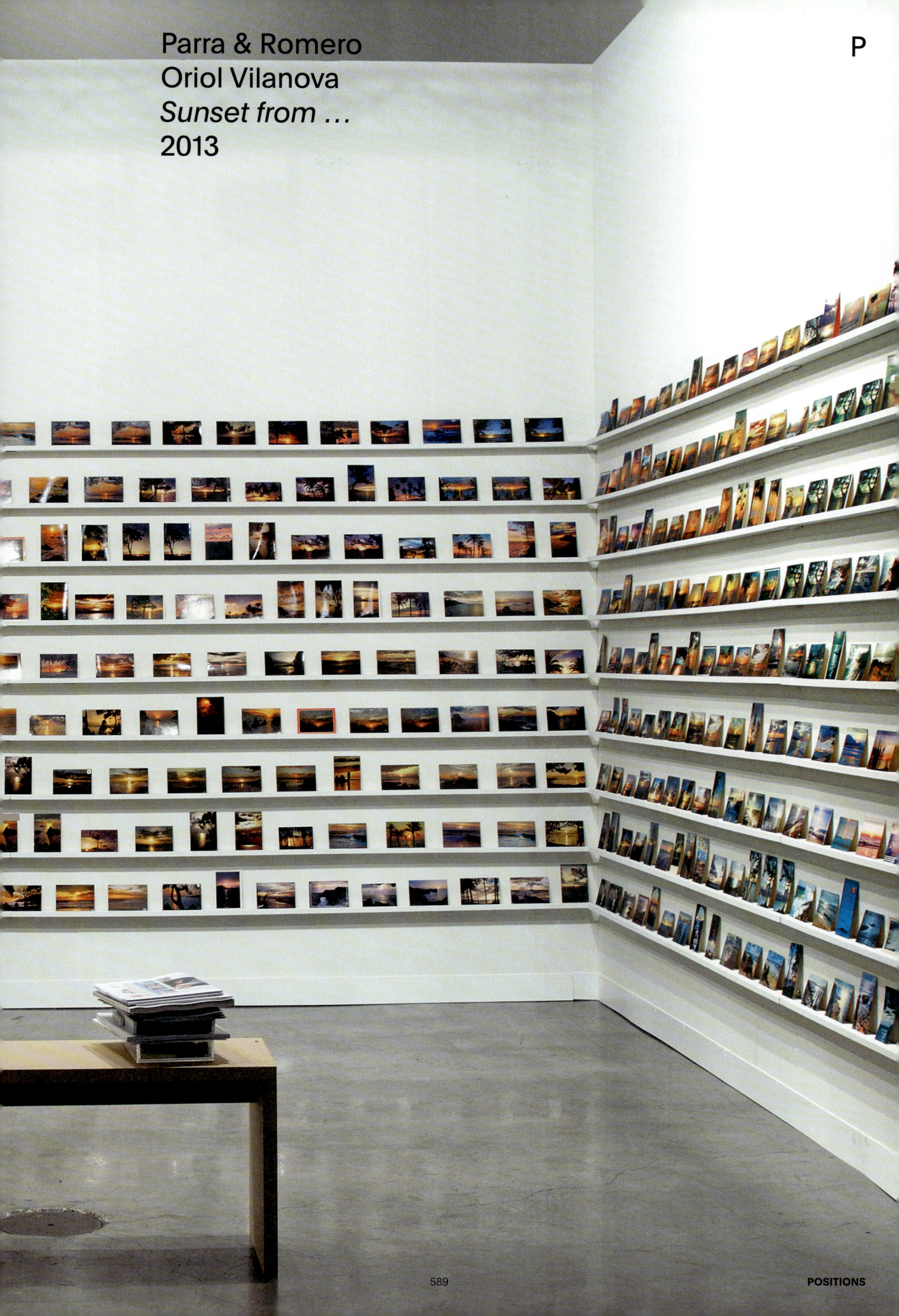

P

Tang Contemporary Art
Wang Yuyang
Breathing Series – Finance Department
2013

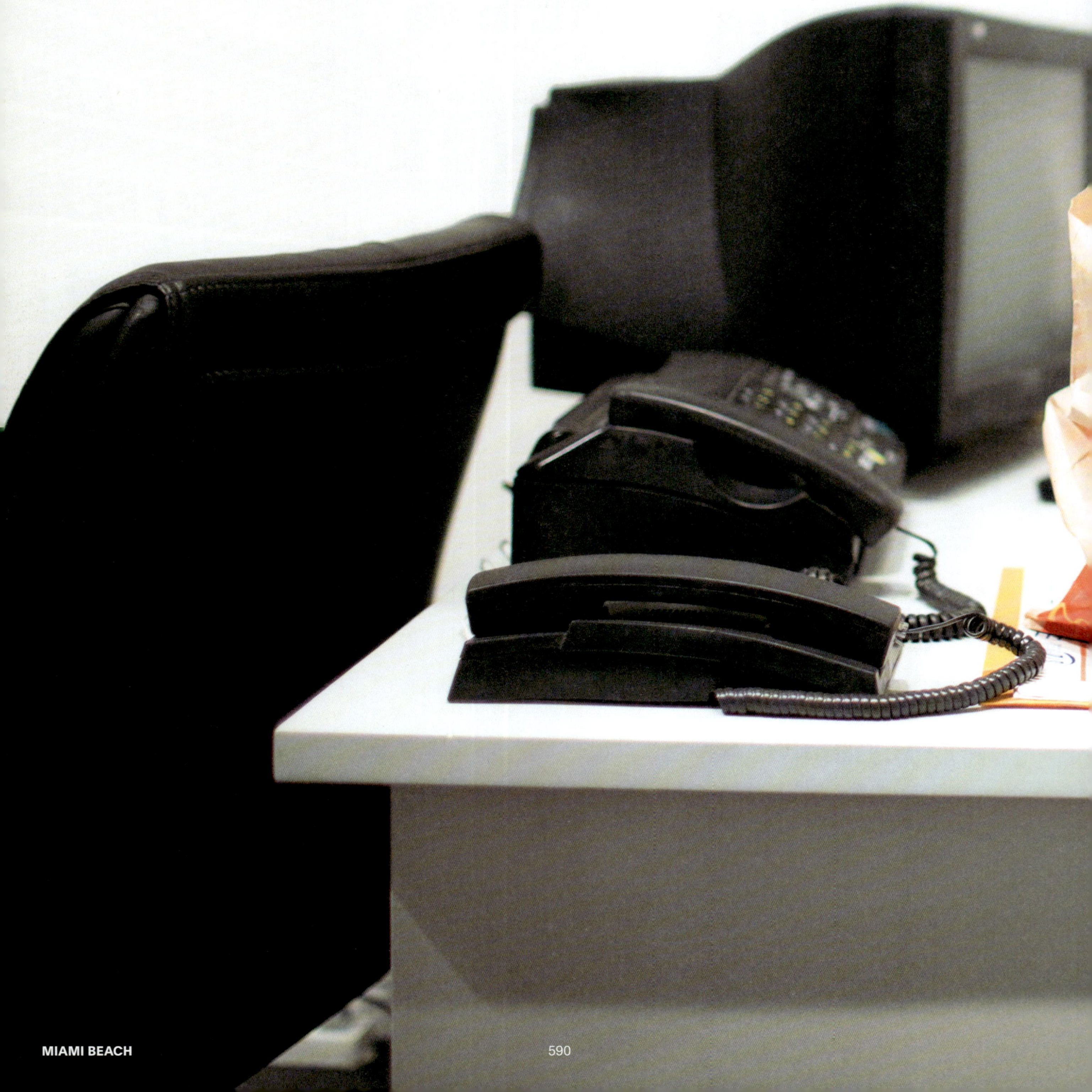

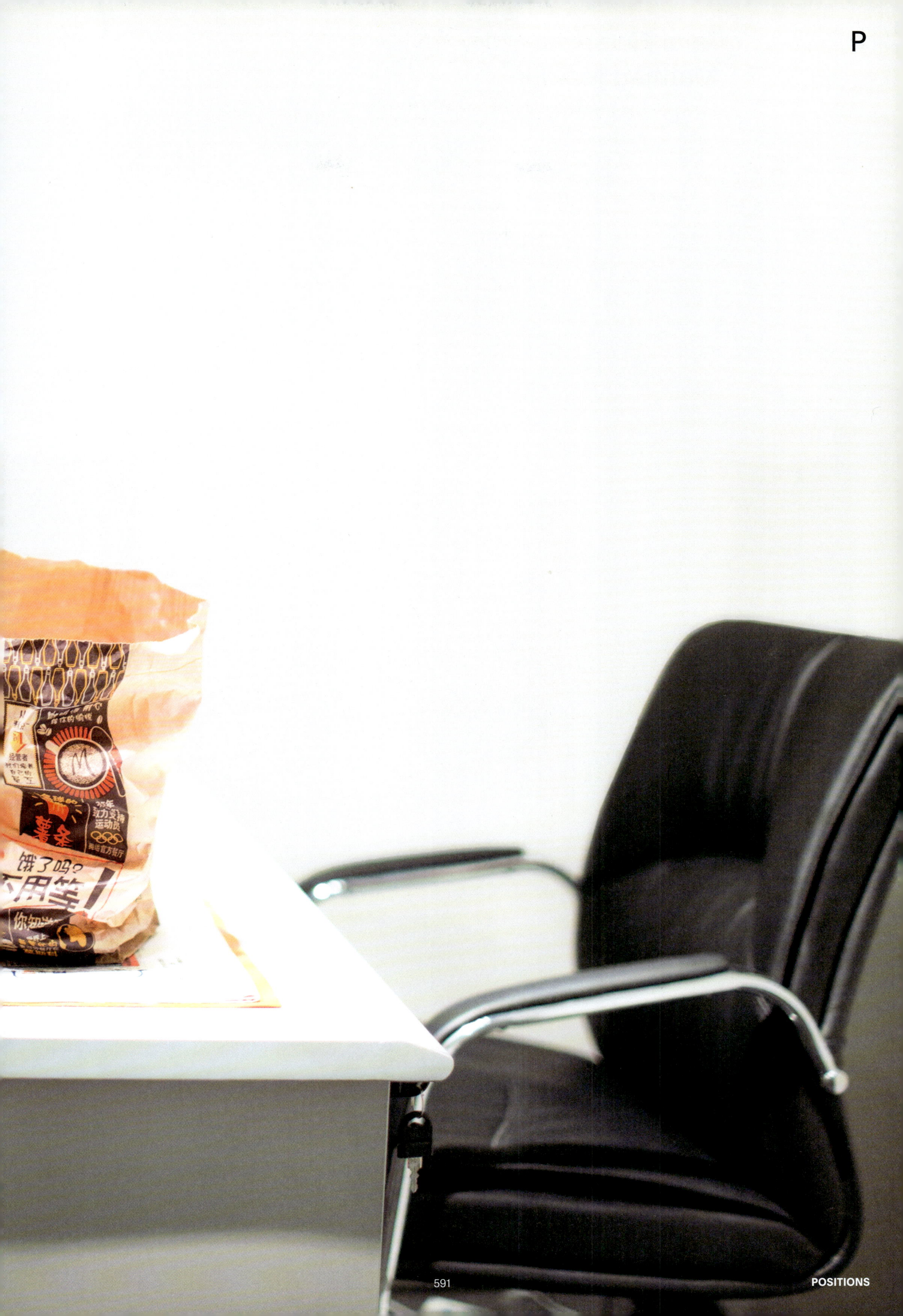
饿了吗?
薯条

P

Real Fine Arts
Mathieu Malouf

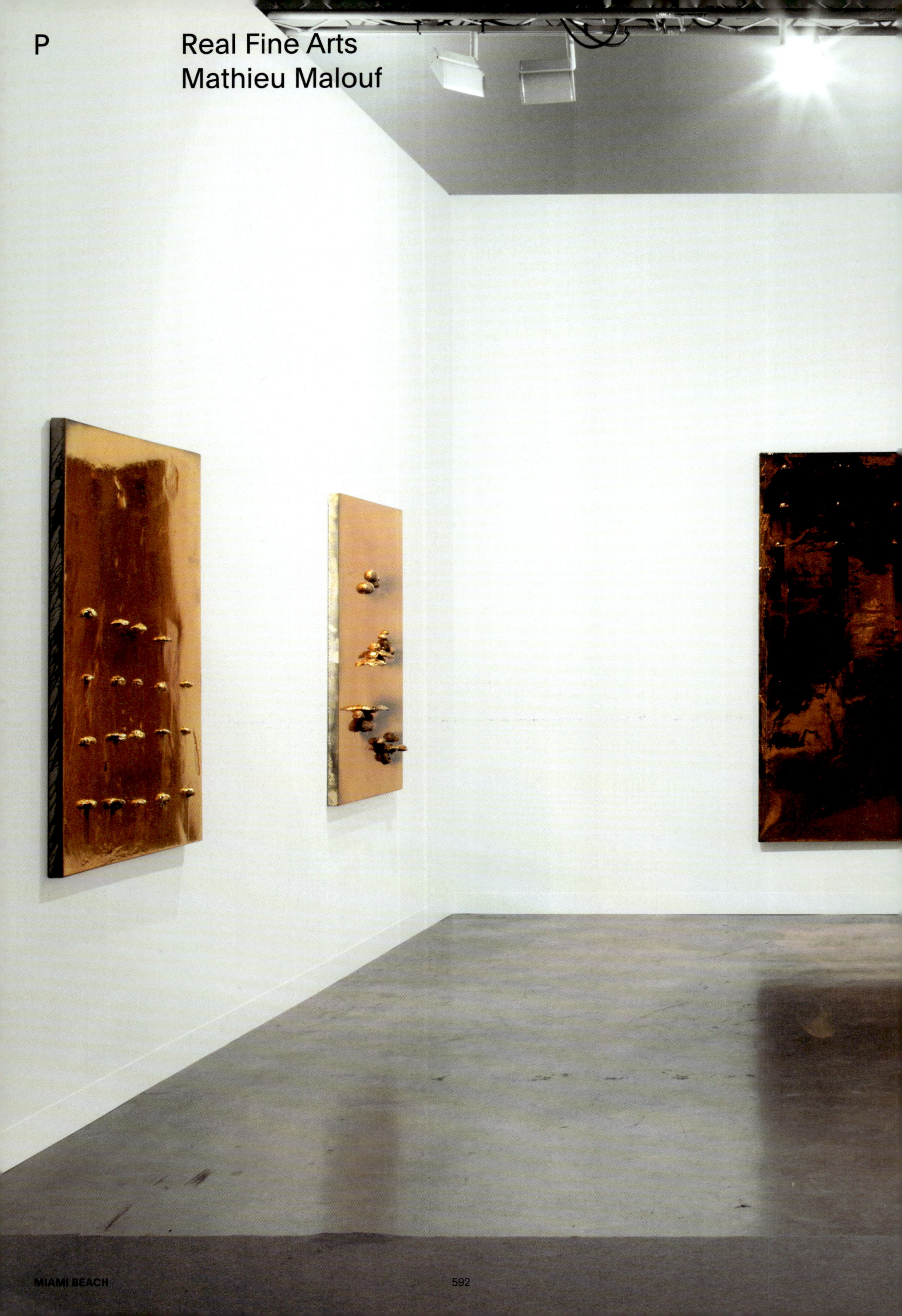

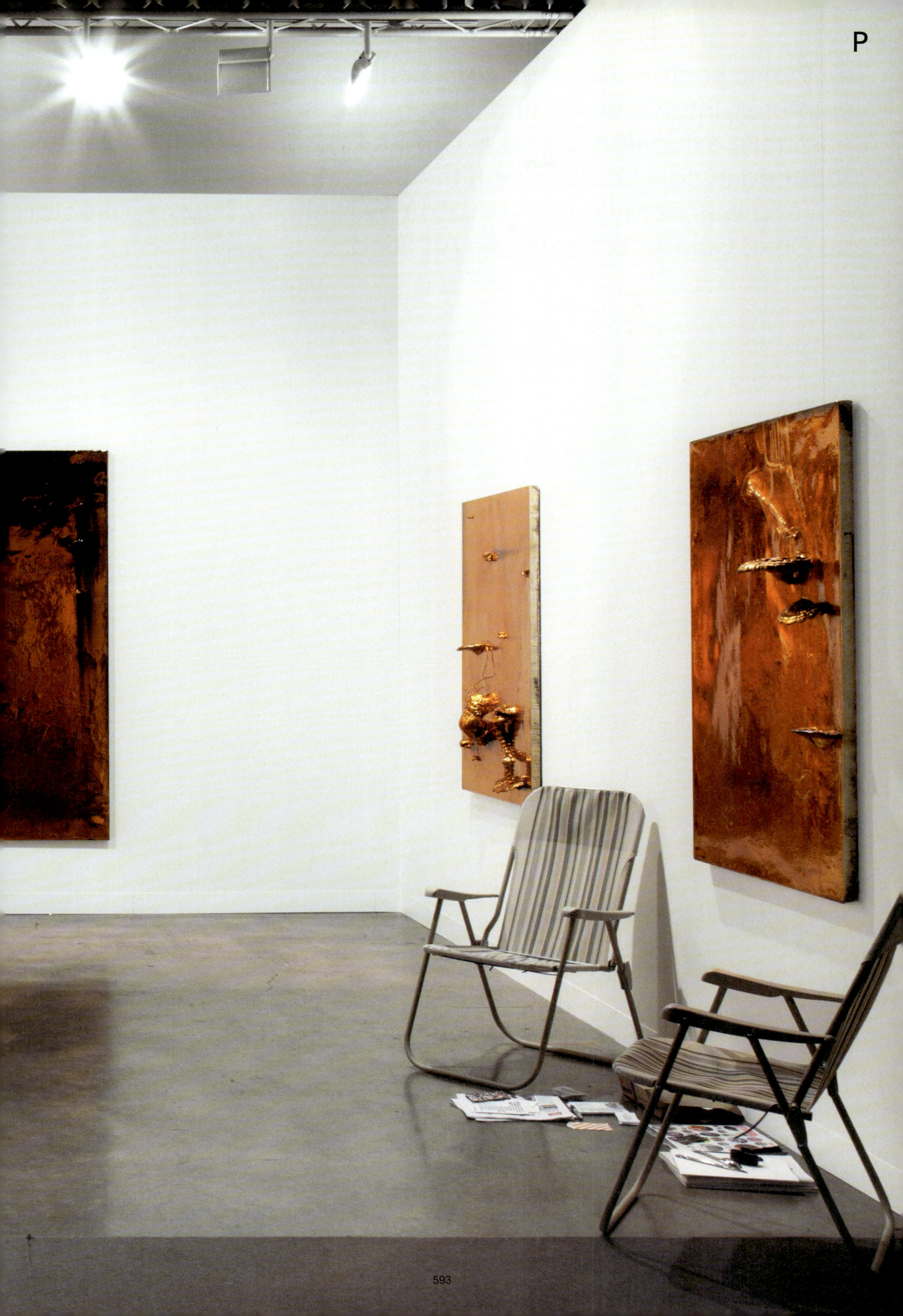

P

The Public sector offered visitors a chance to see outdoor sculptures, interventions, and performances sited within an open and public exhibition format at Collins Park. The sector has been produced in collaboration with the Bass Museum of Art since 2011, and was newly curated in 2013 by Nicholas Baume, Director and Chief Curator of the Public Art Fund.

2013 participants

Huma Bhabha
Salon 94

Carol Bove
Zwirner

Olaf Breuning
Metro Pictures

Aaron Curry
Kordansky

Mark di Suvero
Cooper
Berggruen

Matias Faldbakken
Lee
Cooper

Sam Falls
Presenhuber

Tom Friedman
Luhring Augustine
Friedman

Jeppe Hein
303 Gallery
König
Wallner

Thomas Houseago
Gagosian

Alicja Kwade
König
mennour

Richard Long
Sperone Westwater

Michelle Lopez
Preston

Matthew Monahan
Kern

Charlotte Posenenske
Chouakri
Freeman

Scott Reeder
Gupta

Santiago Roose
80m2

Tony Tasset
Gupta

Pascale Marthine Tayou
Continua

Mungo Thomson
elbaz

Oscar Tuazon
Presenhuber

Maarten vanden Eynde
Meessen De Clercq

Ursula von Rydingsvard
Lelong

Phil Wagner
Untitled

Performances during Public Opening Night by:
Olaf Breuning
David Colman
Kate Gilmore
Ryan McNamara
Mungo Thomson

PUBLIC

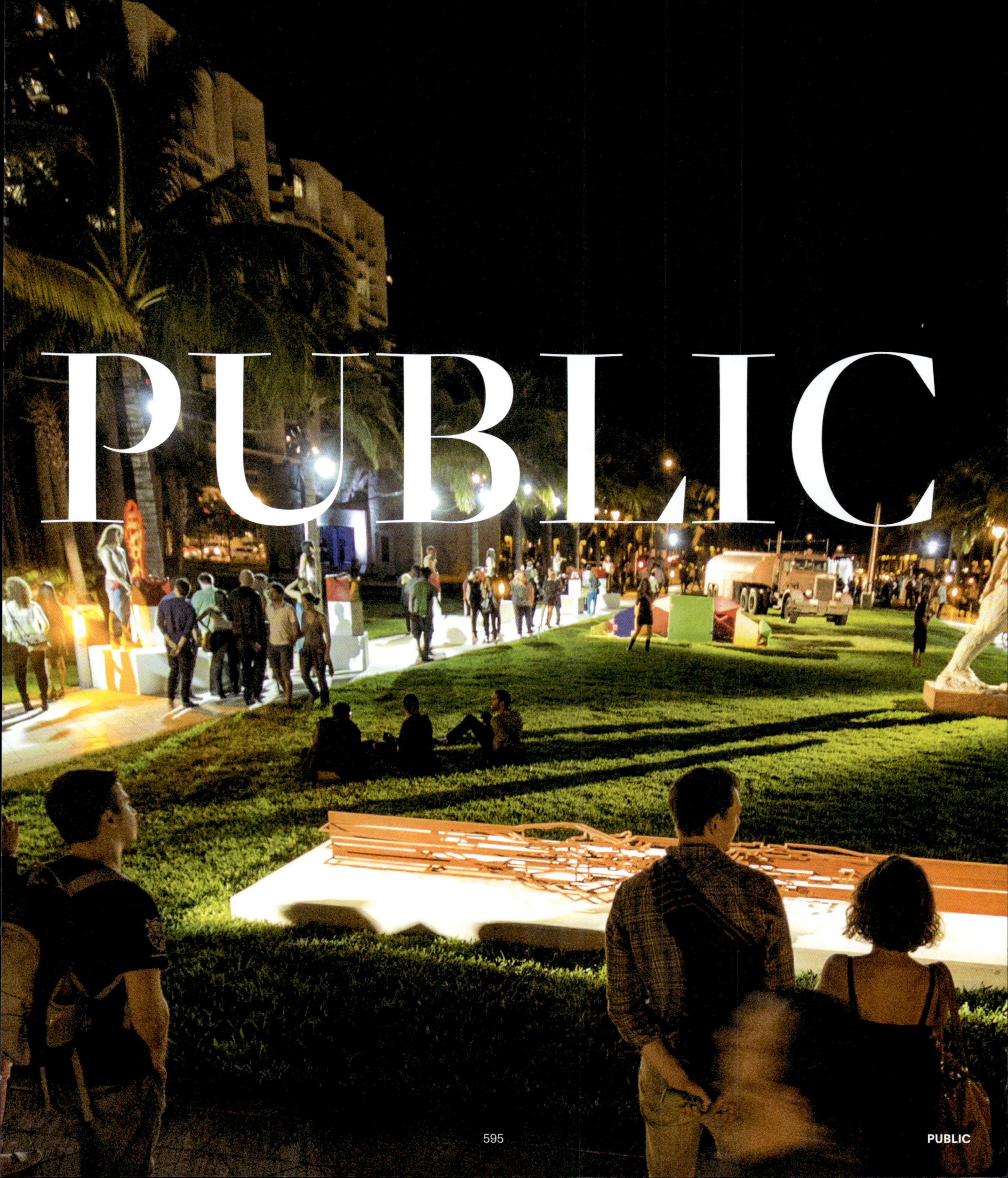

P

Aaron Curry
Untitled
2013

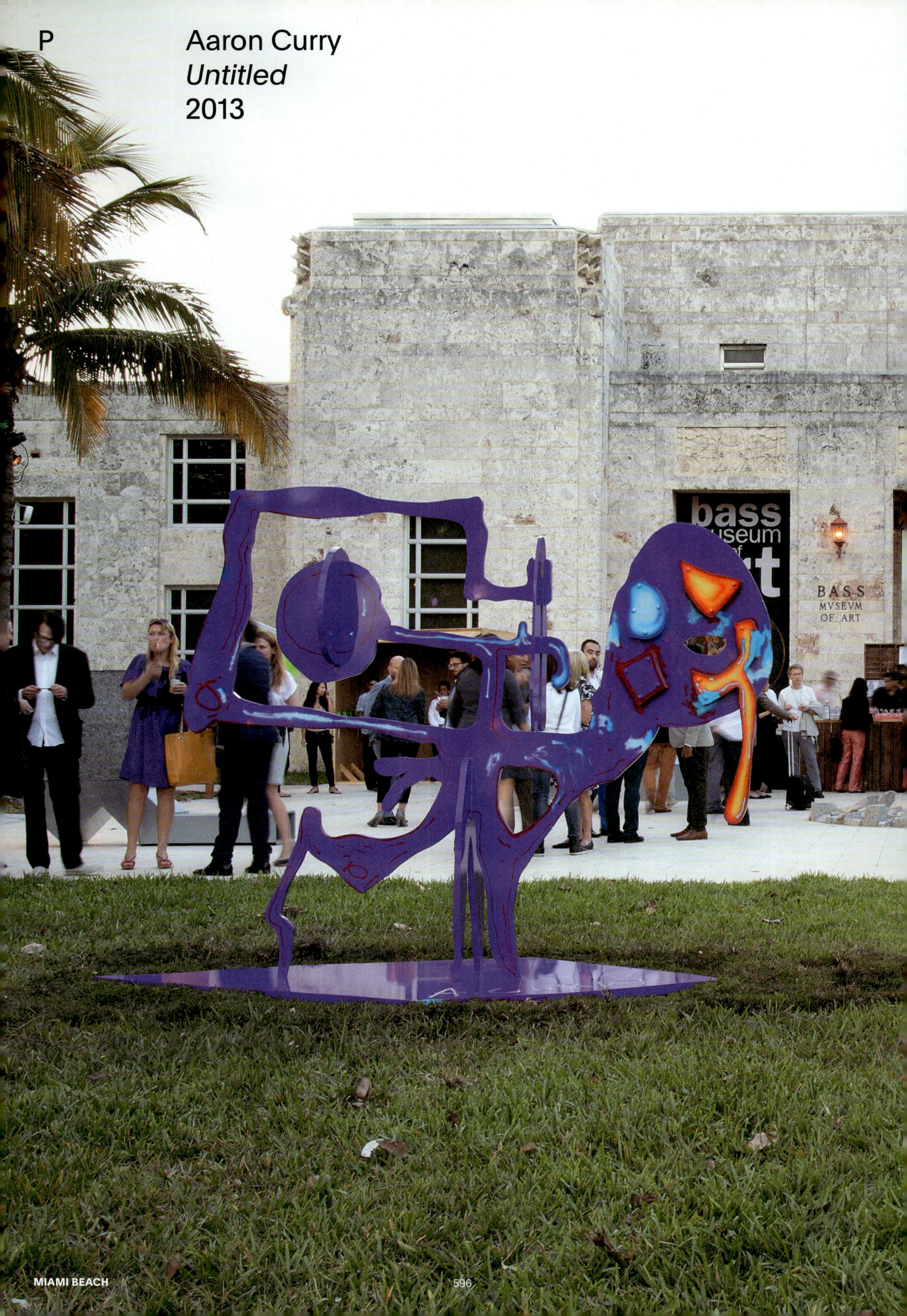

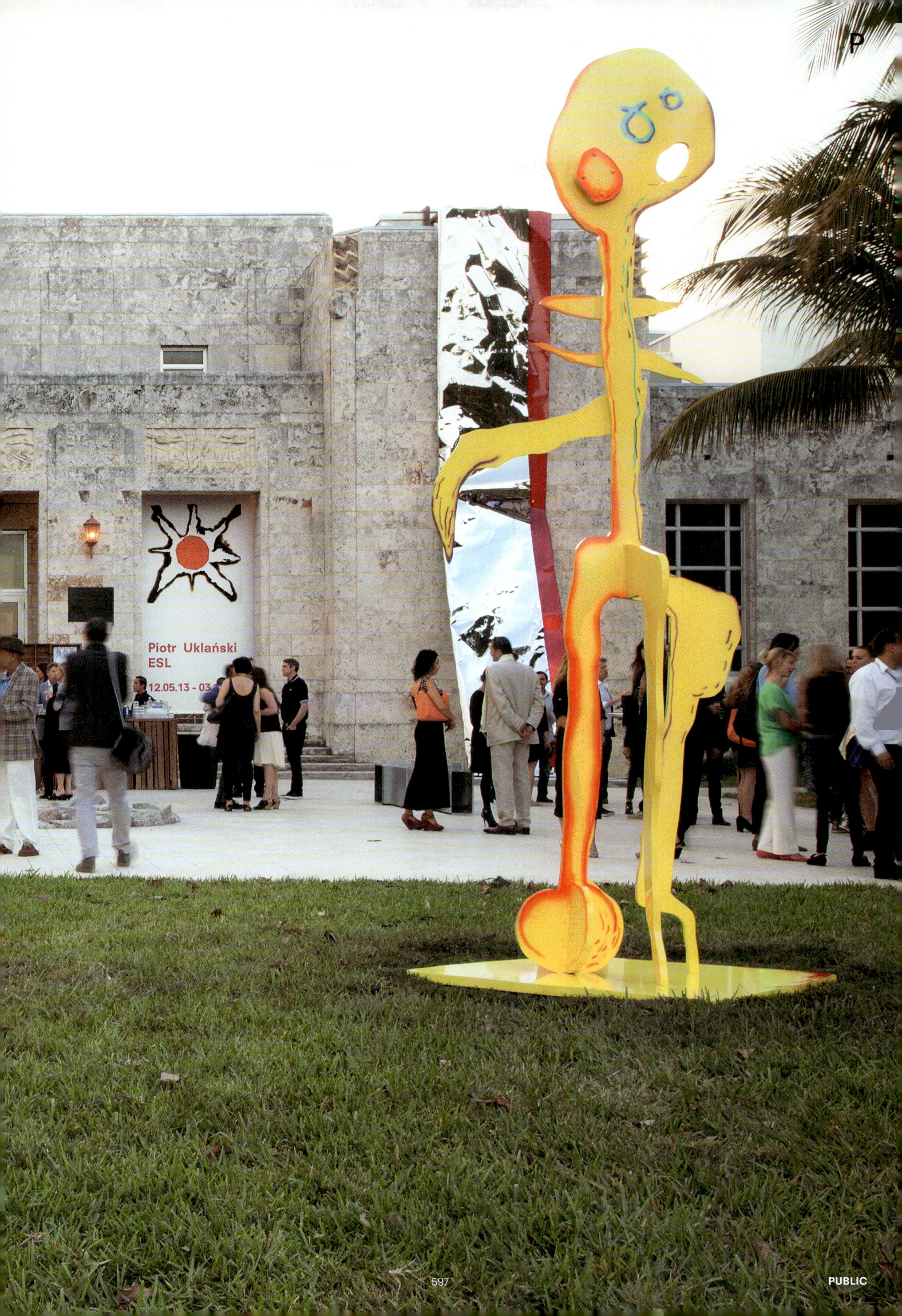
Piotr Uklański
ESL

P

Thomas Houseago
Striding Figure (Rome I)
2013

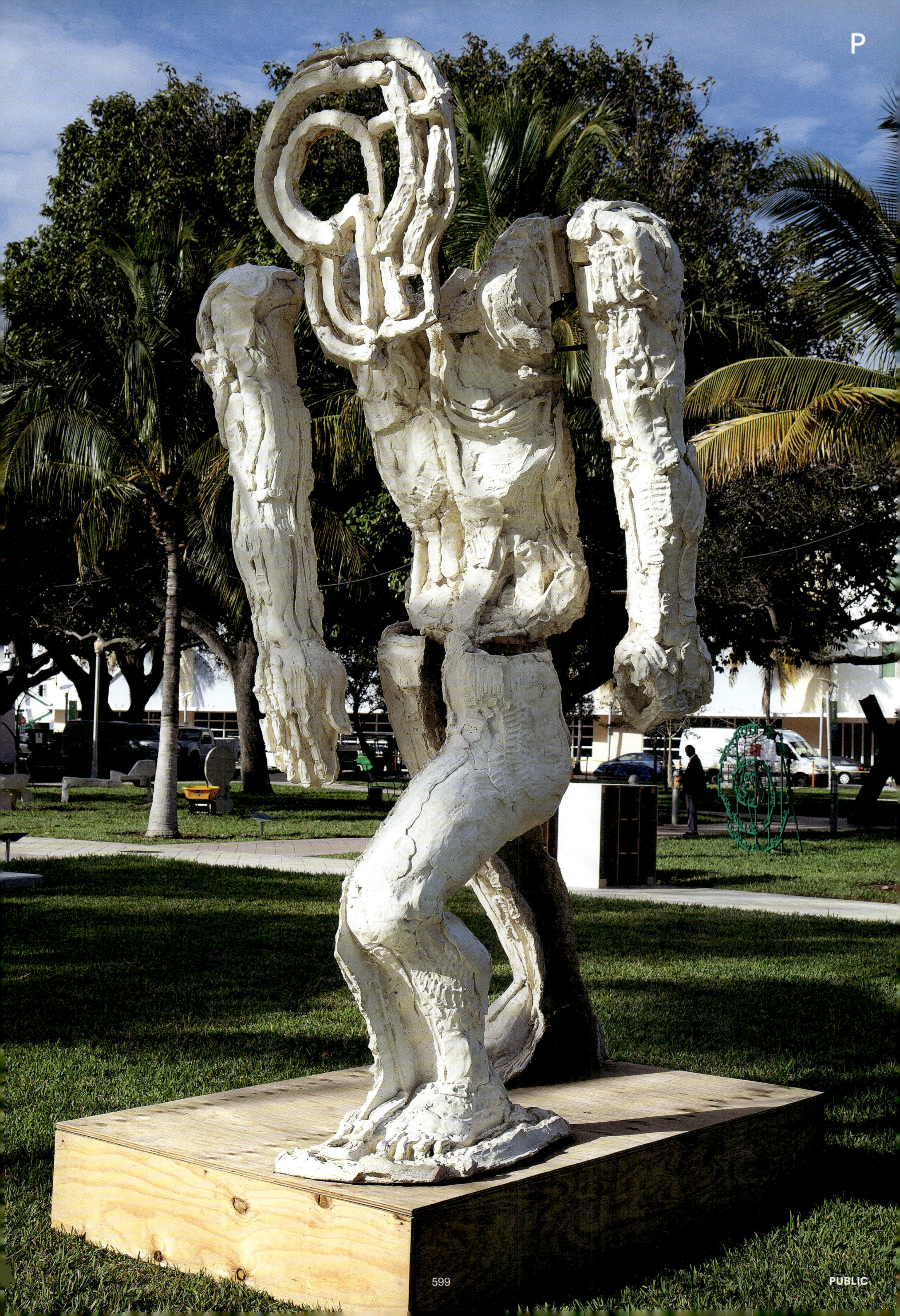

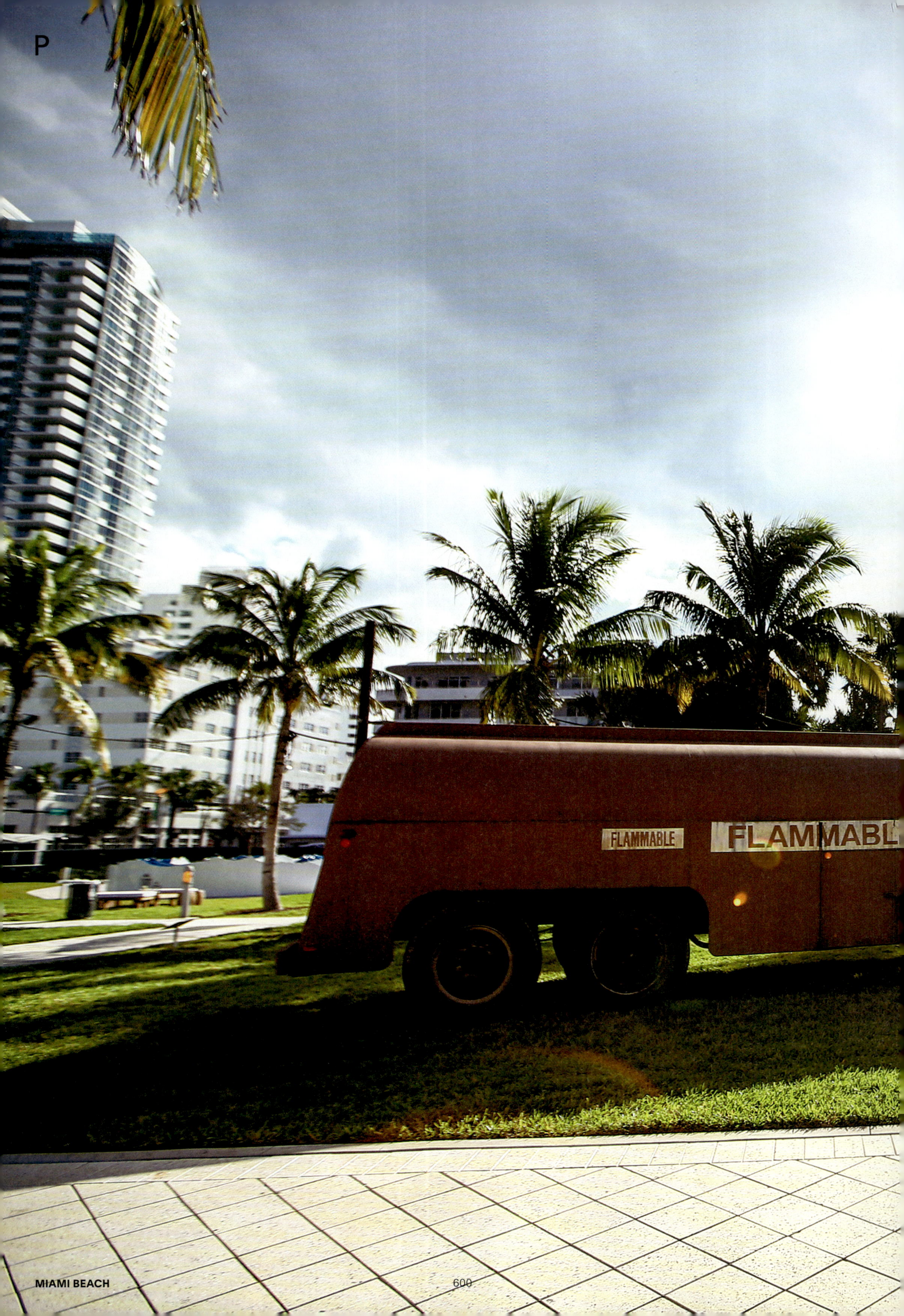
FLAMMABLE
FLAMMABL

Matias Faldbakken
Untitled (Duel Truck)
2013

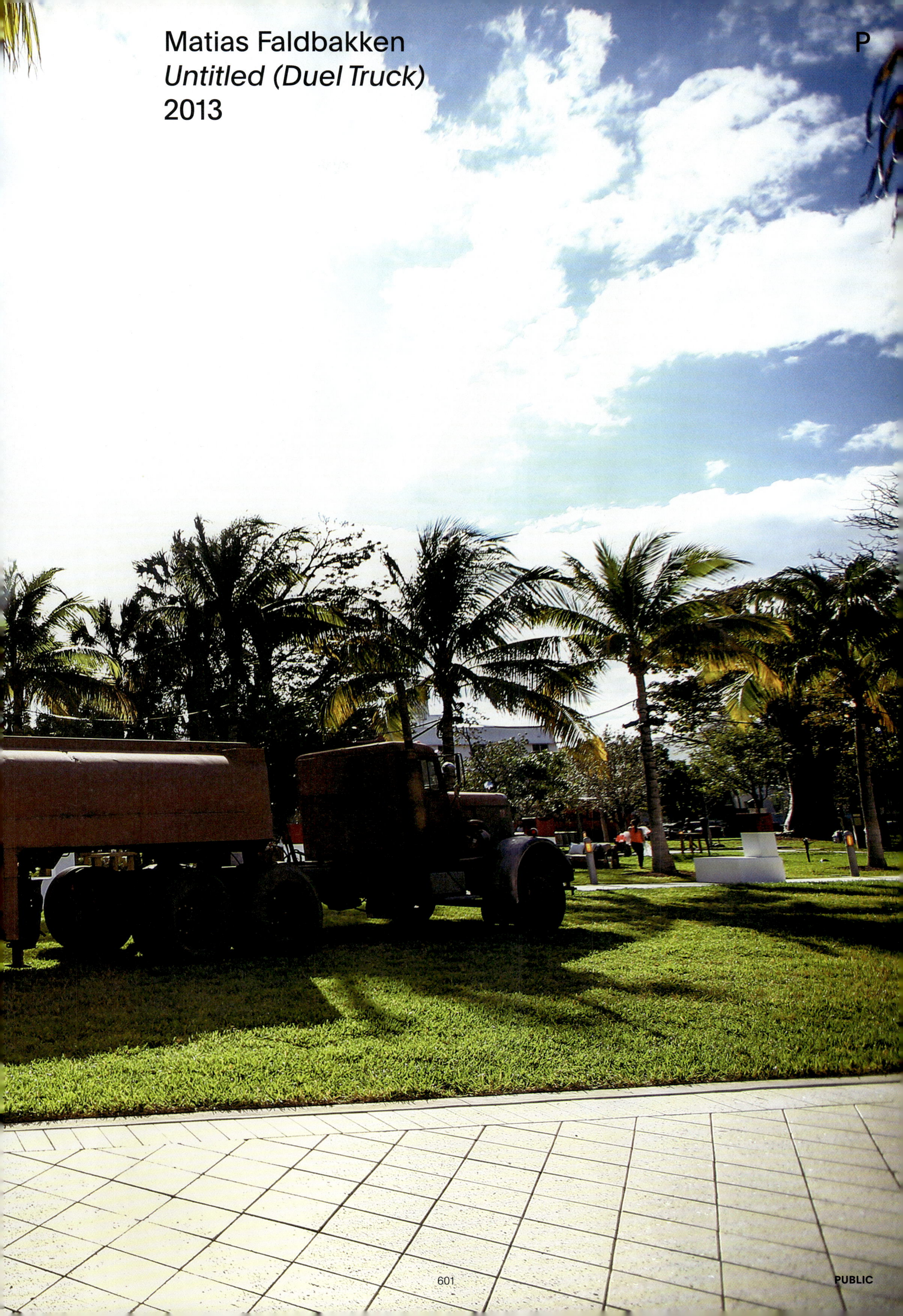

P

Mark di Suvero
Exemplar
1979

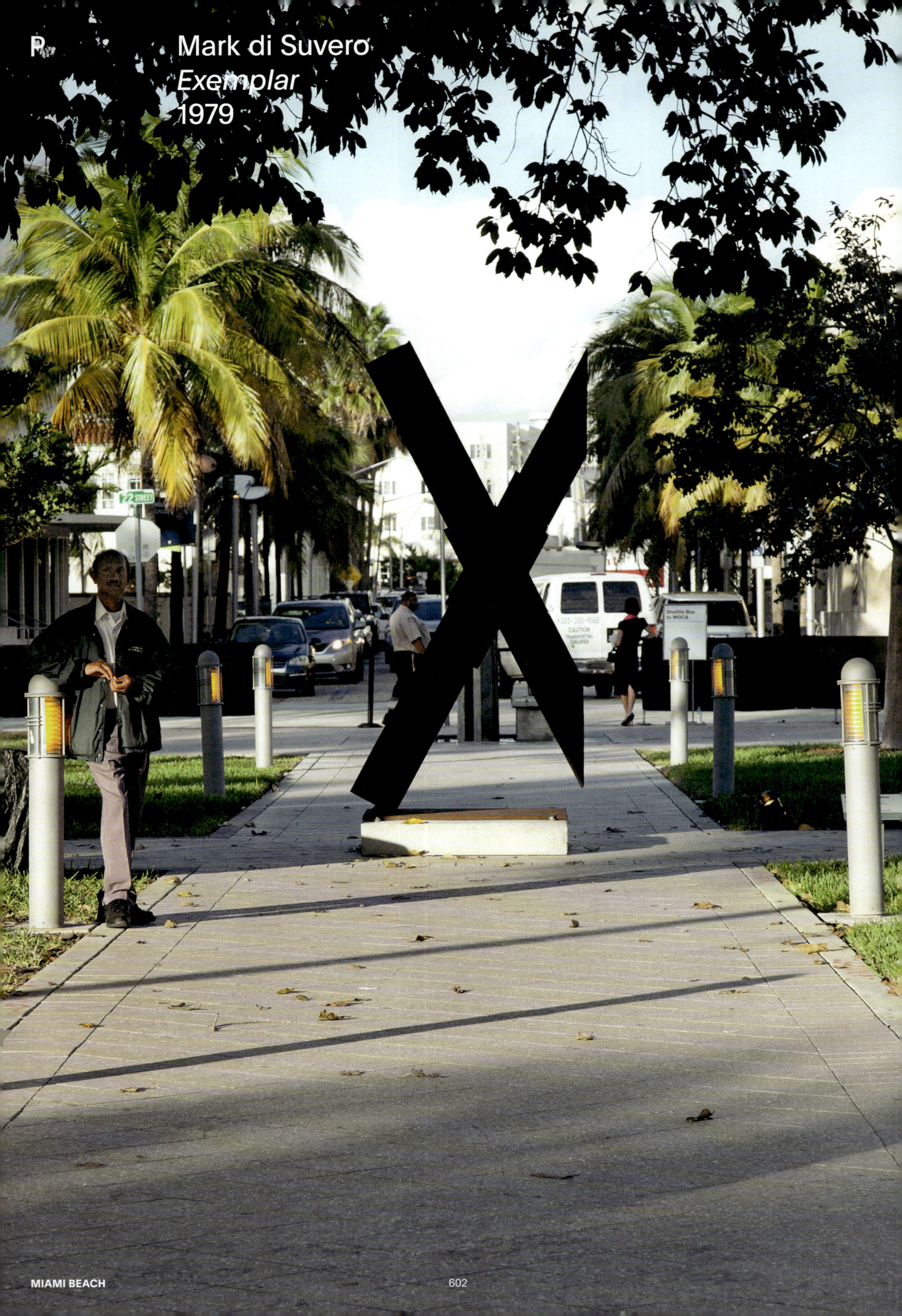

Mungo Thomson
Crickets Solo for Violin
2013

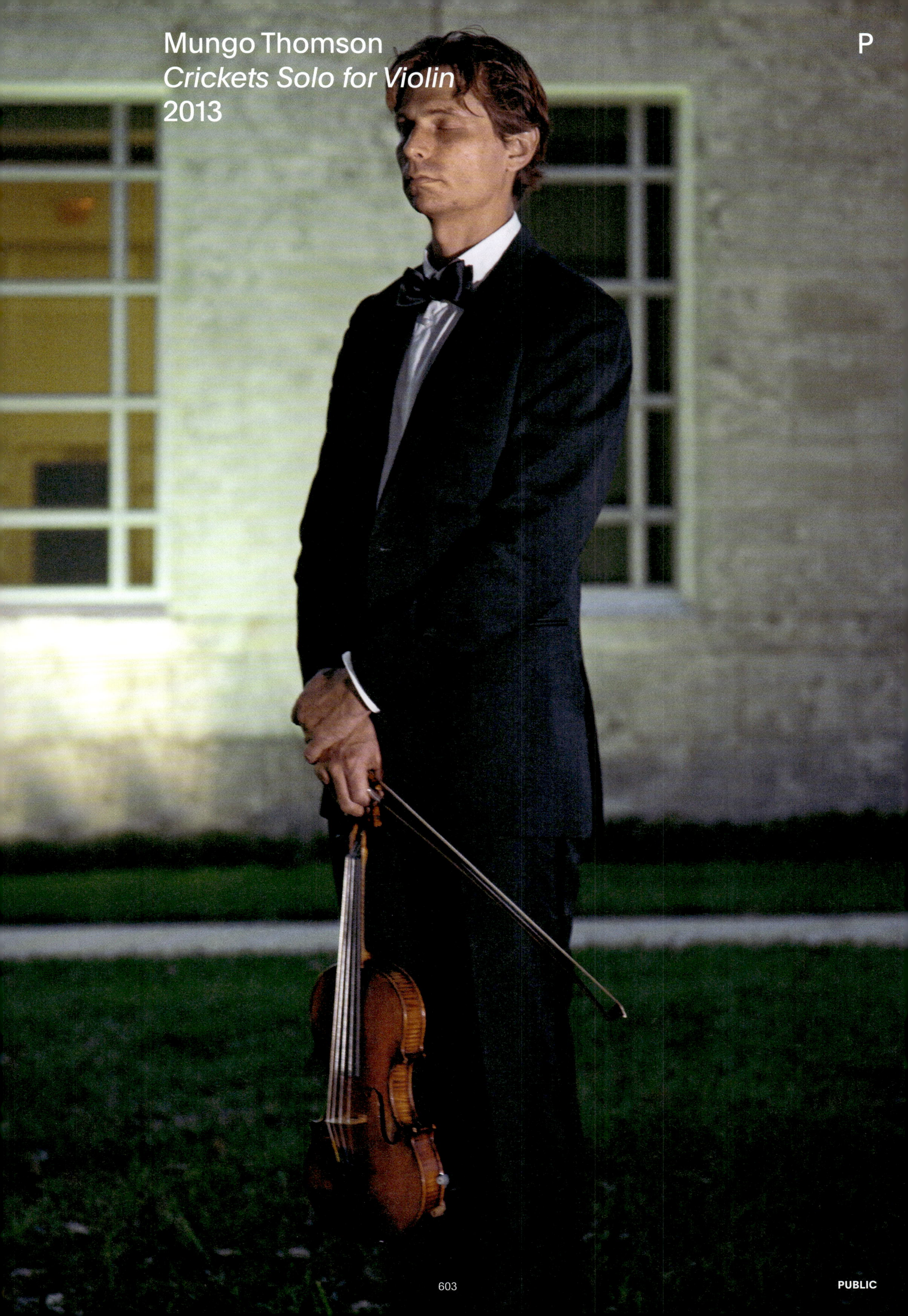

P

Jeppe Hein
Appearing Rooms
2004

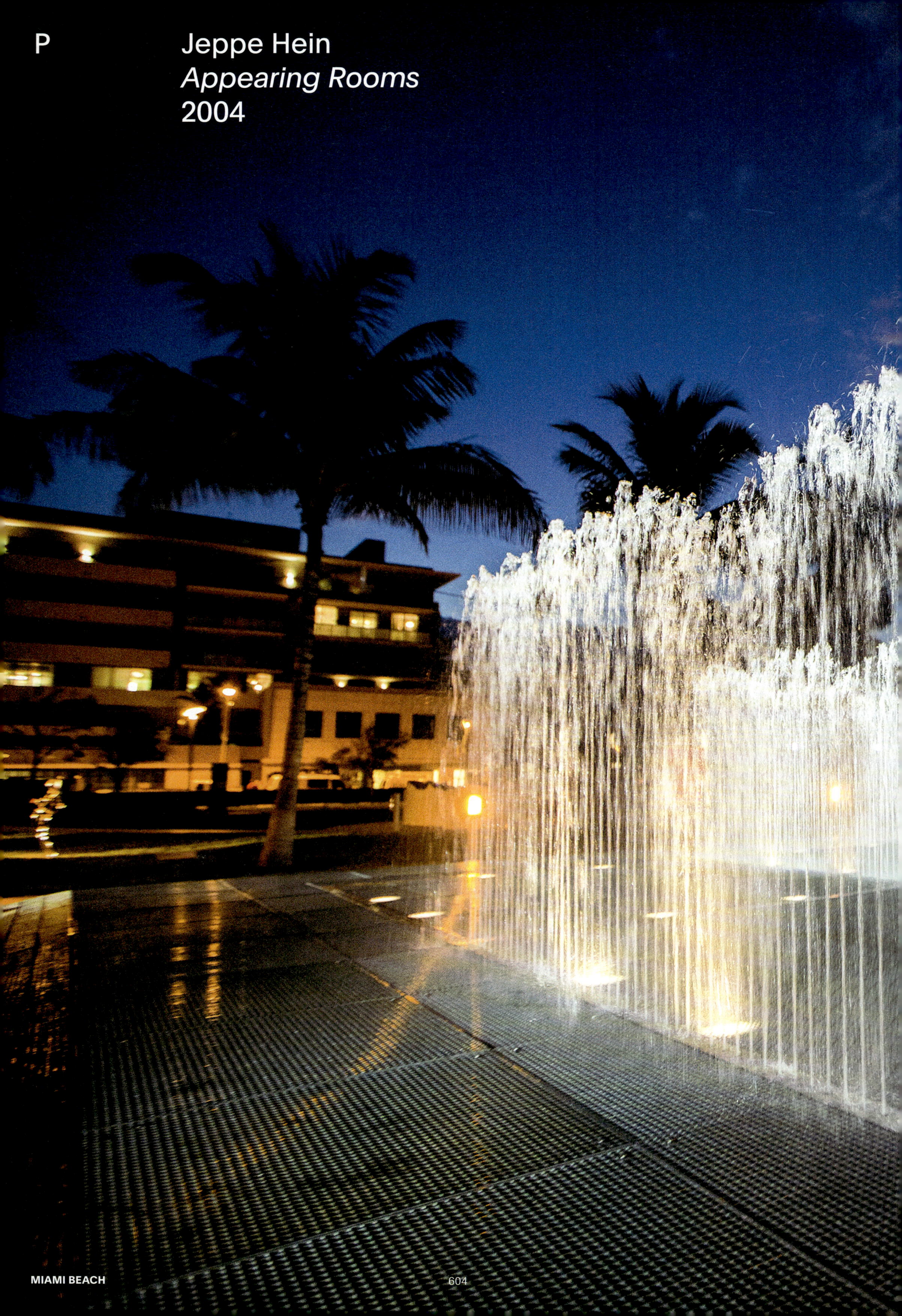

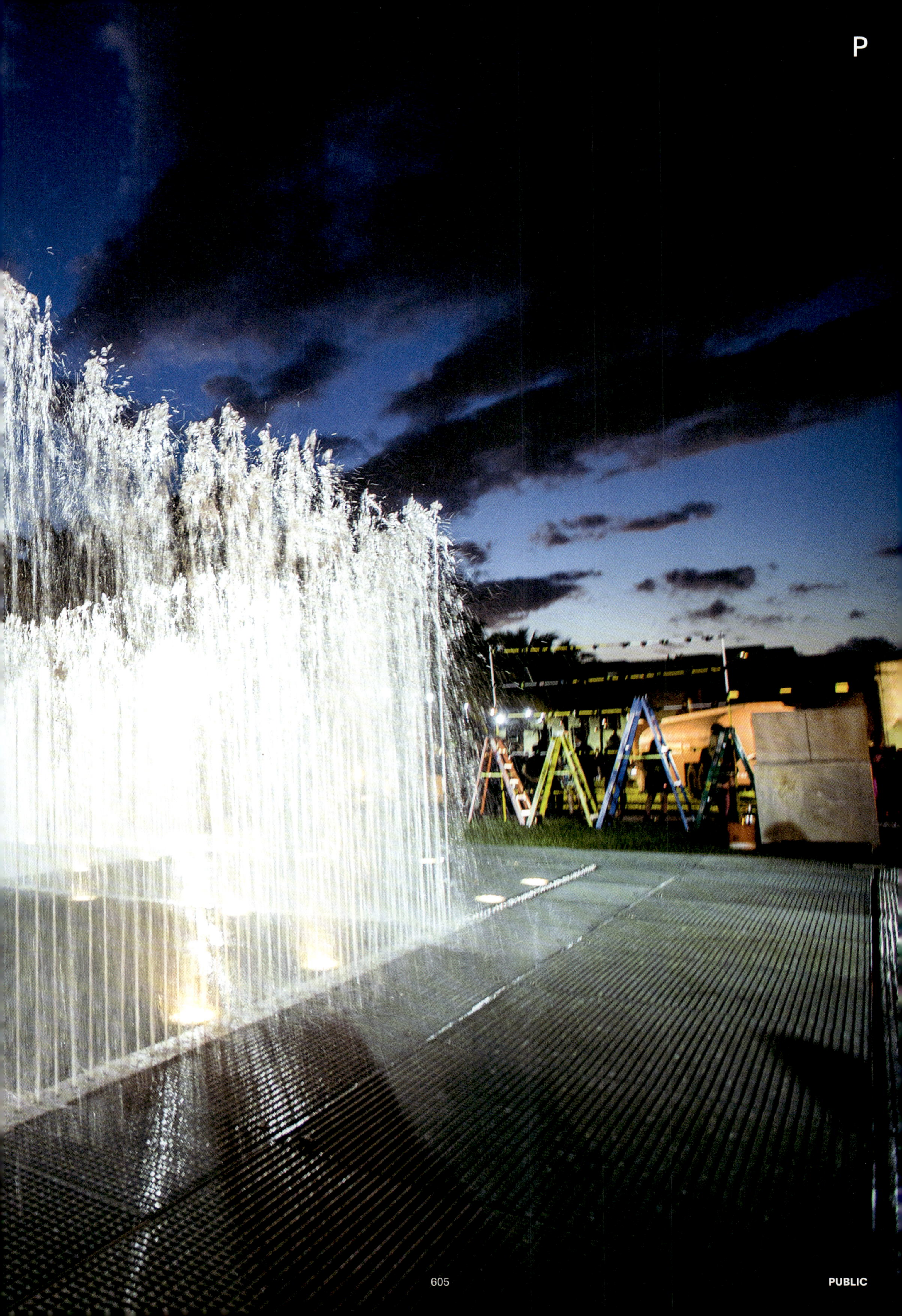

P

Public Art: Social Animals

Kate Gilmore, Alicja Kwade, Mungo Thomson, and Nicholas Baume

Conversations
Artist Talk

Miami Beach
December 5, 2013

Kate Gilmore, Artist,
New York

Alicja Kwade, Artist,
Berlin

Mungo Thomson, Artist,
Los Angeles

Moderator: Nicholas Baume, Curator of Art Basel's Public sector and Director & Chief Curator of Public Art Fund, New York

A complete version of the conversation is available at www.artbasel.com

NICHOLAS BAUME I was approached to curate Public having been a regular visitor to Art Basel in Miami Beach. It was interesting to think about how to curate in an art fair context, because my background is as a museum curator and now at the Public Art Fund in New York City, where we do exhibitions and commissions in the parks, plazas, and public spaces of the city.

Obviously the parameters are a little different: the participants have to be artists represented by galleries who are participating in the fair—the only exception being the performances we organized for the openings. And then, of course, there is Collins Park, which offers unique features: the Bass museum with its beautiful stone facade, the almost sculptural Baobab trees, the tropical feeling, the sense of abandoned nature and of the ocean very nearby, and an interesting layout with that quite classical avenue, flanked on either side by more curvaceous pathways.

So, it turned into thinking about how artists' work could engage and activate those different spaces—some very open and formal others more shaded and intimate—and how to think about the context of an art fair where, by definition, there is a very diverse and heterogeneous selection of works, artists, mediums, generations, and origins. At its best an art fair is about the collision, layering, and juxtaposition of works that you wouldn't normally think of putting together, thus creating dialogues and surprising correspondences.

I was thrilled that so many artists and galleries wanted to participate and bring major pieces. About half of the artists actually made new works for the exhibition. It became a really nice dialogue between classic works, pieces from the 1960s and 1970s, and some young artists. It's like a jigsaw puzzle when you have the work of these artists and you have to think about how you would put them together, not only to show the work to its best advantage, but to create an interesting dialogue with the landscape itself.

I called it *Social Animals*, a playful title. I wanted to think about the context here, because everyone associates Art Basel in Miami Beach with social events. To me it was interesting to think about what that actually means, what the social space is. A public park

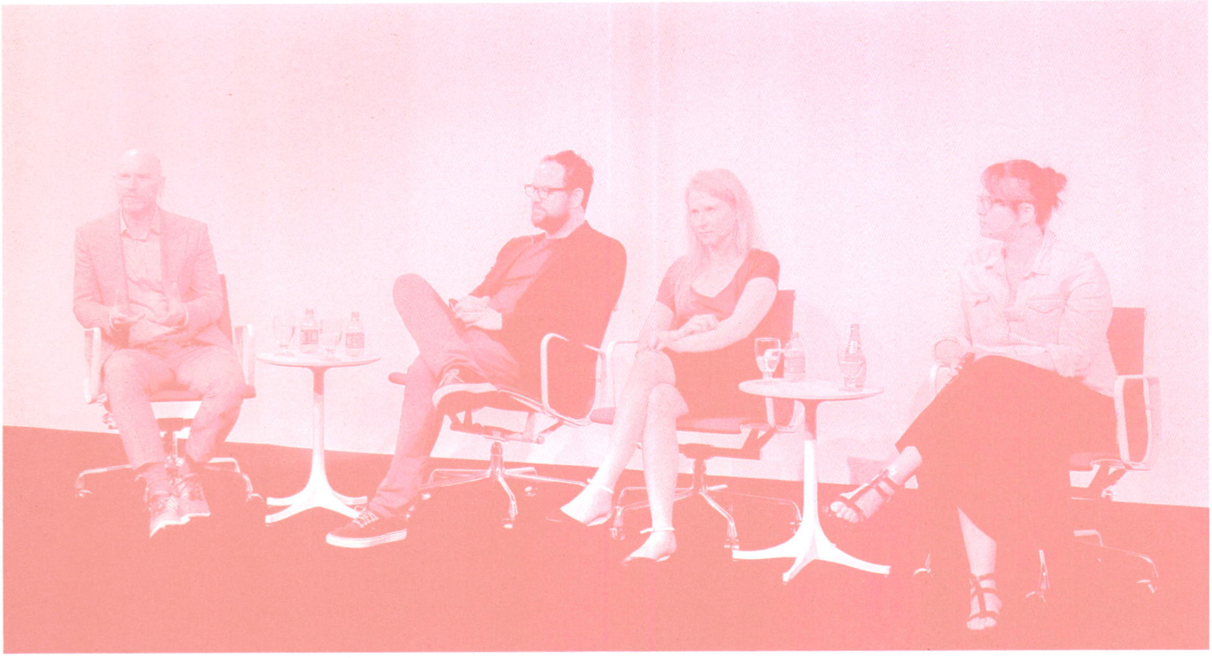

From left to right: Nicholas Baume, Mungo Thomson, Alicja Kwade, Kate Gilmore

of course is the quintessential social space. The work we do with Public Art Fund is all about offering a broad community the opportunity to see and engage with serious and contemporary artists' work. The social is the inherently human as Aristotle pointed out. The exhibition functions as a social space where the artworks speak among themselves, as if they were a community in conversation with each other during the course of the fair. Mungo Thomson's sound-based work is but one of these occurrences.

MUNGO THOMSON My project *Crickets* is a sort of multi-platform musical work that began in 2009. I collaborated with a composer to transcribe a few recordings of crickets from around the world for an ensemble orchestra, and it became an orchestral performance in Los Angeles and in New York. It also produced these "solos": throughout the process of recordings and performances, I managed to get little snippets of a violinist, clarinetist, flutist, or percussionist impersonating a single cricket, making sounds that could be mistaken for the sound of a cricket.

I've been installing these indoors and outside on speakers. When my gallery proposed the speakers for the park (you can hear the clarinet in the bushes and so on), Nicholas said, "let's do a performance, let's get ambitious with it!" Art Basel was kind enough to fly me here with four musicians who all have previously performed the project elsewhere, and we scattered them around the park to play cricket solos.

The significant difference between the audio work and the performance is simply that you can see the player and that this is not a cricket sound, but you still sort of drift into a fantasy state where it might be. The work deals with these distinctions between sound, noise, and music, music as a kind of organized sound, and your position when you experience this phenomenologically.

KATE GILMORE I also did a performance piece [*Only One Like You*, 2013]: we had 12 performers who look alike, men and women, tall, skinny, with long brown hair; the women flat chested, the men rather thin. On the first opening night they were wearing blue jeans, no shirts, work boots, and a red bandanna tied however they wanted. They were on bases where red (the color of vendetta) steel cubes stood, and they sledge hammered these big cubes throughout the evening, for two hours. On the next night, because it was open to the public, they had a white tank top on. The gist of the piece is that these people look alike, performing this action on these objects that are transformed through their physical interaction.

NB What are the differences from your perspective on presenting such a work in a museum or gallery space, compared to places like Collins Park? Do you think people respond to it differently? Does it make you think about the work differently?

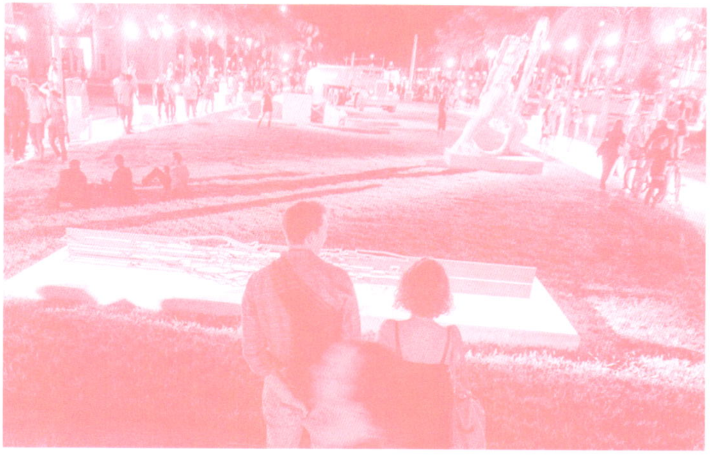

Alicja Kwade, *Pulse of Time*, 2013

KG For me this is an ideal place because you get such a large and diverse group of people to attend. You get a chance to make it a jarring experience, but also an experience that is about talking about what it means to make art. There are no rules in public parks. In museums no one is going to take a sledgehammer after the piece is done and destroy it. You can't control the audience in the same way. There's a major risk factor in it; and often the performers are working with people they don't really know, so you don't know how they will react. You could have some crazy person come up and mess up your entire piece, but in another sense it adds to the excitement of making works in these kind of environments.

ALICJA KWADE I think for me it's always a big challenge to do an outdoor sculpture, because in a museum or gallery you have a secured space around the work. I have this typical white cube in mind, where you just need to place something anywhere and people are expected to go there, most of them are educated about art and know how to read it. In the public space people have no expectations about what they have to think, or about how they should react. Also, in a park elements are unpredictable. To me, that's very interesting and very challenging.

My work is a lot about structures of reality and how social agreement works. *Pulse of Time* (2013) is about time: the bronze lines here refer to the various time zones of the world. The work represents a concept that was invented in the 19th century, when the railway became central to public travel: a system was needed to make it work and the world was divided into 25 zones by straight lines. Because of country borders and trade issues, those lines started to change—they are not straight any-more, they have all these extensions. The system is still not fixed, it changes every year depending on political and economic decisions.

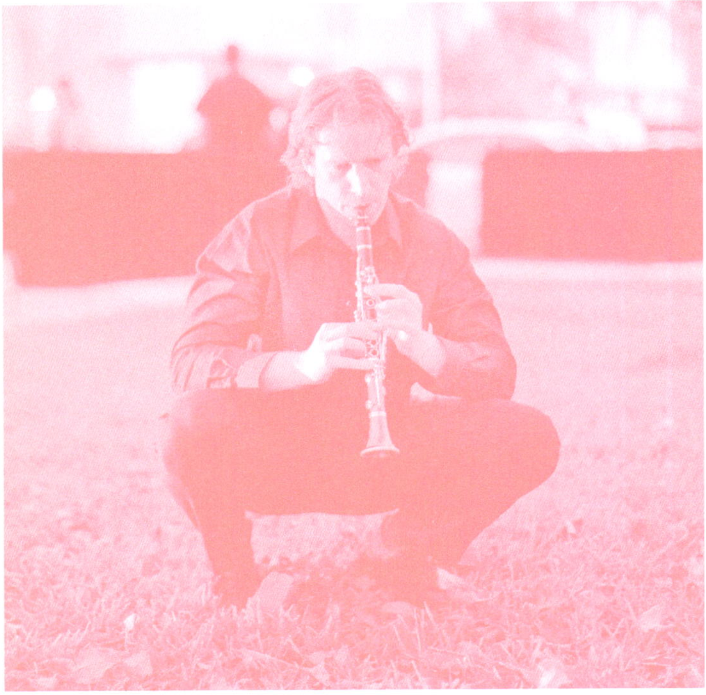

Mungo Thomson, *Crickets Solo for Clarinet*, 2013

NB There's a dynamic in the public space. With a sculpture like yours, Alicja, one gets very different effects depending on the shadows and the sun—if it's bright or cloudy. There's this abstract sense of codifying natural phenomena; how we, as humans, try to classify time.

AK Yes, there's this juxtaposition of natural elements and crazy systematic concepts.

MT I've done a lot of public works, but I'd never done an outdoor sculpture. I work in a pretty context-sensitive way and I try to make things that are adaptable—the *Crickets* piece is a sound work, a video work, there's a written score in a book that will be published, and then some performances, and speaker works, and now these solo performances. It keeps shedding these little organisms. I think there's a distinction to make between outdoor and public. I think of exhibitions as public. But the context of the gallery is of course changing with the art fairs and so on, and they are increasingly less democratic (the way a public park is). I'm interested in all these contexts and in negotiating with them on site, on the ground.

NB Obviously in a gallery you wouldn't expect to hear crickets, whereas when we were figuring out where to put them, I was hearing them for the first time in nature, and some of them were so convincing as crickets I was worried whether anyone would realize that these are not real crickets.

MT But, that's what is interesting! Alicja, you've made a few works that are really difficult to detect, and there's something interesting about that; it's how you find your audience in a way. That is, people who do notice.

NB Something that each of you reveals in different ways is the idea of variations. Mungo, taking one idea and creating variations in lots of different forms is a very classic conceptual strategy. Alicia's piece is all about variations from one time zone to the next. Kate is at first also very much about the similarity between each of the performers, but then the differences become more pronounced.

MT It's all about adaptability. We need to be able to put our work in the public realm, we need to be able to put our work at the fair, and they need to survive in these contexts.

NB Which one is harder to survive in?

MT Maybe the most challenging, the new standard, and, at the same time, the lowest standard as a context is just free walls in an apartment … The lighting is unfortunate but it's increasingly where most people will see your work. And you can play with that.

AK At a fair, people take ten seconds to get it or not. You are also limited by size, weight, and content I think. It's about selling art: it's not about reading, writing, or art philosophy. That's something you have to keep in mind when showing a piece. In an exhibition, you have the chance to create a story, relationships between single works, you can express your whole world and ideas. I like showing in public spaces as well because it's part of normal life in a way …

NB So, if you have five or ten seconds to get people's attention, do you fight that and try to slow them down or do you submit to this limitation?

AK I never plan works like that. I plan doing a work for an art fair, but some are too difficult or too big, and it makes no sense to present them there.

MT I think a lot about reception, and reception as the social field of perception; *Crickets* is the sound of no one paying attention. The comedian makes a joke, no one laughs, you hear crickets. That sort of sensitivity is built into the project, that thinking through what happens to the fair, how it is producing encounters, and what if there are no encounters.

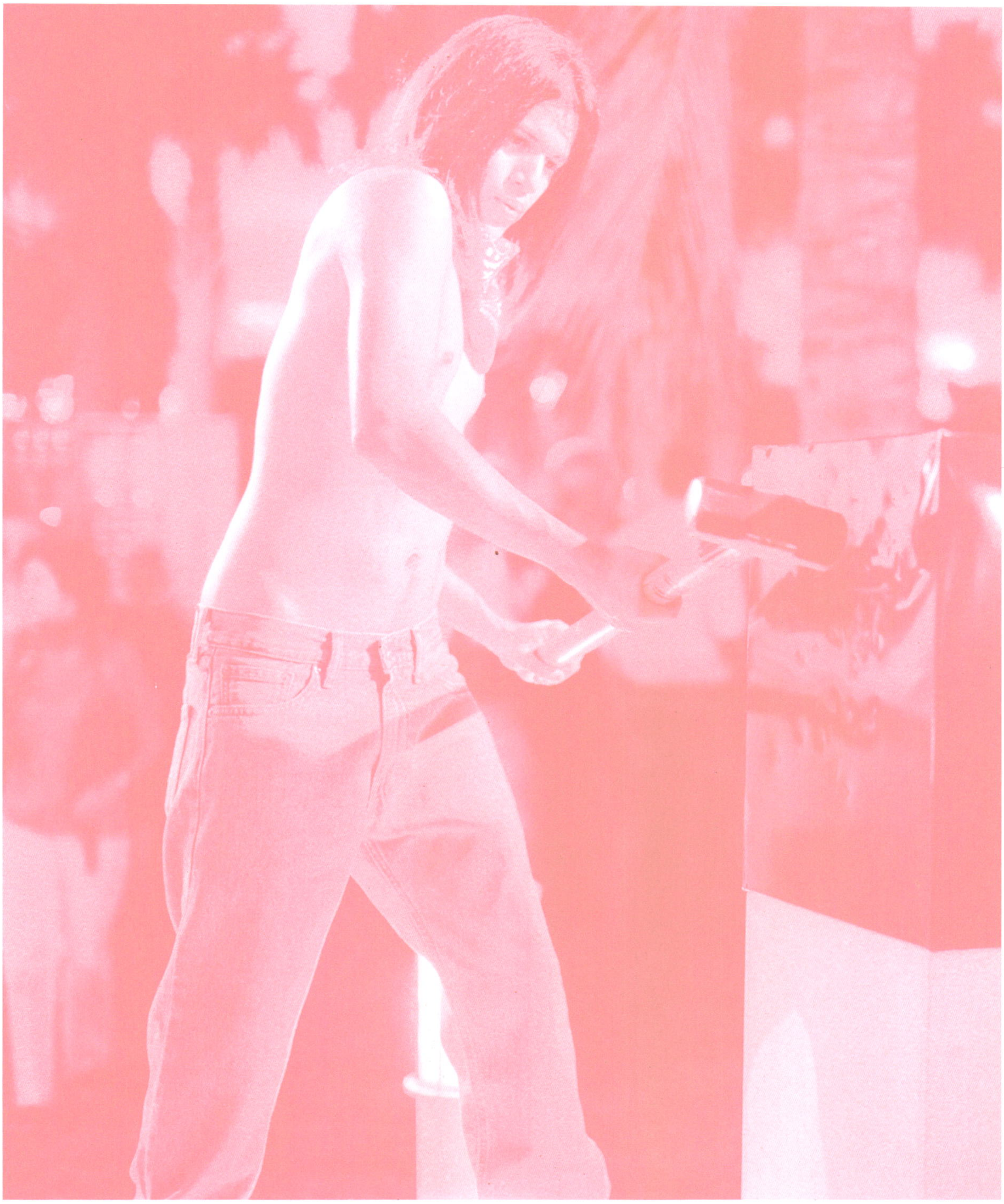

Kate Gilmore, *Only One Like You*, 2013

Q

R

R

- Hong Kong
- Basel
- Miami Beach

RaebervonStenglin

Zurich

- Discoveries
- Feature
- Parcours
- Nova

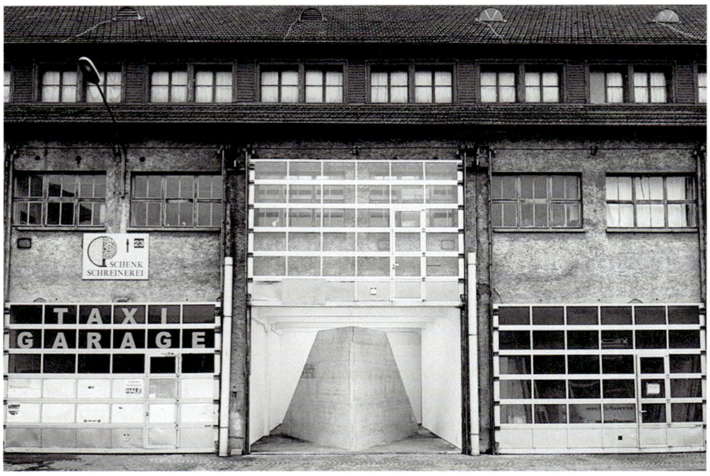

What first compelled you to open a gallery?
The possibility to work with young, emerging artists, to build their careers, and be a platform for challenging, space-related works. And, of course, to do great shows!

Who is the first artist you showed and what was most memorable about that show?
The first show was by German sculptor Karsten Födinger, who installed a giant concrete avalanche-breaker in the gallery, and which was sold to a Swiss collector.

When did you first participate in Art Basel and what was most memorable about that show?
In 2012, in the Statements sector with Karsten Födinger. Födinger won the Baloise Art Prize and had a sensational show at The Hamburger Kunsthalle as a result.

• **Contact**	RaebervonStenglin Matthias von Stenglin info@raebervonstenglin.com
• **Established**	2010
• **Owner(s) / Partner(s)**	Beat Raeber Matthias von Stenglin
• **Space(s)**	120 m² +140 m² (showroom)
• **Artists at Art Basel**	Saâdane Afif Karsten Födinger David Keating Robert Kinmont Kilian Rüthemann
• **Further artists represented**	Andrew Dadson Sofia Hultén Susanne Kriemann Manuela Leinhoss Jill Magid Dane Mitchell Taiyo Onorato & Nico Krebs Ivan Seal Alexander Wagner

Ratio 3

San Francisco

- Galleries

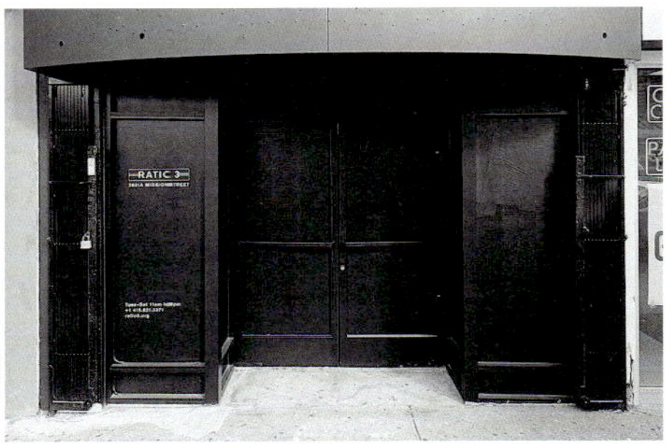

What first compelled you to open a gallery?
I thought it would be fun to produce exciting exhibitions in San Francisco.

Who is the first artist you showed and what was most memorable about that show?
The first artist we showed was Mark Shetabi, from Philadelphia. I remember being shocked and surprised when we sold a painting.

When did you first participate in Art Basel and what was most memorable about that show?
We first participated in Art Basel in the Statements sector in 2009. That year they staged *Il Tempo de Postino*. Amazing and unforgettable!

• **Contact**	Ratio 3 Chris Perez chris@ratio3.org gallery@ratio3.org
• **Established**	2004
• **Owner(s) / Partner(s)**	Chris Perez
• **Team**	4
• **Space(s)**	500 m²
• **Artists at Art Basel**	Lutz Bacher Miriam Böhm Ruth Laskey Barry McGee Mitzi Pederson Noam Rappaport
• **Further artists represented**	Katarina Burin Buck Ellison Matthew Hale Jordan Kantor Danny Keith Margaret Kilgallen Ryan McGinley Takeshi Murata Geof Oppenheimer Ara Peterson Lucy Raven

Raucci/Santamaria

Naples

- Galleries

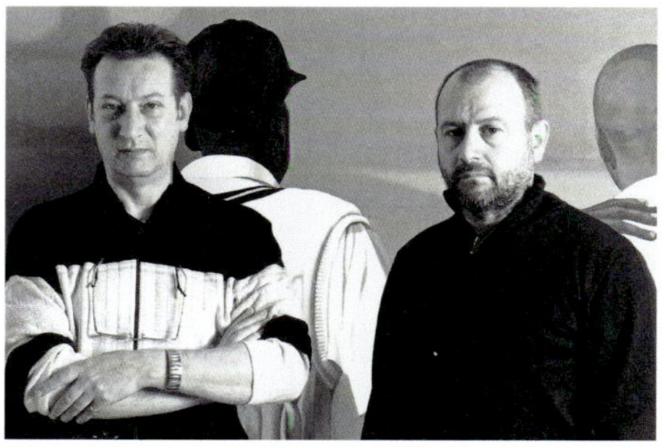

What first compelled you to open a gallery?
To experiment and show new languages in art.

Who is the first artist you showed and what was most memorable about that show?
Sasà Giusto: the exhibition was conceptually very strong and the presentation of the work very direct and clear!

When did you first participate in Art Basel and what was most memorable about that show?
Pádraig Timoney—the reaction of people to the diversity of the works!

- **Contact** Galleria Raucci/Santamaria
  Umberto Raucci
  info@raucciesantamaria.com
- **Established** 1992
- **Owner(s) / Partner(s)** Umberto Raucci
  Carlo Santamaria
- **Team** 3
- **Space(s)** 300 m²
- **Artists at Art Basel** Hany Armanious
  Mat Collishaw
  Danilo Correale
  Karl Haendel
  Tim Rollins and K.O.S.
  Norbert Schwontkowski
  Glenn Sorensen
  Cheyney Thompson
  Pádraig Timoney
- **Further artists represented** Georg Herold
  Evan Holloway
  Hervé Ingrand
  David Robbins
  Ugo Rondinone
  Torbjörn Vejvi
  Cathy Wilkes
  James Yamada

Real Fine Arts

New York — Positions

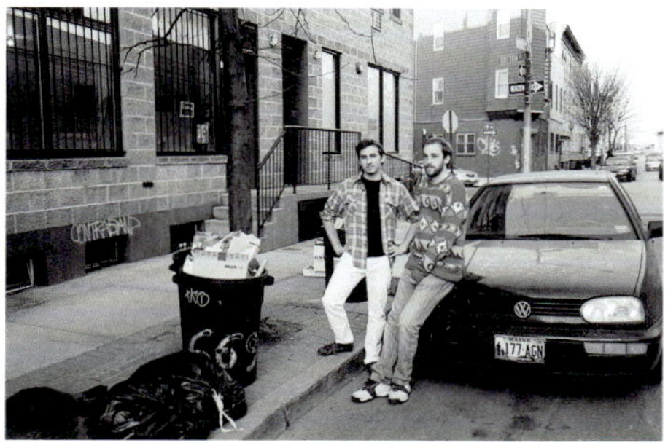

What first compelled you to open a gallery?
We didn't really mean to open a gallery. We found a large space in which to live and realized we could have casual shows with friends. We are artists too and ultimately just wanted to create an arena for things to develop on our own terms. Eventually things just fell into place and here we are now.

Who is the first artist you showed and what was most memorable about that show?
Asher Penn. Certainly we melted at the sight of Asher's optimistic and celebratory heart paintings. They seemed to anticipate the weight and value of the Internet's now widespread usage of the word "like." If only these platforms allowed us to use the word "Love" as Asher did.

When did you first participate in Art Basel and what was most memorable about that show?
In 2013, at Art Basel in Miami Beach.

- **Contact** Real Fine Arts
  Tyler Dobson
  realfinearts@gmail.com
- **Established** 2008
- **Owner(s) / Partner(s)** Tyler Dobson
  Ben Morgan-Cleveland
- **Team** 2
- **Space(s)** 61.5 m²
- **Artists at Art Basel** Mathieu Malouf
- **Further artists represented** Yuji Agematsu
  Nicolas Ceccaldi
  Whitney Claflin
  Jana Euler
  Flame
  Bill Hayden
  Lena Henke
  Chris Kraus
  Caitlin MacBride
  Alissa McKendrick
  Dave Miko
  Jon Pestoni
  Sam Pulitzer
  Heji Shin
  Ned Vena
  Antek Walczak

Rech

Paris
Brussels

Galleries
Galleries Unlimited
Galleries

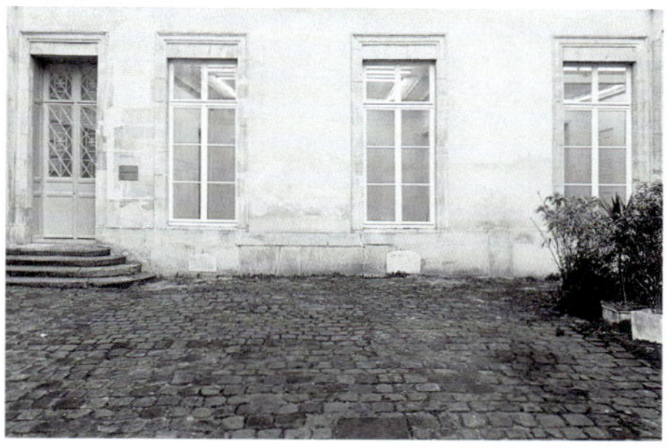

What first compelled you to open a gallery?
I wanted to be involved in the contemporary art creation and discover new artists, and also show more established ones that I thought were important. I wanted to know them, to try to contribute to making art more visible, and offer the artists a space to use as freely as possible.

Who is the first artist you showed and what was most memorable about that show?
The first artist I showed was James Turrell in 1990. He had never shown a light piece in a gallery in Europe and I remember that people close to me thought that I was crazy, but the amazing thing is that it was a tremendous success with a huge line of visitors; and to my great surprise the piece was immediately bought by a great Mexican collector, Mr. Emilio Azcarraga, who had sent his curator Robert R. Littman, for his museum Centro de Televisao.

When did you first participate in Art Basel and what was most memorable about that show?
I was in Art Basel in the early 1990s when I had a gallery in partnership, and I came back to Basel in 2000 with my own gallery. I remember showing a light piece by James Turrell in Unlimited and it was truly challenging.

- **Contact** Almine Rech Gallery
  Marie Jasseron
  marie@alminerech.com
  contact.paris@alminerech.com
- **Established** 1997
- **Owner(s) / Partner(s)** Almine Rech
- **Team** 20
- **Space(s)** 1,075 m²
- **Artists at Art Basel** Matthias Bitzer
  Johan Creten
  Aaron Curry
  Mark Hagen
  Adam Helms
  Gregor Hildebrandt
  Alex Israel
  Erik Lindman
  Liu Wei
  Joel Morrison
  David Ostrowski
  Richard Prince
  Ugo Rondinone
  Taryn Simon
  Eduardo Terrazas
  James Turrell
  Francesco Vezzoli
  Franz West
  Tsuruko Yamazaki
  Yeesookyung
- **Further artists represented** Ziad Antar
  Joe Bradley
  Don Brown
  Tom Burr
  Beatrice Caracciolo
  Philip-Lorca diCorcia
  Teresita Fernández
  Sylvie Fleury
  John Giorno
  Uwe Henneken
  Patrick Hill
  Xylor Jane
  Isaac Julien
  Barbara Kasten
  Thomas Kiesewetter

Jeff Koons
Joseph Kosuth
Jannis Kounellis
Ange Leccia
Daniel Lergon
Curtis Mann
John McCracken
Peter Peri
Anselm Reyle
Matthieu Ronsse
Taryn Simon
Hedi Slimane
Yee Sookyung
Katja Strunz
Su Xiaobai
Tatiana Trouvé
Gavin Turk
Ida Tursic & Wilfried Mille
Not Vital
Gabriel Vormstein
Aaron Young

Reena Spaulings

New York — Galleries

- **Contact** Reena Spaulings Fine Art
reena@reenaspaulings.com
- **Established** 2004
- **Owner(s) / Partner(s)** John Kelsey
Emily Sundblad
Jake Palmert
Carissa Rodriguez
- **Artists at Art Basel** Merlin Carpenter
Michaela Eichwald
Alex Israel
Jutta Koether
Klara Liden
Ken Okiishi
Seth Price
- **Further artists represented** Ei Arakawa
Loretta Fahrenholz
Matias Faldbakken
Shadi Habib Allah
K8 Hardy
Georgie Nettell
Henrik Olesen
Josephine Pryde

Regen Projects

Los Angeles — Galleries Unlimited — Galleries

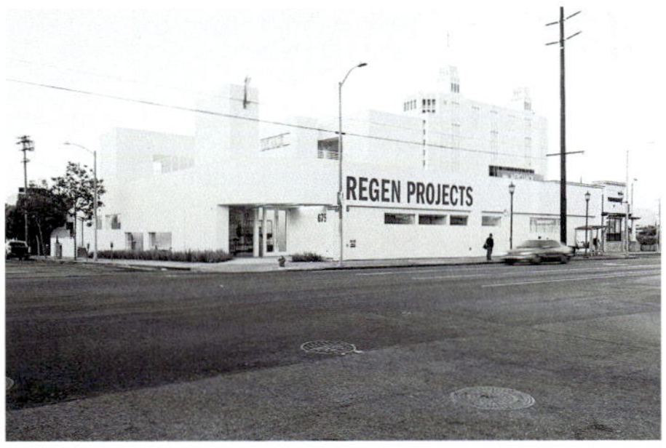

What first compelled you to open a gallery?

In 1989, and new to Los Angeles, there were so many possibilities available. The gallery was opened by my late husband, Stuart Regen, and I was the director of the gallery until we were married in 1991. There were a number of East Coast and European artists that we both admired and were friends with, and Los Angeles seemed like a great frontier to establish a program and start a business. As young dealers, the quality of life was particularly compelling in LA, and artists also loved to come and visit. There was also an amazing community of artists and curators here.

Who is the first artist you showed and what was most memorable about that show?

Lawrence Weiner was our opening show, and we were so proud to have him as our first artist. The show was called *Assuming the Position*, and consisted of one very large work on four walls, and two smaller works in the second room. Lawrence also made a beautiful poster, and the mix of people who came to the opening was a fantastic combination of the art community and his friends in the movie and music community who were living in city. We did very well with the show, and then immediately following it there was a terrible economic downturn. The Margaret Seaworthy gothic font and ampersands, and the silver/black text continue to leave an impression.

When did you first participate in Art Basel and what was most memorable about that show?

In 2000. What impressed me the most was the amount of serious critical and curatorial attention that many of the artists we brought received. And as we tried to make a strong concentration of artists from Los Angeles, it was apparent how little knowledge there was about many of them in Europe at that time.

- **Contact** Regen Projects
Ben Thornborough
benthornborough
@regenprojects.com
office@regenprojects.com
- **Established** 1989
- **Owner(s) / Partner(s)** Shaun Caley Regen
- **Team** 16
- **Space(s)** 1,858 m²
- **Artists at Art Basel** Doug Aitken
Walead Beshty
John Bock
Abraham Cruzvillegas
Willem de Rooij
Lizzie Fitch/Ryan Trecartin
Rachel Harrison
Elliott Hundley
Sergej Jensen
Anish Kapoor
Toba Khedoori
Gabriel Kuri
Liz Larner
Glenn Ligon
Scott McFarland
Marilyn Minter
Catherine Opie
Manfred Pernice
Raymond Pettibon
Jack Pierson
Lari Pittman
Gary Simmons
Wolfgang Tillmans
Ryan Trecartin
Gillian Wearing
Lawrence Weiner
James Welling
Sue Williams
Andrea Zittel
- **Further artists represented** Matthew Barney
Dan Graham
Christian Jankowski
Jennifer Pastor
Elizabeth Peyton
Richard Prince
Daniel Richter

René

Paris — Galleries

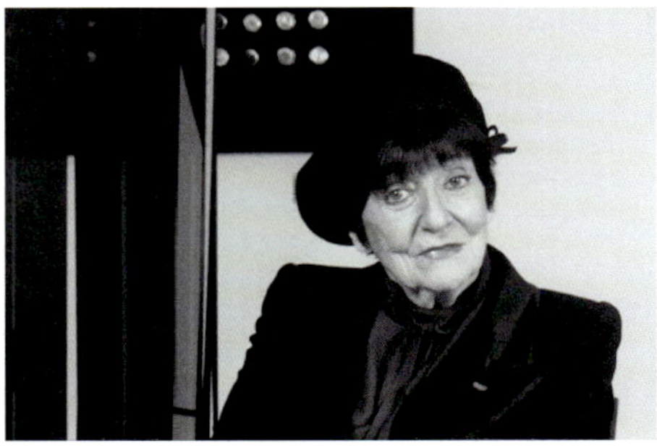

Who is the first artist Denise René showed and what was most memorable about that show?

Victor Vasarely. The Liberation of Paris, and the will to create new exhibition spaces.

When did Denise René first participate in Art Basel?

Since the beginning.

- **Contact** Galerie Denise René
Denis Kilian
denis.kilian@deniserene.com
info@deniserene.com

- **Owner(s) / Partner(s)** Denise René (1944–2012)
Denis Kilian (2012–)
- **Team** 3
- **Space(s)** 200 m²
- **Artists at Art Basel** Yaacov Agam
Jean Arp
David Bill
Jakob Bill
Max Bill
Anne Blanchet
Geneviève Claisse
Elias Crespin
Carlos Cruz-Diez
Emmanuel
Freddy Fraek
Karl Gerstner
Gun Gordillo
Auguste Herbin
Youri Jeltov
Julio le Parc
Aurélie Nemours
Jesús Rafael Soto
Haruhiko Sunagawa
Jean Tinguely
Santiago Torres
Wolfram Ullrich
Victor Vasarely
Zimoun
- **Further artists represented** Josef Albers
Olle Baertling
Marta Boto
Pol Bury
Marcelle Cahn
Walterico Caldas
Chryssa
Dias Cicero
Sonia Delaunay
Hugo Demarco
Jean Dewasne
Jean Deyrolle
Angel Duarte
Equipo 57
Günter Fruhtrunk
Horacio Garcia Rossi
Jean Gorin
Knut Henrik Henriksen
André Heurtaux
Robert Indiana
Robert Jacobsen
Lajos Kassak
Michalis Katzourakis
Frantisek Kupka
Le Corbusier
Walter Leblanc
Richard Paul Lohse
Angel Luque
Macaparana
Heinz Mack
François Morellet
Richard Mortensen
Mehdi Moutashar
Takashi Naraha
Dario Perez-Flores
Maria Carmen Perlingeiro
Ivan Picelj
Serge Poliakoff
Nicolas Schöffer
Francisco Sobrino
Henryk Stazewski
Joël Stein
Sophie Taeuber-Arp
Luis Tomasello
Tsaï Wen-Ying
Gregorio Vardanega
Jean-Pierre Yvaral

Renshaw

Brisbane ● Insights

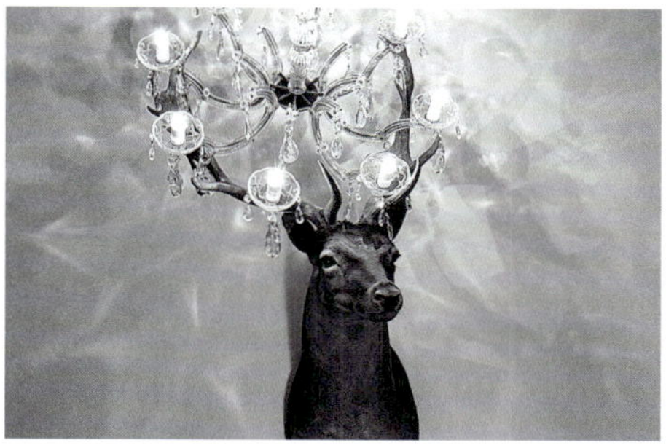

What first compelled you to open a gallery?
To provide a commercial exhibiting platform for artists working in non-traditional mediums.

Who is the first artist you showed and what was most memorable about that show?
We first showed the work of Osaka-based photographer Yoshiro Masuda. The exhibition resulted in a lifelong friendship between ourselves and the artist, and forged a long-standing art relationship between Osaka and Brisbane.

When did you first participate in Art Basel and what was most memorable about that show?
The 2013 Art Basel in Hong Kong. Coming from one of the most geographically isolated countries in the world it was wonderful to feel a part of the international art community.

- **Contact** Ryan Renshaw Gallery
Ryan Renshaw
ryan@ryanrenshaw.com.au
info@ryanrenshaw.com.au
- **Established** 2006
- **Owner(s) / Partner(s)** Ryan Renshaw
Danielle Renshaw
- **Team** 3
- **Space(s)** 150 m²
- **Artists at Art Basel** Rodney Glick
Peter Madden
- **Further artists represented** Peter Alwast
James & Eleanor Avery
Michael Candy
James Cousins
James Dodd
Nicholas Folland
Irene Hanenbergh
Gavin Hipkins
Scott Miles
Bruce Reynolds
Sarah Ryan
Kate Shaw
Martin Smith
Yvonne Todd

Revolver

Lima ● Nova

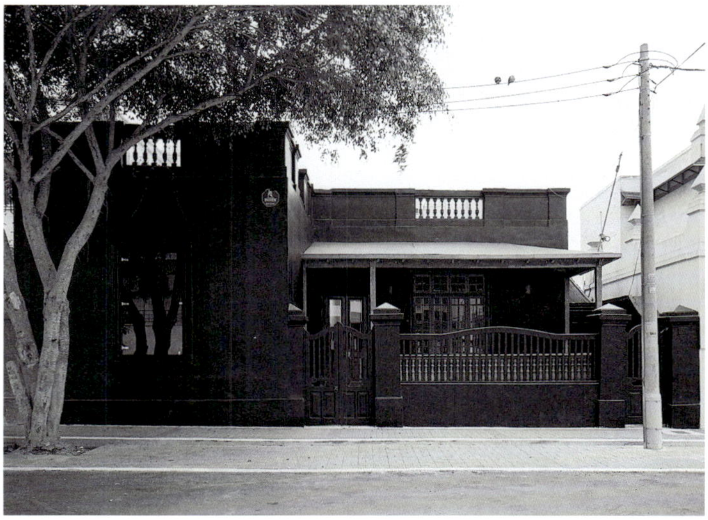

What first compelled you to open a gallery?
It was a time when galleries were not correctly representing artists from my generation. As an artist, I knew what we needed as a gallery.

Who is the first artist you showed and what was most memorable about that show?
Jerry B. Martin, *Blue Pieces*.

- **Contact** Revolver Galería
Maria Fe Gonzalez
mariafe@revolvergaleria.com
contacto@revolvergaleria.com
- **Established** 2008
- **Owner(s) / Partner(s)** Giancarlo Scaglia
- **Team** 4
- **Space(s)** 200 m²
- **Artists at Art Basel** Jerry B. Martin
José Carlos Martinat
Giancarlo Scaglia

Reynolds

London — Galleries

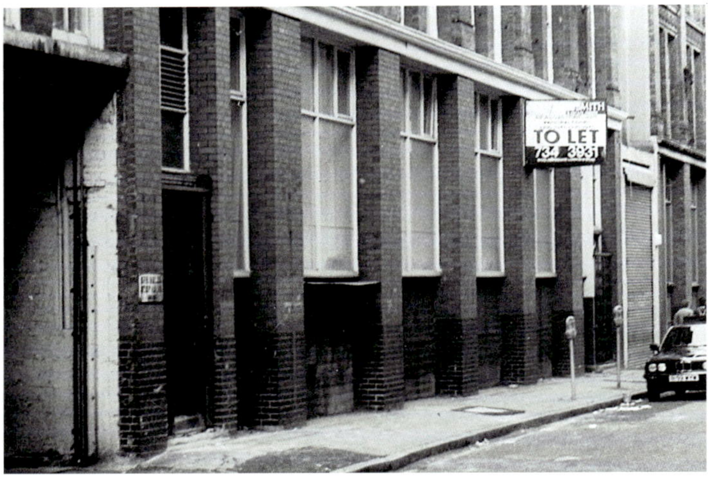

What first compelled you to open a gallery?
The impossibility of representing artists without one.

Who is the first artist you showed and what was most memorable about that show?
Ian Breakwell—that my conviction in his work is now, 28 years later, being vindicated.

When did you first participate in Art Basel and what was most memorable about that show?
In 1992. The combination of pride, excitement, and fear!

- **Contact** Anthony Reynolds Gallery
Anthony Reynolds
ar@anthonyreynolds.com
info@anthonyreynolds.com
- **Established** 1985
- **Owner(s) / Partner(s)** Anthony Reynolds
- **Team** 5
- **Space(s)** 250 m²
- **Artists at Art Basel** David Austen
Richard Billingham
Ian Breakwell
Peter Gallo
Leon Golub
Paul Graham
Lucy Harvey
Emily Jacir
Kai Kaljo
Andrew Mansfield
Asier Mendizabal
Lucia Nogueira
Walid Raad
Georgia Sagri
Nancy Spero
Sturtevant
Jon Thompson
Amikam Toren
Nobuko Tsuchiya
Mark Wallinger

Riis

Oslo
Stockholm — Galleries Unlimited

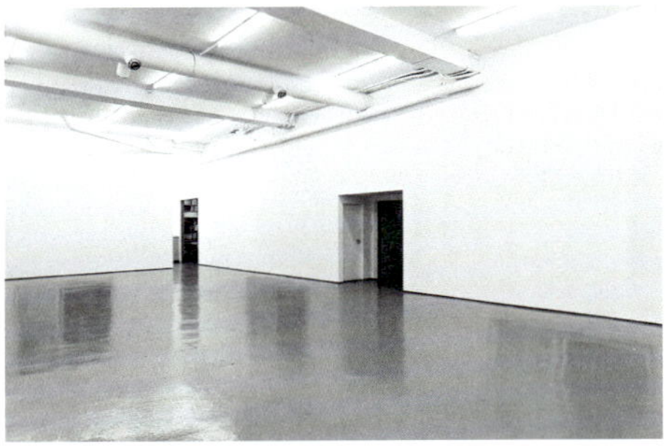

What first compelled you to open a gallery?
We took over the directorship in 1984. The gallery then had a quite established program that was changed throughout the 1980s toward a more contemporary Scandinavian profile.

Who is the first artist you showed and what was most memorable about that show?
We showed the Norwegian artist Bård Breivik's minimalist black stone sculptures *The Collector*, in 1985. For us it was a revelation in how to use the space.

When did you first participate in Art Basel and what was most memorable about that show?
In 1986. Coming from a small art scene in Oslo, it was very inspiring and made a big impression to exhibit our artists alongside many established colleagues with international reputations and world-famous artists.

- **Contact** Galleri Riis
Espen Ryvarden
espen@galleririis.com
info@galleririis.com
- **Established** 1972
- **Owner(s) / Partner(s)** Kristin Elisabeth Bråten
Espen Ryvarden
- **Team** 6
- **Space(s)** 500 m²
- **Artists at Art Basel** Morten Andenæs
Martin Erik Andersen
Signe Marie Andersen
Bård Breivik
Andreas Eriksson
Hamish Fulton
Jan Groth
Håvard Homstvedt
Olav Christopher Jenssen
Marte Johnslien
Daido Moriyama
Eline Mugaas
Christine Ödlund
Paul Osipow
Stein Rønning
Fredrik Söderberg
Günter Umberg
Marijke van Warmerdam
Tone Vigeland
Dan Wolgers
Troels Wörsel
Sverre Wyller

Roberts & Tilton

Los Angeles — Galleries

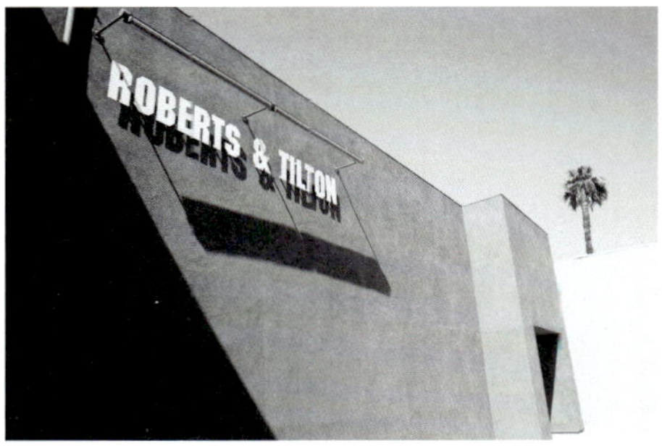

What first compelled you to open a gallery?

In the late 1990s there was an incredible surge of energy in the Los Angeles art scene. Bennett Roberts, Julie Roberts, and Jack Tilton sought to open a gallery that would support the talents of a number of interesting and promising artists, and that would offer opportunities to exhibit unique works, advance practices, and develop careers.

When did you first participate in Art Basel and what was most memorable about that show?

We first participated in 2003 with a Statements booth at Art Basel by Chris Johanson. The most interesting element was assisting Chris in sourcing discarded wood in and around Basel. .

- **Contact** Roberts & Tilton
  Mary Skarbek
  mary@robertsandtilton.com
  info@robertsandtilton.com
- **Established** 1999
- **Owner(s) / Partner(s)** Bennett Roberts (Co-Owner)
  Julie Roberts (Co-Owner)
  Jack Tilton (Co-Owner)
- **Team** 6
- **Space(s)** 300 m²
- **Artists at Art Basel** Michael Dopp
  Egan Frantz
  Jonathan Hartshorn
  Eberhard Havekost
  Thomas Kiesewetter
  Israel Lund
  Daniel Joseph Martinez
  Barry McGee
  Betye Saar
  Ed Templeton
  Kehinde Wiley
  Zhao Zhao

Roesler

São Paulo

Galleries
Galleries

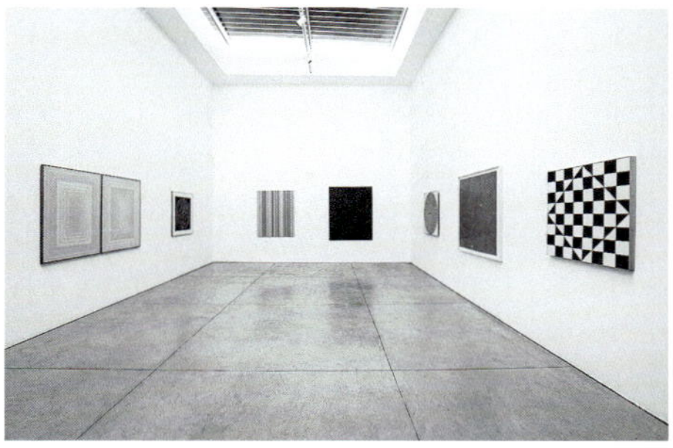

What first compelled you to open a gallery?

I first opened a gallery in my hometown of Recife, in the northeast of Brazil, where there were no galleries, nor a market focused on contemporary art. My first intention was to bring together the two different "Brazils." Thus, in Recife, I showed the work of great artists from other regions—including Tomie Ohtake, with whom I still work today—and invited curators, critics, and journalists from around the country to get to know the local artistic production and to promote cultural meetings, conversations, and lectures to the public of Recife. The gallery served as a bridge, as a center of exchange between these different cultural poles. The dynamics of the gallery remain similar, although they have taken different proportions—today, we promote this exchange at an international level.

When did you first participate in Art Basel and what was most memorable about that show?

Our first participation at Art Basel was in Miami Beach in 2003, with a project for the Statements sector. Laura Vinci presented a development of the exhibition *Estados* (States, 2002), one of the most talked about shows in São Paulo the previous year, at the renowned Centro Cultural Banco do Brasil. The visibility generated by our participation resulted in many institutional invitations to the artist, testifying to the role of Art Basel as an important cultural agent. The audience's response to the aesthetically sensitive works by Laura Vinci was genuine bedazzlement and awe.

- **Contact** Galeria Nara Roesler
  Deborah Moreira
  deborah@nararoesler.com.br
  info@nararoesler.com.br
- **Established** 1989
- **Owner(s) / Partner(s)** Nara Roesler
  Daniel Roesler
  Alexandre Roesler
  Alexandra Garcia Waldman
- **Team** 19
- **Space(s)** 1,200 m²
- **Artists at Art Basel** Brígida Baltar
  Alberto Baraya
  Paulo Bruscky
  Cristina Canale
  Carlito Carvalhosa
  Marcos Chaves
  Eduardo Coimbra
  Antonio Dias
  Bruno Dunley
  O Grivo
  Cao Guimarães
  Jonathan Hernández
  Isaac Julien
  Lucia Koch
  Karin Lambrecht
  Julio Le Parc
  Artur Lescher
  Artur Lescher
  Milton Machado
  Marco Maggi
  Alice Miceli
  Raul Mourão
  Vik Muniz
  Tomie Ohtake
  Hélio Oiticica
  Oscar Oiwa
  Abraham Palatnik
  Rodolpho Parigi
  José Patrício
  Paul Ramírez Jonas
  Marcelo Silveira
  Luzia Simons
  Sérgio Sister
  Melanie Smith
  Laura Vinci
- **Further artists represented** Angelo Venosa

Rokeby

London

Discoveries

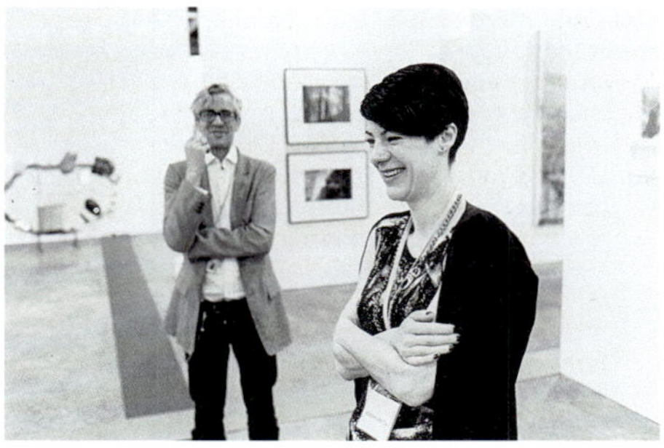

What first compelled you to open a gallery?

This is a question we ask each other regularly and the answer changes as frequently.

Who is the first artist you showed and what was most memorable about that show?

Seven years before we opened the gallery, Beth put together a series of interventions across London by relatively unknown artists; the first was by Michael Samuels, who is now a gallery artist, memorable for the fact that it was in a window.

When did you first participate in Art Basel and what was most memorable about that show?

We first participated in the Statements sector in 2010 with an installation by Bettina Buck. Bettina tiled the booth, and then built a new booth virtually obscuring the considerable effort undertaken; that was memorable for Bettina's commitment and the bravery of the fair.

- **Contact** Rokeby
  Beth Greenacare
  beth@rokebygallery.com
  rokeby@rokebygallery.com
- **Established** 2005
- **Owner(s) / Partner(s)** Beth Greenacre
  Ed Greenacre (Directors)
- **Space(s)** 40 m²
- **Artists at Art Basel** Sam Dargan
- **Further artists represented** Axel Antas
  Raul Ortega Ayala
  Bettina Buck
  Erica Eyres
  Doug Fishbone
  Simon Keenleyside
  Leung Chi Wo
  Ian Pedigo
  Gideon Rubin
  Michael Samuels
  Mathew Sawyer
  Conrad Ventur
  WITH

Ropac

Salzburg
Paris

Galleries
Galleries Unlimited
Galleries

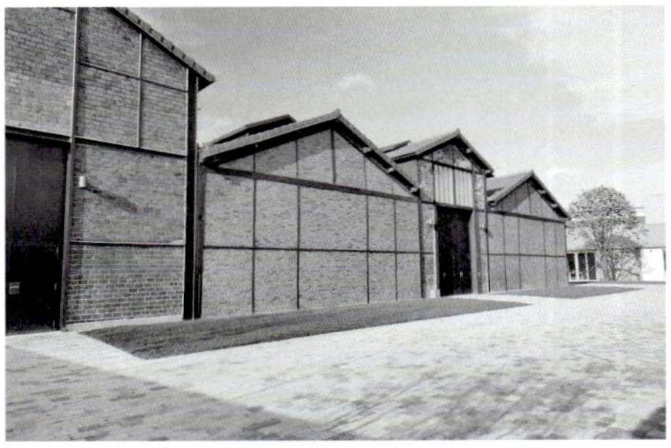

What first compelled you to open a gallery?
As a failed artist, I wanted to stay close to the art world.

Who is the first artist you showed and what was most memorable about that show?
It was Joseph Beuys. The intensity of his presence and his incredible charisma were the most memorable.

When did you first participate in Art Basel and what was most memorable about that show?
In 1984. I was very impressed by the internationality of the fair.

- **Contact** Galerie Thaddaeus Ropac
  Arne Ehmann
  arne.ehmann@ropac.at
  galerie@ropac.net
- **Established** 1983
- **Owner(s) / Partner(s)** Thaddaeus Ropac
- **Team** 60
- **Space(s)** 9,800 m²
- **Artists at Art Basel** Cory Arcangel
  Ali Banisadr
  Georg Baselitz
  Joseph Beuys
  Lee Bul
  Tony Cragg
  Jules de Balincourt
  Sylvie Fleury
  Gilbert & George
  Antony Gormley
  Ilya & Emilia Kabakov
  Alex Katz
  Anselm Kiefer
  Terence Koh
  Wolfgang Laib
  Robert Longo
  Liza Lou
  Jason Martin
  Farhad Moshiri
  Jack Pierson
  Marc Quinn
  Daniel Richter
  Tom Sachs
  David Salle
  Raqib Shaw
  Andreas Slominski
  Sturtevant
  Banks Violette
  Not Vital
  Erwin Wurm
  Yan Pei-Ming
- **Further artists represented** Art & Language
  Claire Adelfang
  Donald Baechler
  Mahmoud Bakhshi
  Stephan Balkenhol
  Philippe Bradshaw
  Marc Brandenburg
  Jean-Marc Bustamante
  Francesco Clemente
  Matali Crasset
  Richard Deacon
  Elger Esser
  Harun Farocki
  Amos Gitai
  Imi Knoebel
  Jonathan Lasker
  Marcin Maciejowski
  Robert Mapplethorpe
  Bernhard Martin
  Nick Oberthaler
  Rona Pondick
  Arnulf Rainer
  Gerwald Rockenschaub
  Hubert Scheibl
  Sandra Vásquez de la Horra
  Andy Warhol
  Lawrence Weiner

Rosen

New York

Galleries Unlimited
Galleries

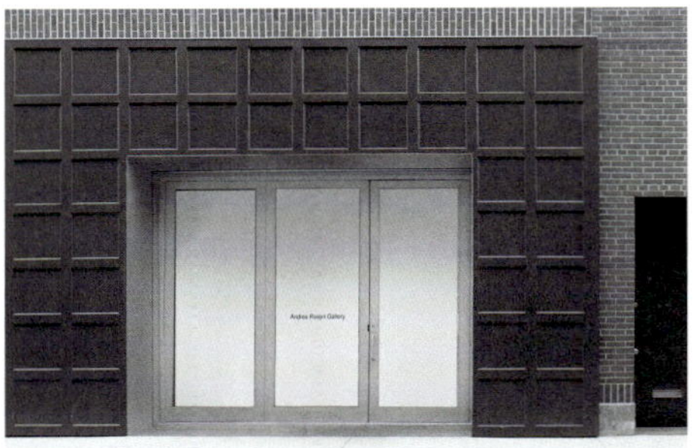

- **Contact** Andrea Rosen Gallery
  Rebekah Bowling
  R.Bowling@rosengallery.com
  andrea@rosengallery.com
- **Established** 1990
- **Owner(s) / Partner(s)** Andrea Rosen (President)
- **Team** 24
- **Space(s)** 800 m²
- **Artists at Art Basel** David Altmejd
  Gillian Carnegie
  Nigel Cooke
  Walker Evans
  Lizzie Fitch/Ryan Trecartin
  Felix Gonzalez-Torres
  Al Hansen
  Elliott Hundley
  Friedrich Kunath
  José Lerma
  Josiah McElheny
  Josephine Meckseper
  László Moholoy-Nagy
  Katy Moran
  Dan Peterman
  Michael Raedecker
  Matthew Ritchie
  Matthew Ronay
  Mika Rottenberg
  Wolfgang Tillmans
  Andrea Zittel
- **Further artists represented** Tetsumi Kudo
  Ryan Trecartin

Rosenfeld

New York — Galleries

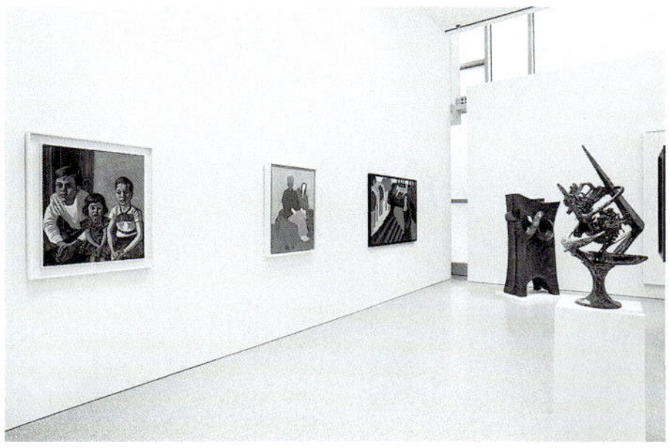

What first compelled you to open a gallery?

After working as a private dealer for several years, Michael Rosenfeld opened his gallery to exhibit and promote artists and movements that he passionately admired, but that few were exhibiting outside of museums. Now celebrating its 25th anniversary, the gallery remains dedicated to its founding commitment to Surrealism, Social Realism, figurative Expressionism, early American abstraction, Abstract Expressionism, and African-American masters.

Who is the first artist you showed and what was most memorable about that show?

As an introduction, the gallery (originally located at 50 West 57 Street) opened with a selection of 20th-century American art and followed with an important survey of American Surrealism/Magic Realism. Having an audience to share our knowledge and love of art was exciting; an enthusiastic audience has continued to motivate us!

When did you first participate in Art Basel and what was most memorable about that show?

Our first participation was in 2007 at Art Basel Miami Beach and we were amazed at the size and diversity of the fair audience. Our presentation was enthusiastically embraced with sales to private collectors and institutions. We could not have anticipated the positive response to our installation, and hence our desire to continue to participate year after year. We take our booth presentation very seriously, trying to unveil masterpieces that are fresh to the market!

- **Contact** — Michael Rosenfeld Gallery
Halley Harrisburg
hkh@michaelrosenfeldart.com
info@michaelrosenfeldart.com
- **Established** — 1989
- **Owner(s) / Partner(s)** — Michael Rosenfeld
Halley K. Harrisburg
- **Space(s)** — 743 m²
- **Artists at Art Basel** — Benny Andrews
Ruth Asawa
Romare Bearden
Jay DeFeo
Beauford Delaney
Burgoyne Diller
Michael Goldberg
Morris Graves
Lee Krasner
Jacob Lawrence
Norman Lewis
Conrad Marca-Relli
Alfonso Ossorio
Richard Pousette-Dart
Anne Ryan
Betye Saar
Charles Seliger
Charles Shaw
Joseph Stella
Alma Thomas
Bob Thompson
- **Further artists represented** — John Biggers
Federico Castellón
Nancy Grossman
Seymour Lipton
Boris Margo
Irving Norman
Theodore Roszak
Louis Stone
Charmion von Wiegand

Rossi & Rossi

London
Hong Kong — Galleries

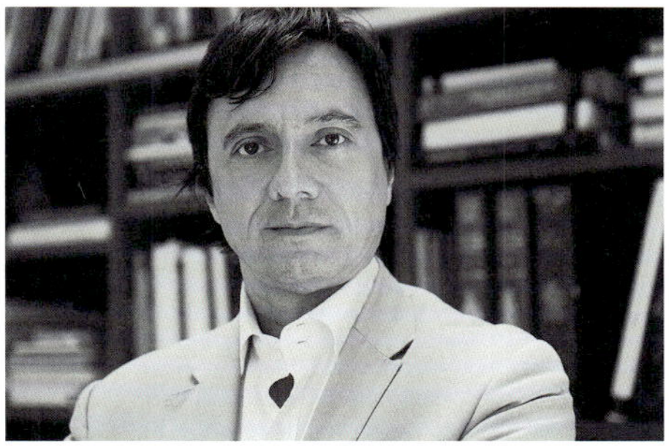

What first compelled you to open a gallery?

Fabio Rossi: My mother, Anna Maria Rossi, started dealing in classical works of art from the Himalayas, specifically Tibet, many years ago. This has more recently expanded into contemporary art from the area, as well as wider Asia. We have always been fascinated by art from the region, traveling there many times over the past 40 years including times when I was a very young child. Becoming a dealer and opening a space was the natural extension of this enthusiasm. In the earlier days the exhibition space was small, but now the demands of the contemporary art we present have seen us move to a much larger space with bigger walls, suitable for the more ambitiously sized works of art our artists are creating.

Who is the first artist you showed and what was most memorable about that show?

The first contemporary exhibition was a group show of Tibetan artists; it was the first time such artists had been shown in the UK, indeed Europe, which proved to be both a critical and commercial success. The most memorable aspect of the show was that we were able to bring the artists over from Tibet, and to share their sudden submergence in the life of a major Western city and all that it involves was a moving and fascinating experience.

When did you first participate in Art Basel and what was most memorable about that show?

We exhibited at ART HK (the precursor to Art Basel in Hong Kong) since its inception and were very happy to continue exhibiting at Art Basel in Hong Kong in 2013. What was most memorable about the show was that we showed the work of one young artist—Tsherin Sherpa—and sold all his paintings.

- **Contact** — Rossi & Rossi
Martin Clist
martin@rossirossi.com
info@rossirossi.com
- **Established** — 1988
- **Owner(s) / Partner(s)** — Anna Maria Rossi
Fabio Rossi
- **Team** — 5
- **Space(s)** — 700 m²
- **Artists at Art Basel** — Tsherin Sherpa
- **Further artists represented** — Jaishri Abichandani
Fereydoun Ave
Benchung
Konstantin Bessmertny
Bhutanese Textile Project
Faiza Butt
Caroline Chiu
Heman Chong
Lois Conner
Shane Cotton
Dedron
Heri Dono
Christopher Doyle
Gade
Naiza H Khan
Kesang Lamdark
Erbossyn Meldibekov
Nortse
Tsering Nyandak
Tenzing Rigdol
Leang Seckon
Tsewang Tashi
Palden Weinreb

Rumma

Milan — Galleries
Naples — Galleries

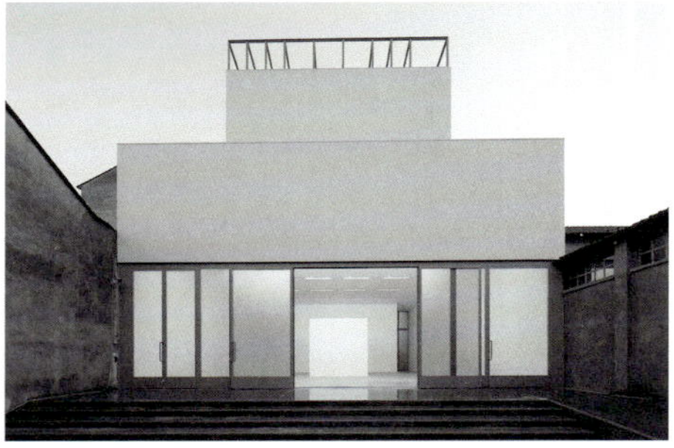

What first compelled you to open a gallery?
Lia Rumma: Before opening the gallery I began collecting art works with my husband Marcello Rumma, and together we started our small art-dedicated publishing house. At that time we supported crucial art projects in Italy, among them *Amalfi '68* curated by Germano Celant. After my husband's death, I decided to carry on my destiny in contemporary art by opening my first gallery in Naples.

Who is the first artist you showed and what was most memorable about that show?
The gallery opened in 1971 with a solo show by Joseph Kosuth. He showed *The Eight Investigation (A.A.I.A.I.)*, a conceptual installation composed of tables, clocks, and notebooks, focusing on time and on the role of language and meaning within art. Thinking of such a conceptual show in Naples at that time was a great challenge.

When did you first participate in Art Basel and what was most memorable about that show?
In 1979 in Basel.

• **Contact**	Lia Rumma Sara Ceroni sara@liarumma.it info@liarumma.it
• **Established**	1971
• **Owner(s) / Partner(s)**	Lia Rumma (Owner) Paola Potena (Partner)
• **Team**	15
• **Space(s)**	1,000 m² (Milan) 150 m² (Naples)
• **Artists at Art Basel**	Ilya & Emilia Kabakov Marina Abramović Vanessa Beecroft Enrico Castellani Gary Hill Alfredo Jaar William Kentridge Joseph Kosuth Hendrik Krawen Marzia Migliora Michelangelo Pistoletto Thomas Ruff Ettore Spalletti Haim Steinbach Tobias Zielony Gilberto Zorio
• **Further artists represented**	Clegg & Guttmann van Bazak Alberto Burri Gino De Dominicis Günther Förg Andreas Gursky Douglas Huebler Anselm Kiefer Ottonella Mocellin Reinhard Mucha Sabah Naim Nicola Pellegrini Franco Scognamiglio Dré Wapenaar

Regen Projects
Interview with Shaun Caley Regen

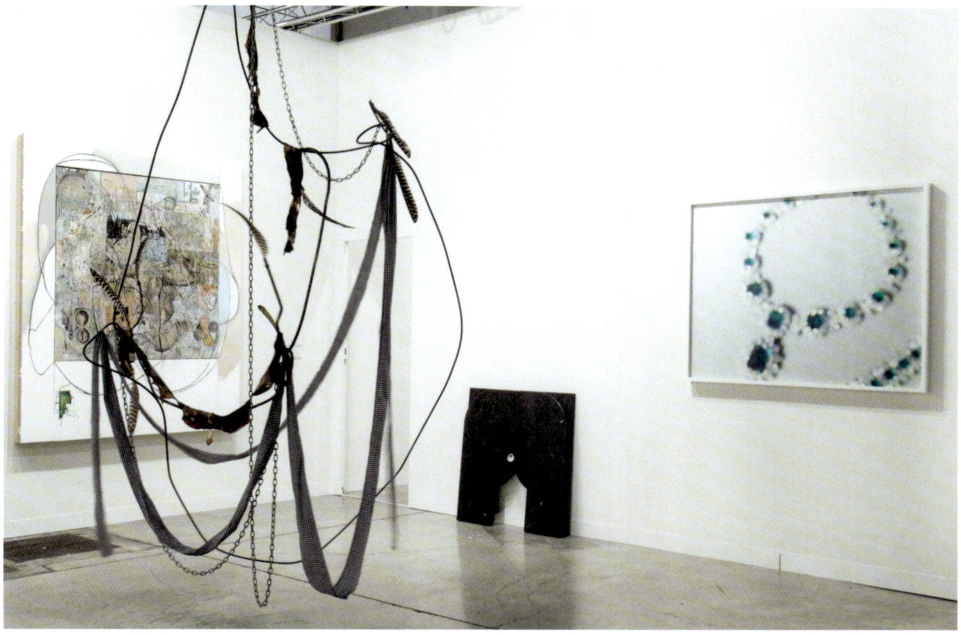

Art Basel in Miami Beach, Nova, 2013

You were on the committee of Art Basel in Miami Beach. How did it start?

Yes, from the beginning. We canceled in 2001 because of 9/11, so the first fair was in 2002. At the time Sam Keller was running the fair. It was fantastic. I think it was also very smart on their part because it really engaged the Latin-American and American artists and markets, a lot of doors were opened …

When did you open your gallery?

We opened the gallery in December 1989, as the Stuart Regen gallery, with a Lawrence Weiner show, and then we moved around that block four times until this recent move to Hollywood. The gallery will be 25 years old next year.

Do you still work with the same artists you originally represented?

Yes, like Lawrence Weiner, Liz Larner, and many others. A lot of people we started with, such as Toba Khedoori, Matthew Barney, Catherine Opie, were in their early, or first, shows. Most of them we still work with.

There's a big sense of continuity.

It's important, loyalty—we have worked with Raymond Pettibon since 1990, and Matthew Barney since 1991. We started working with Glenn Ligon in 2004. Some came along the way.

How would you define the gallery program, starting with a generation like Weiner, and then adding younger artists? How do you combine these different generations and backgrounds?

We opened in 1989 when the market crashed, and it was a time when nobody was selling, so it didn't really matter what you showed. Then, for about two years, we were entirely broke and at the beginning of the 1990s we moved to a very small space that we called Regen Projects. The idea was to do shows around the city. The first project we did was Richard Prince's *First House* (1993), followed by projects with Lawrence Weiner at the Central Market, Matthew Barney, etc. At that point there were new artists in the program like Elizabeth Peyton, Wolfgang Tillmans, Sol LeWitt. It was really about keeping a very low overhead, about surviving and breaking even. The gallery continued that way for a number of years in the 1990s.

I was able to expand again around 2002, and took on another space to do the Charles Ray *Hinoki* piece, the big log. We moved to Hollywood last year because there was an opportunity to buy a large building and to consolidate everything, rather than having three disparate spaces.

The LA scene has changed a lot in terms of relationships with institutions, for instance, and with other galleries. People are increasingly interested in what is happening here artistically, and galleries now tend to prefer opening a gallery in LA than in New York.

Yes, there is a lot of that. Los Angeles has always had a very rich history. It's a place that never writes its own history, but there have always been amazing artists there, and it's a great place for artists to work. I don't know if it's because it's so spread out, so anonymous, or just a great place to have a studio, work, and not have too much on top of you, too much information.

The first Los Angeles show I remember is a show that Lars Nittve did at the Louisiana Museum of Modern Art, *Sunshine & Noir* (1997). Everyone was wondering why an outsider was telling our story, but many of the exhibited artists went at the opening: it was the first time a lot of the younger artists met with the older generations, so Ed Ruscha was meeting let's say Catherine Opie for the first time. It was these funny and weird encounters. At the time they weren't such a community. The community was the art schools.

It is still important for your artists to have a teaching position and to meet the older generation?

I think that the artists have been very generous there. In New York, you usually teach when you're not making enough money selling your works. In LA teaching is more a normal thing to do.

The artist scene has been here for decades; what was the market like 20 years ago?

I've been here almost 25 years and you keep finding things in LA the more you scratch. It is a great collecting community. It's maybe not as evident as in other places. The museums have been a great support too. LACMA is very strong. The Hammer is very strong. MOCA, which was always a great museum, is kind of struggling right now. But their presence within the art community is very consistent.

You also take part in Art Basel in Basel. What differences are there between the two fairs, and what approach do you adopt with each one?

We always try to bring the strongest and most representative works of the artists, because it's not just about selling work, it's also about curators seeing the works in context. I've been doing Basel a bit longer than Miami Beach, since 2000 maybe, and actually I don't think we bring different material to the fairs, but you want to bring challenging works. As an American gallerist I probably know more people in Miami Beach than I naturally know in Basel. But I would say they both are very strong fairs for us.

RY ROCK LEN

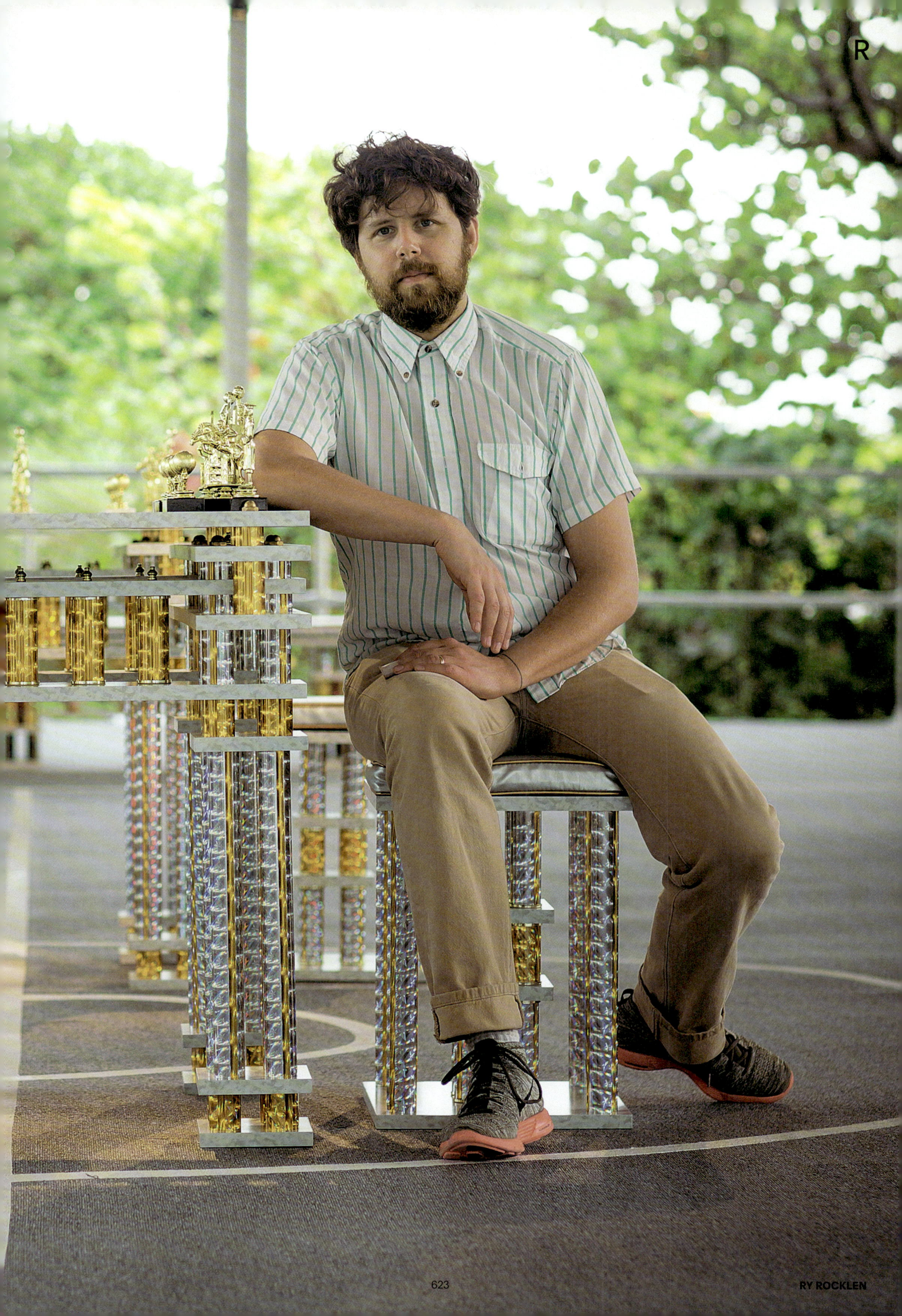

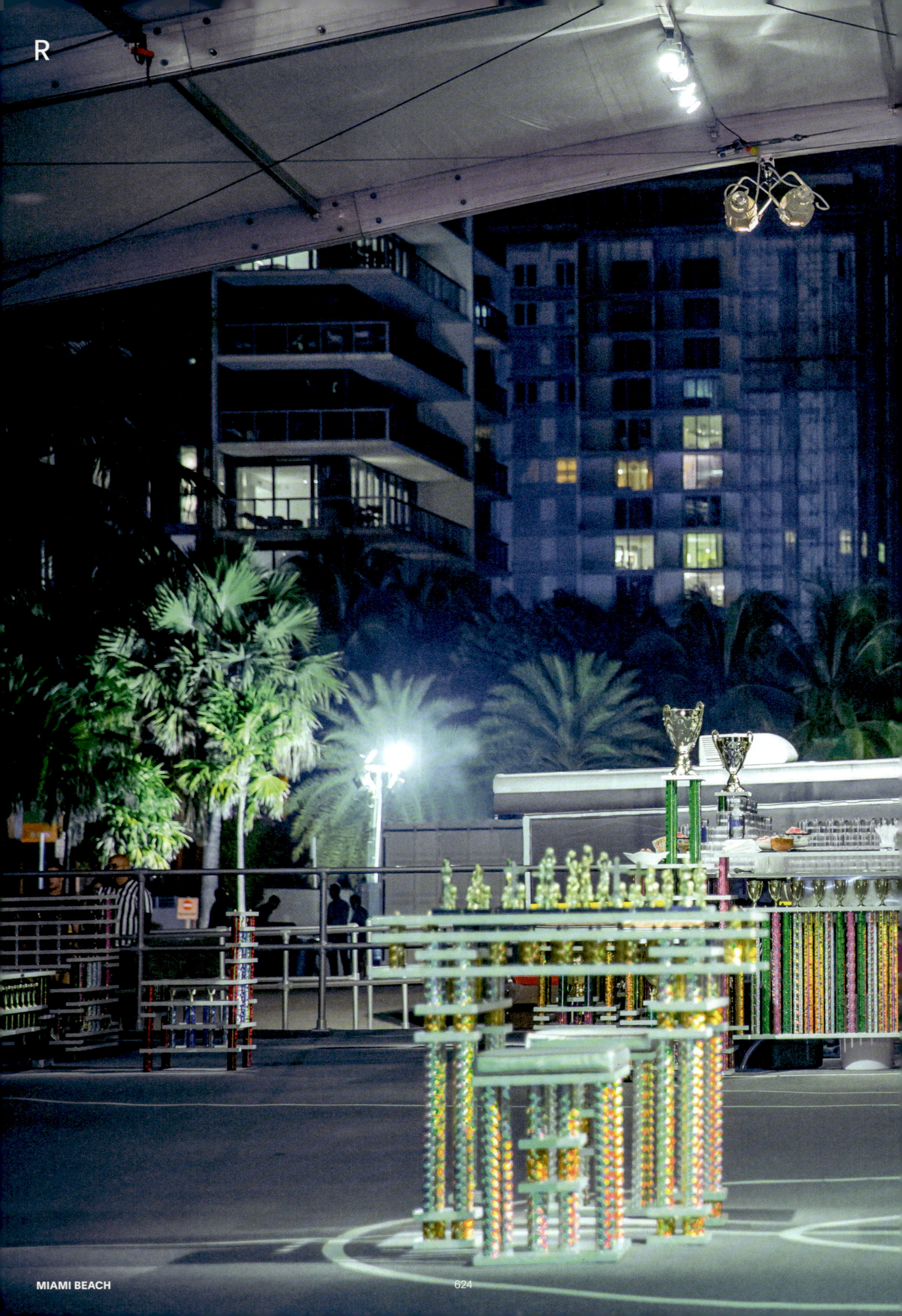

Night Court
2013

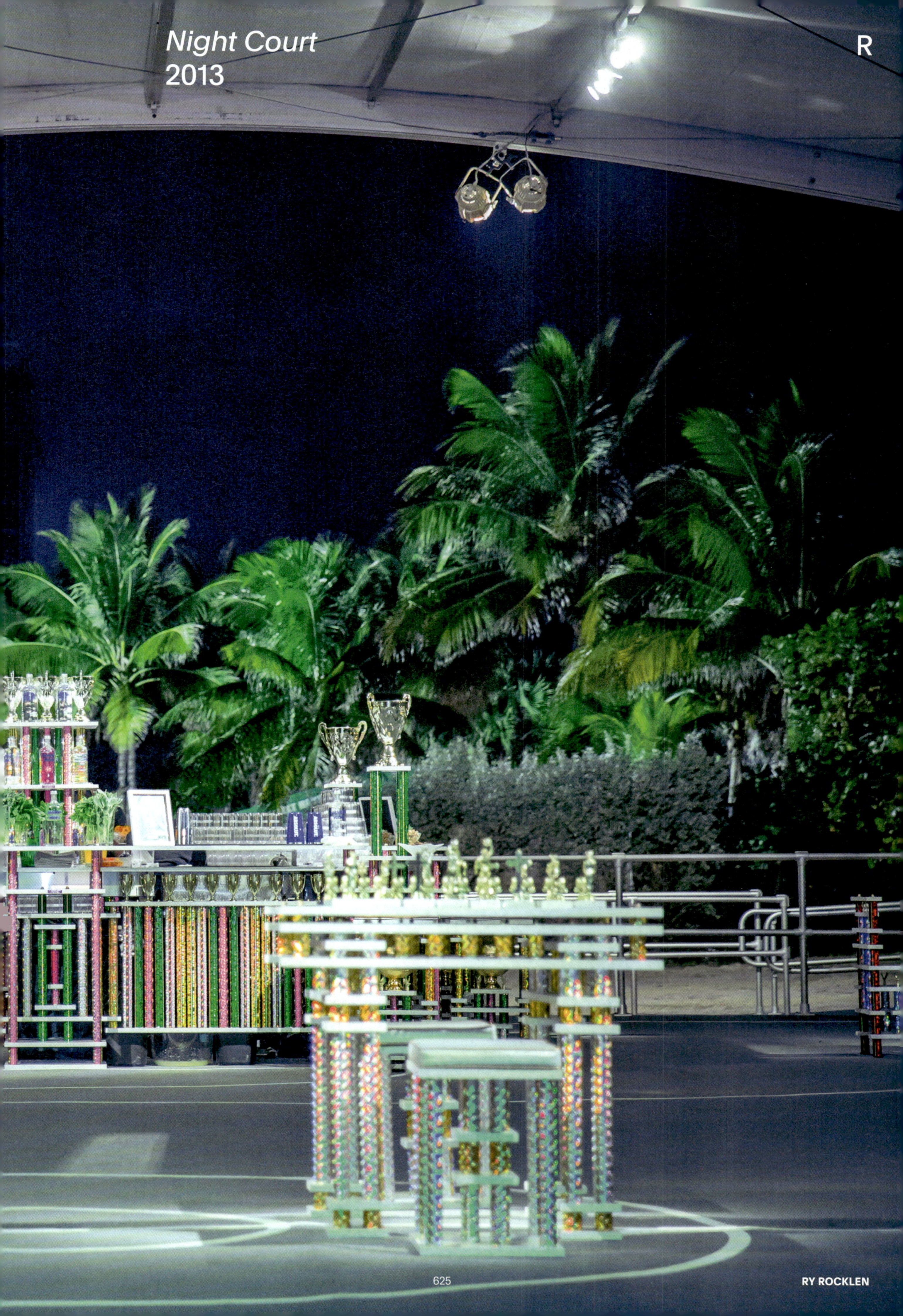

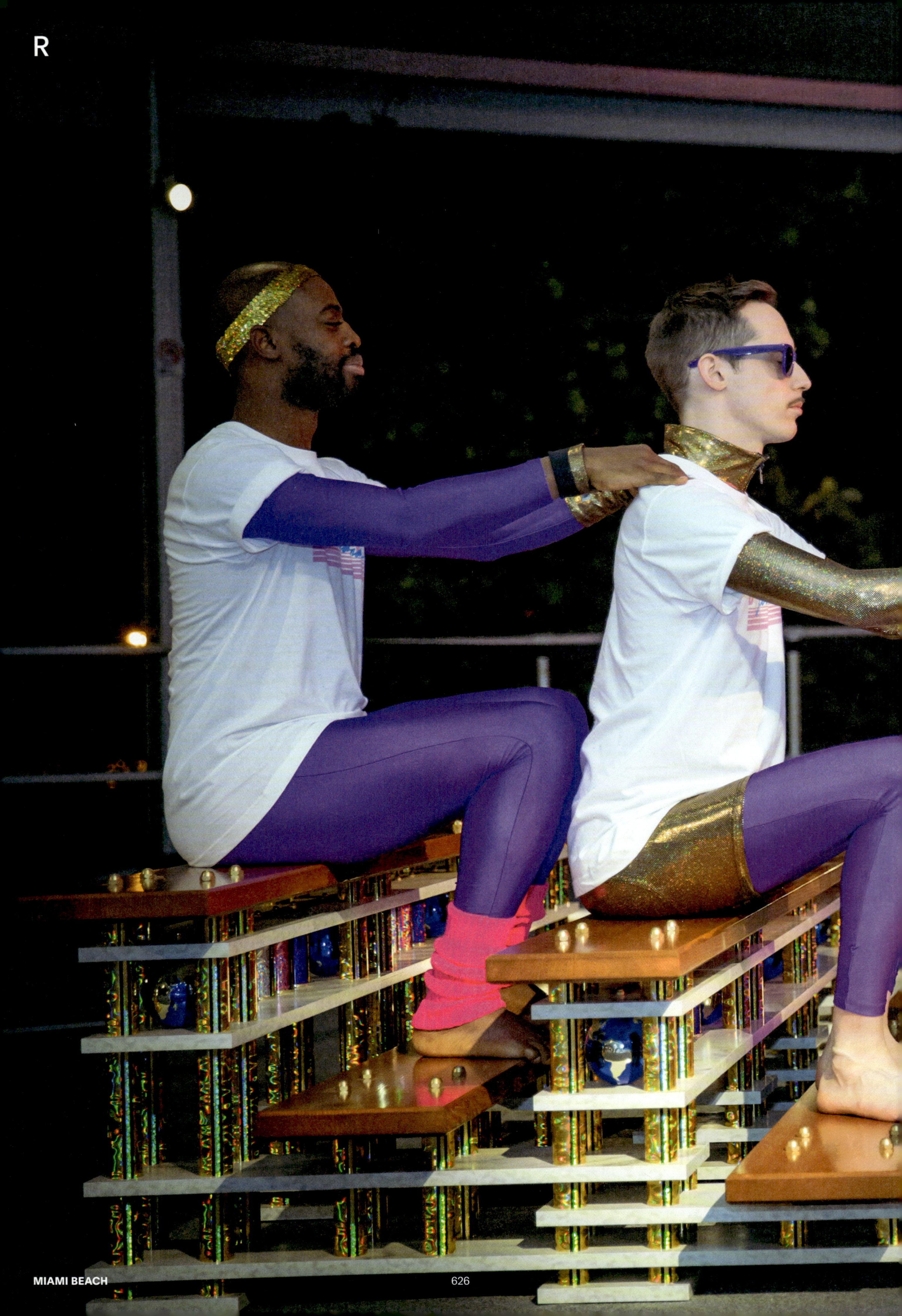

2013
Performance by Bodies International

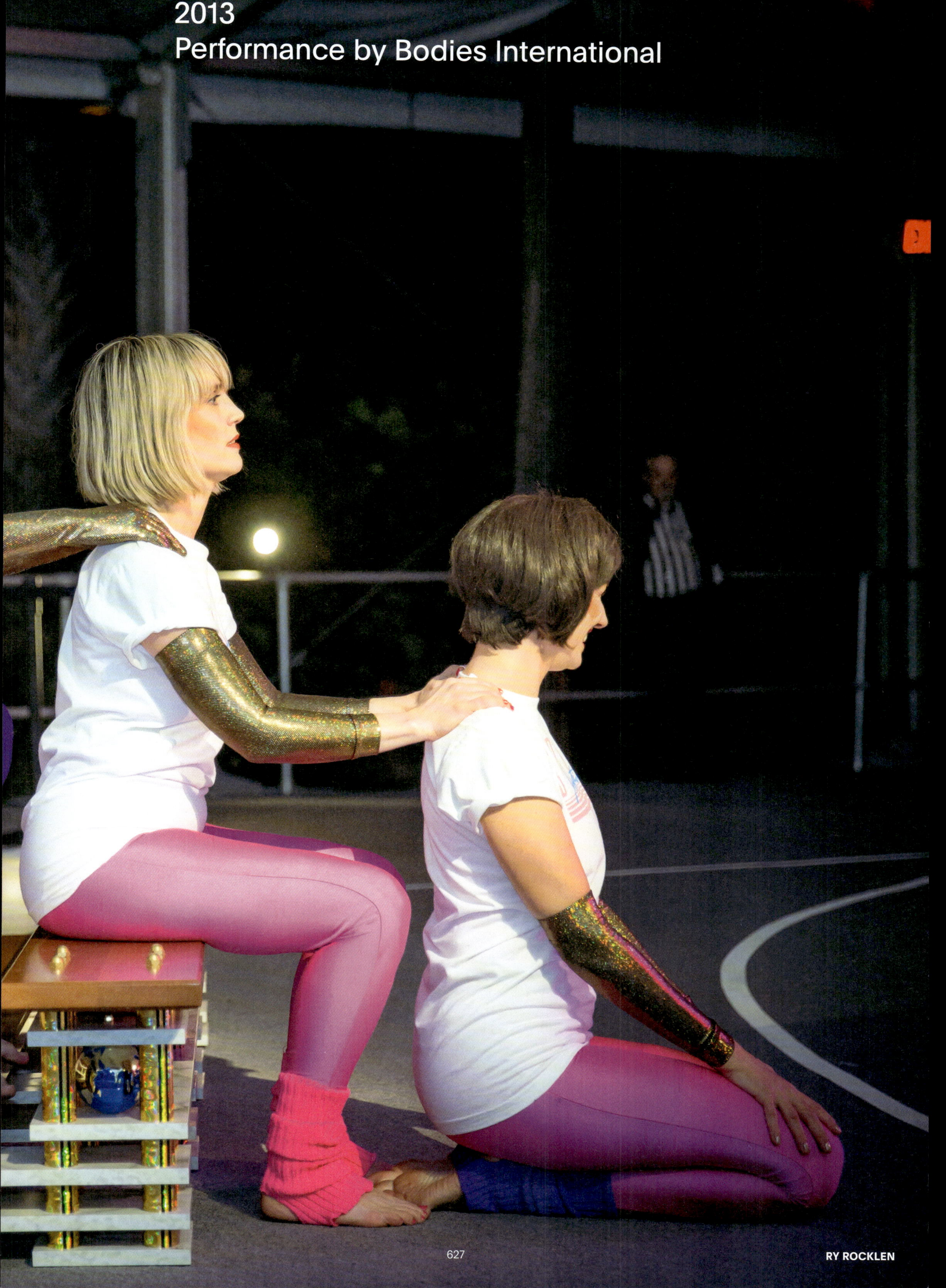

Trophy Modern, or A Drink by Oceanfront, Miami Beach

Conversation with Ry Rocklen on his *Night Court* bar conceived for and presented by Absolut Art Bureau, Art Basel in Miami Beach, December 2013

Miami Beach
Night Court
December 3–7, 2013
Oceanfront

Ry Rocklen
Absolut Art Bureau

CLÉMENT DIRIÉ How did you approach Absolut's proposal to realize this project?

RY ROCKLEN In 2010 I went to a local thrift shop—I often make works from found objects—and they had 150 or so trophies on the shelves. I thought that would be a great material to make a sculpture, maybe because of their odd kind of pathos but also their celebratory look—all the gold and shiny. I put them together into one big sculpture called *Second to None* (2011), which LACMA owns now.

Trophy Modern furniture is just furniture, but the enterprise of Trophy Modern is the art, and somehow this is the conceptual trajectory of the whole project.
— Ry Rocklen

I had finished that sculpture when my art dealer came to town, and we were walking around, looking at furniture shops when he told me: "I wish I had an artist who makes furniture." So I replied, "I have a whole line of furniture made out of trophy parts!" At the time it was just an idea … He said, "Oh that's great, let's do that at an art fair." In January 2013 I thus produced a couch, a coffee table, a club chair, and a dining chair, the first four Trophy Modern pieces, which were exhibited in a solo booth at Art Los Angeles Contemporary. When I had this idea, I was interested in making real furniture, not sculpture. So I came up with a company name. Everything in the Art Basel in Miami Beach installation is "Trophy Modern" furnishing. In a way it's almost a brand partnership: Absolut and Trophy Modern. Trophy Modern furniture is just furniture, but the enterprise of Trophy Modern is the art, and somehow this is the conceptual trajectory of the whole project.

Absolut had scouts on the ground of the LA fair and they contacted me. They came to Los Angeles to visit the studio and to explain the basic parameters of the project to me: the budget, the area where it would be, etc. I built a bar out of trophy parts, added furniture and some games—chess, ping-pong, etc. Part of the interest of Trophy Modern is that it's a system—you can make anything out of it.

In my work I often use tiles on the floor to dictate the space, how the work is arranged within the space by these patterns, so I thought it would be great to have a full-scale basketball court painted on the carpet. I knew that this size of deck would be similar to a basketball court so it would work proportionally—with its beautiful lines. This dictated the arrangement of the bar, the set, the games, etc.

CD You also conceived the cocktails and a music program …

RR Yes. Absolut was very keen for me to do both things. In the cocktail department, I used common sports phrases as my guidelines. "Winning Spirit" is just Absolut on the rocks with a little bit of water. "And one"—a basketball term—is an amazing ginger and blueberry cocktail and comes with a side shot of vanilla-infused vodka. The "Blood of a Champion" is a Bloody Mary and the "Modernade" is inspired by a sports drink and is served in this ridiculous plastic sports bottle with a straw.

As for the music program—well, I am from Los Angeles so I have a lot of incredibly talented friends that are musicians and performance artists. As a general parameter I wanted to have one performance-based and one music-based event every night. We had Mykki Blanco, Dynasty Handbag, Ariel Pink, Nite Jewel, TMO, Bodies International, etc. I made a rap band with my friend Nick Lowe, called The Bushes, and we'll be performing in our classic green outfit. It's a very thematic rap: we have songs about things made in China, about making love to animals, about confessions, etc.

In this kind of curating, I tried to keep it funny. All of these artists have some sense of humor, and their act is not super-serious. Obviously it's a bar, so there must be a bit of a sense of humor! And in general I wanted it to feel distinctly American.

LIONEL BOVIER I'd like to come back to your artistic practice. You said that it started as a sculpture, developed as a furniture concept, and ended up as a company that produces the furniture. You said that the art is the company, right?

RR Yes, the art as an enterprise. Art is a kind of game, in Duchamp's sense: he did a great checkmate for his generation by designating the readymade as an artwork.

LB You know that he made a book about chess … more specifically about the game's irresolution.

RR There is a little bit of that sensibility in Trophy Modern: one of my taglines is "In Trophy Modern, every one's a winner!" No one's a winner and every one is a winner. Try a game, just come, and be happy.

LB Were you thinking of Andy Warhol and his "business art" when making the company?

RR That too. I brought up Duchamp because I think of him as a problem-solver, someone who does this next move or next step; and for me the idea of having this corporation is all about the next step—we start with Trophy Modern and we have our first set of furniture, then we go on, we do the bar here, we develop the brand, open up our furniture store, and then we have some commercials, a good web presence, a logo, etc. It becomes a world onto itself, a Trophy Modern universe, a conceptual enterprise! As part of this project I should go all the way, that's the demand of the conceptual framework, even if I don't really want to go to my furniture store everyday, hoping I'll make sales …

LB Somehow there is a Sottsass and Alchimia aesthetics to it, with faux marble, 1980s-gilt, absurdly overdecorated elements.

RR Sottsass is someone I think about a lot. Memphis design was what I grew up with. It is totally in the furniture, in the faux finishes and the crazy colors, in its absurd functionality. But each element follows a very strict system: everything has to be made in a certain way to comply with how a real trophy would be built. Trophy Modern is crazy-looking furniture, it started as a joke, but I want each piece to look good, and within that aesthetic to be as discerning as possible. Even though the material is very loud, I am not adding to it, I am rather repairing it a bit.

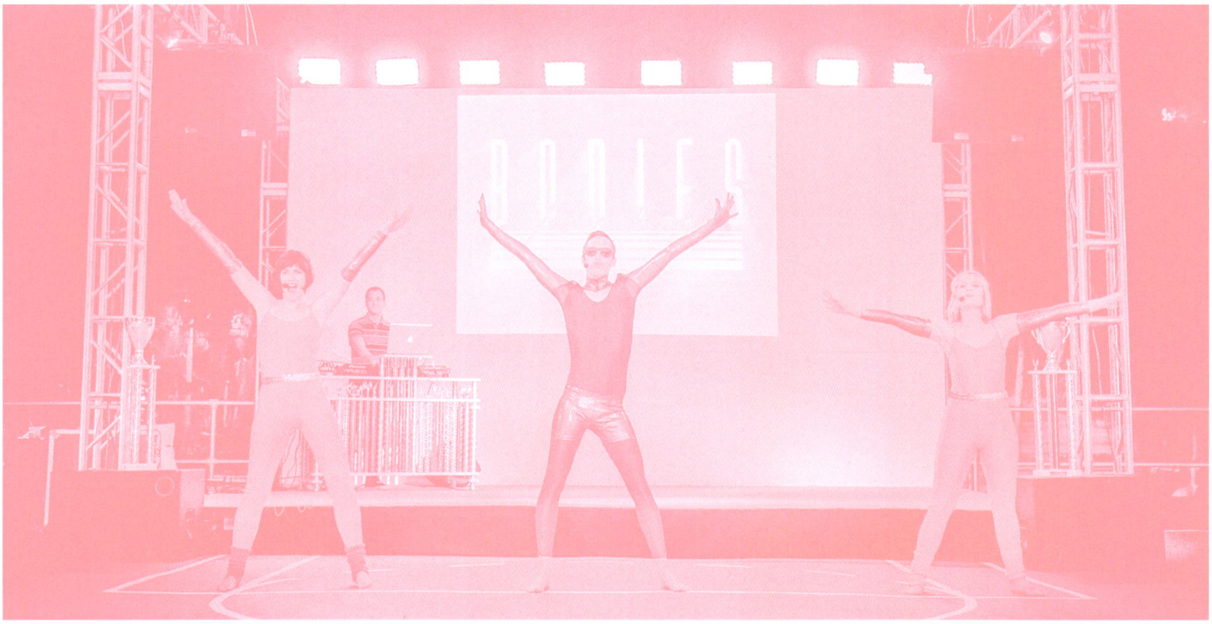

Night Court, 2013
Performance by Bodies International

S

S.A.L.E.S.

Rome

Discoveries
Encounters

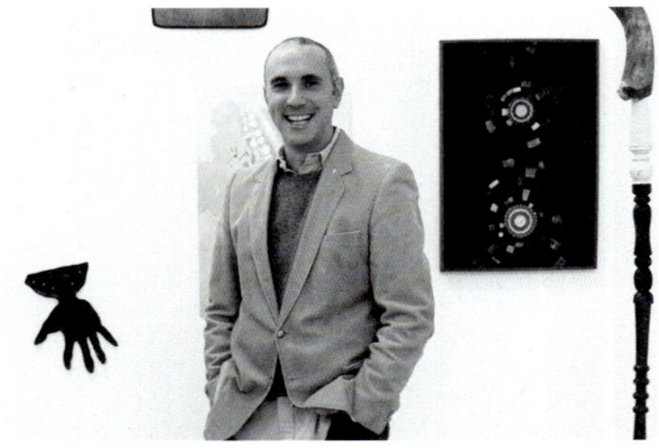

What first compelled you to open a gallery?
Since I was a small child I have always felt a strong passion for contemporary art. When I was a boy I understood that it was not only a passion, but the purpose of my life.

Who is the first artist you showed and what was most memorable about that show?
The first artist I showed was Monica Carocci. I clearly remember the crowd at the gallery and the passionate response the show had.

When did you first participate in Art Basel and what was most memorable about that show?
It was in 2011. The gallery participated in the Feature sector with a project based on a selection of Alighiero Boetti's late works in relation to most recent works of Stefano Arienti. Art Basel gives the chance to meet the most important collectors and curators of the world. And I had this chance! I think this is the most memorable aspect to me.

- **Contact** Galleria S.A.L.E.S.
  Andrea Vancheri
  andrea@galleriasales.it
  info@galleriasales.it
- **Established** 1994
- **Owner(s) / Partner(s)** Norberto Ruggeri
- **Team** 3
- **Space(s)** 200 m²
- **Artists at Art Basel** Avish Khebrehzadeh
  Shahryar Nashat
- **Further artists represented** Mario Airò
  Stefano Arienti
  Charles Avery
  Botto e Bruno
  Matti Braun
  Monica Carocci
  Hansjörg Dobliar
  Flavio Favelli
  Michel François
  Kerstin Kartscher
  Euan Macdonald
  Marta Mancini
  Eva Marisaldi
  Nicola Pecoraro
  Gitte Schäfer
  Wolfgang Tillmans
  Grazia Toderi
  Donald Urquhart
  Marcel van Eeden
  Claudia Wieser
  Richard Woods

Sage

Paris

Galleries

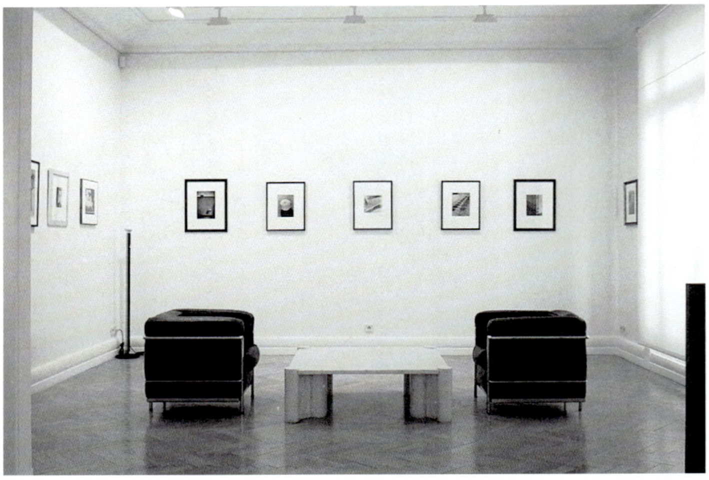

What first compelled you to open a gallery?
Our gallery's committed, above all, to art. Photography has proven to be a current and relevant, provocative, and reflective medium of our time. Sage Paris strives to reinforce these two ideas for the enjoyment and enrichment of the collecting community.

Who is the first artist you showed and what was most memorable about that show?
Karl Blossfeldt, vintage photographs. We sold them all before the opening.

When did you first participate in Art Basel and what was most memorable about that show?
In 2010, at Art Basel in Basel. The emotion we all felt when the show opened and closed.

- **Contact** Sage Paris
  François Sage
  francoissage@wanadoo.fr
  info@sageparis.com
- **Established** 2004
- **Owner(s) / Partner(s)** François Sage
- **Team** 4
- **Space(s)** 130 m²
- **Artists at Art Basel** David Armstrong
  Ilse Bing
  Brassaï
  Naoya Hatakeyama
  André Kertész
  Daido Moriyama
  Scott Peterman
  Josef Sudek
  Hiroshi Sugimoto
- **Further artists represented** Berenice Abbott
  Diane Arbus
  Eugène Atget
  Karl Blossfeldt
  Harry Callahan
  Bernard Dufour
  Walker Evans
  Florence Henri
  Miyako Ishiuchi
  Germaine Krull
  Man Ray
  Robert Mapplethorpe
  Masao Mochizuki
  Nadar
  Takuma Nakahira
  Helmut Newton
  Kazumasa Ogawa
  João Penalva
  Giuseppe Penone
  Stephen Shore
  Arthur Siegel
  Aaron Siskind
  Julia Smirnova
  W.H.F. Talbot
  Else Thalemann
  Cy Twombly
  Andy Warhol
  Tomoko Yoneda
  Zhuang Hui

Sakshi

Mumbai

- Galleries

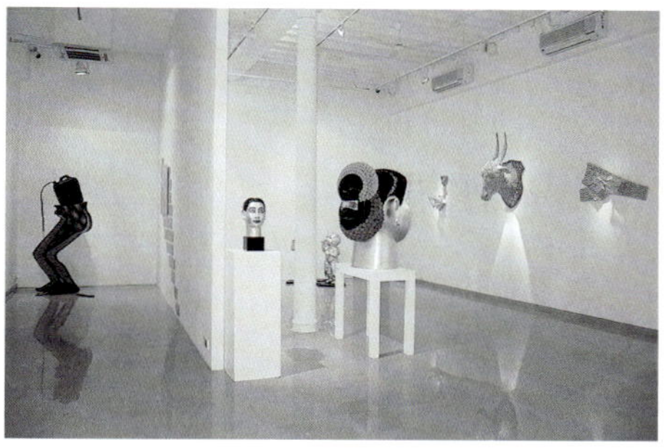

What first compelled you to open a gallery?
Love of art.

Who is the first artist you showed and what was most memorable about that show?
K. K. Hebbar—for his versatility and integrity.

When did you first participate in Art Basel and what was most memorable about that show?
In 2010. Just to be part of Art Basel!

- **Contact** Sakshi Gallery
  Sanyogita Deo
  art@sakshigallery.com
- **Established** 1984
- **Owner(s) / Partner(s)** Geetha Mehra
  Sanjay Kumar
- **Team** 20
- **Space(s)** 278 m²
- **Artists at Art Basel** El Anatsui
  Sunil Gawde
  Valay Shende
- **Further artists represented** Remen Chopra
  N.S. Harsha
  Anirban Mitra
  Surendran Nair
  Julian Opie
  Sudhir Patwardhan
  Ravinder Reddy
  Rekha Rodwittiya
  Chintan Upadhyay
  Nandini Valli Muthiah
  Vivek Vilasini

Salon 94

New York

- Unlimited
- Galleries
  Public

- **Contact** Salon 94
  info@salon94.com
- **Established** 2002
- **Owner(s) / Partner(s)** Jeanne Greenberg Rohatyn (Founder)
  Fabienne Stephan (Partner & Director)
  Alissa Friedman (Partner & Director)
- **Artists at Art Basel** Terry Adkins
  Amy Bessone
  Huma Bhabha
  Liz Cohen
  Gerald Davis
  Jules de Balincourt
  Jimmy DeSana
  Francesca DiMattio
  Dzine (Carlos Rolon)
  Sylvie Fleury
  Katy Grannan
  Kara Hamilton
  Paula Hayes
  Jon Kessler
  Takuro Kuwata
  Matthias Merkel Hess
  Marilyn Minter
  Carlo Mollino
  Takeshi Murata
  Jayson Musson
  Nicolas Party
  Aïda Ruilova
  David Benjamin Sherry
  Laurie Simmons
  Lorna Simpson
  Lucien Smith
  Betty Woodman

SCAI

Tokyo

- Galleries
- Galleries
- Galleries

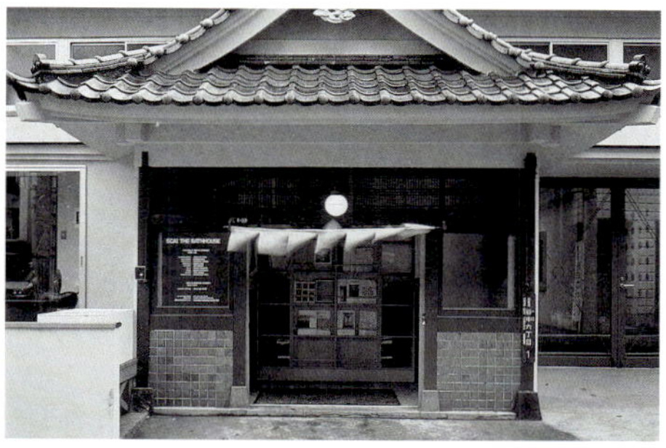

What first compelled you to open a gallery?
Mr. Shiraishi had long been engaged to form and develop the market for contemporary art from Tokyo since the 1980s, and had served various positions such as the Vice-Director of Touko Museum of Contemporary Art, and a founding member of NICAF, the first art fair in Japan with a clear focus on contemporary art. In 1993 he opened the current gallery at a former bathhouse in downtown Tokyo, with a vision to expand its inherent meaning of a coincidental meeting place for local communities. The dimensions of the building and an eight-meter-high ceiling also satisfied the criteria for quality exhibition space. The gallery is located in Old Tokyo, near the national museums.

Who is the first artist you showed and what was most memorable about that show?
The first solo exhibition at the current location was of James Lee Byars.

When did you first participate in Art Basel and what was most memorable about that show?
Our first participation in Basel was in 2001. Since then, SCAI The Bathhouse has been a regular participant at Art Basel in Basel, Miami Beach, and now Hong Kong.

- **Contact** SCAI The Bathhouse
  Koichiro Osaka
  info@scaithebathhouse.com
- **Established** 1989/1993
- **Owner(s) / Partner(s)** Masami Shiraishi (Managing Director)
- **Team** 8
- **Space(s)** 88 m²
- **Artists at Art Basel** Brian Alfred
  Noriko Ambe
  Toshikatsu Endo
  Jeppe Hein
  Anish Kapoor
  Yusuke Komuta
  Tatsuo Miyajima
  Mariko Mori
  Natsuyuki Nakanishi
  Kohei Nawa
  Miwa Ogasawara
  Daisuke Ohba
  Tomoko Shioyasu
  Sputniko!
  Lee Ufan
  Apichatpong Weerasethakul
- **Further artists represented** Genpei Akasegawa
  Darren Almond
  Didier Courbot
  William Eggleston
  Kaoru Hirano
  Jenny Holzer
  Naoki Ishikawa
  Joonho Jeon
  Kentaro Kobuke
  Haruka Kojin
  Yurie Nagashima
  Julian Opie
  Martin Puryear
  Tomoaki Suzuki
  Nobuko Tsuchiya
  Choe U
  Tadanori Yokoo

S

Scheibler

Berlin

Galleries Unlimited

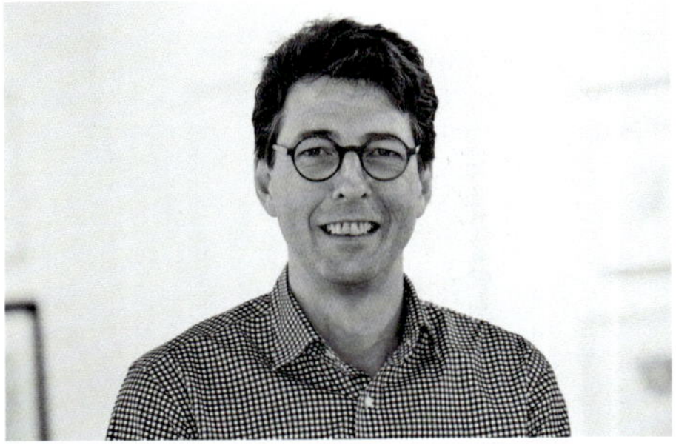

What first compelled you to open a gallery?
Since I was 17, I wanted to be actively involved with art and be a transmitter/ambassador for artists, their ideas, and what they stand for.

Who is the first artist you showed and what was most memorable about that show?
It was Chargesheimer. It was the first exhibition that did not show any of his photography, but instead his photo-chemical experiments from the early 1950s up to his photo-chemical paintings of the 1960s.

When did you first participate in Art Basel and what was most memorable about that show?
I participated for the first time in 1994, with a solo presentation of Jack Pierson. It was the artist's first exposure to an international audience and, despite the bad economy at that time, an almost sold out booth.

- **Contact** Aurel Scheibler
Bendetta Roux
office@aurelscheibler.de
- **Established** 1994
- **Owner(s) / Partner(s)** Aurel Scheibler
- **Team** 4
- **Space(s)** 180 m²
- **Artists at Art Basel** Jonathan Bragdon
Öyvind Fahlström
Norbert Kricke
Stefan Löffelhardt
Ernst Wilhelm Nay
Alice Neel
David Schutter
Curt Stenvert
Gavin Turk
Michael Wutz
- **Further artists** Michel Auder
Wolfgang Betke
Tom Chamberlain
Neil Gall
Anthony Goicolea
Jack Pierson
Thomas Rentmeister
Alessandro Twombly
Christoph Wedding
Erwin Wurm
Joe Zucker

Schipper

Berlin

Galleries Unlimited
Galleries

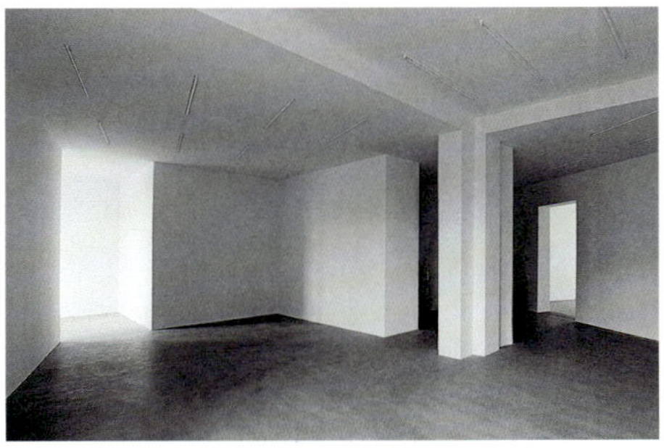

What first compelled you to open a gallery?
In the 1980s, after moving to Germany, in order to finance my studies I worked for Benedikt Taschen, who had just opened a comic book store and started his publishing house. I then took a job at an auction house for Asian antiques and started to work for Monika Sprüth's gallery. Later I began to publish multiples, such as Rosemarie Trockel's *Balaklava*. In 1987 I participated in the program of the École du Magasin, an international curatorial program, in Grenoble. There I met Dominique Gonzalez-Foerster and Philippe Parreno. Both were among the first artists to join the gallery I opened in 1989 in Cologne. I wanted to work for and with artists. At that time, the gallery setting seemed to me the most flexible, but also the most durable structure that allowed for a real relationship with art and its making.

Who is the first artist you showed and what was most memorable about that show?
The first show I did was with the artists' group General Idea. I thought that a gallery should also be a place of production and experimentation. Therefore, for this very first exhibition, I wanted to produce General Idea's *Yen Boutique*, which unfortunately wasn't finished in time. AA, Jorge, and Felix were very indulgent and decided to turn it into a two-part inaugural show: the work was first shown covered, and the opening happened around this mysterious object which then was unveiled a week later.

- **Contact** Esther Schipper
Stefanie Lockwood
lockwood@estherschipper.com
office@estherschipper.com
- **Established** 1989
- **Owner(s) / Partner(s)** Esther Schipper
Florian Wojnar
- **Team** 17
- **Space(s)** 850 m²
- **Artists at Art Basel** Angela Bulloch
Liam Gillick
Dominique Gonzalez-Foerster
Pierre Huyghe
Gabriel Kuri
Ari Benjamin Meyers
Philippe Parreno
Ugo Rondinone
Karin Sander
Tomás Saraceno
- **Further artists represented** Matti Braun
AA Bronson
Nathan Carter
Thomas Demand
Ceal Floyer
Grönlund-Nisunen
Ann Veronica Janssens
Christoph Keller
Isa Melsheimer
Christopher Roth
Julia Scher
The Estate Of General Idea

Schoeni

Hong Kong

Insights

- **Contact** Schoeni Art Gallery
gallery@schoeni.com.hk
- **Established** 1992
- **Owner(s) / Partner(s)** Nicole Schoeni
- **Artists at Art Basel** Hung Keung
- **Further artists represented** Chen Fei
Chen Yu
Fung Lik Yan Kevin
Kum Chi Keung
Li Hongbo
Ling Jian
Tang Zhigang
Xia Xiaowan
Yang Yongliang
Zhang Linhai
Zhao Fang
Zhou Jinhua

Schöttle

Munich
Paris
Cologne
Zurich

● Galleries

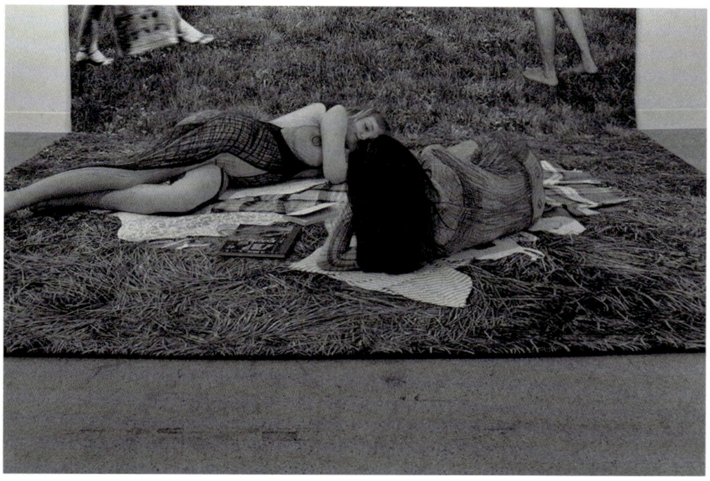

What first compelled you to open a gallery?
The proximity to the artists.

Who is the first artist you showed and what was most memorable about that show?
Arnulf Rainer—the radicality of his works.

When did you first participate in Art Basel and what was most memorable about that show?
In 1972.

- **Contact** Galerie Rüdiger Schöttle
Ingrid Lohaus
info@galerie-schoettle.de
- **Established** 1968
- **Owner(s) / Partner(s)** Rüdiger Schöttle
- **Team** 7
- **Space(s)** 240 m²
- **Artists at Art Basel** Janis Avotinš
Stephan Balkenhol
Maria Bartuszová
Armin Boehm
Martin Boyce
Patty Chang
Chen Wei
David Claerbout
Anders Clausen
Steven Claydon
James Coleman
Martin Creed
Björn Dahlem
Slawomir Elsner
Elger Esser
Liam Gillick
Dan Graham
Rodney Graham
Thomas Helbig
Lorena Herrera Rashid
Candida Höfer
Douglas Huebler
On Kawara
John Knight
Běla Kolářová
Tim Lee
Goshka Macuga
Jan Merta
Alex Mirutziu
Andrew Palmer
Thomas Ruff
Anri Sala
Thomas Schütte
Agathe Snow
Thomas Struth
Florian Süssmayr
Jeff Wall
Thomas Zipp

Schubert

Berlin

● Nova

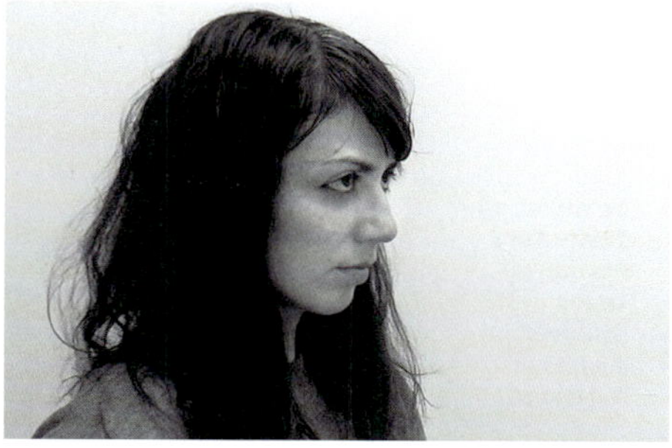

What first compelled you to open a gallery?
Love and passion for art and my ex-boyfriend.

Who is the first artist you showed and what was most memorable about that show?
My ex-boyfriend, Maximilian Zentz Zlomovitz, still an artist of the gallery. It was incredible to see how he changed the complete exhibition space with his installation *Chinese Restaurant*, into a sci-fi-horror movie set.

When did you first participate in Art Basel and what was most memorable about that show?
In 2010, at Art Basel in Miami Beach. It was so exciting to see how people reacted to a then unknown artist I first showed, Marieta Chirulescu.

- **Contact** Galerie Micky Schubert
Mihaela Chiriac
info@mickyschubert.de
- **Established** 2006
- **Owner(s) / Partner(s)** Micky Schubert
- **Space(s)** 110 m²
- **Artists at Art Basel** Lydia Gifford
Sue Tompkins
- **Further artists represented** Ketuta Alexi-Meskhishvili
Marieta Chirulescu
Thea Djordjadze
Graham Fagen
Manuela Leinhoss
Carolin Leszczinski
Barry MacGregor Johnston
Alan Michael
Gerda Scheepers
Daniel Sinsel
Stephen Sutcliffe
Mark Van Yetter
Maximilian Zentz Zlomovitz

Schulte

Berlin

● Galleries Unlimited
● Galleries Kabinett

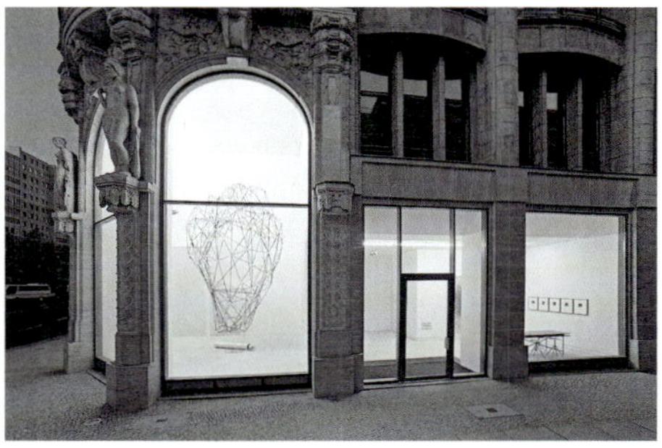

What first compelled you to open a gallery?
The chance to create real change in the German capital after the Wall came down.

Who is the first artist you showed and what was most memorable about that show?
Rebecca Horn. Its tremendous quality, the 4,000 visitors that came to see it, selling the whole show to the Hamburger Kunsthalle within a few weeks, and seeing it installed there in its own special space.

When did you first participate in Art Basel and what was most memorable about that show?
In 1991. Selling almost everything I brought, including the 240 *Plaster Surrogates* by Allan McCollum.

- **Contact** Galerie Thomas Schulte
Gonzalo Alarcón
gonzalo@galeriethomasschulte.de
mail@galeriethomasschulte.de
- **Established** 1991
- **Owner(s) / Partner(s)** Thomas Schulte
Stefan Roepke
- **Team** 9
- **Space(s)** 340 m²
- **Artists at Art Basel** Alice Aycock
Danilo Dueñas
Mark Francis
Alfredo Jaar
Jonathan Lasker
Fabian Marcaccio
David Reed
Iris Schomaker
Juan Uslé
- **Further artists represented** Victor Burgin
Richard Deacon
Idris Khan
Paco Knöller
Iñigo Manglano-Ovalle
Robert Mapplethorpe
Bernhard Martin
Gordon Matta-Clark
Allan McCollum
Michael Müller
Jacco Olivier
João Penalva
Hermann Pitz
Peter Rogiers
Albrecht Schnider
Katharina Sieverding
Stephen Willats
Robert Wilson

Schwartz

Rio de Janeiro — Nova

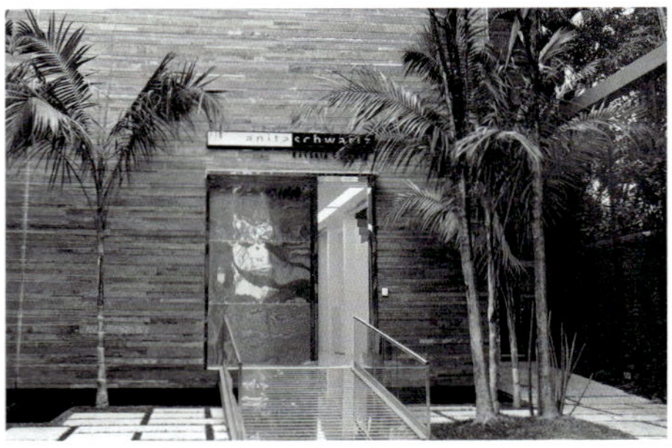

What first compelled you to open a gallery?
Under the influence of my parents and their European heritage (Poland and Lithuania), I always lived surrounded by artworks. When my professional life was at its first stages, it seemed like a natural choice, being aware that it requires constant dedication and commitment. Owing a gallery is, above all, my life project.

Who is the first artist you showed and what was most memorable about that show?
Carlos Zilio was chosen to inaugurate our new space due to his importance in the Brazilian art scene since the 1960s. Being the first building in the city fully designed to host a gallery, a large audience of over 1,000 people attended the exhibition opening.

When did you first participate in Art Basel and what was most memorable about that show?
My first participation was at Art Basel in Miami Beach in 2011 on the Solo Projects, with an installation by young artist Otavio Schipper. For the work titled *Empty Voices*, 20 aphonic diapasons were displayed on an anechoic chamber-like booth. It was an exhibition heavily visited by art critics and important collectors; I was greatly honored to be part of the event.

- **Contact** Anita Schwartz Galeria de Arte
Felipe Pena
felipe@anitaschwartz.com.br
galeria@anitaschwartz.com.br
- **Established** 1998
- **Owner(s) / Partner(s)** Anita Schwartz
- **Space(s)** 700 m²
- **Artists at Art Basel** Carla Guagliardi
Antonio Manuel
Abraham Palatnik
- **Further artists represented** Rochelle Costi
Célia Euvaldo
Ana Holck
Gonçalo Ivo
Artur Lescher
Maria Lynch
Ivens Machado
Everardo Miranda
Germana Monte-Mór
Wagner Morales
José Paulo
Wanda Pimentel
Fernanda Quinderé
Nuno Ramos
Otavio Schipper
Estela Sokol
Gustavo Speridião
Angelo Venosa
Daisy Xavier
Carlos Zilio

Semarang

Semarang — Insights

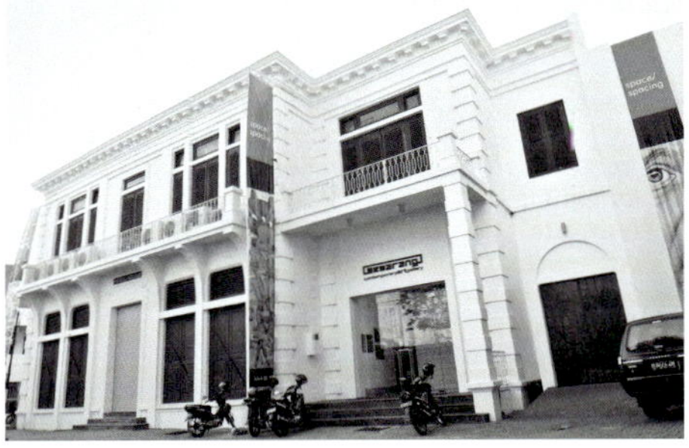

What first compelled you to open a gallery?
A love of art and a commitment to dedicate a venue as an introductory medium for the artworks of Asian contemporary artists, especially those from Indonesia.

Who is the first artist you showed and what was most memorable about that show?
Widayat. Most memorable about the show was the enthusiasm of the public in Semarang, Indonesia.

When did you first participate in Art Basel and what was most memorable about that show?
In Hong Kong in 2013. Most memorable was the chance to meet many collectors from all over the world.

- **Contact** Semarang Gallery
Devi Ariany
galeri_semarang@yahoo.com
- **Established** 2001
- **Owner(s) / Partner(s)** Chris Dharmawan
- **Space(s)** 1,000 m²
- **Artists at Art Basel** Eddie haRA
- **Further artists represented** Samsul Arifin
Bestrizal Besta
Marco Cassani
Andy Dewantoro
Sugiyo Dwiarso
Agapetus A. Kristiandana
Sardono W. Kusumo
Rudi Mantofani
I Made Widya Diputra

Seroussi

Paris • Galleries

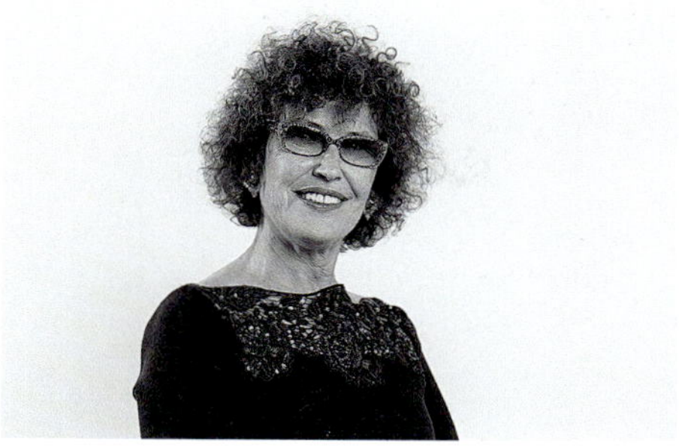

What first compelled you to open a gallery?
The desire to share my artistic passions.

Who is the first artist you showed and what was most memorable about that show?
Sandro Chia. It was the first time I showed a contemporary artist, while I was specialized in the 1920s, and I was impressed by the international success of the exhibition. I sold everything! Which was not the case for the next exhibition with works by Giaccomo Balla!

When did you first participate in Art Basel and what was most memorable about that show?
That was in 1980. I presented a show titled *Black and White* with drawings by Kandinsky, Léger, Delaunay, etc. Art Basel made me discover an international audience and a completely different world from that of my gallery in Paris.

- **Contact** Galerie Natalie Seroussi
  Anne-Sarah Bénichou
  evenements-seroussi@wanadoo.fr
  galerieseroussi@wanadoo.fr
- **Established** 1983
- **Owner(s) / Partner(s)** Natalie Seroussi
- **Team** 4
- **Space(s)** 70 m²
- **Artists at Art Basel** Yaacov Agam
  Carmelo Arden Quin
  Giacomo Balla
  Marcel Louis Baugniet
  Pol Bury
  Alexander Calder
  Lygia Clark
  Philippe Decrauzat
  Marcel Duchamp
  Malachi Farrell
  Fausto Melotti
  Jesús Rafael Soto
  Takis
  Jean Tinguely
- **Further artists represented** Jean Arp
  Evelyne Axell
  Alighiero e Boetti
  Victor Brauner
  Christo
  Jean Dubuffet
  Max Ernst
  Raymond Hains
  Jean Hélion
  Le Corbusier
  Fernand Léger
  André Masson
  Gordon Matta-Clark
  Francis Picabia
  Martial Raysse
  Gil Joseph Wolman

Seven Art

New Delhi • Discoveries

- **Contact** Seven Art
  supriya@sevenartlimited.com
- **Established** 2008
- **Owner(s) / Partner(s)** Aparajita Jain
- **Artists at Art Basel** Rajorshi Ghosh
- **Further artists represented** Amina Ahmed
  Brendan Fernandes
  Suhasini Kejriwal
  Martand Khosla
  Aakash Nihalani
  Saravanan Parasuraman
  Vijai Patchineelam
  Asim Waqif

Sfeir-Semler

Beirut
Hamburg
• Galleries
Unlimited

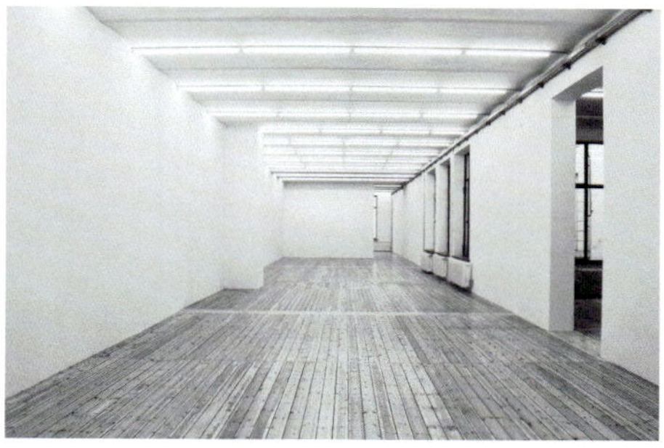

What first compelled you to open a gallery?
I opened my first gallery in the middle of nowhere, in Kiel, in the north of Germany, after I finished my PhD and had my daughter. It was almost a spontaneous decision, but I've loved art for as long as I can remember, and it just felt right at the time.

Who is the first artist you showed and what was most memorable about that show?
My first show was Arnulf Rainer, he had made a series on Bernhard Minetti. It was magical to be around these older artists who had such a strong connection.

When did you first participate in Art Basel and what was most memorable about that show?
I first participated in Art Basel in 1989, or 1990. I had started on the ground floor with the established galleries, and the most memorable thing is really how different the fair and my gallery are today in comparison. I actually left Basel in 2003 after working with strongly established German and European artists, and then came back on the first floor, with a new group of young, developing Middle Eastern artists—and I couldn't be happier.

- **Contact** Sfeir-Semler
  Anna Nowak
  galerie@sfeir-semler.com
  beirut@sfeir-semler.com
- **Established** 1985
- **Owner(s) / Partner(s)** Andree Sfeir-Semler
- **Team** 6
- **Space(s)** 600 m² (Beirut)
  250 m² (Hamburg)
- **Artists at Art Basel** Etel Adnan
  Mounira Al Solh
  Yto Barrada
  Robert Barry
  Günter Haese
  Rabih Mroué
  Timo Nasseri
  Walid Raad
  Khalil Rabah
  Marwan Rechmaoui
  Hassan Sharif
  Wael Shawky
  Rayyane Tabet
  Akram Zaatari
- **Further artists represented** Moritz Altmann
  Taysir Batniji
  Balthasar Burkhard
  Elger Esser
  Ian Hamilton Finlay
  Hans Haacke
  Marwan
  Hiroyuki Masuyama
  Michelangelo Pistoletto
  Ulrich Rückriem
  Christine Streuli
  Hoda Tawakol

Shainman

New York • Galleries

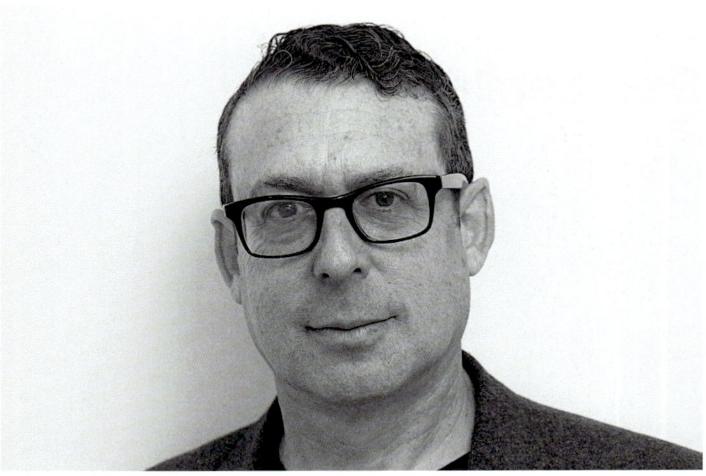

What first compelled you to open a gallery?
The love of art and the inability to make my own.

Who is the first artist you showed and what was most memorable about that show?
My first show was with Claude Simard and it was all very memorable. It was such an exciting time, opening a new gallery with an artist I believed in so strongly. I was able to sell most of the show, which allowed me to stay in the business.

When did you first participate in Art Basel and what was most memorable about that show?
The gallery first participated in Art Basel in Miami Beach in 2003. I never realized that you could place so many artists from museum collections at an art fair.

- **Contact** Jack Shainman Gallery
Joeonna Bellorado-Samuels
joeonna@jackshainman.com
info@jackshainman.com
- **Established** 1984
- **Owner(s) / Partner(s)** Jack Shainman
- **Space(s)** 3,500 m²
- **Artists at Art Basel** El Anatsui
Nick Cave
Gehard Demetz
Vibha Galhotra
Brad Kahlhamer
Hayv Kahraman
Kerry James Marshall
Odili Donald Odita
Toyin Odutola
Susana Solano
Hank Willis Thomas
Lynette Yiadom-Boakye
- **Further artists represented** Shimon Attie
Radcliffe Bailey
Tim Bavington
Yoan Capote
Barkley L. Hendricks
Deborah Luster
Richard Mosse
Zwelethu Mthethwa
Adi Nes
Jackie Nickerson
Claudette Schreuders
Malick Sidibe
Michael Snow
L.N. Tallur
Carlos Vega
Leslie Wayne
Carrie Mae Weems

Shanghai Gallery

Shanghai • Galleries

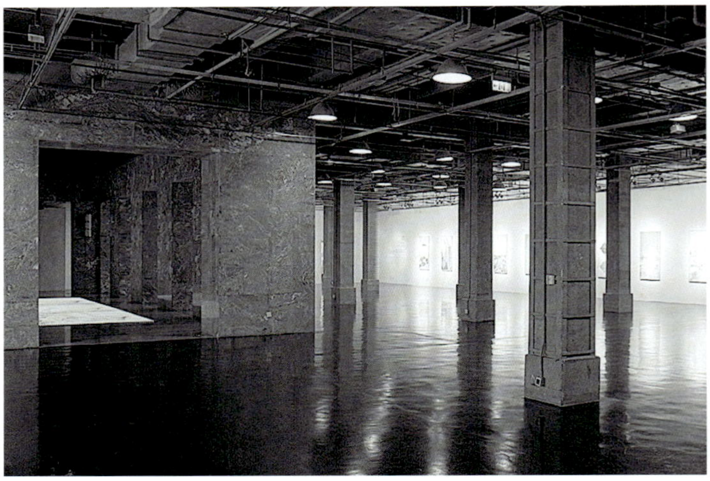

What first compelled you to open a gallery?
When our family bought one of the buildings along the Shanghai Bund, the Bund area was zoned as a financial district. Underlying is a resilient belief that the historic and scenic Bund area is unique as an identity to Shanghai. It has a unique character in which the citizens take pride, and that no other cities possess. We approached the then Shanghai Mayor and presented a new vision to renovate the building to house contemporary Chinese art, culture, and life. We believe that this landmark Bund district in Shanghai beckons as a vibrant round-the-clock center of contemporary culture.

Who is the first artist you showed and what was most memorable about that show?
It was a group show titled *Beyond Boundaries* featuring the most representative Chinese contemporary artists, including Fang Lijun, Gu Dexin, Lin Tianmiao, Sui Jianguo, Wang Guangyi, Wang Jianwei, Xu Bing, Yan Lei, Yang Fudong, Ye Yongqing, Yue Minjun, Zhan Wang, Zhang Peili, Zhang Xiaogang, and Zhou Chunya, etc.

- **Contact** Shanghai Gallery of Art
Cindy Yang
cyang@on-the-bund.com
gr@on-the-bund.com
- **Established** 2004
- **Owner(s) / Partner(s)** Cherie Liem (Chairman)
- **Team** 10
- **Space(s)** 1,200 m²
- **Artists at Art Basel** Gao Weigang
Jiang Zhi
Michael Lin
Map Office
Rirkrit Tiravanija
Wu Di
Xu Bing
Zhao Renhui
- **Further artists represented** Feng Mengbo
Jin Jiangbo
Qiu Jie
Tan Dun
Wu Shanzhuan &
Inga Svala Thorsdottir
Zhao Xuebing

ShanghART

Shanghai — Galleries
Beijing — Galleries
Singapore

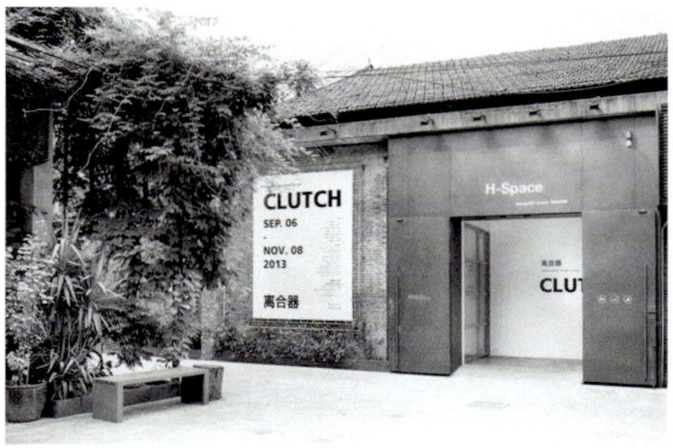

What first compelled you to open a gallery?
Maybe due to my family background.

Who is the first artist you showed and what was most memorable about that show?
Ding Yi. It was an exhibition with no name in a corridor of the Portman Hotel.

When did you first participate in Art Basel and what was most memorable about that show?
In 2000, in the Statements sector with a solo presentation by Zhou Tiehai, *3 Scrolls*.

- **Contact** — ShanghART, Fay Yeong, fay@shanghartgallery.com, info@shanghartgallery.com
- **Established** — 1996
- **Owner(s) / Partner(s)** — Lorenz Helbling
- **Team** — 27
- **Space(s)** — 2,678 m²
- **Artists** at **Art Basel** — BirdHead, Chen Xiaoyun, Ding Yi, Geng Jianyi, Li Shan, Liang Shaoji, Liu Weijian, MadeIn Company, Shen Fan, Sun Xun, Tang Maohong, Xue Song, Yang Fudong, Yang Zhenzhong, Yu Youhan, Zeng Fanzhi, Zhang Ding, Zhang Enli, Zhou Tiehai
- **Further artists represented** — Chen Yanyin, Gu Zhenghua, Hu Jieming, Hu Yang, Huang Kui, Ji Wenyu & Zhu Weibing, Jin Weihong, Li Pinghu, Liang Yue, Lu Chunsheng, Mao Yan, Pu Jie, Shao Yi, Shi Qing, Shi Yong, Song Tao, Tang Guo, Wang Guangyi, Wang Youshen, Wei Guangqing, Wu Yiming, Xiang Liqing, Xu Zhen, Xue Song, Yu Youhan, Zhang Qing, Zhao Biandi, Zhou Zixi, Zhu Jia

Shin

Tokyo — Insights

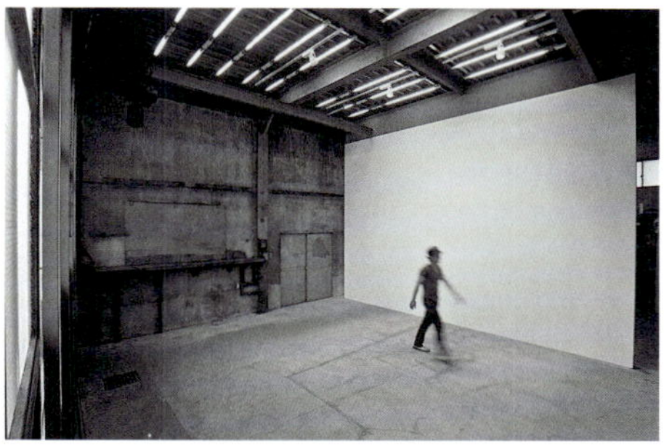

What first compelled you to open a gallery?
We opened to introduce private, public, and corporate clients to cutting-edge exhibitions, introducing both local and international artists who express themselves through a conceptual approach. Our further objective is to seek a relationship between art and other disciplines, such as architecture.

Who is the first artist you showed and what was most memorable about that show?
Ai Weiwei. It was the first solo show of Ai Weiwei at a commercial gallery in Japan. The gallery space is housed in a former iron factory, which makes the space different from a white cube or a museum. Also the size of the space fitted perfectly with the volume of the work, *Cube Light*. It turned into a very unique exhibition. It was widely publicized in the media and attracted lots of visitors.

When did you first participate in Art Basel and what was most memorable about that show?
In 2013, in Hong Kong. Meeting world-class collectors.

- **Contact** — Misa Shin Gallery, Aiko Nakamura, info@misashin.com
- **Established** — 2010
- **Owner(s) / Partner(s)** — Misa Shin
- **Space(s)** — 92 m² (including office and storage)
- **Artists at Art Basel** — Shomei Tomatsu
- **Further artists represented** — Ai Weiwei, Arata Isozaki, Back Seung Woo, Jio Shimizu, Kimsooja, Ken Lum, Momoyo Torimitsu, Shingo Francis, Tsuyoshi Ozawa, Yasuko Iba

ShugoArts

Tokyo — Galleries
Galleries

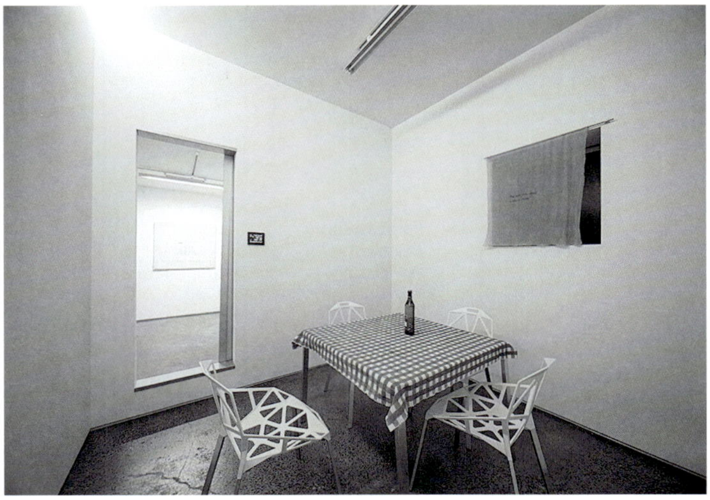

What first compelled you to open a gallery?
Artists with whom Shugo Satani had been working.

Who is the first artist you showed and what was most memorable about that show?
Yasumasa Morimura, *A Hundred Polaroids*. The artist proposed to have a show at ShugoArts when he found out that Shugo had started the gallery. Shugo was very honored, since he had known the artist for years.

When did you first participate in Art Basel and what was most memorable about that show?
In the Statement sector in 2000 with Navin Rawanchaikul. The artist received the Baloise Prize and a lot of attention.

- **Contact** ShugoArts
  Shinichiro Higashi
  shinichiro@shugoarts.com
  info@shugoarts.com
- **Established** 2000
- **Owner(s) / Partner(s)** Shugo Satani (President)
  Satoko Oe (Director)
- **Space(s)** 130 m²
- **Artists at Art Basel** Masaya Chiba
  Chen Chieh-Jen
  Yukio Fujimoto
  Carsten Höller
  Mitsuhiro Ikeda
  Leiko Ikemura
  Takuya Ikezaki
  Tomohito Ishii
  Runa Islam
  Tadasuke Iwanaga
  Ilya Kabakov
  Teppei Kaneuji
  Shinichiro Kano
  Lee Kit
  Masato Kobayashi
  Aki Kondo
  Naofumi Maruyama
  Boris Mikhailov
  Ritsue Mishima
  Yasumasa Morimura
  Takuma Nakahira
  Kazuna Taguchi
  Shigeo Toya
  Jun Yang
  Tomoko Yoneda
- **Further artists represented** Candice Breitz
  Ylva Ogland

Sicardi

Houston • Galleries

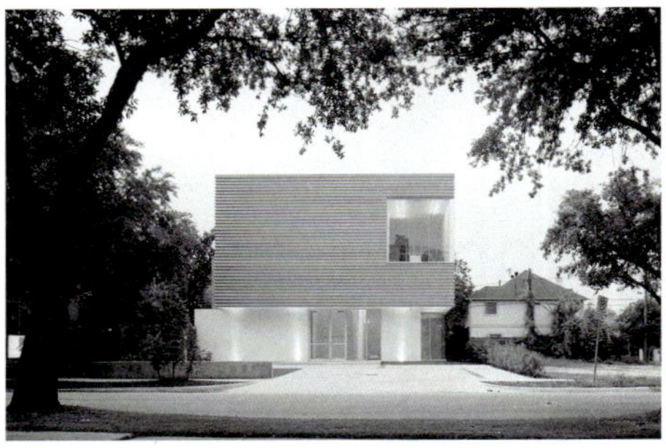

When did you first participate in Art Basel?
In 2005.

- **Contact** Sicardi Gallery
  Laura Wellen
  laura@sicardi.com
  info@sicardi.com
- **Established** 1994
- **Owner(s) / Partner(s)** María Inés Sicardi
  (Owner and Director)
  Allison Ayers
  (Owner and Co-Director)
  Carlos Bacino
  (Owner)
- **Team** 8
- **Space(s)** 548 m²
- **Artists at Art Basel** Antonio Asis
  Martín Blaszko
  Carlos Cruz-Diez
  Jesús Rafael Soto
  Luis Tomasello
- **Further artists represented** María Fernanda Cardoso
  Gabriel de la Mora
  Dias & Riedweg
  Sérvulo Esmeraldo
  Manuel Espinosa
  León Ferrari
  Gego
  Thomas Glassford
  Graciela Hasper
  Marco Maggi
  Oscar Muñoz
  Liliana Porter
  Miguel Ángel Rojas
  Pablo Siquier

Side 2

Tokyo • Insights • Statements

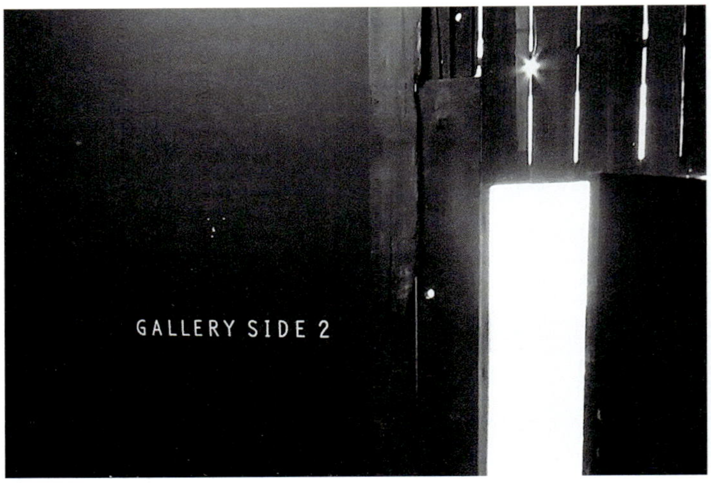

What first compelled you to open a gallery?
When I returned from New York in early 1990s, artists that I had befriend such as Rirkrit Tiravanija, Udomsak Krisanamis, Maureen Gallace, and Karen Kilimnik had not had a gallery show in Tokyo. I really wanted to introduce their work to the Tokyo audience.

Who is the first artist you showed and what was most memorable about that show?
Yutaka Sone. Showing a Japanese artist for our first show was a challenge for myself as I had been away. To talk with Yutaka about the Japanese art scene, its struggles and possibilities, and also about the international art community, was a very important starting point.

When did you first participate in Art Basel and what was most memorable about that show?
In 2001 in the Statements sector in Art Basel. I was really impressed and excited to see and get to know galleries from all over the world, from different generations, but all with the same serious commitment to art.

- **Contact** Gallery Side 2
  Junko Shimada
  junko@galleryside2.net
  info@galleryside2.net
- **Established** 1997
- **Owner(s) / Partner(s)** Junko Shimada
- **Team** 3
- **Space(s)** 80 m²
- **Artists at Art Basel** Takeo Hanazawa
  Udomsak Krisanamis
  Peter McDonald
  Yusuke Saito
- **Further artists represented** Jun Fujita
  Maureen Gallace
  Takahiro Inamori
  Elke Krystufek
  Yuko Murata
  Isabel Nolan
  Steven Pippin
  Rob Pruitt
  Shinzko Sato
  Rirkrit Tiravanija
  Fumito Urabe
  Yasuko Watanabe

Sies + Höke

Düsseldorf

- Galleries
- Galleries
- Galleries

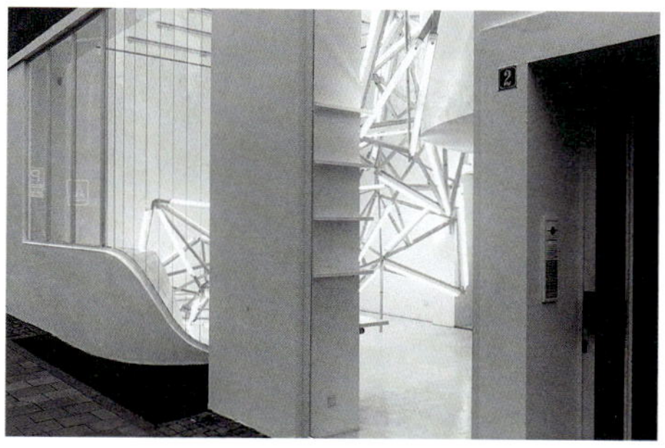

What first compelled you to open a gallery?
We opened the gallery with no list of artists, no collectors, and no money.

Who is the first artist you showed and what was most memorable about that show?
The first show was Florian Slotawa. He built a plywood box that occupied the whole gallery space, and into which we had to move with all the furniture, supply, staff, and art. There was nothing to sell.

When did you first participate in Art Basel and what was most memorable about that show?
The first participation was at Art Basel in Miami Beach in 2003. We showed in one of the containers by the beach.

- **Contact** Sies + Höke
Hanne Tonger-Erk
hanne@sieshoeke.com
post@sieshoeke.com
- **Established** 1999
- **Owner(s) / Partner(s)** Nina Höke
Alexander Sies
- **Team** 10
- **Space(s)** 600 m²
- **Artists at Art Basel** Abel Auer
Etienne Chambaud
Talia Chetrit
Björn Dahlem
Marcel Dzama
Daniel Gustav Cramer
João Maria Gusmão + Pedro Paiva
Federico Herrero
Dorota Jurczak
Thomas Kiesewetter
Kris Martin
Jonathan Meese
Fabrice Samyn
Florian Slotawa
Michael van Ofen
Claudia Wieser
Sam Windett

Sikkema Jenkins

New York

- Galleries
- Galleries
- Galleries

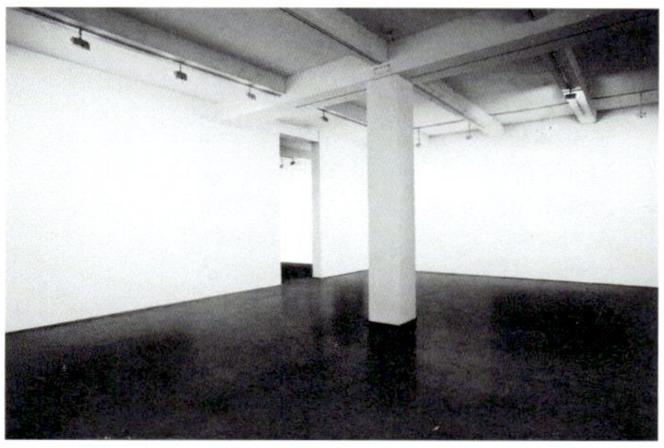

What first compelled you to open a gallery?
When I opened Wooster Gardens gallery in 1991 the art world was in a state of crisis. Numerous galleries were closing and there was a loss of confidence in the transcendent possibilities of art. I wanted to reassert it.

Who is the first artist you showed and what was most memorable about that show?
Our first exhibition was a group show called *Healing*, which included, among others, works by Tom Friedman, Adam Fuss, David Ireland, Donald Moffett, Jack Pierson, Pedro Cabrita Reis, and Felix Gonzalez-Torres. The exhibition started with the notion of healing—to make better, to make oneself better, to make oneself sound and whole again, and then connect it with the idea of making art. I believed in both healing and art as a remaking, a process that leads to change. The AIDS crisis had by necessity taken on a new urgency and gave rise to new and radical forms of art.

When did you first participate in Art Basel and what was most memorable about that show?
In 1998, the gallery participated with a Statements booth by Kara Walker. What was most memorable is that she created one single work and it sold to a major American collection.

- **Contact** Sikkema Jenkins & Co.
Katie Rashid
katie@sikkemajenkinsco.com
gallery@sikkemajenkinsco.com
- **Established** 1991
- **Owner(s) / Partner(s)** Brent Sikkema (Principal)
Michael Jenkins (Senior Partner)
Meg Malloy (Partner)
- **Team** 10
- **Space(s)** 930 m²
- **Artists at Art Basel** Antony
Burt Barr
Trisha Brown
William Cordova
Leonardo Drew
Mitch Epstein
Tony Feher
Josephine Halvorson
Marc Handelman
Jan Henle
Arturo Herrera
Leslie Hewitt
Sheila Hicks
Merlin James
Jennie C. Jones
Nikki S. Lee
Marlene McCarty
Vik Muniz
Elizabeth Neel
Jorge Queiroz
Kay Rosen
Arlene Shechet
Shahzia Sikander
Amy Sillman
Janaina Tschäpe
Kara Walker

Silverlens

Manila
Singapore

- Galleries
- Statements

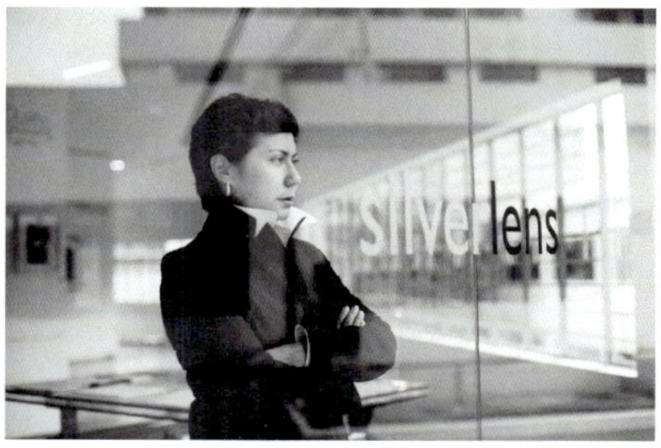

What first compelled you to open a gallery?
The lack of professional galleries in Manila.

Who is the first artist you showed and what was most memorable about that show?
Myself, Isa Lorenzo.

When did you first participate in Art Basel and what was most memorable about that show?
In the first year of Art Basel in Hong Kong, in 2013, but we had participated in ART HK since it began.

- **Contact** Silverlens
  Isa Lorenzo
  isa@silverlensgalleries.com
- **Established** 2004
- **Owner(s) / Partner(s)** Isa Lorenzo (Director)
  Rachel Rillo (Director)
- **Team** 11
- **Space(s)** 850 m²
- **Artists at Art Basel** Mariano Ching
  Gary-Ross Pastrana
  Patricia Perez Eustaquio
  Rachel Rillo
  Maria Taniguchi
- **Further artists represented** Frank Callaghan
  Christina Dy
  Dina Gadia
  Luis Lorenzana
  Isa Lorenzo
  Wawi Navarroza
  Gina Osterloh
  Hanna Pettyjohn
  Ryan Villamael
  Costantino Zicarelli

Silverman

San Francisco — Statements

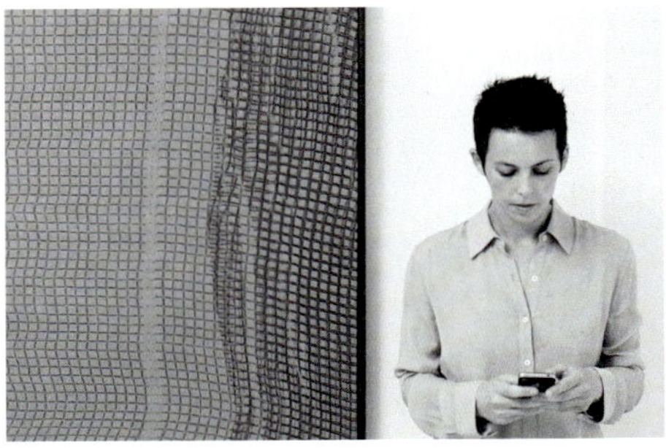

What first compelled you to open a gallery?
From an early age I was interested in the business of art and emergence. The confluence of these two areas of interest allowed me to support artists and educate collectors. That might be the biggest part of the job, especially because I am the primary dealer for most of the artists in my roster and work diligently to promote their work to curators, collectors, and dealers elsewhere.

Who is the first artist you showed and what was most memorable about that show?
We recently moved into a new gallery space that allows us to have an increasingly ambitious, international program of exhibitions. The artists that we represent are already inspired by the space's beauty, distinctiveness, and versatility. I am really pleased that our inaugural show will present important paintings and sculptures from the 1980s and 1990s by Amikam Toren, an Israeli-born, London-based artist, who has never had a solo show in America. This exhibition will hold a special place because it is the beginning of the gallery's new evolution.

When did you first participate in Art Basel and what was most memorable about that show?
We first exhibited at Art Basel in 2013 with Hugh Scott-Douglas in the Statements sector. We presented a cross-sectional view of three new bodies of work, displayed on and in road cases that perform the multiple roles of frame, screen, and architecture. There were many great memories but the one that sticks out most is the relationships and conversations that developed with other dealers participating to the fair.

- **Contact** Jessica Silverman Gallery
  Jessica Silverman
  jessica@jessicasilvermangallery.com
  info@jessicasilvermangallery.com
- **Established** 2007
- **Owner(s) / Partner(s)** Jessica Silverman
- **Team** 4
- **Space(s)** 280 m²
- **Artists at Art Basel** Hugh Scott-Douglas
- **Further artists represented** Christopher Badger
  Luke Butler
  Tammy Rae Carland
  Shannon Finley
  Desiree Holman
  Barbara Kasten
  Matt Lipps
  Dashiell Manley
  Lucas Michael
  Hayal Pozanti
  Yuval Pudik
  Conrad Ruiz
  Susanne M. Winterling

Silverstein

New York — Galleries, Galleries

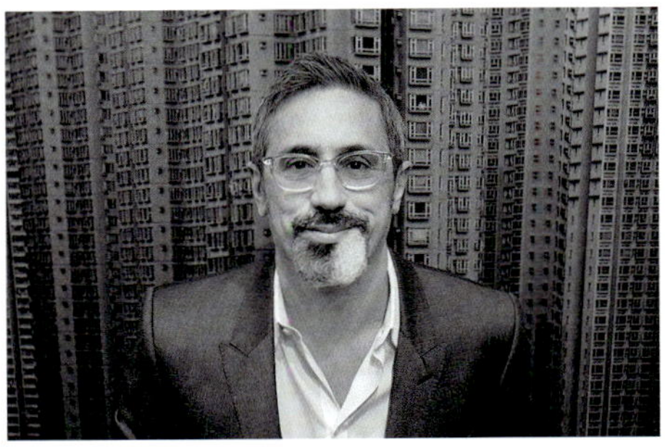

What first compelled you to open a gallery?
As the child of an artist, I was quite creative, having a propensity for drawing and sculpting. Through family visits to museums and looking at art books with my father, I was exposed from a very young age to a variety of art forms and periods, ranging from pre-Columbian pottery to European Renaissance painting through 20th-century American folk art. Yet, like many children of working artists, I chose not to pursue my own artistic passion, but instead follow a more "secure" career path in business. It was not until I approached 30 years old that I realized that I could no longer deny my creative impulses. Despite no previous gallery experience, and the warnings of those who I knew in the field, I decided to open a gallery in 2001. I am grateful to have taken the risk.

Who is the first artist you showed and what was most memorable about that show?
On April 17, 2001, the gallery opened in a 46 m2 Chelsea space with Lucien Aigner: *Picture Stories*. Unlike his Hungarian contemporaries Brassai and Andre Kertesz, who also photographed in Paris in the 1920s and 1930s, Aigner's work was virtually unknown until this exhibition. I remember the absolute pride had in having a role in rediscovering that work, and the great responsibility I had taken in editing works from the archive for this exhibition. Beyond that, I painted the walls, hung the frames, designed the invitation, wrote the press release, and for the first time, began to learn on the job the very basics of having a gallery.

- **Contact** Bruce Silverstein
  Liam van Loenen
  liam@brucesilverstein.com
  inquiries@brucesilverstein.com
- **Established** 2001
- **Owner(s) / Partner(s)** Bruce Silverstein
- **Team** 10
- **Space(s)** 465 m²
- **Artists at Art Basel** Diane Arbus
  Constantin Brancusi
  Bill Brandt
  Brassaï
  Harry Callahan
  Henri Cartier-Bresson
  Mark Cohen
  Marie Cosindas
  Martin Denker
  Robert Doisneau
  Marvin E. Newman
  Walker Evans
  Robert Frank
  Leonard Freed
  Todd Hido
  Emil Otto Hoppé

Nicolai Howalt
André Kertész
Dorothea Lange
Lu Yao
Nathan Lyons
Maria Antonietta Mameli
Robert Mapplethorpe
Shinichi Maruyama
Lisette Model
Barbara Morgan
Max Neumann
Emil Otto
Frank Paulin
Irving Penn
Man Ray
Larry Silver
Aaron Siskind
Keith Smith
Rosalind Solomon
Frederick Sommer
Trine Søndergaard
Edward Steichen
Alfred Stieglitz
Paul Strand
Zoe Strauss
Randy West
Brett Weston
Edward Weston
Joel-Peter Witkin
Michael Wolf
Silvio Wolf
John Wood

Sin Sin

Hong Kong ● Insights

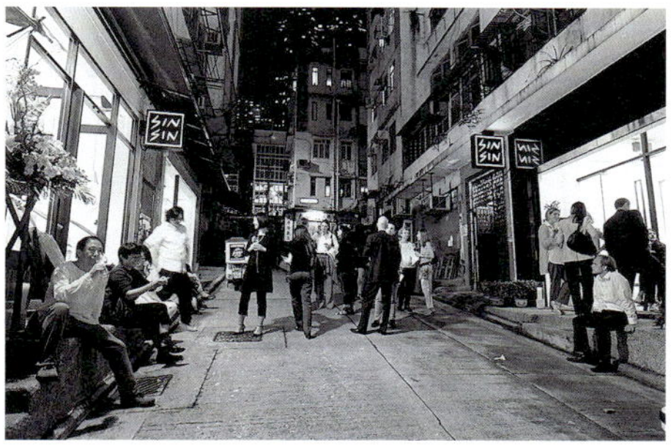

What first compelled you to open a gallery?

It was chance and fate.

Who is the first artist you showed and what was most memorable about that show?

Sin Sin launched her new venture with an inaugural exhibition entitled *Passion*, which featured new contemporary artworks by Chinese (Inner Mongolian) artist Deng Xiao Hong and Thai artist Thaiwijit Poengkasemsomboon, in 2003. Being surrounded by friends, family, and art lovers was very inspiring. Their response to the works gave me such pleasure that I knew I had found what I wanted to do for the next chapter of my life.

When did you first participate in Art Basel and what was most memorable about that show?

Our first participation in Art Basel was in 2013 in Hong Kong. Having mounted so many of my own shows over the years, I think the most memorable thing about the show was the venue and excellent support of the Art Basel organization. I was most gratified by the quality and shared passion of the visitors of this international forum.

- **Contact** Sin Sin Fine Art
  Alisa Fung
  info@sinsinfineart.com
- **Established** 2003
- **Owner(s) / Partner(s)** Sin Sin Man
- **Team** 5
- **Space(s)** 2,200 m² (three locations)
- **Artists at Art Basel** Andy Dewantoro
  Muhamad Irfan
- **Further artists represented** Jumaldi Alfi
  Fauzie As'ad
  Vincent Cazaneuve
  S. Teddy Darmawan
  Peter Dittmar
  Lie Fhung
  Fung Ming Chip
  Roland Hagenberg
  Hanafi
  Eddie Hara
  Tilo Kaiser
  Youri Leroux
  Rick Lewis
  Maria Lobo
  Hiromi Miyakita
  Nasirun
  Pablo Posada Pernikoff
  Kokok P. Sancoko
  Tisna Sanjaya
  Abdi Setiawan
  Sun Guangyi
  Putu Sutawijaya
  Pande Ketut Taman
  Wong Yan Kwai

Skape

Seoul ● Galleries

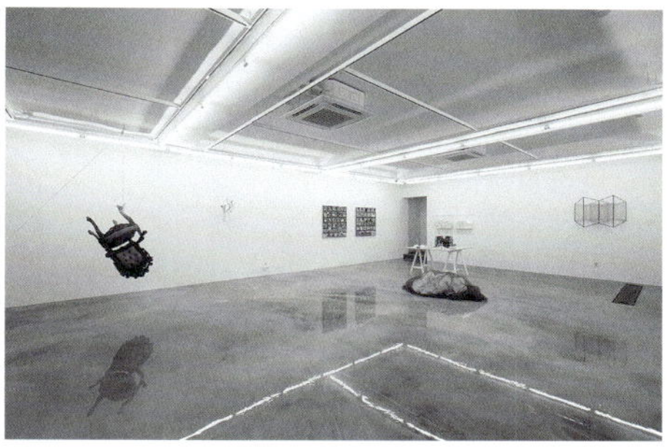

What first compelled you to open a gallery?

Being a painter, I always wanted to contribute to promoting Korean and Asian contemporary art in an international art scene. I have actively introduced many Korean artists abroad and it has been ten wonderful years since I opened the gallery.

Who is the first artist you showed and what was most memorable about that show?

Joonsung Bae, Suejin Chung, Kwangho Cheong, Jungkug Seo, Soojung Han were represented in the first show. Their support and enthusiasm was very impressive, and they were as excited as I was to start a new artistic journey together. It was also a great privilege to have the Korean contemporary art scene's warm support and attention.

When did you first participate in Art Basel and what was most memorable about that show?

I participated in Art Basel for the first time in 2013. I had great pleasure meeting new important collectors—the collectors from Switzerland and Italy especially liked the show very much, they readily accompanied me to other artistic events, and we had long and interesting discussions about the Korean contemporary art scene and art promotion together. That was such a memorable time.

- **Contact** Gallery Skape
  Yunkyong Kim
  kyk@skape.co.kr
- **Established** 2004
- **Owner(s) / Partner(s)** Kyung Ae Sohn
- **Team** 5
- **Space(s)** 110 m²
- **Artists at Art Basel** Yujung Chang
  Suejin Chung
  Jungwook Kim
  Sungsoo Kim
  Hyungkoo Lee
  Sodam Lim
  Youngho Yoo
- **Further artists represented** Changhong Ahn
  Kyuchul Ahn
  Soojung Choi
  Sungmyung Chun
  Sungdo Hong
  Jihyun Jung
  Jungyeob Jung
  Myeongbeom Kim
  Taeheon Kim
  Sun K. Kwak
  Myoungho Lee
  B. G. Muhn
  Reinoud Oudshoorn
  Jeongwon Yoon

Skarstedt

New York, London

- Galleries
- Galleries

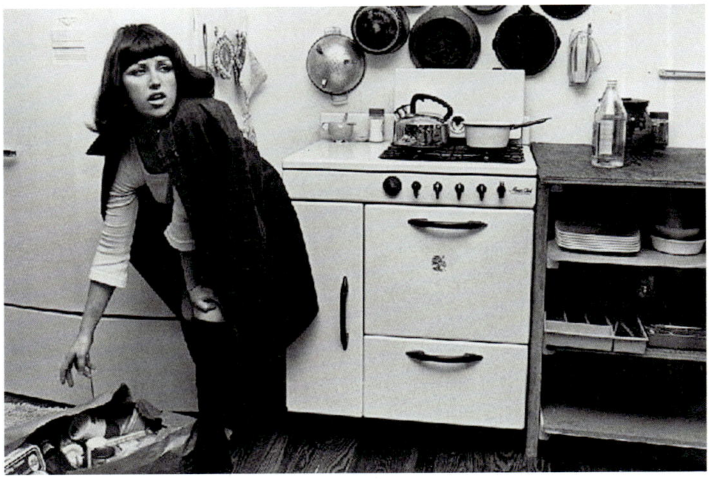

What first compelled you to open a gallery?
To work with living artists.

Who is the first artist you showed?
Richard Prince.

When did you first participate in Art Basel?
In 1998.

- **Contact** Skarstedt Gallery
  Alison Ward
  alison@skarstedt.com
  info@skarstedt.com
- **Established** 1994
- **Owner(s) / Partner(s)** Per Skarstedt (Owner)
  Bona Colonna Montagu (Partner)
- **Team** 15
- **Artists at Art Basel** George Condo
  Carroll Dunham
  Eric Fischl
  Peter Fischli/David Weiss
  Lucio Fontana
  Günther Förg
  Robert Gober
  Keith Haring
  Jenny Holzer
  Mike Kelley
  Martin Kippenberger
  Yves Klein
  Barbara Kruger
  Louise Lawler
  Sherrie Levine
  Robert Mapplethorpe
  Juan Muñoz
  Cady Noland
  Albert Oehlen
  Richard Prince
  David Salle
  Thomas Schütte
  Cindy Sherman
  Rosemarie Trockel
  Andy Warhol
  Christopher Wool

SKE

Bangalore
New Delhi

- Discoveries
- Feature
- Nova

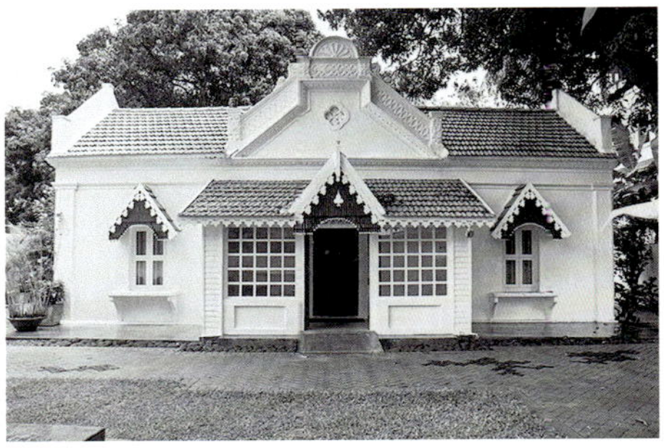

What first compelled you to open a gallery?
I joined a gallery, just out of college, and it taught me what I wanted and did not want to do: I wanted to work with artists of my generation and in a private gallery in the Indian context; after ten years the idea is still evolving.

Who is the first artist you showed and what was most memorable about that show?
Mahendra Sinh, it was a photography show. It will always be memorable for being my first show.

When did you first participate in Art Basel and what was most memorable about that show?
Our first participation was in Art Basel in Miami Beach in 2008; we showed artists Srinivasa Prasad and Sudarshan Shetty. The most memorable part of the fair was all the conversations with gallerists from different parts of the world.

- **Contact** GallerySKE
  Nishi Palnitkar
  nishi@galleryske.com
  post@galleryske.com
- **Established** 2003 (Bangalore)
  2013 (New Delhi)
- **Owner(s) / Partner(s)** Sunitha Kumar Emmart
- **Team** 18
- **Space(s)** 836 m² (Bangalore)
  370 m² (New Delhi)
- **Artists at Art Basel** Sheela Gowda
  Bharti Kher
  Prabhavathi Meppayil
  Sudarshan Shetty
  Mariam Suhail
- **Further artists represented** Krishnaraj Chonat
  Sakshi Gupta
  Abhishek Hazra
  Anup Mathew
  Srinivasa Prasad
  Sreshta Rit Thomas Premnath
  Navin Thomas
  Avinash Veeraraghavan

Skopia

Geneva

- Galleries

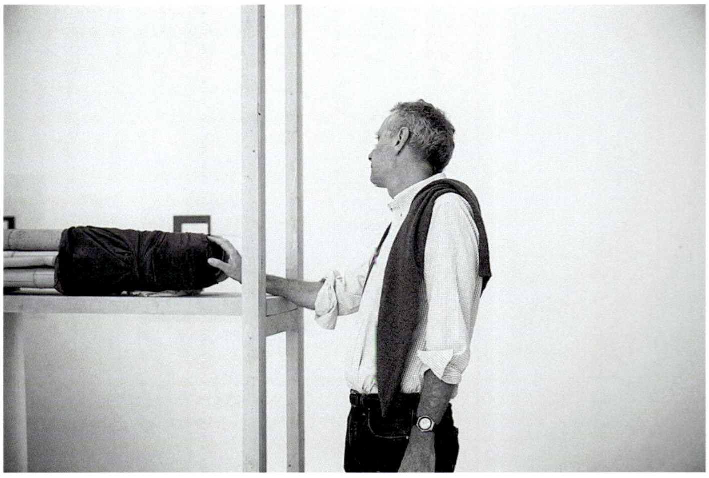

What first compelled you to open a gallery?
A "raison d'être."

Who is the first artist you showed and what was most memorable about that show?
Daniel-Albert Pilloud. Our wedding party took place in the gallery at the same time as the preview.

When did you first participate in Art Basel and what was most memorable about that show?
In 1993. I remember everything, I remember every detail, every feeling. It was both real and unreal.

- **Contact** Skopia P.-H. Jaccaud
Constance Delamadeleine
info@skopia.ch
- **Established** 1989
- **Owner(s) / Partner(s)** Pierre-Henri Jaccaud
- **Team** 5
- **Space(s)** 210 m²
- **Artists at Art Basel** Silvia Bächli
Francis Baudevin
Alexandre Bianchini
Erik Bulatov
Jérémy Chevalier
Jean Crotti
Pierre André Ferrand
Franz Gertsch
Alex Hanimann
Thomas Huber
Alain Huck
Robert Ireland
Stanislaw Koba
Jean-Luc Manz
Claudio Moser
Olivier Mosset
Christoph Rütimann
Hinrich Sachs
Simone Schardt
Pierre Schwerzmann
Marion Tampon-Lajarriette
Vanessa van Obberghen
Franz Erhard Walther

Snitzer

Miami ● Galleries

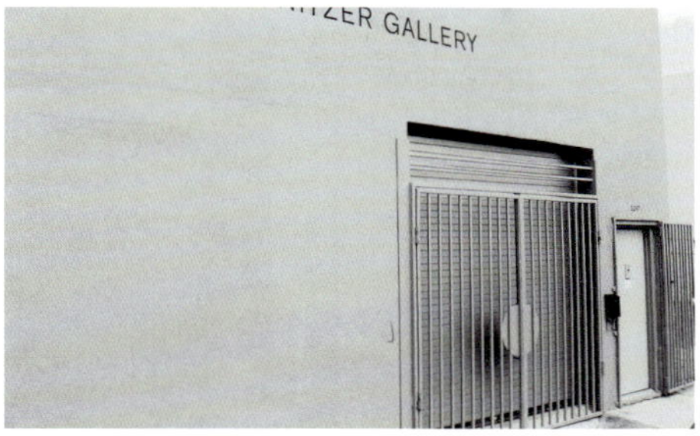

What first compelled you to open a gallery?
I was trained as an artist and couldn't make a go of it. I needed to support my family so I opened the gallery in 1977.

Who is the first artist you showed and what was most memorable about that show?
I had an exhibition of Wifredo Lam's prints. I wanted to embrace the Cuban community. The exhibition was well received, but I had several bomb threats. I had to alert the local police to the situation. Welcome to Miami.

When did you first participate in Art Basel and what was most memorable about that show?
I exhibited in the first Art Basel in Miami Beach in 2001 but it was canceled. I have exhibited every year since.

- **Contact** Fredric Snitzer Gallery
info@snitzer.com
- **Established** 1977
- **Owner(s) / Partner(s)** Fredric Snitzer
- **Team** 4
- **Space(s)** 325 m²
- **Artists at Art Basel** Alice Aycock
Hernan Bas
Ridley Howard
Alexander Kroll
Diego Singh
- **Further artists represented** José Bedia
Timothy Buwalda
Zhivago Duncan
Naomi Fisher
Mauricio Gonzalez
Jessica Laino
Natalya Laskis
Maria Martinez-Cañas
Gavin Perry
Jon Pylypchuk
Bert Rodriguez
Michael Vasquez

Soka

Beijing
Taipei
Tainan ● Galleries

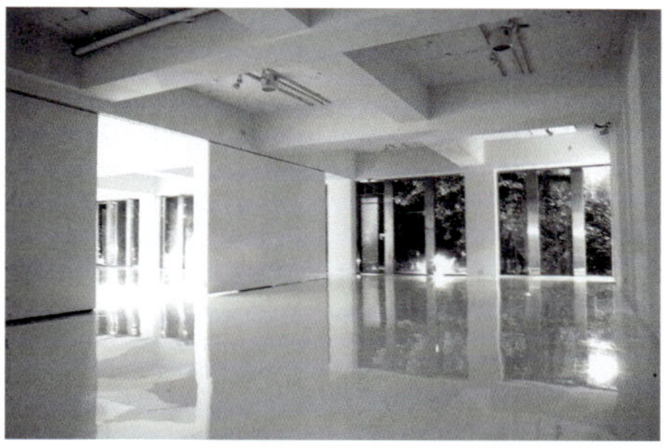

What first compelled you to open a gallery?
Hsiao Fuyuan opened the gallery in 1992 in Taiwan. He transformed his interest in collecting into his main business. This interest resulted in Soka Art becoming one of the galleries in Taiwan and Mainland China with the best reputation.

Who is the first artist you showed and what was most memorable about that show?
The artist Yu Xiaofu from Shanghai, in 1992. Most memorable was that the artist was unknown at the time in Taiwan. However, many visitors came to see the show and were touched by the paintings, which I did not expect at the beginning.

When did you first participate in Art Basel and what was most memorable about that show?
In 2009.

- **Contact** Soka Art
Crystal Cheng
crystal.chengs@gmail.com
info@soka-art.com
- **Established** 1992
- **Owner(s) / Partner(s)** Hsiao Fuyuan
- **Team** 15
- **Space(s)** 2,500 m²
- **Artists at Art Basel** Cai Guo-Qiang
Chu Teh-Chun
Hong Ling
Hsi Shin-Pin
Mao Xuhui
Peng Hs
Ilda Kiriko
Xu Bing
Zao Wou-Ki
- **Further artists represented** Gabriel Barredo
Chen Jieciang
Joyce Ho
Li Chao
Li Tiefu
Lin Baoling
Lin Fengmian
Tzeng Sheng-Hui
Xu Beihong
Xun Guipin
Yan Wenliang
Zhao Bo

S

Statements at Art Basel presents exciting new solo projects by young, emerging artists. Since 1999, each year, two outstanding artists in this sector are awarded the Baloise Art Prize. The Baloise Group also acquires works by the award-winning artists, which it donates to important European art institutions.

STATE MENTS

2013 participants

Beijing Commune
Hu Xiaoyuan

Campbell
Tony Lewis

Campoli Presti
Daniel Lefcourt

Casas Riegner
Mateo López

Chert
David Horvitz

Clages
Olivier Foulon

Gaudel de Stampa
Jonathan Binet

Gitlen
Jessica Jackson Hutchins

Krobath
Jenni Tischer

Meessen De Clercq
Thu Van Tran

Melas Papadopoulos
Kostas Sahpazis

mother's tankstation
Mairead O'hEocha

Murray Guy
Sergei Tcherepnin

47 Canal
Antoine Catala

One and J.
Chosil Kil

Overduin and Kite
Erika Vogt

Side 2
Peter McDonald

Silverlens
Maria Taniguchi

Silverman
Hugh Scott-Douglas

Stevenson
Kemang Wa Lehulere

The Third Line
Laleh Khorramian

Tilton
Egan Frantz

Vavassori
Greg Parma Smith

Winter
Judith Fegerl

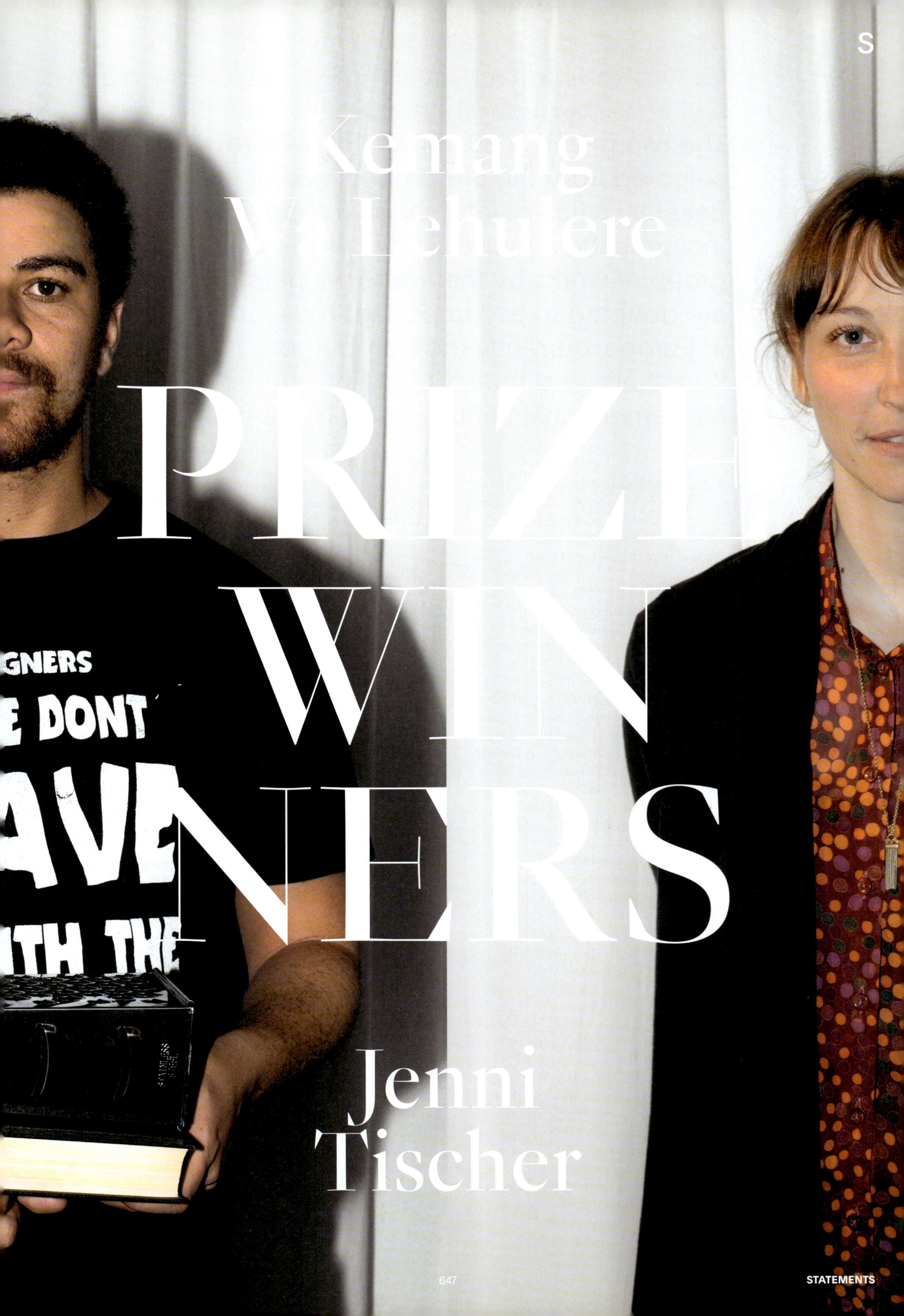

Kemang Wa Lehulere

PRIZE WINNERS

Jenni Tischer

Martin Schwander Talks to Jenni Tischer (Berlin) and Kemang Wa Lehulere (Johannesburg), 2013 Baloise Prize Winners

The two prizes of 30,000 CHF each are selected from the Statements sector of Art Basel by a jury of international experts and includes the acquisition by Baloise of a group of works by the award winners. They are donated to two important museums in Europe: currently the Hamburger Kunsthalle and the MUMOK, Museum Moderner Kunst Stiftung Ludwig, Vienna.

Baloise Prize Jury 2013:

Manuel Borja-Villel, Director Museo Nacional Centro de Arte Reina Sofía, Madrid

Eric Decelle, Collection Eric Decelle, Brussels

Karola Kraus, Director, Museum Moderner Kunst Stiftung Ludwig, Vienna

Petra Roettig, Director, Galerie der Gegenwart, Hamburger Kunsthalle, Hamburg

Martin Schwander, Fine Art Advisor of Baloise, Chairman of the Jury.

MARTIN SCHWANDER I would like to start with your motivation to become an artist. Jenni, you started to study art at 25. Did you already have an artistic practice before that?

JENNI TISCHER Yes, I was already doing drawing, painting, collages, and sculptures. I decided quite late to study art; beforehand I was more interested in biology.

MS Kemang Wa Lehulere, you have quite a different background. In one of your interviews I read that already as a boy you were involved in the art theater world, you wrote plays and made sets. When did the transition from the theater world to the art world take place?

KEMANG WA LEHULERE I had family involved in theater—as writers, directors, actors, and producers. So, I grew up in this environment and it interested me from an early age. I followed theater classes in high school, and I then went to Community Arts Projects to study performing arts. After six months I got bored. So I decided to do something a bit more challenging and continue in the direction of visual arts. That switch was in 2003. At the same time, I took a course in film and television [at the Community Video Education Trust (CVET) in Cape Town], and that's when I began thinking about writing seriously, at least film scripts, which I've been doing since then.

MS You both work with words and literary fragments. What is the function of these elements in your art?

JT I started writing and working with texts when I studied at the Academy in Vienna and was an assistant in art theory. The last text I really got into was a text by Shaftesbury from the 18th century. He was one of the first who dealt with the question of authorship, and he also wrote about the process of becoming an artist: about how to create something, you get in a dialogue with yourself, and how, through expressing and creating something, you develop your thoughts. That was very interesting for me because in my work the process of creation is always part of the work, and remains visible, such as text fragments.

KWL In my work, the use of words came initially from a frustration: I was working within a collective that I co-founded [Gugulective, 2006] and at the same time I was doing documentary films for television; these two practices were too separated. Bringing text into my work was a way of channeling different thought processes into one channel of energy. I really began developing an interest in writing, and also in literary fiction and short stories. I then began to think about how I could incorporate these into the various mediums I was working with, for example I started writing performance scripts, and also used writing to document performance without capturing an image, by rewriting the experience.

MS Another common aspect between your respective works is that you both use stereotypes. What is your aim in dealing with such political, social, racial, or gender stereotypes?

JT That's a big question … Art is more or less working against stereotypes. I work with materials that are most of the time seen in a female context (sewing needles, textiles, fabrics, weaving looms, etc.), and which are related to the history of female work, but I did not plan to bring up gender issues. I was interested in the complexity of the weaving works, and in their conceptual aspect: they are very sensitive, and at the same time very strong.

KWL Usually, the figures I develop are devoid of any gender or race, so they become these collective bodies. I try to go against markers of identity, but I'm also very cautious to talk about these things, because I don't want to be trapped in identity politics.

MS Is Statements at Art Basel a good place for the perception of your work? And did the context here influence its presentation?

JT There's always a question of how your work is seen in different contexts, but I try to focus on the work and make it speak in an autonomous way. Of course it is a great context here!

KWL Yes, it's an important platform. My work is influenced by the context, especially the wall of drawings, because of the format of the booth: it's square and I normally work in more rectangular formats, like a cinematic field. That does affect the drawing itself. Also, performances shift according to the space. If it were outside, I would have to think of different strategies to employ because there are no lights, for example. It impacts the way the work will be seen.

MS In a few minutes you will get a cash prize. Do you already know what you want to do with this cash prize?

JT Well, I want to go on working, and spend the money on my next project.

KWL It's the same for me. It will make possible the realization of projects I have been developing.

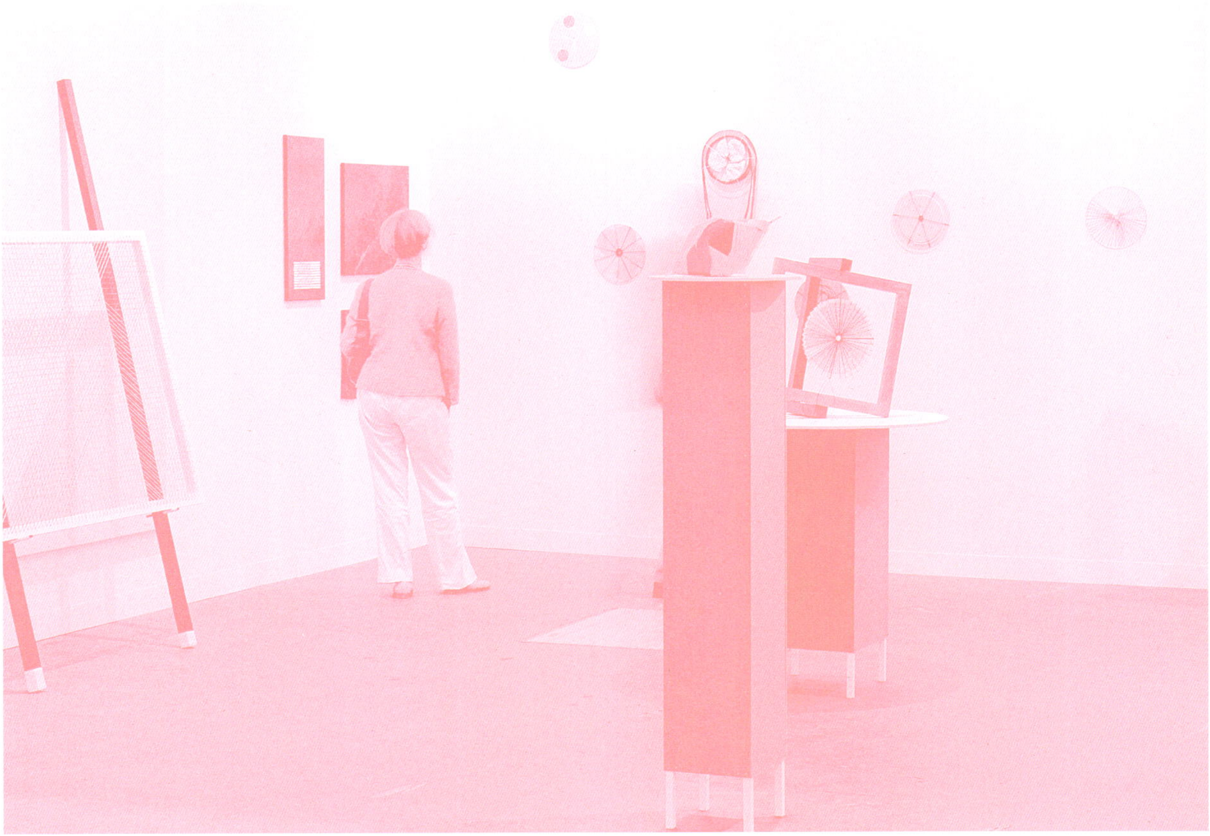

Jenni Tischer, Krobath, Art Basel in Basel (Statements)

Krobath
Jenni Tischer

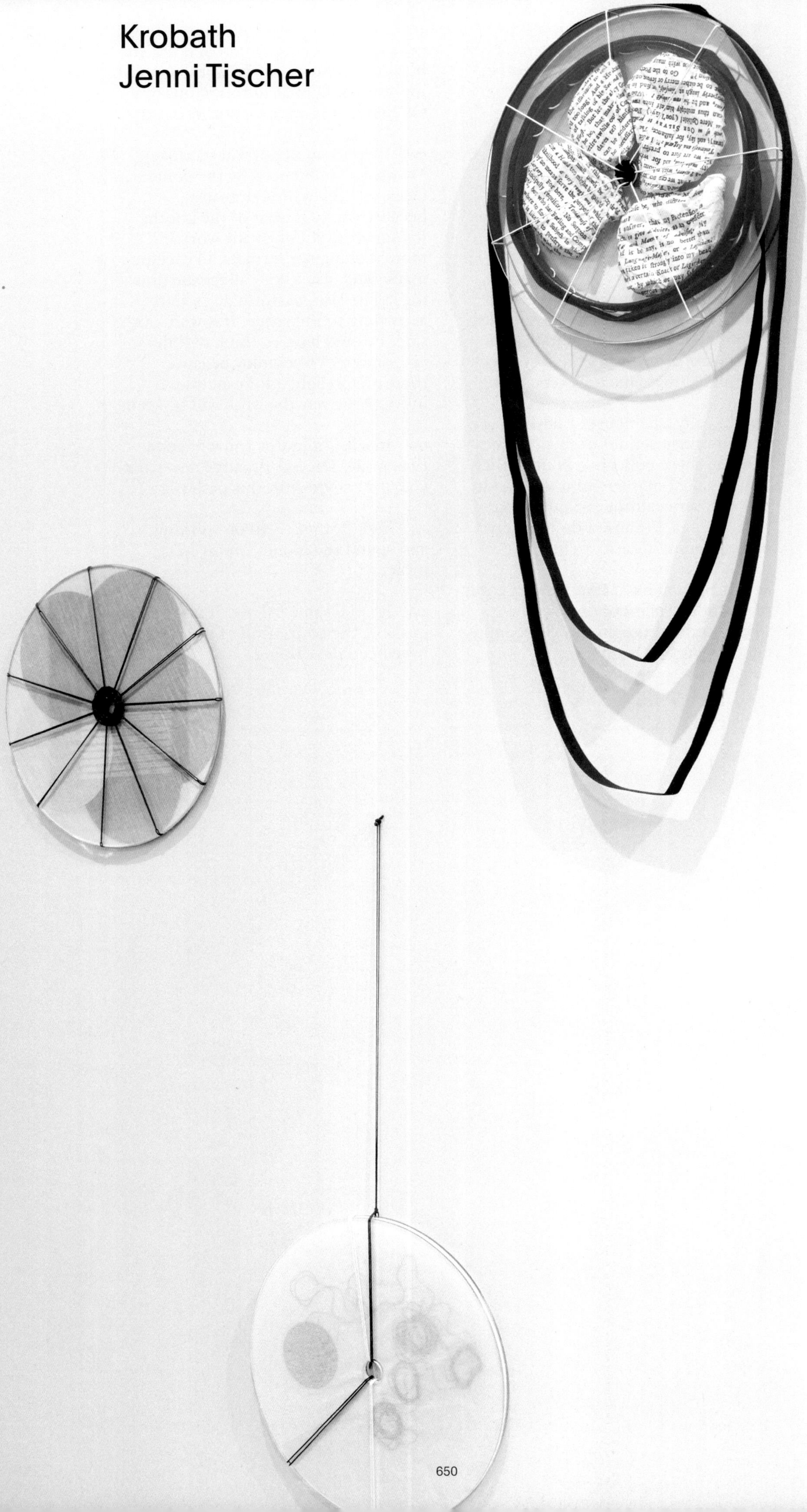

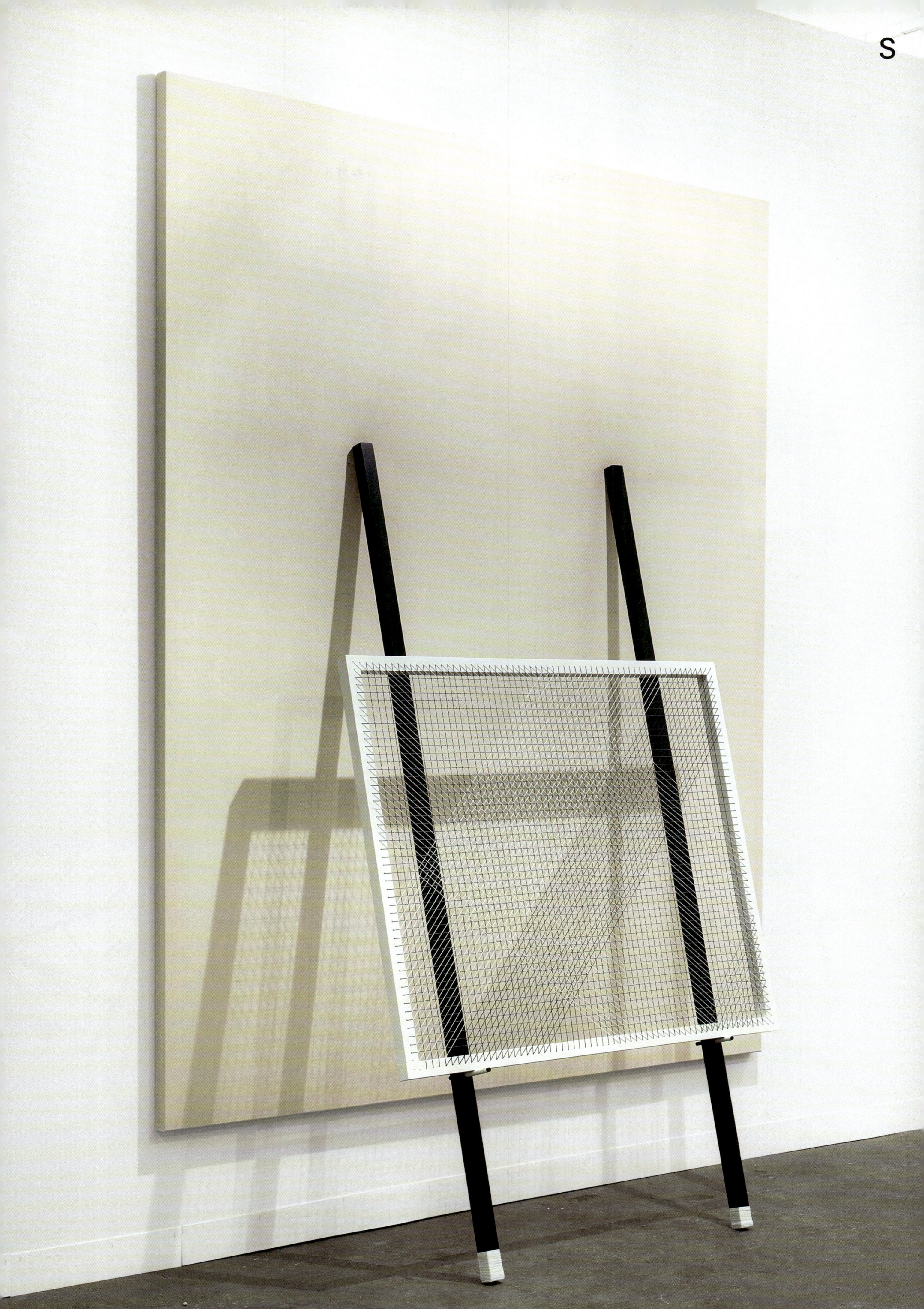

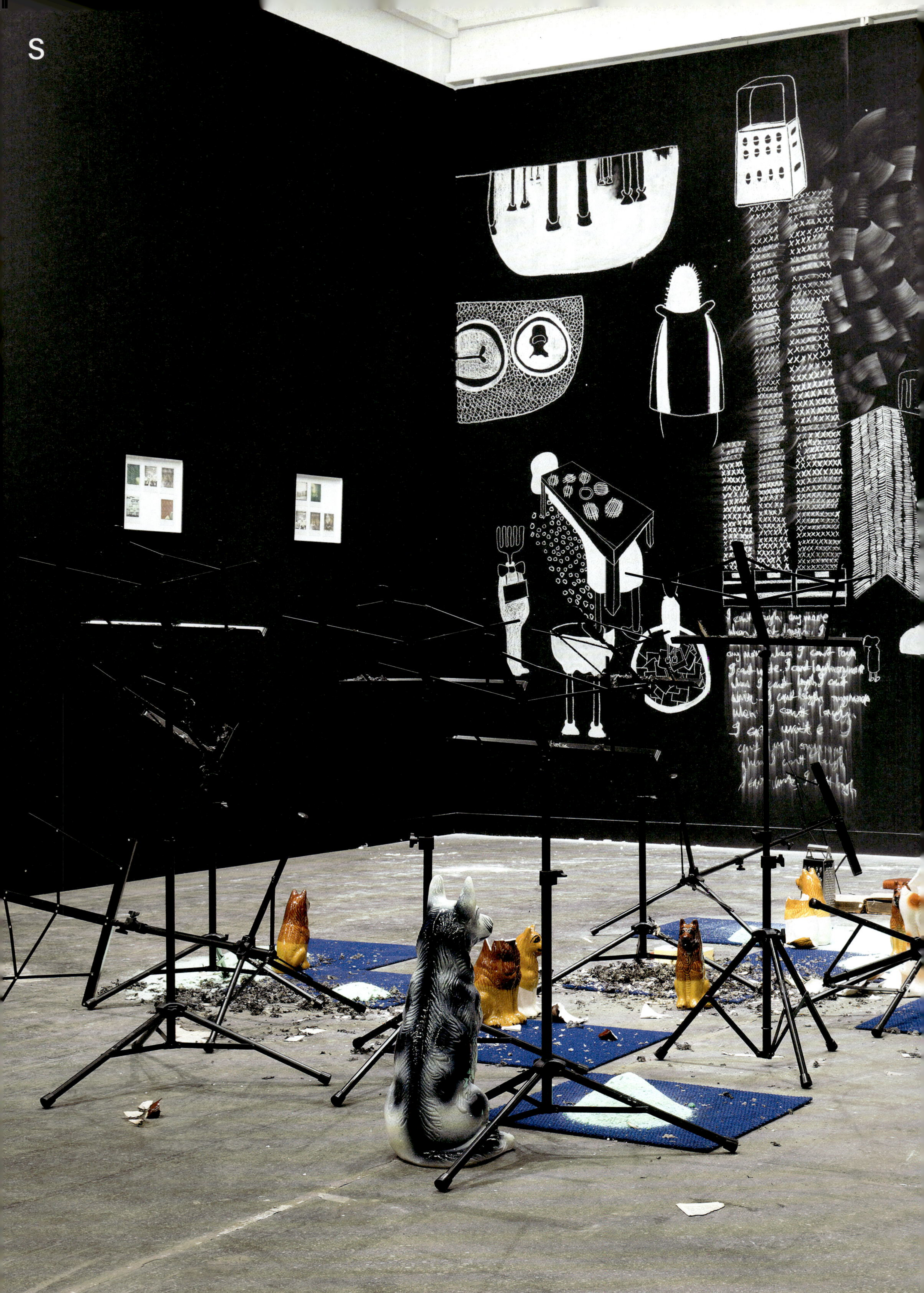

Stevenson
Kemang Wa Lehulere

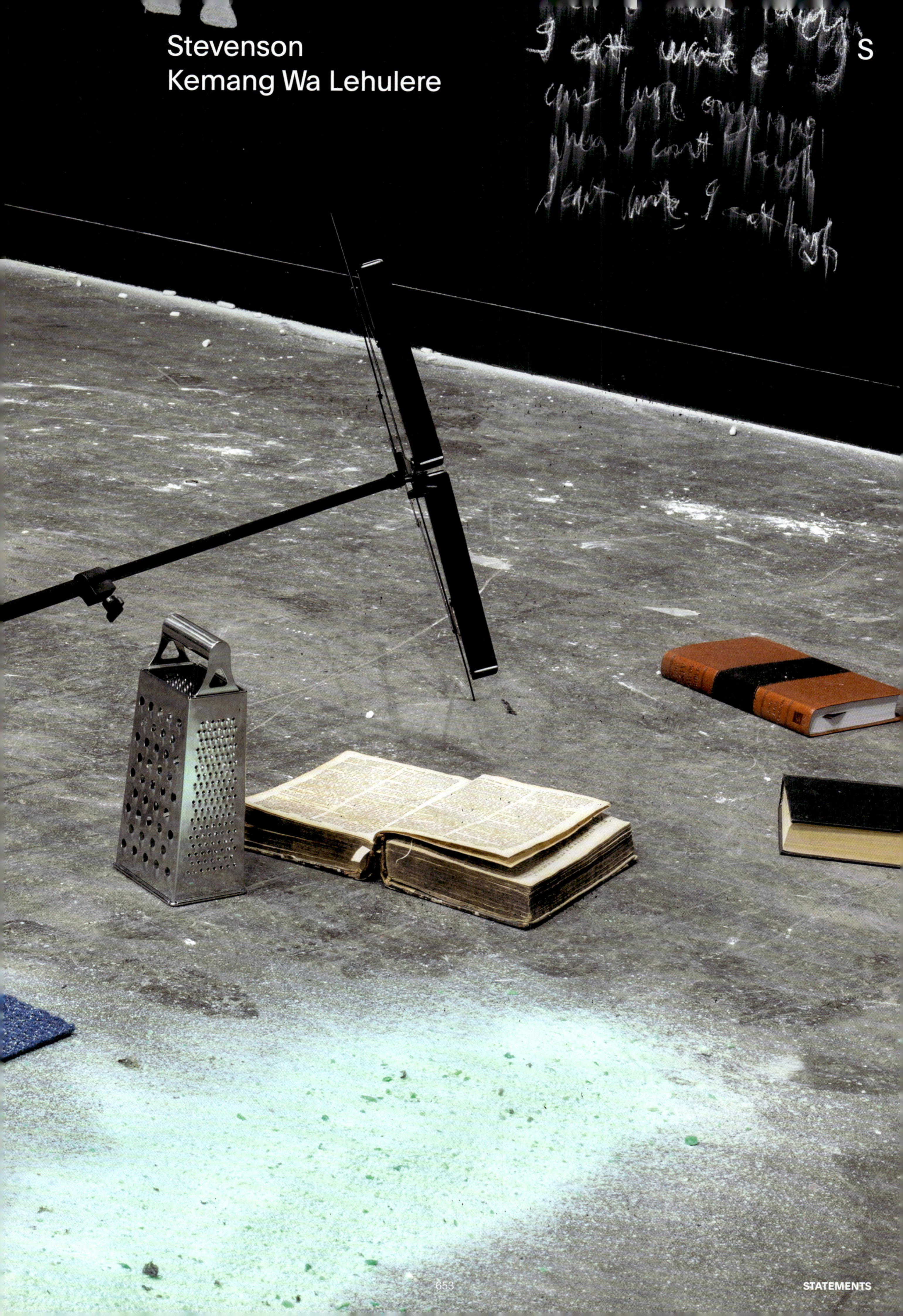

S

Spartà

Chagny

Feature

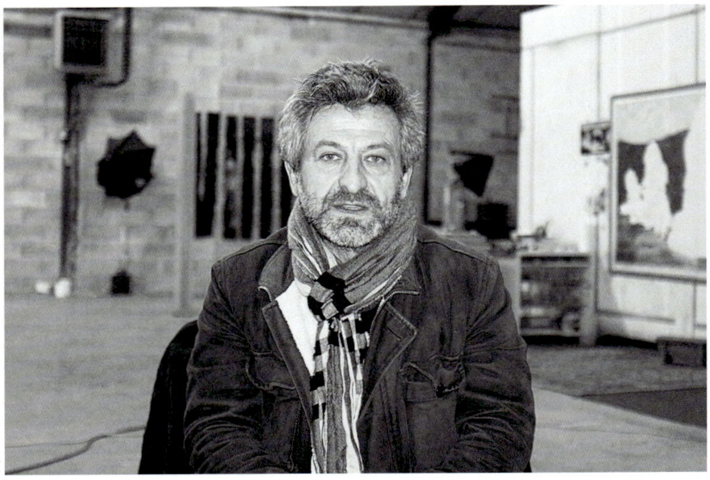

What first compelled you to open a gallery?
The feeling that a rose can grow in a desert.

Who is the first artist you showed and what was most memorable about that show?
The first show was a group show: Christian Boltanski, Victor Burgin, Hans-Peter Feldmann, Paul-Armand Gette, Gilbert & George, Jenny Holzer & Peter Nadin, On Kawara, Joseph Kosuth, Jean Le Gac, Urs Lüthi, Annette Messager, Richard Prince, Arnulf Rainer, Cindy Sherman, John Stezaker, and Lawrence Weiner.

When did you first participate in Art Basel and what was most memorable about that show?
Maybe in 1988. The quality of the works exhibited at the fair and the excellent relationship with international galleries.

- **Contact** Galerie Pietro Spartà
Pietro Spartà
galeriepietrosparta@wanadoo.fr
- **Established** 1982
- **Owner(s) / Partner(s)** Pietro Spartà (Director)
Pascale Petit (Director)
- **Team** 3
- **Space(s)** 900 m²
- **Artists at Art Basel** Mario Merz
Thomas Schütte
Niele Toroni
- **Further artists represented** Daniel Buren
Balthasar Burkhard
Gérard Collin-Thiébaut
Peter Downsbrough
Philippe Droguet
Luciano Fabro
Lee Friedlander
Grout/Mazéas
Jannis Kounellis
Bertrand Lavier
Sol LeWitt
Richard Long
François Morellet
Jean-Luc Moulène
Eric Poitevin
Alain Séchas
Ida Tursic & Wilfried Mille
Didier Vermeiren
Lawrence Weiner
Gilberto Zorio

Sperone Westwater

New York
Lugano

Galleries Unlimited
Galleries Public

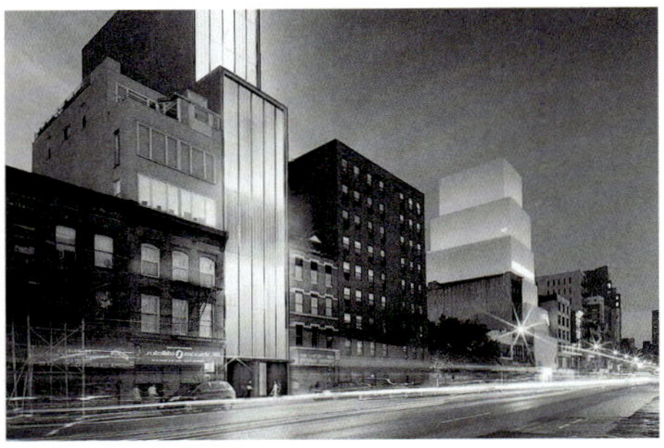

What first compelled you to open a gallery?
Sperone Westwater Fischer was founded in 1975, when Italian art dealer Gian Enzo Sperone, Angela Westwater, and German art dealer Konrad Fischer opened a space at 142 Greene Street in SoHo, New York. The founders' original program showcased a European avant-garde alongside a core group of American artists to whom its founders were committed. Notable early exhibitions include a 1977 show of Minimalist works by Carl Andre, Dan Flavin, Donald Judd, and Sol LeWitt; German artist Gerhard Richter's first solo exhibition in New York, in 1978; seven of Bruce Nauman's seminal early shows; 11 Richard Long exhibitions; and the installation of one of Mario Merz's celebrated glass and neon igloos in 1979—part of the gallery's ongoing dedication to Arte Povera artists, including Alighiero Boetti. Other early historical exhibitions at the Greene Street space include a 1989 group show, *Early Conceptual Works*, which featured the work of On Kawara, Bruce Nauman, Alighiero Boetti, and Joseph Kosuth, among others; a 1999 Fontana exhibition titled *Gold: Gothic Masters and Lucio Fontana*; and selected presentations of work by Piero Manzoni. From 2002 to 2010 the gallery was located at 415 West 13 Street, in a 10,000-square foot space in the Meatpacking District. In 2010 Sperone Westwater inaugurated a new Foster + Partners designed building at 257 Bowery in New York. Today, almost 39 years after its conception, the gallery continues to exhibit an international roster of prominent artists working in a wide variety of media. The gallery has worked with major institutions around the world on a regular basis since it was founded.

- **Contact** Sperone Westwater
Anne Bruder
anne@speronewestwater.com
info@speronewestwater.com
- **Established** 1975
- **Owner(s) / Partner(s)** Gian Enzo Sperone
Angela Westwater
Konrad Fischer
- **Team** 14
- **Space(s)** 1,579.5 m²
- **Artists at Art Basel** Carla Accardi
Kutlug Ataman
Barry X Ball
Ali Banisadr
Bertozzi & Casoni
Alighiero Boetti
Wim Delvoye
Kim Dingle
Lucio Fontana
Mark Greenwold
Guillermo Kuitca
Wolfgang Laib
Charles LeDray
Liu Ye
Richard Long
Emil Lukas
Heinz Mack
Piero Manzoni
Mario Merz
Frank Moore
Malcolm Morley
Nabil Nahas
Bruce Nauman
Evan Penny
Otto Piene
Alexis Rockman

Susan Rothenberg
Tom Sachs
Andrew Sendor
Fabio Viale
Not Vital
William Wegman
Martin Wilner
Jan Worst

- **Further artists represented**
  Braco Dimitrijevic
  Andrew Grassie
  Julian Schnabel
  Richard Tuttle
  Aaron van Erp
  Andy Warhol

Spinello

Miami ● Nova

- **Contact**
  Spinello Projects
  info@spinelloprojects.com
- **Established**
  2005
- **Owner(s) / Partner(s)**
  Anthony Spinello
- **Artists at Art Basel**
  Sinisa Kukec
  Naama Tsabar
  Agustina Woodgate
- **Further artists represented**
  Farley Aguilar
  Abby Double
  Aramis Gutierrez
  Kris Knight
  Manny Prieres
  Santiago Rubino
  Typoe
  Antonia Wright

Sprüth Magers

Berlin ● Galleries
London ● Galleries Unlimited
● Galleries

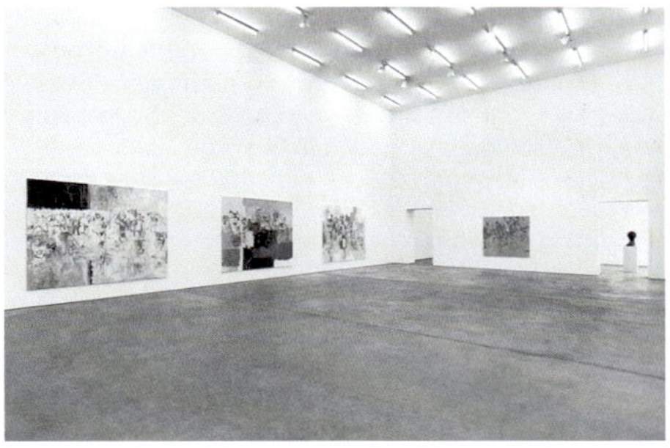

What first compelled you to open a gallery?
Monika Sprüth opened her gallery amid the dynamic scene developing in Cologne in the early 1980s, and immediately focused on a new generation of young artists from both Germany and the US. She also felt that it was important to position female artists such as Barbara Kruger, Cindy Sherman, Rosemarie Trockel, and Jenny Holzer among the more famous, mostly male artists of the period. Between 1985 and 1989 Sprüth published three editions of the experimental magazine *Eau de Cologne*, a publication devoted to the work of women artists and writers. She was also instrumental in developing the early careers of such major figures in conceptualism as Peter Fischli & David Weiss and Louise Lawler, photographers such as Andreas Gursky and Thomas Demand, as well as painters Andreas Schulze, George Condo, Walter Dahn, Axel Kasseböhmer, and Thomas Scheibitz, many of whom have been with the gallery for over 20 years. Philomene Magers took up where her mother left off, starting her own gallery after she had no choice but to close the gallery in Bonn that her mother had started. She noticed at the time that an older generation of conceptual artists was incredibly influential on 1990s art, and yet those artists were underrepresented in Germany, especially in Cologne. In addition to mounting important exhibitions of work by such landmark figures of postwar art as Donald Judd, John Baldessari, Richard Artschwager, and Ed Ruscha, she also showed work by younger European and American artists, including Karen Kilimnik and Andrea Zittel. The relationship the gallery establishes with their artists is built on trust, responsibility, and longevity. A close collaboration with the artists is always the main goal and focus of the gallery.

- **Contact**
  Sprüth Magers
  Sina Deister
  sd@spruethmagers.com
  info@spruethmagers.com
- **Established**
  1983 (M. Sprüth, in Cologne)
  1991 (P. Magers)
  1998 (M. Sprüth & P. Magers)
- **Owner(s) / Partner(s)**
  Monika Sprüth
  Philomene Magers
- **Space(s)**
  550 m² (Berlin)
  140 m² (London)
- **Artists at Art Basel**
  Richard Artschwager
  John Baldessari
  Bernd & Hilla Becher
  George Condo
  Thomas Demand
  Thea Djordjadze
  Peter Fischli/David Weiss
  Cyprien Gaillard
  Andreas Gursky
  Jenny Holzer
  Gary Hume
  Karen Kilimnik
  Joseph Kosuth
  Barbara Kruger
  Louise Lawler
  Robert Morris
  Ed Ruscha
  Analia Saban
  Thomas Scheibitz
  Andreas Schulze
  Cindy Sherman
  Rosemarie Trockel
  Andrea Zittel
- **Further artists represented**
  Siegfried Anzinger
  Alighiero Boetti
  Walter Dahn
  Philip-Lorca diCorcia
  Robert Elfgen
  Sylvie Fleury
  Maureen Gallace
  Donald Judd
  Axel Kasseböhmer
  Astrid Klein
  Kraftwerk
  David Lamelas
  David Maljkovic
  Anthony McCall
  Reinhard Mucha
  Jean-Luc Mylayne
  Michail Pirgelis
  Nina Pohl
  Richard Prince
  Sterling Ruby
  Gerda Scheepers
  Frances Scholz
  Stephen Shore
  Alexandre Singh
  Robert Therrien
  Ryan Trecartin
  Marcel van Eeden
  Andro Wekua

St. Etienne

New York ● Galleries

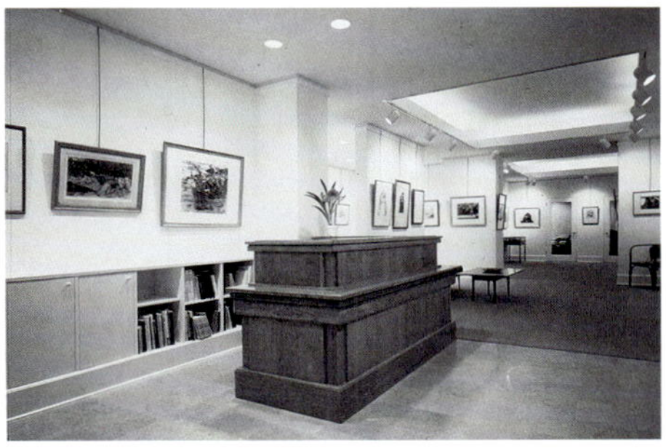

What first compelled you to open a gallery?
The Galerie St. Etienne was founded by Otto Kallir after Hitler's annexation of Austria forced him to abandon his original Vienna gallery, the Neue Galerie (est. 1923).

Who is the first artist you showed and what was most memorable about that show?
The Neue Galerie opened in 1923 with the first posthumous exhibition of the paintings and drawings of Egon Schiele, who has been a gallery mainstay ever since.

When did you first participate in Art Basel and what was most memorable about that show?
In 2004. The quality of the Basel audience was, and still is, unequaled. (Also, that first year, half our stock was inadvertently left in New York by the shipper and arrived only during the vernissage, which created quite a spectacle!)

- **Contact** Galerie St. Etienne
  Jane Kallir
  jkallir@gseart.com
  gallery@gseart.com
- **Established** 1939
- **Owner(s) / Partner(s)** Jane Kallir (Co-Director)
  Hildegard Bachert (Co-Director)
- **Team** 7
- **Space(s)** 1,500 m²
- **Artists at Art Basel** Leonard Baskin
  Max Beckmann
  Sue Coe
  Lovis Corinth
  Otto Dix
  Lyonel Feininger
  George Grosz
  Erich Heckel
  Ernst Ludwig Kirchner
  Paul Klee
  Gustav Klimt
  Oskar Kokoschka
  Käthe Kollwitz
  Alfred Kubin
  Paula Modersohn-Becker
  Marie-Louise Motesiczky
  Otto Mueller
  Emil Nolde
  Hermann Max Pechstein
  Egon Schiele
  Karl Schmidt-Rottluff

Stærk

Copenhagen

Galleries
Galleries

What first compelled you to open a gallery?
I started collecting art when I was 13 years old—prints and drawings was what I could afford. After high school I wanted to become an architect, but I began working for a gallery during my summer vacations and have been working in the gallery business ever since. After some years working for other galleries I became interested in starting my own gallery. Claes Nordenhake was a great inspiration at that time and he encouraged me to go ahead.

Who is the first artist you showed and what was most memorable about that show?
I began the gallery in Copenhagen without my own exhibition space. My first artist was Miriam Bäckström and at that time there was very little interest in Denmark for young artists using photography. I therefore joined forces with two smaller museums in Denmark and one in Sweden and arranged Miriam's first museum show and catalogue. We sent it out all over the world and it became a huge success and a good start for both my and Miriam's career.

When did you first participate in Art Basel and what was most memorable about that show?
The first participation was in 2004. We showed in the Statements sector with Matthew Ronay. It was a big step for the gallery at that time and I was therefore very pleased that the show was so well received and sold out.

- **Contact** Nils Stærk
  nils@nilsstaerk.dk
  gallery@nilsstaerk.dk
- **Established** 1997
- **Owner(s) / Partner(s)** Nils Stærk
- **Team** 6
- **Space(s)** 500 m²
- **Artists at Art Basel** Miriam Bäckström
  Olaf Breuning
  Ingvar Cronhammar
  Gardar Eide Einarsson
  Mads Gamdrup
  Nils Erik Gjerdevik
  Richard Hughes
  Jone Kvie
  Michael Kvium
  Runo Lagomarsino
  Torbjørn Rødland
  Matthew Ronay
  Tom Sandberg
  Tove Storch
  Thaddeus Strode
  SUPERFLEX
  Ed Templeton

Stampa

Basel

Galleries

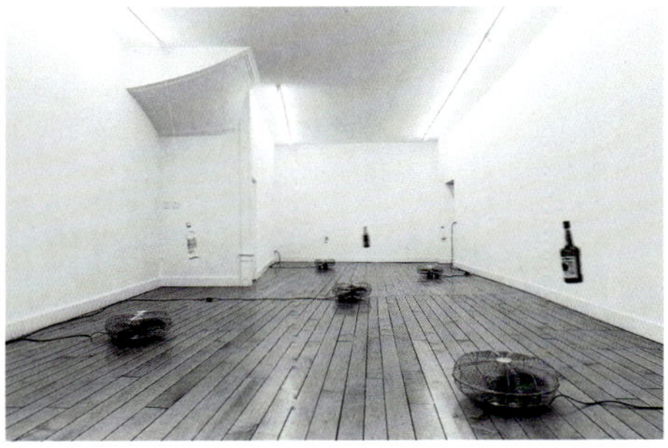

What first compelled you to open a gallery?
The impulse was a sense of pleasure in cultural engagement in a historical situation of change, with the intention to create a new form of exhibition space for upcoming artistic media, such as performance, video, and installation, as well as to offer a platform for cultural interaction in Basel.

Who is the first artist you showed and what was most memorable about that show?
The first exhibition was *Christian Rothacher – Holz, Fell und Flaum (Wood, Fur, and Fuzz)*, a room installation which marked an important shift from painting to new materials and presentation forms. At that time, Rothacher (1944–2007) was a protagonist of the young Swiss avant-garde. In 2011, the Aargauer Kunsthaus, Aarau, dedicated a retrospective exhibition to him.

When did you first participate in Art Basel and what was most memorable about that show?
In 1970. Most impressive was the meeting of international galleries, collectors, artists, and audience. Having the pleasure to get to know these people, this first edition of Art Basel was a useful start and input for our young gallery, as well as for us personally.

- **Contact** Stampa
  Gilli & Diego Stampa
  info@stampa-galerie.ch
- **Established** 1969
- **Owner(s) / Partner(s)** Gilli & Diego Stampa
- **Team** 3
- **Space(s)** 280 m²
- **Artists at Art Basel** Vito Acconci
  Silvia Bächli
  Miriam Cahn
  Christine & Irene Hohenbüchler
  Monika Dillier
  Marlene Dumas
  Ian Hamilton Finlay
  General Idea
  Martina Gmür
  Herzog & de Meuron
  Hanspeter Hofmann
  Daniela Keiser
  Udo Koch

Eva-Fiore Kovacovsky
Zilla Leutenegger
Heinrich Lüber
Dorit Margreiter
Josef Felix Müller
Guido Nussbaum
Marcel Odenbach
Dennis Oppenheim
Pipilotti Rist
Roman Signer
Erik Steinbrecher
Gerda Steiner & Jörg Lenzlinger
Valentina Stieger
Vivian Suter
Ernesto Tatafiore
Rosemarie Trockel
Till Velten

Standard (Oslo)

Oslo

Galleries
Galleries

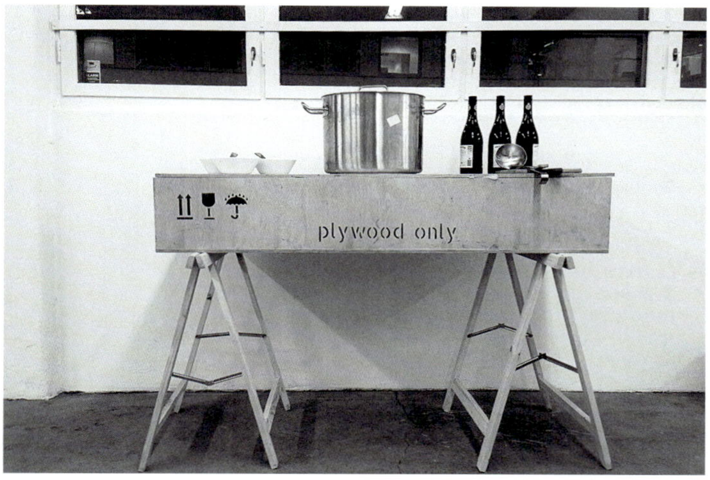

What first compelled you to open a gallery?
Seeing the second exhibition by the artists I had given their first solo exhibition to in a former project space I was running.

Who is the first artist you showed and what was most memorable about that show?
A group exhibition entitled *Start Kapital*, that offered little capital to start with.

When did you first participate in Art Basel and what was most memorable about that show?
In the Statements sector in 2007, and spending a perfect Sunday indoors while waiting for the jury of the Baloise prize to walk around.

- **Contact**: Standard (Oslo)
Eivind Furnesvik
eivind@standardoslo.no
info@standardoslo.no
- **Established**: 2005
- **Owner(s) / Partner(s)**: Eivind Furnesvik
- **Team**: 5
- **Space(s)**: 800 m²
- **Artists at Art Basel**: Tauba Auerbach
Nina Beier
Matias Faldbakken
Aaron Garber-Maikovska
Ann Cathrin November Høibo
Alex Hubbard
Chadwick Rantanen
Fredrik Værslev
- **Further artists represented**: Johanna Billing
Gardar Eide Einarsson
Marius Engh
Ane Graff
Kim Hiorthøy
Michaela Meise
Anders Nordby
Nick Relph
Torbjørn Rødland
Josh Smith
Oscar Tuazon
Emily Wardill

Standing Pine

Nagoya

Insights

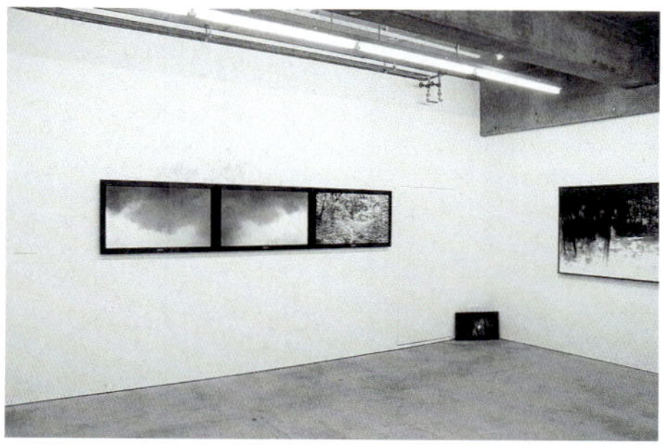

What first compelled you to open a gallery?
Because my father was a painter, I spontaneously became interested in art since I was little, and I finally opened my own gallery.

Who is the first artist you showed and what was most memorable about that show?
It was an unknown young artist in his 20s. I felt very happy to be surrounded by my favorite artworks in a white gallery.

When did you first participate in Art Basel and what was most memorable about that show?
We participated in Art Basel in 2013 in Hong Kong for the first time. The most memorable thing was that Shinji Ogawa's works, which we exhibited alone, were sold out during the VIP preview. Furthermore, Shinji Ogawa was chosen as one of the Top 10 artists by Art Basel curators in Hong Kong.

- **Contact**: Standing Pine
Takeshi Tatematsu
info@standingpine.jp
- **Established**: 2009
- **Owner(s) / Partner(s)**: Takeshi Tatematsu
- **Space(s)**: 99 m²
- **Artists at Art Basel**: Shinji Ogawa
- **Further artists represented**: Masayuki Arai
Youki Hirakawa
Mayumi Inukai
Tomoaki Shitara
Kenji Sugiyama
Kenta Taguchi

Star

Beijing

Insights

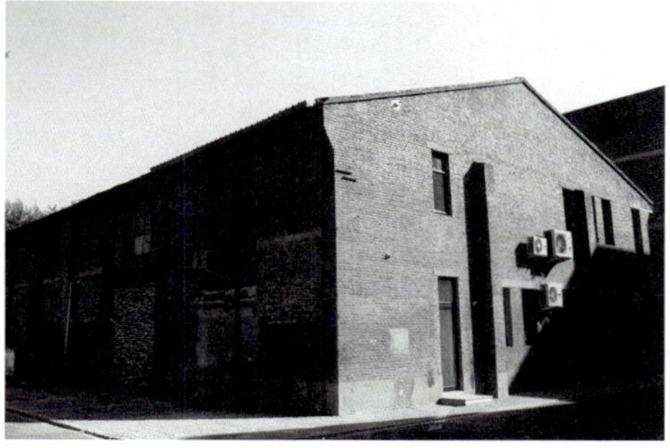

What first compelled you to open a gallery?
To prove my own taste in art. To identify and promote those artists who have not been fully recognized.

Who is the first artist you showed and what was most memorable about that show?
A group show *Next Station: Cartoon?* Not a single work sold. There was no budget for a decent opening dinner, but everyone was very happy.

When did you first participate in Art Basel and what was most memorable about that show?
Hong Kong, in 2013.

- **Contact** Star Gallery
  Patricia Cui
  cuij@stargallery.cn
  ff@stargallery.cn
- **Established** 2005
- **Owner(s) / Partner(s)** Fang Fang (Founding Director)
- **Team** 8
- **Space(s)** 1,000 m²
- **Artists at Art Basel** Chen Ke
- **Further artists represented** Chen Fei
  Gao Yu
  Jin Nü
  Qiu Jiongjiong
  Wang Yifan
  Wei Jia
  Wen Ling
  Xu Maomao
  Yan Cong

Starkwhite

Auckland — Galleries

What first compelled you to open a gallery?
Both directors had worked in the public sector, holding senior positions in major institutions, including the Arts Council of New Zealand and public art galleries. In 2001 we launched Starkwhite as a company working in the creative industries sector, with a project space allowing us to continue working with artists. However, within a couple of years it was clear that staging artists' projects was more rewarding than creative consultancy work and in 2003 we moved to new premises to re-launch Starkwhite as a fully-fledged gallery operation.

Who is the first artist you showed and what was most memorable about that show?
We launched Starkwhite with an "alteration" by conceptual artist Billy Apple. Apple subtly altered our project space by moving one of the interior walls one meter further into the space, which constituted a significant change for the better. The wall remained as a permanent fixture, creating an elegantly proportioned space for future projects and curated exhibitions.

When did you first participate in Art Basel and what was most memorable about that show?
Our first participation was in 2008. We presented two works commissioned for the fair: *Conjuring Form* by Dane Mitchell in the Statements sector, and *altruistic studies* by et al. in Unlimited. In both cases it involved a great leap of faith on our part, allowing the artists a free hand to develop their projects, which was consistent with our general approach to working with artists.

- **Contact** Starkwhite
  John McCormack
  john@starkwhite.co.nz
  starkwhite@starkwhite.co.nz
- **Established** 2003
- **Owner(s) / Partner(s)** Dominic Feuchs (Director)
  John McCormack (Director)
- **Team** 2
- **Space(s)** 780 m²
- **Artists at Art Basel** Billy Apple®
- **Further artists represented** Martin Basher
  Whitney Bedford
  Phil Dadson
  Alicia Frankovich
  Gavin Hipkins
  Jin Jiangbo
  Hye Rim Lee
  Jae Hoon Lee
  Seung Yul Oh
  Grant Stevens
  Clinton Watkins

Starmach

Kraków — Galleries

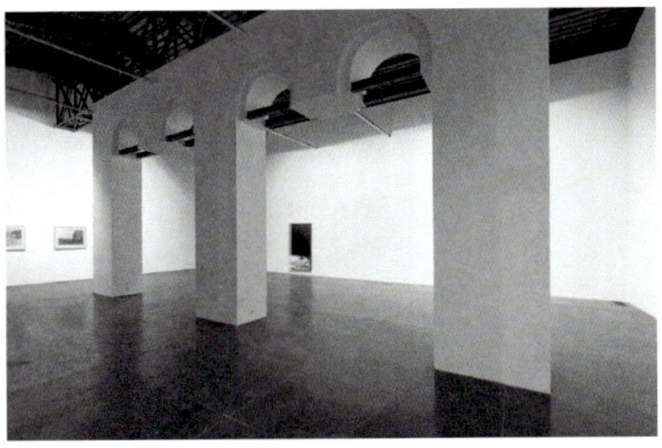

What first compelled you to open a gallery?
Friendship with artists and the particular situation and changeover in Poland in 1989.

Who is the first artist you showed and what was most memorable about that show?
Andrzej Pawłowski and his "photograms." In crowds. All the works were sold.

When did you first participate in Art Basel and what was most memorable about that show?
In 2003. Establishing contact with new collectors.

- **Contact** Galeria Starmach
  Andrzej Szczepaniak
  andrzej@starmach.eu
  galeria@starmach.eu
- **Established** 1989
- **Owner(s) / Partner(s)** Teresa & Andrzej Starmach
- **Team** 4
- **Space(s)** 589 m²
- **Artists at Art Basel** Władysław Hasior
  Tadeusz Kantor
  Edward Krasinski
  Jerzy Nowosielski
  Henryk Stazewski
  Alina Szapocznikow

Stein

Milan — Galleries
Galleries

- **Contact** Christian Stein
  christianstein@iol.it
- **Established** 1966
- **Owner(s) / Partner(s)** Gianfranco Benedetti
- **Artists at Art Basel** Marco Bagnoli
  Domenico Bianchi
  Alighiero Boetti
  Pier Paolo Calzolari
  Paolo Canevari
  Enrico Castellani
  Luciano Fabro
  Lucio Fontana
  Bernard Frize
  Jannis Kounellis
  Piero Manzoni
  Fausto Melotti
  Mario Merz
  Marisa Merz
  Mimmo Paladino
  Giulio Paolini
  Jack Pierson
  Michelangelo Pistoletto
  Remo Salvadori
  Christopher Wool
  Peter Wüthrich
- **Further artists artists represented** Helmut Dorner
  Giuseppe Uncini

Stevenson

Cape Town
Johannesburg

Statements
Unlimited
Galleries

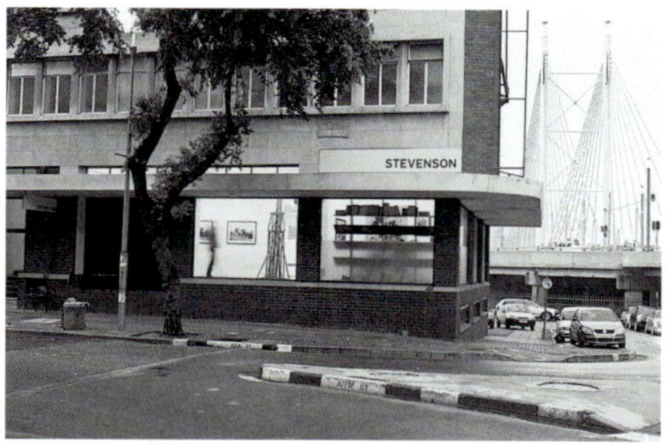

What first compelled you to open a gallery?
A generation of South African artists was coming of age, and the country lacked the gallery infrastructure to support them.

Who is the first artist you showed and what was most memorable about that show?
Guy Tillim was the first artist to have a solo show with us. A former documentary photographer, the context of a gallery immediately made his work more open-ended and expansive, and opened up a whole new way of working—for him, and for us.

When did you first participate in Art Basel and what was most memorable about that show?
In 2011, we showed 63 portraits of black lesbians and transmen by South African activist photographer Zanele Muholi in the Statements sector. It is hard to describe how it felt to see Muholi's uncompromising fight for visibility take her, and us, to the inner sanctum of the international art world.

- **Contact** Stevenson
  Joost Bosland
  joost@stevenson.info
  info@stevenson.info
- **Established** 2003
- **Owner(s) / Partner(s)** Federica Angelucci
  Joost Bosland
  David Brodie
  Andrew da Conceicao
  Sophie Perryer
  Michael Stevenson
- **Team** 25
- **Space(s)** 600 m²
- **Artists at Art Basel** Wim Botha
  Nicholas Hlobo
  Pieter Hugo
  Kemang Wa Lehulere
- **Further artists represented** Zander Blom
  Dineo Seshee Bopape
  Conrad Botes
  Steven Cohen
  Paul Edmunds
  Ângela Ferreira
  Meschac Gaba
  Ian Grose
  Simon Gush
  Anton Kannemeyer
  Michael MacGarry
  Sabelo Mlangeni
  Nandipha Mntambo
  Billy Monk
  Zanele Muholi
  Daniel Naudé
  Serge Alain Nitegeka
  Odili Donald Odita
  Deborah Poynton
  Jo Ractliffe
  Robin Rhode
  Viviane Sassen
  Claudette Schreuders
  Berni Searle
  Lerato Shadi
  Penny Siopis
  Guy Tillim
  Frohawk Two Feather
  Lynette Yiadom-Boakye

Stigter van Doesburg

Amsterdam

Galleries

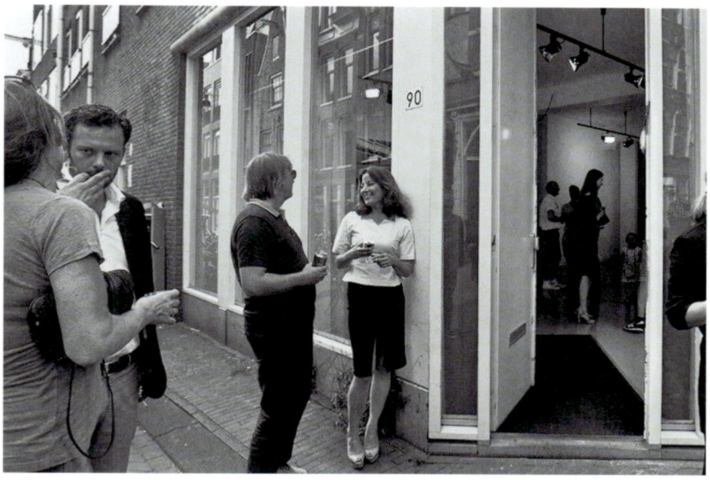

What first compelled you to open a gallery?
Ileana Sonnabend.

Who is the first artist you showed and what was most memorable about that show?
Pierre Bismuth; special guest: Jonathan Monk. The opening was three days after 9/11. While installing the show we went to the local Sony store to buy a television screen for Pierre's work and saw the planes crash into the Twin Towers on multiple screens, thinking at first that we were watching some bizarre action movie.

When did you first participate in Art Basel and what was most memorable about that show?
In 2003, in the Statements sector with Saskia Olde Wolbers. Winning the Baloise Art Prize.

- **Contact** Stigter van Doesburg
  Elisa Sjelvgren
  mail@stigtervandoesburg.com
  mail@dianastigter.nl
- **Established** 2001
- **Owner(s) / Partner(s)** Diana Stigter
  David van Doesburg
- **Team** 4
- **Space(s)** 150 m²
- **Artists at Art Basel** Elspeth Diederix
  Amalia Pica
  Jimmy Robert
- **Further artists represented** Tariq Alvi
  Tjebbe Beekman
  Semâ Bekirovic
  Mark Boulos
  Martha Colburn
  Yael Davids
  Amie Dicke
  Irene Fortuyn
  Tom Gidley
  Thomas Helbig
  Aukje Koks
  Nathaniel Mellors
  Saskia Olde Wolbers
  Maaike Schoorel
  Pilvi Takala
  Sue Tompkins
  Antonio Vega Macotela
  Helen Verhoeven

Stolper

London • Edition

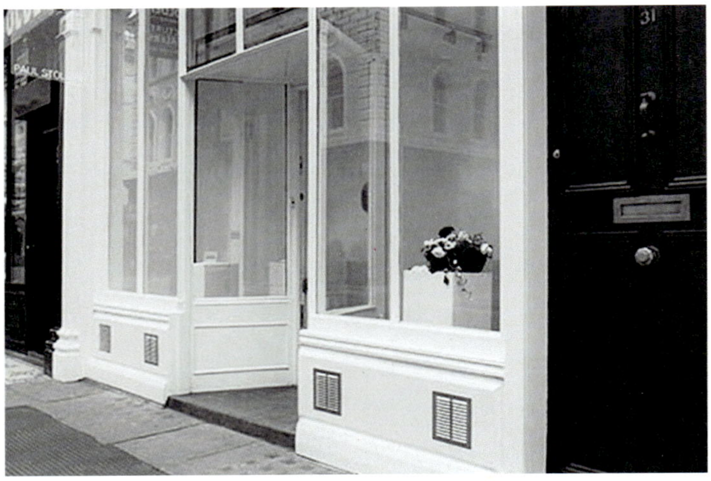

What first compelled you to open a gallery?
I needed a physical space for our clients and audience to visit. Having a gallery allows them to revisit over a period of time to get a real sense of all the projects we initiate and artists we work with.

Who is the first artist you showed and what was most memorable about that show?
The first show was Jeremy Deller's *Boys and Girls* in 1991, in a huge warehouse space, Turtle Keys, in London. Joshua Compston, who set up events such as *Fete Worse than Death*, *Hanging Picnic*, and his gallery Factual Nonsense, appeared at the private view completely naked except for some bubble wrap covering his private parts.

When did you first participate in Art Basel and what was most memorable about that show?
In 2013 in Miami Beach, with a solo presentation by Peter Saville and Anna Blessmann.

- **Contact** Paul Stolper Gallery
  Alexandra Sterling
  alexandra@paulstolper.com
  info@paulstolper.com
- **Established** 1998
- **Owner(s) / Partner(s)** Paul Stolper
- **Team** 5
- **Space(s)** 130 m²
- **Artists at Art Basel** Anna Blessmann
  Peter Saville
- **Further artists represented** David Bailey
  Peter Blake
  Don Brown
  Darren Coffield
  Keith Coventry
  Kevin Cummins
  Jeremy Deller
  John Dove & Molly White
  Shaun Doyle & Mally Mallinson
  Shepard Fairey
  Magne Furuholmen
  Pablo Genovés
  Susie Hamilton
  Sarah Hardacre
  Damien Hirst
  Andrew Hollis
  Rachel Howard
  Grace O'Connor
  Claire Pestaille
  Jamie Reid
  Ray Richardson
  Mit Senoj
  Gavin Turk

STPI

Singapore • Galleries • Edition • Edition

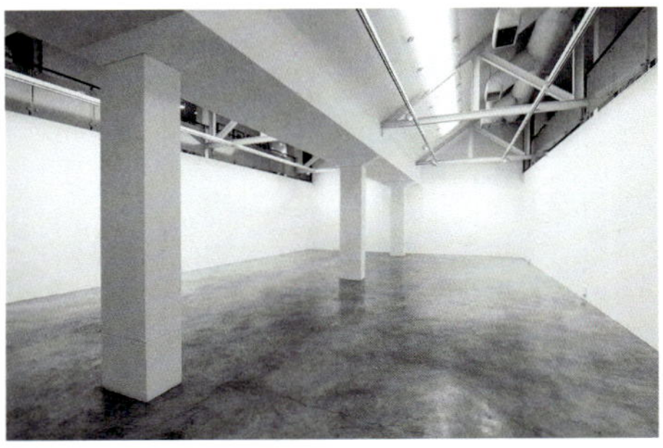

What first compelled you to open a gallery?
STPI Gallery was established together with the Print & Paper workshop in 2002 by the then Ministry of Information, Communication, and the Arts (MITA), to be a catalyst contributing to a vibrant art scene in Singapore, and to nurture future art professionals in Singapore and the region.

Who is the first artist you showed and what was most memorable about that show?
Our very first exhibition was *Frank Stella in 2002*, the renowned American abstract artist's first major solo-exhibition in Asia. We had 23 of his most recent works including mixed media paintings, sculptures, and maquettes directly from the artist himself, and it was a great opportunity for Singaporeans to witness and be inspired by his creativity first-hand. Singapore was still new to contemporary art at that time and it was therefore a huge effort on STPI's part to set the tone for what was to come for the arts industry. As much infrastructure was still being put in place, it was a real challenge for the team both administratively and logistically to install the exhibition.

When did you first participate in Art Basel and what was most memorable about that show?
2013 has been a very significant year for STPI. Not only is it the first year we exhibited at Art Basel in Hong Kong; we participated in all three Art Basel fairs—in Hong Kong, Basel, and Miami Beach.

- **Contact** STPI – Singapore Tyler
  Print Institute
  Yen Hui Teng
  tengyenhui@stpi.com.sg
  stpi@stpi.com.sg
- **Established** 2002
- **Owner(s) / Partner(s)** Emi Eu (Director)
- **Team** 13
- **Space(s)** 400 m²
- **Artists at Art Basel** Ghada Amer & Reza Farkhondeh
  Song-Ming Ang
  Heman Chong
  Genevieve Chua
  Richard Deacon
  Hong Zhu An
  Eko Nugroho
  Wu Shanzhuan &
  Inga Svala Thorsdottir
  Sumir Tagra
  Jiten Thukral
  Haegue Yang
- **Further artists represented** Ashley Bickerton
  Teresita Fernández
  Trenton Doyle Hancock
  Geraldine Javier
  Lin Tianmiao
  Handiwirman Saputra
  Do Ho Suh
  Donald Sultan
  Sun Xun
  Rirkrit Tiravanija
  Ronald Ventura
  Zhan Wang

Strina

São Paulo

- Galleries
- Unlimited
- Galleries

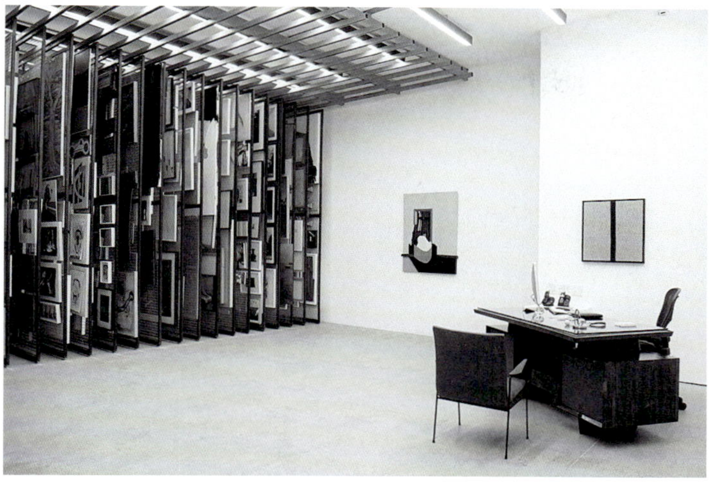

What first compelled you to open a gallery?
In 1970 Luisa began as an art merchant for friends and artists such as Wesley Duke Lee, Fajardo, Baravelli, José Resende, and Babinski.

Who is the first artist you showed and what was most memorable about that show?
In 1974 she opened Galeria Luisa Strina at Baravelli's old studio with a well defined strategy: to show the work of national and international artists, both here in Brazil and abroad.

When did you first participate in Art Basel and what was most memorable about that show?
Luisa Strina was the first Latin-American gallery to exhibit at Art Basel, in 1992.

- **Contact** Galeria Luisa Strina
Patricia Dominguez
patricia@galerialuisastrina.com.br
info@galerialuisastrina.com.br
- **Established** 1974
- **Owner(s) / Partner(s)** Luisa Malzoni Strina
- **Team** 11
- **Space(s)** 200 m²
- **Artists at Art Basel** Pablo Accinelli
Leonor Antunes
Juan Araujo
Alessandro Balteo Yazbeck
Laura Belém
Erick Beltrán
Alexandre da Cunha
Caetano de Almeida
Edgard de Souza
Matías Duville
Olafur Eliasson
Marcius Galan
Carlos Garaicoa
Fernanda Gomes
Brian Griffiths
David Haines
Federico Herrero
Magdalena Jitrik
Marcellvs L.
Luisa Lambri
Tonico Lemos Auad
Laura Lima
Armin Linke
Jarbas Lopes
Jazmín López
Mateo López
Renata Lucas
Jorge Macchi
António Manuel
Marepe
Gilberto Mariotti
Cildo Meireles
Pedro Motta
Muntadas
Bernardo Ortiz
Nicolás Paris
Pedro Reyes
Marina Saleme
Gabriel Sierra
Adrián Villar Rojas

Sullivan+Strumpf

Sydney

- Insights

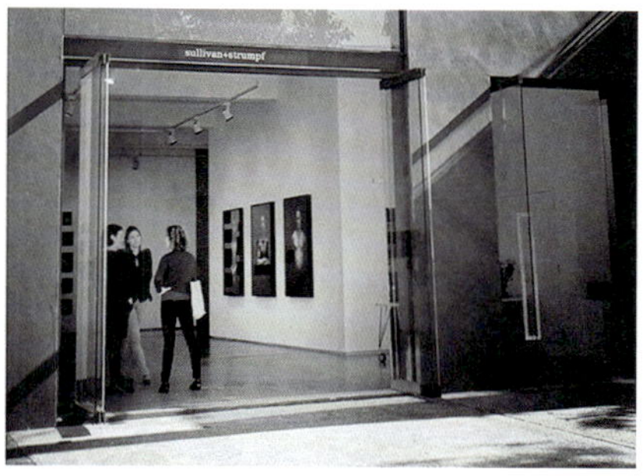

What first compelled you to open a gallery?
A love of art, especially contemporary art, and the desire to work with artists.

Who is the first artist you showed and what was most memorable about that show?
Alasdair Macintyre—he made these very pop *Zeitgeist* sculptures that capture the craziness of what it is to be a person that wants to engage in contemporary art.

When did you first participate in Art Basel and what was most memorable about that show?
Our first Art Basel was in Hong Kong in 2013. We were impressed by the Basel black book, which brought some really serious collectors willing to engage with new artists, new work.

- **Contact** Sullivan+Strumpf
Ursula Sullivan
ursula@sullivanstrumpf.com
art@sullivanstrumpf.com
- **Established** 2005
- **Owner(s) / Partner(s)** Ursula Sullivan
Joanna Strumpf
- **Team** 7
- **Space(s)** 440 m²
- **Artists at Art Basel** Penny Byrne
- **Further artists represented** Tony Albert
Matthew Allen
Sydney Ball
Karen Black
Marc de Jong
eX de Medici
Leah Emery
Juan Ford
Arie Hellendoorn
Gregory Hodge
Sam Jinks
Joanna Lamb
Sam Leach
Michael Lindeman
Dane Lovett
Alasdair Macintyre
Laith McGregor
Judy Millar
Alexander Seton
Kate Shaw
Darren Sylvester
Textaqueen

Sur

Punta del Este
Montevideo

Galleries

- **Contact** Galería Sur
sur@montevideo.com.uy
- **Established** 1984
- **Owner(s) / Partner(s)** Martin Castillo
Jorge Castillo
- **Artists at Art Basel** Pablo Atchugarry
Antonio Berni
Fernando Botero
José Pedro Costigliolo
Wifredo Díaz Valdéz
Maria Freire
José Gurvich
Wifredo Lam
Roberto Matta
Miguel Ángel Pareja
Cándido Portinari
Joaquín Torres García
- **Further artists represented** Eduardo Cardozo
Ignacio Iturria
Marcelo Legrand
Lasar Segall
Ernesto Vila

Szwajcer

Antwerp

Galleries
Unlimited

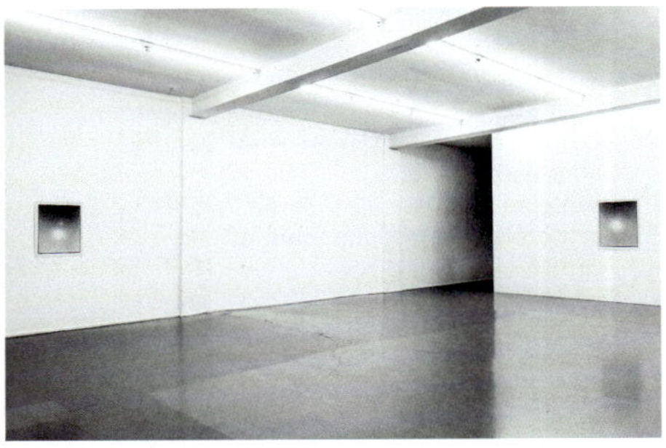

Who is the first artist you showed and what was most memorable about that show?
Sarah Charlesworth.

When did you first participate in Art Basel and what was most memorable about that show?
In 1998.

- **Contact** Galerie Micheline Szwajcer
Nina Serebrenic
nina@gms.be
contact@gms.be
- **Established** 1981
- **Owner(s) / Partner(s)** Micheline Szwajcer
- **Team** 4
- **Space(s)** 250 m²
- **Artists at Art Basel** Stanley Brouwn
Jos de Gruyter & Harald Thys
Koenraad Dedobbeleer
Hans-Peter Feldmann
Lucy McKenzie
Manfred Pernice
Daan van Golden
- **Further artists represented** Giovanni Anselmo
Angella Bulloch
David Claerbout
James Coleman
François Curlet
Luciano Fabro
Bernard Frize
Liam Gillick
Dan Graham
Carsten Höller
Ann Veronica Janssens
On Kawara
Mark Luyten
Guy Mees
Matt Mullican
Tobias Rehberger
Allen Ruppersberg
Lawrence Weiner
Marthe Wéry
Christopher Wool
Heimo Zobernig

Silverlens

Interview with Isa Lorenzo

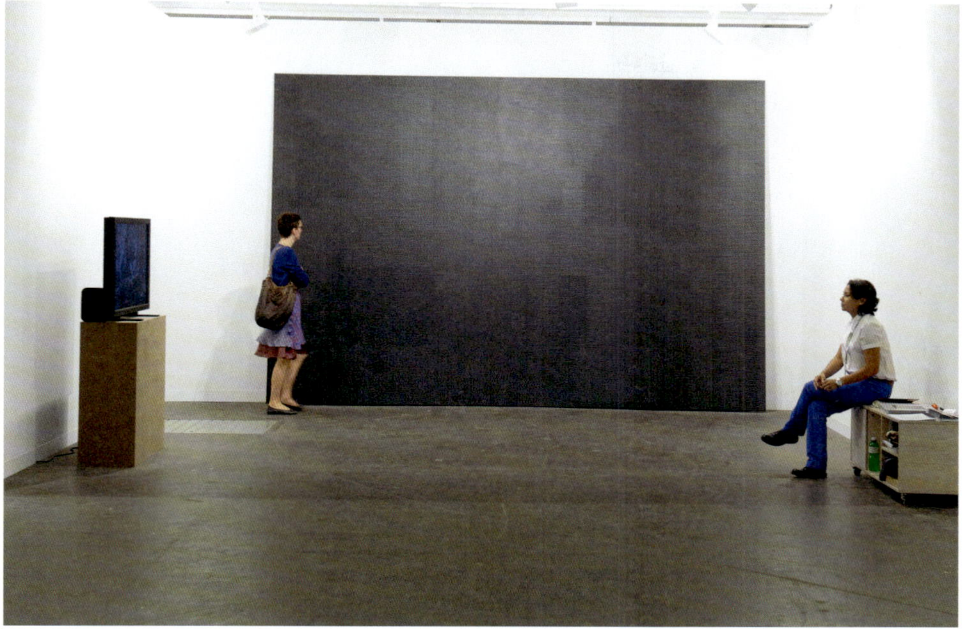

Art Basel in Basel (Statements), 2013

What is the history of the gallery and how did you choose your locations?

Silverlens started in 2004 in Manila. In 2012 we also opened in Singapore. We represent artists from the Philippines and we are slowly integrating Southeast Asian artists into our program. We work mainly with emerging artists and with all kinds of mediums (painting, sculpture, photography, video, performance). We are considered a pioneering gallery in our part of the world. We have been participating in art fairs for the last five years. This is our first time at Art Basel.

Why did you choose to open a new gallery in Singapore after starting in Manila?

There is a new art district called Gillman Barracks, which invited us to be part of the program. That's how we ended up in Singapore. The Philippines is still a very under-represented country. We are at a point where it has become more important for us to just show good artists, wherever they come from, as opposed to making a niche and a local program.

How is the scene in the Philippines for contemporary art?

It's very good. There are maybe 10 to 15 contemporary art galleries. We have a strong local audience of collectors, artists … There's not a lot of institutional support, no museums, no initiatives funded by the government.

What about the project for Statements this year?

The artist is Maria Taniguchi. She's in her mid-30s. Her work has always been about removing variables. She's been making brick paintings for the last five years: she paints a canvas dark gray with acrylic and then, with a pencil, she draws bricks of the same size all over the canvas and paints them in black—any color subtleties come from the different thicknesses of paint. So you get a beautiful collage of black and gray, the same tonalities she uses in her videos. *Figure Study* depicts two men digging in a forest on Negros, the third largest island of the Philippines. It's an island popular for its clay, a dark and compact material, very good for terracotta sculpture, which has been a specific practice of this island for hundreds of years. So, on the first level, it's a film about mining, a sort of anthropological document of digging and mining the ground; but it also has a double meaning, because you don't know if they are digging or burying … It might be connected to a crime rather than to mining. You don't know when it starts or when it ends, it's a repetitive process. You can always imagine that this is happening 50 years ago or today. Because the video is so crisp, you might deduce that it's contemporary, but it sort of shifts in time, since the repetitive action has been happening for many, many years. The conversation between the painting and the video lies in the color scheme and the system of repetition, the subtle differences within the repetition. Maria Taniguchi is a very popular and important artist among collectors in our region, and also a favorite among curators in our area. We thought it was important to show someone who is very active in the scene right now, as opposed to an older or more famous artist.

T

T293

Naples
Rome

- Nova

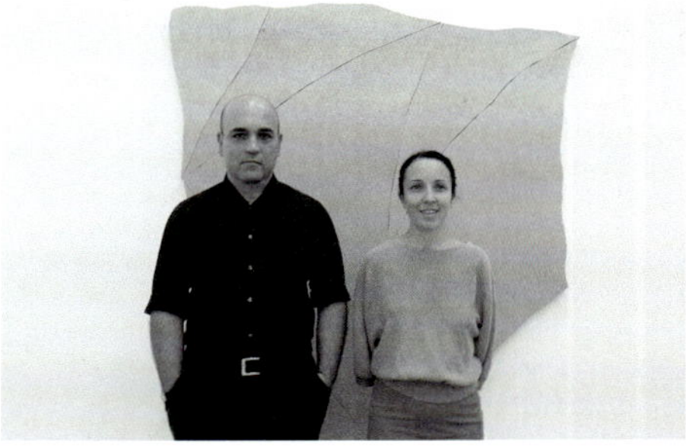

What first compelled you to open a gallery?
The need for a space for emerging artists which was missing in the city before fall 2002, a place that could be a window onto the international art scene.

Who is the first artist you showed and what was most memorable about that show?
The first show featured a group of artists from the School of Art in Naples, who belong to the same generation as we do. It has been incredible and emotional to see the way in which the artworks turned the apartment into a gallery space.

When did you first participate in Art Basel and what was most memorable about that show?
Our first participation was in 2007, with a solo exhibition in the Statements sector by Jordan Wolfson. The most unforgettable thing was the extraordinary beauty of his 16mm film, *Perfect Lover*, which remains among our favorites.

- **Contact** T293
  Alessia Volpe
  alessia@t293.it
  info@t293.it
- **Established** 2002
- **Owner(s) / Partner(s)** Marco Altavilla
  Paola Guadagnino
- **Team** 5
- **Space(s)** 100 m² (Naples)
  200 m² (Rome)
- **Artists at Art Basel** Sam Falls
  Wyatt Kahn
- **Further artists represented** James Beckett
  Simon Denny
  Patrizio Di Massimo
  Claire Fontaine
  John Henderson
  Henrik Olai Kaarstein
  Sonia Kacem
  David Maljković
  Helen Marten
  Pennacchio Argentato
  Dan Rees
  Martin Soto Climent
  Alberto Tadiello
  Tris Vonna-Michell
  Jordan Wolfson

Take Ninagawa

Tokyo

- Discoveries
- Feature

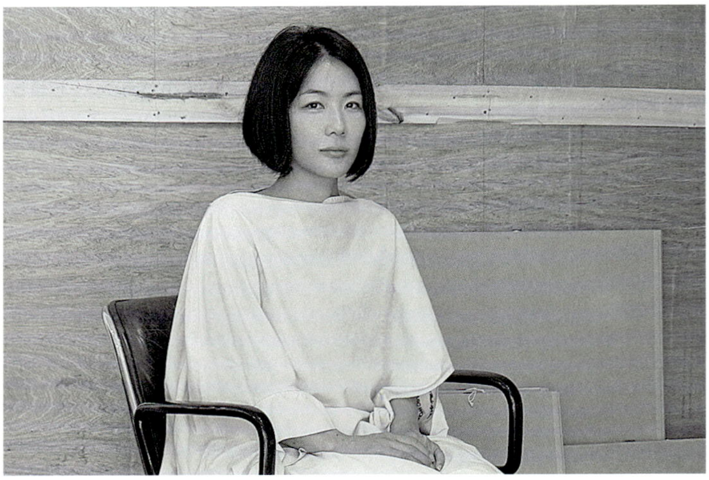

What first compelled you to open a gallery?
I wanted to create a new space for contemporary art and discourse in Japan with the objective of creating a new framework for presenting emerging artists within a historical context.

Who is the first artist you showed and what was most memorable about that show?
Misaki Kawai, who presented new works on canvas and sculptural works in a special installation. Kawai's installation revealed the potential to create a space that would transform from artist to artist and from exhibition to exhibition, and in seeing the other gallerists, curators, artists, and collectors who came to celebrate our inauguration, we were able to find confirmation of the possibility for Take Ninagawa's participation in the Tokyo art scene.

When did you first participate in Art Basel and what was most memorable about that show?
Take Ninagawa's first participation in Art Basel was in the Feature sector, in 2013. We presented a solo show by Tsuruko Yamazaki, one of the founding members of the Gutai Art Association. It was an honor to be able to present historically important works by Yamazaki, including reproductions of works made for the 1955 *1st Gutai Art Exhibition*, at a venue like Art Basel.

- **Contact** Take Ninagawa
  Atsuko Ninagawa
  nina@takeninagawa.com
  info@takeninagawa.com
- **Established** 2008
- **Owner(s) / Partner(s)** Atsuko Ninagawa
- **Team** 5
- **Space(s)** 100 m²
- **Artists at Art Basel** Ryoko Aoki
  Tsuruko Yamazaki
- **Further artists represented** Dale Berning
  Aki Goto
  Shinpei Kageshima
  Misaki Kawai
  Yoriko Kita
  Chikara Matsumoto
  Yuuki Matsumura
  Shinro Ohtake
  Aki Sasamoto
  Yukiko Suto
  Soju Tao

Tang

Beijing
Bangkok

- Galleries
- Encounters
- Positions

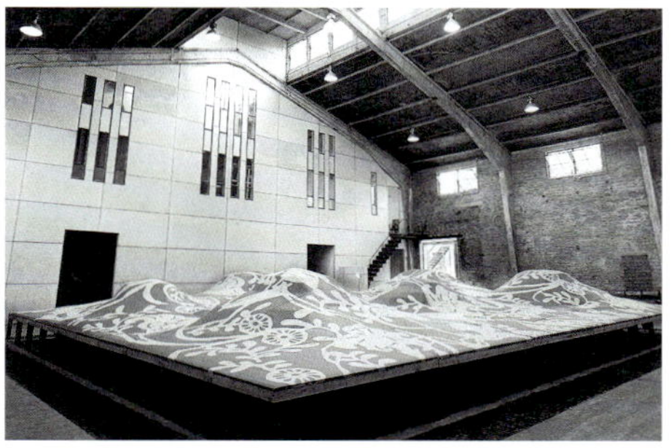

What first compelled you to open a gallery?
I initially began by studying art and was once a young artist who harbored my own hopes for contemporary art. The economy in China during the 1990s was not as good as it is today—there were practically no collectors or institutions. Artists could only have exhibitions or sell works in Europe, the US, or South-East Asia. That was why I originally established Tang Contemporary Art in Bangkok, to help Chinese artists do exhibitions and projects overseas and establish a system for collectors overseas.

Who is the first artist you showed and what was most memorable about that show?
Tang Contemporary Art returned to Beijing in 2006, and after establishing its headquarters in 798, the first exhibition was a group show. The participating artists were all excellent: Yang Jiechang, Michael Lin, Zheng Guogu, and Wu Shanzhuan, for example.

When did you first participate in Art Basel and what was most memorable about that show?
In 2013, at Art Basel in Hong Kong.

- **Contact** Tang Contemporary Art
  Ting Ting Zhao
  zhaotingting@tangcontemporary.com
  info@tangcontemporary.com
- **Established** 2001
- **Owner(s) / Partner(s)** Zheng Lin (President)
- **Space(s)** 600 m²
- **Artists at Art Basel** He An
  Jiang Zhi
  H.H. Lim
  Liu Chuang
  Wang Du
  Wang Yuyang
  Xu Qu
  Yan Lei
- **Further artists represented** Haritorn Akarapat
  Chen Wenbo
  Guo Wei
  Ji Zhou
  Sakarin Krue-On
  Kamin Lertchaiprasert
  Lin Yilin
  Ling Jian
  Liu Xiaodong
  Ken Lum
  Navin Rawanchaikul
  Sakarin Krue-on
  Sun Yuan & Peng Yu
  Rirkrit Tiravanija
  Tawan Wattuya
  Weng Fen
  Yang Jiechang
  Yang Yong
  Zheng Guogu

tanzer

Melbourne
Australia

- Insights

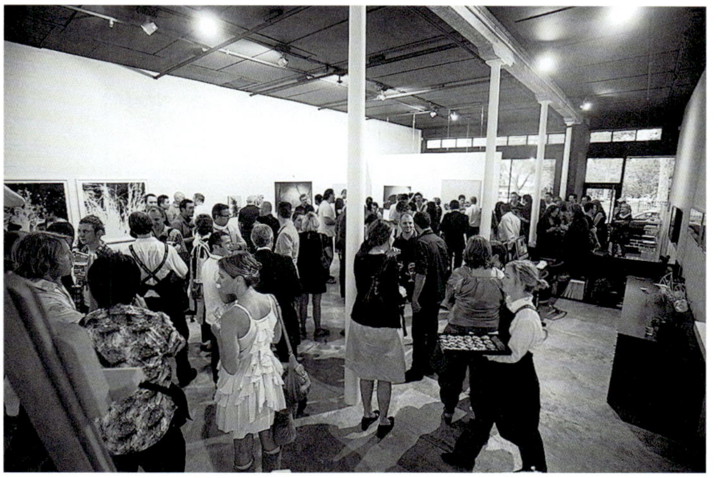

What first compelled you to open a gallery?
I've always understood the fragility of life and the ephemeral nature of things, therefore I've gravitated toward occupations and interests that have longevity and significance. This is a very intellectually challenging career, in which the artists' expectations are great; the disappointments are many, but the rewards can be huge. It all adds up to a pretty heady environment in which to work. Who wouldn't want to spend their life doing this!

Who is the first artist you showed and what was most memorable about that show?
Maryanne Coutts, an emerging Australian painter. To be part of a young artist's first foray into the art world and to experience their overwhelming desire and ambition first-hand was very exhilarating. I knew then that this was a long-term prospect for me.

When did you first participate in Art Basel and what was most memorable about that show?
Art Basel in Hong Kong in 2013. The excitement of meeting and networking with a new array of collectors and galleries was memorable, as were the many compliments our stand and artists received. The reality of exhibiting alongside galleries such as Gagosian, Pace, and other major international galleries was also a bonus.

- **Contact** dianne tanzer gallery + projects
  Dianne Tanzer
  dtanzer@ozemail.com.au
- **Established** 1990
- **Owner(s) / Partner(s)** Dianne Tanzer (Director)
- **Team** 3
- **Space(s)** 200 m²
- **Artists at Art Basel** Juan Ford
- **Further artists represented** Natasha Bieniek
  Michael Cook
  Yvette Coppersmith
  Marian Drew
  Neil Haddon
  Matthew Hunt
  Owen Leong
  Tony Lloyd
  Izabela Pluta
  Victoria Reichelt
  Yhonnie Scarce

Taylor

London

Galleries
Galleries Unlimited
Galleries

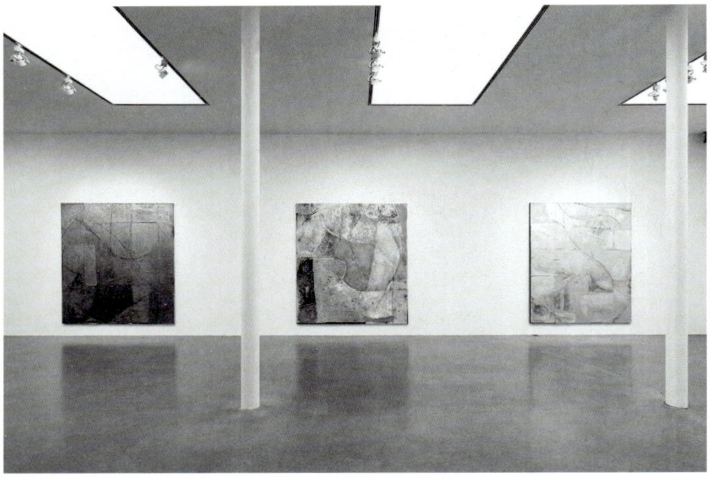

What first compelled you to open a gallery?
I was keen to promote international artists of the highest standard.

Who is the first artist you showed and what was most memorable about that show?
Sean Scully.

When did you first participate in Art Basel and what was most memorable about that show?
The gallery's first participation in Art Basel was in 2004. It was exciting to see such a strong London audience there.

- **Contact** Timothy Taylor Gallery
Carla Borel
carla@timothytaylorgallery.com
mail@timothytaylorgallery.com
- **Established** 1996
- **Owner(s) / Partner(s)** Timothy Taylor Gallery
- **Team** 18
- **Space(s)** 615 m²
- **Artists at Art Basel** Diane Arbus
Jean-Marc Bustamante
Armen Eloyan
Lee Friedlander
Adam Fuss
Ewan Gibbs
Philip Guston
Hans Hartung
Susan Hiller
Volker Hueller
Jessica Jackson Hutchins
Alex Katz
Jonathan Lasker
Agnes Martin
Josephine Meckseper
Richard Patterson
Mai-Thu Perret
Fiona Rae
Bridget Riley
Sean Scully
Kiki Smith
Antoni Tàpies
Liliane Tomasko
Andy Warhol
Lucy Williams
- **Further artists represented** Craigie Aitchison
Ron Arad

team

New York

Galleries

- **Contact** team (gallery, inc.)
office@teamgal.com
- **Established** 1996
- **Owner(s) / Partner(s)** Jose Freire
Miriam Katzeff
Todd von Ammon
Thalassa Balanis
- **Artists at Art Basel** Cory Arcangel
Alex Bag
Pierre Bismuth
Vlassis Caniaris
Brice Dellsperger
Maria Eichhorn
Gardar Eide Einarsson
Massimo Grimaldi
Marc Hundley
Ross Knight
Jakob Kolding
Ryan McGinley
Muntean/Rosenblum
Tam Ochiai
David Ratcliff
Davis Rhodes
Tabor Robak
Sam Samore
Andreas Schulze
Santiago Sierra
Gert & Uwe Tobias
Daniel Turner
Chris Vasell
Banks Violette
Stanley Whitney
- **Further artists represented** Suzanne McClelland

Tega

Milan

Galleries

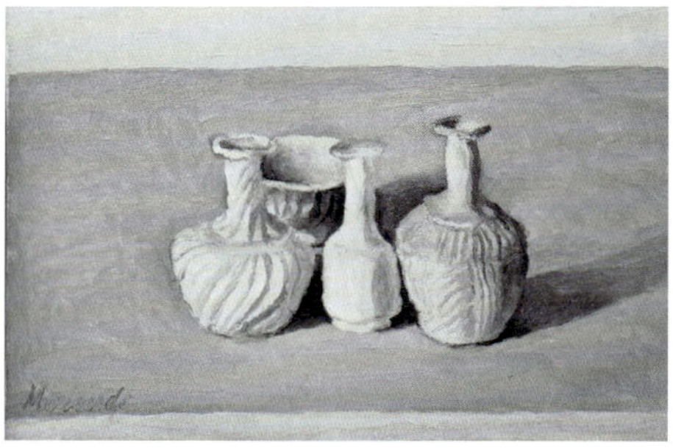

What first compelled you to open a gallery?
In 1964, Dino Tega opened his first gallery in Riccione with an exhibition of Filippo de Pisis. Giulio's son, who had absorbed his father's sensibility, opened his gallery in 1979 in the center of Milan with a show of Giorgio Morandi. Over the following years he presented retrospectives of Alberto Magnelli and of Georges Mathieu. Giulio Tega always privileged choices of high quality, without following the common tendencies. So he presented exhibitions by: Chagall, Tadini, Kolar, Perill, Schneider, Melotti, Tal-Coat, Uncini, Hartung, Licini, Afro. Galleria Tega is one of the few Italian galleries that has for years exhibited in the most important art fair in the world: Art Basel. In the last ten years Galleria Tega has presented high-level shows by Fontana, Manzoni, Burri, Kounellis, Rotella, Christo, Botero, Campigli. The gallery has privileged relationships with Jeanne-Claude and Christo, Fernando Botero, Archivio Campigli, Fondazione Mimmo Rotella, and Achille Perilli. Now my daughters Eleonora and Francesca, as a family tradition, are continuing the gallery with me.

When did you first participate in Art Basel and what was most memorable about that show?
My first participation at Art Basel was 15 years ago. When I first visited the art fair I was impressed by the quality and variety of the art works exhibited.

- **Contact** Galleria Tega
Eleonora Tega
info@galleriatega.it
- **Established** 1979
- **Owner(s) / Partner(s)** Eleonora, Francesca & Giulio Tega
- **Team** 5
- **Space(s)** 160 m²
- **Artists at Art Basel** Carla Accardi
Valerio Adami
Afro
Alighiero Boetti
Fernando Botero
Alberto Burri
Pier Paolo Calzolari
Massimo Campigli
Giuseppe Capogrossi
Enrico Castellani
Christo
Pietro Consagra
Dadamaino
Giorgio de Chirico
Nicola De Maria
Max Ernst
Lucio Fontana
Riccardo Gusmaroli
Damien Hirst
Robert Indiana
Paul Klee
Fernand Léger
Piero Manzoni
Fausto Melotti
Joan Miró
Amedeo Modigliani
Giorgio Morandi
Giulio Paolini
Achille Perilli
Gianni Piacentino
Pablo Picasso
Michelangelo Pistoletto
Mimmo Rotella
Ed Ruscha
Salvatore Scarpitta
Paolo Scheggi
Antoni Tàpies
Cy Twombly
Sophia Vari
Tom Wesselmann
- **Further artists represented** Enrico Baj
Giacomo Balla
Jean-Michel Basquiat
Marc Chagall
Sandro Chia
Ettore Colla
Filippo De Pisis
Nicolas de Stäel
Piero Dorazio
Jean Dubuffet
Luciano Fabro
Jean Fautrier
Piero Guccione
Hans Hartung
Wassily Kandinsky
Kcho
Sol LeWitt
Osvaldo Licini
Alberto Magnelli
Mario Merz
Gastone Novelli
Mimmo Paladino
Claudio Parmiggiani
Giuseppe Penone
Serge Poliakoff
Mel Ramos
Alberto Savinio
Gino Severini
Mario Sironi
Giuseppe Uncini
Andy Warhol
Gilberto Zorio

Templon

Paris
Brussels

Galleries
Galleries Unlimited

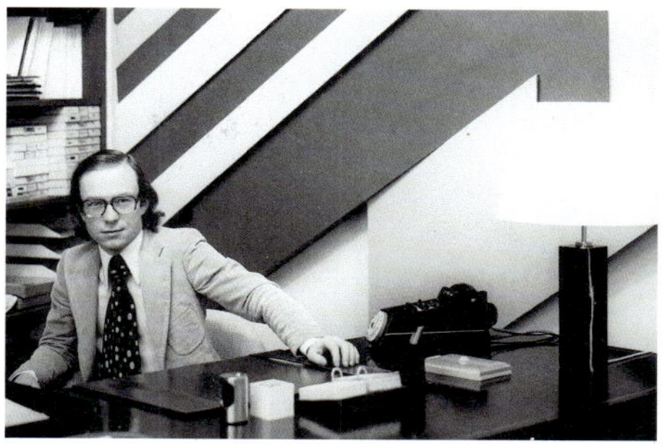

What first compelled you to open a gallery?
At 21, I started in the basement of an antique store on rue Bonaparte, in Saint-Germain-des-Prés. I had a taste for art and adventure.

Who is the first artist you showed and what was most memorable about that show?
My first show was of Marie Raymond, an abstract painter, in the style of the École de Paris and Yves Klein's mother. Everyone came, curious to see who the "mother of the genius" was.

When did you first participate in Art Basel and what was most memorable about that show?
For my first participation, in 1978, I shared a booth with Leo Castelli and Hans Strelow. It was already the most beautiful art fair in the world.

- **Contact** Galerie Daniel Templon
Anne-Claudie Coric
accoric@danieltemplon.com
info@danieltemplon.com
- **Established** 1966
- **Owner(s) / Partner(s)** Daniel Templon (President)
- **Team** 14
- **Space(s)** 660 m²
- **Artists at Art Basel** Norbert Bisky
Anthony Caro
James Casebere
Philippe Cognée
Atul Dodiya
Jan Fabre
Eric Fischl
He An
Oda Jaune
Jitish Kallat
David LaChapelle
Mao Yan
Jonathan Meese
Iván Navarro
Joel Shapiro
Sudarshan Shetty
Chiharu Shiota
Frank Stella
Tunga
Kehinde Wiley
Yue Minjun
- **Further artists represented** Valerio Adami
Jean-Michel Alberola
Arman
Larry Bell
Ben
Saint Clair Cemin
Gregory Crewdson
Daniel Dezeuze
Jim Dine
Anju Dodiya
Gérard Garouste
Clay Ketter
Guillermo Kuitca
Ulrich Lamsfuss
Loïc Le Groumellec
Jonathan Meese
Philip Pearlstein
Julião Sarmento
Joel Shapiro
Victor Vasarely
Claude Viallat

The Guild

Mumbai ● Galleries

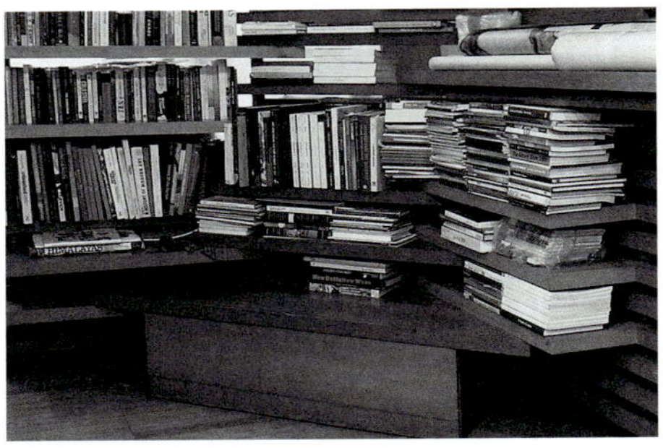

What first compelled you to open a gallery?
Our first exhibition was a group show comprising young eminent, mid-career, and young emerging artists.

Who is the first artist you showed and what was most memorable about that show?
One early most memorable solo show was by T. V. Santhosh, entitled *One Hand Clapping/Siren*, with all monochromatic black and whites. The response from the audience and art professionals was outstanding.

When did you first participate in Art Basel and what was most memorable about that show?
In 2013. Well organized, spacious, with fantastic booth layout, and exciting public projects.

- **Contact** The Guild
  Urvi Shah
  teanattheguild@gmail.com
  theguildart@yahoo.com
- **Established** 1997
- **Owner(s) / Partner(s)** Shalini Sawhney (Director)
- **Team** 10
- **Artists at Art Basel** Ravi Agarwal
  Navjot Altaf
  Sudhir Patwardhan
  K. P. Reji
  T. V. Santhosh
  Praneet Soi
- **Further artists represented** Prayas Abhinav
  Shadi Ghadirian
  G. R. Iranna
  Pooja Iranna
  Vidya Kamat
  Riyas Komu
  Amitabh Kumar
  Sathyanand Mohan
  Baiju Parthan
  Gieve Patel
  Rakhi Peswani
  Balaji Ponna
  Prajakta Potnis
  K. G. Subramanyan
  Charwei Tsai

The Third Line

Dubai ● Statements

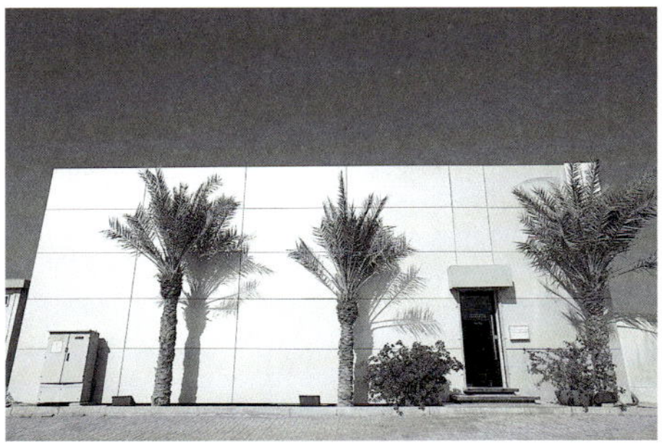

What first compelled you to open a gallery?
The Third Line was created to offer professional representation to regionally-based artists and to bring artists from the diaspora back to the region to exhibit their works.

Who is the first artist you showed and what was most memorable about that show?
Amir H. Fallah, *You Know Where You Came From, You Know Where You Are Going*, in September 2005. Amir H. Fallah displayed a large-scale mural painting that he created on-site. This mural was then presented alongside a selection of smaller works, all of which represented Amir's breakaway from his previous street-art style practice.

When did you first participate in Art Basel and what was most memorable about that show?
The Third Line first showed in the Art Supernova sector of Art Basel Miami Beach in 2008, and in the Statements sector of Art Basel in 2013.

- **Contact** The Third Line
  Gabriella Moore
  gabriella@thethirdline.com
  artfair@thethirdline.com
- **Established** 2005
- **Owner(s) / Partner(s)** Sunny Rahbar (Co-Owner)
  Claudia Cellini (Co-Owner)
  Omar Ghobash (Co-Owner)
- **Team** 14
- **Space(s)** 3,000 m²
- **Artists at Art Basel** Laleh Khorramian
- **Further artists represented** Ebtisam Abdulaziz
  Arwa Abouon
  Abbas Akhavan
  Tarek Al-Ghoussein
  Shirin Aliabadi
  Sophia Al-Maria
  Rana Begum
  Ala Ebtekar
  Fouad Elkoury
  Amir H. Fallah
  Golnaz Fathi
  Lamya Gargash
  Babak Golkar
  Sherin Guirguis
  Joana Hadjithomas & Khalil Joreige
  Hassan Hajjaj
  Sahand Hesamiyan
  Pouran Jinchi
  Hayv Kahraman
  Huda Lutfi
  Farhad Moshiri
  Youssef Nabil
  Monir Shahroudy Farmanfarmaian
  Slavs and Tatars

Thomas

Munich ● Galleries ● Galleries

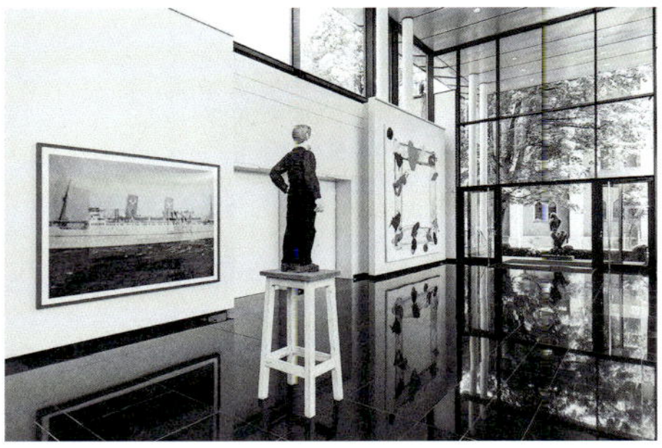

What first compelled you to open a gallery?
My enthusiasm after visiting Munich galleries in 1961.

Who is the first artist you showed and what was most memorable about that show?
Sculptor Paul Isenrath (b. 1936). He was a student of Norbert Kricke and his technique of sculptures in folded steel fascinated me.

When did you first participate in Art Basel and what was most memorable about that show?
In 1972, and I was very impressed to meet so many potential collectors from Basel and from all over the world.

- **Contact** Galerie Thomas
  Barbara Zmeck
  b.zmeck@galerie-thomas.de
  info@galerie-thomas.de
- **Established** 1964 (Galerie Thomas)
  2009 (Galerie Thomas Modern)
- **Owner(s) / Partner(s)** Raimund Thomas
  Silke Thomas
- **Team** 22
- **Space(s)** 180 m² (Galerie Thomas)
  600 m² (Galerie Thomas Modern)
- **Artists at Art Basel** Josef Albers
  Alexander Archipenko
  Jean Arp
  Georg Baselitz
  Max Beckmann
  Joseph Beuys
  Fernando Botero
  Alexander Calder
  Marc Chagall
  Eduardo Chillida
  Willem de Kooning
  Robert Delaunay
  Jim Dine
  Max Ernst
  Lyonel Feininger
  Lucio Fontana
  Sam Francis
  Alberto Giacometti
  Hans Hofmann
  Robert Indiana
  Wassily Kandinsky
  Anselm Kiefer
  Ernst Ludwig Kirchner
  Paul Klee
  Fernand Léger
  Roy Lichtenstein
  August Macke
  Franz Marc
  Henri Matisse
  Joan Miró
  Joan Mitchell
  Otto Mueller
  Gabriele Münter
  Edvard Munch
  Emil Nolde
  Max Pechstein
  Pablo Picasso
  Sigmar Polke
  Robert Rauschenberg
  Gerhard Richter
  Oskar Schlemmer
  Karl Schmidt-Rottluff
  Chaïm Soutine
  Cy Twombly
  Alexej von Jawlensky
  Andy Warhol
  Tom Wesselmann
- **Further artists represented** Arman
  Heinrich Campendonk
  Lovis Corinth
  Wim Delvoye
  Otto Dix
  Günther Förg
  Gotthard Graubner
  Peter Halley
  Erich Heckel
  Imi Knoebel
  Georg Kolbe
  Piero Manzoni
  Takashi Murakami
  Ernst Wilhelm Nay
  Louise Nevelson
  Otto Piene
  Serge Poliakoff
  Marc Quinn
  Jesús Rafael Soto
  George Rickey
  Simon Schubert
  George Segal
  Günther Uecker
  Victor Vasarely

Three Star

Paris ● Edition

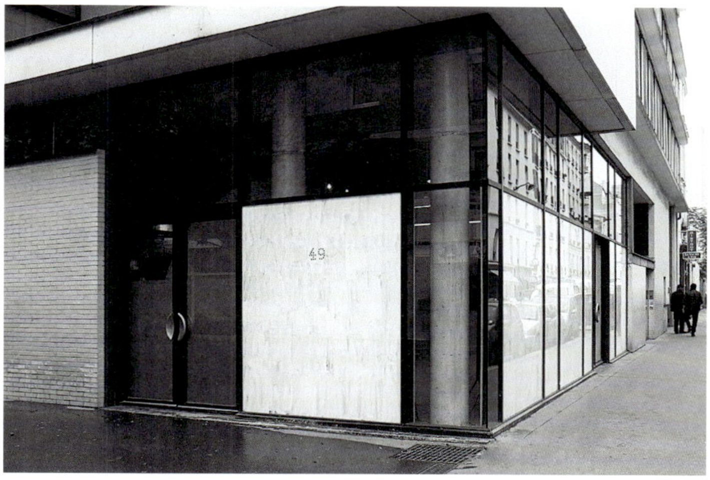

What first compelled you to open a gallery?
We started TSB (Three Star Books) because we felt that the long tradition of Parisian "livres d'artistes, livres de peintres" needed to be freshened up.

Who is the first artist you showed and what was most memorable about that show?
We presented Jonathan Monk's *The Billboard Book Project (Paris)* which was our first successful event.

When did you first participate in Art Basel and what was most memorable about that show?
Our first participation was in 2011. We presented a very special project with Matt Mullican's *88 MAPS* (2010), alongside Jonathan Monk's *Billboard Book Project (Paris)*, Maurizio Cattelan's handmade monograph, and a unique book/sculpture by Tobias Rehberger, among others. Our memorable experience from Art 42 Basel was establishing new relationships with collectors and institutions with whom we still work today.

- **Contact** Three Star Books
  Melanie Scarciglia
  melanie@threestarbooks.com
  info@threestarbooks.com
- **Established** 2007
- **Owner(s) / Partner(s)** Christophe Boutin
  Cornelia Lauf
  Melanie Scarciglia
- **Team** 3
- **Space(s)** 118 m²
- **Artists at Art Basel** John M Armleder
  Tauba Auerbach
  Maurizio Cattelan
  Ryan Gander
  Liam Gillick
  Dominique Gonzalez-Foerster
  Thomas Hirschhorn
  Jonathan Monk
  Olivier Mosset
  Matt Mullican
  Blake Rayne
  Tobias Rehberger
  Slavs & Tatars
  Simon Starling
  Haim Steinbach
  Lawrence Weiner
  Heimo Zobernig
- **Further artists represented** Hubert Damisch
  Alison Knowles & Rirkrit Tiravanija
  Ken Lum

Thumm

Berlin

Galleries

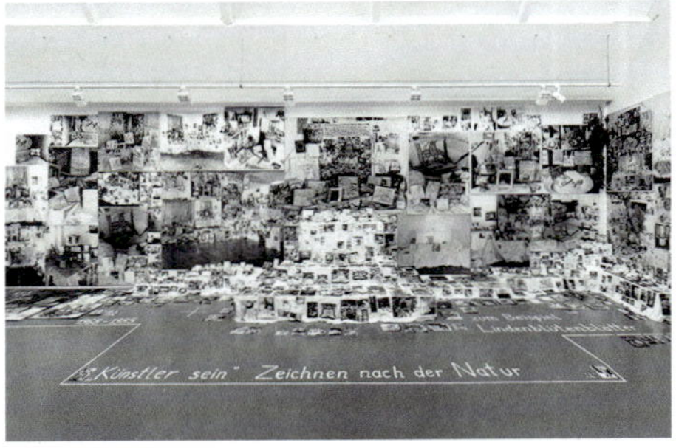

What first compelled you to open a gallery?
Having been a painter myself, I started the gallery very much from an artist's point of view. I was intrigued by the discursiveness of the public space I created. The gallery opened in the pioneering times of the now grown up Berlin gallery scene. I wanted to be part of the cultural formation of the newly united city.

Who is the first artist you showed and what was most memorable about that show?
The first show was with Julian Opie. We showed car sculptures and wall paintings of buildings. It was fascinating how the reductive images of urbanity resonated in the postmodern socialist architecture that surrounded us.

When did you first participate in Art Basel and what was most memorable about that show?
My first participation was in Art Basel in Miami Beach when there was no fair. We had all contributed to support the fair, which was cancelled due to 9/11. The next year, we spent a fantastic time in the containers at the beach. I remember colleagues selling art in their bikinis. My most memorable show in Basel was a presentation of one of the largest pieces by Fernando Bryce in the Unlimited sector in 2005.

- **Contact** Galerie Barbara Thumm
  Barbara Thumm
  info@bthumm.de
- **Established** 1997
- **Owner(s) / Partner(s)** Barbara Thumm
- **Team** 4
- **Space(s)** 270 m²
- **Artists at Art Basel** Jo Baer
  Fernando Bryce
  Teresa Burga
  Simon Cantemir Hausi
  Anna K.E.
  Antonio Paucar
- **Further artists represented** Fiona Banner
  Bigert & Bergström
  Sebastiaan Bremer
  Jota Castro
  Martin Dammann
  Valérie Favre
  Diango Hernández
  Teresa Hubbard
  Alexander Birchler
  Johnny Miller
  Mariele Neudecker
  Anna Oppermann
  Chloe Piene
  Ann-Sofi Sidén
  Anne-Mie van Kerckhoven

Tilton

New York

Statements
Galleries

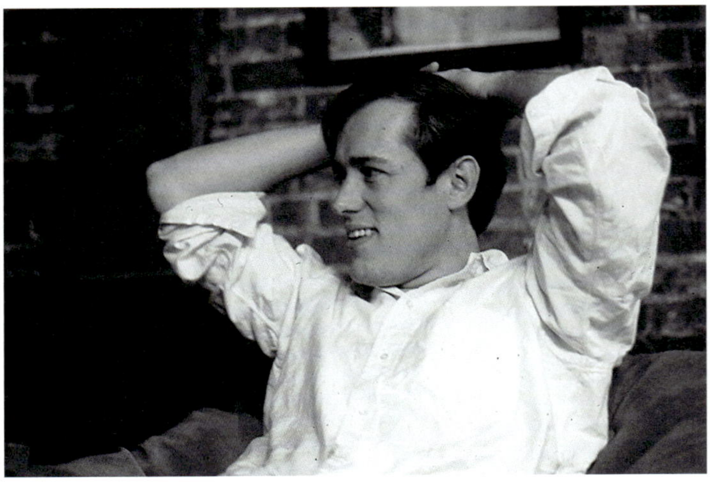

What first compelled you to open a gallery?
I had been working for Betty Parsons for about a decade—when she passed away I decided to open a gallery of my own. I love(d) both art and business. The opportunity to help artists at various stages of their careers was what I suppose made me want to open a gallery most.

Who is the first artist you showed and what was most memorable about that show?
The first show was a group show made up of young American and European artists. In hindsight, what is most noteworthy to me is that the gallery's dedication to showing art from all over the globe was there from the very beginning.

When did you first participate in Art Basel and what was most memorable about that show?
It was early on, sometime in the 1980s. I just remember the energy being great. To see artists and collectors converge in Basel from all over was a really special thing.

- **Contact** Tilton Gallery
  Ryan McKenna
  ryanm@jacktiltongallery.com
  info@jacktiltongallery.com
- **Established** 1983
- **Owner(s) / Partner(s)** Jack Tilton
- **Team** 5
- **Space(s)** 300 m²
- **Artists at Art Basel** Derrick Adams
  Noel Anderson
  Noah Davis
  Luca Dellaverson
  Andreas Diefenbach
  Egan Frantz
  Chitra Ganesh
  Fred Holland
  James Jean
  Yashua Klos
  Simone Leigh
  Jarbas Lopes
  David Lynch
  John Outterbridge
  Rebecca Purdum
  Sudarshan Shetty
  Leonid Sokov
  Jeff Sonhouse
  Berend Strik
  Kianja Strobert
  Ruth Vollmer
  Brenna Youngblood
  Zhang Peili
- **Further artists represented** Matthew Fischer

Tolarno

Melbourne ● Insights

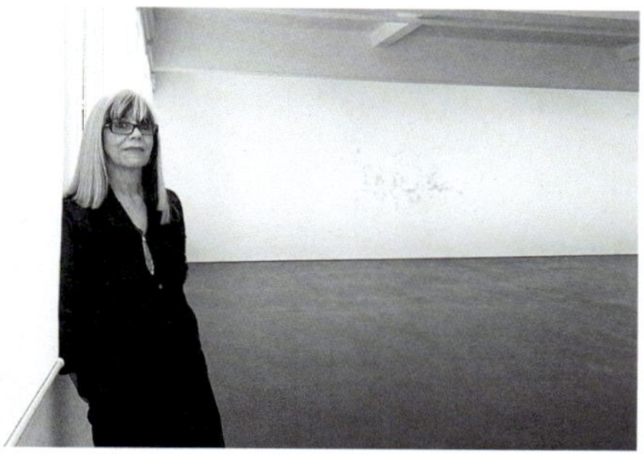

What first compelled you to open a gallery?

I was working as Curator of Australian Art at the National Gallery of Victoria. Stepping into the shoes of the Contemporary Curator while he was on leave, I put together a big show titled *Freestyle*. It focused on individuals rather than on a group of artists. This was the late 1980s and it created a buzz. Shortly after, Georges Mora, the then director of Tolarno Galleries, asked me to join him with a view to taking over when he retired. I left the National Gallery so that I could work directly with artists. After Georges died in 1993, I purchased Tolarno and its exhibition records. I wanted to be right in the middle of what was happening then rather than studying what had occurred 50 years before. I re-located the business to the other side of Melbourne and opened the doors to the new space in February 1993.

Who is the first artist you showed and what was most memorable about that show?

The first artist I showed was Dick Watkins.

When did you first participate in Art Basel and what was most memorable about that show?

In 2013 we presented 43 works by Brendan Huntley at Art Basel in Hong Kong. His "primitive" paintings and sculptures were recognized as free-spirited and full of risk. The response to his distinctive voice was phenomenal. A complete sell-out.

- **Contact** Tolarno Galleries
  Jan Minchin
  janminchin@tolarnogalleries.com
  mail@tolarnogalleries.com
- **Established** 1967
- **Owner(s) / Partner(s)** Jan Minchin (Director)
- **Team** 5
- **Space(s)** 180 m²
- **Artists at Art Basel** Martin Bell, Brendan Huntley
- **Further artists represented** Brook Andrew, Benjamin Armstrong, Peter Atkins, Andrew Browne, Peter Graham, Brent Harris, Louise Hearman, Peter Hennessey, Bill Henson, Tim Johnson, Anastasia Klose, Rosemary Laing, Christopher Langton, Tim Maguire, Patricia Piccinini, Ben Quilty, Robert Rooney, Caroline Rothwell, David Wadelton, Judy Watson

Tonkonow

New York ● Galleries

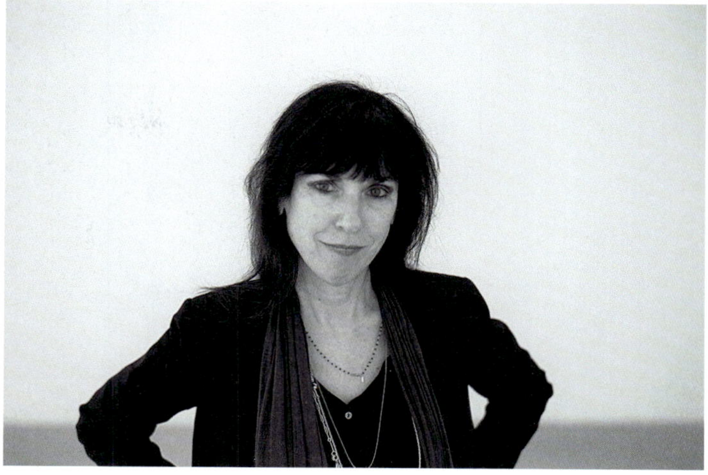

What first compelled you to open a gallery?

In 1984, when I was a young artist, the East Village gallery scene was starting and I was given the use of a small storefront. I didn't know how to sell art, but I had lots of ideas and all my friends were artists. Through them I met other artists, curators, and critics (including my husband who was writing for *Flash Art*). I soon realized that I loved the public discourse of the gallery, preferring it to the solitude of the studio. I learned the business of art by working for two outstanding modern and contemporary dealers (Virginia Zabriskie from 1989 to 1995 and Paula Cooper, briefly afterwards). By 1997 I was ready to be on my own again and opened Leslie Tonkonow Artworks + Projects in Chelsea.

Who is the first artist you showed and what was most memorable about that show?

The first artist I represented was Kunié Sugiura, a Japanese woman who had two exhibitions with me in the East Village.

When did you first participate in Art Basel and what was most memorable about that show?

Our first presentation was in 2009 at Art Basel in Miami Beach; it was extremely successful with very strong sales and attendance. In addition to collectors, we were visited by many museum directors, curators, and trustees. One highlight that year was an extended visit from the Society for Contemporary Art at the Art Institute of Chicago for whom I gave a special presentation on the works of Robert Watts, an early Pop artist and founder of Fluxus.

- **Contact** Leslie Tonkonow
  Artworks + Projects
  Tyler Auwarter
  tyler@tonkonow.com
  info@tonkonow.com
- **Established** 1997
- **Owner(s) / Partner(s)** Leslie Tonkonow
- **Team** 3
- **Space(s)** 200 m²
- **Artists at Art Basel** Dean Byington, Agnes Denes, Laurel Nakadate, Michelle Stuart, Kunié Sugiura, Robert Watts
- **Further artists represented** Tracey Baran, Amy Cutler, Ian Davis, Danny Jauregui, Betsy Kaufman, Malerie Marder, Julia Oschatz, Tokihiro Sato

T

Tornabuoni

Florence	Galleries
Paris	Galleries
Milan	
Forte dei Marmi	
Porto Fino	

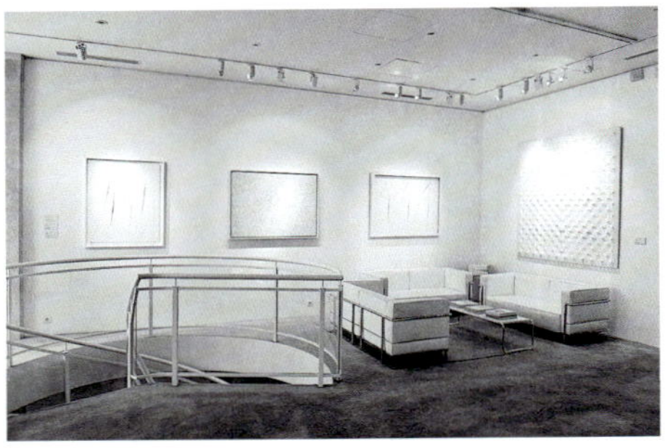

What first compelled you to open a gallery?
Mr. Casamonti decided to open a gallery to show and improve his personal collection.

Who is the first artist you showed and what was most memorable about that show?
Lucio Fontana is the gallery's most historical artist. For every opening of a new space or a new art fair we traditionally present a Lucio Fontana show.

When did you first participate in Art Basel and what was most memorable about that show?
Art Basel in Miami Beach in 2012 was our first art fair in the United States which enabled us to properly enter the American market.

- **Contact** Tornabuoni Art
  Francesca Piccolboni
  fpiccolboni@tornabuoniart.fr
- **Established** 1983
- **Owner** Roberto Casamonti (Founder)
- **Space(s)** 300 m²
- **Artists at Art Basel** Carla Accardi
  Pablo Atchugarry
  Alberto Biasi
  Alighiero Boetti
  Agostino Bonalumi
  Alberto Burri
  Pier Paolo Calzolari
  Giuseppe Capogrossi
  Enrico Castellani
  Dadamaino
  Giorgio de Chirico
  Piero Dorazio
  Lucio Fontana
  Piero Manzoni
  Giorgio Morandi
  Francesca Pasquali
  Salvatore Scarpitta
  Paolo Scheggi
  Turi Simeti
- **Further artists represented** Giacomo Balla
  Jean-Michel Basquiat
  Vanessa Beecroft
  Umberto Boccioni
  Georges Braque
  Mario Ceroli
  Christo
  Tony Cragg
  Enzo Cucchi
  Gino De Dominicis
  Jean Dubuffet
  Jean Fautrier
  Keith Haring
  Hans Hartung
  Nam June Paik
  Wassily Kandinsky
  Jannis Kounellis
  Wifredo Lam
  Sebastian Matta
  Joan Miró
  Giulio Paolini
  Pino Pascali
  Pablo Picasso
  Michelangelo Pistoletto
  Serge Poliakoff
  Arnaldo Pomodoro
  Robert Rauschenberg
  Mimmo Rotella
  Victor Vasarely
  Emilio Vedova
  Andy Warhol
  Tom Wesselmann

Travesía Cuatro

Madrid	Nova
Guadalajara	

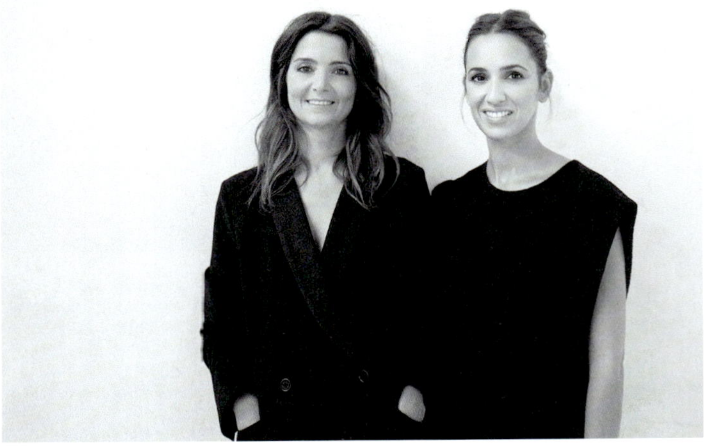

What first compelled you to open a gallery?
After working in different areas of the art world, the partners Silvia Ortiz and Inés López-Quesada saw the necessity of opening their own space, to represent and promote the work of a whole generation. Madrid at that point was a good place for developing a new gallery, as the art scene was managed by an older generation.

Who is the first artist you showed and what was most memorable about that show?
We showed Ana Márcia Varela and Leonardo Villela, two young Brazilian artists. This was our first contact with Latin-America, something that has stayed with us until today.

When did you first participate in Art Basel and what was most memorable about that show?
In 2009, it was a solo show by Mexican artist Jose Dávila in the Nova sector at Miami Beach. This was very important for the gallery, and of course for the career of the artist.

- **Contact** Travesía Cuatro
  Alberto Sanchez
  alberto@travesiacuatro.com
  galeria@travesiacuatro.com
- **Established** 2003
- **Owner(s) / Partner(s)** Inés López-Quesada
  Silvia Ortiz
- **Team** 4
- **Space(s)** 275 m² (Madrid)
  180 m² (Guadalajara)
- **Artists at Art Basel** Gonzalo Lebrija
  Jorge Méndez Blake
- **Further artists represented** Jose Dávila
  Juan de Sande
  John Isaacs
  Yuri Masnyj
  Marco Rountree
  Carolina Silva
  Vicky Uslé

Tschudi

Zuoz ● Galleries

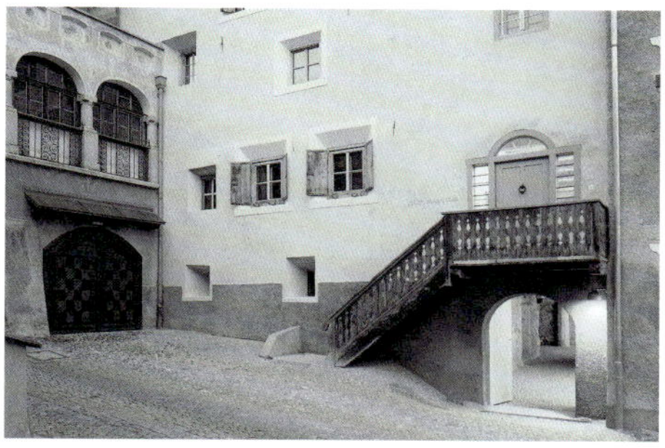

What first compelled you to open a gallery?
The fascination with contemporary art and the possibility of having an insightful view.

Who is the first artist you showed and what was most memorable about that show?
Günther Uecker and his students. The most memorable moments were the controversial reactions provoked by the Punk concert some of the students organized for the opening.

When did you first participate in Art Basel and what was most memorable about that show?
In 1992. Most memorable was that we did not sell anything, and how our booth stood out with the strict and not very colorful artworks.

- **Contact** Galerie Tschudi
  Elsbeth Bisig
  elsbeth.bisig@galerie-tschudi.ch
  info@galerie-tschudi.ch
- **Established** 1985
- **Owner(s) / Partner(s)** Ruedi Tschudi
  Elsbeth Bisig
- **Space(s)** 600 m²
- **Artists at Art Basel** Carl Andre
  Stanley Brouwn
  Balthasar Burkhard
  Alan Charlton
  Hamish Fulton
  Bethan Huws
  Callum Innes
  Kimsooja
  Martina Klein
  Richard Long
  Mario Merz
  Ulrich Rückriem
  Serge Spitzer
  Niele Toroni
  Su-Mei Tse
  Not Vital
  Dan Walsh
  Petra Wunderlich

Tsuruno

Tokyo ● Insights

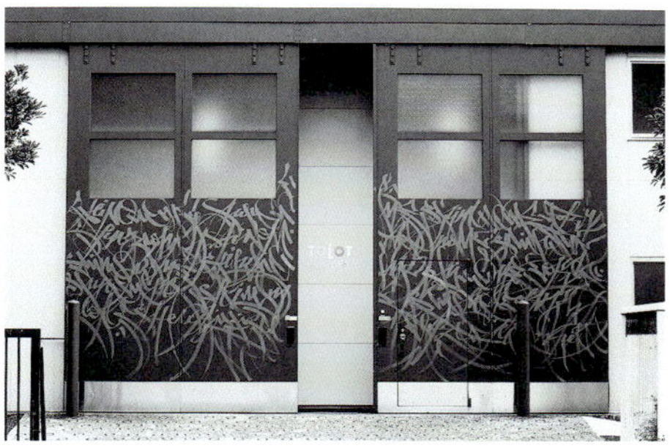

What first compelled you to open a gallery?
I was inspired by Mary Boone through learning about Basquiat.

When did you first participate in Art Basel and what was most memorable about that show?
In 2013.

- **Contact** Yuka Tsuruno
  y@yukatsuruno.com
  info@yukatsuruno.com
- **Established** 2009
- **Owner** Yuka Tsuruno
- **Team** 2
- **Space(s)** 80 m²
- **Artists at Art Basel** Yuichiro Tamura
- **Further artists represented** Tim Barber
  Tetsuro Kano
  Maiko Kasai
  Kwan Sheung Chi
  mamoru
  Manika Nagare
  Tomomi Nitta
  Nobuyuki Osaki
  José Parlá
  Nobuhiro Shimura
  Yu Yasuda

Tucci Russo

Torre Pellice (Turin) ● Galleries

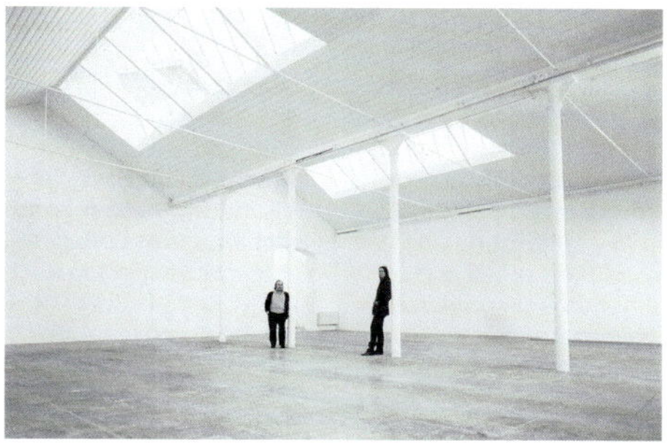

What first compelled you to open a gallery?
During the 1960s I was interested in and engaged with poetry. In doing so I knew and got along with the Arte Povera artists. At that time they were showing their first artworks at Sperone's gallery in Turin. The time I spent with them led me to the desire to deal with their works, as it has subsequently happened. I decided to open my own gallery in 1975 building a kind of cultural bridge between some of the Arte Povera's artists and the new generations.

Who is the first artist you showed and what was most memorable about that show?
The first exhibition that I organized in my gallery was a solo show by Pier Paolo Calzolari with artworks spanning 1966 to 1972. Moreover, a work originally planned for the exhibition *Op Losse Schroeven* at the Stedelijk Museum in Amsterdam was also shown in this exhibition. The museum could not realize the piece. The work comprised a white boxer with red eyes next to four pink melting ice blocks.

When did you first participate in Art Basel and what was most memorable about that show?
In 1985. I remember the very good organization of the fair and the dialogue with the international galleries. There was a strong cultural discussion with them in order to build synergies to help artists within the art system.

- **Contact** Tucci Russo Studio per l'Arte Contemporanea
  Elisabetta Di Grazia
  gallery@tuccirusso.com
- **Established** 1975
- **Owner(s) / Partner(s)** Antonio Tucci Russo
  Elisabetta di Grazia
- **Space(s)** 1,200 m²
- **Artists at Art Basel** Giovanni Anselmo
  Gianni Caravaggio
  Francesco Gennari
  Richard Long
  Giulio Paolini
  Giuseppe Penone
  Robin Rhode
  Jan Vercruysse
- **Further artists represented** Daniel Buren
  Pier Paolo Calzolari
  Tony Cragg
  Harald Klingelhöller
  Mario Merz
  Marisa Merz
  Paolo Mussat Sartor
  Alfredo Pirri
  Paolo Piscitelli
  Thomas Schütte
  Conrad Shawcross

Two Palms

New York

● Edition
● Edition

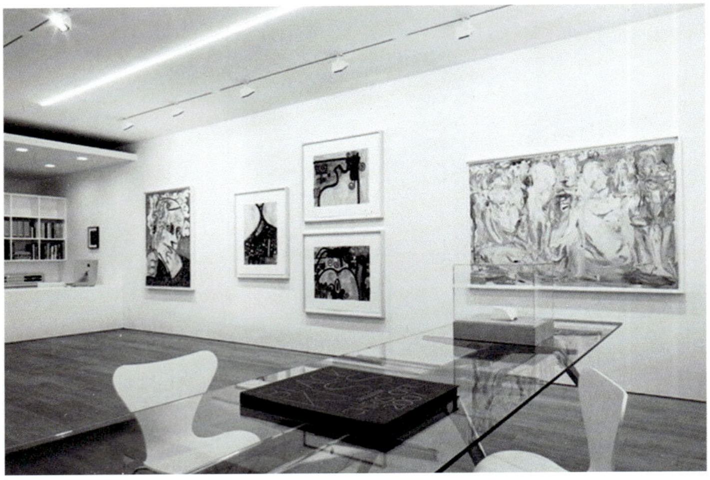

What first compelled you to open a gallery?
We published and produced prints and other artworks with major contemporary artists and needed a space to exhibit the works.

Who is the first artist you showed and what was most memorable about that show?
The first artist we had an exhibition with was Sol LeWitt. It took two years to produce the *Star* prints for the series and the exhibition was the first time it could be seen all together outside of the studio.

When did you first participate in Art Basel and what was most memorable about that show?
Our first Art Basel was in 2004 where we premiered Ellen Gallagher's epic work *DeLuxe* (2004–2005), which is a work composed of 60 separate objects that pushed the definition of what a print could be. It was great to show it at Basel because it exposed the work to curators and collectors from across the world, and has since become known as one of the great print projects of the last 50 years.

- **Contact** Two Palms
David Lasry
david@twopalms.us
info@twopalms.us
- **Established** 1994
- **Owner(s) / Partner(s)** David & Evelyn Lasry
- **Team** 10
- **Space(s)** 185 m²
- **Artists at Art Basel** Mel Bochner
Cecily Brown
Chuck Close
Peter Doig
Carroll Dunham
Chris Ofili
Elizabeth Peyton
Richard Prince
David Row
Dana Schutz
Terry Winters
- **Further artists represented** Ellen Gallagher
Per Kirkeby
Sol LeWitt
Matthew Ritchie
Jessica Stockholder

Take Ninagawa

Three Questions for Atsuko Ninagawa

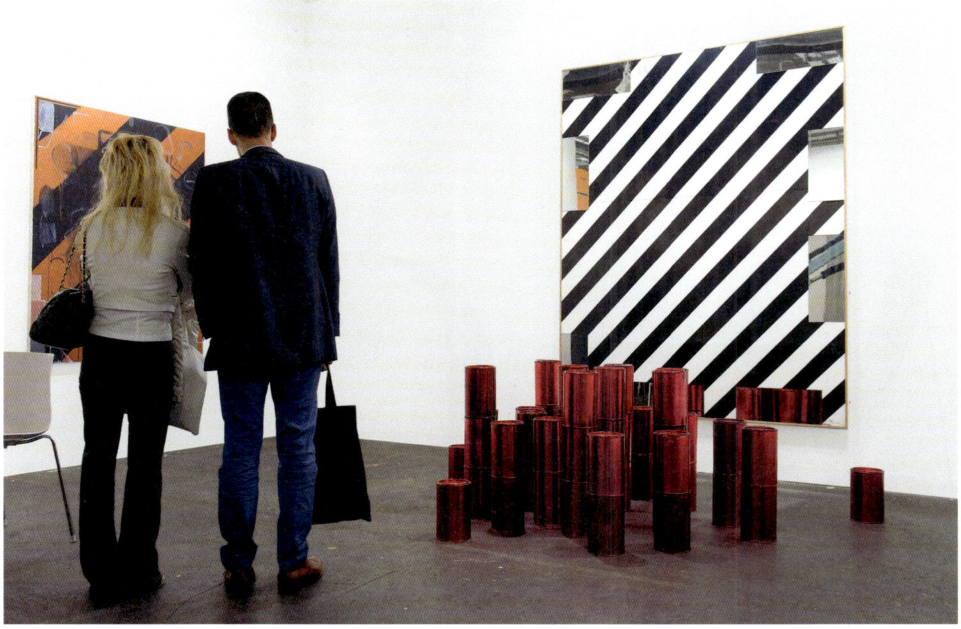

Art Basel in Basel (Feature), 2013

Since 2008 you have elaborated a program recognized throughout Japan as well as internationally, which combines historical artists and younger generations. Could you describe your "policy" and specificity within the many galleries of the Asia-Pacific region?

Take Ninagawa promotes both emerging and established Japanese artists in a cross-generational, international context. We believe the work of past generations informs the experimentation of today's artists, while today's artists open up new perspectives on the experimentation of past generations. For example, although he is by no means indebted to the Gutai Art Association, Shinro Ohtake's use of chance processes and materiality in his paintings, collages, and environments reflects the sensitivity to materials found in Tsuruko Yamazaki's practice, while both Yamazaki and Ohtake resonate with a young artist like Aki Sasamoto, who makes multimedia installations and performances.

What provides the gallery with its specificity is that Japan has over 100 years of avant-garde practice, and we consciously work with this history as a conceptual reference. We are aware not only of the pioneering gallerists who built up the current market for contemporary art in Japan, but also important sites for community and exchange such as Sagacho Exhibit Space, run by independent curator Kazuko Koike in the 1980s, and the Sogetsu Art Center, active from 1958 to 1971.

We also uphold an ethos of collaboration and mutual support with regard to our peers in Japan and the Asia-Pacific region and, indeed, the world. From the viewpoint of Japan, we can see that, even in boom times, contemporary art is under constant threat of marginalization, and we hope to encourage and exchange ideas with anyone who is committed to helping it evolve further.

At Art Basel in Hong Kong you presented a solo show by the young artist Ryoko Aoki in the Discoveries sector. Could you tell us about the artist and her proposition?

Based in Kyoto, Ryoko Aoki is at the forefront of redefining drawing and figuration as a space for conceptual experimentation in Japan. Executed in diverse media on whatever surface is at hand, from note paper to cardboard, her works span all manner of drawing styles, from casual sketches and manga cartoons to botanical studies, cartographic outlines, and geometric patterning, which she combines together in installations to create a landscape of shifting mental states and associations.

While Aoki has exhibited in the US and Europe, including at documenta 12, she has not participated in major exhibitions in Asia, and we felt that a solo exhibition in the Discoveries sector would allow us to introduce her to regional audiences. Aoki made the installation on site, bringing with her works made in charcoal, collage, ink, pencil, watercolor, paper collage, and fabric. We received positive responses from visitors coming from places as diverse as Hong Kong, India, Indonesia, Spain, Switzerland, and the US.

On the other hand, in the Feature sector at Basel you presented a solo show by the artist Tsuruko Yamazaki, born in 1925. Why this choice and what were the reactions to it—was the artist a discovery for most of the visitors?

From her stacked, sculptural arrangements of painted *Tin Cans* (1955) to her use of projected light to create works that blurred the distinctions between painting and environment, Tsuruko Yamazaki's interpretation of the Gutai ethos is truly visionary. As Joan Kee recently wrote in *Artforum*, "[She] understood, perhaps better than any of her colleagues, the generative possibilities of thinking about visual manifestation and substance together."

While remaining sensitive to her position as one of Gutai's founding members, we feel it is necessary to recognize Yamazaki as an individual artist in her own right. We felt that a solo presentation of Yamazaki at Art Basel would be the most effective way to introduce her to a broad, international audience, which is why we included important historic works in the exhibition. It was gratifying to see the extent of institutional interest in her work, both from collecting institutions and from curators working on thematic exhibitions, and also to exchange ideas about Yamazaki with Gutai researchers and experts based in Europe.

MICK ALENE THO MAS

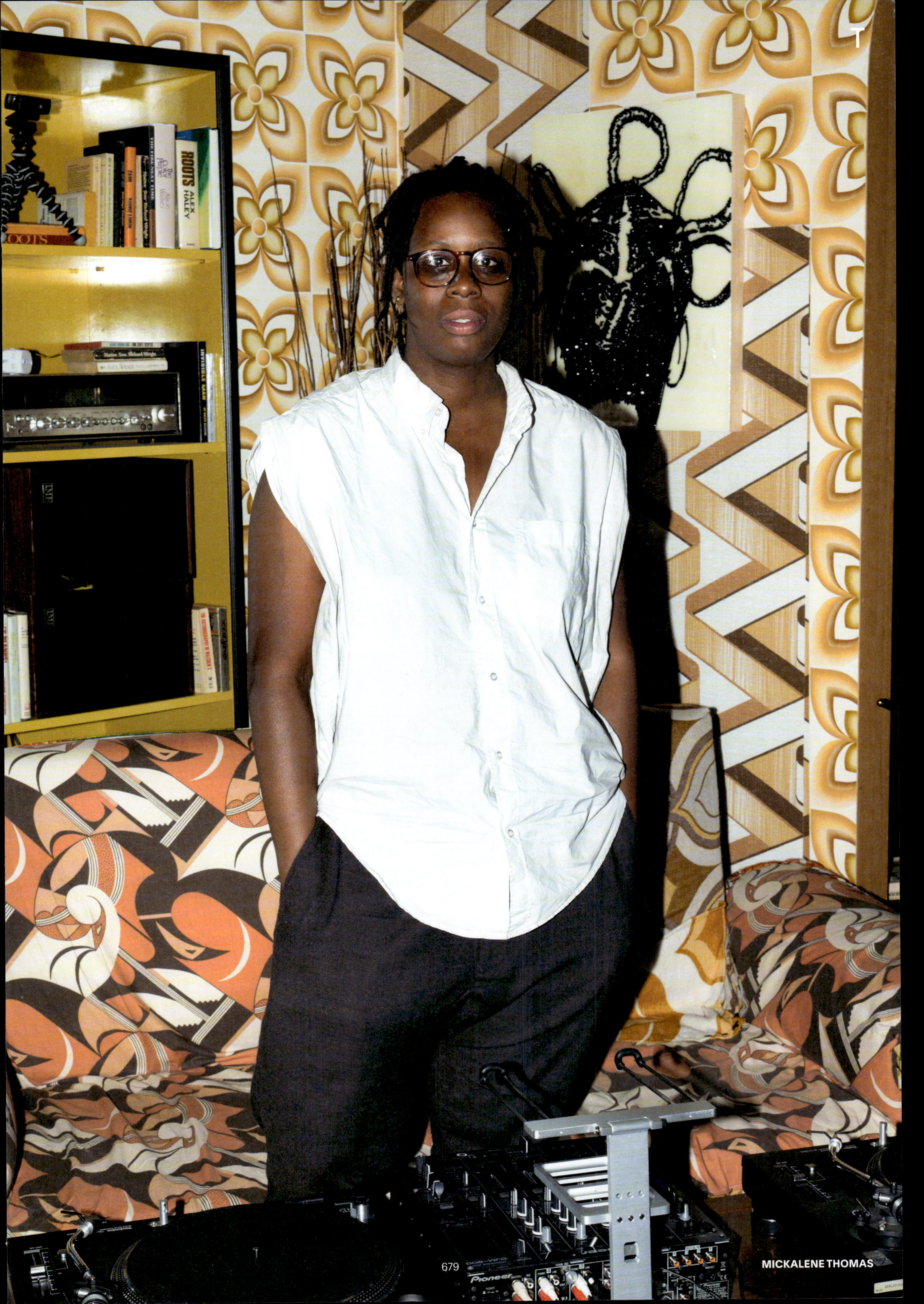
ROOTS
ALEX HALEY
INVISIBLE MAN
Pioneer

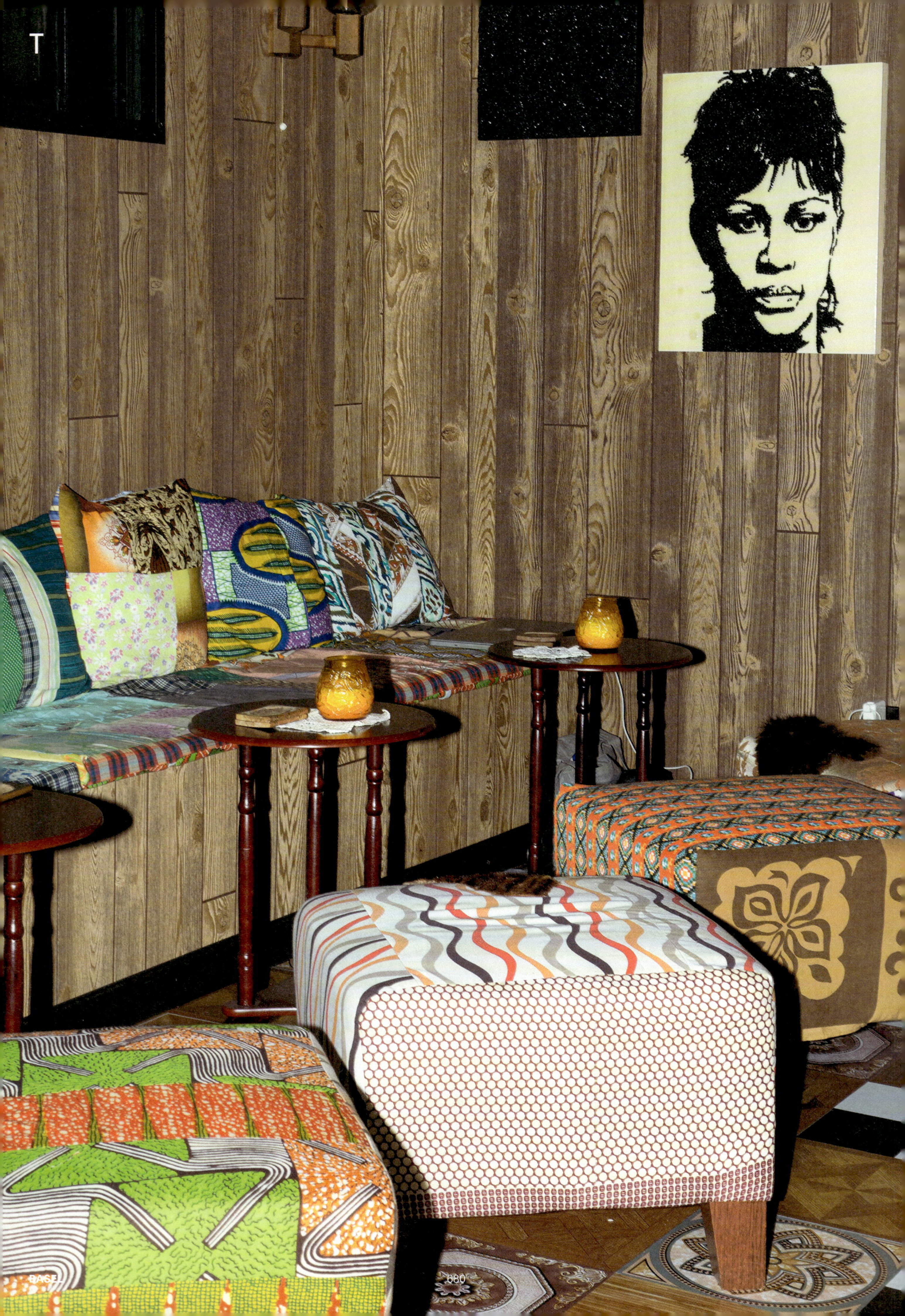

Conversation with Mickalene Thomas

On her *Better Days* bar, conceived for and presented by Absolut Art Bureau, Art Basel, June 2013

Art Basel
Better Days
June 11–15, 2013
Volkshaus

Mickalene Thomas
Absolut Art Bureau

CLÉMENT DIRIÉ Let's start with the origins of the *Better Days* bar project.

MICKALENE THOMAS I was approached by Absolut to develop this project after they saw my exhibition in 2012 at the Brooklyn Museum. In the beginning my idea was to do a very minimal installation with a bar, but when I came here to see the space I realized that I wanted to be much more involved. I thought about particular events (theatrical plays, parties, and fashion shows) that my mother used to draw back in the 1970s with her friends to raise money for a care association. They used to call themselves the "Better Days" group. I wanted to build a bar that would be a composite of various event spaces that they had used.

CD Did Absolut propose the space or did you choose it?

MT Absolut suggested two spaces and I chose this one. I knew I wanted to transform the space and make the viewers feel that they were still part of the Volkshaus, but entering a different type of space: they could feel it is part of the architecture, but also realize that there is a construction—a room within a room. That was very important for me as we built up the space: to leave some of the raw elements exposed.

CD And it's not only about space but also about time, because one feels one is back in the 1970s ...

MT Exactly. It really makes you feel like you are entering a sort of special environment.

CD How did you work to build it? Was it similar to the way you make installations?

MT It was similar to my installations from the faux paneling to the wallpaper to the furniture, to all of the accessories and elements that enhance the space, and everything that I use in my installations and my studio. Maybe just four times as much! The new thing is the bar. *That* was challenging, in the sense of figuring out how to integrate that into my practice. The best thing that came to my mind was to think of it as a house party: you would use your kitchen counter as a bar. That really opened up new ideas of configuring the space: cabinets in the sink, people drinking out of any glass they find in the cupboards, etc. That aesthetic became important to keep up, with the space as a sort of *faux* reality. Even though you know it's a construction, this is a real moment.

CD Will everything disappear after the fair?

MT Yes. We will reclaim things we can take back with us, because 99% of the materials, even the windows and the faux paneling, as well as a lot of the light fixtures, were shipped in a container. So we'll de-install and take everything that we can salvage back with us. I recycle a lot of the materials, a lot of the chairs and accessories, so they'll be fixed up and used for another installation or environment.

> I'm interested in dichotomies of high and low, bringing hierarchical notions to a middle ground where the Western canon of art history can dialogue with pattern and decoration.
> — Mickalene Thomas

CD What about the decoration and the film program?

MT All the art on the walls has been curated by me, either made by some

Better Days, 2013

T

of the DJs that I brought over, or by artists like Lorna Simpson. To activate the space on a different level, I thought it would be interesting to collaborate and have other artists' work and bring a part of New York to this environment. The films I selected work in the same way: they are films that I grew up with or was inspired by. One film in particular is *Killer of Sheep* by Charles Burnett (1977). It's about a middle-class black family in Watts, Los Angeles. The cinematography is extraordinary. There is also a series of features by emergent filmmakers: experimental movies about utopia, the future, in the genre of Afrofuturism. They play on ideas of Afrocentricity, non-Western cosmologies, magic realism, and refer to Sun Ra's *Space Is the Place* (1974). I used them also as a way of liberating the space, to give it another dimension.

CD You also created cocktails for the bar.

MT Yes, I met with Absolut's mixologist, and gave him a list of particular drinks that I thought would be interesting for this space. I chose a series of fruit punch drinks, because a lot of house parties usually have punches as drinks, fruits and juices, and vodka or rum. I wanted to play with that idea, but also create a type of punch that was unexpected. For example, if you had a watermelon punch, it was infused with lavender tea and cardamom seeds, to have a layer of flavor that ignited the punch itself. I also wanted to refer to my favorite musician, Millie Jackson—she did that song called "Fuck you Stephanie," so, I named all the punches after her songs. That's why there's a "Fuck you 1," "Fuck you 2," and "Fuck you 3." And then, the top drinks on the menu are a little more sophisticated: they are mostly Martini, from dry, to sweet, to sour. The first is a rosemary-infused vodka, with a little salt and cucumber taste. The second, called "Mama Fey Clark," is a White Russian, which was one of my mother's favorite drinks. The drinks were actually quite fun to compose.

CD What is the relationship in your work between the way you make paintings, and the way you make furniture and objects with a "useful" meaning, in terms of motifs, decoration, and so on?

MT Whether it's my paintings, photographs, or installations, they all come out of one another. In order to make the paintings, I build these installations to photograph the models in; then I recompose the picture by way of collages, to make images for the paintings. My interest in patterns, their juxtaposition and overlays are bringing in different genres of art making, whether they are considered outsiders or decorative. I've always been interested in working with non-traditional materials, but I'm also interested in these dichotomies of high and low, bringing these hierarchical notions to a middle ground where the Western canon of art history can dialogue with pattern and decoration.

View of Mickalene Thomas' *Better Days*

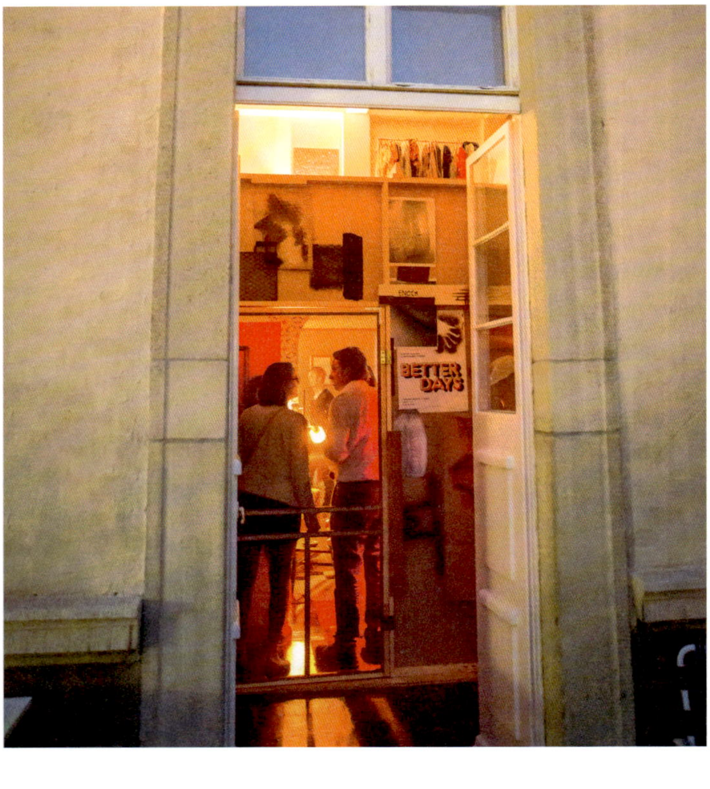

Solange Knowles, performer →

View of Mickalene Thomas' *Better Days*, June 12, 2013 →

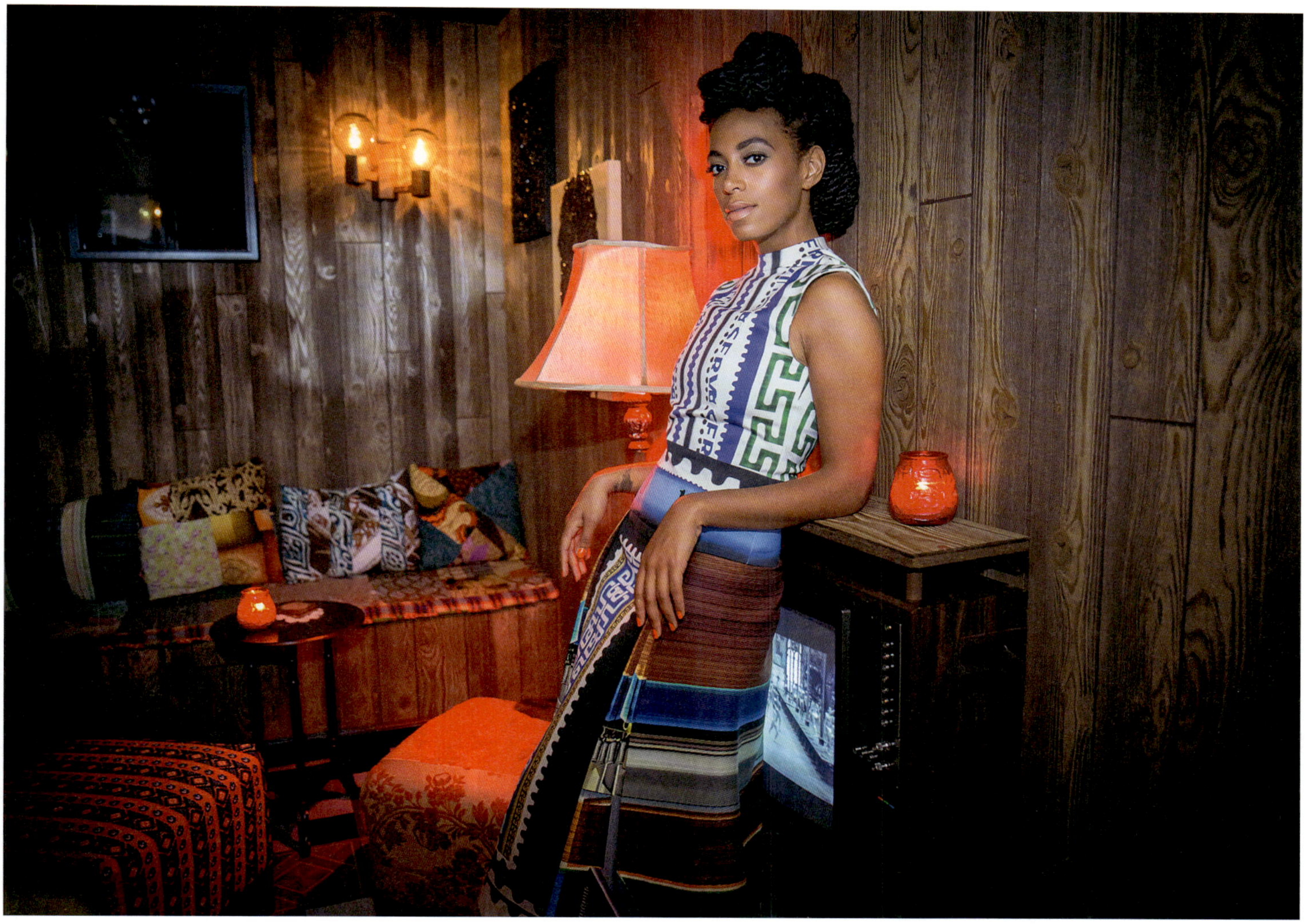

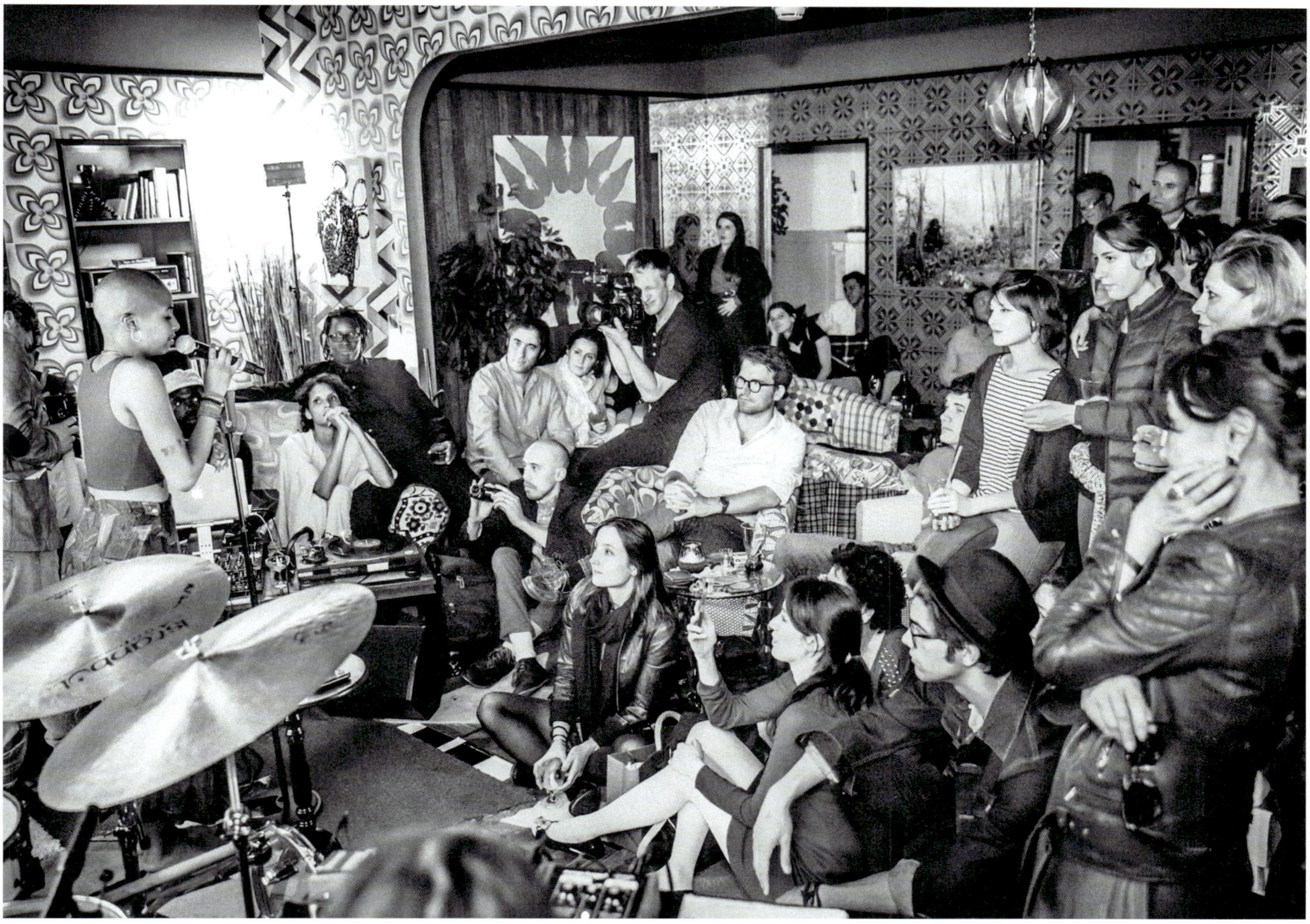

We asked nine art world players for their ten favorite elements present anywhere in the city during the Art Basel week.

TOP

TENS

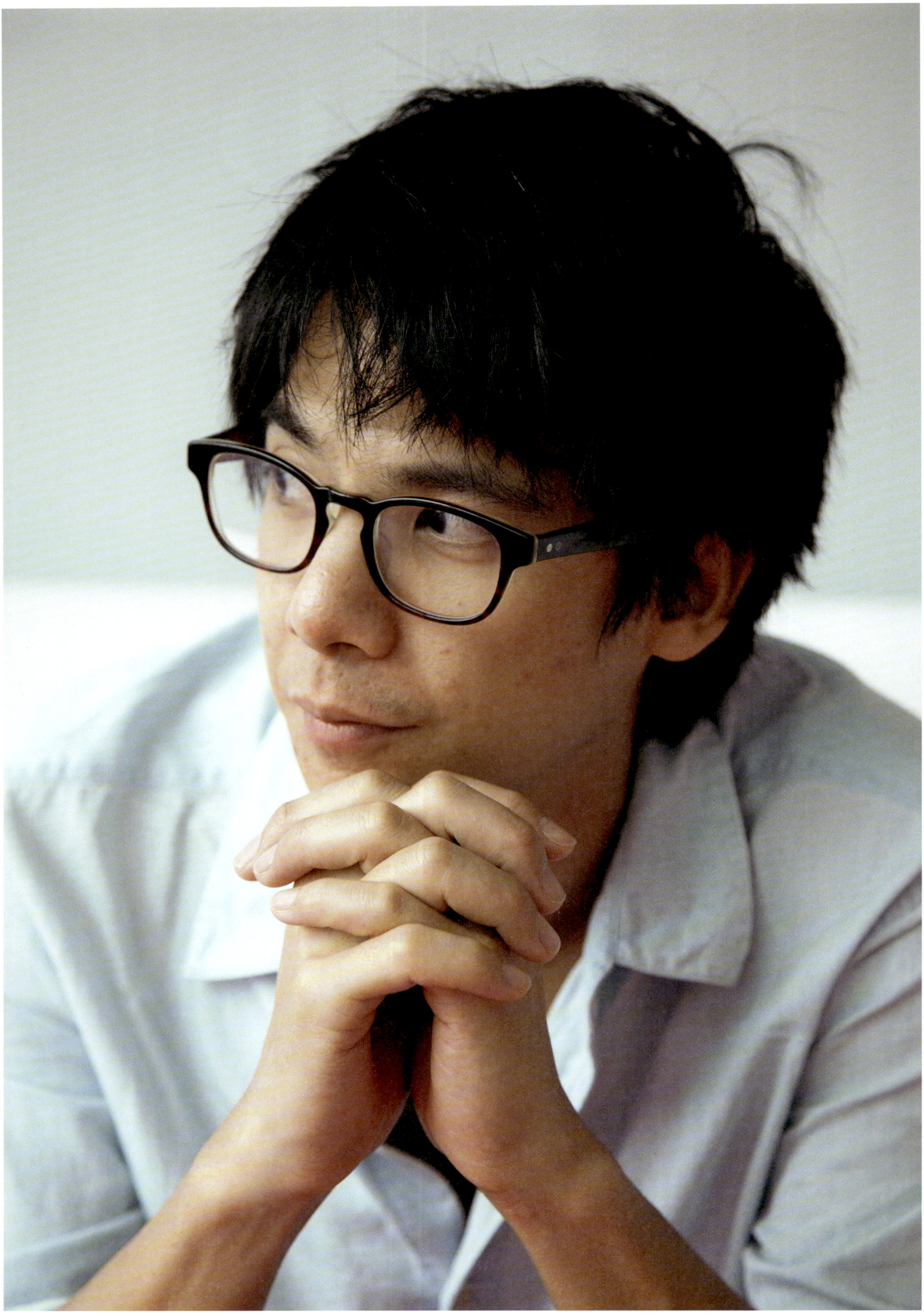

Nadim Abbas

Artist, Hong Kong

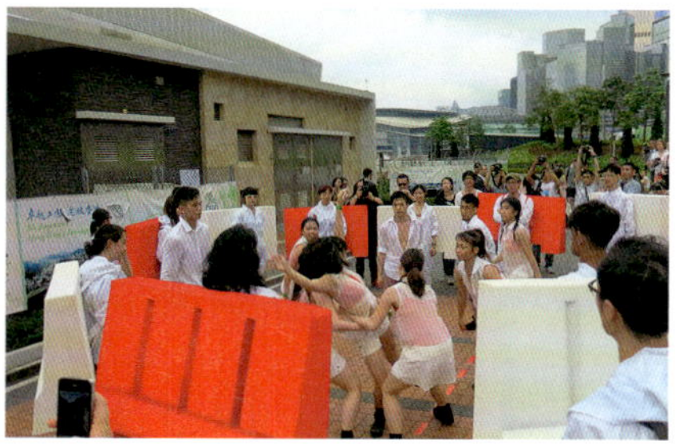

01 *Paper Rain Parade* by Arto Lindsay on the Hong Kong Waterfront, May 23, 2013

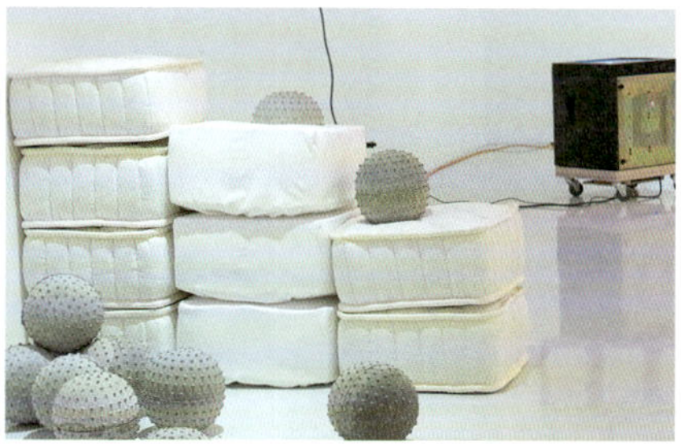

02 Nadim Abbas, *Satellite of ****, 2013
CL3 Architects, Hong Kong Arts Centre

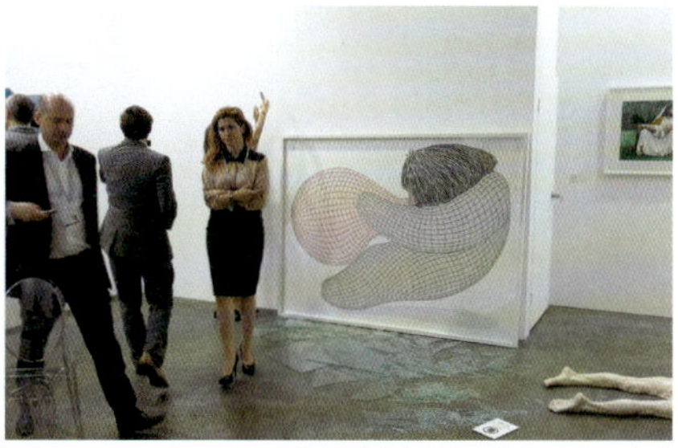

03 Artwork falling off the wall
Galerist

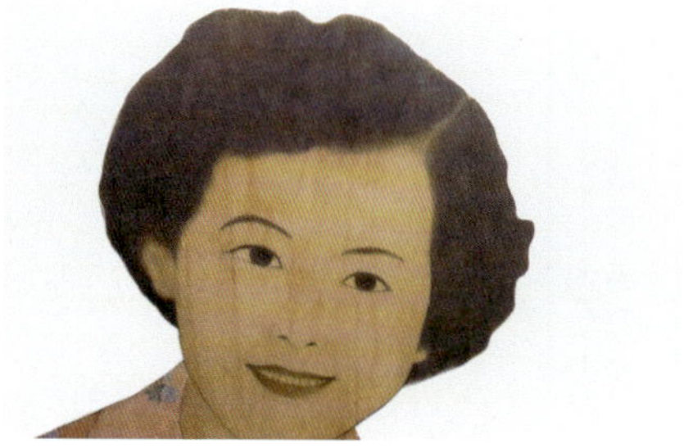

04 Ivy Ma, *Mother*, 2013
Gallery Exit

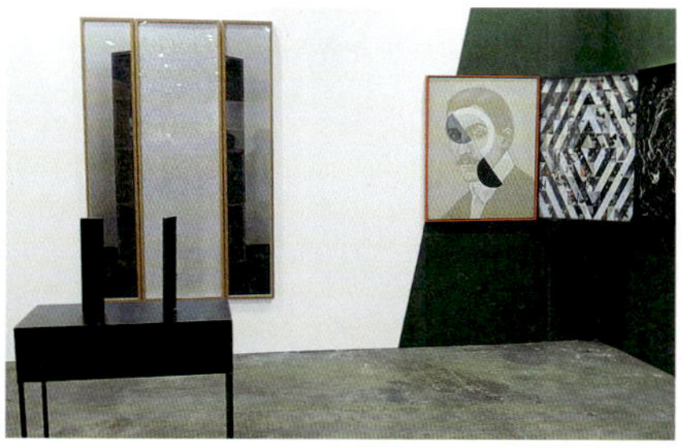

05 Matthias Bitzer & Becky Beasley
Francesca Minini (Discoveries)

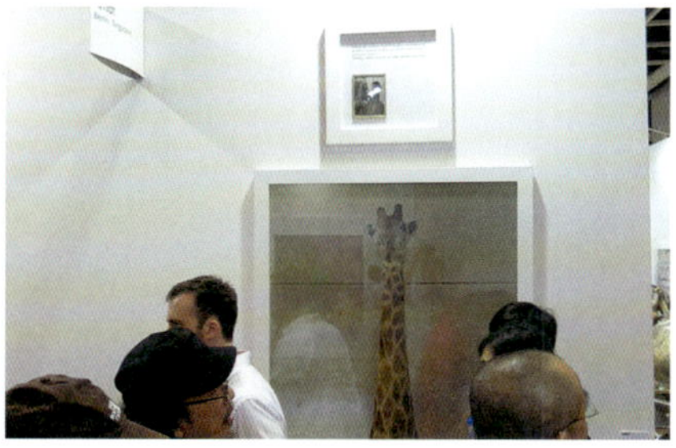

06 Sophie Calle, *The Giraffe*, 2012
Arndt

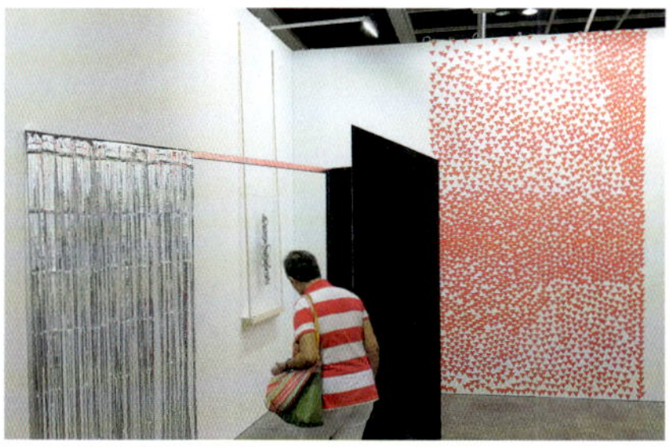

07 Sung Hwan Kim & Heman Chong
Wilkinson

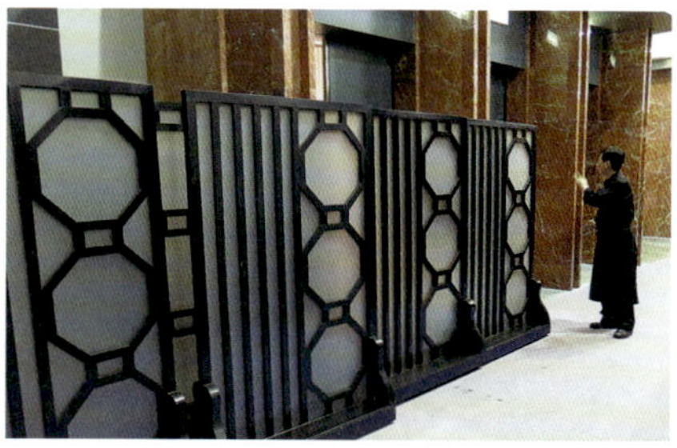

08 Waiter and freestanding screens next to the VIP lounge toilets

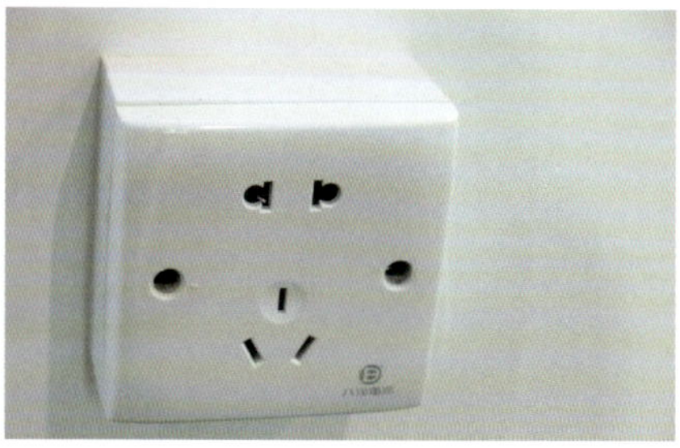

09 Lee Kit, detail of installation
Vitamin Creative Space

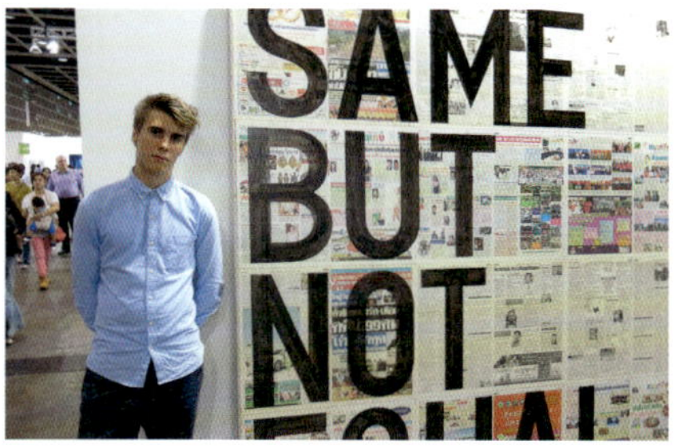

10 Gaspar Gutierrez with Rirkrit Tiravanija work, *Untitled (same but not equal)*, 2013
Shanghai Gallery of Art

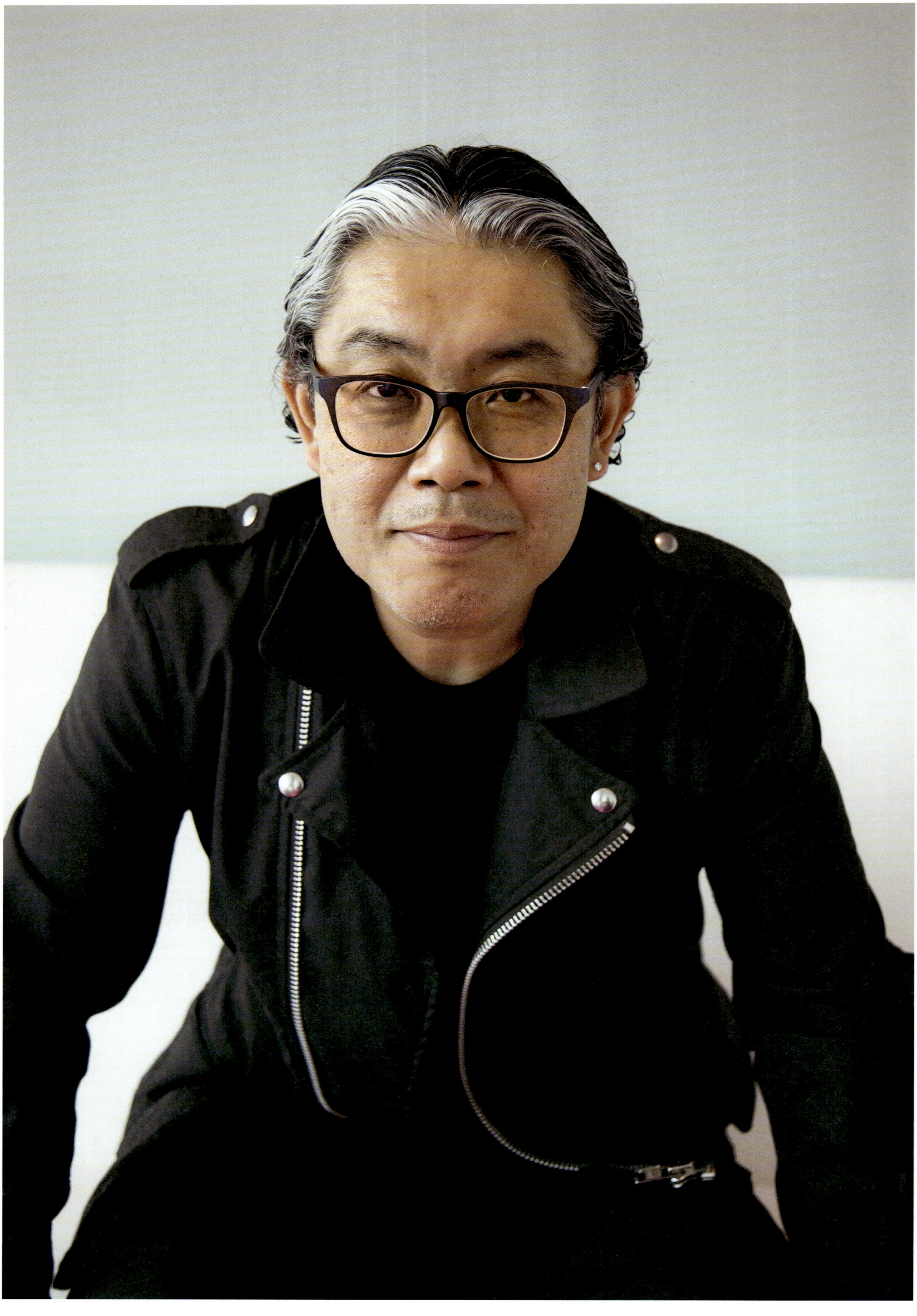

Daisuke Miyatsu

Collector, Tokyo

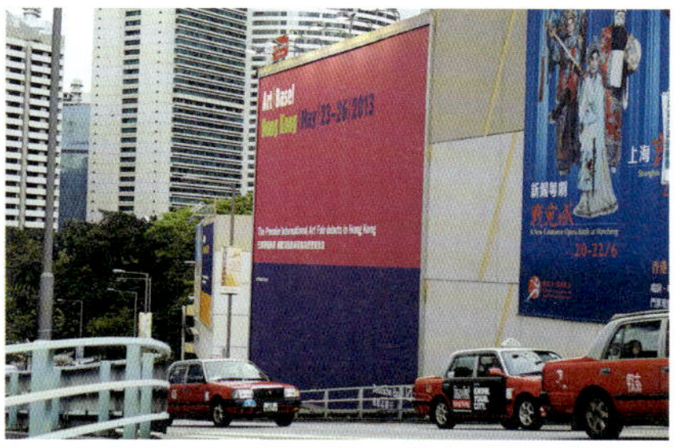

01 Art Basel in Hong Kong

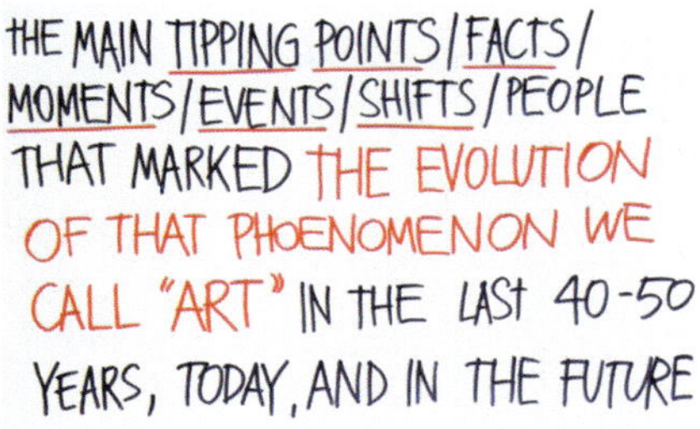

02 24 HRS event

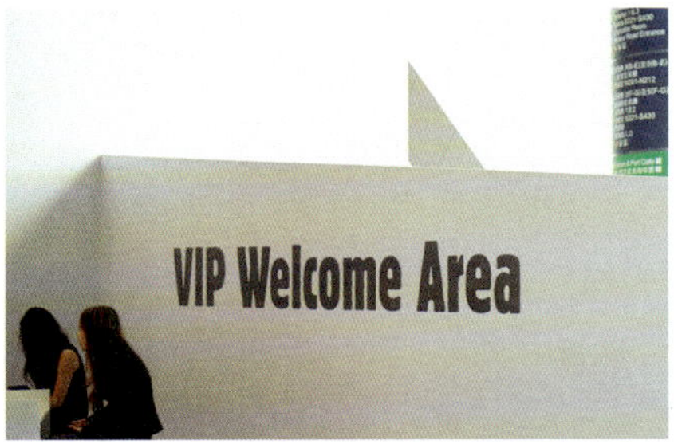

03 VIP relation system

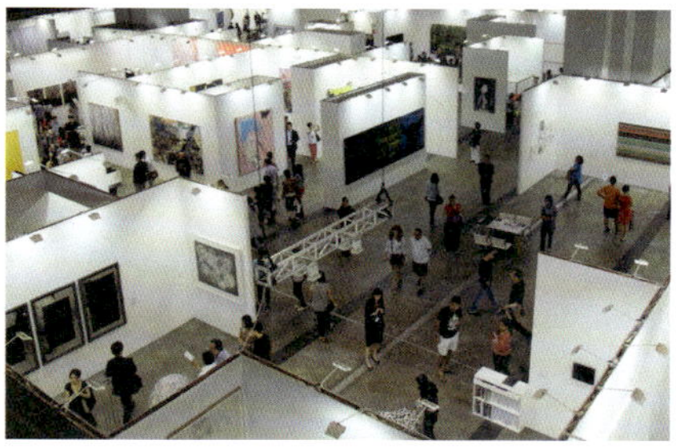

04 Insights sector with new galleries from all over Asia

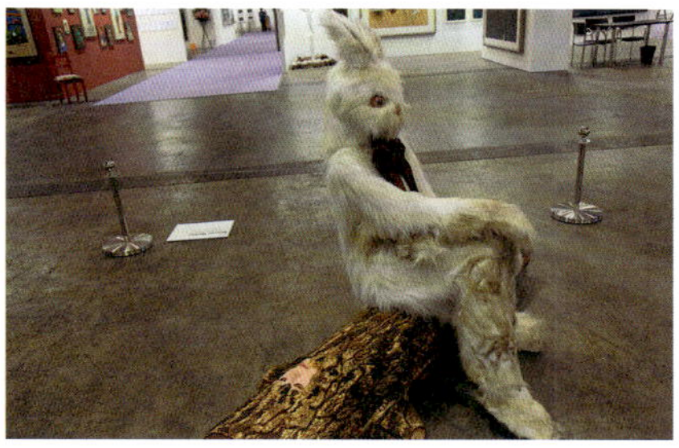

05 Encounters sector

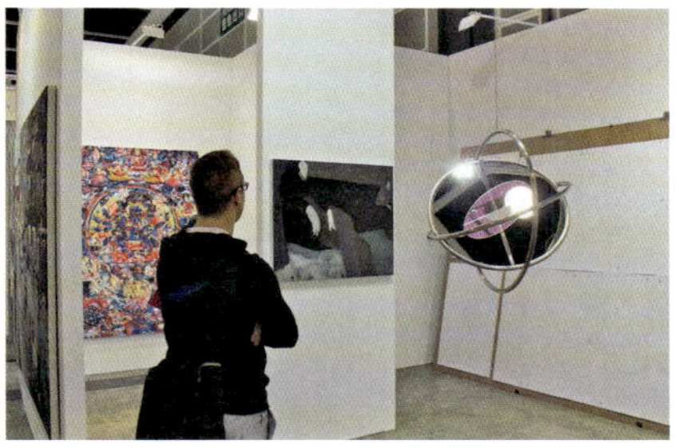

06 Olafur Eliasson, *Your Momentum Device*, 2008
Vitamin Creative Space

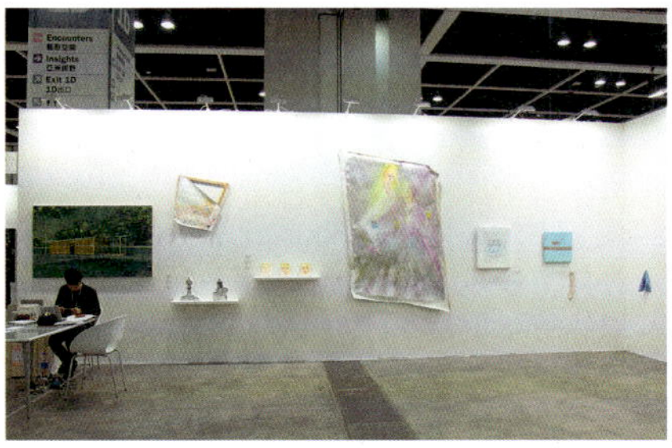

07 ShugoArts

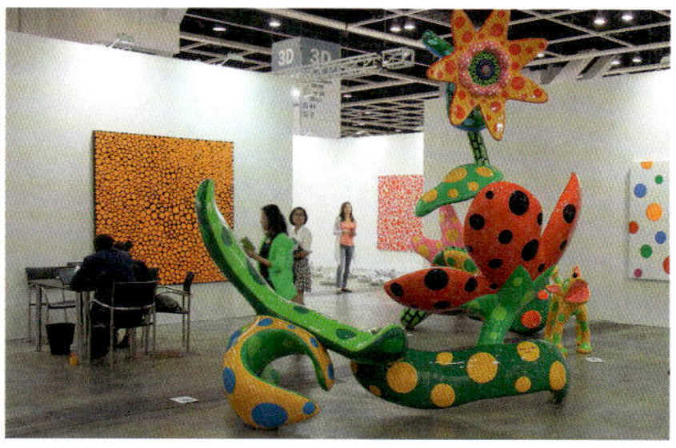

08 Yayoi Kusama
Victoria Miro/Ota Fine Arts

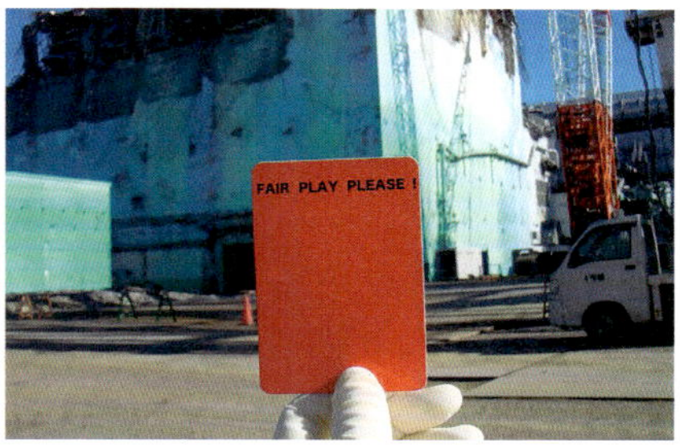

09 Chim↑Pom, *Red Card*, 2011
Mujin-to Production

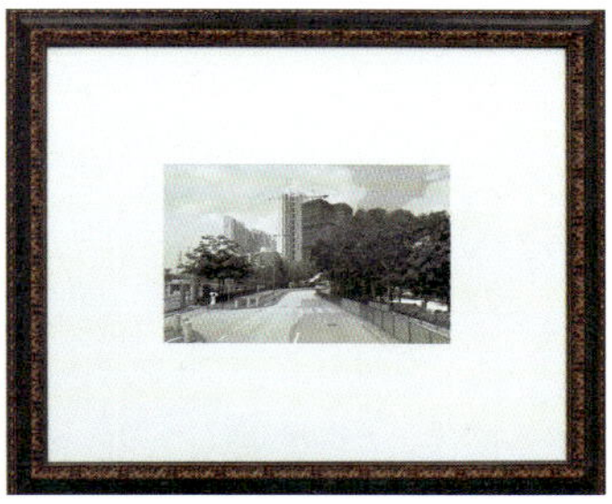

10 Yuichiro Tamura, *A girl with white umbrella*, 2013
Yuka Tsuruno

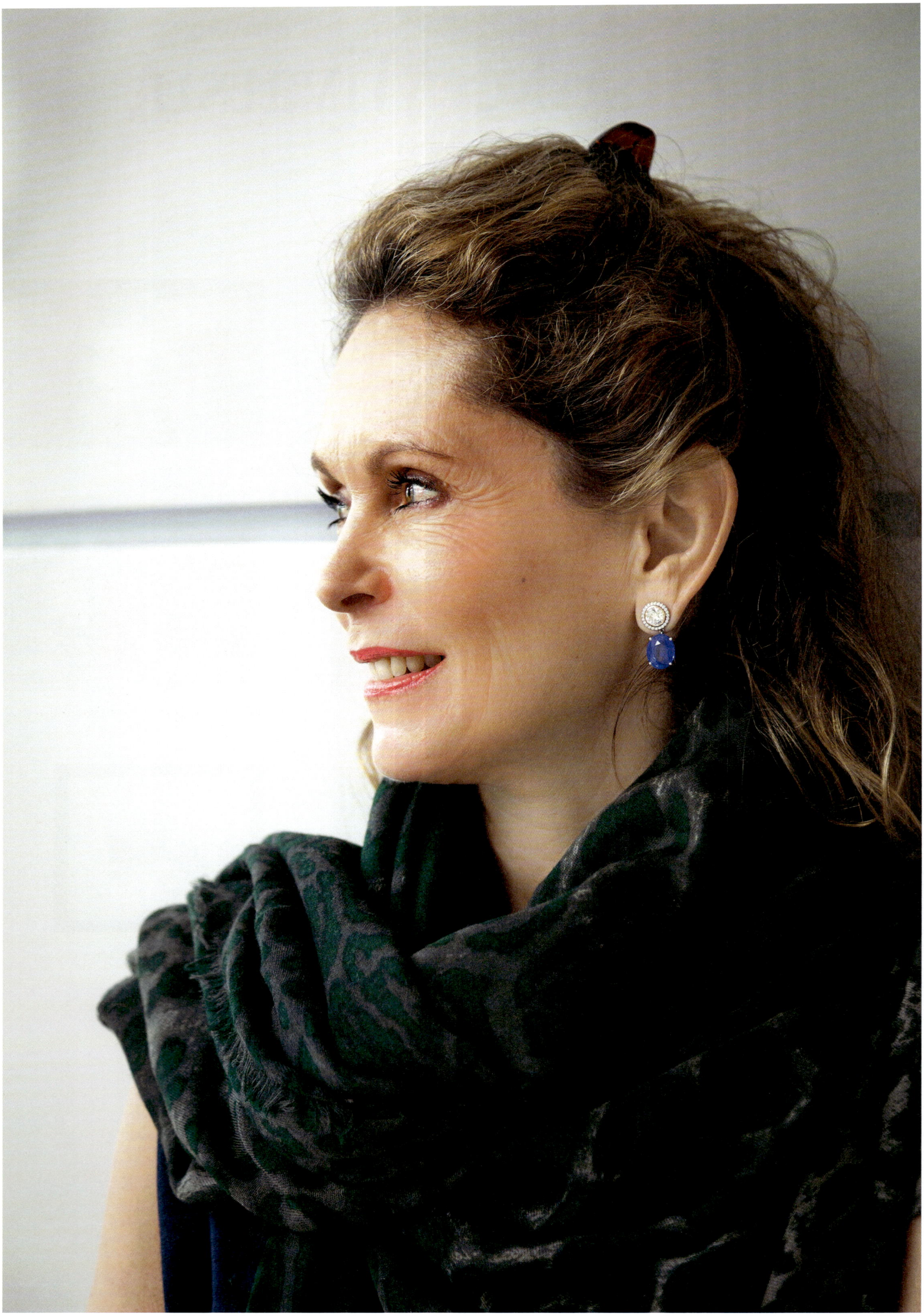

Monique Burger

Collector, Hong Kong

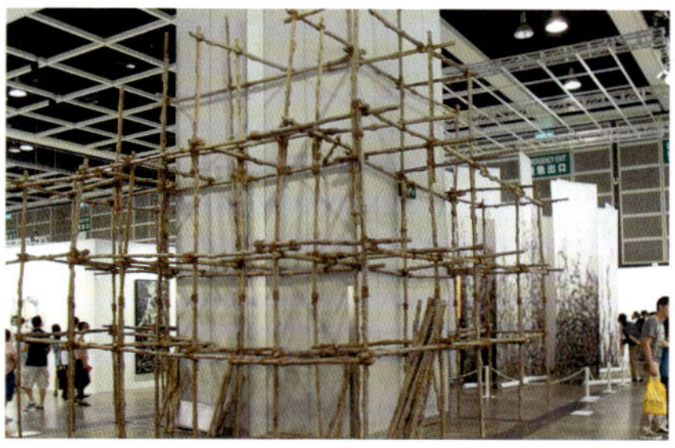

01 Jitish Kallat, *Circa*, 2011
Arndt (Encounters)

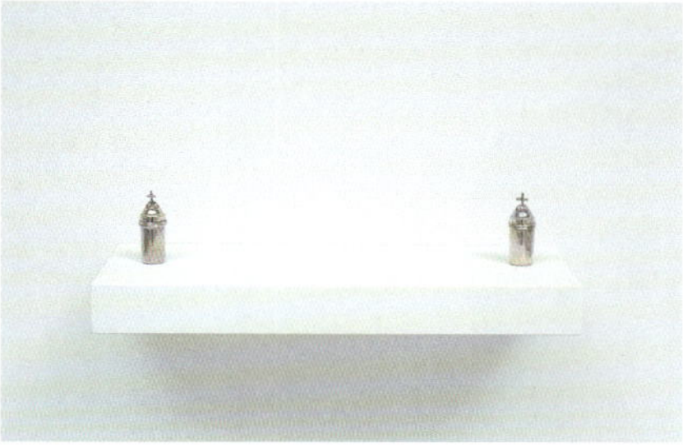

02 Kris Martin, *Selfportrait (christmatories)*, 2008
Sies + Höke

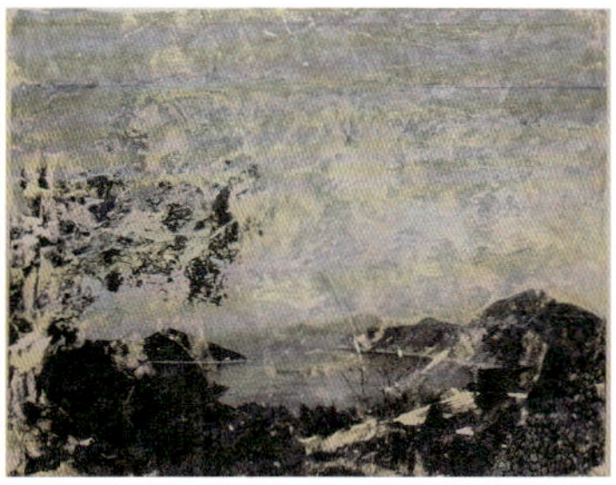

03 Christine Ng Mien Yin, *Remains of the Day*, 2012
Gallery Exit

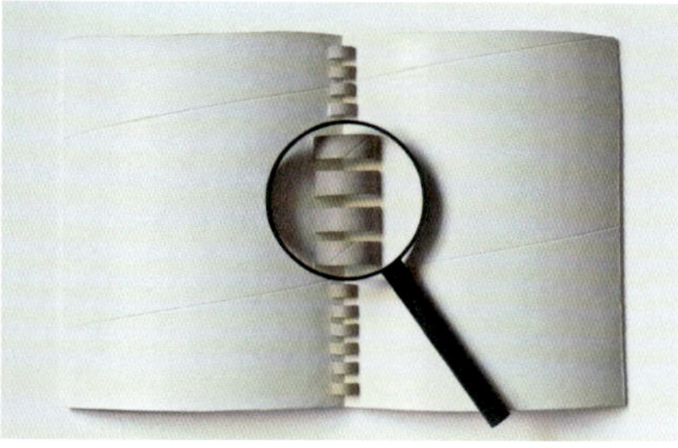

04 Ricky Swallow, *Binder with Magnifying Glass*, 2011
Stuart Shave/Modern Art

05 Li Huasheng, *0546*, 2005
Pearl Lam Galleries

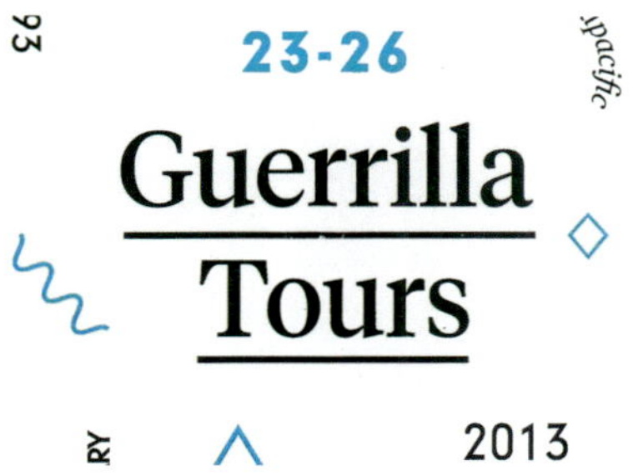

06 *Guerrilla Tours* by Elaine Ng
ArtAsiaPacific magazine

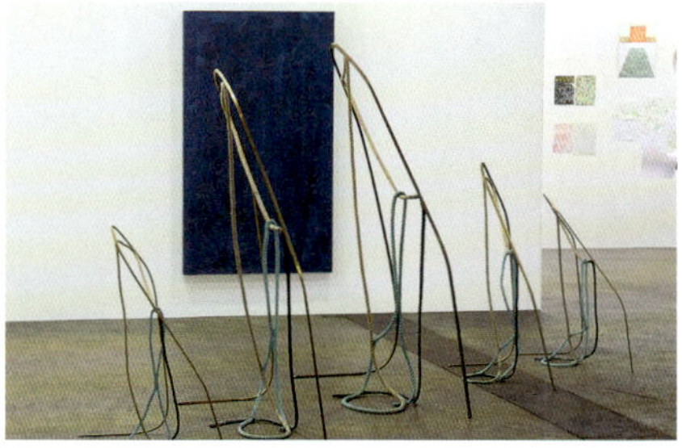

07 David Keating
RaebervonStenglin (Discoveries)

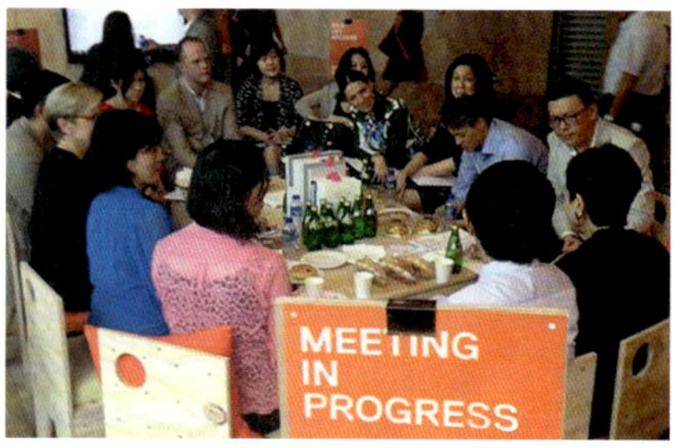

08 AAA Meeting Point
Asia Art Archive Booth

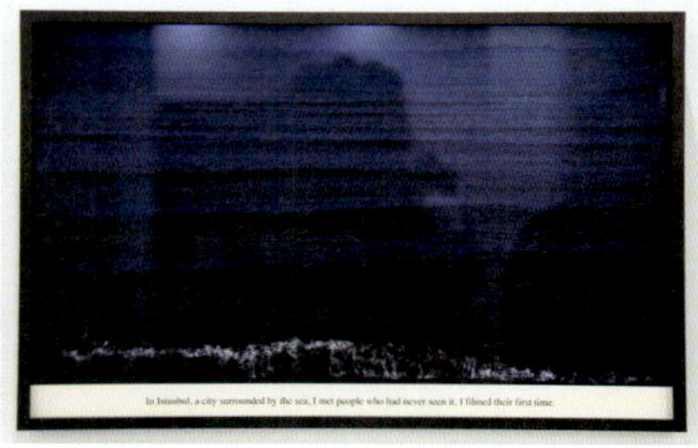

09 Sophie Calle, *L'Homme profond*, 2011
Arndt

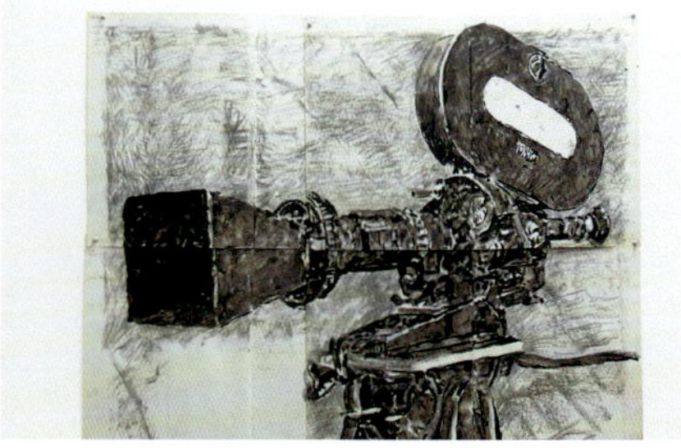

10 William Kentridge, *Camera (Central Boiler Station)*, 2010
Lia Rumma

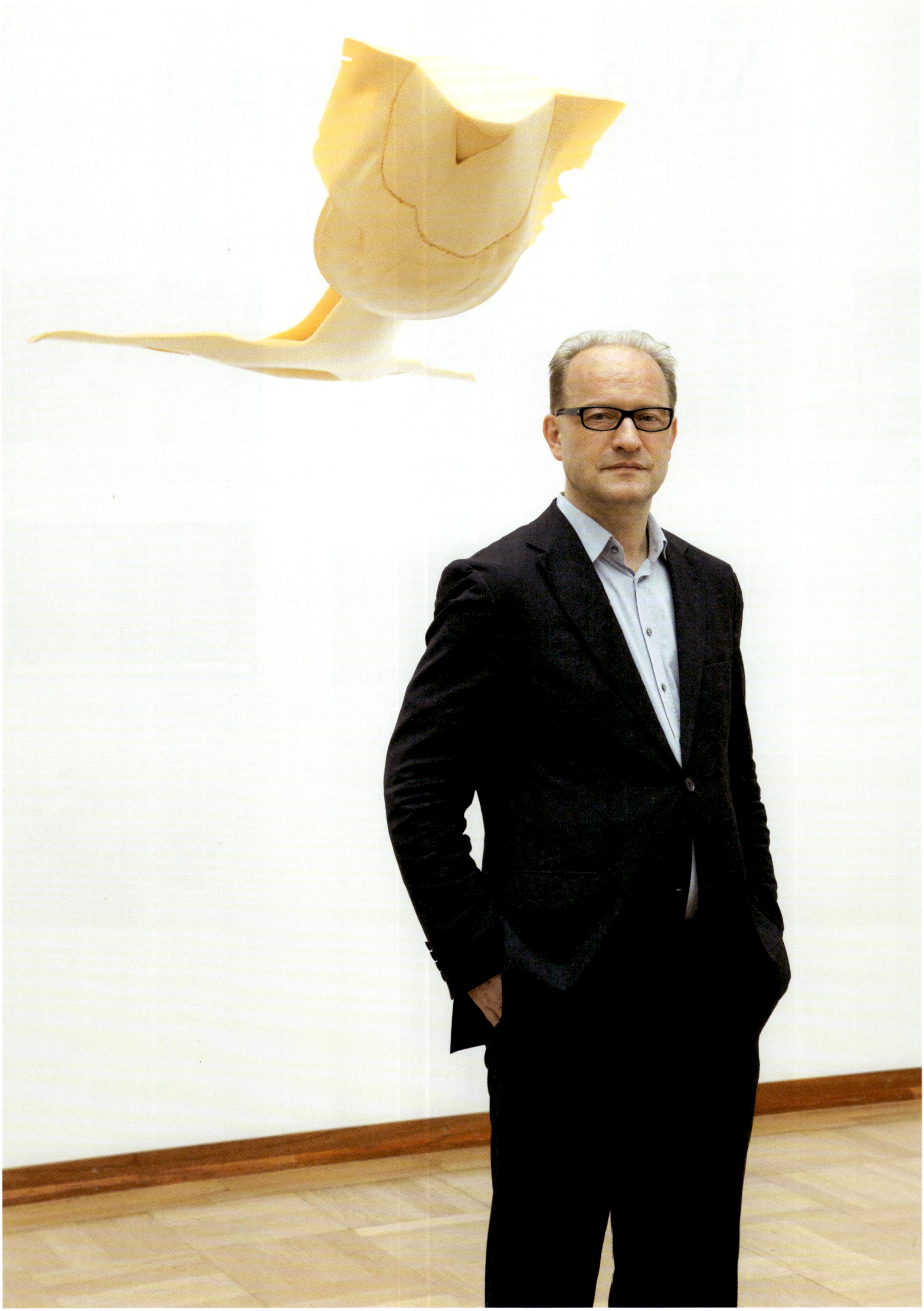

Bernhard Mendes Bürgi

Director, Kunstmuseum Basel

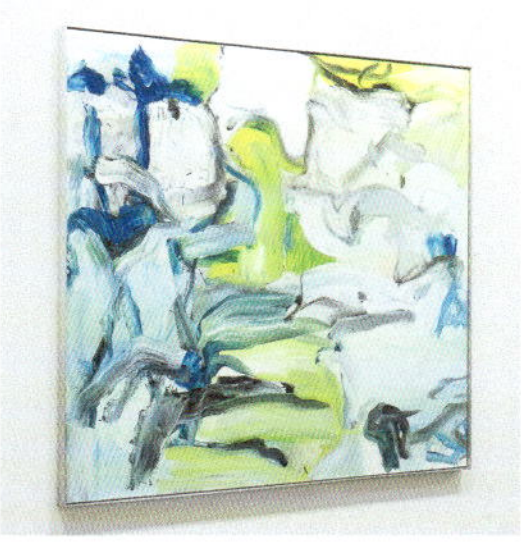

01 Willem de Kooning, *Untitled*, 1978
Hauser & Wirth

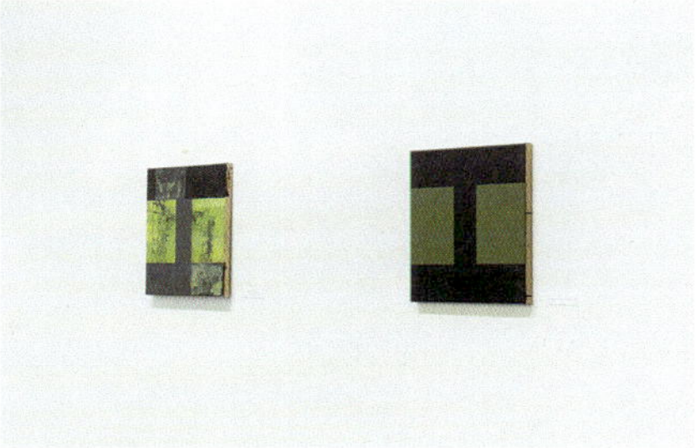

02 Helmut Federle
Peter Blum Gallery

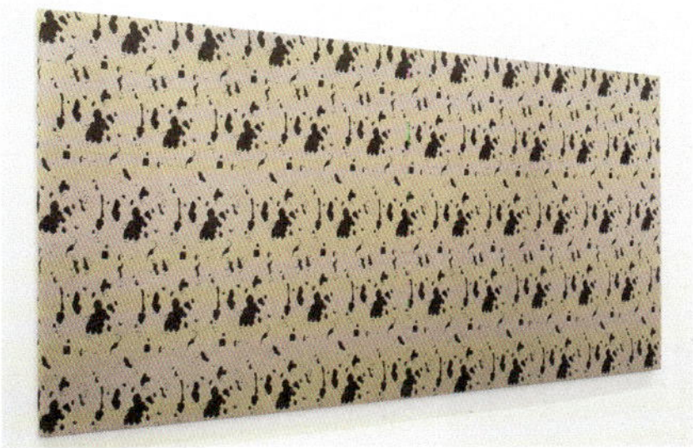

03 Rosemarie Trockel, *Untitled (Fleckenbild)*, 1988
Skarstedt Gallery

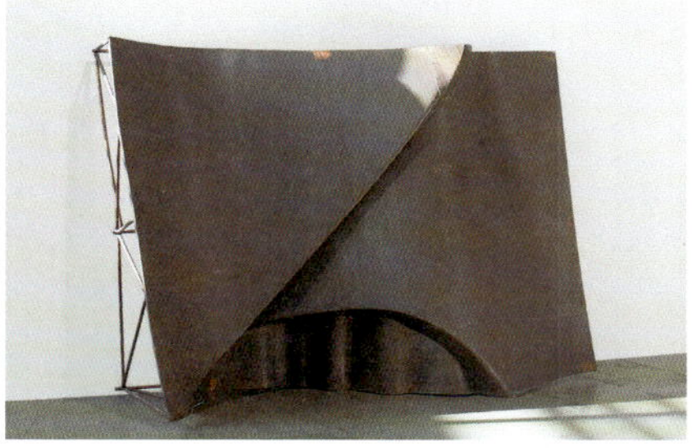

04 Danh Vo, *We The People* (detail), 2011–2013
Galerie Chantal Crousel

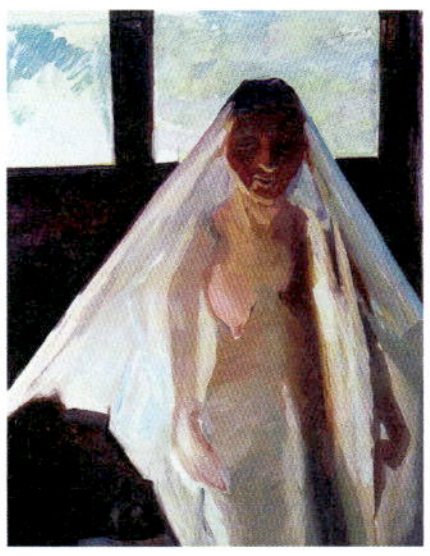

05 Maria Lassnig, *The Illegitimate Bride*, 2007
Friedrich Petzel Gallery

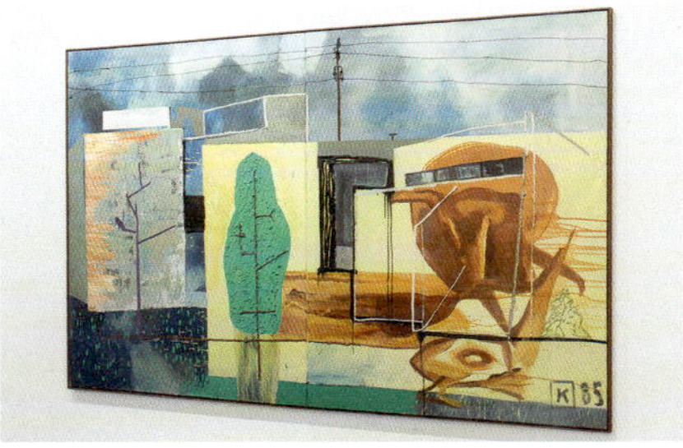

06 Martin Kippenberger, *Betty Ford Clinic*, 1985
Metro Pictures

07 Vija Celmins, *Night Sky #21*, 2009–2013
McKee Gallery

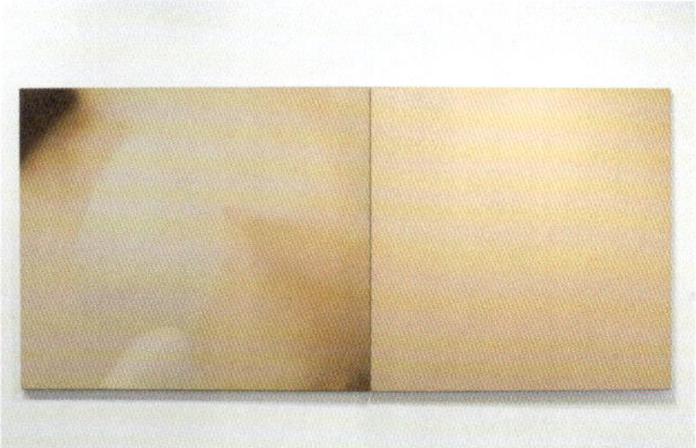

08 Gerhard Richter & Blinky Palermo, *Untitled*, 1970
Richard Gray Gallery

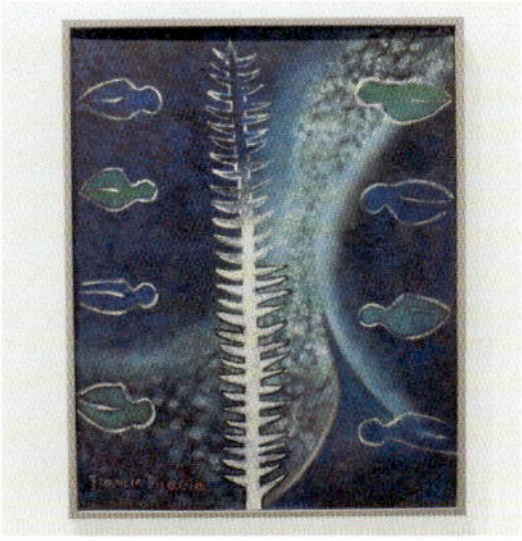

09 Francis Picabia, *La Voie des airs*, 1945
Galerie 1900–2000

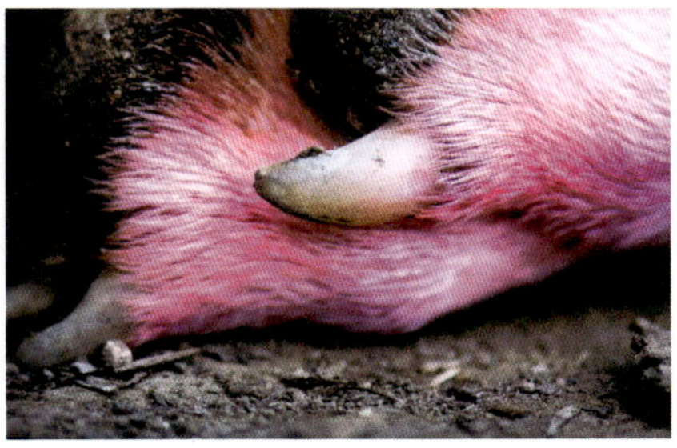

10 Pierre Huyghe, *Untilled Film*, 2013
Marian Goodman Gallery
and Esther Schipper (Unlimited)

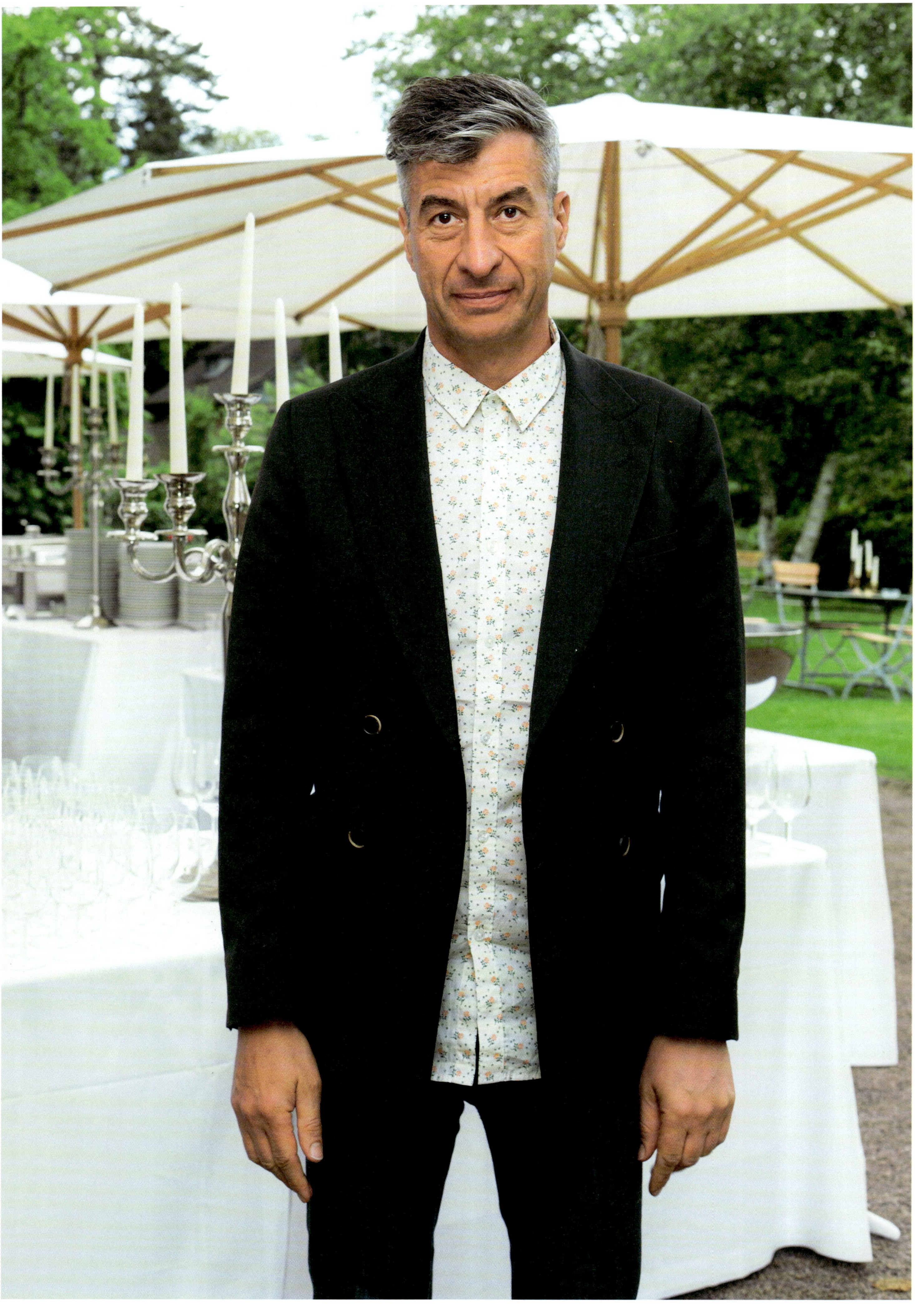

Maurizio Cattelan

Artist, New York

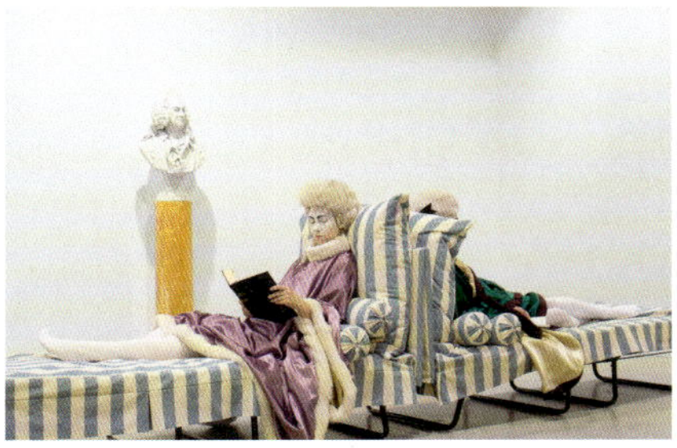

01 Pablo Bronstein, *Marie-Antoinette and Robespierre engage in an irritable post-coital conversation,* 2013
Herald St (Feature)

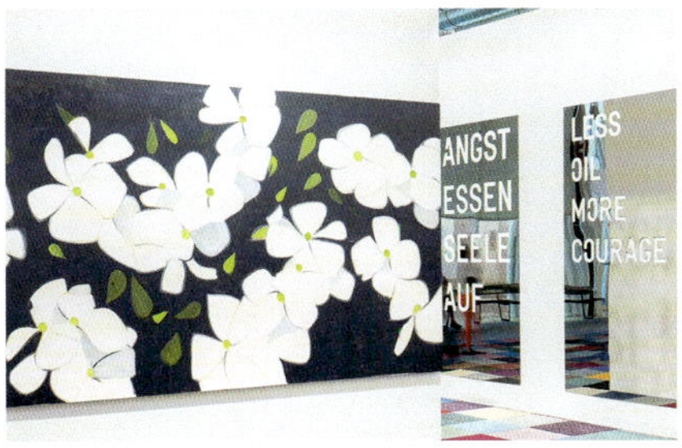

02 Gavin Brown's enterprise booth, with works by Martin Creed, Rob Pruitt, and others

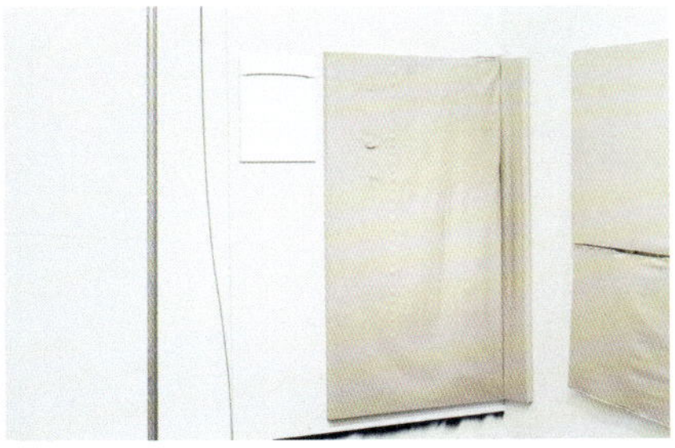

03 Jonathan Binet
Gaudel de Stampa (Statements)

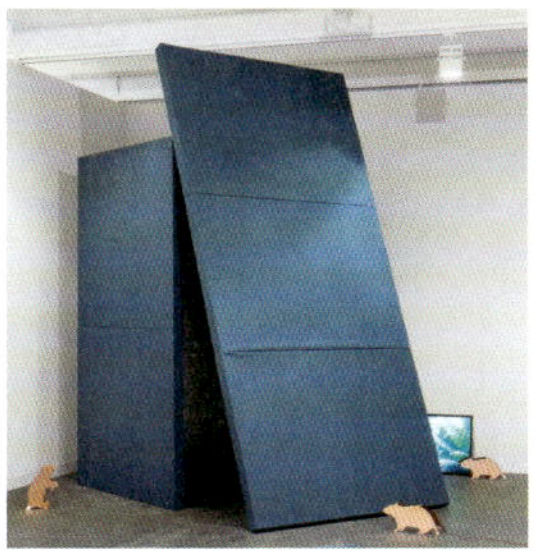

04 Sergei Tcherepnin, *Pied Piper, Part Two: Ringing Rocks*, 2013
Murray Guy (Statements)

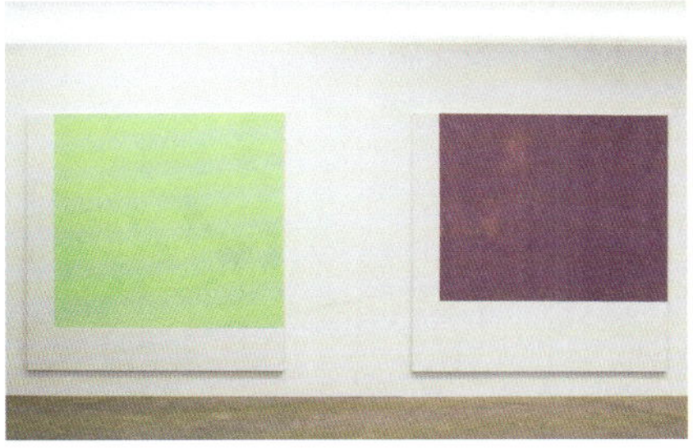

05 Günther Förg, *Untitled*, 1991
Greene Naftali Gallery (Unlimited)

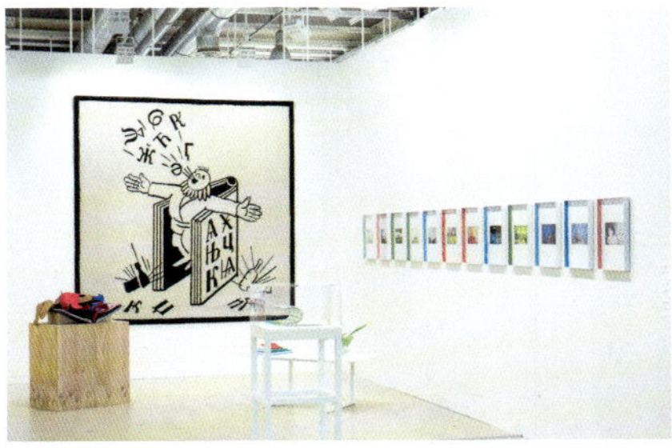

06 Dominique Gonzalez-Foerster, *RGB (Prints)*, 2013
Three Star Books (Edition)

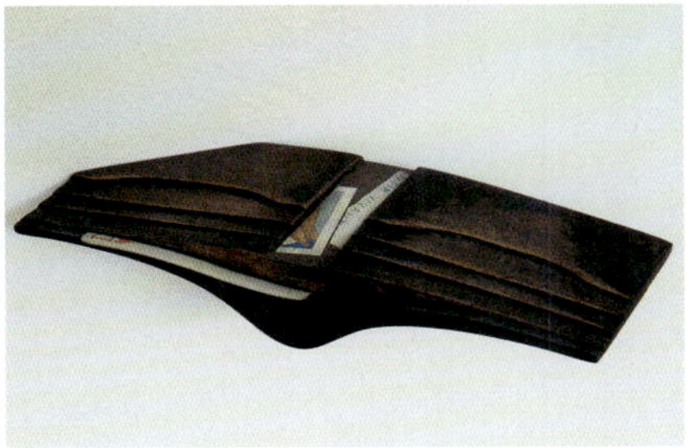

07 Camille Blatrix, *La Lettre d'Alison pour Victor, Portefeuille (détail III)*, 2013
Balice Hertling, Liste Art Fair

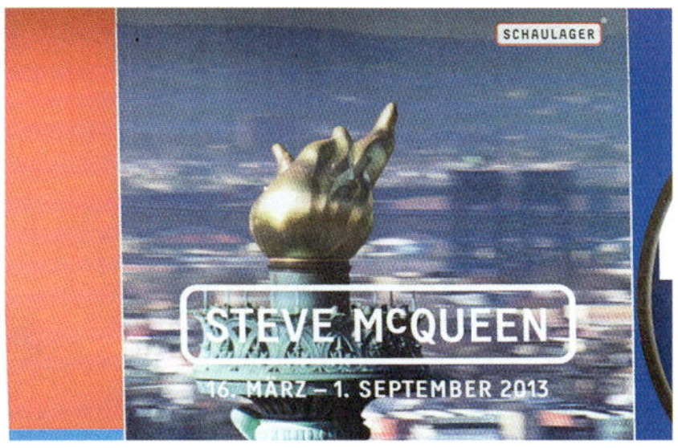

08 Steve McQueen, *Deadpan*, 1997
Schaulager, Basel, solo exhibition

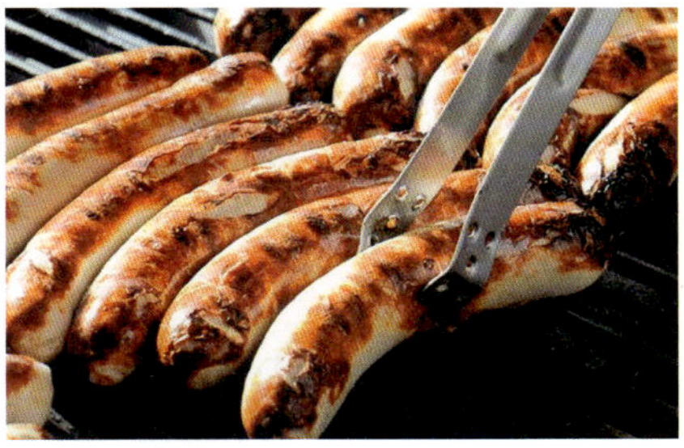

09 Liste 18 Fair's wurst

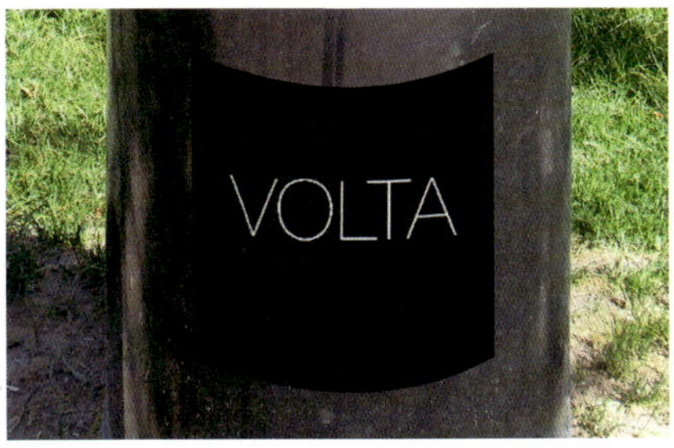

10 Volta Fair advertisement on bins in the city

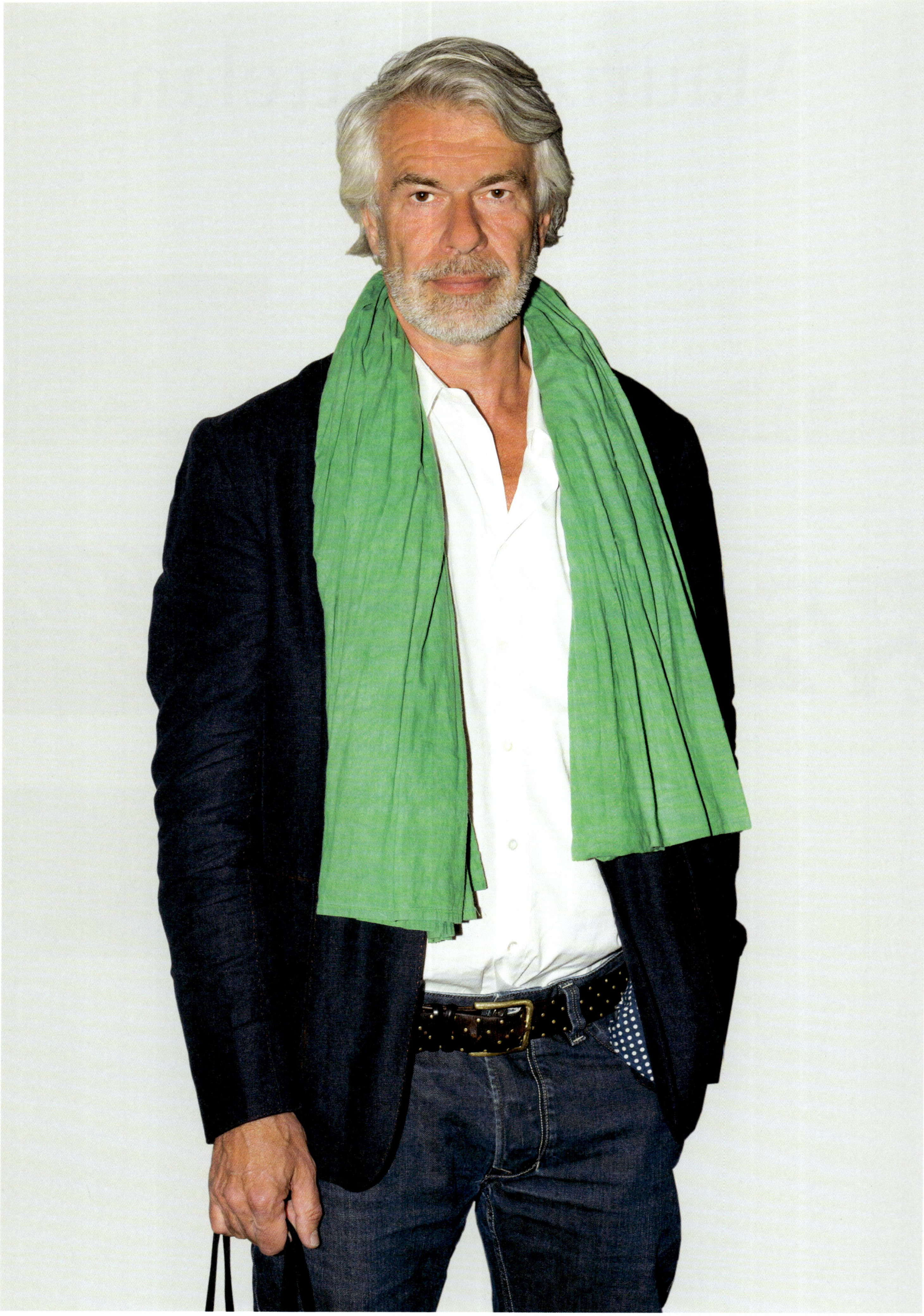

Chris Dercon

Director, Tate Modern, London

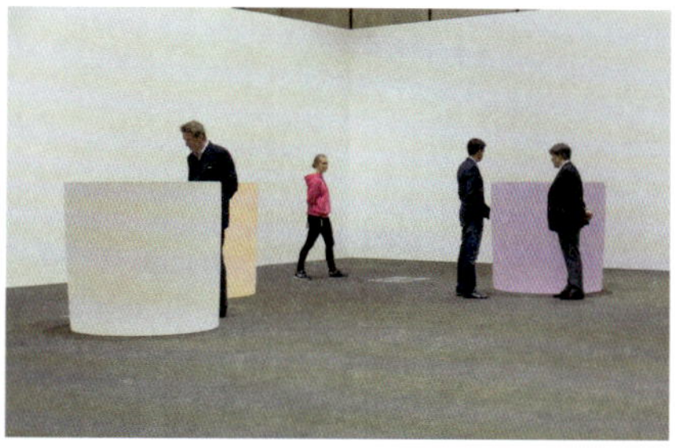

01 Roni Horn, *Untitled*, 2012 (Unlimited)
Hauser & Wirth

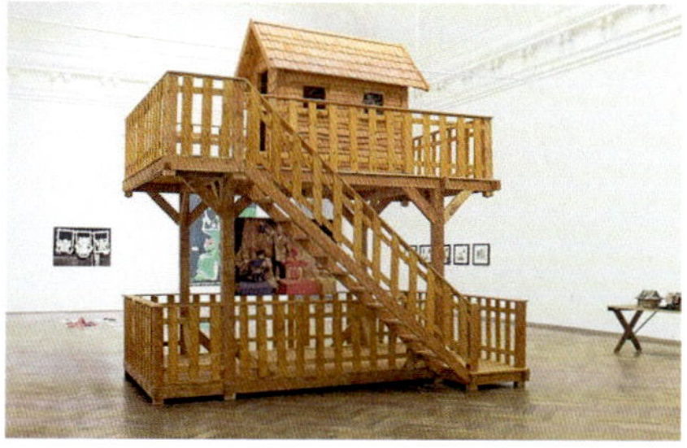

02 *Paulina Olowska: Pavilionesque*,
Kunsthalle Basel, solo exhibition

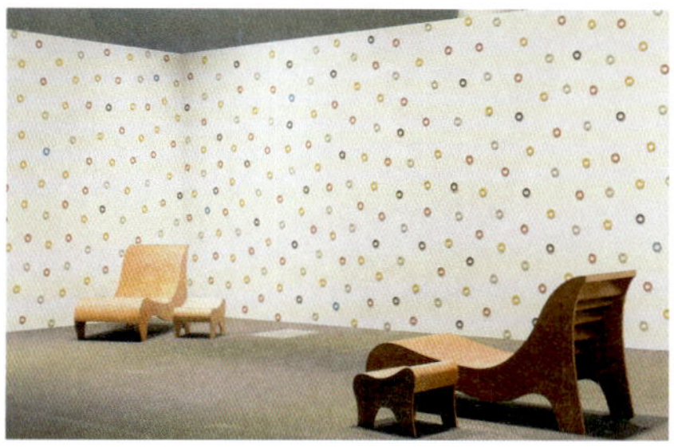

03 Thomas Schütte, *Ringe (Rings)*, 1977–1994
Bernier/Eliades (Unlimited)

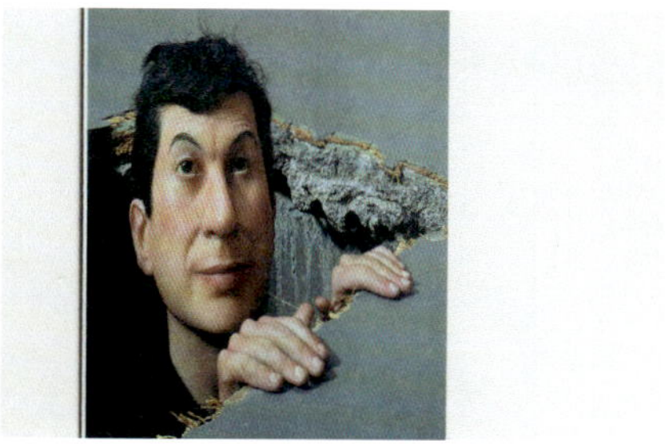

04 *Maurizio Cattelan: Kaputt*, Fondation
Beyeler, Basel, solo exhibition

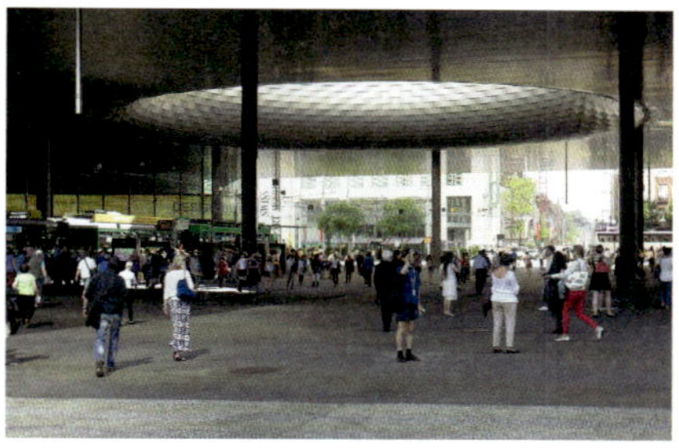

05 Herzog & de Meuron's new architecture for
Messeplatz, Basel

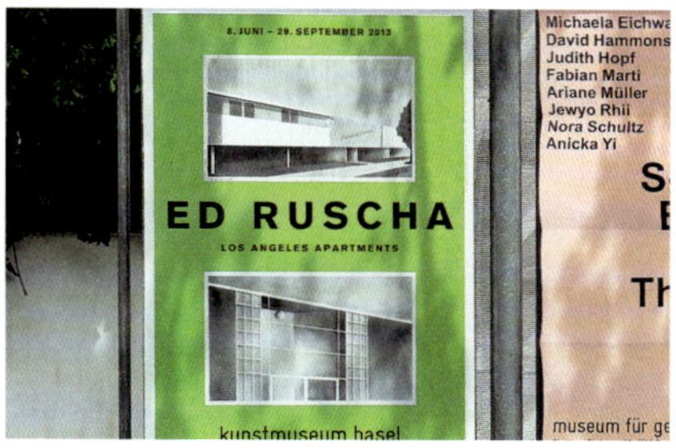

06 *Ed Ruscha: Los Angeles Apartments*,
Kunstmuseum Basel, solo exhibition

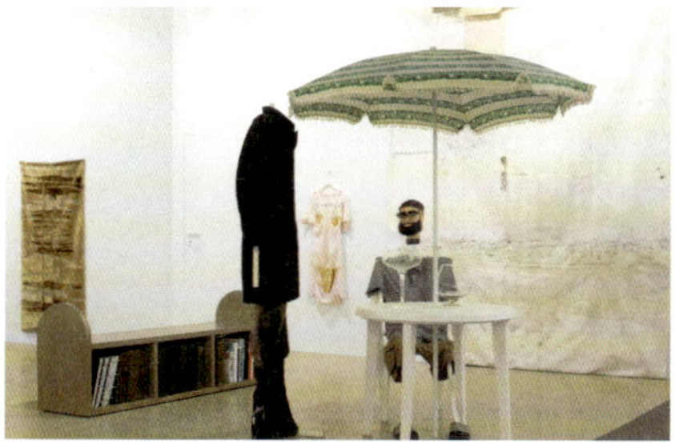

07 Galerie Isabella Bortolozzi booth with works
by Jos de Gruyter & Harald Thys, Juliette
Blightman, Carol Rama, Betty Woodman, and
Oscar Murillo

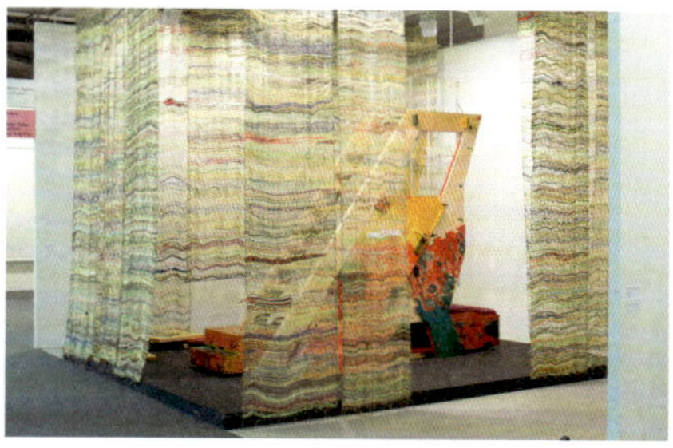

08 Kai Althoff, *Untitled*, 2011
Gladstone Gallery

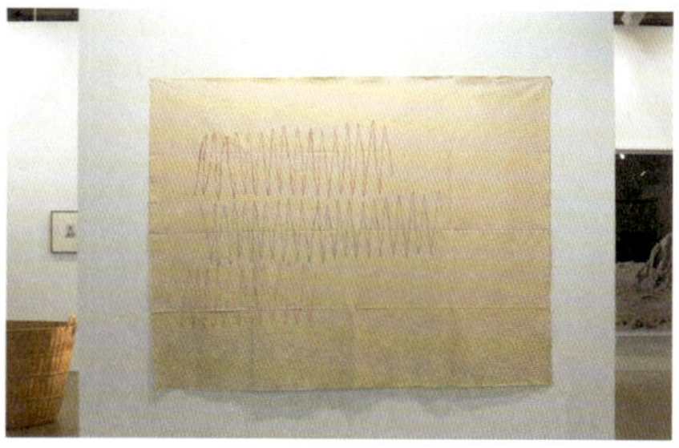

09 Giorgio Griffa, Casey Kaplan

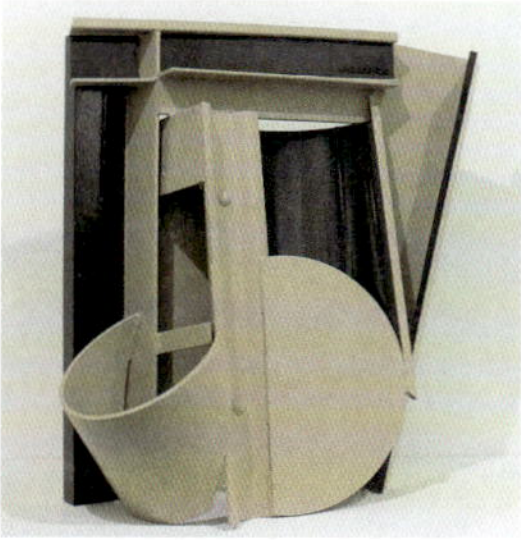

10 Anthony Caro, *Holland*, 1985
New Art Centre

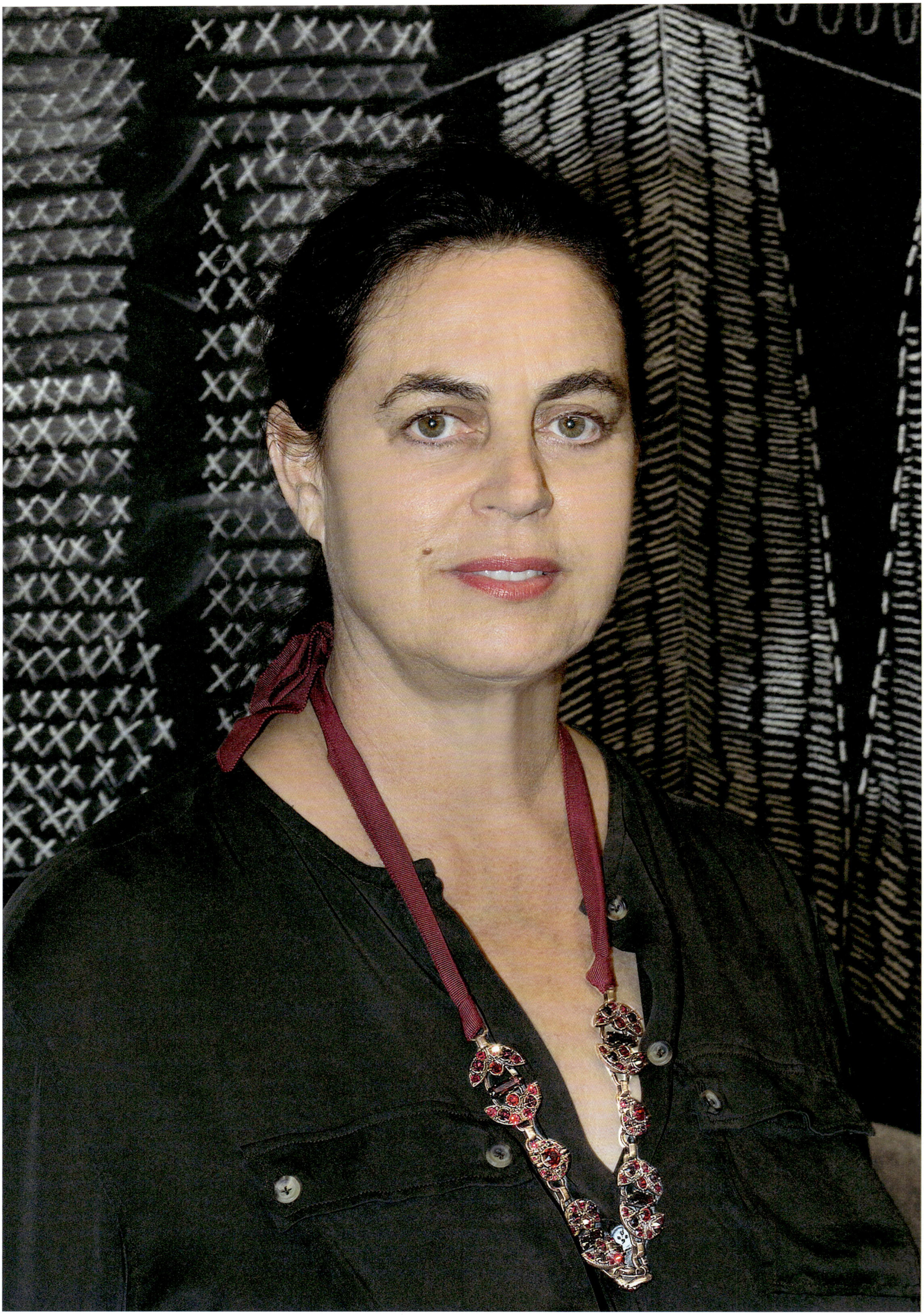

Maja Hoffmann

Collector & Patron (LUMA Foundation), Zurich/London

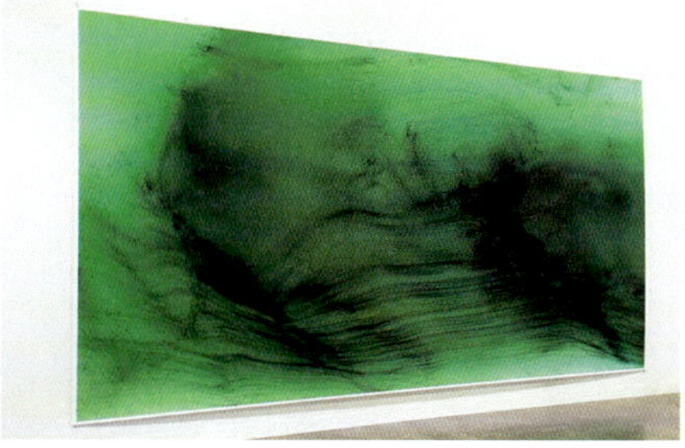

01 Wolfgang Tillmans, *Freischwimmer 155,* 2010
Andrea Rosen Gallery
—"Ever"

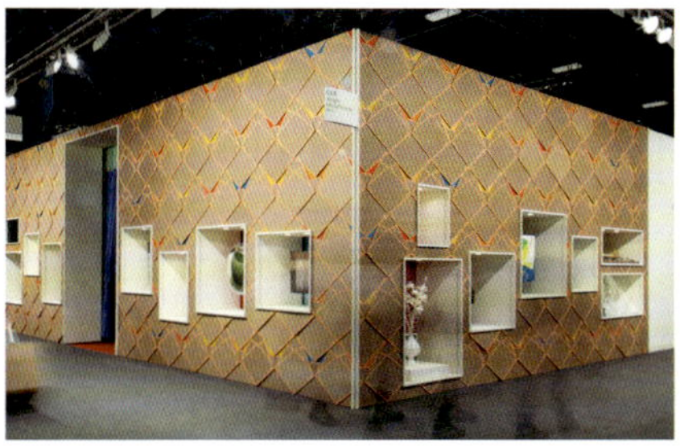

02 Jorge Pardo, *The Booth/El Stand*, 2013
neugerriemschneider
—"Global Latino Gemütlichkeit"

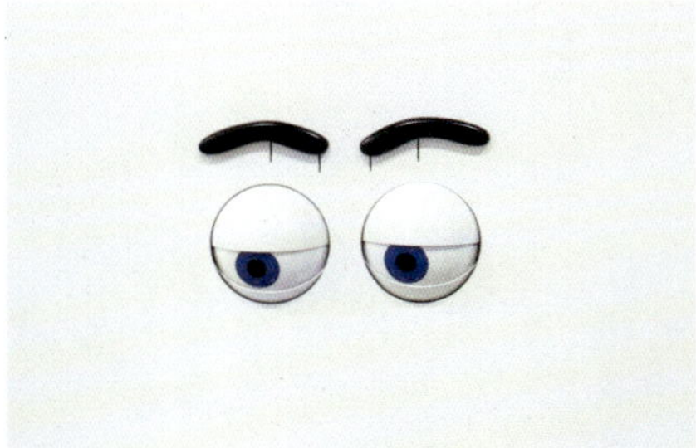

03 Ryan Gander, *Magnus Opus*, 2013
Lisson Gallery
—"Big Brother uncovered"

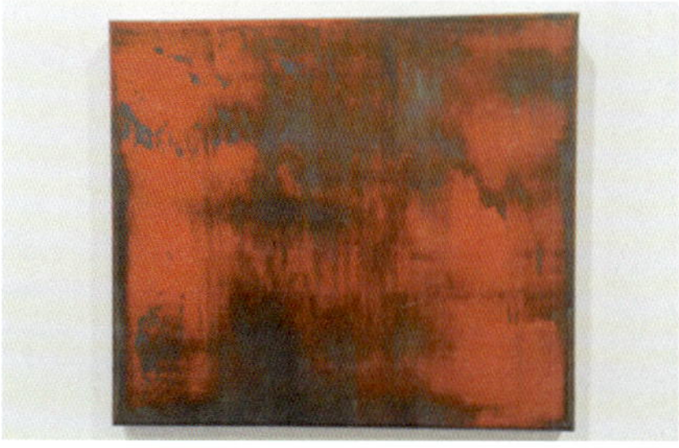

04 Gerhard Richter, *Abstract Painting (744–9),* 1991
Marian Goodman Gallery
—"Our hero"

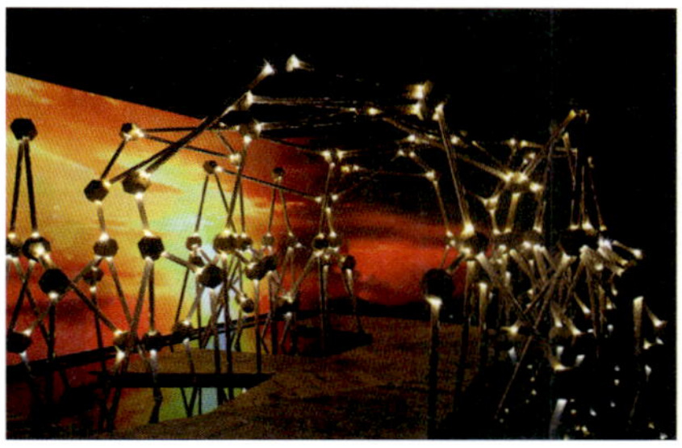

05 Guilherme Torres, *Mangue Groove,* 2013
Swarovski Crystal Palace, Design Miami
—"Based on a mangrove forest"

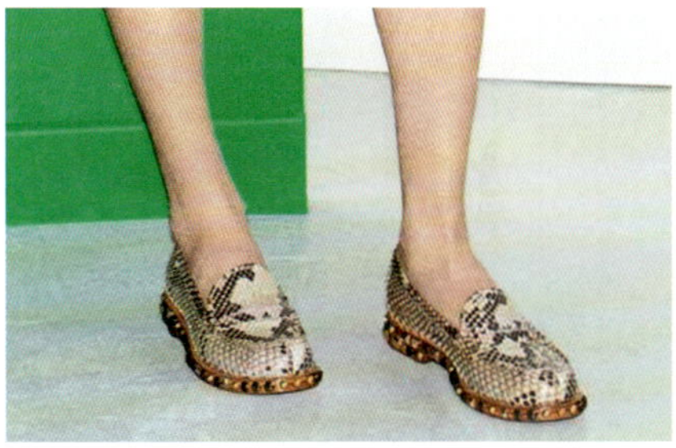

06 Shoe, Louis Vuitton "Icônes" Collection, Spring/Summer 2014, displayed at Charlotte Perriand's *La Maison au bord de l'eau*, 1934–2013, The Raleigh, Miami Beach
—"Give me a break"

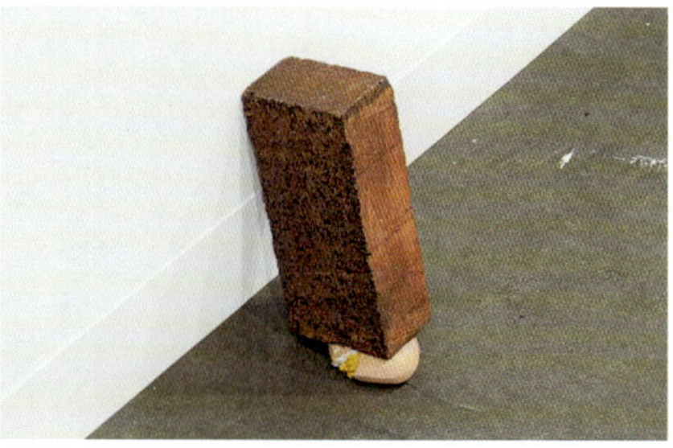

07 Urs Fischer, *Untitled*, 2013
Sadie Coles HQ
—"Fun light/Heavy art"

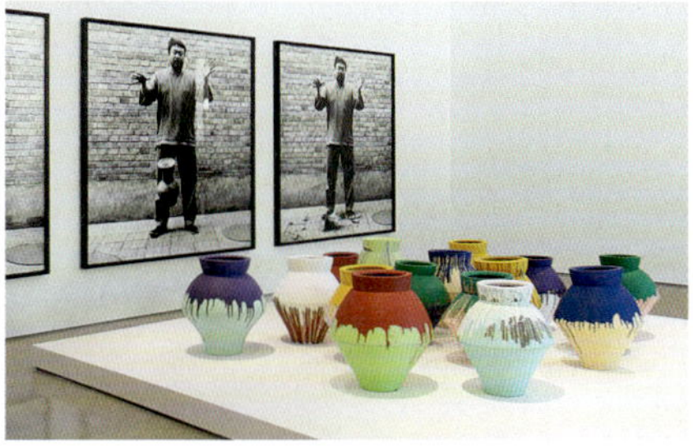

08 Ai Weiwei, *Dropping A Han Dynasty Urn*, 1995–2009; *Coloured Vases*, 2007–2010
Pérez Art Museum Miami
—"A monument"

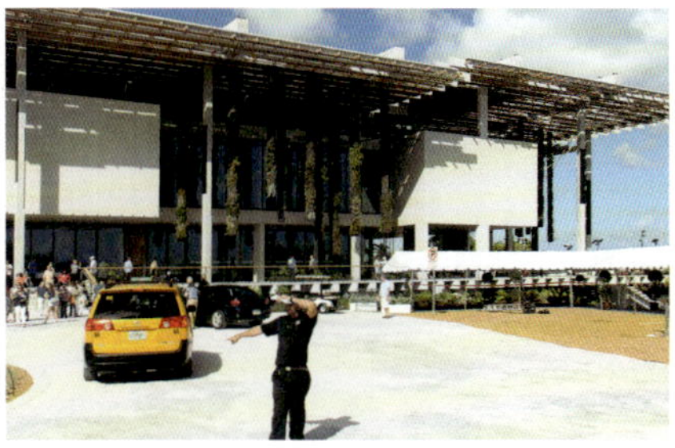

09 Herzog & de Meuron and Christine Binswanger
Pérez Art Museum Miami
—"Brilliant"

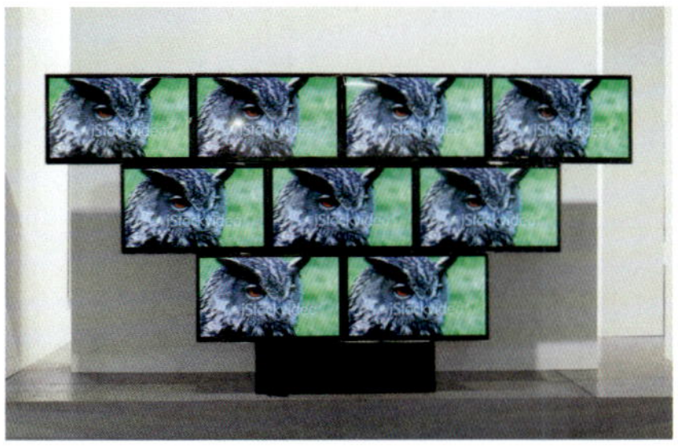

10 Sturtevant, *Elastic Tango*, 2010
Gavin Brown's enterprise
—"My *coup de coeur*"

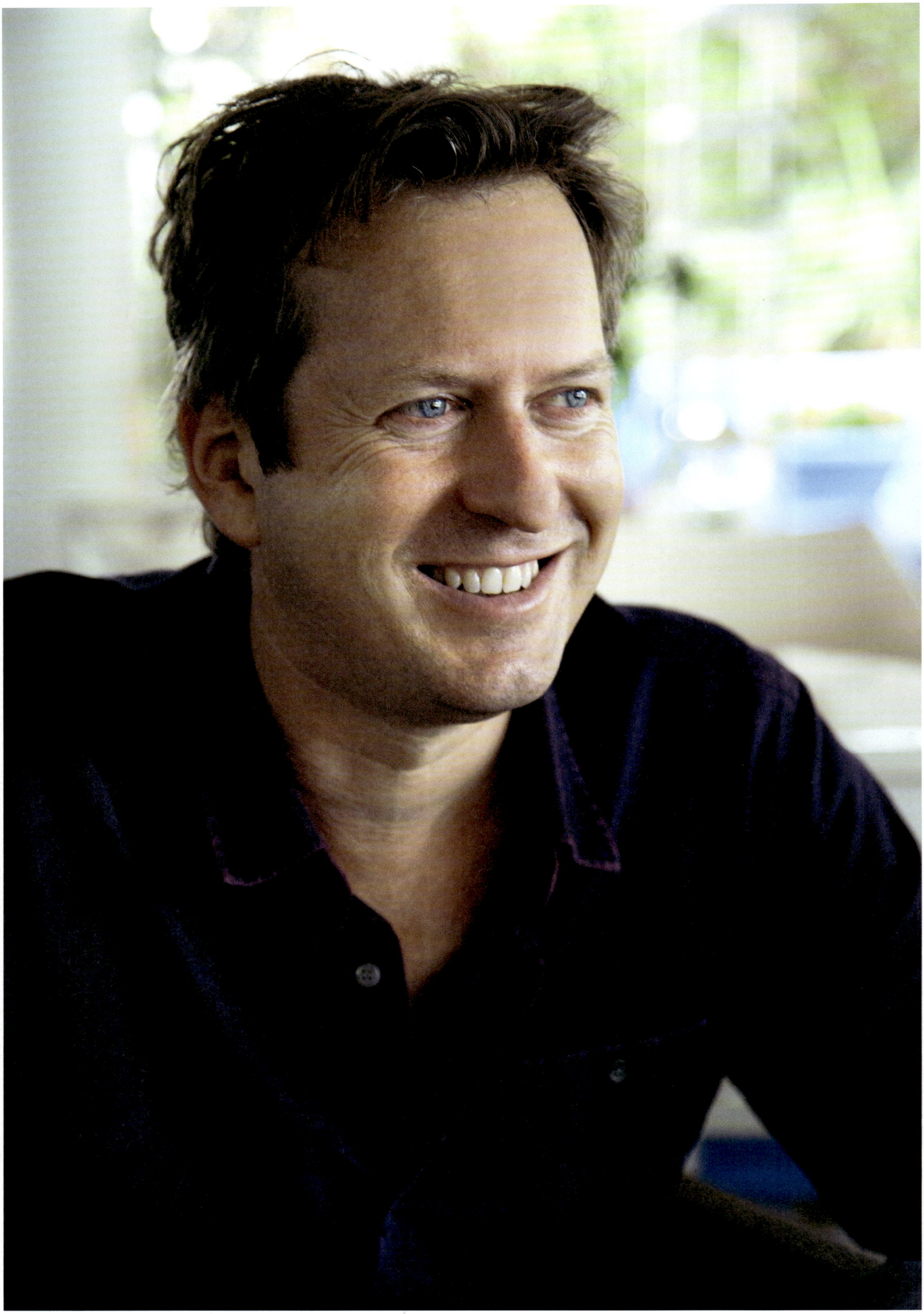

Doug Aitken

Artist, Los Angeles

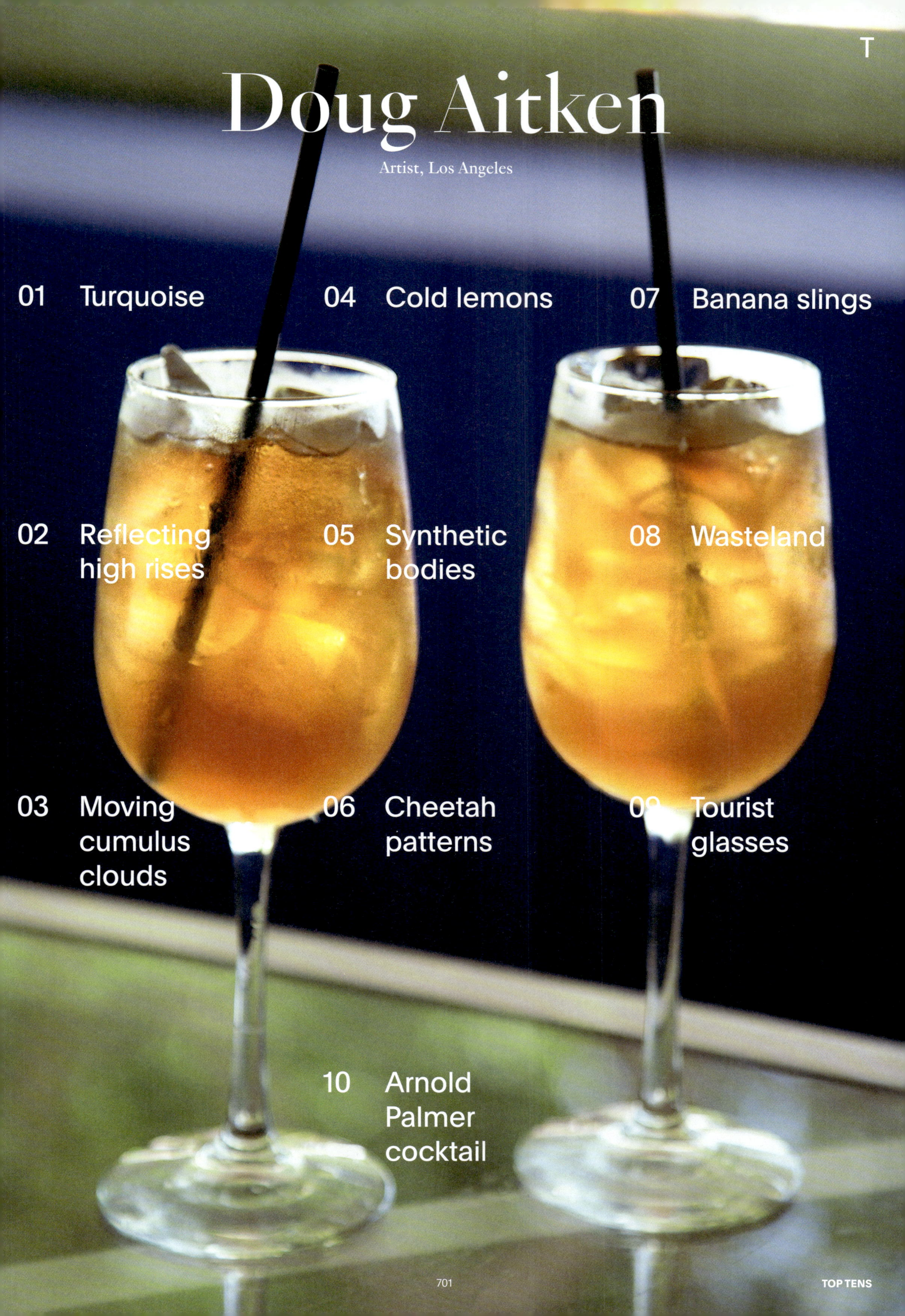

01 Turquoise

02 Reflecting high rises

03 Moving cumulus clouds

04 Cold lemons

05 Synthetic bodies

06 Cheetah patterns

07 Banana slings

08 Wasteland

09 Tourist glasses

10 Arnold Palmer cocktail

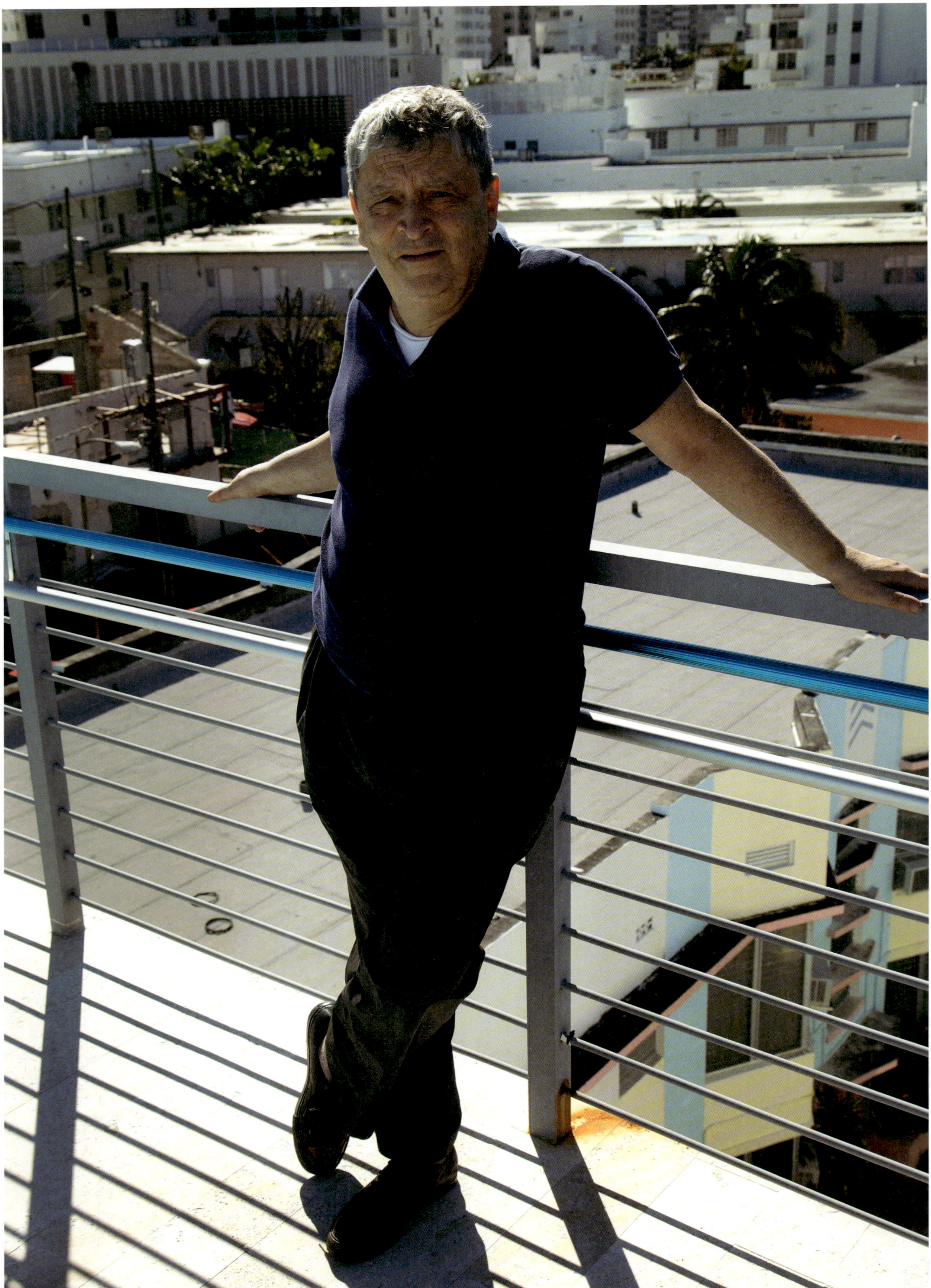

Norman Rosenthal

Independant Curator & Writer, London

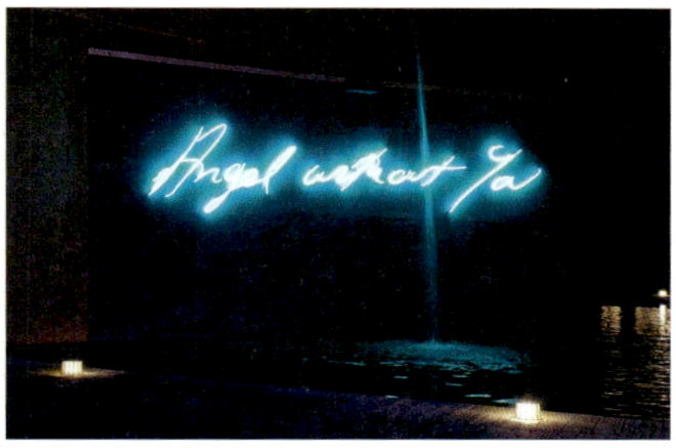

01 Tracey Emin, *Angel Without You* exhibition
Museum of Contemporary Art, North Miami

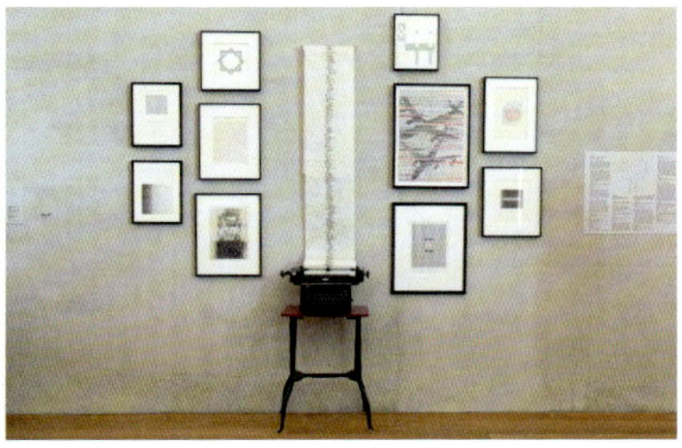

02 *A Human Document: Selections from the Sackner Archive of Concrete and Visual Poetry*
Pérez Art Museum Miami

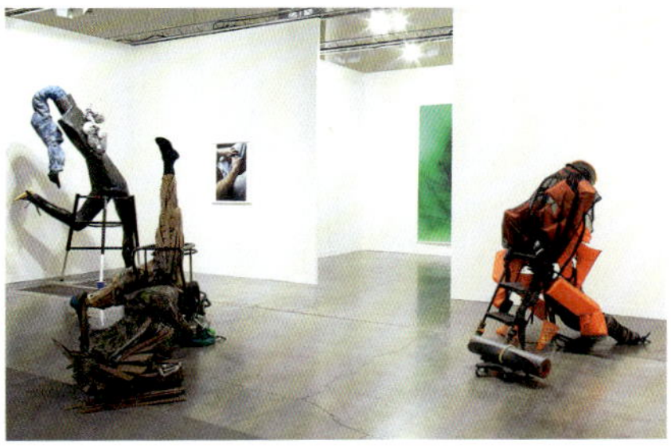

03 Lizzie Fitch/Ryan Trecartin sculptures, 2013
Andrea Rosen Gallery

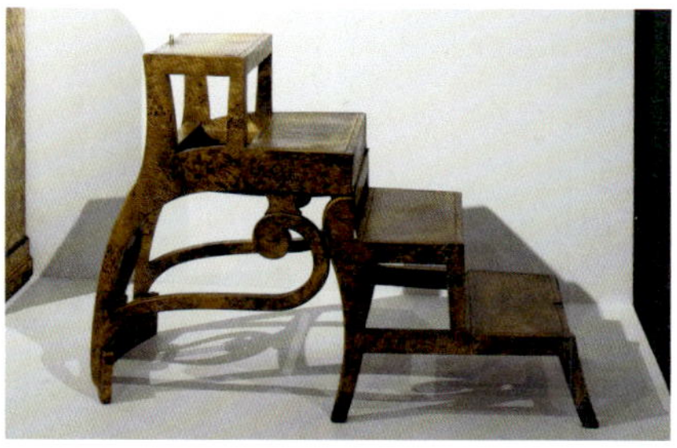

04 Soviet furniture, c. 1940
Heritage International Art Gallery, Design Miami

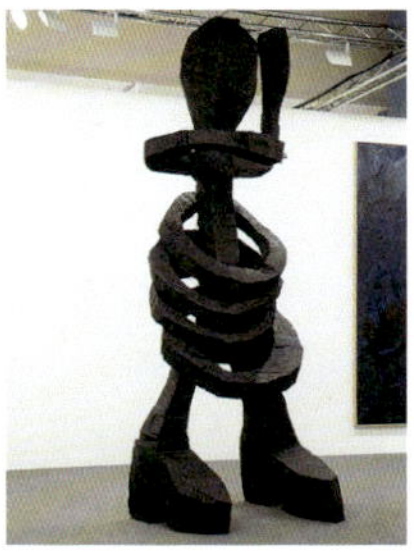

05 Georg Baselitz, *Louise Fuller*, 2013
Galerie Thaddaeus Ropac

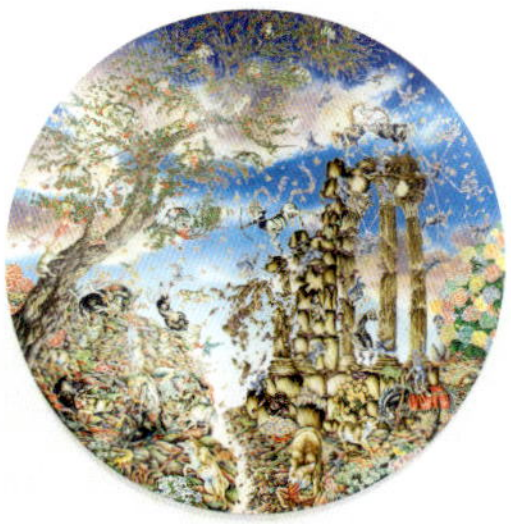

06 Raqib Shaw, *Arrival of the Horse King (Paradise Lost Series)*, 2011–2012
White Cube

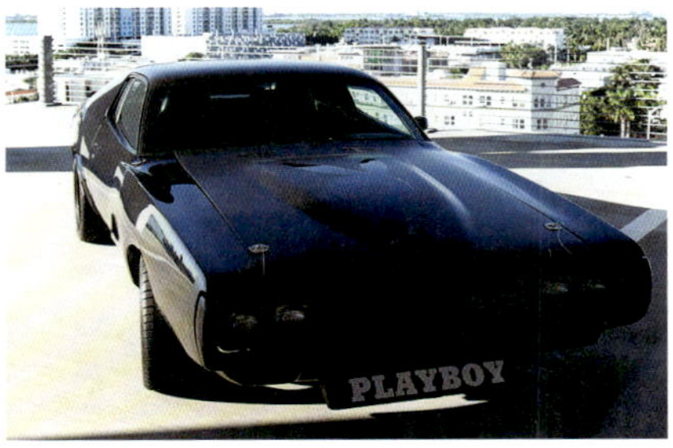

10 Richard Prince, *Vanishing Point (The Artist Cut)*, 2012–2013
Piston Head: Artists Engage The Automobile, Herzog & de Meuron's 1111 Lincoln Road parking, Miami Beach

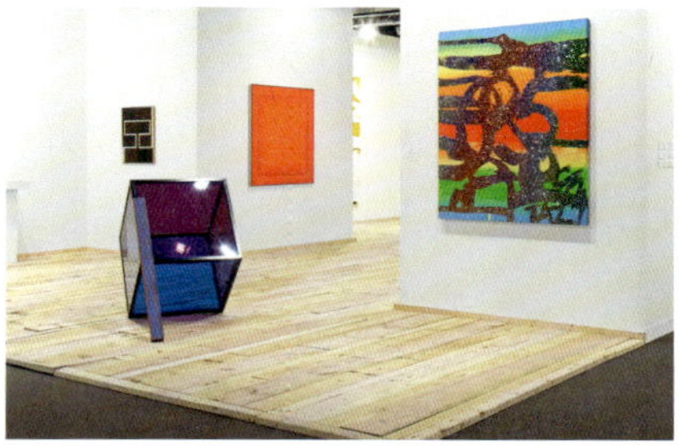

07 Mitchell-Innes & Nash booth with Virginia Overton's floor
"As well as neugerriemschneider booth conceived by Jorge Pardo and Massimo De Carlo booth designed by John M Armleder"

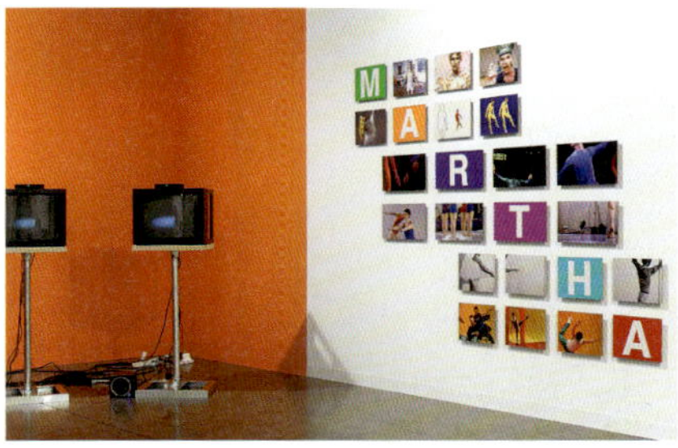

08 Charles Atlas, Vilma Gold (Nova)
"As well as Nick Relph and Math Bass, Overduin & Kite, and Deyson Gilbert and Marina Simão, Mendes Wood" (Nova)

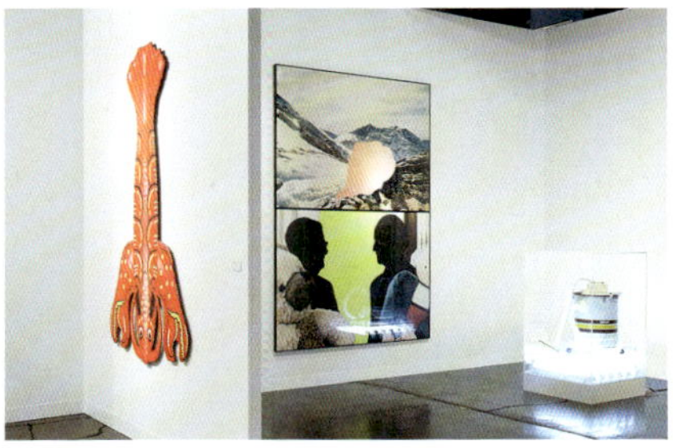

09 *Seeing Double: John Baldessari/Jeff Koons*
Dominique Lévy Gallery

U

U

Untitled

New York

Nova
Public

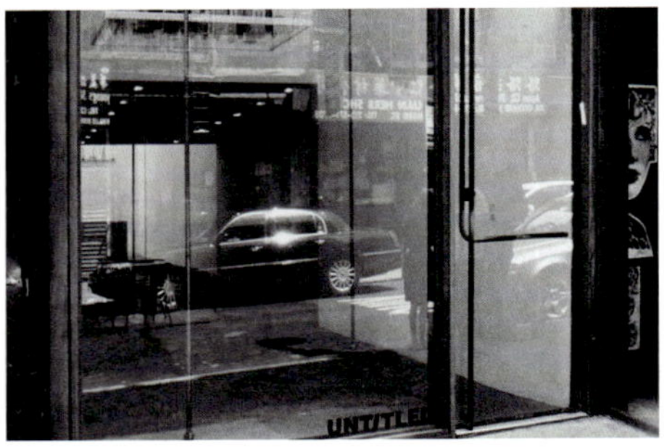

What first compelled you to open a gallery?
Untitled is the partnership between Joel Mesler and Carol Cohen. Previously, Joel founded and ran Rental Gallery. At first aimed at giving out of town galleries an exhibition space in Los Angeles and New York, it soon began representing artists and mounting such as Brendan Fowler's and Matthew Chambers' New York debuts. On her side, Carol ran the secondary market department at White Cube and curated Jay Jopling's personal collection for four years. Since its opening the gallery has continued to nourish the careers of Rental's artists, giving Chambers and Fowler their sophomore New York shows and mounting Henry Taylor's ambitious sculpture show, and has added new blood to this core group with David Adamo, Ian Tweedy, and N. Dash.

Who is the first artist you showed and what was most memorable about that show?
The first show we did was a group show with David Adamo, Heather Cook, Brendan Fowler, Rashid Johnson, Phil Wagner in the fall of 2010. Most memorable were all the "firsts" it entailed: David Adamo's first collaboration with us, Heather Cook's first show in New York, Brendan Fowler's first leaning wall piece, Rashid Johnson's first mirror tile work, Phil Wagner's first neon piece.

When did you first participate in Art Basel and what was most memorable about that show?
We first participated in Art Basel in Miami Beach in 2010 with Phil Wagner in the Positions sector. The most memorable thing about the first Art Basel booth was lying on the grassy hill in the Positions sector with a glass of champagne, having sold Phil's ambitious installation within a few hours of the opening of the fair.

- **Contact** Untitled
  info@nyuntitled.com
- **Established** 2007
- **Owner(s) / Partner(s)** Joel Mesler
  Carol Cohen
- **Team** 4
- **Space(s)** 215 m²
- **Artists at Art Basel** Matthew Chambers
  Phil Wagner
- **Further artists represented** David Adamo
  N. Dash
  Brendan Fowler
  Joshua Neustein
  Anna Plesset
  Ry Rocklen
  Henry Taylor
  Ian Tweedy

Utopian Slumps

Melbourne

Discoveries

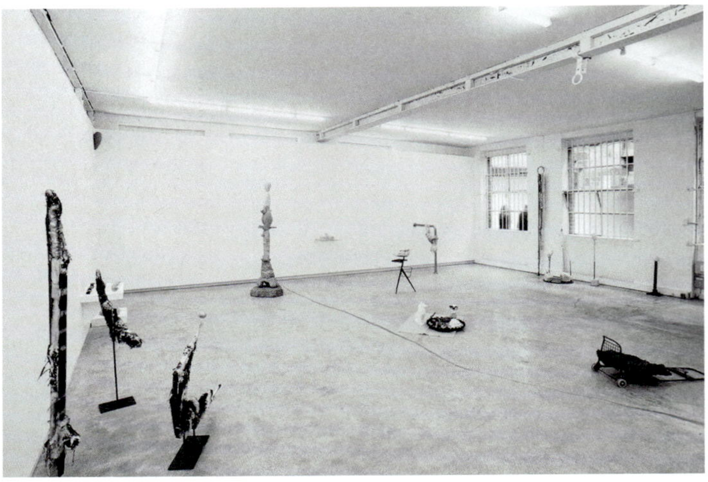

What first compelled you to open a gallery?
I wanted to create more opportunities for local artists, and for myself as an emerging curator.

Who is the first artist you showed and what was most memorable about that show?
I opened Utopian Slumps as a commercial gallery in 2010 with a group exhibition entitled *Territorial Pissings*, featuring the work of Australian and New Zealand artists Sean Bailey, Dan Bell, Nathan Gray, Michelle Hanlin, Matthew Hopkins, Saskia Leek, Rob McHaffie, Toby Pola, Tom Polo, Tim Price, Mark Rodda, Gemma Smith, Masato Takasaka, Jake Walker, and Amber Wallis. The exhibition opening attracted a crowd in the hundreds, so people were spilling out onto the street. It felt like a block party.

When did you first participate in Art Basel and what was most memorable about that show?
My first participation at Art Basel was in Hong Kong in 2013. I exhibited Sanné Mestrom, who made three dimensional, feminist inversions of Giorgio Morandi's still life paintings. Her use of materials and textures—unglazed ceramic, bronze, and steel—formed a truly beautiful combination.

- **Contact** Utopian Slumps
  Melissa Loughnan
  melissa@utopianslumps.com
  info@utopianslumps.com
- **Established** 2010
- **Owner(s) / Partner(s)** Melissa Loughnan (Director)
- **Space(s)** 140 m²
- **Artists at Art Basel** Sanné Mestrom
- **Further artists represented** Lauren Berkowitz
  Fergus Binns
  Starlie Geikie
  Nathan Gray
  Misha Hollenbach
  Thomas Jeppe
  Jess Johnson
  Rhys Lee
  William Mackinnon
  Dylan Martorell
  Mark Rodda
  Caleb Shea
  Jake Walker
  Amber Wallis

Utopian Slumps
Interview with Melissa Loughnan

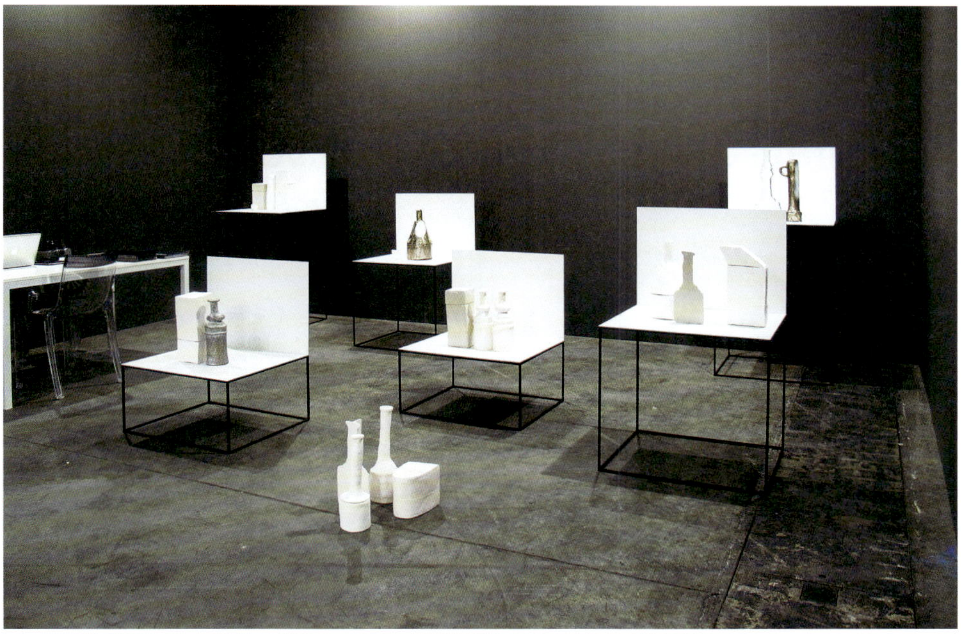

Art Basel in Hong Kong (Discoveries), 2013

As one of the main Australian galleries, could you please tell us about how you see the art scene and the art market in Australia? How do your program and activities fall within this landscape?

The primary market for contemporary Australian art consists of established art dealers, such as Anna Schwartz and Roslyn Oxley, and younger, smaller galleries, such as Utopian Slumps and Neon Parc. As we are a relatively young, geographically isolated country, our market is often inherently self-satisfying. There are not many collectors looking outside our country's borders, and in turn there are not many international collectors looking at Australian art. I am, however, starting to notice a shift, aided by Australian galleries and collectors' increasing presence at Art Basel in Hong Kong and other international art fairs, which is promising for myself and for future generations.

As the director of Utopian Slumps I am motivated to redress this sense of isolation and imbalance through the inclusion of international artists in curated exhibitions within my program, aiming to increase cross-cultural exchange, as well as through the gallery's participation in international art fairs. Utopian Slumps' program and activities aim to assert the significance of Australian art on a global stage, with the ultimate aim of dissolving its limitations of distance and assertions of national identity.

Why did you choose the rather atypical name, Utopian Slumps?

I first opened Utopian Slumps as a non-profit, curator-run gallery in 2007. The entrance was down an alley filled with skip bins, discarded mattresses, broken glass, graffiti, and pigeons. Once you ascended a rusty steel staircase you were met with a pristine white cube. Jess Johnson, an artist friend and now one of the artists I represent, suggested the name "Utopian Slumps." It is the title of one of Ed Ruscha's paintings for the 2005 Venice Biennale. It also for me represents the utopian ideals of pursuing a career in the arts, and the slumps of reality. It is everything and nothing at once, and it perfectly encapsulated the experience of the gallery's first space.

How did you deal with the gallery transformation from a non-profit space into a commercial gallery? And what motivated your decision?

Government arts funding in Australia is quite conservative, and throughout the three years that I operated Utopian Slumps as non-profit I continually received rejection letters to grant applications, with feedback such as "we haven't heard of any of the artists you're working with" and "we haven't heard of your board members." It was a frustrating process, and rather than compromise my vision and the way that the gallery functioned I decided to remove my dependency on public funding and shift to a commercial gallery model. This has been a steep learning curve, but one that has enabled me to stay true to my goals and ideals. Since the gallery's establishment in 2007, and reestablishment as commercial in 2010, I have maintained a strong curatorial focus in my program, and if anything, the only change has been a shift from monumental installation to smaller-scale sculpture and assemblages. I believe, however, that this is represents more of a shift from spectacular and large-scale works to relational aesthetics and unmonumental sculpture; a broader reflection of the art scene than a commercial constraint that I have passed on to my artists.

How does this past curatorial activity influence you current activity?

I recently opened a second non-profit curator-run project space with artist-curator Brooke Babington and writer Helen Hughes, entitled SLOPES—a play on Utopian "Slumps," which is often referenced just as "Slumps," and an allusion to the space we are occupying, which has a sloping floor and large ramp at its center. The gallery will operate for 12 months, presenting the work of Australian artists and curators alongside the work of international artists.

For Art Basel in Hong Kong you presented a solo show by Sanné Mestrom in the Discoveries sector. Tell us about the artist and her proposition.

Sanné Mestrom was born in the Netherlands, grew up in New Zealand, and later immigrated to Australia to complete postgraduate studies. She is now Melbourne-based and a lecturer in fine art at Monash University. Mestrom typically deploys emblems of modernist art and design to inform her materially-driven practice. She translates found objects and imagery through acts of replication and disruption, testing her audience's powers of association with icons of modernism, and investigating notions of lineage, originality and influence through feminized inversions of modernist, traditionally masculine, tropes. For Art Basel in Hong Kong, Mestrom extended a series that she began developing earlier in 2013 for *NEW13* at the Australian Centre for Contemporary Art—three-dimensional interpretations of Morandi's still lives. This was accompanied by a series of collages using found imagery and reproductions of Henry Moore sculptures.

U

Art Basel's pioneering exhibition platform, established in 2000, Unlimited in Basel boasts ambitious contemporary and historical works, including massive sculptures and paintings, video projections, large-scale installations, and live performances. Unlimited was curated in 2013 by Gianni Jetzer of New York.

2013 participants

Eija-Liisa Ahtila
Marian Goodman

Ai Weiwei
Meile

David Altmejd
Hufkens
Modern Art
Rosen

Carl Andre
Fischer

Kutluğ Ataman
Dane
Sperone Westwater

Atelier Van Lieshout
Grimm
Jousse Entreprise
Krinzinger

Kader Attia
Continua

Miroslaw Balka
Gladstone

Karla Black
Capitain
Modern Art

Iñaki Bonillas
Nordenhake

Peter Buggenhout
Fischer

Marc Camille Chaimowicz
Cabinet

Chen Zhen
Continua

Lygia Clark
Jacques

Matt Connors
Cherry and Martin
Herald St

Martin Creed
Gavin Brown
Hauser & Wirth

François Curlet
Air de Paris
Szwajcer

Aaron Curry
Rech

Willem de Rooij
Buchholz
Crousel
Petzel
Regen Projects

Thomas Demand
Marks
Sprüth Magers

Willie Doherty
Alexander and Bonin
Kerlin
Kilchmann

Latifa Echakhch
kaufmann repetto
mennour
Presenhuber

Lionel Estève
Baronian
Bernier/Eliades
Perrotin

Ceal Floyer
303 Gallery
Lisson
Schipper

Günther Förg
Greene Naftali

Michel François
Hufkens
mennour

Jonah Freeman and Justin Lowe
Marlborough

Dara Friedman
Gavin Brown

Meschac Gaba
Stevenson

Theaster Gates
White Cube

Simryn Gill
Williams

Antony Gormley
Continua

Johan Grimonprez
Kelly
mennour

Noriyuki Haraguchi
McCaffrey

He An
Templon

Susan Hiller
Taylor

Roni Horn
Hauser & Wirth

Jonathan Horowitz
Gavin Brown
Coles
Weiss

Huang Yong Ping
Gladstone

Pierre Huyghe
Marian Goodman
Schipper

Alfredo Jaar
Goodman Gallery
Lelong
mennour
Schulte

Michael Joo
Kukje/Kim

Esther Kläs
Blum

Emil Michael Klein
Vavassori

Norbert Kricke
Scheibler

Shakuntala Kulkarni
Chemould

Wolfgang Laib
Ropac

Sean Landers
greengrassi
Petzel

Liu Wei
Long March

Jorge Macchi
Alexander and Bonin
Benzacar
Continua
Kilchmann
Strina

Michel Majerus
Marks
neugerriemschneider

Teresa Margolles
Kilchmann

Justin Matherly
Cooper
König

Mario Merz
Gladstone

Matt Mullican
Klosterfelde
Mai 36

Oscar Murillo
Bortolozzi

Gina Pane
mennour

Giulio Paolini
Lambert

Claudio Parmiggiani
Lee
Meessen De Clercq

Amalia Pica
Foxx
Herald St

Rob Pruitt
Gavin Brown

Florian Pumhösl
Abreu
Buchholz
Lisson

Walid Raad
Cooper
Sfeir-Semler

Thomas Schütte
Bernier/Eliades
Faggionato

Sean Scully
Cheim & Read

Nobuo Sekine
Blum & Poe

Chiharu Shiota
Templon

Dayanita Singh
Frith Street

John Stezaker
Approach

Jessica Stockholder
Mitchell-Innes & Nash
Obadia

L.N. Tallur
Chemould
Nature Morte

Oscar Tuazon
Maccarone
Presenhuber

Tunga
Luhring Augustine
Corrias
Mendes Wood
Meyer Riegger
Noero

Piotr Uklański
Gagosian
De Carlo

Marijke van Warmerdam
Gelink
Ishii
Riis

Adriana Varejão
Fortes Vilaça
Lehmann Maupin
Miro

Betty Woodman
Bortolozzi
Pia
Salon 94

Yan Xing
Meile

David Zink Yi
Hauser & Wirth
König

Marc Camille Chaimowicz
Enough Tyranny
1972

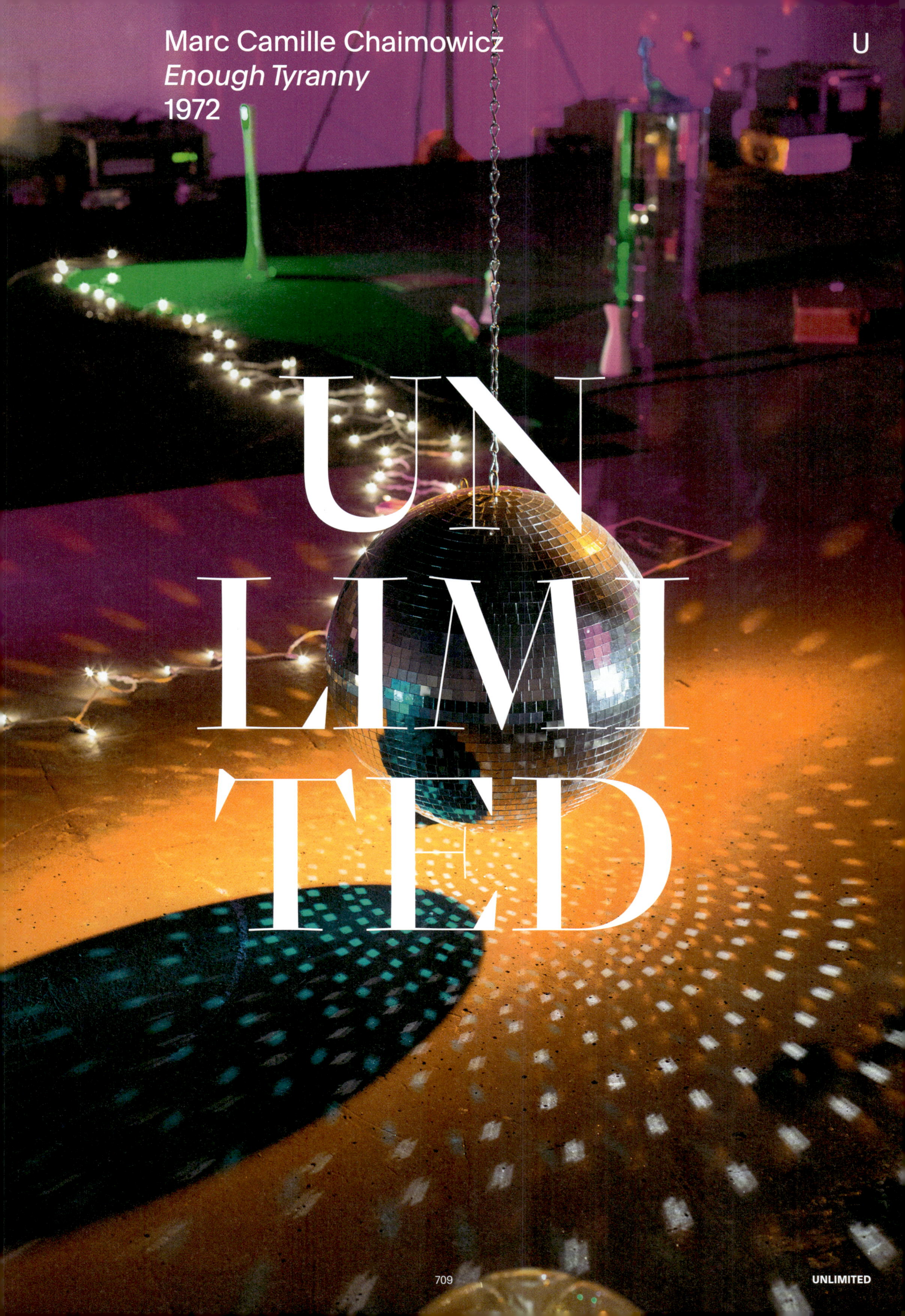

UN
LIMI
TED

U

Noriyuki Haraguchi
A-7E Corsair II
2011

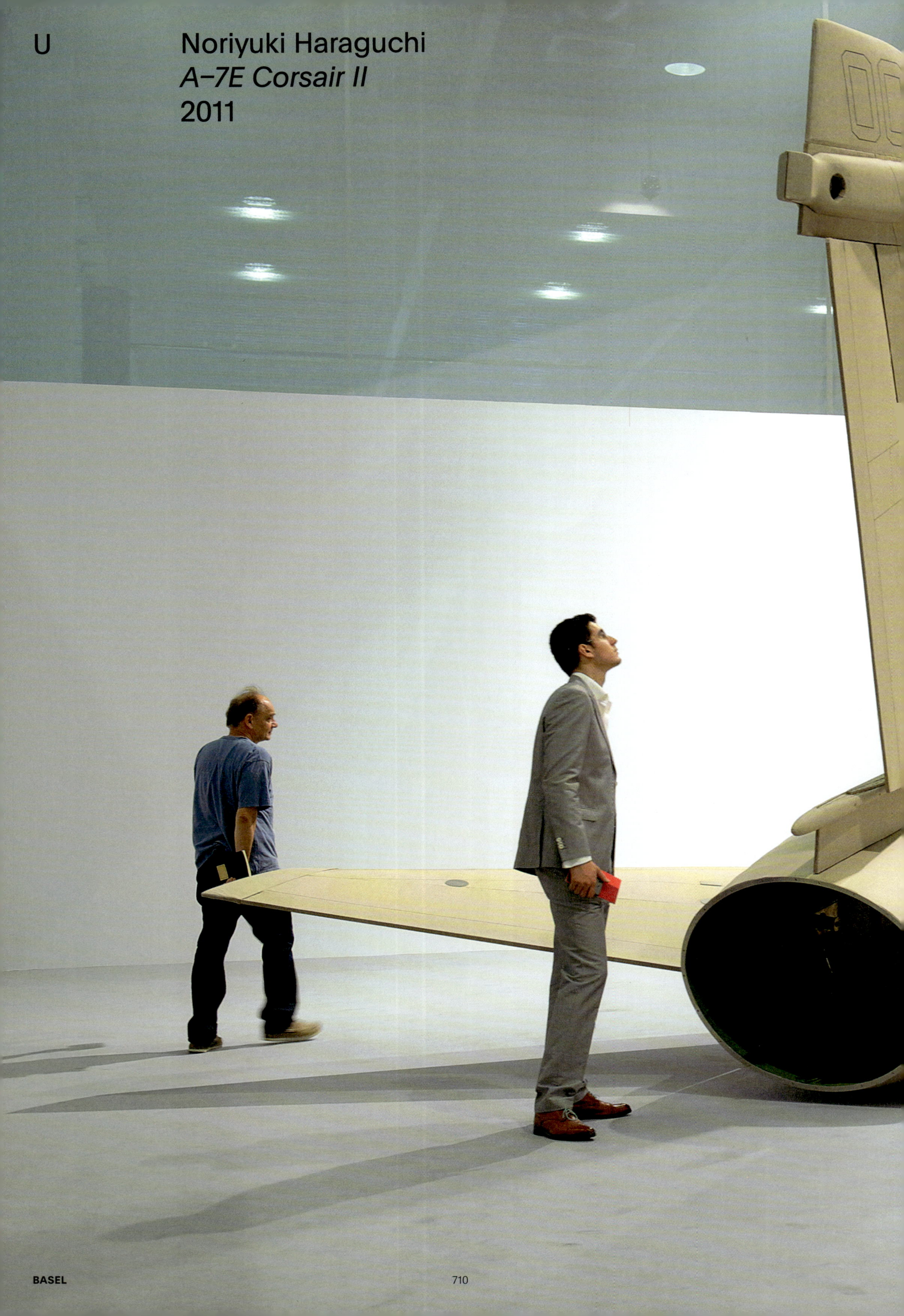

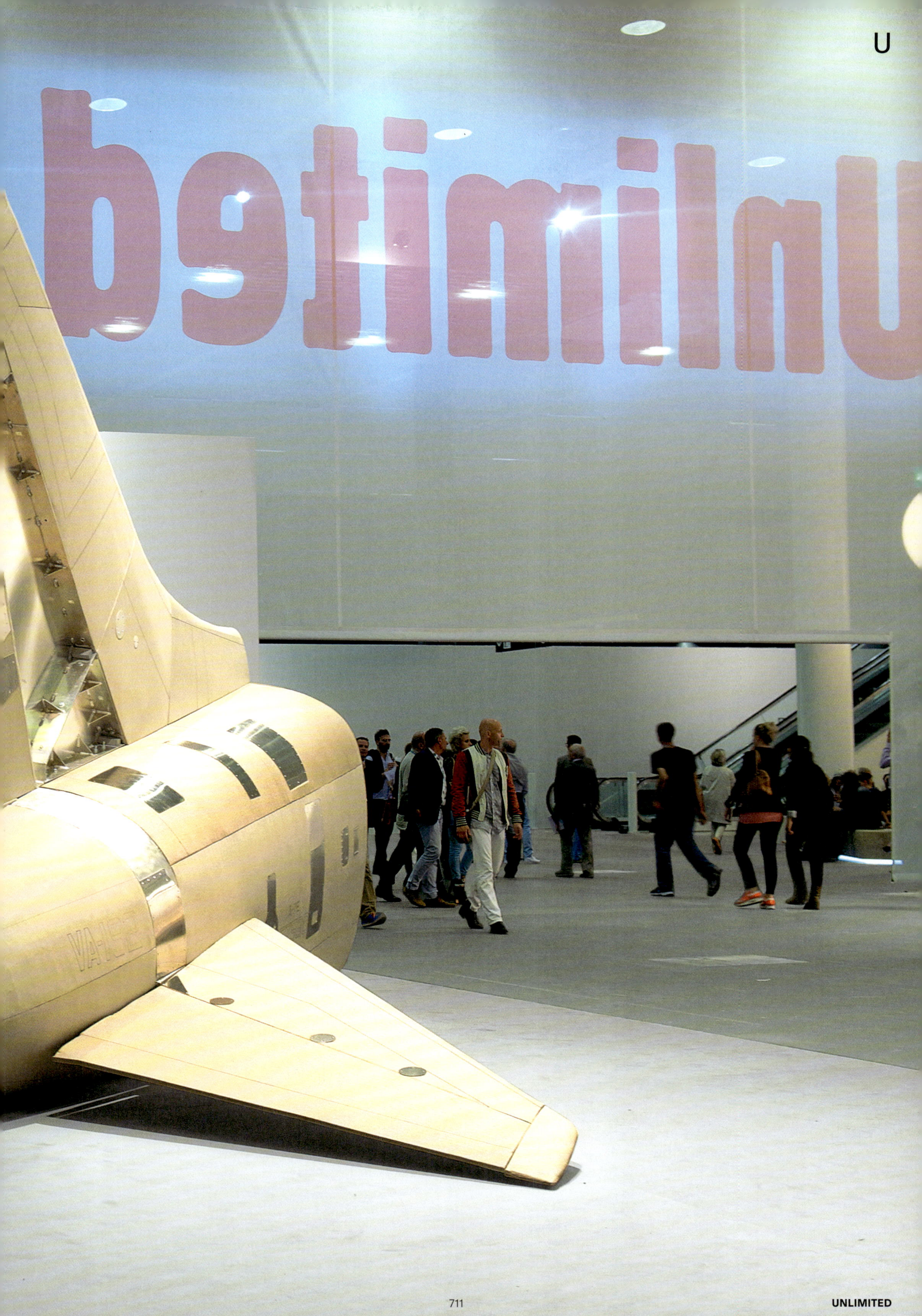

Gianni Jetzer Talks with Matt Connors, Latifa Echakhch, and Oscar Tuazon about Unlimited 2013

Salon
Artist Talk

Basel
June 13, 2013

Matt Connors, Artist, New York

Latifa Echakhch, Artist, Martigny (Switzerland)

Oscar Tuazon, Artist, Paris/Los Angeles

Moderator: Gianni Jetzer, Curator of Art Basel's Unlimited sector and former Director of the Swiss Institute Contemporary Art, New York

A complete version of the conversation is available at www.artbasel.com

GIANNI JETZER Unlimited is an exhibition with a very special format: it's a fair exhibition but also a kind of temporary museum, with its almost 85,000 visitors. What is quite special for me as a curator is that you can build walls, much more walls than in any museum of the world … This year with the whole Hall 1 as an exhibition space, we had roughly two kilometers (or 1.3 miles) of walls. So, you can create a *parcours* and you can try to present the artworks in the best conditions possible. For me, the most important thing remains to rely on great artworks and great artists.

Matt Connors' work, *Demonstration (red and blue)*, has been created for Unlimited. It consists of walls that are quite high (six meters high, five meters wide), double layered: you have a free standing wall and a second wall leaning against it. Matt Connors was born in Chicago and lives in LA. Matt, how did you approach this invitation?

MATT CONNORS Basically, those ideas were born out of painting, from a desire to "theatricalize" the ideas and gestures inside of paintings, and from the (maybe dumb) idea that I wanted to see this juxtaposition of forms in real life, outside of a painting. The first time I did it, it kind of gave me permission to stop thinking about painting as my only venue.

I think objects do not need a human to use them in order to exist.
— Latifa Echakhch

GJ Actually in the show you did at MoMA PS1, you were already leaning canvases, but small ones, against the wall. Is there any relationship between these pieces?

MC I've been very attached to the gesture of leaning. I think I initially just turned a Richard Serra piece into a painting. It then felt very satisfying that instead of pictorializing a relationship I was able to create a physical relationship.

GJ Latifa Echakhch was born in Morocco. She lived many years in France and eventually moved to Martigny in Switzerland. She was presented in the Venice Biennale in 2011, and in the Sydney Biennale in 2012. Usually she explores issues of cultural transfers and the shifts of identity that they entail. Her solo show at the Kunsthaus Zürich last year on circus culture, was surprising, and her piece here relates to that exhibition. Of course there were certain elements that were in sync with your previous works, for example the emptiness, the aspect of something missing, the absence of things, a sense of abandonment. But the circus also represents the idea of a spectacle that lives entirely from the tension of the moment. Could you tell us more about this?

LATIFA ECHAKHCH At the Kunsthaus Zürich it was more about the architecture of the space, because I had to deal with walls, columns, and also a space that is not really a "white cube." I started this kind of work in 2003: this was the first time I built an installation without any direct performance. I really wanted to explore the world of the circus because it's something like a childhood memory, but also because I consider it a radical event: one space, a short period of time, and a succession of acts and sets. It changes very fast, and each event is very short and powerful.

GJ Liberating objects is a key element in your work: you use objects that you detach from their usual function and identity.

LE I think objects do not need a human to use them in order to exist. If you see objects like the horse riding material and the costume of the acrobat I created, you think of the acrobat and the horse without needing the presence of the models. On one hand it's the idea of a still life, like in a painting where you set things on a table for example. On the other hand, it's also about how to prepare a performance without a performance. I did it very seriously and had dialogues with professionals: we talked a lot about the technical aspects of props—for example, about how long it takes to change a costume. So, the costume was really made for dancers. In a sense it was a way to enter into that world but to not finish the action.

GJ Oscar Tuazon (b. in Tacoma, Washington) lived for many years in Paris, before moving to Los Angeles. In Paris he founded the collectively run gallery Castillo/Corrales. You might have seen one of his "Para-Pavilions" at the Venice Biennale in 2011. He presented a new work for Unlimited, *A Free Country* (2013). It's a structure built out of steel, aluminum and concrete. His work generally works with and against the entropic qualities of natural materials. It was quite thrilling to see how intelligently the form was chosen. It's a lot about the dialectic between different metals and different forces, the potential of expression that lies in deformation. In the work of Oscar Tuazon, there are traces of physical labor. Can you tell us a little bit more about the different phases and maybe the problems that you encountered?

OSCAR TUAZON The artwork comes from a series of works that I started about five years ago. They were structures built in a gallery space and suspended from the ceiling. They would collapse in their own way, but be suspended from the ceiling and directly connected to the space of the gallery. To me that was a way of saying that the work is contingent, that it depends on the space, and that it can't exist outside the space, that it really needs the gallery as a protection, a support context, in a physical way. But in this context here, maybe because the ceiling is so high, I wanted to go a little further, and instead of having something collapsing from the ceiling, I wanted things to react dynamically within the work itself—that it could actually be a stand-alone work determined and formed by that physical process. In this case, it's two structures deforming each other.

GJ There are two structures and one slides into the other; with cables you started to pull on one structure and it crashed slightly into the other structure. Obviously the deformation was an important factor from the beginning because of the choice of materials you made, but how much can you control the deformation?

OT I'm getting a bit better, but it's hard to anticipate. That's also part of the strangeness. There's a hypothesis from the beginning and then I try to figure out how that will happen.

Obviously it looks very different from the sketch even if I imagine it while we are building it. It's dealing with gravity and the forces of physics in a very intuitive way. One of the things I thought was interesting from

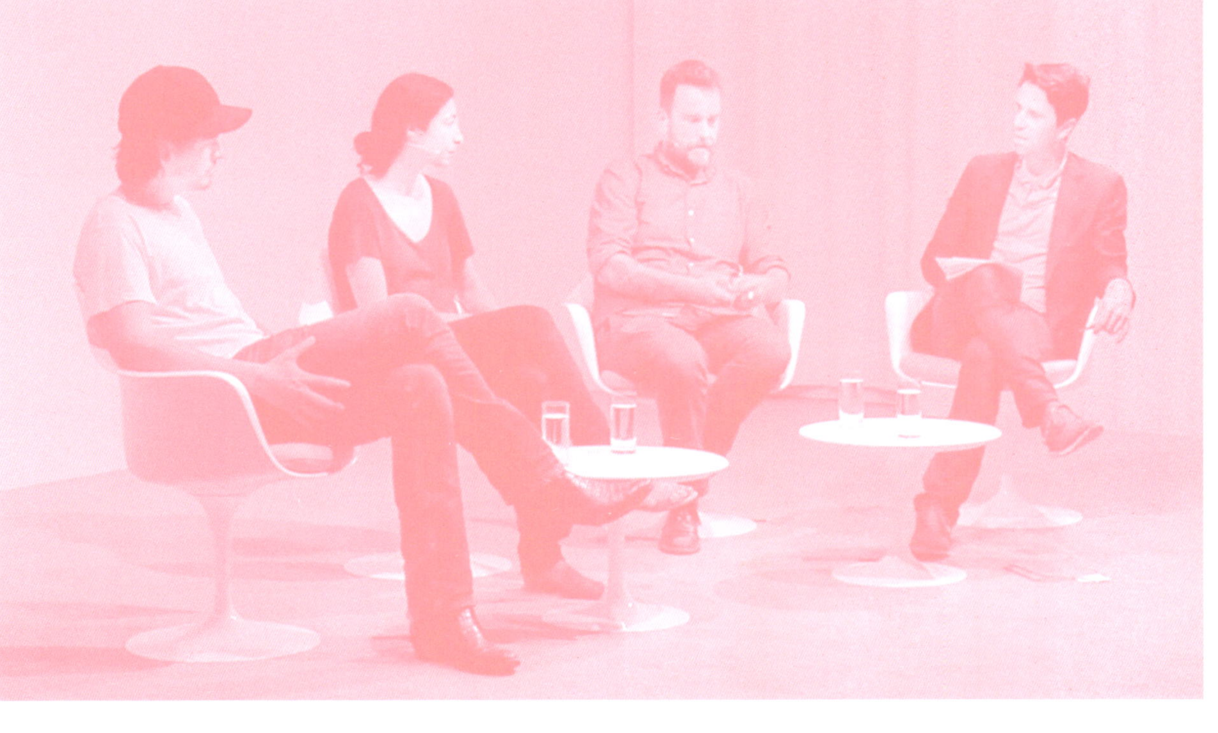

From left to right: Oscar Tuazon, Latifa Echakhch, Matt Connors, Gianni Jetzer

a structural standpoint, or as an engineer, or an architectural standpoint, would be the idea of designing a structure that is meant to collapse, and thereby creates the form of the structure. It really inverses the usual understanding of design.

One person I think about a lot is Scott Burton, an American sculptor and furniture maker who existed on a very vague boundary between architecture, sculpture, and furniture. I guess the simple reason that his work is so compelling to me is that it's always engaging this question of the body, and in not such an easy way—he made very uncomfortable chairs. I've also tried making furniture in the past. Some pieces have been more successful than others. That's the prerogative of making sculpture that looks like a chair—you can really exist in that double space and failure is permitted.

GJ One of the core elements of Unlimited is that it's not a group show built up on similarities but rather on contrasts. It asks the artists to be highly eccentric. What is also very beautiful in Unlimited is how the whole dialogue becomes trans-generational: Marc Camille Chaimowicz's piece from 1972, for example, seems to be timeless, or at least I would expect it to be from the late 1990s, with all its individual mythologies and the use of objects as private objects rather than as readymades ... I think it's really an interesting format because on the one hand it's very competitive, but on the other hand it's also quite protective of the singular positions of the artists. And maybe it reflects what the early 21st century is about: a very competitive open field of many voices and of many possibilities to make contemporary art.

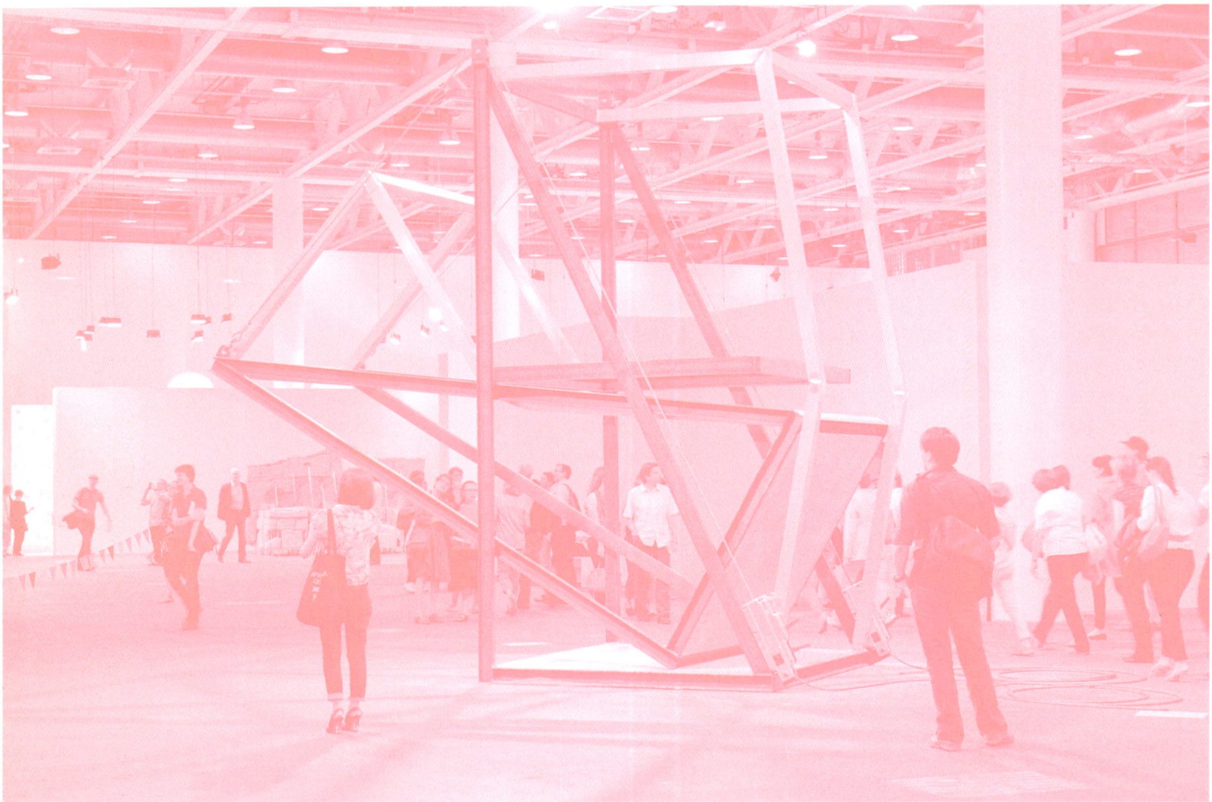

Oscar Tuazon, *A Free Country*, 2013

Matt Connors, *Demonstration (red and blue)*, 2013

Alfredo Jaar
The Sound of Silence
2006

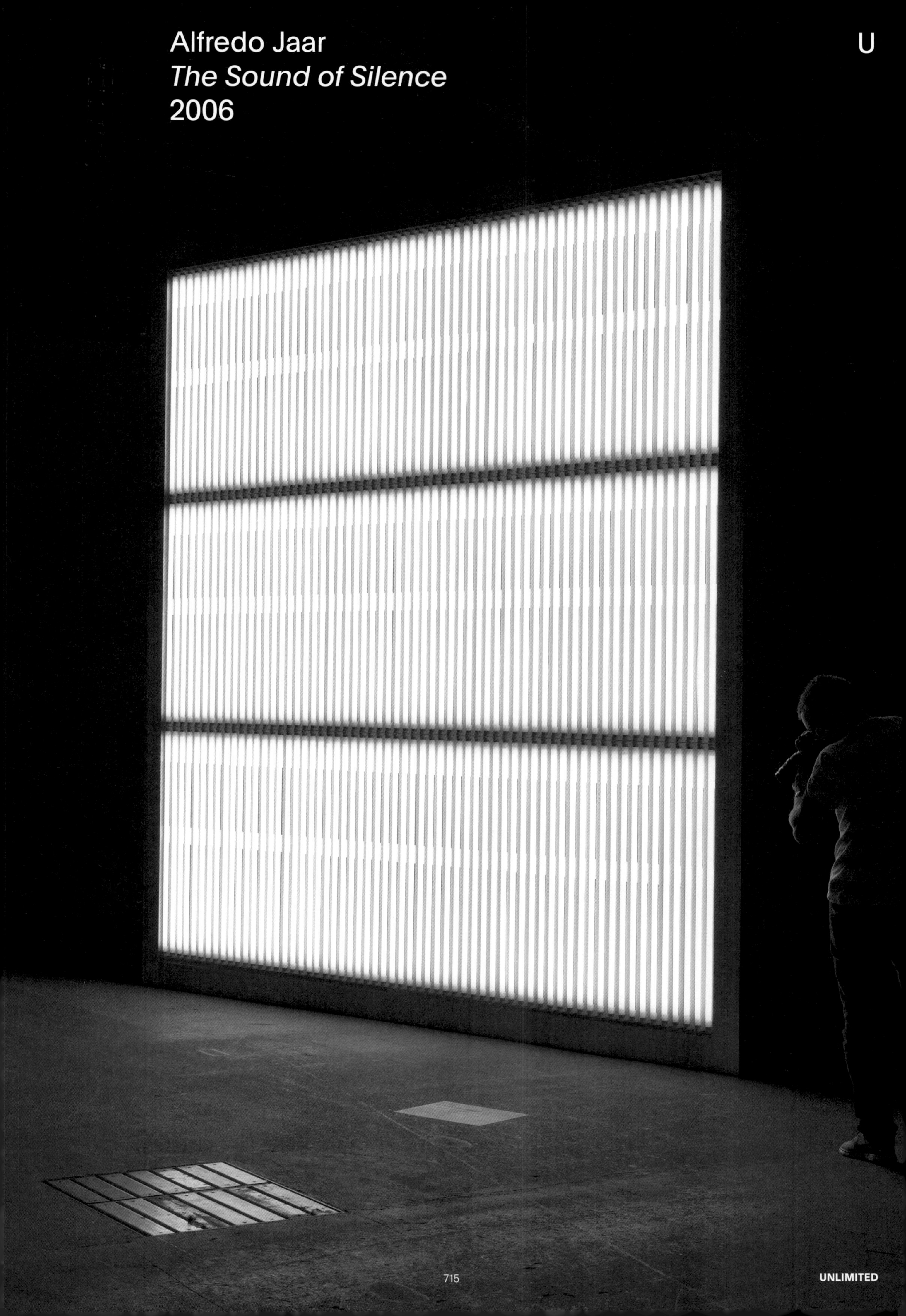

U

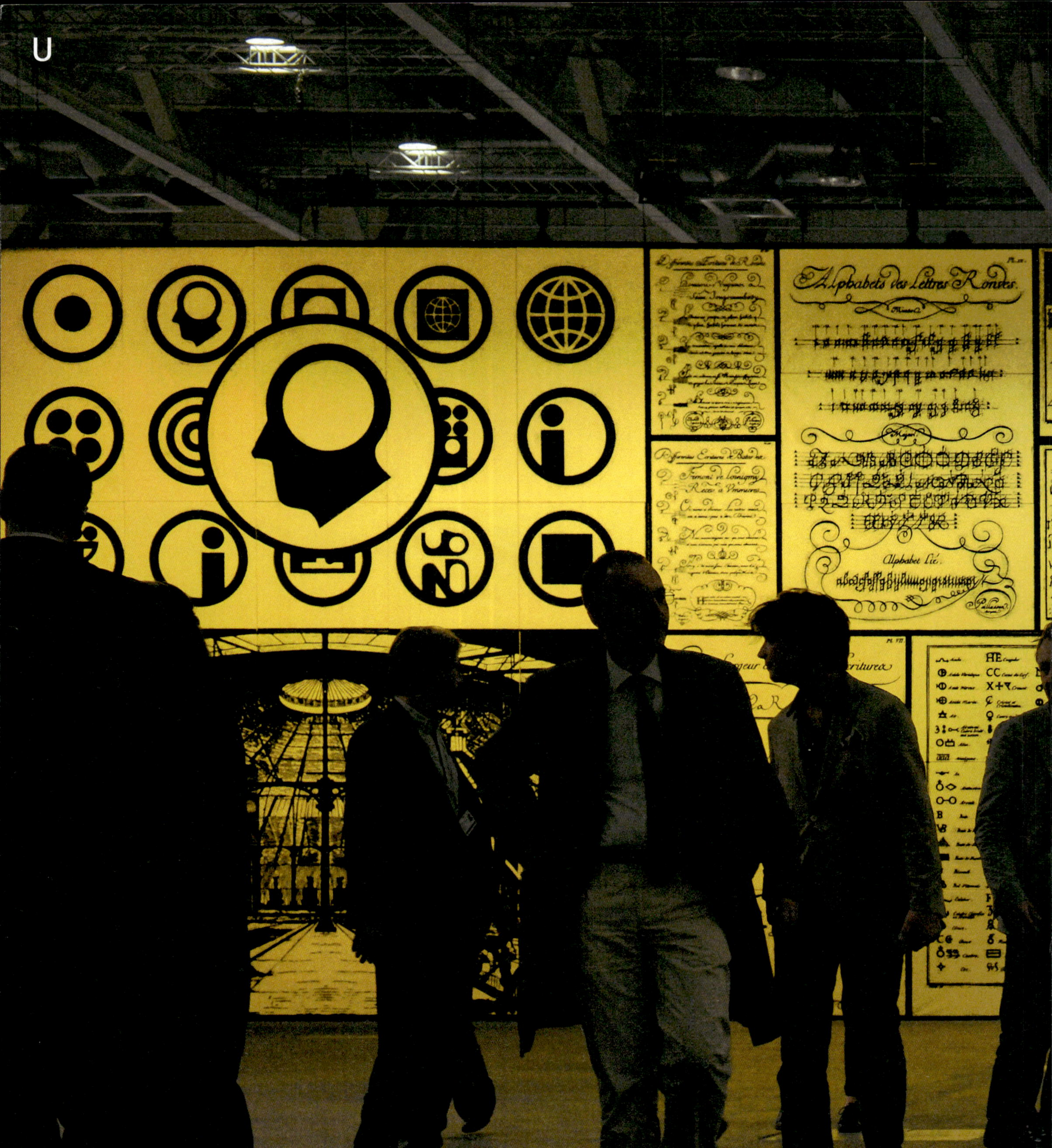

Matt Mullican
Untitled (Two Into One Becomes Three)
2011

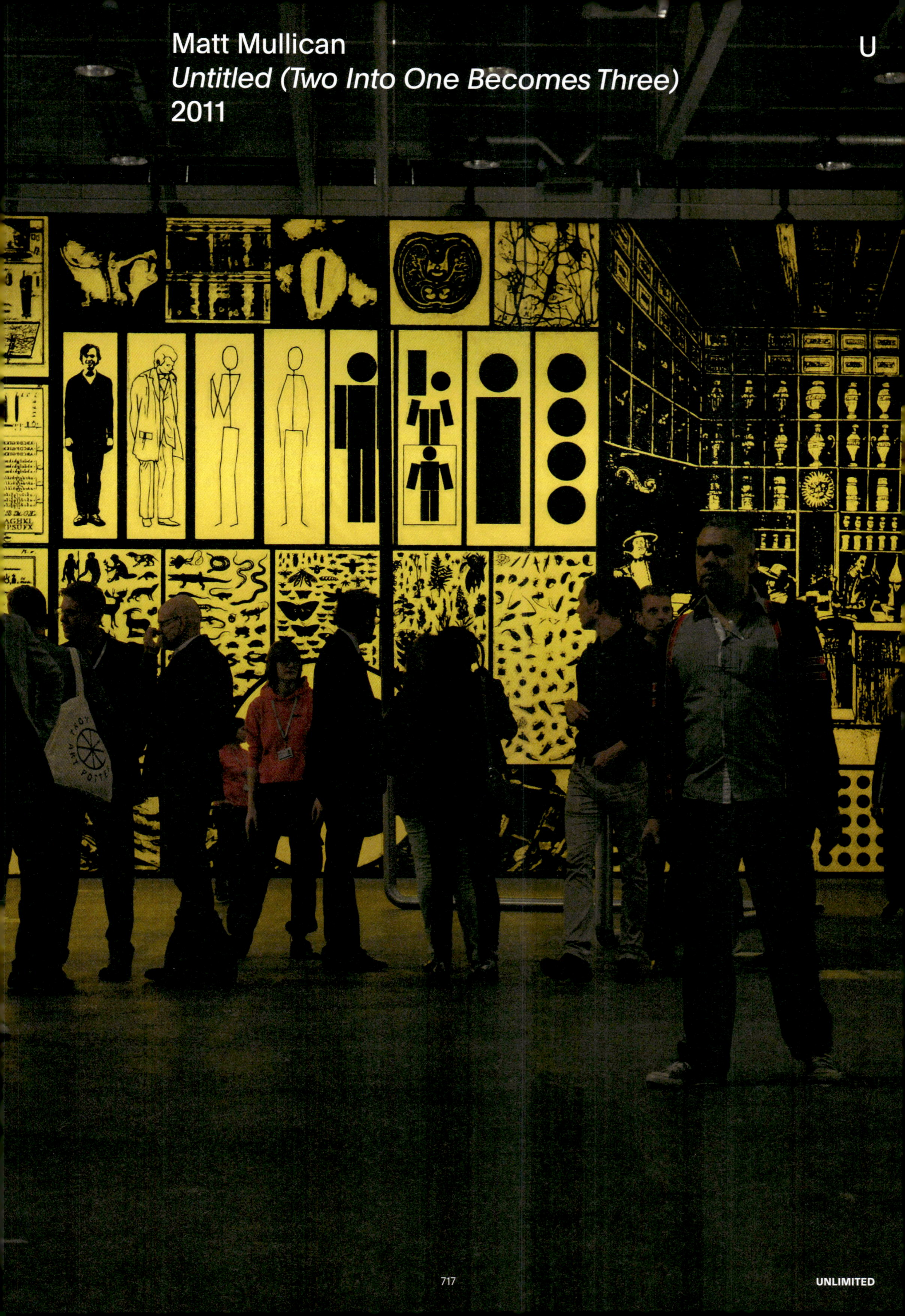

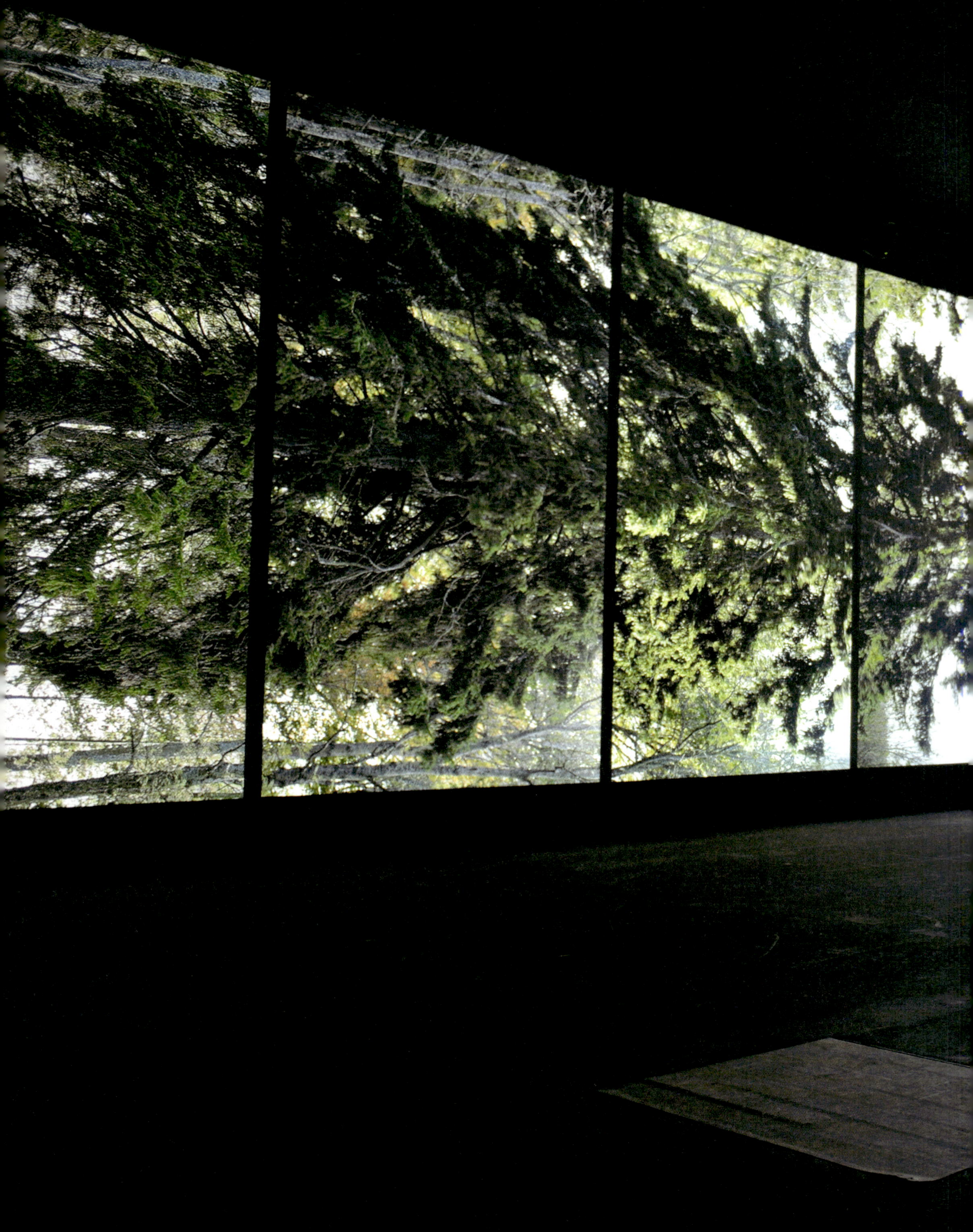

Eija-Liisa Ahtila
Horizontal (Vaakasuora)
2011

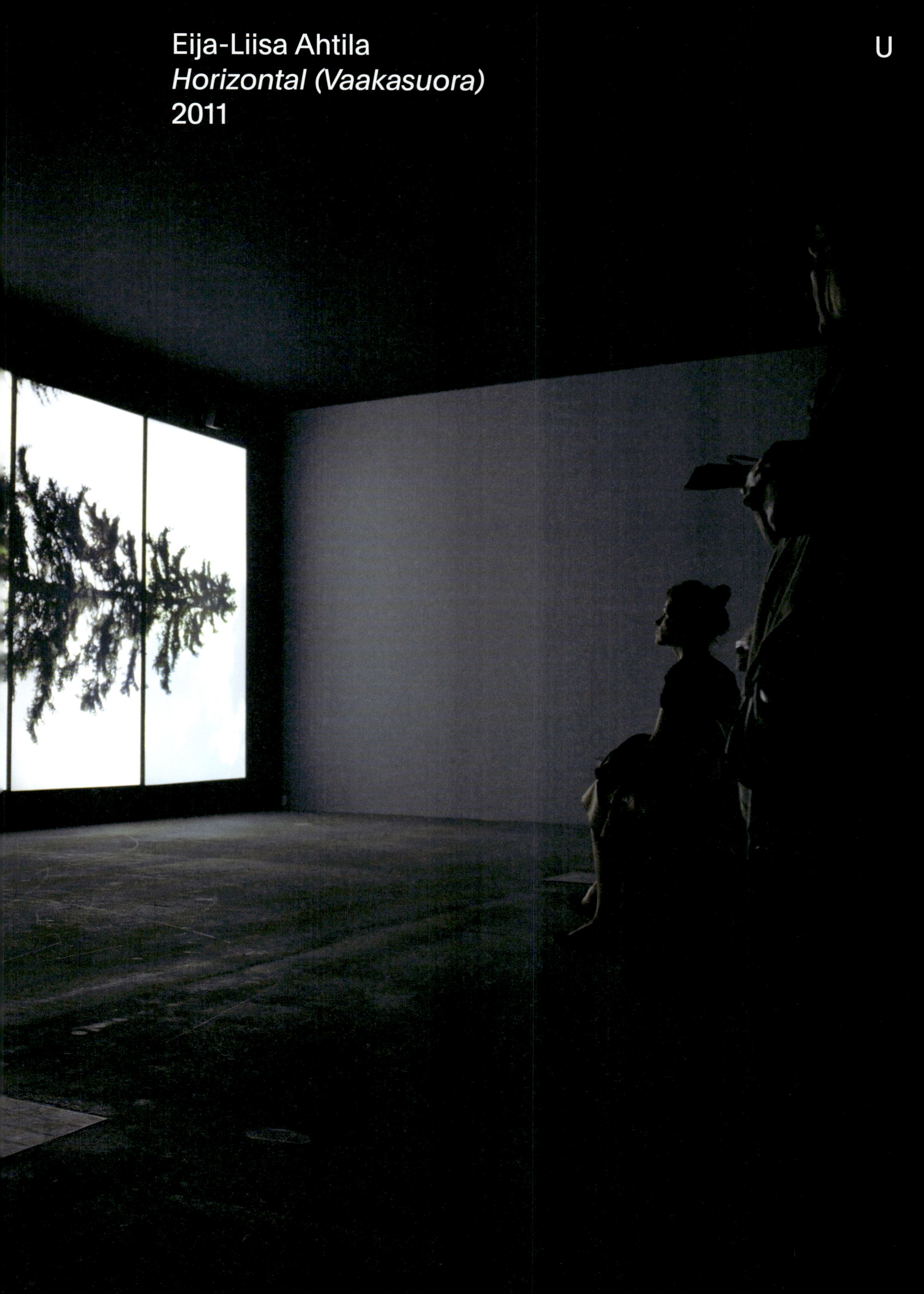

Sean Landers
Moby Dick (Merrilees)
2013

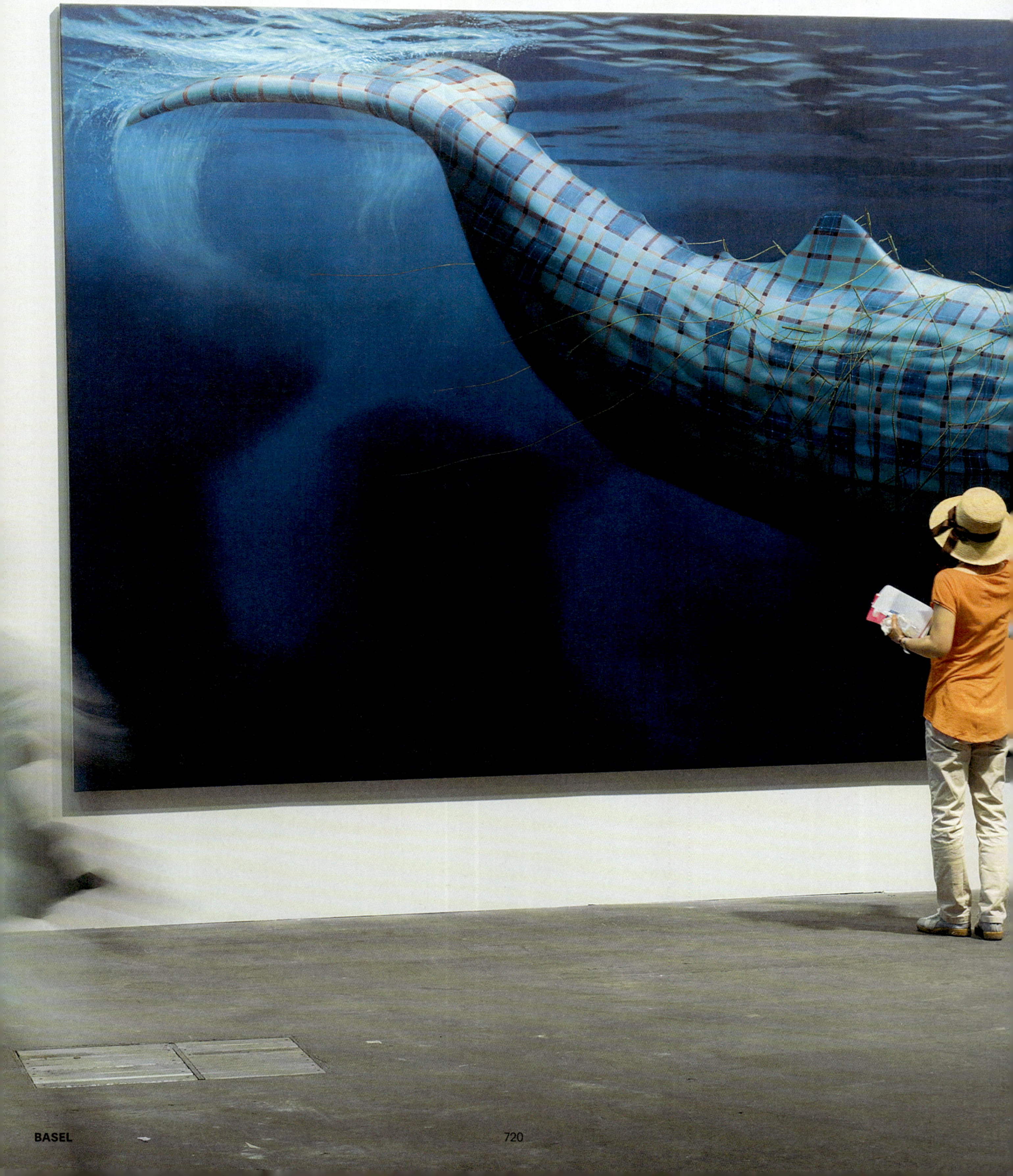

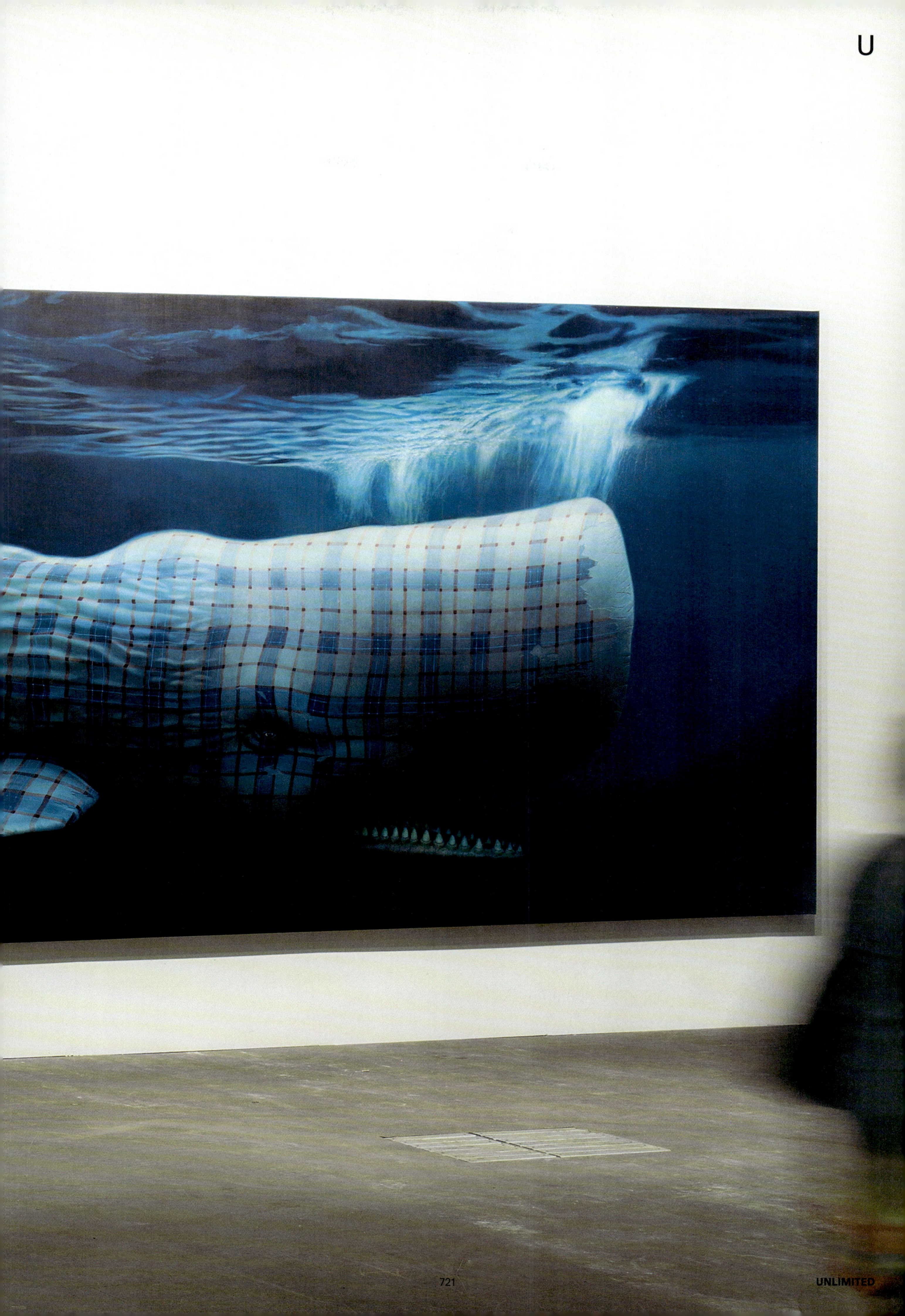

U

Latifa Echakhch
Horse & Figure
2012

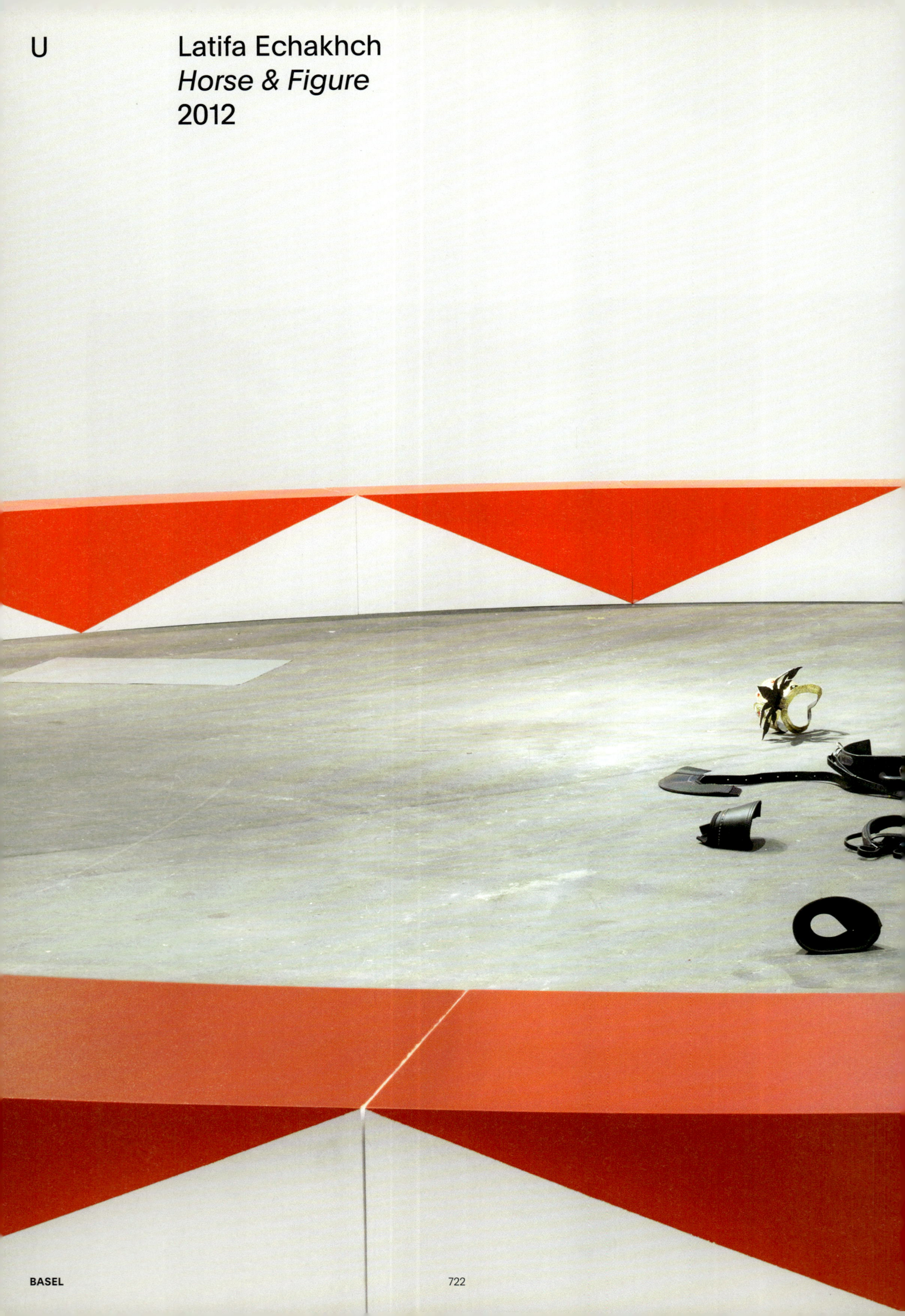

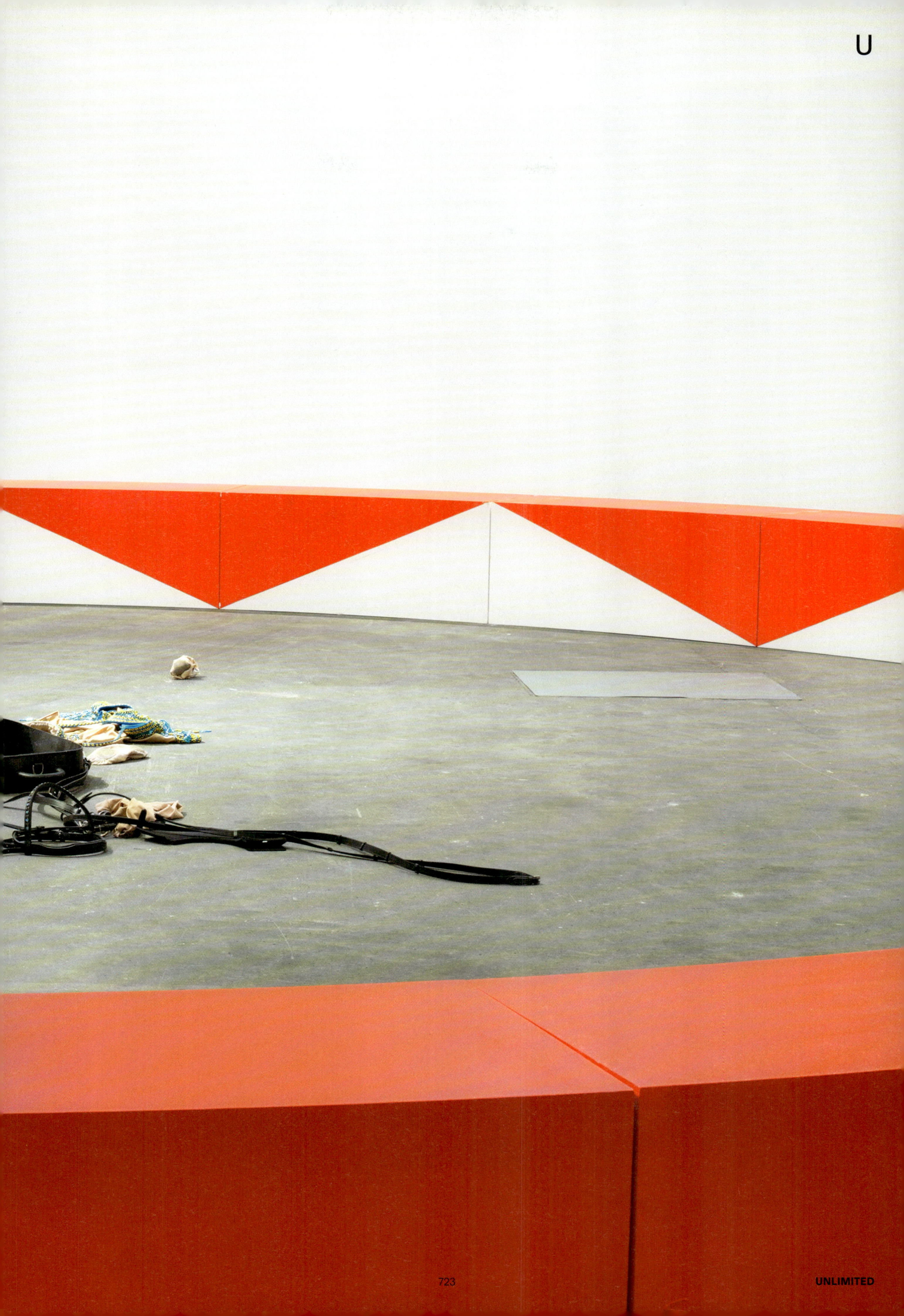

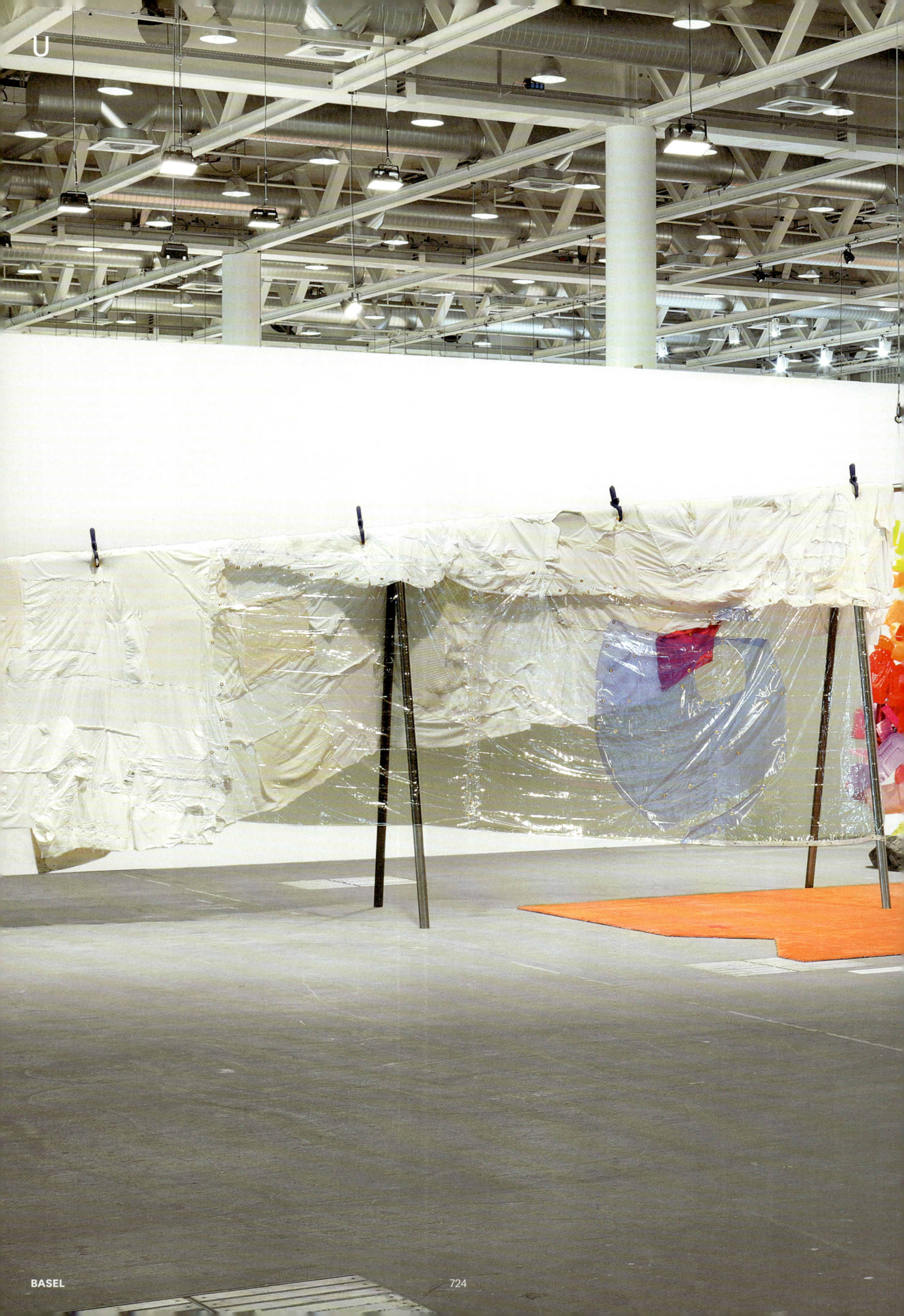

Jessica Stockholder
Wide Eyes Smeared Here Dear
2009

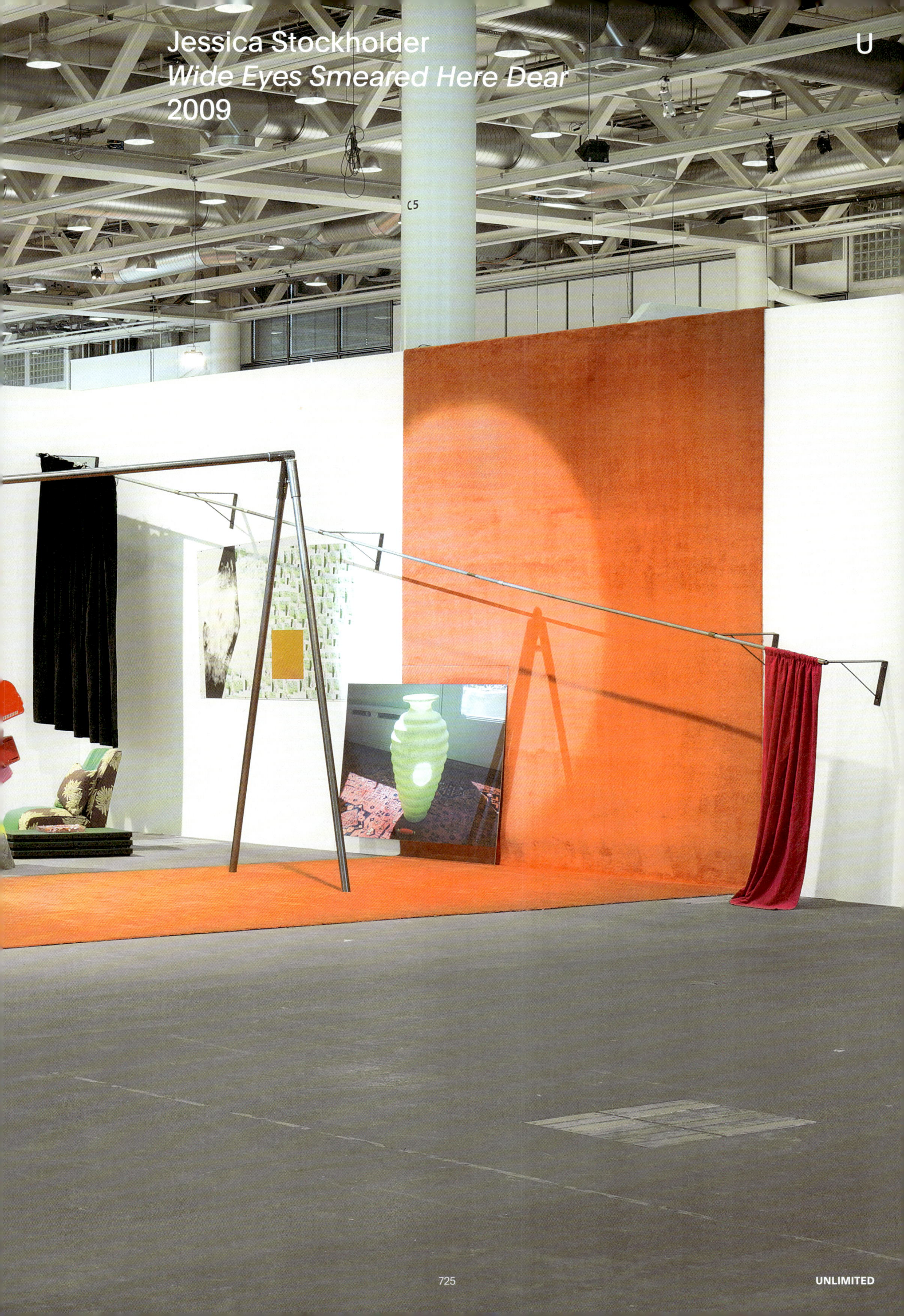

U

Peter Buggenhout
The Blind Leading the Blind/
What the Fuck . . . (Final State)
2009–2013

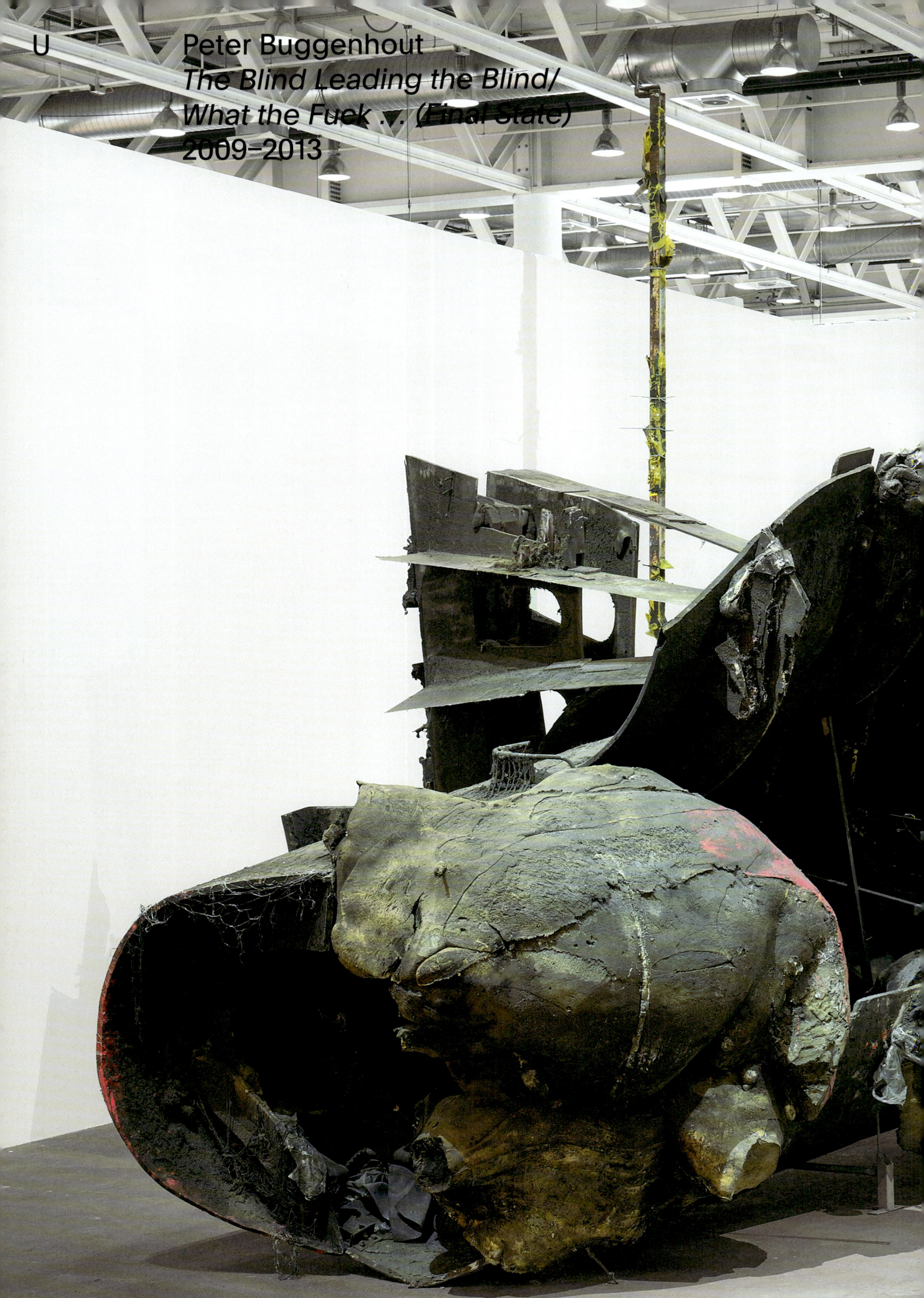

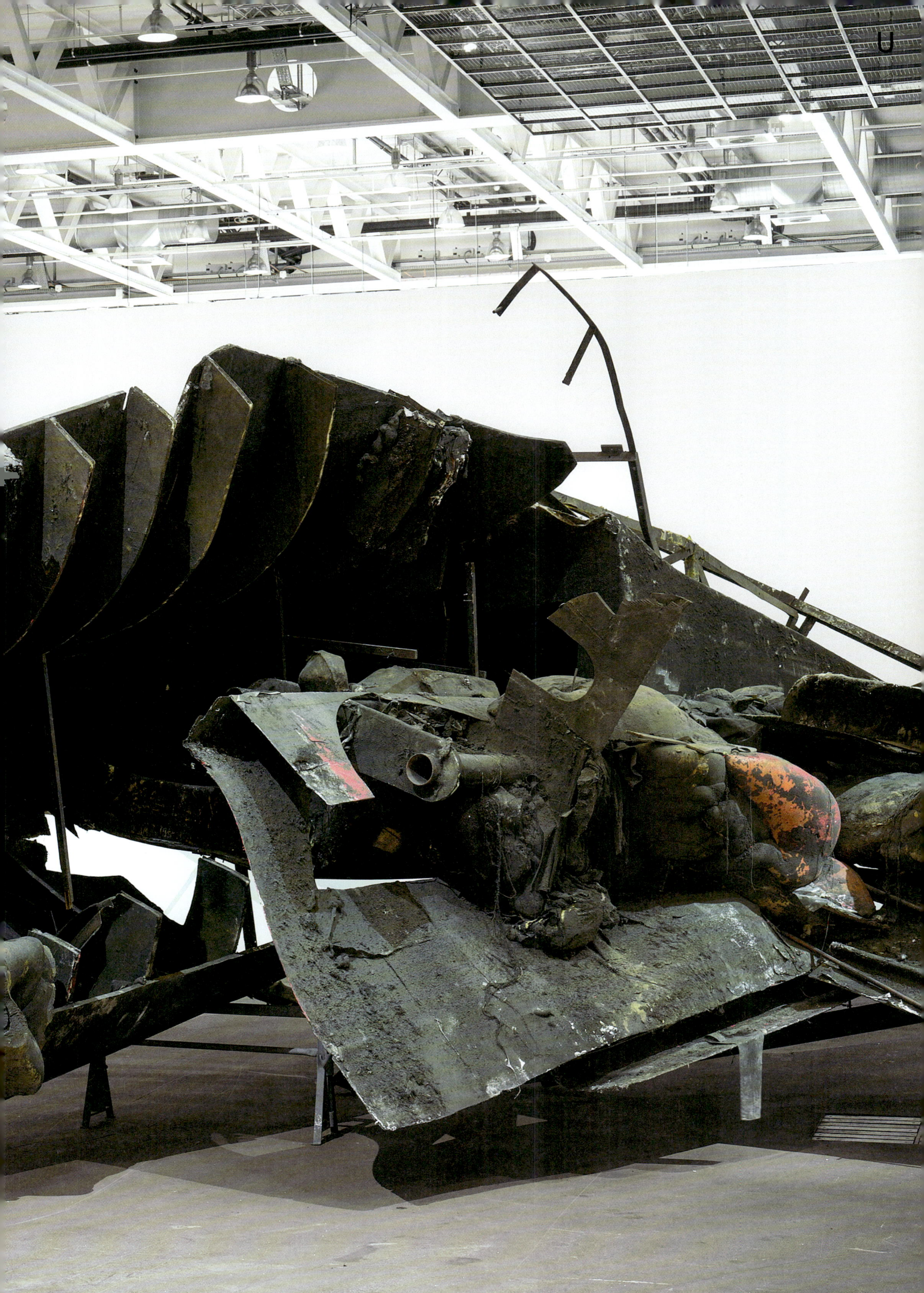

Chiharu Shiota
In Silence
2013

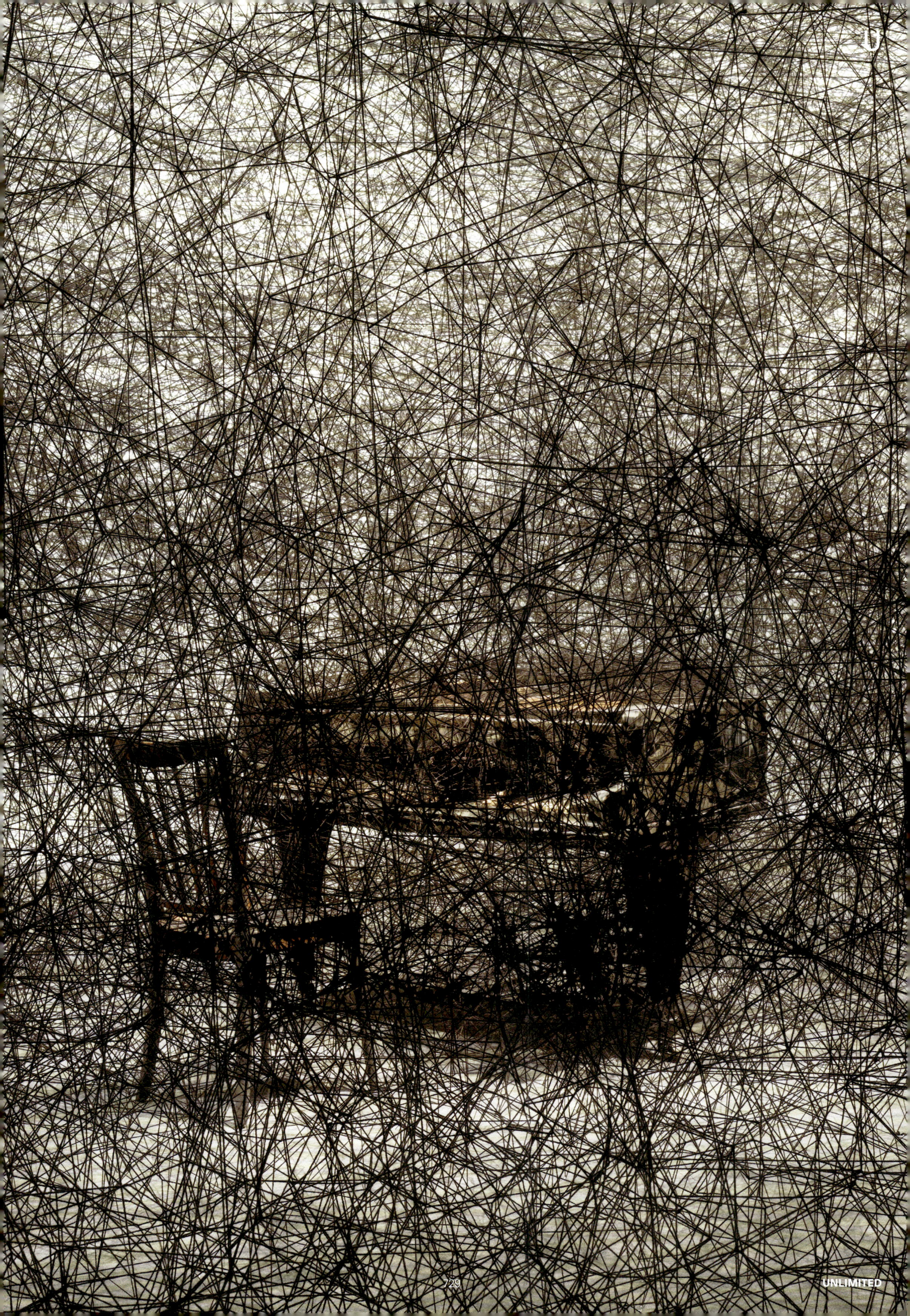

Chen Zhen
Purification Room
2000

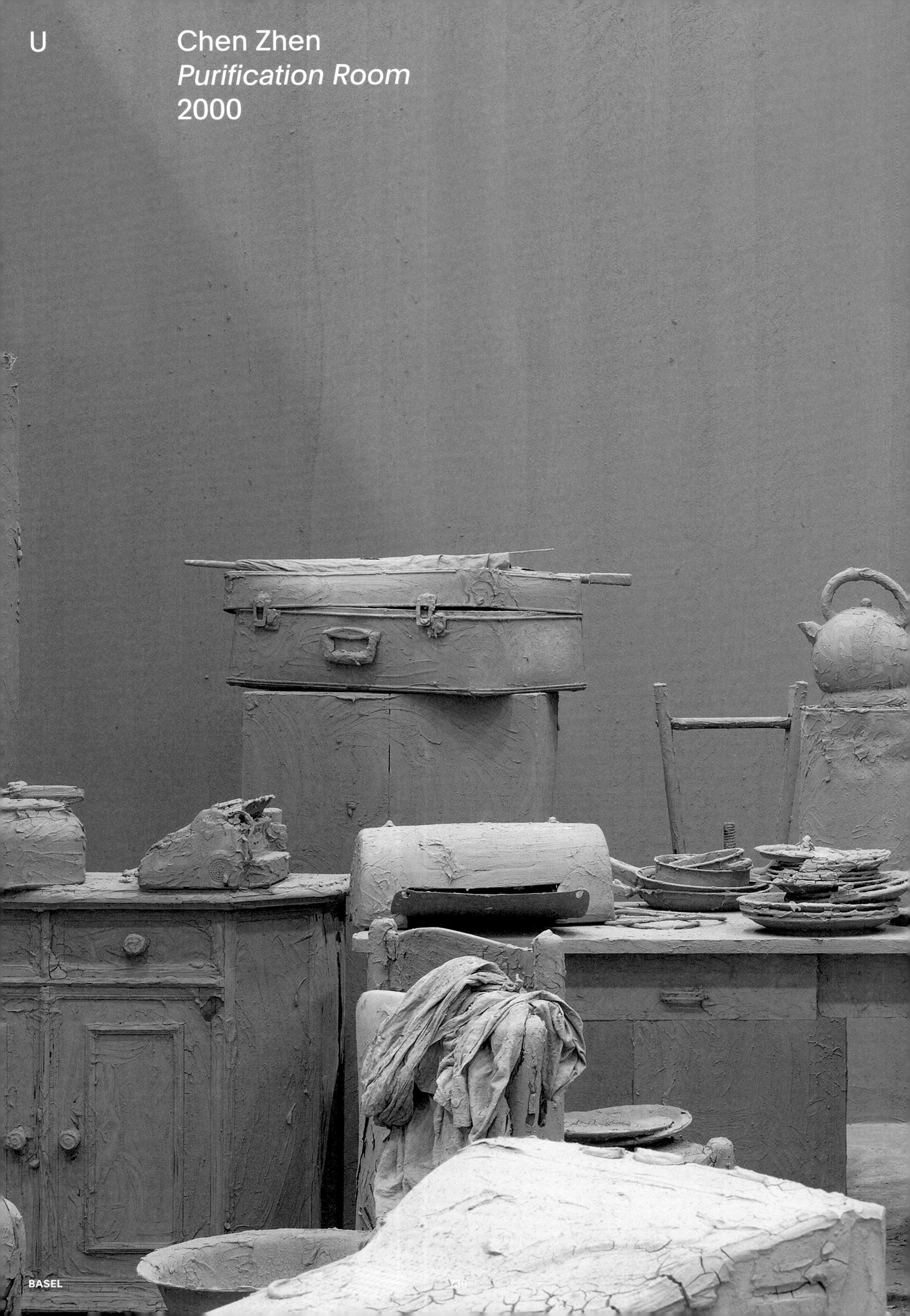

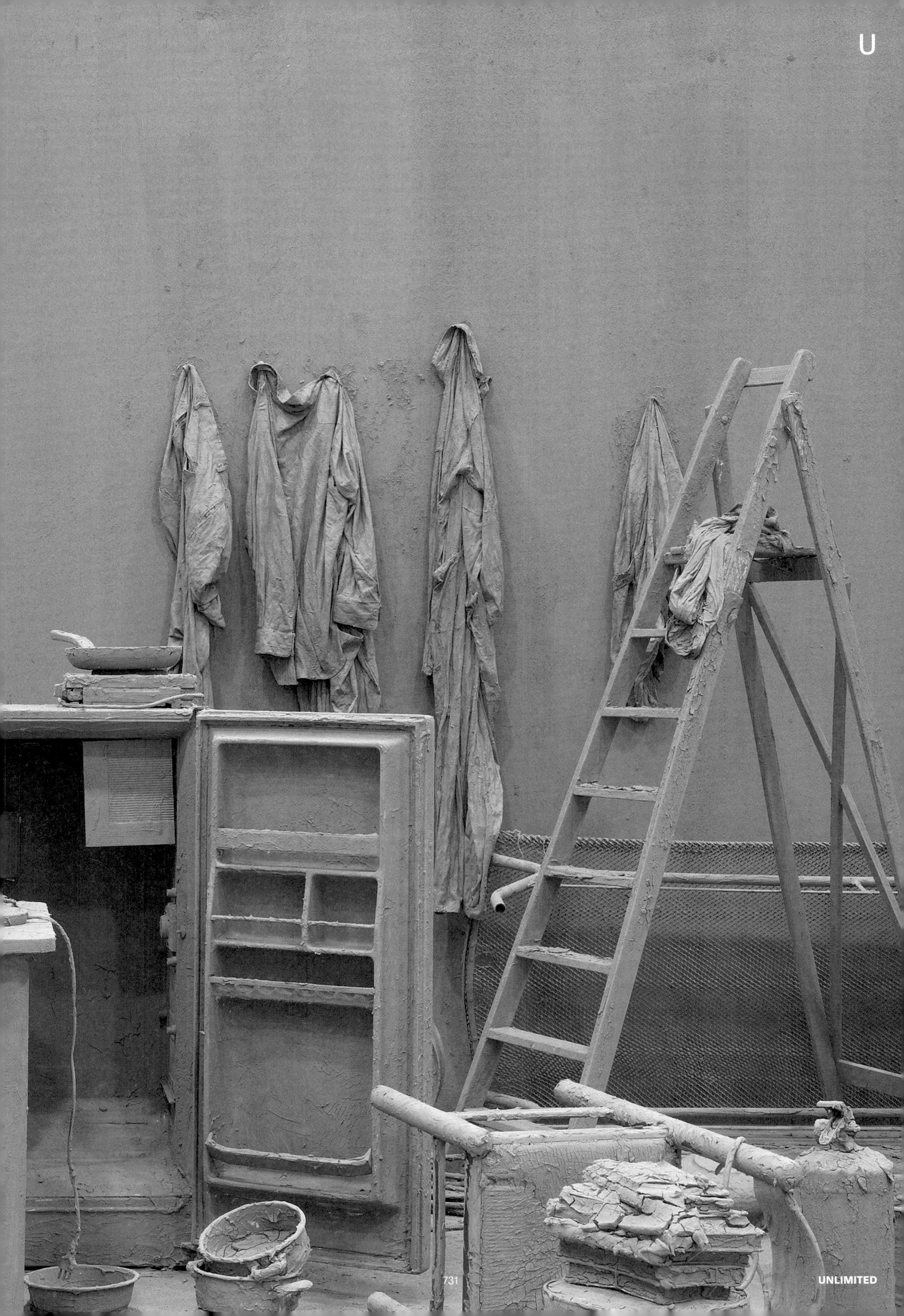

Ai Weiwei
Fairytale
2007

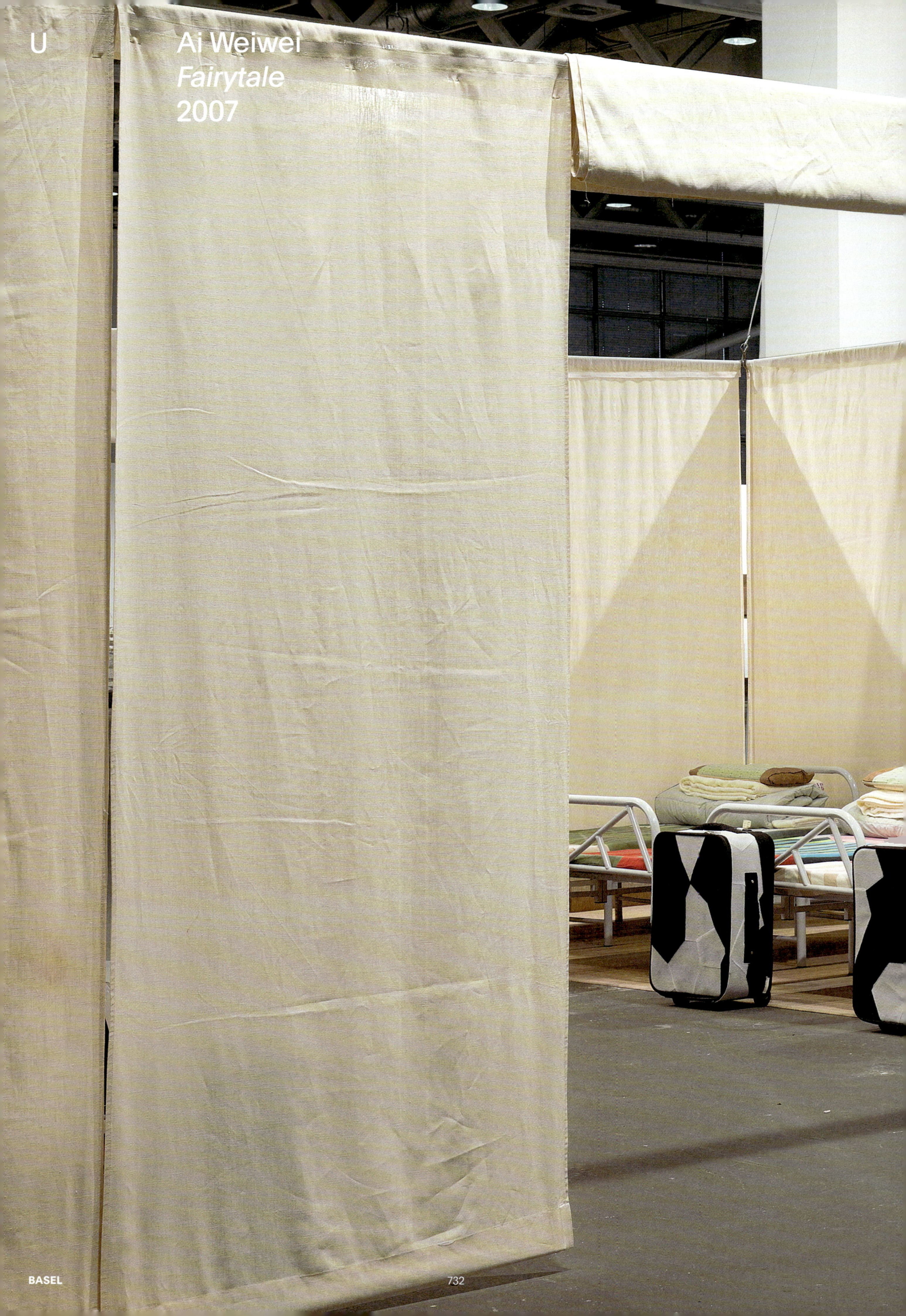

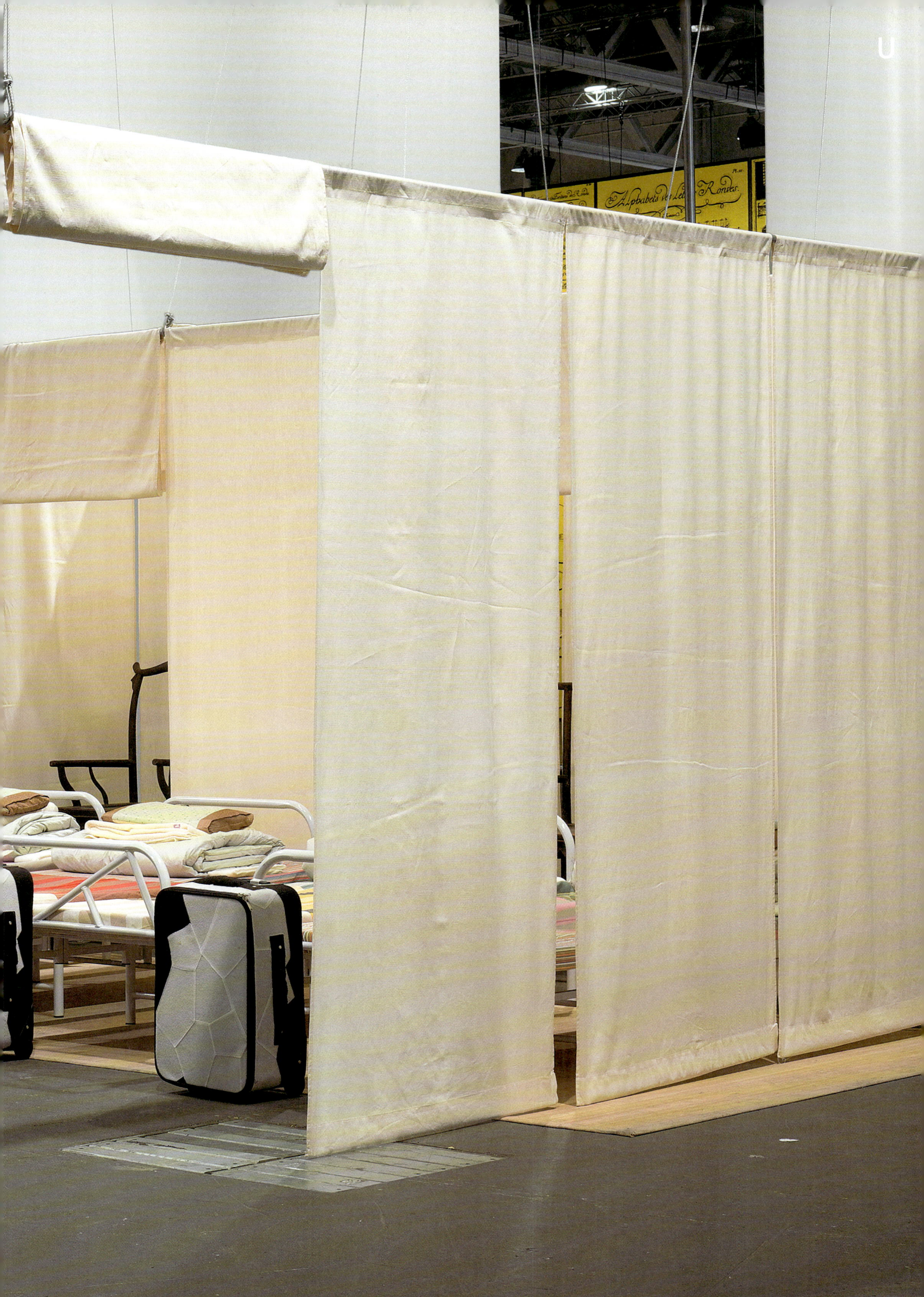

Rob Pruitt
Us
2013

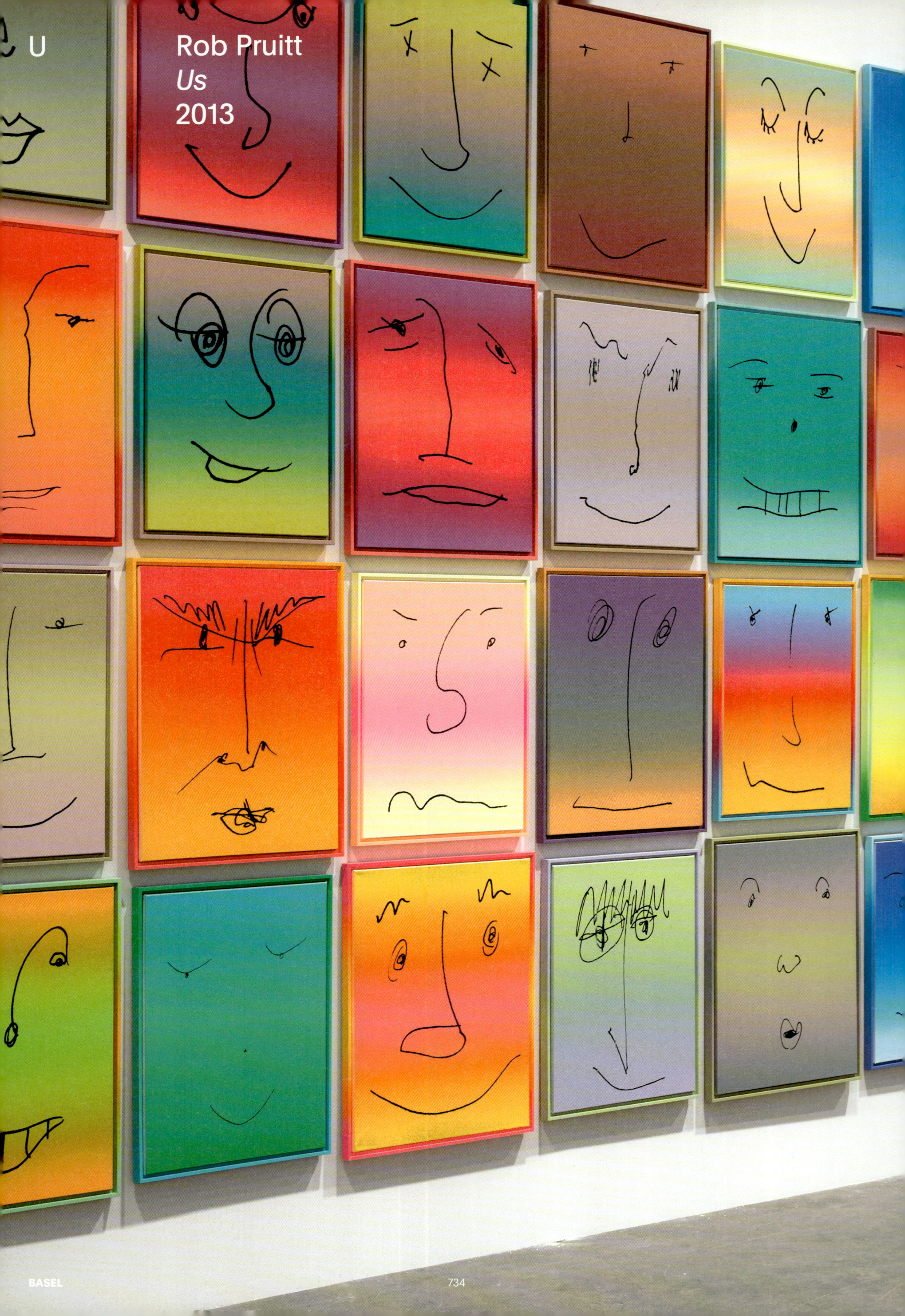

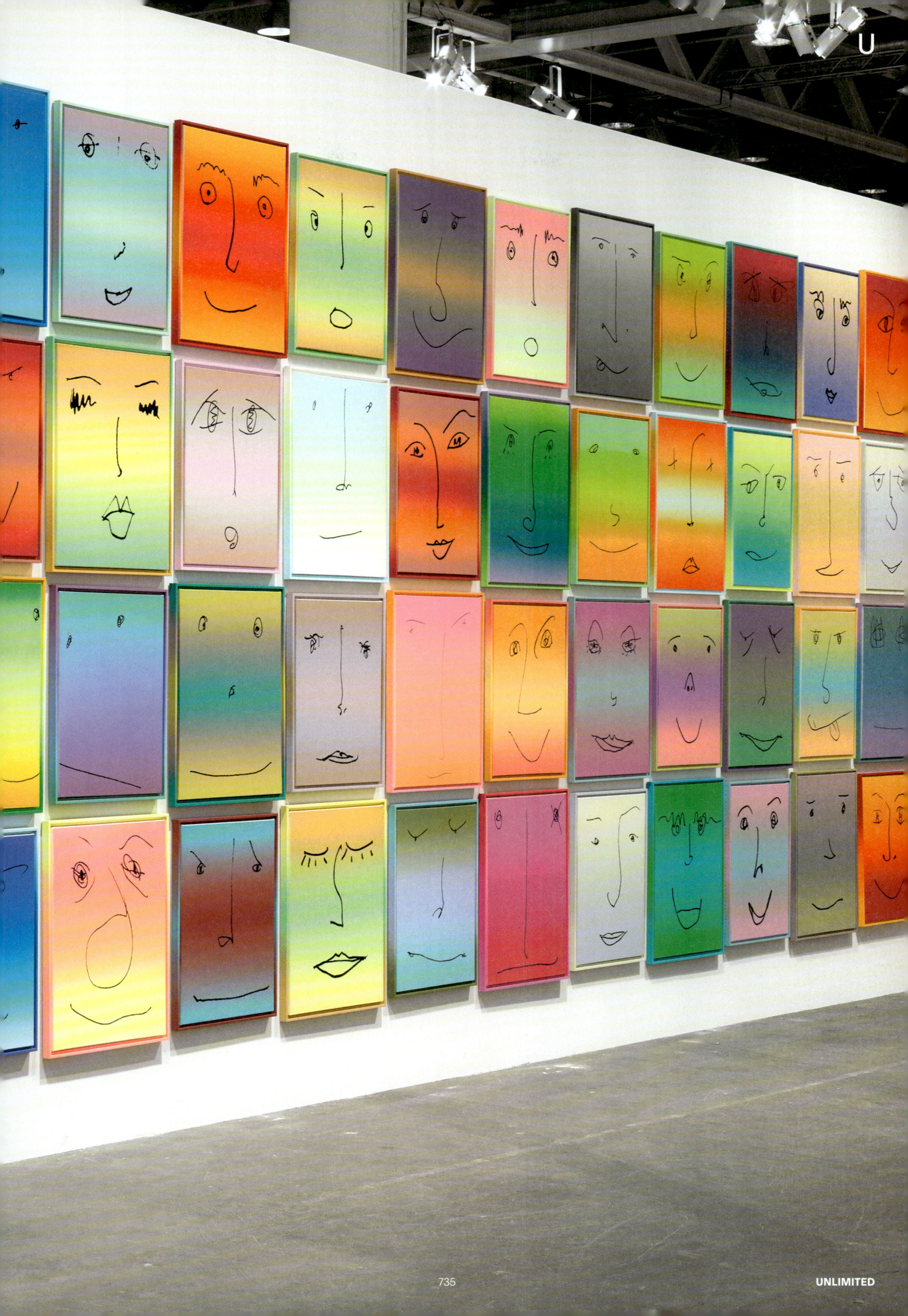

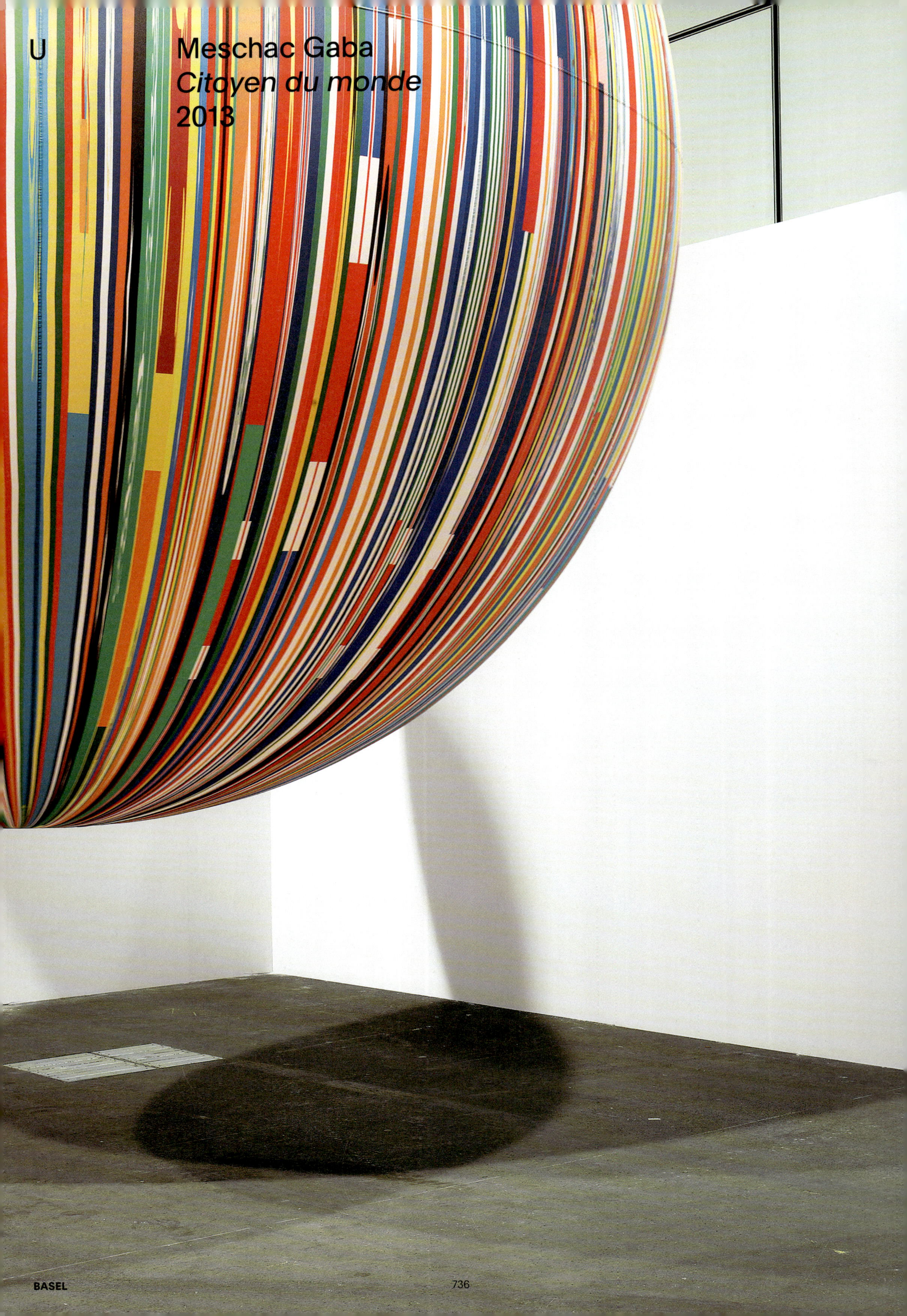

U

Meschac Gaba
Citoyen du monde
2013

V

- Hong Kong
- Basel
- Miami Beach

M.F. Husain
Ram Kumar
Tyeb Mehta
A Ramachandran
SH Raza
Ravinder Reddy
Gulammohammed Sheikh
Arpita Singh
Praneet Soi
FN Souza
Hema Upadhyay

Vadehra

New Delhi
London

Galleries

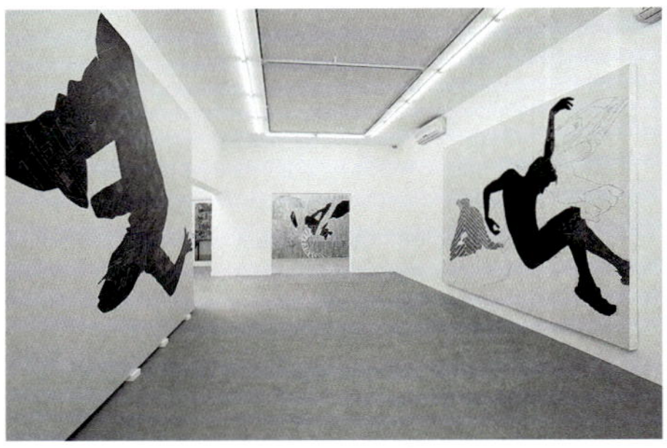

What first compelled you to open a gallery?
The realization that while art production in India was very strong in the 20th century, there was a need to build art institutions to promote and support it. The Vadehra Art Gallery opened in the late 1980s when there was a drop in public sector support for the visual arts and a nascent art industry developed by private players. We were the first to step into this changing scene and develop an art institution that has sustained and promoted modern and contemporary Indian art for more than 25 years now.

Who is the first artist you showed and what was most memorable about that show?
M. F. Husain, India's leading post-Independence modern artist, was one of the earliest people to exhibit at the Vadehra Art Gallery. One of the most significant shows we supported was convincing the public institution, the National Gallery of Modern Art in New Delhi, to hold the first ever solo exhibition of a living artist. Titled *Let History Cut Across Me Without Me*, the exhibition was a grand gesture. With one sweep M. F. Husain's monumental paintings took stock of the 20th century, playing with irreverent ease and facility with its icons, symbols, and mythologies.

When did you first participate in Art Basel and what was most memorable about that show?
Hong Kong in 2012 was our first participation. We really appreciated how well organized the fair was.

- **Contact** Vadehra Art Gallery
  Vidya Shivadas
  vidyashivadas@vadehraart.com
  art@vadehraart.com
- **Established** 1987
- **Owner(s) / Partner(s)** Arun Vadehra
  Roshini Vadehra
  Parul Vadehra
- **Team** 20
- **Space(s)** 500 m²
- **Artists at Art Basel** Faiza Butt
  Anju Dodiya
  Atul Dodiya
  Shilpa Gupta
  Zakkir Hussain
  Juul Kraijer
  Nalini Malani
  Jagannath Panda
- **Further artists represented** Manjit Bawa
  Atul Bhalla
  Rameshwar Broota
  Sunil Gupta

Van de Weghe

New York

Galleries
Galleries

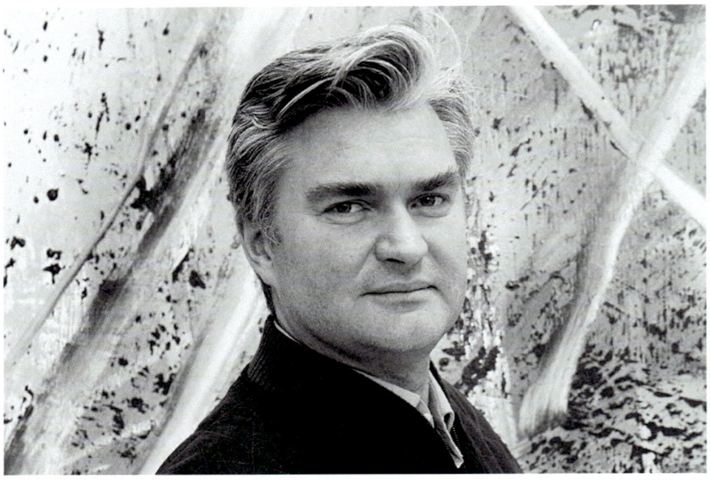

What first compelled you to open a gallery?
I studied the history of art and loved the idea of being in a business where I would be surrounded by art.

Who is the first artist you showed and what was most memorable about that show?
As a secondary market gallery, I don't represent artists, but I was interested in Basquiat in the early 1990s, and the first time I sold a Basquiat was in 1993; it was a very exciting moment

When did you first participate in Art Basel and what was most memorable about that show?
My first participation at Art Basel was in 2007. What was most memorable was the high quality of the fair.

- **Contact** Van de Weghe Fine Art
  Pierre Ravelle-Chapuis
  pierre@vdwny.com
  info@vdwny.com
- **Established** 1999
- **Owner(s) / Partner(s)** Christophe Van de Weghe
- **Team** 4.5
- **Space(s)** 200 m²
- **Artists at Art Basel** Jean-Michel Basquiat
  Alexander Calder
  Salvador Dalí
  Jean Dubuffet
  Duane Hanson
  Donald Judd
  Roy Lichtenstein
  René Magritte
  Henri Matisse
  Pablo Picasso
  Richard Prince
  Gerhard Richter
  Mark Rothko
  Ed Ruscha
  Frank Stella
  Cy Twombly
  Andy Warhol

Van Doren Waxter

New York

Galleries
Kabinett

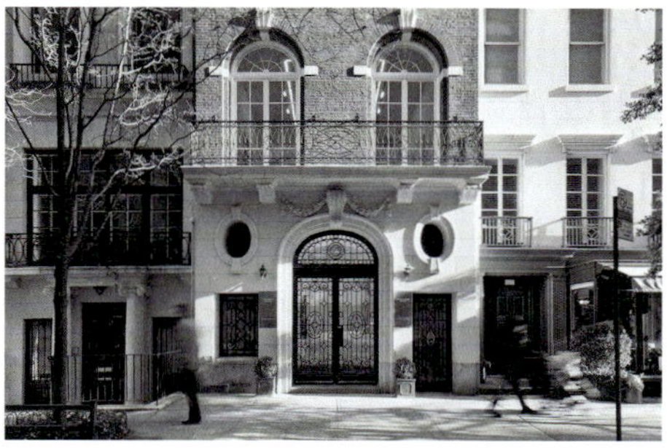

What first compelled you to open a gallery?
Good and trustworthy partners and the Estate of Richard Diebenkorn. We have built on that beginning by showing a number of Californian artists, both living and deceased.

Who is the first artist you showed and what was most memorable about that show?
Richard Diebenkorn was our first show and the works were from the *Ocean Park* series. We could not hope to have such a show again as the material is simply not available. We had seven large canvases.

When did you first participate in Art Basel and what was most memorable about that show?
In 2002. There was tremendous excitement about the debut of the show in the US and great spirit of recovery following 2001.

- **Contact** Van Doren Waxter
  Dorsey Waxter
  dorsey@vandorenwaxter.com
  liz@vandorenwaxter.com
- **Established** 1999
- **Owner(s) / Partner(s)** John Van Doren (Owner)
  Dorsey Waxter (Partner)
- **Space(s)** 276 m²
- **Artists at Art Basel** Lee Bontecou
  James Brooks
  John Chamberlain
  Richard Diebenkorn
  Sam Francis
  Helen Frankenthaler
  Al Held
  Ellsworth Kelly
  John McLaughlin
  Robert Motherwell
  Richard Pousette-Dart
  Dorothea Rockburne
  Alan Shields
  David Smith
  Frank Stella

van Orsouw

Zurich

Galleries

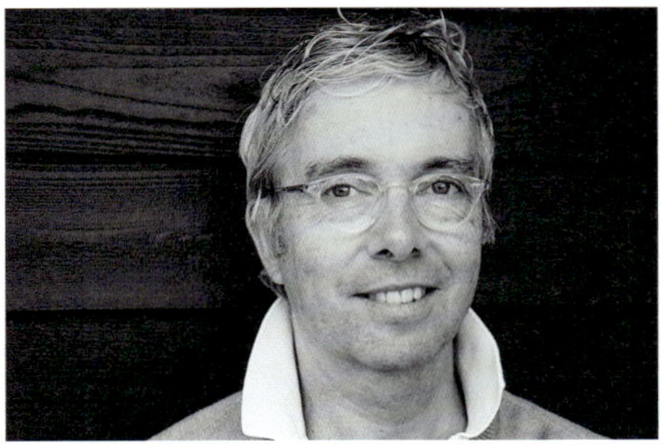

What first compelled you to open a gallery?
Passion, fascination, and curiosity in art.

Who is the first artist you showed and what was most memorable about that show?
The Swiss artist Albrecht Schnider, with whom I still work after 25 years. We showed wonderful black chalk drawings and watercolors and I sold a few. During the show I got to know a Zurich-based collector in a restaurant and gave him my business card. The next morning he visited me, looked around, and said: "hmmm, hmm … so you already sold some." I was very proud of my sales. Afterward he said: "Get your calculator and make me a good price, I'll take the rest!" He became a friend and is still an art collector.

When did you first participate in Art Basel and what was most memorable about that show?
In 1992, after four years of having my gallery. Most of my artists came and helped, and we did the whole transport ourselves with a small van. For all of us this was a premiere and the beginning of a new decade.

- **Contact** Galerie Bob van Orsouw
  Stefanie Zangerl
  stefanie@bobvanorsouw.ch
  mail@bobvanorsouw.ch
- **Established** 1988
- **Owner(s) / Partner(s)** Bob van Orsouw
- **Space(s)** 320 m²
- **Artists at Art Basel** Julia Dault
  Armen Eloyan
  Daido Moriyama
  Ernesto Neto
  Shirana Shahbazi
  Marcel van Eeden
  Ger van Elk
- **Further artists represented** Philip Akkerman
  Nobuyoshi Araki
  Hannah Greely
  Anton Henning
  Teresa Hubbard/Alexander Birchler
  Agnieszka Kurant
  Lutz & Guggisberg
  Paul Morrison
  Muntean/Rosenblum
  Julian Opie
  Walter Pfeiffer
  Albrecht Schnider
  Bernard Voïta

Vavassori

Milan

Statements
Unlimited

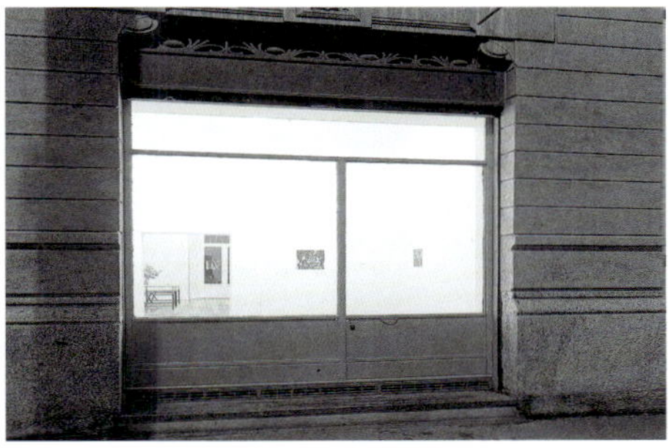

What first compelled you to open a gallery?
The lack of young galleries in Milan. A kind of generational void.

Who is the first artist you showed and what was most memorable about that show?
The first exhibition was a group show titled *Burrata*. Everybody loves burrata. It's so soft and puffy, a sort of goofy mozzarella. There's a whole world in it.

When did you first participate in Art Basel and what was most memorable about that show?
The gallery participated in Art Basel in June 2013, in the Statements and Unlimited sectors. A truly mind-blowing experience.

- **Contact** Federico Vavassori
  federico@vava-milano.com
  info@vava-milano.com
- **Established** 2011
- **Owner(s) / Partner(s)** Federico Vavassori
- **Team** 2
- **Space(s)** 40 m²
- **Artists at Art Basel** Greg Parma Smith
- **Further artists represented** Rossana Buremi
  Caleb Considine
  Emil Michael Klein
  Kaspar Müller
  Max Hooper Schneider

Vermelho

São Paulo ● Galleries

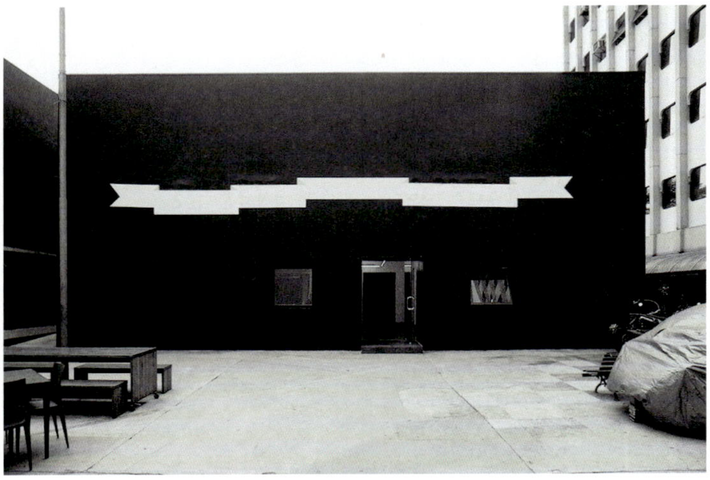

What first compelled you to open a gallery?
Eduardo Brandão was an art teacher at the university and had a small art school.

When did you first participate in Art Basel and what was most memorable about that show?
In 2005.

- **Contact** Vermelho
  Akio Aoki
  akio@galeriavermelho.com.br
  info@galeriavermelho.com.br
- **Established** 2002
- **Owner(s) / Partner(s)** Eduardo Brandão (Artistic Director)
  Jan Fjeld (Finance Director)
  Eliana Finkelstein (Sales Director)
  Akio Aoki (Sales Director)
- **Team** 21
- **Space(s)** 1,200 m²
- **Artists at Art Basel** Chiara Banfi
  Rodrigo Braga
  Cadu
  Lia Chaia
  Marcelo Cidade
  Marilá Dardot
  Jonathas de Andrade
  Detanico Lain
  Enrique Jezik
  André Komatsu
  Dora Longo Bahia
  Cinthia Marcelle
  Odires Mlászho
  Guilherme Peters
  Rosângela Rennó
  Nicolás Robbio
  Daniel Senise
- **Further artists represented** Gabriela Albergaria
  Claudia Andujar
  Ivan Argote
  Rafael Assef
  Nicolás Bacal
  Cia Da Foto
  Maurício Dias/Walter Riedweg
  Chelpa Ferro
  Carmela Gross
  Maurício Ianês
  Clara Ianni
  João Loureiro
  Leya Mira Brander
  Fabio Morais
  Gisela Motta/Leandro Lima
  Ana Maria Tavares
  Carla Zaccagnini

Verna

Zurich ● Galleries

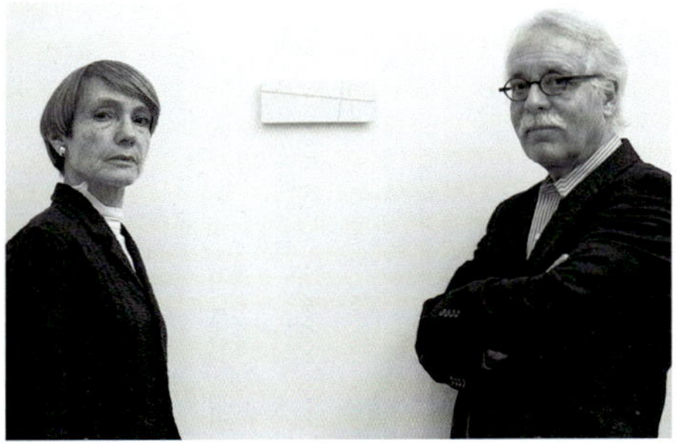

What first compelled you to open a gallery?
To offer a space to the artists.

Who is the first artist you showed and what was most memorable about that show?
Antonio Calderara (1903–1978) and Fred Sandback (1943–2003). Fred Sandback transformed our space into a sculpture.

When did you first participate in Art Basel and what was most memorable about that show?
In 1971. It inspired us to exhibit in Basel every following year.

- **Contact** Annemarie Verna Galerie
  Gianfranco Verna
  office@annemarie-verna.ch
- **Established** 1969
- **Owner(s) / Partner(s)** Annemarie Verna
  Gianfranco Verna
- **Team** 3
- **Space(s)** 100 m²
- **Artists at Art Basel** James Bishop
  Antonio Calderara
  Andreas Christen
  Joseph Egan
  Dan Flavin
  Richard Francisco
  Donald Judd
  Sol LeWitt
  Robert Mangold
  Agnes Martin
  Rita McBride
  Mario Merz
  Ree Morton
  Giulio Paolini
  Sylvia Plimack Mangold
  David Rabinowitch
  Glen Rubsamen
  Fred Sandback
  Richard Tuttle
  Robert Wilson
  Jerry Zeniuk

Vielmetter

Los Angeles ● Galleries

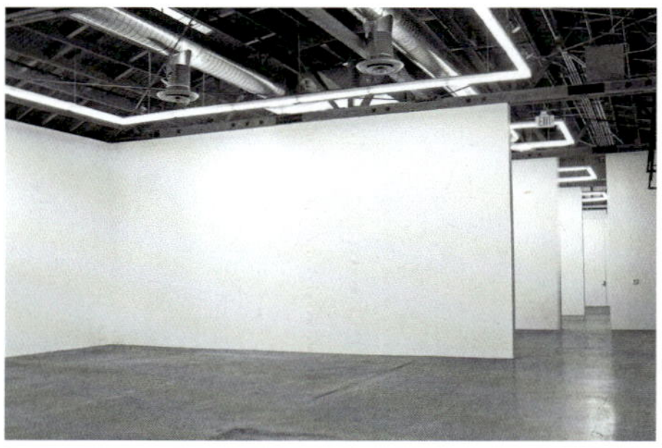

What first compelled you to open a gallery?
I have always been interested in the intersection between visual art and language—and I see the gallery as a place where that intersection is a daily reality. I think that language can make a visual event that is in itself untranslatable, more accessible, and help the viewer to appreciate a work. When I came to Los Angeles I was fascinated with the richly diverse art scene here; opening a gallery to reflect this vibrant cultural reality felt both very exciting and relevant.

Who is the first artist you showed and what was most memorable about that show?

One of the first artists we showed was Tam Van Tran, who was the first artist of my program to be included in the Whitney Biennial two years later.

When did you first participate in Art Basel and what was most memorable about that show?

We first participated in Art Basel in Miami Beach in 2003 and have been participating in this fair ever since. 2014 is an important year for us, as we will for the first time participate at Art Basel in Hong Kong and in Basel. During our first presentation at Art Basel in Miami Beach we showed a sculpture by Rodney McMillian that caused quite a stir. It was a dilapidated chair that the artist had found on the street, and we had it professionally crated and shipped with an art shipper to the fair. It was priced at $2,800, and sold to an important collector in Germany, but visitors to the fair could not quite get their head around the fact that the artist had not "done" anything to the chair other than finding it.

- **Contact** Susanne Vielmetter Los Angeles Projects, Kevin Scholl, kevin@vielmetter.com, info@vielmetter.com
- **Established** 2000
- **Owner(s) / Partner(s)** Susanne Vielmetter
- **Space(s)** 800 m²
- **Artists at Art Basel** Andrea Bowers, Nicole Eisenman, Rodney McMillian, Yunhee Min, Wangechi Mutu
- **Further artists represented** Edgar Arceneaux, Whitney Bedford, Jedediah Caesar, Sean Duffy, Charles Gaines, Karl Haendel, Stanya Kahn, Raffi Kalenderian, Jutta Koether, Olga Koumoundouros, Shana Lutker, Dave McKenzie, Martin McMurray, Elizabeth Neel, Ruben Ochoa, Mary Reid Kelley, Steve Roden, Amy Sillman, Joel Tauber, Mickalene Thomas, Nicola Tyson, Monique van Genderen, Tam Van Tran, Patrick Wilson

Vilma Gold

London ● Nova

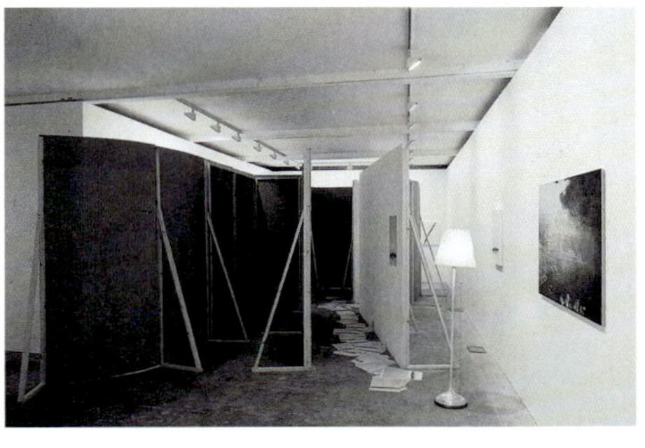

What first compelled you to open a gallery?

The artists' work around me at the time.

Who is the first artist you showed and what was most memorable about that show?

Mark Titchner. Mark's ambition.

When did you first participate in Art Basel and what was most memorable about that show?

In 2006.

- **Contact** Vilma Gold, Martin Rasmussen, martin@vilmagold.com, laura@vilmagold.com
- **Established** 2000
- **Owner(s) / Partner(s)** Rachel Williams
- **Team** 5
- **Space(s)** 3,000 m²
- **Artists at Art Basel** Charles Atlas
- **Further artists represented** Trisha Baga, KP Brehmer, Nicholas Byrne, William Daniels, Vladimir Dubossarsky & Alexander Vinogradov, Michaela Eichwald, Felix Gmelin, Brian Griffiths, HobbypopMUSEUM, Alan Michael, Oliver Osborne, Karthik Pandian, Luther Price, Stephen G. Rhodes, Hannah Sawtell, Markus Selg, Josef Strau, Mark Titchner, Sophie von Hellermann, Julia Wachtel, Jennifer West

Vistamare

Pescara ● Feature

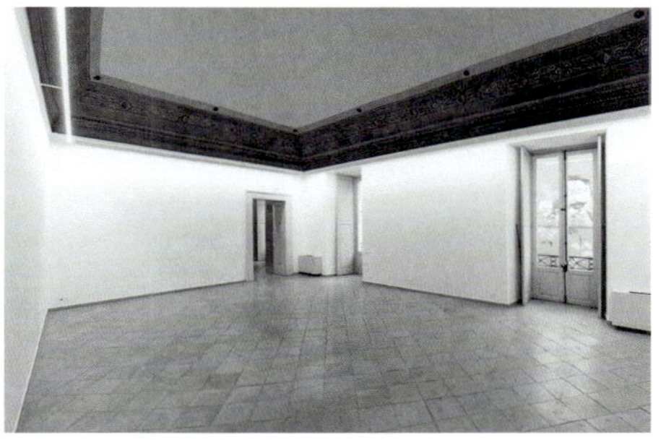

What first compelled you to open a gallery?

Just myself.

Who is the first artist you showed and what was most memorable about that show?

A group show titled *Camera Italia*: 10 Italian artists were invited. The three permanent installations by Enzo Cucchi, Alberto Garutti, and Ettore Spalletti were the most memorable things about the show.

When did you first participate in Art Basel and what was most memorable about that show?

The first participation was in 2013. The most memorable thing was the high level of the organization and the great competence of the collectors.

- **Contact** Vistamare, Arianna Chiriatti, info@vistamare.com
- **Established** 2001
- **Owner(s) / Partner(s)** Benedetta Spalletti
- **Team** 4
- **Space(s)** 500 m²
- **Artists at Art Basel** Pedro Barateiro, Bethan Huws, Joseph Kosuth
- **Further artists represented** Mario Airò, Rosa Barba, Simone Berti, Pavel Büchler, Anna Franceschini, Mimmo Jodice, Armin Linke, Sanna Marander, Ettore Spalletti, Haim Steinbach, Grazia Toderi

Vitamin

Guangzhou — Galleries
Beijing — Galleries

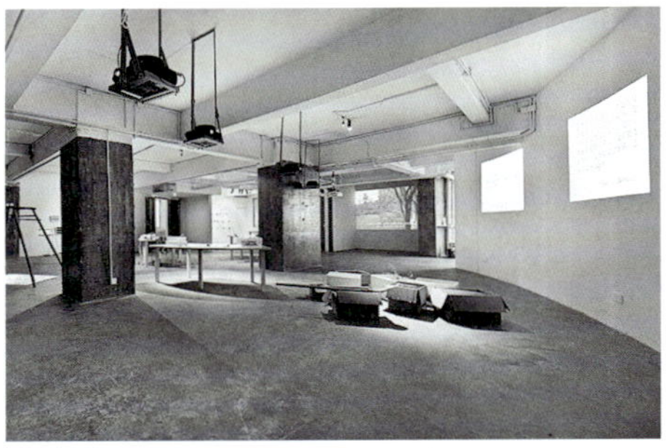

What first compelled you to open a gallery?
The memory of Hans Van Dijk.

When did you first participate in Art Basel and what was most memorable about that show?
In 2007.

- **Contact** Vitamin Creative Space
  Chuan Yan
  brookeyan
  @vitamincreativespace.com
  mail@vitamincreativespace.com
- **Established** 2002
- **Artists at Art Basel** Lee Kit
  Koki Tanaka
  Zhou Tao
- **Further artists represented** Cao Fei
  Heman Chong
  Chu Yun
  Duan Jianyu
  Jun Yang
  Firenze Lai
  Hao Liang
  Ming Wong
  Pak Sheung Chuen
  Xu Tan
  Yangjiang Group
  Zheng Guogu

Volte

Mumbai — Galleries

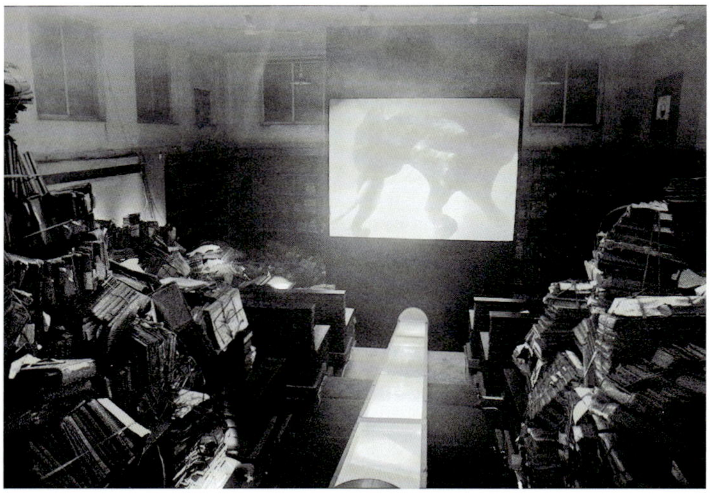

What first compelled you to open a gallery?
I had always been passionate about contemporary art. After working in finance and the technology industries for a decade, I was unfulfilled and burnt out. I took some time off to connect with my real passions, and the first and obvious one was to spend more time in the art world. What better way than to start a gallery?

Who is the first artist you showed and what was most memorable about that show?
Ranbir Kaleka. The most memorable moment was when William Kentridge walked in and saw the show. He loved the show and the gallery, and agreed to do an exhibition with us, which happened in February this year.

When did you first participate in Art Basel and what was most memorable about that show?
My first participation in Art Basel was in Hong Kong in 2013. The most memorable moment was when a major installation of one of our artists was acquired after a two-minute conversation. We ordered a bottle of champagne and celebrated at the booth!

- **Contact** Volte Gallery
  Ameya Dias
  ameya@volte.in
  info@volte.in
- **Established** 2008
- **Owner(s) / Partner(s)** Tushar Jiwarajka
- **Team** 6
- **Space(s)** 300 m²
- **Artists at Art Basel** Sheba Chhachhi
  Wim Delvoye
  Ranbir Kaleka
  William Kentridge
  Raghava KK
- **Further artists represented** James Turrell

Vitamin Creative Space

Two Questions for Hu Fang

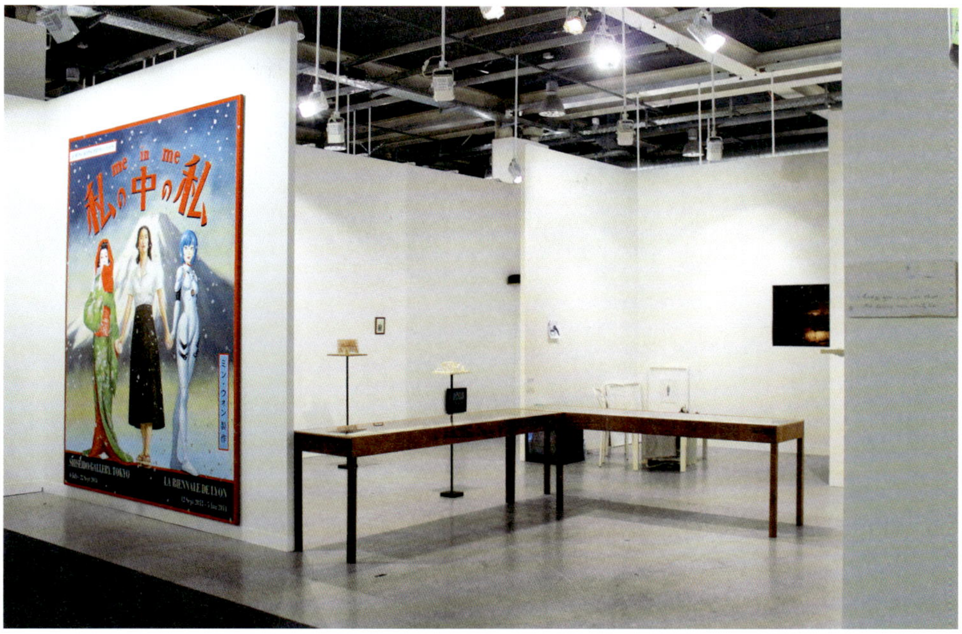

Art Basel in Basel, 2013

Founded in 2002, Vitamin Creative Space has acquired a major role on the Chinese artistic scene and in the current effervescence of the Asia-Pacific area, partly due to its double activities—commercial gallery and not-for-profit space. Could you define your specificity and describe the way you built your program?

To us, it is very important to focus on the artists' creative process, which represents the core of our space's practice and activities.

Given this direction for Vitamin Space, it is difficult to make any arrangements within our program in advance. The mode of working therefore is really organic, it follows the flows and we stay open to every encounter.

We take the creative process as a routine sensory training, from which a heightened sense emerges, which will generate vital energy. This energy, whenever there is an encounter with art, induces currents that drive a moment of intensity, and breaks the dormancy of the creative seedling. This is the moment when we come into play—providing a nurturing ground for germination and facilitating the execution of ideas.

In 2013, you participated in the main sectors of Art Basel and Art Basel in Hong Kong. What was your approach to these two different participations, and how would you define the two fairs?

Actually we did not have a strategy for these two fairs. We have the simplest approach—we review our on-going research, and see if anything already has enough intensity to generate dynamic conversations. If something is powerful enough to hold up to a form of exhibition, we decide where it could be shown—that is the "strategy" that we have been practicing for fairs.

VANI TAS

Andy Warhol
Skull
1976
Dominique Lévy Gallery

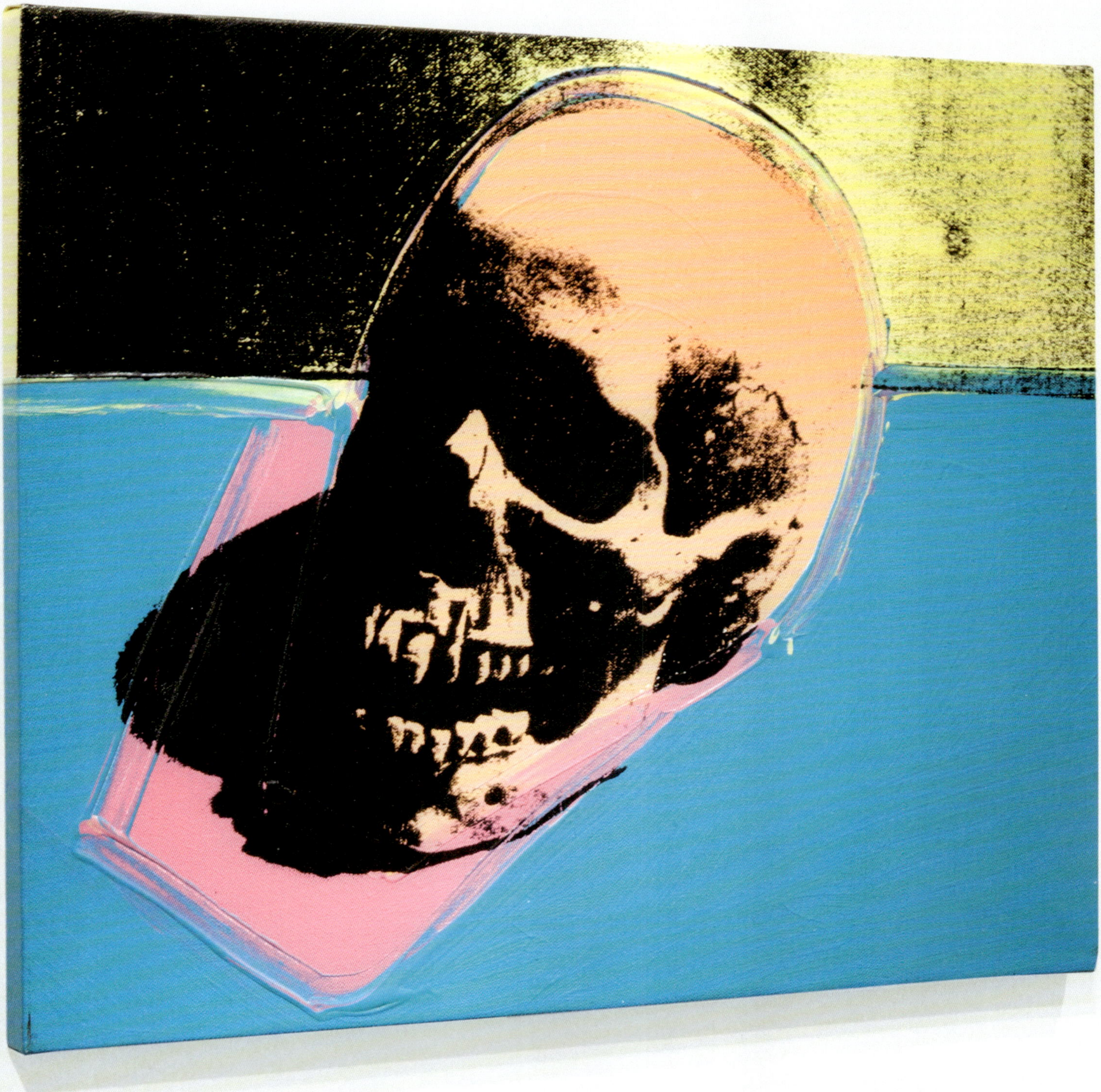

V

John M Armleder
Untitled
2002
Massimo De Carlo

V

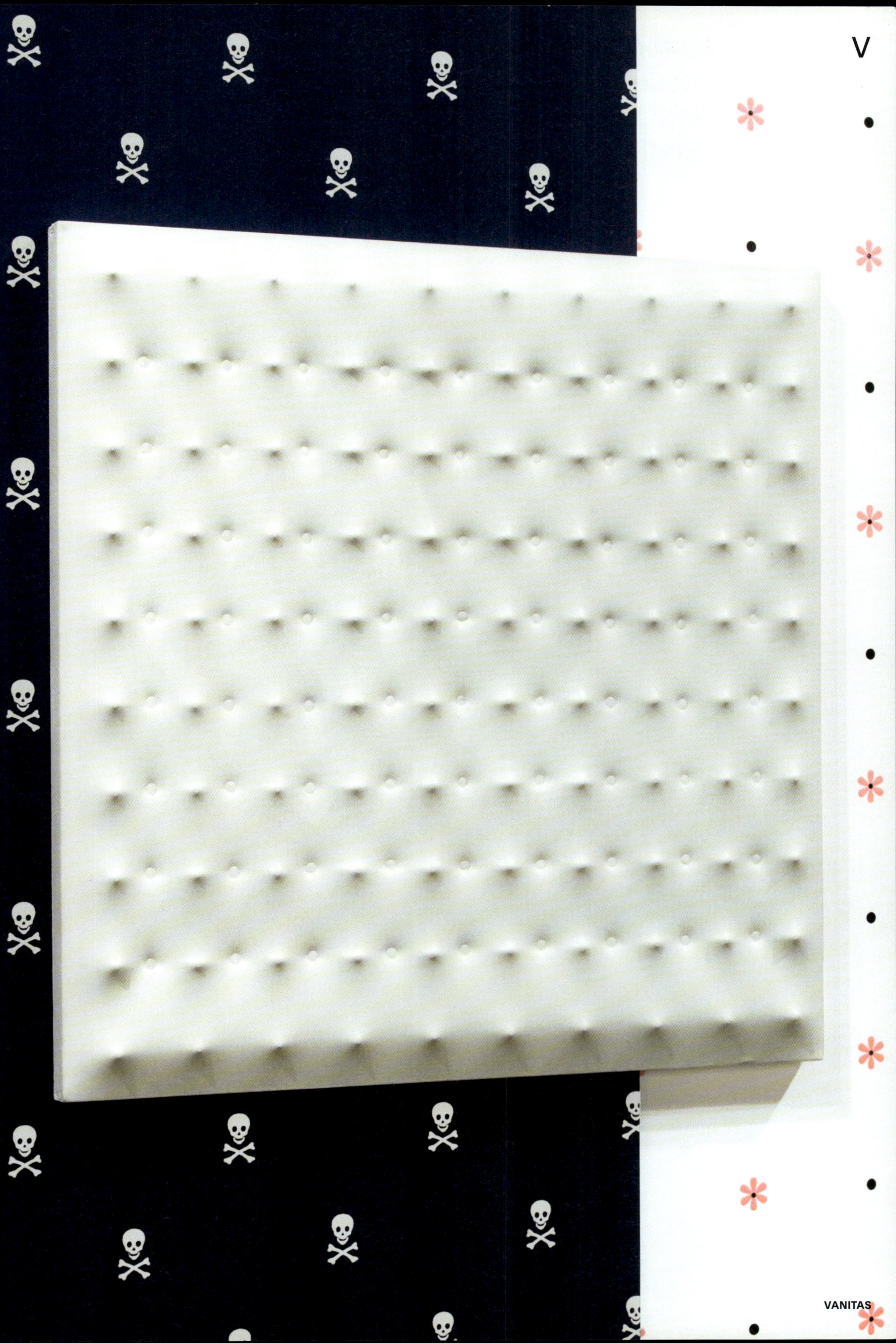

VANITAS

V

Walter Dahn
Immer Trinken
1982
Sprüth Magers

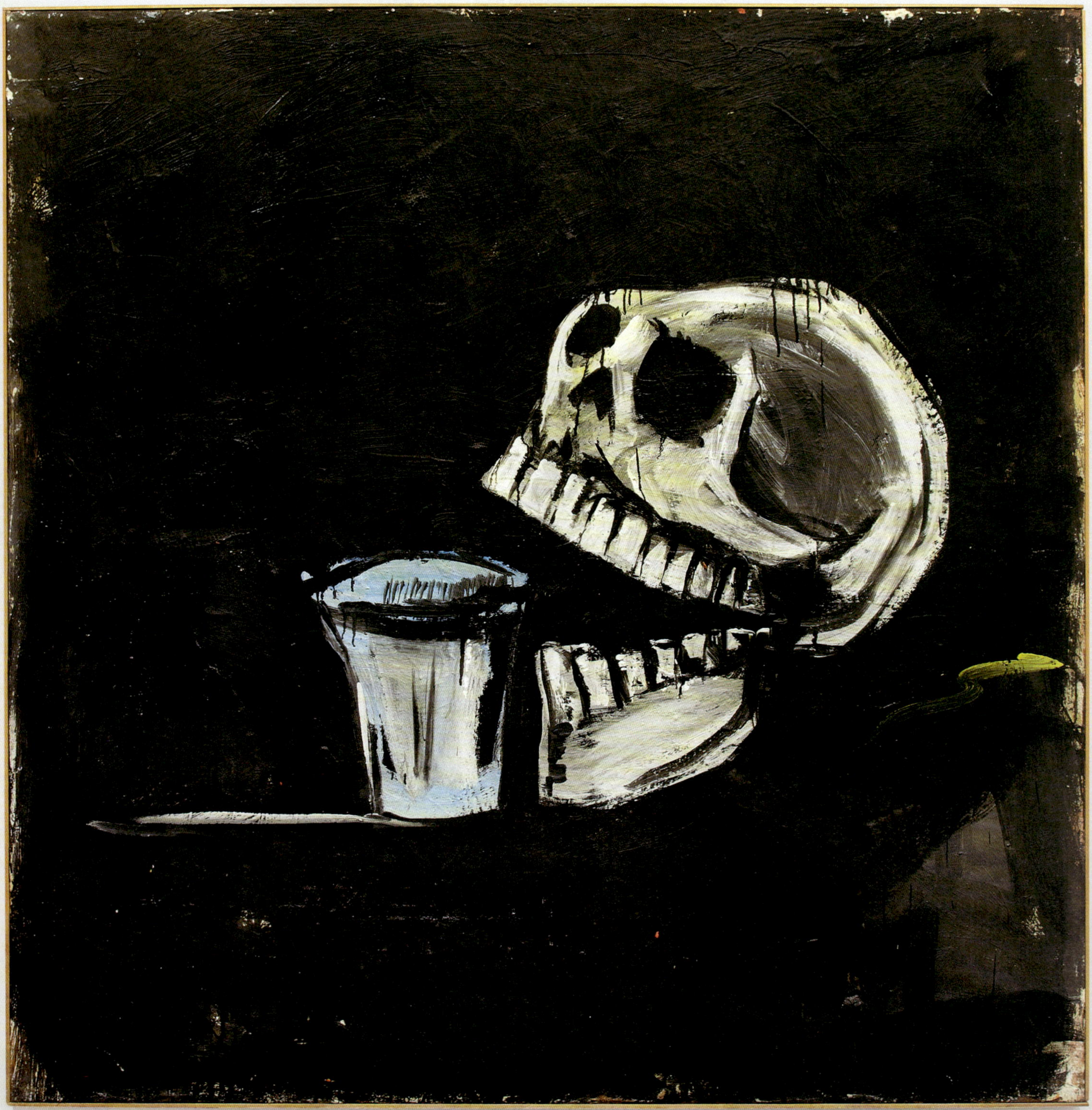

Wilhelm Sasnal
Skull Inside
2012
Anton Kern Gallery

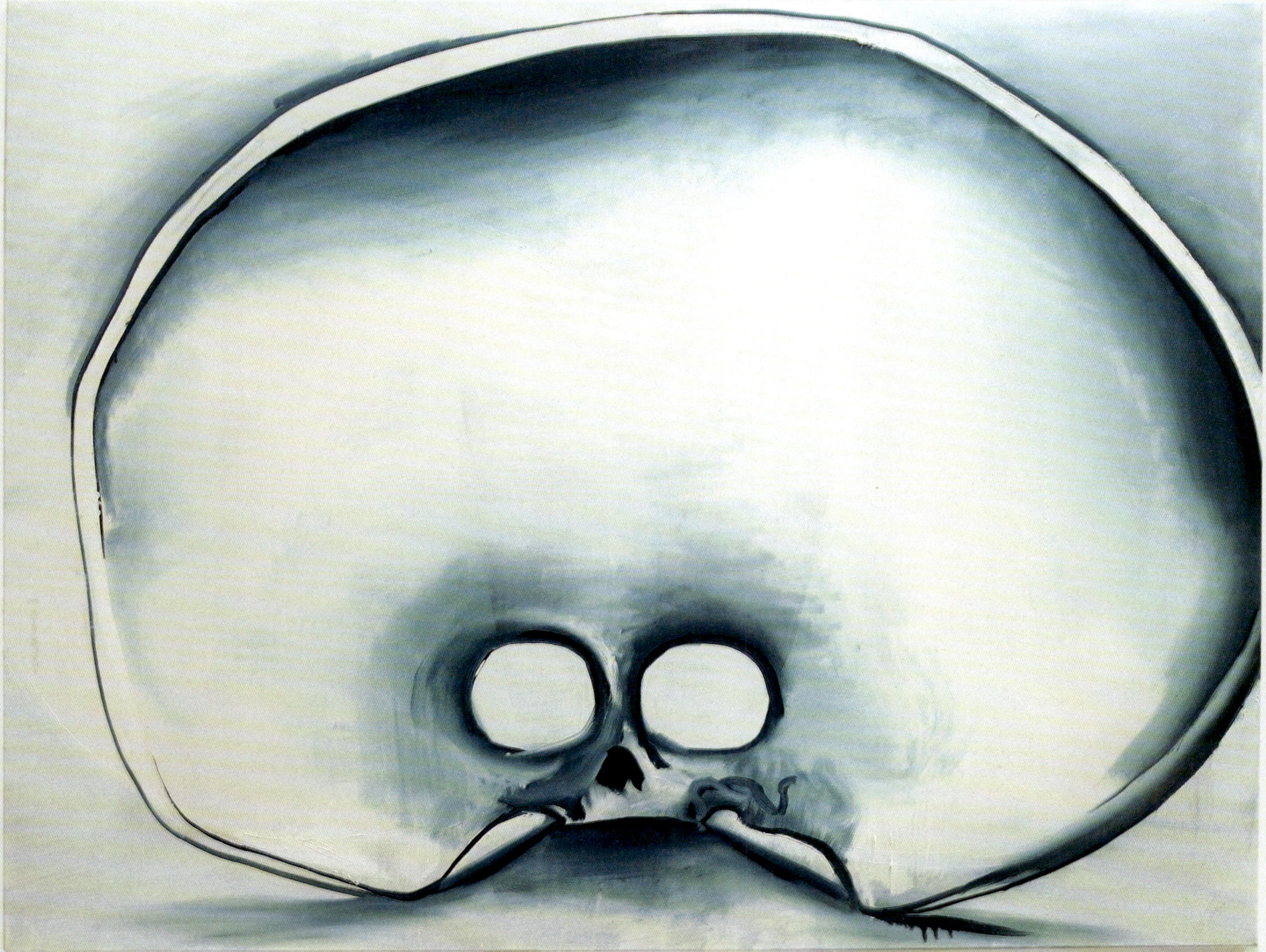

V

Thomas Houseago
Yet To Be Titled
2013
Xavier Hufkens

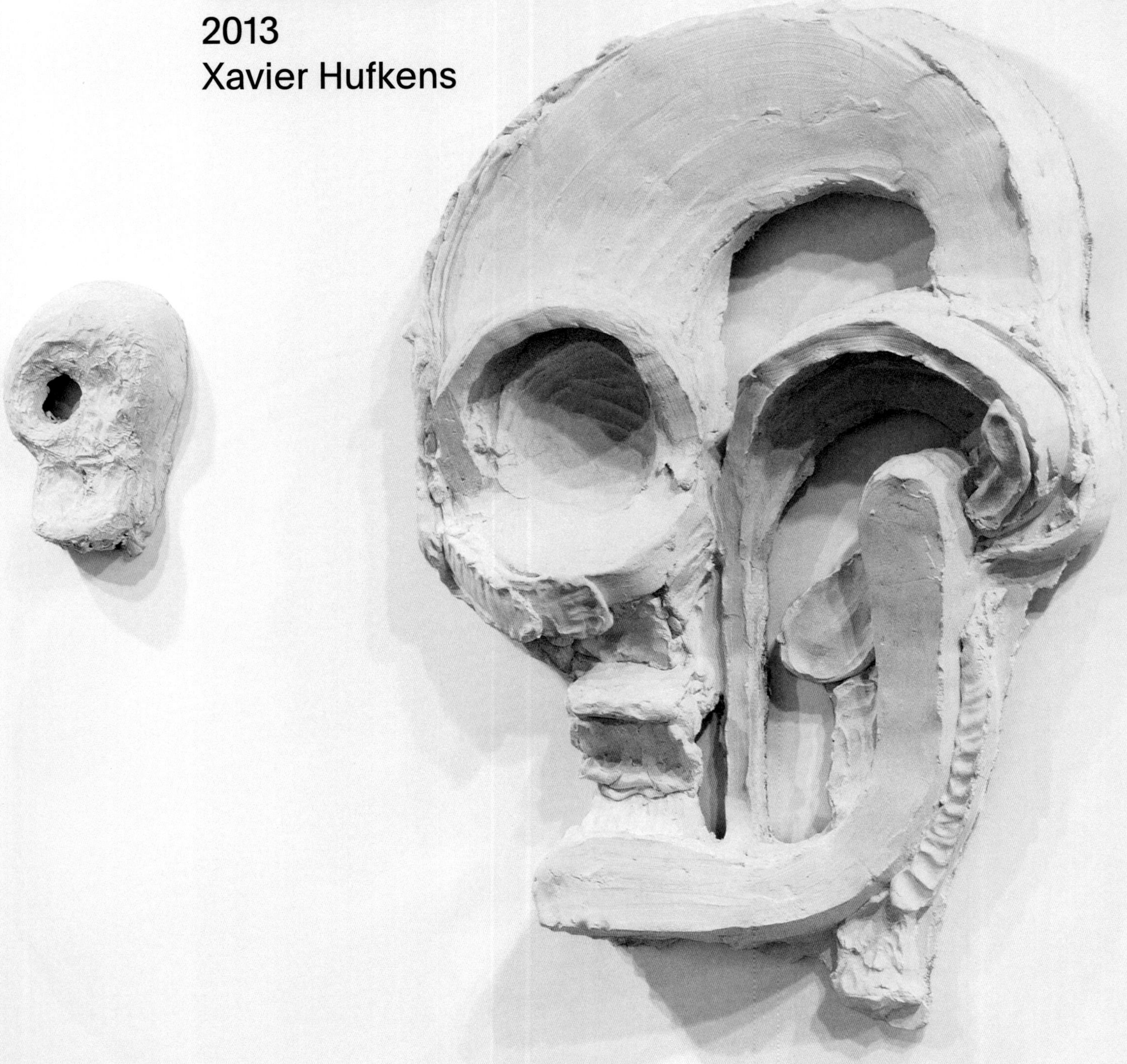

W

Hong Kong
Basel
Miami Beach

Waddington Custot

London

Galleries
Galleries

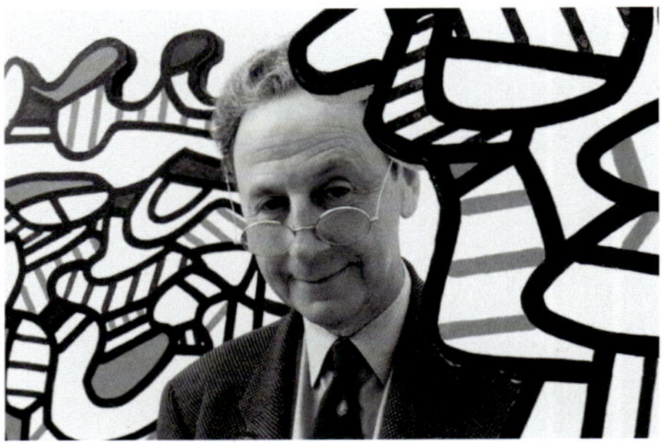

What first compelled you to open a gallery?
My father was a dealer and we initially worked together. I then went on to set up my own gallery in 1966.

Who is the first artist you showed and what was most memorable about that show?
Milton Avery, an American artist who influenced both Rothko and Newman. He is an important artist and we have continued to show his work to this day.

- **Contact** Waddington Custot Galleries
Charlotte Sanguinetti
charlotte@waddingtoncustot.com
mail@waddingtoncustot.com

- **Owner(s) / Partner(s)** Leslie Waddington
Stéphane Custot
- **Team** 10
- **Space(s)** 250 m²
- **Artists at Art Basel** Craigie Aitchison
Josef Albers
Carl Andre
Milton Avery
Clive Barker
Joseph Beuys
Peter Blake
Patrick Caulfield
John Chamberlain
Michael Craig-Martin
Ian Davenport
Jean Dubuffet
Barry Flanagan
Dan Flavin
Joseph Glasco
Julio González
Peter Halley
Patrick Heron
Hans Hofmann
Axel Hütte
Robert Indiana
Donald Judd
Jannis Kounellis
Sol LeWitt
Jacques Lipchitz
Agnes Martin
Henri Matisse
Roberto Matta
Fausto Melotti
Manolo Millares
Joan Miró
Henry Moore
Ben Nicholson
Claes Oldenburg &
Coosje van Bruggen
Mimmo Paladino
Francis Picabia
Pablo Picasso
Marc Quinn
Robert Rauschenberg
James Rosenquist
Susan Rothenberg
Lucas Samaras
Haim Steinbach
Frank Stella
Antoni Tàpies
Joe Tilson
William Turnbull
Meyer Vaisman
Fabienne Verdier
Andy Warhol
John Wesley
H.C. Westermann
Bill Woodrow
Jack B. Yeats

Wako

Tokyo

Galleries

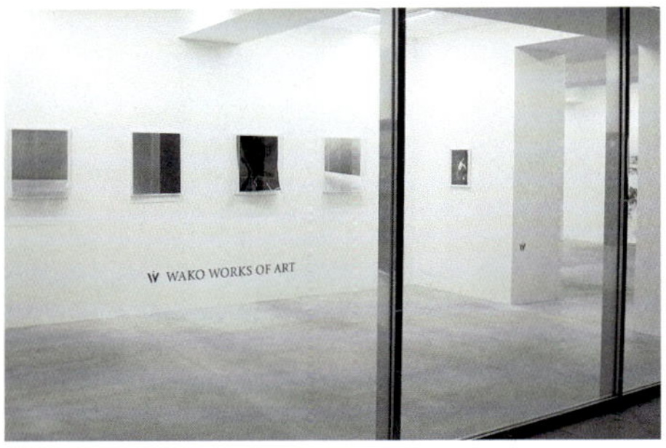

What first compelled you to open a gallery?
We wanted to introduce good artists who were new to Japan, such as Gerhard Richter, Luc Tuymans, etc.

Who is the first artist you showed and what was most memorable about that show?
Yuji Takeoka. We had so many visitors even though it was his very first show in Tokyo, maybe because he had just participated in documenta 9.

When did you first participate in Art Basel and what was most memorable about that show?
Art Basel in Hong Kong in 2013.

- **Contact** Wako Works of Art
Naofumi Osaka
osaka@wako-art.jp
info@wako-art.jp

- **Established** 1992
- **Owner(s) / Partner(s)** Kiyoshi Wako
- **Team** 3
- **Space(s)** 165 m²
- **Artists at Art Basel** Takeshi Masada
Gerhard Richter
Wolfgang Tillmans
Nana Yokoi

- **Further artists represented** Raoul De Keyser
Noritoshi Hirakawa
Joan Jonas
Mike Kelley
Gregor Schneider
Andreas Slominski
Yuji Takeoka
Fiona Tan
Luc Tuymans
Henk Visch
James Welling
Christopher Williams
Shizuka Yokomizo

Wallner

Copenhagen

- Galleries
- Galleries Public

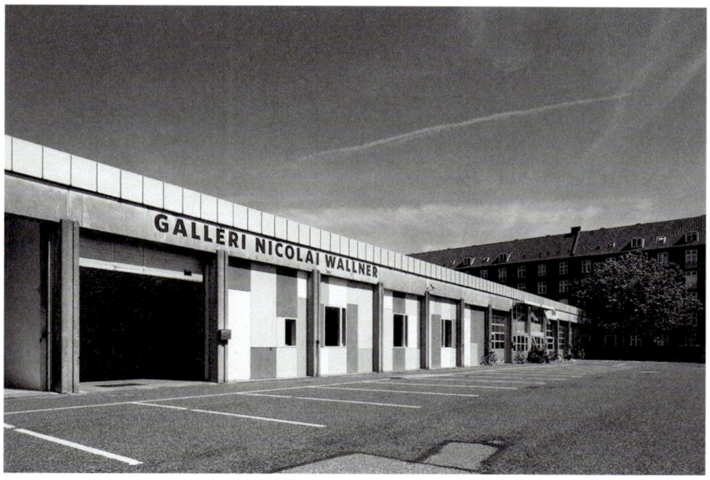

What first compelled you to open a gallery?

Galleri Nicolai Wallner opened in Copenhagen in 1993 to fill a kind of void. At the time, young contemporary Danish artists were being shut out of more established galleries due to a lack of interest. I felt that their work was important and needed to be shown, and I opened the gallery with the goal of communicating this new generation not just within Denmark, but equally on an international scale.

Who is the first artist you showed and what was most memorable about that show?

The first artist shown at the gallery was Joachim Koester. For the exhibition he had made a site-specific work, *Boarded Up Houses (Galleri Nicolai Wallner)* (1993–1994), in which the gallery windows were boarded up on the outside. The effect was beyond what we had expected, and solidified how necessary the gallery was. As the piece was on the outside of the gallery, it worked to contextualize the street—there was a heightened level of interaction between the piece and the average person. People were unsure of what it was, and if it even was an artwork, or rather if there was an alternate reason for the windows being boarded up. This type of intervention was unlike anything else shown by other galleries in Copenhagen.

When did you first participate in Art Basel and what was most memorable about that show?

Galleri Nicolai Wallner first participated in Art Basel in 1999 with works by Joachim Koester, Elmgreen & Dragset, David Shrigley, and Jonathan Monk among others—an immediate buzz.

- **Contact** — Galleri Nicolai Wallner, Marie Gellert Jensen, mgj@nicolaiwallner.com, nw@nicolaiwallner.com
- **Established** — 1993
- **Owner(s) / Partner(s)** — Nicolai Wallner
- **Team** — 6
- **Space(s)** — 800 m²
- **Artists at Art Basel** — A Kassen, Daniel Buren, Elmgreen & Dragset, Dan Graham, Jeppe Hein, Chris Johanson, Jesper Just, Joachim Koester, Jakob Kolding, Peter Land, Jonathan Monk, Clare Rojas, Christoph Ruckhäberle, Christian Schmidt-Rasmussen, David Shrigley, Glenn Sorensen, Alexander Tovborg, Richard Tuttle, Gitte Villesen

Wallspace

New York

- Nova

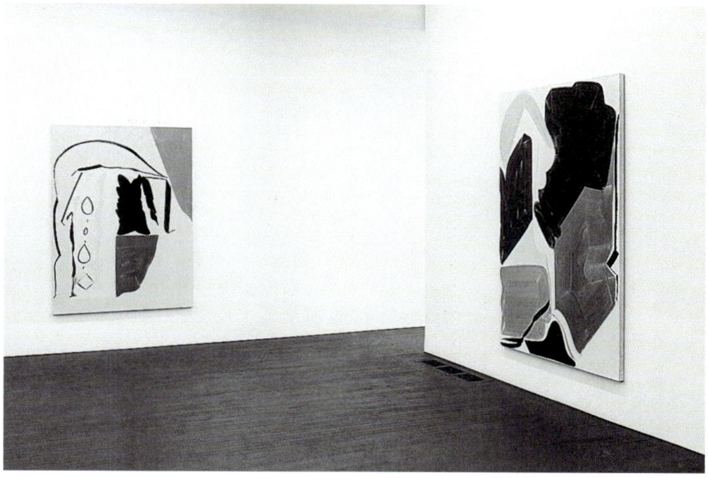

What first compelled you to open a gallery?

The love of curating.

Who is the first artist you showed and what was most memorable about that show?

A group show with Walead Beshty, Michael Queenland, Michael Rashkow, and Brandon Lattu. It was in our first space, which was maybe 12 by 7 feet. All amazing works by then very young and unknown artists just out of graduate school, who have all gone on to do amazing things!

When did you first participate in Art Basel and what was most memorable about that show?

Our first participation in Art Basel was in Miami Beach in 2008. We did Art Positions during the last year it was held in shipping containers on the beach. Martha Friedman installed over 100 giant rubber bands from floor to ceiling within a container.

- **Contact** — Wallspace, Jane Hait, jane@wallspacegallery.com, info@wallspacegallery.com
- **Established** — 2003
- **Owner(s) / Partner(s)** — Janine Foeller, Jane Hait
- **Team** — 5
- **Space(s)** — 214 m² (gallery), 214 m² (basement)
- **Artists at Art Basel**
- **Further artists represented** — John Divola, Gaylen Gerber, Ron Amstutz, Kate Costello, Harry Dodge, Shannon Ebner, Paul Elliman, Martha Friedman, Daniel Gordon, Jiří Kovanda, Scott Olson, Laura Riboli, Helen Verhoeven, Donelle Woolford

Washburn

New York

Galleries
Galleries

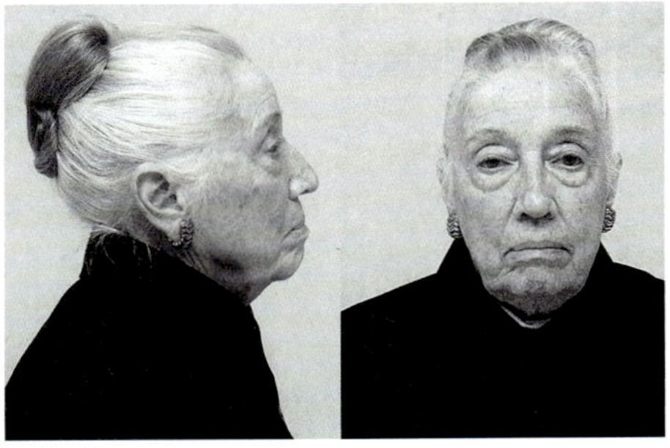

What first compelled you to open a gallery?
Twenty years of experience in galleries.

Who is the first artist you showed and what was most memorable about that show?
Jean Xceron. Most memorable because we sold a painting to a museum for $6,000, which is worth $100,000 to $150,000 today.

When did you first participate in Art Basel and what was most memorable about that show?
The first participation in Art Basel was in 1999. Most memorable was the sale of a drawing by Jackson Pollock to the Kunstmuseum, Basel.

- **Contact** Washburn Gallery
Joan Washburn
jwashburn@earthlink.net
- **Established** 1971
- **Owner(s) / Partner(s)** Joan Washburn (President)
Brian Washburn (Asst. Director)
- **Team** 4
- **Space(s)** 4,018 m²
- **Artists at** Ilya Bolotowsky
Nicolas Carone
Tom Levine
Doug Ohlson
Ray Parker
Leon Polk Smith
Jackson Pollock
David Smith
Richard Stankiewicz
Jack Youngerman
- **Further artists represented** James Abbe
Rosalind Bengelsdorf
Oscar Bluemner
Norman Bluhm
Patrick Henry Bruce
Alexander Calder
Mary Callery
Arthur B. Carles
Marjorie Content
Stuart Davis
Willem de Kooning
Burgoyne Diller
Arthur Dove
Werner Drewes
Albert E. Gallatin
Fritz Glarner
Arshile Gorky
John Graham
Balcomb Greene
Gertrude Greene
Marsden Hartley
William Hill
Joshua Johnson
Paul Kelpe
Conrad Kramer
Man Ray
John Marin
Alice Trumbull Mason
George L. K. Morris
Georgia O'Keeffe
Ammi Phillips
Richard Pousette-Dart
Mark Rothko
Morgan Russell
Anne Ryan
Rolph Scarlett
Louis Schanker
John Sennhauser
Niles Spencer
Alfred Stieglitz
Myron Stout
Jean Xceron

Wei-Ling

Kuala Lumpur
Penang

Insights

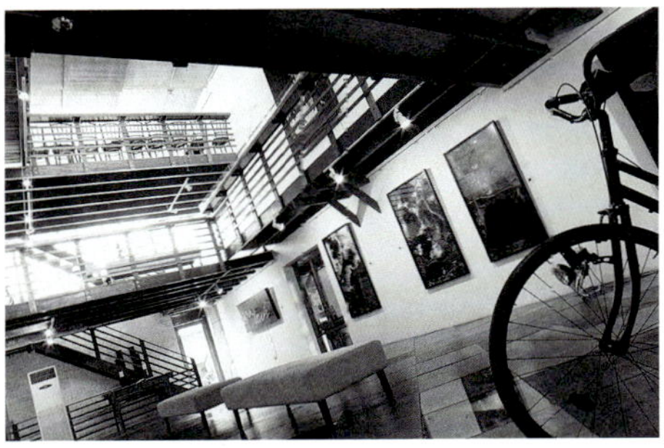

What first compelled you to open a gallery?
I had initially set up the space as a studio for my own work, but obviously there were other plans for me: after my first solo exhibition, several artists approached me to show their works. One thing led to another and before I knew it, my own artistic career had taken a back seat and I was representing and promoting contemporary Malaysian artists. In my first year I only had two exhibitions, then five, and eight in the year after and now, 11 years later, we have a full exhibition program that spreads over three galleries, and have become the largest publisher of art books in the country. This was obviously a calling for me and I cannot imagine doing anything else now.

Who is the first artist you showed and what was most memorable about that show?
Chin Kong Yee. I first visited this artist when he was painting in his mother's kitchen. He had the most incredible body of work but had never had a show, so I took him under my wing and gave him his first show. We were both fledglings at the time and had to have absolute trust in one another, as neither of us had a track record to go by. It was an exhilarating yet challenging time; I had no idea how to go about promoting an artist, but I had faith in him and a good feeling about the works. The show was a huge success; a big corporate collector saw the body of work and booked up most of it for their corporate collection. What I remember most about the show was the fact that the artist was over the moon and was then able to continue on his journey. He has continued showing with us and today has traveled the world showing his works, and has bought himself a new home and studio.

When did you first participate in Art Basel and what was most memorable about that show?
In 2013 at Art Basel in Hong Kong. A wonderful platform for us. We were also the first gallery to ever represent Malaysia in Art Basel.

- **Contact** Wei-Ling Gallery
Shaza Sofi
weilinggallery@gmail.com
- **Established** 2002
- **Owner(s) / Partner(s)** Lim Wei-Ling
- **Team** 6
- **Space(s)** 1,500 m² (three galleries)
- **Artists at Art Basel** Ivan Lam
- **Further artists represented** Chen Wei Meng
Cheng Yen Pheng
Chin Kong Yee
Choy Chun Wei
Amir Gulgee
Hamidi Hadi
Azril Ismail
Anurendra Jegadeva
Stewart MacFarlane
Michal Macku
Munkao
Ng Kim Peow
Noor Azizan Rahman Paiman
Umibaizurah Mahir
Yau Bee Ling
Zulkifli Yusoff

Weingrüll

Karlsruhe ● Discoveries

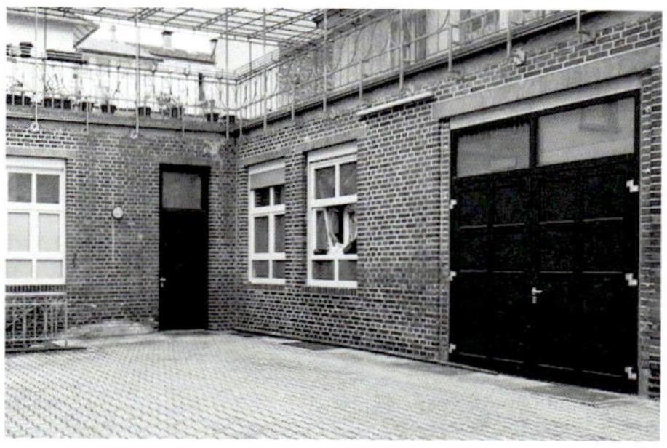

What first compelled you to open a gallery?
I ran a project space in Karlsruhe while I was still at the university. Soon I realized that working in a gallery fits my personality. I showed artists with whom I would love to work for more than just one show. So I re-opened as a gallery before I graduated.

Who is the first artist you showed and what was most memorable about that show?
The opening show of the gallery was a solo presentation of Thomas Geiger's works. It was a very important show for the gallery in many respects. A lot of the people that came to see it are still important parts of the gallery's network. The show also set the course for the program and influenced it very much.

When did you first participate in Art Basel and what was most memorable about that show?
Weingrüll took part in Art Basel's first edition in Hong Kong. What I found especially noteworthy—as I did ART HK twice before—is how Art Basel kept all that made ART HK such an important fair, and at the same time increased quality and international visibility.

- **Contact** Weingrüll
  Florian Weingrüll
  florian@weingruell.com
  info@weingruell.com
- **Established** 2010
- **Owner(s) / Partner(s)** Florian Weingrüll
- **Team** 1
- **Space(s)** 120 m²
- **Artists at Art Basel** Benjamin Appel
- **Further artists represented** Enrico Bach
  Jakup Ferri
  Thomas Geiger
  Otto D. Handschuh
  Eric Hattan
  Stephanie Kiwitt
  Gabriela Oberkofler
  Maeghan Reid
  Cameron Rowland
  Christian Schmuck

Weiss

Berlin ● Galleries Unlimited

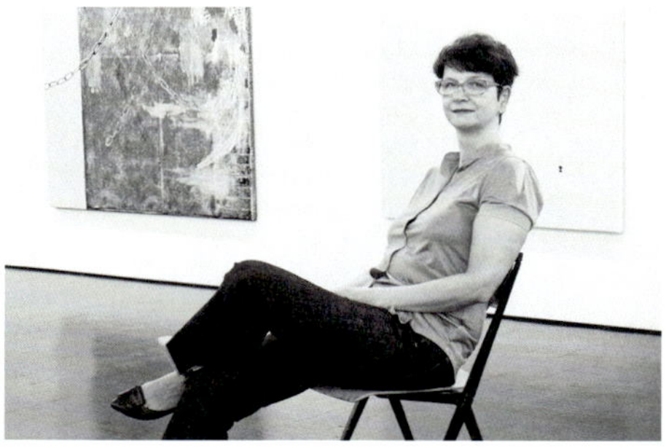

What first compelled you to open a gallery?
I was interested in the collaboration with artists.

Who is the first artist you showed and what was most memorable about that show?
Larry Clark.

When did you first participate in Art Basel and what was most memorable about that show?
In 2000.

- **Contact** Galerie Barbara Weiss
  Sophia von Westerholt
  svw@galeriebarbaraweiss.de
  mail@galeriebarbaraweiss.de
- **Established** 1992
- **Owner(s) / Partner(s)** Barbara Weiss
- **Team** 5
- **Space(s)** 600 m²
- **Artists at Art Basel** Monika Baer
  Heike Baranowsky
  Thomas Bayrle
  Geta Bratescu
  Janet Cardiff & George Bures Miller
  Raoul De Keyser
  Maria Eichhorn
  Nicole Eisenman
  Ayse Erkmen
  Harun Farocki
  Friederike Feldmann
  Berta Fischer
  Mary Heilmann
  Christine & Irene Hohenbüchler
  Laura Horelli
  Jonathan Horowitz
  Boris Mikhailov
  John Miller
  Rebecca Morris
  Deimantas Narkevicius
  Susanne Paesler
  Mai-Thu Perret
  Collier Schorr
  Andreas Siekmann
  Roman Signer
  Niele Toroni
  Suse Weber

Wentrup

Berlin ● Galleries
● Galleries

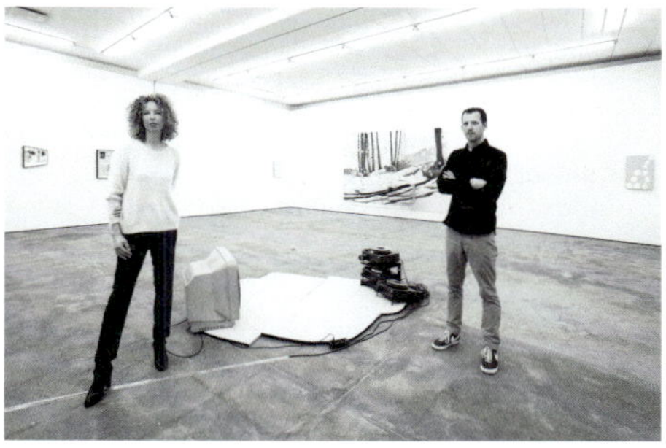

What first compelled you to open a gallery?
When I studied art history I sometimes felt like a paper-shuffler in a Kafka novel. Now I feel like I'm on the road with Jack Kerouac.

Who is the first artist you showed and what was most memorable about that show?
The first show was with the painter Axel Geis, and most memorable is that I was the curator, the host, the framer, the installer, the handyman, the wall painter, the mailman, the press agent, the cleaner, the driver, the barkeeper, and luckily also the dealer.

When did you first participate in Art Basel and what was most memorable about that show?
The first participation was with Gregor Hildebrandt for an Art Basel Statements in 2008 and it was the longest booth installment we ever had. It took six people and four days to install a floor made of 5,653 audiocassettes.

- **Contact** Wentrup
  Sascha Welchering
  sascha@wentrupgallery.com
  mail@wentrupgallery.com
- **Established** 2004
- **Owner(s) / Partner(s)** Tina Wentrup
  Jan Wentrup
- **Space(s)** 300 m²
- **Artists at Art Basel** Miriam Böhm
  Gregor Hildebrandt
  Florian Meisenberg
  David Renggli
- **Further artists represented** Nevin Aladag
  Cristian Andersen
  Axel Geis
  Mathew Hale
  Olaf Metzel
  Jen Ray
  Wawrzyniec Tokarski
  Timm Ulrichs

Werner

New York
London

- Galleries
- Galleries
- Galleries

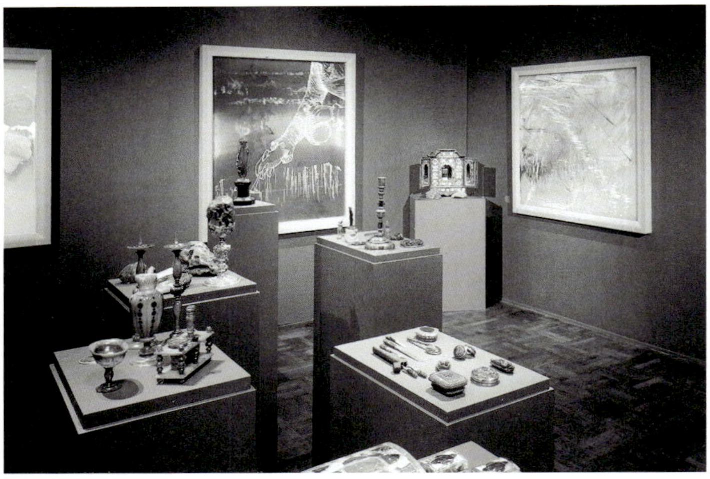

Who is the first artist you showed and what was most memorable about that show?
In 1963, the Galerie Werner & Katz in Berlin opened its doors with George Baselitz's first solo exhibition. A public scandal ensued over the perceived obscenity of the paintings that led to the authorities confiscating two of the paintings.

- **Contact** Michael Werner
  Joe Brittain
  joe@michaelwerner.com
  newyork@michaelwerner.com
- **Established** 1963
- **Owner(s) / Partner(s)** Michael Werner
  Gordon VeneKlasen
- **Team** 19
- **Space(s)** 270 m²
- **Artists at Art Basel** Hurvin Anderson
  Georg Baselitz
  Marcel Broodthaers
  James Lee Byars
  Aaron Curry
  Enrico David
  Peter Doig
  Jörg Immendorff
  Per Kirkeby
  Eugène Leroy
  Markus Lüpertz
  Ernst Wilhelm Nay
  A.R. Penck
  Francis Picabia
  Sigmar Polke
  Kurt Schwitters
  Don Van Vliet

White Cube

London
Hong Kong

São Paulo

- Galleries
- Galleries Unlimited
- Galleries

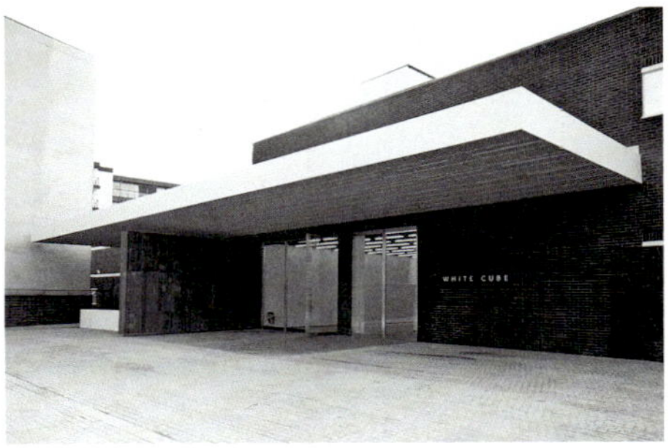

What first compelled you to open a gallery?
White Cube was set up by Jay Jopling in 1993 as a project room for contemporary art. Situated on Duke Street, St James's, one of London's most traditional art dealing streets, the gallery was a perfect white cube, a room within a room. The central concern when establishing the program was to create an intimate space in which an artist could present a single important work of art or a coherent body of work within a focused environment, an idea that, in some way, stemmed from the memorable experience of Walter de Maria's *Earth Room* in New York. The program was singular among commercial galleries in that an artist was invited to exhibit only once. Duke Street closed in 2002.

Who is the first artist you showed and what was most memorable about that show?
White Cube's inaugural exhibition was *The Secret Life and Archaic Times of Mr D* by Israeli-born artist Itai Doron, who at the time was a recent graduate of Goldsmith's in London.

- **Contact** White Cube
  David Chadwick
  davidchadwick@whitecube.com
  enquiries@whitecube.com
- **Established** 1993
- **Owner(s) / Partner(s)** Jay Jopling
- **Team** 126
- **Space(s)** 1,110m² (Mason's Yard)
  5,440 m² (Bermondsey)
  550 m² (Hong Kong)
  298 m² (São Paulo)
- **Artists at Art Basel** Franz Ackermann
  Darren Almond
  Ellen Altfest
  Miroslaw Balka
  Georg Baselitz
  Ashley Bickerton
  Mark Bradford
  Candice Breitz
  Ernesto Caivano
  Jake & Dinos Chapman
  Chuck Close
  Gregory Crewdson
  Tracey Emin
  Katharina Fritsch
  Theaster Gates
  Gilbert & George
  Antony Gormley
  Andreas Gursky
  Mona Hatoum
  Eberhard Havekost
  Damien Hirst
  Gary Hume
  Robert Irwin
  Runa Islam
  Sergej Jensen
  Anselm Kiefer
  Rachel Kneebone
  Friedrich Kunath
  Elad Lassry
  Jac Leirner
  Liu Wei
  Liza Lou
  Christian Marclay
  Kris Martin
  Josiah McElheny
  Julie Mehretu
  Harland Miller
  Sarah Morris

Gabriel Orozco
Damián Ortega
Eddie Peake
Richard Phillips
Magnus Plessen
Marc Quinn
Jessica Rankin
Robin Rhode
Doris Salcedo
Raqib Shaw
Haim Steinbach
Neal Tait
Sam Taylor-Johnson
Fred Tomaselli
Jeff Wall
Cerith Wyn Evans
Zhang Huan

White Room

Melbourne — Galleries

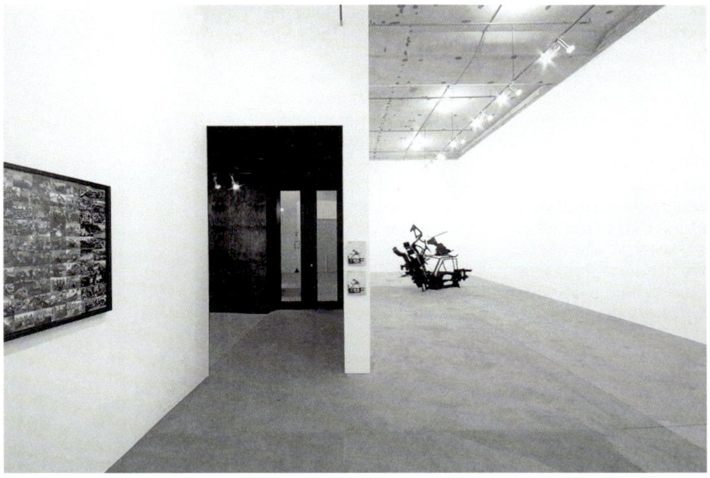

What first compelled you to open a gallery?
The gallery opened with a specific aim to offer a higher level of curatorial advocacy for emerging to mid-career artists. The generational opportunity to professionally exhibit and represent many artists for the first time was also identified, and much over-due in Melbourne at the time.

Who is the first artist you showed and what was most memorable about that show?
Alexander Knox in October 2006. A single impressive sculpture informed by the timely but devastating imagery emerging from the war in Iraq at the time.

When did you first participate in Art Basel and what was most memorable about that show?
In Art Basel in Hong Kong in 2013. First international art fair attendance. Highlights included the gallery appearing on the cover of the daily edition of *The Art Newspaper* and the new audiences, curators, and collectors engaged.

- **Contact** Murray White Room
  Murray White
  email@murraywhiteroom.com
- **Established** 2006
- **Owner(s) / Partner(s)** Murray White (Director)
- **Team** 3
- **Space(s)** 120 m²
- **Artists at Art Basel** Polly Borland
  Tony Clark
  Richard Giblett
  Anne-Marie May
  Alasdair McLuckie
  Sally Ross
  Sangeeta Sandrasegar
  Judith Van Heeren
  Constanze Zikos
- **Further artists represented** Mira Gojak
  Eliza Hutchison
  Alexander Knox
  Alex Pittendrigh

White Space

Beijing — Galleries

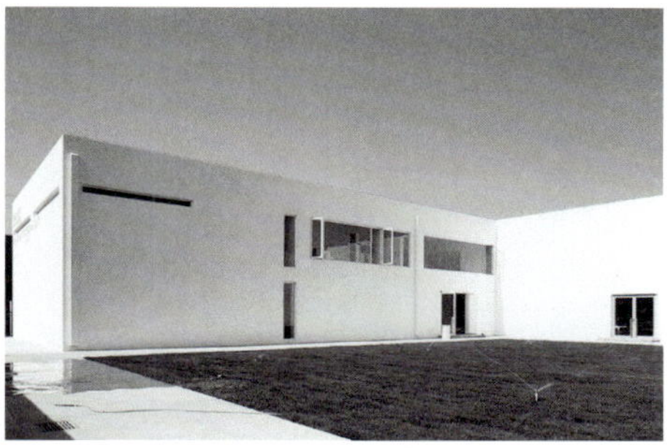

What first compelled you to open a gallery?
To serve the artists.

Who is the first artist you showed and what was most memorable about that show?
He Xiangyu.

When did you first participate in Art Basel and what was most memorable about that show?
In 2012, I was moved by Art Basel's professionalism and organization.

- **Contact** White Space Beijing
  Di Zhang
  zhangdi@whitespace-beijing.com
  info@whitespace-beijing.com
- **Established** 2004
- **Owner(s) / Partner(s)** Tian Yuan
- **Team** 6
- **Space(s)** 1,150 m²
- **Artists at Art Basel** He Xiangyu
  Li Shurui
  Liu Ren
  Liu Wentao
  Liu Xinyi
  Shi Zhiying
  Wang Haiyang
  Wang Qiang
  Xie Fan
  Yang Jian
- **Further artists represented** Chi Peng
  Gao Lei
  Jian Ce
  Su Bo
  Wang Chung-kun
  Wang Min
  Yang Hongwei
  Yangzi
  Zhang Ruyi

Wigram

London — Galleries, Nova

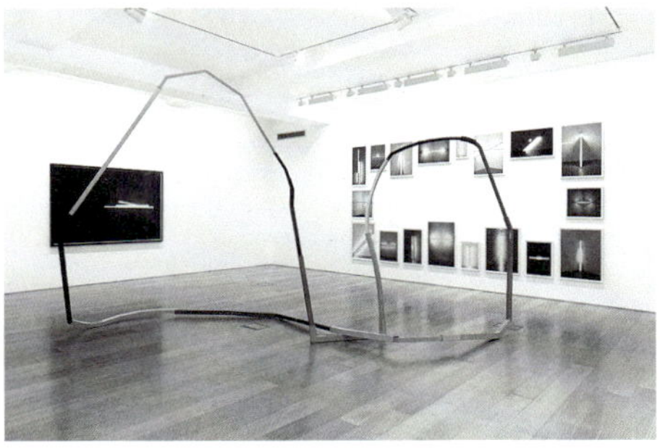

Who is the first artist you showed and what was most memorable about that show?
Marine Hugonnier—memorable because it was a large project which involved flying the artist and a team to Alaska to shoot photographs.

- **Contact** Max Wigram Gallery
  James Fox
  james@maxwigram.com
  info@maxwigram.com
- **Established** 2001
- **Owner(s) / Partner(s)** Max Wigram

- **Team** 8
- **Space(s)** 100 m²
- **Artists at Art Basel** Jose Dávila, Marine Hugonnier, Mustafa Hulusi, Valeska Soares, Richard Wathen, James White, Luiz Zerbini
- **Further artists represented** Athanasios Argianos, Slater Bradley, Pavel Büchler, Edwin Burdis, Ximena Garrida-Lecca, Barnaby Hosking, Julian Rosefeldt

Wilkinson

London — Galleries

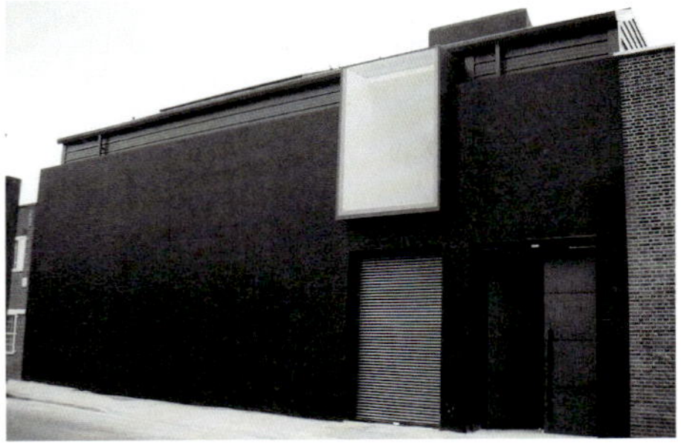

What first compelled you to open a gallery?

To put on exhibitions and work with artists.

Who is the first artist you showed and what was most memorable about that show?

In 2001 the gallery became Wilkinson Gallery and our first show, entitled *I Am Making Art*, was a group show of early video works by Vito Acconci, John Baldessari, Joan Jonas, Paul McCarthy, Bruce Nauman. It was memorable because it began our year-long video project space and was the start of our working relationship with Joan Jonas.

When did you first participate in Art Basel and what was most memorable about that show?

In the Statements sector of Art Basel in 1999 with Bob & Roberta Smith: the project was participatory and people were asked to invent new words for the millennium which were then painted and displayed on the booth. We had a great response to the project.

- **Contact** Wilkinson, Anthony Wilkinson, anthony@wilkinsongallery.com
- **Established** 2001
- **Owner(s) / Partner(s)** Amanda Wilkinson, Anthony Wilkinson
- **Team** 5
- **Space(s)** 550 m²
- **Artists at Art Basel** Mark Alexander, Heman Chong, Joan Jonas, Sung Hwan Kim, Makiko Kudo, Elizabeth Magill, George Shaw, Shimabuku, Laurie Simmons
- **Further artists represented** Tilo Baumgärtel, Dara Birnbaum, Matt Calderwood, Clegg & Guttmann, Jimmy De Sana, A K Dolven, Matthew Higgs, Tillman Kaiser, Thoralf Knobloch, Marcin Maciejowski, Renzo Martens, Ciprian Muresan, Robert Orchardson, Anna Parkina, Barbara Probst, Silke Schatz, Martina Steckholzer, Phoebe Unwin, Harm van den Dorpel

Williams

New York — Feature, Unlimited

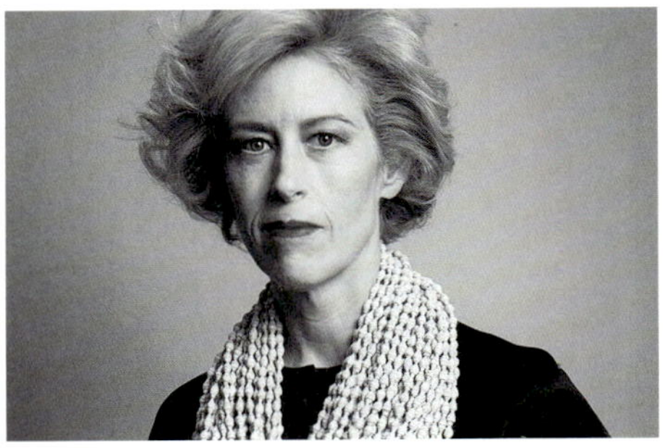

What first compelled you to open a gallery?

Having worked in the contemporary art field for several decades, it was inevitable that I would eventually open a gallery. Following the events of 9/11, I decided the time was now.

Who is the first artist you showed and what was most memorable about that show?

My first gallery exhibition was with Pedro Cabrita Reis in 2004. It may have been one of the few times Cabrita Reis adapted to an intimate environment, as the original gallery was in an 1840s townhouse in the West Village, NYC.

When did you first participate in Art Basel and what was most memorable about that show?

My first participation was in Art 38 Basel, in 2007, with a presentation by Barbara Bloom and Zoe Leonard in the Features sector—both extraordinary artists.

- **Contact** Tracy Williams, Ltd., Rana Saner, rana@tracywilliamsltd.com, info@tracywilliamsltd.com
- **Established** 2004
- **Owner(s) / Partner(s)** Tracy Williams
- **Team** 3
- **Space(s)** 325 m²
- **Artists at Art Basel** Barbara Bloom
- **Further artists represented** Ernst Caramelle, Nicole Cherubini, Anna Craycroft, Simryn Gill, Olav Christopher Jenssen, Judy Ledgerwood, Domingo Milella, Matt Mullican, Murad Khan Mumtaz, Jennifer Nocon, Alyssa Pheobus Mumtaz, Anne-Marie Schneider, Georgina Starr, Peter Stichbury, Astrid Svangren

Winter

Vienna — Statements

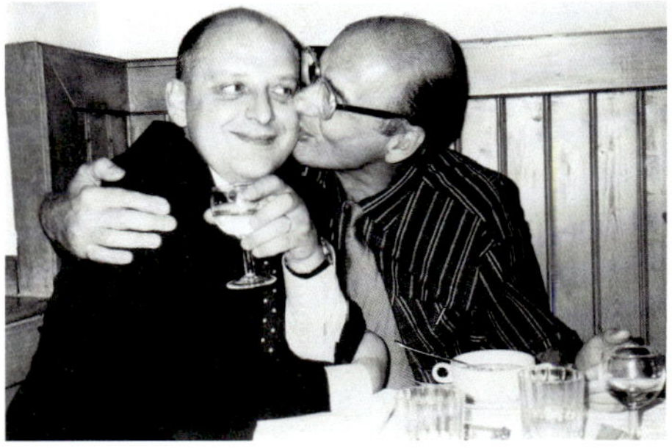

What first compelled you to open a gallery?
I am a trained art and book dealer and I wanted to have my own business as soon as possible.

Who is the first artist you showed and what was most memorable about that show?
Arnulf Rainer. Looking back: aggression and failure.

When did you first participate in Art Basel and what was most memorable about that show?
In 1992.

- **Contact** Galerie Hubert Winter
  Melanie Wagner
  office@galeriewinter.at
- **Established** 1971
- **Owner(s) / Partner(s)** Hubert Winter
- **Team** 5
- **Space(s)** 340 m²
- **Artists at Art Basel** Judith Fegerl
- **Further artists represented** William Anastasi
  Guillaume Bijl
  Mary Ellen Carroll
  Ian Hamilton Finlay
  Marcia Hafif
  Nancy Haynes
  Michael Höpfner
  Birgit Jürgenssen
  Michael Kidner RA
  Lei Xue
  Paul Etienne Lincoln
  Urs Lüthi
  Ingo Nussbaumer
  Richard Nonas
  Danica Phelps
  Katherine Porter
  Laura Ribero
  Fred Sandback
  Stephen Skidmore
  Haim Steinbach
  Franz Vana
  Lawrence Weiner
  Francesca Woodman
  Nil Yalter

Wolff

Paris

● Galleries
● Galleries

What first compelled you to open a gallery?
Visiting galleries like Jennifer Flay, Crousel, Philippe Nelson …

Who is the first artist you showed and what was most memorable about that show?
We opened with a solo exhibition of Clemens von Wedemeyer. Exploring the relationships between art and cinema remains a theme of research in our program.

When did you first participate in Art Basel and what was most memorable about that show?
It is a fascinating but also brutal confrontation with the art market, that so far was something abstract to me.

- **Contact** Galerie Jocelyn Wolff
  Nasim Weiler
  nasim.weiler@galeriewolff.com
- **Established** 2003
- **Owner(s) / Partner(s)** Jocelyn Wolff
- **Team** 6
- **Space(s)** 160 m²
- **Artists at Art Basel** William Anastasi
  Katinka Bock
  Miriam Cahn
  Guillaume Leblon
  Clemens von Wedemeyer
  Franz Erhard Walther
- **Further artists represented** Zbynek Baladrán
  Valérie Favre
  Isa Melsheimer
  Ulrich Polster
  Prinz Gholam
  Hans Schabus
  Philippe Schwinger & Frédéric Moser
  Elodie Seguin
  Francisco Tropa
  Christoph Weber

Workplace

Gateshead
London

● Discoveries

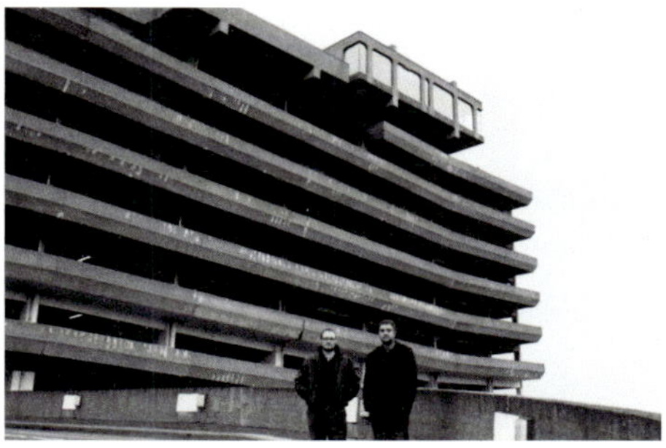

What first compelled you to open a gallery?
Paul Moss and Miles Thurlow: We were both artists and graduates of Newcastle University in 1998 and 2000 respectively. We were making work and showing regularly, but felt increasingly that there wasn't the mechanism to extend our own careers or the careers of our peer group into an international context. At the time, the local art community could easily be categorized in two ways. The importing of high quality contemporary art into the region through organizations such as BALTIC; and a more self-reflexive artist-run community showing to the same audience time and time again. We thought we could add something to the situation here by focusing on trying to present the work to a much wider audience with confidence that it was relevant to a much greater context. The idea of formally representing artists came through our experiences at art fairs when we realized first hand the direct relationship between the critical and the economic and the importance of both in the development of artists' careers. As a gallery that started in a place with no local market we have tried to address the traditional hierarchy between dealer, curator, collector, and artist, involving ourselves in all aspects of art. Our program has sought to investigate intersections between the object and architecture, performance, video and social commentary, painting and photography, exhibiting international artists within the increasingly dynamic art scene in the north east of England alongside positioning the work of our represented artists internationally through art fairs, and recently the opening of a second space in central London.

- **Contact** Workplace Gallery
  Paul Moss
  paul@workplacegallery.co.uk
  info@workplacegallery.co.uk
- **Established** 2005
- **Owner(s) / Partner(s)** Paul Moss
  Miles Thurlow
- **Space(s)** 400 m² (Gateshead)
  157 m² (London)
- **Artists at Art Basel** Marcus Coates
- **Further artists represented** Tanya Axford
  Eric Bainbridge
  Darren Banks
  Sophie Lisa Beresford
  Catherine Bertola
  Cath Campbell
  Hugo Canoilas
  Joe Clark
  Jo Coupe
  Jacob Dahlgren
  Jennifer Douglas
  Peter J. Evans
  Laura Lancaster
  Rachel Lancaster
  Paul Merrick
  Mike Pratt
  Richard Rigg
  Cecilia Stenbom
  Matt Stokes
  Wolfgang Weileder

White Cube

Three Questions for Jay Jopling

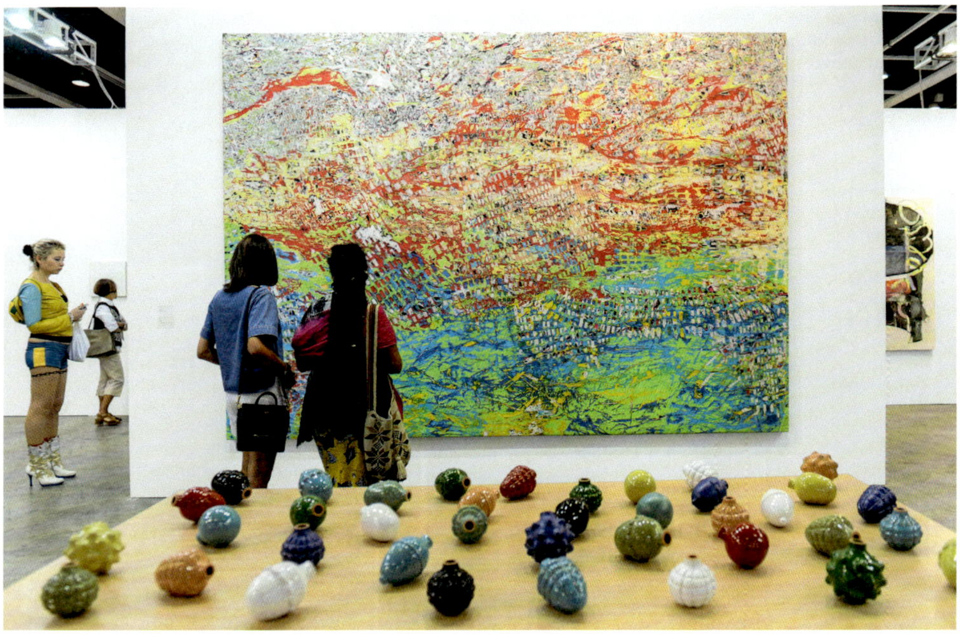

Art Basel in Hong Kong, 2013

With galleries around the world, White Cube is one of the main actors in the art world and art market. Could you briefly present your program and outline the specific qualities of White Cube since the 1990s?

We have four galleries: two in London, one in Hong Kong, and one in São Paulo. Our program is very broad and has always been predicated around the idea of showing those artists whom we believe to be the most interesting and important currently working. The gallery expanded and has been very much associated with the rise of the generation of British artists who came to prominence in the 1990s, led by Damien Hirst. Just as their aspirations were international, so were ours, and the global success of our represented artists, both critical and commercial, is how we measure ourselves. Although we are very much associated with British artists, 70% of all shows at White Cube since it was founded in 1993 have been by artists based overseas.

You have participated in Art Basel in Basel and in Miami Beach for a number of years, and this year you participated in the first edition of Art Basel in Hong Kong—a city where you opened a gallery in 2012. What does the shift of the art world and art market toward the Asia-Pacific area mean to you? How do you deal with your presence in this area?

First, it is important to stress that we still believe London to be unsurpassed as a cultural hub and are proud to be part of that energy. The expanding markets in the Asia-Pacific region are clearly of interest and Hong Kong is a good base from which to explore this, both commercially and culturally. The main purpose of setting up a gallery there is to provide an expanded context for our artists. It is fundamentally not a market-driven decision Art fairs are where markets are focused and cultivated; galleries are where reputations are made and enhanced, and for which the best work is created.

At the end of 2012 you launched a new gallery in São Paulo, almost 20 years after opening the smallest commercial gallery in Europe on Duke Street in London. Why did you choose to open in São Paulo?

Brazil is a difficult place to do business, but a great place to show artists. We wanted to get closer to what is happening there in terms of artists, museums, and collectors. As the first major Western gallery to establish a space in Brazil, we have been very heartened by the response. You could say it's a pioneering venture and a calculated risk, but our lease is for three years and we can reassess the situation at the end of this time.

AD RIAN WONG

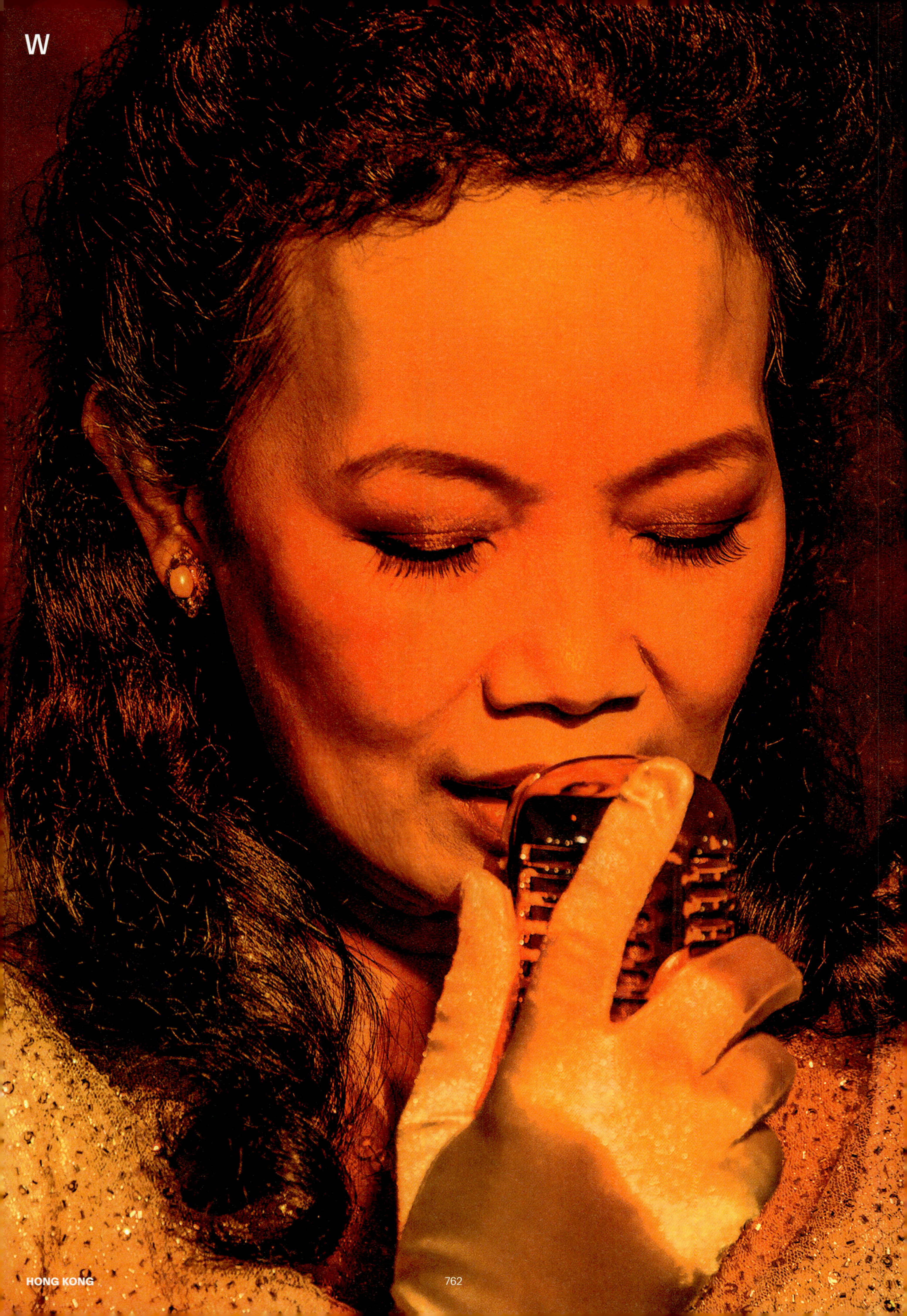

Blowing Cow and a Dancing Sack, or, the Search for a Primordial Hong Kong

by Robin Peckham

Hong Kong
Wun Dun, 2013
Fringe Club

Adrian Wong
Absolut Art Bureau

"There was something featureless yet complete, born before heaven and earth."[1] In the beginning was the bar, and the bar was with god, and the bar was god.[2] "There was a Primal Simplicity, there was a Primal Commencement, there were Primal Beginnings, there was a Primal Material. The Primal Simplicity preceded the appearance of the breath. The Primal Beginnings were the breath beginning to assume shape. The Primal Material was the breath when it began to assume substance. Breath, shape, and substance were complete, but things were not yet separated from each other."[3] Hence the name *Wun Dun*: chaos, confusion. A cosmic gourd; a god in the shape of a yellow sack.

Adrian Wong has devised a mythological space that should not exist but, in a sense, has already existed for millennia. It contains the bones of a bar covered with the skin of a local Cantonese diner, or *cha chaan teng*, an odd combination of social function and aesthetic elaboration that gestures wildly at the fabricated nature of culture and place in Hong Kong, a city where Irish pubs and Chiuchow banquet halls seem to draw their decor from comparably pre-packaged sets of props.

As with many of his projects, Wong began this installation as an attempt to manufacture the aura of a vintage Hong Kong history unmoored from "real" or factual content—only to end up by convincing himself that the experience of the city is, in fact, nothing more than a kaleidoscope of fabrications. The art-bar installation draws its references from the Chinese origin myth of the *hundun*, a featureless sack that brings the living senses into being only after it is struck by lightning, which punctures holes in the sack in the shape of eyes, ears, nostrils, mouth, anus, urethra. The *hundun* is a metaphor for Hong Kong, a placeless and faceless entity, which itself does not exist until it is penetrated and reconstituted through aesthetic projects like this one.

Readers familiar with Wong's past work will have immediately recognized the bar as one of his trademark spaces. Laminated banquettes lined the walls, tile patterns abounded, and a decorative metal grille lined a stage occupied by an animatronic jazz duo in the mold of his talking heads and rolling carpet monsters. One furry figure played the piano and picked at a double bass; the other had a trumpet for a face and a half-dozen appendages put to use on a drum kit.

There was initially an element of cognitive dissonance involved, as the interior united so many disparate threads of Hong Kong design culture. The feeling was akin to taking high tea in a grimy dive bar, or pounding shots at a truckstop breakfast counter. But this feeling quickly faded into the general din produced by the actors and performers whom Wong has hired to bring the space to life. Visitors were met at the door by a greeter, escorted in by a maitre d', and served by a team of waiters and bussers, all of whom were costumed and trained by a professional choreographer to exaggerate the incommensurate walks of life from which they were hired. Many have served at iconic local restaurants of the "soy sauce Western" category, where they catered to a mix of curious tourists and nostalgic locals. Others were security guards and ferry captains.

It is precisely this anxiety of performance and authenticity that Wong intended to provoke. Let there be no confusion: what was staged within the bar was a performance of bar service. But it was no more a performance than the work of the waiter within a soy sauce steakhouse. Hong Kong is a there without a there, a city where the American steak and the Peking duck are equally foreign. Life always wins out in the end, and here the reader is confronted with a sense of the spectacular that settles into

1 See Laozi, *Tao Te Ching: The Classic Book of Integrity and the Way*. Trans. Victor H. Mair. New York: Bantam Books, 1990. p. 90.

2 See *King James Bible Online*, 2008. John 1:1.

3 See Lie Yukou, *The Book of Lieh-tzu: A Classic of Tao*. Trans. Angus C. Graham. New York: Columbia University Press, 1990. pp. 18–19.

the familiar role of the everyday. Move along—there's nothing to see here. Except that there is.

What remains after the many-layered onion of hyperreality is stripped down to the core is a set of techniques, strategies, and instructions for bringing structure to form. This was a semi-conscious mirroring of the other in which no one was quite sure who belongs on which side of the fence. Adrian Wong served up an artificial vision of locality that was perfectly suited for art world tastes in ironic entertainment, slumming, orientalism, and excessive consumption; fortunately, it was equally a vision manufactured for this same locality.

Surly waiters aside, many aspects of the installation should ring true, particularly for those who grew up in Hong Kong or have at least some sense of its aesthetic transformations across the past half century. Singing on the stage to the accompaniment of the two animatronic jazz hands, for instance, were older singers ranging in expertise from professional Cantonese opera to the semi-professional karaoke-style stages of Temple Street, belting out local lounge classics and covers of Western standards from the 1960s. Again, the performance involved hiring very real people to matter-of-factly do what they do—not putting them on display, as though in an art exhibition, but rather simply recreating the cultural circumstances that allowed them to

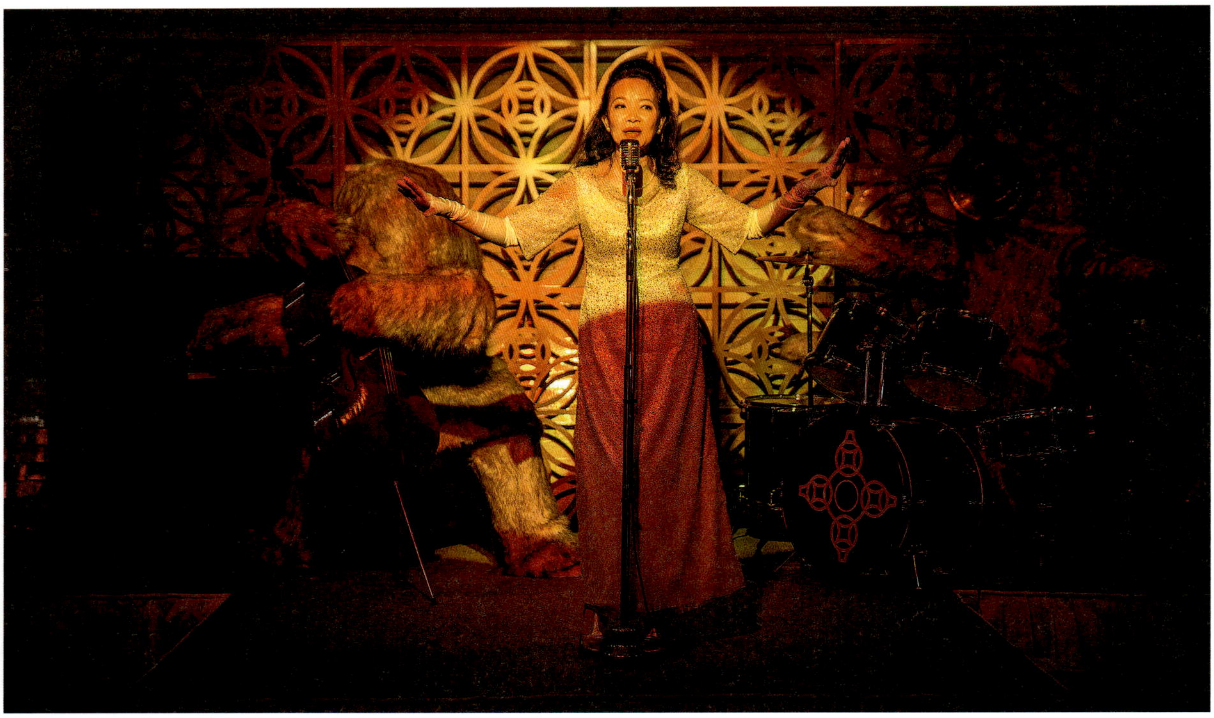

Lilian Chan Shiu San, Wun Dun's resident septuagenarian songstress, was discovered in a seedy karaoke bar in the Yau Ma Tei night market.
— Adrian Wong

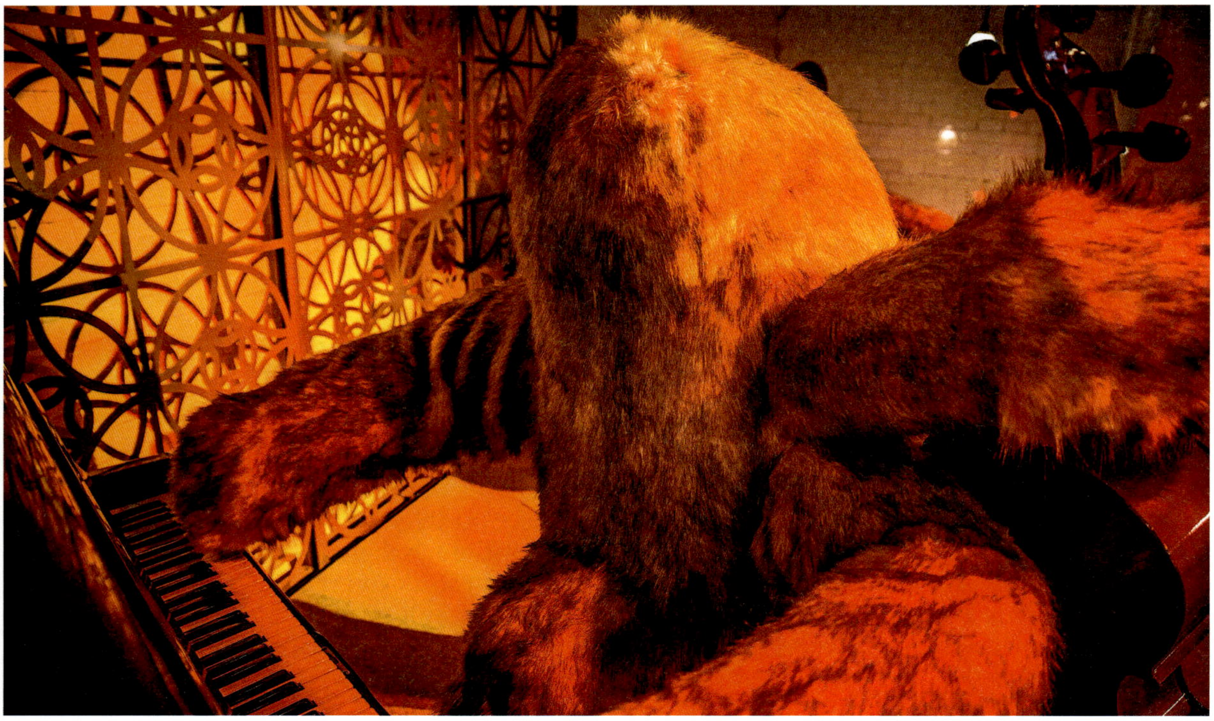

Lilian was supported on stage by two animatronic Wun Dun, one on the piano and double bass, the other on the drums and horn. Sprung from the primordial chaos which existed before the division of heaven and earth, the Wun Dun were said to be yellow sacks with six legs and no sensory orifices—until they were struck by cosmic lightning, creating holes through which the world could be viewed, heard, smelled, and tasted.
— Adrian Wong

be themselves. Even the drinks menu, designed in collaboration with Absolut mixologist Andres Basile-Léon, incorporated the distinctive flavor profiles of the region's cuisine—from roast duck-infused vodka, to cape-gooseberry soup, to monkey-picked oolong martinis.

Wong's recent work has focused on how design and other aesthetic decisions structure lifestyle, and how non-linguistic communication in animals and children can define perception. By situating his bar as a study in anachronistic pastiche, in which clothing, furniture, music, and architecture from multiple periods were brought together, along with non-human actors in the form of both an animatronic jazz band and exotic sea creatures in aquariums, Wong tested his audience's presuppositions around how place and heritage are constructed in a social context. This free-floating, aesthetic approach to our understanding of reality was inspired by Hong Kong, but it is universally applicable. An experienced raconteur, the artist is enamored with the discursive mode best captured by the Cantonese expression, "blowing cow," often sacrificing historical accuracy for narrative impact. The experience of the space between true and false, after all, can be a rich one.

A yellow sack with no limbs and no eyes partial to singing and dancing—a tale told by an idiot, full of sound and fury, signifying nothing.[4]

4 See William Shakespeare, *Macbeth*. MIT Shakespeare Online. Act 5, Scene 5, Lines 26–28.

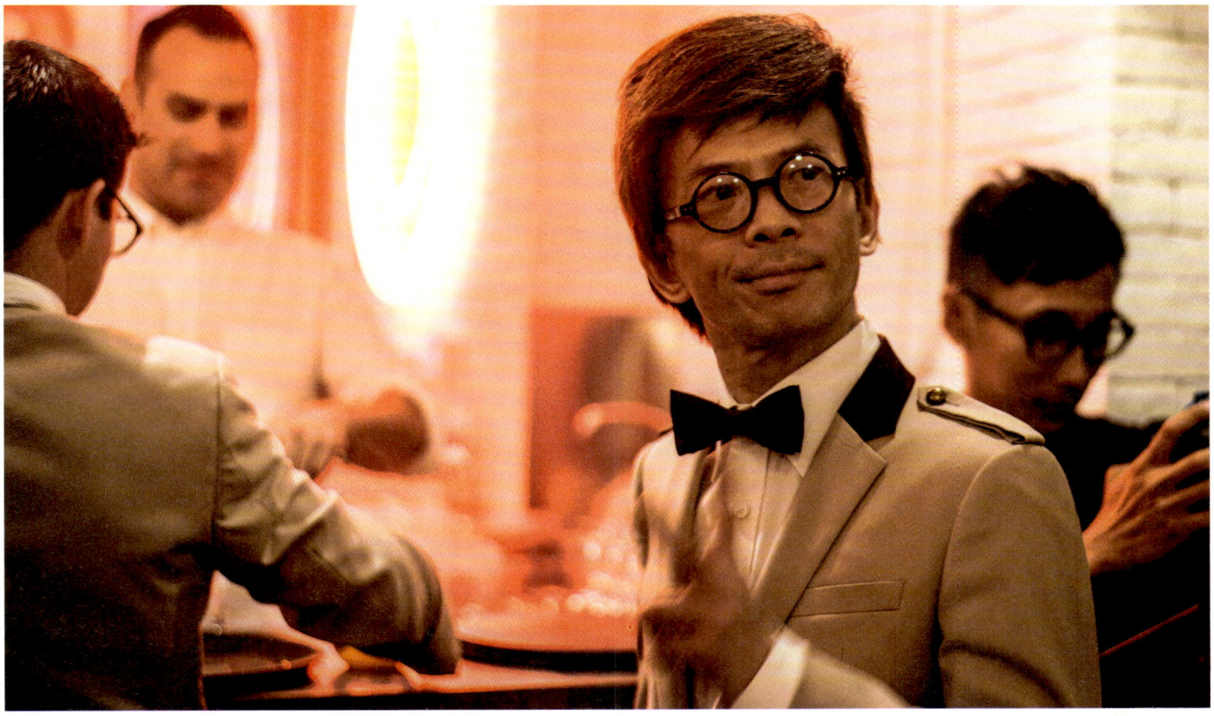

David Lo was poached from the staff of iconic Hong Kong eatery Tai Ping Koon, and encouraged to incorrectly take down drink orders and manifest general incompetence.
— Adrian Wong

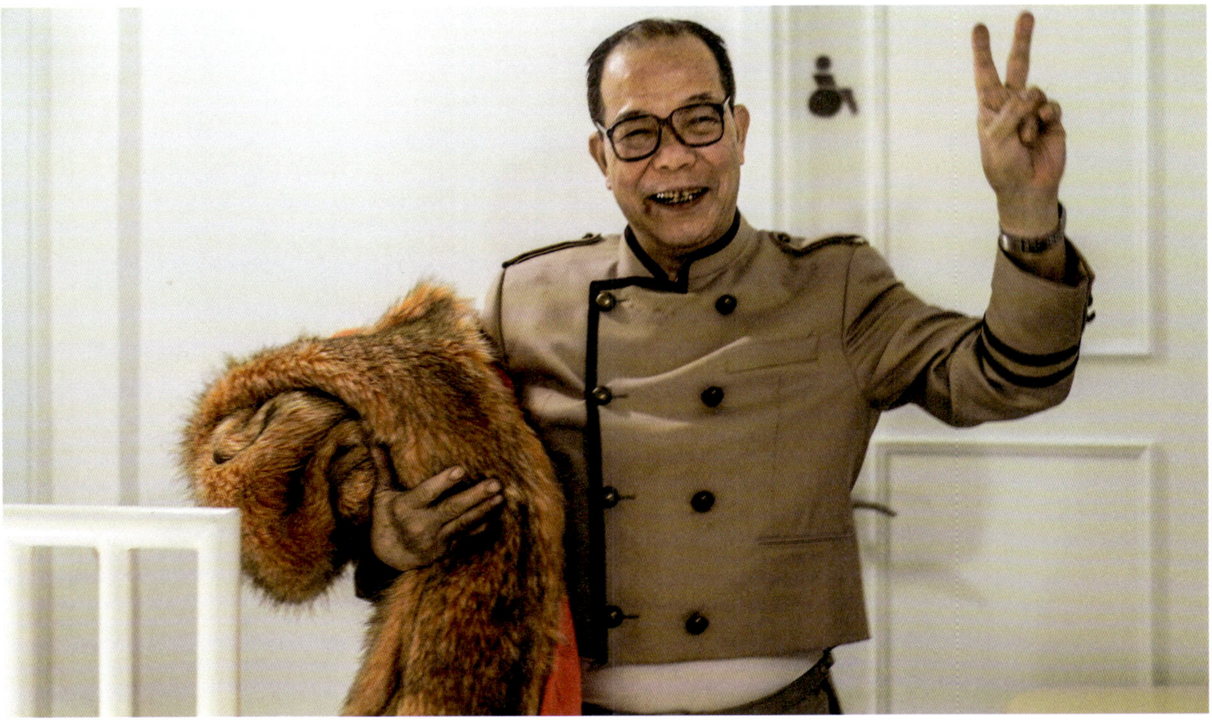

Cheung Kam Fai, the night doorman from my apartment complex, was our bathroom attendant and greeter.
— Adrian Wong

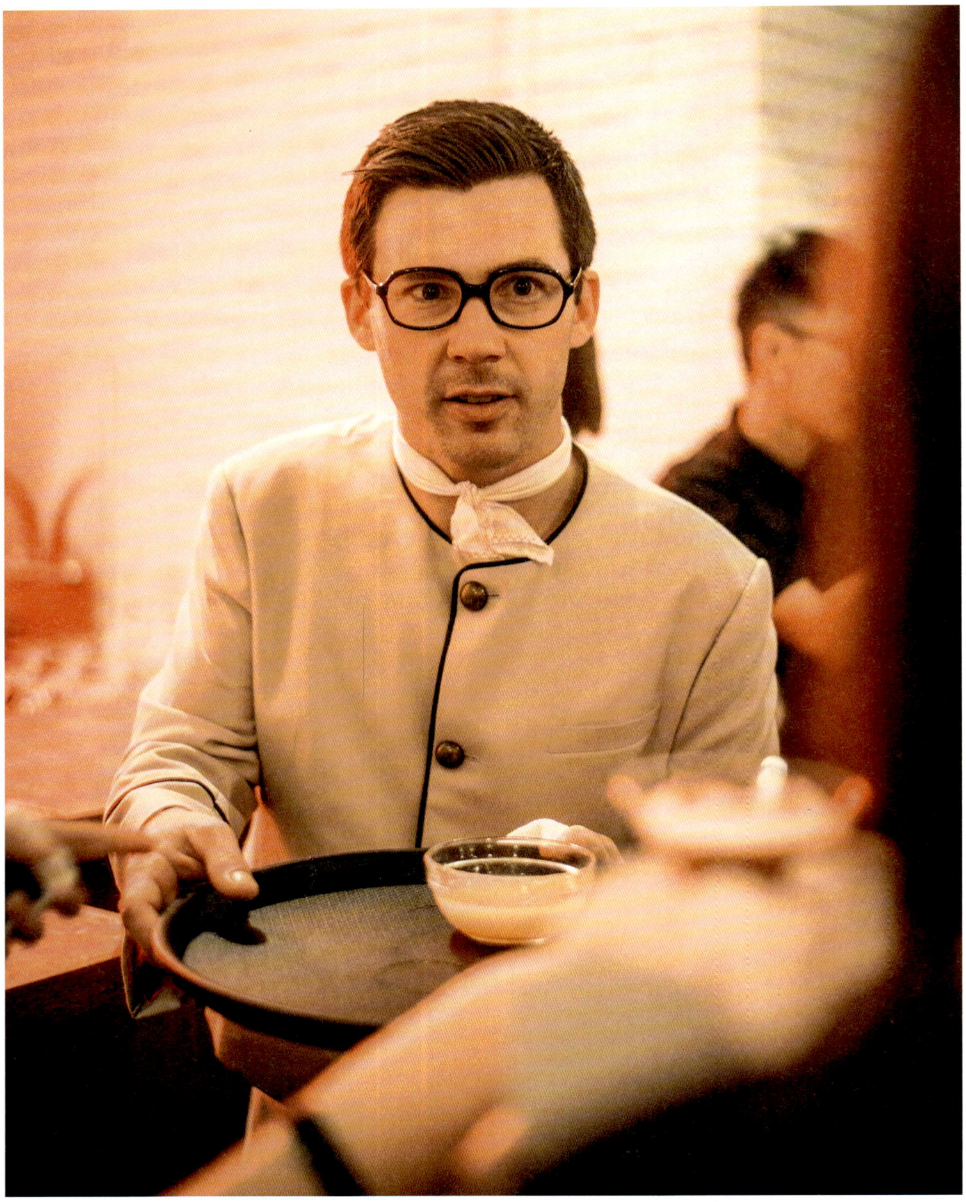

New York based performance artist Jacob Borndal played the role of an aloof busboy, with a penchant for making female patrons uncomfortable and napping on the job.
— Adrian Wong

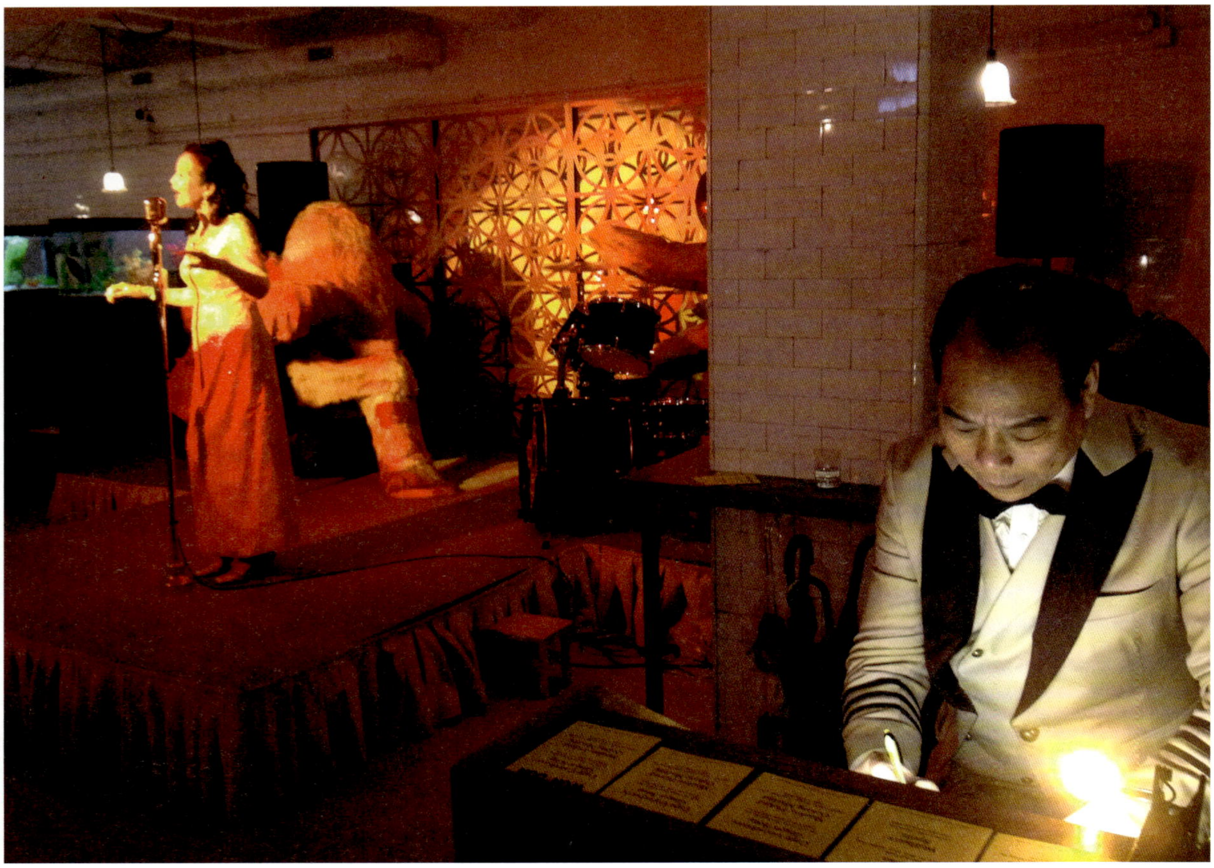

Relieved of his usual duties as captain of Hong Kong's iconic Star Ferry, Ng Kam Shing served as Wun Dun's disgruntled Maître d'. Mr. Ng was very camera shy and eluded photographs throughout the performance.
— Adrian Wong

X

X

x-ist

Istanbul — Insights

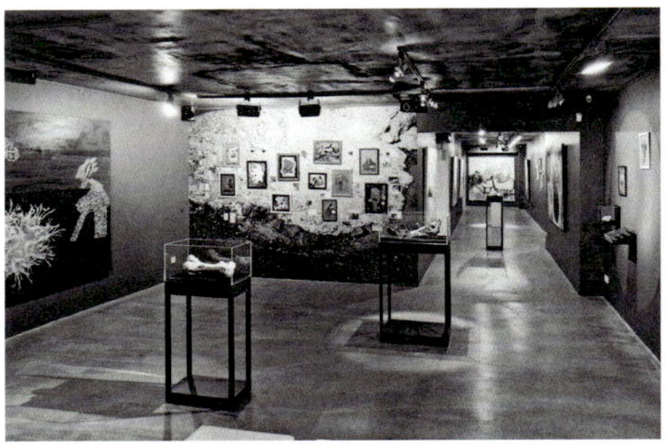

What first compelled you to open a gallery?
When I opened the gallery in May 2004, I had been a postwar Turkish modern art collector for seven years. Then, all of a sudden, I noticed that there was nothing and no one else I was interested in collecting anymore, which led me to the naked truth of the absence of new artists in an era when contemporary art had new things to say every day. Hence I opened x-ist.

Who is the first artist you showed and what was most memorable about that show?
Mehmet Güleryüz. He was (and still is) one of the best contemporary artists that came out of Turkey. He was from the Paris school that many of his contemporaries belonged to, but he couldn't achieve a real success. That was an amazing show at an infant gallery; around 500 visitors attended the opening.

When did you first participate in Art Basel and what was most memorable about that show?
Our first participation in Art Basel was in 2013 in Hong Kong, with two young and acclaimed Turkish artists: Nuri Kuzucan and Ceren Oykut. It was our fourth year of presence at Hong Kong fairs, nevertheless the change in the quality of the organization along with the overall program was really memorable.

- **Contact** Gallery x-ist
  Yasemin Elci
  yasemin@artxist.com
  info@atxist.com
- **Established** 2004
- **Owner(s) / Partner(s)** Davit Beskinazi (Owner and Founder)
- **Space(s)** 180 m²
- **Artists at Art Basel** Nuri Kuzucan
  Ceren Oykut
- **Further artists represented** Serkan Adın
  Fatih Alkan
  Ansen
  Bahadır Baruter
  Banu Birecikligil
  CANAN
  Cem Dinlenmiş
  Ali Elmacı
  Seda Hepsev
  Ahmet Polat
  Ekin Saçlıoglu
  Sena
  Lale Tara
  Erkut Terliksiz
  Nalan Yırtmaç

XL

Moscow — Galleries

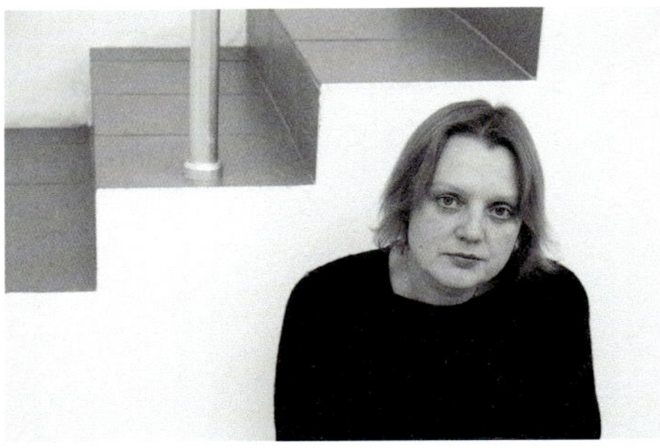

What first compelled you to open a gallery?
The desire to show some of the most interesting moves and trends in Russian contemporary art.

Who is the first artist you showed and what was most memorable about that show?
Marina Chernikova. A mix of performance and photography.

When did you first participate in Art Basel and what was most memorable about that show?
In 2005 in Art Basel and Art Basel in Miami Beach. At Miami we were in the Art Positions sector, in the containers. We changed the exhibition three times every day, and that was really fun.

- **Contact** XL Gallery
  Sergey Khripun
  xlgallery@gmail.com
- **Established** 1993
- **Owner(s) / Partner(s)** Elena Selina
  Sergey Khripun
- **Team** 3
- **Space(s)** 160 m²
- **Artists at Art Basel** Konstantin Belyaev
  Bluesoup group
  Irina Korina
  Mikhail Kosolapov
  Viktor Pivovarov
  Sergei Shekhovtsov
  Anna Zhelud
- **Further artists represented** ABC group
  Aristarkh Chernyshev
  Anna Jermolaewa
  Igor Makarevich
  Igor Moukhin
  Boris Orlov
  Alexandr Povzner
  Aidan Salakhova
  ZIP group
  Konstantin Zvezdochetov

Xu

Shanghai — Discoveries

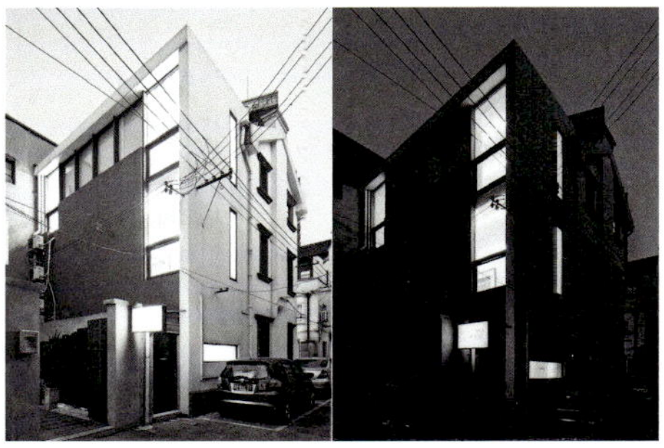

What first compelled you to open a gallery?
The urge to work with a young generation of (Chinese) artists whose art responded to the new media and tech-inspired cultures and policies. The desire to support new ideas and to develop the careers of a new generation defining new cultures.

Who is the first artist you showed and what was most memorable about that show?
Cheng Ran. Cheng's first show with the gallery (*What Why How*, 2012) represented a set of new video/cinematic vocabularies that question the possibilities of 20th-century cinema. A hybrid

product of various disciplines (art house cinema, early video art, music video, among others), the show defied the cliched definition of Chinese video and sought to deliver the voice of his peers who have been strongly inspired by the immediate reality and access to bootleg cultural products since the early 1990s. The vision of the show matched that of the gallery.

- **Contact** Leo Xu Projects
  Leo Xu
  leo.xuyu@gmail.com
  info@leoxuprojects.com
- **Established** 2011
- **Owner(s) / Partner(s)** Leo Xu (Director)
  Private Partners
- **Team** 3
- **Space(s)** 250 m²
- **Artists at Art Basel** Chen Wei
- **Further artists represented** Cheng Ran
  Cui Jie
  Guo Hongwei
  Gabriel Lester
  Li Qing
  Michael Lin
  Liu Chuang

XVA

Dubai

Insights

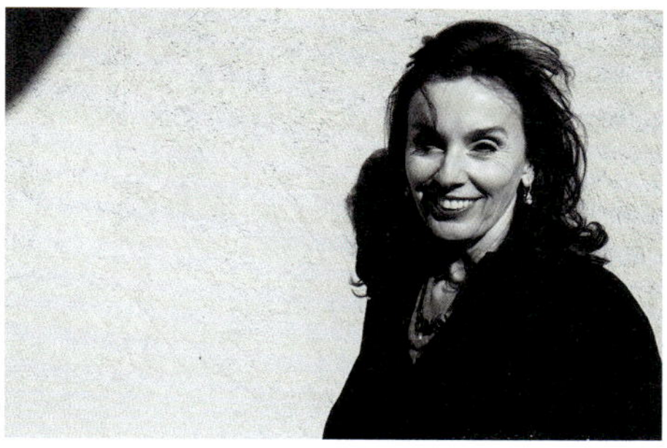

What first compelled you to open a gallery?
I was certain that there was a need to show art of a certain sophistication, which I felt the region was lacking.

Who is the first artist you showed and what was most memorable about that show?
Nelda Gilliam. There was great support for both Gilliam and our fledgling gallery. We had an oud player in the courtyard and the event was very well attended. It was very exciting because at the time there were no contemporary art galleries in Dubai.

When did you first participate in Art Basel and what was most memorable about that show?
In Art Basel in Hong Kong in 2013. The huge crowds of art connoisseurs! It was a thrill to see the collectors that we had met from the year before. The organization of the fair was superb and it has been an honor to be a part of the fair's growth.

- **Contact** XVA Gallery
  Eleanor Smith
  ellie@xvagallery.com
  xva@xvagallery.com
- **Established** 2003
- **Owner(s) / Partner(s)** Mona Hauser
- **Space(s)** 55 m²
- **Artists at Art Basel** Imran Channa
- **Further artists represented** Mohsen Ahmadvand
  Halim Al Karim
  Sami Al Karim
  Hussein Al-Mohasen
  Arezu
  Al Braithwaite
  Faiza Butt
  Simeen Farhat
  Maitha Huraiz
  Meera Huraiz
  Walid Siti
  Morteza Zahedi

Leo Xu Projects

Three Questions for Leo Xu

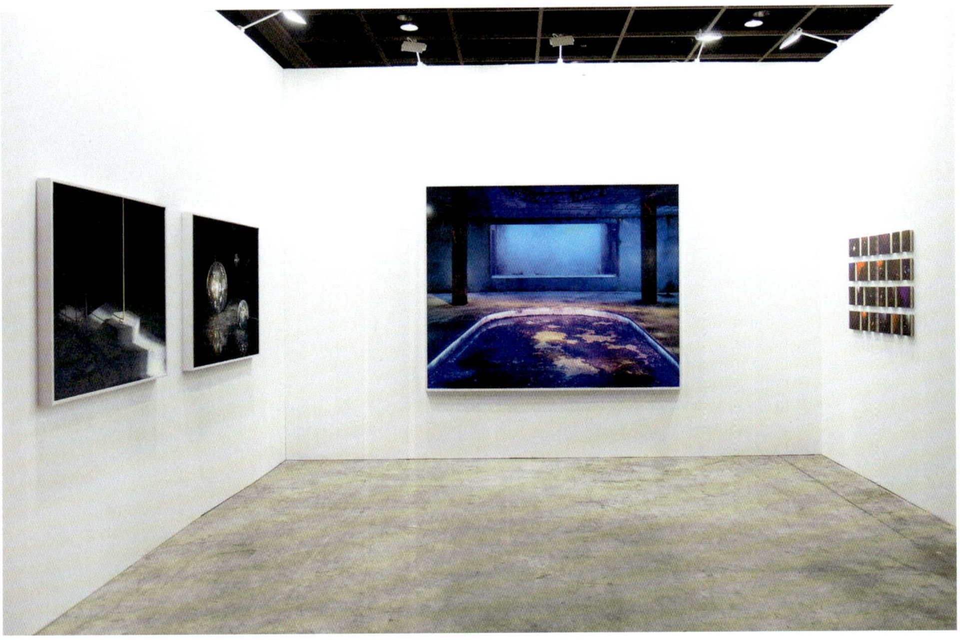

Art Basel in Hong Kong (Discoveries), 2013

Leo Xu Projects is a contemporary art gallery founded in 2011 in Shanghai, which exhibits young Chinese and international artists. How have you chosen to represent the current vitality of the Asia-Pacific art scene? What is your perception of this current dynamism?

Ever-changing socio-political situations, cultural policies, new economies and technologies, the Chinese diaspora, unprecedented and unpredictable factors, have all sent the Asia-Pacific region into seismic artistic activity. Both the gallery artists and our program represent our interest in exploring the layers beneath all this, the new media/tech inspired cultures, and new Chinese/Asian identities in particular.

Could you briefly present your gallery, its program, and its specificities within this art scene?

The gallery sees its mission as developing the careers of our young and mid-career Chinese/Asian artists and bringing our international artists closer to the local communities. In the gallery space every year we have about four solo shows, two thematic or group exhibitions curated by the gallery, and a series of off-site projects with institutions, public spaces, publications, and cyberspace projects.

Taking Shanghai and its semi-colonial past as inspiration, our program is curated to probe the possibilities of new media applied in various disciplines, and to test the new models in urbanism in the Asia-Pacific region. The program of the first two years has delivered an in-depth analysis of China's *shanzhai* (bootleg/piracy) culture, and studies the visualities informed by local urbanism and education.

Located in the heart of the former French Concession, the gallery is neighbor to the city's best cultural establishment institutions, which places our program in a clear context. The gallery space is small, as we understand physical space differently: we have played a lot with social media, the cyber world, and print/digital publications to extend our program into various and unlimited dimensions.

You participated in Art Basel in Hong Kong with a solo show by Chen Wei in the Discoveries sector. Could you tell us about this artist and his proposition?

Chen Wei's solo presentation revisits the youth culture shaped by pop music from the 1990s. It maps an overlooked kinship between Mainland China and Hong Kong in this specific sector. Through reproducing those choreographed and staged moments as a disco scene, our booth translated the clubs into a cultural shelter and monument. The exhibit came at the time when a young generation of Chinese are reflecting on the escalating issues between the Mainland and Hong Kong, and are rethinking their/our identities within a much bigger framework and context.

Y

Y++ Wada

Tokyo — Insights

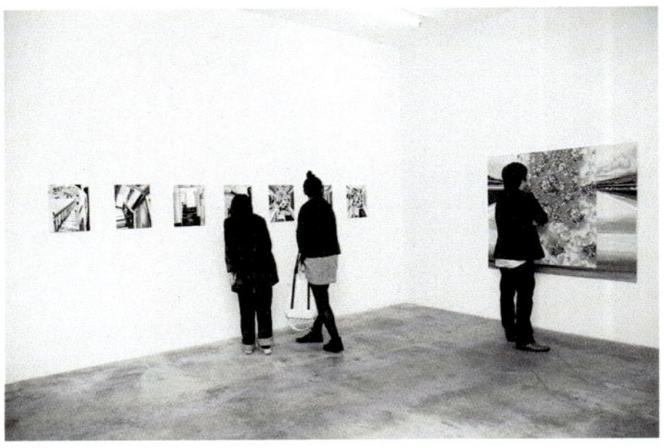

What first compelled you to open a gallery?
I like art very much and graduated from an art university, from one of the most prestigious in Japan. I grew up looking at my father's collection. I developed a network in the art world at the university. My family business has a long history: it is a company making traditional Japanese kimonos. I proposed to launch an art department as a new business brand of the company in 1990; we opened the gallery Iseyoshi within our own building (Ginza, Tokyo). I established Wada Fine Arts in its current form, as an independent art gallery, in 2007.

Who is the first artist you showed and what was most memorable about that show?
Gunji Fukasawa.

When did you first participate in Art Basel and what was most memorable about that show?
In 2013 in Hong Kong.

- **Contact**: Y++ Wada Fine Arts, Yumie Wada, wadayumie@gmail.com, info@wadafinearts.com
- **Established**: 1990
- **Owner(s) / Partner(s)**: Yumie Wada (CEO and Art Director)
- **Space(s)**: 90 m²
- **Artists at Art Basel**: Tetsuya Ishida
- **Further artists represented**: Heri Dono, Yasushi Ebihara, Takafumi Hara, Atsuko Imaizumi, Minori Inata, Shinichiro Kitamura, Takahiro Miura, Yoichi Miyajima, Hiroshi Ohashi, Donna Ong, Anna Oya, Keiko Sakamoto, Takehiko Sugawara, Hisako Sugiyama, Rodel Tapaya, Takafumi Tsuchiya, Yan Heng, Tomoko Yokoyama, Zhao Gang

Yamaki

Kobe — Insights

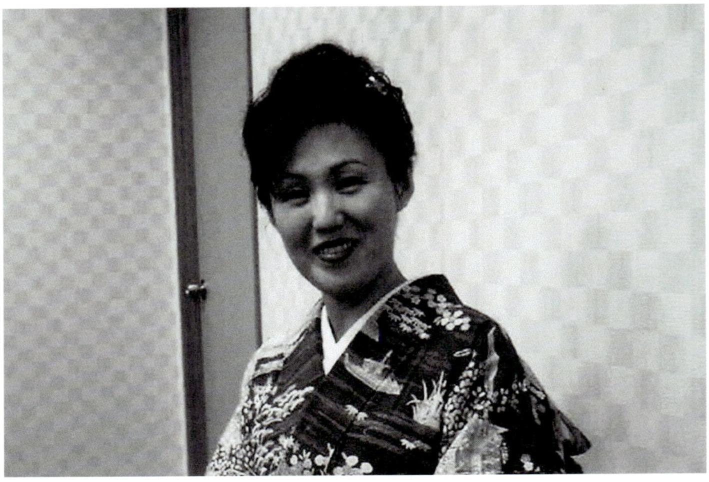

What first compelled you to open a gallery?
Having worked for a prefectural museum, I learned that art museums in Japan mostly hold exhibitions planned by newspaper companies, and only an exhibition or two per year on their own. This made me aware that a gallery might be able to contribute more to the future of an art scene in Japan, at a grassroots level, especially by exhibiting interesting contemporary artworks.

Who is the first artist you showed and what was most memorable about that show?
Louis Cane, a French artist, who belonged to the French art group Supports/Surfaces.

When did you first participate in Art Basel and what was most memorable about that show?
Our first participation in Art Basel was in Hong Kong in 2013. What was most memorable about that show was the installation by Susumu Koshimizu.

- **Contact**: Gallery Yamaki Fine Art, Seika Abe, info@gyfa.co.jp
- **Established**: 2006
- **Owner(s) / Partner(s)**: Kanako Yamaki (Director)
- **Team**: 4
- **Space(s)**: 150 m²
- **Artists at Art Basel**: Susumu Koshimizu
- **Further artists represented**: Louis Cane, Veronika Dovers, Michio Fukuoka, Yuki Hayashi, Sadaharu Horio, Kenji Inumaki, Christian Jaccard, Tatsuo Kawaguchi, Saki Kirizuki, Jean Le Gac, Min-Ho Lee, Jörg Lehmann, Frederique Lucien, Takesada Matsutani, Ringo Tang, Mario Tauchi, Jun Tsukawaki, Keiji Uematsu, Claude Viallat, Nobuko Watanabe

Yamamoto Gendai

Tokyo ● Galleries

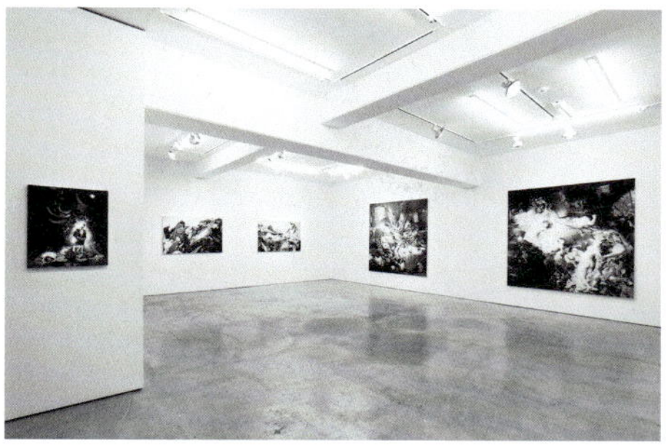

What first compelled you to open a gallery?
Some fortunate coincidences brought me to open my gallery.

Who is the first artist you showed and what was most memorable about that show?
We inaugurated our gallery with a solo exhibition by Motohiko Odani. Two weeks prior to the opening Odani told me that he would be unable to realize the show. I had no other choice, but I understood his situation and said okay. In case that happened I was going to put up a notice on the entrance door, saying that "our first show has been postponed," and I told him how I will manage. He became rather motivated somehow then. He was probably testing my mettle? Anyway, the show opened peacefully and had a splendid success.

When did you first participate in Art Basel and what was most memorable about that show?
At the inaugural edition of Art Basel in Hong Kong in 2013, after exhibiting at the former ART HK every year since 2009.

- **Contact** Yamamoto Gendai
  Kazumasa Nonaka
  n@yamamotogendai.org
  i@yamamotogendai.org
- **Established** 2004
- **Owner(s) / Partner(s)** Yuko Yamamoto
- **Team** 4
- **Space(s)** 100 m²
- **Artists at Art Basel** Kei Imazu
  Erina Matsui
  Yasuyuki Nishio
  Keisuke Tanaka
  UJINO
- **Further artists represented** Yayoi Deki
  Etsuko Fukaya
  Shinichi Hara
  Natsumi Hirakawa
  Kaori Kobayashi
  Kohei Kobayashi
  Sako Kojima
  Li Yan
  Edgar Martins
  Osamu Mori
  Ruriko Murayama
  Hermann Nitsch
  Motohiko Odani
  Tsukasa Ohtake
  Keita Sugiura
  Masakatsu Takagi
  Tiger Tateishi
  Naohiro Ukawa
  Kenji Yanobe

Yang

Beijing ● Insights

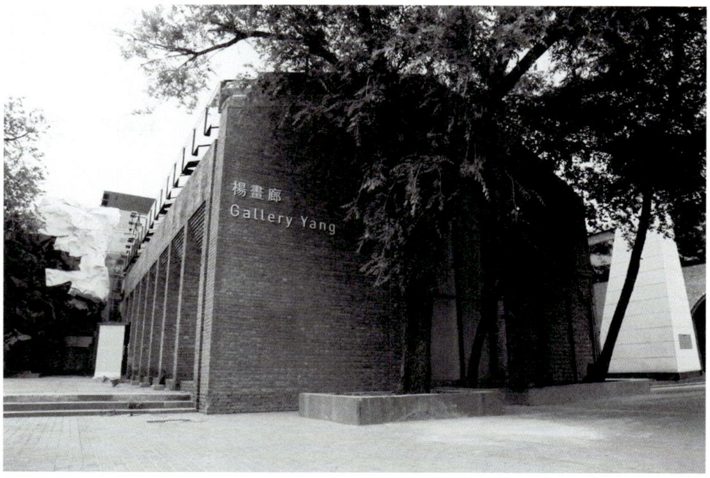

What first compelled you to open a gallery?
To support emerging artists, working on projects and exhibitions, and occasionally with established artists.

Who is the first artist you showed and what was most memorable about that show?
The opening exhibition of Gallery Yang, entitled *Six + Six: Energy, Pass on* in 2010, was curated by Guo Xiaoyan. Each of the participating and established artists (Fang Lijun, Liu Xiaodong, Zhou Chunya, Mao Yan, Yang Shaobin, and Xiang Jing) recommended a young artist, which included Yang Yong, Chen Zhuo, Tu Hongtao, Wu Wen, Qin Qi, and Wu Di.

- **Contact** Gallery Yang
  Jinpeng Mu
  jinpeng.mu@galleryyang.com
- **Established** 2010
- **Owner(s) / Partner(s)** Yang Min
- **Team** 6
- **Space(s)** 200 m²
- **Artists at Art Basel** Yan Bing
- **Further artists represented** Chen Zhuo
  Jiang Pengyi
  Kong Lingnan
  Li Bo
  Wang Yuyang
  Yan Heng
  Ye Linghan
  Zhan Chong
  Zheng Yunhan

Gallery Yang

Three Questions for Jinpeng Mu

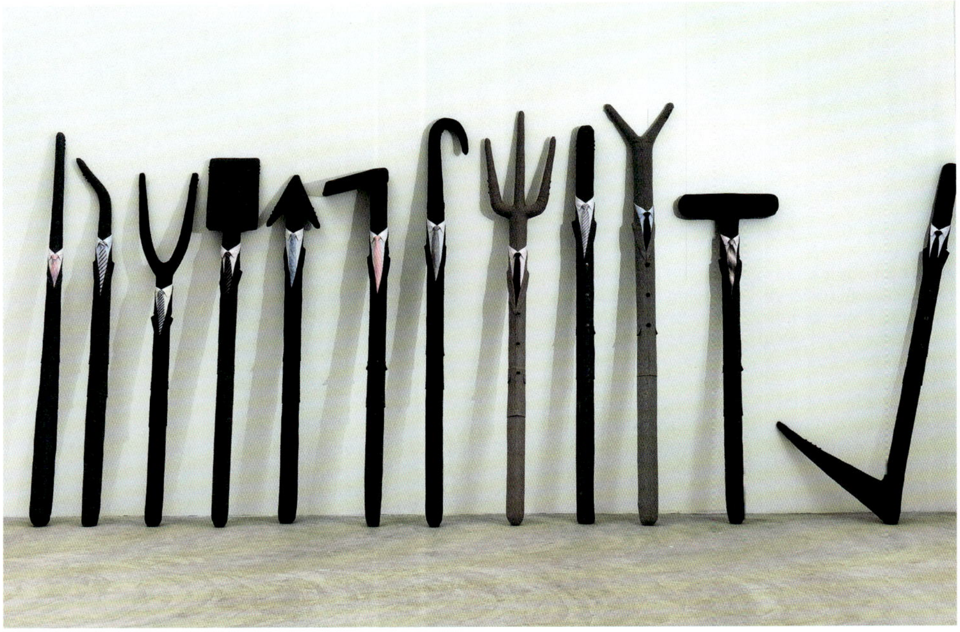

Art Basel in Hong Kong (Insights), 2013

Located in Beijing's famous area, the "798 Art Zone," your gallery has promoted about 50 Chinese artists since its creation in 2010. Could you tell us about your program and exhibition policy …

Gallery Yang usually holds five solo exhibitions and two group exhibitions each year. Its 158 square-meter exhibition hall is perfect for solo exhibitions. Since 2010, many young artists have made their debuts in our solo exhibitions. We do not confine ourselves to painting; in 2013, more experimental works have been shown, such as moving images, installation, performance, etc. The artists we represent often work in collaboration with curators to use to possibilities offered by the space fully, and better present the gist of their works. For example, in 2013, the artist Dong Yuan worked in collaboration with the curator Wei Xing for the exhibition *A Short History of Everything*. Li Binyuan, an artist working with new media and performance art, invited Cui Cancan as the curator of his work in *I Have Issues*. These two exhibitions were very successful.

Furthermore, since 2011, Bao Dong started curating a series of exhibitions called *Painting Lesson*, which became a brand of Gallery Yang with their occurrence for three consecutive years. They give good presentations of Chinese contemporary painting, mainly works by young artists.

How did your booth in Art Basel in Hong Kong reflect this position? Why did you choose to present a focus on the artist Yan Bing?

Gallery Yang has collaborated several times with Yan Bing; the first time was his solo exhibition *My Labor*, in 2011. Convinced by his personality and the quality of his oeuvre, the gallery has worked to build a long-term relationship with him—Yan Bing is an unassuming and uncompromising man, with a serious and deliberate attitude toward art. He graduated from CAFA, with his major in oil painting. Even though he comes from a poor family, Yan Bing then chose to focus on installations, a much less commercial medium—he only came back to painting in 2012. Yan Bing clings to the core of his art without being harassed and influenced by the external world; this is the kind of artist we look for and want to collaborate with in the long term.

For Art Basel in Hong Kong, Yan Bing presented the work *Tools* (2013), a meditation on the relationship between humankind and the land. It reflects the idea that the history of humankind is a history of the development of tools. The questions he explores have been overlooked and ignored by the younger generation. Our booth was visited a lot; we believe that with their direct external forms, Yan Bing's works are closer to the nature and heart of human beings.

What is your view of the effervescent Chinese art scene and its market? How does Art Basel in Hong Kong distinguish itself from the other fairs of the region?

We are confident about the future of Chinese art. The market can give an impetus to art, but any impetus brings some problems. Development always has a phase of disorder. Depression is a sign of self-examination, and a new phase of understanding will ensue. We have cultural roots and population foundation in China, which is our territory. After the pomp of the previous generation, the next one will come back to fundamental questions and establish rules of their own.

Art Basel in Hong Kong is a special event, and the most important exhibition now in Asia. It is a meeting point connecting Chinese contemporary art with the rest of the world. With its increasing commercialization, however, it may more or less reduce the possibilities of the emergence of young artists.

Z

Z

Susanne Zander

Cologne
Berlin (2014)

Galleries

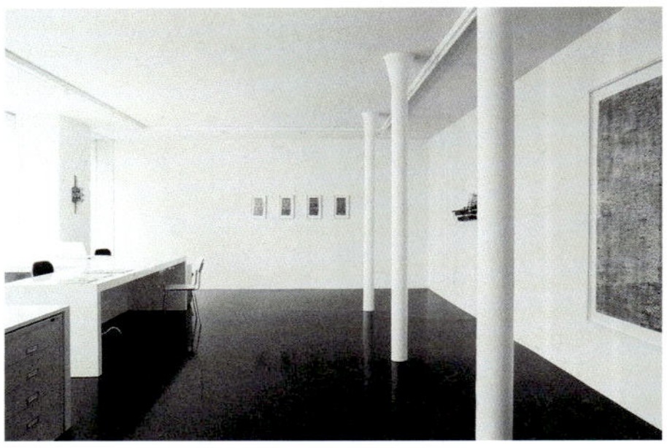

What first compelled you to open a gallery?
A love for Art Brut and Outsider positions in art. And a unique vision for a unique gallery.

Who is the first artist you showed and what was most memorable about that show?
Sava Sekulić. The heartfelt interest of other artists for Outsider art was memorable as well as the great support from gallery-colleagues.

When did you first participate in Art Basel and what was most memorable about that show?
Susanne Zander: It was either 1989 or 1990. I I was very excited about taking part in such a great art fair. There was little sleep, great conversations, a lot of alcohol, and a lot of fun.
Nicole Deimes: My first Art Basel fair was in 2010 when we showed Russian Outsider art at our booth. Despite the risk we took in our choice of artist, we were able to sell works to important international collectors and museeums. As always it was worth taking the risk for passion.

- **Contact** — Galerie Susanne Zander, Susanne Zander, zander@galerie-zander.de
- **Established** — 1988
- **Owner(s) / Partner(s)** — Nicole Deimes, Susanne Zander
- **Team** — 6
- **Space(s)** — 150 m² (Cologne), 130 m² (Berlin)
- **Artists at Art Basel** — Morton Bartlett, Günter K. – 'Margret', Miroslav Tichý
- **Further artists represented** — Horst Ademeit, Martin Erhard, Madge Gill, Paul Goesch, Blalla W. Hallmann, Margarethe Held, Chris Hipkiss, Paul Humphrey, Aurel Iselstöger, Karl Junker, Alexander Lobanov, Dietrich Orth, Bruno Schleinstein, Sava Sekulic, Oswald Tschirtner, Oskar Voll, August Walla, George Widener, Wesley Willis, Agatha Wojciechowsky

Thomas Zander

Cologne

Galleries

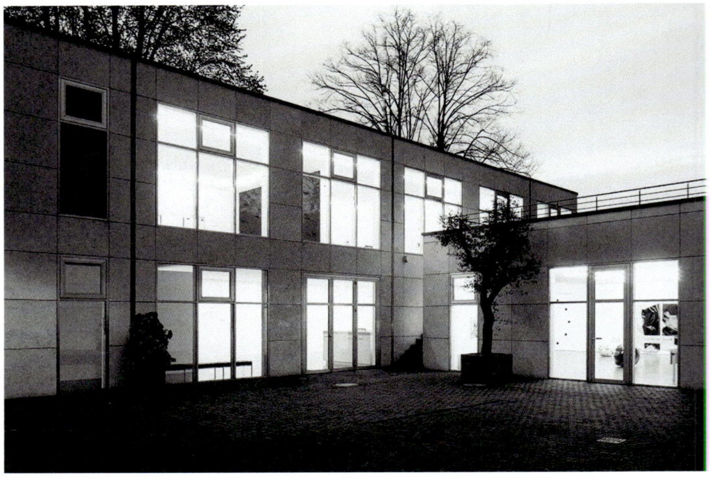

What first compelled you to open a gallery?
There were always many artists among my family friends and I grew up around art. Early on I developed a desire to do more for these artists, represent them in the best sense of the word, and see their work grow. For me it is important to mount exhibitions, publish books, and arrange museum shows for my artists. This is why I became a gallerist rather than an independent art dealer.

Who is the first artist you showed and what was most memorable about that show?
One of the first exhibitions consisted of Ronald B. Kitaj's drawings and graphic work. It took place in my first tiny gallery space outside Cologne. On a Saturday afternoon, one of the most important collectors in Cologne strolled into the gallery and ended up buying a drawing. A few days later a review of the show appeared in the newspaper.

When did you first participate in Art Basel and what was most memorable about that show?
We first participated in 2006 and that was also the first time we presented a solid light installation by Anthony McCall in the Unlimited sector. The Unlimited sector is a unique opportunity to exhibit large-scale works or installations outside the gallery booth Especially for my gallery, which has a focus on photography, this was a fantastic option to show a wider range of works across different media, and promote the idea of expanded photography.

- **Contact** — Galerie Thomas Zander, Frauke Breede, f.breede@galeriezander.com, mail@galeriezander.com
- **Established** — 1996
- **Owner(s) / Partner(s)** — Thomas Zander
- **Team** — 10
- **Space(s)** — 500 m² (excluding storage)
- **Artists at Art Basel** — Lewis Baltz, Lothar Baumgarten, Bernd & Hilla Becher, Victor Burgin, Joe Deal, Peter Downsbrough, Mitch Epstein, Lee Friedlander, Andrea Geyer, Dieter Meier, Trevor Paglen, Tata Ronkholz, Larry Sultan, Henry Wessel
- **Further artists represented** — Diane Arbus, William Christenberry, Jean-Paul Deridder, Don Dudley, William Eggleston, Walker Evans, Anthony McCall, John McLaughlin, Joel Meyerowitz, Gabriele & Helmut Nothhelfer, Max Regenberg, Garry Winogrand

Zeno X

Antwerp

Galleries
Galleries

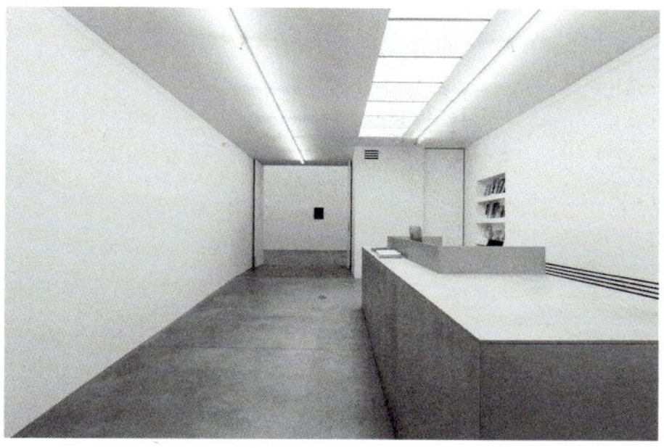

What first compelled you to open a gallery?
I have always been fascinated by art. Actually the gallery started as a hobby; I was quite naive, and wasn't conscious of the art market. After a few years it became more serious and I lost my naivety, but luckily not my passion for art. I am glad we are still working with some artists we have represented from the very beginning. I am thinking of Anne-Mie Van Kerckhoven, Patrick Van Caeckenbergh, Luc Tuymans, and Marlene Dumas.

Who is the first artist you showed and what was most memorable about that show?
In 1981 I planned my first exhibition with Luc Deleu, a Belgian architect and artist, but in the end another artist, Vic Joseph, got the first show at the gallery. *Perspective and Scale* by Luc Deleu followed. In the beginning I focused on Conceptual art and installations. It all felt very avant-garde.

When did you first participate in Art Basel and what was most memorable about that show?
This year we celebrate our 20th participation at Art Basel. In 1994, for the first time, when we were invited to the young section of the fair, we had a special installation by Mark Manders. The whole booth was covered with colored blankets and there was an old wooden stove. The stove was a replica of the one in his parents' house in the Dutch province of Brabant. He installed it above a large surface of blankets which reminded him of his childhood. We also showed *Fox/Mouse/Belt*, also by him. It is nice to look back and see his development. His work is now in major museum collections, which is of course a great fulfillment for all the supporters of his works!

- **Contact** Zeno X Gallery
  Benedicte Goesaert
  info@zeno-x.com
- **Established** 1981
- **Owner(s) / Partner(s)** Frank Demaegd
- **Team** 7
- **Space(s)** 1,200 m²
- **Artists at Art Basel** Michaël Borremans
  Dirk Braeckman
  Anton Corbijn
  Raoul De Keyser
  Jan De Maesschalck
  Marlene Dumas
  Kees Goudzwaard
  Yun-Fei Ji
  Kim Jones
  Johannes Kahrs
  Naoto Kawahara
  John Körmeling
  Mark Manders
  Jockum Nordström
  Grace Schwindt
  Jenny Scobel
  Bart Stolle
  Luc Tuymans
  Patrick Van Caeckenbergh
  Anne-Mie Van Kerckhoven
  Jack Whitten
  Cristof Yvoré

ZERO

Milan

Galleries
Galleries

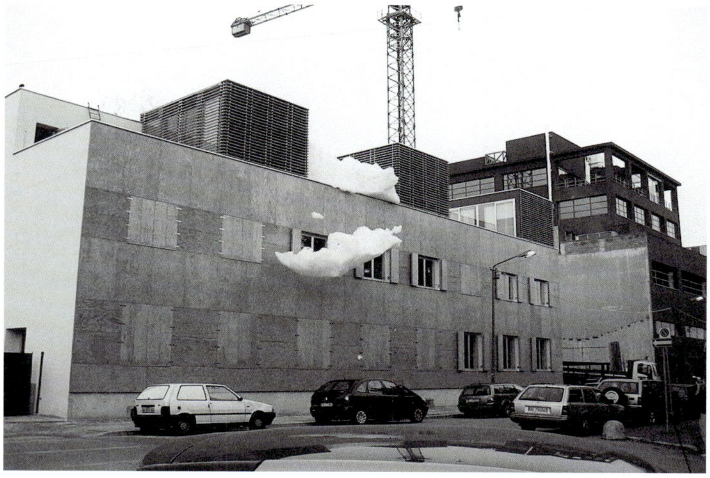

What first compelled you to open a gallery?
The love for human beings and a quite naive vision about art and its system. I am learning about life in general through my experience in the art world. I still love to focus my attention on new directions and I still see art as a possible way to a better future.

Who is the first artist you showed and what was most memorable about that show?
My first exhibition was a group show, entitled *Natural Blues*, a kind of little manifesto in the shape of a prayer. Fischli and Weiss gave me a present in deciding to be in the show.

When did you first participate in Art Basel and what was most memorable about that show?
My first participation was in 2006 in the Art Basel's Premiere sector. I felt I was back home after a long journey and I was happy.

- **Contact** ZERO...
  Paolo Zani
  alberto@galleriazero.it
  info@galleriazero.it
- **Established** 2001
- **Owner(s) / Partner(s)** Paolo Zani
- **Team** 4
- **Space(s)** 330 m²
- **Artists at Art Basel** Yuri Ancarani
  Giorgio Andreotta Calò
  Micol Assaël
  Mark Barrow
  Neïl Beloufa
  Cezary Bodzianowski
  Hubert Duprat
  Christian Frosi
  Giuseppe Gabellone
  Francesco Gennari
  Massimo Grimaldi
  João Maria Gusmão + Pedro Paiva
  Thomas Houseago
  Gavin Kenyon
  Victor Man
  Pietro Roccasalva
  Michael Sailstorfer
  Hans Schabus
  Shimabuku
  Gedi Sibony
  Michael E. Smith

Z

Zwirner

New York
London

Galleries
Galleries
Galleries
Public

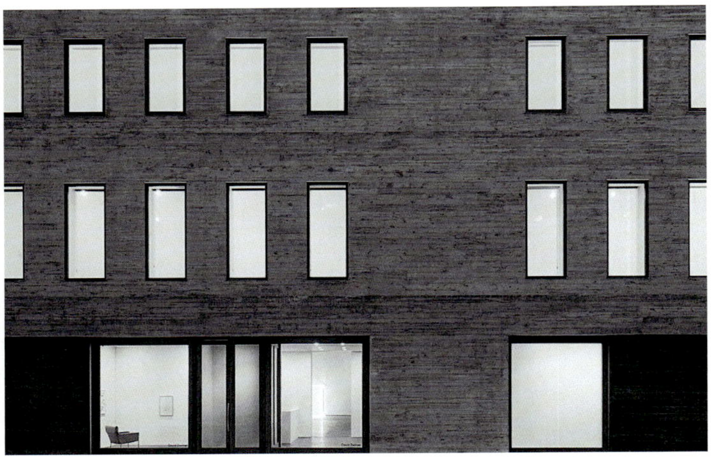

Who is the first artist you showed and what was most memorable about that show?
Franz West.

When did you first participate in Art Basel and what was most memorable about that show?
In 1999.

- **Contact** David Zwirner
Nicollette Eason
nicollette@davidzwirner.com
information@davidzwirner.com
- **Established** 1993
- **Owner(s) / Partner(s)** David Zwirner
Kristine Bell (Partner)
Angela Choon (Partner)
Christopher D'Amelio (Partner)
Bellatrix Hubert (Partner)
Julia Joern (Partner)
Tracy Nolder (Partner)
Ales Ortuzar (Partner)
Hanna Schouwink (Partner)
- **Team** 120
- **Space(s)** 929 m² (19th Street, New York)
2,787 m² (20th Street, New York)
2,787 m² (Grafton Street, London)
- **Artists at Art Basel** Adel Abdessemed
Francis Alÿs
Mamma Andersson
Michaël Borremans
Carol Bove
Raoul De Keyser
Philip-Lorca diCorcia
Stan Douglas
Marlene Dumas
Marcel Dzama
Dan Flavin
Suzan Frecon
Isa Genzken
Donald Judd
Jeff Koons
Yayoi Kusama
John McCracken
Alice Neel
Jockum Nordström
Chris Ofili
Raymond Pettibon
Neo Rauch
Jason Rhoades
Michael Riedel
Thomas Ruff
Fred Sandback
Al Taylor
Luc Tuymans
James Welling
Christopher Williams
Lisa Yuskavage
- **Further artists represented** Tomma Abts
R. Crumb
On Kawara
Toba Khedoori
Gordon Matta-Clark
Daniel Richter
Katy Schimert
Yutaka Sone
Diana Thater
Doug Wheeler
Yan Pei-Ming

Interview with David Zwirner

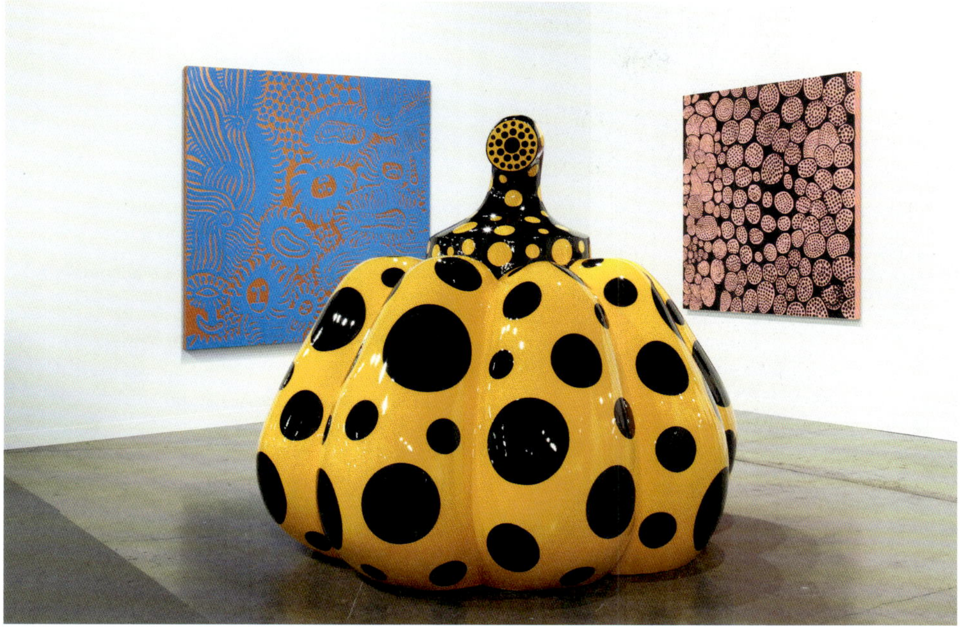

Art Basel in Miami Beach, 2013

Could you tell us about your gallery's program, which is a mix of estates and contemporary artists? How do you deal with this program and how did you construct it?

Ultimately we run two separate businesses. We have two galleries: one on 19th Street and one on 20th Street—and of course we have the gallery in London. The one on 19th Street is the one that primarily deals with artists' management: the primary market and exhibitions by living artists. Not necessarily young, we have a big age range. In the building that we just finished this year on 20th Street, we really focus on estate management—so there we work with the estates of Donald Judd, Dan Flavin, Fred Sandback, and John McCracken, among others.

I think of these jobs as things that very much overlap. Certainly when we come to Art Basel we bring things from both sides of our activities. They are quite different, so I have a two different teams, one working with the estates and one with the artists.

You mentioned the building on 20th Street; it's a quite striking architectural choice within Chelsea. Did you plan it for particular estates, particular works of art?

In retrospect, a lot of people say "oh, you've built this building for Minimalism—it's a temple for Minimalism," and that's great because we have these wonderful Minimalist estates, but I really built it to be able to house, exhibit, and showcase all kinds of art. I really wanted as perfect conditions as possible. I believe that daylight is really the ideal lighting—so, we have this wonderful daylight in all the spaces in which we show the art, even in the viewing rooms—and then the rest is really proportions! We just tried to create a very user-friendly gallery space. It seems to work.

A successful gallery building should be such that you can appreciate the architecture but you also forget about it. I think if you were entering the Ad Reinhardt exhibition you would certainly not think about architecture, you'd think about the art. This is what is wrong with a lot of contemporary museum architecture—it's all about the experience of the facade, or the "skin." We tried to do something that is a little more muted and services the art well.

You have been part of Art Basel in Basel and in Miami Beach for a long time. You also participated in Art Basel in Hong Kong this year. What was it like, and what are your thoughts about the Asia-Pacific market and art scene?

First of all, I think Art Basel has a very strong ground. I'm a believer in art fairs, they are a big part of what we do, and I want to work with very strong and well-managed fairs. So, when I heard the fair was expanding to Hong Kong I was immediately very enthusiastic, because I don't know that much about that part of the market and it gives us a user-friendly entry to a market that needs attention. I think this market is still forming itself and the emphasis on Chinese art overshadows other great art made in the world. And of course we are not a gallery of Chinese artists, we are a gallery for Western artists, so we will keep coming back and hope we can grow an audience, but to be honest that has been slower than I wanted it to be. I would like to find some more active collectors. We also haven't been able to find the museums. That's what's missing in the mix. If I show at Basel, I would talk to major curators or major directors. I know they are coming and I know what they are doing. In Hong Kong, I don't see it. But nonetheless, it's a pioneering fair, and we'll definitely be back next year.

Finally, what was your approach for Miami Beach in 2013?

The art market is very strong and we had record auctions, so there's no need to say that we wanted to come on very strong. We focused on one of the stars of this year, both in my gallery and on the international market: Jeff Koons. We also wanted to feature Isa Genzken who has a show at MoMA this winter, and who has always been under-appreciated. She's one of the greatest artists, and it was wonderful to see a new audience for her work. And last but not least, Yayoi Kusama, a superstar who is now part of the gallery, and who is an artist who translates from East to West, from North to South. We wanted three very strong positions, and it seems to work well so far.

Art Basel Team 2013–2014

EXECUTIVE COMMITTEE

Marc Spiegler
Director

Marco Fazzone
Director Resources & Finance

Magnus Renfrew
Director Asia

Annette Schönholzer
Director of New Initiatives

MANAGEMENT BOARD

Andreas Bicker
Head of General Management

Laura Blagho
Head of Marketing & Communications

Maureen Bruckmayr
General Manager Miami Beach

Patrick Foret
Head of Sponsorship

Andrew Strachan
General Manager Hong Kong

Sven Tresp
Head of Operations & Logistics

Thomas Wüstenhagen
Head of Gallery Relations

DIRECTORS' ASSISTANTS

Janett Schickler
Directors Assistant

Jenny Or
Director's Assistant Asia

Claudia Schachenmann
Assistant of New Initiatives

Aileen Zumstein
Assistant of New Initiatives

GALLERY RELATIONS

Eve Share Banghart
Gallery & Project Manager Asia

François M. Croissant
Gallery & Project Manager

Lucy Crommelin
Gallery & Project Manager Asia

Ursula Diehr
Gallery & Project Manager

Dunja Gottweis
Gallery & Project Manager

Benjamin Grappin
Gallery & Project Manager

Markus Mäder
Gallery & Project Manager

Michael Müller
Gallery & Project Manager

Angelle Siyang-Le
Gallery & Project Manager Asia

Jonas Egli
Gallery & Project Assistant

Dominik Honegger
Gallery & Project Assistant

Muriel Meidinger
Gallery & Project Assistant

Daniela Schimmel
Gallery & Project Assistant

Stefanie Wenger
Assistant Unlimited

OPERATIONS & LOGISTICS

Trevor Hyland
Operations & Logistics Manager Asia

Suez Lui
Associate Operations & Logistics Manager Asia

Zenia Choy
Operations & Logistics Executive Asia

Nour El-Gourany
Operations & Logistics Assistant

MARKETING & COMMUNICATIONS

Kristi D'Arcy
Media Production Manager

Dorothee Dines
Public Relations Manager

Magdalena Dysli
Event Manager

Lucinda Evans
Associate Event Manager Asia

Jennifer Pratt
Marketing & Communications Manager Asia

Claudio Vogt
Associate Event Manager

Janice Ching
Marketing & Communications Assistant Asia

Yoko Choy
Media Production Manager Asia

Myrta Holinger
Public Relations Assistant

Lucy Knight
Content & Channel Manager

Urs Mangold
Media Production Manager

David Meier
Marketing & Events Assistant

Dominic Sutter
Marketing & Events Assistant

Aurélia Thiébaud
Marketing Intern

Helen Homan Wu
Event Manager Asia

SPONSORSHIP

Nadine Marti
Sponsorship Manager

Gerda van den Bergh
Sponsorship Manager Europe

Dovenia Chow
Sponsorship Manager Asia

Hanna Barber
Sponsorship Manager Americas

Lena Walter
Sponsorship Assistant

VIP & VISITOR SERVICES

Olivia Doppler
Visitor Services Manager

Deborah Ehrlich
VIP Relations Manager Asia

Marina Mottin
VIP Relations Manager

Sascha Nikitin
VIP Relations Manager Switzerland & Russia

Isabel Dombos
VIP Relations Assistant

Naoki Fukushima
VIP Relations Assistant

Sarah Huber
CRM Development Coordinator

Nicola Huell
VIP Relations Assistant

Alena Lachmann
VIP Relations Assistant

Verona Zeng
VIP Relations Assistant Asia

VIP RELATIONS

Princess Alia Al-Senussi
Middle East

Stefanie Block Reed
USA

Bambi Blumberg
Australia, New Zealand

Karen Boros
Germany

Mirta d'Argenzio
Italy

Amanda Echeverria/Mariana Munguia Matute
Mexico

Charlotte Bancroft/Sarah Hardin-White
USA, Canada

Luluc Huang
China/Beijing

Jenny Lee
Taiwan

Hélène Mairlot
Benelux

Cecilia Ong/Adeline Ooi
Singapore, Malaysia, Indonesia, Philippines

Anjali Devidayal/Sharmistha Ray
India

Iciar S-Mangas
Latin America, Spain, Portugal

Ricardo Sardenberg
Brazil

Andreas Siegfried
United Kingdom

Natane Takeda
Japan

Denise Vilgrain
France

Euna Yoo
South Korea

Malena Zhang
China/Shanghai

REPRESENTATION

FITZ & CO, New York
USA

Garber + Goodman, Inc., Miami
Florida

Hong Kong

SELECTION COMMITTEE

Massimo De Carlo, Massimo De Carlo, Milan & London
Emi Eu, STPI – Singapore Tyler Print Institute, Singapore
Shireen Gandhy, Chemould Prescott Road, Mumbai
Suzie Kim, Kukje Gallery/Tina Kim Gallery, Seoul & New York
Maho Kubota, SCAI The Bathhouse, Tokyo
David Maupin, Lehmann Maupin, New York & Hong Kong
Urs Meile, Galerie Urs Meile, Beijing & Lucerne
Zhang Wei, Vitamin Creative Space, Guangzhou & Beijing

SECTOR EXPERTS

Discoveries
Finola Jones, mother's tankstation, Dublin
Atsuko Ninagawa, Take Ninagawa, Tokyo

Modern Art
Mathias Rastorfer, Galerie Gmurzynska, Zurich, St. Moritz & Zug

CURATOR

Encounters
Yuko Hasegawa, Tokyo

Basel

SELECTION COMMITTEE

Xavier Hufkens, Xavier Hufkens, Brussels
Jochen Meyer, Meyer Riegger Galerie, Berlin & Karlsruhe
Lucy Mitchell-Innes, Mitchell-Innes & Nash, New York
Tim Neuger, neugerriemschneider, Berlin
Franco Noero, Galleria Franco Noero, Turin
Eva Presenhuber, Galerie Eva Presenhuber, Zurich

SECTOR EXPERTS

Statements and Feature
Miguel Abreu, Miguel Abreu Gallery, New York
Silvia Dauder, ProjecteSD, Barcelona
Sunitha Kumar Emmart, GallerySKE, Bangalore

Edition
Niels Borch Jensen, Niels Borch Jensen Gallery & Edition, Berlin & Copenhagen

Classical Photography
Edwynn Houk, Edwynn Houk Gallery, New York

Appeals Board
Cyrill Häring, President, Basel
Christoph Degen, Basel
Christina Végh, Bonn

CURATORS

Film
This Brunner, Zurich
Marc Glöde, Berlin

Parcours
Florence Derieux, Reims

Unlimited
Gianni Jetzer, New York

HONORARY BOARD

Ernst Beyeler †
Trudi Bruckner
Felix Buchmann †
Pierre Huber
Gianfranco Verna
Annely Juda †
Denise René †
Lucio Amelio †

Miami Beach

SELECTION COMMITTEE

Chantal Crousel, Galerie Chantal Crousel, Paris
Peter Freeman, Peter Freeman, Inc., New York
Martin Klosterfelde, Galerie Klosterfelde, Berlin
José Kuri, kurimanzutto, Mexico City
Friedrich Petzel, Friedrich Petzel Gallery, New York
Jeff Poe, Blum & Poe, Los Angeles
Mary Sabbatino, Galerie Lelong, New York

SECTOR EXPERTS

Nova and Positions
Marcío Botner, A Gentil Carioca, Rio de Janeiro
Joanna Kamm, Galerie Kamm, Berlin
Andrew Kreps, Andrew Kreps Gallery, New York

Florida Galleries
Fredric Snitzer, Fredric Snitzer Gallery, Miami

CURATORS

Film
This Brunner, Zurich
David Gryn, London

Public
Nicholas Baume, New York

Editorial Committee
Laura Blagho
Lionel Bovier
Clément Dirié
Gilles Gavillet
Annette Schönholzer
Marc Spiegler

General Editorial Coordination
Lionel Bovier
Clément Dirié
Eléonor de Pesters

Gallery Data
Muriel Meldinger
Thomas Wüstenhagen

Editing
Lionel Bovier
Clément Dirié
Lucy Knight
Eléonor de Pesters
Clare Manchester

Copyediting and Proofreading
Clément Dirié
Muriel Meldinger
Clare Manchester
Eléonor de Pesters
Jennifer Pratt
Kevin Slide

Art Direction
Gavillet & Rust/Gilles Gavillet

Design
Gavillet & Rust/Vincent Devaud

Assistance
Pauline Piguet, Chi-Long Trieu

Typefaces
Plain, Genath Basel (François Rappo/www.optimo.ch)

Translations
Unless otherwise mentioned: Apostroph AG; Brian Currid (Falckenberg); Judith Hayward (Sebti; Bellet; Ursprung; Weiss); Simon Turner (Minini)

Image Courtesies
All images in the Exhibitors Lists as well as in the Curators' Choices, Top Tens, and Galleries Focus are courtesy of the galleries.

Photo Credits & Courtesies
Unless otherwise noted, the photographs, including portraits, of Art Basel in Hong Kong are by Gabriele Heidecker; those of Art Basel in Basel by Julien Gremaud; and those of Art Basel in Miami Beach by Matthieu Lavanchy.

Additional photography of the three fairs by MCH Messe Schweiz (Basel) AG photographers: p. 57, 61, 157, 158, 159, 201, 248–249, 250–251, 256–257, 317, 318, 320, 379, 390–391, 444–445, 446–447, 460–461, 462–463, 498, 524–525, 572, 573, 577, 580–581, 582–583, 586–587, 590–591, 595, 600–601, 602, 603, 604–605, 606, 607, 608, 609, 652, 709, 710–711, 713, 714, 718–719

Absolut/Roberto Chamorro: p. 623–627, 629, 764b, 682–683/Christian Hagward: 762, 764t–765, 766t; Andreas Angelidakis and The Breeder: 114; Audemars-Piguet: 440–441; Iwan Baan: 482–483, 484–485, 490r, 491; Barford Sculptures Ltd.: 548l; Baruchello Foundation, Rome: 53tl; Cecilia Bengolea & François Chaignaud/Photo: Alain Monot: 115; Ulla von Brandenburg/Art : Concept, Pilar Corrias, and Produzentengalerie: 117t; Eglė Budvytytė/Photo: Ieva Budzeikaite: 117b; CCAA: 147br; Sarah Charlesworth Estate: 552; Ciné-Tamaris, 2000: 53tr; Philippe Dutartre, 1977: 550l; Stichting Egress Foundation, Amsterdam: 546l; Estate Günther Forg/Cécile Huber, Freiburg: 548r; Fundación Augusto y Leon Ferrari: 550r; François Ghebaly Gallery: 549; Zheng Guogu: 54–55; Fritz Haeg: 53b; Serge Hasenböhler: 409; Herzog & de Meuron: 147bl, 490l; Hufton+Crow: 487; Annely Juda Fine Arts: 356; Tadashi Kawamata & Christophe Scheidegger: 394; Malcolm McLaren Estate: 255; Françoise Marquet/D.R., 2012: 547r; Galleria Massimo Minimi: 551; Olivier Nouspikel: 292, 293; Galerie Nathalie Obadia: 386–387; Office Baroque: 187b; Kenneth Price Estate: 547l; Janina Quint, 2009: 545; Peter Ross, 1998/The Dorothea Tanning Foundation: 546r; Fabrice Seixas: 395; Margherita Spiluttini: 486; Wolfgang Tillmans, Berlin/London: 176; Adrián Villar Rojas: 50–51; Robert Wedemeyer: 691(2); Adrian Wong: 766b; Martin Wong: 377; Kurt Wyss: 345, 348–349, 350–351, 352, 354–355, 357, 358–359; Yamaki Fine Art: 143

Acknowledgments
We are grateful to all the authors, artists, and photographers who contributed to this book, as well as to Seika Abe; Derya Akay; Viviana Bertanzetti; Emma-Charlotte Gobry-Laurencin; Julian Cho; Olivier Deger (Audemars Piguet); Richenda Devereux, Abigail Varian, and David Field (Sutton PR); Hu Fang; Noelia Ferretti; Winona Huang; Lu Jia; Dehua Li; Ulrika Lövdahl (Absolut); Klaus Malonek; George Newall; Olivier Nouspikel; Susannah Palmer; Brad Plumb; Lisa Polten; Naima Saidi; Stéphanie Scanvic; Olivia Sophia; Joanna Spice; Chantal Störmer; Carla Subrizi; Nao Tazaki; Zhang Wei; Danica Willi; Tobias Wyss; Zoie Yung, and Boris Zuberbühler.

Color Separation & Print
Musumeci S.p.A., Quart (Aosta)

The information printed in this book is based on the three 2013 Art Basel catalogues (Hong Kong, Basel, Miami Beach) and an online questionnaire answered directly by the exhibitors: gallery name and list of artists, sectors' participations, etc. thus follow Art Basel's formatting and editorial guidelines. Every attempt has been made by the publisher to copyedit and correct this information within the constraints of these guidelines and the timeframe of the publication.

Printed in Europe

Published by
JRP|Ringier
Limmatstrasse 270
CH–8005 Zurich
T +41 (0) 43 311 27 50
F +41 (0) 43 311 27 51
E info@jrp-ringier.com
www.jrp-ringier.com

ISBN 978-3-03764-362-4

JRP|Ringier books are available internationally at selected bookstores and from the following distribution partners:

Switzerland
AVA Verlagsauslieferung AG
Centralweg 16, CH-8910 Affoltern a.A.
verlagsservice@ava.ch, www.ava.ch

France
Les presses du reel
35 rue Colson, F-21000 Dijon
info@lespressesdureel.com
www.lespressesdureel.com

Germany and Austria
Vice Versa Distribution GmbH
Immanuelkirchstrasse 12, D–10405 Berlin
info@vice-versa-distribution.com
www.vice-versa-distribution.com

UK and other European countries
Cornerhouse Publications
70 Oxford Street, UK-Manchester M1 5NH
publications@cornerhouse.org
www.cornerhouse.org/books

USA, Canada, Asia, and Australia
ARTBOOK|D.A.P.
155 Sixth Avenue, 2nd Floor, USA-New York, NY 10013
orders@dapinc.com, www.artbook.com

For a list of our partner bookshops or for any general questions, please contact JRP|Ringier directly at info@jrp-ringier.com, or visit our homepage www.jrp-ringier.com for further information about our program.

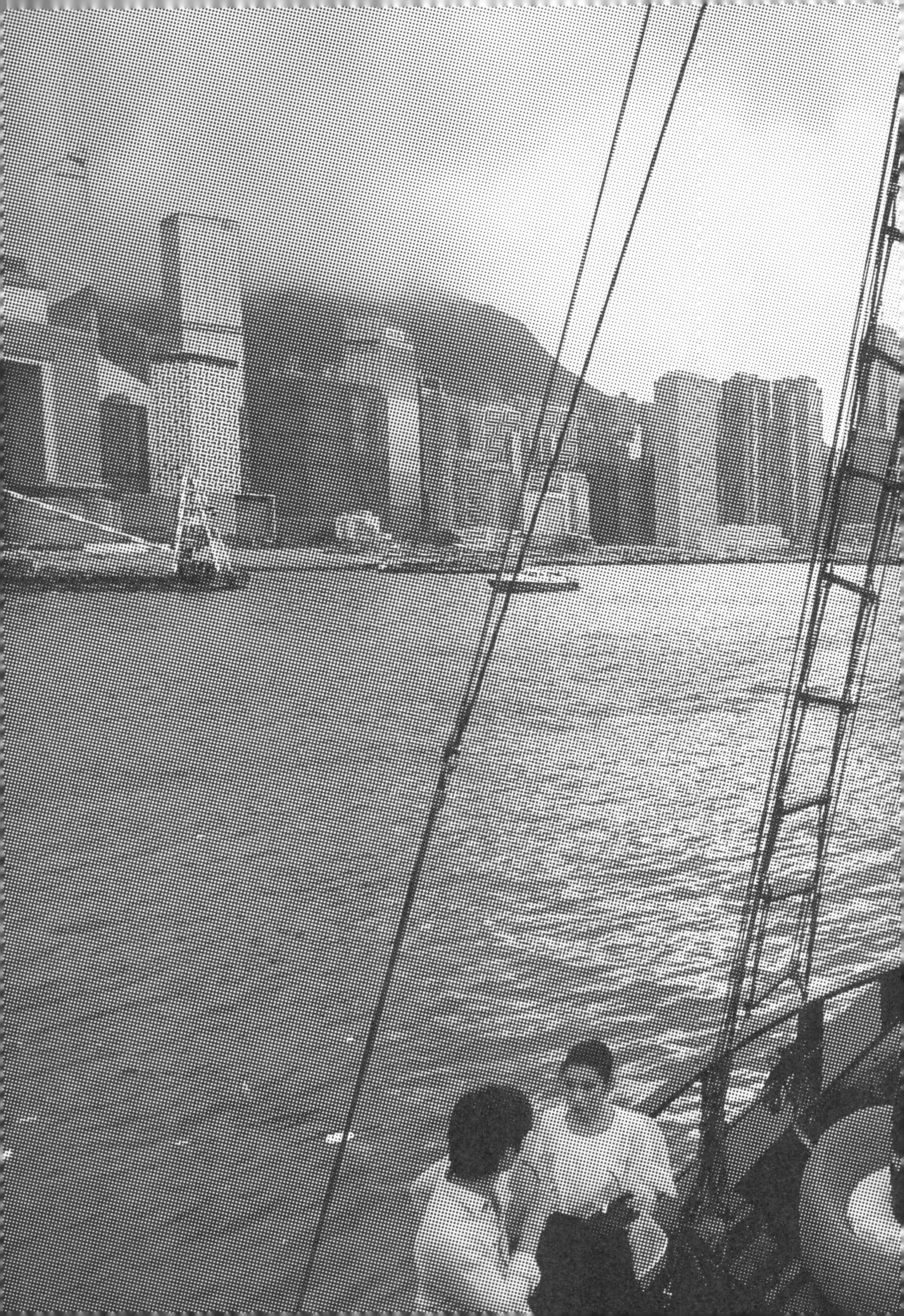